Lecture Notes of the Institute for Computer Sciences, Social Informatics and Telecommunications Engineering 292

More information about this series at http://www.springer.com/series/8197

Xinheng Wang · Honghao Gao ·
Muddesar Iqbal · Geyong Min (Eds.)

Collaborative Computing: Networking, Applications and Worksharing

15th EAI International Conference, CollaborateCom 2019
London, UK, August 19–22, 2019
Proceedings

Springer

Editors
Xinheng Wang
Xi'an Jiaotong-Liverpool University
Suzhou, China

Honghao Gao
Shanghai University
Shanghai, China

Muddesar Iqbal
London South Bank University
London, UK

Geyong Min
University of Exeter
Exeter, UK

ISSN 1867-8211   ISSN 1867-822X (electronic)
Lecture Notes of the Institute for Computer Sciences, Social Informatics
and Telecommunications Engineering
ISBN 978-3-030-30145-3   ISBN 978-3-030-30146-0 (eBook)
https://doi.org/10.1007/978-3-030-30146-0

This Springer imprint is published by the registered company Springer Nature Switzerland AG
The registered company address is: Gewerbestrasse 11, 6330 Cham, Switzerland

Preface

We are delighted to introduce the proceedings of the 15th European Alliance for Innovation (EAI) International Conference on Collaborative Computing: Networking, Applications and Worksharing (CollaborateCom 2019). This conference brought together researchers, developers, and practitioners around the world who are interested in fully realizing the promises of electronic collaboration in terms of networking, technology and systems, user interfaces and interaction paradigms, and interoperation with application-specific components and tools.

This year's conference attracted 121 submissions. All of the submissions were reviewed by at least three reviewers. After a rigorous review process, 40 full papers and 8 short papers were accepted for oral presentation at the main conference sessions. The conference sessions were: Session 1: (a) Cloud, IoT, and Edge Computing and (b) Data Analysis and Recommendation; Session 2: (a) Collaborative IoT Services and Applications, and (b) Artificial Intelligence; Session 3: (a) Security and Trustworthy and (b) Software Development; Session 4: (a) Algorithms, Networks, and Testbeds and (b) Collaborative Applications for Recognition and Classification; and Session 5: Smart Transportation. Along with the main conference, two workshops were organized and 6 papers were accepted for oral presentation at Session 6: the Third International Workshop on Securing IoT Networks (SITN) and Cognitive Computing and Analytics (WCCA). In addition, a panel session, Civil Protection Volunteers Training (CiProVoT), was also organized, where panelists from various backgrounds shared their views and visions for addressing the urgent needs of training volunteers for civil protection. Apart from high-quality technical paper presentations, the technical program also featured three keynote speeches which were delivered by Prof. Niki Trigoni (Oxford University), Prof. Tasos Dagiuklas (London South Bank University), and Mr. Jun Xu (Huawei Technologies Co., Ltd.), as well as three tutorials delivered by Dr. Muddesar Iqbal, Dr. Shancang Li, and Dr. Leandros Maglaras.

Coordination with the steering chair Imrich Chlamtac, and Steering Committee members Song Guo, Bo Li, Xiaofei Liao, Xinheng Wang, and Honghao Gao, was essential for the success of the conference. We sincerely appreciate their constant support and guidance. It was also a great pleasure to work with such an excellent Organizing Committee and we thank them for their hard work in organizing and supporting the conference. In particular, the Technical Program Committee, led by our TPC chair, Dr. Honghao Gao, completed the peer-review process of technical papers with tremendous efforts, enthusiasm, and affection, and complied a high-quality technical program. We are also grateful to conference manager, Karolina Marcinova, for her support and all the authors who submitted their papers to the CollaborateCom 2019 conference and workshops.

We strongly believe that the CollaborateCom conference provides a good forum for all researchers, developers, and practitioners to discuss all science and technology aspects that are relevant to collaborative computing. We also expect that the future

CollaborateCom conferences will be as successful and stimulating, as indicated by the contributions presented in this volume.

August 2019

Xinheng Wang
Honghao Gao
Muddesar Iqbal
Geyong Min

Conference Organization (CollaborateCom)

Steering Committee

Chair

Imrich Chlamtac   Bruno Kessler Professor, University of Trento, Italy

Steering Committee Members

Song Guo	The Hong Kong Polytechnic University, SAR China
Bo Li	The Hong Kong University of Science and Technology, SAR China
Xiaofei Liao	Huazhong University of Science and Technology, China
Xinheng Wang	Xi'an Jiaotong-Liverpool University, China
Honghao Gao	Shanghai University, China

Organizing Committee

General Chairs

Xinheng Wang	Xi'an Jiaotong-Liverpool University, China
Muddesar Iqbal	London South Bank University, UK
Geyong Min	University of Exeter, UK

Program Chair

Honghao Gao   Shanghai University, China

Workshop Chairs

Shahid Mumtaz	Instituto de Telecomunicações, Portugal
Anwer Al-Dulaimi	EXFO Inc., Canada

Publicity Chairs

Andrei Tchernykh	CICESE Research Center, Mexico
Anandakumar Haldorai	Sri Eshwar College of Engineering, India

Sponsorship Chair

Massoud Zolgharni   University of West London, UK

Publication Chairs

Youhuizi Li	Hangzhou Dianzi University, China
Azah Kamilah	Universiti Teknikal Malaysia, Malaysia

Web Chair

Chekfoung Tan   University of West London, UK

Conference Manager

Karolina Marcinova   European Alliance for Innovation, Belgium

Technical Program Committee

Anwer Al-Dulaimi	University of Toronto, Canada
Amjad Ali	Korea University, South Korea
Junaid Arshad	University of West London, UK
Zhongqin Bi	Shanghai University of Electric Power, China
Bin Cao	Zhejiang University of Technology, China
Buqing Cao	Hunan University of Science and Technology, China
Liang Chen	University of West London, UK
Shizhan Chen	Tianjing University, China
Yihai Chen	Shanghai University, China
Ying Chen	Beijing University of Information Technology, China
Fei Dai	Yunnan University, China
Yucong Duan	Hainan University, China
Xiaoliang Fan	Fuzhou University, China
Shucun Fu	Nanjing University of Information Science and Technology, China
Fekade Getahun	Addis Ababa University, Ethiopia
Jiwei Huang	Beijing University of Post and Telecommunications, China
Tao Huang	Silicon Lake University, China
Congfeng Jiang	Hangzhou Dianzi University, China
Malik Ahmad Kamran	COMSATS University Islamabad, Pakistan
Li Kuang	Central South University, China
Rui Li	Xidian University, China
Youhuizi Li	Hangzhou Dianzi University, China
Wenmin Lin	Hangzhou Dianzi University, China
Jianxun Liu	Hunan University of Science and Technology, China
Shijun Liu	Shandong University, China
Xihua Liu	Nanjing University of Information Science and Technology, China
Xuan Liu	Southeast University, China
Yutao Ma	Wuhan University, China
Lin Meng	Ritsumeikan University, Japan
Shunmei Meng	Nanjing University of Science and Technology, China
Elahe Naserianhanzaei	University of Exeter, UK
Yu-Chun Pan	University of West London, UK
Shanchen Pang	China University of Petroleum, China
Lianyong Qi	Qufu Normal University, China

Kuangyu Qin	Wuhan University, China
Stephan Reiff-Marganiec	University of Leicester, UK
Imed Romdhani	Edinburgh Napier University, UK
Changai Sun	University of Science and Technology, China
Xiaobing Sun	Yangzhou University, China
Wenda Tang	Lancaster University, UK
George Ubakanma	London South Bank University, UK
Shaohua Wan	Zhongnan University of Economics and Law, China
Dongjing Wang	Hangzhou Dianzi University, China
Jian Wang	WuHan University, China
Junhao Wen	Chongqing University, China
Yiping Wen	Hunan University of Science and Technology, China
Yu Weng	Minzu University of China, China
Yirui Wu	Hohai University, China
Yunni Xia	Chongqing University, China
Haolong Xiang	University of Auckland, New Zealand
Jiuyun Xu	China University of Petroleum, China
Xiaolong Xu	Nanjing University of Information Science and Technology, China
Yueshen Xu	Xidian University, China
Xiaoxian Yang	Shanghai Polytechnic University, China
Yuyu Yin	Hangzhou Dianzi University, China
Li Yu	Hangzhou Dianzi University, China
Yuan Yuan	Michigan State University, USA
Jun Zeng	Chongqing University, China
Gaowei Zhang	Nanyang Technology University, China
Jie Zhang	Nanjing University, China
Yanmei Zhang	Central University of Finance and Economics, China
Yiwen Zhang	Anhui University, China
Zijian Zhang	Beijing Institute of Technology, China
Xuan Zhao	Nanjing University, China
Zhuofeng Zhao	North China University of Technology, China
Yu Zheng	Nanjing University of Information Science and Technology, China
Ao Zhou	Beijing University of Posts and Telecommunications, China
Guobing Zou	Shanghai University, China

Contents

Security and Trustworthy

Smart Transportation

Recommendation and Social Computing

Cloud, IoT and Edge Computing

Lightweight Computation to Robust Cloud Infrastructure for Future Technologies (Workshop Paper)

Sonia Shahzadi[1], Muddesar Iqbal[2]([✉]), Xinheng Wang[3], George Ubakanma[4],
Tasos Dagiuklas[4], and Andrei Tchernykh[5]

[1] Swan Mesh Networks Ltd, Research and Development, London, UK
[2] School of Computer Science and Electronic Engineering,
University of Essex, Colchester, UK
m.iqbal@lsbu.ac.uk
[3] Department of Electrical and Electronic Engineering,
Xian Jiaotong University, Suzhou, China
[4] School of Engineering, London South Bank University, London, UK
[5] CICESE Research Center, Ensenada, Baja California, Mexico

Abstract. Hardware and software lightweight solutions became the mainstream for current and future emerging technologies. Container-based virtualization provides more efficient and faster solutions than traditional virtual machines, offering good scalability, flexibility, and multi-tenancy. They are capable of serving in a heterogeneous and dynamic environment across multiple domains, including IoT, cloud, fog, and multi-access edge computing. In this paper, we propose a lightweight solution for LCC (Live Container Cloud) that permits the user to access live/remote cloud resources faster. LCC can be embedded as a fog/edge node to permit the users to allocate and deallocate cloud resources. The performance of such a containerization technology is presented.

Keywords: Cloud Computing · Internet of Things · Fog Computing · Docker · OpenStack

1 Introduction

Cloud Computing is shifting from large centralized data centers to the distributed multi-cloud environment to provide more efficient services. It can be integrated into Internet-of-Things (IoT) devices, edge, and fog computing.

To provide computational power, storage capability, reliable connectivity, and other resources for billions of devices, we need lightweight solutions to be run on resource-constrained devices. They should be feasible for smart infrastructures and provide elasticity and flexibility. We have proposed a lightweight

© ICST Institute for Computer Sciences, Social Informatics and Telecommunications Engineering 2019
Published by Springer Nature Switzerland AG 2019. All Rights Reserved
X. Wang et al. (Eds.): CollaborateCom 2019, LNICST 292, pp. 3–11, 2019.
https://doi.org/10.1007/978-3-030-30146-0_1

virtualization solution for cloud services that is more efficient than traditional VMs. Lightweight virtualization based on the container has gained popularity for cloud deployments due to containers are more light and portable compared to VMs [5]. A VM is an emulation of a computer system with the independent OS, while containers are based on the host operating systems and share the same kernel with other containers running in the same machine. That is why containers require fewer resources and smaller in size. It makes them more suitable for resource-constrained devices [6]. Docker is one of the most popular solutions for container deployment and management, providing flexible, extensible, and portable computation [2]. Linux Container (LXC) LXC is a well-known set of tools, templates, library, and language bindings.

In this paper, we present a lightweight, portable infrastructure solution based on LXC to enable on-demand resource provisioning. We provide a performance evaluation of the hypervisors and answer the following questions

1. Which cloud infrastructure is suitable for the public and private sectors?
2. Should we continue to use traditional VM infrastructure on the cloud or move to lightweight technologies for fast robustness?
3. Which type of virtual servers is suitable for future technologies?
4. How do these tools help to provide service migration on future generation technologies?

2 Literature Review

In the last era of computing, virtualization technology plays a vital role, especially in cloud computing. After the evolution of virtualization, the demand for these virtualized resources is increased. Two popular types of virtualization technologies are hypervisor-based virtualization and container-based virtualization [3]. VM can snapshot the whole working environment, including software, applications, dependencies, and more [4]. These snapshot images can be hosted on other servers. This approach facilitates reproducibility [4]. Virtualization is the key part of cloud services as cloud computing provides virtual resources on user demand [1].

This virtual environment can be deployed on physical machines and is completely transparent to the clients.

2.1 Hypervisor Based Virtualization in Cloud Computing

A hypervisor or Virtual Machine Monitor (VMM) is executed on a host or a physical system by splitting and allocating host resources into a guest operating system or VM. There are two types of hypervisor-based architectures. In Type 1, the hypervisor runs directly on the top of the host hardware, while in Type 2, the hypervisor runs on the top of the host operating system. Several hypervisors are used according to deployment and optimization such as KVM, QEMU, Microsoft Hyper-V Server, etc. They provide the following features:

- *Encapsulation:* A virtual hard disk is located in VM to store files. This disk can be easily moved, backed-up, copied, replicated or migrated from one host to another one.

- *Isolation:* User can run multiple virtual machines on the same host without interfering. Each VM has its operating system and software. Failure of one VM does not affect other VM or host operating system.
- *Transparency:* VM and guest operating system are unaware that they are running in a virtual environment and programs run within the virtual environment in the same way as they run on physical machines.
- *Manageability:* Hypervisor is responsible for allocating resources to VMs and execution of VMs through a management interface.

2.2   Container-Based Virtualization in Cloud Computing

In container-based virtualization, all containers share the same operating system, which reduces the runtime and storage overhead. A container image provides a standalone package for container instantiation and execution. It encapsulates everything, including system configuration and applications [8]. Multiple containers can be executed on the same physical server or different servers to provide fault tolerance. Although containers share the same operating system, they are isolated from each other through process IDs, inter-process communication, network interfaces, and directory trees. Control Groups (cgroups) are used for resource management, while namespaces are used for processes isolation. Resource optimization is achieved by providing low overhead with transparency.

2.3   Comparison of VM and Container

OpenStack is one of the open source solutions for cloud implementation that is widely used for private and public sectors. Hypervisors are responsible for providing services for clients. OpenStack mostly used KVM hypervisor. However, Google and IBM are successfully using containerization technology [1]. The main features of VMs and containers are given in Table 1, and in Fig. 1. They show the importance of Docker container adoption.

Table 1. Comparison of VM and container

S.no	Features	VM	Container
1	Isolation	H	L
2	Resources wastage	H	L
3	Transparency	H	H
4	Runtime overhead	H	L
5	Storage overhead	H	L
6	Fault tolerance	L	H

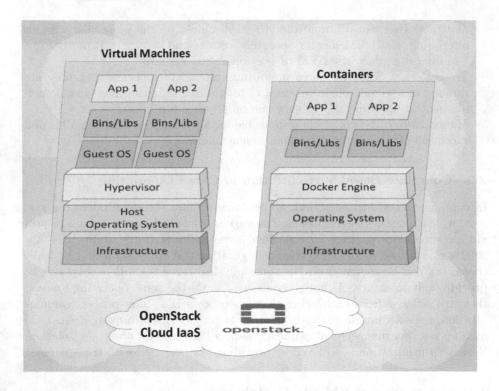

Fig. 1. Virtual Machines vs Containers

3   Use Cases

Millions of devices with sensing and actuators capabilities are connecting with the Internet of Things (IoT) in everyday life, and mostly IoT objects send data to cloud servers for computation purpose and then back to the devices. However, this method is not sustainable due to the rapid growth of IoT objects as a massive quantities of devices creates congestion, security, and latency challenges. Fog Computing introduces a new paradigm to overcome these challenges where edge nodes/devices are deployed at the edge of the network for local capabilities. These edge nodes are resource constraints and varying according to processing and storage. Cloud computing provides a lightweight solution with a container for distributed applications deployment where computation infrastructure can be robust for smart services. Figure 2 demonstrates the proficiency of LXC (Linux Container) for two cases.

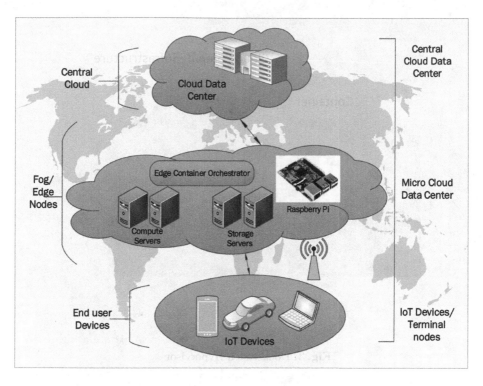

Fig. 2. Lightweight architecture for future technologies

4   Implementation

To implement lightweight technology inside the cloud infrastructure, we have the following steps:

- **Configure Cloud IaaS to enable Docker:** To enable Docker as a hypervisor in OpenStack cloud, we have configure this with compute node and performed several tests to prove its functionality for a production-ready environment.
- **Initiated via Docker Hypervisor:** In this scenario, we have compared multiple hypervisors in cloud computing scenarios where we can compare the performance of cloud servers via Qemu and LXC, as shown in Fig. 3.
- **Live cloud resources deployment from container:** In this scenario, we have compared the performance of live cloud resources that use containers and VMs (Fig. 4).

5   Performance Evaluation

To evaluate the performance of VM and container, we setup a cloud testbed using OpenStack and Docker container integrated with OpenStack. Ubuntu 14.04 is

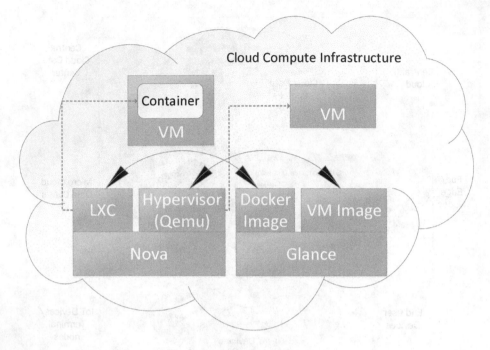

Fig. 3. Docker as a Hypervisor

used as a host OS with 3-tier cloud architecture. We have measure VM hypervisor and LXC performance in following two scenarios.

5.1 Instance/Server Performance Measurement

We have performed these tests under the following environments.

Cloud Platform: OpenStack
Host OS: Ubuntu Server 14.04
VM hypervisor: QEMU
LXC: Docker container
Image: cirros-0.3.3-x86_64 (12.6 MB), tutum/wordpress (485.5 MB)
Image format: qcow2, raw

Docker images are lightweight, but we have chosen 485.5 MB size image for Docker and 12.6 MB size for Qemu. We have started and deleted servers with both VM and Docker images. Booting and deleting times are shown in Fig. 5. We see that Qemu VM is about 3.5 times slower.

5.2 Cloud Performance Measurement

To compare cloud performance of VM vs. Docker, first, we have deployed cloud services from VM and measure parameters. Then, we have deployed live cloud

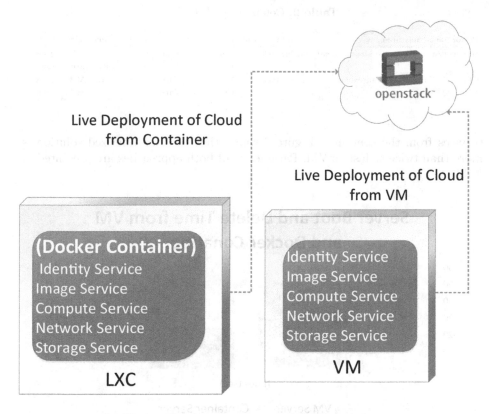

Fig. 4. Cloud resources access from Container

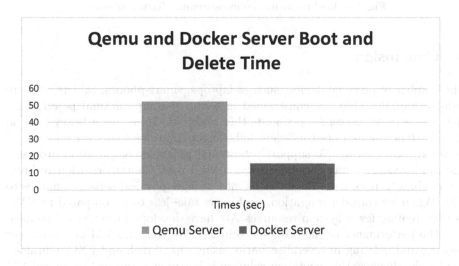

Fig. 5. Docker vs VM server boot and delete time

Table 2. Comparison of results

Performance measurement	Cloud platform	Hypervisor	Image name	Image size	Format
Hypervisor Performance Measurement	OpenStack	Qemu	Cirros	12.6 MB	Qcow
		Docker	Docker Cirros	485.5 MB	Raw
Cloud Performance Measurement	OpenStack	VM	Cirros	12.6 MB	Qcow
		Container	Cirros	12.6 MB	Qcow

services from the container. Figure 6 shows that the containerized solution is more than twice as fast as VM. Parameters of both approaches are presented in Table 2.

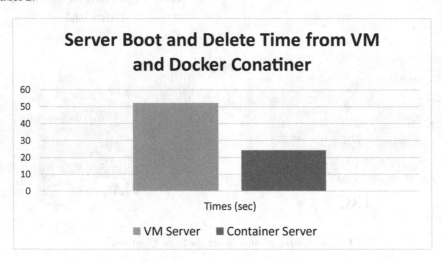

Fig. 6. Cloud performance measurement from container

6   Conclusion

The number of personal devices such as laptops, smart-phones, tablets, etc. are growing rapidly. They are constrained in terms of computational power, storage, connectivity, power supply, and other resources. It creates a heavy load on IT infrastructure and needs efficient lightweight solutions to deliver on-demand resources provisioning. To support robust and portable computation processes and applications, Linux container plays a vital role. Containerization technology enables to pack more applications into a single physical server compares to VM. When we consider migration, containers take less time compared to VMs, as they require fewer system resources. We have developed the testbed to measure the performance of the proposed solution. We compare VM and container booting and deleting in several scenarios using OpenStack and LXC. Obtained results clearly show that container solution is better as compared to typical VM hypervisors in the cloud computing environment.

References

1. Bernstein, D.: Containers and cloud: from LXC to docker to kubernetes. IEEE Cloud Comput. **1**(3), 81–84 (2014)
2. Boettiger, C.: An introduction to docker for reproducible research. ACM SIGOPS Operating Syst. Rev. **49**(1), 71–79 (2015)
3. Bui, T.: Analysis of docker security. arXiv preprint arXiv:1501.02967 (2015)
4. Howe, B.: Virtual appliances, cloud computing, and reproducible research. Comput. Sci. Eng. **14**(4), 36–41 (2012)
5. Pahl, C.: Containerization and the paas cloud. IEEE Cloud Comput. **2**(3), 24–31 (2015)
6. Soltesz, S., Pötzl, H., Fiuczynski, M.E., Bavier, A., Peterson, L.: Container-based operating system virtualization: a scalable, high-performance alternative to hypervisors. In: ACM SIGOPS Operating Systems Review, vol. 41, pp. 275–287. ACM (2007)

A Dynamic Difficulty-Sensitive Worker Distribution Model for Crowdsourcing Quality Management

Miao Zheng$^{(\boxtimes)}$, Lizhen Cui, Wei He, Wei Guo, and Xudong Lu

School of Software, Shandong University, Jinan, China
zheng_miao@outlook.com, {clz,hewei,guowei,dongxul}@sdu.edu.cn

Abstract. Crowdsourcing utilizes the intelligence of people to solve problems that are difficult for machines such as entity resolution, sentiment analysis and image recognition. In crowdsourcing systems, requesters publish tasks that are answered by workers. However, the responses collected from the crowd are ambiguous as the workers on internet with unknown and very diverse abilities, skills, interests and knowledge background. In order to ensure the quality of crowdsourcing results, it is important to characterize worker quality accurately. Many previous works model the worker quality by a fixed value (such as probability value or confusion matrix). But even when workers complete the same type of tasks, the quality is affected by some factors (task difficulty) to varying degrees. Here we propose a dynamic difficulty-sensitive worker quality distribution model. In our model, the worker's ability is affected by task difficulty and fits a functional distribution. This model reflects the relationship between worker reliability and task difficulty. In addition, we utilize Expectation-Maximization approach (EM) to obtain maximum likelihood estimates of the parameters of worker quality distribution model and the true answers to the tasks. We conduct extensive experiments with synthetic data and real-world data. The experimental results show that our method significantly outperforms other state-of-the-art approaches.

Keywords: Crowdsourcing quality management ·
Worker quality distribution model · Maximum likelihood estimation

1 Introduction

Crowdsourcing can utilize the intelligence of the internet workers to solve some problems which are difficult for machine. At present, there are many successful crowdsourcing platforms, such as AMT [1], Upwork [3] and Crowdflow [2]. When requester publish tasks in the crowdsourcing platforms, workers can accept and complete tasks to obtain the corresponding reward. Moreover, many types of tasks can be solved by crowdsourcing, including annotation and tagging of

© ICST Institute for Computer Sciences, Social Informatics and Telecommunications Engineering 2019
Published by Springer Nature Switzerland AG 2019. All Rights Reserved
X. Wang et al. (Eds.): CollaborateCom 2019, LNICST 292, pp. 12–27, 2019.
https://doi.org/10.1007/978-3-030-30146-0_2

images and documents, writing and reviewing software codes, product design and financing. Although corwdsourcing use wisdom of workers enables to solve machine-hard tasks more quickly and accurately, the quality of workers is also uneven due to the different age, education and knowledge background. It is very important to model the quality of workers accurately in crowdsourcing. Worker quality also plays an important role in answer aggregation. When estimating the answer to a task, we mainly rely on the answers from different workers. The quality of workers will have a great impact on estimating the true answer to the task. In addition, quality of workers also be taken into account in the task assignment.

Consider the following example. A machine learning system needs a lot of labeled data. It publishes some Twitter messages on crowdsourcing platforms as emotional analysis tasks. Workers need to judge whether twitter messages express negative or positive emotions, then workers complete tasks and submit answers. Each task may receive multiple answers. Each worker may also answer multiple tasks and the difficulty of each task varies. If a task receives 10 responses from different workers, one of them is "negative" and nine responses are "positive", then we can see that this task is less controversial and simpler. Generally, workers may be better at completing tasks which are easier to identify the answer. On the contrary, their reliability will decrease when answering difficult tasks, and each worker's reliability will be affected differently. In previous works on crowdsourcing quality management, the quality of workers is mostly expressed by the accuracy of task completion or a confusion matrix. However, these worker models can not accurately describe the quality characteristics of workers.

In this paper, we focus on labeling tasks, such as emotional analysis, pattern recognition, image recognition and so on. We propose a worker quality distribution model, in which the worker's quality is a distribution that changes with the task difficulty. It can describe the worker's quality characteristics more accurately, and we also propose a fitting algorithm to form each worker's quality model. In addition, we propose an inference algorithm based on maximum likelihood estimation to estimate the parameters of the worker quality model and the true answer of tasks. Our aim is to estimate the correct answers to the tasks and the quality of the workers more accurately. This paper mainly makes contributions including the following three points.

(1). We propose a dynamic difficulty-sensitive worker quality distribution model, which can describe the worker quality characteristics more accurately. In our worker quality distribution model, we model the task difficulty according to the response received by the task and design a worker quality distribution function.

(2). We propose an inference algorithm based on maximum likelihood estimation. We maximize the likelihood to estimate the parameters of the worker quality model and the true answers to the tasks by EM method. Since there are many unobserved variables in the likelihood function, we also propose a fitting algorithm to get the worker quality distribution model of each worker.

(3). We compare our method with other crowdsourcing quality management algorithms through experiments with synthetic data and real-world data, and results show that our method has higher estimation accuracy than other algorithms.

The rest of this paper is organized as follows. Section 2 reviews the related work. Section 3 describes our conceptual definitions and the problem we study. Section 4 presents the proposed worker quality distribution. We describe our inference algorithms in Sect. 5. Section 6 discusses our experimental evaluation and Sect. 7 concludes this work.

2   Related Work

In order to address the quality management problem in crowdsourcing, various techniques have been proposed to estimate the true answers of tasks based on the worker quality.

The general methods for quality management are majority voting [10,19], The majority voting strategy returns the result with the most votings. In addition, Wang et al. [5] propose a worker quality-aware model is similar to Hidden Markov Models (HMM). Ma et al. [7] propose a fine grained truth discover model to estimate both worker topical expertise and true answers. Before the task is answered, the workers can be evaluated whether they know the relevant knowledge of the task by adding a Qualification test. This can not only eliminate some fraudsters, but also eliminate some workers who do not know the task. It can also make the workers more familiar with the task and improve the quality of the results. Randomly add one in the task. Questions that have the right answers are tested for worker quality [8]. [4] obtained the accuracy of workers' answers by increasing the test questions, and used Bayesian theory to combine the accuracy of workers' answers with the answers given by workers to get the final results.

The Expectation Maximization (EM)-based methods [6,14,21,25,27–29] are the state-of-the-art approaches to estimate task true answers and worker quality. The EM algorithm is primarily used for making up for the lack of data by iteration calculation of maximum likelihood estimate from incomplete data [13]. Each iteration of algorithm includes an expectation step and a maximization step. In Crowdsourcing, the incomplete data is workers responses for tasks and the unobserved latent variables is the task true answer and worker quality. Worker quality can be characterized by worker model, include worker probability [15,20] and confusion matrix [16,24]. EM-based methods iteratively update the parameters of worker model and the true answers of tasks until convergence. Dawid and Skene [12] used EM algorithm in a scene where was similar to Crowdsourcing, for the problem about errors existing in the collected patient records. Later, Ipeirotis et al. [16] Proposed the EM algorithm for crowdsourcing with data from AMT platform, not only estimate the correct answer of tasks, but also get the workers quality represented by the error rate matrix. Moreover, there are many factors that influence the quality of workers. Movellan et al. [30] proposed the method which took task difficulty as parameters into EM algorithm. Hence the iterative process contains three unknown variables, the true answer of tasks, workers' expertise and tasks' difficulties. Afterwards, Kurve et al. [22] proposed to utilize EM algorithm to calculate the task answers and workers quality. They take four latent variables into consideration, the true answer of task, skills of workers, workers intention (i.e. honest worker or dishonest worker) and the task difficulty.

Some workers focus on theoretical guarantees, they provide probabilistic bounds [11,18,26,31] for task answers and worker quality estimates. For example, Dalvi et al. [11]show that the error in their estimates of worker quality is lower by θ under certain assumptions about the graph structure. Das Sarma et al. [26] proposed a technique for globally optimal quality management, finding the maximum likelihood item ratings and worker quality estimates. But its assumptions are not true in reality and the amount of computation increases dramatically as the number of tasks increases.

3   Problem Statement

In this chapter, we first introduce the notation (Table 1) involved in our method, and then describe the problems we study in this paper, some of which will be described in detail in later chapters.

Table 1. Notation table.

Symbol	Explanation
t	Task
w	Worker
r_t^w	Responses from worker w to task t
z_t	The true answer of task
M_t	The task response set
d_t	The task difficulty
$Q(d)$	The worker reliability function
L	Overall likelihood

Task Question and Option. Consider a group of tasks $\{t\}^n$, whose total number is n, these tasks are completed by a group of workers $\{w\}^m$, whose total number is m. Worker w completes task t through k options $\{1, 2, 3..., k\}$ as his response r_t^w. Each worker may accomplish many different tasks, and each task may be accomplished by many different workers. And each task has a true answer z (that is, one of the k options is the correct answer).

Example 1. For example, there is a set of emotional analysis tasks $\{t_1, t_2\}$ with three options: option 1 is positive, option 2 is natural and option 3 is negative. A group of workers $\{w_1, w_2\}$ give responses to the emotional tasks. The real answer to task t_1 is positive, and the real answer to task t_2 is natural.

Task Response Set. After the task receives the worker's responses, we can know the response set of the task $M_t = (v_1, v_2, v_3...v_k)$ refers to the number of responses received by each option of the task.

Example 2. For example, there is a task with three options $\{1, 2, 3\}$, one worker chooses option 1, three workers choose option 2, and seven workers choose option 3. So the response set of this task is $(1, 3, 7)$.

Task Difficulty. We get the task difficulty d_t according to the state of the task's response set. The more difficult a task is, the more difficult it is for workers to distinguish the correct answer for task. Then we can judge the difficulty of a task by the response set. The closer each option of a task receives, the more difficult the task is. The specific method for expressing task difficulty is introduced in Sect. 4.1.

Worker Reliability. Workers have different abilities to accomplish tasks with different difficulties, and the reliability of the answers given by workers is different. We use function $Q(d)$ to express the relationship between worker reliability and task difficulty. We have a detailed introduction in Sect. 4.2.

When a group of tasks $\{t\}^n$ receive the responses r_t^w from a group of workers $\{w\}^m$. We model the task difficulty d_t for each task and build the worker quality distribution model for each worker. Our goal is to estimate the true answer to the task accurately based on the worker quality distribution model.

4   Worker Quality Distribution Model

In this paper, we propose a worker quality distribution model, in which a functional distribution is used to represent the relationship between worker quality and task difficulty. In general, the quality of workers will be affected by the difficulty of the task. The more difficult the task is, the lower probability that workers can correctly answer the task. Here, we consider that the difficulty of tasks has a great relationship with the state of tasks (response set). We propose a method to reflect the difficulty of task according to the state of tasks(response set). In addition, the reliability of workers is affected by the task difficulty. Some workers still have high accuracy even when they complete the difficult tasks, and some workers have poor quality even if they complete simple tasks. We use a functional distribution model to visualize worker's reliability and how worker's reliability is affected by task difficulty.

4.1   Modeling Task Difficulty

We know that the more difficult a task is, the more difficult it is to distinguish the correct answer of task, that is, the more similar the number of answers it receives in different options. Consider an example, the response set of an emotional analysis task is (19, 17, 15). That is to say, 19 workers answered "positive", 17 workers answered "natural" and 15 workers answered "negative". The three options of the task received a similar number of responses. It shows that the task caused great controversy among the workers. It indicates that the task is difficult to estimate the correct answer. We divide tasks into binary task and multi-task, and express the difficulty of tasks according to response set of task, respectively.

In the binary task (tasks with two options), the response set of the task is (v_1, v_2). We use the ratio of the number of answers received by the two options to express the task difficulty. That is, the ratio of a small number to a large number of responses received with two options.

$$d_t = \frac{min(v_1, v_2)}{max(v_1, v_2)} \tag{1}$$

In this way, the task difficulty is controlled between 0 and 1. When the value of task difficulty is 0, it is the easiest to distinguish the answer for the representative task. When the value of task difficulty is 1, the task is the most controversial and the most difficult to estimate the true answer.

Example 3. For example, a task receives 10 responses, in which 2 workers answered 0/no and 8 workers answered 1/yes. Then the value of task difficulty is 0.25.

In multi-task (i.e. the number of task options is greater than two), the task has K options $\{1, 2, 3...k\}$, then the task receives a response set $(v_1, v_2, v_3...v_k)$. We know that variance is a measure of the degree of confusion in a set of numbers. However. if we simply use the variance of the task response set to indicate the difficulty of the task, sometimes there will be some errors. Let's see the following example: a group of tasks $\{t_1, t_2\}$ with three options. The response set of task t1 is (1, 2, 6) and the response set of task t_2 is (1, 5, 6). According to variance formula, the difficulty values of both tasks are 14, and we can easily see that task t_2 is more difficult than task t_1.

Therefore, we propose a difficulty representation method suitable for crowd-sourcing multi-task. In the task response set, the higher degree of the most supported option is, the easier task can identify the true answer.

$$d_t = \sqrt{\frac{(\frac{v_1}{max\{v\}})^2 + (\frac{v_2}{max\{v\}})^2 + ... + (\frac{v_k}{max\{v\}})^2}{k}} \tag{2}$$

We represent task difficulty by the average sum of squares of the ratio of the number of responses received by each option to the highest number of responses. Similarly, task difficulty ranges from 0 to 1. The greater the value of d, the more difficult the task is. When $d = 1$, the task is the most controversial and the most difficult to estimate the true answer.

4.2   Worker Quality Distribution Function

There is a negative correlation between the quality of workers and the difficulty of tasks, that is, the more difficult the task is, the lower the reliability of workers. Here, we assume that the relationship between worker's reliability and task difficulty is bell-shaped distribution. The distribution function is as follows:

$$Q(d) = \mu + e^{-\delta d^2} \qquad (3)$$

The worker quality distribution model can describe worker's quality characteristics more vividly than other worker model. For example, a worker w_1 completes a binary task t_1 with response set $(4, 1)$. If we use a fixed value such as accuracy to represent worker quality. No matter how difficult the task is, the reliability of worker is 0.7. In fact, the worker's reliability may be 0.8 when answering simple tasks. Therefore, the worker quality distribution model can describe the worker's characteristics in more details.

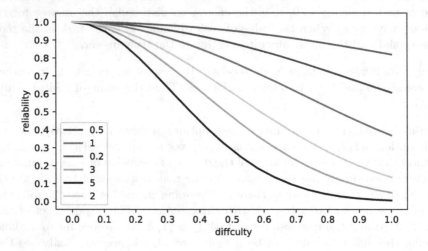

Fig. 1. Worker model

In the Fig. 1, the ordinates indicate the quality of the worker (that is, the ability to answer questions correctly). Where $\mu = 0$, the value of δ is constantly changing. From the figure, we can see that the smaller the value of δ, the smaller the impact of task difficulty on the quality of workers. And the parameters of each worker's quality distribution model are different.

5   Inference Algorithm

After we get the response r_t^w of workers $\{w\}$ to tasks $\{t\}$. We use maximum likelihood estimation to estimate the parameters of the worker model and the true answer to the task. We assume that all worker's responses are independent, then our goal is to maximize the likelihood function.

$$argmax_{z_t, d_t, q_w} \prod_{t,w} p(r_w^t | z_t) \qquad (4)$$

5.1   Parameter Estimation Method

Here we use EM method to obtain maximum likelihood estimates of the parameters. EM method iteratively estimates the parameters of worker quality model and true answers of tasks through E-step and M-step. We know that EM algorithm needs initial parameters. Here, the initial parameter input of EM is task answer or worker model parameter. The initial answers of tasks can be obtained by the rule of majority voting; the initial parameters of the worker quality model can be set to the worker of good quality.

E-step. We get the response r_t^w of workers $\{w\}$ to tasks $\{t\}$. We estimate the probability of the true answer z_t of the task according to the values of the parameters of the worker quality model derived by M-step.

$$P(z^t | r, d, \mu, \delta) = P(z^t | r_t^w, d_t, \mu_w, \delta_w)$$
$$\propto p(z_t) \prod_w p(r_t^w | z^t, d_t, \mu_w, \delta_w) \qquad (5)$$

M-step. We maximize the expectation of likelihood function L log-Likelihood to estimate the parameters of worker quality model δ and μ based on the estimation of the answers to tasks derived by E-step and the workers' responses to tasks.

$$\mathbb{E}(\ln L) = \mathbb{E}\left[\ln p(z, r, d | \mu, \delta)\right]$$
$$= \mathbb{E}\left[\ln \prod_t \left(p(z_t) \prod_w p(r_t^w | z_t, d_t, \mu_w, \delta_w)\right)\right] \qquad (6)$$

Since there are many unobserved variables (z, δ and μ) in the expectation of likelihood function. We estimate the parameters of the worker quality model δ and μ by a fitting algorithm(in Sect. 5.2) based on our worker quality distribution function and the estimation of the answers of tasks derived by E-step.

5.2   Fitting Algorithm for Worker Distribution Model

In our worker quality distribution model, each worker's reliability varies when he or she completes tasks with different difficulty. And reliability of workers will be affected differently by task difficulty. We propose a fitting algorithm (show in Algorithm 1) to derive the parameters of worker quality distribution model. Next, we describe the process of fitting the worker quality distribution function in detail.

Step 1: Finding the discrete data points of each worker model. In the previous chapter, we describe the representation method of task difficulty (i.e. independent variables) in the model. We use the response set of each task to indirectly represent the difficulty of the task. In addition, the reliability of the worker's response to the task represents the worker's ability (i.e. dependent variable).

Step 2: Clustering the discrete points in each worker's quality model. The purpose is to take some outliers into account as well. Because each worker completes many tasks with different difficulties, the data points in the model may be too scattered and there are many abnormal points. As a result, it is difficult to fit the worker model that best fits the characteristics of workers. So, we cluster the discrete data points to find some centroids that best reflect the characteristics of workers. When clustering, we will limit the corresponding task difficulty of data points in the same cluster to a centroid.

Step 3: We use the least square method to fit a curve closest to the worker's quality distribution function according to the centroids obtained by clustering, and get the parameters of each worker quality distribution model.

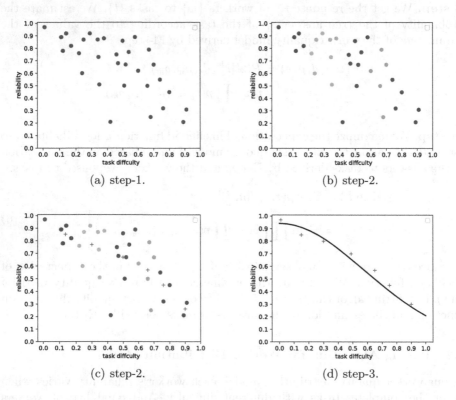

(a) step-1.   (b) step-2.

(c) step-2.   (d) step-3.

Fig. 2. An example of fitting algorithm (Color figure online)

The Fig. 2 shows an example of fitting worker quality model. In the Fig. 2(a), green points represent discrete data points. Figure 2(b) shows the results of our clustering, in which different color points represent different clusters. The red points in Fig. 2(c) represent centroid points obtained by clustering, and Fig. 2(d) shows the worker quality model fitted according to centroid points.

Algorithm 1. Fitting Algorithm.

Input: response set of task, M_t; reliability of worker, Q_w;
Output: Parameters of worker quality model μ, δ;
1: Model task difficulty d_t based on M_t;
2: discrete data points $\{(d_t, Q_w)\}$
3: Initialize k centroids $\{c\}$;
4: **if** cluster of any point changes **then**
5:     **for** each point(d_t, Q_w) **do**
6:         **for** each centroid c **do**
7:             Calculate the Distance between centroid c and point (d_t, Q_w);
8:             Put point into the nearest cluster;
9:         **for** each cluster **do**
10:            new centroid $c \leftarrow$ mean of points;
11:        **end for**
12:    **end for**
13: **end for**
14: **end if**
15: $\mu, \delta \leftarrow$ least squares method with centroids $\{c\}$;
16: **return** μ, δ;

In the fitting algorithm, We first compute all discrete data points in the worker model. Then we cluster the discrete data points to find some centroids that best reflect the characteristics of workers. The time complexity of clustering is related to the number of discrete data points, $O(n)$. At last, we use the least square method to estimate the parameters of each worker quality distribution model.

6 Experiment

In the experimental part, we evaluate our method (WDM) with a set of real-world data and synthetic data, and we compare our method with other algorithms (MV, DS [12], KOS [33], Zen [32]) that are also estimating the true answer of tasks and worker quality.

6.1 Synthetic Data Experiments

In the synthetic experiment, we use a set of data generated by the model itself to explore the performance of our method. In this case, we can know the real values of the parameters of the worker model and the true answers of the tasks. We compare our method with other four algorithms on accuracy of task true answer estimation. In addition, we also evaluate the similarity between estimated and actual parameters of the worker quality model.

Data Generation. In the process of generating synthetic data, we first generate a set of ture answers to tasks. Given a fixed probability value u, we assign a real answer to each task. The probability of task answer 1 is u, and vice versa, the probability is $(1 - u)$. For each task, we set a difficulty value between 0–1. Then, we generate a different worker quality curve for each worker, i. e. setting the parameters of each worker model, the constraints generated are that most workers (more than 90%) are better than random ones. Then, we generate the corresponding workers'responses to the tasks according to the quality of these workers and the difficulty of the task. In the synthetic data, we set the total number of tasks $n = 1000$ and total number of workers $m = 100$, then vary the number of responses received by each task and the number of tasks completed by each worker.

Experimental Process and Results. We evaluate our method on estimating task true answers and parameters of worker quality model. We know that EM algorithm needs to be inputted a set of initial parameters. Here, we set the worker quality $\mu = 0$ and $\delta = 0.5$ as the initial parameters to carry out experiments. We conducted experiments with multiple combinations of data: setting 1, each task receives s response, the total number of workers $m > s$; setting 2, each worker completes h tasks, and each task receives a different number of responses from workers.

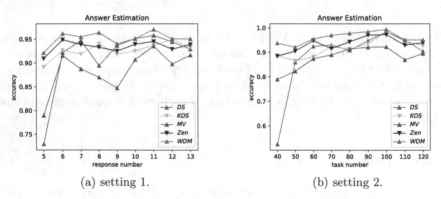

(a) setting 1.   (b) setting 2.

Fig. 3. True answer of task estimation

True Answer of Task Estimation. In Fig. 3(a), (b), we plot the accuracy of task truth estimation, and each algorithm correctly estimates the score of task answer (the higher the score, the better). Here, our strategy estimates the true answer of the task with higher accuracy than other algorithms.

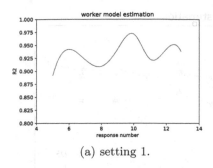
(a) setting 1.

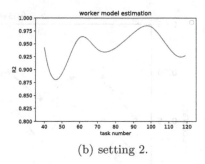
(b) setting 2.

Fig. 4. Worker quality model estimation

Worker Quality Model Estimation. Figure 4(a) and (b) show the gap between estimated and actual worker quality. We calculated the coefficient of determination R^2 (the higher the score, the better) between the estimated worker quality model and the actual worker quality. We observe that the similarity between our estimated worker model and the real worker model is generally high, and with the increase of data, the accuracy of worker quality estimation is on the rise.

Summary. In the synthetic data experiments, our method is superior to other algorithms on estimation for task true answer. In addition, our method can accurately estimate the parameters of the worker quality model.

6.2   Real-World Data Experiments

In our real-world data experiments, data is collecting by publishing a large number of movie reviews as emotional analysis tasks on AMT. The workers on the platform will complete these emotional analysis tasks, that is, to judge whether the movie reviews express positive or negative emotions, and finally collect the responses of workers to the tasks. The data contains a total of 5,000 tasks, which were responsed by about 200 workers.

Experimental Process and Results. In real data experiments, we know the real answers of tasks, but we can not know the real quality of workers in real data. And we randomly extract data from real data sets in three different ways. For each data setting, we compare our method with four algorithms in the accuracy of task true answer estimation.

Data setting 1: We randomly select a certain number of workers from all workers in the data, then select all the response data of these workers, and we constantly change the number of workers selected. In the Fig. 5, we plot the accuracy of task true answer estimation (the higher the score, the better) returned by our method and four other algorithms on varying the number of worker. We observe that our method obtains more accurate estimation results than other methods.

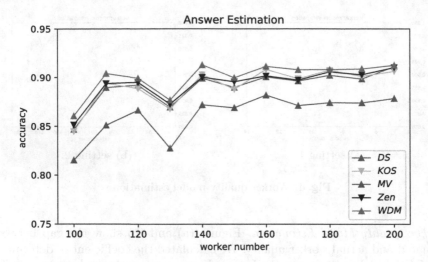

Fig. 5. Data setting 1: true answer of task estimation

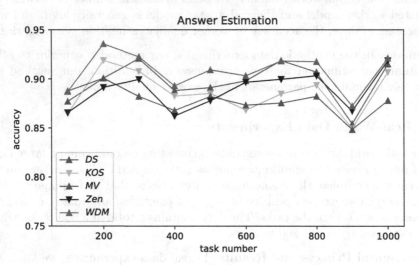

Fig. 6. Data setting 2: true answer of task estimation

Data setting 2: We randomly select a certain number of tasks from all tasks in the data, then extract all the responses received by these tasks, we constantly change the number of tasks extracted. The Fig. 6 shows the accuracy of task truth estimation returned by our method and four other algorithms on varying the number of task. Here, again, our method returns more accurate estimation results in the case of different numbers of tasks.

Data setting 3: We randomly sample a certain number of labels from all data, then we constantly change the number of labels extracted. The Fig. 7 shows the results of comparing our method with four other answer estimation algorithms on

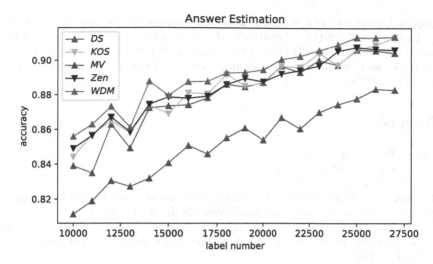

Fig. 7. Data setting 3: true answer of task estimation

varying the number of label. We observe that our method obtain more accurate estimation results than other methods.

Summary. From the results of experiments, we observe that our method always returns more accurate results on the three data setting. And the richer the worker's response data is, the better the estimation result of our method is. Although we can not know the real quality of workers, we believe that our method with worker quality distribution model can estimate the characteristics of workers more accurately.

7 Conclusion

In crowdsourcing, quality management is an important problem because of the uneven ability of workers on internet. The quality of workers can influence the results of crowdsourcing. And the quality of workers will be affected by the difficulty of the task. The more difficult the task is, the lower probability that workers can correctly answer the task. We propose a dynamic difficulty-sensitive worker quality distribution model to improve the quality of results from crowdsourcing. Our model more accurately describes the relationship between worker reliability and task difficulty. We conduct extensive experiments with synthetic data and real-world data. The results show that our method has higher accuracy of task answer estimation than other algorithms. Moreover, our worker quality distribution model can not only describe the characteristics of workers more accurately, but also predict the reliability of workers in tasks they have not done. In the future work, our worker quality distribution model can be applied to other studies of crowdsourcing, such as task allocation. We can assign tasks to the suitable workers based on our worker quality distribution model as the task states change dynamically.

Acknowledgements. The research work was supported by the National Key R&D Program ($No.\,2017YFB1400100$), the Innovation Method Fund of China ($No.\,2018IM020200$), the SDNFSC ($No.\,ZR2017ZB0420, No.\,ZR2018MF014$) and the Science and Technology Development Plan Project of Shandong Province ($No.\,2018YFJH0506$).

References

1. https://www.mturk.com/
2. http://www.crowdflower.com
3. https://www.upwork.com
4. Heymann, P., Garcia-Molina, H.: Turkalytics: analytics for human computation. In: International Conference on World Wide Web DBLP (2011)
5. Wang, H., Guo, S., Cao, J., et al.: MeLoDy: a long-term dynamic quality-aware incentive mechanism for crowdsourcing. IEEE Trans. Parallel Distrib. Syst. **PP**(99), 1 (2018)
6. Hu, H., Zheng, Y., Bao, Z., et al.: Crowdsourced POI labelling: location-aware result inference and task assignment. In: IEEE International Conference on Data Engineering, pp. 61–72. IEEE (2016)
7. Ma, F., Li, Y., Li, Q., et al.: FaitCrowd: fine grained truth discovery for crowdsourced data aggregation. In: ACM SIGKDD International Conference on Knowledge Discovery and Data Mining, pp. 745–754. ACM (2015)
8. Liu, X., Lu, M., Ooi, B.C., Shen, Y., Wu, S., Zhang, M.: CDAS: a crowdsourcing data analytics system. PVLDB **5**(10), 1040–1051 (2012)
9. Bo, P., Lee, L.: Seeing stars: exploiting class relationships for sentiment categorization with respect to rating scales, pp. 115–124 (2005)
10. Cao, C.C., She, J., Tong, Y., et al.: Whom to ask?: jury selection for decision making tasks on micro-blog services. Proc. VLDB Endowment **5**(11), 1495–1506 (2012)
11. Dalvi, N.N., Dasgupta, A., Kumar, R., et al.: Aggregating crowdsourced binary ratings, pp. 285–294 (2013)
12. Dawid, A.P., Skene, A.M.: Maximum likelihood estimation of observer error-rates using the EM algorithm. J. Roy. Stat. Soc. **28**(1), 20–28 (1979)
13. Dempster, A.P., Laird, N.M., Rubin, D.B.: Maximum likelihood from incomplete data via the EM algorithm. J. Roy. Stat. Soc. **39**(1), 1–38 (1977)
14. Feng, J., Feng, J., Feng, J., et al.: QASCA: a quality-aware task assignment system for crowdsourcing applications. In: ACM SIGMOD International Conference on Management of Data, pp. 1031–1046. ACM (2015)
15. Guo, S., Parameswaran, A., Garcia-Molina, H.: So who won?: dynamic max discovery with the crowd. In: ACM SIGMOD International Conference on Management of Data, pp. 385–396. ACM (2012)
16. Ipeirotis, P.G., Provost, F., Wang, J.: Quality management on Amazon mechanical turk. In: ACM SIGKDD Workshop on Human Computation, pp. 64–67. ACM (2010)
17. Karger, D.R., Oh, S., Shah, D.: Iterative learning for reliable crowdsourcing systems. In: International Conference on Neural Information Processing Systems, pp. 1953–1961. Curran Associates Inc. (2011)
18. Karger, D.R., Oh, S., Shah, D.: Efficient crowdsourcing for multi-class labeling. ACM Sigmetrics Perform. Eval. Rev. **41**(1), 81–92 (2013)

19. Kuncheva, L.I., Whitaker, C.J., Shipp, C.A., et al.: Limits on the majority vote accuracy in classifier fusion. Pattern Anal. Appl. 6(1), 22–31 (2003)
20. Liu, X., Lu, M., Ooi, B.C., et al.: CDAS: a crowdsourcing data analytics system. Proc. VLDB Endowment 5(10), 1040–1051 (2012)
21. Marcus, A., Wu, E., Karger, D., et al.: Human-powered sorts and joins. Proc. VLDB Endowment 5(1), 13–24 (2011)
22. Kurve, A., Miller, D.J., Kesidis, G.: Multicategory crowdsourcing accounting for variable task difficulty, worker skill, and worker intention. IEEE Trans. Knowl. Data Eng. 27(3), 794–809 (2015)
23. Parameswaran, A.G., Garciamolina, H., Park, H., et al.: CrowdScreen: algorithms for filtering data with humans, pp. 361–372 (2012)
24. Raykar, V.C., Yu, S., Zhao, L.H., et al.: Supervised learning from multiple experts: whom to trust when everyone lies a bit. In: International Conference on Machine Learning, ICML 2009, Montreal, Quebec, Canada, pp. 889–896. DBLP, June 2009
25. Sarawagi, S., Bhamidipaty, A.: Interactive deduplication using active learning. In: Proceedings ACM SIGKDD Conference on Knowledge Discovery and Data Mining, pp. 269–278 (2002)
26. Das Sarma, A., Parameswaran, A., Widom, J.: Towards globally optimal crowdsourcing quality management: the uniform worker setting, pp. 47–62 (2016)
27. Smyth, P., Fayyad, U., Burl, M., et al.: Inferring ground truth from subjective labelling of venus images. In: International Conference on Neural Information Processing Systems, pp. 1085–1092. MIT Press (1994)
28. Wang, J., Kraska, T., Franklin, M.J., et al.: CrowdER: crowdsourcing entity resolution. Proc. VLDB Endowment 5(11), 1483–1494 (2012)
29. Wang, J., Li, G., Kraska, T., et al.: Leveraging transitive relations for crowdsourced joins. In: ACM SIGMOD International Conference on Management of Data, pp. 229–240. ACM (2013)
30. Whitehill, J., Ruvolo, P., Wu, T., et al.: Whose vote should count more: optimal integration of labels from labelers of unknown expertise. In: International Conference on Neural Information Processing Systems, pp. 2035–2043. Curran Associates Inc. (2009)
31. Zhang, Y., Chen, X., Zhou, D., et al.: Spectral methods meet EM: a provably optimal algorithm for crowdsourcing. Adv. Neural Inf. Process. Syst. 2, 1260–1268 (2014)
32. Demartini, G., Difallah, D.E., CudréMauroux, P.: ZenCrowd: leveraging probabilistic reasoning and crowdsourcing techniques for large-scale entity linking. In: International Conference on World Wide Web. ACM (2012)
33. Karger, D.R., Oh, S., Shah, D.: Iterative learning for reliable crowd-sourcing systems. In: NIPS, pp. 1953–1961 (2011)

Priority-Based Optimization of I/O Isolation for Hybrid Deployed Services

Jiancheng Zhang[1,2], Youhuizi Li[1,2(✉)], Li Zhou[1,2], Zujie Ren[3], Jian Wan[1,4], and Yuan Wang[5]

[1] Key Laboratory of Complex Systems Modeling and Simulation, Ministry of Education, Hangzhou Dianzi University, Hangzhou, China
{huizi,zhouli}@hdu.edu.cn
[2] School of Computer Science and Technology, Hangzhou Dianzi University, Hangzhou, China
[3] Zhejiang Lab, Hangzhou, China
renzj@hdu.edu.cn
[4] School of Information and Electronic Engineering, Zhejiang University of Science and Technology, Hangzhou, China
wanjian@zust.edu.cn
[5] Key Enterprise Research Institute of NetEase Big Data of Zhejiang Province, Netease Hangzhou, Network Co.Ltd, Hangzhou, China

Abstract. With the increasing of software complexity and user demands, collaborative service is becoming more and more popular. Each service focuses on its own specialty, their cooperation can support complicated task with high efficiency. To improve the resources utilization, virtualization technology like container is used and it enables multiple services running in the same physical machine. However, since the host physical machine is shared by several services, the resource competition is inevitable. Isolation is an effective solution, but the weak isolation mechanisms of container cannot handle such complicated scenarios. In the worst situation, the performance of services cannot meet the requirements and the system may crash. In order to solve this problem, we propose a priority-based optimization mechanism for I/O isolation after analyzing the characteristics of typical service workloads. Based on the real-time performance data, priority is automatically assigned to each service and corresponding optimization methods are applied. We evaluate the optimization effects of the priority-based mechanism in both static and dynamic workload cases, besides, the influence of different priority order is also analyzed. The experimental results show that our approach can indeed improve the system performance and guarantee the requirements of all the running services are satisfied.

Supported in part by the Natural Science Foundation of Zhejiang Province under Grant LQ18F020003 and Grant LY18F020014, and in part by the Natural Science Foundation of China under Grant 61802093 and Grant 61572163, in part by the Xi'an Key Laboratory of Mobile Edge Computing and Security (201805052-ZD3CG36) and in part by the Key Research and Development Program of Zhejiang Province under Grant 2018C01098.

Keywords: Priority-based · I/O isolation · Container ·
Hybrid deployment

1 Introduction

With the development of the Internet and computing technology, one service
cannot support the various requirements of users, especially when applications
are becoming more and more complex. For example, the web services nowadays
are often composed of multiple sub-services such as location, video and communication to satisfy users' demands [5]. The cost of developing and maintaining
a "perfect" application/service that has all the functions that users request will
be huge. Hence, collaborative service is applied [18,21]. Each service is responsible for a small portion, the workload is decomposed and distributed to several
services. By cooperating with each other and sharing intermediate data and
resources, the complex task can be finished efficiently. Single service normally is
simple and the resources requirement is low. To improve the resources utilization
of servers, multiple services are deployed on a same physical machine. If these
services are working on a same task, they can use memory/disk to transmit the
data instead of network, which also further improves the service performance
and security.

Virtualization is used to support multiple services running in one physical
server. Container [1,4], as a lightweight virtualization technology which does
not pack the guest operating system, is widely used since it provides high
resources utilization and low overhead. Although we deploy multiple services
in one machine, the services themselves are independent, even they may work
together. To make sure their execution are normal and not influenced by others,
there should be strict resource isolation mechanisms. However, container mainly
relies on the original Namespace and the Cgroups of the Linux to provide isolation feature [16,20]. It cannot properly handle the severe competition situations.
Besides, the workload and functionality of collaborative services are various, the
different behavior/requirements of the services make the resource competition
even more complicated. The worst case is that the requirements of most services
cannot be satisfied and the system will crash. Hence, there is a great challenge
to cope with the resource isolation and performance optimization for hybrid
deployed services.

Existing isolation optimization methods mainly target homogeneous deployment scenario, that is, the deployed services have the same type of performance requirements. So, single optimization method is enough to protect all
services. For latency-sensitive services, the commonly used approaches are sending requests repeatedly and rate limiting [3,9,12,17,19,22,23]. For throughput-
first services, disk allocation and I/O concurrency control are applied [2,6–8,10].
Asides from one-dimensional (latency or throughput) performance restriction,
there are also services that require both metrics to meet the standards. The optimization method [11] is more conservative, and the resources utilization is relatively low. This two-dimensional services situation still belongs to homogeneous

case since all the services are the same type. Hence, the aforementioned solutions can only handle specific type of services, and they are not appropriate for hybrid deployment scenario. In addition, our previous work PINE [13] can cope with one latency-sensitive service plus multiple throughput-first services scenario. It classifies services according to their performance indicators and applies different optimization methods accordingly. By leveraging the idle server resource of a latency-sensitive service (when its workload is light), the enterprise can support other throughput-first services to make extra profits. However, it cannot be guaranteed that PINE also works for multiple latency-sensitive services and multiple throughput services scenario which usually happens in collaborate services.

In this paper, we extend PINE and propose an priority-based I/O isolation optimization mechanism which targets more general hybrid deployed scenarios. First, according to the services characteristics, different optimization methods are applied. For examples, adjusting the I/O concurrency level for latency-sensitive services, and modifying disk allocation for throughput-first services. Then, to support the execution of multiple latency-sensitive services, a prioritization algorithm is developed. The latency-sensitive services are sorted based on their influence to the whole system, and the optimization method is applied accordingly to maintain the status. As far as we know, this optimization mechanism is the first method that effectively handles hybrid deployment scenario and ensures that each service can meet its requirements.

The rest of this paper is organized as follows. Section 2 reviews the related work in the performance optimization field. Section 3 analyzes the characteristics of the hybrid deployment scenario and illustrates the priority-based optimization mechanism. Section 4 comprehensively evaluates the optimization effects and the performance of the prioritization algorithm. Section 5 summarizes the paper and describes the future work.

2   Related Work

Performance optimization is a popular research topic in recent years, especially with the widely-spread virtualization technology. According to the type of the deployed services, previous researches can be divided into the following three categories: one-dimensional homogeneous services, two-dimensional homogeneous services, and single hybrid heterogeneous services.

One-Dimensional Homogeneous Services Scenario: The most common types of performance indicators are 99.9th percentile latency and throughput. The services in this scenario have either latency or throughput as their requirements. For latency-sensitive services, there are three optimization method: (1) Modifying the queue scheduling strategy of the Linux kernel. Li *et al.* [12] believed that the FIFO is a more friendly scheduling strategy for 99.9th percentile latency. (2) Sending requests redundantly to reduce the blocking possibility. Google [3] proposed that the same request can be sent redundantly, and the fastest response will be take. The latency is improved as a result of resource overuse. (3) Integrated scheduling. Wang *et al.* [19] designed Cake, a multi-layer optimization framework, to efficiently schedule several resources together so the performance can be improved. For throughput-first services, disk resource allocation is the commonly used optimization approach. Gulati *et al.* [8] proposed mClock, which sets the upper and lower disk threshold based on the service requirements in advance, to control the disk resource. In one-dimensional homogeneous services scenario, the optimization methods only work for single type of services (latency or throughput), it cannot handle hybrid deployment scenario and will inevitably leads to part of the services failed.

Two-Dimensional Homogeneous Services Scenarios: All the services' type in this scenario are also the same, but each service can contain two performance indicators (latency and throughput) instead of one. The PSLO framework [11] exactly targets this situation. It satisfies the latency and throughput requirements of each service by controlling the I/O rate and concurrency level. However, since there is an obvious trade-off between latency and throughput in some cases, PSLO provides a boundary curve which describes this relationship. If the resource competition is too fierce that exceeds the boundary curve, PSLO will not take any action. Besides, the optimization strategy of PSLO is also conservative, and the resource utilization is relatively low. Hence, the optimization method used in this scenario cannot cope with hybrid deployment either.

Single Hybrid Heterogeneous Services Scenario: In this scenario, services with different requirements are deployed together, specifically, only one service can have a "special" type of requirements that different with all others. For example, one latency-sensitive service with multiple throughput-first services. PINE [13] is developed to handle this scenario, it achieves latency optimization through adjusting I/O concurrency level and throughput optimization using disk allocation. As a result, all services can satisfy their performance requirements. However, PINE has over-optimization problem and resource utilization degradation issue when multiple latency-sensitive services exist.

After analyzing the existing related works, we plan to propose an optimization mechanism which ultimate goal is to efficiently handle general multiple hybrid deployment situations and guarantee all the services' requirements can be satisfied as much as possible.

3   Priority-Based Optimization Mechanism

In this section, we first discuss the general service types in the hybrid deployment scenario, then the performance interference and existing optimization methods are analyzed. Following that, we illustrate the prioritization algorithm and priority-based optimization mechanism.

3.1   Service Type

After analyzing modern collaborative services, we summarized mainly two types of services: latency-sensitive service and throughput-first service.

Latency-Sensitive Service: With the developing of Internet, the response time becomes a critical data that directly influence the user experience, especially for social media service, search engines, online maps [14]. To improve the performance, services normally will split the request to several sub-requests and execute in a parallel way. So, the response time is defined by the longest task. Compare with the average latency, the 99.9th percentile latency is selected as the performance metric for latency-sensitive services. The execution of latency-sensitive services are usually thread-driven or event-driven. Thread-driven services use synchronous blocking I/O and generate a new thread for each new user's I/O request, while event-driven services apply asynchronous non-blocking I/O and handle all I/O requests by several worker threads. The I/O processing speed of a server is commonly fast until there are many request pending. The latency will be amplified in the 99.9th percentile metric, even the interference is very small, which leads to latency performance violation.

Throughput-First Service: Services that need to process batch jobs pay more attention to throughput, such as analyzing working logs [15]. These services can be delayed occasionally or restarted over time. The throughput is the main metric that user cares most, which is decided by the available disk bandwidth. When the disk resource of a service is enough, it can achieve the reasonable performance requirements. If the resource competition is severe, other services may malicious occupy the shared disk, which leads to the failure of the throughput-first service.

3.2   Performance Interference in Hybrid Deployment Scenario

In real usage scenarios, services that deployed on a same physical machine are randomly selected. We target at general hybrid deployed situations where several types of services may mix together and each type also can have multiple services running. Hence, the interference exists in different types of services, and the resource competition also comes from other same-type services. To analyze the performance influence, we did the following experiments. MySQL represents latency-sensitive service, which enables 64 threads to read and write 10 tables together (the initial IO concurrency level is 64); Hadoop MapReduce as the throughput-first service executes the MapReduce operation for 100 files.

Latency-Sensitive Service: Figure 1(a) shows the latency comparison under three cases: running alone, mixed with MapReduce (different service type) and mixed with MySQL (same service type). In the mixed with MapReduce case, the workload of MySQL is constant and the workload of MapReduce gradually increases. Similarly, in the mixed with MySQL case, the workload of one MySQL service increases. The results show that there is no obvious difference of the three cases when the disk bandwidth usage is low (e.g. 50%, 60%, and 70%), which means the competition of disk resource is not intense. While the disk usage rate rises to 80% or more, there is a great delay in mixed cases. The 99.9th percentile latency of MySQL in the mixed with MapReduce case is nearly 6 times higher than running alone, and it is 8 times in the mixed with MySQL case when the disk usage was close to 100%. Hence, the loss of performance will be significant

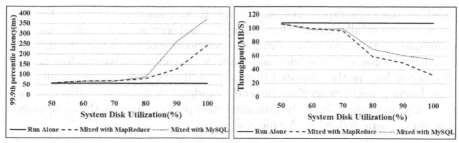

(a) Performance comparison of latency-sensitive services.

(b) Performance comparison of throughput-first services.

Fig. 1. Performance interference in hybrid deployment scenario.

when the disk usage reaches a threshold (like 80% in this experiment), and the impact of the same-type services is greater than different types of services for latency-sensitive services.

Throughput-First Service: The configurations are same with the previous experiments except that the position of MapReduce and MySQL is interchanged, and we focused on the throughput of MapReduce. As the Fig. 1(b) presented, the performance trend of MapReduce was similar with previous MySQL's. The influence of disk resource competition became significant when the disk utilization is around 70%, and the impact of the same type of service is also greater.

The two experiments show that the impact of disk resource competition on service performance will suddenly increase after the system disk utilization reaches a certain threshold. Both latency-sensitive services and throughput-first services will be interfered by the same-type and different types of services, and the influence from same-type services is more serious.

3.3 Existing Isolation Method

To handle the single hybrid heterogeneous services scenario, PINE applies I/O concurrency control for latency-sensitive services and disk resource allocation for throughput-first services. In this section, we first analyze whether the above two optimization methods are still feasible in general hybrid deployed scenarios (multiple hybrid heterogeneous services scenario). Since the limitation of the I/O concurrency control method is illustrated in [13], we focus on the disk allocation method and the combination of the two methods.

Disk Allocation: Docker creates virtual device and assigns distinct device number for each container, so Cgroups can be used to implement disk allocation method. Based on the throughput requirements of the services, we can perform an overall disk resource partition at the operating system level. Throughput-first services can get their own share, which decreases the performance interference caused by the same-type services. For the latency-sensitive services, Cgroups cannot accurately allocate disk for each individual service since they do not have throughput performance value. From the perspective of container, the influence of single latency-sensitive service and multiple latency-sensitive services have no difference as long as the allocated disk is fixed. So the disk resource is allocated for all latency-sensitive services instead of individual latency-sensitive service. Hence, Cgroups can effectively guarantee the performance of throughput-first services in general hybird deployment scenario.

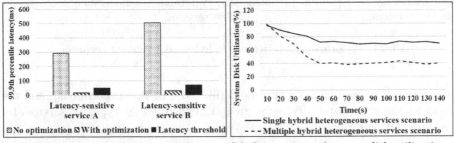

(a) Comparison of 99.9th percentile latency. (b) Comparison of system disk utilization.

Fig. 2. Optimization comparison in hybrid deployed scenarios.

Combination of I/O Concurrency Control and Disk Allocation: After allocating disk resource using Cgroups for each throughput-first service and the group of all latency-sensitive services, the I/O concurrency control algorithm in PINE is applied to each latency-sensitive service. There are two latency-sensitive services (A and B) in the experiment, the optimization comparison results are shown in Fig. 2(a). Comparing with the no optimization case, the I/O concurrency control method successfully decreased the latency of service A and B. After several iteration intervals, the 99.9th percentile latency of service A and B are around 16 ms and 31 ms respectively, which is much lower than the required latency value. However, with the same experimental configuration, the latency value in the single hybrid heterogeneous services scenario is close to its standard latency requirement. To figure out the behind reason, we analyzed the system disk utilization in the two scenarios. Figure 2(b) shows that the disk utilization decreases to a stable value after applying the optimization method in both cases. In the single hybrid heterogeneous services scenario, the disk utilization dropped to around 70%, which is 30% more than the multiple hybrid heterogeneous services scenario. The results indicate that PINE sacrifices the resource utilization to guarantee the latency. But it over-optimized, the latency is less than 50% of the required value. Hence, this method is not appropriate for general hybrid deployed scenarios.

Analysis: In general hybrid deployed scenarios, there are two levels of resource competition: different-type service competition and same-type service. For throughput-first services, their performance directly related to available disk resource. After given fixed disk space, they are total isolated from others (including other throughput-first services and latency-sensitive services) and their performance is also determined. For latency-sensitive services, there is no clear mathematical relationship of I/O concurrency and 99.9th percentile latency. Besides, the allocated disk resource is for all latency-sensitive services. Since the behavior of same-type services are very similar, the resource competition is more intense in this case. As a result, the existing method cannot efficiently handle the same-type service competition of the latency-sensitive services. The I/O concurrency limitation is for all latency-sensitive services, the difference between each service is not considered. So, the over-optimized situation happens. The potential solution is control I/O concurrency of each service one by one. Assuming there are three latency-sensitive services: A, B and C. After we control the I/O concurrency of A, the system needs sometime to react and it also influences the behavior/performance of service B and C. Hence, to eliminate the over-optimization, we can only modify one variable in each iteration and wait for the effects, then decide the next move.

3.4 Prioritization Algorithm

To deal with same-type service competition and over-optimization phenomenon of latency-sensitive services, the asynchronous I/O concurrency control is proposed. If the disk resources of one service changed, it will also influence other services' performance, while the assumption of synchronous I/O concurrency control is the environment keeps constant for all services within the iteration interval. Hence, asynchronous I/O concurrency control method, which considers the interactions of latency-sensitive services and only sets the I/O concurrency level of one service in each iteration, can effectively decrease the optimization time and improve the performance as well as resource utilization.

Prioritization algorithm is designed to automatically select the service whose I/O concurrency should be updated at each iteration interval. The throughput variation after applying the concurrency control is the main factor we consider. If the throughput of a service changes greatly, it will have a huge impact on the shared disk resource, which further influences other latency-sensitive services. Therefore, the idea of the proposed algorithm is that the greater the impact on the disk resource, the higher the priority should be. If concurrency control is applied to small-impact services first, then when it comes to control large-impact services, the latest configuration will total sacrifice the optimized results of small-impact services. Hence, we will adjust the I/O concurrency of the highest priority service, that is, the service whose throughput variation is maximum.

The service throughput variation is decided by the current throughput and the violation degree of 99.9th percentile latency. If the violation degree is high, then the I/O concurrency level control will be stronger, the variation rate of the throughput will be high. Combined with the current throughput value, the throughput variation can be calculated. Assuming L_{cur} represents the current

99.9th percentile latency and L_{SLO} represents the required 99.9th percentile latency, then the violation degree Vio is defined as:

$$Vio = \frac{L_{cur} - L_{SLO}}{L_{SLO}} \tag{1}$$

With the current throughput Th_{cur}, the throughput variation Th_{dif} can be calculated as:

$$Th_{dif} = \frac{Vio}{L_{Now}/L_{SLO}} * Th_{cur} \tag{2}$$

3.5 Priority-Based Optimization Mechanism

Based on the negative feedback regulation, priority-based optimization mechanism collects the performance requirements and real-time data of all running services, then applies the customized optimization strategy according to the difference. The architecture is shown in Fig. 3. The optimization process includes throughput optimization and 99.9th percentile latency optimization. Since it takes some time for the optimization to take effect in the system, the iteration interval of data collection and optimization is set to 10 s based on practical experience.

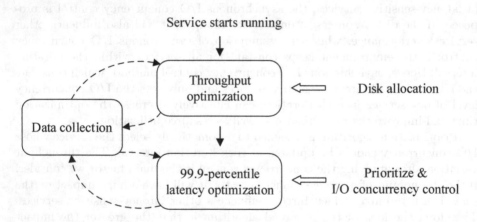

Fig. 3. The architecture of priority-based optimization mechanism.

Throughput-First Services: The performance requirement for this type of services normally is to maintain the throughput above the predefined threshold. As the Fig. 4(a) illustrates, the first step is collecting throughput data. It is necessary to distinguish the different services' traffic since the processes in the container are all running on the host machine. Docker builds a virtual disk volume with an distinct device ID for each container. So, the IOSTAT tool can be used to get the performance data (e.g. IOPS) of each service, and then the real-time throughput value can be calculated. If the throughput does not match the predefined threshold, the violation happens. To control the throughput, Cgroups is leveraged to allocate disk resources for each throughput-first service based on their thresholds.

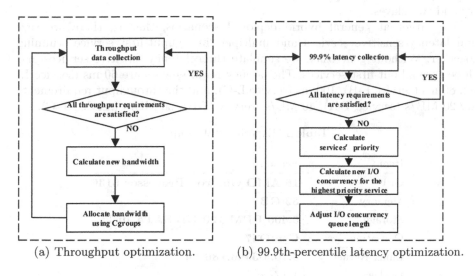

(a) Throughput optimization.   (b) 99.9th-percentile latency optimization.

Fig. 4. The optimization process.

Latency-Sensitive Services: Similar to throughput optimization, Fig. 4(b) describes the process of latency-sensitive services. To calculate the 99.9th percentile latency, the response time of all the requests of the service within the iteration interval is logged. The collected latency is sorted in ascending order, and the data at the 99.9th percentile position in the sequence is tagged as the 99.9th percentile latency of the service. Comparing with the latency threshold, if the violation exists, we need to modify the I/O concurrency level. First, the priority of each service which does not reach the latency requirements is calculated according to the proposed prioritization algorithm. The I/O concurrency level of the highest priority service should be adjusted. The new value of the I/O concurrency level for the next cycle is estimated using a linear fitting equation in a multi-iterate manner. To control the I/O concurrency level, the I/O concurrent queue length of the selected service is set to the calculated new value. If the current number of outstanding requests (i.e., being executed) is less than the queue length, the new request is allowed to enter the queue, otherwise the request is refused.

4   Evaluation

After presenting the experimental setup, we evaluate the optimization effect of the priority-base optimization mechanism and the influence of service priority.

4.1   Experimental Setup

The experimental setup is shown in Table 1, MySQL and Hadoop MapReduce represent 99.9th percentile latency-sensitive service and throughput-first service respectively. The Hadoop cluster is composed of three nodes, including one master and two slaves.

We target at general hybrid deployed scenarios, that is, there are several latency-sensitive services and multiple throughput-first services running together. Without generosity, we simulate three latency-sensitive services and three throughput-first services. The latency requirements are 60 ms (service L-A), 80 ms (service L-B), 100 ms (service L-C), and the throughput requirements are 20 MB/s (service T-A), 40 MB/s (service T-B), 60 MB/s (service T-C).

Table 1. Experimental setup.

Item	Version
CPU	**16 AMD Opteron Processor 6136**
Memory	**32 GB**
Storage	**5,400 RPM 120 GB SATA disks**
Operating System	**CentOS7**
Linux Kernel	**3.10.5-3.el6.x86_64**
Docker	**1.17-ce**
MySQL	**MySQL 5.6**
Hadoop	**Apache Hadoop 1.0**

4.2   Optimization Evaluation

Constant Workload Optimization: All the services' workload are constant in this experiment. The workload of each service is equal to the load amount when the service runs alone and just satisfies its performance requirement. The comparison under the with and without optimization cases is shown in Fig. 5.

Latency-Sensitive Services: As Fig. 5(a) demonstrates, there are serious latency violations of the three latency-sensitive services in the no optimization case. The 99.9th percentile latency of service L-A has reached 243.13 ms, which was 305% worse than its latency threshold (60 ms). The similar situations for service L-B and L-C. On the contrary, the 99.9th percentile latency of the three services can be stabilized at the predefined latency threshold. Taking service L-B as an example, the 99.9th percentile latency was reduced by 65.5% compared to the no optimization case and successfully reached the 60 ms latency requirement.

Throughput-First Service: As Fig. 5(b) shows, there are also serious throughput violations of the three throughput-first services in the no optimization case. Taking service T-A (requirement is 20 MB/s) as an example, its throughput was only 5.42 MB/s, and it is 72.9% lower than the threshold. After applying the optimization, the throughput was stabilized at 21.52 MB/s.

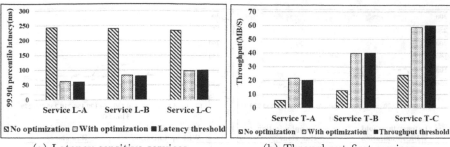

    (a) Latency-sensitive services.   (b) Throughput-first services.

Fig. 5. The performance comparison under constant workload.

The experimental results indicate that the isolation optimization method proposed in this paper can indeed optimize the performance of constant workload services in hybrid deployed scenarios.

Dynamic Workload Optimization: To evaluate the priority-based optimization mechanism in the real-world usage scenarios, we pay more attention to dynamic workload optimization results. The workloads in actual production environment are commonly various with time, especially for latency-sensitive services. Without generosity, the workload changing of the same-type services is happened at the same time, and the transition from non-violation to violation will also occurs simultaneously. In this case, the resources competition is stronger than the workload changes one by one. Besides, based on the previous observation experiments, the performance influence from same-type services is greater than the effects of different-type services. Hence, we dynamically modify the workload of same-type services and the different-type services workload are constant for simplicity.

Latency-Sensitive Services: As can be seen from Fig. 6, there was no latency violation of the three MySQL services due to the low workload before the 30 s. Then the workload increased suddenly to make their 99.9th percentile latency over the thresholds. Take service L-A (threshold is 60 ms) as an example, its 99.9th percentile latency reaches 105.11 ms at the time 30 s. In the with optimization case, the latency dropped back to 60.82 ms after six iteration cycles. The workload increased again at 110 s, which generated another latency violation for all latency-sensitive services. In the with optimization case, the latency of the three services all fall back to the threshold after a few cycles. Hence, no matter how the workload changes, the latency can be kept near the predefined threshold, and even there is a violation, it can also be adjusted back within several iteration cycles. The priority-based optimization mechanism can efficiently cope with the latency-sensitive service isolation problem to guarantee their performance.

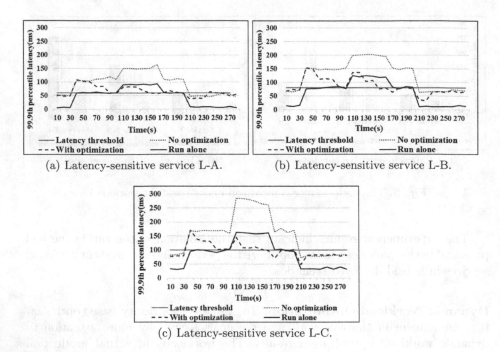

(a) Latency-sensitive service L-A.   (b) Latency-sensitive service L-B.

(c) Latency-sensitive service L-C.

Fig. 6. Performance comparison of latency-sensitive services under dynamic workload.

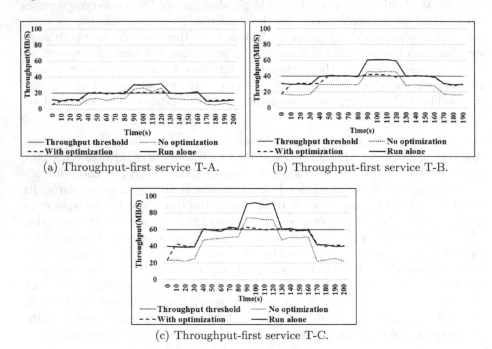

(a) Throughput-first service T-A.   (b) Throughput-first service T-B.

(c) Throughput-first service T-C.

Fig. 7. Performance comparison of throughput-first services under dynamic workload.

Throughput-First Services: Similarly, we modified the workload of the three throughput-first services and keeps latency-sensitive services' constant. As illustrated in Fig. 7, take the service T-A as an example, its throughput was below the threshold due to the low workload in the beginning (before 30 s). Compared to the no optimization case, the throughput in the with optimization case was more close to the value when running alone. When the workload increased and the throughput was higher than the threshold, the optimization mechanism was applied to avoid excessive occupying the resource and the throughput was restricted around the predefined threshold. The experimental results show that the priority-based optimization mechanism can also effectively handle throughput-first services in the hybrid deployed scenarios.

4.3   Priority Influence

To cope with latency-sensitive same-type service competition problem and eliminate over-optimization, we propose prioritization algorithm which assigns priority to each latency-sensitive service based on their impact to the system disk usage and the highest service is selected to apply I/O concurrency control. In this part, we evaluate the influence of different priority sequence on the system performance. Since the priority is calculated for each latency-sensitive service, the experimental configuration is similar to the dynamic workload latency-sensitive services case.

Figure 8 show the performance comparison, we analyzed three cases: Fig. 8(a) uses the order calculated from the proposed prioritization algorithm, Fig. 8(b) does not consider the order and applies I/O control for all latency-services at the same time, and Fig. 8(c) uses the reverse order of Fig. 8(a)'s. In Fig. 8(a), the workload is increased in the 30th second, and the 99.9th percentile latency of the three services took only 2–3 cycles from violation state to normal state. While in Fig. 8(b), it did not consider impact from other same-type services and optimized all three services at the same time, which lead to over-optimization. In order to relief from over-optimization, the system increased the I/O concurrency level. Unfortunately, this action only causes the latency violation in the next cycle. The back and forth process repeatedly happen, and the optimization time is obviously extended. In Fig. 8(c), we actually first controlled the smallest impact latency-sensitive service, service L-A. However, since the impact of service L-A is small, when the system comes to control high impact service, the previous results of modifying service L-A may be affected and service L-A need to be re-optimized again in the subsequent optimization cycle. As a result, although the 99.9th percentile latency of the three latency-sensitive services tends to be stable and reached their respective latency threshold, the optimization cycle is longer compared with Fig. 8(a), and its ability to handle burst high workloads is even worse.

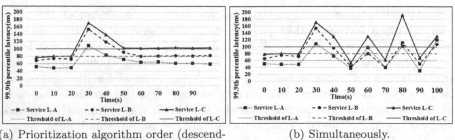

(a) Prioritization algorithm order (descending order).

(b) Simultaneously.

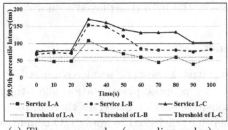

(c) The reverse order (ascending order) .

Fig. 8. The latency comparison under three different priority orders.

In summary, optimizing one latency-sensitive service in each iteration cycle can greatly avoid over-optimization. Besides, applying the optimization based on the impact descending order (calculated according to the prioritization algorithm), the system can effectively decrease the optimization time.

5   Conclusion

To improve the performance of hybrid deployed collaborative services, we focus on the I/O isolation optimization problem. Firstly, we abstract the typical hybrid deployment scenarios by analyzing the execution process and potential interference of collaborative services. Then, we propose a priority-based isolation mechanism, which automatically assigns priority based on the real-time performance data and applies appropriate optimization methods. Comparing with the no-optimization case, for the latency-sensitive services, the 99.9th percentile latency violation can be recovered to the normal value in one or two cycles with a decreasing of 70%; for the throughput-first services, the throughput can achieve 50% higher in one cycle. The experimental results show that the priority-based optimization mechanism can effectively guarantee the performance of hybrid deployed services.

In the future, we will further improve the proposed mechanism from the aspects of more complex usage scenarios, more types of sub-services, optimal priority order and less recovery time.

References

1. Bernstein, D.: Containers and cloud: from LXC to docker to kubernetes. IEEE Cloud Comput. **1**(3), 81–84 (2015)
2. Bruno, J., Brustoloni, J., Gabber, E., Mcshea, M., Silberschatz, A.: Disk scheduling with quality of service guarantees. In: IEEE International Conference on Multimedia Computing & Systems (1999)
3. Dean, J., Barroso, L.A.: The tail at scale. Commun. ACM **56**(2), 74–80 (2013)
4. Felter, W., Ferreira, A., Rajamony, R., Rubio, J.: An updated performance comparison of virtual machines and linux containers. In: IEEE International Symposium on Performance Analysis of Systems & Software (2007)
5. Foster, H., Uchitel, S., Magee, J., Kramer, J.: Model-based verification of web service compositions. In: 18th IEEE International Conference on Automated Software Engineering (ASE 2003), Montreal, Canada, pp. 152–163, 6–10 October 2003. https://doi.org/10.1109/ASE.2003.1240303
6. Gulati, A., Ahmad, I., Waldspurger, C.A.: Parda: proportional allocation of resources for distributed storage access. In: Proceedings of the Conference on File & Storage Technologies (2009)
7. Gulati, A., Shanmuganathan, G., Zhang, X., Varman, P.: Demand based hierarchical QOS using storage resource pools. In: Usenix Conference on Technical Conference (2012)
8. Gulati, A., Varman, P.J.: mClock: handling throughput variability for hypervisor IO scheduling. In: Usenix Conference on Operating Systems Design & Implementation (2011)
9. Jeon, M., et al.: Predictive parallelization: taming tail latencies in web search (2014)
10. Jin, W., Chase, J.S., Kaur, J.: Interposed proportional sharing for a storage service utility. ACM Sigmetrics Perform. Eval. Rev. **32**(1), 37–48 (2004)
11. Li, N., Jiang, H., Feng, D., Shi, Z.: PSLO: enforcing the Xth percentile latency and throughput slos for consolidated VM storage. In: Proceedings of the Eleventh European Conference on Computer Systems, EuroSys 2016, London, United Kingdom, pp. 28:1–28:14, 18–21 April 2016. https://doi.org/10.1145/2901318.2901330
12. Li, N., Jiang, H., Feng, D., Shi, Z.: Customizable slo and its near-precise enforcement for storage bandwidth. ACM Trans. Storage **13**(1), 6 (2017)
13. Li, Y., Zhang, J., Jiang, C., Wan, J., Ren, Z.: Pine: optimizing performance isolation in container environments. IEEE Access **7**, 30410–30422 (2019)
14. Lo, D., Cheng, L., Govindaraju, R., Ranganathan, P.: Heracles: improving resource efficiency at scale. ACM Sigarch Comput. Archit. News **43**(3), 450–462 (2015)
15. Marshall, P., Keahey, K., Freeman, T.: Improving utilization of infrastructure clouds. In: IEEE/ACM International Symposium on Cluster (2011)
16. McDaniel, S., Herbein, S., Taufer, M.: A two-tiered approach to I/O quality of service in docker containers. In: 2015 IEEE International Conference on Cluster Computing, CLUSTER 2015, Chicago, IL, USA, pp. 490–491, 8–11 September 2015. https://doi.org/10.1109/CLUSTER.2015.77
17. Suresh, L., Canini, M., Schmid, S., Feldmann, A.: C3: cutting tail latency in cloud data stores via adaptive replica selection. In: Usenix Conference on Networked Systems Design & Implementation (2015)
18. Touzi, J., Benaben, F., Pingaud, H., Lorré, J.P.: A model-driven approach for collaborative service-oriented architecture design. Int. J. Prod. Econ. **121**(1), 5–20 (2009)

19. Wang, A., Venkataraman, S., Alspaugh, S., Katz, R., Stoica, I.: Cake: enabling high-level SLOs on shared storage systems. In: ACM Symposium on Cloud Computing (2012)
20. Xavier, M.G., Oliveira, I.C.D., Rossi, F.D., Passos, R.D.D., Matteussi, K.J., Rose, C.A.F.D.: A performance isolation analysis of disk-intensive workloads on container-based clouds. In: Euromicro International Conference on Parallel (2015)
21. Li, Y., Zhou, M., You, C., Yang, G., Mei, H.: Enabling on demand deployment of middleware services in componentized middleware. In: Grunske, L., Reussner, R., Plasil, F. (eds.) CBSE 2010. LNCS, vol. 6092, pp. 113–129. Springer, Heidelberg (2010). https://doi.org/10.1007/978-3-642-13238-4_7
22. Zhang, J., Sivasubramaniam, A., Riska, A., Qian, W., Riedel, E.: An interposed 2-level i/o scheduling framework for performance virtualization. In: ACM Sigmetrics International Conference on Measurement & Modeling of Computer Systems (2005)
23. Zhu, T., Tumanov, A., Kozuch, M.A., Harchol-Balter, M., Ganger, G.R.: Prioritymeister: Tail latency QOS for shared networked storage. In: ACM Symposium on Cloud Computing (2014)

Optimal Device Management Service Selection in Internet-of-Things

Weiling Li[1], Yunni Xia[1(✉)], Wanbo Zheng[2,3(✉)], Peng Chen[4], Jia Lee[1], and Yawen Li[1]

[1] School of Computer Science, Chongqing University, Chongqing, China
weilinglicq@outlook.com, xiayunni@hotmail.com, lijia@cqu.edu.cn
[2] Data Science Research Center, Kunming University of Science and Technology, Kunming, China
zwanbo2001@163.com
[3] Faculty of Science, Kunming University of Science and Technology, Kunming, China
[4] School of Computer and Software Engineering, Xihua University, Chengdu, China
Chenpeng1980@163.com

Abstract. In Internet-of-Things (IoT), IoT device management is a challenge for device owners considering the huge amount of devices and their heterogeneous quality of service (QoS) requirements. Recently, IoT device management service (MS) providers are arising to serve device owners. Device owners can now easily manage their devices by using IoT device MSs. It is critical to select suitable MSs from numerous candidates for devices. An optimal service selection must maximize the number of MS managed devices and minimize the total cost while ensuring the QoS requirements of IoT system. To optimize the IoT Device Management Service Selection problem, we propose IDMSS, a Lexicographic Goal Programming (LGP) based approach. However, due to the high computational complexity of the IoT Device Management Service Selection problem, an alternative heuristic-based approach called GA4MSS is proposed. Two series of experiments have been conducted and the experimental results show the performance of our approaches.

Keywords: Internet-of-Things (IoT) · IoT Device Management · Vector bin packing problem · Genetic Algorithm (GA)

This work was supported in part by the International Joint Project through the Royal Society of the U.K., in part by the National Natural Science Foundation of China under Grant 61611130209, in part by the National Science Foundations of China under Grants 61472051/61702060, in part by the Science Foundation of Chongqing under Grant cstc2017jcyjA1276, in part by the China Postdoctoral Science Foundation under Grant 2015M570770, in part by the Natural Science Foundation of Chongqing under Grant cstc2016jcyjA1315, and in part by the National Key R&D Program of China under Grant 2018YFD1100304.

X. Wang et al. (Eds.): CollaborateCom 2019, LNICST 292, pp. 45–57, 2019.
https://doi.org/10.1007/978-3-030-30146-0_4

1 Introduction

1.1 Background

Internet-of-things (IoT) [1], which integrates distributed smart objects, burgeoning technologies and communications solutions [2], e.g., tracking technologies and enhanced communication protocols, has become a promising paradigm for smart systems such as smart cities and healthcare [3].

IoT is the network of devices, e.g., sensors and actuators. The devices sense the physical world and take reactions to specific scenarios. To achieve a smart system, the system builder should (a) deploy sufficient and specific designed IoT devices to specific environment or space, (b) interconnect deployed devices by some cores. However, due to the high difficulty of owning all-round management techniques and resources [4,5], it is not a easy job for many IoT device owners to maintain such huge amount of devices. In such condition, IoT management service providers (MSP) are arising to catch business opportunities. IoT MSPs usually provide rules engine for users which makes it possible to build IoT applications without managing any infrastructure. They also support a wide range of communication protocols and even allow IoT devices to communicate with each other while they are using different protocols. For example. Amazon provides MSs called AWS IoT [6], which provides all aforementioned features and extensions like device shadow for device owners.

1.2 Motivating

According to Ericsson's Mobility Report [7], by 2023, there will be around 32 billion connected devices. Considered to be a growing market, its great economic benefit attracts many organizations to provide their own MS. It is predictable that there will be more and more MSPs. By utilizing cloud computing and edge computing, the MSs are usually convenient, reliable and economical efficiency. Adequate utilization of IoT device MS allows device owners to improve their own business. However, in practical scenarios, the heterogeneous QoS requirements of devices and the heterogeneous capacities of services make IoT device owners more difficult to work out a plan for device management optimization.

Motivated by this need, in this study, our objectives are modeling the problem and providing approaches to solve it. First of all, the constraints in the problem are investigated.

To build a large-scale IoT application, such as smart grid [8], a large amount of IoT devices should be deployed. These devices, such as sensors and monitors are spread among a large space which makes it hard to connect them to one MS due to the nonfunctional requirements like Quality-of-service (QoS) [9].

QoS requirement of an IoT device is multiple dimensional. It is naturally, for example, IoT devices for remote health monitoring and emergency notification systems have stringent demands on performance and reliability for real-time communication, and in smart grid, to satisfy certain security requirements, data collected by video monitors should be transmitted to MS for analysis within a limited time frame to detect potential threats, which demands sufficient throughput. Most of these QoS requirements are quantifiable.

According to the European Telecommunications Standards Institute (ETSI), the typical response times of different IoT functions should meet the values in Table 1.

Table 1. Typical response times of different IoT functions

Function	Response time
Protection	1 to 10 ms
Control	100 ms
Monitoring	1 s
Metering/Billing	1 h to 1 day
Reporting	1 day to 1 year

For any IoT device, there might be list of satisfiable and selectable MSs. However, a MS cannot bear all application devices due to the capacity limitation. It is clear that in the era of edge computing, a MSP can deploy MS on edge servers, whose computing resource such as CPU, bandwidth or memory are limited.

Number of devices, service capacity, QoS requirement of a certain device and the QoS prediction data between any device and service can be obtained or calculated. Based on this information, while fulfilling the above constraints, the number of devices managed by MS must be maximized. Due to the aforementioned constraints, there might be a number of devices that cannot be assigned to MS. Those devices will managed by device owners with extra resource. Additionally, minimize the total cost of renting management service is another optimization objective.

1.3   Our Work

In this study, we refer to the above problem as a Constraint Optimization Problem (COP). The IoT Device Management Service Selection problem is proven to be $\mathcal{NP}$-hard. Two approaches have been proposed to solve it. The main contributions of this work are as follows:

- The IoT Device Management Service Selection problem is modeled as a COP and we have proven its $\mathcal{NP}$-hard;
- we have developed an optimal approach for solving the COP problem using the Lexicographic Goal Programming technique;
- A genetic algorithm (GA)-based method has been proposed as an alternative approach to solve the COP problem.
- we have evaluated our approaches against a baseline approach with experiments to demonstrate their performance.

The remainder of the paper is organized as follows. Section 2 models the problem. In Sect. 3, we prove proposed COP problem is $\mathcal{NP}$-hard and provide a solution. Section 4 proposes an alternative approach. Section 5 evaluates proposed approaches and Sect. 6 concludes this paper.

2   System Modeling

Let $V_1 = \{d_1, d_2, ..., d_m\}$ represent a set of IoT devices, where $m = |V_1|$ is the size of set V_1 and $V_2 = \{s_1, s_2, ..., s_n\}$ a set of candidate MSs, where $n = |V_2|$ is the size of set V_2. Obviously, the vertex sets V_1 and V_2 are two disjoint sets that $V = V_1 \cup V_2$ and $V_1 \cap V_2 = \emptyset$. The potential assignment between IoT devices and services can be presented by a set of edges $E \in V_1 \times V_2$, such that every edge $e \in E$ has one vertex in V_1 and the other in V_2. Therefore, the relationship between IoT devices and device management services can be presented by a Bipartite Graph $G = (V_1, V_2, E)$. Then, the solution space of concerned problem can be presented as a $0 - 1$ matrix.

For any IoT device d_i in V_1, there are totally n potential services and naturally $e_{ij} = 1$ if device i is managed by service j.

The infrastructure of management service can be Cloud data center, 5G base station or other computational resources. Their scales are obviously heterogeneous. Consequentially, the maximum capacity of management services are many and varied. In this study, the maximum connectivity, e.g., c_j, determines the service capacity. Specifically, for a service s_j, the number of connected devices is limited to c_j.

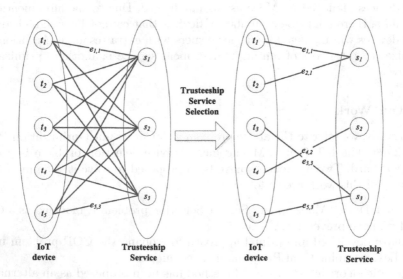

Fig. 1. A brief example of proposed COP problem.

To fulfil its function smoothly, an IoT system requires its components follow the QoS requirements. Therefore, selecting qualified MSs is critical. As aforementioned, different IoT devices have different QoS requirements. Before allocating an IoT device to a management service, the QoS data is required first to support such decision. However, in IoT scenarios, the device-side QoS performance, e.g., response-time and throughput, are highly different due to many factors such as network conditions and deployment environment. Considering the large number of IoT devices and candidate services, the high expense of taking real-world service evaluations is unacceptable. It is a commonly dilemma for QoS-based service selection approaches. Fortunately, these QoS data can be predicted by using QoS prediction techniques, e.g., collaborative filtering (CF)-based approaches [12,13]. Especially, the latent factor (LF)-based predictors [14–16] are proven to be highly accurate.

Suppose an IoT device has z independent QoS requirements. The source data for the QoS predictors is a 3-dimensional matrix, e.g., $H^{m \times n \times z}$ which contains numerous missing entries. The QoS predictors firstly separate $H^{m \times n \times z}$ into z $H^{m \times n}$ matrices, and implement the QoS prediction to complete them. For any QoS $H_k^{m \times n}, 1 \geq k \leq z$, the entry q_{ij}^k indicates the kth predicted QoS data between device i and service j. Suppose k^{th} dimension Qos requirement of device i is $\hat{q}_i^k$. Comparing each q_{ij}^k with $\hat{q}_i^k$ by a specific rule, e.g., $<$ or $>$, we can obtain a selectable service list notated by $g_k(i)$. The intersection of z $g_k(i)$, e.g., $g(i)$, is a list of selectable services for device i.

The price of device management service depends on both device and service. According to AWS IoT Core pricing, the price is determined by Connectivity, e.g. number of devices and duration, Messaging, e.g., message number and message size, and Rules Engine. In this study, a matrix $P^{m \times n}$ contains the price information and p_{ij} denotes the money cost by device i on service j in a unit time.

Additionally, in this study we suppose that any IoT device is only managed by one service, then we have the condition (Fig. 1),

$$\sum_{j=1}^{n} e_{ij} = 1, \forall i \tag{1}$$

Until now, all constraints of our optimization problem are clear. As aforementioned, the optimization has two objectives: (1) maximizing the number of devices connected to MS and (2) minimizing the total cost, while satisfying the capacity constraint and QoS constraint. Then we have modeled the IoT Device Management Service Selection problem as a constraint optimization problem (COP):

$$Maximize.F = \sum_{i=1}^{m} \sum_{j=1}^{n} e_{ij} \tag{2}$$

$$Minimize.R = \sum_{i=1}^{m} \sum_{j=1}^{n} p_{ij} e_{ij} \tag{3}$$

subject to

$$\sum_{j=1}^{n} e_{ij} = 1, \forall i \in \{1, ..., m\} \tag{4}$$

$$\sum_{j \in g(i)} e_{ij} = 1, \forall i \in \{1, ..., m\} \tag{5}$$

$$\sum_{i=1}^{m} e_{ij} \leq c_j, \forall j \in \{1, ..., n\} \tag{6}$$

$$e_{ij} \in \{0, 1\}, \forall i \in \{1, ..., m\}; j \in \{1, ..., n\} \tag{7}$$

where:

$e_{ij} = 1$ if device d_i is allocated to service s_j.

g_j is provided by CF-based QoS predictor.

c_j is provided by MSP.

The objective function (2) maximizes the number of devices that are assigned to management service. The objective function (3) minimizes the total cost of the management. Note that objective (2) has the higher rank compared to objective (3). Constraint family (4) ensures each device is allocated to at most one management service. family (5) ensures the QoS requirement of any device based on the result of QoS predictor. Constraint family (6) ensures the number of devices allocated to any service won't exceed its capacity.

3 IDMSS Approach

In this section, we analyse the aforementioned COP problem and proposed an approach to solve it directly. First, we introduce the definitions of Bin packing (BP) Problem and Vector Bin Packing (VBP) Problem, which are similar with our COP.

Definition 1. *Bin Packing (BP) Problem.* *Given an infinite supply of identical bins $B = \{b_1, b_2, ..., b_m\}$ and the maximum capacity of any bin b_i, C_i, equals 1. And a set of n items $U = \{u_1, u_2, ..., u_n\}$. The size of a item u_j, w_j, satisfies $0 < w_j \leq C$. The objective of **BP** is to pack all the given items into the fewest bins such that the total item size in each bin must not exceed the bin capacity C.*

Definition 2. *Vector Bin Packing (VBP) Problem.* *Given a set of items $U = \{u_1, u_2, ..., u_n\}$, the size of an item u_j is denoted as a k-dimensional vector $w_j = < w_j^1, w_j^2, ..., w_j^k >, w_j \in [0, 1]$. given an infinite supply of identical bins $B = b_1, b_2, ..., b_m$ with maximum capacity $C = < 1^1, 1^2, ..., 1^d >$. The objective is to pack the set U into a minimum number of bins.*

BP problem is known to be an $\mathcal{NP}$-hard combinatorial optimization problem [10]. The size of an item is presented as a single aggregate measure in BP problem. By contrast, the size of an item in the VBP problem is associated with a multi-dimensional vector and the VBP problem is also known as multi-capacity BP problem in some literatures, which is $\mathcal{NP}$-hard.

Proof. In our problem, there is a set of devices $D = \{d_1, d_2, ..., d_m\}$ and a set of management services $S = s_1, s_2, ..., s_i$, the selectable services of a device d_i is denoted as a n-dimensional vector $e_i =< e_{i1}, e_{i2}, ..., e_{in} >, e_{ij} \in 0, 1$. The maximum service capacity $C =< c_j * e_{1j}, c_j * e_{2j}, ..., c_j * e_{mj} >$. The objective is to pack maximum elements in set D into a fix number of bins. VBP requires $d > 2$, in our COP, m is a huge number and $\sum_{i=1}^{M} e_{ij} \gg d$, so our COP is equivalent to VBP.

To solve the Proposed COP, Lexicographic Goal Programming (LGP) [11] technique is a valid solution. LGP is suitable to solve multi-objective optimization problem whose optimization objectives are ranked by their levels of importance, or priorities. The LGP solver first finds optimal solutions satisfied the primary objective and then proceeds to find solutions for the next objective without deteriorating the previous objective(s).

An LGP program can be solved as a series of connected integer linear programs, which can be easily solved by commercial computing tools such as IBM CPLEX Optimizer. This direct approach is named as IDMSS in this study.

4   GA-based Approach

As proven in Sect. 3, the proposed COP problem is $\mathcal{NP}$-hard. The traditional methods are exhausted considering the solution space of proposed COP problem can be very big in practical. Therefore, we proposed an alternative approach called GA4MSS, a Genetic Algorithm-based approach for MS Section.

Genetic algorithms (GAs) [17, 18] belongs to a subset of heuristic algorithms. They are inspired by the natural biological evolution and proven to be robust and performed well in most cases. The GAs operate the solution, which is in the form of chromosome, with genetic operators such as crossover and mutation to boost the evolution. This process may create solutions approximate the optimum. Basic GA components and their relationship are shown in Fig. 2.

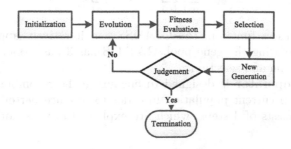

Fig. 2. A flow chart of basic genetic algorithms.

In GAs, solutions are encoded as chromosomes. GA4MSS encodes a possible solution as a single string, as shown in Fig. 3. The index of the string element denotes the device id, e.g., index 1 is device d_1. The values in each position denotes the id of a service. The encoding method promises that each device can only select one service, which makes GA4MSS satisfies the constraint family (4). Moreover, to satisfies the constraint family (5), the value in each position of the chromosome can only choose from the selectable set, e.g., $g(i)$. According to such encoding method, GA4MSS covers all possible QoS-aware solutions and Z solutions are generated as the Initial Population.

d_1	d_2	d_3	d_4	d_5
S_1	S_1	S_3	S_2	S_3

Fig. 3. GA4MSS encoding.

To evaluate the fitness of a solution, a fitness function is required. GA4MSS combines two objectives by punishing the unconnected devices. The punishment is implemented by adding an extra cost to the solution as follows:

$$T = \sum_{i=1}^{m}(\lambda \times p_{ij} \times \hat{e}_i), \forall j \tag{8}$$

where $\hat{e}_i \in \{0, 1\}$ denotes management state of a device, $\hat{e}_i = 1$ if device d_i connects no service, and λ is a $(1, \infty)$ parameter to estimate the potential cost of managing the devices by owners themselves. It is reasonable because if there is no qualified management service, the device owner should manage these devices by themselves, which leads to a higher cost. Moreover, GA4MSS assimilates the capacity constraint into the fitness function by punishing the exceeding devices. The fitness function of GA4MSS is as follows,

$$Minimize.R = \sum_{i=1}^{m}\sum_{j=1}^{n}p_{ij}e_{ij} + \sum_{i=1}^{m}(\lambda \times p_{ij} \times \hat{e}_i) \tag{9}$$

Given the fitness function, the GA4MSS can iteratively approximate the optimum by operating the gene pool. GA4MSS has 3 basic operators, namely crossover, mutation and selection.

Crossover operator is designed to encourage the recombination of individual features in current population in order to produce better offsprings. In GA4MSS, it consists of 4 steps, which are explained in what follows with the help of Fig. 4:

1. generate two replicas of two individuals which are randomly chosen from current population.
2. Randomly generate a 0–1 crossover indicator.
3. swap the ith element of two replicas if i^{th} value in crossover indicator is 1.
4. repeat 1–3 until a number of individuals, e.g., $2Z$, in the population.

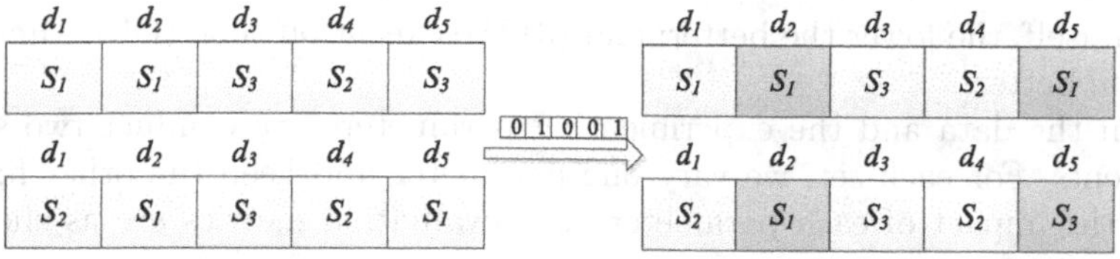

d_1	d_2	d_3	d_4	d_5
S_1	S_1	S_3	S_2	S_3

d_1	d_2	d_3	d_4	d_5
S_1	S_1	S_3	S_2	S_1

0	1	0	0	1

d_1	d_2	d_3	d_4	d_5
S_2	S_1	S_3	S_2	S_1

d_1	d_2	d_3	d_4	d_5
S_2	S_1	S_3	S_2	S_3

Fig. 4. GA4MSS crossover operation

Mutation operator allows an offspring to obtain features which are not owned by its parents. GA4MSS randomly exchange a value in d_i with a element in $g(i)$.

Selection operator works as a filter which allows a part of the operated population into next generation. There are Kinds of selection schemes, GA4MSS implements the truncation. The individuals in current population after crossover and mutation is sorted by their fitness value, and the first Z individuals survive.

5 Experimental Evaluation

5.1 Experiment Settings

We have conducted a range of experiments aiming at evaluating the effectiveness and efficiency of proposed approaches. In this study, all experiments are conducted on a Windows machine with Intel(R) Xeon(R) E5-CPU and 32 GB RAM. The IDMSS approach in Sect. 3 was implemented using IBM ILOG CPLEX Optimizer and the GA4MSS was implemented using Java SE.

Our approaches will be benchmarked against a baseline approach called RANDOM. In RANDOM, each IoT device will be assigned to a random service. A device won't be account to be a MS managed device if it violates the QoS requirement or it exceeds the capacity of assigned service.

Experiment Data. A QoS data set collected by the WS-Dream system is utilized as the experiment data. The data set contains 1873838 response-time data by 339 users on 5825 real world Web-services. To implement our experiment, we first employed INLF [16], a non-negative latent factor QoS predictor to predict the missing QoS data. The price of managing a device by a MS is randomly generated based on the basic price and a random factor τ. In this study, the basic price is 0.10 dollar, which is a standard fee charged by AWS GovCloud for one connection.

Performance Metrics. We evaluate three approaches, namely IDMSS, GA4MSS and the RANDOM baseline approach by following metrics: (1) the percentage of MS managed IoT devices of all IoT devices, the higher the better; (2) total cost including the estimating cost of the devices managed by device owner himself, the lower the better; and (3) the execution time (CPU time), the lower, the better.

Given the data and the experimenting parameters, we conduct two sets of experiments. For each set, we vary one parameter and keep the other fixed to observe the impact of each parameter. The evaluation metrics are as shown in Table 2.

Table 2. Parameter Settings

Set	capacity	Basic unit Price	τ	λ	Number of devices	Number of services
#1	20	0.10	(1, 1.5]	2	100, 200,...,1000	100
#2	20	0.10	(1, 1.5]	2	1000	20, 40,...,100

5.2 Experimental Results

Effectiveness: Figures 5 and 6 show the results obtained from the experiment set 1 and set 2, respectively. The three performance metrics are depicted in each sub-figure: (a) percentage of MS managed devices, (b) total cost, and (c) gives the execution time of each approach.

Figure 5 shows that in experiment set 1, when the number of IoT devices increases from 100 to 1000, the random approach performs poorly in terms of trusteeship device percentage (only 38%–40% of the IoT devices are assigned to the MS) compared to our approaches. Proposed approaches perform approximately equal that most devices having been managed by MS. Comparing to GA4MSS, IDMSS can always find a better solution, although the trusteeship device percentage keep decreasing as the number of devices increases, the decreasing of IDMSS is obviously slower note that the gap between IDMSS and GAMSS is approximately growing from 0.05% to 3.7%.

In experiment set 2, we change the number of candidate services. As depicted in Fig. 6(a), trusteeship device percentage increases while the number of services increases from 20 to 100. IDMSS continues to achieve the best performance. Regarding to Fig. 6(b), the total cost decreasing largely as the service capacity increases.

Efficiency: Experiment set 1 shows that the computation time of IDMSS approach increases considerably while we increasing the number of IoT devices. As shown in Fig. 5(a), when there are 1000 devices, the GA4MSS and random approaches take only approximately 4.3 and 1.4 s while IDMSS takes around 59.0 s to solve an instance of the IoT device management selection problem. In experiment sets 2, where we increase the capacity of service, the IDMSS approach consumes more time to make a decision. Since proposed COP problem is $\mathcal{NP}$-hard, it is expected that IDMSS approach, which optimally solves the problem, will take the most time as opposed to the other approaches.

Increasing number of IoT devices or number of services will increase the complexity of proposed COP problem, which is $\mathcal{NP}$-hard, and thus take more time

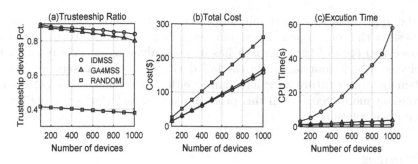

Fig. 5. Results of set #1 (number of devices changing)

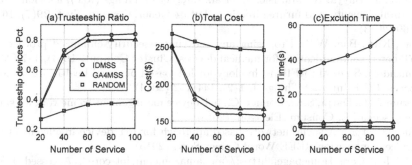

Fig. 6. Results of set #2 (number of services changing)

to find an optimal solution. Our experimental results show that the random approach is not able to optimize the optimization objectives as it can only connect around only 40% of all the IoT devices in the experiments by chance. IDMSS and GA4MSS have similar effectiveness; they are able to assign a similar number of IoT devices to MS. However, as shown in Figs. 5(c) and 6(c), GA4MSS outperforms IDMSS in performance especially while the COP problem is scaling up.

6   Conclusion

IoT device management is a challenge to many device owners considering the huge amount of devices and their heterogeneous characteristics. Recently, IoT device management service (MS) providers raise to serve device owners, e.g., AWS IoT core. IoT device owners can easily do their management work by using IoT device MS. However, it is not a easy job to select suitable service for each devices considering the constraints, e.g., QoS constraint and capacity constraint. An optimal service selection must maximize the number of MS managed devices and minimize the total cost while ensuring the required QoS of devices. To address this problem, we model the IoT Device Management Service Selection problem as a COP and solve it by a Lexicographic Goal Programming (LGP) approach. At the mean time, an alternative approach, GA4MSS, is proposed to find the approximate optimal solution within shorter time. Our experimental results show that our approaches significantly outperforms the baseline random approach and each of the approach has its own advantages. This research has established a basic foundation for the IoT device management service selection problem and in the future we will (a) improve the performance of GA4MSS, and (b) consider more scenarios in this problem, such as IoT devices' mobility and service price volatility.

References

1. Gubbi, J., Buyya, R., Marusic, S., et al.: Internet of Things (IoT): a vision, architectural elements, and future directions. Future Gener. Comput. Syst. **29**(7), 1645–1660 (2013)
2. Han, K.H., Bae, W.S.: Proposing and verifying a security-enhanced protocol for IoT-based communication for medical devices. Cluster Comput. **19**(4), 1–7 (2016)
3. Amendola, S., et al.: RFID technology for IoT-based personal healthcare in smart spaces. IEEE Internet Things J. **1**(2), 144–152 (2014)
4. Perumal, T., Datta, S.K., Bonnet, C.: IoT device management framework for smart home scenarios. Consum. Electron. (2016)
5. Guo, C., et al.: A social network based approach for IoT device management and service composition. IEEE World Congr. Serv. (2015)
6. AwS IoT Core Homepage. https://aws.amazon.com/iot-core/. Accessed 4 Mar 2019
7. Heuveldop, N.: Ericsson Mobility Report. Technical report, Ericsson, November 2017
8. Yun, M., Bu, Y.: Research on the architecture and key technology of Internet of Things (IoT) applied on smart grid. In: International Conference on Advances in Energy Engineering (2010)
9. Aazam, M., et al.: MeFoRE: QoE based resource estimation at Fog to enhance QoS in IoT. In: International Conference on Telecommunications (2016)
10. Garey, M.R., Johnson, D.S.: Computers and Intractability: A Guide to the Theory of NP-Completeness. W. H. Freeman, New York (1979)
11. Kwak, N.K., Schniederjans, M.J.: An alternative solution method for goal programming problems: the lexicographic goal programming case. Socio Econ. Plann. Sci. **19**(2), 101–107 (1985)
12. Zheng, Z., Zhang, Y., Lyu, M.R.: Distributed QoS evaluation for real-world Web services. In: IEEE International Conference on Web Services (2010)
13. Luo, X., et al.: Generating highly accurate predictions for missing QoS data via aggregating nonnegative latent factor models. IEEE Trans. Neural Netw. Learn. Syst. **27**(3), 524–537 (2016)
14. Zheng, Z.B., Ma, H., Lyu, M.R., King, I.: Collaborative web service QoS prediction via neighborhood integrated matrix factorization. IEEE Trans. Services Computing. **6**(3), 289–299 (2012)
15. Luo, X., Zhou, M., Xia, Y., et al.: An efficient non-negative matrix-factorization-based approach to collaborative filtering for recommender systems. IEEE Trans. Industrial Informatics. **10**(2), 1273–1284 (2014)

16. Luo X., et al.: An inherently non-negative latent factor model for high-dimensional and sparse matrices from industrial applications. IEEE Trans. Ind. Inf. (2017)
17. Anderson-Cook, C.M.: Practical genetic algorithms. Publ. Am. Stat. Assoc. **100**(471), 1099 (2004)
18. Canfora, G., et al.: An approach for QoS-aware service composition based on genetic algorithms. In: Conference on Genetic & Evolutionary Computation (2005)

A Dynamic Planning Framework
for QoS-Based Mobile Service Composition
Under Cloud-Edge Hybrid Environments

Honghao Gao[1,2,5], Wanqiu Huang[1], Qiming Zou[2,3],
and Xiaoxian Yang[4(✉)]

[1] School of Computer Engineering and Science,
Shanghai University, Shanghai, China
[2] Computing Center, Shanghai University, Shanghai, China
[3] Shanghai Shang Da Hai Run Information System Co., Ltd., Shanghai, China
[4] School of Computer and Information Engineering,
Shanghai Polytechnic University, Shanghai, China
xxyang@sspu.edu.cn
[5] Shanghai Key Laboratory of Computer Software Evaluating and Testing,
Shanghai, China

Abstract. In cloud-edge hybrid environments, when QoS constraints of the
SOA-based mobile service composition change, a dynamic reconfiguration
needs to be performed. Different from the traditional cloud service, the cloud-
edge hybrid environment has the characteristics of limited resource storage,
limited energy at the edge and uncertain users who move frequently. Dynamic
reconfiguration in this mode is challenging. QoS is an important indicator of
service evaluation. Most studies focus on only the static QoS attributes of the
service. However, the QoS of a service is not statically constant; it changes
dynamically over time. Therefore, to avoid the immediate failure of the service
and ensure the stability of the mobile service composition after dynamic
reconfiguration, an LSTM neural network is applied to predict the future QoS
value for candidate service. This value is used as a service evaluation indicator
during dynamic reconfiguration. Then, attributes such as energy consumption,
traffic and moving track are considered. A cost-reward mechanism is constructed
to calculate the cost and reward of the service when it is invoked. The reasonable restriction conditions are added for controlling dynamic reconfiguration.
Finally, the dynamic reconfiguration problem-solving process and framework
for mobile service composition based on QoS in a cloud-edge hybrid environment is introduced, guiding the mobile service composition dynamic reconfiguration task in cloud-edge hybrid environments.

Keywords: Cloud-edge hybrid environments · Mobile service composition ·
Service QoS · Service failure · Dynamic reconfiguration

© ICST Institute for Computer Sciences, Social Informatics and Telecommunications Engineering 2019
Published by Springer Nature Switzerland AG 2019. All Rights Reserved
X. Wang et al. (Eds.): CollaborateCom 2019, LNICST 292, pp. 58–70, 2019.
https://doi.org/10.1007/978-3-030-30146-0_5

1 Introduction

With the rapid development of mobile devices and cloud computing, cloud-edge hybrid environments have been widely known for its powerful computing capacity [1]. In this model, users can invoke services provided in the cloud or deployed on edge devices to achieve high-performance, low-latency, and high-bandwidth service interaction experiences [2]. However, due to the heterogeneity, openness and synergy of the network in cloud-edge hybrid environments, the reliability and correctness of service-oriented applications are seriously affected [3]. For example, as the geographic location of a mobile device changes dynamically, there will be unpredictable latency in the communication process, resulting in application failure behavior. Therefore, it is necessary to propose a dynamic reconfiguration scheme for the application of mobile service composition in cloud-edge hybrid environments [4].

QoS is an essential indicator for evaluating services in dynamic reconfiguration [15]. If quality of service (QoS) constraints need to be improved, the dynamic reconfiguration process [16] can be completed by replacing the service with a higher QoS value in the application. The existing research mainly focuses on the dynamic reconfiguration problem of the static QoS value of traditional services [5]. This method mainly has the following shortcomings: (1) Because of the instability of network environments in mobile environments, the attributes such as signal strength, response time and reliability of mobile devices are affected, and dynamic fluctuations in service QoS will occur [14]. Dynamic reconfiguration of a service based on the current QoS value will cause the application to be in an unstable and unreliable state. (2) Another unavoidable problem with cloud-edge hybrid environments is decreasing the energy consumption of mobile terminal devices [6–8]. With the exponential growth of mobile devices, an increasing number of mobile applications are attempting to accomplish more complex logic functions [9]. In addition, to improve application performance and reduce energy consumption of mobile devices, it is necessary to address the energy consumption problem [11].

To solve the above problems and ensure the stability of the application in the running process. We use a long short-term memory (LSTM) neural network to predict the dynamic QoS of the service [12, 13] and build the service value attributes as an optimization selection target. The service cost and reward attribute that guide service dynamic reconfiguration process are evaluated. Finally, the dynamic reconfiguration problem is formalized, a suitable solution is obtained, and a framework to unify the above processes is built.

The remainder of this paper is organized as follows. Section 2 presents the formal definition of cloud-edge services. Section 3 describes the quantitative calculation of service-related attributes in the dynamic reconfiguration process. Section 4 uses the LSTM prediction model to predict the QoS value of services. Section 5 integrates previous papers and builds a dynamic reconfiguration framework for mobile service composition under cloud-edge hybrid environments. Section 6 presents conclusions and provides future research directions.

2 Formal Definition

In this section, according to the characteristics of the cloud-edge hybrid environment, the definitions of cloud-edge service, service plan, service invocation and composite services are given first for clearly showing the related concepts.

2.1 Definition of Cloud-Edge Service

Definition 1 (Cloud-Edge Service): A cloud-edge service can be represented as a triple $(i, o, \{QoS_t\})$, where:

1. i is the input parameters;
2. o is the output parameters;
3. $\{QoS_t\}$ is a chronological sequence of quality of service.

The cloud-edge service can be either a traditional web service or an edge-end service deployed on a variety of sensors. The service QoS value records the quality of service sequence for a certain period. It can effectively reflect the dynamic change trend of service quality.

Definition 2 (Service Plan): A service plan can be represented as a triple (T, P, B), where:

1. $T = \{t_i\}_{i=1}^{n}$ is a set of tasks, including two mutually disjoint subsets FT and CT, where FT is the functional task subset, and CT is the control task subset;
2. P is a set of settings in the service plan (e.g., execution probabilities of the branches and loops structures);
3. B provides the structural information of the service plan, which can be specified by XML-based languages such as the business process execution language (BPEL).

The service plan is an abstract description of the business process. There are two types of tasks in a service plan: functional tasks to imply functional requirements, and control tasks to flow directions. The control tasks can coordinate and monitor the structure of the service and ensure the relationship between functional tasks. Given the two tasks, t1 and t2, the four compositional structures are shown in Fig. 1. The structure of the service plan is divided into four categories: sequence, choice, parallel, and iteration. In different structures, each service attribute is calculated differently.

Definition 3 (Cloud-Edge Service Invocation): A cloud-edge service invocation can be represented as a tetrad $(t, s, cost, reward)$, where:

1. t indicates the tasks performed in the service plan;
2. s is the service invoked to realize t;
3. $cost$ is the cost during the invocation of s;
4. $reward$ is the cost during the invocation of s.

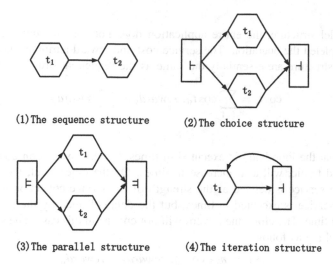

(1) The sequence structure   (2) The choice structure

(3) The parallel structure   (4) The iteration structure

Fig. 1. Compositional structures.

In a cloud-edge hybrid environment, the service plan is implemented by a set of service invocations, each corresponding to a service invocation and an appropriate service. In the process of calling a cloud-edge service, a certain number of costs and rewards will be generated. For example, the energy consumption and traffic expense of calling a service are service costs. However, while data redundancy requires a large budget, more data can improve data quality to some extent [18]. So, we define the strength of the service collection data as a reward for calling the service.

In addition, the cost and reward calculations for composition services are not the same for different workflow structures in the service plan [15]. Given a structure S consisting of S1, S2, ..., Sn, and n subservices, we give the calculation of cost and reward properties under four service portfolio structures.

1. Sequence

$$\cos t_s = \sum_{i=1}^{n} \cos t_{si}, \ reward_s = \sum_{i=1}^{n} reward_{si}$$

2. Choice

Assume the probability of selecting the first branch in the selection structure is P_i, and $\sum_{i=1}^{n} p_i = 1$.

$$\cos t_s = \sum_{i=1}^{n} \cos t_{si} p_i, \ reward_s = \sum_{i=1}^{n} reward_{si} p_i$$

3. Parallel

In a parallel structure, the entire application does not continue until all branches have completed the operation. The service cost and reward attribute calculations in a parallel structure are essentially the same as the sequential structure, as follows:

$$\cos t_s = \sum_{i=1}^{n} \cos t_{si}, \ reward_s = \sum_{i=1}^{n} reward_{si}$$

4. Iteration

Assume that the loop body is executed m times. Service invocation costs, such as energy and traffic, will also increase m times. On the other hand, the reward for calling the service is defined as the strength of the service collection data. In this case, the service is executed m times, but the data collected by the service is the same each time. Therefore, the reward will not change in this case. The service cost and reward are as follows:

$$\cos t_s = m * \cos t_{si}, \ reward_s = reward_{si}$$

Definition 4 (Cloud-Edge Composite Service): A cloud-edge composite service can be represented as a triple (S, B, QoS), where:

1. S is the set of web services and edge service set constituting the composite service;
2. B provides the structural information of the service plan;
3. QoS expresses the quality of the composite service.

A cloud-edge composition service is a collection of services that consist of edge services and web services. A cloud-edge composite service is implemented through a set of service invocations where the appropriate service implementation is selected for each task.

3 Quantitative Calculation for Service Properties

3.1 Service Value

The value property of the service is used as a measure of service availability in dynamic reconfiguration. In determine that the service does not expire and reduce the potential operational risk, it is necessary to accurately predict the future QoS value of it [19, 20]. Therefore, taking into account the QoS attribute value and the predicted QoS property value of the service, we assign a value property to each service, which represents the importance of the service to the application's dynamic reconfiguration. Based on the above description, we model the value function of the service $s_i \in S$ as follows:

$$
value_k(Q(T_i), Q(T_{(i+1)}), Q(T_{(i+2)})) = \frac{\int_{T_i}^{T_{(i+2)}} f(x)dx}{T_{i+2} - T_i}
$$
$$
= \frac{\frac{T_{i+2} - T_i}{6}[Q(T_i) + Q(T_{i+1}) * Q(T_{i+2})]}{T_{i+2} - T_i}
$$

Among them, $value_k$ represents the value function of service k. Its value is determined by the $Q(T_i)$, $Q(T_{i+1})$ and $Q(T_{i+2})$. Where, $Q(T_i)$ is the service QoS value at the current moment, $Q(T_{i+1})$ is the QoS value at T_{i+1} moments and $Q(T_{i+2})$ is the QoS value at T_{i+2} moments. $Q(T_{i+1})$ and $Q(T_{i+2})$ are predicted using the LSTM neural network. $value_k$ is an improved service metric. It is determined not only by the current QoS of the service but also by the possible QoS values of the service in the coming period.

3.2   Cost-Reward Mechanism

The mobile service composition in the cloud-edge hybrid environments has many complex characteristics. When the dynamic reconfiguration problem of service is formalized, it is not enough to improve the QoS value of service composition. It does not guarantee the efficient and reliable operation of the application after dynamic reconfiguration. Therefore, the different characteristics and the specific factors of mobile service composition are considered to define the service cost and reward attributes. The attributes can improve the efficiency and reliability of the application after dynamic reconfiguration.

3.2.1   Service Cost

We define a cost attribute for each service. It can be divided into two parts, energy consumption cost and traffic cost. For a service $s_i \in S$, its cost is defined as:

$$c_i(E_i, D_i) = \alpha_i E_i + \beta_i D_i$$

where c_i represents the cost, E_i represents the energy consumption and D_i represents the traffic expense in the process of calling service i. α_i and β_i represent the weight of the traffic expenses and energy consumption, respectively.

First, for traffic consumption D_i, the calling environment is dynamically changing, and the user is frequently moving. However, the traffic calling the service is fixed and does not change dynamically as the service objects and the service providers may move. Therefore, the definition of D_i is as follows:

$$D_i = ud_i + dd_i$$

where ud_i is the quantity of upload data required to invoke service i, and dd_i is the quantity of download data required to invoke service i.

Second, we focus on the impact of the mobile environment on energy consumption during service invocation. The calculation of energy consumption in traditional cloud-edge hybrid environments is usually static [14]. However, due to the dynamic change in the location of the service caller, the network signal strength is unstable. It leads to fluctuations in the transfer rate when the data are uploaded and downloaded. As well as the response time changes a lot. Ultimately, the energy consumption of the device is also in the process of dynamic change. The energy consumption computation model in paper [17] is used to calculate the energy consumption E_i of service i in a mobile environment. The definition of the mobile path of the service caller is given below.

Definition 5 (Mobile Path): A mobile path is represented by a triple (T, L, F), where:

1. $T = \{(t_i, t_{i+1})\}_{i=0}^{n-1}$ is a set of discrete time intervals, with as the start time and as the stop time;
2. L is a set of discrete location points;
3. F is a function representing the correspondence between time and location: $\forall t \in (t_0, t_n) F(t) \rightarrow L$.

Where function $F(t)$ represents the correspondence between time and position. Given a point in time, we can obtain the position that corresponds to the user at that point in time.

Although the signal strength in the mobile environment changes dynamically, the signal strength of the same path segment after the path is refined is usually stable and can be measured. We define the formula for the energy consumption E_i of service i in a mobile environment as follows:

$$E_i = uc + sc + dc$$

The energy consumption of uc when uploading data in the process of calling service i is calculated as follows:

$$uc = \frac{D(i)}{H(G(l_1))} \times (R(G(l_1)) + sp)$$

where $D(i)$ is the data size; $l_1 = F(t_1)$, which is the corresponding path point for the user at time t_1; $H(G(l_1))$ is the data transfer rate at location l_1 at the time of the upload. The signal strength is $G(l_1)$. Similarly, $R(G(l_1))$ is the location l_1 where the data are uploaded. The radiation power of the device when the signal strength is $G(l_1)$. The standby power for the mobile device is sp. And, sc is the standby energy consumption of the device while waiting to execute the service; the calculation method is as follows:

$$sc = sp \times rt$$

Among them, rt is the response time of the service, and the energy consumption of dc for downloading data is calculated as follows:

$$dc = \frac{D(o)}{H(G(l_2))} \times (R(G(l_1)) + sp)$$

$$l_2 = F(t_1 + \frac{D(i)}{H(G(l_1))} + rt)$$

Therefore, we use the energy consumption computation model to calculate the energy consumption of service calls in a mobile environment. Furthermore, the cost of the service is calculated. During the dynamic reconfiguration process, the cost attribute value for each candidate service represents the costs of calling the service. The higher the cost value of a service, the greater the cost of calling the service.

3.2.2 Service Reward

The cost of calling different services is different, but this does not mean that a service with a lower cost should be invoked as a priority. The relationship between the quantity of data uploaded and downloaded by the service and the QoS is subject to the marginal benefit rule to some extent [18]. In other words, when the service receives more upload and download data, to a certain extent, it will improve the accuracy of the data to ensure the quality of the service. However, as a result of the reduction in the marginal increase of the data quality, data redundancy is generated. It inevitably leads to a waste of resources. For service $s_j \in S$, D_j represents the quantity of data that the service uploads and downloads. The corresponding reward for the service is:

$$r_j(d_j) = \gamma_j \times e^{-\lambda_j d_j}$$

Among them, λ_j is the initial reward of service J, which is a parameter to control the marginal decreasing effect of the data. A larger λ_j indicates that the reward of the service decreases faster as the quantity of uploaded and downloaded data increases.

3.2.3 Formal Dynamic Reconfiguration

The value property of the service is used as a metric to evaluate whether the service is available. As described earlier, the value property of a service is an important parameter for applying the current and future QoS property values. The greater the value of the service, the greater its effect on improving the current and future QoS values. Therefore, the goal of dynamic reconfiguration is to maximize the values of the mobile service composition application.

In addition, for mobile service composition applications, the cost and reward of calling each service are different. From the user's point of view, the cost of calling services should be no higher than its value. In summary, the application of dynamic reconfiguration in mobile service composition under cloud-edge hybrid environments can be formalized in the following form:

$$\max. \sum_{k=1}^{s} value_k$$

$$s.t. \sum_{s_i \in S} c_i \leq \sum_{s_i \in S} r_i$$

Among them, the first formula indicates that the goal of dynamic reconfiguration is to maximize the value of the application. The second formula is the constraint condition of the dynamic reconfiguration problem, that is, the application cost should not be greater than the reward. Note that S is a collection of all services in the mobile services composition app.

4 LSTM Model for Predicting Service QoS

In a mobile environment, the quality of service will change as the location of the service changes dynamically. This may cause the service to fail. To ensure the stability of dynamic reconfiguration and reduce the risk in application operation, an LSTM neural network is employed to predict service QoS.

As shown in Fig. 2, this paper constructs an LSTM prediction model with an LSTM loop layer and two full-connection layers. The service response time, throughput, current signal strength and other parameters are selected to predict the service QoS value. The predictive model framework of the LSTM neural network is similar to conventional fully connected neural networks, except that some hidden layers in the network are replaced with LSTM structures. The input of the model is a sequence of attributes. It affects the change of service QoS value and the output predictive service QoS sequence in the cloud-edge hybrid environment.

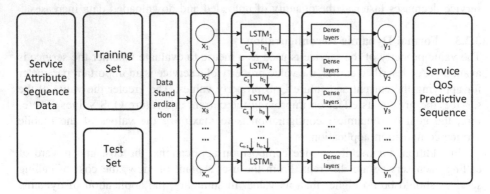

Fig. 2. LSTM neural network predictive model framework

The training process of the LSTM neural network is similar to conventional fully connected neural network. First, the feedforward propagation is used to input the training data into the network. The output value of the LSTM unit is calculated. Then the feature is extracted by two layers of the fully connected layer so that the layer is trained to the output layer. The "predictive estimate" of the sample data is obtained. Second, the error value of each neuron is calculated backward. The reverse propagation of the LSTM neural network consists of two functions. One function is the reverse propagation along time; that is, the error entry at each moment is calculated from the current T moment. The other function propagates the error item to the upper layer, according to the corresponding error item. By calculating the gradient of each weight, the model parameters are adjusted so that the prediction results are close to the optimization target. Through the above iteration, the training obtains the required optimization objectives to establish an LSTM neural network prediction model to meet the error requirements.

5   Framework

As shown in Fig. 3, the mobile service composition dynamic reconfiguration framework includes the candidate service value solving process, the service constraint condition solving process and the service dynamic reconfiguration process. The process of solving the service value is the process of calculating the importance parameters of the candidate service to the dynamic reconfiguration of the application. The process of solving the cost and reward of each service is measured by the service constraint condition. Finally, the final dynamic reconfiguration process selects the appropriate scheme in the candidate service to satisfy the new QoS constraint process.

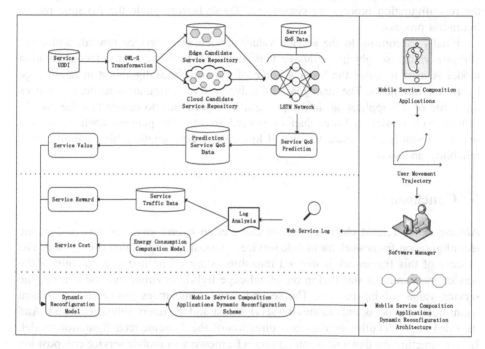

Fig. 3. Mobile service composition application dynamic reconfiguration framework

Solving the importance parameters of the candidate service for dynamic reconfiguration of the application is divided into two steps. The first step trains the LSTM neural network using the web service QoS dataset and the service invocation information collected from the sensor. The candidate service dataset from the cloud and edge end is the input variable to predict its QoS property value. The input dataset primarily contains a sequence of properties that have a greater impact on applications in cloud-edge hybrid environments, such as response time, throughput, and signal strength of the service. The second step combines the QoS property values at the current time and the predicted QoS property values for a future period of time to calculate the importance value of the service for this dynamic reconfiguration. It is based on the value function calculation formula.

In the second phase of the dynamic reconfiguration framework, we first analyze and process the log information of the candidate service. Then, the available information is extracted. We collect the mobile user's trajectory and place it into a grid to build the mobile trajectory model. The model is used to further handle changes in the signal strength of the user's device during the invocation of the service. The dynamic fluctuation of service-related property values caused by the changing environment of the user is one of the factors considered in this step. Finally, the mobile trajectory data and service upload and download, response time, signal strength and other attributes are combined. The service flow consumption, energy consumption and service reward are calculated according to the traffic calculation formula and energy consumption computation model, respectively. In this step, the factors that have a significant impact on the reconfiguration process are considered. Those factors guide the dynamic reconfiguration process.

Finally, according to the service value, service cost, service reward, and other attribute values sought in the above two stages. A formal dynamic reconfiguration model is used to solve the better scheme of dynamic reconfiguration in cloud-edge hybrid environments. The main goal of the dynamic reconfiguration model maximizes the value of the application. In the process, it is necessary to ensure that the cost of calling each service is lower than its reward so that the planned application as a returned result has the characteristics of low energy consumption, high stability, high reliability and so on.

6 Conclusion

Aiming at the related characteristics in cloud-edge hybrid environments, a dynamic reconfiguration framework for mobile service composition application is proposed. The process of this framework is divided into three stages. The first stage quantifies the service measurement standard in the cloud-edge hybrid environment and clarifies the service value solving process. The second stage summarizes the service constraint quantification process and clarifies the service cost and the return solution process. And the third stage identifies the data flow direction of the dynamic reconfiguration model. By constructing the dynamic reconfiguration framework of mobile service composition in the cloud-edge hybrid environment, the dependence of each module and the reconfiguration process are shown clearly.

In the next step, the dynamic reconfiguration framework proposed in this paper will be implemented and transformed into a real application, and the dynamic reconfiguration problem under this model will be standardized. In addition, structural optimization and loss function of the neural network will be considered to further improve its performance, such as using user collaboration and Microservice deployed in mobile App.

Acknowledgment. This work is supported by the National Key Research and Development Plan of China under Grant No. 2017YFD0400101, the Natural Science Foundation of Shanghai under Grant No. 16ZR1411200, and CERNET Innovation Project under Grant No. NGII20170513.

References

1. Cai, Y., Yu, F.R., Bu, S.: Cloud computing meets mobile wireless communications in next generation cellular networks. IEEE Netw. **28**(6), 54–59 (2014)
2. Deng, S., Huang, L., Wu, H., et al.: Toward mobile service computing: opportunities and challenges. IEEE Cloud Comput. **3**(4), 32–41 (2016)
3. Gao, H., Miao, H., Zeng, H.: Service reconfiguration architecture based on probabilistic modeling checking. In: International Conference on Web Services (2014)
4. Gao, H., Miao, H.: Research on the dynamic reconfiguration of Web application using two-phase compatibility verification. Int. J. Comput. Math. **90**(11), 2265–2278 (2013)
5. White, G., Nallur, V., Clarke, S.: Quality of service approaches in IoT: a systematic mapping. J. Syst. Softw. **132**, 186–203 (2017)
6. Kumar, K., Liu, J., Lu, Y.H., Bhargava, B.: A survey of computation offloading for mobile systems. Mob. Netw. Appl. **18**(1), 129–140 (2013)
7. Yang, Y., Zhao, H., Gu, X.: Improve energy consumption and packet scheduling for mobile edge computing. In: Liang, Q., Mu, J., Jia, M., Wang, W., Feng, X., Zhang, B. (eds.) CSPS 2017. LNEE, vol. 463, pp. 1659–1666. Springer, Singapore (2019). https://doi.org/10.1007/978-981-10-6571-2_201
8. Liu, P., Xu, G., Yang, K., Wang, K., Li, Y.: Joint optimization for residual energy maximization in wireless powered mobile-edge computing systems. KSII Trans. Internet Inf. Syst. **12**(12), 5614–5633 (2018)
9. Lane, N.D., Miluzzo, E., Lu, H., Peebles, D., Choudhury, T., Campbell, A.T.: A survey of mobile phone sensing. IEEE Commun. Mag. **48**(9), 140–150 (2010)
10. Palacin, M.R.: Recent advances in rechargeable battery materials: a chemist's perspective. Chem. Soc. Rev. **38**(9), 2565–2575 (2009)
11. Chen, X., Jiao, L., Li, W., Fu, X.: Efficient multi-user computation offloading for mobile-edge cloud computing. IEEE/ACM Trans. Network. **24**(5), 2795–2808 (2016)
12. White, G., Palade, A., Clarke, S.: Forecasting QoS attributes using LSTM networks. In: 2018 International Joint Conference on Neural Networks, IJCNN, pp. 1–8 (2018)
13. Madariaga, D., Panza, M., Bustos-Jimenéz, J.: I'm only unhappy when it rains: forecasting mobile QoS with weather conditions. In: 2018 Network Traffic Measurement and Analysis Conference, TMA, pp. 1–6. IEEE (2018)
14. Miorandi, D., Sicari, S., De Pellegrini, F., Chlamtac, I.: Internet of things: vision, applications and research challenges. Ad Hoc Netw. **10**(7), 1497–1516 (2012)
15. Li, Y., Lu, Y., Yin, Y., Deng, S., Yin, J.: Towards QoS-based dynamic reconfiguration of SOA-based applications. In: 2010 IEEE Asia-Pacific Services Computing Conference, pp. 107–114. IEEE (2010)
16. Zeng, L., Benatallah, B., Ngu, A.H., Dumas, M., Kalagnanam, J., Chang, H.: QoS-aware middleware for web services composition. IEEE Trans. Software Eng. **30**(5), 311–327 (2004)
17. Deng, S., Wu, H., Tan, W., Xiang, Z., Wu, Z.: Mobile service selection for composition: an energy consumption perspective. IEEE Trans. Autom. Sci. Eng. **14**(3), 1478–1490 (2017)
18. Tao, X., Song, W.: Location-dependent task allocation for mobile crowdsensing with clustering effect. IEEE Internet Things J. (2018)

19. Labbaci, H., Medjahed, B., Aklouf, Y.: A deep learning approach for long term QoS-compliant service composition. In: Maximilien, M., Vallecillo, A., Wang, J., Oriol, M. (eds.) ICSOC 2017. LNCS, vol. 10601, pp. 287–294. Springer, Cham (2017). https://doi.org/10.1007/978-3-319-69035-3_20
20. Deng, S., et al.: Toward risk reduction for mobile service composition. IEEE Trans. Cybern. **46**(8), 1807–1816 (2016)

A Security Framework to Protect Edge Supported Software Defined Internet of Things Infrastructure

Wajid Rafique[1,2], Maqbool Khan[1,2], Nadeem Sarwar[3], and Wanchun Dou[1,2(✉)]

[1] State Key Laboratory for Novel Software Technology, Nanjing University,
Nanjing, People's Republic of China
rafiqwajid@smail.nju.edu.cn, douwc@nju.edu.cn
[2] The Department of Computer Science and Technology, Nanjing University,
Nanjing, People's Republic of China
[3] Department of Computer Science, Bahria University, Lahore, Pakistan

Abstract. Managing the huge IoT infrastructure poses a vital challenge to the network community. Software Defined Networking (SDN), due to its characteristics of centralized network management has been considered as an optimal choice to manage IoT. Edge computing brings cloud recourses near the IoT to localize the cloud demands. Consequently, SDN, IoT, and edge computing can be combined into a framework to create a resourceful SDIoT-Edge architecture to efficiently orchestrate cloud services and utilize resource-limited IoT devices in a flexible way. Besides a wide adoption of IoT, the vulnerabilities present in this less secure infrastructure can be exploited by the adversaries to attack the OpenFlow channel using Distributed Denial of Service (DDoS) attacks. DDoS on OpenFlow channel have the ability to disrupt the whole network hence, providing security for the OpenFlow channel is a key challenge in SDIoT-Edge. We propose a security framework called SDIoT-Edge Security (SIESec) against the security vulnerabilities present in this architecture. SIESec prototype employs machine learning-based classification strategy, blacklist integration, and contextual network flow filtering to efficiently defend against the DDoS attacks. We perform extensive simulations using Floodlight controller and Mininet network emulator. Our results proclaim that SIESec provides extensive security against OpenFlow channel DDoS attacks and pose a very less overhead on the network.

Keywords: SDN · IoT · Edge computing · Security · DDoS

1 Introduction

Information technology (IT) has revolutionized the lifestyle of human-beings where ubiquitous computing has been widely adopted affirming Mark Weiser's prediction of extraordinary IT involvement in everyday life, which he proposed

© ICST Institute for Computer Sciences, Social Informatics and Telecommunications Engineering 2019
Published by Springer Nature Switzerland AG 2019. All Rights Reserved
X. Wang et al. (Eds.): CollaborateCom 2019, LNICST 292, pp. 71–88, 2019.
https://doi.org/10.1007/978-3-030-30146-0_6

28 years ago [28]. Cisco Systems claims that more than 50 billion devices will be connected to the internet until 2020 [4]. Internet of Things (IoT) has been deployed in all the fields of life, including industry, agriculture, health, transport, homes, and many others. The revenue for IoT vendors, service providers, and software solution developers is expected to reach $1 trillion until 2025 [19]. Besides, such lucrative benefits, managing such a huge repository of connected objects is a vital challenge. The resource-limitation in IoT devices makes it challenging to deploy a security solution onto the IoT infrastructure. Software Defined Networking (SDN) offers a layered architecture to enable flexible control, management, and programmability of the network. Therefore, the research community believes that SDN is an optimal choice to manage decentralized IoT infrastructure [13,15].

Since IoT devices are limited in resources, therefore cloud services facilitate compute-intensive tasks on IoT. Edge cloudlets are placed between the traditional cloud and the IoT infrastructure to offload the computations. Moreover, edge cloudlets also act as data filtering and classification resource, which only transmit the mandatory data to the traditional cloud data center and redeem vital network resources, including bandwidth, energy, and storage. Similarly, edge computing can effectively help resource-limited and latency-sensitive IoT applications by providing computation infrastructure near the edge of IoT. As SDN and edge are more powerful resources as compared to IoT, they are combined to devise a sustainable infrastructure of Software Defined Internet of Things using Edge computing (SDIoT-Edge) for efficient IoT service orchestration [16].

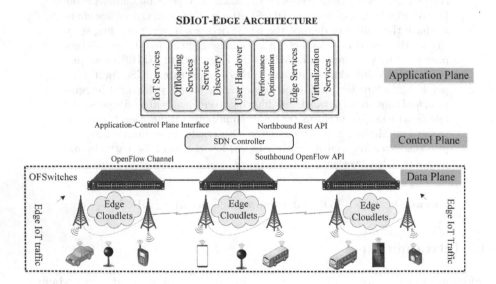

Fig. 1. An architecture of SDIoT-Edge.

Fig. 1 illustrates the integration of SDN, edge computing, and IoT to devise an SDIoT-Edge architecture where IoT devices are connected with the edge cloudlets at the data plane. The application plane contains novel edge services, including service discovery, user handover, offloading, and virtualization to facilitate edge resource provisioning. The figure also represents the OpenFlow channel, which connects the control plane and the data plane of the SDIoT-Edge framework. Although the integration of IoT-Edge infrastructure in the SDN paradigm seems a promising solution, this architecture is vulnerable toward countless novel security challenges and attacks including Link Flooding Attack (LFA) [18] and Distributed Denial of Service Attacks (DDoS) [11]. For example, in a recent Mirai botnet attack, the adversary leveraged the security vulnerabilities in IoT to prepare a huge army of compromised devices to attack internet infrastructure. The attackers used the open Teletype Network (Telnet) ports of IoT devices and tried to login using 61 different combinations of user-name and passwords that were mostly used as default credentials and never changed. After acquiring access to these devices, the attackers were able to manipulate 500,000 IoT botnets to attack internet infrastructure [11]. In another similar incident, vulnerabilities present in IoT architecture were exploited by adversaries to attack Dyn's [2] Domain Name Server (DNS)[1] causing massive information and revenue loss [8].

OpenFlow channel is a vital resource in SDIoT-Edge architecture as all the control information, e.g., flow rule installation, traffic management, and policy enforcement need to pass through this channel [12]. Consequently, the security of the OpenFlow channel is of prime importance in SDIoT-Edge ecosystem. Any attack on the OpenFlow channel can provoke management inconsistencies in the network and in severe circumstances, bring down the whole network. For example, in a DDoS attack, a malicious adversary can exploit the resource-limitation vulnerabilities in IoT to employ them as bots to attack the OpenFlow channel. In such an incident, 100,000 IoT devices were compromised, which attacked individual systems and enterprise servers around the globe, which provoked a huge revenue loss [22]. Therefore, providing security in SDIoT-Edge infrastructure is of prime importance to safeguard current networks. IoT devices are limited in memory, which makes it challenging to provide security solutions on these devices, therefore, network-based security solutions are highly needed.

Due to these vulnerabilities, there is a high need to provide security solutions for the OpenFlow channel protection in SDIoT-Edge. Therefore, we propose a network-level security solution against OpenFlow channel DDOS attacks named as SDIoT-Edge Security (SIESec). We develop this as a solution at the application plane of the SDN controller. We simulate the DDoS attack from IoT devices to demonstrate their vulnerabilities to be manipulated and provide a defense. SIESec employs an unsupervised machine learning classifier based on Self Organizing Maps (SOM) and includes blacklisting of malicious hosts, contextual traffic filtering, and customized flow rule generation for the identified malicious flows. SIESec performs SDN-oriented flow measurements therefore, no

---

[1] This attack targeted DNS systems of Dyn which caused major network services outage in Europe and North America.

extra hardware or measurement agents are required at the data plane of SDN. We perform extensive simulations using Mininet network emulator and Floodlight open-source controller to demonstrate the effectiveness of detection and mitigation of the SIESec. We present the contributions of this research in the following.

- We propose an architecture of SDIoT-Edge and highlight DDoS vulnerabilities on the OpenFlow channel of this architecture where any attack on this channel disrupts the whole network infrastructure.
- We devise a SIESec solutions, which utilize an unsupervised SOM-based classification and malicious traffic filtering based on blacklists and contextual information to detect and eliminate DDoS attacks in SDIoT-Edge.
- A comprehensive experimental evaluation and comparison demonstrate that SIESec provides efficient security against the OpenFlow channel DDoS attacks and induces a negligible overhead on the network.

Rest of the paper is organized as follows. Section 2 elaborates the architecture of the SDIoT-Edge and its security vulnerabilities. Section 3 discusses the SIESec solution, its components, and the working principle of all these components. Section 4 illustrates the experimental evaluation of the solution using different performance parameters. Section 5 presents the related work and comparison analysis, and finally, Sect. 6 concludes the paper and provides some future insights.

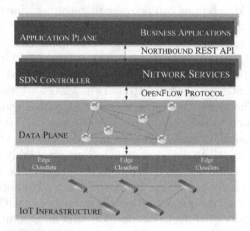

Fig. 2. A high-level architecture of SDIoT-Edge which extends the traditional SDN architecture [1].

2   SDIoT-Edge Architecture

The SDIoT-Edge architecture encompasses SDN, IoT, and edge computing to provide seamless infrastructure management and service orchestration. In this architecture, the cloudlets provide the offloading capability to the resource-limited IoT devices. These cloudlets are placed between the IoT infrastructure and the central cloud data center to facilitate the IoT devices in performing compute-intensive tasks. A high-level architecture of SDIoT-Edge is provided in Fig. 2, which illustrates three SDN planes and an IoT infrastructure plane facilitated by edge cloudlets. The data plane includes OpenFlow-enabled switches which forward the IoT traffic by exploiting three flow rule installation strategies including reactive, proactive, and hybrid. The application plane of the controller enables programmability where the administrators can develop and deploy innovative applications to provoke a wide range of services, including customized traffic forwarding, security, and management. In this architecture, the application plane includes edge services to effectively manage the IoT-service orchestration by using cloud infrastructure at the edge.

Due to the presence of immense security vulnerabilities in the resource-limited IoT devices, they can be effortlessly manipulated by the adversaries, which can deploy them as bots and attack the sophisticated network infrastructure. A few examples of such attacks generated by the IoT in SDIoT-Edge infrastructure includes information spoofing using Man-in-the-Middle (MiTM) attacks, policy switch attacks, flow table overflow attacks, and OpenFlow channel attacks. A taxonomy of these attacks is presented in Fig. 3. The most lethal of these attacks is the OpenFlow channel flooding attack where the controller can be disconnected from the infrastructure plane by DDoS traffic. The adversaries exploit IoT vulnerabilities and devise a manipulated army of bots to generate new flow rule installation requests at the data plane switches which continuously communicate with the controller for the flow rules. A higher number of flow rule installation requests congest the OpenFlow channel and disconnect it from the data plane in severe cases. This attack has lethal consequences on the network where it can shut down the whole network in severe cases. We present a defense solution to mitigate DDoS attacks on the SDIoT-Edge infrastructure. The characteristics of the novel SDIoT-Edge architecture are illustrated in the following.

1. **Resource Limitation:** IoT encompasses resource-limited infrastructure having the lower processing speed, memory, energy, and storage capacities. Therefore, these devices cannot support complex algorithms and defense strategies such as endpoint encryption and security solutions against the attacks. Meanwhile, this resource-limitation can be exploited by the adversary to manipulate them as bots in many devastating attacks.

2. **IoT Big Data:** A large number of IoT devices produce a huge amount of data which renders the basic requirement for DDoS attacks exertion and propagation. Although the same amount of data can be generated by other powerful infrastructures, the data generating resources in IoT are countless, which become a potential enabler for a security threat toward the network infrastructure.

3. **Flow Rule Installation:** In SDIoT-Edge the controller uses OpenFlow channel to communicate with the infrastructure, which is the backbone

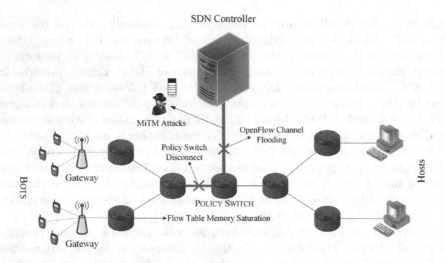

Fig. 3. Attack vulnerabilities in SDIoT-Edge.

SDIoT-Edge. When a flow arrives at the switch, it performs a flow table lookup and processes the flow using one of the three modes, including proactive, reactive, and hybrid. In the proactive mode, the network administrators proactively install the intended flow rules on the data plane switches to reduce the packet processing time. In a reactive mode, the flow rules are installed after the packets arrive at the switch using a PACKET_OUT message from the controller, whereas the hybrid mode uses both strategies to manage the flow rules. Although the choice of proactive flow rule installation method seems promising, the switches possess a meager Ternary Content Addressable Memory (TCAM) which cannot store a huge number of flow rules. Therefore, the reactive flow rule installation method is necessary to serve diverse traffic in the network. However, the reactive flow rule installation method can be exploited by the adversaries to transmit the flood of specially crafted flows to the switches which continuously transfer the requests to the controller for the flow rule installation and congest the OpenFlow channel.

4. **Offloading:** Although IoT devices are equipped with sophisticated sensors which continuously collect and transmit data, they do not possess the resources to perform compute-intensive tasks. The latency-sensitive applications in IoT suffer due to long waiting time induced by the central cloud data center in serving their requests. Alternatively, edge nodes encompass the resources to perform the offloaded tasks from the latency-sensitive IoT infrastructure. Moreover, data filtering and classification can be performed on the edge nodes to avoid unnecessary resource consumption in terms of bandwidth, storage, and energy. However, offloading and downloading of data incorporate many security, privacy, and data provenance issues.

Keeping in view the above-mentioned vulnerabilities in the SDIoT-Edge infrastructure, we propose SIESec solution to secure this infrastructure against DDoS attacks.

3 SIESec Solution

In this section we present SIESec solution, which provides defense against Open-Flow channel DDoS attacks on SDIoT-Edge architecture.

3.1 Adversary Model

The IoT-based DDoS have become one of the most devastating attacks against the current data center networks [8,11]. In the OpenFlow channel DDoS attack, the adversary exploits the vulnerabilities present in the IoT devices and flood the OpenFlow channel of the SDIoT-Edge infrastructure. We assume that the IoT manipulating adversary has the following capabilities.

- The adversary can access the IoT devices attached to an SDN, moreover, it can manipulate these devices to send attack packets to the other hosts in the network.
- The adversary can program IoT devices to send carefully crafted flood packets which cause packet miss in the switches at the infrastructure plane.
- The adversary ascertains the information of the victim's network using probing packets, including topology, network hierarchy, ingress switches, and packet miss information.
- The SDIoT-Edge network employs a reactive flow rule installation mechanism which has been widely used to provide flexible network provisioning [21,24].
- The adversary attacks the data plane switches using carefully crafted flood packets which cause packet miss and trigger new flow rule installation.

The adversary initially exploits topology discovery commands to inspect the network structure. Then it sends probing packets to the attached hosts to analyze the packet miss strategy by changing the packet header information and analyzing the Round Trip Time (RTT). When a packet miss occurs, its RTT increases as for a packet miss, the switch needs to request the controller to install a new flow rule using a PACKET_IN message. Subsequently, the controller replies with a PACKET_OUT message containing the flow rule for the packet, which increases the RTT. The adversary analyzes maximum different packet header combinations which cause packet miss and stores this information to attack the network. Furthermore, the adversary sends a flood of specially crafted attack packets to the network, which causes packet miss in the OpenFlow switches. Consequently, the controller is forced to install flow rules for a large number of new packets which causes extra overhead on the controller and impedes the flow rule installation process. With a further increase in the attack traffic, the controller becomes irresponsive, and OpenFlow channel turns into a congestion state. The attack invokes increase in delay, RTT, extra utilization of controller CPU, and bandwidth saturation of the OpenFlow channel.

SIESec performs collaborative network measurements by exploiting the centralized control strategy of SDN and then deploys an unsupervised machine learning SOM algorithm to classify the network traffic. We explain the SOM classification strategy in the next section.

1. Initiate $\overrightarrow{w}_j$ for every j^{th} neuron.
2. For each x_i in the training dataset, identify the neuron having smallest Euclidean distance to $\overrightarrow{x}_i$

   $min(\|\overrightarrow{x}_i - \overrightarrow{w}_j\})\|$
3. Update weight of all neurons extracted in step 2.
4. For each training vector repeat from step 2.

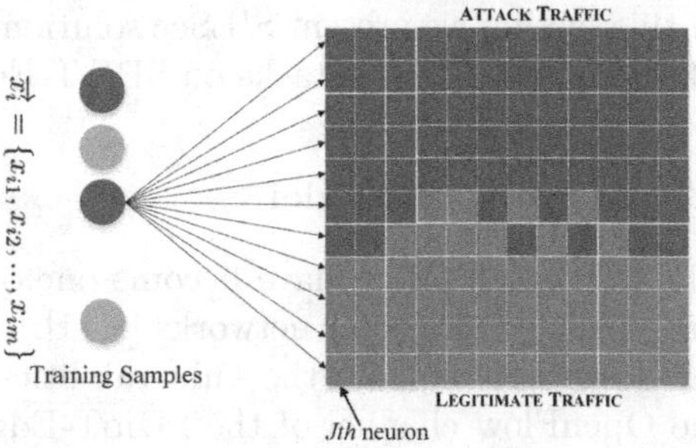

Fig. 4. Steps in SOM classification and a two dimensional graphical representation of training samples.

3.2   Self Organizing Maps Classification Algorithm

We employ an artificial neural network-based machine learning algorithm called SOM for the traffic classification. It first creates a randomized two-dimensional map of the training dataset. Then a data point is randomly selected on the map whereas a neuron called as Best Matching Unit (BMU) is chosen based on lowest Euclidean Distance and brought closer to the data point. The distance that the BMU covers is called the learning rate, which decreases after every iteration. Subsequently, the neighbors of the BMU are also moved closer to the data point to complete the first iteration. Furthermore, the learning rate and Euclidean Distance of BMU are recomputed for the next iteration. This process continues until the neurons in the grid take the shape of the data and finally reveal the intrinsic clusters in the dataset.

The SOM machine learning algorithm represents the network training samples to a set of neurons at a higher dimension and align them to a lower dimension during the classification task. The training process builds a model based on input features, and the mapping process classifies the traffic based on the lowest Euclidean Distance values. The algorithm to compute SOM is illustrated in Fig. 4 which describes four steps to classify the DDoS traffic. A two-dimensional SOM strategy is employed where the weight vector at j_{th} neuron having an m dimension is computed by the Eq. 1.

$$\overrightarrow{w_j} = [w_{j1}, w_{j2}, ..., w_{jm}] \tag{1}$$

The weight value of every neuron is assigned in a random manner where the feature values are constrained in a 0 to 1 range. The BMU neuron is selected using the Eq. 2.

$$\vec{w_i^*} = \min_{\forall \vec{wj} \in W} \sqrt{\sum_{k=1}^{m}(x_{ik} - x_{ik})^2} \qquad (2)$$

Where x_i is the i_{th} training sample which can be represented by the Eq. 3.

$$\vec{x_i} = [x_{j1}, x_{j2}, ..., x_{jm}] \qquad (3)$$

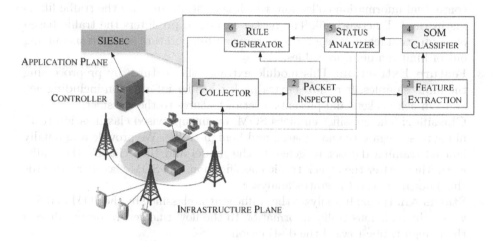

Fig. 5. Workflow of SIESec solution.

The weight of the competing neurons is finally computed in order to bring their values close to the training samples. The input to the SOM in SIESec is 6 features as discussed in the next section whereas the benign training samples were labeled manually.

3.3 Work-Flow of SIESec

SIESec is composed of six modules, as illustrated in Fig. 5. Overall, network security is ensured using the security solution. The detail of all the modules is discussed in the following.

1. **Collector:** This module continuously collects the network statistics by exploiting Representational Estate Transfer (REST) API of the open-source Floodlight controller, including the switch, packet, and flow-level statistics. It stores 6 statistics including source IP, average packet loss rate, time duration per flow, bandwidth consumption, overall link bandwidth, and packet drop rate.
2. **Packet Inspector:** The packet inspector performs two packet matching operations, including blacklist and contextual information inspection. The adversary tries to inject malicious traffic continuously using the compromised

IoT devices during the attack. Therefore, we employ a malicious packet identification database for the already identified adversaries to speed up the detection process. We keep updating the database as and when an adversary is identified. The traffic from the collector comes to the blacklist inspector, which matches the packet source with the database entries. If the incoming packet source is matched with an entry in the database, the control is forwarded to the flow rule generator, which requests the controller to generate a flow rule to drop this packet. The packet inspector also incorporates the contextual information collection, which is a vital source for the traffic filtering in the IoT network [6]. The packet inspector pre-filters the traffic based on contextual features, e.g., a compromised temperature sensor transmitting out of limit temperature values.

3. **Feature Extraction:** This module extracts the features by preprocessing the input samples. It removes extra packet header information including ack and syn-ack packets and presents a set of features to the classifier.

4. **Classifier:** The classifier employs SOM, an unsupervised classification technique to segregate the adversarial and benign traffic. We provide a manually labeled training dataset to generate the model and then classify the traffic at runtime. After the attack traffic classification, the SOM classifier forwards this information to the status analyzer.

5. **Status Analyzer:** It analyzes the traffic status classified by the SOM and forwards the malicious traffic information to the flow rule generator and directs the benign traffic toward the destination.

6. **Rule Generator:** This is the final operation in the SIESec solution, it requests the controller with the malicious flow packet identity to generate a flow rule to drop this packet. Many techniques can be applied to block or mitigate the flooding flows, including null routing, scrubbing, and dropping a flow. However, we utilize the flow-drop strategy to eliminate the malicious packets because it poses only a minor computation overhead on the network. Subsequently, the source IP of the malicious flow is added to the blacklist database, which can be utilized for future traffic filtering. An important feature of SIESec solution is that it advocates reuse, where the information of a malicious adversary can be stored and reused in the future. Therefore, it saves extra effort on the classification of already identified adversaries.

The collector module continuously collects network statistics using the REST API and provide the features to the SOM classifier. All the traffic from the SDIoT-Edge should pass through the SDN switches where the surveillance is performed using the security solution. The collector obtains network statistics from the infrastructure plane and provides it to the packet inspector, which filters the traffic packets for the identification of blacklists and contextual information. If any of the two filtering operations is true, a notification is transmitted to the flow rule generator with the packet information, which requests the controller to drop the identified flow. Subsequently, the traffic is forwarded to the feature extraction module which performs the pre-processing on the data and forwards the traffic to the SOM classifier. This module classifies the DDoS traffic and transfers the results to the status analyzer, which moves the benign traffic toward the hosts and malicious traffic to the flow rule generator. The controller is requested to generate flow-drop rules for the identified malicious flows. It is pertinent to note here that when an adversary is detected, the source is added to the blacklists to enhance the traffic filtering in the future.

In this section, we elaborated the SIESec solution. In the next section, we discuss the experimental evaluation of SIESec.

4   Experiment Evaluation

SIESec acts as an application in the application layer of SDN. All the network measurements have been performed using the SDN controller, which poses a minimal network overhead. We use iperf tool to generate traffic from the IoT hosts, moreover, we utilize Mininet network emulator and Floodlight open-source controller for experimentation. The controller was running on a Windows 10 machine with an Intel Core i7 processor and 16 GB of RAM, whereas the Mininet emulator was configured on a Ubuntu 16.0.4 operating system running on an Oracle-Virtualbox, virtual machine manager. The input parameters for the SOM classifier includes 6 features, 2 output neurons, and a learning rate of 0.4. The training features have been manually labeled in both legitimate and DDoS traffic scenario. We emulate the network topology, as shown in Fig. 6. Moreover, we employ the following traffic features.

1. Source IP
2. Average of packet loss rate
3. Time duration per flow
4. Bandwidth consumption
5. Overall link bandwidth
6. Packet received rate.

4.1   Attack Setup

We employ the network topology represented in Fig. 6 for the experimentation, which represents four clusters of IoT devices connected with the edge gateways. The adversary utilizes a huge repository of IoT devices at three clusters to send DDoS traffic on the network. Similarly, a cluster of legitimate devices sends benign traffic toward the destination hosts in the network. Therefore, the network contains both legitimate and DDoS attack flows. The bandwidth of the OpenFlow channel was set to 1 Gbps, and the attack rate varied from o to 1000 Packets Per Second (PPS).

4.2   Results

We use four performance metrics to evaluate SIESec as represented in Fig. 7. When the attack occurs on the network, it decreases the available bandwidth of the OpenFlow channel, increases delay, RTT, and CPU utilization. The results of the experimentation are illustrated in the following.

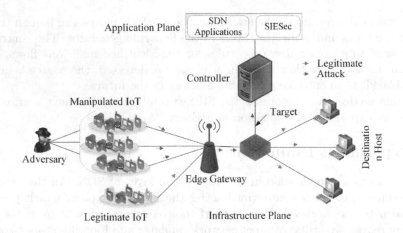

Fig. 6. The experimental topology illustrating a huge number of compromised IoT devices sending DDoS traffic to the network.

4.3 Available Bandwidth

In this experiment, we send a flood of specially crafted packets to the switches in the data plane causing packet miss with an attack packet rate from 0 to 1000 PPS. The bandwidth is measured during each round of the experiment. The experiment was conducted with and without SIESec solution. In the presence of SIESec, the available bandwidth drops initially due to the flow rule installation for the benign traffic, which further becomes stable. In the second experiment, we run the attack without SIESec solution, and the bandwidth is measured after 100 PPS attack intervals. The results demonstrate that the bandwidth of the channel dropped to 0 when the attack rate reached 900 PPS. It can also be observed in Fig. 7a that the bandwidth of OpenFlow channel saturates rapidly with the increase in the attack packets. However, it remained stable throughout the experiment when SIESec solution was deployed. The evaluation using available bandwidth demonstrates the effectiveness of the SIESec to comprehensively maintain the available bandwidth of the OpenFlow channel during the attack.

4.4 Round Trip Time

We perform RTT experiment with and without SIESec and measure the RTT as represented in Fig. 7b. We analyze the RTT using ping command at the benign host during the attack. The graph without SIESec solution illustrates that the value of RTT increased significantly when the attack rate reached to 200 PPS, which further increased continuously and reached a value peak at 1000 PPS attack rate. Experiment with the SIESec solution demonstrates that the RTT increased slightly when the attack rate was 300 PPS, the reason behind this fluctuation was the training of the classifier which induced a slight time delay and increased the RTT. Subsequently, the RTT graph became stable, and the

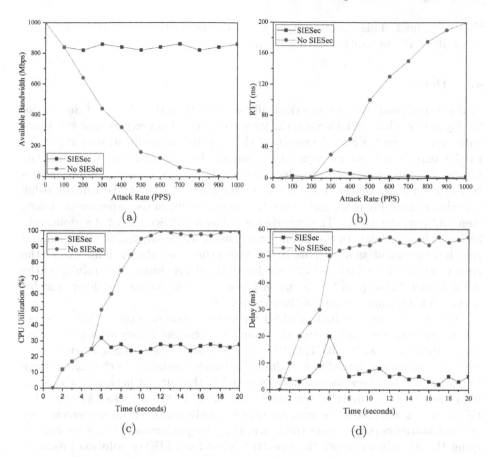

Fig. 7. Evaluation of SIESec using different evaluation measures.

RTT values remained closer to 0. This experiment demonstrates that the SIESec solution efficiently minimizes RTT during the OpenFlow channel DDoS attacks.

4.5   CPU Utilization of Controller

In this experiment, the CPU utilization of the controller is observed with and without SIESec solution, as illustrated in Fig. 7c. The CPU utilization during the attack increased from around 25% at 5 s to a peak value of up to 100%. The CPU utilization was around 25% at the start of the attack due to the normal traffic. However, with the increase in the attack traffic, the utilization continuously increased and reached to 100%. Alternatively, we perform the experiment with SIESec solution, as we can observe from Fig. 7c that the CPU utilization was stable and remained around 25% throughout the experiment. There is a slight increase in the utilization ratio near 6 s, where it reached around 33% due to the initial attack detection latency. However, further utilization remained stable until the end of the experiment, other than a negligible uplift at the start of the experiment. This experiment demonstrates that SIESec efficiently manages controller CPU utilization during the attack.

4.6 Delay

In this experiment, we measure the traffic delay with and without SIESec during the OpenFlow channel DDoS attack. We perform the delay experiment two times with and without SIESec, the results of the experiment are illustrated in Fig. 7d. In this experiment, we measured the delay of the legitimate traffic during the attack, for this, we exploit the legitimate IoT devices to send traffic packets to the other hosts at the destination and measure the delay. We run the delay experiment multiple times and record the average value of the experiment at each step and plot the graph. The experiment without SIESec revealed significantly higher values of delay. In the second experiment, we deploy SIESec solution and run the experiment again. Figure 7d illustrates that the delay increased when the time was 6 s and reached up to 20 ms due to the delay during the training of the SOM model. Subsequently, the graph becomes stable where the delay remains around 5 ms during the rest of the experiment.

The experimental evaluation of SIESec solution portrays that SIESec is effective in systematically alleviating the OpenFlow channel DDoS attacks based on the available bandwidth, RTT, CPU utilization, and delay. SIESec actively mitigates the attack and introduces a minimal network overhead. As the SDIoT-Edge infrastructure has been increasingly deployed in the current networks, this technique provides a comprehensive solution against DDoS attacks. As the other DDoS attack mitigation techniques deploy hardware-based measurements for network statistics collection or traffic rerouting, we perform all the measurements using the SDN-based centralized control. Therefore, SIESec solution invokes a minimal overhead and efficiently provides security against OpenFlow channel DDoS attacks.

5   Related Work and Comparison Analysis

IoT is capturing tremendous attention from academia and industry during the past few years. However, the security vulnerabilities in IoT pose a vital challenge for the network community and effective realization of IoT. With the widespread adoption of IoT, the issues of security assessment and devising defense mechanisms are of prime concern for the network security researchers. SDN provides centralized network management by separating infrastructure and control planes. This separation provokes a flexible network evolution and programmability. Therefore, SDN is considered as the best choice for IoT-Edge networks [13,15]. However, the adoption of SDN for IoT management also impels numerous security challenges [3,10,22].

The integration of IoT with fog computing using SDN has been proposed by [20] whereas the security vulnerability assessment in IoT has been performed by [25]. Authors in [10] propose MiTM attacks in SDN IoT-fog infrastructure.

They provide an experimental evaluation on how the vulnerabilities in IoT can be exploited by the adversaries to attack the OpenFlow channel, including information spoofing, topology faking, and information theft attacks. A security solution employing multi-hop routing technique has been proposed in [26] where a multi-path route can be computed by identifying the neighbors, their location, and energy of the sensory devices.

In the DDoS reflection attack, the source sends a minimal query to the IoT device, which replies with a long message to the victim. In [17], authors propose that the IoT devices suffer from the vulnerability of DDoS reflection attacks. They demonstrate that the household devices can be exposed to these attacks besides being protected by the gateways. Authors in [9] propose a DDoS solution against IoT using a fast communication channel to actively detect and defend these attacks. An attack graph can be used to identify probable attack routes, where securing the route can proactively mitigate the DDoS attack. A graph-based method to detect the sequence of paths that the adversary follows during an attack in Industrial internet of things has been provided in [14]. A lightweight solution against bandwidth attacks using intrusion prevention technique in IoT has been presented in [5]. However, this mechanism is hard to implement in IoT as it needs high computation power, which is not available in the current IoT infrastructure.

Defense techniques against security in SDN can be divided into two categories, including data plane security [7] and the control plane defense [27]. FloodDefender [21] is a security solution against resource saturation attacks on both control and data planes. It employs traffic filtering, table miss analysis, and flow migration to defend against DoS attacks. However, this technique induces more delay in the network traffic due to the complex analysis and time-consuming rule migration. Similarly, FloodGuard considers DoS attack strategy where only one adversary sends flood packets. However, SIESec provides defense against DDoS attacks in SDIoT-Edge, where a huge number of IoT devices flood the OpenFlow channel. SGuard [23] provides access control using a classification strategy, however, the complex measurements in this technique increase overhead on the network. BWManager [27] provides defense against DoS attacks on the controller by using a scheduling strategy to process the flow requests. However, this technique also induces traffic overhead by directing the traffic to follow the round-robin scheduling strategy. Moreover, CyberPulse [18] provides defense against OpenFlow channel LFA using machine learning techniques. However, this solution follows a direct attack strategy on the OpenFlow channel, which differs from our proposed attack and defense mechanism.

The difference between the previous techniques and SIESec is that the previous solutions do not consider the complex SDIoT-Edge paradigm. Similarly, these techniques perform complex network measurements using specialized hardware or software agents. However, SIESec provides comprehensive security without posing extra overhead on the network. Besides, SIESec employs blacklist and contextual information filtering to mitigate DDoS traffic interactively. Although the SIESec provides promising benefits, the actual implementation of SDIoT-

Edge will precisely reveal the efficiency in a practical paradigm. Moreover, SOM classification strategy may suffer in some cases as it needs sufficient training samples to classify the attack traffic accurately. However, the cost-benefit analysis of SIESec makes it an efficient solution against DDoS attacks in SDIoT-Edge paradigm.

6   Conclusion and Future Work

The huge proliferation of decentralized IoT devices poses a vital challenge in the network management. Software defined networking due to its capability of flexible network management has been proposed to manage IoT infrastructure. Edge computing brings cloud resources near to the IoT devices to overcome resource-limitation bottleneck in IoT. Therefore, SDIoT-Edge integration provides a resourceful platform to enable efficient IoT service orchestration.

In this research, we first proposed the architecture of SDIoT-Edge infrastructure and then provided a novel security solution against DDoS attacks in SDIoT-Edge. Nevertheless, the SDN infrastructure of IoT-Edge provides promising features, the integration of diverse platforms pose several security challenges. To overcome the vulnerability of DDoS attacks on the OpenFlow channel, we presented a security solution named as SIESec. The proposed SIESec solution employs machine learning-based SOM classification algorithm, blacklist integration, and contextual information filtering of the malicious IoT traffic to provide defense against DDoS attacks. The experiments performed using Mininet network emulator, and Floodlight open-source controller demonstrates that SIESec provides an efficient solution against OpenFlow channel DDoS attacks and poses a minimal network overhead.

A scalable solution can be developed for large-sized SDIoT-Edge networks by extending SIESec using SOM filtering on smaller SDIoT-Edge network segments, and then a centralized security solution for the global network can be implemented. In future work, we plan to implement this solution using multiple algorithms and provide the evaluation using a physical testbed.

Acknowledgment. This research is supported by the National Science Foundation of China under Grant No. 61672276 and 61702277 and the Collaborative Innovation Center of Novel Software Technology and Industrialization, Nanjing University.

References

1. SDN architecture. https://www.opennetworking.org/wp-content/uploads/2013/02/
2. DNS products trusted by the worlds most admired digital brands (2019). http://dyn.com/dns/
3. Administrator: MMD-0056-2016 - Linux/Mirai, how an old ELF malcode is recycled (2016). http://blog.malwaremustdie.org/2016/08/mmd-0056-2016-linuxmirai-just.html

4. Afshar, V.: Cisco: Enterprises are leading the internet of things innovation (2017). https://www.huffingtonpost.com/entry/cisco-enterprises-are-leading-the-internet-of-things_us_59a41fcee4b0a62d0987b0c6
5. Aldaej, A.: Enhancing cyber security in modern internet of things (IoT) using intrusion prevention algorithm for IoT (IPAI). IEEE Access (2019, In press)
6. Aleroud, A., Karabatis, G.: Contextual information fusion for intrusion detection: a survey and taxonomy. Knowl. Inform. Syst. **52**(3), 563–619 (2017)
7. Ambrosin, M., Conti, M., De Gaspari, F., Poovendran, R.: LineSwitch: tackling control plane saturation attacks in software-defined networking. IEEE/ACM Trans. Netw. **25**(2), 1206–1219 (2017)
8. Baker, C.: Recent IoT-based attacks: what is the impact on managed DNS operators? (2016), http://dyn.com/blog/dyn-analysis-summary-of-fridayoctober-21-attack/
9. Bhardwaj, K., Miranda, J.C., Gavrilovska, A.: Towards IoT-DDoS prevention using edge computing. In: {USENIX} Workshop on Hot Topics in Edge Computing (HotEdge 2018), Boston, MA (2018)
10. Cheng, L., Qin, Z., Novak, E., Li, Q.: Securing SDN infrastructure of IoTfog networks from MitM attacks. IEEE Internet Things J. **4**(5), 1156–1164 (2017)
11. De Donno, M., Dragoni, N., Giaretta, A., Spognardi, A.: DDoS-capable IoT malwares: comparative analysis and Mirai investigation. Secur. Commun. Netw. **2018** (2018)
12. Deng, S., Gao, X., Lu, Z., Li, Z., Gao, X.: Dos vulnerabilities and mitigation strategies in software-defined networks. J. Netw. Comput. Appl. **125**, 209–219 (2019)
13. Farris, I., Taleb, T., Khettab, Y., Song, J.: A survey on emerging SDN and NFV security mechanisms for IoT systems. IEEE Commun. Surv. Tutor. **21**(1), 812–837 (2019)
14. George, G., Thampi, S.M.: A graph-based security framework for securing industrial IoT networks from vulnerability exploitations. IEEE Access **6**, 43586–43601 (2018)
15. Jararweh, Y., Al-Ayyoub, M., Benkhelifa, E., et al.: An experimental framework for future smart cities using data fusion and software defined systems: the case of environmental monitoring for smart healthcare. Future Gener. Comput. Syst. (2018, In press)
16. Jararweh, Y., et al.: Software-defined system support for enabling ubiquitous mobile edge computing. Comput. J. **60**(10), 1443–1457 (2017)
17. Lyu, M., Sherratt, D., Sivanathan, A., Gharakheili, H.H., Radford, A., Sivaraman, V.: Quantifying the reflective DDoS attack capability of household iot devices. In: Proceedings of the 10th ACM Conference on Security and Privacy in Wireless and Mobile Networks, pp. 46–51. ACM, Montreal (2017)
18. Rasool, R.U., Ashraf, U., Ahmed, K., Wang, H., Rafique, W., Anwar, Z.: Cyberpulse: a machine learning based link flooding attack mitigation system for software defined networks. IEEE Access **7**, 34885–34899 (2019)
19. Sabet, K.A.: IoT revenue opportunity to exceed $1 trillion by 2025 (2018). https://www.itpro.co.uk/internet-of-things-iot/31218/iot-revenue-opportunity-to-exceed-1-trillion-by-2025
20. Salman, O., Elhajj, I., Chehab, A., Kayssi, A.: IoT survey: An SDN and fog computing perspective. Comput. Netw. **143**, 221–246 (2018)
21. Shang, G., Zhe, P., Xiao, B., Hu, A., Ren, K.: FloodDefender: protecting data and control plane resources under SDN-aimed DoS attacks. In: IEEE Conference on Computer Communications (INFOCOM), Atlanta, GA, USA, pp. 1–9 (2017)

22. Sunnyvale, C.: Proofpoint uncovers internet of things (IoT) cyberattack (2014). https://docplayer.net/16470381-Proofpoint-uncovers-internet-of-things-iot-cyberattack.html

23. Tao, W., Chen, H.: SGuard: a lightweight sdn safe-guard architecture for DoS attacks. Chin. J. **14**(6), 113–125 (2017)

24. Wang, H., Xu, L., Gu, G.: FloodGuard: a DoS attack prevention extension in software-defined networks. In: IEEE/IFIP International Conference on Dependable Systems and Networks, Washington, DC, USA (2015)

25. Wang, H., Chen, Z., Zhao, J., Di, X., Liu, D.: A vulnerability assessment method in industrial internet of things based on attack graph and maximum flow. IEEE Access **6**, 8599–8609 (2018)

26. Wang, J., Miao, Y., Zhou, P., Hossain, M.S., Rahman, S.M.M.: A software defined network routing in wireless multihop network. J. Netw. Comput. Appl. **85**, 76–83 (2017)

27. Wang, T., Guo, Z., Chen, H., Liu, W.: Bwmanager: mitigating denial of service attacks in software-defined networks through bandwidth prediction. IEEE Trans. Netw. Serv. Manage. **15**(4), 1235–1248 (2018)

28. Weiser, M.: The computer for the 21st century. IEEE Pervasive Comput. **1**(1), 19–25 (2002)

Data Analysis and Recommendation

SMART: A Service-Oriented Statistical Analysis Framework on Spatio-Temporal Big Data (Short Paper)

Jie Zhou[1,3]([⊠]), Weilong Ding[1,2], Zhuofeng Zhao[1,3], and Han Li[1,2]

[1] Data Engineering Institute,
North China University of Technology, Beijing 100144, China
136139154@qq.com
[2] Beijing Key Laboratory on Integration and Analysis of Large-Scale Stream
Data, Beijing 100144, China
[3] Beijing Urban Governance Research Center, Beijing 100144, China

Abstract. Spatio-temporal data is one of the most important assets in the context of smart cities. Spatio-temporal big data comes from a variety of sensor devices, implies the state of urban operation, insight into the development trend. Due to the multidimensional characteristics and diverse analysis needs of spatial-temporal data, data analysis based on spatial-temporal data must take into account the large capacity, diversity and frequent changes of data. This makes spatial and temporal data analysis more difficult. In order to simplify the analysis of spatio-temporal data, a service-oriented intelligent framework is proposed. Firstly, the concept of spatio-temporal data service is introduced into the framework, and several common spatio-temporal data service models are defined. Then, a configurable scripting language was proposed to define the analytic application. We also developed a prototype tool to implement spatio-temporal data services on Hadoop. In order to prove the applicability of our method, we demonstrate the effectiveness of our work through a practical application-based study.

Keywords: Spatio-temporal data · Service composition · Configurable

1 Introduction

In nowadays, various sensors are adopted in modern cities [1], such as recognition cameras on the trunk roads, smart-card readers in the buses, GPS equipped devices in taxis, RFID tags embedded on freights, inductive loops at the toll stations, and transducer in the power plants. The accumulated sensory data with attributes of space and time [2, 3] can reflect the urban rhythm.

Spatio-temporal data is a multidimensional continuum and always accumulated as big data. It is crucial to understand the dependencies across time and space [4] during the analysis. Considering their large amount and high velocity, the data analyses are intrinsically challenging. (1) First, traditionally it is a long cycle to describe requirements, complete programming, and plot the results. To balance the programming availability and analysis complexity is not trivial. It is urgent to find ways to depict

X. Wang et al. (Eds.): CollaborateCom 2019, LNICST 292, pp. 91–100, 2019.
https://doi.org/10.1007/978-3-030-30146-0_7

requirements easily in domain specific manner. (2) Second, for common descriptive statistical analysis, it is inconvenient to configure multiple steps of preprocessing, statistical processing and visualization. Each step would contain various configurable parameters. (3) Third, for such a statistical analysis application, collaborate multiple steps in a complete and rigorous manner is inefficient. In current solutions, only limited capabilities (e.g., processing through Hadoop MapReduce and storage on NoSQL) are supported, but the association with preprocessing or visualized is ignored.

In this paper, SMART is presented for typical descriptive statistics with the following contributions. (1) In view of the process of spatio-temporal data preprocessing, descriptive statistic and visualization, this paper summarizes the extraction of different types of service requirements, and on this basis, the corresponding service model is designed. (2) A method of implementing spatio-temporal descriptive statistic service in Hadoop environment is proposed. Statistics service program based on big data environment can be realized automatically through configuration. (3) The spatio-temporal data service composition language and the implementation engine are used to constrain and describe the behavior of the spatio-temporal data service composition.

The organizational structure of this article is as follows. Section 2 introduces the related work. Section 3 introduces the system structure of SMART. Section 4 presents the implementation of specific cases.

2 Related Work

Web service is a technology based on standard network protocol, which is an important means to realize the mutual access operation of application services between heterogeneous systems on the Internet. In the implementation of Web services, because the implementation and operation of REST-based Web services are easier and simpler than those based on SOAP and XML-RPC [5], REST has attracted wide attention in the industry since it was proposed. Amazon has also put REST principles into practice. It has implemented RESTFul services with XML as data exchange format [6], as well as social platform FaceBook and Paypal, which provide REST-style Web services.

Current research on service composition is mostly based on service discovery and service composition of the Internet of Things, and few studies are focused on service discovery and modeling under the background of multidimensional analysis of large spatial and temporal data. The literature [7] proposes a four-tier architecture, namely, storage layer, online and historical data processing layer, analysis layer and decision layer. This architectural approach can be used to handle large static data streams as well as large online data streams.

3 Architectural Design and Realization

3.1 Architectural Design

The architecture of SMART is presented as Fig. 1. On the virtualized infrastructure, data analyses as configurable applications would be built as these steps. We will explore and study these three steps in the next work.

(1) In the process of spatio-temporal data analysis, this paper summarizes different types of services for data preprocessing, statistical calculation and visualization. On this basis, the service model is studied. Following the characteristics of spatio-temporal data analysis, the statistical application of spatio-temporal data can be constructed quickly.

(2) A method of spatio-temporal description of statistical service in Hadoop environment is proposed, and the statistics service based on big data environment can be quickly realized through configuration

(3) Declarative configuration languages can describe the multidimensional characteristics of spatio-temporal data. It can also be used to constrain the behavior of services and service composition.

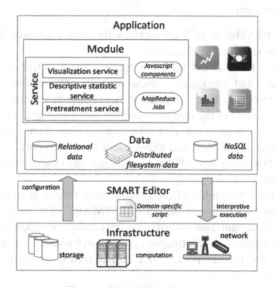

Fig. 1. SMART architecture

3.2 Spatio-Temporal Data Service Recognition and Modeling

According to the characteristics of spatio-temporal large data and multidimensional data, this paper studies the methods of spatio-temporal large data analysis, and preliminarily designs several common services: pretreatment service, descriptive statistic service and visualization service. The model of spatio-temporal data service is designed.

The service model of spatio-temporal data can be expressed as a quintuple <Prefix, Type, Service ID, Parameter, Result>:

Prefix: Universal prefix for basic services, defined here as http://ip:port/hn/jsps/service;

Types: Types of service. Three types are defined here: pretreatment service, descriptive statistic service and visualization service. These three types correspond to preprocess, statistics, visualized.

Service ID: Service ID, the unique service identification generated by a user when creating a service on a Web page.

Parameters: A list of parameters. The different parameters of the services accessed are different. Specific parameters are related to the content of each service. For example, the parameters of pretreatment service are optional processing methods, the parameters of descriptive statistic service are attributes of different dimensions such as space, time and object, and the parameters of visualization service are optional visual graphical effects.

Result: The result returned by the service is displayed in the JSON string. Specific results are designed according to HTTP requests.

3.3   Fast Implementation of Descriptive Statistic Service Based on Big Data Environment

SMART provides RESTful style Web services for data communication and service invocation of spatio-temporal data services.

Pretreatment Service: Pretreatment service extracts some data from massive redundant spatio-temporal data and eliminates erroneous data. Pretreatment service mainly includes three functions. (1) Data integration: According to the needs of multidimensional analysis, extract part of the data from multidimensional space-time data. (2) Data revision based on spatio-temporal correlation: excluding data with cross temporal attributes, invalid spatial attributes and inconsistent spatio-temporal attributes. (3) Data filtering based on business rules: eliminating illegal attributes, invalid null attributes and duplicate redundant data.

The configuration information of the pretreatment service is obtained through the method of selecting preconfigured services by SMART. The preprocessing module obtains the URI of configuration information, executes corresponding preprocessing jobs according to configuration information, and sends the address where the results are stored to SMART. The pretreatment service API design is shown in Table 1 below.

Table 1. Pretreatment service API design

Request mode	GET			
Request path	/HN/jsps/service/getpre?serviceID&type=ptype			
Request parameters	Name	Position	Type	Description
	serviceID	URL Route	string	Service ID, which is automatically generated by the system according to the service type.
	type	URL Route	string	Service type, automatically added by the system.
URL example	http://localhost:8080/HN/jsps/service/getpre?serviceID=01&type=prepro			
Reponse Body	JSON format adds result sets for operations			

Descriptive Statistic Service: The function of descriptive statistic service is to analyze the data obtained by preprocessing and get the statistical results. After the pretreatment service is executed, the MapReduce model of Hadoop platform is used to realize the multidimensional descriptive statistical service. The descriptive statistic service API design is shown in Table 2 below.

Table 2. Descriptive statistic service API design

Request mode	GET			
Request path	/HN/jsps/service/getsta?serviceID&type=stype			
Request parameters	Name	Position	Type	Description
	serviceID	URL Route	string	Service ID, which is automatically generated by the system according to the service type.
	type	URL Route	string	Service type, automatically added by the system.
URL example	http://localhost:8080/HN/jsps/service/getsta?serviceID=11&type=statistics			
Reponse Body	Result Set from Data Statistical Job in JSON format			

The descriptive statistic service obtains the URI of the configuration information of the data statistics jobs configured by SMART, and executes the corresponding data statistics jobs according to the configuration information. The address stored in the statistical results is sent to SMART. Our innovative work is to design a data statistics template based on MapReduce model of Hadoop platform for multidimensional data statistics. When data statistics are needed, there is no need to repeat coding. We only need to get the parameter list of descriptive statistic service and then we can get the data statistics results in different dimensions through the template. The flow chart for MapReduce template execution is shown in Fig. 2.

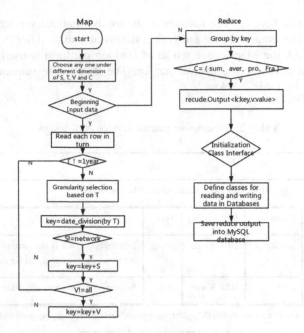

Fig. 2. MapReduce diagram

Visualization Service: Each visualization service may correspond to multiple data statistics services. As required, we get the results of the descriptive statistic service and select the configurable component style to display the results. The visualization service API design is shown in Table 3 below.

Table 3. Visualization service API design

Request mode	GET			
Request path	/HN/jsps/service/getview?serviceID&type=vtype			
Request pa-rameters	Name	Position	Type	Description
	serviceID	URL Route	string	Service ID, which is automatically generated by the system according to the service type.
	type	URL Route	string	Service type, automatically added by the system.
URL example	http://localhost:8080/HN/jsps/service/getview?serviceID=21&type=view			
Reponse Body	JSON format to query data table fields, field types and other information result sets			

3.4   Configurable Spatio-Temporal Data Service Composition

An application can be built using the services provided by SMART, such as Qingming Festival vehicle travel. The application involves three services: (1) pretreatment service extracts data from three-day traffic data and cleans data, extracts spatio-temporal related data, and eliminates erroneous data that do not conform to spatio-temporal correlation. (2) Descriptive statistic service performs corresponding data statistics jobs according to the dimension information of time, space and object selected by users, and obtains the data statistics results. (3) Visualization service obtains the results of descriptive statistic service and prediction service, and displays them visually.

SMART provides configurable options for three types of services. Users can select the specific information corresponding to the three types of services through SMART. The configuration files for each service are given below:

Configuration file1 Pretreatment service Information

---

1.   `<prepro>`

2.   `<period>2018-06-16--2018-06-18</period>`

3.   `<preproccess>Time attribute out of bounds</preproccess>`

4.   `<preproccess>Invalid space attribute</preproccess>`

5.   `<preproccess>Inconsistent time and space attributes</preproccess>`

6.   `<preproccess>Illegal license plate attribute</preproccess>`

7.   `<preproccess>license</preproccess>`

8.   `<data>`

9.   `<url>http://localhost:8080/HN/jsps/service/enc?serviceID=10&type=encapsulate</url>`

10.   `</data>`

11.   `</prepro>`

Configuration file2 Descriptive statistic service Information

---

12.   `<item>`

13.   `<ID>d1</ID>`

14.   `<space>network</space>`

15.   `<date>day</date>`

16.   `<vehicle>MTC</vehicle>`

17.   `<data>`

18.   `<input_url>hdfs://10.61.8.230:8020/user/hnetl/input</input_url>`

19.   `<output_url>jdbc:mysql://10.61.4.120:3306/hnfreeway</output_url>`

20.   `</data>`

21.   `</item>`

Configuration file3 Visualization service Information

22.	\<view\>
23.	\<form\>pie plot\</form\>
24.	\<serviceID\>d1,d2\</serviceID\>
25.	\<data\>
26.	\<input_url\>jdbc:mysql://10.61.4.120:3306/hnfreeway\</input_url\>
27.	\<tb_structure\>tb_PerStaOneDayEM:stationID,date,type,volume\</tb_structure\>
28.	\</data\>
29.	\</view\>

4 Case Study

Any service as a job runs on the infrastructural resources, and it is an instance parameterized from an abstract MapReduce template in our previous work [8]. Taking the mentioned highway domain as an example, an application for the traffic flow analysis during Dragon Boat Festival is presented as Fig. 3. The toll data used is typical spatio-temporal one with attributes vehicle license, entry (exit) timestamp, and entry (exit) station. The toll data of three-day vacation includes four modules: ETC and MTC traffic flow, daily traffic flow statistics, station traffic flow ranking, daily peak hours. Five corresponding MapReduce jobs are instantiated to execute, and the results are displayed as defined configuration scripts.

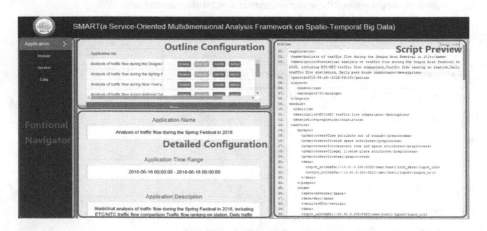

Fig. 3. SMART editor.

Next, we introduce the configuration process of the tool. (1) Fill in the basic information of the whole application on the web page, and apply the time range of title, description and statistics. (2) The number and arrangement of configuration modules and the statistical methods of each module. (3) The third step is to configure the services used for each module. Taking ETC and MTC traffic statistics as examples, we first choose the method of pretreatment service. Here we choose according to our needs. Then, in order to compare traffic flow, two traffic descriptive statistic services are needed: the spatial dimension of the whole network, the time dimension of one day and the object type of ETC vehicles and so on. MTC traffic statistics: the spatial dimension of the whole network, the time dimension of one day, the object dimension of MTC vehicles. Finally, visualization service method is selected as pie chart. After configuring the corresponding services of each module in turn, an application configuration file is obtained. (4) Submit a complete application configuration file to the engine for execution, and the results are shown in Fig. 4.

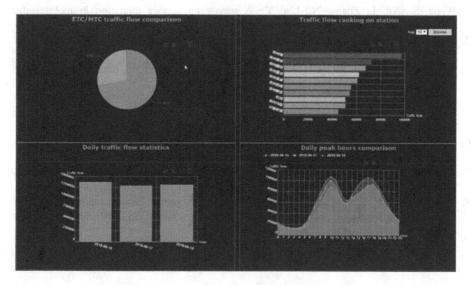

Fig. 4. An example data analysis application.

5 Summary

Three services are provided to support the multidimensional analysis of massive redundant spatial and temporal data. Pretreatment services extract keyword fields, eliminate erroneous data and correct available data. Descriptive statistic service conducts offline data statistics to obtain statistical results. Visualization services display statistical results with configurable composite visualized components.

A declarative language script is designed for describing the related information and service composition of three basic services. The script combines basic services into data analysis module, and data analysis module into data analysis application. The platform provides a series of data analysis, which can show some existing data analysis results, and can also be configured according to the platform to get new data analysis results.

SMART proposes the application of typical descriptive statistical analysis to spatio-temporal data only by configuration. Practice proves that the method is feasible and effective.

Acknowledgments. This work was supported by the Youth Program of National Natural Science Foundation of China (No. 61702014), Beijing Natural Science Foundation (No. 4192020), Youth Innovation Foundation of North China University of Technology (No. XN018022), and the R&D General Program of Beijing Education Commission (Grant No. KM201810009004).

References

1. Wang, S., Xu, J., Zhang, N., Liu, Y.: A survey on service migration in mobile edge computing. IEEE Access **6**, 23511–23528 (2018)
2. Zheng, Y.: Trajectory data mining: an overview. ACM Trans. Intell. Syst. Technol. **6**, 1–41 (2015)
3. Wikle, C.K.: Modern perspectives on statistics for spatio-temporal data. Wiley Interdisc. Rev.: Comput. Stat. **7**, 86–98 (2015)
4. Cressie, N., Wikle, C.K.: Statistics for Spatio-Temporal Data. Wiley, New York (2015)
5. Sheehy, J., Vinoski, S.: Developing RESTful web services with webmachine. IEEE Internet Comput. **14**(2), 89–92 (2010)
6. Maleshkova, M., Pedrinaci, C., Domingue, J.: Investigating web APIs on the world wide web. In: IEEE European Conference on Web Services. IEEE (2011)
7. A Four-Layer Architecture for Online and Historical Big Data Analytics. DASC/PiCom/DataCom/CyberSciTech (2016)
8. Ding, W., Zou, J., Zhao, Z.: A multidimensional service template for data analysis in highway domain. In: 11th International Conference on Service Science (ICSS 2018), Shanghai, China (2018)

Extracting Topics from Semi-structured Data for Enhancing Enterprise Knowledge Graphs

Neda Abolhassani(✉) and Lakshmish Ramaswamy

Department of Computer Science, University of Georgia, Athens, GA 30602, USA
{neda,laks}@cs.uga.edu

Abstract. Unifying information across the organizational data silos that lack documentation, structure and automated semantic discovery has been of an intense interest in the recent years. Enterprise knowledge graph is a common tool of data integration and knowledge discovery and it has become a backbone to APIs that demand access to structured knowledge. A piece which was previously unnoticed in building enterprise knowledge graph, is adding an abstract layer of themes and concepts which is mapped to various documents stored as semi-structured files in databases. Augmenting enterprise knowledge graphs by concepts will help companies to find the trends in their data and get a holistic view over their entire data stores. Extracting topics from semi-structured data suffers from lack of corpus or description as its major challenge. In this research, we investigate the impact of self-supplementation of words and documents on probabilistic topic modeling upon semi-structured data. Another contribution of this paper is finding the best tuning of probabilistic topic modeling that fits semi-structured data. The extracted topics are potential summaries and concepts about the dataset. Moreover, they can be mapped to their sources of origin in order to extend the enterprise knowledge graph. We consider 2 inferencing techniques and demonstrate the results on real data pools from Open City data and Kaggle data containing 7.5 GB and 1.15 GB of data stored in MongoDB collections, respectively. We also propose a selection heuristic for effective identification of topics hidden in various data sources.

Keywords: Topic modeling · Knowledge graphs ·
Semi-structured data · MongoDB · Gibbs Sampling · Variational Bayes

1 Introduction

In recent years, many organizations have focused on discovering insight from data that is isolated in various sources. The expensive task of knowledge discovery, performed by data experts, faces several key issues. Analyzing the ever increasing and rapidly produced amount of data, particularly the data with heterogeneous structures, is a true bottleneck. Constructing knowledge graphs is a

© ICST Institute for Computer Sciences, Social Informatics and Telecommunications Engineering 2019
Published by Springer Nature Switzerland AG 2019. All Rights Reserved
X. Wang et al. (Eds.): CollaborateCom 2019, LNICST 292, pp. 101–117, 2019.
https://doi.org/10.1007/978-3-030-30146-0_8

potential solution to this problem. A knowledge graph consists of metadata information about the data sources. It holds the relationships and semantics which is hidden in the raw data. In addition, it can capture data governance and lineage information for security and documentation purposes. In terms of structure, knowledge graphs are compatible with RDF data model which has an ontology as its schema. The ontology makes knowledge graphs highly extensible [1].

Integrating information of different files and databases plays a key role in knowledge graph construction. The information integration, summarizing the topics (covered in all the collections), and detecting the documents containing similar themes, make knowledge graph an excellent tool for metadata exploration. Adding these topics to the knowledge graphs is important for monumental tasks such as finding trends, recommending relevant contents, and getting insight on the organization's dataset without reading every document.

Concept extraction and summarization of the growing volume of isolated and semi-structured data stored in files or NoSQL databases -which is the focus of this paper- is essential in identifying and connecting contextually related data elements. These operations, in turn, demand vast amounts of domain knowledge and complex tools. The following challenges are also faced:

- Schema-less nature of semi-structured data or NoSQL databases leads to serious difficulties in detecting logical connections and overlaps among different datasets.
- The data fields has no rich corpus or description and the values are sparse and distributed among different collections as short strings and numbers.
- The data fields usually do not have the natural structure of a sentence and they do not have additional context for understanding words.

For example, consider a data analyst who is interested in analyzing the U.S. cities data stored in various MongoDB collections. MongoDB collections do not have explicit linkage points and they can store sparse and semi-structured contents. There are thousands of documents covering miscellaneous topics such as health care facilities, government jobs, health benefits of employees, school, crime, student loans, local weather archives, etc. Categorizing the dataset to general topics such as education, employment, weather, and health along with connecting the topics to their associated data sources summarizes the dataset contents. The summaries will help the data analyst to get a holistic view about the dataset and find trends in it. In case of the semi-structured data, most of the records contain short strings or numerical values and the short terms do not provide adequate term co-occurrence information. Figure 1 is a sample of a JSON document describing employee wage's data of the city San Jose stored in a MongoDB collection. The same keys are repeated in all documents of the collection and the values are too short to contain enough term co-occurrences. The other collections that are not about the employee wages have also similar keys such as *name* and *department*. This makes it difficult to distinguish between the collection themes.

To the best of our knowledge, this work is the first to consider the challenges of the concept extraction from the semi-structured sparse data. This research

```
"_id" : ObjectId("599b6b9bc87166670e03b9dc"),
"Name" : "Lee,Alan M",
"Department" : "Police",
"Job Title (as of 12/31/16)" : "Police Sergeant",
"Total Cash Compensation" : "216,251.46",
"Base Pay" : "127,441.60",
"Overtime" : "73,253.61",
"Sick and Vacation Payouts" : "",
"Other Cash Compensation" : "15,556.25",
"Defined Contribution Plan Contributions - City Paid" : "",
"Medical Dental Vision" : "16,430.04",
"Retirement Contributions - City Paid*" : "119,803.25",
"Long Term Disability, Life, Medicare" : "2,970.36",
"Misc Employment Related Costs" : "" }
```

Fig. 1. Example records of cities' data set

evaluates the benefits of the concept extraction over real world data for the purpose of knowledge graph construction. Latent Dirichlet Allocation (LDA) [2] is often used for topic modeling and concept extraction from large corpus of text documents. However in the case of semi-structured data, scanning files and data collections word by word does not lead to effective topic extraction using LDA, because of the lack of enough textual words in the files that convey a specific concept. Therefore, we design various configurations of words and documents related to the semi-structured nature of data. The proposed approach is to augment the base data and emphasize more on descriptive words. Furthermore, we do a comparative study on the designed word-document configurations in order to figure out which one creates the appropriate corpus that leads to a correct topic modeling from semi-structured data. In summary, this paper makes the following contributions:

- Proposes a corpus self-supplementation approach based on the nature of semi-structured files in order to solve the short text topic modeling problem.
- Does a comparative study about applying LDA topic modeling based on four different word and document configurations, two feature extraction methods and two inferencing algorithms in order to find the best tuning that fits the semi-structured data.
- Advocates a simple proposed heuristic topic selection approach in order to choose the best topics from the non-replicable LDA results.

The rest of the paper is organized as follows: In the next section, emerging industrial use cases and related literature are highlighted. In Sect. 3, the preliminary steps of topic extraction from semi-structured data are explained. Section 4, gives a detailed description of the concept extraction procedure. Multiple experiments are run and evaluated in Sect. 5. We conclude the paper with some future works in Sect. 6.

2   Motivation and Related Work

Developments in the industry research is still ongoing in the data integration and knowledge discovery field. According to Gartner [3], knowledge graphs are included in the hype cycle for blooming technologies. In this section, we cover some emerging use cases and complementary enterprise knowledge graph tools. Since concept extraction and topic modeling is a focus of this paper and we are dealing with the short and sparse data in semi-structured files, a section is devoted to the related works in short text topic modeling.

2.1 Modern Knowledge Graph Tools

There have been a number of recent developments in metadata integration. Google Knowledge Graph is a significant example of linked data knowledge bases that enhances the Web search. It provides a short summary about the searched topic in a structured format along with a list of contextually related websites. Knowledge graphs for Web search engines were the inspiration to solve the data silos integration problem in enterprises. One of these solutions is Google Goods [4]. It is a platform for metadata integration across heterogeneous datasets of Google's data lake. Its main storage is the temporal key-value store, BigTable [5], that keeps the linkages between datasets as a catalog. Another metadata integration system is Ground [6], a UC Berkeley developed open-source data context service, which extracts and manages the metadata over the various versions of data. A recent development is CoreKG [7,8] which offers a Rest API for extracting metadata, enriching the extracted information by providing more features (e.g. synonyms and stems), linking the extracted features to the external knowledge bases, and querying data using available data virtualization tools. Where-Hows [9] is another example of enterprise knowledge graphs. It is a LinkedIn product which helps employees to find the answers to questions, such as who owns a workflow, what datasets were aggregated to form a view, when was the last ETL, where is a specific profile data, and how was the dataset originally created. The connections to the backend repository of schedulers and a strict schema context help WhereHows extracts and stores its operational metadata. In another study, we have introduced UMR [10] which is a metadata integration platform providing data reconciliation, single logical view, traceability and data lineage. In UMR, the technical and business metadata is extracted via various profiler tools. These modern tools cover many aspects of hidden knowledge in heterogeneous data sources. A missing piece that we are covering in this paper is adding summaries and concepts about the semi-structured data to the enterprise knowledge graphs.

2.2 Emerging Use Cases

Concept extraction from semi-structured data introduces several use cases in different industries, specifically, the industries that support enterprise knowledge graphs. Concept extraction enables companies, such as Amazon that work in various industries (online shopping, web services, media), to segment their technical data into each of their sections and products. Categorizing technical data, which is declared in semi-structured format via clustering it into distinct topical groups, provides a logical view about the data and reduces the manual tasks of data experts.

Figure 2 demonstrates an example knowledge graph which integrates document stores containing JSON documents about open city data. The collected data can help an urban planner understand city's problems and conduct city services. There are nodes in the knowledge graph for different collections in databases (e.g. *Police_Reports*) and different data fields along with their data types (e.g. *Location, String*). There are also edges connecting database nodes to data field nodes and data field nodes to other data field nodes that have overlapping information. In order to query this knowledge graph, the user must know the address of each data field and its parent database. A single abstract layer containing the summary of concepts in each data source (e.g. *Crime*) and connecting it to its data source of origin has various benefits. The user can search for her topic of interest, and the knowledge graph will automatically resolve the address of its data source (through the dotted lines shown in Fig. 2). Moreover, the user can get a global view about various data silos and monitor their data trends.

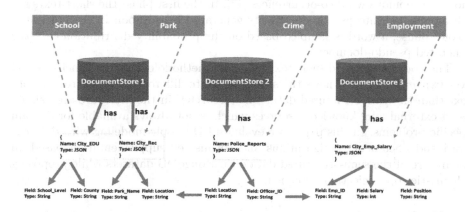

Fig. 2. Example knowledge graphs augmentation with concepts

Strategic planning and data monitoring are other use cases for the topic extraction from semi-structured data that exist in any data driven company. An organization can monitor the state of its semi-structured data and discover the trends in them more effectively using the discovered topics. There is always a demand to track documents that relate to decisions and recommendations in business planning. There are business nodes in an enterprise knowledge graph which should be linked to their correspondent technical documents. Discovering the topics and concepts while keeping track of the data sources that contain those topics connects the business and the technical nodes of an enterprise knowledge graph.

2.3   Short Text Topic Modeling

Existing topic modeling approaches such as, LDA and PLSA [11] have shown great achievements on long texts. However, uncovering the latent topics within the short and sparse texts which do not have a rich corpus and sufficient word co-occurrence is challenging. There are some methodologies proposed in the literature to solve the short text topic modeling problem. In [12] authors clustered twitter messages based on Probase which is Microsoft's probabilistic taxonomy obtained from billions of web pages [13]. They have developed a Baysian inference model to draw out concepts according to instances and attributes detected in Probase. Another conceivable approach is to enrich the short texts with auxiliary long documents [14]. [15] studies how word embedding for vector representation of words based on external knowledge sources like Wikipedia enhances the extraction of latent topics. However, finding relevant external long documents are not always feasible. [16] proposes a biterm topic modeling approach in which the topic assignments are drawn on corpus level distribution instead of the document level and the unordered biterms of a document are sampled from the same topics. Another approach is a two phase topic modeling which provides more autonomous word co-occurrences [17]. In the first phase the short texts are self aggregated into pseudo-documents generated based upon LDA, and in the second phase, a word is sampled based on the probability distribution over the generated pseudo-documents.

The above mentioned short text modeling methodologies were bench-marked over twitter datasets or news titles that are quite different in structure and context than the semi-structured data. The researches in the literature are usually using external long knowledge sources which is not always available for domain specific problems. In this paper, we evaluate LDA topic modeling with different word and document configurations and corpus self-supplementation based on the nature of the semi-structured data over MongoDB datasets while proposing a heuristic topic selection approach.

3   Preliminaries

The Latent Dirichlet Allocation (LDA) topic modeling technique is a generative probabilistic model where documents of a corpus are assumed to be probability distributions over latent topics $p(z|d)$ and topics are assumed to be distributions over words $p(w|z)$ [2]. The model also considers two Dirichlet priors for the per document topic distribution α and the per topic word distribution β. LDA uses posterior distribution to uncover the latent variable z which explains the topic. The following equation shows the LDA posterior distribution of the hidden variables given the words in the documents.

$$p(\phi_{1:K}, \theta_{1:D}, z_{1:D}|w_{1:D}) = \frac{p(\phi_{1:K}, \theta_{1:D}, z_{1:D}, w_{1:D})}{p(w_{1:D})} \qquad (1)$$

Where K is the number of topics, D is the number of documents, θ is the distribution of topics in document d, and ϕ is the distribution of words in topic

k. Since the denominator of the above equation is not tractable, the solution is to approximate the posterior inference. Two representative inferencing methodologies in this area are Gibbs Sampling [18] and Variational Bayes [19].

Gibbs Sampling finds the posterior approximation based on an empirical distribution using Markov Chain Monte Carlo approach. It starts with random initialization of each word to one of the K topics and it samples a new topic assignment iteratively using the following equation while it assumes that all topic assignments except for the current one are correct.

$$p(z_i = k | w_i = w, z_{-i}, w_{-i}, \alpha, \beta) =$$

$$\frac{n_{k,-i}^{(d)} + \alpha}{\sum_{k'=1}^{K} n_{k',-i}^{(d)} + K\alpha} \times \frac{v_{w,-i}^{(k)} + \beta}{\sum_{w'=1}^{W} v_{w',-i}^{(k)} + W\beta} \tag{2}$$

Where z_i is word i topic assignment and z_{-i} is all topic assignments to other words. $n_{k,-i}^{(d)}$ is the number of times document d uses topic k excluding the current assignment and $v_{w,-i}^{(k)}$ is the number of times topic k uses word w excluding the current assignment. The above equation finds how much a document likes topic k and how much a topic likes word w in each iteration.

Variational Bayes approximates $p(z|w)$ by a simpler distribution $q(z)$ for which marginalization is tractable. Variational inference turns into an optimization problem which assumes a variational family of distributions over the latent variables $q(z; v)$. It fits the variational parameters v to be close in Kullback Leibler (KL) distance to the exact posterior $KL(q||p)$. It approximates $p(\phi, \theta, z|w, \alpha, \beta)$ with the below equation.

$$q(\phi, \theta, z | \lambda, \gamma, \eta) = \Pi q(\phi_k | \lambda_k) \Pi q(\theta_d | \gamma_d) \Pi q(z_{d,n} | \eta_{d,n}) \tag{3}$$

Where λ, γ, and η are the hidden variables of the variational distribution. For further theoretical overview on Variational Bayes see [19].

Each input document to the LDA can be represented based on its word occurrences. Bag of Words (BoW) model and Term Frequency Inverse Document Frequency (TFIDF) model are two feature extraction methods that convert text documents to vectors representing the frequency of all the distinct words in documents. BoW only considers the term frequencies. However, TFIDF reduces the impact of words with higher frequencies in all documents. Since LDA shows topics as clusters of high ranked words, the association between a word and its data source of origin is necessary in building conceptualized layer of enterprise knowledge graphs. Therefore, another preliminary step to concept extraction is to store the mapping between the words that are ingested to LDA and their associated data sources while creating the feature vectors. The concept abstract layer will be connected to its data source of origin using this association map.

4   Corpus Self Augmentation-Based Topic Extraction

Our framework for concept extraction takes semi-structured data as inputs and returns a set of ranked word clusters that describe the hidden topics existing in the entire dataset. The two novel aspects of the framework are its corpus creation and topic selection filtering. The corpus creation component results in building the best corpus that fits the semi-structured nature of data for better topic modeling and the topic selection filtering finds the most distinctive topic word clusters. The result concepts can further be visualized using topic visualization tools such as LDAviz [20]. The framework is illustrated in Fig. 3.

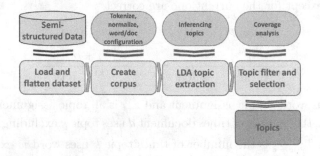

Fig. 3. An overview of the topic extraction framework for semi-structured documents.

Load and Flatten Dataset. This module ingests a variety of semi-structured datasets such as, JSON, CSV, and etc. Documents in a semi-structured file such as a JSON document in MongoDB or a column family in HBase can have nested formats. In a JSON example, a key can hold another set of key value pairs as its value. In this case, flattening the files can help in reducing the complexity of the analysis. In our experiments, we focused on MongoDB databases that contain collections of JSON documents. Therefore, flattening is a mandatory step. For instance, when we have *Key*1 with another document as its value containing two keys called *Key*2 and *Key*3, JSON flattening will result in generating new keys called *Key*1.*Key*2 and *Key*1.*Key*3. The new generated keys still keep their unique association to the values in the subsumed document.

Corpus Creation. This component makes different word-document config-urations. First, each document of the data sources should be scanned, tok-enized, and normalized. Next, the words and documents should be declared based on the contents of the semi-structured file. Table 1 shows the LDA con-figurations which include 4 different word-document settings. In case of Mon-goDB data, either a document or a collection can be considered as LDA input document. Attribute names, such as keys in JSON documents can be iden-tified as words all by themselves. This setting is denoted as *Keys-MongoDB Collection* in Table 1. Values subsumed by the keys play a significant role in finding topics from the data. Therefore, in the other settings we makes long pseudo documents based on corpus self-supplementation. We take advantage of adding values to the LDA input words. If a key is appeared in multiple doc-uments, the key is included once besides all the N values associated with it. This setting is denoted as *1Key_NValue-MongoDB Collection*. In this setting, the semi-structured document is ingested after the normalization without any corpus self-supplementation. Corpus self-supplementation is another word-document configuration which helps in creating long pseudo documents. In this configuration, each value can be accompanied by its key although the same key may appear in the collection multiple times. *1Key_1Value-MongoDB Collection* refers to this setting. The last configuration is *1Key_1Value-MongoDB Document* which takes all the words of each MongoDB document as input words to LDA. Since keys are unique in each document, they appear only once in the *1Key_1Value-MongoDB Document* setting. Finally the corpus of words can be vectorized using BoW or TFIDF models.

Table 1. Summary of 16 different experimental LDA settings. The proposed word-document configurations are designed for the semi-structured data based on MongoDB terminology.

Inferencing technique	Feature extraction	Word-document configuration
Variational Bayes	BoW	Keys - MongoDB Collection
		1Key_Nvalues - MongoDB Collection
		1Key_1Value - MongoDB Document
		1Key_1Value - MongoDB Collections
	TFIDF	Keys - MongoDB Collection
		1Key_Nvalues - MongoDB Collection
		1Key_1Value -MongoDB Document
		1Key_1Value - MongoDB Collections
Gibbs sampling	BoW	Keys - MongoDB Collection
		1Key_Nvalues - MongoDB Collection
		1Key_1Value - MongoDB Document
		1Key_1Value - MongoDB Collections
	TFIDF	Keys - MongoDB Collection
		1Key_Nvalues - MongoDB Collection
		1Key_1Value - MongoDB Document
		1Key_1Value - MongoDB Collections

LDA Topic Extraction. This component runs LDA topic modeling based on two inferencing methods, Gibbs Sampling and Variational Bayes. The inferencing methods are well discussed in Sect. 3.

Topic Filter and Selection. The inferencing methods applied to LDA are based on random initiation. Thus each time LDA is run, it shows different words in the topic's top words cluster. We know intuitively that distinct data sources have higher chance of covering different topics and we want each topic word cluster to be as distinct as possible from the other topics. Therefore, based on the word-data source map, the number of times each data source appears in a topic's top word cluster can be calculated. We define the coverage filter as the set of topics that have minimum similarity in their associated data sources, i.e.:

$$Coverage = min \sum_{i<j} sim(t_i, t_j) \tag{4}$$

Where each topic $t_i = [C_1, C_2, ..., C_n]$ and C_k is the number of times data source k appears in topic t_i. Here, n is the number of distinct data sources. The coverage filter can be applied to the topic results in two ways. In the first approach, a single LDA run generates a set of top ranked words as topics for the coverage filter. Afterwards, the filter is applied to all runs one by one and the run with the highest coverage is selected. In the second approach, all LDA runs generate sets of top ranked words as topics and then all possible combinations of sets of top ranked words are generated from the extracted topics. Next, the coverage filter will find the combination with the highest coverage. Using the coverage, we filter out the topic word clusters that only select their words from quite a few data sources and keeps the topic word clusters that covers as many data sources as possible.

5   Evaluations and Results

In this section, we present the results of running 16 different configurations of LDA on real world data pools of Kaggle data [21] and Open City data. Table 2 shows some statistics over these datasets. Open City data is collected from 18 different cities of the United States. The collected data is about various topics such as, employment, crime, schools, and recreations. The dataset is stored in MongoDB databases as JSON documents and it has a total size of 7.5 GB. The Kaggle data, which is about movie and political elections, includes various JSON files stored in MongoDB databases with the total size of 1.15 GB. We compared the 16 different LDA configurations and the heuristic topic selection using the precision metric while considering the top 8 words in each topic. The precision is represented as follows:

$$Precision = \frac{|top\,relevant\,words\,in\,all\,topics|}{|top\,retrieved\,words\,in\,all\,topics|} \tag{5}$$

Table 2. Dataset statistics for the experiments

Data source	DB size	# Collections	# Documents
Kaggle data	1.15 GB	12	1, 246, 310
Open city data	7.5 GB	45	5, 823, 732

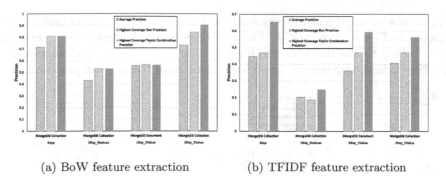

(a) BoW feature extraction   (b) TFIDF feature extraction

Fig. 4. Evaluation of the experimental analysis based on Variational Bayes Inferencing on Open City data.

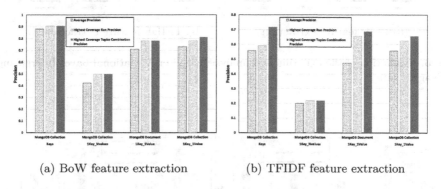

(a) BoW feature extraction   (b) TFIDF feature extraction

Fig. 5. Evaluation of the experimental analysis based on Gibbs Sampling Inferencing on Open City data.

As an alternative evaluation, we compared all of the configurations and the heuristic topic selection using the UMass coherence proposed by Mimno et al. [22]. Given the T top words of a topic z the coherence score is defined as:

$$Coherence_{UMass} = \Sigma_{i=2}^{T}\Sigma_{j=1}^{i-1}log\frac{D(w_i^{(z)}, w_j^{(z)}) + 1}{D(w_j^{(z)})} \qquad (6)$$

Where $D(w)$ is the document frequency of term w and $D(w, w')$ is the number of documents containing both words w and w'. Based on the above equation, when the words co-occurred within the same document of the corpus and they belong to the same topic, the coherence score is high. This metric is more intrinsic in nature because it compares words of the original corpus and it does not need any external source of knowledge.

In our experiments, the number of iterations for Gibbs Sampling inferencing is set to 1000. Each LDA configuration is run for 10 times because the applied inferencing methods are based on random initiation. The average precision of the LDA topic modeling based on the Variational Bayes and Gibbs Sampling with their associated feature extraction and word-document configurations are depicted in Figs. 4, 5, 6, and 7. The precisions of the heuristic topic selection which belong to the run with the highest coverage and the topic combination with the highest coverage are also shown along with the average precision.

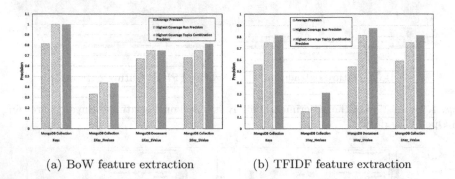

(a) BoW feature extraction   (b) TFIDF feature extraction

Fig. 6. Evaluation of the experimental analysis based on Variational bayes Inferencing on Kaggle data.

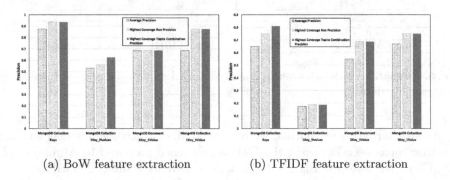

(a) BoW feature extraction   (b) TFIDF feature extraction

Fig. 7. Evaluation of the experimental analysis based on Gibbs Sampling Inferencing on Kaggle data.

Keys in JSON files, headers in CSV files, column names in columnar databases, and elements in XML files, summarize the meaning of their subsumed content. The subsumed contents can be numbers, named entities, and short text descriptions. Therefore, corpus self-supplementation, which is accompanying keys with values as the input words of the LDA topic modeling for semi-structured data, shows higher precision in our results compared to the *1Key_NValue-MongoDB Collection* in which the semi-structured document is ingested as it is. The high precision of *Keys - MongoDB Collection* corpus also is a proof of the impact of Keys in the quality of topic extraction. The experiments show lower average precision when key and values both are considered as words (*1Key_1Value*) and MongoDB documents are considered as LDA documents compared to the case where MongoDB collections are LDA documents with the same word configuration. The reason is considering MongoDB documents as LDA documents results in fewer words in each document of the corpus.

The TFIDF feature extraction reduces the impact of words such as, *id* which occur in most of the collections and have less semantical value. However, the precision of the configurations which include TFIDF approach are lower than the precision of BoW model in all the different setting. TFIDF feature extraction is slightly shrinking the corpus and this can justify the result. The results also show better precision for average Gibbs Sampling inferencing compared to average Variational Bayes. Figures 4, 5, 6, and 7 also demonstrate the precision of our heuristic topic selection approach which is even more than the average precision or very close to it in all of our experiments. This proves that the LDA results which cover heterogeneous data sources define more reasonable topics.

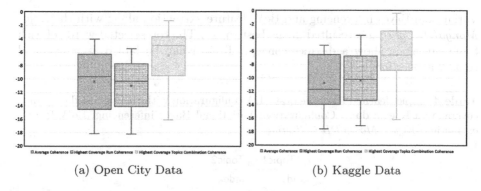

(a) Open City Data   (b) Kaggle Data

Fig. 8. Coherence evaluation of the two approaches of implementing topic selection heuristic compared to the average coherence upon the 16 different topic modeling configurations.

Figure 8 shows the coherence result of the two datasets. In both of the datasets, the second approach of implementing the heuristic topic selection which finds the best topic combination from the LDA models generated from all runs demonstrates the best coherence. The minimum (worst) coherence among all the 16 different LDA configurations belongs to the *1Key_NValue*-MongoDB Collection in which the semi-structured document is ingested as it is without any self-supplementation.

Tables 3 and 4 illustrate the top words of LDA topic modeling approach for both datasets. In Open City data, Variational Bayes inferencing and BoW feature extraction along with the *1Key_1Value-MongoDB Collection* corpus self-supplementation resulted in the best topics. The top selected words of each topic can clearly show a distinct concept. Topic 1 can be labled as *school*, topic 2 as *crime*, topic 3 as *recreation/park*, and topic 4 as *employment*. In Kaggle data,

Table 3. Topics learned from the best LDA configuration with the highest data source coverage on Open City data. Configuration: Variational Bayes inferencing, BoW feature extraction, *1Key_1Value - MongoDB Collection*

Topic1	Topic2	Topic3	Topic4
id	id	Park	Total
School	Type	id	id
Address	Address	Objectid	Job
Objectid	Victim	Zone	Contribution
Elementary	Offense	Thegeom	Department
City	Name	Acre	Name
X	Crime	Parkname	Code
Name	Date	Location	Pay

Variational Bayes inferencing and BoW feature extraction along with the *Keys-MongoDB Collection* resulted in the best topics. The top selected words of each topic can again show a distinct concept. Topic 1 can be labled as *movie*, and topic 2 as *election*.

Table 4. Topics learned from the best LDA configuration with the highest data source coverage on Kaggle data. Configuration: Variational Bayes inferencing, BoW feature extraction, *Keys - MongoDB Collection*

Topic1	Topic2
id	Index
Rating	Election
Year	Fair
Runtime	Voter
Genre	Vote
Director	Electoral
Score	Law
Title	Ballot

Table 5 shows precision and elapsed running time of the two of the word-document settings that resulted in the highest precision among the average of 10 runs. This table captures the trade off between running time and precision of the two evaluated inferencing techniques. Although Gibbs Sampling perform with higher quality, it takes longer than the Variational Bayes to run. Table 5 compares only 4 of the experiments. However, Variational Bayes has almost 50% time performance improvement in the average case of all the 16 different settings compared to Gibbs Sampling. According to the results shown in Figs. 4, 5, 6, and 7 and the running time performance, Variational Bayes accompanied by the BoW feature extraction and the topic selection heuristic filter (the second implementation approach which find the best topics combination) provide the high quality tuning for LDA with more time efficiency.

Table 5. Average running time and average precision of the best performing algorithms for each scenario

Setting	Precision		Elapsed time (Seconds)	
	Kaggle data	Open city data	Kaggle data	Open city data
Variational Bayes Keys MongoDB Collection BoW	81%	71%	0.54	1.94
Gibbs Sampling Keys MongoDB Collection BoW	87%	88%	30.90	30.96
Variational Bayes IKey_IValue MongoDB Collection BoW	68%	73%	8.36	58.02
Gibbs Sampling IKey_IValue MongoDB Collection BoW	68%	73%	33.09	58.62

6   Conclusion and Future Work

In light of the results presented in Sect. 5, we conclude that the LDA model performs with the highest precision (above 80%) for semi-structured data when considering keys only as the words. The second highest precision is provided when using the corpus self-supplementation. It allows more impact on the keys while considering their subsumed values from an entire collection. This configuration accompanied by BoW model has an average precision of 73% on the Open City data. The heuristic coverage filter for topic selection also improves the precision to 90%. Regarding the inferencing techniques, we often see higher precision for Gibbs Sampling. However, the Variational Bayes inferencing is more time efficient and has almost 50% time performance improvement in the average case of all the 16 different settings. The trade off between the precision and the time performance in Variational Bayes and Gibbs Sampling upon semi-structured data match the results of the same techniques upon the unstructured data in the literature. The results also show the same trends on the Kaggle dataset regarding the precision and time performance.

Considering the fact that we have the word-data source mapping as explained in the preliminary step, each topic can be connected to its relevant data sources when we build an enterprise knowledge graph. This work has applications in recommendation systems and data trend discovery. It also allows enterprises to explore and understand their large scale semi-structured data with less effort. Our research in finding optimal concept extraction approach for semi-structured data has been very promising and can add another level of knowledge to the knowledge graph systems. However, an engaging direction for future work is adding state-of-the-art automatic topic labeling to our framework for describing the cluster of words selected as concept representatives in a more extensive way.

Acknowledgments. The authors would like to thank Dr. Pouya Asrar and Kamal Shadi for their valuable feedback in this project. This research has been partially funded by the National Science Foundation (NSF) under grants CCF-1442672 and SCC-1637277 and gifts from Accenture Research Labs. Any opinions, findings, and conclusions or recommendations expressed in this material are those of the authors and do not necessarily reflect the views of the NSF or other funding agencies and companies mentioned above.

References

1. Pan, J.Z., Vetere, G., Gómez-Pérez, J.M., Wu, H.: Exploiting Linked Data and Knowledge Graphs in Large Organisations. Springer, Cham (2017). https://doi.org/10.1007/978-3-319-45654-6
2. Blei, D.M., Ng, A.Y., Jordan, M.I.: Latent Dirichlet allocation. J. Mach. Learn. Res. **3**(Jan), 993–1022 (2003)
3. Hype cycle for emerging technologies. https://www.gartner.com/smarterwithgartner/5-trends-emerge-in-gartner-hype-cycle-for-emerging-technologies-2018/. Accessed 22 Oct 2018
4. Halevy, A.Y., et al.: Managing Google's data lake: an overview of the goods system. IEEE Data Eng. Bull. **39**(3), 5–14 (2016)
5. Chang, F., et al.: Bigtable: a distributed storage system for structured data. ACM Trans. Comput. Syst. (TOCS) **26**(2), 4 (2008)
6. Hellerstein, J.M., et al.: Ground: a data context service. In: CIDR (2017)
7. Beheshti, A., Benatallah, B., Nouri, R., Tabebordbar, A.: CoreKG: a knowledge lake service. Proce. VLDB Endowment **11**(12), 1942–1945 (2018)
8. Beheshti, A., Benatallah, B., Nouri, R., Chhieng, V.M., Xiong, H., Zhao, X.: CoreDB: a data lake service. In: Proceedings of the 2017 ACM on Conference on Information and Knowledge Management, pp. 2451–2454. ACM (2017)
9. Data discovery and lineage for big data ecosystem. https://github.com/linkedin/WhereHows. Accessed 22 Jan 2018
10. Abolhassani, N., et al.: Universal metadata repository: integrating data profiles across an organization. In: 2018 IEEE International Conference on Information Reuse and Integration (IRI), pp. 452–459. IEEE (2018)
11. Hofmann, T.: Probabilistic latent semantic analysis. In: Proceedings of the Fifteenth conference on Uncertainty in artificial intelligence, pp. 289–296. Morgan Kaufmann Publishers Inc. (1999)
12. Song, Y., Wang, H., Wang, Z., Li, H., Chen, W.: Short text conceptualization using a probabilistic knowledgebase. In: Proceedings of the Twenty-Second International Joint Conference on Artificial Intelligence-Volume Volume Three, pp. 2330–2336. AAAI Press (2011)
13. Wu, W., Li, H., Wang, H., Zhu, K.Q.: Probase: a probabilistic taxonomy for text understanding. In: Proceedings of the 2012 ACM SIGMOD International Conference on Management of Data, pp. 481–492. ACM (2012)
14. Jin, O., Liu, N.N., Zhao, K., Yu, Y., Yang, Q.: Transferring topical knowledge from auxiliary long texts for short text clustering. In: Proceedings of the 20th ACM International Conference on Information and Knowledge Management, pp. 775–784. ACM (2011)

15. Qiang, J., Chen, P., Wang, T., Wu, X.: Topic modeling over short texts by incorporating word embeddings. In: Kim, J., Shim, K., Cao, L., Lee, J.-G., Lin, X., Moon, Y.-S. (eds.) PAKDD 2017. LNCS (LNAI), vol. 10235, pp. 363–374. Springer, Cham (2017). https://doi.org/10.1007/978-3-319-57529-2_29

16. Yan, X., Guo, J., Lan, Y., Cheng, X.: A biterm topic model for short texts. In: Proceedings of the 22nd International Conference on World Wide Web, pp. 1445–1456. ACM (2013)

17. Quan, X., Kit, C., Ge, Y., Pan, S.J.: Short and sparse text topic modeling via self-aggregation. In: IJCAI, pp. 2270–2276 (2015)

18. Griffiths, T.L., Steyvers, M.: Finding scientific topics. Proc. Nat. Acad. Sci. **101**(suppl 1), 5228–5235 (2004)

19. Hoffman, M., Bach, F.R., Blei, D.M.: Online learning for latent Dirichlet allocation. In: Advances in Neural Information Processing Systems, pp. 856–864 (2010)

20. Sievert, C., Shirley, K.: LDAvis: a method for visualizing and interpreting topics. In: Proceedings of the Workshop on Interactive Language Learning, Visualization, and Interfaces, pp. 63–70 (2014)

21. Kaggle open datasets. https://www.kaggle.com/datasets/. Accessed 02 Oct 2019

22. Mimno, D., Wallach, H.M., Talley, E., Leenders, M., McCallum, A.: Optimizing semantic coherence in topic models. In: Proceedings of the Conference on Empirical Methods in Natural Language Processing, pp. 262–272. Association for Computational Linguistics (2011)

Collaborative Contextual Combinatorial Cascading Thompson Sampling

Zhenyu Zhu, Liusheng Huang[✉], and Hongli Xu

University of Science and Technology of China, Hefei, Anhui Province, China
zzy7758@mail.ustc.edu.cn
{lshuang,honglixu}@ustc.edu.cn

Abstract. We design and analyze collaborative contextual combinatorial cascading Thompson sampling (C^4-TS). C^4-TS is a Bayesian heuristic to address the cascading bandit problem in the collaborative environment. C^4-TS utilizes posterior sampling strategy to balance the exploration-exploitation tradeoff and it also incorporates the collaborative effect to share information across similar users. Utilizing these two novel features, we prove that the regret upper bound for C^4-TS is $\tilde{O}(d(u + \sqrt{mKT}))$, where d is the dimension of the feature space, u is the number of users, m is the number of clusters, K is the length of the recommended list and T is the time horizon. This regret upper bound matches the theoretical guarantee for UCB-like algorithm in the same settings. We also conduct a set of simulations comparing C^4-TS with the state-of-the-art algorithms. The empirical results demonstrate the advantage of our algorithm over existing works.

1 Introduction

Most recommendation systems recommend an ordered list of candidate items to users due to the limited space. The user examines the recommended list sequentially, clicks on the first satisfying item and stops examining further. The click of the user reveals that the items before the clicked item are not satisfying and the items after the clicked item are unexamined. The recommendation systems observe this feedback and adjust its recommendation strategy accordingly. This kind of interaction is often formulated as the cascading model, which is simple, intuitive and effective in characterizing user behaviours.

We consider the contextual combinatorial cascading model in a collaborative environment. In the stochastic contextual settings, the expected reward of an item is assumed to be a linear function of the item features and a stationary but unknown user vector. At each time step, the learning agent recommends a combination of items to the user. It then observes the cascading feedback of the user and adjusts its recommendation strategy accordingly. The goal of the learning agent is to maximize the cumulative reward in T rounds. As the expected rewards of the items are unknown to the learning agent, it has to balance between exploring new information to improve future performance and exploiting the best empirical items so far. This tradeoff is modelled by the bandit problems which have been well studied in the literature. While effective, standard

X. Wang et al. (Eds.): CollaborateCom 2019, LNICST 292, pp. 118–132, 2019.
https://doi.org/10.1007/978-3-030-30146-0_9

bandit algorithms often work in a content-dependent regime, so that any collaborative effects among users are ignored. This drawback hinders the practical deployment of bandit algorithms in highly dynamic and large-scale domains, in which incorporating collaborative effects often helps to accumulate information more efficiently. Thus, exploiting collaborative effects into bandit algorithms can be one of the most promising approaches to further improvement of the recommendation performance. But it also raises new challenges in the design and analysis of the algorithm.

In this paper, we propose collaborative contextual combinatorial cascading Thompson sampling (C^4-TS) algorithm. Following the approaches in [8, 13], C^4-TS maintains a dynamic graph to represent the partition of users. If two users are connected, they are considered to be in the same cluster. The graph is fully-connected at the beginning, and the edges are gradually removed as the algorithm accumulates more information about user preference. At each round, the algorithm considers both the historical feedbacks of the user and the collaborative information to make decisions. It applies posterior matching strategy by recommending the items according to their probability of being optimal. The feedback of the users is then used to update the user vector and the graph.

Our algorithm is based on Thompson sampling because of its advantage over UCB in both empirical performance [5, 6, 15, 17, 18] and computational efficiency [3, 16]. Although the regret upper bound of UCB-like algorithm in similar settings has been studied [13], the randomness of Thompson sampling presents additional challenges. Under some reasonable assumptions, we utilize the matrix martingale theory to bound the variance of the reward estimator and quantify the exploration-exploitation tradeoff. We prove an upper bound of $\tilde{O}(d(u + \sqrt{mKT}))$ for the expected cumulative regret, where u is the number of users, m is the number of clusters, d is the dimension of feature space, K is the length of the recommended list, and T is the time horizon. The notation $\tilde{O}$ ignores dependence on the logarithmic factors. This bound matches the regret upper bound for UCB-like algorithm. We also conduct experiments on a synthetic dataset to demonstrate the advantage of the model and algorithm over existing studies.

The rest of this paper is organized as follows. Section 2 introduces the related works in similar settings. Section 3 introduces the basic model settings (learning model, notations and assumptions) and presents a detailed description of C^4-TS algorithm. Section 4 provides the theoretical analysis of its regret bound. Section 5 reports the result of simulations. Section 6 concludes this paper.

2   Related Work

Cascading bandit was first introduced by Kveton and Branislav [10]. They also proposed CascadeUCB1 and CascadeKL-UCB to solve the problem and provided gap-dependent regret upper bound of the algorithms. The regret upper bound of CascadeKL-UCB matches the lower bound of the problem within a logarithmic factor. Zong and Ni [18] then generalized the cascading bandit with linear payoff and proposed CascadeLinUCB and CascadeLinTS. They also provided an upper bound on the regret of CascadeLinUCB and suggested that the same theoretical guarantee should hold for CascadeLinTS. The work [12] by Li and Wang generalized the contextual combinatorial cascading setting with position discounts and more general reward functions and provided a similar theoretical guarantee. The first theoretical analysis of Thompson sampling for non-contextual cascading bandit is provided by Cheung and Tan [6]. They proved that the regret upper bound of CascadeTS matches the state-of-the-art regret bounds for UCB-like algorithms.

Beyond the general settings of cascading bandit and Thompson sampling, our work is also closely related to the dynamic clustering of bandits. Clustering over bandits to utilize collaborative information has been studied in a series of works. These works are based on the assumption that the algorithm servers a large set of users and these users can be partitioned into several groups. All users in the same group can share feedbacks to facilitate customizing personal recommendation. The work [8] first considered online clustering of contextual bandits. It used the confidence interval of the user vector to estimate user similarity and share information across similar users. The work [14] incorporates dynamic clustering to divide users into groups and customizes the bandits to each group. They first used the K-means clustering algorithm within the contextual bandit framework. In [19], the authors developed a collaborative contextual bandit algorithm and leveraged the adjacency graph to share information and feedbacks among similar users while online updating. In [11], the authors extended the work [19] by performing online clustering at both the user side and the item side. They also used a sparse graph to represent the clusters to avoid expensive computation. The work [7] considered a variant of online clustering where the clusters over users are estimated in a context-dependent manner.

The most similar work to ours is [13]. In this paper, the authors first formulated the problem of dynamic clustering of contextual cascading bandits. They designed UCB-like algorithm CLUB-cascade to address the problem and provided an upper bound for its cumulative regret. Our work is based on Thompson sampling which tends to outperform UCB-like algorithms empirically [18]. We also give an alternative proof of the convergence rate of online clustering and provide a theoretical analysis of Thompson sampling in the contextual cascading settings.

3 Preliminaries

3.1 Problem Settings

We first formulate the collaborative contextual combinatorial cascading problem. In this problem, there are u users and these users can be partitioned into m clusters where $n \gg m$. The clusters are fixed but unknown to the learning agent. All users in the same cluster share the same preference which is encoded by a user vector $\theta \in \mathbb{R}^d$. For any users i and j, if they are not in the same cluster, then $\|\theta_i - \theta_j\| \geq \gamma$.

At each round t, the learning agent interacts with user i_t to customize personal recommendation. It first selects an ordered list of items $X_t = (X_{t,1}, X_{t,2}, ..., X_{t,k})$ from item set $\mathcal{X} \subset \mathbb{R}^d$ to recommend. The user checks the recommended list sequentially, clicks the first satisfying item and stops checking further. The learning agent observes the index of the clicked item C_t. It reveals that the first $C_t - 1$ items are not satisfying, the payoff of the C_t-th recommended item is 1, and the rest items are not checked by the user. If no item is clicked, the observed payoff will be $C_t = \infty$. The observed payoff $r(x)$ of an item x is generated by sampling from a Bernoulli distribution with mean $\mathbb{E}[r(x)]$. The expected reward $\mathbb{E}[r(x)]$ of an item x is calculated by a linear function $\mathbb{E}[r(x)] = x^T\theta$. We assume that the probability of the user clicking each item is independent. Thus, the expected reward of a list X is

$$\mathbb{E}[r(X)] = 1 - \prod_{x \in X}(1 - x^T\theta).$$

It is worth noting that rearrangement of the items does not change the expected reward of a list. We define the optimal item list X^* as the list with maximum expected reward $X^* = \arg\max_{X \subset \mathcal{X}} \mathbb{E}[r(X)]$.

The instantaneous expected regret $R(t)$ at round t is defined as the gap between the expected reward of the optimal item list and that of the recommended list. The objective of the algorithm is to minimize the expected cumulative regret in T rounds:

$$\mathbb{E}[\mathcal{R}(T)] = \mathbb{E}[\sum_{t=1}^{T}(r(X^*) - r(X_t))],$$

where the expectation is taken over the randomness in selecting the recommended list X_t and the noise of the feedbacks.

3.2 Notations

We use $\|x\|_p$ to denote the p-norm of $x \in \mathbb{R}^d$. For matrix $M \in \mathbb{R}^{d \times d}$ and vector $x \in \mathbb{R}^d$, we denote by $\|x\|_M = \sqrt{x^T M x}$ the weighted 2-norm. We use $\lambda_{min}(M)$ and $\lambda_{max}(M)$ to denote the smallest and the largest eigenvalue of matrix M respectively.

Assumption 1 (Contextual vector and user vector). The contextual vectors and the user vector are in a closed subset of $\mathbb{R}^d$ such that $0 < \|x\|_2^2 \le 1$ for all $x \in \mathcal{X}$ and θ. This assumption is required so that the regret bound does not depend on the scale of the vectors. If $0 < \|x\|_2^2 \le L$, the regret bound would increase by a factor L.

Assumption 2 (Eigenvalues). For any round t, there exists a constant λ_{min} such that $\forall t, \lambda_{min} \le \lambda_{min}(\mathbb{E}(x_t x_t^T))$. In standard contextual bandit algorithms, this assumption is often violated. The probability of selecting the optimal item will be 1 after enough rounds. Thus the smallest eigenvalue will be $\lambda_{min}(\mathbb{E}[x_t x_t^T]) = \lambda_{min}(x^* x^{*T}) = 0$. But in cascading settings, if the expected reward of the optimal item is smaller than 1, then the suboptimal items will be checked by the user with at least constant probability, thus $\lambda_{min}(\mathbb{E}[x_t x_t^T]) > \lambda_{min}$ is a reasonable assumption.

3.3 Collaborative Contextual Combinatorial Cascading Thompson Sampling

Our algorithm maintains a posterior distribution $\mathcal{N}(\hat{\theta}_t, V_t)$ of user vector θ for each user. The posterior distribution is updated with the recommended lists and the feedbacks. Let $(X_1, X_2, ..., X_n)$ be the sequence of lists recommended to one user and

$(C_1, C_2, ..., C_n)$ be the observed rewards until round t , the posterior distribution of user vector θ at round $t+1$ is $\mathcal{N}(\hat{\theta}_t, V_t^{-1})$, where $K_i = \min(K, C_i)$ and

$$V_t = \sum_{i=1}^{n} \sum_{k=1}^{K_i} X_{i,k} X_{i,k}^T, \quad f_t = \sum_{i=1}^{n} \sum_{k=1}^{K_i} X_{i,k}^T \mathbb{I}\{k = C_i\}, \quad \hat{\theta}_t = (\lambda I + V_t)^{-1} f_t. \quad (1)$$

Our algorithm also maintains an undirected graph $G_t(|u|, E_t)$ to store the cluster information. The graph is initialized as a fully-connected graph and the edges are removed gradually. At each round t, the algorithm first selects a user i_t to serve. It then finds the connected component set of i_t in graph G_{t-1}, which is referred to as M_t. The posterior distribution is then calculated by all the checked items and the feedbacks of the cluster M_t. The algorithm then samples $\tilde{\theta}_{i_t, M_t}$ from the distribution and generates the list by $X_{t,k} = \max_{x \in \mathcal{X} \setminus \{X_{t,1}, X_{t,2}, ... X_{t,k-1}\}} x^T \tilde{\theta}_{i_t, M_t}$. The algorithm then observes the feedback of the user and updates the user vector and the graph respectively.

Theorem 1. *For the collaborative contextual combinatorial cascading bandit problem, under Assumptions 1 and 2, the expected regret bound for C^4-TS algorithm within time horizon T is*

$$\mathbb{E}[R(T)] = O(d\sqrt{mKT} \ln KT + ud \ln duT)$$

Algorithm 1. C^4-Thompson sampling

Input: Set of items $\mathcal{X}, \lambda, \alpha, \beta > 0$
Init: $G_0 = (|u|, E_0)$ is a fully-connected graph over the user set $|u|$, for any user $i \in [u]$, $f_{i,0} = 0_d, V_{i,0} = \lambda I_d, \hat{\theta}_{i,0} = (V_{i,0} + \lambda I)^{-1} f_{i,0}$.
for $t = 1, 2, 3..., T$ **do**
 Select user i_t to serve and find the user set $M_t \subset |u|$ from graph G_{t-1} so that all users in M_t are connected to i_t
 Compute the following variable:
  $V_{i_t, M_t} = \lambda I + \sum_{j \in M_t} V_{j,t-1}$
  $f_{i_t, M_t} = \sum_{j \in M_t} f_{j,t-1}$
  $\hat{\theta}_{i_t, M_t} = V_{i_t, M_t}^{-1} f_{i_t, M_t}$
 Sample $\tilde{\theta}_{i_t, t}$ from distribution $\mathcal{N}(\hat{\theta}_{i_t, M_t}, \alpha V_{i_t, M_t}^{-1})$
 for $k \in [K]$ **do**
  Extract $X_{t,k} = \arg\max_{x \in \mathcal{X} \setminus \{X_{t,1}, X_{t,2}, ... X_{t,k-1}\}} x^T \tilde{\theta}_{i_t, t}$
 end for
 Recommend list X_t to user i_t and observe payoff C_t
 Set $r_t = \mathbb{I}(C_t \leq K)$ and $C_t = \min(C_t, K)$
 Update $f_{i_t, t}, V_{i_t, t}, \hat{\theta}_{i_t, t}$ and $N_{i_t, t}$ as in Equation (1)
 for $l \in [u]$ **do**
  if $\|\hat{\theta}_{i_t, t} - \hat{\theta}_{l,t}\|_2 \geq \beta(\frac{\sqrt{1+\ln(1+N_{i_t,t})}}{1+N_{i_t,t}} + \frac{\sqrt{1+\ln(1+N_{l,t})}}{1+N_{l,t}})$ **then**
   Delete the edges $(i_t, l) \in E_{t-1}$
  end if
 end for
end for

4 Regret Analysis

4.1 Proof Outline

The proof of Theorem 1 can be split into two parts. In the first part, we bound the expected number of rounds the algorithm need to partition the users into the right clusters, which is $O(ud \ln duT)$. In the second part, we prove that when the users are correctly partitioned, the expected regret bound is $O(d\sqrt{mKT} \ln KT)$. Thus the total regret is $\mathbb{E}[R(T)] = O(d\sqrt{mKT} \ln KT + ud \ln duT)$.

We follow three steps to show that the algorithm needs at most $O(ud \ln duT)$ rounds to partition the users into the right clusters. First, we notice that for any user, the 2-norm distance between $\hat{\theta}_t$ and θ decreases very fast [13]:

$$\|\hat{\theta}_t - \theta\|_2^2 \le \frac{\|\hat{\theta}_t - \theta\|_{V_{t-1}}^2}{\lambda_{min}(V_{t-1})} = O(\frac{d \ln N_{t-1}}{N_{t-1}}),$$

where $\|\hat{\theta}_t - \theta\|_{V_{t-1}}^2$ is the weighted 2-norm and $\lambda_{min}(V_{t-1})$ is the smallest eigenvalue of matrix V_{t-1}. Second, we prove that under Assumption 2, the smallest eigenvalue of the cumulative matrix V_{t-1} grows linearly with the number of checked arms $N_{t-1} = \sum_{i=1}^{t-1} C_i$ with high probability. Third, we model C_t as a truncated Poisson variable and show that after serving the user for $O(d \ln udT)$ rounds, the confidence interval for user vector will be smaller than $\gamma/2$, where the γ is the constant in the assumption of clusters. Thus, after $O(ud \ln udT)$ rounds, the edges between different clusters will be removed.

After the clusters are correctly partitioned, the recommendation is based on the estimates of cluster vector and its covariance matrix. We follow three steps to bound the expected cumulative regret up to round T. First, we define event $F_k = \{$the k-th item in X_t is examined$\}$ for any time t and $k \in [K]$, and decompose the regret as [18]:

$$\mathbb{E}[R(t)] \le \mathbb{E}[\sum_{k=1}^{K} \mathbb{I}(F_k)(r(X_k^*) - r(X_{t,k}))]$$

Thus, the instantaneous regret can be bounded by the difference between expected rewards of the best items and the checked items. Second, We define event $E^\mu(t)$, $E^\theta(t)$ and prove that these events happen with high probability. If both events are true, we further decompose the regret as

$$\mathbb{E}[R(t)] \le \mathbb{E}[\sum_{k=1}^{C_t}(\alpha_t + \beta_t)(s_t(X_k^*) + s_t(X_{t,k}))],$$

where $s_t(x) = \|x\|_{V_{t-1}}$.

Finally, we show that under assumption 2, the smallest eigenvalue of the matrix V_{t-1} grows linearly with the number of items the user has observed, which is referred to as N_{t-1} in the algorithm. We can then prove that the sum of the variance $\sum_{t=1}^{T} \sum_{k=1}^{C_t} s_t(X_k^*)$ is of order $\sqrt{dKT \ln KT}$. Then, substituting this result along with Lemma 2, we obtain the desired expected regret bound:

$$\mathbb{E}[R(T)] = O(d\sqrt{mKT} \ln KT + ud \ln duT)$$

4.2   Proof of Part 1

Definition 1. *Define* $\mathbb{E}^\lambda(t)$ *as the event that the smallest eigenvalue of* V_t *grows linearly with* N_t, *where* N_t *is the number of checked items after* t *rounds. Formally, define* $\mathbb{E}^\lambda(t)$ *as the event that*

$$\lambda_{min}(V_t) \geq 1/2 N_t \cdot \lambda_{min}, \quad \forall N_t \geq \left(\frac{8}{\lambda_{min}^2} + \frac{4}{3\lambda_{min}}\right) \ln \frac{dut^2}{\delta},$$

We prove that event $\mathbb{E}^\lambda(t)$ holds with probability at least $1 - \frac{\delta}{ut^2}$ by substituting $\delta = \delta'/ut^2$ into Lemma 6.

Definition 2. *Define* $\mathbb{E}^\theta(t)$ *as the events that the estimator* $\hat{\theta}$ *is close to its real value* θ. *More precisely, define* $\mathbb{E}^\theta(t)$ *as the event that*

$$|\hat{\theta}_{t+1} - \theta|_{V_t} \leq \alpha_t,$$

where $\alpha_t(\delta) = R\sqrt{d \ln \frac{ut^2(1+N_t/\lambda)}{\delta}} + \sqrt{\lambda}$.

We prove that event $\mathbb{E}^\theta(t)$ holds with probability at least $1 - \frac{\delta}{ut^2}$ by substituting $\delta = \delta'/ut^2$ into Lemma 5.

If the events $\mathbb{E}^\lambda(t)$ and $\mathbb{E}^\theta(t)$ both hold for all users, then for any user,

$$\|\hat{\theta}_{t+1} - \theta\|_2 \leq \frac{\|\hat{\theta}_{t+1} - \theta\|_{V_t}}{\sqrt{\lambda_{min}(V_t)}} \leq \frac{\sqrt{2}\alpha_t}{\sqrt{N_t\lambda_{min}}} \leq \frac{\gamma}{2},$$

where the last inequality is valid when

$$N_t \geq \frac{8d}{\lambda_{min}\gamma^2} \ln \frac{uT^2}{\delta}.$$

Combining with the condition in $\mathbb{E}^\lambda(t)$, it is required that

$$N_t \geq \max\left\{\frac{8d}{\lambda_{min}\gamma^2} \ln \frac{uT^2}{\delta}, \left(\frac{8}{\lambda_{min}^2} + \frac{4}{3\lambda_{min}}\right) \ln \frac{duT^2}{\delta}\right\}.$$

If the user has been served in t rounds, where

$$t \geq \frac{2K^2}{q^2} \ln \frac{8duT}{\delta} + \frac{2}{q}\left\{\frac{8d}{\lambda_{min}\gamma^2} \ln \frac{uT^2}{\delta}, \left(\frac{8}{\lambda_{min}^2} + \frac{4}{3\lambda_{min}}\right) \ln \frac{duT^2}{\delta}\right\} := t_0,$$

the algorithm will be able to partition the user into the real cluster with probability at least $1 - 4\delta/u$. The above inequality is proven by modeling C_t as a truncated Poisson variable with mean q where $q = O(K/p)$. And the lower bound of t is calculated by using Lemma 4.

It reveals that the after ut_0 rounds, the user clusters are correctly partitioned with probability at least $1 - 4\delta$. Thus the cumulative regret before all the users are correctly partitioned is

$$\mathbb{E}[R'(T)] = O(ud \ln duT)$$

4.3 Proof of Part 2

After the users are correctly clustered, the information learned by a user is shared by all users in the same cluster. And the users in different clusters are independent. We consider the cumulative regret of one cluster. Suppose the users in the cluster are served in T rounds.

Following the previous approach [10, 11], we rearrange the elements of the optimal list X^* so that if $x \in X^*$ and $x \in X_t$, then $index(X^*, x) = index(X_t, x)$. Under this arrangement, for all round t,

$$\forall k \in [K], \quad X_k^{*T}\theta \geq X_{t,k}^T\theta \quad and \quad X_k^{*T}\tilde{\theta}_t \leq X_{t,k}^T\tilde{\theta}_t.$$

The algorithm uses the user feedbacks and contextual vector to update the estimator $\hat{\theta}_t$ and the covariance matrix V_t^{-1}. As the algorithm accumulates more information each round, $\hat{\theta}$ approaches θ gradually and the variance of expected reward of each item decreases. If $\tilde{\theta}$, $\hat{\theta}$, and θ are close enough, the algorithm is likely to select the optimal list and the regret can be bounded by the variance. This intuition leads to the definition of the following two events.

Definition 3. *Define $\mathbb{E}^\theta(t)$ and $\mathbb{E}^\mu(t)$ as the events that $x^T\hat{\theta}_t$ and $x^T\tilde{\theta}_t$ are concentrated around $x^T\theta$ and $x^T\hat{\theta}_t$ respectively. Formally, define $\mathbb{E}^\theta(t)$ and $\mathbb{E}^\mu(t)$ as*

$$Event \quad \mathbb{E}^\theta(t) : \forall x \in \mathcal{X} : |x^T\hat{\theta}_t - x^T\theta| \leq \alpha_t s_t(x)$$

$$Event \quad \mathbb{E}^\mu(t) : \forall x \in \mathcal{X} : |x^T\tilde{\theta}_t - x^T\hat{\theta}_t| \leq \beta_t s_t(x),$$

where $\alpha_t(\delta) = R\sqrt{d \ln \frac{t^2(1+N_t/\lambda)}{\delta}} + \sqrt{\lambda}$, $\beta_t = \sqrt{4d \ln \frac{t}{\delta}}$ and $s_t(x) = \|x\|_{V_{t-1}^{-1}}$.

We prove in Lemma 5 that both events hold with probability at least $1 - \delta/t^2$. And if events $\mathbb{E}^\mu(t)$ and $\mathbb{E}^\theta(t)$ are both true, the instantaneous expected regret can be decomposed as:

$$\mathbb{E}[R(t)] = \mathbb{E}[\prod_{k \in [K]}(1 - r(X_k^*)) - \prod_{k \in [K]}(1 - r(X_{t,k}))]$$

$$\leq \mathbb{E}[\sum_{k=1}^{K}\prod_{j=1}^{k-1}(1 - r(X_{t,j}))](r(X_k^*) - r(X_{t,k}))]$$

$$\leq \mathbb{E}[\sum_{k=1}^{K}\mathbb{I}(F_{t,k})(r(X_k^*) - r(X_{t,k}))]$$

$$\leq \mathbb{E}[\sum_{k=1}^{K}\mathbb{I}(F_{t,k})(\alpha_t + \beta_t)(s_t(X_k^*) + s_t(X_{t,k}))], \tag{2}$$

where $F_{t,k}$ is defined as the event that the item $X_{t,k}$ is checked by the user. Equation (2) is by

$$r(X_k^*) - r(X_{t,k}) \leq (X_k^{*T} - X_{t,k}^T)\tilde{\theta}_t + (\alpha_t + \beta_t)(\|X_k^*\|_{V_{t-1}^{-1}} + \|X_{t,k}\|_{V_{t-1}^{-1}})$$

$$\leq (\alpha_t + \beta_t)(s_t(X_k^*) + s_t(X_{t,k})).$$

If event $\mathbb{E}^\lambda(t)$ holds, then the expected cummulative regret is

$$\mathbb{E}[R(T)] \leq \sum_{t=1}^{T}\mathbb{E}[\sum_{k=1}^{K}\mathbb{I}(F_{t,k})(\alpha_t + \beta_t)(s_t(X_k^*) + s_t(X_{t,k}))]$$

$$\leq (\alpha_T + \beta_T)\sum_{t=1}^{T}\mathbb{E}[\sum_{k=1}^{C_t}s_t(X_k^*)] + \mathbb{E}[\sum_{k=1}^{C_t}s_t(X_{t,k})]$$

$$\leq (\alpha_T + \beta_T)(\sqrt{\frac{2d}{\lambda_{min}}}(2\sqrt{TK\ln TK} + K) + \sqrt{2dTK\ln(1 + \frac{KT}{\lambda d})}).$$

$$(3)$$

If event $\mathbb{E}^\lambda(t)$ is true for any round t, then $\lambda_{min}(V_{t-1}) \geq 1/2N_{t-1}\lambda_{min}$. It implys that for any item $x \in \mathcal{X}$, $\|x\|_{V_{t-1}^{-1}} \leq \sqrt{\frac{2d}{N_{t-1}\lambda_{min}}}$, where $N_{t-1} = \sum_{i=1}^{t-1}C_i$ is number of checked items. Thus applying Lemma 7, we get that

$$\sum_{t=1}^{T}\sum_{k=1}^{C_t}s_t(X_k^*) \leq \sqrt{\frac{2d}{\lambda_{min}}}(C_1 + \sum_{t=2}^{T}\frac{C_t}{\sqrt{\sum_{i=1}^{t-1}C_i}})$$

$$= \sqrt{\frac{2d}{\lambda_{min}}}(\sqrt{2KT\ln KT} + K).$$

And the second term of Eq. (3) follows from Lemma 2.

Substituting the value of α_T and β_T in $\mathbb{E}[R(T)]$, we obtain that for one cluster, if the users in the cluster are served in T rounds, the cumulative regret is:

$$\mathbb{E}[R(T)] = O(d\sqrt{KT}\ln KT).$$

Suppose the users are partitioned into m clusters and each cluster is served in $T_1, T_2, ..., T_m$ rounds where $\sum_{i=1}^{m}T_i = T$, the total regret is

$$\mathbb{E}[R''(T)] = \sum_{i=1}^{m}\mathbb{E}[R(T_i)]$$

$$\leq d\ln KT\sum_{i=1}^{m}C_i\sqrt{KT_i}$$

$$= O(d\sqrt{mKT}\ln KT)$$

Combining the results of part 1 and part 2 completes the proof of Theorem 1.

4.4 Technique Lemmas

In this section, we introduce the technique lemmas used in the proof of Theorem 1.

Lemma 1. *(Confidence Ellipsoid [1]). Let $(x_t : t \geq 0)$ be a sequence of d-dimensional vectors and $\|x_t\|^2 \leq 1$. Let $r_t = x_t^T\theta + \epsilon_t$ where ϵ_t is R-sub-Gaussian for some constant*

R, $V_t = \lambda I + \sum_{i=1}^{t} x_t x_t^T$ and $\hat{\theta}_t = V_t^{-1} \sum_{i=1}^{t} x_i r_i$. Then, for any $0 < \delta < 1$ and $t \geq 1$,

$$\|\hat{\theta}_t - \theta\|_{V_t} \leq \alpha_t(\delta)$$

holds with probability at least $1 - \delta$, where

$$\alpha_t(\delta) = R\sqrt{d \ln \frac{1 + t/\lambda}{\delta}} + \sqrt{\lambda}.$$

Lemma 2. *(Sum of standard deviation [13]). Let $\lambda > 1$, for any sequence $(X_1, X_2, ..., X_T)$, let $V_t = \lambda I + \sum_{i=1}^{t} \sum_{k=1}^{C_t} X_{i,k} X_{i,k}^T$ where $C_t \leq K$. Then*

$$\sum_{t=1}^{T} \sum_{k=1}^{C_t} \|X_{t,k}\|_{V_{t-1}^{-1}} = O(\sqrt{dTK \ln(1 + \frac{TK}{\lambda d})}).$$

Lemma 3. *(Azuma-Hoeffding inequality [4,9]). If $(Y_t : t \geq 0)$ is a super-martingale process, and for all $t \in [T]$, $|Y_{t+1} - Y_t| \leq c_t$ for some constant c_t, then for any $a \geq 0$,*

$$P(Y_T - Y_0 \geq a) \leq 2e^{-\frac{a^2}{2\sum_{t=1}^{T} c_t^2}}.$$

Lemma 4. *(Sum of variables) Let $(C_t : t \geq 1)$ be a sequence of truncated Poisson variables with mean $1 \leq q_i \leq K$ and $q = \min_{i \in [t]}\{q_i\}$. Let $\delta > 0$ and $B > 0$, then*

$$\sum_{i=1}^{t} C_i \geq B$$

holds for all $t \geq \frac{2B}{q} + \frac{2}{q^2}k^2 \ln \frac{2}{\delta}$ with probability at least $1 - \delta$.

Proof. We construct a super-martingale process by defining $X_i = C_i - q_i$ and $Y_i = \sum_{j=1}^{i} X_j$. By the Azuma-Hoeffding inequality (Lemma 3), we obtain that for all $t \geq \frac{2B}{q} + \frac{2}{q^2}k^2 \ln \frac{2}{\delta}$,

$$P(\sum_{i=1}^{t} C_i \leq B) = P(\sum_{i=1}^{t}(q_i - C_i) \geq \sum_{i=1}^{t} q_i - B) \leq 2e^{-\frac{(tq-B)^2}{2tk^2}} \leq \delta.$$

Lemma 5. *(High probability property of the events). For all t and $0 < \delta < 1$, event $\mathbb{E}^\mu(t)$ happends with probability at least $1 - \frac{\delta}{t^2}$. And for any possible filtration event $\mathbb{E}^\theta(t)$ happens with probability at least $1 - \frac{1}{t^2}$.*

Proof. The proof of this lemma follows from previous work on linear Thompson sampling [3]. The high probability property of $\mathbb{E}^\mu(t)$ is proven by applying the concentration inequality stated as Lemma 7 in [1]. The probability bound for $\mathbb{E}^\theta(t)$ is obtained by applying the concentration inequality of Gaussian random variables [2].

Lemma 6. *(Lower bound of the smallest eigenvalue of sum of hermitian matrices). Let $(x_t x_t^T : t \geq 1)$ be a sequence of $d \times d$ matrices generated sequentially from random distribution $x_t x_t^T \in \mathbb{R}^{d \times d}$. Suppose that for all t, $\mathbb{E}[x_t x_t^T]$ is full rank Hermitian matrix and $\mathbb{E}[x_t x_t^T] \geq \lambda_{min}$ (Assumption 2) and $\|x\| \leq 1$ (Assumption 1). Let $V_t = \sum_t x_t x_t^T$, then for any $t \geq (\frac{8}{\lambda_{min}^2} + \frac{4}{3\lambda_{min}}) \ln \frac{d}{\delta}$, event $\lambda_{min}(V_t) \geq 1/2t\lambda_{min}$ holds with probability at least $1 - \delta$.*

Proof. We first define three random sequences:

$$X_t = \mathbb{E}[x_t x_t^T] - x_t x_t^T$$

$$Y_t = \sum_{k=1}^{t} X_k = \sum_{k=1}^{t} \mathbb{E}[x_k x_k^T] - \sum_{k=1}^{t} x_k x_k^T$$

$$W_t = \sum_{k=1}^{t} \mathbb{E}_{k-1}[X_k^2].$$

As $\mathbb{E}X_t = \mathbb{E}[\mathbb{E}[x_t x_t^T] - x_t x_t^T] = 0$, Y_t is a matrix martingale whose values are Hermitian matrices with dimension $d \times d$ and X_t is the difference sequence. Note that $\lambda_{max}(X_t) \leq 1$, then by the Matrix Freedman's inequality, for any a and b:

$$\mathbb{P}(\lambda_{max}(Y_t) \geq a \quad and \quad \lambda_{max}(W_t) \leq b) \leq d \cdot \exp^{-\frac{a^2/2}{b+a/3}}.$$

We define that $V_t = \sum_{k=1}^{t} x_k x_k^T$ and $G_t = \sum_{k=1}^{t} \mathbb{E}[x_k x_k^T]$, then $V_t + Y_t = G_t$. By the Wely's Theorem $\lambda_{min}(V_t) + \lambda_{max}(Y_t) \geq \lambda_{min}(G_t)$, then

$$\mathbb{P}(\lambda_{min}(V_t) \geq \frac{1}{2}t\lambda_{min}) \geq \mathbb{P}(\lambda_{min}(G_t) - \lambda_{max}(Y_t) \geq \frac{1}{2}t\lambda_{min})$$

$$= \mathbb{P}(\lambda_{max}(Y_t) \leq \lambda_{min}(G_t) - \frac{1}{2}t\lambda_{min})$$

$$= 1 - \mathbb{P}(\lambda_{max}(Y_t) \geq \lambda_{min}(G_t) - \frac{1}{2}t\lambda_{min})$$

$$\geq 1 - \mathbb{P}(\lambda_{max}(Y_t) \geq \frac{1}{2}t\lambda_{min}) \qquad (4)$$

$$= 1 - \mathbb{P}(\lambda_{max}(Y_t) \geq \frac{1}{2}t\lambda_{min} \quad and \quad \|W_t\| \leq t) \qquad (5)$$

$$\geq 1 - d \cdot \exp(-\frac{\lambda_{min}^2 t^2/8}{t + 1/6\lambda_{min}t}).$$

Equation (4) holds because of the assumption that $\lambda_{min}(\mathbb{E}[x_t x_t^T]) \geq \lambda_{min}$ and the Wely's inequality and Equation (5) holds because of the fact that $\lambda_{max}(W_t) = \lambda_{max}(\sum_{k=1}^{t} \mathbb{E}[(x_k x_k^T)^2] - \mathbb{E}[x_k x_k^T]^2) \leq t$ holds with probability 1.

Thus, for any $t \geq (\frac{8}{\lambda_{min}^2} + \frac{4}{3\lambda_{min}}) \ln \frac{d}{\delta}$, $\mathbb{P}(\lambda_{min}(V_t) \geq 1/2t\lambda_{min}) \geq 1 - \delta$, which completes the proof.

Lemma 7. *Suppose $S = (a_t : t \in [T])$ is a finite sequence of positive integer and $1 \leq a_i \leq K$ for any $i \leq T$. Let $f(S) = a_1 + \sum_{t=2}^{T} \frac{a_t}{\sqrt{\sum_{j=1}^{t} a_j}}$. Then, $f(S) = O(K + \sqrt{KT \ln KT})$.*

Proof. We first prove that for any sequence $S_1 = (a_1, a_2, ..., a_T)$, if there exist $1 \leq i \leq T$ that $a_i \geq a_{i+1}$, we can switch these two elements a_{i+1} and a_i so that we get another sequence $S_2 = (a_1, a_2, ..., a_{i+1}, a_i, ... a_T)$ and $f(S_2) \geq f(S_1)$. We set that $\sum_{j=1}^{i-1} a_j = M$, then

$$f(S_2) - f(S_1) = \frac{a_{i+1}}{\sqrt{M}} + \frac{a_i}{\sqrt{M + a_{i+1}}} - \frac{a_i}{\sqrt{M}} - \frac{a_{i+1}}{\sqrt{M + a_i}}$$

$$= \frac{a_{i+1} - a_i}{\sqrt{M}} + \frac{a_i}{\sqrt{M + a_{i+1}}} - \frac{a_{i+1}}{\sqrt{M + a_i}}$$

We define a function $g(x) = \frac{1}{\sqrt{M+x}}$, as $g''(x) = \frac{3}{4}(M + x)^{-\frac{5}{2}} \geq 0$, $g(x)$ is a convex function. Then,

$$\forall x_1, x_2 \geq 0 \quad and \quad t \in [0, 1], \quad g(tx_1 + (1 - t)x_2) \leq tg(x_1) + (1 - t)g(x_2).$$

We substitute $x_1 = 0$, $x_2 = a_{i+1}$, $t = 1 - a_i/a_{i+1}$ into above inequality, and we obtain

$$g(a_i) \leq (1 - \frac{a_i}{a_{i+1}})g(0) + \frac{a_i}{a_{i+1}}g(a_{i+1})$$

Thus,

$$\frac{a_{i+1}}{\sqrt{M + a_i}} \leq \frac{a_{i+1} - a_i}{\sqrt{M}} + \frac{a_i}{\sqrt{M + a_{i+1}}},$$

so that $f(S_2) \geq f(S_1)$.

For any sequence S, if the elements of the sequence are fixed, we can recursively switch the elements to get the maximum value of $f(S)$. The maximal value is obtain when $a_1 \leq a_2 \leq ... \leq a_T$. As the value of the elements can only be selected from K positive integers, we assume that the integer $1 \leq k \leq K$ is selected T_k times and $\sum_{k=1}^{K} T_k = T$, thus

$$a_1 + \sum_{i=2}^{T} \frac{a_i}{\sqrt{\sum_{i=1}^{i} a_i}} \leq K + \sqrt{(\sum_{i=1}^{T} a_i)(\sum_{i=2}^{T} \frac{a_i}{\sum_{j=1}^{i} a_j})} \tag{6}$$

$$\leq K + \sqrt{KT(\sum_{i=2}^{T} \frac{a_i}{\sum_{j=1}^{i} a_j})}$$

$$\leq K + \sqrt{KT(\sum_{k=1}^{K} \sum_{j=1}^{T_k} \frac{k}{\sum_{h=1}^{k-1} hT_h + (j - 1)k})} \tag{7}$$

$$\leq K + \sqrt{KT(\sum_{k=2}^{K} \ln \frac{k}{k - 1} + \ln \sum_{k=1}^{K} \frac{k}{K} T_k)} \tag{8}$$

$$= O(K + \sqrt{KT \ln KT}),$$

where Eq. (6) follows from the Cauchy–Schwarz inequality and $a_i \leq K$, Eq. (7) follows from the fact that after the rearrangement of the sequence, $a_i \leq a_{i+1}$ holds for any $1 \leq i \leq T - 1$, and $\sum_{k=1}^{K} T_k = T$. Equation (8) holds because $\sum_{j=1}^{T_k} \frac{k}{\sum_{h=1}^{k-1} hT_h + (j-1)k} \leq \ln \sum_{i=1}^{k} \frac{i}{k} T_i - \ln \sum_{i=1}^{k-1} \frac{i}{k} T_i$.

5   Experiment

We evaluate our algorithm C^4-TS on a synthetic dataset. Its performance is compared with CLUB-cascade, CascadeLinUCB and CascadeLinTS, which are the most related algorithms. The empirical results demonstrate the advantage of using Bayesian heuristic and online clustering.

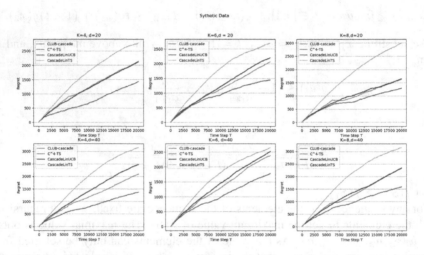

Fig. 1. These figures compare C^4-TS with CLUB-cascade, CascadeLinUCB and CascadeLinTS on Synthetic dataset. Plots reporting the cummulative regret over time step T. The basic setting is that there are 200 items, 20 users and 2 clusters. The users in different clusters have orthogonal user vectors. The dimension of feature space is $d = \{20, 40\}$. The length of recommended list is $K = \{4, 6, 8\}$

In all the subfigures, we generate a candidate set with $N_{items} = 200$ items, each item is represented by a d-dimensional feature vector $x \in \mathbb{R}^d$ with $x^T x \leq 1$ and $d \in \{20, 40\}$. We then generate $N_{users} = 20$ users and the users can be grouped into two clusters. We set that the users in the same cluster share the same user vectors $\theta \in \mathbb{R}^d$. And for users in different clusters, we set that their user vectors are orthogonal so that $\gamma = \sqrt{2}$ in these settings. The observed payoff for user θ to item x is a Bernoulli random variable, whose mean is the linear function $x^T \theta$. At each round, the algorithm selects a user to serve and recommends $K = \{4, 6, 8\}$ items to the user. The algorithm then observes the cascading feedback and updates its parameters accordingly.

In Fig. 1, we plot the cumulative regret as a function of time step T for C^4-TS, CLUB-cascade, CascadeLinUCB and CascadeLinTS. It is obvious that our algorithm outperforms other algorithms in all settings. We compare the performance of the collaborative algorithms and the standard bandit algorithm. It can be seen that the collaborative algorithms significantly outperform those algorithms without online clustering in all settings, which demonstrates the advantage of utilizing collaborative effect in these algorithms. We can also compare the performance of Thompson sampling and UCB-like algorithms. Although CascadeLinTS does not perform as well as CascadeLinUCB, our algorithm outperforms CLUB-cascade in all settings. In fact, we can tune CascadeLinTS by adjusting the exploration rate so that CascadeLinTS performs as well as CascadeLinUCB, but Fig. 1 is a clear proof of the collaborative effect on Thompson sampling. It can be seen that the collaborative algorithms benefit from collaborative effects after several rounds. This observation is empirical evidence of part 1 that the algorithm can find the cluster structure efficiently. Another important property of Thompson sampling is that it often has higher variance than UCB. An explanation is that Thompson sampling requires additional randomness because it samples from the posterior distribution of θ to explore information. In contrast, UCB-based algorithms explore by adding a deterministic positive bias.

6 Conclusion

We design and analyze C^4-TS algorithm for the stochastic cascading bandit in a collaborative environment. We prove that the regret bound of our algorithm matches the regret bound for UCB-like algorithms. And the experiments conducted on a synthetic dataset demonstrate the advantage of our algorithm over existing UCB-like algorithms and standard Thompson sampling algorithm. Further investigations include deriving the lower regret bound for cascading bandit and the frequentist regret bound for Thompson sampling algorithms.

Acknowledgments. This paper is supported by the National Science Foundation of China under Grant 61472385 and Grant U1709217.

References

1. Abbasi-Yadkori, Y., Pál, D., Szepesvári, C.: Improved algorithms for linear stochastic bandits. In: Advances in Neural Information Processing Systems, pp. 2312–2320 (2011)
2. Abramowitz, M., Stegun, I.: Handbook of mathematical functions with formulas, graphs, and mathematical tables (applied mathematics series 55). National Bureau of Standards, Washington, DC (1964)
3. Agrawal, S., Goyal, N.: Thompson sampling for contextual bandits with linear payoffs. In: International Conference on Machine Learning, pp. 127–135 (2013)
4. Azuma, K.: Weighted sums of certain dependent random variables. Tohoku Math. J. **19**(3), 357–367 (1967). Second Series
5. Chapelle, O., Li, L.: An empirical evaluation of Thompson sampling. In: Advances in Neural Information Processing Systems, pp. 2249–2257 (2011)
6. Cheung, W.C., Tan, V.Y.F., Zhong, Z.: Thompson sampling for cascading bandits (2018)
7. Gentile, C., Li, S., Kar, P., Karatzoglou, A., Etrue, E., Zappella, G.: On context-dependent clustering of bandits. arXiv preprint arXiv:1608.03544 (2016)

8. Gentile, C., Li, S., Zappella, G.: Online clustering of bandits. In: International Conference on Machine Learning, pp. 757–765 (2014)
9. Hoeffding, W.: Probability inequalities for sums of bounded random variables. J. Am. Stat. Assoc. **58**(301), 13–30 (1963)
10. Kveton, B., Szepesv, C., Wen, Z., Ashkan, A.: Cascading bandits: learning to rank in the cascade model (2015)
11. Li, S., Karatzoglou, A., Gentile, C.: Collaborative filtering bandits. In: Proceedings of the 39th International ACM SIGIR Conference on Research and Development in Information Retrieval, pp. 539–548. ACM (2016)
12. Li, S., Wang, B., Zhang, S., Chen, W.: Contextual combinatorial cascading bandits. In: Proceedings of the 33rd International Conference on Machine Learning, pp. 1245–1253 (2016)
13. Li, S., Zhang, S.: Online clustering of contextual cascading bandits (2018)
14. Nguyen, T.T., Lauw, H.W.: Dynamic clustering of contextual multi-armed bandits. In: Proceedings of the 23rd ACM International Conference on Conference on Information and Knowledge Management, pp. 1959–1962. ACM (2014)
15. Russo, D., Van Roy, B.: Learning to optimize via posterior sampling. Math. Oper. Res. **39**(4), 1221–1243 (2014)
16. Russo, D., Van Roy, B.: An information-theoretic analysis of Thompson sampling. J. Mach. Learn. Res. **17**(1), 2442–2471 (2016)
17. Russo, D.J., Van Roy, B., Kazerouni, A., Osband, I., Wen, Z., et al.: A tutorial on Thompson sampling. Found. Trends Mach. Learn. **11**(1), 1–96 (2018)
18. Shi, Z., Hao, N., Sung, K., Nan, R.K., Kveton, B.: Cascading bandits for large-scale recommendation problems. In: Conference on Uncertainty in Artificial Intelligence (2016)
19. Wu, Q., Wang, H., Gu, Q., Wang, H.: Contextual bandits in a collaborative environment. In: Proceedings of the 39th International ACM SIGIR Conference on Research and Development in Information Retrieval, pp. 529–538. ACM (2016)

Multi-label Recommendation of Web Services with the Combination of Deep Neural Networks

Yanglan Gan[1], Yang Xiang[2,3], Guobing Zou[2,3(✉)], Huaikou Miao[2,4],
and Bofeng Zhang[2(✉)]

[1] School of Computer Science and Technology,
Donghua University, Shanghai 201620, China
ylgan@dhu.edu.cn
[2] School of Computer Engineering and Science,
Shanghai University, Shanghai 200444, China
guobingzou@gmail.com, bfzhang@shu.edu.cn
[3] Shanghai Institute for Advanced Communication and Data Science,
Shanghai University, Shanghai 200444, China
[4] Shanghai Key Laboratory of Computer Software Evaluating and Testing,
Shanghai, China

Abstract. With the increasing number of web services on the Internet, how to effectively classify and recommend service labels has become a research issue. It plays an important role in web service organization and management. However, the deficiency of current approaches is that they either recommend only a single label for a web service or a set of independent labels without order ranking that is still difficult for service providers to publish their web services. In this paper, together with label embedding techniques, we propose a novel approach for service multi-label recommendation using deep neural networks. Unlike traditional approaches, the predicted service labels of our approach not only satisfy the demands of service multi-label recommendation, but also provide the importance with an ordered label ranking. The experiments are conducted to validate the effectiveness on a large-scale dataset from ProgrammableWeb, involving 13,869 real-world Web services. The experimental results demonstrate that our approach for multi-label recommendation of web services outperforms the competing approaches in terms of multiple evaluation metrics.

Keywords: Web service · Multi-label recommendation · Label embedding · Deep neural networks

1 Introduction

With the rapid advancement of web technology and the increasing demands on service-oriented applications, more and more software vendors publish their applications on the Internet as web services. Web services are platform-independent, modular, loosely coupled and self-describing distributed software components. As of 2019, the world's largest online web service registration platform, ProgrammableWeb, has registered 20,230 APIs and 7,937 mashup services. Those services significantly accelerate

X. Wang et al. (Eds.): CollaborateCom 2019, LNICST 292, pp. 133–150, 2019.
https://doi.org/10.1007/978-3-030-30146-0_10

machine-to-machine interactions and promote the development of service-oriented applications. They can be published, discovered and selected [1], automatically composed [2, 3], scheduled [4], recommended [5, 6] and invoked over the Internet.

As the increasing number of web services published on the Internet and their diverse functionalities across different application domains, there are always hundreds of service categories in an online RESTful service repository. This makes it difficult to effectively organize and manage web services in a manual manner. As a result, it tends to be a labor-intensive challenging task for service providers to search and find one or multiple appropriate categories from registered ones, when publishing their API services on a service management platform [7]. Therefore, how to design a novel approach for service providers and help them effectively and automatically recommend appropriate service labels have become a challenging research topic.

In recent years, correlative research efforts have been posed to support automated organization and management of web services. Machine learning methods have been adopted for web service classification and recommendation. In the traditional approaches [7–15] for service classification and recommendation, only a single service label is recommended for a web service. However, in service-oriented software system applications, a web service often holds cross-domain characteristics. Thus, a service provider is required to choose multiple labels for a web service when it is published to a service management platform. Moreover, unlike the traditional multi-label classification problem, service multi-label recommendation aims at recommending a sorted sequence of service labels, instead of a set of independent ones. For example, each web service in the ProgrammableWeb has a sorted sequence of service domain labels with different priorities. Therefore, as the number of services increases dramatically, how to recommend ordered multiple labels for web services is an urgent research issue to be solved.

To handle above research issue, we proposed a novel approach for service multi-label recommendation using deep neural networks. First, a convolutional neural network [16] is applied to extract service general and sequence features. Then, by using the relationship among service labels, a label embedding model is proposed to generate label feature representation of a web service. Finally, together with label embedding and attention mechanism [17], a Gated Recurrent Unit (GRU) deep neural network is used to recommend a sorted sequence of service labels. Consequently, the predicted service labels not only satisfy the demands of service multi-label recommendation, but also provide the importance with an ordered label ranking.

To test the performance of service multi-label recommendation, extensive experiments are conducted on a large-scale real-world dataset from ProgrammableWeb, involving 13,869 real-world web services with 474 service labels. We compare our approach with the state-of-the-art three existing machine learning-based approaches on service multi-label recommendation. The experimental results demonstrate that our approach can outperform those competing approaches in terms of multiple evaluation metrics. The main contributions of this paper are summarized as follows.

- We propose a novel service multi-label recommendation framework with the combination of deep neural networks, where convolutional and recurrent neural networks are combined together to predict an ordered sequence of service labels, instead of a set of independent ones without label ranking.

- We propose a novel model for service label embedding. With the consideration of the associations among different service labels, a label embedding model is trained to support more accurate generation of service multi-label recommendation.
- We design and implement a prototype system and conduct extensive experiments on a real-world dataset from ProgrammableWeb. The experimental results demonstrate that our approach for multi-label recommendation of web services is superior to existing completing approaches.

The remainder of this paper is organized as follows. Section 2 presents the overall framework. Section 3 presents the details of our approach for service multi-label recommendation. Section 4 shows extensive experiments and analyzes the results. Section 5 reviews the related work. Finally, Sect. 6 concludes the paper.

2 Framework of the Approach

To recommend multiple labels for a Web service, we propose an approach using deep neural networks. It mainly consists of two components, including service feature extraction and service label generation. Figure 1 shows the overall framework of service multi-label recommendation.

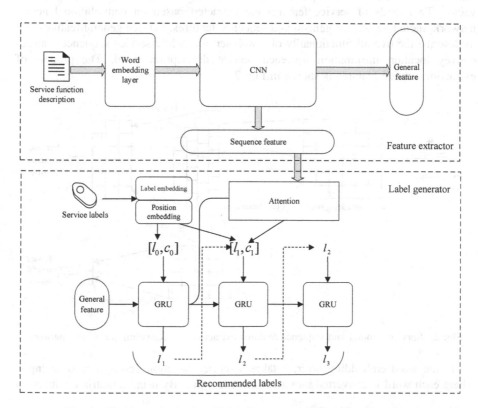

Fig. 1. The framework of multi-label recommendation of web services

In the stage of extracting service features, taking the functional description of web services as inputs, it is converted into a matrix representation through the layer of word embedding. Convolutional neural network (CNN) is then used to extract service general and sequence features respectively, where service general feature is a feature vector to reflect the whole feature of service functional description and sequence features correspond to each service description word.

In the stage of service multi-label recommendation, the extracted service features are taken to the label generator that is a recurrent neural network based on GRU. Specifically, service general feature is used as the initialization of the hidden feature of GRU model. Service labels and their positions are converted to a vector by the label embedding model. Then, the attention layer converts service sequence features to a vector. By merging service feature vector and label vector as the input of the GRU unit, it outputs the label probability of a web service. Through the iterative process, a sequence of sorted service labels is generated recommended.

3 Service Multi-label Recommendation

3.1 Service Feature Extraction

In order to extract service features, convolutional neural network (CNN) is applied to transform functionality description of a web service into a low-dimensional feature vector. Two kinds of service features are extracted based on convolutional neural network, including service general and sequence features. Service general features aim to describe the overall functionality of a web service, while service sequence features convey location information for each service description word. The process of extracting service features is shown in Fig. 2.

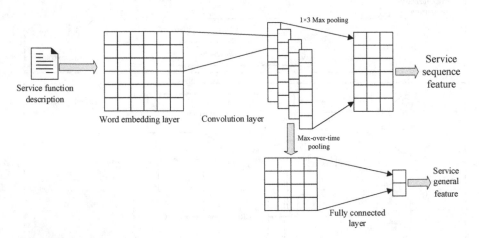

Fig. 2. Service general and sequence features extraction by convolutional neural network

In the word embedding layer, it takes a service function description as an input, where each word is converted into a vector of length t. By using a matrix e with $n \times t$

dimension, where each row represents a representation of a word, the embedded feature of a service description word is expressed as

$$We(w_i) = onehot(w_i)^T e \tag{1}$$

Where $onehot(w_i)$ is an n dimension vector, and the value of the i-th is 1 and the rest of the values are 0. $We(w_i)$ is the embedded representation of w_i. e is initialized by the trained word embedding model.

Definition 1 (Service Embedding Representation). Given a service function description D_s, word embedding representation of a web service s is denoted as $e(D_s) = (We(w_1), We(w_2), \ldots, We(w_m))^T$, where, $w_1, w_2, \ldots, w_m \in D_s$ and $e(D_s)$ is a matrix with the dimension $m \times t$.

In the convolutional layer, three different scales of convolutional kernels with the representation of parameter matrix W are used for one-dimensional convolution, which is expressed as

$$Y_{conv} = e(D_s) * W \tag{2}$$

In the convolutional operation, the value of each point in the convolution result vector is calculated by

$$y_i = \sigma\left(\sum_{k=1}^{m} w_k^T e_{i-k+1}\right) \tag{3}$$

Where y_i is value of the i-th point on the convolution result Y_{conv}, w_k is the parameters of the k-th line in the convolutional kernel matrix W, and e_k is the k-th line of the embedding matrix of service function description. σ is a nonlinear function that determines activation degree of each neural unit. For faster convergence, an activation function ReLU is used to improve the model learning efficiency.

When extracting service features, maximum pooling is applied to generate sequence features with the same length as the input sequence. For service general features extraction, max-over-time pooling is used based on a fully connected layer.

3.2 Service Label Embedding

To improve of the accuracy of service multi-label recommendation, service labels are embedded from the idea of Word2vec. Embodying service label semantics and label relationships, a service label is converted into an embedding vector. The training process of service label embedding is illustrated in Fig. 3, which is divided into pre-training stage and actual training stage.

In the pre-training stage, a Word2vec model is first trained through Wikipedia corpus, and then service function descriptions from web service library are selected as training data to boost the accuracy of Word2vec model. In the actual training stage, all of the service labels extracted from web service library and their relationships are taken into account to learn service label embedding model, when trained based on the generated Word2vec model.

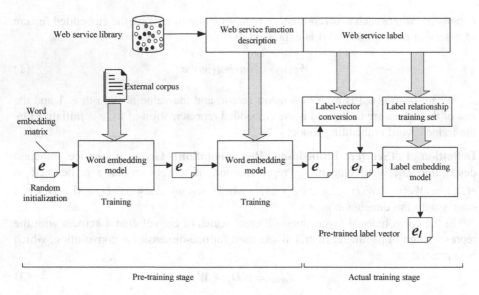

Fig. 3. The two-stage training process of service label embedding

Based on the pre-trained word embedding model, the pre-trained service label vector can be obtained. When a service label contains only one word, its vector can be directly obtained by pre-trained word embedding model. However, if a service label that is composed of multiple words, its corresponding vector is equal to the sum of the vectors of all the words in the label. For each position of the word embedding vector, it is divided by the number of words in the label. It is expressed as

$$e(l_i) = \frac{1}{|Words(l_i)|} \sum_{w_j \in Words(l_i)} e'(w_j) \tag{4}$$

Where $Words(l_i)$ represents the list of words contained in the label l_i, e is the pre-trained service label vector with multiple words, and e' is the pre-trained word embedding vector.

To learn a label embedding model, a training set based on the relationship between web services and their corresponding labels is generated. Assume that each web service in the training set has multiple labels. The process of training label embedding aims at applying the model to predict correlative service labels. Accordingly, a set of labels pairs are generated as training set of label embedding. Given a web service s_i that has j number of service labels $l_1, l_2, \ldots, l_j$, j group of service labels can be generated, including $(l_1|l_2, \ldots, l_j), (l_2|l_1, l_3 \ldots, l_j), \ldots, (l_j|l_1, \ldots, l_{j-1})$. As a result, each service label group $(l_x|l_1, \ldots, l_{x-1}, l_{x+1}, \ldots, l_{j-1})(1 \leq x \leq j)$, where a set of service label pairs $(l_x, l_1), (l_x, l_2), \ldots, (l_x, l_j)$ are generated. For example, suppose that there is a web service with labels on news, web, and mapping, six pairs of training data are generated, as shown in Table 1.

Table 1. A motivating example of six pairs of training data generated by a web service

Input label	Predicted label
News	Web
News	Mapping
Web	News
Web	Mapping
Mapping	News
Mapping	Web

After the above two steps, we construct a Word2vec model that is a simple fully connected network for service label embedding. Specifically, a vector representation of one of the service labels is used to predict the vector representation of the other service label. The objective function of the label embedding training process is

$$L = \sum_{w_i \in \mathbb{D}} \sum_{w_j \in Context(w)} \log P(w_i | w_j) \tag{5}$$

$$P(w_i | w_j) = \frac{\exp(e'(w_i)^T e(w_j))}{\sum\limits_{w' \in \mathbb{V}} \exp(e'(w')^T e(w_j))} \tag{6}$$

Where L represents the objective function, $\mathbb{D}$ and $\mathbb{V}$ represent the entire corpus and dictionary. e and e' represent a word vector matrix to be trained and a word vector matrix to be generated as output, respectively. e and e' are updated using the stochastic gradient descent method to maximize the objective function.

After completing the training, we discard e' and use e as the finally pre-trained label embedding model. It converts a service label into a vector representation that contains both label semantics and inter-label associations. Thus, taking label embedding vectors as inputs for service label generation can improve the accuracy of service multi-label recommendation.

3.3 Service Label Sequence Generation

Based on the service feature extraction and service label embedding, a sorted sequence of service labels can be generated by service label generator, as illustrated in Fig. 4. It initializes the hidden feature by using the service general feature and GRU unit outputs the first label and the hidden state. They are then used as inputs to generate a subsequent sequence of service labels. The generation process is finished until it reaches the convergence condition. The service label generator consists of five correlative layers for multi-label recommendation of web services.

(1) Service Label Embedding Layer. When service label sequence generator predicts the t-th label, it receives the t-1 label that is converted into a label vector through service label embedding layer. It is constructed the same as the word embedding layer. Here, the weight matrix directly adopts the pre-trained label embedding model.

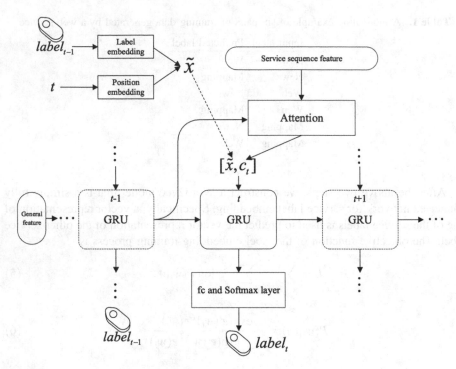

Fig. 4. The model of service label sequence generation with recurrent neural networks

(2) Position Embedding Layer. Together with service label embedding, we take into account position embedding to enable recurrent neural network to better capture location information to promote the multi-label recommendation. Position embedding is a technique for vectorizing position numbers in a sequence, which is defined as

$$\begin{cases} PE_{2i}(p) = \sin(p/10000^{2i/d}) \\ PE_{2i+1}(p) = \cos(p/10000^{2i/d}) \end{cases} \tag{7}$$

Where PE_i is the value of the i-th element of the position vector PE, d is the dimension of the position embedding vector, and p is the number of the current position. Here, it takes the same dimension as the label embedding vector. The connection of label embedding vector and position embedding vector is fed into the next GRU unit that is expressed as

$$\tilde{x} = [e(label), PE(t)] \tag{8}$$

(3) Attention Layer. In order to solve the problem that a single feature vector lacks of enough information, the attention mechanism is applied to calculate the attention weight vector by the hidden state h_t and service sequence feature Z at the previous moment. After connecting with $\tilde{x}$, it is used as the input of the GRU layer.

$$x = [Attention(h_t, Z), \tilde{x}] \tag{9}$$

The attention layer uses the attention mechanism to generate a vector that activates the input sequence portion. The guided model focuses only on a portion of the input sequence, which is express as

$$u_i^t = v^T \tanh(W_1 h_t + W_2 Z_i) \tag{10}$$

Where u_i^t is the current attention score calculated by the input sequence and feature vector at the current time step t of the recurrent neural network, W_1, W_2 and v are internally adjustable weight matrices of the attention model, h_t is the hidden layer feature vector, Z_i is the output of the input sequence processed by the feature extractor at each time step. Since u_i^t is used as a weight, it is normalized using softmax so that the sum of the weights equals to 1.

$$a_i^t = \text{softmax}(u_i^t) \tag{11}$$

Where a_i^t is the attention weight vector at the current time step t. After Z_i and a_i^t are weighted and summed, they are used as input to the recurrent neural network as

$$c_t = \sum_{i=1}^{|Z|} a_i^t Z_i \tag{12}$$

Where c_t is used as the input to our GRU unit at time step t, and h_t is the hidden state input of the recurrent neural network.

(4) GRU and Fully Connected with the Softmax Layer. In the structure of the recurrent neural network, GRU is used in the layer and its operation is subjected to service multi-label recommendation through the fully connected with softmax layer.

3.4 Model Training

As the service multi-label recommendation is an end-to-end learning model, the two crucial stages including service feature extraction and service label generation need to be combined together for training. Here, the loss function of the model for the t-th service label is evaluated by calculating a cross entropy as

$$J_t = -\frac{1}{n} \sum_{i=1}^{n} (y_i^t \log Model(x)_i^t + (1 - y_i^t) \log(1 - Model(x)_i^t)) \tag{13}$$

Where n is the dimension of the output service label and $Model(x)$ is the predicted label of the model for input x. y is the real service label and t is the t-th service label predicted by the model. The total loss for one piece of data is the average of the loss predicted by the label at each location, which is expressed as

$$J = \frac{1}{m} \sum_{t=1}^{m} J_t \qquad (14)$$

Upon the preset maximum number of training, the loss function J is calculated by comparing with the real output service labels. Here, stochastic gradient descent method is used to iteratively optimize the objective loss function that can be minimized by backpropagation and updating the parameters in the model.

4 Experiments

4.1 Experimental Data Set

We have designed and implemented a prototype system and conducted the extensive experiments to validate the effectiveness of our proposed approach for service multi-label recommendation. All the experiments are run on Linux Operating System and carried out on a platform with an NVIDIA GTX1080Ti*2 GPU, Intel(R) Xeon(R) Gold 6132*2 CPU and 192 GB RAM.

The data set used in the experiments was collected from a web service management platform ProgrammableWeb[1], the world's largest online API and mashup service repository. As of 2019, there are 20,230 web APIs, 7,937 mashups, 545 web services development frameworks, 1,698 development libraries, and 14,325 SDKs. The Web APIs included in ProgrammableWeb are web services actually used in the real world applications. In the experiments, we have crawled API services, including service name, function description and labels that can be visualized and downloaded from our lab[2]. After the preprocessing, we obtained a collection of 13,869 API services. The statistics of experimental data set is shown in Table 2.

Table 2. The statistics of experimental data set crawled from ProgrammableWeb

Data set item	Value
Number of API services	13,869
Total number of labels	474
Total number of main labels	375
Average number of service labels	3.16
Minimum number of service labels	1
Maximum number of service labels	69
Total number of words of API services	932,450

---

[1] https://www.programmableweb.com/
[2] http://dmis.shu.edu.cn/ProgrammableWebData

In the experimental data set, API services have different number of labels. The distribution of the number of service labels is shown in Fig. 5. The majority of API services correspond to the number of labels ranging from 1 to 5, while the number of API services with 10 or more labels is 61, accounting for 0.44% of the total number of API services.

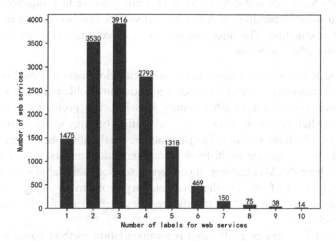

Fig. 5. Distribution of the number of service labels in experimental data set

In terms of the domain of service labels, each of which consists of the number of API services. The distribution of the number of API services within each service label is illustrated in Fig. 6. From the experimental data set, we can find that Tools, Financial, eCommerce, Messaging, Enterprise, Social, Payments, Mapping, Government, and Science correspond to the most number of API services.

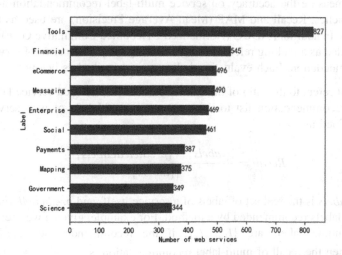

Fig. 6. Distribution of the number of API services within each service label

4.2   Competitive Methods

In order to show the feasibility and effectiveness of our approach, we carried out experiments and compared with three competing approaches for multi-label recommendation of web services, including multi-label Bayesian classifier (ML-Bayes), multi-label SVM classifier (ML-SVM), and convolutional neural network multi-label classifier (CNN-ML). Our self-developed and the comparative methods both have used the pre-trained word embedding model to convert service function description to vector and matrix representation. The three comparative service multi-label recommendation methods are described as below.

- **ML-Bayes.** It is a service multi-label recommendation method based on Bayesian classifier. It converts a multi-label recommendation problem into a set of naive Bayes classifiers of one-vs-other binary classification problem. Each classifier determines whether a web service to be classified belongs to the current label or other labels, which are combined to generate the final multi-label recommendation.
- **ML-SVM.** It is a service multi-label recommendation method based on Support Vector Machine (SVM) classifier. It converts a service multi-label recommendation problem into a set of one-vs-other two-category problem by using SVM classification. All of the classification results are integrated to obtain the final multiple service labels.
- **CNN-ML.** It is a service multi-label recommendation method based on convolutional neural network. We use Text-CNN deep learning model to extract service features. Followed by the fully connected layer of Text-CNN, the Sigmoid layer normalizes the output probability between 0 and 1. The output of each value of the output layer indicates the probability that a label is marked. By choosing the predefined number of recommended results, it generates a series of service labels.

4.3   Evaluation Metrics

In order to measure the accuracy on service multi-label recommendation among different approaches, Recall and MAP (Mean Average Precision) are used as the evaluation metrics. In addition, NDCG (Normalized Discounted Cumulative Gain) value is u is also provided as a ranking reference for evaluating the performance of service multi-label recommendation. Each evaluation indicator is described as below.

(1) Recall. It refers to the ratio of the correct number of predicted service labels in the multi-label recommendation list to the total number of labels of web service itself, which is defined as

$$Recall = \frac{|\{labels\} \cap \{predictedLabels\}|}{|\{labels\}|} \tag{15}$$

Where *labels* is the real set of labels of a service itself, and *predictedLabels* is a set of predicted labels recommended by a method. For example, given a web service s and its corresponding labels are $\{l_1, l_2, l_3\}$, if the recommended service labels are $\{l_1, l_3, l_5\}$, then the recall of multi-label recommendation is $\frac{|\{l_1, l_3\}|}{|\{l_1, l_2, l_3\}|} = \frac{2}{3} \approx 0.667$.

Recall@n refers to the rate when the total number of labels of web service itself $|\{labels\}| = n$. That is, the first n service labels are used to calculate the recall rate. Here, recall measures the degree of the recommendation results that cover all of the original service labels.

(2) MAP. It is the expected average of the precision that is the ratio of the correct number of predicted service labels in the recommendation list, which is defined as

$$P = \frac{|\{labels\} \cap \{predictedLabels\}|}{|\{predictedLabels\}|} \tag{16}$$

In order to measure precision of the service multi-label recommendation more accurately, the value of the precision corresponds to the Pr function that is defined as the value of the recall. The Pr function reflects the change in precision when the recall rate changes from 0 to 1. Integrating Pr function in the 0-1 interval yields the expectation of multi-label recommendation precision. It is defined as

$$MAP@n = \int_0^1 Pr(r)dr = \frac{\sum\limits_{k=1}^{n} P(k)rel(k)}{|\{labels\}|} \tag{17}$$

Where $P(k)$ is the precision of the first k service multi-label recommendation results, $P(k) = \frac{|\{labels\} \cap \{predictedLabels(k)\}|}{k}$, and $rel(k)$ indicates whether the k-th service label prediction is correct. That is, if it is correctly predicted, $rel(k)$ is set as 1, otherwise it is set as 0.

(3) NDCG. It reflects the impact of the service multi-label recommendation at each location in the overall recommendation. It is a location-sensitive evaluation metric, that is, for the recommended results at each location, the value is decremented accordingly. It is defined as

$$NDCG@n = \frac{DCG@n}{IDCG@n} \tag{18}$$

Where $DCG@n = \sum\limits_{k=1}^{n} \frac{2^{rel(k)}-1}{\log_2(k+1)}$ and $IDCG@n$ represents the idealized DCG value.

That is, DCG value is calculated according to the optimal ranking in the current recommendation.

4.4 Experimental Results and Analyses

To test the performance of our proposed approach, the extensive experiments on service multi-label recommendation are conducted among four competitive approaches, where GRU LabelsGen is used to represent our self-developed one. Table 3 shows the experimental results on three different evaluation metrics.

Table 3. Experimental results of service multi-label recommendation among four approaches

	MAP@5	Recall@5	NDCG@5
ML-Bayes	0.168	0.129	N/A
ML-SVM	0.209	0.113	N/A
CNN-ML	0.331	0.188	N/A
GRU LabelsGen	**0.762**	**0.591**	**0.432**

It can be seen from the experimental results that our proposed service multi-label recommendation approach is superior to the existing ones among the three evaluation metrics. Therefore, our approach with the combination of deep neural networks for multi-label recommendation of web services is effective in large-scale data set with a set number of service labels.

In the experiments, ML-Bayes and ML-SVM convert a label prediction task into training a large number of classifiers. Thus, they both have high time complexity as the number of service labels increases. Also, the performance on MAP@5 and Recall@5 of SVM-based service multi-label recommendation approach outperforms that of Bayes-based approach. Furthermore, the proposed approaches have better performance on MAP@5 compared to Recall@5 in MAP. The main reason is that the order of the results of service multi-label recommendation has no absolute impact on the MAP, although it is partially related to the order when predicting the main service labels can improve the accuracy of the experimental results. Therefore, our approach holds a higher MAP score by recommending a sorted sequence of service labels.

As for NDCG evaluation index, it can further test the correctness of the order of recommended service labels for our proposed approach. Since the competitive three service multi-label recommendation approaches cannot output an ordered sequence of service labels, the corresponding NDCG value cannot be calculated. In our proposed approach, NDCG represents the overall ranking accuracy of the predicted sequence of service labels. From the results, it indicates that the proposed approach can recommend a reasonable label sequence of web services.

In order to further test the parameter influence on the service multi-label recommendation, a set of experiments are carried out among four competitive approaches. The experimental results of parameter tuning are illustrated in Figs. 7 and 8.

Along with the changes of parameter for the number of recommended service labels, Figs. 7 and 8 illustrate the experiments results on MAP@n and Recall@n among four competitive approaches. In the experiments, the parameter of MAP@n and Recall@n ranges from 1 to 5 and the results are calculated with different values. Compared to the existing approaches, Fig. 7 shows that the experimental results of our proposed approach has better MAP@n along with the changes of n. Specifically, as n of MAP@n changes from 1 to 5, the experimental results of each approach have a certain decrease, and reach the best multi-label recommendation at MAP@1. Therefore, as the number of service labels to be evaluated increases, the predictive power of each multi-label recommendation approaches declines. However, our self-developed approach has the lowest decline compared with the other three approaches. From the results, it is observed that the proposed method is more suitable for service multi-label recommendation with short function text description.

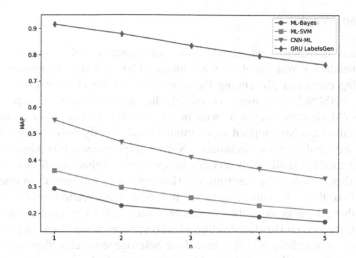

Fig. 7. The experimental results of MAP@n affected by the parameter n

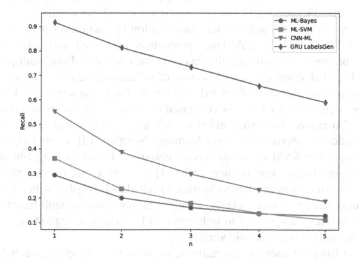

Fig. 8. The experimental results of Recall@n affected by the parameter n

Figure 8 compares the experimental results on Recall@n among four approaches. From the results, it is concluded that CNN-ML approach is better than the traditional two approaches without deep neural networks on Recall@1. However, along with the increase of parameter, the difference becomes smaller and smaller. It indicates that CNN-ML approach is more suitable for service single-label recommendation. The downward trend of our self-developed approach is lower than the other three approaches, indicating that the effectiveness of our proposed approach for multi-label recommendation is superior to the existing competitive approaches for recommending a sequence number of service labels.

5   Related Work

In recent years, correlative research has been investigated on web service classification and recommendation. Wang et al. took advantage of SVM to classify web services into corresponding categories [8]. During the process of service classification, a standard taxonomy, UNSPSC, was used to model the feature space of web services. Although SVM algorithm performs well in service classification, only a single classification method has been applied to recommend and classify web services. Based on the WSDL service description documents, Nisa et al. proposed a text mining approach [9] to automatically classify web services to specific domains and discover key concepts from their functionality descriptions. However, it is still subject to one classification method that still cannot achieve the best classification performance. To overcome above limitations of the conventional techniques for service classification, Qamar et al. focused on the classification of web services using a majority vote based classifier ensemble technique [10], where three heterogeneous classifiers Naïve Bayes, decision tree (J48), and Support Vector Machines are applied to vote for more effective classification of web services.

Recently, more sophisticated techniques are exploited to classify services. Since huge service classification taxonomies at multiple hierarchical levels, Syed et al. proposed a novel approach for web service classification by multi-layer perceptron neural network (MLPNN) [11]. A multi-layer perceptron optimized with tabu search for learning is proposed to automatically classify web services from multiple service categories. Lee et al. developed an IoT service classification and clustering system [12], which classifies the operation of an IoT service by their characteristics. Classic EM algorithm is used to cluster IoT services based on their classification in terms of their similarities. To reduce the human effort on labeling services, Liu et al. proposed a service classification approach by active learning algorithm [13], where LDA is applied to learn an optimum SVM model as service classifier. Based on [13], Shi et al. proposed a multi-label active learning approach [14] for web service tag recommendation, where active learning was considered to train a multi-label classifier with a correlation-aware learning strategy. More recently, Liang et al. presented a graph-based approach [15] to automatically assign tags to unlabeled API services by exploiting both graph structure information and semantic similarity.

Observed from the above investigations, we propose a novel approach for multi-label recommendation of web services with the combination of convolutional and recurrent deep neural networks. By considering the relationships of service labels, it achieves better service recommendation accuracy compared to the existing competitive approaches, where a sorted sequence of labels is recommended.

6   Conclusion

To effectively predict multiple labels of web services with order ranking, we proposed an approach for multi-label recommendation of web services using deep neural network. First, a convolutional neural network Text-CNN has been applied to extract general and sequence features of web services. Taking the associations of service labels, a label embedding model is then proposed to provide label feature representation. Finally, together with web services and their label embedding features, a recurrent neural network GRU is used to recommend a sorted sequence of service labels. Extensive experiments have been conducted on large-scale web service repository. The results demonstrate that our proposed approach outperforms the competitive ones for multiple labels recommendation of web services.

Acknowledgment. This work was partially supported by Shanghai Natural Science Foundation (No. 18ZR1414400, 17ZR1400200), National Key Research and Development Program of China (No. 2017YFC0907505), National Natural Science Foundation of China (No. 61772128, 61602109), and Shanghai Sailing Program (No. 16YF1400300).

References

1. Hwang, S., Hsu, C., Lee, C.: Service selection for web services with probabilistic QoS. IEEE Trans. Serv. Comput. **8**(3), 467–480 (2015)
2. Laleh, T., Paquet, J., Mokhov, S., Yan, Y.: Constraint adaptation in web service composition. In: IEEE International Conference on Services Computing, pp. 156–163 (2017)
3. Deng, S., Wu, H., Taheri, J., Zomaya, A., Wu, Z.: Cost performance driven service mashup: a developer perspective. IEEE Trans. Parallel Distrib. Syst. **27**(8), 2234–2247 (2016)
4. Li, W., Xia, Y., Zhou, M., Sun, X., Zhu, Q.: Fluctuation-aware and predictive workflow scheduling in cost-effective Infrastructure-as-a-Service clouds. IEEE Access **6**, 61488–61502 (2018)
5. Bai, B., Fan, Y., Tan, W., Zhang, J.: DLTSR: a deep learning framework for recommendation of long-tail Web services. IEEE Trans. Serv. Comput. (2017). https://doi.org/10.1109/tsc.2017.2681666
6. Shi, M., Tang, Y., Liu, J. Functional and contextual attention-based LSTM for service recommendation in mashup creation. IEEE Trans. Parallel Distrib. Syst. (2018). https://doi.org/10.1109/tpds.2018.2877363
7. Pang, S., Zou, G., Gan, Y., Niu, S., Zhang, B.: Augmenting probabilistic topic model for web service classification. Int. J. Web Serv. Res. **16**(1), 93–113 (2019)
8. Wang, H. B., Shi, Y. Q., Zhou, X., Bouguettaya, A.: Web service classification using support vector machine. In: IEEE International Conference on TOOLS with Artificial Intelligence, pp. 3–6 (2010)
9. Nisa, R., Qamar, U.: A text mining based approach for Web service classification. Inf. Syst. e-Business Manage. **13**(4), 751–768 (2015)
10. Qamar, U., Niza, R., Bashir, S., Khan, F.: A majority vote based classifier ensemble for Web service classification. Bus. Inf. Syst. Eng. **58**(4), 249–259 (2016)
11. Syed, A., Kumara, S.: Web service classification using multi-layer perceptron optimized with tabu search. In: IEEE International Advance Computing Conference, pp. 290–294 (2015)
12. Lee, D., Lee, H.: IoT service classification and clustering for integration of IoT service platforms. J. Supercomputing **74**(12), 6859–6875 (2018)
13. Liu, X.M., Agarwal, S., Ding, C., Yu, Q.: An LDA-SVM active learning framework for web service classification. In: IEEE International Conference on Web Services, pp. 49–56 (2016)
14. Shi, W.S., Liu, X.M., Yu, Q.: Correlation-aware multi-label active learning for web service tag recommendation. In: IEEE International Conference on Web Services, pp. 229–236 (2017)

15. Liang, T.T., Chen, L., Wu, J., Bouguettaya, A.: Exploiting heterogeneous information for tag recommendation in API management. In: IEEE International Conference on Web Services, pp. 436–443 (2016)
16. Gehring, J., Auli, M., Grangier, D., et al.: Convolutional sequence to sequence learning. In: International Conference on Machine Learning, pp. 1243–1252 (2017)
17. Vaswani, A., Shazeer, N., Parmar, N., et al.: Attention is all you need. In: Advances in Neural Information Processing Systems, pp. 5998–6008 (2017)

An Approach for Item Recommendation Using Deep Neural Network Combined with the Bayesian Personalized Ranking

Zhongqin Bi[1], Siming Zhou[1], Xiaoxian Yang[2,3(✉)], Ping Zhou[1], and Jiale Wu[1]

[1] School of Computer Science and Technology,
ShangHai University of Electric Power, Shanghai, China
[2] School of Computer and Information Engineering,
Shanghai Polytechnic University, Shanghai, China
xxyang@sspu.edu.cn
[3] Shanghai Shang Da Hai Run Information System Co., Ltd., Shanghai, China

Abstract. This paper proposes a deep neural network model (SDAE-BPR) based on Stack Denoising Auto-Encoder and Bayesian Personalized Ranking for the problem of accurate product recommendation. First, we use the Stack Denoising Auto-Encoder (SDAE) as the input of the item's rating data and obtain the hidden features after encoding. Second, the Bayesian personalized Ranking (BPR) method is used to learn the hidden feature vector of the corresponding item. This model can avoid the influence of the sparseness of the matrix. Therefore, this model achieves the effect of more accurate recommendations of items. Third, to reduce the cost of model training, a unique pretraining and fine-tuning strategy is proposed in the deep neural network. Finally, based on the Movielens 20M dataset, the results of the SDAE-BPR, a traditional item-based collaborative filtering model and a user-based collaborative filtering model are compared. It is shown that the SDAE-BPR has higher accuracy. This method improves the accuracy of parameter estimation and the efficiency of model training.

Keywords: Recommendation · Stack Denoising Auto-Encoder · Bayesian Personalized Ranking · Deep learning · The sparseness of matrix

1 Introduction

The recommendation system plays an extremely important role in e-commerce platforms, because it helps the platform promote advertisements and products to users and leads to greater commercial benefits [1]. Currently, collaborative filtering is the most widely used commercial recommendation algorithm. This algorithm learns to build a rating matrix based on the existing item-user ratings to predict the user ratings of unknown items [2, 3]. With the advent of the era of big data, the number of users and products has soared. Most of the products have been rated by only a small number of users. Thus, the sparsity of the rating matrix seriously affects the quality of the recommendation results [4].

© ICST Institute for Computer Sciences, Social Informatics and Telecommunications Engineering 2019
Published by Springer Nature Switzerland AG 2019. All Rights Reserved
X. Wang et al. (Eds.): CollaborateCom 2019, LNICST 292, pp. 151–165, 2019.
https://doi.org/10.1007/978-3-030-30146-0_11

Therefore, to improve the accuracy, this paper proposes a new method. uses Stack Denoising Auto-Encoder based on Bayesian Personalized Ranking to determine the relevance ranking table for each unique item. This method is different from the previous method that relies on specific context information. For each item, we choose the automatic encoder method in the feature extraction step. This approach has the generalization capability due to adding the noise to the input data, achieving greater robustness [5]. Additionally, by ranking the similarity probabilities of other items and itself, it is guaranteed that these similar items are ranked higher than the dissimilar items, and this sorting method is proved to be effective and can solve the imbalance problem. To address the large computational cost, we proposed a pre-training + fine-tuning strategy [6] for the model.

In this paper, the proposed model integrates the advantages of the BPR and the SDAE into a deep learning model. Compared with the traditional collaborative filtering recommendation algorithm, this model has some unique advantages. First, the rating vector of each item can obtain a more complex representation of the hidden features after extracting the deep network through the SDAE. Meanwhile, the addition of noise also improves the anti-interference property of the model, making the extracted features more reliable. Second, the final BPR ranking part can better capture the unique characteristics of each item and give the probability of the similarity between each item to reduce the impact of data sparsity effectively. Thus, this approach helps to improve the accuracy of recommendation. Third, in order to avoid poor parameter estimation, we design a pre-training and fine-tuning strategy based on the Bernoulli probability model. In the last part of this paper, the experiments carried out on real commodities datasets are described. The results show that this model obtains more accurate recommendation results than the classical collaborative filtering algorithm. Figure 1 shows an overview of our method.

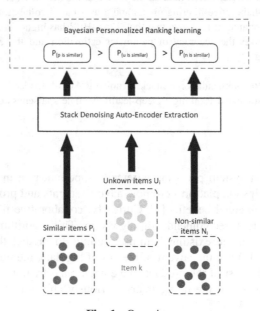

Fig. 1. Overview

The remainder of this paper is organized as follows. In Sect. 2, we introduce the deep neural network model based on Stack Denoising Auto-Encoder and Bayesian Personalized Ranking. Section 3 presents the details and results of the experiments. Section 4 reviews the related works. Section 5 states the conclusions and describes future research directions.

2 Model Framework

This section first describes a pairwise raking task in the commodity recommendation problem. Then, we propose a Bayesian deep neural network model based on the BPR and describe the pre-training strategy. Figure 2 shows the architecture of the model.

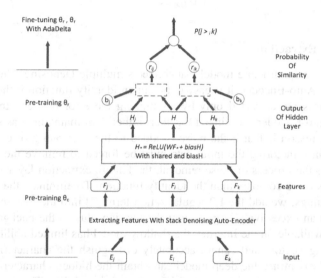

Fig. 2. SDAE-BPR

2.1 Preliminaries

User $u \in R^N$, item $I \in R^I$. $E \in \{0,1\}^{I \times N}$ is the rating matrix formed by all of the user's scores on all of the items. Notation $e_{iu} = E(i,u) = 1$ indicates that user u is interested in item i, and $e_{iu} = E(i,u) = 1$ indicates that user u is not interested in item i. In most e-commerce platforms, the rating matrix E is usually sparse because most users can only obtain access to a small part of the entire item database.

Define a similarity probability matrix $R \in [0,1]^{I \times I}$, with notation $r_{ij} = R(i,j)$ representing the similarity probability of items i and j. Thus, for each item i, it can be divided into two disjoint sets that include the set of items with similar relations $P_i = \{j \mid r_{ij} = 1\}$ and the set of items with uncertain similar relations $M_i = \{j \mid r_{ij} < 1\}$. Here, we seek to recommend the ranking task learning model. This model ensures that all of the items with a similar relationship are in front of the of missing items. We can also divide the missing items M_i into the unknown U_i and dissimilar N_i, implying

$M_i = U_i \cup N_i$. In the training process of ranking tasks, $j \in P_i$ and $k \in M_i$, or $j \in U_i$ and $k \in N_i$ should be guaranteed, and the probability of item similarity r_{ij} should be greater than r_{ik}. In Bayesian personalized sorting, this relation is called partial relation $j >_i k$.

Based on the above definition, the product recommendations in this paper can be divided into two types of partial relations: $\{j >_i k | j \in P_i \cup k \in M_i\}$ and $\{j >_i k | j \in U_i \cup k \in N_i\}$. The set of all partial relations for item i is expressed as $R_i = \{(j,k) | j >_i k\}$. Therefore, it is observed that the ranking task is the essence of the product recommendation task in this paper. Compared with the classification and fitting, the sorting task can better avoid the imbalance problem. The final goal of this ranking task is to maximize the likelihood probability of the ranking given by:

$$\max \prod_{i \in R^I} \prod_{(j,k) \in R_i} P(j >_i k) \tag{1}$$

2.2 Feature Extraction

The SDAE is a deep structure model that connects multiple Denosing Auto-Encoders. For a common Auto-Encoder, it is easy to obtain an identity function if the features of the rating vectors are extracted only by minimizing the error between the input and output. The Auto-Encoders are linked together, rather than maintained as single Auto-Encoders. The reason is that if the noise is added to the user rating of each item, the encoder used in refactoring the input data must be forced to remove the noise. After training, due to the process of noise removal, the feature extraction layer will obtain a function that is more complex than the identity function. To eliminate the influence of noise in the ratings, we add the L2 regularization term [7] into the loss function. This term penalizes an excessively large weight. In addition, due to the background of the massive data available on the Internet, the shallow model has limited ability to express numerous rating vectors and cannot accurately distinguish the characteristics of different items. By contrast, the deep model can obtain the hidden characteristics behind each item's rating due to its more powerful deep extraction ability. The deep model can extract results more vividly and representatively than the shallow model. The design of the SDAE is described in Table 1.

Table 1. Algorithm of SDAE for feature extraction

Algorithm 1 SDAE for Feature Extraction
Input: Rating vector x
Output: Extracted feature F_i
Initialization: Randomly generate $W^{(1)}$, $b^{(1)}$, $\nabla J(\theta)$, $f^0 = x$, $h = 1$
1: while $\nabla J(\theta) \mathrel{!}= 0$
2:      for $h < 3$
3:          Calculate result f^h by taking f^{h-1} through h layer
4:          Update $W^{(h)}$, $b^{(h)}$, by BP method in h layer
5:          $h = h + 1$
6:      Calculate $\nabla J(\theta)$ by equation (3)
7: $F_i = f^h$
8: return F_i

In Table 1, $H = 3$ layers. The structure of the SDAE is U-A-B. Here, U is the input layer of each rating vector. A and B are the first hidden layer and the second hidden layer, respectively. For the original rating x, assign value 0 to some of the data before inputting into the network to obtain $x^\wedge$ in proportion. Then, $x^\wedge$ is input, and a greedy strategy is used in the training network of each layer step by step. All of the above steps comprise the pre-training of the SDAE layer. Finally, we use the results of the last layer as hidden characteristics. Considering that the input data are nonlinear and negative, it will be better to choose a sigmoid function as the activation function. Here, W is the weight matrix, and B is the bias vector. The training process is as follows: first, to obtain f^1, $x^\wedge$ is used as the input into the first hidden layer. Then, put f^1 into the decoding function in order to obtain $x'^{(1)}$. For each rating of the items, its reconstruction error function in any layer is given by Eq. (2).

$$l(x, x') = -\sum_{n=1}^{N} x_n \log(x') + (1 - x_n) \log(1 - x'_n) \tag{2}$$

For the whole training set with I items, the error function of the integration in this layer is given by Eq. (3).

$$J(\theta) = -\frac{1}{I}\left[\sum_{i=1}^{I}\sum_{n=1}^{N} x_n^{(i)} \log(x_n'^{(i)}) + (1 - x_n^{(i)}) \log(1 - x_n'^{(i)}) + \frac{\lambda}{2N}\sum_{h=1}^{H-1}\sum_{i=1}^{I_h}\sum_{n=1}^{I_{h+1}} (\theta_{ni}^{(h)})^2\right] \tag{3}$$

The goal of training is to minimize the error function in each step of the iteration. Therefore, to prevent over-fitting, the regularization parameter λ is introduced to avoid the weight becoming too large. For the error function of each layer, the Back-Propagation method and the Stochastic Gradient Descent method are combined to obtain the parameter θ^l of this layer. Under this parameter, the output f^l of this layer is the input of the hidden layer of the next layer. Repeat the above training process and keep the parameters of each training layer.

2.3 Learning to Rank

The rest of the deep model proposed in this paper is based on the hidden layer H. In the final output layer, the BPR is adopted to rank and learn an output so that the most similar items are ranked at the top, and the final recommended items are selected from the top k items. The training model maximizes the likelihood probability specified by Notation (1), and the loss function of the whole model is given by Eq. (4).

$$L(\theta_c, \theta_r) = -\sum_{i}\sum_{(j,k\in R')} P(j >_i k) + \lambda_1 \|\theta_c\|^2 + \lambda_2 \|\theta_r\|^2 \tag{4}$$

Here, $\theta_c = \{W_1^1, W_1^2, b_1^1, b_1^2\}$ is the weight and bias of the SDAE part. $\theta_r = \{W_2, b_2, b_3\}$ is the parameter of the other parts. After the pre-training in the SDAE layer, θ_c and θ_r were determined again by the Backward Propagation Stochastic Gradient Descent method. When the gradient is stable, the probability that all other items are similar to itself is calculated. Then, a ranking list can be created easily. Then, the system recommends items to users according to this list. After the training, the user rating vector of any two items is used as input, and the probability value of similarity $r_{ij} = P(e_{ij} = 1)$ between two items is determined. This probability value is the reason why we recommend these items.

Hidden Layer. The input part is F_i, F_j, F_k, which is the feature extracted by i j, k through the SDAE. The purpose of the hidden layers is to embed them in H_i, H_j, H_k for further calculation. In this layer of the network, we select the ReLU function as the activation function. The hidden layer effect here is not to extract features, so we choose the ReLU function with relatively less information but faster convergence Eq. (5).

$$H_i = ReLU(W^2 F_i + b_2) \tag{5}$$

Predicting Layer. The input is H_i, H_j, H_k, the output is r_{ij} and r_{ik}, and the activation function is given by Eq. (6)

$$r_{ij} = \sigma(b_3^i + b_3^j + H_j H_i^T) \tag{6}$$

Sigmoid is chosen as the activation function because the probability of the final output should be within [0, 1]. In the previous hidden layer, to improve the efficiency of training, all of the items use the same parameter $\{W_2, b_2\}$, but each item has its own unique parameter b_3^i in the predicting layer. Therefore, it is more likely to explore the inherent potential of each item and to improve the accuracy of the recommendation. The probability of the partial relation between j and k is defined by Eq. (7).

$$P(j >_i k) = \frac{r_{ij} - r_{ik}}{2} + 0.5 \tag{7}$$

2.4   Pre-training of θ_r and Fine-Tuning

In the feature extraction section above, the pre-training method of θ_c was described. Here, the pre-training method of θ_r and the fine-tuning method of the whole model are mainly introduced. Table 2 describes the flow of these two algorithms. Later, we will provide a detailed explanation of how each step in the algorithms is implemented in combination with this chart.

Pre-training θ_r. The feature F_i generated after training in the part of the SDAE is used as the input, and the output is r_{ij}, r_{ik}. To estimate the parameter, set $\theta_r = \{W_2, b_2, b_3\}$ of project i, and the remaining structural parts must be pre-trained. The similarity relation e_{ij} between the items in the training set is regarded as a sample of the Bernoulli distribution with a parameter r_{ui} given by Eq. (8).

$$p(e_{ij}|r_{ij}) = r_{ij}^{e_{ij}} (1 - r_{ij})^{1 - e_{ij}} \tag{8}$$

The likelihood probability corresponding to the above equation is defined as follows:

$$L = \sum_{i,j} (e_{ij} \log r_{ij} + (1 - e_{ij}) \log(1 - r_{ij})) \tag{9}$$

To estimate θ_r, let us define a function $r_{ui} = g\,(F_i, F_j)$ that goes from F_i, F_j to r_{ui}. Item i and item j are sampled from the positive example set P_i and the negative example set N_i, respectively. The negative examples are collected from set N_i rather than from U_i because this approach can greatly improve the training efficiency. Therefore, the logarithmic likelihood probability θ_r is defined using Eq. (10)

$$L(\theta_r) = \sum_i \sum_{i \in P_i} \log g(F_i, F_j) + \sum_{j \in N_i} \log[1 - g(F_i, F_j)] - \lambda \|\theta_r\|^2 \tag{10}$$

For the above equation, we use the Stochastic Gradient Descent optimization. In each iteration of the SGD, the updating method of θ_r is given by Eq. (11), where η is the learning rate and λ is the regularization parameter.

$$\Delta\theta_r = \eta \cdot ([e_{ij} - g(F_i, F_j) \cdot \frac{\partial g}{\partial \theta_r}] - \lambda\theta_r) \tag{11}$$

Fine-Tuning. Fine-tuning is necessary if the pre-training parameters are separately trained. To give the whole entire parameter a better initial space, we adopted the AdaDelta algorithm [8] that is based on the history of the gradient and weight to scale the SGD learning rate and can accelerate the convergence speed of the neural network in the first stage of the training process.

Table 2. Algorithm of pre-training θ_r and fine-tuning.

Algorithm 2 Pre-training θ_r and Fine-tuning
Initialization: Randomly generate θ_r
1: repeat (Pre-training θ_r)
2:    for all $i, j \in$ batch
3:       Calculate r_{ij} from F_i and F_j
4:       Back propagation through SDAE-BPR
5: until Convergence
6: for Epoch in AdaDelta (Fine-tuning)
7:    Random select a partial relation i, j, k
8:    Calculate r_{ij}, r_{ik} from E_i, E_j, E_k
9:    Update SDAE-BPR with AdaDelta
10: end

3   Experiments and Analysis

3.1   Data Sets and Evaluation Indicators

In the experimental part of this work, the proposed model is compared with some existing classical collaborative filtering recommendation algorithms. The following experiments are based on the movielens 20M dataset and movielens 1M dataset, respectively. For each method, 10-fold cross-validation is performed on the data set, and the average result is shown at the end.

To measure the performance of the different methods on the specified data sets, we use AUC as an indicator to evaluate the performance of different recommended methods and draw Precision-Recall graphs for intuitive comparison.

Movielens 20M Dataset [9]. This dataset is a stable benchmark dataset. A total of 238,000 users made 27,000 comments on 27,000 movies. These 27,000 movies come with attribute tags and 12 million movie correlation scores.

Movielens 1M Dataset. This dataset is a small dataset with 600 users applying 100,000 ratings and 3,600 attribute tags to 9,000 movies.

UB – CF [10]. User-based collaborative filtering is a collection of similar users based on the user's rating of the item that measures the similarity between the users, and then organizes them into a sorted catalogue for recommendation based on their favourite items. However, due to the large number of items in the Internet, most users only evaluate a few items, so there is a problem of sparsity that is difficult to solve.

IB – CF [11]. Item-based collaborative filtering uses the interactive information between the users and items to make recommendations for the users. Currently, IB-CF is the most widely used recommendation algorithm. However, the adopted shallow model cannot learn the deep features of users and items.

AUC [12]. Formally, AUC considers the ranking quality of sample prediction, while the ROC curve represents the comparison between the TPR and FPR as the classification threshold standard changes. Therefore, the AUC area is used here instead of the ROC curve as the measurement index. AUC values range from 0.5 to 1, with higher values indicating better performance. To evaluate the recommendation performance, we use the AUC between P and U to measure the model's ability to rank.

Precision-Recall Curve [13]. We can rank the samples according to the prediction result of the learner. The samples in the first place are the examples that the learner considers "most likely" to be positive, and the samples in the last place are the examples that the learner considers "least likely" to be positive. By taking samples as the positive examples one by one in this order for prediction, the current accuracy and recall can be calculated each time. Equations (12) and (13) are formula definitions, where TP, FP, FN represents true positive samples, false positive samples, and false negative samples, respectively. The Precision-Recall curve is obtained by plotting the accuracy ratio on the vertical axis and the recall ratio on the horizontal axis. If the Precision-Recall curve of one learner is completely wrapped by the curve of another learner, the latter can be asserted to have better performance than the former.

$$P = \frac{TP}{TP + FP} \tag{12}$$

$$R = \frac{TP}{TP + FN} \tag{13}$$

In order to evaluate the ranking quality of the recommendation results, we also adopted NDCG@n as one of the recommendation indicators.

NDCG [14]. Normalized Discounted Cumulative Gain (NDCG) is the ratio of the DCG to the described Ideal DCG, which means its similar items P are always ranked before the rest of the items. The higher NDCG value indicates a better learning performance. Commonly, the NDCG@n that calculates the NDCG result over the top ranked n items are used in the recommendation tasks. The NDCG result is described as follows:

$$N(n) = Z_n \sum_{j=1}^{n} (2^{r(j)} - 1) / \log(1 + j) \tag{14}$$

In formula 14, j represents the number of goals we want in the results and Z_n represents the normalization. In our experiments, we calculate NDCG@5 for each item and average them as a metric. Meanwhile, we also try different n for detailed estimation.

3.2 Result Analysis

To measure the performance of these models on datasets of different sizes, these models are validated using the movielens 20M dataset and the movielens 1M dataset, respectively. This validation is performed by calculating the AUC of the results and drawing P-R graphics to compare the comprehensive performance of the model. It was found that the AUC of the SDAE-BPR and the P-R curve are is higher than those of the classical algorithms. At the same time, the NDCG@n of the SDAE-BPR is also larger than those for the other two classical collaborative filtering algorithms.

Table 3. Comparison of AUC and NDCG@6 results.

	Movielens 20M		Movielens 1M	
	AUC	NDCG@6	AUC	NDCG@6
UB-CF	0.926	0.883	0.913	0.839
IB-CF	0.941	0.892	0.927	0.874
SDAE-BPR	0.967	0.971	0.944	0.958

AUC. As observed from the examination of the data presented in Table 3, the AUC of the SDAE-BPR is 2.6% higher than that of the IB-CF. The AUC of the SDAE-BPR is also 4.1% higher than that of UB-CF for the movielens 20M dataset. For the movielens 1M dataset, the AUC of SDAE-BPR was 1.7% higher than that of IB-CF and 3.1% higher than that of UB-CF. Based on the horizontal comparison, with the increase in the size of the training samples, the model can fit better. Therefore, all of these three methods perform better for large datasets than for small datasets. From a longitudinal perspective, the SDAE-BPR has the best performance in each training set followed by the IB-CF and the UB-CF. UB-CF shows the worst performance because when the number of items is too large, each user can only evaluate a few items. Thus, it is difficult to find enough users who are very similar in the training set. Because it measures the similarity between the items, the IB-CF can find many similar items in the training set. In addition to calculating the similarity of the items, the SDAE-BPR also deeply extracted the user evaluation vector to obtain the unique characteristics of each item. This deep extraction ensures the higher accuracy of the recommendation results. Furthermore, we can easily find that the difference in AUC is larger than that in NDCG@6. Here, we can assume that the main function of the SDAE-BPR is to rank a better result.

Precision-Recall Curve. In Fig. 3, the P-R curve of SDAE-BPR basically wraps the curves of the other two models. This finding is also observed in Fig. 4. According to the definition of the P-R curve in the previous paper, we can conclude that the comprehensive performance of the SDAE-BPR is the best in both large and small data sets. The conclusions drawn here are in accordance with the results of the AUC. By comparing these two results, we can clearly determine that the SDAE-BPR has better comprehensive performance than the classical collaborative filtering algorithm. However, in Fig. 4, the P-R curve of all methods nearly overlap. Even with the increasing amount of training data sets, in Fig. 3, their Precision-Recall curves were not becoming sufficiently different. Based on this phenomenon, we infer that significantly improving the performance of the model is not the advantage of the SDAE-BPR. To verify this assumption, analysis of the NDCG must be performed as described in the next section.

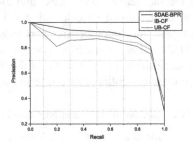

Fig. 3. Precision-Recall curves on movielens 20M

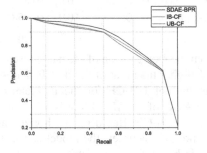

Fig. 4. Precision-Recall curves on movielens 1M

NDCG@n. First, we need to choose a value of n, that is, to ensure that the NDCG can be as large as possible, while the training cost is as small as possible. It is observed from Fig. 5 that the NDCG will be stable when n equals 6. This condition is also observed for the results presented in Fig. 6. Therefore, we choose 6 as the value of n. From Table 2, in each dataset, the NDCG@6 is much larger than other two classical collaborate filtering algorithms. The curve of the SDAE-BPR in Fig. 5 is much higher than the other two curves. In Fig. 6, the differences still stay the same. This result means the SDAE-BPR always has more accurate rank results than the classic methods. Therefore, the SDAE-BPR has the highest rank quality among these three algorithms. In addition, the difference of the NDCG@6 among all methods is also much larger than that of the AUC. This result is because the goal of the SDAE-BPR in training is to maximize the difference between the positive example probability and the negative example probability, rather than simply to calculate the similarity of each item after fitting. It was found that the SDAE-BPR model is more suitable for a small number of precise recommendation application scenarios. In addition, for each different item i, the bias b_i belonging to this item is added, also contributing to improving the quality and accuracy of the recommendation ranking results.

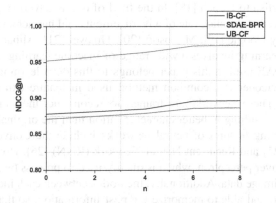

Fig. 5. NDCG@n on movielens 20M

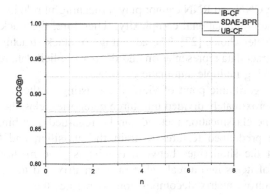

Fig. 6. NDCG@n on movielens 1M

4 Related Work

The most popular model for the recommender system is k-nearest neighbour (kNN) collaborative filtering. [15] Recently, matrix factorization (MF) has become very popular in recommender systems both for implicit and explicit feedback. In early work, [16] singular value decomposition (SVD) has been proposed to learn the feature metrics. The MF models learned by SVD have been shown to be highly prone to overfitting. Below, we review some of the better methods mentioned in this paper.

Deep Learning. Deep learning has become highly popular on the Internet for big data and artificial intelligence [17]. Deep learning, by combining low-level features to form denser high-level semantic abstracts, can automatically discover the distributed feature representation of data. Deep learning can solve the problem of manual design features in traditional machine learning and has achieved breakthroughs in image recognition, machine translation, speech recognition, online advertising and other fields. In the field of image recognition, the accuracy rate of deep learning exceeded 97% in the 2016 ImageNet image classification competition. In the field of machine translation, the Google neural machine translation system (GNMT) based on deep learning has achieved a translation level close to that of humans in the field of English to Spanish and English to French [18]. In the field of online advertising, deep learning is widely used to predict the click rate of advertisements and has achieved great success in its application by Google [19], Microsoft [20], Huawei [21], Alibaba [22] and other enterprises. Deep learning involves a wide range of machine learning technologies and structures. The SDAE used in this paper belongs to this deep learning structure.

SDAE. Auto-Encoder is a common method used in feature extraction by neural network [23, 24]. These networks are trained to reconstruct their inputs by dimensionality reduction, resulting in better characterization than the original data. Common methods for extracting features of neural networks include the Convolutional Neural Network (CNN) [25] and Recurrent Neural Network (RNN) [26]. However, the CNN is a kind of multi-layer perceptron, which is mainly used to process two-dimensional or three-dimensional image data. Additionally, the nodes between each hidden layer of the RNN are connected and able to memorize the past information, so that this method is more suitable for sequence modelling. Considering that the scoring data in the recommendation system are all one-dimensional values without sequence relations, methods such as the CNN and RNN cannot play a meaningful role in feature extraction but will increase the computational complexity. Therefore, the stack denoising auto-encoder may be a better choice [27]. The advantage of stack structure [28, 29] is that multi-hierarchy abstract data representation and deeper implicit data representation can be obtained by stacking multiple automatic encoders.

BPR. From an algorithmic point of view, the existing methods of recommending problems can be approximately divided into three categories: classification, fitting, and ranking. [30, 31] The classification method can be regarded as a binary classification problem, using the predefined features to train the classifier, and finally using the classifier to predict the similarities between the items. The method of fitting is to convert the scores of items into a real value rating matrix and to use a collaborative filtering method such as matrix decomposition to predict the similar probability of items without scoring. The problem of data sparsity will make classification or fitting methods be biased towards dissimilarity. [32] The sorting method considers the recommendation as a sort of learning task. For each item, by ranking the similarity probabilities of other items and itself, it is guaranteed that these similar items are ranked higher than the dissimilar items, and this sorting method proved to be effective and can solve the imbalance problem. Among these models, the BPR model [33, 34] defines the Bayesian pairwise ranking relationship between the items. The relationship is that probabilities of similar items should be greater than those of the non-similar items. This model has been verified to achieve good performance.

5   Conclusions

In this paper, the existing BPR model and the SDAE are combined to recommend products. The SDAE is used to extract the implicit characteristics of the user evaluation vector, and the already extracted BPR is based, in part, on deep hidden features to obtain the features of the products and, on the basis of the entire model, to propose a set that is suitable for the preliminary training of the model; then, an optimization strategy is used to speed up the training efficiency and improve the recommendation accuracy. As demonstrated in the experimental verification, the model proposed in this paper has better performance than the existing classical collaborative filtering commodity recommendation algorithm, obtaining higher accuracy and better sorting of the results and avoiding the impact of sparsity. However, this model still has some shortcomings. For example, when the data volume is large, features are extracted for each item, and the similarity probability of any two items must be calculated. The model learning and data preservation may encounter some difficulties. However, the application of deep learning in the recommendation system has been studied by many researchers and has been proven to be feasible. Therefore, we believe that this research direction is promising.

In the future, we will study the interpretability of the algorithm. Currently, we can only provide the answer about probability to the user. It is not yet possible to convincingly show why the probability should have this value. Furthermore, the users' interest in different goods on e-commerce platforms changes rapidly with time. It will be useful to connect our methods to the changes in user interest.

Acknowledgments. This paper is supported by the Youth Foundation of Shanghai Polytechnic University under Grant No. EGD18XQD01; the CERNET Innovation Project No. NGII2017 0513.

References

1. Xie, F., Chen, Z., Xu, H., et al.: Threshold based similarity transitivity method in collaborative filtering with cloud computing. Tsinghua Sci. Technol. **18**(3), 318–327 (2013)
2. Stanford University's machine learning course on courser. https://www.coursera.org/learn/machine-learning/lecture/2WoBV/collaborative-filterin. Accessed 29 Mar 2019

3. Li, W., Yeung, D., Zhang, Z.: Generalized latent factor models for social network analysis. In: Proceedings of the 22nd International Joint Conference on Artificial Intelligence, Barcelona, Spain, pp. 1705–1710 (2011)
4. Bobadilla, J., Ortega, F., Hernando, A., et al.: Recommender systems survey. Knowl.-Based Syst. **46**, 109–132 (2013)
5. Vincent, P., Larochelle, H., Bengio, Y., et al.: Extracting and composing robust features with denoising autoencoders. In: Proceedings of the 25th International Conference on Machine Learning, Helsinki, Finland, pp. 1096–1103 (2008)
6. Ding, D., Zhang, M, Li, S., et al.: BayDNN: friend recommendation with bayesian personalized ranking deep neural network. In: ACM (2017)
7. Wang, H., Shi, X., Yeung, D.: Relational stacked denoising autoencoder for tag recommendation. In: Proceedings of the 29th Conference on Artificial Intelligence, Austin, USA, pp. 3052–3058 (2015)
8. Zeiler, M.D.: ADADELTA: an adaptive learning rate method. Comput. Sci. (2012)
9. Recommend for new research. http://grouplens.org/datasets/movielens. Accessed 30 Mar 2019
10. Zhao, Z., Shang, M.: User-based collaborative-filtering recommendation algorithms on Hadoop. In: WKDD 2010 Third International Conference on IEEE, pp. 478–481 (2010)
11. Su, X., Khoshgoftaar, T.: A survey of collaborative filtering techniques. Adv. Artif. Intell. **2009**(4), 421425:1–421425:19 (2009)
12. Bradley, A.P.: The use of the area under the ROC curve in the evaluation of machine learning algorithms. Pattern Recogn. **30**(7), 1145–1159 (1997)
13. Boyd, K., Eng, Kevin H., Page, C.D.: Area under the precision-recall curve: point estimates and confidence intervals. In: Blockeel, H., Kersting, K., Nijssen, S., Železný, F. (eds.) ECML PKDD 2013. LNCS (LNAI), vol. 8190, pp. 451–466. Springer, Heidelberg (2013). https://doi.org/10.1007/978-3-642-40994-3_29
14. Yilmaz, E., Kanoulas, E., Aslam, J.: A simple and efficient sampling method for estimating AP and NDCG In: Proceedings of the 31st Annual International ACM SIGIR Conference on Research and Development in Information Retrieval, pp. 603–610. ACM (2008)
15. Deshpande, M., Karypis, G.: Item-based top-n recommendation algorithms. ACM Trans. Inform. Syst. **22**(1), 143–177 (2004)
16. Sarwar, B., Karypis, G., Konstan, J., Riedl, J.: Incremental singular value decomposition algorithms for highly scalable recommender systems. In: Proceedings of the 5th International Conference in Computers and Information Technology (2002)
17. Silver, D., Huang, A., Maddison, C., et al.: Mastering the game of Go with deep neural networks and tree search. Nature **529**(7587), 484–489 (2016)
18. Wu, Y., Schuster, M., Chen, Z., et al.: Google's neural machine translation system: Bridging the gap between human and machine translation. arXiv preprint arXiv:1708.05123 (2017)
19. Cheng, H., Koc, L., Harmsen, J., et al.: Wide & deep learning for recommender systems. In: Proceedings of the 1st Workshop on Deep Learning for Recommender System, Boston, USA, pp. 7–10 (2017)
20. Shan, Y., Hoens, T., Jiao, J., et al.: Deep crossing: web-scale modeling without manually crafted combinatorial features. In: Proceedings of the 22nd ACM SIGKDD International Conference on Knowledge Discovery and Data Mining, San Francisco, USA, pp. 255–262 (2017)
21. Guo, H., Tang, R., Ye, Y., et al.: DeepFM: A factorization-machine based neural network for CTR prediction. In: Proceedings of the 26th International Joint Conference on Artificial Intelligence, Melbourne, Australia, pp. 1725–1731 (2017)
22. Zhou, G., Song, C., Zhu, X., et al.: Deep interest network for click-through rate prediction. arXiv preprint arXiv:1708.05123 (2017)

23. Wu, Y., DuBois, C., Zheng, A., et al.: Collaborative denoising auto-encoders for top-n recommender systems. In: Proceedings of the 9th ACM International Conference on Web Search and Data Mining, San Francisco, USA, pp. 153–162 (2016)
24. Vasile, F., Smirnova, E., Conneau, A.: Meta-Prod2Vec: product embeddings using side-information for recommendation. In: Proceedings of the ACM Conference on Recommender Systems, Boston, USA, pp. 225–232 (2016)
25. Krizhevsky, A., Sutskever, I., Hinton, G.: ImageNet classification with deep convolutional neural networks. In: Proceedings of the Advance in Neural Information Processing Systems, Lake Tahoe, USA, pp. 1097–1105 (2012)
26. Graves, A., Jaitly, N.: Towards end-to-end speech recognition with recurrent neural networks. In: Proceedings of the 31st International Conference on Machine Learning, Beijing, China, pp. 1764–1772 (2014)
27. Strub, F., Mary, J.: Collaborative filtering with stacked denoising AutoEncoders and sparse inputs. In: Proceedings of the NIPS Workshop on Machine Learning for E-Commerce, Montreal, Canada (2015)
28. Vincent, P., Larochelle, H., Lajoie, I., et al.: Stacked denoising autoencoders: learning useful representations in a deep network with a local denoising criterion. J. Mach. Learn. Res. 11(12), 3371–3408 (2010)
29. Bengio, Y., Lamblin, P., Popvici, D., et al.: Greedy layer-wise, training of deep networks. In: Proceedings of the Advances in Neural Information Processing Systems, Vancouver, Canada, pp. 153–160 (2007)
30. Li, Z., Fang, X., Sheng, O.R.L.: A survey of link recommendation for social networks: methods, theoretical foundations, and future research directions. Comput. Sci. (2015)
31. Han, S., Yan, X.: Friend recommendation of microblog in classification framework: using multiple social behavior features. In: International Conference on Behavior, Economic and Social Computing, pp. 1–6 (2014)
32. Jeni, L., Cohn, J., Torre, F.: Facing imbalanced data recommendations for the use of performance metrics. In: Humaine Association Conference on Affective Computing and Intelligent Interaction, pp. 245–251 (2012)
33. Qiu, S., et al.: Item group based pairwise preference learning for personalized ranking. In: Proceedings of the 37th International ACM SIGIR Conference on Research and Development in Information Retrieval, pp. 1219–1222 (2014)
34. Rendle, S., Freudenthaler, C., Gantner, Z., et al.: BPR: Bayesian personalized ranking from implicit feedback In: Conference on Uncertainty in Artificial Intelligence. AUAI Press (2009)

Itinerary Recommendation for User Groups in Temporary Social Network

Jing Xia[1,2], Yu Li[1,2], and Yuyu Yin[1,2(✉)]

[1] School of Computer, Hangzhou Dianzi University, Hangzhou 310018, China
[2] Key Laboratory of Complex Systems Modeling and Simulation of Ministry of Education, Hangzhou 310018, China
yinyuyu@hdu.edu.cn

Abstract. Temporary social network has been a increasing popular field in the last few years where people form a temporary social group for a short time period with common interests or purposes in the same area. When a user attends an event or conference in a new city, he/she can join the temporary social networks with his/her social account. Users who attend the same academic conference or activity may have similar interests and time schedules, so they are willing to travel together. Recently, renting cars to travel has become very common, since it helps improve user experience as well as save travel costs (e.g., renting and oil costs). Thus, we propose a group-wise itinerary planning framework to minimize the travel costs for each user in a temporary social network. Experimental results conducted on real-world data sets confirm the efficiency and effectiveness of our proposed framework.

Keywords: Travel planning · Spatial temporary social network · Mobile computing

1 Introduction

Temporary social network has been a increasing popular field in the last few years where people form a temporary social group for a short time period with common interests or purposes in the same area. When a user attends an event or conference in a new city, he/she can join the temporary social networks with his/her social account. They can send message to all group members, share locations and pictures, set up sub-groups, etc. All the records of her actions in the temporary social network will be deleted after the guest checks out of the hotel.

Supported by the National Key Research and Development Program of China (No. 2017YFB1400601), National Natural Science Foundation of China (No. 61802098), Natural Science Foundation of Zhejiang Province (No. LY16F020017), Shaanxi Province (No. 2018JQ6050), and Fundamental Research Funds for Central Universities (JBX171007).
The two authors Jing Xia and Yu Li contribute equally to this paper, and they are co-first authors.

© ICST Institute for Computer Sciences, Social Informatics and Telecommunications Engineering 2019
Published by Springer Nature Switzerland AG 2019. All Rights Reserved
X. Wang et al. (Eds.): CollaborateCom 2019, LNICST 292, pp. 166–179, 2019.
https://doi.org/10.1007/978-3-030-30146-0_12

Travel is a core function of temporary social networks. For instance, in a hotel social network, guests may attend the same conference in a new city, but they did not know each other before. Guests may have common interests and thus be willing to travel together with their new friends, thereby improving user satisfaction. More importantly, guests prefer to travel together to share travel costs (e.g., car-renting and oil costs). However, organizing guests into temporary social groups may negatively affect user experience, thus driving the users away from the application. Because, although the guests are coming to the same conference/business activity/concert, their time schedules and interest preferences may vary greatly.

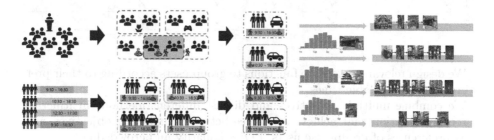

Fig. 1. Example of the framework

In this paper, we propose a framework for temporary social networks to group users and recommend group-wise itineraries. When a guest checks in at a commercial activity/academic conference, we will obtain his or her interest preferences and available time periods for traveling via his/her social network account. As showed in Fig. 1, we first group similar guests with similar hobbies, then we allocate users into car groups whose size are limited by the car capacity (e.g., four). Then, we recommend an itinerary to each group with crowdedness-aware. This itinerary will meet all group members' interest preferences and time constraints. To measure the similarity of two guests, we consider the overlapping of their available time slots and their common interest preferences.

Some research has been conducted to examine similar problems to those presented herein. Our problem formulation presents major differences from those current studies. For comparison, the differences between our system and the earlier works are illustrated in Table 1.

In this paper, we consider the deadline and interest preference of each user while grouping users, as well as the group size (car capacity). Then we also take the popularity and crowdedness of each POI into consideration during itinerary recommendation. In this way, we improve the quality of the generated groups and recommended itineraries. To our knowledge, no paper has studied this same problem.

This paper has the following four contributions.

– We propose a group-wise itinerary planning framework, which can be used to improve users' travel experience in a temporal social network.

Table 1. Difference between prior work and our system

Paper	User's deadline	User's preference	POI's category	POI's popularity	POI's crowdedness	Group recommendation	Group size limit
[20]	✓	✓	✗	✗	✗	✗	✗
[5]	✗	✓	✓	✗	✗	✓	✗
[13]	✓	✓	✓	✓	✗	✓	✗
[19]	✓	✓	✓	✓	✓	✗	✗
[2]	✓	✓	✓	✓	✓	✗	✗
[11]	✓	✓	✓	✓	✓	✗	✗
ours	✓	✓	✓	✓	✓	✓	✓

- We design relevance measure functions to group users according to their preferences and available times.
- We combine multiple objectives and discuss different methods in itinerary recommendation that achieve a balance between conflicting objectives such as preferences of group-wise users, POI popularity and crowdedness.
- We evaluate the efficiency and effectiveness of our proposed framework and methods by extensive experiments using real road network data sets.

For the remaining paper: Sect. 2 formally formulates the preliminary definitions and propose our three-step framework. Section 3.1 trains the city model by cluster method. Section 3.2 presents a greedy-based user allocating algorithm. Section 4.2, we compare two algorithms to recommend itinerary avoiding crowdedness. Section 5 gives the experimental study. Section 6 discusses related work; and Sect. 7 concludes this paper.

2   Problem Statement

In this section, we first introduce the main symbols used in this paper and then formally formulate the framework proposed in this paper.

$U = \{u_1, \ldots, u_n\}$ be the set of users and $V = \{v_1, \ldots, v_l\}$ be the set of POIs. Given that $C = \{c_1, \ldots, c_o\}$ as POI category set, each POI v belongs to one category. The popularity of POI v is defined as $Pop(v)$.

We assume $Int_u(c)$ be the user's interest preference for category c. In our implementation, we estimate user interest preference using the total number of check-ins from user history data. The user interest preference of every user is defined as $I_u = \langle Int_u(c_i), \ldots, Int_u(c_o) \rangle$.

We aim to address the problem in terms of its two sub-problems of user grouping and route recommendation. As illustrated in Fig. 2, our three-step framework includes offline city model train, car group allocation and itinerary recommendation with crowdedness. We use the cluster method train the different city travel pattern then part users into pattern groups and then each group query runs car group allocation method in parallel. For each small groups, we unified group members' interests and time schedules. Finally, we use route recommender calculate the itinerary for each group to satisfy the group's preferences and time constraints, at the same time, help users avoid crowdedness. The objective of *group-wise itinerary planning* is to recommend traveling partners and traveling routes for users in the temporal social network, such that: ($\mathcal{O}1$) all users' time constraints are satisfied, ($\mathcal{O}2$) users' preferences are satisfied, and ($\mathcal{O}3$) each user's traveling cost is minimized.

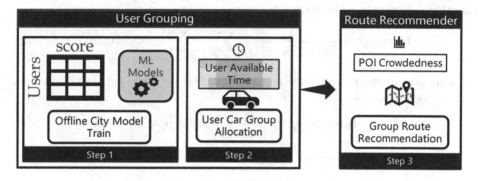

Fig. 2. Framework

3 User Grouping

In this section, we illustrate how to group users in a temporal social network. First, we train offline city model to find the distinguished interest patterns in the city so as to divide users into pattern groups according to these interest patterns. Then, we further divide each pattern group based on users' available time periods and car capacities. As the time complexity of car group allocation is quite high, we obtain the user groups by the greedy method at the end of this section.

3.1 Step 1: Offline City Model Train

According to the history travel itinerary, the kinds of different interest preferences among users are limited. A natural approach to group by interest preferences in a city is to use some clustering method. We train the offline city model by clustering history users interest preferences in the city to find all key interest patterns.

In our case, however, the number of clusters is not known in advance. In the following discussion, we assume there are k interest patterns in a city, i.e., $P = \{p_1, \ldots, p_k\}$, where p_i represents a city interest preference pattern. Each interest preference pattern p_k consists of a cluster of users $p_k = \{u_1, \ldots, u_q\}$, and users in the same pattern have similar interest preferences. The k patterns are as follows:

$$p_k = \frac{1}{|p_k|} \sum_{u \in p_k} I_u, \forall p \in P. \tag{1}$$

In this paper, we represent discrete travel patterns by Gaussian mixture model(GMM) [15] which is a set of continuous density functions. Effective clustering minimizes inter-cluster and maximizes intra-cluster similarities [3]. We use cosine similarity $Cos(u_i, u_j)$ of interest preference measure the interest preference similarity between two users.

Intra-cluster similarity is the average cosine similarity of all pair-wise combinations of users in a cluster p.

$$Intra(p_k) = \frac{1}{(|p_k| \cdot (|p_k| - 1))} \sum_{u_i \in p_k} \sum_{u_j \in p_k, u_j \neq u_i} Cos(u_i, u_j) \tag{2}$$

The inter-pattern similarity is the similarity between patterns, which is defined as follows:

$$Inter(p_i, p_j) = \frac{\boldsymbol{p_i} \cdot \boldsymbol{p_j}}{\|\boldsymbol{p_i}\| \cdot \|\boldsymbol{p_j}\|}, \forall p_i, p_j \in P \tag{3}$$

Formally, we find a best set of k patterns P such that:

$$Max \frac{\frac{1}{k} \sum_1^k Intra(p_k)}{\frac{1}{(k \cdot (k-1))} \sum_{p_i \in P} \sum_{p_j \in P, p_j \neq p_i} Inter(p_i, p_j)} \tag{4}$$

After we model those k patterns, and part users' queries into k pattern groups. In subsequent steps, users in the same pattern group can be allocated by their available time in parallel. In this way, we can reduce the server-side response time and improve system efficiency.

3.2 Step 2: Car Group Allocation

We allocate similar users into car groups, help them to save costs and find travel partners, even if they need to adjust their travel schedules slightly. We need to group users according to interest preferences and the overlap of their available time, as well as the group size which is limited by car capacity.

User's query: $u = \{I, l, u, v_s\}$, where $u.I$ is the user's interest preference. $u.t = [t_s, t_e]$ is the user's available time period. $u.v_s$ is the user's start position. We assign the users into k pattern groups by comparing $u.I$ with each k pattern center and then mark them with the label $u.l$.

Time Similarity: The time period similarity between users u_i and u_j calculated by the Jaccard similarity, which is also known as the intersection over the union.

$$TS(u_i, u_j) = \frac{u_i.t \cap u_j.t}{u_i.t \cup u_j.t} \tag{5}$$

User Similarity: Then, we define the similarity between u_i, u_j using

$$Sim(u_i, u_j) = \mu TS(u_i, u_j) + (1 - \mu) Cos(u_i, u_j) \tag{6}$$

Thresholds: DT be the maximum start/end time difference between two users, TT be the lowest time overlap and CT be the lowest interest similarity of group members based on Cosine.

Occupancy Rate: Car Capacity CA. The lowest car occupancy rate OR means the group size is least $OR \times CA$ users in a group, otherwise renting a car is too wasteful.

Car Group: $\mathcal{G} = \{g_1, \ldots, g_m\}$ is the set of car groups, whose size $|g|$ is smaller than CA and larger than $OR \times CA$. Each query is defined by $g = (I, t_s, t_e, v_s)$, where $g.I$ is the group's interest preference.

$$I_g = \langle Int_g(c_1), \ldots, Int_g(c_o) \rangle, \forall \{c_1, \ldots, c_o\} \in C \qquad (7)$$

$g.t_s$ is the group's start time which is the start time of the latest start user in the group. $g.t_e$ is group's end time which is the end time of the earliest end user in the group. $g.v_s$ is the group's start position. We assume users are in the same hotel.

Group's Interest Preference: One major challenge in the group-wise itinerary recommendation is the diverse interest preferences among group members. We define a collective group interest preference to meet all members demand. The group interest preference for category c as follows:

$$Int_g(c) = \omega \cdot rel(u, c) + (1 - \omega) \cdot (a_{max} - dis(u, c)), \forall u \in g \qquad (8)$$

where a_{max} is maximum interest preference among group members for category c and $rel(u, c)$ is the average preference score among group members for category c; $dis(u, c)$ is the pairwise interest preference difference of group members for category c.

Problem Define: The (1) car capacity CA, (2) occupancy rate OR, and (3) users' queries U are given. Allocating users into different car groups whose size is limited by CA and OR. Our goal is to group more people to travel together, and the maximum total average user similarity in each group includes people who should travel alone.

3.3   Method

Since the optimal solution requires the assessment of all possible combinations with very high complexity, we design a greedy strategy with following rules to allocate each pattern group users into small car groups. We use *queries* queue to receive more user queries.

Rule 1. If u and u' both send a query, and the start time of u is earlier than that of u', u is serviced first. We sort the users' queries by start time and end time.

Algorithm 1. Car Group Allocation

Input: a level-1 group g, CA,OR,DT,TT,CT
Output: $\mathcal{G} = \{g_1, g_2, \cdots, g_m\}$
  1: $queries \leftarrow \emptyset$, $\mathcal{G} \leftarrow \emptyset$, $single \leftarrow \emptyset$
  2: $used \leftarrow \emptyset$
  3: **while** $g \setminus used \neq \emptyset$ **do**
  4:    $u' \leftarrow$ first $u \in g \setminus used$, $candi \leftarrow$ empty $MaxHeap(CA - 1)$
  5:    **for** $u'' \in g \setminus \{used \cup u'\}$ **do**
  6:       **if** $isGroup(u', u'')$ **then**
  7:          $candi \leftarrow candi \cup u''$
  8:       **end if**
  9:    **end for**
 10:    **if** $OR \times CA - 1 \leq |candi| \leq CA - 1$ **then**
 11:       $g' \leftarrow u' \cup candi$, $\mathcal{G} \leftarrow \mathcal{G} \cup g'$, $used \leftarrow used \cup u' \cup candi$
 12:    **else**
 13:       $used \leftarrow used \cup u'$, $queries \leftarrow u'$
 14:    **end if**
 15: **end while**
 16: $g \leftarrow queries$ **go to** line 2
 17: **for** $u \in queries$ **do**
 18:    $single \leftarrow single \cup u$
 19: **end for**
 20: **return** $\mathcal{G} \cup single$

Lemma. Suppose $u_1.t_s = 9:00, u_2.t_s = 9:10, u_3.t_s = 9:20, u_4.t_s = 9:30, u_5.t_s = 9:40$, and u_1 is the earliest user according to the start times among users. We find similar users to u_1 starting from 9:00, and then find similar users to u_2 starting from 9:10, excluding u_1 with a start time earlier than himself or herself. If u_2 can be grouped with u_1, after the previous identification of similar users to u_1, we will group u_1 with u_2. Then when we consider u_2, u_1 and u_2 are already in the same group, so there is no need to consider u_2 with u_1.

Rule 2. For u and u', we use function $isGroup(u, u')$ to validate if u and u' could travel together. $isGroup(u, u')$ returns $true$ if u and u' satisfy TT, CT and DT.

Furthermore, the number of similar users is too little to generate a group, and similar itineraries are recommended for them. Instead of querying *exact* itinerary recommendation for every single person, which may generate a lot of computational overhead, we send their queries as a batch and response a same recommendation.

4   Step 3: Itinerary Recommendation with Crowdedness

In this section, we use route recommender calculate the itinerary for each group to satisfy the group's preferences and time constraints, at the same time, help users avoid crowdedness.

4.1 POI Crowdedness

The crowdedness $Crd(v,t)$ of POI v at time t is the number of users visiting POI v at time t normalized to between zero and one. We can model the POI crowdedness in the future prediction as a time series forecasting problem. In our work, we use the average number of people per hour at each POI from data set as a prediction.

4.2 Itinerary Profit and Constraints

For each group g with a category preference $g.I$, start time $g.t_s$, end time $g.t_e$ and start point $g.v_s$, we recommend an itinerary $R_g = \{v_1, v_2, \dots, v_n\}$ which maximize the following object function:

$$Score(R_g) = \sum_{v \in R_g} pr_g(v) \tag{9}$$

where the $pr_g(v,t)$ evaluate the profit that gained when group members g visit POI v(category c) at time t, which is defined as:

$$pr_g(v,t) = \frac{(\rho \cdot Pop(v) + (1 - \rho) \cdot I_g(c))^\gamma}{Crd(v,t)} \tag{10}$$

The itinerary constraints are as follows:

Rule 1. Each itinerary can visit the same POI only once, avoiding blind searches back and forth among POIs or rounding in the cycle, which is time-consuming and not beneficial.

Rule 2. The itinerary time cost $\sum_{v_i \in R} (Dur(v_i) + Dist(v_{i+1})) + Dist(v_s, v_1) + Dist(v_n, v_s)$ should not exceed $g.t_e - g.t_s$, where $Dur(v_i)$ is the average visit duration for a POI v. $Sat(v_i, v_j, t)$ returns $true$ if leaving from v_i at time t to visit v_j provides sufficient time to reach destination v_s within the budget time.

4.3 Methods

Due to the irregular profit changes with time, then backtrack with pruning approach is to perform an exhaustive search which finds the optimal itinerary. To avoid the expensive backtrack with pruning search, the greedy method also proposed.

Backtrack with Pruning. We use depth-first backtrack to enumerate all the feasible arrangements of POI within time budget. And we use *visited* set to record the POI which is already visited in current partial itinerary. During the search we update the current best itinerary score.

Algorithm 2. Backtrack with Pruning

1: $R \leftarrow \emptyset$, $r' \leftarrow \langle v_s \rightarrow \emptyset \rightarrow v_s \rangle$, $visited \leftarrow \emptyset$
2: **for** $v_j \in V \setminus visited$ **do**   // Rule 1
3:     **if** $Sat(v_i, v_j, \pi_i)$ **then**   // Rule 2
4:         $r' \leftarrow r' \cup v_j$; $visited \leftarrow visited \cup v_j$;
5:         **if** $Score(r') > Score(R)$ **then**
6:             $R \leftarrow r'$;
7:         **end if**
8:         $backtrack(r', visited)$;
9:         $r' \leftarrow r' \setminus v_j$; $visited \leftarrow visited \setminus v_j$;
10:    **end if**
11: **end for**
12: **return** R

Greedy. Backtrack with Pruning search has too much time complexity, we use greedy method to select next POI v_j iteratively appending to current partial itinerary until the time budget is not enough. We use a strategy function $f(v_j) = \frac{pr(v_j,t)}{Dist(v_i,v_j)+Dur(v_j)+Dist(v_j,v_s)}$ where v_i is last visited POI and t is the access time at v_j to choose the next POI. The next POI should have maximal $f(v_j)$ and users can back to v_s within budget.

5   Experiment and Evaluation

5.1   Experimental Settings

We evaluate our framework on a real-life datasets extracted from Flickr photos [18] in Toronto, Osaka, and Edinburgh, with the statistics shown in Table 2. All datasets are provided by Lim et al. [12,13,19].

We implement our framework and algorithms by Python sklearn packages and Java. All experiments are run on a 3.6 GHz Intel i7 Quad-Core and 16 GB of RAM PC.

Table 2. A summary of the datasets

City	No. of POIs	No. of photos	No. of users	POI visits	Travel sequences
Toronto	30	157,505	1,395	39,419	6,057
Edinburgh	29	82,060	1,454	33,944	5,028
Osaka	29	392,420	450	7,747	1,115

5.2 Effect of Offline City Model Train

We use users' geo-photos as the approximation as a user visit to each POI in real-life. First, we construct the interest preference vector I for each user $u \in U$ by counting each user's photo number in different POI category and the POI popularity $Pop(v)$ by counting total photo number at different POI.

The best k represents the goal in Eq. 3 is maximum when we use the GMM model to identify the best cluster partition based on historical data. The $Inter(P)$ line illustrates the average inter-cluster similarity of the k pattern pairwise combinations. Table 3 shows the results. The intra-cluster similarity is very high, suggesting good cluster compactness. The inter-cluster similarity is low which shows the groups are not redundant. In this way, we get k travel pattern in a city and people are parted to pattern groups with label u_l.

Table 3. Evaluation of Step 1

	Toronto	Edinburgh	Osaka
best k	7	6	5
$Intra(P)$	0.9172	0.9179	0.9109
$Inter(P)$	0.1101	0.1357	0.1809
CT	0.4203	0.5077	0.5547

Table 4. Average evaluation result of Step 2

	Toronto	Edinburgh	Osaka
$Tu(\mathcal{G})$	0.9372	0.9439	0.9436
$Cu(\mathcal{G})$	0.9699	0.9505	0.8889
$Cos(\mathcal{G})$	0.9534	0.9590	0.9727
single person	8/1395	14/1454	10/450
runtime(s)	9.6000	12.4001	1.0024

5.3 Effect of Car Group Allocation

We use average cosine similarity ,time utilization, and car utilization of all generated groups to evaluate the effect of car group allocation.

Time utilization: $Tu(\mathcal{G}) = \frac{1}{|\mathcal{G}|} \sum_{g \in \mathcal{G}} \frac{1}{|g|} \sum_{u \in g} \frac{g.t_e - g.t_s}{u.t_e - u.t_s}$

Car utilization: $Cu(\mathcal{G}) = \frac{1}{|\mathcal{G}|} \sum_{g \in \mathcal{G}} \frac{|g|}{CA}$

Users' check-in timestamps are scattered in the datasets, and their travel are too short to simulate our problem. We generated users' start times $u.t_s$ and end times $u.t_e$ from 9:00 to 11:00 and 16:00 to 18:00 randomly. We set $Ca = 5$, $OR = 0.8$, $DT = 60$ min, $TT = 0.75$, $\mu = 0.5$, $\omega = 0.5$. We use the minimum intra-similarity in city models as (CT).

Figure 3 shows the evaluation results for each small car group on each dataset. Table 4 shows the average evaluation results on each dataset. Our car group allocation algorithm is a greedy solution, the average time utilization $Tu(\mathcal{G})$ is greater than 90% on each dataset, indicating that the each user waits up to one hour (less than DT) for other users. Additionally, the average cosine similarity $Cos(\mathcal{G})$ is higher than the minimum lowest cosine similarity in pattern groups (Step 1). $Cu(\mathcal{G})$ and the single person shows our method group most people. In addition, the runtime on single-threaded shows the efficiency.

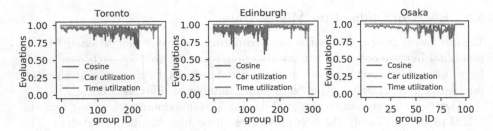

Fig. 3. Evaluation results of all groups in Step 2

5.4 Effect of Itinerary Recommendation

We use the time difference between the photos taken by the user for the first and last visit at a POI as user's visit duration and use the average time of all users as $Dur(v)$. For the cold spots, we replace the duration with the average duration of all POI in the city. We assume that all users' start locations (hotel v_s) are one of the most popular attractions in the city. We use euclidean distance estimate $Dis(v_i, v_j)$ between two POIs. If the distance between the two POI is less than 1 km, we use the walking speed (4 km/hour), consistent with literature [12]; otherwise the driving speed will be used. We estimate the time cost using Google Maps[1].

Figure 4 The upper row shows the recommended itinerary score by Backtrack and Greedy. The y-axis score of 1 represents the optimal result of the backtracking method. The line in the figure shows the ratio of the profit score obtained by the greedy method to the optimal solution. x-axis is the time budget(hours) of each group. As can be seen from the figure, the greedy method can achieve approximately 90% of the optimal solution.

The lower row is the runtime of the two algorithms. The y-axis is the run time in seconds. x-axis is the time budget(hours) of each group. Greedy has a fast and stable runtime. When the available POI is more than 29, the backtrack algorithm running for more than 300 seconds. However, backtracking is still suitable for finding the optimal itinerary in a large attraction or in a city with a small number of POI.

6 Related Work

Group-wise Itinerary Planning. Recently, the study of group-wise itinerary planning has gained growing attention. The problem is looking for a path that covers the set of user input points and minimizes the travel distance of the group. For instance, author in [1] analyzes the needs of group recommendation and proposes a formula that considers the correlation between individuals and the group, as well as the differences between members. [4,5] find the route with the maximum group interest preference and recommend it to multiple users. In [17], a

---

[1] https://www.google.com/maps.

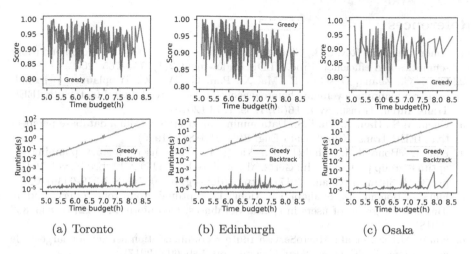

(a) Toronto   (b) Edinburgh   (c) Osaka

Fig. 4. Effect of itinerary recommendation

novel group path query problem is proposed, in which users can dynamically join a new group or leave the original group while traveling. Lim et al. [13] clustered similar tourists into tour groups. Then recommend routes to each group. Finally, assigned an appropriate tour guide to each group.

Route Recommendation. There have also been numerous studies associated with recommending itineraries for a single tourist. [2,10] consider the orienteering problem with time windows(OPTW). These works are aimed at finding the best itinerary to maximize the user's experience under a traffic-conscious time budget constraint. And [11,20] consider the congestion of peak hours and queue time to choose the best time to access the POI. In addition, [6,8,9,16] provided other forms of search problems including optimal route for crowdsourcing works, finding a optimal access sequence. Those works calculate the shortest route passing through specific categories of POIs. Recent works [7,14] analyze interest preferences in user history data to recommend paths for them.

7   Conclusion

In this paper, we propose a group-wise itinerary planning framework which including offline city model train, car group allocation and itinerary recommendation with crowdedness. For improving happiness of the group members and reducing travel costs in the temporary social network, we design relevance measure functions to group users in terms of their interest preferences, time schedule and the group size limit. We use the cluster method to part users into pattern groups and then each group runs car group allocation in parallel. For each group, we design an itinerary score function which combines the group interest preference, the crowdedness and the popularity of each POI in order to achieves a balance between conflicting objectives. An recommended itinerary achieve maximum group satisfaction. The experiment based on a real-world social network data set shows the effectiveness of our framework.

References

1. Amer-Yahia, S., Roy, S.B., Chawlat, A., Das, G., Yu, C.: Group recommendation: semantics and efficiency. Proc. VLDB Endowment **2**(1), 754–765 (2009)
2. Chen, C., Zhang, D., Guo, B., Ma, X., Pan, G., Wu, Z.: Tripplanner: personalized trip planning leveraging heterogeneous crowdsourced digital footprints. IEEE Trans. Intell. Transp. Syst. **16**(3), 1259–1273 (2015)
3. Chen, M.S., Han, J., Yu, P.S.: Data mining: an overview from a database perspective. IEEE Trans. Knowl. Data Eng. **8**(6), 866–883 (1996)
4. Fan, L., Bonomi, L., Shahabi, C., Xiong, L.: Multi-user itinerary planning for optimal group preference. In: Gertz, M., et al. (eds.) SSTD 2017. LNCS, vol. 10411, pp. 3–23. Springer, Cham (2017). https://doi.org/10.1007/978-3-319-64367-0_1
5. Fan, L., Bonomi, L., Shahabi, C., Xiong, L.: Optimal group route query: finding itinerary for group of users in spatial databases. GeoInformatica **22**(4), 845–867 (2018)
6. Khan, M.U.S., et al.: MacroServ: a route recommendation service for large-scale evacuations. IEEE Trans. Serv. Comput. pp. 589–602 (2017)
7. Kurashima, T., Iwata, T., Irie, G., Fujimura, K.: Travel route recommendation using geotags in photo sharing sites. In: Proceedings of the 19th ACM International Conference on Information and Knowledge Management, pp. 579–588. ACM (2010)
8. Li, F., Cheng, D., Hadjieleftheriou, M., Kollios, G., Teng, S.H.: On trip planning queries in spatial databases. In: SSTD, pp. 273–290 (2005)
9. Li, W., Guan, J., Lian, X., Zhou, S., Cao, J.: Probabilistic time-constrained paths search over uncertain road networks. IEEE Trans. Serv. Comput. **11**(2), 399–414 (2018)
10. Li, Y., Yiu, M.L., Xu, W.: Oriented online route recommendation for spatial crowdsourcing task workers. In: Claramunt, C., et al. (eds.) SSTD 2015. LNCS, vol. 9239, pp. 137–156. Springer, Cham (2015). https://doi.org/10.1007/978-3-319-22363-6_8
11. Lim, K.H., Chan, J., Karunasekera, S., Leckie, C.: Personalized itinerary recommendation with queuing time awareness. In: Proceedings of the 40th International ACM SIGIR Conference on Research and Development in Information Retrieval, Shinjuku, Tokyo, Japan, 7–11 August 2017, pp. 325–334 (2017)
12. Lim, K.H., Chan, J., Leckie, C., Karunasekera, S.: Personalized tour recommendation based on user interests and points of interest visit durations. In: Proceedings of the Twenty-Fourth International Joint Conference on Artificial Intelligence, IJCAI 2015, Buenos Aires, Argentina, 25–31 July 2015, pp. 1778–1784 (2015)
13. Lim, K.H., Chan, J., Leckie, C., Karunasekera, S.: Towards next generation touring: Personalized group tours. In: Proceedings of the Twenty-Sixth International Conference on Automated Planning and Scheduling, ICAPS 2016, London, UK, 12–17 June 2016, pp. 412–420 (2016)
14. Lu, X., Wang, C., Yang, J.M., Pang, Y., Zhang, L.: Photo2trip: generating travel routes from geo-tagged photos for trip planning. In: Proceedings of the 18th ACM International Conference on Multimedia, pp. 143–152. ACM (2010)
15. Nasrabadi, N.M.: Pattern recognition and machine learning. J. Electron. Imaging **16**(4), 049901 (2007)
16. Sharifzadeh, M., Kolahdouzan, M.R., Shahabi, C.: The optimal sequenced route query. VLDB J. **17**(4), 765–787 (2008)
17. Tabassum, A., Barua, S., Hashem, T., Chowdhury, T.: Dynamic group trip planning queries in spatial databases. In: Proceedings of the 29th International Conference on Scientific and Statistical Database Management. SSDBM 2017, pp. 38:1–38:6. ACM, New York (2017). https://doi.org/10.1145/3085504.3085584

18. Thomee, B., et al.: The new data and new challenges in multimedia research. CoRR abs/1503.01817 (2015)
19. Wang, X., Leckie, C., Chan, J., Lim, K.H., Vaithianathan, T.: Improving personalized trip recommendation by avoiding crowds. In: Proceedings of the 25th ACM International Conference on Information and Knowledge Management, CIKM 2016, Indianapolis, IN, USA, 24–28 October 2016, pp. 25–34 (2016)
20. Zhang, C., Liang, H., Wang, K., Sun, J.: Personalized trip recommendation with POI availability and uncertain traveling time. In: Proceedings of the 24th ACM International Conference on Information and Knowledge Management, CIKM 2015, Melbourne, VIC, Australia, 19–23 October 2015, pp. 911–920 (2015)

Collaborative IoT Services and Applications

An Integrated and Intelligent Dental Healthcare System with Mobile Services

Yueshen Xu[1,2], Yi Lu[3], Rui Li[1(✉)], Lin Niu[3], Wenzhi Du[3], Ni An[3,4],
Yaning Liu[1], Xinyi Liu[1], Yan Jiang[1], Zhenhua Li[1], Jin Guo[1],
and Xiangdong Wang[5]

[1] School of Computer Science and Technology,
Xidian University, Xi'an 710071, China
{ysxu,rli}@xidian.edu.cn,
{ynliu1,liuxinyi,yjiang_2,zhli_4,jguo_2}@stu.xidian.edu.cn
[2] Provincial Key Laboratory for Computer Information Processing Technology,
Soochow University, Suzhou 215006, Jiangsu, China
[3] Stomatological Hospital, Xi'an Jiaotong University,
Xi'an 710004, People's Republic of China
{luyi1962,niulin}@xjtu.edu.cn, duwenzhi@163.com, 595704542@qq.com
[4] Clinical Research Center of Shaanxi Province for Dental and Maxillofacial Diseases,
College of Stomatology, Xi'an Jiaotong University, Xi'an, China
[5] Shaanxi Lishengruihui Technology Co., Ltd., Xi'an 710075, China
xdwang@intunlp.com

Abstract. Medical informatization takes a key role in medical and healthcare industries, which is a necessary way of improving service quality and treatment experience in a hospital. In this paper, we design and implement an integrated and intelligent healthcare system with mobile services, specific to dental healthcare. The developed system contains four components, including WeChat official account, intelligent question and answering (Q&A) system, mobile follow-up care mini program and AI speech assistant. The developed WeChat official account and intelligent Q&A system provide a large amount of professional knowledge on dental health, which can help narrow the knowledge gap between doctors and patients. The two components facilitate patients to follow up our applications without downloading any extra softwares, as the developed functions (e.g., voice service) are provided through mobile services. These two components also facilitate follow-up management, decreasing manpower and resource usage in hospital. Our system is developed to serve patients as well as dentists, and provides a group of interactive healthcare services in a low cost. In this paper, we elaborate the whole system architecture and implementation detail of each component. We also report the performance test result and training process of the classifier.

Keywords: Dental healthcare · Intelligent information system ·
Mobile service · Neural network · Voice service

Y. Liu, X. Liu, Y. Jiang, Z. Li and J. Guo—contribute equally to this paper.

1   Introduction

The need for dental healthcare or oral healthcare is common nowadays. With the improvement of medical level, an increasing number of people begin to pay attention to their dental health. At the same time, dental healthcare has a great demand for medical informatization. For ordinary people, there is a need for professional knowledge to evaluate their dental problems and seek potential treatment that they intend to receive. The key reasons for the need of medical informatization in dental healthcare are as follows. First, the process of dental medical treatment is complicated. The cycle of treatment is long, usually lasting for several weeks. During the treatment, a patient needs to be treated many times. Second, dental diseases are usually highly professional and most people lack the way to acquire such professional knowledge of dental healthcare. Third, follow-up care is required after dental operation. Patients need a stable and effective way to give feedbacks about their dental problems along with each treatment.

However, the existing dental healthcare information systems have three major defects. First, the existing systems are not intelligent enough, which cannot intelligently answer patients' professional questions related to dental healthcare. Meanwhile, the existing systems cannot provide voice service or information retrieval service. Second, the existing systems are not comprehensive enough, which only provides a small part of necessary services. For example. Some existing dental healthcare systems only provide follow-up care service, and some other systems only provide knowledge retrieval service. Third, there are few existing systems that provide dental healthcare with mobile services. Lacking mobile applications, patients cannot keep sustained attention to their dental conditions in mobile phone platform anytime or anywhere, and are hard to complete the follow-up care to give feedback of their subsequent dental problems.

To solve the problem of the lack of a comprehensive dental healthcare information system, we developed an integrated and intelligent dental healthcare platform providing mobile services. The developed system is based on the tool and framework provided by WeChat and Web service platform, and contains four components, including WeChat official account, question and answering (Q&A) system, the follow-up care mini program and AI speech assistant. WeChat official account provides dental knowledge for patients by retrieval portal. The Q&A system can answer questions raised by patients related to dental health. The follow-up care mini program and AI speech assistant are developed for patients' subsequent dental problems after medical treatment. Patients can give feedbacks on their dental health conditions anytime and anywhere, which also help hospitals improve service quality. We built such a comprehensive system containing the above four modules, and the developed system has been deployed in a high-level dental hospital, i.e., *the affiliated Stomatological Hospital of Xi'an Jiaotong University*[1]. Besides the provided services, the developed system is also used to collect real data generated during the process of dental healthcare, and further analyze and visualize the data, and then guide the hospital to improve treatment quality.

---

[1] http://www.dentalxjtu.com/index_en.php.

The remaining sections of this paper are organized as follows. Section 2 summarizes the work related to dental information systems and mobile medical applications. Section 3 presents the whole framework of our mobile-oriented dental healthcare system. Section 4 elaborates the four developed components of the system. Section 5 describes the system configuration, deployment and application. Section 6 concludes the whole paper.

2   Related Work

With the development of computer technology, dental healthcare information systems have developed rapidly and undergone several phases. With the popularity of electronic medical records, HIS (hospital information system) has gradually involves intelligent elements. In recent years, the emergence of mobile medical care has become a new direction. Nowadays, various mobile medical applications have emerged and are expected to have a promising future. Here we focus on two types of related systems, including dental healthcare information system and mobile medical application.

Dental Information System. Medical information systems have developed for more than 20 years, and have already achieved some progress [16]. However, the existing medical information systems are still in the early stage of development, and most existing systems are in low informatization level, insufficient management and defective function [7]. Most of existing medical information systems only have desktop terminals, and do not support mobile services [10]. The staff operation mode is usually rigid, and medical records are hard to be obtained anytime or anywhere. The intelligent development of existing medical information systems is not enough, although some hospital information systems have also introduced several intelligent techniques. For example. The affiliated hospital of Zhejiang University employs data mining technique to achieve real-time integration and classification of hospital information. Medical staff can understand medical status of a patient in a real-time manner [17]. But the system in the affiliated hospital of Zhejiang University is not fully intelligent. In contrast, our developed system provides voice service and information retrieval service, further improving the efficiency of medical staff.

Mobile Medical Application. Mobile medical healthcare refers to the use of wireless computers or communication devices (e.g., smart phone and tablet computer) that can be carried around to meet the healthcare needs of hospital staff and patients [11]. In [11], the author analyzed and evaluated the function and development of mobile medical applications in China. In [5], the author takes Chunyu healthcare system [1] as an example to study the sustainable development of mobile health network. Let us further take the Good doctor healthcare system [3] and Chunyu healthcare system as two examples. An investigation showed that doctors commented that Good doctor healthcare system and Chunyu healthcare system specialized in online doctor-patient interaction. The existing mobile medical applications do not provide professional dental medical services, and the resources and materials on dental healthcare are limited. Our dental information system combines the advantages of existing healthcare systems and develops a group of mobile medical services for dentists and patients. Our system also provides a humanistic pre-diagnosis mobile counseling service platform to enhance the patient's service depth.

3   The Architecture of the Developed System

Figure 1 presents the whole architecture of the built dental healthcare system with mobile services, which contains four components and each component is given a brief explanation as follows.

1. **WeChat official account.** The developed WeChat official account is an mobile assistant and extension of the intelligent medical system. For the developed mini program, the WeChat official account can send instant follow-up reminding message to patients, and popularize the mini programs to patients. WeChat official account provides access to the intelligent dental healthcare Q&A system, which takes a role of an interface to users. The developed WeChat official account also provides patients a variety of dental healthcare articles and procedures of dental treatment.
2. **Follow-up care mini program.** The main service of the developed mini program is post-diagnosis follow-up care. The follow-up care is conducted according to different types of patients and different time intervals, such as 24 h, 72 h, one week, one month and one year. The developed mini program matches different follow-up problems database, presenting to patients in a user-friendly way. Such a design can save patient's time, and send follow-up message instantly. Patients' feedbacks are sent to the doctor through WeChat official account. After receiving the message, doctors will make a phone call to the patient to improve the medical diagnosis. After all follow-up care feedbacks are stored in the database, the system will generate a follow-up care report in .pdf (portable document format) format, which can be exported for analysis at any time.
3. **AI smart speech assistant.** In order to cover patients of all ages in follow-up care, in the case that some patients do not use the mini program for follow-up care, our intelligent medical care system is capable of automatically dialing the AI smart voice phone, generating professional words requiring to ask for follow-up care. This component is capable of automatically recording and identifying the conversation, and asking the next question based on the patient's answer. Similar to the mini program, the AI smart speech assistant records the information for follow-up care and automatically generates a follow-up care report.
4. **Doctor-patient question and answering (Q&A) system.** The developed Q&A system can scientifically answer the medical questions raised by a patient, as the Q&A system undergoes sufficient training on a large doctor-patient dialogue corpus. After a patient asks a question to our system, a

classifier will first make a decision on whether the patient's question is a problem in dental healthcare field or not. The part-of-speech tagging and dependency parsing can extract the key phrases from the question. We build an answer retrieval engine, and can find the most suitable answers with the highest scores. The answers with the top scores will return to the patient. The developed doctor-patient Q&A system can improve the patient's knowledge level in dental healthcare, and help patients better understand the doctor's treatment.

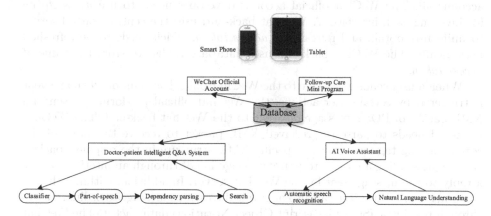

Fig. 1. The architecture of the developed dental healthcare system

4 The Developed Four Components

4.1 The Developed WeChat Official Account

The WeChat official account platform[2] is a platform for operators to provide information and services to WeChat users. The official platform development interface is the basis for providing services [4]. Developers can create WeChat official accounts and obtain administrator right in official platform websites.

The Web framework selected by WeChat is the Flask micro-framework [2], and the recommended programming language is Python. Typically developers will use Flask to build a WSGI application (Web server gateway interface, WSGI for short). The simplest version is to verify the server URL configured in WeChat official platform. The Flask micro-framework is easy to extend, and we can use Flask to build a complete WeChat back-end service. We use the recommended server Waitress[3] that is designed to be stable and secure to run the WSGI application. The server URL configured on WeChat official platform must be *http://* or *https://*, supporting ports 80 and 443 [4]. With the reverse proxy function of Nginx[4], we appoint a proxy *http://URL:80* to the server's local

---

[2] https://mp.weixin.qq.com/?lang=en_US.
[3] https://pypi.org/project/waitress/.
[4] http://nginx.org/en/.

http://localhost:port. Such a strategy prevents the WeChat back-end from being suspended when the common ports 80 and 443 are occupied.

When a user interacts with the WeChat official account, the server address is configured on WeChat official platform website. For example. If a user sends a message to WeChat official account and clicks on the menu, the WeChat official platform will push a message or an event to the server. Then the WeChat back-end can respond according to its own business logic, such as replying messages. The *access_token* is the globally unique interface credential of the WeChat official account [4]. The WeChat official account developer needs to use *access_token* for invoking each interface. A WeChat back-end uses the central control server to uniformly obtain and refresh the *access_token*, which needs to be refreshed periodically. The WeChat back-end uses database Redis[5] to store the value of *access_token*.

When a user sends a message to the WeChat official account or when an event is triggered by certain user actions, the WeChat official platform will send an XML packet of POST message or event to the WeChat back-end. The WeChat back-end needs to parse the received XML packet to receive the value of the corresponding tag and return a specific XML structure in the response packet. Note that, sending a passive response message is not through an interface, but is a reply to the message sent by the WeChat server. In addition, within 12 h, the customer service interface can also be invoked to send a message to ordinary users through posting a JSON (Javascript Object Notation) data packet. The WeChat official account encryption and decryption are a new mechanism provided by the official platform to further strengthen the security of WeChat official account. After the encryption and decryption are enabled, the invocation interface will not be affected. Message encryption and decryption are required only when there is a passive reply to the user's message. Template messages can only be used in service scenarios that meet their requirements. A user will trigger a template message after performing a specific action on the developed WeChat official account. From the above process, it can be seen that the template message is a way of passive reply.

4.2   The Developed Intelligent Dental Healthcare Q&A Sub-system

The intelligent dental healthcare Q&A sub-system is a key component of our developed system. The main function of Q&A system is to answer the patient's questions. The developed Q&A component contains several modules, including a classifier, sentence parsing module and search engine. The proposed classifier classifies the questions raised by users. In the developed dental healthcare Q&A system, we classify all questions into two categories, i.e., ordinary chatting questions and professional dental related questions. After classifying, the Q&A system will pass the question to the sentence parsing module for parsing. The parsed sentences will be further filtered, and be passed to the search engine to return the correct answer.

---

[5] https://redis.io/.

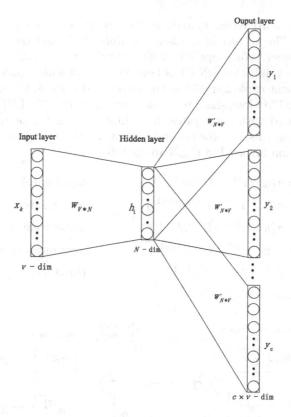

Fig. 2. The network structure of the implemented skip-gram model

The Built Neural Network-Based Classifier. Word2vec contains a collection of models that are capable of generating distributed representation of words or word vectors. The word2vec models are typically neural network-based models that can learn contexts of words in a corpus [14]. Word2vec takes a corpus of texts as input and generates distributed representation of words. The produced vectors typically contain several hundred dimensions, and each word in the corpus is learned to be assigned to a vector. Skip-gram and CBOW (continuous bag-of-words) are two typical models in word2vec. The input of CBOW is the context words around the central word. The idea of skip-gram is opposite to that of CBOW, that is, the input is a central word, and then the task is to generate the vectors of the context words around the central word. In the developed Q&A system, we choose the skip-gram model as it works well for uncommon words when the computing power is sufficient. The developed system implements the skip-gram model that is trained with a 200-dimensional vector on Chinese Wikipedia corpus. Figure 2 shows the network architecture of the implemented skip-gram model.

In Fig. 2, x is the one-hot embedding of a word, v is the vocabulary size, and N is the dimension of word vector. c is twice of the size of the word vector window,

w is the central word vector matrix, and w' is the matrix formed by context words' vectors. The vectors of words are trained first, and the next task is to design the classifier. We adopt recurrent neural network (RNN) as the basic classifier. As the traditional RNN has been verified to suffer from gradient vanishing and gradient explosion [15], in the developed system, we adopt a variant of RNN, i.e., LSTM (long-short term memory) network [6]. LSTM is a neural network configured with three gates, including input gate, forgotten gate and output gate. Figure 3 shows the network structure of the implemented LSTM.

The calculation involved in Fig. 3 are as follows.

$$
\begin{aligned}
i^{(t)} &= \sigma(w^{(i)}x^{(t)} + U^{(i)}h^{(t-1)}) && \text{(input gate)} \\
f^{(t)} &= \sigma(w^{(f)}x^{(t)} + U^{(f)}h^{(t-1)}) && \text{(forget gate)} \\
o^{(t)} &= \sigma(w^{(o)}x^{(t)} + U^{(o)}h^{(t-1)}) && \text{(output gate)} \\
\tilde{c}^{(t)} &= \sigma(w^{(c)}x^{(t)} + U^{(c)}h^{(t-1)}) && \text{(new memory cell)} \\
c^{(t)} &= i^{(t)} \circ \tilde{c}^{(t)} + f^{(t)}c^{(t-1)} && \text{(final memory cell)} \\
h^{(t)} &= o^{(t)} \circ tanh(c^{(t)})
\end{aligned}
\tag{1}
$$

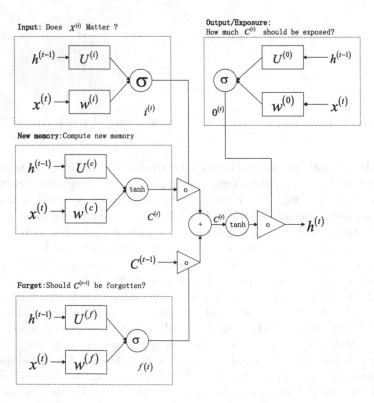

Fig. 3. *Input* denotes the input gate, and *New memory* denotes the new memory cell. *Forget* denotes the forget gate, and *Output* denotes the output gate. t denotes the current moment, $t-1$ represents the last moment, x denotes input, and h denotes the output of the hidden state.

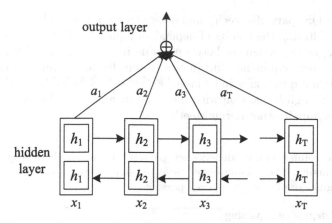

Fig. 4. "hidden layer" is the network structure of bi-directional LSTM. $a_1, a_2, a_3, \ldots, a_T$ are parameters in attention mechanism.

The calculation process of LSTM is as follows. The new memory cell uses $x^{(t)}$ and $h^{(t-1)}$ to generate $c^{(t)}$. So the new memory contains the attributes of the current word. The input gate uses $x^{(t)}$ and $h^{(t-1)}$ to determine how much the attribute of the word at the current moment should be kept, and this amount is represented by $i^{(t)}$. The forget gate uses $x^{(t)}$ and $h^{(t-1)}$ to determine how much the past memory should be forgotten, and this amount is represented by $f^{(t)}$. The final memory cell adds up the new memory retained by input gate and the past memory forgotten by forgotten gate to generate the final memory $c^{(t)}$. The output gate uses $x^{(t)}$ and $h^{(t-1)}$ to determine how much new memory $tanh(c^{(t)})$ should be output, and the output amount is represented by $o^{(t)}$.

In order to improve the accuracy of developed classifier, we build bi-directional LSTM network in the developed system, and the network structure is shown in Fig. 4. In the built bi-directional LSTM, the jth hidden state $h_j \rightarrow$ carries the jth word itself and a part of information in previous words. If the input is in reverse, the jth hidden state $h_j \leftarrow$ carries the jth word and a part of information in posterior words. So combining $h_j \rightarrow$ and $h_j \leftarrow$, $h_j[h_j \rightarrow, h_j \leftarrow]$ can contain the information before and after the jth word. The built classifier aims to classify the questions raised by users, most of which are short sentences, so our system adds the attention mechanism to the basic LSTM network. The attention mechanism is to assign different weights to different words in a sentence, which is likely to improve the accuracy of the classifier, especially in the case of short sentences. In detail, a layer of parameters after hidden layer are added, and are continually trained to be optimized. Figure 4 shows the bi-directional LSTM network with attention mechanism.

Sentences Parsing Module. After classifying the raised questions, if the question is classified into the professional dental healthcare category, we build a sentence parsing module that is used to finish a series of NLP tasks, including segmenting, POS (part-of-speech), and dependency parsing. The final results are generated by filtering the results of dependency parsing. Dependency parsing is to determine the dependencies between words in a sentence. Table 1 shows the result of dependency parsing built in our system for an example of user's question. The original question is in Chinese "戴活动假牙会戴坏其他牙吗？", and the corresponding English question with the same meaning is "Will wearing removable dentures impair other normal teeth?"

Table 1. The column below "dependency parsing" is the result of a question after dependency parsing. The column below "selected_dep" is the result after this system filters the original results of dependency parsing.

The result of dependency parsing
(root, ?#PU,戴#VV) (compound:nn,假牙#NN, 活动#NN) (dobj,戴#VV, 假牙#NN) (aux:modal,坏#VA, 会#VV) (aux:ba,坏#VA,把#BA) (det,牙#NN, 其他#DT) (dep,坏#VA, 牙#NN) (xcomp,坏#VA,戴#VV) (conj,戴#VV,坏#VA) (discourse, 戴#VV,吗#SP) (discourse, ?#PU, 吗#SP)

The result of selected_dep
(dobj, 戴#VV,假牙#NN) (compound:nn, 假牙#NN, 活动#NN) (det,牙#NN, 其他#DT) (dep, 坏#VA, 牙#NN)

In our system, only eight types of dependencies are remained, including *amod* (adjective modified noun), *compound:nn* (noun modified noun), *advmod* (adverb modified adjective), *nsubj* (noun subject), *dobj* (direct modified object), *det* (qualified modification), *parataxis* (parallel relationship) and *assmod* (association modification). For the complete list of the abbreviation in dependency parsing, please refer to paper [9]. Our system does not completely use all these eight dependencies, but adds some constraints to each dependency. For example. For the dependency *advmod*, two constraints are added. We only keep the lengths of the modifier and the modified word are both longer than 1, because in *advmod*, the valuable information contained by the object and the adjective with the length less than 1 is quite limited. Table 2 gives an example of the result of a sentence that is segmented, parsed and filtered.

Table 2. "keywords_filtering" refers to the result with sentence parsing and filtering

The result of keywords_filtering
戴 活动 假牙 其他 牙 坏

Query Module. The query module is built on the basis of an open-source text retrieval engine, i.e., Lucene[6], which provides a complete query engine and index engine. First, we build a Web crawler that is used to collect questions and answers related to dental healthcare from Internet. The collected questions and answers are checked, reviewed and corrected by professional dentists in *the affiliated Stomatological Hospital of Xi'an Jiaotong University.* Then we build indexes with Lucene's index engine for the checked questions and answers. We use Lucene's query engine to return the answer to the question raised by a user. In the search process, our system also adds extra resources, such as synonym dictionary. If a keyword of the question is in the synonym dictionary, the related synonym will also be searched together.

4.3   The Developed WeChat Follow-Up Care Mini Program

The WeChat follow-up care mini program adopts the B2C (business-to-customer) architecture, and the development adopts the architecture mode of server, client, and data management. The server uses Node.js[7] to build the RESTful API. The client uses the WeChat mini program to obtain data by sending an HTTP communication request to the server API. The data management module is the data management back-end for administrators to log in. This subsection introduces the key techniques used by WeChat mini program, including the MINA framework, Node.js framework, construction of RESTful API and MongoDB database.

The MINA framework[8] consists of three parts, including logical layer, view layer, and system layer. The MINA framework provides a set of JavaScript API for the upper layer by encapsulating the basic functions of file system and network communication provided by WeChat mini program. The MINA framework provides a set of language WXML (WeiXin Markup Language) similar to HTML tags and basic components at the view layer [8]. The view layer is a collection of .wxml and .wxss files. For users, the view layer is an interface that directly interacts with each user.

There are nine pages in the mini program, which are the dental classification page, doctor page, home page, patient information page, patient landing page, patient satisfaction survey page, patient message page, tooth type page, and end page. Each page has a life-cycle corresponding to its business logic, which is implemented by *page()* function in page's logical layer. The logical layer of the WeChat mini program development framework is implemented by JavaScript. On the basis of JavaScript, the *app()* and *page()* methods are added to register the program and the page. As the mini program does not run in a browser, some JavaScript's capabilities specific to Web development cannot be used, such as *document()* and *window()* [18]. The system layer contains temporary data, file storage, and network storage.

---

[6] http://lucene.apache.org/.
[7] https://nodejs.org/en/.
[8] https://developers.weixin.qq.com/miniprogram/dev/framework/MINA.html.

Representational state transfer (REST) refers to a constraint and paradigm in communication. REST defines all entities on the Internet as resources, and each resource corresponds to at least one URL. Each URL represents a type of operation, so REST makes Web resources and services addressable. The interaction between a client and a server accessing network resources through standard HTTP requests, such as GET, POST, PUT and DELETE. The following Fig. 5 shows an example of a part of POST code.

For database, we employ a NoSQL database MongoDB[9]. The MongoDB database system is a type of transitional database, between the typical NoSQL database and traditional relational database [13]. The MongoDB database system uses BSON (Binary JSON) format to store data, which is similar to JSON format. Based on BSON format, the database system can store more complex data types and implement complex key-value nesting operation [12]. For WeChat mini program, the database structure follows the standard structure of MongoDB. The advantages of high-speed reading and writing, big data processing, and distributed scalability of MongoDB database meet the needs of mini program.

4.4   The Developed AI Speech Assistant

The developed AI speech assistant is used for patients who do not participate in the follow-up care of WeChat mini program. The AI speech assistant is built as a robot system based on RASA[10] and a speech recognition conversion layer based on hierarchical attention network. The service flow of the AI speech assistant is to convert the text into a speech call for follow-up care, then convert the patient's speech follow-up results into text and store the results in database. First, the raised questions are carefully designed. These designed questions are applied to the robot assistant system with RASA as the core part. The whole text follow-up care process is realized by training the RASA core module and NLU (natural language understanding) module. We develop a hierarchical attention network to convert text into speech, and make phone calls to patients. Second, the system automatically records and uploads the records of the conversation to server. Finally, the hierarchical attention network can convert the speech into text in the back-end and output the details of each phone call.

---

[9] www.mongodb.org/.
[10] https://www.rasa.com/.

```
infoPost: {
        method: 'POST',
        path: '/api/info',
        handler: async (request, h) => {
                let appId = config.wxappid
                let encryptedData = request.payload.foruid.encryptedData
                let sessionKey = request.payload.foruid.sessionKey
                let iv = request.payload.foruid.iv
                let pc = new WXBizDataCrypt(appId, sessionKey)
                let Encrydata = pc.decryptData(encryptedData , iv)
                request.payload.unionid = Encrydata.unionId
                delete request.payload.foruid
                let entity = new inforModel(request.payload)
                let existModle = await inforModel.findByOpenId(request.payload.openId)
                if (existModle.length == 0) {
                        let crOne = await inforModel.create(entity)
                        if (crOne) {
                                return {
                                        status: 201 //Created successfully
                                }
                        }
                        else {
                                return {
                                        status: 400
                                }
                        }
                }
                else {
                        let upOne = await inforModel.updateOne({ openId:
                                        request.payload.openId }, { $set: request.payload })
                        return {
                                status: 200 //update completed
                        }
                }
        },
        config: {
                tags: ['api', 'info'],
                description: 'update'
        },
}
```

Fig. 5. An example of POST code

5   System Configuration, Deployment and Test

5.1   System Running Environment

The front-end of the integrated and intelligent dental healthcare system is mobile
devices, such as smart phones and tablets. Three of the developed modules,
including WeChat official account, follow-up mini program and AI speech assistant, are all based on mobile WeChat platform.

The system back-end is built on Tencent cloud server, running Ubuntu Server 16.04.1 64-bit system with four CPUs, 8G memory and 5 Mbps bandwidth. We applied Nginx server[11], a high-performance HTTP and reverse proxy service. The Flask framework, a lightweight Web application framework is also adopted. MongoDB and Redis are employed as databases. We deployed and applied the developed dental healthcare system in a real dental hospital, that is, *the affiliated Stomatological Hospital of Xi'an Jiaotong University.*

5.2   System Implementation

WeChat Official Account. As shown in Fig. 6, the "post-diagnosis reminder" is a template message.

Fig. 6. The developed WeChat official account

After the user completes the teeth repair, the WeChat back-end triggers a follow-up care template message to the user. The "introduction to the department of prosthodontics" is a passive reply message. When the user clicks on the menu of WeChat official account menu, the WeChat official platform sends a click event to the WeChat back-end, and the WeChat back-end responds to the message "introduction to the dental restoration section". After the user sends a text message to WeChat official account, the WeChat back-end invokes the customer service message interface to reply to the user within 12 h.

---

[11] http://nginx.org/en.

Intelligent Dental Healthcare Q&A System. There is a classifier module in our dental healthcare Q&A system, which was introduced in Sect. 4.2. The training process and classification accuracy of the built classifier are shown in Table 3. The classification accuracy of our classifier can achieve 87.73%.

Table 3. The training process of the built classifier

Iter:0,   Training Loss: 0.72, Training Acc: 49.00%, Val Loss: 0.76, Val Acc: 36.36%
Iter: 50,   Training Loss: 0.3, Training Acc: 91.00%, Val Loss: 0.43, Val Acc: 79.55%
Iter: 100, Training Loss: 0.23, Training Acc: 92.00%, Val Loss: 0.32, Val Acc: 86.82%
Iter: 150, Training Loss: 0.22, Training Acc: 91.00%, Val Loss: 0.31, Val Acc: 87.73%
Iter: 200, Training Loss: 0.2, Training Acc: 95.00%, Val Loss: 0.29, Val Acc: 88.64%
Iter: 250, Training Loss: 0.14, Training Acc: 95.00%, Val Loss: 0.33, Val Acc: 88.64%
Iter: 300, Training Loss: 0.12, Training Acc: 98.00%, Val Loss: 0.36, Val Acc: 87.73%
Iter: 350, Training Loss: 0.29, Training Acc: 87.00%, Val Loss: 0.34, Val Acc: 89.09%
Iter: 400, Training Loss: 0.13, Training Acc: 96.00%, Val Loss: 0.37, Val Acc: 87.73%
Iter: 450, Training Loss: 0.18, Training Acc: 93.00%, Val Loss: 0.38, Val Acc: 87.73%
Iter: 500, Training Loss: 0.22, Training Acc: 93.00%, Val Loss: 0.43, Val Acc: 87.73%
Iter: 550, Training Loss: 0.18, Training Acc: 93.00%, Val Loss: 0.42, Val Acc: 87.73%
Iter: 600, Training Loss: 0.21, Training Acc: 90.00%, Val Loss: 0.43, Val Acc: 87.73%
Iter: 650, Training Loss: 0.19, Training Acc: 90.00%, Val Loss: 0.43, Val Acc: 87.73%

In Table 3, "Iter" is the number of iterations, "Training loss" is the value of the loss function on training set, and "Training Acc" is the accuracy on training set. "Val Loss" is the value of the loss function on validation set, and "Val Acc" is the accuracy on validation set. The built classifier stops training when the accuracy of the validation set is not updated for more than five times. The intelligent doctor-patient Q&A system provides a RESTful API for other authorized access. We evaluated the response time for sentences with different lengths. The sentences of different lengths refer to the contained different numbers of Chinese characters. The interval in the horizontal axis is five words. The results are shown in Fig. 7. From Fig. 7, it can be seen that along with the sentences' lengths increasing, the response time becomes larger smoothly.

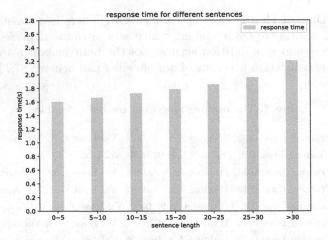

Fig. 7. Response time for sentences with different lengths

The Developed AI Speech Assistant and WeChat Mini Program. Fig. 8 shows the developed AI speech assistant, and Fig. 9 shows the developed WeChat mini program.

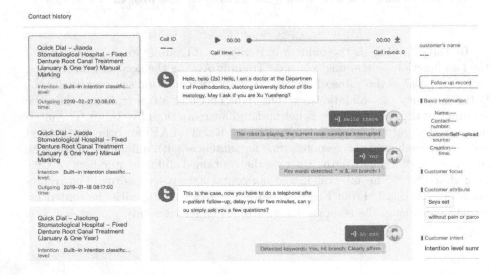

Fig. 8. The developed AI speech assistant

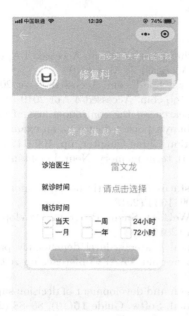 

(a) Example page 1 in WeChat
mini program

(b) Example page 2 in WeChat
mini program

Fig. 9. The developed WeChat mini program

6   Conclusion and Future Work

In this paper, we present four developed components to form a complete intelligent dental medical system with mobile services. The developed system consists of four modules, including WeChat official account, intelligent Q&A system, follow-up care mini program and AI speech assistant. The key function of our system is to provide follow-up care service for patients. Also, the system makes a lot of efforts to provide service in both sides of patients and dentists, reducing the manpower of traditional follow-up care services. Our system provides an interactive healthcare service for patients, also easing dentists' burden. Our system has been deployed and applied in a real dental hospital. We are continuously monitoring the status of system running and are improving system functionality, performance and robustness according to the feedbacks collected from patients and dentists.

The built system also gives several future directions for exploration. In the future, we will continue to collect users' comments and use text mining techniques to analyze those comments. We also plan to expand the dental knowledge database enlarging the resources of our system.

Acknowledgements. This paper is granted by National Natural Science Fund of China (No. 61702391 and No. 61502374) and Natural Science Foundation of Shaanxi province (No. 2018JQ6050).

References

1. Chunyu healthcare system. https://www.chunyuyisheng.com. Accessed 4 Apr 2019
2. Flask. http://docs.jinkan.org/docs/flask. Accessed 28 Mar 2019
3. Good doctor healthcare system. https://www.haodf.com. Accessed 4 Apr 2019
4. Wechat official account. https://mp.weixin.qq.com. Accessed 4 Apr 2019
5. Gu, D., Zhang, Y., Gu, Z., Zeng, S.: Research on the continuous use of mobile health care network community-taking Chunyu pocket doctor as an example. In: International Information System Association China Chapter, pp. 106–112 (2015)
6. Hochreiter, S., Schmidhuber, J.: Long short term memory. Neural Comput. **9**(8), 1735–1780 (1997)
7. Huang, W.: Review of the development status of domestic hospital information system. Comput. Knowl. Technol. **21**, 1009–1044 (2018)
8. Lei, L.: Introduction and Practice of WeChat Small Program Development. Tsinghua University Press, Beijing, China (2017)
9. Li, H., Zhang, Z., Ju, Y., Zhao, H.: Neural character-level dependency parsing for Chinese. In: Proceedings of the Thirty-Second AAAI Conference on Artificial Intelligence (AAAI), pp. 5205–5212 (2018)
10. Li, Y., Jun, Z., Xie, Y., Liu, L., He, J.: Design and development of decision support system for hospital based on mobile terminal. Softw. Guide **16**(10), 85–88 (2017)
11. Li, Y.: Functions of domestic interrogation mobile medical app. Chin. J. Med. Libr. Inf. Sci. **24**(12), 63–65 (2015)
12. Li, Z.: Research on bidirectional mapping algorithm of NoSQL database and relational database based on bson document tree. Jiangxi Norm. Univ. J. (Nat. Sci. Ed.) **5**, 476–480 (2016)
13. Lv, Q., Xie, W.: A real-time log analyzer based on MongoDB. Appl. Mech. Mater. **571–572**, 497–501 (2014)
14. Mikolov, T., Sutskever, I., Chen, K., Corrado, G.S., Dean, J.: Distributed representations of words and phrases and their compositionality. In: Advances in Neural Information Processing Systems (NIPS), pp. 3111–3119 (2013)
15. Pascanu, R., Mikolov, T., Bengio, Y.: On the difficulty of training recurrent neural networks. In: International Conference on Machine Learning (ICML), vol. 28, pp. 1310–1318 (2013)
16. Xing, M.: The status quo and development ideas of hospital information management system. Manag. Obs. **10**, 172–173 (2011)
17. Xu, J.: Research on data mining technology in hospital information system. Zhejiang University (2006)
18. Zhang, X.: WeChat Mini Program: Sharing WeChat Entrepreneur 2.0 Era 100 Million Bonus. Tsinghua University Press, Beijing, China (2017)

An Edge Computing-Based Framework for Marine Fishery Vessels Monitoring Systems

Fengwei Zhu[1], Yongjian Ren[1], Jie Huang[1(✉)], Jian Wan[1], and Hong Zhang[2]

[1] School of Computer Science and Technology, Hangzhou Dianzi University, Hangzhou 310018, China
huangjie@hdu.edu.cn
[2] Institute of Science and Technology Information Research of Zhejiang Province, Hangzhou 310006, China

Abstract. Vessel Monitoring Systems (VMS) have been adopted by many countries which provide information on the spatial and temporal distribution of fishing activity. Real-time communication and interaction between fishing vessels and shore-based systems is a weakness of traditional vessel monitoring systems. This paper proposes a novel framework of edge computing-based VMS (EC-VMS). The framework of EC-VMS mainly consists of four layers. An edge computing terminal is used on each vessel, and the BeiDou navigation satellite system (BDS) is adopted for communication. Meanwhile, edge computing servers interact with corresponding management vessels and the cloud. In order to decrease the communication cost, a data transmission policy called Adaptable Trajectory Transmission Model (ATTM) is presented in this paper. The experimental results illustrate the efficiency of the proposed EC-VMS, with the average communication time significantly decreased in a typical scenario. Moreover, EC-VMS improves the real-time performance of the system.

Keywords: VMS · Edge computing · BDS · Marine fishery

1 Introduction

Currently Vessel Monitoring Systems (VMS) are widely adopted by many countries around the world to allow fisheries administrators to control and monitor fishing activity. The electronic modules are installed on-board vessels which can automatically send data to a base station on shore by satellite communication. The fisheries monitoring center receives the transmitted data and processes it to get vessel trajectories and other information. Utilizing information on the vessels near-real time location, along with the vessel movements information that the VMS gives many benefits such as improving the quantity and quality of logbooks recovered, obtaining access to fishery-independent fishing effort estimates and prompt catch/effort re-porting, enabling the possibility of regional management and understanding both fleet dynamics and vessel behavior, and increasing efficiency of vessel safety protection [1].

© ICST Institute for Computer Sciences, Social Informatics and Telecommunications Engineering 2019
Published by Springer Nature Switzerland AG 2019. All Rights Reserved
X. Wang et al. (Eds.): CollaborateCom 2019, LNICST 292, pp. 201–214, 2019.
https://doi.org/10.1007/978-3-030-30146-0_14

Nevertheless, VMS still has some shortcomings in real-time and maritime communications. For instance;

(1) The development of marine communication networks is much slower than that on land, marine communication systems available today only provide the bare minimum essential services such as ship identification, positioning, location, course, heading, destination, tonnage and speed etc. This is provided in the form of AIS (Automatic Identification System) using VHF radio frequencies. Inter ship satellite communication is possible but is a costly option when compared to conventional wireless communications and not affordable for most small to medium seagoing vessels [2]. Sensor devices deployed on vessels can generate huge volumes of useful data that require significant portions of bandwidth for dissemination but it not utilized due to the deficiencies of the communication network.

(2) Fishing activity is monitored to detect vessels committing infringements, which requires near real time information dissemination so that the suspected infringements can be immediately detected. The processing of such data in the cloud faces additional delay due to wide area network latency that hinders the real-time response [3].

To address the problem, vessel monitoring systems are adopting more intelligent technologies to manage all the vessels. This paper proposes an edge computing-based intelligent VMS (EC-VMS) for smart vessel management. Every vessel has a perception platform to interact with the vessel terminal, sensors and other condition data collectors. Therefore, it can monitor itself in real-time and provide the data to the server. As the BeiDou navigation satellite system (BDS) can be used for positioning and communication through short messaging, the EC-VMS adopts it for communication. Thus, all the vessels can communicate with a server. Moreover, an edge computing-based (EC) server is established to handle all the data for the vessels, including their locations and status values, in real time. So, the processing of the collected data on the EC server can help in making quick responses to abnormalities. The administrators on land communicate through the server, scheduling jobs, noticing abnormalities, and so on.

An experimental system was built on the existing VMS in in the East China Sea, which showed improved performance over current vessel monitoring systems. The average communication times was reduced and the real-time performance of the system improved. Moreover, the EC-VMS could improve the quality of data that is transmitted to shore.

The main contributions of this paper are as follows;

(1) Propose an edge computing-based framework of VMS, which can efficiently transmit the fishing vessels data and reduce the time of the network communication.
(2) A method based on Edge Computing is adopted to improve the real-time performance of the system in the case of marine restricted communication.
(3) Higher performance VMS compared to current systems.

2   Related Work

VMS can provide high resolution data on the spatial and temporal distribution of fishing effort. In Europe, the European Commission has introduced legislation to monitor fishing activity so that all vessels >15 m long are required to transmit their locations, estimated by GPS, at intervals of 2 h or less, so that the data is comparable with data provided by remote animal sensing [1].

The main drawback of VMS is that the data transmission is not in real-time. A large amount of sensor data can be generated on board, but cannot be fully transmitted to shore in time. So, VMS research is mostly focused on VMS data post-processing, to distinguish the employed fishing gear type [4], to detect potential fishing behavior from different gear types [5], to create fish abundance indices [6], to identify and characterize trips made by fishing vessels [7], and to improve fishing efficiency [8]. The other source of information was integrated to improving the uniformity of VMS Data, such as spaceborne high-resolution radar satellite data, satellite automatic identification system (sat-AIS) tracking data, and some vessel detection system (VDS) data [9].

Currently satellite communication is used in the maritime industry, however due to the limitations of satellite bandwidth, real time communications are affected and thus the performance of vessel monitoring systems degraded.

Recently, lots of progress has been made to improve the low-bandwidth communication in satellite positioning and satellite communication [10]. BDS was developed by China which can provide functions such as high precision positioning, short message communication, and Time services etc. In China, BDS is widely used in marine fishing vessels because of its low cost of short message communication [11]. Although there are many applications of marine communication system at present, there are still bottlenecks in the network, and the real-time performance is much worse than that on land [12–14].

Edge computing is becoming a new computing paradigm which combines edge IoT devices and cloud computing [15]. It processes data at the edge of the network, which has the potential to provide a better response time, battery life, bandwidth cost, data safety, and privacy. In edge computing, the computing occurs in the proximity of the data sources. Therefore, it has some advantages compared to cloud computing [16]. The results of some research have demonstrated these advantages [17–20]. The emerging edge computing technologies is the most important technique in our EC-VMS, which could achieve the goal of improving the response time and reduce the communication traffic.

The proposed framework of this paper has benefited from the edge computing paradigm to make the marine fishing management more real-time and intelligent.

3   Architecture

3.1   The Framework of EC-VMS

As shown in Fig. 1, the framework of EC-VMS mainly consists of four layers.

Perception Layer. There are many heterogeneous sensors, video surveillance, navigation and communication equipment in the ship. The perceptive layer refers to the

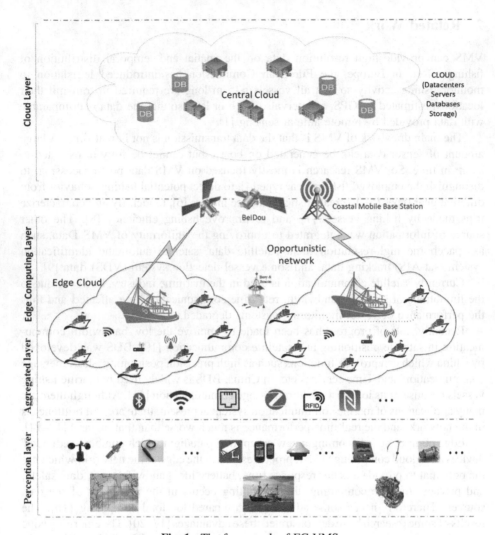

Fig. 1. The framework of EC-VMS

physical sensors and their running platforms. Through these devices, the perception layer gets the data of the operational state and the working environment of the ship.

Aggregated Layer. Shipborne data centers obtain the data for all the ship equipment through various application interfaces, preprocesses and stores them accordingly. The connection with the perceptive layer can be wired or wireless.

Edge Computing Layer. An edge computing-based management system is established between the ships, which can store and make decision immediately and in addition decides whether to forward information to cloud layer. The edge computing layer can run on only one ship, and it can also run in the form of ship network through a marine self-organizing mesh network.

Cloud Layer. A cloud computing-based management system is built on shore, which can store large amounts of ships data and manage the whole system. Moreover, the cloud layer can track all the ships in real time, make decisions and generate emergency commands.

3.2 Perception Layer

The Perception layer collects data mainly on three aspects of fishing vessels; marine environmental data, including meteorological, hydrological, sea surface temperature, humidity and salinity etc. Fishery production data including ship location, fishing conditions, fishing gear, fish catch, materials, personnel and video surveillance of operation etc. Equipment condition data including engine condition, oil quantity and the internal network etc.

Recently, RFID tags and various kinds of sensor technology are adopted by vessel builders. The RFID tag has a self-perception ability, which allows it to report its own status. The sensors can sample numerical values, which reflect the states of the monitored objects. Table 1 shows a part of the data that could be obtained from different sensors and devices onboard. These sampled numerical values reflect the states of the monitored objects.

Table 1. A part of the data from sensors and devices onboard.

Data	Category	Data type
Positioning & navigation	Fishery production	Numeric, characters, dates
Meteorological	Marine environmental	Numeric, image
Hydrological	Marine environmental	Numeric, image
Video surveillance	Fishery production	Video, audio
Power monitoring	Equipment condition	Numeric
Fishery administration	Fishery production	Numeric, characters, image

3.3 Aggregation Layer

The aggregation layer is an adaptor layer to connect the devices of perception layer, which is responsible for sensor node configuration, initialization, data acquisition, data caching and network manager. On modern vessels, the data sensors are shared over an Ethernet network available on the ship. All the local data obtained from sensors or devices onboard can be encapsulated and transmitted to the aggregated layer data storage center using different wireless protocols (e.g. WIFI, Bluetooth, ZigBee and UWB etc.). The aggregated layer has a data cache corresponding to the data cache of perception layer for each device, which is used to facilitate powerful distributed optimizations for communication.

There is an aggregated database to receive, store, and process the raw sampling data from the connected sensors, and then send the processed data to the edge computing layer. The database contains the basic data of vessels information, crew, navigation information, marine geographic information and fishery facilities etc. Moreover, it sets up the scheme for multi-source heterogeneous perception data (e.g. image data from video monitoring and trajectory data from GPS etc.). The aggregated layer exchanges and shares data with other vessels and provides data support for the edge computing layer.

3.4   Edge Computing Layer

The Edge Computing layer represents an abstract edge computer dedicated and responsible for a group of vessels. The Edge Computing layer and aggregation layer can overlap in their functions and both can co-exist within a network of vessels or on a single vessel. Data from the aggregation layer can be sent to the Edge Computing layer for storage, processing and analysis. In an edge computing environment, an aggregation layer can transmit data to its Edge Computing layer rapidly for analysis and respond to the perception device in a few seconds.

A larger aggregation Edge Computing layer that manages the services of local vessel networks is established in a selected vessel called Vessels Edge Computing Server (VECS), which can receive the data from a single aggregation layer in a vessel and make some advanced data analysis. In the larger aggregation edge computing network, vessels can also perform specific computations and communicate with each other. VECS decides which tasks go to the local edge computing node and which go to the cloud center.

In the EC-VMS, few sensor devices will transmit data directly to the cloud. The Edge Computing layer is mainly devoted to the vessel's local data processing and analyzing facilities for real-time needs such as emergency response services. Like the aggregation layer, the Edge Computing layer maintains both data and application caches which allow optimizations to be carried out by analyzing the interactions between sensor data and applications. Figure 2 shows the communication of EC-VMS.

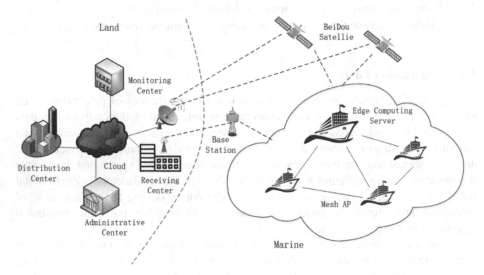

Fig. 2. The communication of EC-VMS

3.5 Cloud Layer

A Cloud layer is designed to provide central control, which delivers elastic computing power and storage at a low cost. However, cloud computing systems are shore based and therefore have an intrinsic delay due to processing and communication links. A local server allows for real time responses due the reduction in communications delay and its exclusive use for running the management system.

It is important to respond to the abnormal condition when the edge node becomes invalid. For example, if a vessel meets with a mishap, and the communication module is damaged, the ECS cannot receive the help message, but the cloud layer can give an alarm by running an anomaly detection service periodicity.

All the vessels in the EC-VMS are shown on the GIS for visualization. In addition, every vessel has its own information on the marine map, consisting of its name, unique ID, location, status and other attributes. Different colors are used to easily distinguish the different states. This makes it easy for administrative staff to see the abnormal vessels. Moreover, the situation must be display in real time. If one vessel is out of touch for a specified time, the vessel on the map must immediately be set to the color of the out of touch state. If a vessel is sailing into prohibited fishing areas, the vessel on the map should synchronously blink, and the message reported to relevant staff.

3.6 Interactivity Policy of EC-VMS

In this work vessel trajectory data was used to validate the EC-VMS, we use a transmission model called the Adaptable Trajectory Transmission Model (ATTM). ATTM combines the LDR algorithm [21], SQUISH trajectory compression algorithm [22] and reliable transmission strategy to establish a unified communication mechanism based on the EC-VMS. The model was divided into two parts in the edge computing layer; data tracking and data simplification.

In order to ensure that the trajectory can be transmitted to the ground monitoring center in time for real time analysis, the trajectory tracking and simplification must be synchronized. The ATTM uses synchronization mode so that when the tracking mechanism sends an updated trajectory, trajectory simplification will also be implemented.

Fishing vessels have a randomness in the process of operation, and its fishing behavior is complex. Therefore, the algorithms such as Neural Networks and Gauss Regression Processes are not suitable for track estimation. The LDR algorithm only needs base points and velocity vectors to estimate track.

This is a linear predictive function of the edge computing layer for the current position of fishing vessels.

$$\vec{l}(t) : t = l_b.\vec{p} + (t - l_b.t)\vec{l_V} \tag{1}$$

where l_b is the prediction base point, $\vec{l_V}$ is velocity vector. For a given error threshold θ_d, LDR guarantees that when the predicted trajectory point P_t' are close to the observation trajectory point P_t, that is $\mathrm{ED}(P_t, P_t') < \theta_d$, the edge computing layer will not produce update messages, and the shore-based monitoring center uses the predicted points instead of the observation points. If the observed trajectory deviates from the predicted trajectory then the prediction base point and velocity vector need to be updated.

In the case of frequent trajectory changes, the edge computing layer needs to send more trajectory points. However, the BDS communication protocol has strict restrictions on message length and transmission time interval, so we need to select a fixed-length trajectory sequence (adapted to the BDS protocol packet) T' from the original observation trajectory T, and send it to cloud layer. ATTM uses SQUISH algorithm for selection, because SQUISH runs fast, has good real-time performance, and can preset the size of the approximate trajectory sequence. The edge computing layer adds the observed trajectory points to the buffer of the SQUISH algorithm. When the transmission condition is reached, the fixed size trajectory sequence T' is obtained from the buffer and sent to the cloud layer together with the update message.

Algorithm 1: ATTM (edge computing layer)

Input:

(1) error threshold θ_d

(2) observation trajectory point P_t

Function:

   send messages

Begin

1: initial uncompressed queue;

2: initial sending queue;

3: **while** (received data)

4:    **if** received a retransmit signal **then**

5:       adding missing messages to the sending queue
         based on message number;

6:    **if** received the observation trajectory points **then**

7:       **if** the uncompressed queue is empty **then**

8:          estimate trajectory points by LDR;

9:          **if** estimated value greater than threshold **then**

10:            add observation point to uncompressed queue;

11:      **else** add observation point to compressed queue;

12:   **if** it's time window for data transmission **then**

13:      **if** sending queue is not empty **then**

14:            send message;

15:      **else if** uncompressed queue is not empty **then**

16:            compress trajectory by SQUISH;

17:            generate message into sending queue;

18:            send message;

End

The cloud layer uses the same trajectory estimation algorithm as the edge computing layer to display the ship's position in real time. In order to reduce the number of satellite communications, the cloud layer will not send a communication receipt for each received message. The Cloud layer updates existing trajectory data according to the new messages.

4 Result and Analysis

4.1 Experimental Setup

The experimental data was collected from the trajectory data of four fishing vessels in the VMS that took place in the East China Sea, near Zhoushan City, Zhejiang Province, China. The VMS manages more than 3,000 vessels. This trajectory data is generated by the shipborne BDS terminal module, and the device can collect positional data once a second, but the minimum interval of satellite transmission is limited to 60 s. Trajectory data contains information such as device number, time, longitude and latitude. In order to control the experimental variables and improve the accuracy of the experiment, we chose four vessels and installed edge computing nodes. The edge computing nodes collected complete trajectory data of four fishing vessels from March 2018 to May 2018, totaling 1018412 trajectories' points. The spatial distribution of the four vessels are shown in Fig. 3.

Fig. 3. Spatial distribution of four vessels' trajectory.

This paper uses the ATTM algorithm to verify the framework proposed in this work, which considers the limitation of the BDS communication protocol on message length and minimum transmission interval. When the transmission interval does not reach the minimum transmission interval, it is not allowed to send messages. When the message length exceeds the maximum transmission length, the data beyond the maximum transmission length will be discarded. Meanwhile, this paper also considers the situation of message distortion and packet loss.

4.2 Experimental Results

The experiment is analyzed from three aspects; the number of trajectory data transmission, the real-time performance and the trajectory quality. Figure 4 shows the comparison of ATTM transmission times with the traditional fixed-interval transmission mode (FITM) of VMS in three cases: 30-m threshold, 50-m threshold and 70-m threshold. FITM transferred data at each time interval. The abscissa represents the minimum communication interval of the VMS, and the ordinate represents the number of communications. As can be seen from the figure, the communication times of FITM and ATTM decrease with an increase in the communication interval.

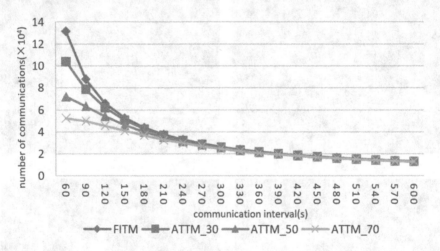

Fig. 4. Comparison of transmission times.

ATTM has a low probability of predicting all observation trajectory points accurately when the communication interval is large. It needs to communicate every time when it reaches the communication window, so the number of transmissions decreases slightly, which is close to FITM. Meanwhile the criterion of accurate prediction is that the distance between the observation trajectory point and the prediction trajectory point is less than the threshold, so the larger the threshold, the less the number of communications. ATTM has less communication times than FITM protocol under different communication intervals and error thresholds, so it has obvious effect in saving communication resources. Under the typical 60-s transmission interval and 50-m threshold, the network traffic is reduced by 45.22%.

Real-time trajectory query is another important indicator of EC-VMS. FITM transmits data at fixed time intervals. When the cloud layer receives data at time t1, it needs to wait for data at time t1 + 1. Therefore, the minimum delay time of FITM query is 0 s, the maximum delay time is the transmission time interval Δt, and the average delay time is $\Delta t/2$ s. The ATTM protocol can be used for real time analysis, however there is an intrinsic delay in the system as the trajectory data will only be updated when the cloud service receives the updated data. In order to compare with FITM, this paper uses statistics to analyze the trajectory data correction time.

As can be seen from Fig. 5, the correction time of ATTM increases with the communication time interval. This is because when the communication interval is large, the ATTM cannot send the correction information in time, which leads to a higher delay time. The higher the error threshold is, the fewer trajectory points are needed to be corrected, so the real-time performance is better. The communication interval and error threshold directly affect the real-time performance of ATTM. It can be seen from Fig. 5 that the correction time of ATTM is obviously lower than FITM, so we can conclude that the real-time performance of ATTM is better than FITM.

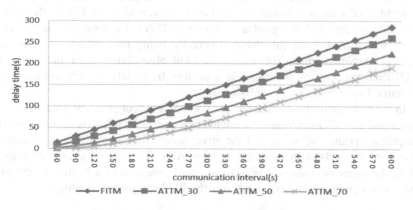

Fig. 5. Comparison of real-time performance.

In order to compare the trajectory data quality of ATTM and FITM, we use the Average of Pairs Distance (APD) as the evaluation criterion. Given trajectories A and B, APD calculates the distance between the points corresponding to the two trajectories and calculates the average value. The calculation formula is as follows:

$$\text{APD}(A, B) = \frac{1}{n} \times \sum_{i=1}^{n} ED(a_1, b_1) \tag{2}$$

In this experiment, A is the trajectory queried in VMS and B is the original observation trajectory. The results are shown in Fig. 6.

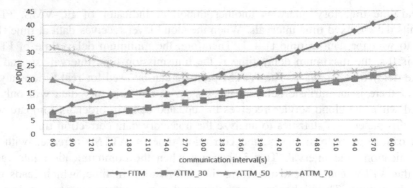

Fig. 6. Comparison of trajectory quality.

We set the error threshold of ARTT to 30 m, 50 m and 70 m, and compared it with FITM.

The APD of FITM increases as the communication interval gets larger due to the lower number of trajectory points in the FIFM transmission. In Fig. 6, the ADP of ARTT decreases first and then gradually increases. This is the result of a large number of points which have been calculated incorrectly being transmitted when the communication interval is small. This means the LDR algorithm is used more frequently and SQUISH compression algorithm is used less frequently, which makes the prediction error larger than the compression error.

With the increase of the communication interval, the proportion of prediction points decreases and the APD decreases. As the interval continues to increase, the proportion of compressed points increases, and the error caused by compression also increases, which eventually leads to an increasing trend of ADP. The larger the error threshold of ARTT is, the larger the value of the ADP will be. In the case of a 30 m error threshold, ATTM has a significant improvement over the FITM trajectory quality.

5   Conclusion

In order to reduce the communication cost and improve real-time efficiency of the VMS, we propose a framework of edge computing-based VMS in this paper. In the EC-VMS, firstly, in order to get more data, a perception platform is established on every vessel to interactive with the data collector. Therefore, it can monitor itself in real-time and provide the data support for the server. Secondly, the EC-VMS adopts the BDS for communication because of its low price and wide coverage. Thus, all the vessels can communicate with the server. Thirdly, an edge computing-based server is established to handle all the data for the vessels, including their locations and status values, in real time. So, the processing of the collected data on the edge computing server can help in making a quick response. Moreover, a data transmission model called ATTM was established to interact between the cloud and edge. The experiment is based on the data of an existing VMS that runs in the East China Sea, Zhoushan City. Results show that it is better than the original VMS in real-time, efficiency and usability. In the future work, more types of vessels data and edge computing methods will be investigated.

Acknowledgment. This work was supported in part by the Key Research and Development Project of Zhejiang Province (Grant No. 2017C03024), the National Natural Science Foundation of China (Grant No. 61572163) and the Zhejiang Province Research Program (Grant No. 2017C3 3065).

References

1. Stephen, C.V., Stuart, B., Matthew, J.W., Richard, I., David, T., Jason, N.: Individual responses of seabirds to commercial fisheries revealed using GPS tracking, stable isotopes and vessel monitoring systems. J. Appl. Ecol. **47**(2), 487–497 (2010)
2. Lee, J., South, A.B., Jennings, S.: Developing reliable, repeatable, and accessible methods to provide high-resolution estimates of fishing-effort distributions from vessel monitoring system (VMS) data. ICES J. Mar. Sci. **67**(6), 1260–1271 (2010)
3. Ejaz, A., Mubashir, H.R.: Mobile edge computing opportunities, solutions, and challenges. Future Gener. Comput. Syst. **70**, 59–63 (2017)
4. Marzuki, M.I., Gaspar, P., Garello, R.: Fishing gear identification from vessel-monitoring-system-based fishing vessel trajectories. IEEE J. Oceanic Eng. **43**(3), 689–699 (2018)
5. de Souza, E.N., Boerder, K., Matwin, S.: Improving fishing pattern detection from satellite AIS using data mining and machine learning. PLOS ONE **11**(7), e0158248 (2016)
6. Ducharme-Barth, N.D., Shertzer, K.W., Ahrens, R.N.M.: Indices of abundance in the Gulf of Mexico reef fish complex: a comparative approach using spatial data from vessel monitoring systems. Fish. Res. **198**, 1–13 (2018)
7. Watson, J.T., Haynie, A.C.: Using vessel monitoring system data to identify and characterize trips made by fishing vessels in the United States North Pacific. PLOS ONE **11**(10), e0165173 (2016)
8. Watson, J.T., Haynie, A.C., Sullivan, P.J.: Vessel monitoring systems (VMS) reveal an increase in fishing efficiency following regulatory changes in a demersal longline fishery. Fish. Res. **207**, 85–94 (2018)
9. Longepe, N., Hajduch, G., Ardianto, R.: Completing fishing monitoring with spaceborne Vessel Detection System (VDS) and Automatic Identification System (AIS) to assess illegal fishing in Indonesia. Marine Pollution Bulletin **131**(SI), 33–39 (2018)
10. Al-Zaidi, R., Woods, J., Al-Khalidi, M.: Next generation marine data networks in an IoT environment. In: Second International Conference on Fog and Mobile Edge Computing 2017, FMEC, pp. 50–55. IEEE, Valencia (2017)
11. Lu, C., Li, X., Nilsson, T.: Real-time retrieval of precipitable water vapor from GPS and BeiDou observations. J. Geodesy **89**(9), 843–856 (2015)
12. Zhang, Y., Chen, S., Hong, Z.: Feasibility of oil slick detection using BeiDou-R coastal simulation. Math. Prob. Eng. **4**, 1–8 (2017)
13. Yu, F., Hu, X., Dong, S.: Design of a low-cost oil spill tracking buoy. J. Mar. Sci. Technol. **23**(1), 188–200 (2018)
14. Wang, L., Li, L., Qiu, R.: Edge computing-based differential positioning method for BeiDou navigation satellite system. KSII Trans. Internet Inf. Syst. **13**(1), 69–85 (2019)
15. Satyanarayanan, M.: The emergence of edge computing. Computer **50**(1), 30–39 (2017)

16. Shi, W., Cao, J., Zhang, Q.: Edge computing: vision and challenges. IEEE Internet Things J. **3**(5), 637–646 (2016)
17. Zeydan, E., Bastug, E., Bennis, M.: Big data caching for networking: moving from cloud to edge. IEEE Commun. Mag. **54**(9), 36–42 (2016)
18. Rahmani, A.M., Gia, T.N., Negash, B.: Exploiting smart e-Health gateways at the edge of healthcare Internet-of-Things: a fog computing approach. Future Gener. Comput. Syst. **78**, 641–658 (2018)
19. Taleb, T., Dutta, S., Ksentini, A.: Mobile edge computing potential in making cities smarter. IEEE Commun. Mag. **55**(3), 38–43 (2017)
20. Premsankar, G., Di Francesco, M., Taleb, T.: Edge computing for the internet of things: a case study. IEEE Internet Things J. **5**(2), 1275–1284 (2018)
21. Trajcevski, G., Cao, H., Scheuermann, P., Wolfson, O., Vaccaro, D.: On-line data reduction and the quality of history in moving objects databases. In: Proceedings of the 5th ACM International Workshop on Data Engineering for Wireless and Mobile Access, MobiDE 2006, pp. 19–26. ACM, Chicago (2006)
22. Muckell, J., Hwang, J., Patil, V., Lawson, C., Ping, F., Ravi, S.: SQUISH: an online approach for GPS trajectory compression. In: Proceedings of the 2nd International Conference and Exhibition on Computing for Geospatial Research & Application, COM. Geo 2011. ACM, Washington DC (2011)

A Mobile and Web-Based Approach for Targeted and Proactive Participatory Sensing

Navid Hashemi Tonekaboni(✉), Lakshmish Ramaswamy,
and Sakshi Sachdev

Department of Computer Science, University of Georgia, Athens, GA, USA
{navidht, sssll759}@uga.edu, laks@cs.uga.edu

Abstract. Participatory sensing applications have gained popularity due to the increased use of mobile phones with embedded sensors. One of the main issues in participatory sensing applications is the uneven coverage of areas, i.e., some areas might be covered by multiple participants while there is no data for other areas. In this paper, we design mobile and web-based infrastructure to enable domain scientists to effectively acquire crowd-sensed data from specific areas of interest (AOIs) to support the goal of even coverage for data collection. Scientists can mark the AOIs on a web-portal, then volunteers will be proactively informed about the participatory sensing opportunities near their current location. We presented a caching algorithm to increase the performance of our proposed system and studied the performance of the caching algorithm for different real-world scenarios on different mobile phones. We observed that prefetching data improves the performance to some extent; however, it starts to degrade after a certain point depending upon the number of nearby AOIs.

Keywords: Participatory sensing · Mobile caching · Citizen science · Crowdsensing

1 Introduction

Mobile phones have evolved from merely being a medium of audio communication to a means of improved information exchange between individuals or groups using the Internet, along with accessing the GPS, microphones, cameras, accelerometer, and other sensors. Due to these additional features, mobile phones are being widely used by users in their day-to-day lives. The increase of mobile phones with embedded sensors has introduced a paradigm called participatory sensing [1]. The main idea of participatory sensing is empowering citizens for collecting data from ubiquitous, handheld mobile phones [2], and it is used in various domains such as urban planning, public health, and natural resource management [3, 4]. Participatory sensing can also be referred to as crowdsensing, urban sensing, community sensing, people-centric sensing, opportunistic sensing, or citizen sensing [5, 6].

Participatory sensing has many advantages over traditional sensor networks. First, due to the mobility of users, broad areas can be covered [7]. Secondly, more often than

X. Wang et al. (Eds.): CollaborateCom 2019, LNICST 292, pp. 215–230, 2019.
https://doi.org/10.1007/978-3-030-30146-0_15

not, there is no need to deploy and maintain sensors as they are integrated into mobile phones. Lastly, the availability of software development tools for mobile phones makes application development and deployment relatively easy [7]. Advantages of participatory sensing have led to an increase in mobile sensing applications. Maintaining user's privacy, recruiting and training participants, incentivizing them, dealing with low-quality data, and interpreting the data are some of the challenges in such applications [1].

There are many different challenges in participatory sensing applications. Quality of the crowd-sensed data, the anonymity of users, incentivization mechanisms, and resource consumption are all different factors to be taken into account in designing such applications. This study focuses on collecting data only from the areas where domain scientists are interested in, as an essential step towards efficient resource consumption. The data collected from the same area by different participants waste participants' resources. On the other hand, the resource consumption of mobile applications plays an essential role in keeping or losing users. Therefore, our approach can significantly benefit different participatory sensing applications. Most of the current participatory sensing applications are passive, and there is a little or even no communication between the participants and domain scientists. In passive participatory sensing, participants install the application and submit the geotagged data to the backend server, while they have no idea whether the geo-tagged data is redundant or not. Passive mode of operation causes data disparity; too much data may get collected from specific locations, while the data acquired from many other locations are insufficient.

In this study, we propose a mobile and web-based approach for leveraging domain scientists' areas of interest to address this shortcoming of many participatory sensing applications. A web portal is developed through which researchers can specify the AOIs to enable proactive participatory sensing. We have also designed and implemented a mobile caching algorithm to prefetch the AOIs as participants are collecting data. To analyze the caching performance, different implementations of the algorithm have been tested on three mobile devices under different scenarios. Our analysis shows the caching performance starts to degrade after a certain threshold depending upon the number of nearby AOIs.

2 Background

In this section, we briefly discuss some of the existing participatory sensing applications and also illustrate the system model of the typical applications. Participatory sensing applications can be classified into three areas based on the type of data being collected [1]:

Environment Centric Applications. In this type of applications, sensors collect data from a surrounding environment of participants. For instance, Youdale et al. [11] introduced a participatory sensing application called Haze Watch in which a mobile phone is interfaced with a pollution sensor to measure carbon monoxide, oxygen, and nitrogen dioxide in the air as well as the temperature and wind speed. This information is uploaded to a server along with the time and location of the participant, which is used by environmental scientists and ecologists. Another application called Ikarus [12] collects thermal information of the atmosphere during flights by paraglider pilots, which is used by other pilots to gain the required heights. It uploads this information along with the time and location of pilots to be used for navigation purposes. Noise Tube [13] and Noise Spy [14] are two other applications of this category which are used to monitor noise pollution. Participants record the audio and upload it to the server. These data are used by specialists to understand the relationship between noise exposition and behavioral problems. Another example is Creek Watch [15], an application that is used for water and trash management. In this application, users take pictures of creeks at various locations and upload this information to the server. All the applications mentioned above are designed to monitor and analyze a specific environmental phenomenon.

Urban Centric Applications. These applications focus on infrastructure and urban information. ParkNet [8] is one of such applications that provides information about parking space occupancy to users through an ultrasonic device installed on the cars. As a result, users can find the nearest vacant parking spots. Nericell [9] is another location-based service app which monitors road traffic conditions through smartphones. It uses microphones, accelerometer, GSM radio, and GPS sensors to detect potholes and bumps. These data are reported to the server to be aggregated for annotating maps and allowing users to search for best driving directions.

Community Centric Applications. These are people-centric applications which use sensor devices to collect data about users. Diet Sense [17] is one such application which captures the image of foods that users eat along with the time, date, and location. Participants share these images with community members to compare their eating habits. The primary use case of this application is for diabetic patients and the ones who want to lose weight using the suggestions from other people with the same conditions. MobAsthma [21] is a personalized asthma-monitoring application which lets asthma specialists and allergists explore the relationship between respiratory symptoms and exposure to different air pollutions. It also monitors the person's asthma condition and remotely alerts the medical staff if the patient experiences an asthma attack. BikeNet [18] is another application that monitors sports exercise of participants by analyzing location information, speed, and burnt calories. It also measures the carbon dioxide on the route taken by the cyclists to find the most suitable routes for cycling. In another application of this category called Live Compare [10], participants take pictures of products' price and barcode. The app searches the stores in that proximity to display the current price of that product in other stores.

Overview of Typical Participatory Sensing Model. Typical participatory sensing applications have a client- server architecture in which mobile devices act as clients through which the participants collect sensor data and submitted to the application server. In the backend server, the data are stored, analyzed, and made available in various forms to the end users as shown in Fig. 1. Various stakeholders are involved in participatory sensing applications as follows:

Participants/Citizen Scientists. Participants act as information providers. They gather sensor data for participatory sensing application and submit it through Wi-Fi or wireless operators to the infrastructure provider.

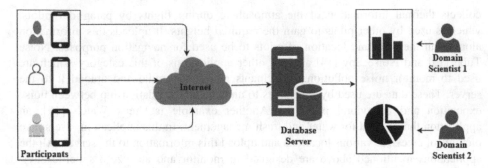

Fig. 1. Conventional model for participatory sensing applications

Domain Scientists. Domain scientists subscribe to the service and access the data gathered by participants. They are experts who use the data collected by participants to analyze the target phenomenon.

Participatory Sensing Infrastructure Provider. Application infrastructure providers are initiators of participatory sensing campaigns. They are responsible for designing, implementing, deploying, and managing the applications.

3   System Architecture

We developed a web-based platform for domain scientists such as social researchers, ecologists, and environmentalists. Using this platform domain scientists can specify AOIs on a map (i.e., the areas from which they are interested in collecting data). Along with AOIs, stop limit (i.e., the number of data entries required for each targeted area) can be specified to prevent additional data collection from a particular area. As depicted in Fig. 2, marked AOI along with stop limits are stored in a database server. When participants collect data using the mobile application, the nearby AOIs are shown on the map as a guide to the participants.

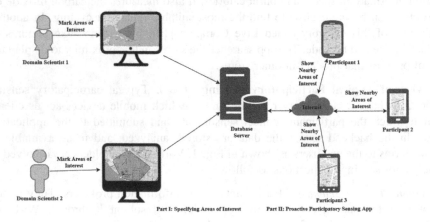

Fig. 2. System architecture

This system is divided into two parts. The first part is designed to identify AOIs by domain scientists, and the second part is designed to obtain data from targeted areas. To identify the AOIs, a web portal is implemented where domain scientists provide the coordinate of their targeted areas upon authorization. They can search for any region on the map and mark the areas, in the form of rectangles as depicted in Fig. 3. Identification of AOIs also allows domain scientists to specify the number of required entries for that area as the stop limit. This information is passed to the server to be stored in a spatial database. PostgreSQL along with PostGIS as a spatial database extender is used to store the spatial and non-spatial data.

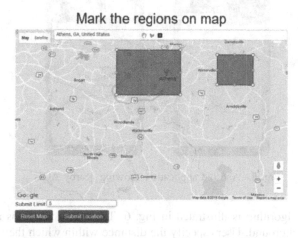

Fig. 3. Identifying Areas of Interest (AOIs)

Proactive participatory sensing approach obtains data from the database server and enables targeted and proactive participatory sensing by showing nearby AOIs to participants. As shown in Fig. 4, this system consists of three modules: data collection platform for mobile applications on the left, web service for AOIs retrieval, and a database server.

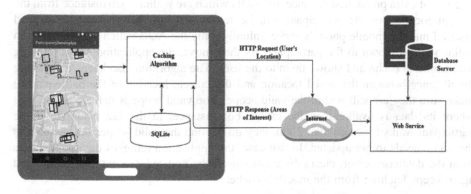

Fig. 4. Proactive participatory sensing

Our data collection platform for mobile application is developed using Android SDK. As depicted in Fig. 5, the app allows participants to specify the radius (from now on, we call it "specified distance") and then shows the AOIs within that radius to the users. Considering that the participants are constantly moving, repeatedly updating the AOIs requires continuous connection and querying from the database which leads to performance degradation. To overcome this challenge, we prefetch targeted areas on the clients' device and present a caching algorithm to improve the performance.

Fig. 5. Android application showing nearby AOIs

The caching algorithm is illustrated in Fig. 6. The user's locations are constantly tracked in the background. Users specify the distance within which they are willing to see the available AOIs (it is called "specified distance"). In addition, we use the term "extra-prefetched distance" to refer to the extra amount of data which the application retrieves from the database server and prefetches to the cache to have a better performance. In other words, the application retrieves more data than required from the database so as to perform more efficiently while the users are moving. In the next step, the whole data, i.e., all the AOIs within a circle that its radius is equal to the specified distance plus the extra-prefetched distance, are inserted into the cache. For example, if a participant specifies to see all the AOIs within 1 km radius and the application is set to 2 km of extra prefetched distance, the AOIs which are within 3 km distance from the current location of the participant will be retrieved from the database server and inserted into the mobile phone's cache. Initially, only the AOIs which are within 1 km radius will be shown to the participant. As they move, the application keeps fetching data from the cache and shows them to the user. The algorithm also keeps calculating the distance between the initial location and the current location of the participant to make sure they are still within the valid scope. The valid scope is defined as the area where its data is available in the cache. For instance, in the last example, if the participant walks for more than 2 km, they go beyond the valid scope, and the data in the cache needs to get updated. In that case, the application retrieves the updated data from the database server, clears the cache, insert the updated data into the cache, and again keeps fetching from the mobile's cache.

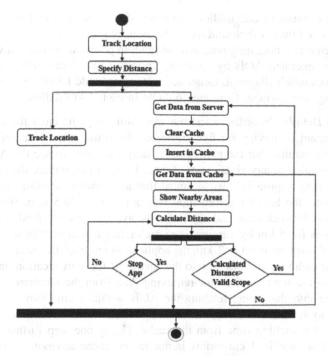

Fig. 6. Basic caching algorithm

For caching targeted areas on the client side, we used SQLite on mobile phones as an embedded relational database. It is serverless, highly portable, easy to use, efficient, and reliable. SQLite is used in numerous applications such as in Apple's Aperture photography software and the Safari web browser. We also used SpatiaLite as a spatial extender of SQLite for caching AOIs (i.e., rectangles) that are retrieved from the database server.

4   Experimental Study

In this section, we discuss the performance of our system for varying extra prefetched distances. We show the performance of our algorithm on three smartphones with different configurations for different caching scenarios.

Experimental Setup. Three mobile phones used for our analyses are OnePlus 3T with 6 GB RAM and 64 GB of internal memory, Samsung Galaxy Note 4 with 4 GB RAM and 32 GB of internal memory, and Nexus-5 with 2 GB RAM and 16 GB of internal memory. We tested the results of our algorithm on a backend server using PostgreSQL v9.6 with spatial extender PostGIS v2.4, and MongoDB v3.6. Our database resides on a Windows server with 8 GB memory using Intel Core i5 2.7 GHz processor. It should be mentioned that we used the geometry data type in SQLite to store each AOI which is 120 bytes. Considering that the primary key associated with each AOI is of type integer (2 bytes), therefore, each row in the cache takes 122 bytes.

Our dataset consists of one million rectangles (i.e., domain scientists' AOIs). We randomly generated twenty thousand rectangles in each state of the United States. Each state is considered as a bounding box, and the random points are generated within each box. Then, we generated AOIs by randomly choosing two points which are the two ends of each rectangle's diagonal. Generated rectangles could be either overlapping or non-overlapping. On average, there are 46 AOIs in each 1 km radius.

Experimental Details. In order to test our algorithm, we simulated the scenarios in which a participant is moving for five kilometers from the initial location while collecting data. We assume that the participant is only interested to see the AOIs within 1 km of their location at any given point of time. In order to compare the performance of different caching approaches, we assumed that the number of AOIs updates every 0.5 km (therefore, the location information is captured every 0.5 km). We created an array of locations for each route and calculated the average time required to show AOIs if the user moves for 5 km by varying extra prefetched distances. For instance, if the extra prefetched distance is set to 2 km, the application retrieves the AOIs within 3 km radius from the database and inserts into the cache. At the start location, the response time is equal to the time required for retrieving data from the database, clearing the cache, inserting into the cache, fetching the AOIs within 1 km from the cache, and showing them to the user. At locations 0.5 km, 1 km, 1.5 km, and 2 km, the response time equals to the fetching time from the cache. Going one step further, at 2.5 km, some of the AOIs within 1 km radius is not in the cache anymore. Therefore, the application needs to retrieve the new data from the database server again and follow the steps depicted in Fig. 6. We continue the same steps up to the 5th kilometer of the route and average the response time of all 11 points (start point, end point, and the 9 points in the middle). We assign this average response time to that route. We compared the results of our algorithm by varying the extra prefetched distances for which the data were cached. Table 1 shows the percentage of cache misses associated with different prefetched distances for the routes used for the following experiments.

We perform the following three experiments to test the caching on different mobile phones on LTE network.

Table 1. Prefetched distance and cache misses.

Prefetched distance (km)	Percentage of cache misses
0	100%
1	36%
2	27%
3	18%
4	18%

4.1   First Approach: Basic Caching

In the first experiment, we test the performance of the caching algorithm exactly as explained in Fig. 6. In other words, this experiment includes the following steps:

1. Retrieving the data (both the specified and extra- prefetched distance) from the database.
2. Clearing the cache.
3. Inserting into the cache.
4. Fetching the required data from the cache.
5. Showing the results for the specified distance to the user.

In this experiment, the x-axis represents the extra prefetched distances, and the y-axis shows the average response time to show the AOIs. As shown in Fig. 7, we observed that the performance of the algorithm improves as the extra prefetched distance increases up to a certain point, then it degrades for 4 km of extra prefetched data. We can find the reason in Table 1, which shows the percentage of the cache misses for 3 km and 4 km extra prefetched distance is the same. Therefore, inserting more data into the cache and fetching from it takes more time. In Fig. 7, the depicted values for the extra prefetched distance of zero shows the time required to retrieve the data from the database server (at that step, the cache is still empty).

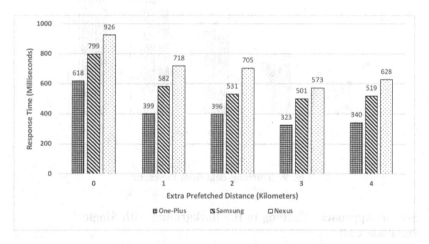

Fig. 7. Performance of the basic caching

To have a better understanding of the caching performance, we calculated the cache insertion and fetching time on different phones. Figure 8 depicts the time it took to insert the AOIs into the cache of different mobile phones. There is a considerable increase in the insertion time as the number of AOIs increases. Figure 9 depicts the fetching time for the same number of AOIs. The difference between the insertion and fetching time is noticeable. On average, the insertion time is 7.5 times more than the fetching time. Therefore, we got to know that cache insertion is a very expensive operation and to improve the total response time in such applications, we need to mainly focus on the insertion operation.

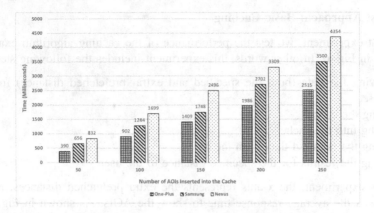

Fig. 8. Inserting data into the cache

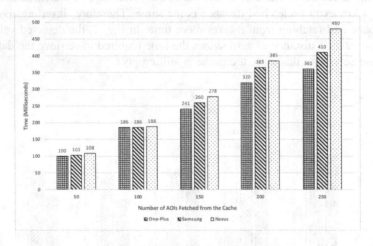

Fig. 9. Fetching data from the cache

4.2 Second Approach: Caching in the Background with Single Database Call

In the second experiment, we test the performance of the algorithm by inserting the data into the cache in the background. In other words, this experiment includes the following steps:

1. Retrieving data (both the specified and extra-prefetched distance) from the database. This step consists of two queries in one database hit, i.e., one query for the whole data and the other one for the specified distance only.
2. Showing the results for the specified distance to the user.

3. Clearing the cache in the background.
4. Inserting into the cache in the background (insertion is an expensive operation).
5. Fetching the required data from the cache for the following locations of the user.

Instead of inserting the data into the cache (which is an expensive operation) and then showing it to the user, in this experiment we first retrieve both extra prefetched and specified distance AOIs from the database server. Then, the application shows the specified distance AOIs directly to the user, and the extra prefetched distance AOIs are inserted into the cache in the background as participants are moving. As shown in Fig. 10, there is a drastic increase in the performance of this approach compared to the first approach. In this figure, when the extra prefetched distance in zero, it means that the application retrieves the data from the database server and nothing is inserted into the cache yet.

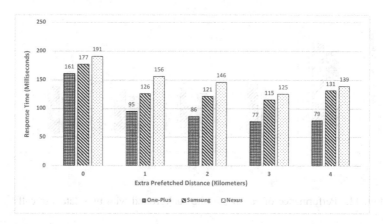

Fig. 10. Performance of caching in the background with single database call

4.3   Third Approach: Caching in the Background with Two Database Calls

In the third experiment, we test the performance of the algorithm same as previous experiment, and the only difference was the fact that instead of retrieving the whole data in the first step, we only retrieved AOIs within the specified distance to be shown to the users. In the next step, we query the database for the second time to retrieve the whole data. In other words, this experiment includes the following steps:

1. Retrieving data (specified distance only) from the database.
2. Showing the results for the specified distance to the user.

3. Retrieving data (both the specified and extra-prefetched distance) from the database in the background.
4. Clearing the cache in the background.
5. Inserting into the cache in the background.
6. Fetching the required data from the cache for the following locations of the user.

In this approach, while the application is showing the AOIs to the users, retrieving the whole data and the other steps happen in the background. As depicted in Fig. 11, we can see a performance increase on all the phones. In this figure again, the extra prefetched distance of zero shows that there is no data in the cache and the depicted numbers show the time it took to retrieve the data from the database server.

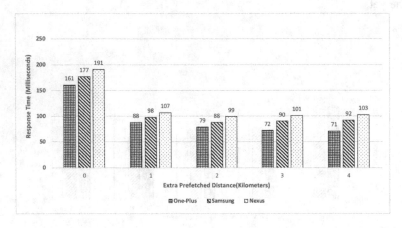

Fig. 11. Performance of caching in the background with two database calls

Comparing the Three Approaches. In order to make an unbiased conclusion, we repeated the experiments associated with each of the three caching approaches on 10 different routes. Figure 12 depicts the average response time to show the AOIs to the users. We observed that the third approach performs 5.48 times faster than the first approach and 10% faster than the second approach. Therefore, for proactive and targeted participatory sensing applications, the third caching approach would be the best choice. Although it is reasonable to have a limit for caching the data, we cannot generalize the observation in our experiments which shows going beyond 3 km of extra prefetched distance leads to performance degradation. In fact, the optimum cache limit is application- specific, and it pretty much depends on the number of nearby AOIs.

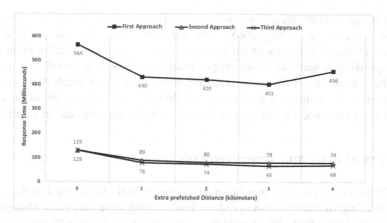

Fig. 12. Performance comparison of the three approaches

5 Related Works

In this section, we review some related studies. Caching the data has been widely used in mobile environments for improving access time. However, cached data becomes obsolete due to the movement of users known as location-dependent data invalidation [20]. Several approaches are proposed to overcome this challenge.

Zheng et al. [19] proposed location dependent data cache invalidation and replacement under a geometric model. They introduced polygon endpoints and app circle invalidation schemes for representing the valid scopes (i.e., regions within which data values are valid). Polygon endpoint records coordinates of polygons representing the valid scope. However, when there are a large number of endpoints, they will consume a substantial portion of the cache space. They also introduced an alternative approximation scheme, which uses inscribed circles to approximate a polygon. However, this scheme treats valid data as invalid for data points which are outside the circle but within the polygon. In order to make a balance between the overhead and precision, a caching-efficiency-based method was proposed. Various cache replacement policies such as probability area and probability area inverse distance in location-dependent services were also proposed in this paper. Access probability, data distance, and valid scope were three factors considered for cache replacement. In the probability area, valid scope and access probability were considered for calculating the cost function, whereas, in the probability area inverse distance, all three factors, i.e., access probability, valid scope, and data distance were considered for calculating the cost function. Both policies choose data with least cost as the victim.

Xu et al. [22] addressed the issue of location-dependent cache invalidation under a cell-based systems location model. Bit vector with compression grouped vector with compression, and implicit scope information is the three methods that were proposed. In this study, it is assumed that each geographical area is partitioned into service areas and each service area can cover one or multiple cells. Also, each service area is associated with an ID for identification purposes which is broadcasted periodically to all mobile clients in that service area. Bit Vector with compression uses bit vector, and its length is equal to the service areas in a system. Every cache item is associated with a bit vector; however, associating every cache item with bit vector is an overhead for a large system. Grouped vector with compression was proposed as a solution to bit vector with compression, where the whole geographical area is divided into disjoint districts and all the data service areas within a district form a group. In Implicit Scope Information model, the database is divided into multiple logical sections based on a valid scope. Data in the same logical section has the same location validation information.

6 Future Works and Improvements

MongoDB is one of the most popular open-source NoSQL databases. For the sake of performance improvement, we analyzed the third caching approach using MongoDB to compare with PostgreSQL. We created the same dataset for MongoDB and performed the same experiments. As depicted in Fig. 13, the performance is consistently better on MongoDB as opposed to PostgreSQL. Therefore, for future work, we are migrating to MongoDB.

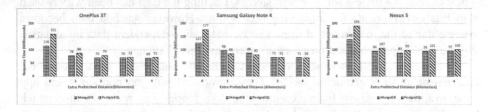

Fig. 13. Performance of the third approach on different database servers

We would also like to compare the performance of the discussed approaches by updating the cache rather than clearing the cache and inserting data into it again. Considering that in participatory sensing applications users often take a loop-like trajectory where they end up near their start location, there are some overlaps with the previously visited AOIs. As a result, updating the cache may outperform our current approaches.

7 Conclusion

Widespread use of mobile phones with embedded sensors has introduced the term participatory sensing. Despite the many advantages of such frameworks, there are some challenges and limitations. Most of the participatory sensing applications are passive, and there is little or no communication between the domain scientists and the participants. In this study, we present a mobile and web-based approach to enable domain scientists to acquire crowd-sensed data from particular areas of interest adequately. Domain scientists mark the areas and participants are proactively informed about the sensing opportunities near their current location. In order to show the nearby AOIs to the participants, data need to be retrieved from a database server frequently, which leads to performance degradation. In order to increase the performance, we introduce a caching approach that stores and prefetches the nearby AOIs locally from the participant's mobile phones. We analyze the performance of the algorithm for three different caching approaches on different mobile phones and present the approach with the best performance.

Acknowledgment. This research has been partially funded by the National Science Foundation (NSF) under grants CCF-1442672 and SCC-1637277 and gifts from Accenture Research Labs. Any opinions, findings, and conclusions or recommendations expressed in this material are those of the authors and do not necessarily reflect the views of the NSF or other funding agencies and companies mentioned above.

References

1. Christin, D., Reinhardt, A., Kanhere, S.S., Hollick, M.: A survey on privacy in mobile participatory sensing applications. J. Syst. Softw. **84**(11), 1928–1946 (2011)
2. Shilton, K., Estrin, D.: Participatory sensing and new challenges to US privacy policy
3. Guo, B., Yu, Z., Zhou, X., Zhang, D.: From participatory sensing to mobile crowd sensing. In: 2014 IEEE International Conference on Pervasive Computing and Communication Workshops (PERCOM WORKSHOPS), pp. 593–598. IEEE (2014)
4. Tonekaboni, N.H., Kulkarni, S., Ramaswamy, L.: Edge-based anomalous sensor placement detection for participatory sensing of urban heat islands. In: 2018 IEEE International Smart Cities Conference (ISC2), pp. 1–8. IEEE (2018)
5. Ganti, R.K., Ye, F., Lei, H.: Mobile crowdsensing: current state and future challenges. IEEE Commun. Mag. **49**(11), 32–39 (2011)
6. Kapadia, A., Kotz, D., Triandopoulos, N.: Opportunistic sensing: security challenges for the new paradigm. In: 2009 First International Communication Systems and Networks and Workshops, pp. 1–10. IEEE (2009)
7. Kanhere, S.S.: Participatory sensing: crowdsourcing data from mobile smartphones in urban spaces. In: Hota, C., Srimani, Pradip K. (eds.) ICDCIT 2013. LNCS, vol. 7753, pp. 19–26. Springer, Heidelberg (2013). https://doi.org/10.1007/978-3-642-36071-8_2
8. Mathur, S., et al.: Parknet: drive-by sensing of road-side parking statistics. In: Proceedings of the 8th International Conference on Mobile Systems, Applications, and Services, pp. 123–136. ACM (2010)
9. Mohan, P., Padmanabhan, V.N., Ramjee, R.: Nericell: rich monitoring of road and traffic conditions using mobile smartphones. In: Proceedings of the 6th ACM Conference on Embedded Network Sensor Systems, pp. 323–336. ACM (2008)
10. Deng, L., Cox, L.P.: Livecompare: grocery bargain hunting through participatory sensing. In: Proceedings of the 10th Workshop on Mobile Computing Systems and Applications, p. 4. ACM (2009)
11. Youdale, N.: Haze watch: database server and mobile applications for measuring and evaluating air pollution exposure. Electrical Engineering and Telecommunication School, University of New South Wales, Sydney, NSW, Australia, Technical report (2010)
12. Von Kaenel, M., Sommer, P., Wattenhofer, R.: Ikarus: large-scale participatory sensing at high altitudes. In: Proceedings of the 12th Workshop on Mobile Computing Systems and Applications, pp. 63–68. ACM (2011)

13. Maisonneuve, N., Stevens, M., Niessen, M.E., Steels, L.: NoiseTube: measuring and mapping noise pollution with mobile phones. In: Athanasiadis, I.N., Rizzoli, A.E., Mitkas, P. A., Gómez, J.M. (eds.) Information Technologies in Environmental Engineering. Environmental Science and Engineering. Springer, Berlin (2009). https://doi.org/10.1007/978-3-540-88351-7_16

14. Kanjo, E.: NoiseSPY: a real-time mobile phone platform for urban noise monitoring and mapping. Mob. Netw. Appl. 15(4), 562–574 (2010)

15. Kim, S., Robson, C., Zimmerman, T., Pierce, J., Haber, E.M.: Creek watch: pairing usefulness and usability for successful citizen science. In: Proceedings of the SIGCHI Conference on Human Factors in Computing Systems, pp. 2125–2134. ACM (2011)

16. Ganti, R.K., Pham, N., Ahmadi, H., Nangia, S., Abdelzaher, T.F.: GreenGPS: a participatory sensing fuel-efficient maps application. In: Proceedings of the 8th International Conference on Mobile Systems, Applications, and Services, pp. 151–164. ACM (2010)

17. Reddy, S., Parker, A., Hyman, J., Burke, J., Estrin, D., Hansen, M.: Image browsing, processing, and clustering for participatory sensing: lessons from a DietSense prototype. In: Proceedings of the 4th Workshop on Embedded Networked Sensors, pp. 13–17. ACM (2007)

18. Eisenman, S.B., Miluzzo, E., Lane, N.D., Peterson, R.A., Ahn, G.-S., Campbell, A.T.: BikeNet: a mobile sensing system for cyclist experience mapping. ACM Trans. Sens. Netw. (TOSN) 6(1), 6 (2009)

19. Zheng, B., Xu, J., Lee, D.L.: Cache invalidation and replacement strategies for location-dependent data in mobile environments. IEEE Trans. Comput. 51(10), 1141–1153 (2002)

20. Ren, Q., Dunham, M.H.: Using semantic caching to manage location dependent data in mobile computing. In: Proceedings of the 6th Annual International Conference on Mobile Computing and Networking, pp. 210–221. ACM (2000)

21. Kanjo, E., Bacon, J., Roberts, D., Landshoff, P.: MobSens: making smart phones smarter. IEEE Pervasive Comput. 8(4), 50–57 (2009)

22. Xu, J., Tang, X., Lee, D.L., Hu, Q.: Cache coherency in location-dependent information services for mobile environment. In: Leong, H.V., Lee, W.-C., Li, B., Yin, L. (eds.) MDA 1999. LNCS, vol. 1748, pp. 182–193. Springer, Heidelberg (1999). https://doi.org/10.1007/3-540-46669-X_16

Forecasting Long-Term Call Traffic Based on Seasonal Dependencies

Longchun Cao, Kui Ma, Bin Cao$^{(\boxtimes)}$, and Jing Fan

Zhejiang University of Technology, Hangzhou, China
bincao@zjut.edu.cn

Abstract. How to use future call traffic for scheduling different staffs to work in a month or a week is an important task for call center. In this problem setting, the call traffic should be predicted in a long-term way where the forecasting results for different periods are required. However, it is very challenging to solve this problem due to the randomness nature of the call traffic and the multiple forecasting in long term. Current methods cannot solve this problem since they either merely focus on short-term forecasting for the next hour or next day, or ignore call-holding time for call traffic prediction. In this paper, we propose an effective method for predicting long-term call traffic with multiple forecasting results for different future periods, e.g., every 15 min, and take both call arrival rate and call-holding time into consideration through the Erlang. In our method, the seasonal dependencies are summarized by performing data analysis, then different features based on these dependencies are extracted for training the prediction model.In order to forecast call traffic of multiple time buckets, we propose two strategies based on different features. The evaluation results show that the features, the prediction models and the strategies are feasible.

Keywords: Long-term · Multiple · Call traffic · Forecasting · Seasonal dependence

1 Introduction

Nowadays, more and more companies set up call centers to help them process customer requests through the telephone. Knowing future call traffic in different time buckets in advance can help call centers to further improve their service quality. However, it is far from trivial to perform effective long-term call traffic forecasting: First, the call arrival process is very complicated and it may be affected by different causes in different time buckets [1–3], e.g., many people may make calls to the taxi service center when they want to take rides to their offices in the morning. Second, some tasks in the call center usually require the awareness of call traffic in different time buckets within a future long term, e.g., the call center wants to schedule the staffs to different time buckets based on the corresponding call traffic for the next week, and as far as we know, the problem of forecasting call traffic of multiple time buckets haven't been well studied. Most existing solutions for call traffic forecasting merely focus on the prediction for the single time bucket of the next hour or day [3–5].

© ICST Institute for Computer Sciences, Social Informatics and Telecommunications Engineering 2019
Published by Springer Nature Switzerland AG 2019. All Rights Reserved
X. Wang et al. (Eds.): CollaborateCom 2019, LNICST 292, pp. 231–246, 2019.
https://doi.org/10.1007/978-3-030-30146-0_16

In this paper, based on the observed seasonal dependencies of historical call traffic data, we propose an effective method for predicting long-term call traffic with multiple forecasting results for different future time buckets. It is important to note that the call traffic here is calculated by Erlang formula [6] where both the call arrival rate and the average holding time are considered. In our method, we first extract the following three types of seasonal features: (1) Date time features, like the year, month, day, and the beginning of the time bucket, (2) Special days features, such as the day of week, whether it is the weekend, the beginning, middle or end of a month, (3) Intraday and interday features, which correspond to the call traffic of the same time buckets in the past few days and the call traffic of previous time buckets. Then, in order to forecast call traffic of multiple time buckets, we propose two strategies based on whether taking into account the third feature type, i.e., intraday and interday features. The first strategy that merely considers first two types of the feature is to directly use supervised classification method, i.e., train the model that connect features and corresponding call traffic, and then perform the prediction by inputting the corresponding features. The second strategy performs the prediction in an incremental way, i.e., we first forecast the next call traffic, and then use the predicted result as the intraday and interday feature values for the next time bucket.

The classification method used in our work is the Random Forests (RF) [7] due to its robustness in real applications. Moreover, to demonstrate the effectiveness of our method, we use the real-world dataset from a China Telecom branch throughout the paper. The experimental evaluation shows that considering different correlated dependencies play an important role in the call traffic forecasting. The contributions in this paper can be summarized as follows:

- We extract a variety of features based on different types of seasonal dependencies, including date time type features, special days features, and the intraday and interday features.
- We propose an incremental strategy for forecasting call traffic of multiple time buckets when intraday and interday features are considered.
- We perform extensive experiments and prove the effectiveness of the proposed method.

The rest of the paper is organized as follows. In Sect. 2, we briefly introduce the dataset. The feature construction based on the seasonal dependencies is detailed in Sect. 3. Then we present the method for forecasting call traffic in Sect. 4. Section 5 shows the experimental results. Related work is reviewed in Sect. 6. Finally, in Sect. 7, we conclude the paper and describe future work.

2   Dataset

The data we use is from a call center of China Telecom which has millions of customers, and its background database records all the information about the call center service. Note that the original data we get from the background database of the call center is from 1 January 2016 to 31 December 2018, and each time bucket that collects call traffic is 15-min intervals.

In order to settle down our problem with minimal cost, we only extract the following five fields from the original database:

- *callID*, the unique identification for the call services in each time bucket.
- *callDate*, the begin date of each time bucket.
- *callTime*, the begin time of each time bucket.
- *callArrivals*, the volume of the call arrivals which are collected in each time bucket.
- *callDuration*, the average call-holding time (the average time of a phone call) in each time bucket.

For the sake of describing the records of the call service more simply and effectively, we generate a new filed to identify the records. We name *callDate* plus *callTime* as *callDatetime* as the unique identification for the call services over 15-min intervals. Furthermore, we name the result of multiply *callArrivals* per second by *callDuration* as *callTraffic*. Finally, we get two fields that we need through data preprocessing: *callDatetime* and *callTraffic*, which can be computed by Eqs. 1 and 2, respectively.

$$callDatetime = callDate + callTime \tag{1}$$

$$callTraffic = \frac{callArrivals}{15 \times 60} \times callDuration \tag{2}$$

3   Feature Engineering

In this section, firstly, we analyze the data and introduce what features to be extracted. The rest of the section, we describe how to extract the features.

3.1   Data Analysis

The call traffic is different in different years, months, days and time buckets, and exhibit intraday, daily, weekly monthly and yearly seasonalities on the influence of people's normal routine and scheduling of the call center. We put the year, the month, the day and the time bucket into the features of the call traffic. Furthermore, we found that call traffic of some special days such as the day of the week, the weekend, the beginning, middle or end of a month, and holidays will suddenly increase or decrease. Therefore, we also take these factors as features. Moreover, under the influence of external factors like the weather or promotions, the impact will last for a period of time or days. As a result, the call traffic is related to the call traffic of previous time buckets, and the call traffic of the same time buckets in the past few days. Undoubtedly, we also consider these two factors as features. Taking these effective features which are related to the call traffic into consideration will make the forecasting more accurate.

Due to the call traffic influenced by date, time, external factors, and based on the analysis of the data mentioned above, we extract the following three types of features:

- Date time features, which have the date time dependencies, like the year, month, day, and total minutes of the begin time of the time bucket.
- Special days features, such as the day of the week, whether it is the weekend, the beginning, middle or end of a month, and whether it is a festival. Note that, the festival is the Spring Festival in this paper.
- Intraday and interday features, that is the call traffic of previous time buckets and the call traffic of the same time buckets in the past few days.

3.2 Date Time Features

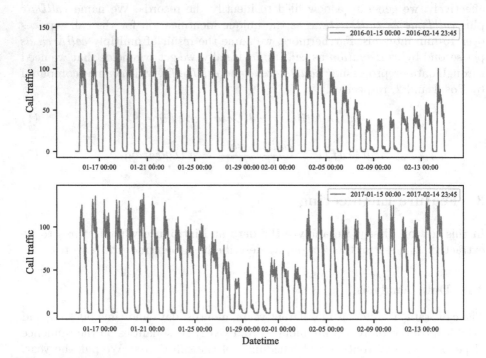

Fig. 1. 15-min call traffic from 15 January, 2016 to 14 February, 2016 and 15 January, 2017 to 14 February, 2017.

Figure 1 provides examples of the two time series. We plot 15-min call traffic from 15 January, 2016 to 14 February, 2016 and 15 January, 2017 to 14 February, 2017. Observe from different years, months, days and time buckets, we can easily find that the call traffic is completely different. So that we take the year, month, day and time bucket as the features. By calculating the timestamp, we can get the values of the date time features. For example, the timestamp is "2016-01-15

07:30", and the values of the year, month, day and total minutes of the time are "2016", "1", "15" and "450". Note that we named *totalMinuetes* as the total minutes of the begin time of the time bucket, which can be calculated by Eq. 3. To sum up, the date time features are the *year, month, day* and *totalMinuetes*.

$$totalMinuetes = hour \times 60 + minute \tag{3}$$

3.3   Special Days Features

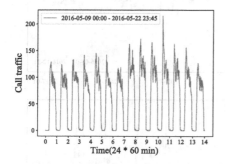

Fig. 2. 15-min call traffic over two consecutive weeks from 9 May 2016 to 22 May 2016.

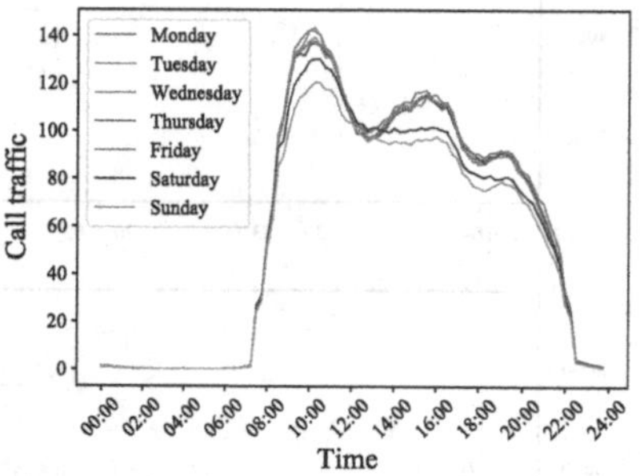

Fig. 3. Intraday profiles of call traffic by weekday and weekend from 1 January, 2016 to 31 December, 2017.

Weekly Features. From Fig. 2, we illustrate weekly seasonality by plotting daily call traffic from 9 May, 2016 to 22 May, 2016 including weekends. It is not hard to find that the call traffic is not equal every day of a week and less on weekends than other days, such as 14 May, 2016 and 15 May, 2016. In order to make this view more convincing, we analyze the data from 1 January, 2016 to 31 December, 2017 and plot 15-minutely average call traffic every day of the week, in Fig. 3. Although the call traffic of every day has a similar distribution, the call traffic at the same time bucket is still not equal and less on weekends than other days. We named *dayofweek* as the day of the week and *isweekend* as whether it is the weekend. The values are given in Table 1. To sum up, the weekly features are *dayofweek* and *isweekend*.

Monthly Features. In Fig. 4 we plot the call traffic per day arriving at the call center from 1 January, 2016 to 31 December, 2016 and from 1 January, 2017 to 31 December, 2017. It is very clear that the volumes of call traffic are particularly large at the beginning and end of every month and the call traffic at the middle of the month is also larger than the other days of the month. In Fig. 5, we plot the average daily call traffic of the same day of the different month from 1 January, 2016 to 31 December, 2017. Through the analysis of call traffic

Table 1. The values of the weekly features in the day of week.

	Mon.	Tues.	Wed.	Thurs.	Fri.	Sat.	Sun.
dayofweek	1	2	3	4	5	6	7
isweekend	0	0	0	0	0	1	1

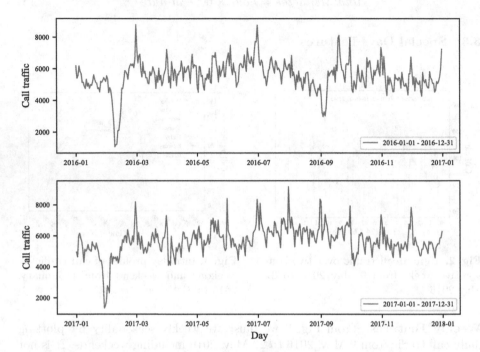

Fig. 4. Daily call traffic over successive months from 1 January, 2016 to 31 December, 2016 and 1 January, 2017 to 31 December, 2017.

distribution and the experience of staffs, The values of the beginning, middle, and end of the month are generated by Eq. 4, and the monthly feature here is named *sectionofmonth*.

$$sectionofmonth = \begin{cases} 0, & otherwise \\ 1, & day \in [1,5] \\ 2, & day \in [16,22] \\ 3, & day \in [days-2, days] \end{cases} \tag{4}$$

where *day* is the day of a month, *days* is the total days of a month.

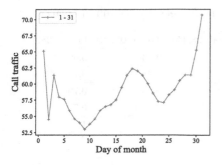

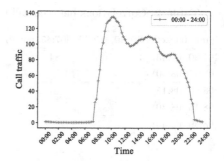

Fig. 5. Average daily call traffic of the same day of the different month from 1 January, 2016 to 31 December, 2017.

Fig. 6. Intraday profiles of average call traffic per day from 1 January, 2016 to 31 December, 2017.

Yearly Features. Observe from Figs. 1 and 4, the call traffic in the Spring Festival from 7 January, 2016 to 13 January, 2016 and from 27 January, 2017 to 2 February, 2017 is obviously less than the other days. The reason for the sharp decline in call traffic during the Spring Festival is that most people are on holiday and only a few staffs are on duty. Furthermore, the annual Spring Festival is not on fixed days. We refer to those days with unusual call traffic as special days of the year. In this paper, the special days we mainly consider is the Spring Festival. The yearly feature here is named *isfestival*, and the value can be calculated by Eq. 5.

$$isfestival = \begin{cases} 1, & is\ during\ the\ Spring\ Festival \\ 0, & otherwise \end{cases} \tag{5}$$

3.4 Intraday and Interday Features

Intraday Features. From the Figs. 1, 2 and 3, we know that intraday profiles of call traffic in every day is similar to each other. For a more microscopic view of intraday calll traffic, we plot intraday profiles of average call traffic per day from 1 January, 2016 to 31 December, 2017, in Fig. 6. We find that the trend of call traffic is almost the same for a consecutive period of time, e.g., from *07:00* to *11:00*, the call traffic increase at an almost same rate. In addition to the schedule of the call center, we divide the day into several sections with a similar trend. According to the trend of increase and decrease, here the sections are [22:30, 07:30), [07:30, 11:00), [11:00, 13:00), [13:00, 16:30), [16:30, 18:00), [18:00, 19:30) and [19:30, 22:30). The minimum duration is [16:30, 18:00) and [18:00, 19:30), and the count of the time buckets is *6*. Hence, the intraday features are the call traffic in the past up to *6* time buckets. For example, if we want to forecast the call traffic of [10:00, 10:15), the intraday features are the call traffic of [09:45, 10:00), [09:30, 09:45), [09:15, 09:30), [09:00, 09:15), [08:45, 09:00) and [08:30, 08:45). In Table 2, we illustrate the intraday correlation in consecutive 15-min intervals from *07:30* to *08:30*. The measure to be used to capture intraday

Table 2. Correlations between call traffic in consecutive 15-min intervals.

Time bucket	[07:30, 07:45)	[07:45, 08:00)	[08:00, 08:15)	[08:15, 08:30)	[08:30, 08:45)
[07:30, 07:45)	1	0.84	0.76	0.73	0.69
[07:45, 08:00)		1	0.81	0.78	0.76
[08:00, 08:15)			1	0.88	0.79
[08:15, 08:30)				1	0.79
[08:30, 08:45)					1

dependence in call traffic is Pearson's correlation coefficient. Table 2 illustrate two properties which are observed very commonly in reality:

- Correlations between the adjacent time buckets within a day are strong and positive.
- Intraday correlations are slightly smaller, with longer lags.

Interday Features. In Figs. 2 and 3, the call traffic exhibit daily and weekly seasonalities. The volumes and trend of call traffic are similar at the same time bucket on each day of the week. The interday features are the call traffic at the same time bucket in past up to 7 days. For instance, if we want to forecast the call traffic of [10:00, 10:15) on 8 January, the interday features are the call traffic of [10:00, 10:15) on 7 January, 6 January, 5 January, 4 January, 3 January, 2 January and 1 January. In Table 3, we illustrate the interday correlation in consecutive days from Monday to Sunday. The measure to be used to capture interday dependence in call traffic is Pearson's correlation coefficient. Table 3 illustrate two properties which are observed very commonly in reality:

- Correlations between successive days are strong and positive.
- Interday correlations are slightly smaller, with longer lags.

Table 3. Correlations between call traffic in consecutive days.

The day of the week	Mon.	Tues.	Wed.	Thurs.	Fri.	Sat.	Sun.
Mon.	1	0.89	0.80	0.74	0.72	0.64	0.60
Tues.		1	0.87	0.79	0.79	0.72	0.62
Wed.			1	0.85	0.81	0.75	0.63
Thurs.				1	0.87	0.78	0.65
Fri.					1	0.87	0.73
Sat.						1	0.83
Sun.							1

4   Forecasting Call Traffic

In this section, we will introduce the process of forecasting call traffic, including call traffic model training and call traffic forecasting. Firstly, we select the training data that we need from the existing call traffic data. Then we use the training data to train the model. Finally, input the features of the time buckets to be forecasted into the model to obtain the call traffic.

4.1   Call Traffic Model Training

Call traffic model training includes the training data preparation and model training. Firstly we introduce how to prepare the training data, then show the way of the model training.

Training Data Preparation. For the reason that the call traffic exhibit yearly and monthly dependencies, the training data we have prepared is the data for the first few months of the forecast month and the same months in the previous years. For example, in Fig. 7, if we want to forecast the call traffic of September 2018 and set the number of previous years to 2, the number of previous months to 3, the training data is from June 2018 to August 2018, from June 2017 to September 2017 and from June 2016 to September 2016.

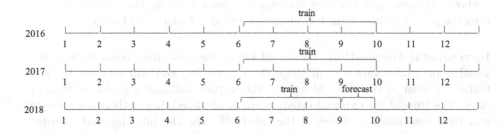

Fig. 7. Training data for September 2018.

Model Training. In this paper, we choose the RF to train model, which is a flexible and easy to use machine learning algorithm that always produces a good result even without hyper-parameter tuning. Since the RF is a supervised learning algorithm, we should know the features and target of each time bucket. Firstly, we can get the training data of the forecast month according to Sect. 4.1, then get the preprocessed data according to Sect. 2. Note that, if you select intraday and interday features to train the model, make sure the values are not null. Because the first few data has no intraday or interday features. Next, we can get the features of each training data according to Sect. 3, and the corresponding target is the call traffic of each time bucket. See Table 4, $tb_{d,i}$ is the ith time bucket on the dth day, $dt_{d,i}$ is the corresponding features of date time, $sd_{d,i}$

is the corresponding features of special days, and $t_{d,i}$ is the corresponding call traffic. Finally, we can select several of the features and target of each time bucket to train the model by using the RF. After training, we can get the model for forecasting call traffic.

Table 4. Features and target of each time bucket.

Time bucket	Features			Target
	Date time	Special days	Intraday and interday	
$\vdots$	$\vdots$	$\vdots$	$\vdots$	$\vdots$
$tb_{d,i}$	$dt_{d,i}$	$sd_{d,i}$	$t_{d,i-1}, t_{d,i-2}, \cdots, t_{d-1,i}, t_{d-2,i}, \cdots$	$t_{d,i}$
$tb_{d,i+1}$	$dt_{d,i+1}$	$sd_{d,i+1}$	$t_{d,i}, t_{d,i-1}, \cdots, t_{d-1,i+1}, t_{d-2,i+1}, \cdots$	$t_{d,i+1}$
$\vdots$	$\vdots$	$\vdots$	$\vdots$	$\vdots$
$tb_{d+1,i}$	$dt_{d+1,i}$	$sd_{d+1,i}$	$t_{d+1,i-1}, t_{d+1,i-2}, \cdots, t_{d,i}, t_{d-1,i}, \cdots$	$t_{d+1,i}$
$tb_{d+1,i+1}$	$dt_{d+1,i+1}$	$sd_{d+1,i+1}$	$t_{d+1,i}, t_{d+1,i-1}, \cdots, t_{d,i+1}, t_{d-1,i+1}, \cdots$	$t_{d+1,i+1}$
$\vdots$	$\vdots$	$\vdots$	$\vdots$	$\vdots$

4.2   Call Traffic Forecasting

This section firstly introduces the incremental forecasting, then presents two strategies to forecast the call traffic. The first strategy uses the model trained without intraday and interday features to forecast, while the second strategy uses the model trained with intraday and interday features to forecast.

Incremental Forecasting. As we all know, the external events such as the weather or promotions will influence the call traffic, and will increase the call traffic for most of the time. Moreover, the impact will last a period of time or days. The time of the external events occur is not fixed, hence there are no date and time seasonalities. However, the call traffic has the intraday and interday dependencies, i.e., it related to the call traffic of previous time buckets and the call traffic of the same time buckets in the past few days. Therefore, we can forecast the call traffic according to the previous. For one month forecast, we can forecast the first call traffic based on the previous call traffic, and the remaining call traffic should be forecasted in an incremental way. Since when we forecast the first call traffic, the previous call traffic has been given, but the previous call traffic of the rest call traffic to be forecasted is unknown. Consequently, before forecasting the next call traffic, we must first forecast the previous. For example, the month to be forecasted is September, we first forecast the call traffic of [00:00, 00:15) on 1 September according to the previous call traffic that is given, then we forecast the call traffic of [00:15, 00:30) on 1 September, according to the call traffic of [00:00, 00:15) on 1 September that has been forecasted and the previous call traffic that is given. So that we can forecast the next call traffic in this incremental way. Finally, we get the call traffic of every time bucket in the month.

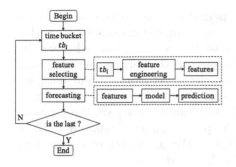

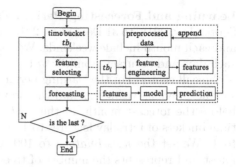

Fig. 8. The flowchart of forecasting without intraday and interday features.

Fig. 9. The flowchart of forecasting with intraday and interday features.

Forecasting Without Intraday and Interday Features. In this method, the features of each time bucket we can get by calculating the beginning timestamp of the time bucket as we mentioned in Sect. 3. Then we can forecast the call traffic of each time bucket by the model trained without intraday and interday features in Sect. 4.1. The flowchart of Fig. 8 details the adopted forecast strategy.

Forecasting with Intraday and Interday Features. As we mentioned in Sect. 3.4, the associations between the call traffic of adjacent time bucket play a role in forecasting the next call traffic. The call traffic is related by the previous call traffic. Hence, the incremental forecasting method we mentioned above is a good choice. First of all, we could forecast the first time bucket of call traffic, because it's features could be extracted from the preprocessed data. Then, before we forecasting the second time bucket of call traffic, we should append the call traffic of the first time bucket to the preprocessed data so that when extracting the features for the second time bucket, we can get the intraday features. Hence, we can forecast the next in the same way. In the end, we could forecast all the call traffic using the incremental method. The flowchart of Fig. 9 details the adopted forecast strategy.

5   Experimental Evaluation

In this section, we conduct an empirical study using the data set described in Sect. 4 and quantify the accuracy of the forecasts generated by the candidate models. To analyze the impact of each group of features, we compare the models with different features based on their forecasting performance. We perform detailed experimental evaluations from the following models:

- *model_d*, trained by date time features.
- *model_ds*, trained by date time and special days features.
- *model_di*, trained by date time features, intraday and interday features.
- *model_dsi*, trained by date time features, specials days, intraday and interday features.

Learning and Forecasting Period. The period we want to forecast is from 1 September, 2018, to 31 December, 2018. That is, we make forecasts for 4 months, and each month include weekends. We generate $24 \times 4 = 96$ predicted values for each day, and accuracy from *07:30* to *22:30*, which is the normal operating time of the call center. For the learning period, in order to get more training data, we set the previous years to 2 and the previous months to 11, that is all the data before the forecast month. In the *model_di* and *model_dsi*, we set the previous time buckets of intraday features to 1 and the previous days of interday features to 1. We set the *n_estimators* to 100, which is the parameter of the random forest and represents the number of trees in the forest.

Performance Measures. We quantify the accuracy of a point prediction by computing the *mean squared error* (MSE) per 15-min intervals, defined by

$$MSE = \frac{1}{N} \sum_{d,i} (V_{d,i} - \hat{V}_{d,i})^2, \tag{6}$$

where N is the total number of predictions made, $V_{d,i}$ is the volume of call traffic in the ith 15-min intervals of a given day d and $\hat{V}_{d,i}$ is the predicted value of $V_{d,i}$. Consistent with standard practice, we also consider the square root of the MSE, the *root mean squared error* (RMSE), given by

$$RMSE = \sqrt{MSE} = \sqrt{\frac{1}{N} \sum_{d,i} (V_{d,i} - \hat{V}_{d,i})^2}. \tag{7}$$

In addition to the MSE and RMSE, we compute, for a relative measure of accuracy, the *mean absolute percentage error* (MAPE) defined by

$$MAPE = \frac{1}{N} \sum_{d,i} \frac{\left| V_{d,i} - \hat{V}_{d,i} \right|}{V_{d,i}}. \tag{8}$$

Forecasting Performance. With the same parameter and training data, Table 5 shows the performance of all the models in different forecast months. In the performance of these four forecast months, *model_ds* always generates the most accurate point forecasts among all models considered. It means that the *model_ds* trained by date time features and special days fit well with the call traffic data which exhibit different types of seasonal dependencies. Compare *model_d* with *model_ds*, although *model_d* has considered the year, month, day and period of the day, and the performance is also very good, it has not considered the specials days. And the performance proves that special days features could help improve the accuracy of the forecasting. Compare *model_d* with *model_di*, the performance in November, 2018 shows that intraday and interday features have a positive effect on improving accuracy, but has no significant effect in the other three months. Hence, we can know that the call traffic mainly depends on date and time and associations between the adjacent call traffic have a little effect from the performance of *model_d*, *model_ds* and *model_di*. The *model_dsi* has the lowest accuracy in three months, it can be inferred that the specials days and intraday, interday features have conflicting relationships, which lead to a decrease in accuracy.

Table 5. Performance of each model in different months

n_estimators	Month	Model	MSE	RMSE	MAPE
100	2018.09	*model_d*	159.7	12.6	13.4
		model_ds	**133.7**	**11.7**	**12.1**
		model_di	141.2	11.9	13.5
		model_dsi	178.9	13.4	15.2
	2018.10	*model_d*	239.5	15.5	20.0
		model_ds	**170.6**	**13.1**	**17.2**
		model_di	242.9	15.6	20.9
		model_dsi	276.2	16.6	22.2
	2018.11	*model_d*	237.6	15.4	15.6
		model_ds	164.6	12.8	**13.1**
		model_di	172.3	13.1	14.1
		model_dsi	**135.9**	**11.7**	13.6
	2018.12	*model_d*	213.3	14.6	18.6
		model_ds	**147.9**	**12.2**	**16.4**
		model_di	168.3	13.0	18.4
		model_dsi	203.4	14.3	19.8
	average	*model_d*	212.5	14.5	16.9
		model_ds	**154.2**	**12.5**	**14.7**
		model_di	181.2	13.4	16.7
		model_dsi	198.6	14.0	17.7

The results of this section show that the model trained by date time and special days features usually lead to the more accurate point than the other models.

6   Related Work

As far as we know, there is little work directly related to forecasting call traffic for a month. However, call arrivals forecasting has been studied in a variety of other research. The call arrivals process can be modeled as a Poisson arrival process, and has been shown to possess several features [1,2,8–10]. Moreover, call center arrivals typically exhibit a significant dispersion relative to the Poisson distribution. Thus, a doubly stochastic Poisson arrival process may be more appropriate [3,11–14]. The method based on Poisson is modeled in a day, and do not consider the seasonal dependencies. The call center arrivals exhibit different types of dependencies. A reasonable forecasting model needs to account appropriately for some or all of the types of dependencies that exist in real data [3]. In the case where the call arrival rate has intraday and interday dependencies, standard time series models may be applied for forecasting call arrivals [3], such as *autoregressive integrated moving average* (ARIMA) models and *exponential smoothing* [15]. It forecast the next value, but in our problem, we should forecast the values of each time bucket in a month. In addition, some studies have proposed fixed-effects models [13,16–18] and mixed-effects models [12,13] to account for the intraday dependence, interday dependence, and inter-type dependence of call arrivals. Dimension reduction [17,19,20] and Bayesian techniques [16,21,22] have also been adopted in the literature. Although it takes the intraday and interday features into consideration, the other seasonal dependencies, e.g., date time dependencies, are ignored. Many forecasting models assume that specials days are outliers, and remove such days [23], or describe the application of singular vector decomposition for outlier detection but provide no empirical evaluation [20]. However, many other studies avoid this problem by assuming the data pre-cleansed [11,18,24–26]. However, in our problem, the period we forecast is one month, including special days, such as weekends, holidays.

In summary, the problem we want to solve in this paper could be distinguished from previous research from four main aspects:

- As far as we know, there is little work had been done on the problem of forecasting long-term call traffic of multiple time buckets.
- Different types of seasonal dependencies are not all considered.
- We choose the RF to train model, which is a supervised learning algorithm.

7   Conclusions

In this paper, we proposed the problem of forecasting long-term call traffic of multiple time buckets, which has not been well addressed so far. In order to solve this problem, we first take the call arrival rate and the average holding time into consideration. Then we extracted three groups of features, named date time features, special days features, intraday and interday features. Next we trained the models based on the features by using the method of the RF. At last, we proposed two strategies to forecast the call traffic based on whether taking into account the intraday and interday features. According to the experiments, we obtained following conclusions:

- All features we extracted work well in our problem;
- The intraday and interday features have a little effect on the performance.
- The second model, trained by date time and special days features is the best choice for our problem.

For future work, we are going to further study the dependencies of the call traffic and explore more reliable features to improve the quality of forecasting.

Acknowledgment. This research was partially supported by the National Key Research and Development Program of China (2018YFB1402802).

References

1. Aksin, Z., Armony, M., Mehrotra, V.: The modern call center: a multi-disciplinary perspective on operations management research. Prod. Oper. Manage. **16**(6), 665–688 (2007)
2. Cezik, M.T., L'Ecuyer, P.: Staffing multiskill call centers via linear programming and simulation. Manage. Sci. **54**(2), 310–323 (2008)
3. Ibrahim, R., Ye, H., L'Ecuyer, P., et al.: Modeling and forecasting call center arrivals: a literature survey and a case study. Int. J. Forecast. **32**(3), 865–874 (2016)
4. Oreshkin, B.N., Réegnard, N., L'Ecuyer, P.: Rate-based daily arrival process models with application to call centers. Oper. Res. **64**(2), 510–527 (2016)
5. Barrow, D.K.: Forecasting intraday call arrivals using the seasonal moving average method. J. Bus. Res. **69**(12), 6088–6096 (2016)
6. Rowlett R.: How many?: A dictionary of units of measurement (1999)
7. Breiman, L.: Random forests. Mach. Learn. **45**(1), 5–32 (2001)
8. Garnett, O., Mandelbaum, A., Reiman, M.: Designing a call center with impatient customers. Manuf. Serv. Oper. Manage. **4**(3), 208–227 (2002)
9. Gans, N., Koole, G., Mandelbaum, A.: Telephone call centers: tutorial, review, and research prospects. Manuf. Serv. Oper. Manage. **5**(2), 79–141 (2003)
10. Wallace, R.B., Whitt, W.: A staffing algorithm for call centers with skill-based routing. Manuf. Serv. Oper. Manage. **7**(4), 276–294 (2005)
11. Avramidis, A.N., Deslauriers, A., L'Ecuyer, P.: Modeling daily arrivals to a telephone call center. Manage. Sci. **50**(7), 896–908 (2004)
12. Aldor-Noiman, S., Feigin, P.D., Mandelbaum, A.: Workload forecasting for a call center: methodology and a case study. Ann. Appl. Stat. **3**(4), 1403–1447 (2009)
13. Ibrahim, R., L'Ecuyer, P.: Forecasting call center arrivals: fixed-effects, mixed-effects, and bivariate models. Manuf. Serv. Oper. Manage. **15**(1), 72–85 (2013)
14. Ding, S., Koole, G.: Optimal call center forecasting and staffing under arrival rate uncertainty. working paper (2014)
15. Hyndman, R., Koehler, A.B., Ord, J.K., et al.: Forecasting with Exponential Smoothing: The State Space Approach. Springer, Heidelberg (2008). https://doi.org/10.1007/978-3-540-71918-2
16. Weinberg, J., Brown, L.D., Stroud, J.R.: Bayesian forecasting of an inhomogeneous Poisson process with applications to call center data. J. Am. Stat. Assoc. **102**(480), 1185–1198 (2007)
17. Shen, H., Huang, J.Z.: Interday forecasting and intraday updating of call center arrivals. Manuf. Serv. Oper. Manage. **10**(3), 391–410 (2008)
18. Taylor, J.W.: A comparison of univariate time series methods for forecasting intraday arrivals at a call center. Manage. Sci. **54**(2), 253–265 (2008)
19. Shen, H., Huang, J.Z.: Forecasting time series of inhomogeneous Poisson processes with application to call center workforce management. Ann. Appl. Stat. **2**(2), 601–623 (2008)
20. Shen, H., Huang, J.Z.: Analysis of call centre arrival data using singular value decomposition. Appl. Stoch. Models Bus. Ind. **21**(3), 251–263 (2005)
21. Soyer, R., Tarimcilar, M.M.: Modeling and analysis of call center arrival data: a Bayesian approach. Manage. Sci. **54**(2), 266–278 (2008)

22. Aktekin, T., Soyer, R.: Call center arrival modeling: a Bayesian state-space approach. Naval Res. Logist. (NRL) **58**(1), 28–42 (2011)
23. Taylor, J.W., De Menezes, L.M., McSharry, P.E.: A comparison of univariate methods for forecasting electricity demand up to a day ahead. Int. J. Forecast. **22**(1), 1–16 (2006)
24. Pacheco, J., Millán-Ruiz, D., Vélez, J.L.: Neural networks for forecasting in a multi-skill call centre. In: Palmer-Brown, D., Draganova, C., Pimenidis, E., Mouratidis, H. (eds.) EANN 2009. CCIS, vol. 43, pp. 291–300. Springer, Heidelberg (2009). https://doi.org/10.1007/978-3-642-03969-0_27
25. Taylor, J.W.: Triple seasonal methods for short-term electricity demand forecasting. Eur. J. Oper. Res. **204**(1), 139–152 (2010)
26. Jongbloed, G., Koole, G.: Managing uncertainty in call centres using Poisson mixtures. Appl. Stoch. Models Bus. Ind. **17**(4), 307–318 (2001)

Attention-Based Bilinear Joint Learning Framework for Entity Linking

Min Cao[1], Penglong Wang[1], Honghao Gao[2]([✉]), Jiangang Shi[3],
Yuan Tao[2], and Weilin Zhang[1]

[1] School of Computer Engineering and Science,
Shanghai University, Shanghai, China
mcao@staff.shu.edu.cn, penglongwang@shu.edu.cn,
zeroized@i.shu.edu.cn
[2] Computing Center, Shanghai University, Shanghai, China
gaohonghao@shu.edu.cn
[3] Shanghai Shang Da Hai Run Information System Co., Ltd,
Shanghai 200444, China
lukepro@163.com

Abstract. Entity Linking (EL) is a task that links entity mentions in the text to corresponding entities in a knowledge base. The key to building a high-quality EL system involves accurate representations of word and entity. In this paper, we propose an attention-based bilinear joint learning framework for entity linking. First, a novel encoding method is employed for coding EL. This method jointly learns words and entities using an attention mechanism. Next, for ranking features, a weighted summation model is introduced to model the textual context and coherence. Then, we employ a pairwise boosting regression tree (PBRT) to rank candidate entities. As input, PBRT takes both features constructed with a weighted summation model and conventional EL features. Finally, through the experiment, we demonstrate that the proposed model learns embedding efficiently and improves the EL performance compared with other state-of-the-art methods. Our approach achieves superior result on two standard EL datasets: CoNLL and TAC 2010.

Keywords: Entity linking · Embedding model · Modeling context · Modeling coherence · Entity disambiguation

1 Introduction

Entity linking (EL) is a key technique for discovering knowledge in a text which is highly important for building Semantic Web. EL is a task to link entity mentions in text with corresponding entities in a knowledge base [1]. EL can help computers find important semantic information in sentences and determine how the meanings of words differ in different contexts, which is indispensable for helping computers understand natural language. EL has been widely adopted in applications such as information extraction, information retrieval, question answering system, and knowledge base population (KBP).

© ICST Institute for Computer Sciences, Social Informatics and Telecommunications Engineering 2019
Published by Springer Nature Switzerland AG 2019. All Rights Reserved
X. Wang et al. (Eds.): CollaborateCom 2019, LNICST 292, pp. 247–259, 2019.
https://doi.org/10.1007/978-3-030-30146-0_17

The challenge of EL is that human natural language is ambiguous. For example, in Fig. 1, more than five entities are likely to be related to mention "Bill Russell", however, the fact is that only one actual reference exists. The meaning of entity is decided by its context dynamically. For instance, as shown in Fig. 1, the context (rookie center) and mentions (Boston Celtics, Bob Cousy, Red Auerbach, NBA) are all valid basis for disambiguating the "Bill Russell" mention.

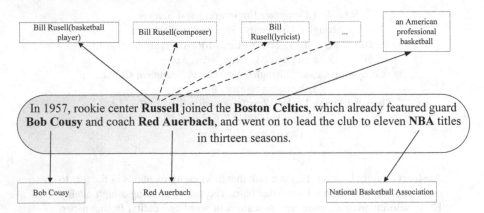

Fig. 1. An example of EL.

In recent years, the study of distributed representation for word and entity has become increasingly interested among researchers. Some works have proposed using embedding of word and entity in entity linking. Huang [2] studied entity embedding to calculate the correlation between entities. Hoffart [3] proposed taking contextual information into account. Yamada [4] assumed that word and entity are distributed in the same space and proposed a special joint learning word and entity embedding model. Chen [5] believed that words and entities should be embedded into different spaces. Hence, he developed a bilinear joint learning model (BJLM). Sun [6] put words and entities into different spaces and employed a neural tensor network to learn the interactions between word and entity. Nevertheless, none of the methods above capture different information aspects of word and entity context, which can result in a loss of information. Therefore, this paper mainly investigates how to effectively embed and combine word and entity with their context, and generates the precise embedding for these words and entities.

The semantic of a word is derived primarily from its context and relationships with other words in the same document. Most previous methods have assumed that all words and mentions in a context have the same weight. Obviously, these approaches result in bias regarding the meanings of words and mentions. In this paper, an attention-based bilinear joint learning model (ABJL) is proposed. When mapping words and mentions to different distributed spaces, ABJL focuses on the different impact of the words and mentions in the context of the target word and mention. Moreover, two EL features are constructed with learned embedding: textual context feature and entity coherence feature. Finally, the constructed EL features as well as the traditional EL features are fed into a pairwise boosting regression tree (PBRT) [7] for candidate ranking.

The remainder of this paper is organized as follows. Section 2 reviews related works. Section 3 presents the bilinear joint learning method with an attention mechanism. Section 4 introduced the application of the proposed embedding method on EL task. Section 5 describes the experimental settings and result and Sect. 6 presents conclusions and provides the directions of future study.

2 Related Work

In past decades, EL has been widely studied and applied in academia. EL involves linking entity mentions in the text to corresponding entities in a knowledge base. There are three main categories of EL algorithms. First, the EL algorithms that adopt an independent paradigm use a single mention and its context information and compare its similarities with candidate entities in a knowledge base. Second, the collective EL algorithms utilize correlations between mentions in the same document to link multiple mentions to knowledge base simultaneously. Third, the collaborative EL algorithms extend contextual information associated with entity mention by means of cross-documentation and then use extended entity mention information to address EL. Here we review some recent works related to our approach.

The conventional representation approach of word named one-hot encoding encounters sparsity problems. Word-to-vector (word2vec) is an effective word representation method that has become increasingly welcome in academia. Word2vec uses a continuous vector of low-dimension to represent a word. Skip-gram [8] is another word embedding method whose goal is to train a word embedding to effectively predict its surrounding words. Given a word w and a context w_c, skip-gram tries to maximize the conditional probability $P(w_c|w)$ through a softmax process. Whereas, this approach has a problem. To calculate $P(w_c|w)$, it involves scanning the whole vocabulary, which is usually large. Therefore, the full calculation is computationally expensive. Skip-gram approximates this conditional probability value using negative sampling (NEG) method which is a simplified method from noise contrastive estimation (NCE) [9] method. Our embedding model is an extension based on skip-gram.

Some works have solved EL tasks using neural networks. Huang [2] used a deep neural network (DNN) to train entity embedding and sorted candidate entities using a semi-supervised graph regularization model. Hu [10] improved entity embedding using a structured knowledge which is derived from Wikipedia's catalogue and construct a model to maximize global consistency between predicted entities. Whereas, these approaches learn entities embedding separately and do not interact with words. Yamada [4] proposed a joint learning model that maps word and entity to the same contiguous vector space and then ranked candidate entities using a gradient boosting regression tree (GBRT) [13] model. Chen [5] developed a bilinear joint learning model (BJLM) that mapped word and entity to different distribution spaces, and then used a pairwise boosting regression tree (PBRT) [7] model to evaluate candidate entities. Sun [6] proposed a tensor neural model to imitate the interactions between mentions, contexts, and entities, and then used a local method to sort candidate entities. Francis-Landau

[14] used a convolutional neural network (CNN) to model semantic correspondence between the context of entity mention and candidate entities and then used a logistic regression layer to rank candidate entities. However, neural networks are overly complex and computationally expensive.

Most previous methods have assumed that all the words in a context have equal importance. In contrast, ABJL model considers the diverse contextual impacts of words on the target word or entity so that more fine-grained learning on word and entity embedding can be performed. In addition, textual context features and entity coherence features are also studied via the proposed ABJL model. PBRT [7] is investigated for candidate entities ranking with new features as well as conventional features.

3 Methodology

In this section, our model for joint learning word and entity embedding is proposed. Additionally, the training method of the proposed model is explained in detail.

3.1 Attention-Based Bi-Linear Joint Learning Model

BJLM [5] does not consider the influences of different words on the target word in context that it is a coarse-grained type of learning. To solve the problem, during the BJLM training process, the different effect of each word in the context of target word is considered in our method. Therefore, we propose an attention-based bilinear joint learning model (ABJL) as an extension of BJLM. The so-called attention mechanism addresses different weight for the words in the context. First, word and entity are embedded into different spaces through an initial matrix mapping method. Then the attention mechanism is integrated into the model to calculate the impacts of context words on the target word and entity training. In such as two-stage method, a more elaborate embedding learning on target word or entity is performed. The attention is calculated via Dot-Product method [15] as follows:

$$Attention(C, E) = softmax(\frac{CE^T}{\sqrt{d_k}})E \tag{1}$$

where C is a matrix of all words vector in context. In addition, E is the vector of entity mention or word. In Eq. (1), $C \in R^{n \times d_k}$ and $E \in R^{1 \times d_k}$. In entity linking, C is the context words vector sequence where entity mention located and E is the vector representation of entity mention.

When training the embedding for a word or entity mention, we consider the values of different influences for each word in its context. Formally, given a sequence of N word and entity string $s_1, s_2, ..., s_N$. ABJL's goal is to maximize the following function:

$$\mathcal{L}_A = \sum_{t=1}^{N} \sum_{s_c \in context(s_i)} \log P_A(s_c|s_i) \tag{2}$$

where S_i represents target string and *context(s_i)* is the context string for s_i. The conditional probability is calculated as follows:

$$P_A(s_c|s_i) = \frac{1}{2}((P_B(s_c|s_i) + Attention(C_{s_i}, s_c))) \qquad (3)$$

where C_{S_i} represents a matrix constructed from vectors of context words of s_i.

The training objective of ABJL is to learn word and entity representations that do best in predicting the nearby words and entities. For example, Fig. 2(a) uses the target word w_t to predict context strings which contain two words (w_{t-1} and w_{t+2}) and an entity e_{t+1}. The attention scores of w_{t-1}, w_{t+2} and e_{t+1} are considered to create a more fine-grained representation of w_t. Figure 2(b) uses the target entity e_t to predict context strings which contain two words (w_{t-1} and w_{t+2}) and an entity e_{t+1}. Again, the attention scores of w_{t-1}, w_{t+2} and e_{t+1} are considered to create a more fine-grained representation of e_t. The projection matrix M is used to bridge the space gap when the target string and the context string are in different embedding types; in contrary, when the target and the context exist in the same embedding types, projection matrix M becomes an identity matrix and does nothing.

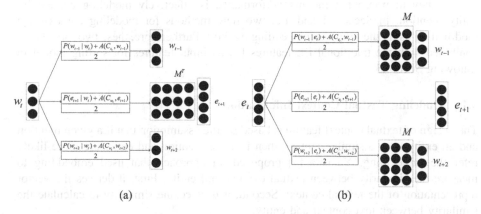

Fig. 2. An example of an ABJL.

3.2   Training

Maximize the function Eq. (2) is the training objective of the proposed model and the result matrix V is used to embed word and entity. One problem is that the computational cost of normalizers contained in $P_A(S_C|S_i)$ is hugely expensive that occurs when training the model because they involve calculating all the words and entities. To solve this problem, negative sampling (NEG) [8] is used to transform the original objective function into a computationally flexible objective function. NEG is defined as follows:

$$\log \sigma(V_{w_t}^T U_{w_{t+j}}) + \sum_{i=1}^{g} E_{w_i} \sim P_{neg(w)}[\log \sigma(-V_{w_t}^T U_{w_i})] \qquad (4)$$

where $\sigma(x) = 1/(1 + \exp(-x))$, and g represents the number of negative samples. Equation (4) is used instead of $log(P_A(S_C|S_i))$ in Eq. (2). Therefore, the objective function Eq. (2) is transformed into a simple binary classification objective function, which distinguishes observed word w_t from the word extracted from the noise $P_{neg(w)}$. Wikipedia is used to train the proposed model and stochastic gradient descent (SGD) [16] is applied for optimization. Maximize the transformed objective function by iterating over Wikipedia page multiple times.

4 Entity Linking Using Embedding

In this section, how to apply the proposed embedding model to EL task is explained in detail. First, a formal definition of EL is given: Given a knowledge base, the goal of EL is to match each entity mention to its corresponding entity in the knowledge base. Note that a named entity mention is a token sequence in a text. The mention may refer to an entity and is pre-identified. EL task usually consists of two subtasks: generation of candidate entities and ranking of candidate entities. Thus, we also discuss the candidate entity ranking.

The key to improving ranking performance is effectively modeling context by entity mention. In Sects. 4.1 and 4.2, two new methods for modeling contexts are modified by using the proposed embedding method. Furthermore, these two models are combined with the traditional EL features [1] as input features for sorting model in following Sect. 4.3.

4.1 Modeling Textual Context Information

The design of textual context feature is based on the assumption that if a given mention and an entity have a similar context, then that the mention and entity are more likely refer the same thing. Yamada [4] proposed an approach that used embedding to measure the similarity between textual context and entity. First, it derives the vector representation of the textual context. Second, it uses cosine similarity to calculate the similarity between text context and entity.

When calculating the context vector, Yamada simply uses an averaging method to sum the word vectors in context. This ignores the greater impact of the more important words in the context and elevates the importance of unimportant words to the average, which is obviously unreasonable. To avoid the problem, the cosine similarity in this paper is calculated between the word in the context and target entity instead of in this stage, where the importance of the entity is determined by the cosine similarity. The textual context vector is derived by weighted summation of the context word vector:

$$\overrightarrow{v_{c_m}} = \sum_{w \in W_{c_m}} \frac{a_{c_{m_i}}}{\sum_1^M a_{c_{m_j}}} \overrightarrow{v_{m_i}} \tag{5}$$

where W_{c_m} is a set of entity mention's context words. M denotes the size of the set, $\overrightarrow{v_{m_i}} \in V$ is the vector representation of word w, and $a_{c_{m_i}}$ represents the similarity between the i_{th} words in context and target entity mention which is calculated by cosine similarity.

Next, similarity between each candidate and the obtained textual context is calculated, which is obtained by calculating the cosine similarity of textual context vector $\overrightarrow{v_{c_m}}$ and the entity vector $\overrightarrow{v_e}$.

4.2 Modeling Entity Coherence

Milne [17] found that effectively modeling coherence of entities is certainly important for assigning entities to mentions in EL. Since most texts deal with one or several semantically related topics, entity consistency becomes a key metric, such as rock music, Internet technology, or global warming. However, not all content is together.

We use a simple two-step approach [18] to solve this problem: First, a coherence score is used to train machine learning models that are among unambiguous mentions. Then, in the second step, the model is retrained using the coherence score between predicted entities. To calculate entity coherence value, our method computes context entities vector, and then measures the similarity between context entities vector and target entity vector. It should be noted that context entities in the first step are unambiguous entities, while the second step uses the predicted entities. Based on this idea, the context entity vector is derived via a weighted summation using cosine similarity:

$$\overrightarrow{v_{c_e}} = \sum_{e \in E_{c_m}} \frac{a_{c_{e_i}}}{\sum_1^N a_{c_{e_j}}} \overrightarrow{v_{e_i}} \tag{6}$$

where E_{c_m} represents the set of entities in the context of m, N is the size of the set, and $a_{c_{e_i}}$ represents the similarity between the i_{th} entity in context and target entity mention.

4.3 Pairwise Ranking Model

Given an entity mention, a ranking score is assigned to each candidate entity by the ranking model. EL system selects the candidate entity with the highest score as the referential entity. Shen [19] regarded EL as a pairwise ranking problem and presented a method based on SVM ranking [16]. Yamada [4] ranked candidate entities using a GBRT with a pointwise loss function. Yet, the pointwise sorting method may cause label deviation problems because there are many candidate entities for a given mention but only one is correct. However, this paper does not intend to study various ranking methods for EL. In our work, a supervised PBRT [7] model is adapted to rank candidate entities.

5   Experiments

In this section, the experimental settings and result are discussed. First, the training method and training tools are explained. Then, the experimental details on two standard EL data sets are introduced. At last, the experimental result is comprehensively analyzed. To demonstrate the effectiveness of the proposed model, we compared the accuracy with those of other state-of-the-art methods on the CoNLL and TAC 2010 datasets.

5.1   Prerequisites

To train our proposed model, Wikipedia dump of September 2018 version is used. The dump file is parsed with JWPL [20], where navigation, maintenance, discussion, redirected and disambiguated pages are initially removed. All page titles and anchors from each page are extracted as reference entities. Through Wikipedia links, the anchor on the page is replaced with the title of the page that it points to.

In the experiments, the dimension size of embedding is 300, the size of the context window c is 10 and the number of negative samples g is 20. Learning rate α is 0.025 and is linearly decreased during the iteration. The model iterates all pages in Wikipedia dump 10 times online.

For the CoNLL dataset, mentions only with legal corresponding entities in the knowledge base are selected. Standard micro-accuracy which aggregates over all mentions and macro-accuracy which aggregates over all documents are used for the measurements of the algorithm. For TAC2010 dataset, the preprocess is the same as CoNLL dataset but only micro-accuracy is used.

Evaluation Metrics. *Precision, recall, F1-measure,* and *accuracy* are usually used as the evaluation metrics to perform the assessments of EL systems. The *precision* of the entity linking system is calculated as the percentage of correctly linked mentions that are generated by the system [1]:

$$precision = \frac{|\{correctly\ linked\ entity\ mentions\}|}{|\{linked\ mentions\ generated\ by\ system\}|} \quad (7)$$

Precision considers all entity mentions linked by the system and determines the percentage of correct entity mentions linked by the EL system. *Precision* is usually used in conjunction with the *recall* metric, which is the fraction of correctly linked entity mentions that should be linked [1]:

$$recall = \frac{|\{correctly\ linked\ entity\ mentions\}|}{|\{entity\ mentions\ that\ should\ be\ linked\}|} \quad (8)$$

Recall considers all the entity mentions that should be linked and determines how correctly linked entity mentions are with regard to total entity mentions that should be linked. These two measures are sometimes used together in F_1-*measure* to provide a single measurement for a system. F_1-*measure* is defined as the harmonic mean of *precision* and *recall* [1]:

$$F_1 = \frac{2 \cdot precision \cdot recall}{precision + recall} \tag{9}$$

For our experiment, entity mentions that should be linked are provided as the input of EL system; consequently, the number of linked mentions generated by the experiment always equals the number of entity mentions that should be linked. In this situation, researchers usually use *accuracy* to assess the system's performance. *Accuracy* is calculated as the number of correctly linked entity mentions divided by the total number of all entity mentions. Therefore, here *precision* = *recall* = F_1 = *accuracy*. Moreover, accuracy is also regarded as the official evaluation measure in the TAC-KBP track.

5.2   Entity Link

Set Up. We test our proposed model's performance on two standard EL datasets: The CoNLL dataset and the TAC 2010 dataset. The details of the two data sets are described below.

CoNLL. The CoNLL dataset is constructed by Hoffart [3] which is a popular EL dataset. The CoNLL dataset includes three parts: training, development, and test sets. The training set is used to train our learning model and the performance of our approach is measured using the test set. In the CoNLL dataset, each mention is annotated with an entity.

TAC 2010. The TAC 2010 dataset is another popular EL dataset. The dataset was constructed by Ji [21] for the Text Analysis Conference (TAC). This data set was constructed based on news articles from various proxy and weblog data, and it contains two collections: the training set and test set. We only use entity mentions where a matching valid entity exists in the knowledge base. The training set is adopted to train our model. And the test set is used to evaluate its performance. In most included documents, a query mention has been annotated with an entity.

Baseline Methods. We compare our method with the following recently proposed state-of-the-art methods:

- Globerson [12] proposed a coherence model with a multi-focal attention mechanism.
- PPRsim [11] is a graph-based EL approach based on Personalized PageRank.
- Yamada [4] presented a joint embedding model and utilized a GBRT model to rank candidate entities.
- Chen [5] developed a bilinear joint learning model and utilized a PBRT model to rank candidate entities.

Knowledge Base and Candidate Entity Generation. We used the Wikipedia of September 2018 version as our reference database. Wikipedia is a free, online, decentralized, multi-language encyclopedia that was created by thousands of volunteers from all over the world. In Wikipedia, each basic entry is an article. The article defines and describes an entity or a topic. And each article is uniquely referenced by an identifier. Besides, Wikipedia has high coverage of named entities and contains a wealth of knowledge for well-known entities. In addition, a rich set of features is provided by the structure of Wikipedia for entity linking. The features include article directories, entity pages, disambiguation pages, redirect pages, and hyperlinks in Wikipedia articles. These features are highly beneficial for EL tasks.

The way we construct a set of candidate entities for mentions that appear in the TAC 2010 dataset is to construct a candidate entity dictionary. We use the title of Wikipedia entity page and the text of bold font in the first paragraph to construct the dictionary. Then we use all the anchors as keys and the corresponding Wikipedia titles as values to construct a key-value dictionary. Finally, we use this dictionary to generate candidate entities. To perform candidate generation for the CONLL data sets, we use a publicly available third-party dictionary [11].

5.3   Experimental Result

In this section, we analyze our experimental results, the prediction errors, and features. A detailed analysis of the above aspects for CoNLL data set is conducted.

$PBRT_A$ refers to the proposed model are all the models are trained with the features derived from ABJL. Table 1 shows the experimental results of our model and the compared baseline model in two data sets. $PBRT_A$ achieves a micro-precision of 0.947 and a macro-precision of 0.943 on CoNLL dataset and achieves a micro-precision of 0.893 on TAC-KBP 2010 dataset. $PBRT_A$ performs better than the baselines on both datasets.

Table 1. Accuracy scores on CoNLL and TAC-KBP 2010 datasets

	CoNLL (micro)	CoNLL (macro)	TAC2010 (micro)
$PBRT_A$	**0.947**	**0.943**	**0.893**
Chen	0.938	0.935	0.881
Yamada	0.931	0.926	0.855
PPRSim	0.918	0.899	-
Globerson	0.927	-	0.872

Our model not only achieves good experimental results but results that are statistically significant. On the CoNLL and TAC datasets, our model achieves advanced EL results and improves the accuracy of EL. This result occurs because ABJL constructs more accurate representations of words and entities. When ABJL trains word and entity embeddings, it considers the different impacts of the words and entities in the context which causes the trained embedding to more accurately represent the semantics of words and entities. More accurate embeddings yield more realistic results when calculating the similarity between words and between entities.

In the experiments, we primarily encountered the following two typical errors. The first type error is one of common sense. For example, when the context is limited, a country name that appears after another person's name usually refers to a country. One sentence *"Warcraft-17-Jack Stimulus (America) played very well"*. The mention *America* has two candidate entities, the *National Football League* and the *United States*. We can infer that the intent of the sentence is nationality when *America* comes after a name. The second type error is also a common sense error but is more difficult to correct. For example, in the sentence *"Santa Fe has mining and mining operations in Nevada, California, Montana, Canada, Brazil, Australia, Chile, Kazakhstan, Mexico and Ghana."* [5], when no additional information is available, it is also difficult for people to understand whether *Mexico* means the country of *Mexico* or the *city of Mexico*. Solving the preceding types of errors is a difficult challenge. Understanding sentences by applying real-world common sense is a more appropriate approach.

6 Conclusion

In this paper, we proposed a new bilinear joint learning model with an attention mechanism (ABJL). When ABJL trains target word or entity embeddings, it expresses the target word and entity more finely and accurately by capturing the various influences and contributions of the contextual words around the target. Embedding trained by the proposed model is used to construct two types of features that are inputted into the PBRT along with traditional EL features. An excellent result is achieved on two standard EL databases showing that ABJL produces efficient embedding that improve the performance of our EL method.

In future work, we plan to further study the application of our model on large-scale datasets and to evaluate the use of distributed clustering methods to address the challenges of large-scale datasets. In addition, because it is still a challenge for computers to acquire real-world common sense knowledge, we want to apply real-world common sense and its relations in a knowledge graph to improve our model.

Acknowledgements. This work is supported by the National Key Research and Development Plan of China under Grant No. 2017YFD0400101, the Natural Science Foundation of Shanghai under Grant No. 16ZR1411200, and the CERNET Innovation Project under Grant No. NGII201 70513.

References

1. Shen, W., Wang, J., Han, J.: Entity linking with a knowledge base: issues, techniques, and solutions. IEEE Trans. Knowl. Data Eng. 27(2), 443–460 (2015)
2. Huang, H., Heck, L., Ji, H.: Leveraging deep neural networks and knowledge graphs for entity disambiguation. arXiv preprint arXiv:1504.07678 (2015)

3. Hoffart, J., Yosef, M.A., Bordino, I., et al.: Robust disambiguation of named entities in text. In: Proceedings of the Conference on Empirical Methods in Natural Language Processing, pp. 782–792. Association for Computational Linguistics (2011)
4. Yamada, I., Shindo, H., Takeda, H., Takefuji, Y.: Joint learning of the embedding of words and entities for named entity disambiguation. arXiv preprint arXiv:1601.01343 (2016)
5. Chen, H., Wei, B., Liu, Y., Li, Y., Yu, J., Zhu, W.: Bilinear joint learning of word and entity embeddings for entity linking. Neurocomputing **294**, 12–18 (2018)
6. Sun, Y., Lin, L., Tang, D., et al.: Modeling mention, context and entity with neural networks for entity disambiguation. In: Twenty-Fourth International Joint Conference on Artificial Intelligence, pp. 632–639 (2015)
7. Chen, T., Guestrin, C.: XGBoost: a scalable tree boosting system. In: Proceedings of the 22nd ACM SIGKDD International Conference on Knowledge Discovery and Data Mining, pp. 785–794. ACM (2016)
8. Mikolov, T., Sutskever, I., Chen, K., et al.: Distributed representations of words and phrases and their compositionality. In: Advances in Neural Information Processing Systems, pp. 3111–3119 (2013)
9. Gutmann, M.U., Hyvärinen, A.: Noise-contrastive estimation of unnormalized statistical models, with applications to natural image statistics. J. Mach. Learn. Res. **13**, 307–361 (2012)
10. Hu, Z., Huang, P., Deng, Y., et al.: Entity hierarchy embedding. In: Proceedings of the 53rd Annual Meeting of the Association for Computational Linguistics and the 7th International Joint Conference on Natural Language Processing (Volume 1: Long Papers), pp. 1292–1300 (2015)
11. Pershina, M., He, Y., Grishman, R.: Personalized page rank for named entity disambiguation. In: Proceedings of the 2015 Conference of the North American Chapter of the Association for Computational Linguistics: Human Language Technologies, pp. 238–243 (2015)
12. Globerson, A., Lazic, N., Chakrabarti, S., et al.: Collective entity resolution with multi-focal attention. In: Proceedings of the 54th Annual Meeting of the Association for Computational Linguistics (Volume 1: Long Papers), pp. 621–631 (2016)
13. Friedman, J.H.: Greedy function approximation: a gradient boosting machine. Ann. Stat. **29**, 1189–1232 (2001)
14. Francis-Landau, M., Durrett, G., Klein, D.: Capturing semantic similarity for entity linking with convolutional neural networks. arXiv preprint arXiv:1604.00734 (2016)
15. Vaswani, A., Shazeer, N., Parmar, N., et al.: Attention is all you need. In: Advances in Neural Information Processing Systems, pp. 5998–6008 (2017)
16. Laporte, L., Flamary, R., Canu, S., et al.: Nonconvex regularizations for feature selection in ranking with sparse SVM. IEEE Trans. Neural Netw. Learn. Syst. **25**(6), 1118–1130 (2013)
17. Milne, D., Witten, I.H.: Learning to link with wikipedia. In: Proceedings of the 17th ACM Conference on Information and Knowledge Management, pp. 509–518. ACM (2008)
18. Ratinov, L., Roth, D., Downey, D., et al.: Local and global algorithms for disambiguation to wikipedia. In: Proceedings of the 49th Annual Meeting of the Association for Computational Linguistics: Human Language Technologies-Volume 1, pp. 1375–1384. Association for Computational Linguistics (2011)
19. Shen, W., Wang, J., Luo, P., et al.: Linden: linking named entities with knowledge base via semantic knowledge. In: Proceedings of the 21st International Conference on World Wide Web, pp. 449–458. ACM (2012)

20. Ferschke, O., Zesch, T., Gurevych, I.: Wikipedia revision toolkit: efficiently accessing wikipedia's edit history. In: Proceedings of the 49th Annual Meeting of the Association for Computational Linguistics: Human Language Technologies: Systems Demonstrations, pp. 97–102. Association for Computational Linguistics (2011)
21. Ji, H., Grishman, R., Dang, H.T., et al.: Overview of the TAC 2010 knowledge base population track. In: Third Text Analysis Conference (TAC 2010), vol. 3, no. 2, pp. 3 (2010)

Collaborative Computing of Urban Built-Up Area Identification from Remote Sensing Image

Chengfan Li[1,2(✉)], Lan Liu[3], Yongmei Lei[1], Xiankun Sun[3], and Junjuan Zhao[1]

[1] School of Computer Engineering and Science,
Shanghai University, Shanghai 200444, China
david-0904@163.com
[2] Shanghai Institute of Advanced Communication and Data Science,
Shanghai University, Shanghai 200444, China
[3] School of Electronic and Electrical Engineering,
Shanghai University of Engineering Science, Shanghai 201620, China

Abstract. Urban built-up area is one of the important criterions of urbanization. Remote sensing can quickly acquire dynamic temporal and spatial variation of urban built-up area, but how to identify and extract urban built-up area information from massive remote sensing data has become a bottleneck arousing widespread concerns in the field of the data mining and application for remote sensing. Based on the traditional urban built-up area identification and data mining of remote sensing, this paper proposed a new collaborative computing method for urban built-up area identification from remote sensing image. In the method, the normalized difference built-up index (NDBI) and the normalized differential vegetation index (NDVI) feature images were constructed firstly from the spectrum clustering map; and then the urban built-up area was identified and extracted by the map-spectrum synergy and mathematical morphology methods. Finally, a case of collaborative computing of urban built-up areas in Chongqing city, China is presented. And the experimental results show that the total accuracy of urban built-up area identification in 1988 and 2007 reached 92.58% and 91.41%, the Kappa coefficient reached 0.8933 and 0.8722, respectively, and the good results in the temporal and spatial variation monitoring of urban built-up area are achieved.

Keywords: Remote sensing image · Collaborative computing · Urban built-up area · Map-spectrum synergy

1 Introduction

In recent years, with the sustained and rapid growth of China's economy, the urbanization continues to increase. Statistically, the total area of urban built-up area in China was about 2×10^5 km^2 by 2017, and the urbanization rate reached 58.52% [1]. How to accurately obtain the dynamic range of urban built-up area has become an urgent task of urban construction and management [2–4]. There are many methods to identify and

© ICST Institute for Computer Sciences, Social Informatics and Telecommunications Engineering 2019
Published by Springer Nature Switzerland AG 2019. All Rights Reserved
X. Wang et al. (Eds.): CollaborateCom 2019, LNICST 292, pp. 260–278, 2019.
https://doi.org/10.1007/978-3-030-30146-0_18

extract the urban built-up area at present, among the methods, the nighttime lighting monitoring from remote sensing image is the most influential and representative [5–7]. However, the traditionally methods which rely on a single means to identify urban built-up area is unrealistic and impractical because of the influence by saturation diffusion and threshold selection. In addition, the urban built-up area is a complex affected by human political, economic and social activities. There are many types of land objects, e.g., buildings, roads, grasslands, rivers, mountains, construction sites, forest land, etc., and the random confusion of different types of objects is obvious. Meanwhile, how to identify and extract the urban built-up area has become a focus of the authorities and the related department.

With the development of space-to-earth observation and the continuous improvement of sensor performance, remote sensing can quickly capture the change information of earth surface with advantages of multi-source, multi-angle and multi-resolution, and has the characteristics of fast data acquisition, short update period and strong timeliness. Accordingly, the amount of remote sensing data has shown an exponential growth trend and has entered the era of big data [8–10]. However, it has a relatively weak ability of data processing in the remote sensing big data and causes data redundancy and dimensional disaster, how to accurately analyze the massive remote sensing data and find out the urban built-up area has become the main focus of urban built-up area dynamic monitoring from remote sensing images. The collaborative computing was first used in the fields of computer networks, resource scheduling, communication, and multimedia, etc. At present it has been widely used in many fields and industries [11]. It has been introduced into the remote sensing only in decades. Limited by the accuracy and efficiency of remote sensing data mining, Chen et al. [12] firstly proposed the idea of geoscience information map-spectrum, and laid the foundation for the full implementation of collaborative computing of remote sensing data mining with the formation of remote sensing big data. Luo et al. [13] explored the cognitive theory of remote sensing map-spectrum and calculation, and pointed out that it is feasible to develop remote sensing cognitive theory and methods combined with visual cognition. Shen et al. [14] extract the Baiyangdian wetland information from the remote time data by the collaborative computing method, and pointed out that the area of Baiyangdian wetland began to reduce firstly and later increase the science 1973. Li et al. [1] extracted the urban built-up area of Beijing-Tianjin-Hebei region from remote sensing images by the comprehensive utilization of multi-source remote sensing data and DMSP/OLS data, and the effectiveness of collaborative computing in the extraction of urban built-up area is verified by the overall accuracy and Kappa coefficient. In general, although collaborative computing can provide a new perspective for remote sensing data mining and information identification of interest, collaborative analysis from multiple data, methods and knowledge enables the extraction and analysis of hidden information [15, 16], so far, the collaborative computing in remote sensing image data mining is still in its infancy, and the related achievements are few.

As the youngest municipality in China, Chongqing has experienced rapid economic development in recent years. At the same time, the urban built-up area covers an area of 150 km^2 in 1988 and 700 km^2 in 2018, respectively. On the basis of the systematic summarization of the map and spectrum information in remote sensing, taking Chongqing main urban area as an example, this paper presented a new collaborative computing method integrating into different levels of knowledge to identify urban built-up area from remote sensing images. The specific collaborative computing includes algorithms, computing resources and computing modes in the process of the calculation, remote sensing data, information, features and knowledge. It can identify accurately the dynamic change information of urban built-up area and improve effectively the remote sensing data mining.

Work in this study is focused on the collaborative computing of map-spectrum synergy for urban built-up area from remote sensing images. The rest of the paper is constructed as follows: Sect. 2 describes brief collaborative computing method of urban built-up area identification and extraction. Section 3 presents a case of collaborative calculation of urban built-up area from remote sensing image. Section 4 devotes the results and analysis. Finally, the discussions and conclusions are separately drawn in Sects. 5 and 6.

2 Collaborative Computing Method of Urban Built-Up Area Identification and Extraction

2.1 Collaborative Computing Mode of Remote Sensing Information

(1) Map-Spectrum Collaborative Computing

Remote sensing images contain plentiful map and spectrum information [17, 18]. The map, also known as spatial information, refers to the shape of the research unit and the spatial relationship and configuration among different units, i.e., pixels, parcels. The spectrum contains spectral, band information, time spectrum, feature attribute spectrum, knowledge spectrum and other forms of the same unit in different dimensions, i.e., spectral performance and long-term phase change information. Map-spectrum collaborative computing is an important basis for the classification and thematic information extraction from remote sensing image.

(2) Multi-resolution and Multi-temporal Collaborative Computing

It is the manifestation of map-spectrum collaborative computing. Multi-resolution synergy realizes collaborative computing of multi-source and multi-resolution data by comprehensively utilizing high-resolution, medium-resolution and low-resolution remote sensing images. Multi-temporal synergy detects changes by collaborative computing multiple time-point remote sensing images [19–22]. Synthesizing remote sensing image information of different resolutions and multi-temporal can provide more accurate and rich map-spectrum information, and it is easy to improve the accuracy of classification and thematic information extraction and change detection from remote sensing images.

(3) Multi-knowledge and Multi-algorithm Collaborative Computing

In the course of remote sensing image processing, on the basis of assisting different levels of prior knowledge, it is necessary to improve the accuracy of remote sensing image classification and thematic information extraction by collaborative computing of multiple knowledge [23, 24]. Such as the spatial relationship between the earths surfaces objects, the reasoning mechanism, the configuration method, the causal relationship and other knowledge models, etc. In addition, the collaborative computing of multiple algorithms improves the efficiency and reliability of remote sensing image mining to a certain extent. There are many usual varieties of indices in the collaborative computing and classification of remote sensing image, i.e., normalized differential vegetation index (NDVI), ration vegetation index (RVI), difference vegetation index (DVI), etc.

2.2 Collaborative Computing of Urban Built-Up Area Identification

The specific collaborative computation method of urban built-up areas from remote sensing images in this paper mainly includes the following steps:

(1) Data Preprocessing

In this study, data preprocessing mainly contains geometric correction and cloud removal. In the data processing, the parameters from geographic position data set were first extracted and used to perform the geometric correction, and then the calibration data set was obtained. Next, the respectively bands R(red), B(blue) and G(green) were selected from remote sensing dataset and further generated a sample dataset, and then a corrected total dataset was obtained by stacking. For the ETM and TM remote sensing data with thin cloud, the cloud removal was performed by cloud mask data.

(2) From Spectrum Clustering Map, Constructing Feature Images of Normalized Difference Built-Up Index (NDBI) and NDVI

Due to the NDBI has a good recognition characteristics of the global built-up area, and it is easy to identify the urban built-up area as a whole. The NDBI computation is as shown below:

$$NDBI = \frac{MIR - NIR}{MIR + NIR} \qquad (1)$$

where MIR and NIR are pixel luminance values in the mid-infrared and near-infrared bands, respectively. For the TM sensor, it corresponds to Band 5 and Band 4, respectively.

Similarly, the NDVI is an effective indicator for the coverage of ground vegetation and is widely used in the field of vegetation information extraction. The specific NDVI computation is as shown below:

$$NDVI = \frac{NIR - \mathrm{Re}\,d}{NIR + \mathrm{Re}\,d} \qquad (2)$$

where NIR and Red are the pixel luminance values of the near-infrared band and the red-light band, which correspond to the band 4 and band 3 of the TM sensor, respectively.

(3) Map-Spectrum Collaborative Computing, Preliminary Identification of Urban Built-Up Area

Based on the administrative boundary of the study area, the total area of the built-up area within the administrative boundary is statistically calculated. Then the regional segmentation method is used to calculate the optimal segmentation threshold of the different administrative units in NDBI feature images, and the spatial distribution information of the urban built-up zone boundaries is obtained. The specific calculation formula is as shown below:

$$\Delta S_k(T_i) = S_k - S_k(T_0 - i) \tag{3}$$

where T_0 is initial threshold value, i is the step size, and $i = 0.1, 0.2, 0.3 \cdots$; k is the k-th administrative boundary in the research area, and $k = 1, 2, 3, \cdots$; S_k is the statistical value of area of administrative boundary, $S_k(T_0 - i)$ is the identified area from feature images, $\Delta S_k(T_i)$ is the difference between identification area and statistical area of the same administrative boundary. If $\Delta S_k(T_i)$ satisfy the condition $\Delta S_k(T_i) < \Delta S_k(T_{i+0.1}) \cap \Delta S_k(T_i) < \Delta S_k(T_{i-0.1})$, then T_i is the optimal segmentation threshold of k-th administrative boundary.

(4) Map-Spectrum Collaborative Computing, Further Identification of Urban Built-Up Area

Based on the preliminary identification of urban built-up areas, multi-scale segmentation algorithm is used to further identify the urban built-up areas from remote sensing image. And the specific calculation formula is as shown below:

$$dH = dH_{color}w_{color} + dH_{shape}w_{shape} \tag{4}$$

where dH is the heterogeneity index of multi-scale segmentation; dH_{color} and w_{color} is the spectral heterogeneity index and weight value, respectively; dH_{shape} and w_{shape} is the shape heterogeneity index and weight value, respectively.

Subsequently, the regional loop identification method is used to number the results of the newly identified urban built-up areas, and the maximum and minimum values of NDVI in each unit are calculated and regarded as the upper and lower thresholds of the urban built-up area. The specific formula is as shown below:

$$\begin{cases} NDVI_{A_i threshold\_max}(x) = \max\{NDVI_{S_i}(x)\} \\ NDVI_{A_i threshold\_min}(y) = \min\{NDVI_{S_i}(y)\} \end{cases} \tag{5}$$

where A_i is the i-th administrative unit, S_i is the identified i-th urban built-up area, $NDVI_{A_i threshold\_max}(x)$ and $NDVI_{A_i threshold\_min}(y)$ are the upper and lower value of segmentation threshold, respectively. And then the attribute of earth object is acquired by the judging criteria. That is to say, when $S_i(t)$ is judged as the type of the urban built-up area $NDVI_{S_i(t)} \in (NDVI_{A_i threshold\_min}(y), NDVI_{A_i threshold\_max}(x))$.

(5) Mathematical Morphology Post Processing

The mathematical morphology operators used in this study are mainly composed of open operations and expansion operations. And the specific calculation formula is as shown below:

$$\begin{cases} A \circ B = (A \ominus B) \oplus B \\ A \oplus B = \left\{ x | ((\hat{B})_y \cap A) \neq \emptyset \right\} \end{cases} \tag{6}$$

where A and B are two non-empty sets, $\hat{B}$ is the mapping of sets B, $\hat{B} = \{x|x = -b, b \in B\}$, y is the displacement of $\hat{B}$, namely, $\hat{B}_y = \{y|y = b + x, b \in B\}$.

The expansion operation was used to the later identified urban built-up area, and the gaps and breaks in the middle of the image and some broken maps of the walk were deleted. Meanwhile, the expansion image was refined further by the open operation. And then the distribution and statistical information of the urban built-up area are finally obtained.

3   Collaborative Calculation Case of Urban Built-Up Area

3.1   General Situation of Research Area

Chongqing is located in the eastern part of the Sichuan Basin, China. It is situated in the junction zone between the eastern part of China and the western part. The main urban area in Chongqing is shown in Fig. 1. The urban area of Chongqing usually includes the area among the Yangtze River, Jialing River, Zhongliang Mountain and Tonglu Mountain. The total area is about 700 km². The terrain in the area is dominated by low mountains and hills, and has an average elevation of about 400 m. Since the establishment of the municipality in 1997, the economy in Chongqing has developed rapidly and the scale of the urban built-up area has expanded rapidly. And now it has formed a new spatial distribution pattern with multi-center and group.

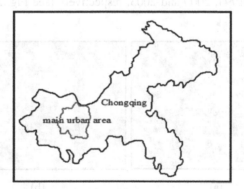

Fig. 1. Geographical location of the main urban area.

3.2   Data Collection

(1) Remote Sensing Data

The remote sensing data contains the medium resolution thematic mapper (TM) images in 1988 and 2007, respectively, and the imaging season is roughly the same. Due to the sixth band in TM sensor is a thermal infrared band and has low spatial resolution of 120 m. it usual affected severely by the atmosphere, so in this study it is not involved in band synthesis. The main parameters of TM sensor are shown in Table 1.

Table 1. Performance of sensors

Time	Band	Resolution (m)	Wavelength (μm)	min	max	avg	med	Standard deviation
1988	1	30	0.45–0.52	77	254	107.21	104	11.48
	2	30	0.52–0.60	26	145	44.60	43	5.60
	3	30	0.63–0.69	21	179	46.07	44	9.66
	4	30	0.76–0.90	15	208	66.45	66	14.67
	5	30	1.55–1.75	2	254	59.72	61	19.45
	7	30	2.08–2.35	1	254	24.05	25	8.14
2007	1	30	0.45–0.52	73	196	96.24	96	8.05
	2	30	0.52–0.60	28	105	42.08	41	4.69
	3	30	0.63–0.69	24	134	42.20	40	8.05
	4	30	0.76–0.90	24	128	64.42	65	13.44
	5	30	1.55–1.75	13	255	63.58	66	16.57
	7	30	2.08–2.35	3	255	29.231	28	11.00

(2) Thematic Data

The thematic data includes the digital topographic maps in Chongqing with 1:50000 scales and the digital elevation model (DEM) in Chongqing. Social data includes the natural and socioeconomic survey statistics. The collected thematic data is usual used to the geometric correction, verification and correction after the classification of remote sensing image. In addition, in this study we also involved in the landuse map of Chongqing in 1983, 1994, 2000 and 2003, respectively (see Fig. 2).

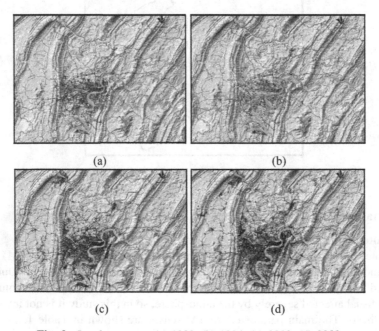

(a)   (b)

(c)   (d)

Fig. 2. Landuse maps, (a) 1983, (b) 1994, (c) 2000, (d) 2003.

(3) Data Preprocessing

Remote sensing image preprocessing process mainly includes filtering noise, radiation correction, geometric correction, image registration, fusion and enhancement. Therinto, the key is geometric correction and image registration.

In addition, for remote sensing images with different imaging time, in order to make the pixels brightness of remote sensing image in different phases consistent and have the comparable and same geospatial coordinate reference and spatial resolution, it is also necessary to perform radiation correction, normalization and resampling processing so as to make. The preprocessed TM remote sensing images are shown in Fig. 3.

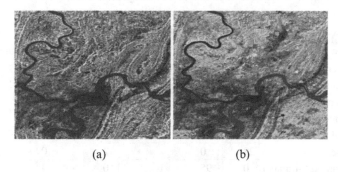

(a)   (b)

Fig. 3. Preprocessed TM images, (a) 1988, (b) 2007.

As can be seen from Fig. 3, there is a brilliant color and a strong sense of layering in the preprocessed TM remote sensing images. The image contrast and inter-class differences are also maximized. It is easy to identify the urban built-up area by visual interpretation and computer collaborative computing.

4   Results and Analysis

4.1   Collaborative Computing Results and Precision Evaluation

The urban built-up area and other three types of land covers (i.e., water, green land and agriculture) are obtained by the proposed collaborative calculation method in this paper, and the results is shown in Fig. 4.

In order to test the effect of urban built-up area extracted by the collaborative computing method, in the next, the confusion matrix is used to evaluate the accuracy of classification results of TM remote sensing image in 1988 and 2007, respectively. The results are shown in Tables 2 and 3.

As shown in Tables 2 and 3, the total accuracy of TM image classification in 1988 reached 92.58%, and the Kappa coefficient reached 0.8933. Meanwhile, the total accuracy of TM image classification in 2007 reached 91.41%, and the Kappa coefficient reached 0.8722, respectively. In Fig. 4(a), the water type information is basically

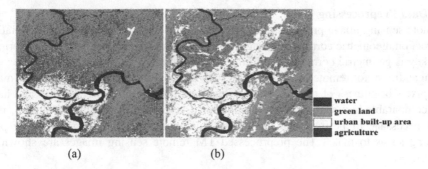

(a)   (b)

Fig. 4. Classification results of TM images, (a) 1988, (b) 2007.

Table 2. Error matrix

Time	Type	Water	Urban built-up area	Green land	Agriculture	Total
1988	Water	23	0	0	0	23
	Urban built-up area	0	94	0	9	103
	Green land	0	0	80	4	84
	Agriculture	0	4	2	40	46
	Total	23	98	82	53	256
2007	Water	28	0	2	0	30
	Urban built-up area	0	95	0	4	99
	Green land	0	7	90	5	102
	Agriculture	0	2	2	21	25
	Total	28	104	94	30	256

Table 3. Classification accuracy

Time	Type	Number of reference pixels	Number of classified pixels	Number of corrected classified pixels	Production accuracy	User accuracy
1988	Water	23	23	23	100.00%	100.00%
	Urban built-up area	98	103	94	95.92%	91.26%
	Green land	82	84	80	97.56%	95.24%
	Agriculture	53	46	40	75.47%	86.96%
	Total	256	256	237	–	–
	Total accuracy	92.58%		Kappa coefficient	0.8933	
2007	Water	28	30	28	100.00%	93.33%
	Urban built-up area	104	99	95	91.35%	95.96%
	Green land	94	102	90	95.74%	88.24%
	Agriculture	30	25	21	70.00%	84.00%
	Total	256	256	234	–	–
	Total accuracy	91.41%		Kappa coefficient	0.8722	

extracted accurately, and the accuracy of the producer and the user accuracy reached 100.00%, respectively. There was a certain misclassified between the urban built-up area and the agricultural land, but there are very few mistakes between the green land and agricultural. According to the analysis, it may be caused by the conversion from the initial cultivated land type to the urban built-up area. At the same time, the misclassification between agriculture and green land maybe caused not by some green land but corn and vegetables in agriculture land. In Fig. 4(b), it is similar to the situation in 1988 that the misclassification occurred in the TM remote sensing image (see Fig. 4a). As a whole, with the expansion of urbanization, the landuse type has become more complicated; it led to a slight decrease in the accuracy of TM remote sensing image classification from 92.58% in 1988 to 91.41% in 2007.

(2) Dynamic Changes of Urban Built-Up Area over Time

①*Rate of Urban Built-Up Change*
    Landuse information dynamic changes can usually be expressed by the rate of landuse type over time. It can accurately describe the rate of landuse type change, especially in the urban built-up area, and predict the future changes of the landuse information. In fact, there is single landuse dynamic rate and comprehensive landuse dynamic rate.
    Single landuse dynamic rate refers to the quantitative change in landuse types over a period of time in an area. And the calculation formula is as shown below:

$$K = (U_b - U_a)/(U_a \times T) \times 100\% \tag{7}$$

where U_a is the number of the initial landuse types, U_b is the number of the end landuse types, T is the time period (i.e., year, month and day). In reality it is also the annual gradient.
    Table 4 clearly illustrates the changes in urban built-up areas and other three landuse types obtained during the period 1988–2007 by formula (7).

Table 4. Changes of landuse types during the 1988–2007

	Time	Changes	Water	Urban built-up area	Green land	Agriculture
Divided period	1988–1994	Area (km²)	−0.13	24.74	−5.21	−19.4
		Proportion (%)	−0.04	2.53	−0.23	−1.00
	1994–2000	Area (km²)	−2.16	65.34	−22.45	−40.73
		Proportion (%)	−0.61	5.81	−1.00	−2.24
	2000–2003	Area (km²)	−2.15	34.86	−13.28	−19.43
		Proportion (%)	−1.25	4.60	−1.25	−2.46
	2003–2007	Area (km²)	−0.22	37.42	−18.87	−18.33
		Proportion (%)	−0.10	3.25	−1.39	−1.88
Whole period	1988–2007	Area (km²)	−4.66	162.36	−59.81	−97.89
		Proportion (%)	−0.41	5.25	−0.83	−1.59

As shown in Table 4, from the overall change point of view, there is only the urban built-up area increased as well as the other three types of landuse decrease, the area of urban built-up area increased to 162.36 km² and the annual change rate reached 5.25%, which is also the largest change rate of the four types of landuse. Thereinto, the water area only slightly decreased, only reduced 4.66 km², and the annual change rate reached 0.41%. It can be concluded that in the expansion of urbanization some dispersed and small-sized pools and pits transformed into the urban built-up area. It is also shown in Fig. 5. Second only to the type of urban built-up area, the area of agriculture and green land has decreased by 97.89 km² and 59.81 km², respectively, and the annual change rates reached 1.59% and 0.83%, respectively. From another point of view, the decrease area of green land and agriculture is basically close to the increased area of urban built-up area. To some extent, it can be considered that the green land and agriculture are the most important sources of urban built-up area transformation in the urbanization.

Table 5. TPM of urban built-up area and other type's landuse

Type		Water	Urban built-up area	Green land	Agriculture	Total
Water	Area (km²)	48.27	2.94	1.94	1.80	54.95
	Transition probability (%)	87.84	5.35	3.53	3.28	100
Urban built-up area	Area (km²)	8.27	128.24	77.72	110.83	325.06
	Transition probability (%)	2.54	39.45	23.91	34.10	100
Green land	Area (km²)	1.49	12.23	181.31	125.55	320.58
	Transition probability (%)	0.46	3.82	56.56	39.16	100
Agriculture	Area (km²)	1.58	19.29	119.42	84.87	225.16
	Transition probability (%)	0.70	8.57	53.04	37.69	100
Total		59.61	162.70	380.39	323.05	925.75

②*Conversions of Urban Built-up Area and Other Types of Landuse*
In order to calculate and analyze the mutual transformation between urban built-up area and other type's landuse during the period 1988–2007, the transition probability matrix (TPM) method was introduced, and the statistical results are shown in Table 5 and Fig. 5.

As shown in Table 5 and Fig. 5, for the urban built-up area, it has small transfer probabilities to agricultural land, green space and water due to the policy influence of greening construction and overall planning. The conversion between water and urban built-up area, green land and agriculture is small, and the transfer probabilities reached 2.54%, 0.46% and 0.70%, respectively. Meanwhile, the transfer area and probabilities from green land and agriculture to urban built-up area are relatively large, and reached

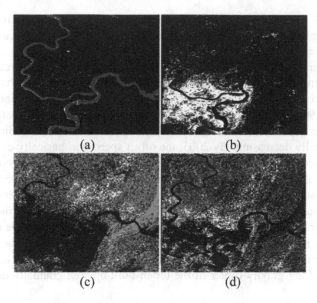

Fig. 5. Transition probability results, (a) water, (b) urban built-up area, (c) green land, (d) agriculture.

77.72 km^2 and 110.83 km^2, respectively, accounting for 23.91% and 34.10% of the total transfer. It also can be verified in Fig. 5(c) and (d). For example, the transfer proportion from green land to agriculture is also large and reached a total of 119.42 km^2, accounting for 53.04% of the total agriculture transfers. In addition, the transferred area from agriculture to the green land reached space by 125.55 km^2, accounting for 39.16% of the total green land transfers. Compared with the field reference data, these transferred area are mainly affected the actual geographical conditions, i.e., topography, slope and environment factors.

(3) Spatial Change in Urban Built-Up Area

①*Gravity Center Changes of Urban Built-Up Area*
    The gravity center change model is a commonly used model to describe the spatial distribution of geospatial targets. The center of gravity usually refers to the radial position of the target object, which can keep the target features evenly distributed. In this study, the gravity center change model of urban built-up area distribution is used to invert the whole landuse change in spatial distribution. The spatial center of gravity model can be obtained by weighted averaging of geographic coordinate values, map latitude and longitude. The specific formula is as shown below:

$$\begin{cases} X_t = \sum (C_{ti} \times X_i) / \sum C_{ti} \\ Y_t = \sum (C_{ti} \times Y_i) / \sum C_{ti} \end{cases} \tag{8}$$

where X_t and Y_t are the geographical coordinates of urban built-up area in t-th year, X_i and Y_i are the geometric center coordinate in i-th area, C_{ti} is the area of urban built-up area in i-th area.

Figure 6 demonstrates the gravity center shifting of urban built-up area distribution in study area from 1988 to 2007. It can be clearly seen from Fig. 6 that the gravity center of the urban built-up area has been shifted to the north-east direction. During the period 1988–1994, the offset speed was less than the speed of the matching speed. Since 1994, the offset speed has begun to increase, and reached its maximum by 2000 and then gradually decreasing. By 2003, the offset speed was basically consistent with the matching speed and then again less than the matching speed. According to the analysis, the scale of urban built-up areas expanded at a small rate before 1997 and the distribution center of the built-up areas also changed little. However, the size of the urban built-up area in the study area has expanded dramatically with the strategy of establishing a municipality directly under the central government and the development of the western region, and reached its peak in 2003. Subsequently, the government began to systematically control the expansion speed and scale of the urban built-up area, so the shifting gravity center of the urban built-up area gradually decreased.

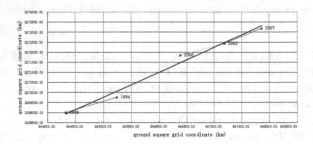

Fig. 6. The shifting gravity center of urban built-up area during the period 1988–2007.

As shown in Fig. 6, the gravity center of the urban built-up area in the study area was shifted by 5.48 km from the north to the east during the period 1988–2007, and the offset angle was 49.7° east. The average offset of the gravity center of the urban built-up area was 0.13 km during the period 1988–1997 as well as the average offset was as high as 0.42 km during the period 1997–2007. It means the urban built-up area has expanded rapidly since the establishment of the Chongqing municipality in 1997.

②*Fractal Feature of Urban Built-Up Area*

Assuming that the urban built-up area is a closed structural unit, the fractal dimension can be expressed by the following formula:

$$D_t = \frac{2\ln(P_t/4)}{\ln(S_t)} \qquad (9)$$

where D_t is the fractal dimension, t is the certain time (e.g., year) of statistical urban built-up area, P is perimeter of the unit, S is the area of the unit.

Based on TM images in 1988 and 2007 and assistant data in 1994, 2000 and 2003, respectively, the area and perimeter of urban built-up area of different periods are calculated, and then the corresponding fractal dimension are calculated and counted. In order to systemically research the fractal dimension change of urban built-up area during the periods, the earlier and corrected landuse map in 1983 as well as the latest Chongqing statistics in 2010 published by the bureau were introduced and used in the study. And the fractal dimension of urban built-up area during the period 1988–2007 is shown in Table 6 and Fig. 7.

Table 6. Fractal dimension of urban built-up area

	1983	1988	1994	2000	2003	2007	2010
Fractal dimension	1.5347	1.5411	1.5483	1.5876	1.6324	1.7145	1.7032

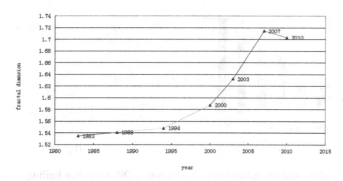

Fig. 7. Fractal feature of urban built-up areas in the study area.

It can be clearly seen from Table 6 and Fig. 7 that the fractal dimensions of the urban built-up area of the study area is greater than 1.5, it indicates that the shape of the urban built-up area is more complicated. In addition, with the large-scale expansion of the urban built-up area and the gradual increase of the fractal dimension, the complexity of the graphic shape of the urban built-up area unit will further increase.

The fractal dimension of the graphic shape of the urban built-up area unit has been floating around 1.54 before 1994. However, it increased rapidly to 1.5876 in 2000, and increased to 1.6324 in 2003 and 1.7145 in 2007. The range of increase was enlarging year by year. When the fractal dimension increases, it indicates that the urban built-up area is dominated by epitaxial expansion. In contrast, when the fractal dimension falls, it indicates that the urban built-up area is dominated by internal filling. Thereinto, the urban built-up area has been in the stage of epitaxial expansion with a slower pace during the period 1983–2007. After the establishment of the Chongqing municipality and the western development strategy, especially in the period 1994–2000, the scale of the urban built-up area in the study area expanded rapidly, and the expansion mode of the urban built-up area was accompanied by simultaneously the extension and internal filling, only the extension of the extension was more obvious. After a period of rapid expansion, the expansion focus of urban built-up areas began to shift to internal filling by 2007. Meanwhile, the fractal dimension of the graphic shape of the urban built-up area began to show a trend of slight downward.

(4) Affecting Factors of Urban Built-Up Area Change

The socio-economic development and population increase are the most important driving factors for the expansion of urban built-up areas. Among them, economic development is the fundamental driving factor for the expansion of urban built-up areas, and the increase of population is the external driving factor for the expansion of built-up areas.

①*Economic Factors*

The relationship between urban built-up area and gross domestic product (GDP) in the study area during the period 1988–2010 is shown in Fig. 8.

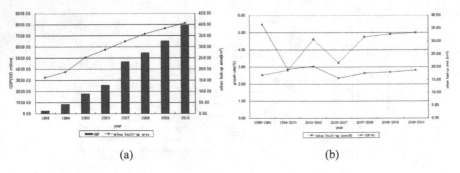

(a)   (b)

Fig. 8. Relationship between urban built-up area and GDP, (a) urban built-up area and GDP, (b) growth rate of urban built-up area and GDP.

As shown in Fig. 8, the urban built-up area and GDP have grown at a high speed from 1988. Although there are differences between different years, the overall growth trend tends to be the same. On the one hand, the growth rate of urban built-up area during the period 1988–1994 was relatively small. After 1994, especially the establishment of municipality in 1997, the economy developed rapidly and the urban built-up area also maintained a high growth rate. When the urban built-up area has expanded to a certain scale, its growth rate has slightly decreased, and then it has begun to stabilize. On the other hand, the GDP growth rate during the period 1988–1994 was much higher than that of earlier years, and the GDP growth is basically in line with the growth of urban built-up areas since 1994. Subsequently, GDP had a small peak in growth in 1997 and 2000; meanwhile, the GDP began to grow at a relatively steady rate.

②*Population Factors*

Figure 9 shows the relationship between the population and the built-up area during the period 1988–2007.

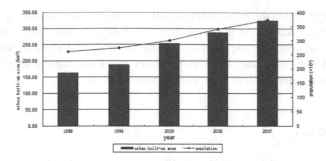

Fig. 9. Relationship between population and urban built-up area.

As shown in Fig. 9, there is a clear positive correlation between the population and the urban built-up area during the period 1988–2007. Similar to the expansion of the urban built-up area, the population growth rate of the study area is relatively low before the establishment of municipality in 1997. By 1997, especially in 2000, there has been a corresponding inflection point in population growth, and then it has entered a high-speed increase phase. At present, with the implementation of the reform of the urban and rural areas policy, as well as the increasing attractiveness of the city itself, it is estimated that the rapid growth in population can continue for some time.

5 Discussions

Aiming at the current insufficiency of identification accuracy of urban built-up area from remote sensing data and selecting thresholds, this paper proposed a new method for collaborative computing of urban built-up area from remote sensing image. It successfully introduced the idea of collaborative computing into the remote sensing data mining. Compared with the traditional identified methods, the proposed collaborative computing method has a great improvement in space-time accuracy and computational efficiency. And the value is mainly reflected in the following aspects:

(1) Combining with the idea of collaborative computing, the map-spectrum synergy, multi-temporal and multi-source remote sensing data synergy are introduced in the identification an extraction of urban built-up area from remote sensing image. The application value of the collaborative computing proposed in this paper is proved by the specific built-up area identification and extraction in Chongqing case.

(2) Aiming at the segmentation threshold in the extraction of urban built-up area, the automatic identification of urban built-up area by map-spectrum collaborative computing, and finally realizes the statistics of urban built-up area by mathematical morphology method are completed. To a certain extent, it avoids the selection of segmentation threshold in the traditional method. The experimental results show that the identification of the urban built-up area by proposed method are not only high overall accuracy and have small errors, but also the results are basically consistent with the visual interpretation range.

(3) This study realizes the rapid, efficient and accurate identification of urban built-up area at small scales. At the same time, by analyzing the spatial and temporal dynamic changes, development trends and influencing factors of urban built-up areas in Chongqing case, it has certain reference value for the identification and extraction of other district from remote sensing data.

6 Conclusions

Based on the traditional identification and extraction methods of urban built-up area, this paper proposed a collaborative computing method for urban built-up area identification from remote sensing image. The NDVI and NDBI are constructed by the collaborative computing of map-spectrum, multi-temporal remote sensing data, multi-knowledge and auxiliary data, and further the urban built-up area in 1988 and 2007 was identified an extracted from TM remote sensing images by mathematical morphology. The experimental results show that:

(1) The total accuracy of urban built-up areas identification of Chongqing municipality in 1988 and 2007 reached 92.58% and 91.41%, respectively, and the Kappa coefficients reached 0.8933 and 0.8722, respectively.
(2) The increased area of urban built-up area reached 162.36 km^2, and the annual change rate is 5.25%. The enlarged area is mainly transformed from cultivated land, woodland, grassland and waters.
(3) The gravity center of the urban built-up area in Chongqing municipality was shifted by 5.48 km from the north to the east during the period of 1988–2007, and the offset angle reached 49.7°.
(4) The fractal dimension of the urban built-up area during the period of 1988–2007 is greater than 1.5; it indicates that the graphic shape of the urban built-up area is more complicated. With the large-scale expansion of the urban built-up area, the fractal dimension of the urban built-up area will be further increased.
(5) It is further verified that socioeconomic development and population increase are the most important driving factors for the expansion of urban built-up area. And there is a clear positive correlation between urban built-up area and the growth of economy and population.

On the basis of collaborative computing proposed in this paper, the collaborative computing mode combined multi-source, multi-temporal, multi-knowledge and computing resources with the characteristics of remote sensing images will be our focus in the future.

Acknowledgements. This research was supported by the National Natural Science Foundation of China under Grant No. U1811461, Graduate Innovation and Entrepreneurship Program in Shanghai University in China under Grant No. 2019GY04, Science and Technology Development Foundation of Shanghai in China under Grant No. 16dz1206000 and 17dz2306400.

References

1. Li, Z., Yang, X.M., Meng, F., Chen, X., Yang, F.S.: The method of multi-source remote sensing synergy extraction in urban build-up area. J. Geo-Inf. Sci. **19**(11), 1522–1529 (2017)
2. Cheng, Y., Zhao, L., Wan, W., Li, L.L., Yu, T., Gu, X.F.: Extracting urban areas in china using DMSP/OLS nighttime light data integrated with biophysical composition information. J. Geogr. Sci. **26**(3), 325–338 (2016)
3. Li, G.D., Fang, C.L., Wang, S.J., Zhang, Q.: Progress in remote sensing recognition and spatio-temporal changes study of urban and rural land use. J. Nat. Resour. **31**(4), 703–718 (2016)
4. Xu, Z.N., Gao, X.L.: A novel method for identifying the boundary of urban built-upareas with POI data. Acta Geographica Sinica **71**(6), 928–939 (2016)
5. Li, X.M., Zheng, X.Q., Yuan, T.: Knowledge mapping of research results on DMSP/OLS nighttime light data. J. Geo-Inf. Sci. **20**(3), 351–359 (2018)
6. Ma, T., Zhou, C.H., Pei, T., Fan, J.: Quantitative estimation of urbanization dynamics using time series of DMSP/OLS nighttime light data: a comparative case study from China's cities. Remote Sens. Environ. **124**(1), 99–107 (2012)
7. Small, C., Elvidge, C.D., Balk, D., Montgomery, M.: Spatial scaling of stable night lights. Remote Sens. Environ. **115**(2), 269–280 (2011)
8. Gong, P., Li, X., Xu, B.: Interpretation on theory and application method development for information on extraction from high resolution remotely sensed data. J. Remote Sens. **10**(1), 1–5 (2006)
9. Zhang, T., Yang, X.M., Tong, L.Q., He, P.: Selection of best-fitting scale parameters in image segmentation based on multiscale segmentation image database. Remote Sens. Land Resour. **28**(4), 59–63 (2016)
10. Li, D.R., Zhang, L.P., Xia, G.S.: Automatic analysis and mining of remote sensing big data. Acta Geodaetica Cartographica Sinica **43**(12), 1211–1216 (2014)
11. Li, C.F., Liu, L., Sun, X.K., Zhao, J.J., Yin, J.Y.: Image segmentation based on fuzzy clustering with cellular autimata and features weighting. EURASIP J. Image Video Process. **1**, 36 (2019)
12. Chen, S.P., Yue, T.X., Li, H.G.: Studies on geo-informatic Tupu and its application. Geogr. Res. **19**(4), 337–343 (2000)
13. Luo, J.C., Wu, T.J., Xia, L.G.: The theory and calculation of spatial-spectral cognition of remote sensing. J. Geo-Inf. Sci. **18**(5), 578–589 (2016)
14. Shen, Z.F., Li, J.L., Yu, X.J.: Water information extraction of Baiyangdian wetland based on the collaborative computing method. J. Geo-Inf. Sci. **18**(5), 690–698 (2016)
15. Ming, D.X., Luo, J.C., Shen, Z.F., Wang, M.M., Sehng, H.: Research on information extraction and target recognition from high resolution remote sensing image. Sci. Surveying Mapp. **30**(3), 18–20 (2005)
16. Li, S.J., Tao, J., Wan, D.S., Feng, J.: Content-based remote sensing image retrieval using co-training of multiple classifiers. J. Remote Sens. **14**(3), 493–506 (2010)
17. Ma, Y., et al.: Remote sensing big data computing: challenges and opportunities. Future Gener. Comput. Syst. **51**(1), 47–60 (2015)
18. O'Callaghan, J.F., Mark, D.M.: The extraction of drainage networks from digital elevation data. Comput. Vis. Graph. Image Process. **28**(2), 323–344 (1984)
19. Lu, D., Tian, H., Zhou, G., Ge, H.L.: Regional mapping of human settlements in southeastern China with multisensor remotely sensed data. Remote Sens. Environ. **112**(9), 3668–3679 (2008)

20. Iounousse, J., Er-Raki, S., Chehouani, H.: Using an unsupervised approach of probabilistic neural network (PNN) for land use classification from multitemporal satellite images. Appl. Soft Comput. **30**(1), 1–13 (2015)
21. Knight, A., Tindall, D., Wilson, B.: A multitemporal multiple density slice method for wetland mapping across the state of Queensland, Australia. Int. J. Remote Sens. **30**(13), 3365–3392 (2009)
22. Zhou, Y., Qiu, F.: Fusion of high spatial resolution WorldView-2 imagery and LiDAR pseudo waveform for object-based image analysis. ISPRS J. Photogramm. Remote Sens. **101** (1), 221–232 (2015)
23. Zhao, R.B., Zhao, S.H., Hu, X.L.: A CPU-GPU collaboration based computing parallel algorithm for MTF degradation of remote sensing simulation images. Comput. Eng. Sci. **37**(7), 1258–1264 (2015)
24. Zhang, Q., Schaaf, C., Seto, K.C.: The vegetation adjusted NTL urban index: a new approach to reduce saturation and increase variation in nighttime luminosity. Remote Sens. Environ. **129**(1), 32–41 (2013)

A Collaborative Anomaly Detection Approach of Marine Vessel Trajectory (Short Paper)

Zejun Huang[1], Jian Wan[1,2], Jie Huang[1(⊠)], Gangyong Jia[1], and Wei Zhang[1]

[1] School of Computer Science and Technology,
Hangzhou Dianzi University, Hangzhou 310018, China
huangjie@hdu.edu.cn
[2] School of Information and Electronic Engineering,
Zhejiang University of Science and Technology, Hangzhou 310023, China

Abstract. Trajectory anomaly detection plays a very important role in navigation safety. Most trajectory anomaly detection methods mainly detect the spatial information of the vessel's trajectory. These methods neglect a vessel's dynamic behavior characteristics, such as course, speed, and acceleration. In this paper, a vessel trajectory multi-factor collaborative anomaly detection (VT-MCAD) approach is proposed to realize the anomaly detection of vessels at sea by studying the trajectory characteristics of vessels. Firstly, the trajectory behavior of historical vessels is identified, and the trajectory characteristics, such as course, speed, and acceleration, are extracted for different trajectory behaviors. Then, the current trajectory behavior is identified when the trajectory anomaly is detected. Based on the TRAjectory Outlier Detection (TRAOD) method, the corresponding trajectory feature model components, including instantaneous angle acceleration, average angle acceleration, instantaneous velocity, and the average velocity and acceleration, are used to detect the anomaly trajectory, and trajectory's suspicious degree of each component in VT-MCAD are obtained. Finally, the suspicious degree of each component is combined to calculate the final suspicious degree. VT-MCAD can change the weight of components according to the detection effectiveness of different components and avoid excessive dependence on one component, which results in better robustness and reliability. The experimental results based on real-world vessel data showed that VT-MCAD could effectively capture anomaly trajectories.

Keywords: Vessel trajectory · Collaborative anomaly detection · Multi-factor · Marine

1 Introduction

With the development of vessel monitoring systems in recent years, more and more maritime surveillance data is collected. Among them, vessel trajectory data is one of the most important data. The loss of personnel and property can be reduced through the detection and analysis of trajectory data by not only making early warnings for piracy, drug smuggling, and other situations but also aiding in timely rescues when vessels encounter bad weather, reef strikes, collisions, or other situations. Due to the large

© ICST Institute for Computer Sciences, Social Informatics and Telecommunications Engineering 2019
Published by Springer Nature Switzerland AG 2019. All Rights Reserved
X. Wang et al. (Eds.): CollaborateCom 2019, LNICST 292, pp. 279–294, 2019.
https://doi.org/10.1007/978-3-030-30146-0_19

number of vessels, the number of historical trajectories generated by them is also very large, and thus it is difficult to detect abnormalities manually. Therefore, it is necessary to use an intelligent algorithm to automatically analyze the abnormalities of the trajectories to help the monitors realize the abnormal monitoring of vessels.

A spatial trajectory is a trace generated by a moving object in geographical spaces, usually represented by a series of chronologically ordered points, where each point consists of a geospatial coordinate set and a time stamp, such as $p = (x, y, t)$. Trajectory anomalies can be items that are significantly different from the other items in terms of some similarity metric. They can also be events or observations that do not conform to an expected pattern [1]. Existing trajectory clustering or frequent pattern mining methods are usually used in trajectory anomaly detection. A trajectory may be abnormal if it cannot adapt to any cluster, or if it is infrequent. The factors affecting trajectory anomalies are not only reflected in unusual location points or sub-trajectories in the spatial domain but also hidden in the sequence of movements associated with a moving object [2].

In the maritime domain, most research of trajectory anomaly detection only considers the trajectory's spatial information and ignores the characteristics of vessel motion. These motion characteristics are the key attributes that describe the behavior of vessels and they become important factors for the anomaly detection of vessel trajectories. This paper proposes a collaborative anomaly detection approach of marine vessel trajectory, called vessel trajectory multi-factor collaborative anomaly detection (VT-MCAD). Based on TRAjectory Outlier Detection (TRAOD) [3], VT-MCAD takes the motion characteristics of the vessel's speed, direction, and acceleration as the components of vessel trajectory anomaly detection, and the anomaly detection result of each component is finally integrated into the trajectory's comprehensive anomaly trend score to achieve anomaly detection. The proposed method combines the spatial models and motion models of the trajectories in a multi-factor framework to generate more accurate detection.

2   Related Work

Most existing anomaly trajectory detection techniques are based on the distance, direction, and density of trajectories. However, classification and historical similarity-based techniques have also been proposed [4].

A distance-based approach was originally proposed by Knorr [5]. Lee [3] proposed the TRAOD algorithm which consists of two phases: partitioning and detection. In the first phase, each trajectory is partitioned first in coarse granularity and then in fine granularity. In the second phase, the outlying trajectory partitions are detected mainly using distance, and thus this phase is intuitive and efficient.

Ge [6] considered outliers in terms of direction and density. An evolving trajectory outlier detection method was provided, named TOP-EYE, which continuously computes the outlying score for each trajectory in an accumulating way. In TOP-EYE, a decay function is introduced to mitigate the influence of the past trajectories on the evolving outlying score, which is defined based on the evolving moving direction and density of trajectories. This decay function enables the evolving computation of the accumulated outlying scores along the trajectories.

Classification-based approaches establish a normal trajectory model and abnormal trajectory model through statistical information of the historical trajectory and generate a trajectory classifier. Li [7] proposed a Motion-Alert classification method for trajectory outlier detection that consists of the following three steps: (1) Object movement features, called motifs, are extracted from the object paths. Each path consists of a sequence of motif expressions associated with the values related to time and location. (2) Motif-based generalization is performed to discover anomalies in object movements, which clusters similar object movement fragments and generalizes the movements based on the associated motifs. (3) With motif-based generalization, objects are put into a multi-level feature space and are classified by a classifier that can handle high-dimensional feature spaces.

The historical similarity-based approach establishes a global feature model according to the frequent patterns of historical data mining, and then the data different from the global feature model are identified as abnormal trajectories. This method can usually be used for training data sets without labels. The historical similarity-based approach is widely used in navigation, road network traffic, and other fields. Lei [2] proposed a framework for maritime trajectory modeling and anomaly detection, called MT-MAD. The model considers the fact that anomalous behavior manifests in unusual location points and sub-trajectories in the spatial domain as well as in the sequence and manner in which these locations and sub-trajectories occur.

Currently, there is little research on trajectory anomaly detection for marine vessels and its application to the real world is still at an immature stage [8–12]. To promote the safety of marine navigation, there is an urgent need to design a more robust trajectory anomaly detection method.

3 Collaborative Trajectory Anomaly Detection Framework

3.1 The Framework

The framework of VT-MCAD is shown in Fig. 1. It may be quite difficult to directly identify whether a trajectory is an anomaly trajectory since anomalous trajectories are rare in the trajectory data set. Therefore, VT-MCAD assumes that each vessel trajectory is suspicious to varying degrees and it achieves anomaly detection by identifying the vessel trajectory's degree of suspiciousness [2]. When a trajectory anomaly detection is performed, VT-MCAD intercepts a trajectory segment of the vessel's adjacent time, and then recognizes the behavior of the trajectory segment, calculates the suspicious degree of its location, speed, direction, acceleration and so on, and integrates them to realize anomaly detection. As shown, the VT-MCAD method can be divided into two phases (shown in Fig. 1): trajectory modeling and anomaly detection.

3.2 TRAOD

TRAOD [3] is a basic component of VT-MCAD. The algorithm divides the trajectory into a set of trajectory segments and then calculates the distance between the trajectory segments to realize trajectory anomaly detection.

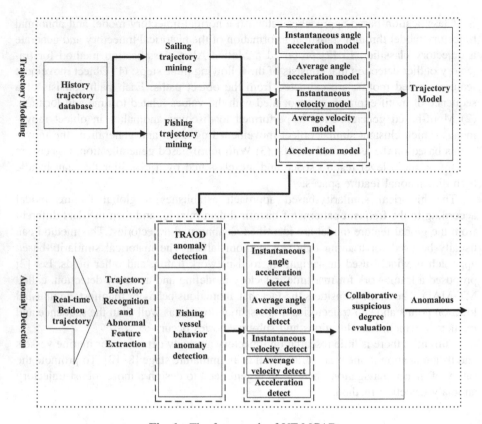

Fig. 1. The framework of VT-MCAD

TRAOD uses the Hausdorff distance, commonly used in pattern recognition, to define the distance between trajectory segments [13], which mainly consists of the perpendicular distance $(d_\perp)$, parallel distance $(d_\parallel)$, and angle distance (d_θ).

Suppose there are two trajectory segments $S_1 = s_1 e_1$, $S_2 = s_2 e_2$, where s_i and $e_i (i = 1, 2)$ are the starting and ending points of the trajectory segment, respectively. S_1 is the shorter one of the two trajectory segments. $d_\perp$, $d_\parallel$, and d_θ are shown in Formulas (1), (2), and (5), respectively. Among them, suppose that the projection points of the points s_1 and e_1 onto S_2 are p_s and p_e, respectively. $l_{\perp 1}$ is the Euclidean distance between s_1 and p_s and $l_{\perp 2}$ is the Euclidean distance between e_1 and p_e. $\|S_1\|$ is the length of S_1 and $\theta (0^\circ \leq \theta \leq 180^\circ)$ is the smaller intersection angle between S_1 and S_2. Finally, the distance between the two trajectory segments can be determined through Formula (6).

$$d_\perp(S_1, S_2) = \frac{l_{\perp 1}^2 + l_{\perp 2}^2}{l_{\perp 1} + l_{\perp 2}} \tag{1}$$

$$d_\parallel(S_1, S_2) = MIN(l_{\parallel 1}, l_{\parallel 2}) \tag{2}$$

$$l_{\|1} = \text{MIN}(\|p_s s_2\|, \|p_s e_2\|) \tag{3}$$

$$l_{\|2} = \text{MIN}(\|p_e s_2\|, \|p_e e_2\|) \tag{4}$$

$$d_\theta(S_1, S_2) = \begin{cases} \|S_1\| \times \sin(\theta), & \text{if } 0° \le \theta < 90° \\ \|S_1\|, & \text{if } 90° \le \theta \le 180° \end{cases} \tag{5}$$

$$\text{dist}(S_1, S_2) = w_\perp \cdot d_\perp(S_1, S_2) + w_\| \cdot d_\|(S_1, S_2) + w_\theta \cdot d_\theta(S_1, S_2) \tag{6}$$

The adjacent trajectory, anomaly segment and anomaly trajectory are defined respectively below. Table 1 introduces the notation meanings used in the following definitions.

Table 1. Notation meanings

SYMBOL	Meaning
$len(S_i)$	The length of the segment S_i
$P(TR_i)$	The set of all segments of TR_i
$CP(TR_i, S_j, D)$	The set of TR_i's segments within the distance D from $S_j \in P(TR_j)$ $(TR_i \ne TR_j)$, i.e., $\{S_i | S_i \in P(TR_i) \wedge \text{dist}(S_i, S_j) \le D\}$
$CTR(S_i, D)$	The set of trajectories close to S_i
$OP(TR_i, D, p)$	The set of outlying segments of TR_i

Definition 1: Adjacent Trajectory. TR_i is S_j's adjacent trajectory when inequality (7) is true, where $S_j \in P(TR_j)(TR_i \ne TR_j)$.

$$\sum_{S_i \in CP(TR_i, S_j, D)} len(S_i) \ge len(S_j) \tag{7}$$

Definition 2: Anomaly Segment. $S_i \in P(TR_i)$ is an anomaly segment when inequality (8) is true. Here, $|\Gamma|$ denotes the total number of trajectories, and p is a parameter given by a user.

$$|CTR(S_i, D)| \le (1 - p)|\Gamma| \tag{8}$$

Definition 3: Anomaly Trajectory. TR_i is an anomaly trajectory when inequality (9) is true. In other words, when the proportion of the anomaly segments in the trajectory is not less than the threshold F (defined by the user), TR_i is an anomaly trajectory.

$$\frac{\sum_{S_i \in OP(TR_i, D, p)} len(S_i)}{\sum_{M_i \in P(TR_i)} len(M_i)} \ge F \tag{9}$$

3.3 Trajectory Behavior Recognition

Trajectory behavior recognition of a fishing vessel is the basis of trajectory modeling [14–17]. In this study, the MSC-FBI algorithm proposed by Zhang et al. [18] is used to recognize fishing vessel behavior. The biggest difference between MSC-FBI and other fishing vessel behavior recognition algorithms is that the time distance between the trajectory points is added to the trajectory point distance measurement, and the distance between the trajectory points is considered comprehensively through the four dimensions of time, space, velocity, and direction. The time distance between two points is shown in Formula (10); the closer the time interval between the trajectory points P_i and P_j is, the smaller their time distance is. The spatial distance, velocity distance, and direction distance between P_i and P_j are shown in Formulas (11), (12), and (13), respectively, where $d(i)$ is the direction change times within a given period of time $\{time_i - t_d, time_i + t_d\}$. Finally, the temporal-spatial distance between P_i and P_j is shown in Formula (14), where W is a weight vector.

$$T(i,j) = \frac{|time_i - time_j|}{\max(T) - \min(T)} \tag{10}$$

$$S(i,j) = \frac{\sqrt{(lon_i - lon_j)^2 + (lat_i - lat_j)^2}}{\max(S) - \min(S)} \tag{11}$$

$$V(i,j) = \frac{|Speed_i - Speed_j|}{\max(V) - \min(V)} \tag{12}$$

$$DIR(i,j) = |d(i) - d(j)| \tag{13}$$

$$D(i,j) = W[T(i,j)\ S(i,j)\ V(i,j)\ DIR(i,j)]^T \tag{14}$$

The following is a brief introduction to the implementation steps of the MSC-FBI algorithm. Data set D contains a historical trajectory that needs behavioral recognition. The specific steps are as follows:

(1) Use DBSCAN and the space-time distance measurement method to cluster the trajectory in D and obtain the trajectory segments of the different behaviors.
(2) Use K-Means to cluster the trajectory segments that were obtained in Step (1), and the trajectory segments of the same behavior pattern are clustered into one cluster.
(3) After obtaining the trajectory segments of same behavior pattern, model the trajectory of different behavior patterns.
(4) Use the behavior model obtained in Step (3) to identify the trajectory behavior.

3.4 Trajectory Modeling

Trajectory modeling is used to establish the behavior model of the fishing vessels, including five trajectory characteristic models: instantaneous angle acceleration, average angle acceleration, instantaneous velocity, average velocity, and acceleration. It is necessary to distinguish between behaviors when modeling due to the different behavior patterns of fishing vessels' sailing state and fishing state. Figure 2 shows the trajectory modeling process of the fishing vessel, in which the behavior of the fishing vessel is divided into two categories: sailing behavior and fishing behavior.

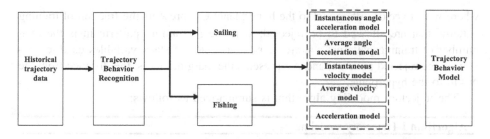

Fig. 2. Trajectory modeling process of the fishing vessel

The trajectory data of the fishing vessel discussed in this paper were positioned and transmitted by the BeiDou navigation satellite system (BDS). The trajectory information includes longitude, latitude, timestamp, direction, speed, and temperature of the fishing vessel. The behavior patterns of fishing vessels in different states can be extracted and the trajectory model can be established through the study and analysis of these attributes.

Traditional anomaly detection modeling methods can be divided into supervised learning and unsupervised learning. Supervised learning needs to label the data in the training set before training the model, and then the anomaly detection model is built by classifying training set labels. In contrast, unsupervised learning does not need to label the training set data before beginning training but implements anomaly detection through data features. Because anomalies are rare in the trajectory data of this study, it was not possible to construct a rich training set for supervised learning, and therefore an unsupervised one-class SVM was used to establish the trajectory model.

One-class SVM [19] is a common method in the field of anomaly detection. It is a variant of the SVM algorithm. SVM is a supervised algorithm, and its essence is to find a hyperplane with the largest classification interval to realize data classification. SVM's training set is divided into two parts: metadata and the classification label. One-class SVM is an unsupervised algorithm in which the metadata does not need any data labels in its training set. The goal of one-class SVM is to find a hyperplane in the feature space so that most of the training patterns are in front of the hyperplane and the distance between the hyperplane and the origin is maximized. In other words, one-class SVM actually finds a hyperplane in the feature space to separate the origin and training patterns, and the distance between the hyperplane and the origin is maximized.

The maximum edge problem is the core of one-class SVM. Therefore, the problem can be formulated as follows:

$$min_{w,\varepsilon,\rho} \frac{1}{2} \|w\|^2 + \frac{1}{mC} \sum_i \varepsilon_i$$
$$w \cdot \emptyset(x_i) \geq \rho - \varepsilon_i, \varepsilon_i \geq 0, \forall i = 1, \ldots, m \tag{15}$$

where w is a vector orthogonal to the hyperplane; C represents the fraction of training patterns that are allowed to be rejected; x_i is the ith training pattern; m is the total number of training patterns; $\varepsilon = \varepsilon_1, \ldots, \varepsilon_m$ is a vector of slack variables used to "penalize" the rejected patterns; and ρ represents the margin, that is, the distance from the origin to the hyperplane.

The trajectory modeling algorithm is summarized as follows:

Algorithm 1 Trajectory modeling.

Input: Sailing trajectory training set $D_s = \{ST_1, ST_2, \ldots, ST_n\}$,
    Fishing trajectory training set $D_f = \{FT_1, FT_2, \ldots, FT_n\}$

Output: Trajectory Model M

1: // Using instantaneous direction, average direction,
2: // instantaneous velocity, average velocity and acceleration
3: // established corresponding models respectively.
4: for each $ST_i(FT_i)$ in $D_s(D_f)$:
5:    for each P_j in $ST_i(FT_i)$:
6:      $S_{MD}^s(S_{MD}^f)$ ← Calculate Moment Direction for P_j
7:      $S_{AD}^s(S_{AD}^f)$ ← Calculate Average Direction for P_j
8:      $S_{MS}^s(S_{MS}^f)$ ← Calculate Moment Velocity for P_j
9:      $S_{AS}^s(S_{AS}^f)$ ← Calculate Average Velocity for P_j
10:     $S_A^s(S_A^f)$ ← Calculate Acceleration for P_j
11:   // Modeling instantaneous angle acceleration by
12:   // instantaneous direction
13:   M_{MD}^s, M_{MD}^f ← Model(S_{MD}^s), Model(S_{MD}^f)
14:   // Modeling average angle acceleration by average
15:   // direction
16:   M_{AD}^s, M_{AD}^f ← Model(S_{AD}^s), Model(S_{AD}^f)
17:   // Modeling of Instantaneous velocity
18:   M_{MS}^s, M_{MS}^f ← Model(S_{MS}^s), Model(S_{MS}^f)
19:   // Modeling of average velocity
20:   M_{AS}^s, M_{AS}^f ← Model(S_{AS}^s), Model(S_{AS}^f)
21:   // Modeling acceleration
22:   M_A^s, M_A^f ← Model(S_A^s), Model(S_A^f)
23:   M ← $\{M_{MD}^s(M_{MD}^f), M_{AD}^s(M_{AD}^f), M_{MS}^s(M_{MS}^f),$
24:   $M_{AS}^s(M_{AS}^f), M_A^s(M_A^f)\}$
25:   return M

The instantaneous angle acceleration model M_{MD}^s, average angle acceleration model M_{AD}^s, instantaneous velocity model M_{MS}^s, average velocity model M_{AS}^s, and acceleration model M_A^s are the five independent components of the trajectory model. When the anomaly trajectories of fishing vessels are detected, the suspicious degree of each component (including TRAOD) are calculated separately, and then the suspicious degrees are combined to realize anomaly detection.

3.5 Anomaly Trajectory Detection of Vessels

In the anomaly detection phase, this method integrates the suspicious degree of the trajectory model's different components to obtain more reliable anomaly detection results. Among them, the suspicious degree of the TRAOD component is calculated using Formula (16), and the suspicious degrees of the other components are calculated by Formula (17), where $OPS(TR_i)$ represents the anomaly point set in trajectory TR_i and $PS(TR_i)$ represents all the points in TR_i.

$$\text{Suspicious Degree}_{TRAOD} = \frac{\sum_{S_i \in OP(TR_i, D, p)} len(S_i)}{\sum_{M_i \in P(TR_i)} len(M_i)} \tag{16}$$

$$\text{Suspicious Degree}_{others} = \frac{OPS(TR_i)}{PS(TR_i)} \tag{17}$$

Different from the traditional anomaly detection algorithm, the motion characteristics of vessel trajectory data are modeled and treated as different components of VT-MCAD. After obtaining the suspicious degree of each component, the final anomaly detection results are obtained by using the predefined combination strategy. In addition, in the process of suspicious degree combination, different characteristic models of the algorithm are given different weights according to the model availability so as to deal with the anomaly detection sensitivity of different characteristics.

Specifically, the different characteristics of vessel trajectory have different meanings. It is necessary to effectively deal with the suspicious degrees while combining them. Traditional combination methods mainly include cumulative sum and sorting methods, but both methods have shortcomings. For example, the cumulative sum method may cause the final result to be excessively dependent on the component and weaken the influence of other components when the suspicious degree of a component is abnormally large. Additionally, the sorting method may cause conflicts in the individual component results. To solve these problems, each component of VT-MCAD is weighted based on the cumulative sum. The weight of each component is determined by the availability of the component in different application scenarios. The weighted cumulative sum algorithm is as follows:

Algorithm 2 Weighted cumulative sum.

Input: Component suspicious degree set $S = \{S_1, S_2, ..., S_n\}$
Output: Final suspicious degree S_f

1: Foreach i=1 to n
2:   Assign w_i to S_i
3:   $S_f = \sum_{i=1}^{n} w_i \cdot S_i$
4: Return S_f

The above algorithm assigns a weight w to the suspicious degree obtained by the different components in VT-MCAD, and $w_1 + w_2 + \ldots + w_n = 1$, where n is the number of VT-MCAD components. Figure 3 shows a flow chart of the vessel trajectory anomaly detection. After inputting the trajectory of the vessel, the six component models of VT-MCAD calculate the suspicious degree separately, and then the components of each component are integrated to acquire the final suspicious degree of the current trajectory.

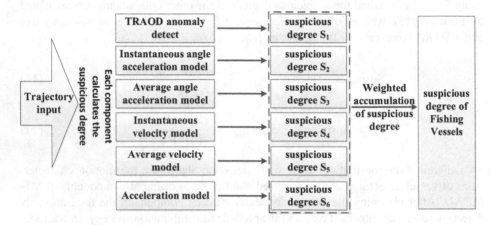

Fig. 3. Flow chart of vessel trajectory anomaly detection

4 Experiments

The experiment used the trajectory data set in a dynamic fishing vessel management system operated in Zhoushan, China. The system utilizes BDS to locate vessels and transmit real-time data. Its main functions include vessel inquiry, track playback, alarm rescue, and voyage statistics. The experimental data were collected from December 22, 2016, to November 8, 2018, from a total of 220 vessels, and was about 0.6 GB in size.

The effectiveness of the VT-MCAD method proposed in this paper was verified by comparing the effect of TRAOD and VT-MCAD on anomaly detection of the above trajectory dataset. Since the detection methods of the two algorithms are basically the same under the two behaviors of fishing vessel sailing and fishing, this study only detected anomalies of the fishing vessel's sailing trajectory.

4.1 TRAOD Anomaly Detection

After cleaning and filtering the trajectory data, 6,110 trajectory data were obtained. The TRAOD trajectory anomaly detection effect was verified on a test set containing 50 normal trajectories and eight anomaly trajectories. During the experiment, the parameter p was set to 0.9 and the parameter F was set to 0.2. Figure 4(a) shows the accuracy of TRAOD for the detection of different parameters D values. As the value of D increases, the detection accuracy of the normal trajectory continuously increases, and the detection accuracy of the anomaly trajectory continuously decreases. Figure 4(b) shows the anomaly detection accuracy of the parameter D from 2 to 3 interval 0.1. As shown, when the parameter D is greater than 2.4, the normal trajectory detection accuracy is 100%, and the accuracy of anomaly trajectory detection is 25%–37.5%.

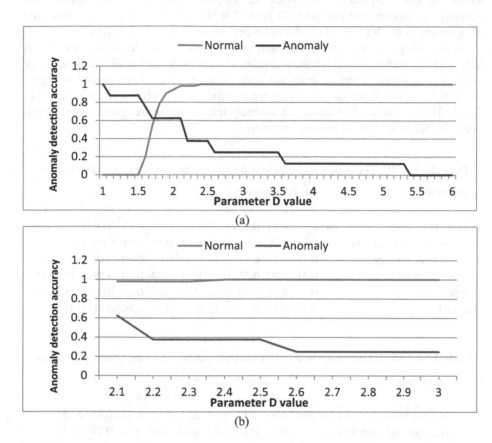

(a)

(b)

Fig. 4. Anomaly detection accuracy of TRAOD with different parameter D values

The experimental results showed that TRAOD is not ideal for anomaly detection of a fishing vessel's trajectory. In the case of not tolerating the misjudgment of the normal trajectory, the final detection ratio of the TRAOD to the anomaly trajectory was only 37.5%, and the risk of the algorithm erroneously judging normal trajectories was large. When the parameter D was increased to reduce misjudgment, the accuracy of the anomaly trajectory detection was further reduced to 25%. Therefore, TRAOD can detect a part of the anomaly trajectory, but the detection accuracy is low and the effect is poor.

4.2   VT-MCAD Anomaly Detection

Tables 2 and 3 show the suspicious degree of VT-MCAD's different components. There were ten normal trajectories and eight anomaly trajectories in the test set, of which the table respectively describes the suspicious degree for the normal and anomaly trajectories. The parameter D in the TRAOD component was 2.6. Since the components in the VT-MCAD had similar performances under the experimental scenario, this study used the simple averaging method to integrate the component results [20]. It can be seen that although the trajectory suspicious degrees of different trajectory features were different, the anomaly detection accuracy of each component was generally higher. Finally, the suspicious degree distribution of each trajectory is shown in Fig. 5. The suspicious degrees of the anomaly trajectories in the graph were significantly higher than those of normal trajectories.

Table 2. VT-MCAD components suspicious degree distribution of the normal trajectory

Components	Normal trajectory									
	1	2	3	4	5	6	7	8	9	10
Instantaneous angle acceleration	0.31	0.05	0.19	0.07	0.07	0.07	0.11	0.00	0.15	0.05
Average angle acceleration	0.31	0.05	0.00	0.21	0.27	0.00	0.17	0.00	0.05	0.32
Instantaneous velocity	0.23	0.21	0.43	0.07	0.33	0.07	0.00	0.19	0.10	0.05
Average velocity	0.31	0.05	0.25	0.07	0.27	0.07	0.00	0.38	0.15	0.16
Acceleration	0.23	0.26	0.38	0.00	0.13	0.07	0.00	0.00	0.15	0.11
TRAOD	0.28	0.32	0.22	0.22	0.21	0.54	0.19	0.41	0.47	0.43

Table 3. VT-MCAD components suspicious degree distribution of the anomaly trajectory

Components	Anomaly trajectory							
	1	2	3	4	5	6	7	8
Instantaneous angle acceleration	0.35	0.17	1.00	0.38	0.50	0.21	0.64	0.23
Average angle acceleration	0.24	0.28	0.33	0.44	0.38	0.14	0.27	0.15
Instantaneous velocity	0.41	0.11	0.67	0.88	0.88	0.79	0.72	0.62
Average velocity	0.29	0.06	1.00	0.81	1.0	0.36	0.91	0.54
Acceleration	0.29	0.06	0.07	0.31	0.25	0.50	0.27	0.38
TRAOD	0.87	0.09	0.21	0.40	0.63	0.24	0.59	0.95

The experimental results showed that compared with TRAOD, the VT-MCAD algorithm proposed in this paper had a higher accuracy of anomaly detection, and the algorithm considers various trajectory features, such as position, speed, and direction, which make VT-MCAD more robust and reliable.

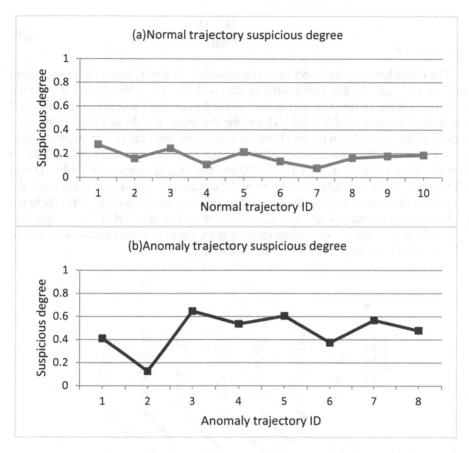

Fig. 5. VT-MCAD suspicious degree

4.3   Algorithm Evaluation

To compare the effectiveness of TRAOD and VT-MCAD, the Precision, Recall, and F-measure evaluation criteria are used, as shown in Formulas (18), (19), and (20), where R represents the known anomaly trajectory data set; D represents the anomaly result set obtained after the algorithm is executed; Precision and Recall are used to evaluate the accuracy and completeness of the algorithm anomaly detection result, respectively; and the F-measure index integrates the Precision and Recall evaluation results.

$$\text{Precision} = \frac{|R \cap D|}{|D|} \tag{18}$$

$$\text{Recall} = \frac{|R \cap D|}{|R|} \tag{19}$$

$$\text{Recall} = \frac{|R \cap D|}{|R|} \tag{20}$$

The algorithm anomaly detection performance evaluation is based on the maximum order of the anomaly detection results in Tables 2 and 3 and Fig. 5, and the top ten trajectories of the maximum ordering were defined as anomaly trajectories. Figures 6, 7 and 8 show the results of VT-MCAD and the Precision, Recall, and F-measure of its various components. It can be seen from the figure that under the current trajectory data set, the anomaly detection accuracy of the TRAOD was 0.5, which was 0.2–0.3 lower than the other components of VT-MCAD, and the final accuracy of VT-MCAD was 0.2 higher than that of TRAOD. In terms of the completeness of anomaly detection, the proportion of anomaly trajectories detected by other components of VT-MCAD to the total number of anomaly trajectories exceeded 0.8 while that of TRAOD was only 0.6. By combining the above two evaluation indicators, the F-measure evaluation results of VT-MCAD were significantly better than TRAOD.

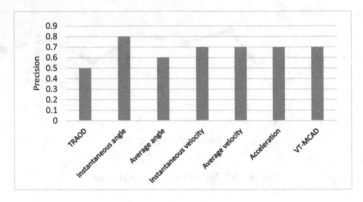

Fig. 6. Precision evaluation

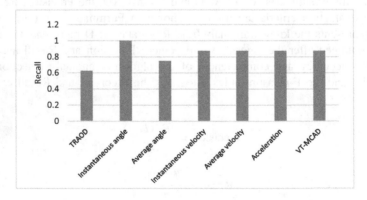

Fig. 7. Recall evaluation

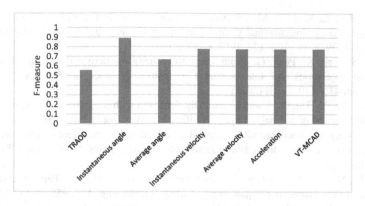

Fig. 8. F-measure evaluation

5 Conclusion

In this paper, a multi-factor collaborative approach to detecting anomaly trajectories of marine vessels is proposed. This approach simultaneously considers the vessel's speed, direction, and acceleration. Our VT-MCAD approach was evaluated using data from the Zhoushan fishing vessel management system. Results showed that the accuracy and completeness of the VT-MCAD in the experiments trajectory dataset were significantly better than the TRAOD, which verifies the effectiveness of the VT-MCAD. Future work shall consider more factors by exploiting the knowledge of marine meteorology and hydrology.

Acknowledgment. This work was supported in part by the Key Research and Development Project of Zhejiang Province (Grant No. 2017C03024) and the National Natural Science Foundation of China (Grant No. 61572163, No. 61872119).

References

1. Zheng, Y.: Trajectory data mining: an overview. ACM Trans. Intell. Syst. Technol. **6**(3), 29 (2015)
2. Lei, P.R.: A framework for anomaly detection in maritime trajectory behavior. Knowl. Inf. Syst. **47**(1), 189–214 (2016)
3. Lee, J.G., Han, J., Li, X.: Trajectory outlier detection: a partition-and-detect framework. In: IEEE International Conference on Data Engineering, Cancun, pp. 140–149. IEEE (2008)
4. Gupta, M., Gao, J., Aggarwal, C.C.: Outlier detection for temporal data: a survey. IEEE Trans. Knowl. Data Eng. **26**(9), 2250–2267 (2014)
5. Knorr, E.M., Raymond, T.N., Vladimir, T.: Distance-based outliers: algorithms and applications. VLDB J. **8**(3–4), 237–253 (2000)
6. Ge, Y., Xiong, H., Zhou, Z., Ozdemir, H., Yu, J., Lee, K.: Top-Eye: top-k evolving trajectory outlier detection. In: Proceedings of the 19th ACM Conference on Information and Knowledge Management, Toronto, pp. 1733–1736. ACM (2010)

7. Li, X., Han, J., Kim, S.: Motion-Alert: automatic anomaly detection in massive moving objects. In: IEEE International Conference on Intelligence and Security Informatics, San Diego, vol. 3975, pp. 166–177. IEEE (2006)

8. Chang, S., Yeh, K., Peng, G.: From safety to security - pattern and anomaly detections in maritime trajectories. In: International Carnahan Conference on Security Technology, Taipei, pp. 415–419. IEEE (2015)

9. Zhen, R., Jin, Y., Hu, Q.: Maritime anomaly detection within coastal waters based on vessel trajectory clustering and naive bayes classifier. J. Navig. 70(3), 648–670 (2017)

10. Tu, E., Zhang, G., Rachmawati, L.: Exploiting AIS data for intelligent maritime navigation: a comprehensive survey from data to methodology. IEEE Trans. Intell. Transp. Syst. 19(5), 1559–1582 (2018)

11. Zhao, L., Shi, G.: A trajectory clustering method based on Douglas-Peucker compression and density for marine traffic pattern recognition. Ocean Eng. 172, 456–467 (2019)

12. Pallotta, G., Vespe, M., Bryan, K.: Vessel pattern knowledge discovery from AIS data: a framework for anomaly detection and route prediction. Entropy 15(6), 2218–2245 (2013)

13. Chen, J., Leung, M.K., Gao, Y.: Noisy logo recognition using line segment Hausdorff distance. Pattern Recogn. 36(4), 943–955 (2003)

14. Marzuki, M.I., Gaspar, P., Garello, R.: Fishing gear identification from vessel-monitoring-system-based fishing vessel trajectories. IEEE J. Oceanic Eng. 43(3), 689–699 (2018)

15. Fernando, T., Mercedes, V., Antonio, F.S.: A complex event processing approach to detect abnormal behaviours in the marine environment. Inf. Syst. Front. 18(4), 765–780 (2016)

16. Dabrowski, J.J., de Villiers, J.P., Beyers, C.: Context-based behaviour modelling and classification of marine vessels in an abalone poaching situation. Eng. Appl. Artif. Intell. 64, 95–111 (2017)

17. de Souza, E.N., Boerder, K., Matwin, S.: Improving fishing pattern detection from satellite AIS using data mining and machine learning. PLoS ONE 11(7), e0158248 (2016)

18. Zhang, J., Geng, J., Wan, J., et al.: An automatically learning and discovering human fishing behaviors scheme for CPSCN. IEEE Access 6, 19844–19858 (2018)

19. Perdisci, R., Gu, G., Lee, W.: Using an ensemble of one-class SVM classifiers to harden payload-based anomaly detection systems. In: International Conference on Data Mining, Hong Kong, pp. 488–498. IEEE (2006)

20. Zhou, Z.H.: Ensemble Methods - Foundations and Algorithms. Taylor & Francis, Milton Park (2012)

Classification of Skin Lesions Based on Data Collaboration Under Imbalance Dataset

Weijia Ji[1,2], Lizhi Cai[1,2], Mingang Chen[2(✉)], and Naiqi Wang[1,2]

[1] School of Information Science and Engineer,
East China University of Science and Technology, Shanghai, China
asdfvl929@gmail.com, slytherinwnq@163.com
[2] Laboratory of Computer Software Testing and Evaluating,
Shanghai Development Center of Computer Software Technology,
Shanghai, China
{clz, cmg}@ssc.stn.sh.cn

Abstract. Imbalance data is a common problem in machine learning task, which often impacts the accuracy of models. An effective way to solve it is to increase the number of minority class samples in the dataset. Many methods are put forward to solve the problem of imbalance data in machine learning. But these are all for low-dimensional data. For high-dimensional data, such as images, these methods are not well applicable. In this paper, an image generation method based on generative adversarial network is introduced to do pattern learning for samples of minority class in the dataset, so as to realize the expansion of data for minority class. And finally the classification networks for skin lesions are trained by data collaboration which consist of real images and generated images. The experimental results indicate that the accuracy of networks are further improved by the addition of generated images while alleviating the imbalance problem to some extent.

Keywords: Imbalance data · Generative adversarial network ·
Data collaboration · Skin image classification

1 Introduction

Classification task is always being a research hotspot in machine learning field. The existing classification methods have been able to achieve good performance on the classification task of conventional dataset. However, the research of these classifiers are based on an assumption that the distribution of sample categories is roughly the same. That means the dataset used for training is balanced. In simple, the number of data samples contained in each category is basically equal. But this assumption does not exist in many practical problems. The truth is the number of samples in one or even several categories in dataset is much smaller than that of other categories. For example, imbalance data exists in these application scenarios, such as information retrieval, credit card illegal transaction [1], medical diagnosis [2, 3], etc. And the recognition rate of minority class in these tasks appears to be more important. As far as medical diagnosis task is concerned, if a normal person is misdiagnosed as a patient, it will

X. Wang et al. (Eds.): CollaborateCom 2019, LNICST 292, pp. 295–306, 2019.
https://doi.org/10.1007/978-3-030-30146-0_20

bring him some mental burdens, but the fact is that the person is healthy. However, if a patient is misdiagnosed as a normal person, it may bring about the patient to miss the best treatment period and some serious consequences. So it often fails to achieve satisfied results when applying the model based on imbalance data to the above scenarios.

The reason for this problem is that the classification model with the overall classification accuracy as the learning target pays too much attention to the majority class samples. That means the model has a high recognition rate of the majority class samples, resulting in the degradation of performance about minority class samples. So it is particularly necessary to solve the problem of imbalance data in some specific fields.

When performing a lesion recognition study on the skin images dataset, we found that the number of image samples for skin cancer diseases was far less than that of benign lesions. This leads to the model's accuracy in predicting malignant lesions is much lower than that of benign lesions. Thus in order to improve the recognition accuracy of skin cancer diseases, it is first necessary to solve the problem that the sample numbers differ greatly, that is, sample imbalance problem.

We firstly adopt the methods [4] commonly used in machine learning to solve the imbalance problem in skin lesion images, such as random sampling, SMOTE, Borderline-SMOTE. But most of these methods are aimed at low-dimensional sample data. For high-dimensional data such as skin images, these solutions cannot play their due role well, and cannot improve the classification accuracy of malignant diseases.

Therefore, this paper introduces an image generation method based on generative adversarial network (GAN) [5]. The images of the same distribution as the corresponding class are generated by learning the pattern features of minority class samples in the dataset. The model is then trained in a way of data collaboration with real images and generated images, thereby further improving the accuracy of lesion classification, especially the prediction of skin cancer.

2   Related Methods

Many methods have been proposed to solve the problem of imbalance data in machine learning classification tasks. We list several commonly used methods here.

2.1   Random Sampling

The sampling algorithm uses some strategies to change the class distribution in the dataset to convert the imbalanced sample into a relatively balanced sample. The random sampling method is the simplest and most intuitive one of the sampling algorithms. There are two types of random sampling: RandomUnderSampling and RandomOverSampling. RandomUnderSampling refers to the random deletion of some data from majority class, so that the data amount of majority class and minority class is basically the same. Another random sampling method, RandomOverSampling, is to achieve the relative balance of classes by adding data to minority class. The method of adding is generally to randomly extract data from and put them back into the minority class, and finally make the number of minority and majority class equal. The essence of RandomOverSampling is to copy some samples from minority class to achieve the effect of increasing the dataset size.

2.2 SMOTE

SMOTE (Synthetic Minority Oversampling Technique) [6] is an improved method based on random oversampling algorithm. Due to random oversampling method uses a strategy of simply copying data form the minority class to increase the sample size of the minority class. It is easy to cause over-fitting problem in the training process of network. So the SMOTE algorithm has made an effective improvement to this problem. Its basic idea is to analyze minority class samples and synthesize new samples, then add them to the dataset.

The operation flow of SMOTE is as follows:

(1) For each sample x in minority class, calculating the distance to all other samples in minority class $S_{minority}$ by the Euclidean distance, and obtain k neighbor samples;
(2) Setting a sampling ratio according to the sample imbalance ratio to determine the sampling magnification N. For each sample x from minority class, randomly selecting several samples from its k neighbors, assuming that the selected neighbor is xn;
(3) For each randomly selected neighbor xn, constructing new sample data with the original sample according to the following formula:

$$x_{new} = x_i + \delta * (\widehat{x_i} + x_i) \tag{1}$$

where $x_i \in S_{minority}$; $\widehat{x_i}$ represents a sample of the k-nearest neighbors of x_i, $\widehat{x_i} \in S_{minority}$ and δ is a random number with a range [0, 1]. The specific operation is shown in Fig. 1, (a) indicates the k-nearest neighbor ($k = 7$) of x_i are found, and then the new data is generated according to formula (1), as in (b) The rhombus shows a sample of the newly synthesized data.

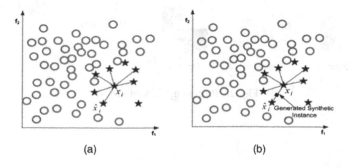

(a)   (b)

Fig. 1. SMOTE [4]

However, the SMOTE algorithm is prone to excessive generalization and high variance, and it is also easy to generate overlapping data. Besides, the SMOTE method produces the same amount of synthesized data for each original sample in minority class without considering the distribution characteristics of its neighboring sample data. So in order to solve the problems in SMOTE, the Borderline-SMOTE [7] is proposed. Unlike SMOTE, which generates new samples for each of the minority class sample, Borderline-SMOTE only generates new data for the minority class samples close to the boundary. That is to say, a minority class sample is selected, in which the number of majority class samples in its adjacent sample set is greater than half of the total. So the data in such a sample set are used to generate the new synthetic samples to increase classification accuracy.

2.3 GAN

The Generative Adversial Network (GAN) is a deep learning-based generation model. It has been paid more and more attention by academics and industry since it was proposed by Ian Goodfellow et al.

Inspired by the zero-sum game in game theory, GAN regards the generation problem as the game between the two networks of generator and discriminator: the generator continuously produces synthetic data from a given random noise and finally outputs an image, the discriminator is to distinguish whether the output image of the generator is a real image. The former tries to produce data that is closer to the real image, while the latter tries to distinguish between the true and false of the generated data. The basic process of GAN is shown in Fig. 2. As a result, the data obtained by the generator become more and more "perfect" and closer to the statistical distribution of real data. So the generator can generate the data we want, such as images, sequences, videos, and others.

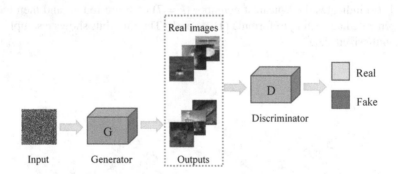

Fig. 2. Processing flow of GAN.

3 Method

The generative adversarial network used in this paper is PG-GAN [8] network. Compared with the previous generative adversarial network like DCGAN [9], WGAN [10] and others [11, 12], PG-GAN has obvious advantages in image generation and can train stably and generate the high-resolution images.

The key idea of PG-GAN is to gradually increase the number of layers of generator and discriminator, that is, to adopt a progressive growing training method. The general process is shown in Fig. 3. Starting from low resolution, the network begins to train and learn. The generator is still used to learn the data mode to generate the corresponding images, while the discriminator is used to judge the authenticity of the generated data. After the low-resolution image is trained, new layers are added to the network structure. And the higher-resolution image is gradually transferred into the training process. Then the network trains the current resolution image stably, and transition to the next higher resolution image by degrees. This new method not only speeds up the training speed of the model, but also greatly stabilizes the training process, so that the model can learn to generate high-quality images, such as the skin lesion images required in this paper.

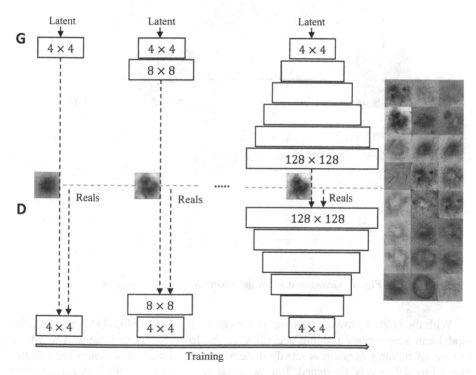

Fig. 3. Training process of PG-GAN on skin lesion images.

Figure 4 shows the operation of PG-GAN network in the growing stage of (a) generator and (b) discriminator. When the generator is in a transitional stage, the image with the resolution 4 × 4 is converted to the output of the same size as the next operation resolution (8 × 8) through resize and convolution. Then the two part outputs make weighted operation. The final output is obtained by to_rgb operation again. The advantage of such a training method is that it can make full use of the results of the previous resolution training, and go through a slow transition (the weight w gradually increases), making the network generated by the training of the next resolution more stable.

The growing stage of the discriminator is shown in Fig. 4(b). The overall detail operation is similar to that in the generator. At the current resolution (8 × 8), the network obtains the output of the same size as that of the next resolution (4 × 4) through pooling and convolution operations. Then the two outputs are weighted, and finally the output is obtained through the to_rgb operation.

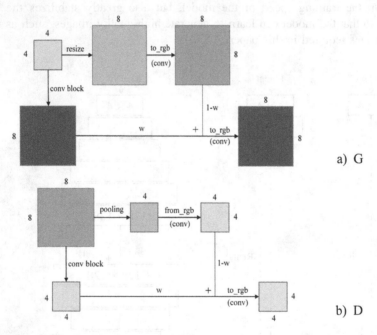

Fig. 4. Growing stage of the generator and discriminator

With the help of growing training, in the early period of the PG–GAN training, the model can keep steady training according to the low resolution images. The whole process of training iteration is mostly done at low resolution, this makes the training time of model greatly shortened. But the generated results are still high-quality. The specific samples can be seen in the experimental part of the paper.

4 Experiments

4.1 Metrics

The following metric methods are used to evaluate the experimental results.
  Specificity:

$$Specificity = \frac{TN}{TN+FP} \tag{2}$$

  Sensitivity:

$$Sensitivity = \frac{TP}{TP+FN} \tag{3}$$

  TP represents the number of True Positive images, that is, in the classification of skin image diseases, the number of sample images that originally belong to the positive class and actually divided into the positive class. TN refers to the number of True Negative images, that is, the number of samples that are originally belong to the negative class and actually classified as negative. FP refers to the number of False Positive images, that is, the number of samples that are originally belong to the negative class and wrongly classified as positive class. FN represents the number of False Negative images, i.e. the number of original positive samples wrongly divided into negative ones.
  Confusion matrix:

Confusion matrix		Predicted label	
		Positive	Negative
True label	Positive	TP	FN
	Negative	FP	TN

  Precision represents the number of samples in which the model prediction is positive.

$$P = \frac{TP}{TP+FP} \tag{4}$$

  Recall indicates the number of correct predictions for the model in the sample whose real label is positive.

$$R = \frac{TP}{TP+FN} \tag{5}$$

  $F1$ measure, a special form of F-measure, is the harmonic average of precision and recall. The average value is equal to all the values, while the harmonic average will give more weight to the smaller values, so it can better reflect the effect of the model in the case of data imbalance. $F1$ is defined as follows:

$$F1 = \frac{2*P*R}{P+R} \tag{6}$$

In addition, AUC (Area Under Curve) evaluation metric is introduced in this paper to evaluate classifiers learned from data sets more accurately.

4.2 Result Analysis

The experimental data in this paper mainly come from two places: one is the open source dataset of ISIC 2018 [13, 14], and the other is the dermatology departments of the Shanghai 9th People's Hospital, 6th People's Hospital, and other medical institutions. The types of skin lesions contained in these data include nevus, seborrheic keratosis, melanoma, and so on.

All of the methods mentioned above are implemented with Python and TensorFlow [15]. In addition, an Nvidia Quadro P5000 GPU is used in the experiment to speed up our training on models.

The comparison of the images generated by PG-GAN with real images is shown in Fig. 5, where (a) represent the real images, (b) represent the generated images. It seems that it's not easy to tell them apart. They have great similarity in the shape, color, texture and so on. So the data generated by the GAN can be used as a part of the training set. Then a model can be trained through the data collaboration of real images and generated images. And finally making experiments to verify its feasibility.

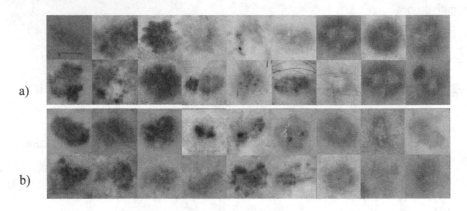

Fig. 5. Real image and generated image

When studying the skin images dataset, it can been easily found that benign nevus and malignant melanoma account for the majority of the dataset. Furthermore, nevus and melanoma have great similarities in appearance, color, etc. see Fig. 6 for details. Therefore, the classification problem of these two classes are mainly analyzed in the experiment, i.e., the classification of nevus and melanoma. In the experiment, our original training set has 5000 images of nevus and 1000 images of melanoma.

Model training is performed on the dataset composed of nevus and melanoma above. The prediction accuracy values of the models obtained by each method on the test set can be seen in Table 1. Among them, Exp-1 refers to the case where 1000 generated images of melanoma are added to the training set, Exp-2 add 4000 generated

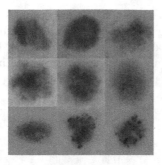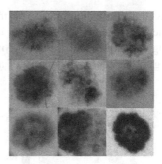

Fig. 6. Nevus and melanoma

melanoma images. It can be found that the accuracy of the random sampling methods, SMOTE and Borderline-SMOTE on the test set is lower than that of the original model which take no methods. The reasons for this may be the under-fitting and over-fitting of the models under these methods. For example, in RandomUnderSampling, the image of nevus is down-sampled to the same number as melanoma, which leads to insufficient training of the model and results in under-fitting problem. In addition, SMOTE and Borderline-SMOTE are methods that are suitable for small size datasets. When they are applied to a large-scale image dataset, there is a high probability that the new data generated by image pixel features is not a skin image. So the accuracy of the model trained by this type of data on the test set will not be high. The numerical results here also prove this.

The models trained on the training set containing the generated images have the higher accuracy than the original model. Besides, the Exp-2 model has the highest accuracy value, reaching 83.231%, which is 1.172% higher than the original model. The explains to some extent that the model trained in data collaboration has a higher accuracy. That is to say, the skin images generated by GAN do have an accuracy improvement in the classification of skin lesions.

Table 1. The prediction accuracy on test set.

Method	Test Acc
Origin	0.82059
RandomOverSampling	0.80843
RandomUnderSampling	0.77627
SMOTE	0.78413
Borderline-SMOTE	0.79414
Exp-1	0.82130
Exp-2	0.83231

However, the accuracy above refers to the accuracy of the overall data, namely that the nevus with a larger number of samples has an advantage in model prediction, and its prediction accuracy for malignant melanoma is difficult to judge.

Therefore, the confusion matrix of the model on the test samples are further observed under each method, as shown in Fig. 7. Here only show the confusion matrix about the original model and the Exp-2 model. The values of TP, FN, FP and TN corresponding to the confusion matrix of all models have been recorded in Table 2.

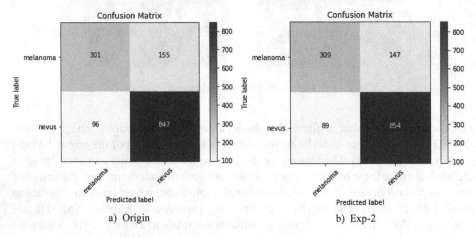

a) Origin   b) Exp-2

Fig. 7. Confusion matrix of the Origin and Exp-2.

Table 2. The values of TP, FN, FP, TN.

Method	TP	FN	FP	TN
Origin	847	96	155	301
RandomOverSampling	849	94	174	282
RandomUnderSampling	723	220	93	363
SMOTE	822	121	181	275
Borderline-SMOTE	851	92	196	260
Exp-1	839	104	146	310
Exp-2	854	89	147	309

At this moment, the corresponding Specificity, Sensitivity, P, R and F1 values can be calculated according to the formulas. The values obtained after their calculation can be seen in Table 3.

In addition to the above metrics, the ROC curves for each method are also plotted, as shown in Fig. 8. The area value on the graph indicates the value of AUC corresponding to the ROC curve. The AUC values of Exp-1 and Exp-2 belong to the highest two of the AUC values of all methods, and the Exp-2's AUC is the largest, which is 0.792.

It can be seen from the above evaluation metrics that the melanoma images generated by GAN do help in improving the overall accuracy of the model and the prediction accuracy of melanoma.

Table 3. The value of metrics.

Method	Sp	Se	P	R	F1
Origin	0.6601	0.8982	0.8453	0.8982	0.8710
RandomOverSampling	0.6184	0.9003	0.8299	0.9003	0.8637
RandomUnderSampling	0.7961	0.7667	0.8860	0.7667	0.8221
SMOTE	0.6031	0.8717	0.8195	0.8717	0.8448
Borderline-SMOTE	0.5702	0.9024	0.8128	0.9024	0.8553
Exp-1	0.6798	0.8897	0.8518	0.8897	0.8703
Exp-2	0.6777	0.9056	0.8531	0.9056	0.8786

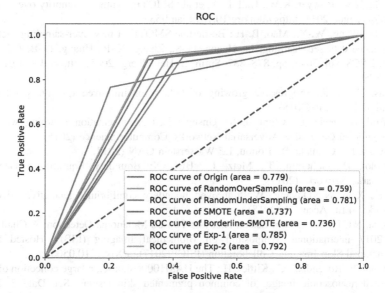

Fig. 8. ROC curves of all methods.

5 Conclusion

The commonly used methods for imbalance data are generally aimed at low-dimensional data, which do not perform well on high-dimensional data such as image. This paper introduces an image generation method based on GAN to realize data expansion for some classes in the training set of skin images. Then a new classifier model is trained by the way of data collaboration. The results show that the high quality skin images generated by the GAN do contribute to improve the overall accuracy of the model and the accuracy of the malignant lesions.

Acknowledgment. This work was funded by Science and Technology Commission of Shanghai Municipality Program (No. 17411952800, No. 18441904500, 18DZ1113400) and Science and Technology Department of Hainan Province (No. ZDYF2018022).

References

1. Chan, P., Stolfo, S.: Toward scalable learning with non-uniform class and cost distributions: a case study in credit card fraud detection (1998)
2. Choe, W., Ersoy, O.K., Bina, M.: Neural network schemes for detecting rare events in human genomic DNA. Bioinformatics **16**(12), 1062–1072 (2000)
3. Plant, C., et al.: Enhancing instance-based classification with local density: a new algorithm for classifying unbalanced biomedical data. Bioinformatics **22**(8), 981–988 (2006)
4. He, H., Garcia, E.A.: Learning from imbalanced data. IEEE Trans. Knowl. Data Eng. **21**(9), 1263–1284 (2009)
5. Goodfellow, I.J., et al.: Generative adversarial nets. In: International Conference on Neural Information Processing Systems. MIT Press (2014)
6. Chawla, N.V., Bowyer, K.W., Hall, L.O., et al.: SMOTE: synthetic minority over-sampling technique, June 2011. https://doi.org/10.1613/jair.953
7. Han, H., Wang, W.-Y., Mao, B.-H.: Borderline-SMOTE: a new over-sampling method in imbalanced data sets learning. In: Huang, D.-S., Zhang, X.-P., Huang, G.-B. (eds.) ICIC 2005. LNCS, vol. 3644, pp. 878–887. Springer, Heidelberg (2005). https://doi.org/10.1007/11538059_91
8. Karras, T., et al.: Progressive growing of GANs for improved quality, stability, and variation. In: ICLR (2018)
9. Radford, A., Metz, L., Chintala, S.: Unsupervised Representation Learning with Deep Convolutional Generative Adversarial Networks. Computer Science (2015)
10. Arjovsky, M., Chintala, S., Bottou, L.: Wasserstein GAN (2017)
11. Berthelot, D., Schumm, T., Metz, L.: BEGAN: Boundary Equilibrium Generative Adversarial Networks (2017)
12. Li, Y., Xiao, N., Ouyang, W.: improved boundary equilibrium generative adversarial networks. IEEE Access 1 (2018)
13. Codella, N.C.F., et al.: Skin Lesion Analysis Toward Melanoma Detection: A Challenge at the 2017 International Symposium on Biomedical Imaging (ISBI), Hosted by the International Skin Imaging Collaboration (ISIC) (2017). arXiv:1710.05006
14. Tschandl, P., Rosendahl, C., Kittler, H.: The HAM10000 dataset, a large collection of multi-source dermatoscopic images of common pigmented skin lesions. Sci. Data **5**, 180161 (2018). https://doi.org/10.1038/sdata.2018.161
15. Abadi, M., et al.: TensorFlow: a system for large-scale machine learning (2016)

Artificial Intelligence

A Next Location Predicting Approach Based on a Recurrent Neural Network and Self-attention

Jun Zeng$^{(\boxtimes)}$, Xin He, Haoran Tang, and Junhao Wen

School of Big Data and Software Engineering, Chongqing University,
Chongqing, China
{zengjun,hexin,tanghaoran,jhwen}@cqu.edu.cn

Abstract. On most location-based social applications today, users are strongly encouraged to share activities by checking-in. In this way, vast amounts of user-generated data can be accumulated, which include spatial and temporal information. Much research has been conducted on these data, which enables heightening the understanding of human mobility. Therefore, the next location problem has attracted significant attention and has been extensively studied. In this paper, we propose a next location prediction approach based on a recurrent neural network and self-attention mechanism. Our model can explore sequence regularity and extract temporal feature according to historical trajectories information. We conduct our experiments on the location-based social network (LBSN) dataset, and the results indicate the effectiveness of our model when compared with the other three frequently-used methods.

Keywords: Trajectory patterns · Next location prediction · Self-attention · Neural network

1 Introduction

In recent years, user can share their activities whenever and wherever, and it owes to a diversity of location-based services in social media applications. Meanwhile, vast amounts of user-generated data can be accumulated, which include spatial and temporal information. For a given user, the check-in data can reflect the underlying patterns which govern his behavior. Finding these patterns can help us to build a model to predict the next location he may visit. Previous studies [1–5] demonstrated that human's behaviors have the features of random and variation. Researchers also exhibit that human mobility follows reproducible [6] under the influence of social and geographic information. Understanding human trajectory patterns and making next location prediction have been widely applied to various tasks, including urban computing [5], the spread of disease [7], traffic congestion prediction [8], personalized recommendation [9], abstractive summarization [10] and semantic role labeling [11].

Nowadays, the next location prediction problem has attracted significant attention and has been extensively studied. Many methods have been proposed in the last ten years. The most commonly used approaches include enhanced Markov model [1], MF

X. Wang et al. (Eds.): CollaborateCom 2019, LNICST 292, pp. 309–322, 2019.
https://doi.org/10.1007/978-3-030-30146-0_21

model [13], Recurrent Neural Network [14], and Bayesian model [15]. Spurred on these approaches, some researchers [1, 16, 17] considered temporal and spatial regularity when making a prediction. However, it still fails to address the two significant challenges well in predicting. Firstly, users are always willing to check in the locations which they are most interested in [12]. However, it can be difficult to identify consistent human mobility patterns according to the sporadic check-ins. In addition, human behavior is affected by several contextual factors like time, weather, emotion, and other factors.

In this paper, we propose a next location prediction approach based on a recurrent neural network and self-attention mechanism. An embedding architecture is used to convert sparse data (e.g., timestamp, location ID, user ID) into dense latent representations. Then, these latent representations are fed into a recurrent neural network to model complicated and long-time dependencies in trajectory sequences. In this way, discrete user check-in data are combined into a continuous sequence, and the relationship among check-ins which are separated by long periods can be extracted.

The output of the recurrent neural network will process into "Self-Attention" mechanism, with the aim of "understanding" the inner relationship of the original sequence. "Self-Attention" mechanism was proposed by Vaswani [18] at 2017 and was initially used to solve Machine Translation problem. Meanwhile, the importance of different contextual factors which influence the transition laws of human behavior can be captured. Then, combined with historical trajectories information [19], the next location is predicted. We conduct our experiments on a real-world dataset, and the results indicate the effectiveness of our model when compared with the other three frequently-used methods.

The rest of the paper is organized as follows. Section 2 summarizes the related work which is highly relevant to our research. Section 3 describes the preliminaries, which includes the definition of the next location prediction problem. Section 4 presents experiments and the results. Section 5 concludes this paper and outlines prospects for future work.

2 Related Work

Location-based services collect massive user-generated data, which contains detailed geo-location information. Researchers attempted to find out whether some basic laws governing human mobility or not. Gonzalez [6] suggested human mobility followed significant regularity like reproducible pattern and believed trajectory could roughly reflect human behavior during a fixed time interval. Zheng [16] introduced trajectories can be transformed into graphs, tensors, matrices, or other data formats. After processing, more data mining and deep learning methods can be applied to extract underlying patterns, which will help researchers analyze human behavior more accurately. In recent years, researchers do not only focus on mining human trajectory but also attempt to predict the next location according to the mined patterns.

Meanwhile, researchers realized the mined patterns could help heighten the understanding of human mobility, and it has a great significance in urban computing, the spread of disease, and personalized recommendation. Chen [20] discovered human movement patterns have a periodic feature, and considered user and collective mobility periodic patterns simultaneously. Liu [21] extracted stay points according to the mined trajectories of users, leveraging the Hidden Markov model predict the next location, and make recommendations. Yao [4] profiled temporal patterns of point-of-interest (POI) and modeled temporal matching user-POI pair to improve the prediction accuracy of POI recommendation.

Nowadays, neural network technology has matured development, and traditional methods are gradually being replaced. Researchers utilized neural networks for predicting which achieved better performance compared with the traditional methods. Kim [22] employed Deep Belief Network (DBN) and Deep Neural Network (DNN) to mine the relationship between human personality and mobility information, then they took this relationship into account when analyzing human mobility and predicting human mobility patterns. Song et al. [23] employed DBN for learning the latent feature representation of heterogeneous data and introduced a DeepMob model to predict the next locations more accurately. Yang [24] demonstrated trajectory records were meaningful for understanding human mobility and presented a neural network model which combined mobility trajectories and social networks. To characterize short-term sequential contexts and long-term sequential contexts, they employed the recurrent neural network (RNN) and Gated Recurrent Unit (GRU) to capture the relationship among sequences from short-term and long-term aspects.

In our paper, we follow these simple patterns that researchers have mined, predicting next locations with RNN and self-attention. Especially, GRU is applied as a methodology to capture complex information of sequences.

3 Preliminaries

In this section, we shed light on problem formulation and introduce GRU. Then Self-attention mechanism is described. Next, the deep connection and positional encoding method are described in detail. Finally, the framework of our model is illuminated.

3.1 Problem Formulation

This section will present the concepts which are referred to in this paper and introduce the research objective.

Definition 1: (check-in). It refers to an event that user records a particular location via location-based services. Each check-in record is unique and includes user ID, timestamp, location information geocoded by <longitude, latitude>. For example, the m-th check-in record c at time t in location l of a given user can be described as $c_m = (t, l)$

Definition 2: (check-in sequence). A user u generates lots of check-ins, and these records can be described as a time-ordered sequence: $S_u = c_1c_2c_3...c_n$

Definition 3: (trajectory). Given a time window w, check-in sequence S_u can be divided into subsequences: $S_u = s_{w1}s_{w2}...s_{wk}$, each subsequence s_{wi} ($i \in \{1,2,3...k\}$): $s_{w1} = c_1c_2c_3...c_j$, $s_{w2} = c_{j+1}c_{j+2}...c_{j+m}$ ($1 < j < j + m < n$) is defined as a trajectory including all the check-ins during the fixed time window w. The window w is the time interval between two subsequences, and its value can be set as an hour, one day, one week or any other threshold which depends on demands.

Goal: (next location prediction). Given check-in sequence $Su = c_1c_2c_3...c_n$ of a given user, the goal is to discover a location where he may visit. That is, given S_u, to obtain a ranked list includes c_{n+1}, c_{n+2} or more locations that user u would like to visit next.

3.2   Gated Recurrent Unit: Extracting the Relationship Among Each Location of Check-in Sequence

In order to mine users' behavior patterns and conduct accurate predicting, a large number of check-in data are necessary. User would like to check in the location where they may be interested in. The sporadic check-ins result in data sparsity. It is difficult to identify the relationship among check-in locations with more extended time intervals. Each location a user will go to is relevant to other locations he visited. RNN is an effective way to extracting the relationship among each location.

GRU and Long Short-Term Memory (LSTM) are the most popular variants of RNN. Different from LSTM, GRU [25] combines *forget gate* and *input gate*, and forms a *reset gate*. Meanwhile, the network no longer gives an extra memory state c_t but regards the output result h_t as the memory state in a continuous backward loop. In this way, GRU can extract the relationship among check-ins that are separated by long periods. The relationship can reflect a user's preference to some extent. For example, a user would like to go to a bookstore after lunch in a restaurant or to a cafe after shopping in a mall. The calculation of GRU is shown as follows:

$$z_t = \sigma(W_t \cdot [h_{t-1}, x_t]) \tag{1}$$

$$r_t = \sigma(W_r \cdot [h_{t-1}, x_t]) \tag{2}$$

$$c_t = \tanh(W \cdot [r_t * h_{t-1}, x_t]) \tag{3}$$

$$h_t = (1 - z_t) * h_{t-1} + z_t * c_t \tag{4}$$

where x_t is the input at timestamp t, h_{t-1} is the network output at time $t - 1$, W is weight matrix which is learned. z_t and r_t are updated gate and reset gate, respectively. σ is a logistic sigmoid function. c_t is a new hidden state, and h_t means the output of the network.

3.3   Self-attention: "Understanding" the Relationship of Each Location Under the Influence of Different Contextual Factors

Human mobility is affected by weather, emotion, and other contextual factors. User may not record the contextual factors when checks. Though GRU can mine the relationship among check-in locations with more extended time intervals. However, it cannot capture the relationship between user behavior and different contextual factors.

Self-attention, which was initially used to improve the accuracy of machine translation, is a particular type of attention mechanism. In this paper, it is utilized for "understanding" the relationship of each location under the influence of different contextual factors.

Vaswani et al. introduced the multi-head attention mechanism and chose a particular attention calculating method called "Scaled Dot-Product Attention". Firstly, we will detail the Scaled Dot-Product Attention. Its formulation is as Eq. (5)

$$Attention(Q, K, V) = soft \max\left(\frac{QK^T}{\sqrt{d_k}}\right)V \tag{5}$$

where d_k is the dimension of hidden units of our neural network. Q, K, V are queries, keys, and values, respectively. They are the outputs of the previous layer in the neural network.

Multi-head attention allows the model to focus on information from different representations of subspaces at different positions. The output of GRU can be divided into eight parts and each part calculates the score of each location under the influence of eight different factors. The formulation of multi-head attention is shown as Eq. (6):

$$head_i = Attention\left(QW_i^Q, KW_i^K, VW_i^V\right) \tag{6}$$

where the projections are parameter matrices $W_i^Q \in \mathbb{R}^{dmodel \times d_k}$, $W_i^K \in \mathbb{R}^{dmodel \times d_k}$, $W_i^V \in \mathbb{R}^{dmodel \times d_k}$ which are denoted as the learned linear maps for the i-th ($i \in \{1, 2, 3...n\}$) head.

$$score_{att}(Q, K, V) = \\ Concat(head_1, head_2, ..., head_n)W^o \tag{7}$$

All the vectors that are produced by parallel heads are concatenated together to form a single vector. Then, different channels from different heads are sent to a linear transformation. The output of multi-head attention has the same shape as the input. Finally, dropout, residual connections, and layer normalization strategies are employed on our network to achieve better performance.

3.4 Positional Encoding

Machine Translation task only requires to explore the relationship among every word. However, check-in sequence demonstrates temporal features. The self-attention mechanism cannot distinguish the connection among locations involved time in different trajectories. It is crucial to consider the time when encoding positions of each location in a given check-in sequence. Vaswani et al. proposed a position encoding method to encode positions of each input word for Machine Translation task. In the process of predicting the next location, the accuracy not only associates with locations' position in a fixed sequence but also correlates with the temporal feature. Though positional encoding works well on Machine Translation task, it is to a little avail on next locations prediction because of check-in sequence involving temporal feature.

Feng et al. proposed a method considering historical trajectories to predict human mobility with an attentional recurrent network, and the core idea of this method is suitable for position encoding at the time level. In this paper, we utilize this idea to explore the relationship among locations involved temporal feature, and $Score_{att}$ can be calculated in this way.

3.5   Framework

In this apart, we will introduce the framework of our model in detail. Figure 1 shows the main architecture of our proposed model.

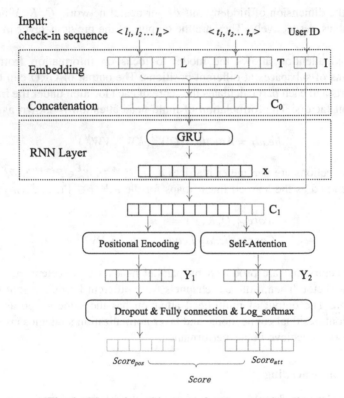

Fig. 1. The main architecture of our proposed mode

Data Processing and Get the Input Data. Check-in sequence of a fixed user has already divided into some trajectories. Each trajectory includes user ID, geographic location information <longitude, latitude> and timestamp. In this paper, geographic location information will be numbered as location ID, using l_i ($i \in \{1, 2, 3...n\}$) to represent each location. In check-in sequence of a given user, location ID, the timestamp, and user ID have been encoded latent vectors representation, then are processed by Embedding layer.

Embed Each Feature Into Latent Representation. Check-in record has three kinds of context information, the timestamp, location ID, and user ID. The timestamp reflected when the user checked. Location ID manifested where the user visited. User ID was the unique identification of a user. Timestamps ($t_1, t_2...t_n$), locations ($l_1, l_2...l_n$) and user ID can be embedded into real-valued vectors L, T, I respectively. For a given user, these vectors include information about his behaviors over a while.

Extract the Relationship Among each Location of Check-in Sequence. As Fig. 1 shows, we concatenate the embedding vectors L and T into C_0. Then C_0 includes the information what the location is and the time when the user visits it. GRU processes the real-valued vectors C_0, aiming to capture the sequential and structure information of a given user's check-ins sequence. The pseudo-code of how GRU works in our method is described in Table 1.

Table 1. The pseudo-code of how GRU works in our method

Input: The real-valued vectors C_0 which is a concatenation of L and T
Output: The vectors which reflect the relationship among each location of check-in sequence

1	$L \leftarrow$ embedding vectors of locations
2	$T \leftarrow$ embedding vectors of timestamps
3	$C_0 \leftarrow$ embedding vectors which are a concatenation of L and T
4	$W_t \leftarrow$ the weight matrices from input to update gate z, $\forall W_t \in (0,1)$
5	$W_r \leftarrow$ the weight matrices from input to reset gate r, $\forall W_r \in (0,1)$
6	$W \leftarrow$ the weight matrices from input to new hidden state c_t, $\forall W \in (0,1)$
7	for all C_0:
8	$\quad z_t = sigmoid (W_t \cdot [h_{t-1}, C_0])$
9	$\quad r_t = sigmoid (W_r \cdot [h_{t-1}, C_0])$
10	$\quad c_t = tanh (W \cdot [r_t \cdot h_{t-1}, C_0])$
11	$\quad h_t = (1 - z_t) * h_{t-1} + z_t * c_t$
12	end until all C_0 are processed

"Understanding" the Relationship of Each Location Under the Influence of Different Contextual Factors. As Fig. 2 shows, X includes the relationship among each location of check-in sequence, and I reflects the unique identification of a user.

We concatenate I and X into C_l to add the user feature. The vectors C_l are regarded as the input of self-attention, and C_l is a concatenation of the output vectors X of GRU and embedded vectors I. C_l not only can reflect the relationship among each location of check-in sequence but also include user information in terms of the user ID that embedded vectors. Multi-head mechanism split the input vectors into eight parallel parts in this paper, and each part called $head_i$ ($\{i \mid 1 \leq i \leq 8, i \in N*\}$).

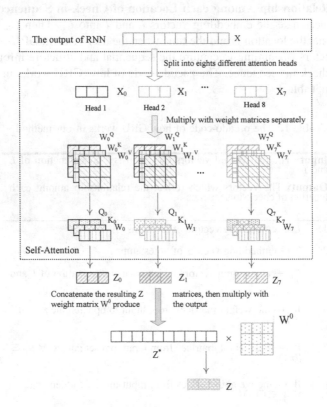

Fig. 2. How Self-attention mechanism works in our proposed model

Each part will multiply with different weight matrices respectively. Users who went to one location could be affected by other locations where he has already gone. Additionally, their behaviors are also influenced by weather, emotion, and other factors. These weight matrices can help the network learn the importance of each location for a given user from different representation subspaces. The path length of the self-attention mechanism is 1. The path length is short enough, which is much easier to learn long-range dependencies and achieve much powerful performance. The output of this step indicates the latent representation of one given location to other locations in the sequential level. The pseudo-code of Self-attention is described in Table 2.

Table 2. The pseudo-code of how self-attention works in our method

Input: The output vectors X and the embedding vectors I
Output: The vectors $Score_{att}$ which the relationship of each location under the influence of different contextual factors

1    $X \leftarrow$ the output vectors of GRU

2    $I \leftarrow$ embedding vectors of user ID

3    $C_I \leftarrow$ embedding vectors which are a concatenation of X and I

4   split C_I into 8 equal parts ($head_1$, $head_2$... $head_8$)

5   queries/Q, keys/K, values/V $\leftarrow C_I$

6    $W_i^Q, W_i^K, W_i^V, W^o \leftarrow$ the weight matrices of each $head_i$, $\forall$ $W_i^Q, W_i^K, W_i^V, W^o \in (0,1)$, $\{i | 1 \leq i \leq 8, i \in N^*\}$

7   for all $head_i$:

8        $head_i = attention(QW_i^Q, KW_i^K, V W_i^V)$

9   end until all $head_i$ are processed

10    $head_1$, $head_2$... $head_8$ are concatenated and multiply with W^o

11   output $Score_{att}$

Positional Encoding. Self-attention was initially used to solve Machine Translation task, and it can capture long-range dependencies among each word. Machine Translation task is essentially a sequence problem. Until now, a given user's check-in data have processed into a sequence. Therefore, it can be solved as a sequence like Machine Translation task. Machine Translation does not have a temporal feature compared with the next location prediction. It is necessary to add positional encoding with temporal feature into prediction problem.

Positional Encoding mechanism will extract human mobility regularities in time. The output of positional encoding indicates the latent representation of one given location to other locations. The DeepMove model proposed by Feng et al. can capture historical trajectories information. We take the main idea of this method to replace the Positional Encoding mechanism proposed by Vaswani. The original Positional Encoding mechanism aims to solve machine translation task. However, it only considers the position of each word. Next locations prediction should take temporal factor into account. Moreover, historical trajectories with time factor can help us to measure the importance of each location.

Dropout and Full Connection and Log-softmax. By taking the concatenation of Self-attention and user ID embedding as the input, dropout strategy can prevent overfitting, and full connection can synthesize the extracted features. Then, the output is processed by log-softmax function to get $score_{att}$. It indicates the transition probabilities from one given location to another in a sequential level. Similarly, the output of Positional Encoding is also projected in the same way to get $Score_{pos}$.

We set $Score$ to represent the final result which is composed of two parts: $Score_{att}$ calculated by Self-attention mechanism and $Score_{pos}$ calculated by Positional mechanism. Its calculation formula is as Eq. (8):

$$Score = \alpha \cdot Score_{att} + \beta \cdot Score_{pos} \tag{8}$$

4   Experiments and Results Analysis

4.1   Experimental Objective

1. Set the different value of α and β, to explore the relationship between two kinds of methods, finding the (α, β) pair that maximizes the Score value, and optimizing the performance of the model.
2. Compared with our proposed method and three frequently-used methods, it aims to measure the predicting performance of our method.

4.2   Dataset

The dataset we choose is Foursquare, which has amassed check-ins in New York City, and these data were collected for about ten months from 12 April 2012 to 16 February 2013. It contains 227,428 check-ins generated by 1083 users. Each check-in is associated with its timestamp, and its GPS coordinates consist of <longitude, latitude> and the unique user ID which represents the corresponding user. We remove users with fewer than 10 check-in records. The time difference between two neighbor trajectories is set as 72 h based on the practice. We also drop the trajectories with fewer than 5 records and users who have trajectories less than 5.

4.3   Experimental Setup

Firstly, we take 70% of each user's trajectory data as a training set and the rest of the data as a testing set.

To evaluate our proposed model on the accuracy of the next locations prediction, we compared our model with some popular methods:

1. **Markov.** It is a widely used method for the next locations prediction. Specifically, the Markov model regards a fixed location as a state, then calculates state transition matrix which corresponds to moving from one given location to other locations.
2. **RNN.** In recent years, RNN attracts increasing attention and is used to predict the next locations. The variants of RNN can capture relationship among sequences at short-term or long-term aspects.

3. **RNN with Attention.** Attention mechanism derives from Computer Vision and Pattern Recognition. Feng et al. proposed an attention-based RNN model called DeepMove to predict human mobility with historical information.

4.4   Experimental Results and Analysis

Here we introduce prediction accuracy to evaluate the performance of our proposed model, which can be described as Eq. (9):

$$prediction\ accuracy = \frac{number\ of\ correct\ prediction\ locations}{total\ number\ of\ prediction\ locations} \qquad (9)$$

where *total number of prediction locations* means how many locations or top-k locations that we predict next time interval, e.g., 1/top-1 location, 5/top-5 locations, or more locations/top-n depend on practical demand.

In this paper, the final score reflects the probabilies from one given location to other locations is described as Eq. (8). $Score_{att}$ indicates the latent representation of one given location to other locations in trajectory level; $Score_{pos}$ indicates the same latent representation in time level. Here we set the different value of α and β ($\beta = 1 - \alpha$) to explore the relationship between two kinds of methods. It also means the importance of discovering the sequence regularity and temporal regularity.

We can conclude Fig. 3 when α equals 0.4 and β equals 0.6, then the model achieves the best prediction performance. According to the experimental results, we consider the importance of sequence regularity takes account forty percent approximately. In previous studies, many researchers indicated human mobility patterns not only associated with temporal information but also related to sequence regularity. In this paper, we explore sequence regularity using Self-attention mechanism and extract temporal feature based on the method proposed by Feng. The experimental results precisely accord with that viewpoint.

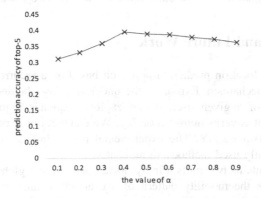

Fig. 3. Prediction accuracy of different α and β value

Figure 4 shows the prediction accuracy of top-k, and k equals to 1 and 5, respectively.

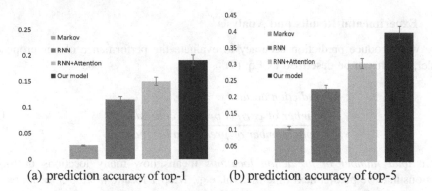

(a) prediction accuracy of top-1   (b) prediction accuracy of top-5

Fig. 4. Prediction accuracy

Figure 4 also shows the experimental results on prediction accuracy and illustrates the proposed model achieves better performance compared with other popular methods. Base on the knowledge of previous researches, though we explore traditional Markov chain can build the transition matrix by taking the sequence of locations a user last visited, it ignores the temporal features. RNN can capture temporal feature compared with the Markov model, and its recurrent units present a solution for long-range dependencies. However, it may pay little attention to historical information. Attention-based RNN model extends RNN with historical information, which illuminates human periodical pattern from long length historical trajectories, and an attention mechanism can capture the information a user pays more attention to some locations. The model we proposed utilizes historical trajectories information to capture the relationship between temporal feature and locations a user has already visited. The Self-attention mechanism helps us to explore the inner relationship of trajectories from different contextual factors. In conclusion, our model achieves better performance on prediction accuracy when compared with the other three frequently-used methods.

5   Conclusion and Future Work

We propose a next location prediction approach based on a recurrent neural network and self-attention mechanism. Exploring the underlying laws behind historical trajectories information of a given user, it can explore sequence regularity and extract temporal feature that governs human mobility. We conduct our experiments on a real-world dataset, Foursquare NY. The experimental results indicate our model outperforms other frequently-used methods significantly.

Future work contains two parts. Firstly, local attention and global attention can be considered, because the mobility pattern of a user will change with time goes by. Secondly, semantic information like reviews can reflect a user's preference. Therefore, we consider predicting the following locations with semantic information, then recommend locations where a user has not visited before while he may be interested in.

Acknowledgment. This research is supported by the National Natural Science Foundation of China (Grant No. 61502062, Grant No. 61672117 and Grant No. 61602070), the China Postdoctoral Science Foundation under Grant 2014M560704, the Scientific Research Foundation for the Returned Overseas Chinese Scholars (State Education Ministry), and the Fundamental Research Funds for the Central Universities Project No. 2015CDJXY.

References

1. Qiao, Y., Si, Z., Zhang, Y., et al.: A hybrid Markov-based model for human mobility prediction. Neurocomputing **278**, 99–109 (2017)
2. Chen, X., Kordy, P., Lu, R., Pang, J.: MinUS: mining user similarity with trajectory patterns. In: Calders, T., Esposito, F., Hüllermeier, E., Meo, R. (eds.) ECML PKDD 2014. LNCS (LNAI), vol. 8726, pp. 436–439. Springer, Heidelberg (2014). https://doi.org/10.1007/978-3-662-44845-8_29
3. Chen, C., Kuo, C., Peng, W., et al.: Mining spatial-temporal semantic trajectory patterns from raw trajectories. In: International Conference on Data Mining, pp. 1019–1024 (2015)
4. Yao, Z.: Exploiting human mobility patterns for point-of-interest recommendation. In: Web Search and Data Mining, pp. 757–758 (2018)
5. Altomare, A., Cesario, E., Comito, C., et al.: Trajectory pattern mining for urban computing in the cloud. IEEE Trans. Parallel Distrib. Syst. **28**, 586–599 (2017)
6. Gonzalez, M.C., Hidalgo, A.R., Barabasi, A., et al.: Understanding individual human mobility patterns. Nature **453**, 779–782 (2008)
7. Ajelli, M., Litvinova, M.: Estimating contact patterns relevant to the spread of infectious diseases in Russia. J. Theor. Biol. **419**, 1–7 (2017)
8. Gao, J., Sun, Y., Liu, W., et al.: Predicting traffic congestions with global signatures discovered by frequent pattern mining. In: Green Computing and Communications, pp. 554–560 (2016)
9. Gao, H., Tang, J., Liu, H., et al.: Personalized location recommendation on location-based social networks. In: Conference on Recommender Systems, pp. 399–400 (2014)
10. Paulus, R., Xiong, C., Socher, R., et al.: A Deep reinforced model for abstractive summarization. In: International Conference on Learning Representations (2018)
11. Tan, Z., Wang, M., Xie, J., et al.: Deep Semantic role labeling with self-attention. In: National Conference on Artificial Intelligence, pp. 4929–4936 (2018)
12. Joseph, K., Tan, C.H., Carley, K.M.: Beyond local, categories and friends: clustering foursquare users with latent topics. In: ACM Conference on Ubiquitous Computing, pp. 919–926. ACM (2012)
13. Wang, Y., Shang, W., Li, Z.: The application of factorization machines in user behavior prediction. In: International Conference on Computer and Information Science, pp. 1–4. IEEE (2016)
14. Liu, Q., Wu, S., Wang, L., et al.: Predicting the next location: a recurrent model with spatial and temporal contexts. In: Thirtieth AAAI Conference on Artificial Intelligence. AAAI Press (2016)
15. Jia, Y., Wang, Y., Jin, X., et al.: Location prediction: a temporal-spatial Bayesian model. ACM Trans. Intell. Syst. Technol. 1–25 (2015)
16. Zheng, Y.: Trajectory data mining: an overview. ACM (2015)

17. Zhenjiang, D., Jia, D., Xiaohui, J., et al. RTMatch: real-time location prediction based on trajectory pattern matching. 84–95 (2017)
18. Vaswani, A., Shazeer, N., Parmar, N., et al.: Attention is all you need. In: Neural Information Processing Systems, pp. 5998–6008 (2017)
19. Feng J.: DeepMove: predicting human mobility with attentional recurrent networks. In: The Web Conference, pp. 1459–1468 (2018)
20. Chen, M., Yu, X., Liu, Y.: Mining moving patterns for predicting next location. Inform. Syst. **54**, 156–168 (2015)
21. Liu, H., Wu, G., Wang, G.: Tell me where to go and what to do next, but do not bother me, pp. 375–376 (2014)
22. Kim, D.Y., Song, H.Y.: Method of predicting human mobility patterns using deep learning. Neurocomputing **280**, 56–64 (2017)
23. Song, X., Shibasaki, R., Yuan, N.J., Xie, X., Li, T., Adachi, R.: DeepMob: learning deep knowledge of human emergency behavior and mobility from big and heterogeneous data. ACM Trans. Inform. Syst. **35**, 1–19 (2017)
24. Yang, C., Sun, M., Zhao, W.X., Liu, Z., Chang, E.Y.: A neural network approach to joint modeling social networks and mobile trajectories. ACM Trans. Inform. Syst. (2016)
25. Cho, K,. Van Merrienboer, B., Gulcehre, C., et al.: Learning phrase representations using RNN encoder-decoder for statistical machine translation. Comput. Sci. 1724–1734 (2014)

A Food Dish Image Generation Framework Based on Progressive Growing GANs

Su Wang[1], Honghao Gao[2($\boxtimes$)], Yonghua Zhu[3], Weilin Zhang[1], and Yihai Chen[1]

[1] School of Computer Engineering and Science,
Shanghai University, Shanghai, China
{wongsou, zeroized, yhchen}@shu.edu.cn
[2] Computing Center, Shanghai University, Shanghai, China
gaohonghao@shu.edu.cn
[3] Shanghai Film Academy, Shanghai University, Shanghai, China
zyh@shu.edu.cn

Abstract. The generative adversarial networks (GANs) have demonstrated the ability to synthesize realistic images. However, there are few researches applying GANs into the field of food image synthesis. In this paper, we propose an extension to GANs for generating more realistic food dish images with rich detail, which adds a food condition that contains taste and other information. That makes the model generate images with rich details. To improve the quality of the generated image, the taste information condition is added to each stage of the generator and discriminator. First, the model learns embedding conditions of food information, including ingredients, cooking methods, tastes and cuisines. Secondly, the training model grows progressively, and the model learns details increasingly during the training process, which allows the model to generate images with rich details. To demonstrate the effectiveness of our proposed model, we collect a dataset called Food-121, which includes the names of the food, ingredients, cooking methods, tastes, and cuisines. The results of experiment show that our model can produce complex details of food dish image and obtain high inception score on the Food-121 dataset compared with other models.

Keywords: GANs · Food dish image synthesis · Food dataset

1 Introduction

Generative Adversarial Networks (GANs) [1] were first proposed by I. Goodfellow and some pioneer researchers in 2014. Since then, they have been successfully used in the image generation area. GANs perform well on datasets with single object in the image, such as human faces in the CelebA dataset [2], birds images in the CUB dataset [3] and flowers images in the Oxford-102 dataset [4]. But the generated images are not realistic enough when multiple irregularly shaped objects exist in the images. The images do not have realistic and rich details, and this is especially obvious in food dish image generation, as there are often many ingredients in food images, and the ingredients have various visual effects. Hence, GANs can probably not generate realistic food dish image only through image data.

© ICST Institute for Computer Sciences, Social Informatics and Telecommunications Engineering 2019
Published by Springer Nature Switzerland AG 2019. All Rights Reserved
X. Wang et al. (Eds.): CollaborateCom 2019, LNICST 292, pp. 323–333, 2019.
https://doi.org/10.1007/978-3-030-30146-0_22

The GANs-based approach is too uncontrollable; therefore, conditional constraints are added to GANs, which is called conditional GANs (CGANs) proposed by Mirza [5]. Karras [6] proposed progressive growing GANs (PGGANs) which generate images by progressively increasing the resolution. PGGANs learn the structure of images at first and then focus on details so that the images look realistic and have higher resolution. Hamada [7] proposed a PGGAN to generate full-body high-resolution anime images by adding a structure condition.

Fig. 1. Different images of ingredients with different cooking methods

The visual appearance of the food is usually determined by the ingredients. However, the relationship between the ingredients and the corresponding food image is complicated, so simply generating food images from the ingredients may cause large deviations. Figure 1 shows the food images of chicken and potatoes cooked using different cooking methods. As shown in Fig. 1, when chicken is cooked by different methods, the colors and textures are quite different. Such phenomena can also be seen on potatoes. On the other side, when chicken and potatoes are cooked separately using the same method, their images share many visual features. Other ingredients in the recipes also have this similarity. Therefore, the cooking method has a great impact on the food dish image and plays an important role in determining the appearance of cooked food.

In addition to the cooking method, taste and cuisine of the food also impact the appearance of the image. Therefore, it is necessary to take food information that contains ingredients, cooking method, taste, and cuisine into account when generating images. To deal with textual food information, Salvador [8] separately processes the ingredients and instructions, where ingredients are represented as a vector with word2vec method and instructions are encoded with skip-thought [14]. The recipe representation is thus obtained through concatenating the ingredient and the instruction representation.

In this paper, we propose a generative adversarial network specialized for food image generation, and collect a dataset, Food-121, that contains full food information and its corresponding image. We describe its comparison with other datasets in Sect. 4. Our model uses the architecture of CGANs, where food information representation works as the condition so that the model can utilize ingredients, cooking method, taste, and cuisine to generate better food images.

The remainder of this paper is organized as follows. Section 2 briefly introduces the preliminary and the related works. Section 3 explains our method in detail. In Sect. 4, our proposed dataset Food-121 is presented, and the experimental results are discussed. Finally, the conclusion and future works are given in Sect. 5.

2 GANs

2.1 Preliminary

The framework of GANs consists of two competitors, generator and discriminator. The task of the generator is to generate a sample that the discriminator cannot discriminate between real and fake. At the same time, the task of the discriminator is to discriminate between the real image and the sample generated by the generator [1]. In training, generator G that inputs the random noise vector and outputs the fake data. Discriminator D inputs the real data or fake data and outputs the possibility that it is real data or fake data. To generate a fake image, the training method achieves the best results by pitting generator G and discriminator D against each other. The process makes the sample data distribution close to the true data distribution. The value function of GANs is:

$$\min_{G} \max_{D} V(D, G) = \mathbb{E}_{x \sim p_{data}(x)}[\log D(x)] + \mathbb{E}_{z \sim p_z(z)}[\log(1 - D(G(z)))] \quad (1)$$

The value function of GANs is shown in (1) [1]; G represents the generator, D represents the discriminator, p_{data} represents for the real data distribution, and p_z represents the noise distribution. The goal of D is to maximize $V(D, G)$, and the goal of G is to minimize $V(D, G)$. G and D are trained at the same time. Finally, G can estimate the distribution of the real samples.

CGANs are an extension of the GANs that are used to solve the problem of uncontrollable image in GANs. In CGANs, conditional information is added to both the generated model G and the discriminant model D to guide the training of the model when using GANs [5]. The difference between GANs and CGANs is that CGANs add a conditional input vector y to the random noise z.

$$\min_{G} \max_{D} V(D, G) = \mathbb{E}_{x \sim p_{data}(x)}[\log D(x|y)] + \mathbb{E}_{x \sim p_z(z)}[\log(1 - D(G(z|y)))] \quad (2)$$

As is shown in (2) [5], the value function of conditional GANs is a two-person minimax game with a condition. The conditional constraint y is simultaneously added to both the generator model G and the discriminator model D to guide the data generation process. The condition can be any additional information. The noise z and the condition y are input to the generator. The data x and the condition y are input as inputs simultaneously to the discriminator. After the conditional input vector y concatenate is in the noise vector z, the generated vector is input to the generator G. Then training is in the same way as GANs.

2.2   Related Works

Salvador [8] established a large-scale, structured recipe dataset, Recipe1 M, which contains more than 1,000,000 recipes and 800,000 food images. As the largest public recipe dataset, Recipe1 M provides the ability to train high-performance models. Using these data, they trained a neural network to find the joint embedding of recipes and images to complete the image-recipe retrieval task. In addition, it was demonstrated that regularization via the addition of a high-level classification objective both improves retrieval performance to rival that of humans and enables semantic vector arithmetic.

To solve the problem of generating images by words, Reed [9] proposed a GAN with learning interpolation and a matching aware generator GAN-INT-CLS model. GAN-INT-CLS generates images through descriptive text. El [10] proposed a GAN to generate food images through recipes. Zhang [11] proposed the stacked GAN model to improve the resolution of generated images. Zhang [12] proposed a GAN model that combined the attention mechanism with GANs.

3   Methodology

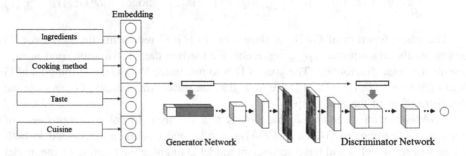

Fig. 2. The overall architecture of our model.

Figure 2 shows the architecture of our model. There are three parts in our model: food text encoder, generator network, and discriminator network. In the training process, food text encoder first transforms the four parts of an input text to vectors, concatenate these vectors to a feature map and feed the feature map into the generator network. Next, the generator network generates an intermediate image. Finally, the discriminator network compares the image and the true image concatenated with food condition and outputs the probability of the image being faked.

3.1   Food Text Encoder

The food information contains four parts: the ingredients, the cooking method, the taste, and the cuisine. For ingredients, the food information encoder learns an ingredient level word2vec representation. The cooking method is encoded by a skip-instruction model.

The skip-instructions [8] model is proposed to obtain the representation of the instructions. Skip-instructions is a kind of sequence-to-sequence [13] models and is based upon skip-thoughts technique. Skip-thoughts encodes a sentence and uses that encoding as context when decoding the previous and next sentences. Skip-instruction adds a start and end to the instructions and uses an LSTM instead of a gated recurrent unit (GRU).

Skip-thought [14] is an unsupervised learning sentence encoder, and sentences with similar semantics are mapped to similar vector representations. The encoder uses the following function:

$$r^t = \sigma(W_r x^t + U_r h^{t-1}) \tag{3}$$

$$z^t = \sigma(W_z x^t + U_z h^{t-1}) \tag{4}$$

$$\bar{h}^t = \tanh(W x^t + U(r^t \odot h^{t-1})) \tag{5}$$

$$h^t = (1 - z^t) \odot h^{t-1} + z^t \odot \bar{h}^t \tag{6}$$

where $\bar{h}^t$ is the proposed state update at time t, z^t is the update gate, r_t is the component-wise product of reset gate $\odot$.

The decoder uses the following formula:

$$r^t = \sigma(W_r^d x^{t-1} + U_r^d h^{t-1} + C_r h_i) \tag{7}$$

$$z^t = \sigma(W_z^d x^{t-1} + U_z^d h^{t-1} + C_z h_i) \tag{8}$$

$$\bar{h}^t = \tanh(W^d x^{t-1} + U^d(r^t \odot h^{t-1}) + C h_i) \tag{9}$$

$$h_{i+1}^t = (1 - z^t) \odot h^{t-1} + z^t \odot \bar{h}^t \tag{10}$$

The decoder is a natural language model with the condition on the output h_i of the encoder. Matrix C_z, C_r and C are used to bias the update gate, reset gate, and hidden state computation by the sentence vector.

For taste and cuisine, we use the word2vec level representation. The cooking method is embedded by a skip-instruction encoder. Then, we obtain the food condition vector by concatenating four representations.

3.2   Conditional Progressive Growing Generator and Discriminator Network

Our model is trained in a progressively increasing manner [6]. To generate higher resolution images, the model starts with training resolution of 4×4 pixels in generator and discriminator, then incrementally add layers to generator and discriminator and evaluate the resolution.

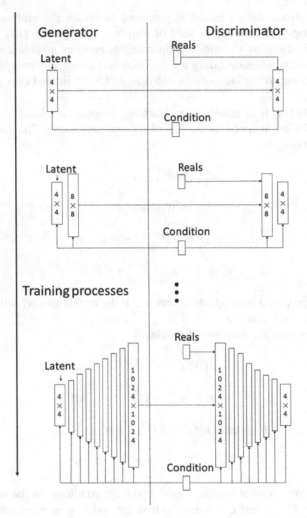

Fig. 3. Generator (G) and Discriminator (D) architecture of our model

Figure 3 illustrates the training process of the generator and the discriminator of our model. A latent vector concatenated with food information condition is input to the initial generator, where at the beginning a low-resolution image is generated. Then the generated image, the truth image, and with the food information condition are fed to the discriminator network together, and the discriminator outputs the possibility that the generated image is not faked. In the subsequent epochs, the generator progressively generates images of higher resolution. Therefore, the quality of the generated food images is gradually improved, and the details of the images become clearer and richer during the process.

4 Experiment

4.1 Dataset

Table 1. Comparison between datasets

	Recipes	Images	Difference
Food-121	121,478	121,478	with taste and cuisine information
Recipe1 M	1,000,000	800,000	–
Food-101	–	101,000	–
VIREO Food-172	65284	110241	only Chinese cuisine

In this section, we introduce our dataset, Food-121, which contains full food information. There are a few datasets about recipes and food images, such as Recipe1 M dataset [8], Food-101 dataset [15], and VIREO Food-172 dataset [16]. Recipe1 M consists of over 1,000,000 recipes and 800,000 food images, but the recipes are only about ingredients and cooking instructions. Food-101 contains 101,000 images in 101 ingredients. But VIREO Food-172 does not have taste and cuisine information. And it is only for Chinese cuisine.

To explore the impact of taste and cuisine on the food images, data are collected from websites. The texts of ingredients, cooking method, taste, and cuisine are extracted from raw HTML and download the corresponding food images. Samples with unclear expression of food information or with blurred images are removed. Eventually, Food-121 dataset contains 121,478 pieces of food information and image. The statistical data of Food-121 and three prior datasets are listed in Table 1, and an example of Food-121 data item is shown in Fig. 4.

Name: Fried chicken wings
Ingredients: Chicken wings, salt, cooking wine, soy sauce, fried chicken powder, ginger, chili
Cooking method: Cut the chicken wings, put the ginger, garlic, cooking wine, salt and sprinkle the fried chicken powder and mix. Marinate for half a day. Pour the chicken wings into oil which is burned to the 80% heat. Fried for five minutes.
Taste: Spicy, salty
Cuisine: Fast food

Fig. 4. An example of Food-121 date item

4.2 Evaluation Metrics

It is necessary to evaluate the generation model in two aspects: whether the generated image is clear and whether the generated image is diverse. If the generated image is not clear enough, this obviously shows that the generated model is not performing well. When the generated image is clear enough, it still need to determine whether the model can generate enough of variety. Therefore, the inspection score (IS) [17] is used to evaluate our model in both aspects.

Considering the above two aspects, the formula of Inception Score is:

$$\mathbf{IS}(G) = \exp(E_{x \sim p_g} D_{KL}(p(y|x) \| p(y))) \tag{11}$$

The generated sample image x is input into Inception V3. Vector y of 1,000 dimensions is output. The basis for the IS to determine the authenticity of the data is derived from the training set of Inception V3.

However, IS also has problems. Only the generated samples are considered, and the real data are not considered because the IS cannot evaluate the distance between the real data and the sample. Therefore, the Fréchet inception distance (FID) [18] is also calculated. The FID calculates the distance between the real image and the fake image at the feature level. The formula for the FID is as follows:

$$\mathbf{FID} = \|m_r - m_g\|^2 + Tr(C_r + C_g - 2(C_r C_g)^{1/2}) \tag{12}$$

Where m_r and m_g are the mean of the features of the real images and generated images, C_r and C_g are the covariance matrix of the features of the real images and the generated picture. The FID is a measure of the distance between two multivariate normal distributions.

Multiscale structural similarity (MS-SSIM) scores [19] represent a set of randomly sampled pairs of images within a given class.

$$\mathrm{SSIM}(x,y) = [l_m(x,y)]^{\alpha M} \cdot \prod_{j=1}^{M} [c_j(x,y)]^{\beta_j} [s_j(x,y)]^{\gamma_j} \tag{13}$$

The exponents αM, β_j and γ_j are used to adjust the relative importance of different components. The mean of the MS-SSIM scores is used, in which a high mean MS-SSIM indicates mode collapse or low sample diversity.

4.3 Experiment Settings

The model uses the same loss function as [6]. Constricted by the graphics processing unit (GPU), the model trains networks with 10 k images and food conditions for each stage. The model uses a mini-batch size 12 and Adam [20] with $\beta 1 = 0$, $\beta 2 = 0.99$ to train the networks.

4.4 Results

In this section, experimental results are discussed. Figure 5 shows some generated images of our method and baseline methods. From these images, it can be seen that when there are multiple objects in the image, our model outperforms the baseline methods. That means our model can generate more realistic images with rich details with the help of food information. Our model can also learn various ingredients visuals in different tastes.

(a)   (b)   (c)

Fig. 5. Food image generation: comparison between GAN-INT-CLS (left), DCGAN (middle), and our model (right)

Figure 5 shows the results of our model and deep convolutional GAN (DCGAN) [21]. Our model learns the composition of the image that there is a dish with various foods because progressive growing GANs architecture is used. The training helps the model learn the rough composition of the images first. Then, the model focused on the details. Therefore, food images generated by our model look more realistic (Table 2).

Table 2. Inception and Fréchet inception distance between DCGAN and our model

	Inception score	Fréchet inception distance	MS-SSIM
DCGAN	3.32 ± 0.15	109.3248 ± 10.0526	0.1256
Our model	**4.56 ± 0.18**	**85.2194 ± 9.2543**	**0.0612**

The IS, FID, and MS-SSIM of DCGAN and our model are evaluated. The higher IS for the model is, the more realistic the generated images are. The smaller the FID is, the smaller distance between the generated images and the real images. In addition, MS-SSIM reflects the seriousness of the mode collapse problem of the model. A high MS-SSIM means a low sample diversity. Our model obtains a higher IS and a lower FID and MS-SSIM on the Food-121 dataset, which means that our model can generate more realistic and various food dish images (Table 3).

Table 3. Inception and Fréchet inception distance between PGGAN and our model

	Inception score	Fréchet inception distance	MS-SSIM
Progressive growing GAN	4.25 ± 0.12	95.7254 ± 8.4682	0.0965
Our model	**4.56 ± 0.18**	**85.2194 ± 9.2543**	**0.0612**

The IS, FID, and MS-SSIM of PGGAN and our model are evaluated. Our model obtained a higher IS and a lower FID and MS-SSIM on the Food-121 dataset, which means that our model can probably generate more realistic and various food images than PGGAN. Besides, compared with DCGAN, the IS, FID, and MS-SSIM did not increase as much as the experiment between DCGAN and our model. Therefore, we hypothesize that the progressive growing training architecture can greatly increase the quality of generation. However, with the condition of the ingredients, cooking method, taste, and cuisine, the model can generate food images with more details.

However, our model is not sufficient for generating a background for the food image, probably because the background of the image has not been dealt with in the Food-121 dataset.

5 Conclusion

In this paper, we demonstrate the effectiveness of adding food information conditions to GANs to generate realistic food images. The quality of the generated food image can be improved by adding food information conditions to the generator and discriminator. It increases the resolution slowly, and adds the embedding of ingredients, taste, cuisine and cooking method to the generator and discriminator in each step, which makes it possible to generate controllable food images. The experimental result shows that our model performs better on the food dataset Food-121. The model's IS and FID are evaluated. Table 1 shows that our model has a higher IS and lower FID on the Food-121 dataset, which means our model performs food image generation well.

Our experiment was restricted by GPU memory constraints, so the model will be trained with more food images in the future. Our model sometimes generates some strange backgrounds. Thus, the image data in Food-121 are planned to clean and retain only the food portion in the picture. More high-resolution food images will be collected from websites to improve the quality of image generation. In addition, every food dish image will be tagged by its ingredients, taste, cooking method and cuisine, extract features from the image in each tag or multi-tag to make our model learn more about the food dish image features.

Acknowledgments. This work is supported by the National Key Research and Development Plan of China under Grant No. 2017YFD0400101, the Natural Science Foundation of Shanghai under Grant No. 16ZR1411200, and CERNET Innovation Project under Grant No. NGII201 70513.

References

1. Goodfellow, I., et al.: Generative adversarial nets. In: Advances in Neural Information Processing Systems, pp. 2672–2680 (2014)
2. Liu, Z., Luo, P., Wang, X., Tang, X.: Deep learning face attributes in the wild. In: Proceedings of the IEEE International Conference on Computer Vision, pp. 3730–3738 (2015)
3. Welinder, P., et al.: Caltech-UCSD birds 200 (2010)
4. Nilsback, M.E., Zisserman, A.: Automated flower classification over a large number of classes. In: 2008 Sixth Indian Conference on Computer Vision, Graphics & Image Processing, pp. 722–729

5. Mirza, M., Osindero, S.: Conditional generative adversarial nets. arXiv preprint arXiv:1411. 1784 [cs.LG] (2014)
6. Karras, T., Aila, T., Laine, S., Lehtinen, J.: Progressive growing of GANs for improved quality, stability, and variation. In: 6th International Conference on Learning Representations (2018)
7. Hamada, K., Tachibana, K., Li, T., Honda, H., Uchida, Y.: Full-body high-resolution anime generation with progressive structure-conditional generative adversarial networks. In: European Conference on Computer Vision, pp. 67–74 (2018)
8. Salvador, A., et al.: Learning cross-modal embedding for cooking recipes and food images. In: Proceedings of the IEEE Conference on Computer Vision and Pattern Recognition, pp. 3020–3028 (2017)
9. Reed, S., Akata, Z., Yan, X., Logeswaran, L., Schiele, B., Lee, H.: Generative adversarial text to image synthesis. In: 33rd International Conference on Machine Learning, pp. 1060–1069 (2016)
10. El, O.B., Licht, O., Yosephian, N.: GILT: generating images from long text. arXiv preprint arXiv:1901.02404 (2019)
11. Zhang, H., et al.: Stackgan: Text to photo-realistic image synthesis with stacked generative adversarial networks. In: Proceedings of the IEEE International Conference on Computer Vision, pp. 5907–5915 (2017)
12. Zhang, H., Goodfellow, I., Metaxas, D., Odena, A.: Self-attention generative adversarial networks. arXiv preprint arXiv:1805.08318 (2018)
13. Sutskever, I., Vinyals, O., Le, Q. V.: Sequence to sequence learning with neural networks. In: Advances in Neural Information Processing Systems, pp. 3104–3112 (2014)
14. Kiros, R., et al.: Skip-thought vectors. In: Advances in Neural Information Processing Systems, pp. 3294–3302 (2015)
15. Bossard, L., Guillaumin, M., Van Gool, L.: Food-101–mining discriminative components with random forests. In: European Conference on Computer Vision, pp. 446–461 (2014)
16. Chen, J., Ngo, C.W.: Deep-based ingredient recognition for cooking recipe retrieval. In: Proceedings of the 24th ACM International Conference on Multimedia, pp. 32–41 (2016)
17. Salimans, T., Goodfellow, I., Zaremba, W., Cheung, V., Radford, A., Chen, X.: Improved techniques for training gans. In: Advances in Neural Information Processing Systems, pp. 2234–2242 (2016)
18. Heusel, M., Ramsauer, H., Unterthiner, T., Nessler, B., Hochreiter, S.: Gans trained by a two time-scale update rule converge to a local nash equilibrium. In: Advances in Neural Information Processing Systems, pp. 6626–6637 (2017)
19. Wang, Z., Simoncelli, E.P., Bovik, A.C.: Multiscale structural similarity for image quality assessment. In: The Thrity-Seventh Asilomar Conference on Signals, Systems & Computers, pp. 1398–1402 (2003)
20. Kingma, D.P., Ba, J.: Adam: a method for stochastic optimization. arXiv preprint arXiv: 1412.6980 (2014)
21. Radford, A., Metz, L., Chintala, S.: Unsupervised representation learning with deep convolutional generative adversarial networks. arXiv preprint arXiv:1511.06434 (2015)

Integration of Machine Learning Techniques as Auxiliary Diagnosis of Inherited Metabolic Disorders: Promising Experience with Newborn Screening Data

Bo Lin[1], Jianwei Yin[1(✉)], Qiang Shu[2(✉)], Shuiguang Deng[1], Ying Li[1], Pingping Jiang[2], Rulai Yang[2], and Calton Pu[3]

[1] College of Computer Science and Technology, Zhejiang University, Hangzhou 310027, China
{rainbowlin,dengsg,cnliying}@zju.edu.cn, zjuyjw@cs.zju.edu.cn
[2] The Children's Hospital, Zhejiang University School of Medicine, Hangzhou 310058, China
{shuqiang,ppjiang,chsczx}@zju.edu.cn
[3] Department of Electrical and Computer Engineering, Georgia Institute of Technology, Atlanta, GA 30332, USA
calton.pu@cc.gatech.edu

Abstract. Tandem mass spectrometry is an advanced biochemical analysis method and has been widely used in screening of inherited metabolic disorders (IMDs). Obtained examination results are filtered by cutoff values and then interpreted based on doctor's knowledge to get diagnoses. However, cutoff-based approaches have difficulties with the correlations of multiple metabolites. Doctor's experiences affect the diagnostic decision-making as well. The rapidly increasing availability of newborn screening data (1.5M cases in this study) enables the application of machine learning (ML) techniques to provide more accurate diagnoses of IMDs compared to simple cutoff values. We investigated two tasks in this study, i.e. complicated patterns between metabolites and better auxiliary diagnostic means. Experimental results show that novel metabolic patterns found in the study are effective and meaningful. Integrating ML techniques with these patterns improved predictive performance compared to existing diagnostic methods, suggesting ML techniques are becoming valuable as auxiliary diagnostic tools.

Keywords: Newborn screening · Machine learning · Metabolic patterns · Auxiliary diagnosis

X. Wang et al. (Eds.): CollaborateCom 2019, LNICST 292, pp. 334–349, 2019.
https://doi.org/10.1007/978-3-030-30146-0_23

1 Introduction

Inherited metabolic disorders (IMDs) are a class of genetic diseases causing mentally disabled, deformity and even death. Systematic screening and treatment to IMDs of newborn can significantly improve prognosis. Research shows that untreated patients tend to spend more money on avoiding neurological sequelae while early intervention is cost-effective over the whole life [18]. Tandem mass spectrometry (MS/MS) is a sensitive, selective and high-throughput technique for concentration detection of various amino acids and acylcarnitine in blood samples, which was first applied to newborn screening in 1990s [15]. A laboratory testing can simultaneously screen out dozens of IMDs, such as amino acid metabolism disorders and fatty acid oxidation disorders, in a few minutes [5]. The existing process of newborn screening is mainly dependent on cutoff-based methods and subjective diagnosis of pediatricians. Setting precise cutoff values for each metabolite or the ratio of two metabolites is the first step to filter out most negative cases. The remaining indistinguishable examination results of MS/MS are interpreted by experienced pediatricians. In practice, cutoff-based methods are hard to deal with complex relationships among metabolites, which bring a large number of false positive cases. As a result, the clinical diagnose still relies on doctor's experience.

In this study, over 1.5M newborn screening data were analyzed by machine learning (ML) techniques, which have proved to be effective for many medical tasks, such as diabetic retinopathy diagnosis [7] and autism spectrum disorder prediction [11]. With enough samples, ML techniques can achieve high performance in the task of disease prediction and act as auxiliary diagnostic means to provide accurate diagnosis. Such diagnostic tool has great social and economic significance. For instance, reducing substantial false alarms not only avoid unnecessary psychological and expenditure burden of families, but improve utilization of medical resources [8]. A refined screening system can be employed in remote districts to enhance the overall quality of medical care in those places. To this end, we aim to answer following two questions: *What is the maximum predictive performance that can be achieved by introducing ML to newborn screening* and *What kind of metabolic patterns can help improve diagnostic accuracy.*

Some related newborn screening projects have explored ML application in IMD diagnosis [2–4]. Compared to these researches, which focus only a few common diseases, we analyzed 16 disorders and evaluated 9 ML algorithms on our dataset. The experimental results demonstrate that more than 20 positive samples are required for a disease to achieve stable performance. Besides common used biomarkers, we discover several metabolites are also contributive to identify diseases. Novel metabolic patterns of their combination outperform existing diagnostic biomarkers. Based on our analysis, ML techniques are effective to be integrated as auxiliary diagnostic tools under certain conditions. Our main contributions are as follows:

- Sixteen IMDs were covered in this study including both common and rare disorders. Extensive experiments with more suitable ML techniques were applied on a large dataset for analysis of practical screening problems.
- We identify a boundary that dividing the applicable situation of ML methods and existing approaches based on the number of positive samples. Possible solutions are provided in both situations.
- We discover novel metabolic patterns in several disorders that achieve higher predictive performance than existing biomarkers.
- Compared to diagnostic methods in existing screening process, we proved integrating ML techniques as auxiliary diagnostic tools can improve predictive accuracy.

To the best of our knowledge, there are few researches that integrating ML techniques into auxiliary diagnosis for dozens of IMDs. We point out strength and weakness of both ML techniques and existing screening approaches in this paper. What's more, further researches can build customized models on the basis of our analyses to improve the screening efficiency (Table 1).

Table 1. List of 16 IMDs investigated in our study.

Abbr.	Disorders
PKU	Phenylketonuria
PTPSD	Tetrahydrobiopterin deficiency
MMA	Methylmalonic acidemia
NICCD	Neonatal intrahepatic cholestasis caused by citrin deficiency
MSUD	Maple syrup urine disease
IVA	Isovaleric acidemia
GA-I	Glutaric acidemia type I
PA	Propionic acidemia
ASS	Citrullinemia type I
VLCAD	Very long-chain acyl-CoA dehydrogenase deficiency
SCAD	Short long-chain acyl-CoA dehydrogenase deficiency
MET	Hypermethioninemia
IBD	Isobutyryl-CoA dehydrogenase deficiency
GA-II	Glutaric acidemia type II
CPT-I	Carnitine palmitoytransferase I deficiency
PRO	Proline acidemia

2   Methods

In this section, we first introduce details of the dataset applied in this study and describe our preprocessing strategies including standardization and train-test split. Various evaluation metrics are then discussed for our imbalanced data.

They are employed reasonably in latter analysis. The experiment was performed on a server with an Intel Xeon E5-2603 1.8 GHz CPU and 16 GB memory. The implementations of ML techniques involved in the experiment are based on the Scikit-learn machine learning framework [16] and imbalanced-learn from its community [14].

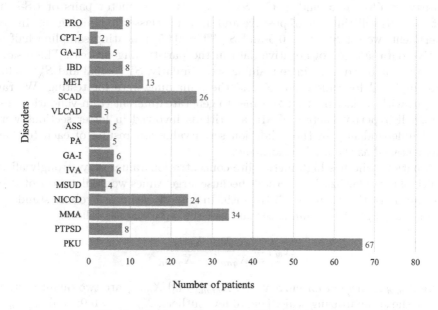

Fig. 1. Number of patients with each disease.

2.1 Data and Preprocessing

The dataset is obtained from the Children's Hospital, Zhejiang University School of Medicine. It consists of 1,506,098 biochemical examination results of neonatus by using MS/MS technique during the period between December, 2011 to December, 2016. Totally 43 biomarkers measured by MS/MS are used in our study (Table A1 in Appendix A), including 11 amino acids, 31 carnitines and a ketone. After excluding diseases with less than two confirmed patients, we obtained 16 IMDs of newborn listed in Tabel 1. Corresponding number of patients in our dataset are shown in Fig. 1. It is worth noting that the actual incidences of disorders are different while total 224 positive cases are only screened by MS/MS. To study the impact of positive sample size on prediction performance, we set two groups, i.e., $G_5 = \{PKU, MMA, NICCD, SCAD, MET\}$ and $G_{16} = \{all\ 16\ disorders\}$, whose average number of positive cases are 32.8 and 14, respectively.

One-Versus-Rest (OVR) strategy, a frequently-used multiclass learning approach, was applied to study each disease separately. That is, one disease was selected as the positive class in each time while others were regarded as negative classes. Common sample splitting strategies, e.g., shuffle split and stratified split, may lead insufficient positive samples when setting small training size or bring redundant negative samples with large size of training set because the splitting almost follows positive-negative sample ratio. Thus, we design an unequal stratified split method called US-split for train-test set generation. The US-split method has a list of class-size parameter $< C, S >$, where S is training size corresponding to target class C. For binary classification problem under OVR strategy, $< C_P, S_P >$ and $< C_N, S_N >$ are two parameter pairs of US-split that controls splitting size of positive and negative classes in training set. In our experiment, we set $S_P^{train} = 0.5$ and $S_N^{train} = 0.05$ indicating sampling half of positive data and 5% of negative data in the partitioning process. These samples were combined as a single training set. Similarly, $S_P^{val} = 0.3$ and $S_N^{val} = 0.1$ were employed for validation set and the remaining were for testing. We ran US-split with replacement for 20 times to generate different train-validation-test splits. All hyperparameters of ML algorithms involved in latter sections were tuned independently in the validation set. Evaluation results of each test set were averaged as the final performance.

A patient who has high metabolite concentration values may strongly affect traditional standardization methods because large values would flat most of samples and make them hard to distinguish. In case of outliers, a robust standardization was applied to training set and test set separately as follows:

$$X_{std} = \frac{X - X_{mid}}{X_{qmax} - X_{qmin}} \tag{1}$$

where X_{mid} is median for current set, X_{qmax} and X_{qmin} are two quantiles that specify the standardizing scale. Due to few outliers, $X_{qmax} = 0.95$ and $X_{qmin} = 0.05$ were chose to cover most of normal samples.

2.2   Evaluation Metrics

We adopted various metrics to evaluate predictive performance from different perspectives. Minimizing false positive rate (FPR) is the primary goal to improve quality of newborn screening while keeping other performances unchanged. Along with this, positive predictive value (PPV), sensitivity (SEN) and specificity (SPE) were considered as basic evaluation metrics. Furthermore, F_β score and G-mean were used for comprehensive ability evaluation.

$$F_\beta = (1 + \beta^2) \frac{PPV \times SEN}{\beta^2 \times PPV + SEN} \tag{2}$$

$$G\text{-}mean = \sqrt{SEN \times SPE} \tag{3}$$

Newborn screening dataset is a typical imbalanced dataset and the details will be discussed in Sect. 3. To better evaluating performance of predictors on this kind of dataset, many researches use F_β to avoid being deceived by a single basic metrics with good results due to preference of models. However, small cardinality of patients would bring impact to PPV if the number of false alarms change slightly. In Eq. (2), it is difficult to choose an appropriate β that balancing

PPV and SEN to fairly reflect the model ability. As an alternative metrics that is useful for imbalanced data, *G-mean* in Eq. (3) utilizes SPE to reduce instability brought by PPV. Specificity is the complementary set of FPR so it satisfies our top priority as well. Therefore, *G-mean* is more accord with this study and chose as major evaluation metrics. We also calculate F_1 score as a reference where $\beta = 1$.

3   Results

3.1   Model Comparison

To validate feasibility of introducing ML techniques to newborn screening, we selected nine suitable classification algorithms as shown in Table 2 to compare their performances based on different evaluation metrics. Basically, these algorithms can be categorized into various types such as weighted-bagging and boosting of ensemble methods, linear or nonlinear mapping, tree-based models and so on. Some special configurations of algorithms should be mentioned to avoid misunderstanding. The gradient boosting in our experiment indicates gradient boosting decision tree that using decision trees as weak learners. As for adaptive boosting (adaboost for short), we choose decision stump, or called one-level decision tree [12] as the weak learner.

Table 2. List of nine machine learning algorithms evaluated in our study.

Abbr.	Models
LR	Logistic regression
LDA	Linear discriminant analysis
DT	Decision trees
RF	Random forest
ET	Extremely-randomized tree
GB	Gradient boosting
ADA	Adaptive boosting
SVM	Support vector machine
kNN	k Nearest neighbors

Hyperparameter optimization applied grid search measured by *G-mean* to choose best configuration P_{best} for diverse diseases and models. Other evaluation metrics including PPV, SEN, and SPE were calculated based on the same P_{best}. Interestingly, we set three kernels, i.e., linear, polynomial and radial basis function for SVM classifier in grid search and P_{best} of SVM for different diseases are all configured by the linear kernel. Thus, LSVM is treated as a synonym of the SVM model equipped with linear kernel in the remainder of this paper. During the test, all classifiers are equipped with corresponding P_{best}. Average evaluation results of diseases on group G_5 and G_{16} are treated as their performances.

Table 3. Average evaluation results of nine machine learning algorithms on group G_5 and G_{16}.

Metrics	ADA	LR	GB	DT	ET	LDA	RF	SVM	KNN
GM	**.7201**	**.6114**	**.5519**	.5347	.4988	.4549	.4050	.3235	.2282
	.4549	**.5397**	.3872	.3768	.2973	**.5071**	.1892	.4387	.1225
F1	**.5710**	**.3819**	.3205	**.3818**	.2200	.2730	.3417	.1784	.1769
	.3731	.2768	.2645	.2818	.1543	**.3408**	.1604	**.2976**	.1015
SEN	.5906	**.6585**	.4498	.3937	.3523	**.8851**	.2679	**.9130**	.1146
	.3814	**.7066**	.3301	.3053	.2218	**.7399**	.1327	**.7647**	.0712
SPE	**.9994**	.8563	.9460	.9980	.9688	.5277	**.9999**	.3636	**.9999**
	.9998	.7714	.9763	.9938	.9806	.7282	**.9999**	.6297	**.9999**
PPV	**.7013**	.4877	.3715	**.4905**	.2791	.2747	**.6083**	.1929	.4658
	.4408	.3031	.2962	**.3299**	.2039	**.3420**	.2614	.3016	.2164

Note: The Metrics GM, F_1, SEN, SPE, PPV are G-mean, F_1 score, sensitivity, specificity, positive predictive value, respectively

As we can see in Table 3, the top three best performances for each metrics are in bold. The result in the upper line represents the performance on G_5 and the lower line is on G_{16}. There are some conclusions can be inferred according to the observation of experimental results.

(a) In ensemble-based methods, boosting models especially adaboost have good generalization on G_5, but bagging methods including extremely-randomized tree and random forest perform relatively poor. The reason is that positive cases are insufficient to represent the real distribution. Inconsistent probability distributions are estimated by base classifiers, which affect bagging methods. Their diverse opinions tend to misclassify samples hovering over the border because of the independence between these base classifiers. That is why sensitivity becomes a weakness for bagging models. As for boosting methods, although their base estimators have high bias, the misclassification is considered and passed to next iteration to repair errors. This propagation pays more attention to indistinguishable samples to avoid missed diagnosis. Some false alarms occur but with limited sensitivity degradation, hence keeping high comprehensive performance.

(b) Unlike ensemble methods, linear models such as LR, LDA and LSVM behave well in G_{16}. Specifically, linear models have the three best sensitivity yet their specificity are the worst. The reason is these models have a less complex decision boundary. Under the constraint of avoiding missed diagnosis, they naturally bring false alarms when searching more positive cases. Also, insufficient positive samples reduce generalization of trained models. No matter how to partition training and testing set, the diversity of positive cases is still low. Theoretically, the cutoff-based method is a kind of naïve linear model. Thus, this evidence proves the shortcoming of traditional cutoff-based decisions as well.

(c) Similarity-based methods such as kNN require adequate decision supports from data points nearby. For rare data problem, this kind of method is not able to obtain enough information to distinguish positives from negatives so it is not suitable in application of IMD diagnosis.

In general, most of evaluation results in G_5 are better than G_{16}. It is consistent with the opinion that too few positive samples have impact on predictive accuracy. In our scenario, ML algorithms require approximately 20 positive samples of a disorder to achieve stable performance. With the positive sample grows, models would have higher accuracy for the disease prediction. Among these algorithms, adaboost outperforms all other methods. If a dataset contains only a few positive samples, existing cutoff-based methods or some linear classifiers could be a good choice.

Table 4. Best algorithms for each disease in auxiliary diagnosis.

Disorders	LR	ADA	SVM	LDA	DT
PKU	△	△			
MMA		△			
NICCD	△	*			
SCAD		△		△	
MET		△			
PTPSD	△				
MSUD			△	*	
IVA	△		*		
GA-I	△				
PA				△	
ASS	△	*			
VLCAD	△		*	△	
IBD		*			
GA-II	△			△	
CPT-I			△		△
PRO			△		

Note: The symbol △ denotes a model with at least one highest score on G-mean or F1 metrics, and * indicates a model performs both second best on two metrics. Disorders belonging to G_5 are in bold.

Based on the analysis results, Table 4 lists recommended ML algorithms that achieve relative good predictive performance for each disease. An algorithm is selected if it has one of the highest scores or both second-best in G-$mean$ and F_1 metrics. Otherwise, models are omitted in the table. Adaboost is quite appropriate for predicting IMDs if owning enough data of patients. It has preferable comprehensive ability and performs well in other basic metrics especially in PPV. Besides, linear models cover nearly all diseases so they can be alternatives when lack of positive data.

3.2 Feature Selection

Feature selection methods are designed to automatically filter out irrelevant variables while retaining important features to accomplish certain tasks. Popular feature selection methods are usually as viable options for dataset with tens of thousands of variables, such as gene segments or personalized recommendation, to avoid curse of dimensionality. Although our dataset owns relatively few features, other functionalities of those methods are still helpful for newborn screening data analysis. In this section, we mainly focus on answering *How much performance improvement can a feature selection method brings to predictors* and *Are those selected features reasonable enough to act as a supplement for diagnostic guidance.*

Wrapper-based, filter-based and embedded-based were described as three typical types of feature selection methods [9]. We do not intend to analyze all these methods for the former question, instead, we chose five popular feature selection methods as listed in Table 5. Their selected features were compared to existing diagnostic markers. Other feature construction methods, for instance, principal component analysis (PCA), would not be involved because of interpretable requirements constrained by the latter question.

Table 5. List of five feature selection methods and two baselines compared in this study.

Types	Methods (Abbr.)
Statistics	χ^2 test (Chi2)
	Analysis of variance (ANOVA)
Information theory	Mutual information (MI)
Model oriented	L1-norm (L1-SVM)
	Tree-based (ET)
Baseline	None (origin)
	General standard (existing)

Note: In model-oriented methods, L1-Norm indicates using L1 regularization term to get sparse solution based on SVM classifier and Tree-based uses extremely-randomized tree as the model to fetch important features. We set two baselines: "None" means using all 43 biomarkers without any feature selection and "General Standard" applies metabolic patterns in existing newborn screening.

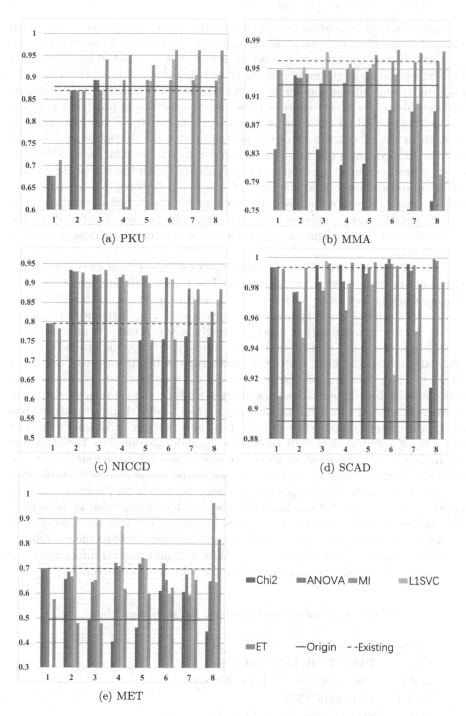

Fig. 2. Predictive performance comparison on G_5 before and after applying feature selection methods and existing diagnostic biomarkers. X-axis represents the number of selected features and Y-axis is average G-mean for all subgraphs.

Figure 2 shows evaluation results of feature selection methods on G_5. Each subgraph consists of two parts: bar graphs are the highest *G-mean* score can be achieved after using different selection algorithms; the dashed line represents the best predictive performance based on existing diagnostic markers and the solid line applies all metabolites in disease prediction. Two lines are treated as baselines to explore effectiveness of these feature selection approaches. Features were selected based on their own criterion such as statistical value or informativeness. In the experiment, we took out the most valuable features considered by different algorithms one at a time and put it into a candidate set $\mathcal{B}$. We iteratively compared changes in prediction performance with the size of $\mathcal{B}$ increase, which are drawn in x-axis as the number of selected features. Up to eight most valuable metabolites are analyzed that account for about 20% of total features. It is remarkable that we enlarge y-axis for better observation of detailed results. Information loss in the figure is inevitable but our primary purpose focuses on higher scores.

From view of differences between two baselines, biomarkers used in newborn screening are truly effective for diagnosis. The results validate the correctness of using existing metabolic patterns. As for feature selection methods, features selected by statistics-based approaches achieve a similar performance to diagnostic markers in general situation. More concretely, ANOVA tends to pick more features, which would not lead to significant improvement or bring any side effects. Chi2 can find out the most relevant features rapidly but is narrowly beaten by ANOVA. Those information theory or model oriented methods greatly outperform statistics-based approaches in some case while keeping similar performance in others. Especially in MET prediction, MI and L1-SVM improve more than 20% performance compared to existing metabolic patterns. Although the first two or three features selected by L1-SVM are usually meaningless, the algorithm can rapidly locate the most valuable features in several more searching steps. Selection criterion based on mutual information performs relatively stable with the size of candidate set changes and the selected metabolic patterns would be useful for diseases prediction. Similarly, the tree-based approach is quite powerful and even the best in the most cases because it involves the idea of both mutual information and bagging in the algorithm. According to the experimental results, model oriented method, especially ET, and mutual information are recommended as auxiliary diagnostic tools for selecting biomarkers.

Table 6. Novel metabolic patterns found by algorithms.

Disorders	Metabolic patterns
PKU	**PHE**, **TYR**, LEU, VAL, PRO, ALA
MMA	C16:1-OH, **C3**, MET, C0, C2, C18:1
NICCD	**CIT**, PHE TYR
SCAD	**C4**, C3, C5:1, C2, SA, C8, C10:1, C6DC
MET	C4, C16:1-OH, C6, C5, PHE, C18:1-OH, C4DC+C5-OH, C18

The most discriminating metabolic patterns found by ML techniques are listed in Table 6. Biomarkers are ranked in the order of their importance. Metabolites are in bold if they are involved in existing diagnostic patterns. For the first four disorders, we can find that these biomarkers are also considered valuable by feature selection algorithms, which verifies correctness of existing patterns. Beyond that, some extra features are deemed to have potential relationships to the cause of disorders. Surprisingly, mutual information approach does not recommend methionine as the top important biomarker to MET. The deeper reason requires further researches by medical experts.

3.3 Rare Data

Many existing ML algorithms assume input data have satisfied the hypothesis of good quality, quantity and representation. Quite the contrary, incompleteness, noise and other data issues in the real application scenarios are completely different from ideal condition. Among these, the class imbalance problem is one of big and common challenges. The term *majority class* denotes the number of samples in a class are overwhelming, otherwise is called *minority class*. There is no definite boundary to distinguish whether a class is considered as majority or not, but in general, the ratio of majority to minority usually reaches hundreds to thousands. Furthermore, rare data problem is a extreme case of imbalance problem, whose ratio is over ten thousand and more. For instance, the majority-minority ratio of our dataset is from 22 thousand to 75 thousand according to data description in Sect. 2. Thus, the absolute quantity of positive samples is rare essentially and it is impractical to solve the insufficiency by increasing overall sample size.

Balancing data by generating simulated samples in minority class or reducing less useful samples in majority class is a natural way to solve this kind of issue. Correspondingly, over-sampling and under-sampling are two types of solutions. We selected two random sampling methods and six advanced works to solve rare data problems, as listed in Table 7. On the basis of metabolic patterns shown in Table 6, re-sampling algorithms are employed to explore possible performance improvements. These algorithms only act on training set without any change in testing set.

Figure 3 shows performance comparisons between before and after applying re-sampling algorithms, which are represented as red lines and bar graphs, respectively. Red lines are used as baselines indicating the highest *G-mean* achieved in Fig. 2. However, it seems these algorithms incur a slight performance degradation in some cases. Two random methods are not stable as expected but still useful in some situation. In general, under-sampling methods perform a little bit better than over-sampling method except One-Sided Selection. But for MET, over-sampling methods are beyond the baseline and achieve higher performance. Core concept of re-sampling techniques utilizes neighbors in the adjacent area to generate simulated samples or drop redundancy. Simulated samples are lack of novelty and informativeness if minor classes provide only a few samples as seeds. Thus, over-sampling methods are not recommended for rare data in

Table 7. List of resampling algorithms for rate data learning.

Types	Methods
Under sampling	Random under sampling
	Tomek links [17]
	One-sided selection [13]
	Edited nearest neighbors [19]
Over sampling	Random over sampling
	SMOTE [6]
	Borderline-SMOTE [10]
Mixed	SMOTE + ENN [1]

general circumstances. However, it could be effective if positive samples have a dense distribution. Generated cases are able to represent relative small sample space with less seed samples. Although under-sampling methods are not helpful for performance improvement, they are also valuable in other applications. For instance, these methods exclude many redundant samples without too much performance degradation, hence selected samples can be used to describe the profile of normal population and new classifiers can be designed based on it.

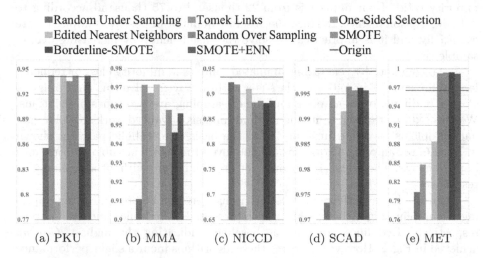

Fig. 3. Predictive performance in G_5 after using re-sampling algorithms. The red line in each subgraph is a baseline representing highest G-mean after applying feature selection algorithms. (Color figure online)

4   Conclusion

Simple cutoff values and doctor's experiences in existing process of newborn screening have limitations on dealing with large-scale MS/MS examination results. To provide more accurate diagnosis of IMDs, we analyze samples of 1.5M neonates and apply several techniques, including ML algorithms, feature selection and re-sampling methods, to improve accuracy in disorder prediction. Experimental results show that adaptive boosting achieves the best comprehensive performance compared to other ML algorithms. Furthermore, feature selection methods are able to find more discriminating metabolites than existing cutoff values on biomarkers. Our analyses also demonstrate that ML algorithms require at least 20 positive samples to achieve stable prediction. For disorders with more than twenty patients, ML techniques can become effective auxiliary diagnostic means for IMDs.

Acknowledgement. This work was supported in part by the National Key Research and Development Program of China (Grant No. 2017YFC1001703, 2018YFC1002700), in part by the National Natural Science Foundation of China (Grant No. 61825205, 61772459) and in part by the National Science and Technology Major Project of China (Grant No. 50-D36B02-9002-16/19).

A   MS/MS Biomarkers

Table A1. Overview of 43 biomarkers measured by MS/MS in this study.

Amino acid	Carnitine
Alanine (ALA)	Free (C0)
Arginine (ARG)	Acetyl (C2)
Citrulline (CIT)	Propionyl (C3)
Glutamate (GLU)	Malonyl+Hydroxybutyryl (C3DC+C4OH)
Leucine (LEU)	Butyryl (C4)
Methionine (MET)	Methylmalonyl+Hydroxyisovaleryl (C4DC+C5OH)
Ornithine (ORN)	Isovaleryl (C5)
Phenylalanine (PHE)	Tiglyl (C5:1)
Proline (PRO)	Glutaryl+Hydroxyhexanoyl (C5DC+C6OH)
Tyrosine (TYR)	Hexanoyl (C6)
Valine (VAL)	Methylglutaryl (C6DC)
	Octanoyl (C8)
Ketone	Octenoyl (C8:1)

(continued)

Table A1. (*continued*)

Amino acid	Carnitine
Succinylacetone (SA)	Decanoyl (C10)
	Decenoyl (C10:1)
	Decenoyl (C10:2)
	Dodecanoyl (C12)
	Dodecenoyl (C12:1)
	Myristoyl (C14)
	Myristoleyl (C14:1)
	Tetradecadienoyl (C14:2)
	Hydroxytetradecadienoyl (C14OH)
	Hexadecanoyl (C16)
	Hexadecenoyl (C16:1)
	Hydroxypalmitoyl (C16OH)
	Hydroxypalmitoleyl (C16:1OH)
	Octadecanoyl (C18)
	Octadecenoyl (C18:1)
	Linoleoyl (C18:2)
	Hydroxystearoyl (C18OH)
	Hydroxyoleyl (C18:1OH)

References

1. Batista, G.E., Prati, R.C., Monard, M.C.: A study of the behavior of several methods for balancing machine learning training data. ACM SIGKDD Explor. Newslett. **6**(1), 20–29 (2004)
2. Baumgartner, C., Böhm, C., Baumgartner, D.: Modelling of classification rules on metabolic patterns including machine learning and expert knowledge. J. Biomed. Inform. **38**(2), 89–98 (2005)
3. Baumgartner, C., et al.: Supervised machine learning techniques for the classification of metabolic disorders in newborns. Bioinformatics **20**(17), 2985–2996 (2004)
4. Van den Bulcke, T., et al.: Data mining methods for classification of medium-chain Acyl-CoA dehydrogenase deficiency (MCADD) using non-derivatized tandem MS neonatal screening data. J. Biomed. Inform. **44**(2), 319–325 (2011)
5. Chace, D., DiPerna, J., Naylor, E.: Laboratory integration and utilization of tandem mass spectrometry in neonatal screening: a model for clinical mass spectrometry in the next millennium. Acta Paediatr. **88**, 45–47 (1999)
6. Chawla, N.V., Bowyer, K.W., Hall, L.O., Kegelmeyer, W.P.: SMOTE: synthetic minority over-sampling technique. J. Artif. Intell. Res. **16**, 321–357 (2002)
7. Gulshan, V., et al.: Development and validation of a deep learning algorithm for detection of diabetic retinopathy in retinal fundus photographs. JAMA **316**(22), 2402–2410 (2016)

8. Gurian, E.A., Kinnamon, D.D., Henry, J.J., Waisbren, S.E.: Expanded newborn screening for biochemical disorders: the effect of a false-positive result. Pediatrics **117**(6), 1915–1921 (2006)
9. Guyon, I., Elisseeff, A.: An introduction to variable and feature selection. J. Mach. Learn. Res. **3**, 1157–1182 (2003)
10. Han, H., Wang, W.-Y., Mao, B.-H.: Borderline-SMOTE: a new over-sampling method in imbalanced data sets learning. In: Huang, D.-S., Zhang, X.-P., Huang, G.-B. (eds.) ICIC 2005. LNCS, vol. 3644, pp. 878–887. Springer, Heidelberg (2005). https://doi.org/10.1007/11538059_91
11. Hazlett, H.C., et al.: Early brain development in infants at high risk for autism spectrum disorder. Nature **542**(7641), 348 (2017)
12. Iba, W., Langley, P.: Induction of one-level decision trees. In: Machine Learning Proceedings 1992, pp. 233–240. Elsevier (1992)
13. Kubat, M., Matwin, S., et al.: Addressing the curse of imbalanced training sets: one-sided selection. In: International Conference on Machine Learning, Nashville, USA, vol. 97, pp. 179–186 (1997)
14. Lemaître, G., Nogueira, F., Aridas, C.K.: Imbalanced-learn: a python toolbox to tackle the curse of imbalanced datasets in machine learning. J. Mach. Learn. Res. **18**(1), 559–563 (2017)
15. Millington, D., Kodo, N., Norwood, D., Roe, C.: Tandem mass spectrometry: a new method for acylcarnitine profiling with potential for neonatal screening for inborn errors of metabolism. J. Inherit. Metab. Dis. **13**(3), 321–324 (1990)
16. Pedregosa, F., et al.: Scikit-learn: machine learning in python. J. Mach. Learn. Res. **12**, 2825–2830 (2011)
17. Tomek, I.: Two modifications of CNN. IEEE Trans. Syst. Man Cybern. **6**, 769–772 (1976)
18. Venditti, L.N., et al.: Newborn screening by tandem mass spectrometry for medium-chain Acyl-CoA dehydrogenase deficiency: a cost-effectiveness analysis. Pediatrics **112**(5), 1005–1015 (2003)
19. Wilson, D.L.: Asymptotic properties of nearest neighbor rules using edited data. IEEE Trans. Syst. Man Cybern. **3**, 408–421 (1972)

Nemesis: Detecting Algorithmically Generated Domains with an LSTM Language Model

Dunsheng Yuan[1,2], Ying Xiong[3], Tianning Zang[2(✉)], and Ji Huang[1,2]

[1] School of Cyber Security, University of Chinese Academy of Sciences,
Beijing, China
[2] Institute of Information Engineering, Chinese Academy of Sciences, Beijing, China
{yuandunsheng,zangtianning}@iie.ac.cn
[3] National Computer Network Emergency Response Technical Team/Coordination
Center of China, Beijing, China

Abstract. Various malware families frequently apply Domain Generation Algorithms (DGAs) to generate numerous pseudorandom domain names to communicate with their Command and Control (C&C) servers. Security researchers make a lot of efforts to detect Algorithmically Generated Domains (AGDs) for fighting Botnets and relevant malicious network behaviors. In this paper, we propose a new AGD detection approach, Nemesis, based on a Long Short-Term Memory (LSTM) language model. Nemesis can identify whether given domain names are AGDs according to their string compositions, and without additional information. Nemesis first leverages an n-gram dictionary, which is built on real domain names, to tokenize domain names into n-grams. Then a pretrained detector is used to classify domain names as real ones or AGDs according to the tokenized results. We evaluate Nemesis' abilities to detect domain names generated by known DGAs and to discover new DGA families. It turns out that Nemesis can accurately detect AGDs with the precision of 98.6% and the recall of 96.7%. Besides, we verify that Nemesis largely outperforms several existing effective approaches.

Keywords: Domain Generation Algorithm · LSTM ·
Language model · Deep learning

1 Introduction

The Domain Name System (DNS), which resolves domain names into IP addresses, is an important public infrastructure and significant for the collaboration of the Internet. However, this mechanism can also be abused by malware to communicate with their Command and Control (C&C) servers. Since it can be easily blocked by blacklists to use hard-coded IP addresses or domain names to establish C&C connections, a variety of malware families apply a more sophisticated mechanism known as Domain Generation Algorithms (DGAs) to hide

© ICST Institute for Computer Sciences, Social Informatics and Telecommunications Engineering 2019
Published by Springer Nature Switzerland AG 2019. All Rights Reserved
X. Wang et al. (Eds.): CollaborateCom 2019, LNICST 292, pp. 350–363, 2019.
https://doi.org/10.1007/978-3-030-30146-0_24

their C&C servers [1]. In a botnet, such as Conficker and Mirai, each compromised computer (bot) algorithmically generates a large set of domain names and queries each of them until one of them is resolved successfully, and then the bot contacts the resolved domain name, which is typically corresponding to the IP address of the C&C server (botmaster). Once the connection is established, the bots can be controlled by the botmaster to launch distributed denial-of-service (DDoS) attacks, steal data and privacy, mine digital currency illegally, *etc* [2]. For example, on October 21, 2016, a large DDoS attack on Dyn, a DNS provider was performed through a Mirai botnet, which involved 100,000 malicious endpoints. The Mirai botnet sent superfluous DNS requests to overload the DNS servers, and the serious consequences of this attack caused dozens of popular websites unreachable for the users in North America. Besides botnets, spammers also generate pseudorandom domain names in spam emails to avoid detection by regular expression based domain blacklists [3].

Since Algorithmically Generated Domains (AGDs) are involved in various malicious network behaviors mentioned above, it becomes a crucial topic of concern for researchers to detect AGDs automatically and accurately. Some traditional AGD detection approaches leverage the distribution of characters in the domain [3]. These approaches are simple but hard to achieve good effects. Others utilize human engineered lexical features [4,5], nevertheless, it is time-consuming to construct effective features.

Motivated by these reasons, we propose a new AGD detection approach called Nemesis[1], which is implemented based upon an LSTM language model. Nemesis first tokenizes a domain name into n-grams and then classifies it as a real domain name or an AGD according to these n-grams. The key insight of Nemesis lies in the truth that domain names are composed of syllables or acronyms for easy readability, and n-grams can represent both of them. Nemesis only mines the n-gram information of domain names but can still keep high precision and recall. Specifically, we make the following key contributions:

- Nemesis can identify whether a single domain name is an AGD according to its string composition. It does not need extra data or the association information of multiple domain names.
- Nemesis can detect AGDs of known DGA families with high precision of 98.6%, recall of 96.7%, an F1-Score of 97.6%, and it largely outperforms detection approaches based on KL, ED, and JI.
- We verified that Nemesis is also able to discover new DGA families, which are not seen in the training data. Specifically, we test Nemesis on AGDs of 10 new DGA families individually, and it can achieve high recall values for every DGA family.

The rest of the paper proceeds as follows. Section 2 summarizes related work in DGA detection and discusses their limitation. Section 3 introduces an overview of our approach and then describes how to implement each module in detail. Section 4 presents the experimental setup, including datasets and evaluation metrics. After that, we compare Nemesis with a typical prior work in Sect. 5. Finally, we conclude our work in Sect. 6.

---

[1] Nemesis is the goddess of retribution for evil deeds in ancient Greek mythology.

2   Related Work

Researchers propose a variety of approaches [3–10] to detect AGDs. Anton-akakis *et al.* [4] develop a detection system called Pleiades to identify DGA-based bots. Their insight is that most DGA-generated domains queried by bots will result in Non-Existent Domain (NXDomain) responses, and that bots using the same DGA algorithm will generate similar NXDomain traffic. Pleiades is implemented based on a combination of clustering and classification algorithms. At first, Pleiades clusters domains based on the similarity in the lexical features of domain names and the groups of machines that queried these domains. Then Pleiades uses the classification algorithm to assign the generated clusters to models of known DGAs. A new model indicating a new DGA family will be produced if a cluster cannot be assigned to a known model.

Schiavoni *et al.* [5] propose Phoenix, a mechanism to detect and classify AGDs. Phoenix first proceeds a binary classification to identify AGDs and real domains based on two linguistic features, namely, the meaningful character ratio and the N-gram normality score. These features are able to measure the meaning and pronounceability of domain names. Then they calculate the probabilistic distribution for legitimate domains based on those linguistic features, and cluster suspicious domain names with known AGDs to classify them as belonging to specific malware families.

Although previous work mentioned above can obtain good effects in terms of detection precision or accuracy, they rely strongly on string-based and host-based features of domain names. These features are time-consuming to construct and extract, and host-based features, such as IP addresses, may change over time. Thus, to build a simple AGD detection approach based on string-based information only, Yadav *et al.* [3] leverage three metrics of distance to detect AGDs, including Kullback-Leibler (KL) distance, Edit distance (ED) and Jaccard Index (JI). These metrics can be easily calculated based solely on sets of domain name strings, and researchers do not need to spend a lot of time on feature engineering for domain names. Although detection method based on these metrics can achieve high accuracy for some DGA families, they have two essential shortcomings. On the one hand, approaches based on KL and JI only leverage the character distributions of domain names. Therefore, the can hardly work on AGDs that have different character patterns but similar distribution as real domain names. On the other hand, approaches based on ED can only detect domain names generated with regular grammar.

3   Proposed Approach

As discussed above, some existing AGD detection approaches are not efficient enough since they spend a lot of time and resources on constructing string-based and host-based features. Thus, in this paper, we propose a new AGD detection system called Nemesis, which does not rely on human-engineered features. Specifically, Nemesis is implemented based upon an LSTM language model, and it only leverages the string-based information of domain names. In this section, we first introduce the architecture of Nemesis, then describe the implementation of each component in detail.

3.1 Architecture of Nemesis

The ultimate purpose of Nemesis is to identify whether unlabeled domain names are real ones or AGDs. Nemesis takes unlabeled domain names as the input, then it outputs the corresponding class label of each unlabeled domain name. To this end, Nemesis first tokenizes each domain name into n-grams according to a predefined n-gram dictionary, then trains an LSTM neural network based on the tokenized results, and uses this network to identify unlabeled domain names at last. As shown in Fig. 1, Nemesis generally consists of three modules: the Modeling module, the Training module, and the Detecting module.

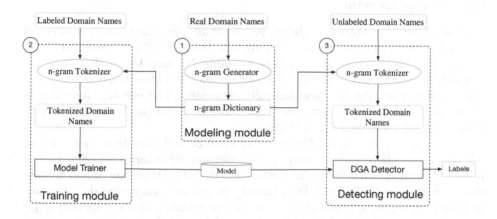

Fig. 1. The architecture of Nemesis.

Modeling Module. The purpose of the Modeling module is to build an n-gram dictionary which includes common n-grams of real domain names. The input to this module is a set of known legitimate domain names, and the output is an n-gram dictionary. This dictionary will be used by the n-gram Tokenizer in the Training module and the Detecting module. The only component of this module is the n-gram Generator, which will be detailly described in Sect. 3.2.

Training Module. The input to the Training module is a set of labeled domain names consisting of known AGDs and legitimate domain names, and the output is a trained LSTM network model. There are two important components in this module: the n-gram Tokenizer and the Model Trainer. We use the n-gram Tokenizer, which is implemented based on the n-gram dictionary obtained in the Modeling module, to tokenize domain names into n-grams, and then employ the

Model Trainer to train the LSTM network. The trained model can automatically distinguish AGDs in unlabeled domain names and will be used as the DGA Detector in the Detecting module.

Detecting Module. The input to the Detecting module is a set of unlabeled domain names, and the output is the corresponding class label of each domain name. This module contains two major functional components, the n-gram Tokenizer and the DGA Detector. The former is the same as the n-gram Tokenizer in the Training module, and the latter is the LSTM model trained in the Training Module. They will be described in Sects. 3.3 and 3.4 respectively. We classify unlabeled domain names in two steps. First, we utilize the n-gram Tokenizer to tokenize unlabeled domain names into n-grams. Second, we leverage the DGA Detector to label these tokenized unlabeled domain names as real ones or AGDs.

3.2 *n*-gram Generator

For readability and pronounceability, real domain names are usually composed of syllables or acronyms. Since it is hard to collect all syllables and acronyms, we compromise to represent them with n-grams. Nemesis learns the rules that how syllables or acronyms form real domain names and identifies domain names that disobey the rules as algorithmically generated. The n-gram Generator is tasked with extracting n-grams from real domain names and build a dictionary containing the most common n-grams.

The input to the n-gram Generator is a set of real domain names, such as Alexa top 1 million, and the output is an n-gram dictionary providing for the n-gram Tokenizer. First, we count the occurrences of each n-gram in real domain names, with n = $\{1, 2, 3, 4\}$. For example, in domain name "google", 1-grams include $\{$'g', 'o', 'l', 'e'$\}$, and the corresponding occurrences are respectively $\{2, 2, 1, 1\}$. 2-grams include $\{$'go', 'oo', 'og', 'gl', 'le'$\}$, and the corresponding occurrences are respectively $\{1, 1, 1, 1, 1\}$. Similarly, 3-grams and 4-grams can be counted in this way. Next, we sort all these n-grams by their occurrence frequencies in ascending order and collect the top 5000 into a dictionary. By extracting n-grams from domain names, we are trying to acquire the most frequent combinations of characters (including lower-case letters, digits, and hyphens) in domain names.

For a fully qualified domain name (e.g. www.example.com), the rightmost segment (e.g. *com*) is the top-level domain (TLD), and *example.com* is the second-level domain name (2LD). Since legitimate TLDs come from a well-known list [11], it is unnecessary for DGAs to generate a TLD. Therefore, we refer to effective 2LD (e.g. *example*) as "domain name" in this paper.

3.3 *n*-gram Tokenizer

The n-gram Tokenizer splits domain names into n-grams according to the dictionary obtained from the n-gram Generator. The input to the n-gram Tokenizer is unlabeled domain names, and the output is the corresponding tokenized domain names (i.e., an n-gram list) for each of the unlabeled domain names.

In this paper, we adopt the Bi-direction Maximum Matching (BMM) Method to tokenize domain names into n-grams. The BMM Method fits languages that have no space to delimit words or characters, such as Chinese and Japanese. The principle of the BMM Method is a combination of the Forward Maximum Matching Method and the Backward Maximum Matching Method. The Forward Maximum Matching Method aims to partition a sentence into words from left to right as long as possible. In contrast, the Backward Maximum Matching Method partitions a sentence into words from right to left as long as possible. For the same sentence, the BMM Method compares the results from the Forward Maximum Matching Method and the Backward Maximum Matching Method, and chooses the better one according to the following rules:

- If the segmentation results from those two methods are the same, choose either of the two.
- If the number of words in the segmentation results from those two methods are not equal, choose the result that has fewer words.
- If the number of words in the segmentation results from those two methods are equal but these two results are not the same, choose the result that has less individual characters.

As we know, a domain name is a contiguous string without spaces, which is similar to the writing convention of Chinese and Japanese. Thus, in the n-gram Tokenizer, we regard domain names and n-grams as sentences and words respectively, then we can apply the BMM Method to domain names. In practice, the n-gram dictionary produced by the n-gram Generator contains all individual characters (1-gram) that appear in real domain names. Therefore, it is unnecessary to worry about meeting an n-gram that does not exist in the dictionary.

3.4 DGA Detector

The purpose of the DGA Detector is to distinguish AGDs from real domain names. After getting tokenized domain names from the n-gram tokenizer, we input them to the DGA Detector and expect it to output the corresponding class label of each domain name. The DGA Detector is implemented mainly based on an LSTM neural network which is widely used in natural language processing. The architecture of the DGA Detector is shown in Fig. 2.

The Numeric Encoder is employed to convert the tokenized domain name (an n-gram list) to a numeric vector since the neural network can only deal with tensors but not strings. It can be simply accomplished by replacing each n-gram with its sequence number (range from 1 to 5,000) in the n-gram dictionary to form a numeric vector. Then we pad the vector with 0 to make all of them have the same length l. The parameter l is the maximum number of n-grams in a single tokenized domain name.

The embedding layer converts the l-length vector to a 2-D tensor in the shape of $l * d$. The tunable parameter d is the output dimension of this layer. We

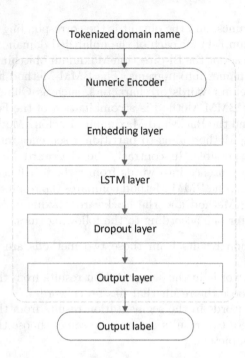

Fig. 2. The architecture of DGA detector

conduct several experiments with different parameter d and find the detection results are not very sensitive to it. Thus it is not important to choose the best parameter d and we set a proper value $d = 64$ to provide enough degrees of freedom to the model in subsequent experiments.

LSTM can capture meaningful temporal relationships among tokens in a sequence [12]. The LSTM cell consists of a state that can be read, written or reset via a set of programmable gates, thereby mitigating the vanishing gradients problem [13]. The LSTM layer can implicitly extract features of domain names and learn the contextual information of n-grams. This layer takes the output of the embedding layer as input, and a dropout layer is applied to the output to avoid overfitting when training the neural network.

The fully connected output layer is a simple logistic regression. It outputs the probability that the input domain name is algorithm generated. At last, the DGA Detector can label the domain name by comparing the probability with a proper threshold. We describe how to choose the optimal threshold in Sect. 5.1.

4   Experimental Evaluation

In this section, we design two experiments to evaluate the effectiveness of Nemesis. We first introduce the data sets used in our experiments, then define the evaluation metrics, and finally describe the experimental setup in detail.

4.1   Data Sets

To evaluate Nemesis, we collect 30 typical DGA families used by live botnets and select ten of them (i.e., Conficker, Banjori, Corebot, Cryptolocker, Dircrypt, Kraken_v1, Locky_v2, Pykspa, Qakbot, and Simda) that are more difficult to detect. We build two data sets for subsequent experiments:

- *malicious dataset*: We use each of these ten DGA families to generate 10k AGDs respectively, and regard all of these 100 k AGDs as the *malicious dataset*.
- *legitimate dataset*: We randomly sample 100 k domain names from Alexa top 1 million on 28th, Oct 2018 as *legitimate dataset*.

4.2   Evaluation Metrics

To evaluate the effectiveness of an AGD detection approach, we first make three definitions for further analysis:

- True Positives (TP): the number of domain names that are classified as AGDs by a detection approach and are indeed AGDs;
- False Positives (FP): the number of domain names that are classified as AGDs by a detection approach but are real ones in fact;
- False Negatives (FN): the number of domain names that are classified as real ones by a detection approach but are AGDs in fact.

Based on these definitions, we use three evaluation metrics, Precision (P), Recall (R) and the F1-Score (F1), to measure the effectiveness of a certain AGD detection approach. They can be calculated as follows:

$$P = \frac{TP}{TP + FP} \tag{1}$$

$$R = \frac{TP}{TP + FN} \tag{2}$$

$$F1 = \frac{2 \times P \times R}{P + R} \tag{3}$$

Precision and recall reflect the ability of the detection system in two aspects respectively. We expect the two values to reach the maximum. However, these two metrics are often contradictory, so we use F1-Score as a compromise between the two.

4.3   Experimental Setup

We conduct two different experiments, Experiment I and Experiment II, to evaluate Nemesis from two aspects.

Experiment I. The purpose of this experiment is to evaluate the ability of Nemesis to accurately identify domain names generated by known DGAs. Specifically, We use 90% of the domain names in *legitimate dataset* and *malicious dataset* as the training dataset, and the rest 10% as the test dataset. We use precision, recall, and F1-Scores to evaluate Nemesis in this experiment. At the same time, we compare Nemesis with previous work in this experiment.

Experiment II. The purpose of this experiment is to evaluate the ability of Nemesis to identify AGDs generated by new DGA families which does not appear in the training dataset. To this end, we apply the leave-one-out cross-validation (LOOCV) method at the level of DGA families. Specifically, for each DGA family, we collect domain names generated by this DGA as test dataset, and the training dataset consists of domain names from *legitimate dataset* and those generated by nine other DGA families. Since we only care about the proportion of domain names that are correctly identified, only recall is used to evaluate Nemesis in this experiment. Similarly, we also compare Nemesis with previous work in this experiment.

The results of Experiments I and II will be presented in Sect. 5.

5   Comparisons

To show the effectiveness of Nemesis, we compare it with a prior AGD detection approach in the process of Experiment I and II. In this section, we introduce the prior work at first, then presents the results of Experiment I and II.

5.1   Prior Work

As described in Sect. 2, Yadav *et al.* [3] use Kullback-Leibler (KL) Distance, Edit Distance (ED) and Jaccard Index (JI) to detect AGDs. Recently, Fu *et al.* [14] also apply these three forms of distance to detect real-life DGA families and achieve good results for five of them. This approach only requires the string-based information of domain names, which is similar to Nemesis, thus we compare it with Nemesis. The main idea of this approach is easy to understand. Given an unlabeled domain name d, the detection procedure can be divided into three steps: (1) Calculate the distance between d and a set of real domain names. (2) Calculate the distance between d and a set of AGDs. (3) Classify d as a real one or an AGD according to which distance is closer. Next, we will describe how to calculate these distances in detail.

Kullback-Leibler Distance. KL distance is a metric to measure the divergence between one probability distribution diverges and a reference probability distribution. In terms of a domain name, the probability distribution refers to the distribution of occurrence frequencies of all valid characters. For simplification, suppose that the list of valid characters in domain names is [a, b, c, d, e, f], then the probability distribution of domain name "*faddec*" is [1/6, 0, 1/6, 1/3, 1/6, 1/6]. For discrete probability distributions P and Q defined on the same probability space, the KL distance between them can be calculated as follows:

$$D_{\mathrm{KL}}(P\|Q) = \sum_i P_i \log \frac{P_i}{Q_i} \tag{4}$$

where i is the index of the value in a discrete random variable. It is evident that KL distance between P and Q is not symmetric, so we can define a symmetric KL distance for uniformity:

$$D_{\mathrm{KL_{sym}}}(PQ) = \frac{1}{2}(D_{\mathrm{KL}}(P\|Q) + D_{\mathrm{KL}}(Q\|P)) \tag{5}$$

Edit Distance. The Edit Distance [15] between two strings A and B are defined as the minimum times of edit operations required to convert A to B. Only three edit operations are allowed: insertion, deletion, and substitution of single characters. ED is symmetric and can be easily calculated by dynamic programming methods.

Jaccard Index. JI [16] is a metric to measure the similarity between two finite sets A and B. It is defined as:

$$JI(A, B) = \frac{|A \cap B|}{|A \cup B|} \tag{6}$$

In our experiments, we can refer the sets of characters in two domain names as set A and B respectively. Note that JI measures similarity while KL and ED measures dissimilarity, we can define JI Distance for uniformity:

$$d_{JI}(A, B) = 1 - JI(A, B) = 1 - \frac{|A \cap B|}{|A \cup B|}. \tag{7}$$

After figuring out the meaning of each metric, we now focus on how to detect AGDs with them. Given a test domain name d_t, we can use one of the three statistical distances to determine whether it is an AGD by following steps:

(1) Calculate $d(L)$ and $d(M)$ which denote respectively the average distance from d_t to each domain names in the *legitimate dataset* and the average distance from d_t to each domain names in the *malicious dataset*.
(2) Calculate Δd which denotes the difference between $d(L)$ and $d(M)$, namely $\Delta d = d(L) - d(M)$. The greater Δd, the more likely d_t is legitimate than malicious.
(3) Select a proper threshold t_{opt} for Δd and build a classifier. If Δd is greater than or equal to t_{opt}, the classifier will judge d_t as real. Otherwise, d_t is judged as an AGD.

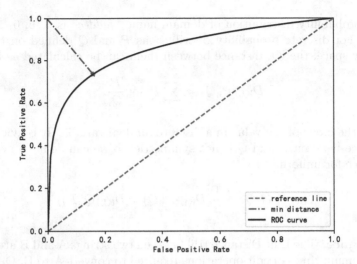

Fig. 3. An ROC curve demo

Then we leverage the Receiver Operating Characteristic (ROC) curve [17] to select the optimal threshold t_{opt} as follows: (1) Sample nine-tenth of the training dataset in Experiment I to train the classifier and use the rest one-tenth as the test dataset. (2) Select different t to calculate true positive rates (TPRs) and false positive rates (FPRs). (3) Draw the ROC curve based on the series of TPRs and FPRs, as shown in Fig. 3. (4) Find the closet point A on the ROC curve to the point $(0,1)$, and the corresponding threshold is the optimal threshold t_{opt}.

5.2 Experimental Results

Experiment I. This experiment compares the ability of several approaches to accurately detect domain names generated by known DGA families. Figure 4 shows the results comparison among Nemesis and previous approaches based on KL, ED and JI. As illustrated in Fig. 4, Nemesis reaches the highest values of precision (98.6%), recall (96.7%) and the F1-Scores (97.6%), while those of the other approaches range from 72% to 83%. Obviously, the experiment result suggests that Nemesis has a considerable advantage in terms of detecting AGDs generated by known DGAs over approaches based on KL, ED and JI.

Experiment II. This experiment compares the ability of several approaches to discover new DGA families. Table 1 displays the recall values of Nemesis and approaches based on KL, ED and JI. In terms of certain DGAs, previous approaches are even inferior to an untrained binary classifier since they get recall values lower than 50%, though they may achieve better results than Nemesis on

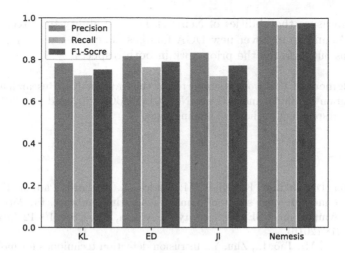

Fig. 4. Results of Experiment I

Table 1. Recall of four detection approaches on 10 DGA families in Experiment II

DGA name	Nemesis	KL	ED	JI
Conficker	0.833	0.879	0.402	0.902
Banjori	0.945	0.876	0.922	0.884
Corebot	0.975	0.572	0.743	0.473
Cryptolocker	0.903	0.821	0.835	0.794
Dircrypt	0.968	0.901	0.873	0.893
Kraken_v1	0.994	0.912	0.822	0.904
Locky_v2	0.983	0.886	0.929	0.813
Pykspa	0.985	0.473	0.895	0.402
Qakbot	0.942	0.899	0.793	0.845
Simda	0.834	0.858	0.729	0.784

other DGAs. In contrast, recall values of Nemesis are all greater than 83%, which means Nemesis has better stability in discovering different DGA families. In a word, Nemesis is stable and effective to discover unknown DGAs.

6   Conclusion

This paper represents a new AGD detection approach, Nemesis, which is implemented based on an LSTM language model. It takes unlabeled domain names as inputs, and outputs whether the domain names are AGDs or not. Nemesis employs theories and techniques in natural language processing and deep learning. It can learn from labeled domain names automatically and does not require any other additional information. We conduct two experiments on ten DGA families to measure the abilities of Nemesis, i.e., the ability to detect AGDs of known DGAs and to discover new DGA families. The experiment results show that Nemesis outperforms the prior work in both respects.

Acknowledgments. This work is supported by the National Key Research and Development Program of China under Grant No. 2018YFB0804702 and No. 2018YFB080 4704. The corresponding author is Tianning Zang.

References

1. Plohmann, D., Yakdan, K., Klatt, M., Bader, J., Gerhards-Padilla, E.: A comprehensive measurement study of domain generating malware. In: 25th USENIX Security Symposium, USENIX Security 16, Austin, TX, USA, 10–12 August 2016, pp. 263–278 (2016)
2. Gai, K., Qiu, M., Tao, L., Zhu, Y.: Intrusion detection techniques for mobile cloud computing in heterogeneous 5G. Secur. Commun. Netw. **9**(16), 3049–3058 (2016)
3. Yadav, S., Reddy, A.K.K., Reddy, A.L.N., Ranjan, S.: Detecting algorithmically generated domain-flux attacks with DNS traffic analysis. IEEE/ACM Trans. Netw. **20**(5), 1663–1677 (2012)
4. Antonakakis, M., et al.: From throw-away traffic to bots: detecting the rise of DGA-based malware. In: Proceedings of the 21th USENIX Security Symposium, Bellevue, WA, USA, 8–10 August 2012, pp. 491–506 (2012)
5. Schiavoni, S., Maggi, F., Cavallaro, L., Zanero, S.: Phoenix: DGA-based botnet tracking and intelligence. In: Detection of Intrusions and Malware, and Vulnerability Assessment - 11th International Conference, DIMVA 2014, Egham, UK, 10–11 July 2014, Proceedings, pp. 192–211 (2014)
6. Sharifnya, R., Abadi, M.: Dfbotkiller: domain-flux botnet detection based on the history of group activities and failures in DNS traffic. Digit. Invest. **12**(12), 15–26 (2015)
7. Woodbridge, J., Anderson, H.S., Ahuja, A., Grant, D.: Predicting domain generation algorithms with long short-term memory networks. CoRR, vol. abs/1611.00791 (2016)
8. Huang, J., Wang, P., Zang, T., Qiang, Q., Wang, Y., Yu, M.: Detecting domain generation algorithms with convolutional neural language models. In: TrustCom/BigDataSE, pp. 1360–1367 (2018)
9. Yu, B., Pan, J., Hu, J., Nascimento, A.C.A., Cock, M.D.: Character level based detection of DGA domain names. In: 2018 International Joint Conference on Neural Networks, IJCNN 2018, Rio de Janeiro, Brazil, 8–13 July 2018, pp. 1–8 (2018)
10. Sood, A.K., Zeadally, S.: A taxonomy of domain-generation algorithms. IEEE Secur. Priv. **14**(4), 46–53 (2016)
11. Root zone database. https://www.iana.org/domains/root/db
12. Bengio, Y., Boulanger-Lewandowski, N., Pascanu, R.: Advances in optimizing recurrent networks. In: IEEE International Conference on Acoustics, Speech and Signal Processing, ICASSP 2013, Vancouver, BC, Canada, 26–31 May 2013, pp. 8624–8628 (2013)
13. Gers, F.A., Schmidhuber, J., Cummins, F.A.: Learning to forget: continual prediction with LSTM. Neural Comput. **12**(10), 2451–2471 (2000)
14. Fu, Y., et al.: Stealthy domain generation algorithms. IEEE Trans. Inf. Forensics Secur. **12**(6), 1430–1443 (2017)

15. Levenshtein, V.I.: Binary codes capable of correcting deletions, insertions, and reversals. Sov. Phys. Dokl. **10**(8), 707–710 (1966)
16. Small, H.: Co-citation in the scientific literature: a new measure of the relationship between two documents. J. Am. Soc. Inf. Sci. **24**(4), 265–269 (1973)
17. Fawcett, T.: An introduction to ROC analysis. Pattern Recogn. Lett. **27**(8), 861–874 (2006)

Positive-Unlabeled Learning for Sentiment Analysis with Adversarial Training

Yueshen Xu[1,2]($\boxtimes$), Lei Li[1], Jianbin Huang[1], Yuyu Yin[3], Wei Shao[4], Zhida Mai[5], and Lei Hei[6]

[1] School of Computer Science and Technology, Xidian University,
Xi'an 710071, China
{ysxu,jbhuang}@xidian.edu.cn, lli_3@stu.xidian.edu.cn
[2] Provincial Key Laboratory for Computer Information Processing Technology,
Soochow University, Suzhou 215006, Jiangsu, China
[3] School of Computer, Hangzhou Dianzi University, Hangzhou 310018, China
yyy718@gmail.com
[4] School of Science, RMIT University, Melbourne, VIC 3001, Australia
wei.shao@rmit.edu.au
[5] Xanten Guangdong Development Co., Ltd., Foshan 528200, China
top.mark@e-live.cn
[6] Center of Journal Publication, Xidian University, Xi'an 710071, Shaanxi, China
heilei@xidian.edu.cn

Abstract. Sentiment classification is a critical task in sentiment analysis and other text mining applications. As a sub-problem of sentiment classification, positive and unlabeled learning or positive-unlabeled learning (PU learning) problem widely exists in real-world cases, but it has not been given enough attention. In this paper, we aim to solve PU learning problem under the framework of adversarial training and neural network. We propose a novel model for PU learning problem, which is based on adversarial training and attention-based long short-term memory (LSTM) network. In our model, we design a new adversarial training technique. We conducted extensive experiments on two real-world datasets. The experimental results demonstrate that our proposed model outperforms the compared methods, including the well-known traditional methods and state-of-the-art methods. We also report the training time, and discuss the sensitivity of our model to parameters.

Keywords: Sentiment analysis · PU learning problem ·
Adversarial training · LSTM · Attention mechanism

1 Introduction

Sentiment analysis is one of key tasks in natural language processing (NLP) and has received a lot of attention in recent years [21,26]. As a basic problem of

© ICST Institute for Computer Sciences, Social Informatics and Telecommunications Engineering 2019
Published by Springer Nature Switzerland AG 2019. All Rights Reserved
X. Wang et al. (Eds.): CollaborateCom 2019, LNICST 292, pp. 364–379, 2019.
https://doi.org/10.1007/978-3-030-30146-0_25

sentiment analysis, *sentiment classification* aims to classify reviews or comments into different sentimental polarities [16]. Along with the rapid development of e-commerce sites and social networking sites, the volumes of reviews and comments increase dramatically, and those online sites are in need of analyzing the polarities from large volumes of reviews and comments with high accuracy [5, 6].

Many works have tried to address sentiment classification using various techniques, including K-Nearest Neighbor (KNN), Support Vector Machine (SVM), Naïve Bayes, neural networks and some other methods [3, 29]. Meanwhile, as an effective technique for improving the robustness of machine learning methods, *adversarial training* has been also studied in tasks of text mining and natural language processing. In this paper, we exploit adversarial training in sentiment analysis, and there are few works exploiting adversarial training in sentiment analysis. For adversarial training, we have the following observations.

1. Traditional classifiers are likely to suffer from overfitting problem [8]. That is, a classifier overwhelmingly fits a certain words distribution in training reviews set and is trained to obtain a collection of parameters, but fails to fit the words distribution in test reviews set or new reviews set.
2. Adversarial examples are inputs formed by adding small perturbations with the intent of causing classifiers (e.g., neural networks) to misclassify [23], and can attack the generalization and fitness of classifiers. It can be inferred that a new classifier that is capable of resisting the attack of adversarial examples can achieve promising performance.

In this paper, we aim to solve the positive and unlabeled learning (PU learning) problem. In PU learning problem, there only exist positive labeled and unlabeled reviews, without any negative labeled reviews. PU learning problem indeed exists in real-world cases, and takes an important role in sentiment analysis [17]. PU learning problem was studied by previous works [13, 25]. In real-world cases, e-commerce sites and social networking sites can indeed confront PU learning problem. In this paper, we aim to solve PU learning problem based on adversarial training and neural network. Note that, there are several obstacles to exploit adversarial training in PU learning problem, including

1. Adversarial training requires that all training data have been labeled, but there are no negative labeled reviews in PU learning problem.
2. The evaluation metric for PU learning problem is usually F1-score, precision or recall, which cannot be modeled in the current loss function of adversarial training, which increases the difficulty in optimization during training process.

In this paper, we aim to solve PU learning problem comprehensively under the framework of adversarial training and neural network. In the proposed solution, we first identify negative reviews from unlabeled reviews. Then, we build an attention-based LSTM (Long Short-Term Memory) network, enhanced with an improved adversarial training method. We evaluate our models in two real-world datasets. The experimental results demonstrate that our models achieve the best performance, compared to a series of existing methods.

In summary, the contributions of this paper are as follows.

1. We propose a comprehensive solution to solve PU learning problem. The proposed solution is based on adversarial training and attentive LSTM network.
2. In PU learning problem, the procedure that distinguishes negative labels from unlabeled texts, is likely to introduce noise into training review texts, which can further hurt the classification performance. To tackle this issue, we propose an enhanced adversarial training method, adding a new perturbation to the word embeddings in LSTM network.
3. We conduct comparison experiments in two real-world datasets, and the experimental results demonstrate that our models can achieve better performance than compared methods. We also conduct sensitivity experiment to give instructions for selecting optimal parameter.

The rest of this paper is organized as follows. Section 2 discusses the related work. Section 3 elaborates the detail of our proposed model. Section 4 presents the experimental results and gives further analysis. Section 5 reports the sensitivity experimental result. Section 6 concludes the whole paper.

2   Related Work

There have been many works studying sentiment classification, which employ a variety of methods, including machine learning methods (e.g., KNN, SVM and Naïve Bayes) and neural network methods [15]. PU learning (positive and unlabeled learning) problem is a sub-problem of sentiment classification, where there are no negative labels in corpus, but only positive and unlabeled reviews. PU learning problem also exists in real-world e-commerce sites and social networking sites. As for adversarial training, it has been verified to be effective to improve the robustness of models in many applications.

PU learning problem was first studied in [17]. In PU learning problem, there is a preliminary task to construct a classifier to identify negative labeled reviews from positive and unlabeled review texts. [14] proposed a whole framework and identified negative labeled reviews using Rocchio technique. [4] studied the design of the loss function in PU learning problem. The authors established the generalization error bounds for loss function in PU learning problem. [25] and [13] focused on a specific but valuable problem, that was, to detect deceptive reviews from positive and unlabeled reviews. In this paper, we aim to solve PU learning problem based on adversarial training and attentive neural network. The procedure of identifying negative labeled reviews is highly likely to bring erroneous labels, and we design a new adversarial training method to attack these erroneous labels, further improving the classification performance.

Adversarial training aims to improve the robustness of machine learning models by exposing a model to adversarial examples during training process. Adversarial training was first introduced in the problem of image classification, where the input image pixels were continuous values [8], and researchers studied adversarial training technique from many aspects [7,12]. [23] proposed a new algorithm of crafting adversarial examples. [20] adapted adversarial training to solve text classification in a semi-supervised setting. [27] employed adversarial training in relation extraction problem and proposed an improved neural network architecture. As a prevailing tool in many artificial intelligence tasks, the generative adversarial net (GAN) proposed by [7] also borrows ideas from adversarial training. In this paper, we exploit the potential of adversarial training in improving the performance of PU learning problem.

3   Adversarial Training for Sentiment Classification

In this section, we first state the base models employed in our methods, and then elaborate the proposed model for PU learning problem.

3.1   The Base Models

LSTM Network. Recurrent neural network (RNN) takes sequential data as input, and finishes the computation via recursive cells. Standard RNN has several problems in training process, such as gradient vanishing and gradient exploding. To address these issues, LSTM network is developed and achieves superior performance [9]. Formally, each cell in LSTM is computed as follows.

$$X = \begin{bmatrix} h_{t-1} \\ x_t \end{bmatrix} \tag{1}$$

$$f_t = \sigma(W_f \cdot X + b_f) \tag{2}$$

$$i_t = \sigma(W_i \cdot X + b_i) \tag{3}$$

$$c_t = f_t \odot c_{t-1} + i_t \odot tanh(W_c \cdot X + b_c) \tag{4}$$

$$o_t = \sigma(W_o \cdot X + b_o) \tag{5}$$

$$h_t = o_t \odot tanh(c_t) \tag{6}$$

At time step t, the previous hidden output h_{t-1} and the current input x_t together form the input X (see Eq. 1). There are three gates in an LSTM cell, which are forget gate, input gate and output gate. Forget gate outputs a value in $[0,1]$, to indicate the amount of information from previous cell that need to be dumped in Eq. 2. Input gate first decides those values that LSTM will update by i_t in Eq. 3, and further computes a candidate cell state c_t using Eq. 4. Finally, the output gate decides which part of the candidate cell states will be outputted, and the cell output h_t is computed by Eq. 6.

Let T be a piece of review represented by a sequence of m words, as $T = \{w_t|t = 1, \ldots, m\}$, and T is tagged with a label as y. Each word w_t is embedded into a k-dimensional word vector $v_t = \mathbf{W} \times w_t$, where $\mathbf{W} \in \mathbb{R}^{k \times |V|}$ is a word embedding matrix to be learned, and V denotes the vocabulary. Figure 1 shows the basic LSTM model for classification task in NLP. w_{eos} denotes the end mark of a review, and v_{eos} is the word embedding result of w_{eos}.

Attention Mechanism. In recent years, attention mechanism has become a compelling technique in sequence models, which can improve the capability of

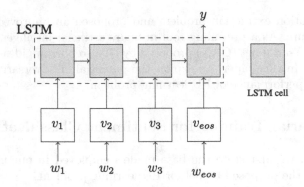

Fig. 1. The basic LSTM model for classification task in NLP

models in handling long-range dependencies [2]. In NLP tasks, attention mechanism gives the model a chance to capture the important part of the input that needs more attention. Guided by a weight vector learned from the input text and the result that is produced so far, attention-based model captures more information based on a more comprehensive modeling of the input. In detail, we learn an attention vector α as follows.

$$u_i = tanh(W_s h_i + b_s), \tag{7}$$

$$\alpha_i = \frac{\exp(u_i^T u_s)}{\sum_i \exp(u_i^T u_s)}, \tag{8}$$

$$\omega = \sum_i \alpha_i h_i \tag{9}$$

where α_i denotes each element in α. The final output of an attentive LSTM is ω (see Eq. 9), which can be treated as a weighted sum over all outputs of all cells in LSTM. With the output ω of the attentive LSTM network, a fully connected layer and a softmax non-linear layer are used to map ω to the probability distribution over each class, and further to obtain the label y.

3.2   The Proposed Model for PU Learning Problem

Compared to traditional sentiment classification, in PU learning problem, there is one extra step before conducting classification. The step is to distinguish the reviews or comments with negative labels from the positive and unlabeled review texts. We adopt a two-step strategy to finish this task, following the suggestions in [17]. In detail, we use the Rocchio technique [19] to generate positive and potential negative review texts from unlabeled review texts. In Rocchio technique, each document is represented by a vector, and each element in the vector is the value that is computed with tf-idf (term frequency-inverse document frequency).

Let D denote the whole set of training texts, and let C_j denote the set of training reviews in class c_j. In this paper, we have two classes, that is, j being

1 represents the positive review and j being -1 represents the negative review. To build a Rocchio classifier, a representative vector c_j of C_j is constructed for each class c_j first, which is as follows.

$$c_j = \eta \frac{1}{|C_j|} \sum_{d \in C_j} \frac{d}{\|d\|} - \rho \frac{1}{|D - C_j|} \sum_{d \in D - C_j} \frac{d}{\|d\|} \qquad (10)$$

where η and ρ are parameters that control the weights of similar and dissimilar training examples. d denotes a piece of review, and $\|d\|$ denotes the norm of review d (i.e., the number of words in d). Then for each test review td, the similarity of td with each representative vector is measured by cosine similarity. Finally, td is assigned to the class, the representative vector of which is the most similar to td. We use P to denote the positive set and U to denote the unlabeled set. The overall procedure of Rocchio technique is stated as follows.

1. Assign each review in P to class label 1;
2. Assign each review in U to class label -1;
3. Build a Rocchio classifier using P and U;
4. Use the classifier to classify U. Those reviews in U that are classified to be negative will form the negative reviews set.

Although the dataset is fully formed, the potential unreliability of the identified negative labeled texts increases the noise that is likely to harm the performance of neural networks. More specifically, the noise refers to the positive reviews which are labeled to be negative by the Rocchio classifier. To tackle those noise data in PU learning problem, we add a new random perturbation r to word embedding results E, due to the following two reasons.

1. The first is that adding a new random perturbation can help the gradient computation escape from the non-smooth surrounding area of each word embedding [12].
2. The second is that a random perturbation on word embeddings input can take the role of regularization to defend the potential overfitting.

The added random perturbation in current word embedding results E generates new perturbed word embedding results E', which are as follows.

$$r = \beta \times sign(\mathcal{N}(\mathbf{0}^k, \mathbf{I}^k)) \qquad (11)$$

$$E' = E + r \qquad (12)$$

$$e_{adv} = \epsilon \frac{g}{\|g\|}, \quad \text{where } g = \nabla_{E'} L(E'; \hat{\Theta}) \qquad (13)$$

We choose Gaussian distribution to generate the random adversarial perturbation (Eq. 11). $\mathcal{N}(\mathbf{0}^k, \mathbf{I}^k)$ is the Gaussian distribution, where $\mathbf{0}^k$ is the mean vector and $\mathbf{I}^k$ is the covariance matrix (k is the dimension of word embedding). β controls the extent of trusting Gaussian distribution to generate the adversarial perturbation. $sign(\cdot)$ is the multi-dimensional indicator function, and the input of $sign(\cdot)$ is a k dimensional vector. The loss function for PU learning problem is constructed as follows.

$$L_{cls} = L(E'; \Theta) \tag{14}$$

$$L_{adv} = L(E' + e_{adv}; \Theta) \tag{15}$$

$$\hat{L}(\Theta) = \alpha L_{cls} + (1 - \alpha)L_{adv} \tag{16}$$

where e_{adv} and Θ are two parameters in adversarial training. α is a parameter to control the ratio of classification loss and adversarial loss. We name the proposed model as *PU learning problem with Adversarial Training* (PUAT for short). Figure 2 demonstrates the model of PUAT, where $r^{(i)}$ $(i = 1, 2, \ldots)$ denotes the element in r and $e^{(i)}$ $(i = 1, 2, \ldots)$ denotes the element in e_{adv}. h_i $(i = 1, 2, \ldots)$ is the hidden output of each LSTM cell.

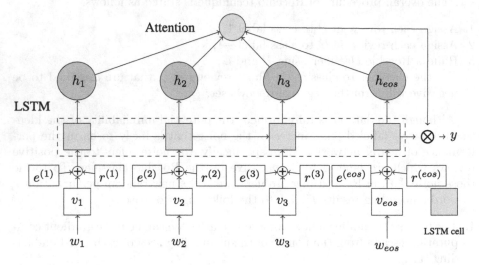

Fig. 2. The PUAT model with perturbed and random word embeddings and attentive LSTM

4 Experiment and Evaluation

4.1 Experimental Setting

Datasets. We evaluated our methods on two real-world datasets, i.e. IMDB dataset and Elec dataset. The IMDB dataset contains movie reviews and has been widely used in evaluation of sentiment classification [18]. The Elec dataset contains electronic product reviews collected from Amazon and has been also widely used in sentiment classification tasks [10]. The statistics of the two datasets are shown in Table 1.

In Table 1, *#label* denotes the number of classes, and there are two sentiment classes in both datasets, including positive class and negative class. *#training*

Table 1. Statistics of IMDB dataset and Elec dataset

Dataset	#label	#training	#test	Avg.	Max
IMDB dataset	2	25000	25000	239	2506
Elec dataset	2	25000	25000	107	4983

and #test represent the number of reviews in the training set and test set. *Avg.* is the average length of reviews in each dataset, and *Max* denotes the maximum length of the reviews. We randomly selected 90% reviews from training reviews set to form the training set and the remained 10% reviews form the validation set.

Implementation. We implemented our codes in TensorFlow [1]. We compare our models to the following models that can be used to solve the classification problem on review texts, including

1. SVM and Naïve Bayes. SVM and Naïve Bayes are two classic classification methods that are also commonly used in text mining and natural language processing applications. [22] showed that the two methods can be used in sentiment classification problem.
2. LSTM (Long-Short Term Memory) and GRU (Gated Recurrent Unit). LSTM and GRU are two popular variants of RNN, and have been also applied on sentiment classification tasks. We built an LSTM network with the hidden size being 128. The parameters and configuration of GRU network are the same as those in LSTM.
3. Attention-based LSTM or attentive LSTM. This model is proposed in [28], as a hierarchical attention-based LSTM network, and achieves good performance on a series of text classification tasks.
4. Adversarial LSTM. This model is proposed in [20], which adapts adversarial training in basic LSTM network and achieves the state-of-the-art performance on semi-supervised classification problem.

Regarding the preprocessing, the words whose document frequencies are less than 2 are removed from the reviews in both datasets. The reason is that, those words that less frequently appear will enlarge the whole vocabulary size, and further obviously increase training time. In our proposed model PUAT, the LSTM network is configured with 128 hidden units.

Parameter Setting. The parameters are set based on the evaluation results on the validation set. The word embeddings are initialized by GloVe [24], and the dimension of word embedding vector k is 200. The parameter α in Eq. 16 is set to 0.5. The parameter ϵ in Eq. 13 is set to 1.0.

For the optimization of model parameters, we used Adam optimizer [11]. Based on the results on validation set, we set the learning rate to 0.001, batch size to 256 and dropout rate to 0.8. The parameters of the compared methods are set according to the default settings in referred papers.

4.2   The Generation of Training Sets in PU Learning Problem

Similar to [17], we take the following steps to generate PU learning problem dataset from the training set. We randomly select p percent of positive reviews as the positive set P, and the remaining positive reviews and negative reviews are disassociated with their labels, and are used to form the unlabeled set U. The task is to classify negative reviews from unlabeled set U. We change the value of p in the range from 20% to 40% to provide a comprehensive evaluation.

As stated in Sect. 3.2, we used $tf\text{-}idf$ to compute the weight of each word and further to form feature vectors. We then built a Rocchio classifier on the positive set P and unlabeled set U. The reviews in set U that are classified to

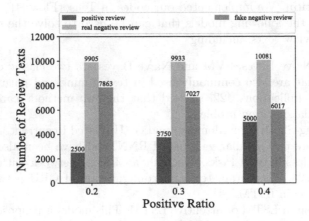

Fig. 3. The number of review texts of the three different review types in IMDB dataset. The bars from left to right represent the positive review, real negative review and fake negative review respectively.

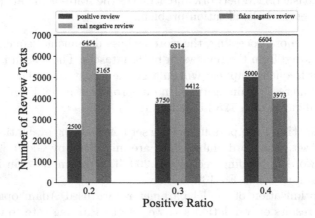

Fig. 4. The number of review texts of the three different review types in Elec dataset. The bars from left to right represent the positive review, real negative review and fake negative review respectively.

be negative form the negative set N. Figure 3 (IMDB dataset) and Fig. 4 (Elec dataset) show the details of negative reviews generated by Rocchio classifier with different positive ratios (0.2, 0.3 and 0.4). It can be seen that the whole training set is divided into positive set and negative set. The negative set consists of two parts, including real negative review texts and fake negative review texts. The fake negative review texts are the original positive reviews but misclassified as negative reviews by Rocchio classifier. Also, it can be found that along with the positive ratio increasing (0.2 to 0.4), the proportion of fake negative review texts decreases.

4.3   Experimental Results in PU Learning Problem

We conduct the experiments under three cases of positive ratios (0.2, 0.3 and 0.4), which correspond to the positive ratio settings in Sect. 4.2. We will report the test performance of each method. The evaluation metrics include F1-score, recall and test accuracy. F1-score is a widely used metric in classification problem and tends to give an integrated evaluation, as F1-score combines recall and precision. The reported F1-score is computed on positive class, as in PU learning problem, there are only positive labeled reviews. F1-score is computed as

$$F1 = \frac{2 * Precision * Recall}{Precision + Recall} \tag{17}$$

To give a comprehensive evaluation, we also report the results of recall and test accuracy. Furthermore, we will discuss the relationship between the positive ratio and test performance. In the generation of training sets, we have generated positive labeled sets P and negative labeled sets N under different cases of positive ratios (0.2, 0.3 and 0.4). Different positive ratios decide different proportions of positive reviews and negative reviews in final training set.

Table 2. Test performance in IMDB dataset and Elec dataset in PU learning problem with positive ratio being 0.2.

Method	IMDB dataset			Elec dataset		
	F1-score	Recall	Test accuracy	F1-score	Recall	Test accuracy
Naïve Bayes	0.159	0.086	0.509	0.608	0.480	0.595
SVM	0.341	0.207	0.599	0.777	0.706	0.797
GRU	0.526	0.368	0.655	0.760	0.673	0.783
LSTM	0.512	0.354	0.647	0.772	0.706	0.779
Attentive LSTM	0.609	0.458	0.695	0.775	0.721	0.786
Adversarial LSTM	0.530	0.370	0.665	0.799	0.739	0.808
PUAT	**0.650**	**0.502**	**0.723**	**0.804**	**0.772**	**0.814**

Table 3. Test performance in IMDB dataset and Elec dataset in PU learning problem with positive ratio being 0.3.

Method	IMDB dataset			Elec dataset		
	F1-score	Recall	Test accuracy	F1-score	Recall	Test accuracy
Naïve Bayes	0.280	0.164	0.527	0.704	0.626	0.670
SVM	0.509	0.347	0.666	0.824	0.807	0.824
GRU	0.676	0.531	0.742	0.815	0.796	0.823
LSTM	0.683	0.539	0.747	0.820	0.805	0.825
Attentive LSTM	0.719	0.588	0.772	0.815	0.806	0.822
Adversarial LSTM	0.689	0.544	0.764	0.819	0.779	0.828
PUAT	**0.815**	**0.751**	**0.832**	**0.825**	**0.808**	**0.839**

Table 4. Test performance in IMDB dataset and Elec dataset in PU learning problem with positive ratio being 0.4.

Method	IMDB dataset			Elec dataset		
	F1-score	Recall	Test accuracy	F1-score	Recall	Test accuracy
Naïve Bayes	0.421	0.270	0.565	0.732	0.686	0.696
SVM	0.626	0.464	0.723	0.829	**0.831**	0.828
GRU	0.752	0.639	0.788	0.821	0.813	0.830
LSTM	0.774	0.675	0.792	0.825	0.803	0.832
Attentive LSTM	0.775	0.681	0.793	0.831	0.823	0.839
Adversarial LSTM	0.799	0.716	0.813	0.830	0.819	0.838
PUAT	**0.818**	**0.749**	**0.824**	**0.835**	**0.831**	**0.845**

Tables 2, 3 and 4 present F1-score, recall and test accuracy results of all methods in PU learning problem. It can be found that the proposed PUAT method achieves the highest F1-score, recall and test accuracy values in all three positive ratio settings (0.2, 0.3 and 0.4). Furthermore, we can have following observations.

1. First, in all three positive ratio settings, the proposed PUAT method achieves better F1-score and test accuracy results than the traditional classifiers, including SVM and Naïve Bayes. Take SVM as an example. In the case of positive ratio being 0.2, SVM achieves a 0.341 F1-score and a 0.599 test accuracy in IMDB dataset and a 0.777 F1-score and a 0.797 test accuracy in Elec dataset. In contrast, PUAT achieves a higher performance of a 0.650 F1-score and a 0.723 test accuracy in IMDB dataset and a 0.804 F1-score and a 0.814 test accuracy in Elec dataset, also in the case of positive ratio being 0.2.
2. PUAT also outperforms the state-of-the-art methods. For example, in the case of positive ratio being 0.3, adversarial LSTM achieves a 0.689 F1-score and a 0.764 test accuracy in IMDB dataset, and achieves a 0.819 F1-score

and a 0.828 test accuracy in Elec dataset. In contrast, the proposed PUAT achieves a superior performance of a 0.815 F1-score and a 0.832 test accuracy in IMDB dataset, along with a 0.825 F1-score and a 0.839 test accuracy in Elec dataset.

3. Compared to the performance achieved by LSTM and GRU, the F1-score results of SVM are competitive, especially in Elec dataset. That is, the F1-score results of SVM are close to those of LSTM and GRU or even better than those of LSTM and GRU.

   An important reason is in the existence of misclassified reviews (noise), i.e., the true positive review texts that are misclassified to be negative. The LSTM network is easy to suffer from overfitting on such kind of noise. As for SVM, the positive set P and negative set U have been generated by Rocchio classifier, and such data separation provides a preliminary preparation for SVM to find a strong margin to separate positive and negative classes. The noise also leads to bad performances of Naïve Bayes, and Naïve Bayes tends to predict all reviews in test set to be negative.

4. For the analysis of recall, let us start from the computation of recall, which is given by

$$recall = \frac{\text{TP}}{\text{TP} + \text{FN}} \tag{18}$$

   where TP (short for **true positive**) denotes the number of positive reviews that are correctly predicted as positive labeled reviews. FN (short for **false negative**) denotes the number of positive reviews that are misclassified to be negative reviews. In our model, adversarial training improves the ability of distinguishing true negative reviews from fake negative reviews, which decreases the number of fake negative reviews.

5. Besides, we can make some interesting observations on the positive ratio p. When p is equal to 1.0, PU learning problem turns to a case that all positive labeled reviews in training set are reserved. When p is near to 0, it indicates that there are few positive review texts, and it will be difficult to build an effective classifier purely using unlabeled review texts. From Tables 2, 3 and 4, it can be found that there is a positive correlation between the evaluation metrics and positive ratio p. The reason is that the increasing number of positive review texts can help the classifier learn more useful features.

4.4   Training Time Comparison

Training time is another concern when people deploy neural network models. In this section, we compare the training time of different models in IMDB dataset and Elec dataset. As neural network models are usually trained by iterations of epochs, we report the average training time of one epoch when positive ratio p is 0.4. All experiments were conducted on a machine equipped with a Xeon E5-2680 v4 CPU and a single NVIDIA Telsa M40 GPU. The compared results are present in Table 5.

Table 5. Training time comparison with positive ratio p being 0.4

Model	Average training time of one epoch	
	IMDB dataset	Elec dataset
Attentive LSTM	7.28 s	6.43 s
Adversarial LSTM	16.85 s	15.06 s
PUAT	19.38 s	17.05 s

From Table 5, it can be found that the models using adversarial training techniques (adversarial LSTM and PUAT) require more training time. The reason is that the models using adversarial training techniques require to compute the adversarial perturbations. As for our model, PUAT needs to compute the gradients also on E in Eq. 13.

Furthermore, it can be seen that the average training time of our models is slightly higher than that of adversarial LSTM model. Note that, our proposed models achieve better performances, which have been verified by the experimental results in previous sections. Take PUAT as an example. Compared to adversarial LSTM in IMDB dataset, PUAT achieves higher F1-score, recall and test accuracy (see Table 4), while PUAT only spends 2.53 s more in one epoch (19.38 s for PUAT and 16.85 s for adversarial LSTM). The results indicate that considering the superior performances, the training time of our proposed models is acceptable.

5   Impact of β

The parameter β controls the trust extent of the adversarial perturbation generated from Gaussian distribution (see Eq. 11 in Sect. 3.2). If β is equal to 0, the proposed PUAT model degenerates into the ordinary adversarial training method. If β is a large value, the random perturbations may exert too much impact on word embeddings, which probably further harms the result of word embedding. We study the sensitivity of PUAT model to β, and take the case that the positive ratio is equal to 0.3 as an example. The experimental results are shown in Fig. 5, where the horizontal axis is set as the logarithmic coordinate ranging from 10^{-3} to 10^1.

It can be found that the optimal value of β is achieved around the value of 10^0 (i.e., 1.0) in both datasets. The change trend of β in IMDB dataset is smoother than the change trend in Elec dataset. These observations mean that the value of β should be set not too large or too small. In our experiments, β is set to 1.0 in all experiments.

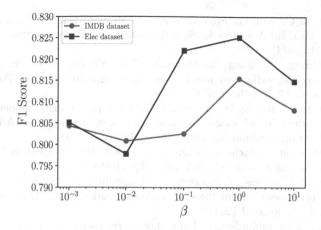

Fig. 5. F1-score varies with β when the positive ratio is equal to 0.3

6 Conclusion

In this paper, we give a comprehensive study of adversarial training in PU learning problem. The proposed model is built based on adversarial training and attentive LSTM network, and is named as PUAT (*PU learning with Adversarial Training*). To the best of our knowledge, this is the first paper that conducts fully study of adversarial training in PU learning problem.

In two datasets, the experimental results demonstrate that our proposed models achieve superior performance than the compared models. Such superiority verifies the effectiveness of the proposed way of using attention mechanism and adversarial training in our model. We gave a detailed discuss on experimental results. We also discussed the parameter sensitivity and reported the comparison results of training time.

Acknowledgements. This paper is granted by Fundamental Research Fund for Central Universities (No. JBX171007), National Natural Science Fund of China (No. 61702391), Natural Science Foundation of Shaanxi province and Zhejiang province (No. 2018JQ6050, No. LY12F02003). Meanwhile, the authors would like to thank Minhao Ni for her valuable suggestions in experiment design.

References

1. Abadi, M., Agarwal, A., Barham, P., Brevdo, E., Chen, Z., et al.: TensorFlow: large-scale machine learning on heterogeneous distributed systems (2015)
2. Bahdanau, D., Cho, K., Bengio, Y.: Neural machine translation by jointly learning to align and translate. In: Proceedings of the International Conference on Learning Representations (ICLR) (2015)
3. Dey, L., Chakraborty, S., Biswas, A., Bose, B., Tiwari, S.: Sentiment analysis of review datasets using naïve bayes and k-nn classifier. Int. J. Inf. Eng. Electron. Bus. **4**, 54–62 (2016)

4. Du Plessis, M.C., Niu, G., Sugiyama, M.: Analysis of learning from positive and unlabeled data. In: Advances in Neural Information Processing Systems (NIPS), pp. 703–711 (2014)

5. Gao, H., Huang, W., Yang, X., Duan, Y., Yin, Y.: Toward service selection for workflow reconfiguration: an interface-based computing solution. Future Gener. Comput. Syst. **87**, 298–311 (2018)

6. Gao, H., Mao, S., Huang, W., Yang, X.: Applying probabilistic model checking to financial production risk evaluation and control: a case study of Alibaba's Yu'e Bao. IEEE Trans. Comput. Soc. Syst. **5**(3), 785–795 (2018)

7. Goodfellow, I., et al.: Generative adversarial nets. In: Advances in Neural Information Processing Systems (NIPS), pp. 2672–2680 (2014)

8. Goodfellow, I.J., Shlens, J., Szegedy, C.: Explaining and harnessing adversarial examples. In: Proceedings of the International Conference on Learning Representations (ICLR), pp. 1–11 (2015)

9. Hochreiter, S., Schmidhuber, J.: Long short-term memory. Neural Comput. **9**(8), 1735–1780 (1997)

10. Johnson, R., Zhang, T.: Semi-supervised convolutional neural networks for text categorization via region embedding. In: Advances in Neural Information Processing Systems (NIPS), pp. 919–927 (2015)

11. Kingma, D.P., Ba, J.: Adam: a method for stochastic optimization. In: Proceedings of the International Conference on Learning Representations (ICLR) (2015)

12. Kurakin, A., Boneh, D., Tramèr, F., Goodfellow, I., Papernot, N., McDaniel, P.: Ensemble adversarial training: attacks and defenses. In: Proceedings of the International Conference on Learning Representations (ICLR) (2018)

13. Li, H., Liu, B., Mukherjee, A., Shao, J.: Spotting fake reviews using positive-unlabeled learning. Computacióny Sistemas **18**(3), 467–475 (2014)

14. Li, X.-L., Liu, B.: Learning from positive and unlabeled examples with different data distributions. In: Gama, J., Camacho, R., Brazdil, P.B., Jorge, A.M., Torgo, L. (eds.) ECML 2005. LNCS (LNAI), vol. 3720, pp. 218–229. Springer, Heidelberg (2005). https://doi.org/10.1007/11564096_24

15. Lin, J., Mao, W., Zeng, D.D.: Personality-based refinement for sentiment classification in microblog. Knowl.-Based Syst. **132**, 204–214 (2017)

16. Liu, B.: Sentiment Analysis: Mining Opinions, Sentiments, and Emotions. Cambridge University Press, Cambridge (2015)

17. Liu, B., Dai, Y., Li, X., Lee, W.S., Yu, P.S.: Building text classifiers using positive and unlabeled examples. In: Third IEEE International Conference on Data Mining (ICDM), pp. 179–186 (2003)

18. Maas, A.L., Daly, R.E., Pham, P.T., Huang, D., Ng, A.Y., Potts, C.: Learning word vectors for sentiment analysis. In: Proceedings of the 49th Annual Meeting of the Association for Computational Linguistics (ACL), pp. 142–150 (2011)

19. Manning, C.D., Raghavan, P., Schütze, H.: Introduction to Information Retrieval. Cambridge University Press, Cambridge (2009)

20. Miyato, T., Dai, A.M., Goodfellow, I.: Adversarial training methods for semi-supervised text classification. In: Proceedings of the International Conference on Learning Representations (ICLR) (2017)

21. Pang, B., Lee, L.: Opinion mining and sentiment analysis. Found. Trends Inf. Retrieval **2**(1–2), 1–135 (2007)

22. Pang, B., Lee, L., Vaithyanathan, S.: Thumbs up?: sentiment classification using machine learning techniques. In: Proceedings of the Conference on Empirical Methods in Natural Language Processing (EMNLP), pp. 79–86 (2002)

23. Papernot, N., McDaniel, P., Jha, S., Fredrikson, M., Celik, Z.B., Swami, A.: The limitations of deep learning in adversarial settings. In: IEEE European Symposium on Security and Privacy (EuroS&P), pp. 372–387 (2016)
24. Pennington, J., Socher, R., Manning, C.: GloVe: global vectors for word representation. In: Proceedings of the Conference on Empirical Methods in Natural Language Processing (EMNLP), pp. 1532–1543 (2014)
25. Ren, Y., Ji, D., Zhang, H.: Positive unlabeled learning for deceptive reviews detection. In: Proceedings of the Conference on Empirical Methods in Natural Language Processing (EMNLP), pp. 488–498 (2014)
26. Wang, Y., Huang, M., Zhao, L., Zhu, X.: Attention-based LSTM for aspect-level sentiment classification. In: Proceedings of International Conference on Empirical Methods in Natural Language Processing (EMNLP) (2016)
27. Wu, Y., Bamman, D., Russell, S.: Adversarial training for relation extraction. In: Proceedings of the Conference on Empirical Methods in Natural Language Processing (EMNLP), pp. 1778–1783 (2017)
28. Yang, Z., Yang, D., Dyer, C., He, X., Smola, A., Hovy, E.: Hierarchical attention networks for document classification. In: Proceedings of NAACL, pp. 1480–1489 (2016)
29. Yuan, Z., Wu, S., Wu, F., Liu, J., Huang, Y.: Domain attention model for multi-domain sentiment classification. Knowl.-Based Syst. **155**, 1–10 (2018)

CNASV: A Convolutional Neural Architecture Search-Train Prototype for Computer Vision Task

Tianbao Zhou$^{(\boxtimes)}$ (ID), Yu Weng (ID), and Guosheng Yang

College of Information Engineering, Minzu University of China, Beijing 100081, China
tianbaochou@163.com

Abstract. Neural Architecture Search (NAS) has become more and more prevalent in the field of deep learning in the past two years. Existing works often focus on image classification, and few works recently extend NAS to another computer vision task, such as semantic image segmentation. The semantic image segmentation is essentially a dense prediction for each pixel on whole image. Therefore, we choose the same basic primitive operations to build the search space for the two computer vision task respectively. Searching good neural network architectures and then training them from scratch is a regular procedure for NAS. In this paper, we design a prototype system that deploy search module and train module to collaborate with each other. Follow the former research, we initialize over-parameterized cells architecture and then transform to the continuous relaxation of the architecture to derive the good subnetwork by gradient descent. Our system can support any differential search algorithm, such as one-shot, DARTS or ProxylessNAS. We illustrate the effectiveness of our chosen primitive operations in the image classification and ability to transfer these operations to build search space for semantic image segmentation.

Keywords: CNASV · Image classification · Image segmentation

1 Introduction

How to automatically design a good neural network architecture for dataset on hand? We may fit the pre-trained network model to custom dataset which denoted transfer learning. However, a more nature way is to customize a network architecture to the dataset from different fields. Neural architecture search (NAS), a subfield of AutoML, has proposed to solve this problem. Image classification is the start point for NAS to show it's power on searching neural network architectures exceed human-designed architecture. NAS can be categorized three components: search space, search algorithm and the model evaluation [9]. The search space defines what architectures can be found during the search process. Incorporating prior knowledge about properties well-suited for task can reduce

© ICST Institute for Computer Sciences, Social Informatics and Telecommunications Engineering 2019
Published by Springer Nature Switzerland AG 2019. All Rights Reserved
X. Wang et al. (Eds.): CollaborateCom 2019, LNICST 292, pp. 380–393, 2019.
https://doi.org/10.1007/978-3-030-30146-0_26

the size of the search space and simplify the search. For example, in image classification, the search space including the selection of primitive operations at each search step and the prior backbone architecture used to define outer network.

The search strategy details how to explore the search space. The objective of NAS is typically to find architectures that have high evaluated performance on unseen data (e.g. split training datasets into training and validation, and search architecture on training but evaluated by validation) [9]. Recent works have introduced many effective search algorithm, including reinforcement learning (RL) [2,5,20,32,33], evolutionary algorithms [22,28–31], Bayesian optimization [14,15], and gradient based algorithms [11,21,27].

Reinforcement learning methods usually encode whole network architecture as RNN sequence or cell architecture and update RNN weights to derive next candidate architecture by Q-Learning or another update strategy. Besides the RL algorithm, evolutionary algorithms represented by the genetic algorithm (GA) describe the architecture as a gene string, and then perform crossover and mutation. Each string represents a network architecture, and by training and putting it on the validation set, those with good evaluation results are more likely to be retained. Bayesian optimization is a good method to optimize the parameters of the machine learning algorithm model. In recent years, some scholars have used it to speed up the evaluation of the performance of currently searched which improving the search progress. The previous methods are all based on the discrete search space. Recently, Liu et al. extend the works of Grathwohl et al. [11,27] by proposing a continuous relaxation of the search space to enable gradient-based optimization [21], denoted DARTS. The authors initialize an over-parameterized network, similar to densenet [13] but replace fix a single operation o_i (e.g. convolution) to calculated as a specific layer with mixing N operation from a set of operations $o_1, o_2, \cdots o_N$. More specifically, given a layer input x, the layer output y is computed $y = MixO(x) = \sum_{i=1}^{N} w_i o_i(x), w_i \geq 0$, where the w_i indicates how important does o_i contribute to the layer output. Cai et al. [6] propose ProxylessNAS which introduces a binary gate to reduce the N candidate path to two at each update.

Model evaluation is a vital step to tell the search algorithm whether current candidate architecture is good or not and decide whether to keep it at next update. The traditional way to evaluate a network performance is train from scratch, but cost too much time. Model performance prediction is a natural idea to speed up the process of searching network architecture. Klein et al. design a Bayesian Neural Network to predict the learning curve of the network searched and early terminated the worse network if the curve is bad [17]. Baker et al. use an additional hand-designed features on the basis of Klein et al. to predict the learning curve in the v-SVR (Sequential regression model) [3]. Liu et al. choose a LSTM network as the surrogate predictor. Each time the network predicts the performance of the model, it selects the k best performance network architectures and train them from scratch to get the real performance, and then updates the surrogate predictor parameters [19]. Peephole encodes the layer of the network architecture into vectors and put it into a LSTM surrogate function.

This function can predict performance based only on the previous network architecture, without additional training [8].

Since Zoph et al. proposed the RL-based NAS method obtained competitive performance on the CIFAR-10 and Penn Treebank benchmarks. Many researchers have focused on improving search methods to speed up the search process. As we mentioned before, lots of search algorithms have successfully reduce the search time from 800 GPUs for three to four weeks to 1 GPUs several days even one days. Weight-sharing is a major factor to accelerate the entire search procedure for these search algorithms. In DARTS, One-Shot and ProxylessNAS the mixed operation is actually a weight sharing trick, which avoids retraining the currently generated network architecture by sharing the sub-network architecture's weights in the search process.

Image classification lays a good foundation for the development of NAS. A logical next step is extending to another computer vision task, such as semantic image segmentation and object detection. A few work recently applied NAS to image segmentation. Chen et al. [7] first introduce NAS to solve image segmentation. The authors show that even with random search on constructing a recursive search space, the architecture search outperforms human-invented architectures and achieves better performance on many segmentation datasets. However, this work does not use one-shot searching, which focused on search a small Atrous Spatial Pyramid Pooling (ASPP) module called DPC (similar as decoder) and fix the pre-trained backbone (modified Xception) as encoder. Liu et al. [18] propose Auto-DeepLab: a general-purpose network level search space, and jointly search across two-level hierarchy (network level and cell level architecture). The authors indicate that search space includes various existing designs such as DeepLabv3, Conv-Deconv and Stacked Hourglass. However, the search space of Auto-DeepLab does not include U-Like architectures (eg. U-net), which are the most famous architectures in the field of medical image segmentation.

In this paper, we attempt to find a set of primitive operations for computer vision problems, such as image classification and image segmentation, and then we build two different search space for image classification and semantic image segmentation. After that, we design a prototype of search-train system using NAS for image classification and semantic image classification. Our system supports any type of differential architecture search algorithms to search on our search space. In summary, our contributions are as follows:

1. We build two different search space for image classification and semantic image segmentation.
2. We design a prototype of search-train system for automatically search good architecture on specific dataset and train that model.
3. We speed up the forward passing of cell-based architecture search on our system by parallel non-topology order nodes in our cell architecture.

2 The NAS Methods

2.1 Search Space

CNN Architecture Representation. A directed acyclic graph (DAG) is used to represent the network topology architecture, in which each node h_i represents input image or a feature map and each edge e_{ij} is associated with an operation (e.g. convolution operation, a pooling operation and a skip connection) between node h_i and node h_j. When the generation method of the DAG is unrestricted, its network architecture space will be very large, which will bring great challenges to the present search algorithms. Therefore, we use cell-based architecture [33]. When determining the best cell architecture, we can stack the cells into a deeper network on the backbone network (we will describe below). In other words, the architecture of cell is shared by entire network.

Primitive Operation Sets. How to choose suitable primitive operations? We have investigated the popular CNN architecture and the former NAS that has great success on image classification, and choose the primitive operations as Fig. 1 shown.

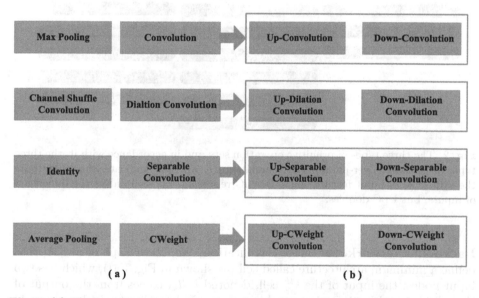

Fig. 1. (a) The basic primitive operations for image classification and image segmentation (b) the up and down operations derived from four basic primitive operations. CWeight operation indicates squeeze-and-excitation operation [12].

We can see from Fig. 1(b) that when the sliding step (stride value) greater than 1, the convolution operation can halve the dimension of feature map or double the dimension (we simply set stride as 2), the former denoted 'Down'-Convolution and the later called 'Up'-Convolution. This indicates that the down operation and up operation can be derived from the same base operation. In contrast, different from the primitive operations in image classification, the 'up'-version of some operations make no sense (e.g. the identity operation) and the 'up'-version of pooling operations (e.g. the average pooling and max pooling) do not exist. In our work, based on these primitive operations, we design three types of primitive operation set: Normal POs, Down POs and Up POs. In accordance with it, the three types of cell-based over-parameterized architecture are formed. As shown in the Fig. 2, the Normal POs and Down POs form NormalC and DownC, Up POs constitute UpC. All the operations is 3×3.

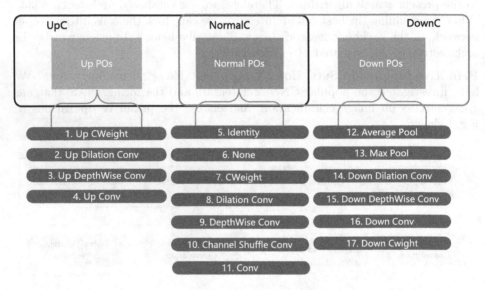

Fig. 2. The three types of primitive operation sets and in accordance with it, the three types of cell-based over-parameterized architecture. NormalC indicates the cell outputs the same size of input feature maps. DownC represents the cell halves the dimension of inputs, but UpC doubles.

Backbone Network. For image classification, We follow Zoph et al. [32] that define a minimum architecture called cell (as shown in Fig. 3(a)), which has two input nodes: the input of the kth cell, denoted $cell_k$, comes from the output of the cell $k-1$ and $k-2$. During searching, we stack the cells into shadow network, but when finish searching, we stack more cells into deep network. Inspired by the success of encoder-decoder network in semantic image segmentation, we use an encoder-decoder architecture as our backbone (Fig. 3(b)) for semantic image segmentation. Different from the image classification, the input of the kth cell either comes from the output of the cell $k-1$ (FCN-like networks) or $k-1$ and $k-2$ in the encoder parts, but the decoder parts are $L-k+1$, where $L = \#DownC + \#UpC$ is total number of cells (U-Like networks).

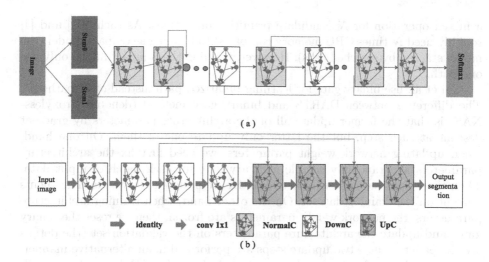

Fig. 3. (a) The backbone network used for image classification. The Stem0 and Stem1 is a Conv-ReLU-BN with stride 2 for reduce the image dimension (b) The backbone network used for semantic image segmentation.

2.2   Search Algorithm

In this section, we frist describe the way to construct an over-parameterized network [4,6,18,21]. After that we introduce two differential architecture search method into our work: DARTS and ProxylessNAS, and describe the smility and difference between them below.

Over-Parameterized Cell Architecture. Given a cell architecture $C(e_1, \cdots, e_E)$ where e_i represents a certain edge in the DAG. Let $O = o_i$ be a set of operations in the above with N candidate operations. Instead of setting each edge associates with definite operation, we set each edge to be a mixed operation that has N parallel paths (As shown in Fig. 4(a), the green arrows indicate the output of cell which simply the concatenation of the blocks' output tensors $\sum_{i=1}^{M} h_i$, where M is the number of intermediate Nodes), denoted as $MixO$. Therefore, the over-parameterized cell architecture can be expressed as $C(e_1 = MixO_1, \cdots, e_E = MixO_E)$. The output of a mixed operation $MixO$ is defined based on the output of its N paths:

$$MixO(x) = \sum_{(i=1)}^{N} w_i o_i(x). \tag{1}$$

As shown in Eq. 1, w_i represents the weight of o_i, in One-Shot [4] is constant value 1, but in DARTS [21] is calculated by applying softmax to N real-valued architecture parameters $\{\alpha_i\} : e^{\alpha_i} / \sum_j e^{\alpha_j}$. The initial value of α_i is $1/N$.

In the above, the ouput feature maps of all N paths is calculated when all operations are loaded into GPU memory. Because the output of each edge is a mixed operation for N candidate primitive operations. As such, [21] and [4] roughly need N times GPU memory compared to training a compact model (the model stacked by searched cells). However, training the compact model only use one path.

Cai et al. use binary gate for learning binarized path instead of N paths [6]. The difference between DARTS and binary gate method (denoted Proxyless-NAS) is that the former update all of the architecture parameters by gradient descent at each step, but the latter only update one of them. On one hand, when updating network weight parameters, we need first fix the architecture parameters and randomly sample a binary gate for each batch of input data. Then the weight parameters of active paths are updated via standard gradients descent on the training dataset. On the other hand, when training architecture parameters, the network weight parameters are frozen, then we reset the binary gates and update the architecture parameters on the validation set (the details see the paper). These two update steps are performed in an alternative manner. Once the training of architecture parameters is done, we need derive the our cell-based architecture by pruning redundant paths. In this work, we simply choose the path with the k ($k = 2$, for our works) highest path weight (Fig. 4(b)). In this way, the memory requirement is reduced to the same level of training a compact model. Since only considers two paths for updating at each update step, the trained-level of operation not on current two paths being much lower than the operation on (it is unfair to compare the contribution of a well-trained operation and another insufficiently trained operation to the output.). Therefore, we need more iterations for updating util all of the operations is well-trained and a extra time will cost at moving feature map not in GPU memory to GPU.

2.3 Parallel the Operations Calculation

As we mentioned before, a cell is a DAG consisting of an ordered sequence of M nodes. Therefore, the $Node_i$ always be produced before $Node_j$. However, the $Node_i$ and $Node_j$ may not exist data correlation ($Node_j$ can only be created after $Node_i$ has done). It means we can parallel output $Node_i$ and $Node_j$. For example, in Fig. 4(b), $Node_1$ and $Node_2$ has not data correlation, and we can produce $Node_1$ and $Node_2$ simultaneously. In our implementation, before training a network architecture searched, we first seperate each topology-path and parallel compute them between cells. On this way, we can accelerate the efficiency of our network.

3   A Prototype of Search-Train System

In this section, We design a search-training prototype for image classification and semantic image segmentation (which can also be used to other computer vision tasks, such as object detection). It is useful when user need find a good network architecture for new image dataset without any high-performance equipment at hand and it is easy to use. Combing with binary gate search algorithm [6]

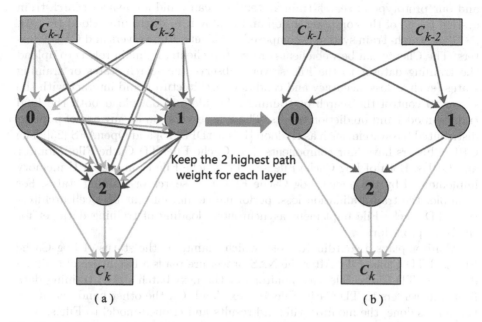

Fig. 4. (a) The over-parameterized architecture (b) Choose the path with the two highest path weight.

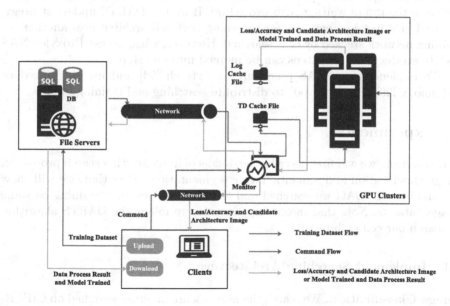

Fig. 5. A prototype of search-train system, notice that the Clients can be web clients or desktop clients (such as Qt clients).

and our prototype of search-train system, we can build a one-shot search-train system for all of the computer vision and deploy it in distributed cloud (Fig. 5).

The Search-Train system is composed of Clients, File Servers and GPU Clusters. The Clients can be web clients or desktop clients. Its main role is to upload the training dataset to the File servers, observe the search states or training states (such as loss, accuracy and candidate architecture), and interact with the server to control the search or training schedule and download both the final trained-model and prediction results. The File servers can be any one of popular distributed file system, such as Hadoop [1], FastDFS [25] and OpenAFS [23]. The GPU Clusters have four components: Log Cache File, TD Cache File, Monitor and GPUs. Both of Log Cache File and TD Cache File is on the CPU memory implemented by the queue. Log Cache File store search or training states. For example, the train/validation loss, performance and current best cell architecture. TD Cache File implement asynchronous loading of training data set for the NAS procedure.

Monitor plays a coordinator role, which maintains the status of Log Cache File and TD Cache File. After the NAS procedure reads a batch size of training data from TD Cache File, the monitor put the next batch size of training data from File servers to TD Cache File for next load. On the other hand, when the training is done, the monitor will send results and trained-model to File servers and notifies Clients to download. Similarly, the monitor gets the data from Log Cache File and send it to Clients. In addition, the Monitor also manages the status of NAS procedure, including new a NAS procedure to waiting queue, close the error or stopped NAS procedure to recycle the GPU resources and assign free GPUs to the top of waiting NAS procedure. If we use DARTS update strategy, we need clearly two steps, one for searching best cell architectures another for training network stacked by cells searched. However, when we use ProxylessNAS update strategy, the two steps can be merged into one step.

We implement our NAS procedure in Pytorch [24] and use ring-allreduce technology [26] (e.g. Horovod) to distribute searching and training models.

4   Experiments

In this section, we will first describe the details of implementing search process on image classification and semantic image segmentation. After that, we will show the architecture DAG we searched and the performance after training on some image datasets. Note that in our experiments, we follow the DARTS algorithm to search our cell architecture.

4.1   Implement Searching Architecture

Image Classification. We search the network architecture searched on CIFAR-10 dataset. We keep half of the training data as the validation set, and a small network obtained by stacking 6 cells is trained for 50 epochs with batch size 64, and we use the classification error rate on the validation set as the performance

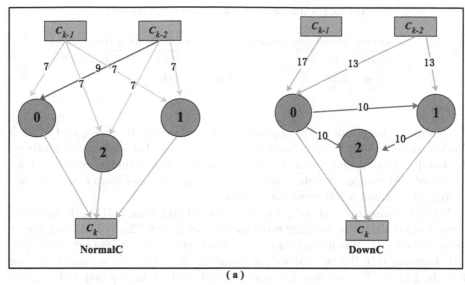

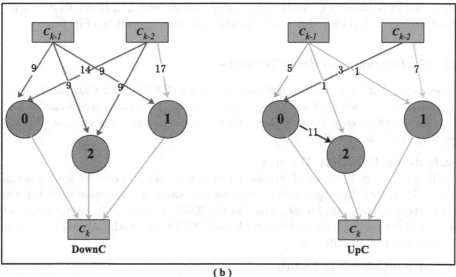

Fig. 6. (a) The Down Cell and Normal Cell architectures searched on CIFAR 10 for image classification (b) The Down Cell anb Up Cell architectures on PASCAL VOC2012 for semantic image segmentation. The operation represented by the specific Node numbering can be found in Fig. 2

of the cells we searched. Cells located at 1/3 and 2/3 of the total depth of the network are Down Cells.

Semantic Image Segmentation. We search our image segmentation network architecture on PASCAL VOC 2012 dataset [10]. Similiar to Image Classification,

Table 1. Comparison with Darts on CIFAR-10

Model	Model size (million)	Accuracy	Evaluation time
Darts	3.16	4.74	18 h
Ours	**2.12**	**4.96**	9 h

We randomly keep half of the training data as the validation set, and stack 3 DownC and UpC into U-like backbone. When we use DARTS search strategy, the batch size is 2 and the architecture search optimization is conducted for a total of 120 epochs. A batch size can be 8 when we use binary gate update strategy, but a much 200 epochs is needed.

When learning network weight w, we follow DARTS use SGD optimizer with momentum 0.95, cosine learning rate that decays from 0.025 to 0.01, and weight decay 0.0003 [21]. When learning the architecture, we use Adam optimizer [16] with learning rate 0.0003 and weight decay 0.0001. The cell architectures are show in Fig. 6. We can that the node 0 and node 1 in Normal Cell can be calculated in parallel (Fig. 6(a)). All of intermediate nodes in Down Cell or node 0 and node 1 in Up Cell also can be calculated simultaneously (Fig. 6(b)).

4.2 Performance on Some Datasets

We evaluate our two network architectures on CIFAR10 and Camvid dataset. The error rate is selected as the evaluation metric for image classification and Mean Intersection over Union (mIoU) for semantic image segmentation. We will describe the train details below.

Evaluate on CIFAR10 Dataset

We use a large network of 20 cells for training over 200 epochs with a batch size of 64. Other hyperparameters remain the same as the ones used for the architecture search, similar to Darts. As the Table 1 shown, our performance of our classification network is comparable to DARTS but with halves parameters size and much more efficient.

Evaluate on CamVid Dataset

From the Table 2, we can see that the origin U-net has a much bad performance in Camvid dataset but with larger parameters. Which reveals that the more network parameters may not improve network performance. Our network achieve a comparable performance with FC-DenseNet103 but a much less parameters and 3 time faster owing to our parallel computation technology. It is worth to noticing that the FC-DenseNets cost over 2 times GPU memory than U-Net and Ours network.

Table 2. Results on CamVid dataset.

Model	Model size (million)	mIoU	Evaluation time
U-Net	31.4	54.3	15 h
FC-Densenet56	1.5	58.9	2 day-12 h
FC-Densenet67	3.5	65.8	2 day-21 h
FC-Densenet103	9.4	**66.9**	3 day-10 h
Ours	**1.09**	66.1	18 h

5   Conclusion

In this paper, we select eight basic primitive operations for both image classification and image segmentation. Moreover, we create three types of primitive operation set base on them. We search our cell-based architectures on different backbone networks for image classification and image segmentation respectively. To implement our experiments, we design a prototype called CNASV for search good architectures and train them in a shot. Owing to our parallel calculation of operations cell architectures, our networks are more efficient than other comparison networks. In the future, we will integrated binary gate for allowing use more batch size to accelerate prune over-parameterized network and improve each module in our system.

References

1. Apache Hadoop. https://hadoop.apache.org/
2. Baker, B., Gupta, O., Naik, N., Raskar, R.: Designing neural network architectures using reinforcement learning. In: International Conference on Learning Representations (ICLR), pp. 1–18 (2017). https://doi.org/10.1080/0305215042000274942. http://arxiv.org/abs/1611.02167
3. Baker, B., Gupta, O., Raskar, R., Naik, N.: Accelerating neural architecture search using performance prediction. In: ICLR Workshop, vol. 2, pp. 1–7 (2018). http://metalearning.ml/papers/metalearn17_baker.pdf
4. Bender, G., Kindermans, P.J., Zoph, B., Vasudevan, V., Le, Q.: Understanding and simplifying one-shot architecture search. In: 35th International Conference on Machine Learning (ICML), vol. 80, pp. 549–558 (2018). https://doi.org/10.1109/TDEI.2009.5211872. http://proceedings.mlr.press/v80/bender18a.html
5. Cai, H., Chen, T., Zhang, W., Yu, Y., Wang, J.: Efficient architecture search by network transformation. In: AAAI (2018). http://arxiv.org/abs/1707.04873
6. Cai, H., Zhu, L., Han, S.: ProxylessNAS: direct neural architecture search on target task and hardware. In: 2019 International Conference on Learning Representations (ICLR) (2019)
7. Chen, L.C., et al.: Searching for efficient multi-scale architectures for dense image prediction. In: NeurIPS (2018)
8. Deng, B., Lin, D., Yan, J., Lin, D.: Peephole: predicting network performance before training (2017). http://arxiv.org/abs/1712.03351

9. Elsken, T., Metzen, J.H., Hutter, F.: Neural architecture search: a survey. CoRR abs/1808.05377 (2018)
10. Everingham, M., Eslami, S.M.A., Van Gool, L., Williams, C.K.I., Winn, J., Zisserman, A.: The Pascal visual object classes challenge: a retrospective. Int. J. Comput. Vis. 111(1), 98–136 (2015). https://doi.org/10.1007/s11263-014-0733-5
11. Grathwohl, W., Creager, E., Kamyar, S., Ghasemipour, S., Zemel, R.: Gradient-based optimization of neural network architecture. In: International Conference on Learning Representations (ICLR), pp. 1–6 (2018)
12. Hu, J., Shen, L., Sun, G.: Squeeze-and-excitation networks. In: 2018 IEEE/CVF Conference on Computer Vision and Pattern Recognition, pp. 7132–7141 (2018)
13. Huang, G., Liu, Z., van der Maaten, L., Weinberger, K.Q.: Densely connected convolutional networks. In: 2017 IEEE Conference on Computer Vision and Pattern Recognition (CVPR), pp. 2261–2269 (2017)
14. Jin, H., Song, Q., Hu, X.: Efficient neural architecture search with network morphism. CoRR abs/1806.10282 (2018)
15. Kandasamy, K., Neiswanger, W., Schneider, J., Poczos, B., Xing, E.: Neural architecture search with bayesian optimisation and optimal transport (2018). http://arxiv.org/abs/1802.07191
16. Kingma, D.P., Ba, J.: Adam: A method for stochastic optimization. CoRR abs/1412.6980 (2014). http://arxiv.org/abs/1412.6980
17. Klein, A., Falkner, S., Springenberg, J.T., Hutter, F.: Learning curve prediction with bayesian neural networks. In: International Conference on Learning Representations (ICLR), pp. 1–16. MCMC (2017)
18. Liu, C., et al.: Auto-DeepLab: hierarchical neural architecture search for semantic image segmentation. CoRR abs/1901.02985 (2019)
19. Liu, C., et al.: Progressive neural architecture search. In: ECCV (2018)
20. Liu, H., Simonyan, K., Vinyals, O., Fernando, C., Kavukcuoglu, K.: Hierarchical representations for efficient architecture search. In: 2018 International Conference on Learning Representations (ICLR) (2018). https://openreview.net/forum?id=BJQRKzbA-
21. Liu, H., Simonyan, K., Yang, Y.: DARTS: differentiable architecture search. In: 2019 International Conference on Learning Representations (ICLR) (2019). https://openreview.net/forum?id=S1eYHoC5FX
22. Miikkulainen, R., et al.: Evolving deep neural networks. In: Kozma, R., Alippi, C., Choe, Y., Morabito, F.C. (eds.) Artificial Intelligence in the Age of Neural Networks and Brain Computing. Elsevier, Amsterdam (2018). http://nn.cs.utexas.edu/?miikkulainen:chapter18
23. Milicchio, F., Gehrke, W.A.: Distributed Services with OpenAFS: For Enterprise and Education, 1st edn. Springer, Heidelberg (2010). Incorporated
24. Paszke, A., et al.: Automatic differentiation in PyTorch. In: NIPS, pp. 1–4 (2017)
25. Qing, Y.: FastDFS is an open source high performance distributed file system (DFS) (2013). https://github.com/happyfish100/fastdfs/tree/master
26. Sergeev, A., Balso, M.D.: Horovod: fast and easy distributed deep learning in TensorFlow. CoRR abs/1802.05799 (2018). http://arxiv.org/abs/1802.05799
27. Shin, R., Packer, C., Song, D.: Differentiable neural network architecture search. In: International Conference on Learning Representations (ICLR), pp. 1–4 (2018). No. 2017
28. Stanley, K.O., D'Ambrosio, D.B., Gauci, J.: A hypercube-based encoding for evolving large-scale neural networks. Artif. Life 15(2), 185–212 (2009). https://doi.org/10.1162/artl.2009.15.2.15202. http://www.mitpressjournals.org/doi/10.1162/artl.2009.15.2.15202

29. Stanley, K.O., Miikkulainen, R.: Evolving neural networks through augmenting topologies. Evol. Comput. **10**(2), 99–127 (2002). https://doi.org/10.1162/106365602320169811

30. Elsken, T., Metzen, J.H., Hutter, F.: Simple and efficient architecture search for convolutional neural networks. In: 2018 International Conference on Learning Representations (ICLR) (2018). https://openreview.net/forum?id=SySaJ0xCZ

31. Xie, L., Yuille, A.L.: Genetic CNN. In: 2017 IEEE International Conference on Computer Vision (ICCV), pp. 1388–1397 (2017)

32. Zoph, B., Le, Q.V.: Neural architecture search with reinforcement learning. In: International Conference on Learning Representations (ICLR), pp. 1–16 (2017). https://doi.org/10.1016/j.knosys.2015.01.010

33. Zoph, B., Vasudevan, V., Shlens, J., Le, Q.V.: Learning transferable architectures for scalable image recognition. In: 2018 IEEE/CVF Conference on Computer Vision and Pattern Recognition, pp. 8697–8710 (2018)

Web Services Classification with Topical Attention Based Bi-LSTM

Yingcheng Cao[1,2], Jianxun Liu[1,2(✉)], Buqing Cao[1,2], Min Shi[1,2],
Yiping Wen[1,2], and Zhenlian Peng[1,2]

[1] Hunan University of Science and Technology, Xiangtan, China
caoyingcheng12138@gmail.com, ljx529@gmail.com
[2] Key Laboratory of Knowledge Processing and Networked Manufacturing,
HNUST, Xiangtan, China

Abstract. With the rapid growth of the number of Web services on the Internet, how to classify web services correctly and efficiently become more and more important in the development and application of Web services. Existing function-based service clustering techniques have some problems, such as the sparse document semantics, unconsidered word order and the context information, so the accuracy of service classification needs to be further improved. To address this problem, this paper exploits the attention mechanism to combine the local implicit state vector of Bi-LSTM and the global LDA topic vector, and proposes a method of Web services classification with topical attention based Bi-LSTM. Specifically, it uses Bi-LSTM to automatically learn the feature representation of Web service. Then, it utilizes the offline training to obtain the topic vector of Web service document and performs the topic attention strengthening processing for Web service feature representation, and obtains the importance or weight of the different words in Web service document. Finally, the enhanced Web service feature representation is used as the input of the softmax neural network layer to perform the classification prediction of Web service. The experimental results validate the efficiency and effectiveness of the proposed method.

Keywords: Web services · Bi-directional Long Short-Term Memory ·
LDA topic model · Web service classification · Attention model

1 Introduction

Web service is an application that exposes to the outside world as an API that can be called over the Web. With the rapid development of the Internet, a large number of Internet applications based on SOA (Service-oriented Architecture) have been created, and Web services have gradually become the mainstream technology for implementing SOA. Web services are published by service providers on private or shared Internet platforms. Users search in a flood of Web services in order to find those Web services can meet their actual business needs. In this process, users do not need to know the specific implementation of the Web services to get satisfactory results [1, 2].

© ICST Institute for Computer Sciences, Social Informatics and Telecommunications Engineering 2019
Published by Springer Nature Switzerland AG 2019. All Rights Reserved
X. Wang et al. (Eds.): CollaborateCom 2019, LNICST 292, pp. 394–407, 2019.
https://doi.org/10.1007/978-3-030-30146-0_27

With the rapid growth of the number and diversity of Web services on the Internet, it is necessary to manage Web services through Web services-based applications such as service discovery [3, 4] and service composition or Mashup [5, 6]. Hence, it is unrealistic to organize Web services manually. For such a large number of Web services, how to enable machines to automatically recognize, manage, and use Web services has been attracted from many researchers [7]. The first step in implementing automated management is to classify Web services correctly and efficiently. At present, the research on Web service classification mainly includes function-based service clustering and QoS-based service clustering. Among them, the main techniques of function-based service clustering are keyword extraction based on TF-IDF algorithm [8, 9], Web service document clustering based on K-Means algorithm [10], and document topic modelling based on LDA [11], etc. These methods and techniques improve the accuracy of service clustering, but we are still facing the following two problems:

- Considering the Web service description document is usually short and their corpus is limited, some investigations exploit the auxiliary information, such as tags and word clustering, to augment the service description document to optimize the service clustering process. However, the relevance of the expanded content is insufficient and semantics sparsity problem of service document still exists.
- Document modeling techniques, such as TF-IDF and LDA, only perform statistical learning on the probability of occurrence of each word in the service document, and do not utilize the word order and context information between words, which are essential to fully characterize services functional semantics.

In recent years, neural network models have been proved with great potential in various information processing tasks. They can learn effective feature representation of documents and achieve optimal performance in many natural language processing (NLP) tasks. Among a variety of neural network models, Bi-directional Long Short-Term Memory Network (BiLSTM) [12] is widely used since it can comprehensively consider context information in sequence information learning. Here, we hope to use the Bi-LSTM model to learn the feature representation of Web service documents via taking into account word order and contextual information. For this reason, inspired by the work of Li et al. [13], when learning the feature representation of Web services, we improve Bi-LSTM by incorporating topic modeling into the Bi-LSTM architecture through an attention mechanism. The topic distribution of Web service documents is incorporated into the learning process to discriminate the importance of different words in Web service documents. To this end, we propose a novel topical attention based Bi-LSTM for Web services classification, called as LAB-Bi-LSTM. This method firstly takes the description document and the topic distribution of the Web service as input and then outputs the feature vector of the Web service. Finally, a softmax neural network is used for the classification prediction of the feature vector of the Web service.

The rest of the paper is structured as follows. Section 2 presents the proposed model. The experiment is described in the Sect. 3. Section 4 introduces related work of service classification methods. Section 5 concludes this paper and gives the future work.

2 Proposed Model

In this paper, we consider the Web services classification as a text multi-classification problem. A common practice is to use Bi-LSTM to learn vector representations of Web service documents, and then to classify Web service documents based on this vector representation. However, a potential problem with this approach is that all the necessary information in the Web service document needs to be compressed into a vector with fixed-dimension size. The existing method is to perform an average pooling operation on the hidden state vector of Bi-LSTM. Despite great promise, we argue that Bi-LSTM can be hindered by its modelling of all words in Web service documents with the same weight which means that each word in the Web service document contributes to the generation of the document vector equally. In real-world applications, different words usually have different representation capability, not all words contain useful information for generation of the document vector. As such, the words with less useful features should be assigned a lower weight as they contribute less to the generation of the document vector. Nevertheless, Bi-LSTM lacks such capability of differentiating the importance of words, which may result in sub-optimal document vector. In this work, we improve Bi-LSTM by discriminating the importance of different words. We propose a novel model, named as LAB-BiLSTM, which utilizes the recent advance in neural network - the attention mechanism [14] to enable words to contribute differently to the generation of the document vector. More importantly, the importance of a word is automatically learned from data without any human domain knowledge. Firstly, through Bi-LSTM, the eigenvector representation of the Web service description document is learned. Next, the attention mechanism is used to capture the topic relevance of different words in the document. Finally, by modeling the local interactions between the words and the global topics, the proposed model can learn effective representations of services for classification. As shown in Fig. 1, the LAB-BiLSTM architecture is a multi-layer feedforward neural network. It includes five specific function layers: Input layer, Embedding layer, Bi-LSTM layer, Topical attention layer, and Output layer. In its forward propagation process, the output of each layer is used as the input of the next layer. The following parts describe each layer and its processing in detail.

2.1 Input Layer

Considering that Web services' tags contain a wealth of functional information, we take the Web Services' tags together with the description documents as the input of LAB-BiLSTM model. The description document of Web service a is denoted as $W^{(a)} = \left\{ w_1^{(a)}, w_2^{(a)}, \cdots, w_{|W^{(a)}|}^{(a)} \right\}$, where $w_i^{(a)}$ is the i-th word of the document, and $|W^{(a)}|$ is the number of words. Tags annotated with Web service a are defined as $T^{(a)} = \{t_1, t_2, ..., t_m\}$, where t_i is the i-th tag of the Web service, and m is the number of tags. $Z^{(a)} = \left\{ z_1^{(a)}, z_2^{(a)}, \cdots, z_K^{(a)} \right\}$ is the topic distribution of a, where K represents the number of topics, and $Z^{(a)}$ is a vector with a length K. Since the number of words and the number of tags in each Web service are all different, we fix the length of input sequence to N.

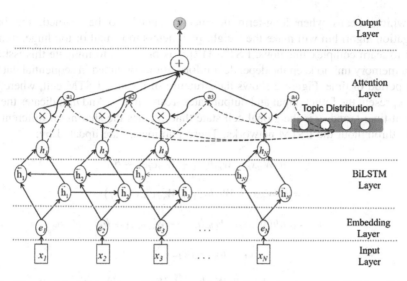

Fig. 1. The graphical illustration of the proposed topical attention-based BiLSTM model (LAB-BiLSTM)

Given an input sequence, it will be filled with the word "null" for a length less than N and the part whose length is greater than N will be truncated.

2.2 Embedding Layer

The embedding layer is above the input layer. Given a service document consisting of N words $S = \{x_1, x_2, ..., x_N\}$, every word x_i is converted into a real-valued vector e_i. For each word in S, we first look up the embedding matrix $w^{wrd} \in R^{d^w|V|}$, where V is a fixed-sized vocabulary, and d^w is the size of word embedding. The matrix w^{wrd} is a parameter to be learned, and d^w is a hyper-parameter to be chosen by user. We transform a word x_i into its word embedding e_i by using the matrix-vector product shown in the below formula:

$$e_i = W^{wrd}v^i \tag{1}$$

where v^i is a vector with size $|V|$ which has value 1 at index e_i and 0 in all other positions. Then the sentence is feed into the next layer as a real-valued vectors $emb_s = \{e_1, e_2, ..., e_N\}$.

2.3 Bi-LSTM Layer

Recurrent Neural Network (RNN) is a special kind of feed-forward neural networks that has gained significant success to tackle many problems in the NLP area, such as question answering [15] and sentiment prediction [16]. It is famous for its ability to process sequential data of arbitrary length like text. However, during the gradient computation step, RNN tends to suffer from the vanishing/exploding gradient problem

[17], which means when long-term dependency needs to be learned, the back-propagation algorithm will make the weight parameters too small or too huge, making it hard to learn complex functions. LSTM [12] was proposed to mitigate this issue by using a memory unit to keep the dependent information contained in sequential data for a long period of time. Figure 2 shows the structure of a single LSTM cell, where f_t, i_t and i_t represent the forget, input and output gates, respectively. And h_t indicates the cell output at time t, and o_t is the global cell state that enables the sharing of different cell outputs throughout the LSTM networks. These parameters are updated by:

$$i_t = \sigma(W_{xi}x_t + W_{hi}h_{t-1} + W_{ci}c_{t-1} + b_i) \tag{2}$$

$$f_t = \sigma(W_{xf}x_t + W_{hf}h_{t-1} + W_{cf}c_{t-1} + b_f) \tag{3}$$

$$g_t = tanh(W_{xc}x_t + W_{hc}h_{t-1} + W_{cc}c_{t-1} + b_c) \tag{4}$$

$$c_t = i_t g_t + f_t c_{t-1} \tag{5}$$

$$o_t = \sigma(W_{xo}x_t + W_{ho}h_{t-1} + W_{co}c_t + b_o) \tag{6}$$

$$h_t = o_t tanh(c_t) \tag{7}$$

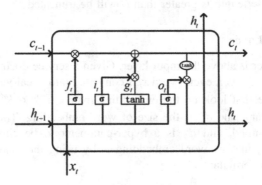

Fig. 2. Structure of the LSTM memory block

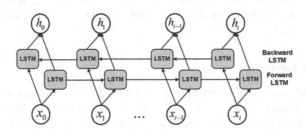

Fig. 3. The Bi-LSTM networks

However, in some situations like modeling description documents in this paper, it is beneficial to capture both the past and future dependencies of words. Bi-directional LSTM (Bi-LSTM) [12] is proposed for this purpose by introducing a second LSTM layer, where the hidden connections flow from the opposite direction. Figure 3 presents the network structure of Bi-LSTM, which contains two LSTM layers to model the sequential data from the opposite directions. For the t-th time step, the forward LSTM and the backward LSTM process the input from the opposite direction, and then output the hidden state vectors $\vec{h}_t$ and $\overleftarrow{h}_t$, respectively. There are many ways to combine $\vec{h}_t$ and $\overleftarrow{h}_t$. Here, we concatenate $\vec{h}_t$ and $\overleftarrow{h}_t$ to form the final representation h_t.

$$h_t = \vec{h}_t + \overleftarrow{h}_t \tag{8}$$

The output of Bi-LSTM layer is a sequence of hidden vectors $[h_1, h_2, ..., h_N]$. Each annotation h_t contains information about the whole input document with a strong focus on the parts surrounding the t-th word of the input document.

2.4   Topical Attention Layer

Since the attention mechanism has been introduced to neural network modelling, it has been widely used in many tasks [14]. Its main idea is to allow different parts to contribute differently when compressing them to a single representation. Motivated by the limitation of Bi-LSTM, we propose to employ the attention mechanism on hidden vectors $[h_1, h_2, ..., h_N]$ by introducing a series of attention-weighted combinations of these hidden vectors using the external topic distribution.

Taking all hidden states $[h_1, h_2, ..., h_N]$ and the external topic vector $\theta_s \in R^{K \times 1}$ as input, the topical attention layer outputs a continuous context vector $vec \in R^{d \times 1}$ for each input document. The output vector is computed as a weighted sum of each hidden state h_j:

$$vec = \sum_{j=1}^{N} a_j h_j \tag{9}$$

where d is the hidden dimension of Bi-LSTM, $a_j \in [0, 1]$ is the attention weight of h_j and $\sum_j a_j = 1$.

Next, we will introduce how we obtain $[a_1, a_2, ..., a_N]$ in detail. Specifically, for each h_j, we use the following equation to compute scores on how well the inputs around position j match the topic distribution θ_s:

$$g_j = v_a^T \tanh(W^a \theta_s + U^a h_j) \tag{10}$$

where K is the number of topics, $W^a \in R^{d \times K}$, $v_a \in R^{d \times 1}$ and $U^a \in R^{d \times d}$ are the weight matrices. After obtaining $[g_1, g_2, ..., g_N]$, we feed them to a softmax function to calculate the final weight scores $[a_1, a_2, ..., a_N]$.

2.5 Output Layer

Finally, we use the output from the topical attention layer as the embedding of the service document from our LAB-BiLSTM. We feed the output vector *vec* to a linear layer whose output length is the number of service categories. Then a softmax layer is added to output the probability distributions of all candidate categories. The softmax function is calculated as follows, where M is the number of services categories:

$$softmax(m_i) = \frac{exp(m_i)}{\sum_i^M exp(m_i)} \tag{11}$$

3 Experiment

3.1 Dataset Description

To evaluate the proposed approach, we crawled a Web service dataset from ProgrammableWeb.com and obtained 12919 API services as well as their related information, and basic statistics of it are shown in Table 1. This crawled dataset is available at http://kpnm.hnust.cn/xstdset.html. There are totally 384 categories for 12919 Web services and the average size of each category is 33.73. The number of Web services in each category is severely uneven. For example, the category Tools contains 790 Web services while the category law contains 1 service only. Table 2 shows the detailed distribution data of the top 10 Web services categories.

Table 1. APIs statistics in the web service dataset

Items	Values
Number of APIs	12919
Number of categories	384
Average number of member APIs per category	33.64
Average number of tags per APIs	3.46
Total number of tags	44734

Table 2. Top 10 categories order by number

Category	Number	Category	Number
Tools	790	Messaging	388
Financial	586	Payments	374
Enterprise	487	Government	306
eCommerce	435	Mapping	295
Social	405	Science	287

3.2 Evaluation Metrics

In our experiments, we evaluate the clustering performance by three metrics, *i.e.*, precision, recall, and F-smeasure. Suppose the standard classification of Web services in top M categories as $RSC = \{RC_1, RC_2, ..., RC_M\}$, which is available in the crawled dataset. We represent the experimental Web services classification results as $ESC = \{EC_1, EC_2, ..., EC_V\}$. The precision and recall metrics are defined as follows:

$$recall(EC_i) = \frac{|EC_i \cap RC_i|}{|RC_i|} \tag{12}$$

$$precision(EC_i) = \frac{|EC_i \cap RC_i|}{|EC_i|} \tag{13}$$

where $|EC_i|$ is the number of Web services in category EC_i, $|RC_i|$ is the number of Web services in RC_i and $|EC_i \cap RC_i|$ is the number of Web services successfully placed into category RC_i.

The average precision and average recall for all Web service categories are respectively:

$$Precison = \frac{1}{M}\sum_{C=1}^{M} precison(EC_i) \tag{14}$$

$$Recall = \frac{1}{M}\sum_{C=1}^{M} recall(EC_i) \tag{15}$$

F-measure: a tradeoff value between the recall and precision, which is denoted as:

$$F - measure = \frac{2 \times Precision \times Recall}{Precision + Recall} \tag{16}$$

3.3 Baselines

In this section, we compare our approach with the following approaches to verify the effectiveness of the proposed approach.

[1] **Naive Bayes:** The Naive Bayes classifier is a simple classification method based on Bayes theory, which shows excellent performance in many fields. Here, all the words in the Web service description document are one-hot encoded, then the description document of the Web service is converted into a digital sequence as input to the classifier.

[2] **LDA-SVM:** Support vector machine is a common classification method. It is a supervised learning model that is commonly used for pattern recognition, classification, and regression analysis. First, the description text of the Web service is modeled by the LDA topic model, and the topic distribution vector of each Web service document is obtained, then they are used as the input of the SVM for classification prediction.

[3] **Bi-LSTM:** We regard the last hidden vector from Bi-LSTM as the service document representation. Then we feed it to a linear layer whose output length is the number of categories. Finally, a softmax layer is added to output the probability distributions of all candidate categories.

[4] **Tag-BiLSTM:** On the basis of Bi-LSTM, it exploits tags as auxiliary information of the Web service description document to perform Web services classification. The tag contains a wealth of information about the Web service features, which helps improve the result of service classification.

[5] **LAB-BiLSTM:** The proposed method in this paper, which incorporates topic modeling into the Bi-LSTM architecture through an attention mechanism for service classification.

3.4 Experimental Results

Experimental Setup. In the experiment, we chose 30% data as the training set and 70% data as the test set. As for Bi-LSTM, Tag-BiLSTM and LAB-BiLSTM, we use a same minibatch stochastic gradient descent (SGD) algorithm together with the Adam method to train their model [18]. The hyperparameters β_1 is set to 0.9 and β_2 is set to 0.999. The learning rate is equal to 0.001, and the batch size is equal to 100. For LAB-BiLSTM, we test with different numbers of LDA topic size K and find an optimal setting when $K = 20$.

Performance Comparison. In this section, we select the top 10, 20, 30, 40, and 50 categories of Web services to conduct performance comparison, respectively. The experimental results are shown in Fig. 4. It can be seen that the method proposed in this paper LAB-BLSTM is superior to the other four methods in terms of precision, recall and F-measure. When the number of service categories is 20, LAB-BiLSTM has 38%, 32%, 24%, and 14% improvement in F-measure compared to Naive Bayes, LDA-SVM, BiLSTM, and Tag-BiLSTM, respectively. Specially, we have the following observations:

- The neural network-based models (*i.e.*, Bi-LSTM, Tag-BiLSTM, and LAB-BiLSTM) are far superior to Naive Bayes and LDA-SVM. It indicates that deep neural networks can achieve better classification results than traditional machine learning methods.
- Tag-BiLSTM has a significant increase in F-measure value of nearly 10% compared to Bi-LSTM. This is because the tags of the Web service are added as auxiliary information to the service description document, which greatly improves service classification performance.
- Compared to Tag-BiLSTM, LAB-BiLSTM has an increase of 14% in F-measure, which indicates that the introduction of LDA topic attention mechanism is indeed beneficial to Web services classification. In the LAB-BiLSTM method, words in the Web service description document that are highly relevant to the topic are gained greater attention weight, and these words become keywords in generating document-level feature vector representations.

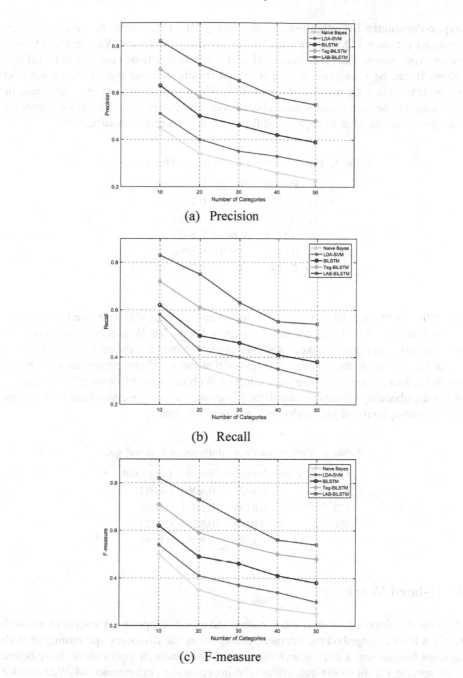

(a) Precision

(b) Recall

(c) F-measure

Fig. 4. Performance comparisons of all the baseline methods listed.

Hyper-Parameter Investigation. Firstly, taking 10 service categories as an example, we select different LDA topics (i.e., 10, 15, 20, 30, and 50) for Web service classification experiments. The precision, recall, and F-measure obtained are shown in Table 3 below. It can be seen from the experimental results that our model shows the best performance when the number of topics is 20. When the number of topics decreases or increases, the service classification effect decreases accordingly. Therefore, choosing the appropriate number of topics is still important for service classification.

Table 3. Performance *w.r.t* different number of topics K

K	Precision	Recall	F-measure
10	0.7777	0.7764	0.7770
15	0.7963	0.7806	0.7883
20	0.8106	0.8074	0.8071
30	0.8012	0.8001	0.8006
50	0.7837	0.7769	0.7802

Secondly, taking top 10 service categories as an example, different word embedding dimensions (i.e., 64, 128, 256 and 512) are selected for Web service classification experiments. The precision, recall and F-measure obtained are shown in Table 4 below. It can be seen from the experimental results that the word embedding dimension has limited influence on the classification effect of Web services. Moreover, the increasing of word embedding dimension can slightly improve the service classification effect, but the time complexity of the model will also increase greatly.

Table 4. Performance *w.r.t* different embedding size

Embedding size	Precision	Recall	F-measure
64	0.8077	0.8064	0.8037
128	0.8106	0.8074	0.8071
256	0.8249	0.8219	0.8224
512	0.8289	0.8284	0.8281

4 Related Work

With the development of service computing and cloud computing, a variety of network services have emerged on the Internet. Among them, the discovery and mining of Web services has become a hot research direction. Some research works show that efficient Web service classification can effectively improve the performance of Web service discovery [19]. As investigated, the researches on automatic Web services classification have attracted the attention of many researchers, mainly based on function-based service clustering and QoS-based service clustering.

At present, there are a lot of researches on function-based service clustering methods. Among them, Web service clustering method based on functional similarity [8, 9], which uses the key features of Web services extracted from WSDL documents to discriminate the similarity between Web services according to the cosine similarity. Liu et al. [20] proposed to extract content, context, host name and service name from Web service description document to perform Web service clustering. Huang et al. [10] proposed a K-Means algorithm based on Mashup service similarity for service clustering based on the description document and corresponding tags of Mashup service. Shi et al. [11] proposed an enhanced LDA topic modeling algorithm for Web service clustering. The word vectors trained by word2vec [21] were clustered to obtain clusters of words and merged into LDA training process. However, some obvious issues of the above approaches exist: (1) only utilizing services description documents; or (2) do not utilize the word order and context information between words, which are essential to fully characterize services functional semantics. Our approach incorporates topic modeling into the Bi-LSTM architecture through an attention mechanism and takes over the advantages of the both.

In addition, QoS-based Web service clustering mainly used the QoS (Quality of Service), which includes throughput, availability, execution time, and so on, to perform service clustering. Xia et al. proposed to cluster large number of atomic Web services into many groups according to their QoS properties [22], which takes non-functional properties such as cost, execution time and reliability into account. Xiong et al. [23] used the long short-term memory neural network LSTM model and collaborative filtering algorithm to predict the QoS value of Web services from the historical call records of services. Wang et al. [24] designed an online QoS prediction method that uses the LSTM model to learn and predict the reliability of the service system in the future. However, QoS of services are dynamic with time and many existing methods fail to take this property into account. In addition, QoS are usually hard to be obtained. Therefore, there are many works focus on content-based or functional-based services clustering, as we do in this paper.

5 Conclusion and Future Work

This paper proposes a novel topical attention-based Bi-LSTM model for Web service classification. We first adopt the architecture of Bi-LSTM to capture the most important semantic information in a service document. Then, our model incorporates topic modeling into the Bi-LSTM architecture through an attention mechanism and takes over the advantages of the both. We evaluate the proposed approach on a real-world dataset and the experimental results show it has an improvement of 34% in F-measure over the standard Bi-LSTM model. In the future, we will consider to exploit other valuable auxiliary information, such as service relationship information, into our model to further improve the accuracy of service classification.

Acknowledgment. This work was supported in part by the National Natural Science Foundation of China under Grant 61572187, Grant 61872139, and Grant 61702181, in part by the Natural Science Foundation of Hunan Province under Grant 2017JJ2098, Grant 2018JJ2136, and Grant 2018JJ2139, and in part by the Educational Commission of Hunan Province of China under Grant 17C0642.

References

1. Zhang, L., Zhang, J., Hong, C.: Service-oriented architecture. Serv. Comput. 89–113 (2007)
2. Gottschalk, K., Graham, S., Kreger, H.: Introduction to web services architecture. IBM Syst. J. **41**(2), 170–177 (2002)
3. Nayak, R., Lee, B.: Web service discovery with additional semantics and clustering. In: International Conference on Web Intelligence, pp. 555–558 (2007)
4. Zhang, X., Yin, Y., Zhang, M.: Web service community discovery based on spectrum clustering. In: International Conference on Computational Intelligence and Security, pp. 187–191 (2009)
5. Zhang, L.J., Li, B.: Requirements driven dynamic services composition for web services and grid solutions. J. Grid Comput. **2**(2), 121–140 (2004)
6. Dustdar, S., Schreiner, W.: A survey on web services composition. Int. J. Web Grid Serv. **1**(1), 1–30 (2005)
7. Bruno, M., Canfora, G., Penta, M.D.: An approach to support web service classification and annotation. In: IEEE International Conference on E-Technology, E-Commerce and E-Service, pp. 138–143 (2005)
8. Chen, L., Hu, L., Zheng, Z., Wu, J., Yin, J., Li, Y., Deng, S.: WTCluster: utilizing tags for web services clustering. In: Kappel, G., Maamar, Z., Motahari-Nezhad, Hamid R. (eds.) ICSOC 2011. LNCS, vol. 7084, pp. 204–218. Springer, Heidelberg (2011). https://doi.org/10.1007/978-3-642-25535-9_14
9. Elgazzar, K., Hassan, A.E., Martin, P.: Clustering WSDL documents to bootstrap the discovery of web services. In: IEEE International Conference on Web Services, pp. 147–154 (2010)
10. Huang, X., Liu, X., Cao, B.: MSCA: mashup service clustering approach integrating K-means and agnes algorithms. J. Chin. Mini-Micro Comput. Syst. **36**(11), 2492–2497 (2015)
11. Shi, M., Liu, J., Zhou, D.: WE-LDA: a word embeddings augmented LDA model for web services clustering. In: IEEE International Conference on Web Services, pp. 9–16 (2017)
12. Zhou, P., Shi, W., Tian, J.: Attention-based bidirectional long short-term memory networks for relation classification. In: Meeting of the Association for Computational Linguistics, pp. 207–212 (2016)
13. Li, Y., Liu, T., Jiang, J., Zhang, L.: Hashtag recommendation with topical attention-based LSTM. In Proceedings of COLING, pp. 943–952 (2016)
14. Chen, J., Zhang, H., He, X., Nie, L., Liu, W., Chua, T.: Attentive collaborative filtering: Multimedia recommendation with feature- and item-level attention. In: Proceedings of the 40th International ACM SIGIR Conference on Research and Development in Information Retrieval, pp. 335–344 (2017)
15. Feng, M., Xiang, B., Glass, M.R., Wang, L., Zhou, B.: Applying deep learning to answer selection: a study and an open task. In: IEEE Workshop on Automatic Speech Recognition and Understanding, pp. 813–820 (2015)

16. Tang, D., Qin, B., Liu, T.: Document modeling with gated recurrent neural network for sentiment classification. In: Conference on Empirical Methods in Natural Language Processing (EMNLP), pp. 1422–1432 (2015)
17. Bengio, Y., Simard, P., Frasconi, P.: Learning long-term dependencies with gradient descent is difficult. IEEE Trans. Neural Netw. **5**, 157–166 (1994)
18. Kingma, D.P., Ba, J.: Adam: a method for stochastic optimization. Comput. Sci. (2014)
19. Chen, L., Wang, Y., Yu, Q., Zheng, Z., Wu, J.: WT-LDA: user tagging augmented LDA for web service clustering. In: Basu, S., Pautasso, C., Zhang, L., Fu, X. (eds.) ICSOC 2013. LNCS, vol. 8274, pp. 162–176. Springer, Heidelberg (2013). https://doi.org/10.1007/978-3-642-45005-1_12
20. Liu, W., Wong, W.: Web service clustering using text mining techniques. Int. J. Agent-Oriented Softw. Eng. **3**(1), 6–26 (2009)
21. Mikolov, T., Chen, K., Corrado, G.: Efficient estimation of word representations in vector space. Comput. Sci. (2013)
22. Xia, Y., Chen, P., Bao, L., Wang, M., Yang J.: A QoS-aware web service selection algorithm based on clustering. In: IEEE 9th International Conference on Web Services, pp. 428–435 (2011)
23. Xiong, W., Wu, Z., Li, B.: A learning approach to QoS prediction via multi-dimensional context. In: International Conference on Web Services, pp. 164–171 (2017)
24. Wang, H., Yang, Z., Yu, Q.: Online reliability prediction via long shortterm memory for service-oriented system. In: International Conference on Web Services, pp. 81–88 (2017)

Relation Extraction Toward Patent Domain Based on Keyword Strategy and Attention+BiLSTM Model (Short Paper)

Xueqiang Lv[1], Xiangru Lv[1], Xindong You[1(✉)], Zhian Dong[1], and Junmei Han[2]

[1] Beijing Key Laboratory of Internet Culture
and Digital Dissemination Research, Beijing Information Science
and Technology University, Beijing, China
youxindong@bistu.edu.cn
[2] Laboratory of Complex Systems, Institute of Systems Engineering,
AMS, PLA, Beijing, China

Abstract. Patent terminology relation extraction is of great significance to the construction of patent Knowledge graph. In order to solve the problem of long-distance dependency in traditional depth learning, a new method of patent terminology relation extraction is proposed, which combines attention mechanism and bi-directional LSTM model and with keyword strategy. Category keyword features in each sentence obtained by the improved TextRank with the patent text information vectorization added. BiLSTM neural work and attention mechanism are employed to extract the temporal information and sentence-level global feature information. Moreover, pooling layer is added to obtain the local features of the text. Finally, we fuse the global features and local features, and output the final classification results through the softmax classifier. The addition of category keywords improves the distinction of categories. Substantial experimental results demonstrate that the proposed model outperform the state-of-art neural model in patent terminology relation extraction.

Keywords: Patent terminology relation extraction · Patent knowledge graph · Keyword features · BiLSTM · Attention mechanism

1 Introduction

Automatic extraction of patent terminology relationship plays an important role in patent information retrieval, patent similarity detection, patent domain ontology construction, patent knowledge graph construction and latent semantic analysis.

In this paper, a new method of patent terminology relation extraction is proposed, which combines BiLSTM with Attention and keyword strategy and pooling layer are also added. The improved TextRank algorithm is used to extract the class keyword features, then the BiLSTM neural network and attention mechanism are used to extract the temporal information and sentence-level important information, then the key

X. Wang et al. (Eds.): CollaborateCom 2019, LNICST 292, pp. 408–416, 2019.
https://doi.org/10.1007/978-3-030-30146-0_28

features of each sentence are selected under the action of the pool layer, and finally the classification results are obtained through the full connection layer into the classifier. As a whole, the main contributions of this paper are as follows:

(1) *The class keyword features of each sentence are extracted by improved TextRank algorithm, which is combined with the patent information.*
(2) *The pooling layer is added parallel with the attention mechanism after the Bi-LSTM, which is fused as the input of Softmax classifier.*
(3) *Substantial experiments are conducted on different neural network model, which confirm the superiority of our proposed methods than the state-of-art neural network model.*

2   Related Work

At present, many scholars have done a lot of research on relationship extraction, and under the impetus of the actual needs, the relationship extraction technology has made great progress and has been widely used. Relationship extraction methods include pattern matching method, dictionary-driven method, statistics-based machine learning method and multi-method hybrid method [1]. Rink and Harabagiu [2] extracted semantic and lexical features from external corpus, and extracted semantic relations using Support Vector Machines (SVM) classifier. Zhang et al. [3] used Kernel method to extract entity relations, and discussed various Kernel methods to extract relations from free text.

In recent years, the use of depth learning method for entity relationship extraction has become the mainstream. In depth learning, we can automatically learn and acquire effective text features. This method achieves better performance than the traditional methods in many natural language processing tasks without using the basic natural language processing tools [4]. Liu et al. [5] proposed a new convolutional neural network, introduced a new coding method, which used the synonym lexicon to encode the input words and combined with lexical features to extract relations. Zeng et al. [6] proposed a convolution neural network method based on entity location information for entity relationship extraction. The problem of long-distance dependency is alleviated to some extent. Santos et al. [7] proposed a new pairwise ranking loss function in the task of using convolution neural networks to deal with relational classification. The network is categorized by rankings and achieved the best classification performance at the time. Zhang et al. [8] use RNN based on word position information to complete the task of relation extraction, which makes better use of the context information of entities. Zhou et al. [9] used Attention+BiLSTM model for relation extraction. After the BiLSTM model got the high-level semantics of sentences, Attention mechanism was used for high-level semantics representation, which improved the performance of relation extraction.

3   Patent Terminology Relation Extraction Model

This paper extracts patent terms based on BiLSTM. At first, the patent text is severed by commas, semicolons and periods, and the terminology features in each sentence are identified, and the location information is added, and the features of the category keywords in each sentence are obtained by the improved TextRank keyword extraction algorithm, and then the sentences and the extracted features are formed into a final vector matrix. Vector matrix is imported into BiLSTM model and attention probability is calculated by attention mechanism. The whole feature of text information is obtained to highlight the importance of specific words to the whole sentence. At the same time, the key feature of each sentence is selected as a local feature by using the maximum pooling layer. Finally, the whole feature and the local feature are fused, and the final classification result is output through the classifier. The complete framework of the model is shown in Fig. 1.

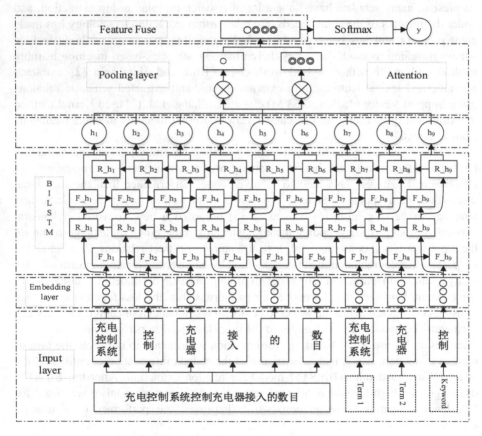

Fig. 1. Model complete framework

3.1   Position Vector Feature

In the task of patent term relation extraction, the words that can highlight the term relation are often distributed near the term, so adding the distance from each word to the two terms into the model can improve the effect of term relation extraction. For each word w_i in a sentence $s = \{w_1, w_2, w_3, \ldots, w_k\}$ containing k words, the relative distance to the two terminologies is $i - i_1$ and $i - i_2$. Where i is the index of the position of the current word in the sentence, i_1 and i_2 are the index of the position of the two terms in the sentence, respectively.

3.2   Sentence-Level Category Keyword Feature Extraction

TextRank algorithm is simple and easy to use, which makes use of the relevance between words. But TextRank only relies on the document itself and the importance of each word is the same when initialized, so it is difficult to extract the keywords from the text accurately. TF-IDF algorithm relies on the corpus environment and can get the importance of a word in advance Therefore, combing the idea of TF-IDF algorithm to TextRank algorithm is helpful to improve the efficiency and accuracy of the algorithm. The improved Text-Rank (IMTR) algorithm is described as follows:

(1) Input patent text information set $S = \{s_1, s_2, s_3, \ldots, s_n\}$, and set parameters: damping factor is d, sliding window size is w, maximum iteration number is I, iteration stop threshold is σ;
(2) The TF-IDF value of each word in the patent text information set S is calculated by a TF-IDF algorithm; And a keyword graph G_i composed of the words in s_i is constructed;
(3) According to the formula:
$$W(v_i) = (1 - d) + d \times W'(v_i)_{TF-IDF} \times \sum_{j \in In(v_i)} \frac{w_{ji}}{\sum_{v_k \in Out(v_j)} w_{jk}} W(v_j),$$ the weight of
each word in the keyword graph G_i is calculated iteratively until it converges;
(4) Each word in the keyword graph G_i is sorted by its weight, and the words with the largest weight and the verb part of speech are selected as the category characteristic keywords.

In the algorithm, $W(v_i)$ is the weight of node v_i; d is damping factor; $In(v_i)$ is the set of nodes pointing to node v_i; $Out(v_j)$ is the set of nodes pointing from node v_j; w_{ji} is the weight of the edges of nodes v_j to v_i, and $W'(v_i)_{TF-IDF}$ is the TF-IDF value of node v_i.

3.3   Attention+BiLSTM Model

In the task of semantic relation extraction of patent terms, the historical information and future context information of the text should be taken into account. However, the LSTM model only records historical information and knows nothing about the future. Unlike the LSTM model, the bi-directional LSTM model considers both the characteristics of the past and those of the future. Simply understood, the bi-directional LSTM model is equivalent to two LSTMs, one forward output sequence and one reverse output sequence, and the outputs of the two are combined as the final result.

The bi-directional LSTM model effectively uses the context information of the patent text, and can extract more hidden features in the patent text.

In this part, we use the attention mechanism of relational classification task to calculate the output of Bi-LSTM model, and get the distribution of attention probability. From the distribution of attention probability, we can get the importance of the output state of LSTM unit to relational classification at each time, and then improve the final classification performance. In this model, the following formula is used for the attention layer:

$$M = tanh(H) \tag{1}$$

$$\alpha = \text{softmax}\left(w^T M\right) \tag{2}$$

$$h^* = \tanh\left(H\alpha^T\right) \tag{3}$$

Where $H = [h_1, h_2, h_3, \ldots, h_T]$ is a matrix output by that Bi-LSTM lay at T times and $H \in R^{d^w \times T}$. d^w is the dimension of the word vector; w is the training parameter vector and w^T is the transpose of w; α is the probability distribution vector of attention; h^* is the expression of a learned sentence.

For the output $H = [h_1, h_2, h_3, \ldots, h_T]$ of the BiLSTM model, besides the attention mechanism, the maximum pool method is used to compute the output, and the most relevant feature representation of the classification task is obtained, which is $h' = maxpool(H)$.

Feature fusion is to merge the computational results of attention layer and pooling layer to achieve the performance of complementary advantages among multiple features, which is $F = h^* \otimes h'$. Where $\otimes$ represents vector splicing.

4 Experiment

4.1 Experimental Data and Evaluation Criteria

The data used in this experiment was a patent text of 9,978 new energy vehicles crawled from the patent search and analysis website. The ultimate goal of this experiment is to extract the terminology relation used in the patent text of the new energy automobile field. Since there are domain terms in each part of the patent text, the title, abstract, specification and claims in the patent are used as corpus. Patent text data were preprocessed and 6912 corpora were selected as experimental data, of which 5248 corpora were used as training data and 1664 corpora as test data. The data processing steps as follows:

(1) The patent terminology is extracted from the patent corpus by our previous proposed algorithm [10]. Dividing patent data into commas, semicolons and periods, each of which belongs to a corpus;
(2) Select a sentence that contains only two patent terms to form the final data set;
(3) Mark the selected data to determine the final experimental data.

There are 7 relationships in 6912 pieces of data selected in this experiment. The instance sample is shown in Table 1.

In order to verify the correctness and validity of the model proposed in this paper, the macro_averagedF1 (macro_F1) was used as experimental evaluation criteria. To calculate the macro-averaged F1 value, first calculate the Precision, Recall, and F1 value for each category. The formula is as follows:

$$P_i = \frac{TP_i}{TP_i + FP_i} \times 100\% \tag{4}$$

$$R_i = \frac{TP_i}{TP_i + FN_i} \times 100\% \tag{5}$$

$$F1_i = \frac{2 \times P_i \times R_i}{P_i + R_i} \times 100\% \tag{6}$$

TP_i is the number of data correctly predicted in the i-th relationship type. FP_i is the number of data erroneously predicted in the i-th relationship type. FN_i is the number of data belonging to the i-th relationship type that is incorrectly predicted to be of another relationship type. $macro_{averaged}F1$ is calculated as follows:

$$\text{macro\_averagedF1} = \frac{1}{M} \sum_{m=1}^{M} F1_m \tag{7}$$

Where M is the number of relationship types.

Table 1. Sample Instance.

Relation	Samples Content
Whole-Component	【驱动电机】装有两套【定子绕组】
Component-Whole	每组【动力电池】固定于一个【电池箱】中
Product-Material	其特征在于【转子】是用【稀土钴永磁】材料制作的
Spatial	【励磁绕组】与【电子控制器】相连接
Control	【操作手柄】控制【主轴】转动
Belongs to	所述【发动机】作为【动力单元】

4.2 Parameter Setting and Result Analysis

The experiments are conducted on a 64-bit Ubuntu 16.04 operating system installed on a Dell server with an NVIDIA Tesla K40 GPU and running memory of 64 GB. The model was implemented using the TensorFlow framework and python language. The experimental results of this model are closely related to the parameters in the model. Through a large number of parameter adjustment experiments, the local optimal value of each parameter is obtained. The Dimension of Word Vector is 300, the Dimension of Distance Vector is 50, the Batch_size is 128, the Learning Rate is 1e-5, the Hidden Layer is 256, the BiLSTM Layer is 2, the Droupout is 0.85. The overall results of this experiment are shown in Table 2.

Table 2. Overall experimental results.

Relation	Precision (%)	Recall (%)	F1 value (%)
Whole-component	95.97	93.53	94.73
Component-whole	87.55	95.61	91.40
Product-material	77.78	93.33	84.93
Control	97.06	83.90	90.00
Spatial	99.35	95.64	97.46
Belongs to	82.86	87.88	85.30
Other	95.38	84.62	89.68
Macro-averaging	90.85	90.64	90.50

From the experimental results for each relationship type in Table 2, from which we can be seen that the simplicity and complexity of the relationship types affect the final performance of the relationship extraction. This is because simple relationship types are easily learned by the model, and can be identified more accurately. It is difficult for the proposed model to learn the semantic association of complex relationship types, which result in low recognition accuracy.

4.3 Internal Comparison Experiment of the Model

In order to validate the effectiveness of keyword features and pooling layer adding Attention+BiLSTM model for patent terminology relationship recognition, four sets of internal comparison experiments are designed. The original input of the model is sentence vector, position vector and terminology vector. The experimental results are shown in Table 3.

Table 3. Comparative results of internal experiments of the model.

No.	Models	Evaluation criteria (%)		
		macro_P	macro_R	macro_F1
1	Attention+BiLSTM (ABL)	87.98	89.19	88.39
2	Keyword+Attention+BiLSTM (KABL)	89.50	89.63	89.34
3	Attention+BiLSTM+Pooling (ABLP)	88.77	89.32	88.81
4	Keyword+Attention+Bi-LSTM+Pooling (KABLP)	90.85	90.64	90.50

From the accuracy rate, recall rate and F1 value of each group of experiments shown in Table 3, we can see that the model of designed in this paper has got relatively good results and new energy vehicle patent terminology relation can be effectively extracted. In Experiment 1, only the Attention+Bi-LSTM model was used. Although performance has improved to some extend, the problem of terminology relation extraction in the patent field could be solved to a certain extent, but the final extraction result still needs to be improved. Experiment 2 added the keyword features on the basis of Experiment 1, and Experiment 3 added the pooling layer on the basis of Experiment 1. These two groups of experiments have improved experimental results compared to Experiment 1. It can be concluded that the keyword features and pooling layer have played a role in improving the efficiency of extraction of terminology relation in the patent domain. Compared to Experiment 1, the F1 value in Experiment 2 is increased by 0.95% and the F1 value in Experiment 3 increased by 0.42%. It can be concluded that the keyword features has played a greater role than the pooling layer in improving the efficiency of extraction of terminology relation in the patent domain. This is because the addition of category keyword features improves the distinction of categories of patent terminology relation, and also makes up for the shortage of Attention +BiLSTM model automatic learning features, therefore, the explicit addition of keyword features can play a certain role in patent terms relationship extraction.

Therefore, a method of adding keyword features and pooling layer to Attention +BiLSTM model is designed in this paper. It can be concluded from Experiment 4 that the KABLP can achieve a better performance than the general deep learning model.

4.4   Comparative Experiments of Different Classification Methods

In order to verify the advantages of Attention+BiLSTM model in patent terminology relation extraction, Attention+BiLSTM model is compared with RNN, LSTM and Bi-LSTM model on the same dataset. In order to unify the experimental standards, the input word vectors of all the models are the same, and the pooling layer is added to the models. The experimental results are shown in Table 4.

Table 4. Experimental results of different methods

NO.	Models	Evaluation criteria (%)		
		macro_P	macro_R	macro_F1
1	Attention+BiLSTM (ABL)	84.18	83.39	84.18
2	Keyword+Attention+BiLSTM (KABL)	86.24	88.96	87.54
3	Attention+BiLSTM+Pooling (ABLP)	87.18	89.19	88.12
4	**Keyword+Attention+Bi-LSTM+Pooling (KABLP)**	**90.85**	**90.64**	**90.50**

Comparisons of the different methods in Table 4 show that the BiLSTM method exhibits better performance than the LSTM and RNN methods. This is because the Bi-LSTM model not only considers the past characteristics but also the future characteristics, and effectively uses the context information of the patent text, which can extract more hidden features in the patent text. By adding Attention mechanism to Bi-LSTM model, the performance is further improved, because attention mechanism can highlight the importance of a particular word to the whole sentence by calculating the probability of attention, which can make the model pay more attention to the important information in patent text.

5   Conclusion and Future Work

In this paper, we mainly focus on relationship extraction from the new energy vehicle patent terminology, and propose an Attention+BiLSTM combined with keyword strategy and pooling layer of patent terminology relationship extraction method. However, this model can only extract the preset patent terms relationship types, how to extract the open domain relationship and automatically discover new patent terms relationship will be our main future work.

Acknowledgments. This work is supported by National Natural Science Foundation of China under Grants No. 61671070, National Science Key Lab Fund project 6142006190301, National Language Committee of China under Grants ZDI135-53, and Project of Three Dimension Energy Consumption Saving Strategies in Cloud Storage System in Promoting the Developing University Intension–Disciplinary Cluster No. 5211910940.

References

1. Rong, B., Fu, K., Huang, Y., Wang, Y.: Relation extraction based on multi-channel convolutional neural network. Appl. Res. Comput. **34**(03), 689–692 (2017)
2. Rink, B., Harabagiu, S.: UTD: classifying semantic relations by combining lexical and semantic resources. In: International Workshop on Semantic Evaluation, pp. 256–259. Association for Computational Linguistics (2010)
3. Zhang, X., Gao, Z., Zhu, M.: Kernel methods and its application in relation extraction. In: International Conference on Computer Science and Service System, pp. 1362–1365. IEEE (2011)
4. Collobert, R., Weston, J., Bottou, L., et al.: Natural language processing (almost) from scratch. J. Mach. Learn. Res. **12**(1), 2493–2537 (2011)
5. Liu, C.Y., Sun, W.B., Chao, W.H., et al.: Convolution neural network for relation extraction. In: Motoda, H., Wu, Z., Cao, L., Zaiane, O., Yao, M., Wang, W. (eds.) ADMA 2013. LNCS, vol. 8347, pp. 231–242. Springer, Berlin (2013)
6. Zeng, D., Liu, K., Lai, S., et al.: Relation classification via convolutional deep neural network. In: Proceedings of the 25th International Conference on Computational Linguistics, pp. 2335–2344 (2014)
7. Santos, C.N.D., Xiang, B., Zhou, B.: Classifying relations by ranking with convolutional neural networks. Comput. Sci. **86**(86), 132–137 (2015)
8. Zhang, D., Wang, D.: Relation classification via recurrent neural network [EB/OL]. https://arxiv.org/pdf/1508.01006.pdf. Accessed 05 Apr 2015
9. Zhou, P., Shi, W., Tian, J., et al.: Attention-based bidirectional long short-term memory networks for relation classification. In: Meeting of the Association for Computational Linguistics, pp. 207–212 (2016)
10. Lv, X.: Patent domain terminology extraction based on multi-feature fusion and BILSTM-CRF model. Front. Artif. Intell. Appl. **309**, 495–500 (2018)

Security and Trustworthy

Application and Implementation of Multivariate Public Key Cryptosystem in Blockchain (Short Paper)

Ruping Shen[1(✉)], Hong Xiang[2], Xin Zhang[1], Bin Cai[1], and Tao Xiang[3]

[1] School of Big Data and Software Engineering, Chongqing University,
Chongqing, China
{shenruping,zhang.x,caibin}@cqu.edu.cn

[2] Key Laboratory of Dependable Service Computing in Cyber Physical Society
Chongqing University, Ministry of Education, Chongqing, China
xianghong@cqu.edu.cn

[3] School of Computer Science, Chongqing University, Chongqing, China
txiang@cqu.edu.cn

Abstract. Blockchain is one of the most revolutionary and innovative technologies in recent years. The traditional asymmetric encryption algorithms guarantee the security of data on blockchain. However, with the rapid development of quantum computing technologies, as long as large-scale quantum computers appear, these kind of encryption systems can be deciphered by shor algorithm in polynomial time. Therefore, blockchain technologies are going to face potential security threats. To solve this problem, the best solution at present is to replace the asymmetric encryption algorithms in the blockchain with post-quantum cryptosystems. In this paper, we apply the Rainbow algorithm with high signature efficiency to the existing Ethereum platform, and test the feasibility of the scheme by building a private chain. In addition, we compare the signature efficiency of Rainbow algorithm with ECDSA, which is expected to provide direction and inspiration for future research on blockchain resistance to quantum computing.

Keywords: Blockchain · Quantum computers ·
Post-quantum cryptosystems

1 Introduction

Blockchain [1,2] has attracted increasing attention because of its decentralization in recent years. Blockchain emerges originally as the core technology of Bitcoin [3]. Subsequently, in 2015, the emergence of blockchain platforms represented by Ethereum [4] and Hyperledger [5] has once again pushed blockchain technology to a climax of research. However, as a new technology, blockchain will inevitably face various problems and challenges [6]. The security of data on the

X. Wang et al. (Eds.): CollaborateCom 2019, LNICST 292, pp. 419–428, 2019.
https://doi.org/10.1007/978-3-030-30146-0_29

blockchain mainly depends on the traditional asymmetric cryptosystems. For example, the most popular Bitcoin and Ethereum use the Elliptic Curve Digital Signature Algorithm (ECDSA) [7]. However, with the rapid development of quantum computing technologies, as long as large-scale quantum computers appear, the Shor algorithm [8] can decipher the ECDSA in a short time, thus the blockchain technologies face a huge security threat [9].

Although the current blockchain security issue is particularly important, everyone is still on the stage of theoretical analysis stage. Until 2017, the UK released Quantum-Resistant Ledger [10], which uses an encryption algorithm that can resist quantum attacks, and successfully combines blockchain technologies with post-quantum cryptosystems. However, if post-quantum cryptosystems want to be widely used, which requires the formulation of relevant international standards.

In 2017, NIST published the results of the first batch of post-quantum cryptosystems [11,12]. It can be seen that post-quantum cryptographic design schemes have been officially put on the agenda, which means that blockchain technologies relying on the traditional cryptosystems must make an alternative plan to the advent of quantum computers. There are mainly five categories of post-quantum cryptosystems [13]: Hash-based, Code-based, Lattice-based, Isogeny-based and Multivariate Public Key cryptosystems. Compared with other post-quantum cryptosystems, the research on multivariate public key cryptosystems started relatively early. Thus, there are many mature multivariate public key cryptosystems. Apart from resisting the attack of quantum computers, it also has the advantages of fast computing speed and less computing resource, which is consistent with the real-time needs of blockchain. Therefore, combining multivariate public key cryptosystems with blockchain technologies is of great significance.

Based on the above backgrounds, we apply the most popular Rainbow signature scheme to Ethereum. The rest of this paper is organized as follows: Sect. 2 introduces the knowledge of Blockchain, Multivariate Public Key Cryptosystem and Rainbow signature scheme; In Sect. 3, we introduce the details of experiments; Sect. 4 analyzes the experimental results and Sect. 5 summarizes the full text.

2   Preliminaries

2.1   Blockchain

This section takes Ethereum as an example to introduce related technologies of blockchain. The total architecture of Ethereum is shown in Fig. 1.

Smart contract [14] is the main innovation of Ethereum. It is a collection of code and data (state), and can also be understood as a contract written in code that can be executed automatically on blockchain.

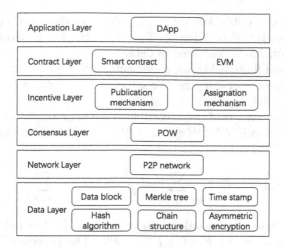

Fig. 1. Ethereum overall architecture.

2.2 Multivariate Public Key Cryptosystem

Multivariate Public Key Cryptosystem [15] aims to design a secure encryption and signature scheme by constructing a multivariate quadratic equation as a public key. Its key compositions are respectively: $pk = P = S \circ F \circ L, sk = \{S, F, L\}$. This paper focuses on the multivariate signature scheme. Its process of signature and verification is shown in Fig. 2.

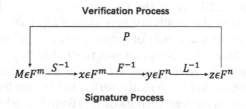

Fig. 2. Process of Multivariate Signature Scheme.

Signature: Suppose $M \in F^m$, one calculates sequentially $x = S^{-1}(M) \in F^m, y = F^{-1}(x) \in F^n$ and $z = L^{-1}(y) \in F^n$. z is the signature of M.

Verification: One calculates $M' = P(z) \in F^m$, if $M' = M$, the signature is accepted; otherwise, reject the signature.

2.3 Rainbow Signature Scheme

In 2005, Ding and Schmidt [16] improved the Unbalanced Oil-Vinegar (UOV) scheme and proposed Rainbow [17], which is a multilayer UOV scheme. Due to its high signature efficiency, Rainbow signature scheme is considered as one of the most promising multivariate signature schemes. The core difference between different multivariate public key cryptographic algorithms is that the construction of the private key F is different. Therefore, the key generation process of the Rainbow algorithm is described in detail:

Let $F = F_q$ be a finite field with q elements, $n \in N$ and $v_1 < v_2 < \cdots < v_l < v_{l+1} = n$ be a sequence of integers. We set $m = n - v_1, O_i = \{v_i + 1, \ldots, v_{i+1}\}$ and $V_i = \{1, \ldots, v_i\}(1, \ldots, l)$

The private key consists of two invertible affine map $S : F^m \to F^m, L : F^n \to F^n$ and a central map $F(f^{(v_1+1)}(x), \ldots, f^{(n)}(x)) : F^n \to F^m$. The expression of the polynomials $f^{(i)}(i = v_1 + 1, \ldots, n)$ is

$$f^{(i)} = \sum_{k,l \in V_j} \alpha_{k,l}^{(i)} \cdot x_k \cdot x_l + \sum_{k \in V_j, l \in O_j} \beta_{k,l}^{(i)} \cdot x_k \cdot x_l + \sum_{k \in V_j \cup O_j} \gamma_k^{(i)} \cdot x_k + \eta^{(i)}$$

Here, the coefficients are randomly selected from F. The public key is composed of the map $P = S \circ F \circ L : F^n \to F^m$. The process of signature and verification is the same as in Sect. 2.2, so there is no longer a description.

3   Experiment

Ethereum offers several open source projects on github, Go-ethereum [18] project based on Go is currently the most widely used Ethereum Geth client. It provides an interactive command console that includes all functional interfaces, such as building a private chain, mining, deploying smart contracts and so on.

This experiment made full use of the convenience brought by open source thinking. We replaced ECDSA in the Go-ethereum project by Rainbow algorithm. Finally, we tested the feasibility by building a private chain.

Each Ethereum's user has a pair of secret keys, one public and one private. By using Rainbow algorithm, users can use the public key hash as address of the account to identify different users. When the transaction is sent, in order to prove that the transaction is actually carried out by sender itself, the sender must sign the transaction content with its own private key, while other recipients can verify the legality of the signature. On the one hand, this can guarantee that the user's account is not impostor. On the other hand, the senders can't deny the transaction they have signed.

Next, this paper will introduce the experimental environment, the implementation of Rainbow algorithm API and the specific application of it in Ethereum's account generation and transaction transmission and the experimental results.

3.1   Environmental Environment

All the experiments in this paper are executed on a PC with an Intel Core i5 processor and 8GB of RAM. The Operating System is Windows 10 Professional, 64-bit. As for the software, we take Eclipse 4.8.0 as IDE and *go* as the development language.

3.2   API of Rainbow Signature Algorithm

Since Rainbow signature algorithm essentially performs matrix operations on a finite field, we need to complete the implementation of the library that the Rainbow algorithm relies on:

- Element operations on the specific finite field $GF(256)$, such as addition and multiplication.
- Matrix operations on the specific finite field $GF(256)$, such as transposition, inversion and so on.

On this basis, the main functions of Rainbow signature algorithm are implemented: key generation, signature, signature verification, address generation and recover public key. The external interfaces are shown in Table 1.

Table 1. Rainbow Algorithm External Interfaces and its Introduction

Function	Introduction
func GenerateKey() (*PrivateKey)	Generate a public-private key pair
func SignMPKC(hash []byte, prv *mpkc.PrivateKey) ([]byte, error)	Calculate signature by private key and hash of message
func VerifySignatureMPKC(pubkey, mpkc.PublicKey,hash []byte,, signature []byte) bool	Verify signature according to public key, hash of message and signature
func EcrecoverMPKC(hash,sig []byte), ([]byte, error)	Recover public key according to hash of message and signature
func PubkeyToAddressMPKC(pub, mpkc.PublicKey) common.Address	Generate an address based on the public key

3.3   Account Generation Process

When creating a new account, users first need to enter a passphrase. Then the program internally generates a public-private key pair by calling the *GenerateKey()* function of Rainbow algorithm. After the public key is hashed, it is used as an account address, and the public key-address pair is stored in public key storage server, so that the public key is queried according to address information. The private key is encrypted by using passphrase as a password of AES-CTR algorithm. Finally, the account address and randomly generated parameters in the encryption process are written to the wallet file. Among them, Mac values are used to verify the legitimacy of passphrase for preventing others tampering when decrypting. It actually has an effect of signature. This detailed procedure is shown in Fig. 3.

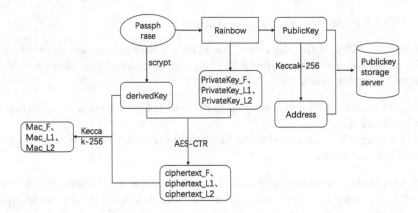

Fig. 3. Account Generation Process.

3.4 Transaction Transmission Process

When a transaction is sent, in order to prove that the transaction was actually carried out by sender itself, the sender must sign this transaction with its own private key. When signing a transaction, first call RLP encoding this transaction, then perform a Keccak-256 hash; next, call *SignMPKC()* function of Rainbow algorithm to sign the hash value of transaction; after that, the signature and sender address are respectively encapsulated into this transaction. This procedure is explained by Fig. 4. Hereafter, the sender broadcasts this signed transaction to each node in the network. When receiving a transaction, node can index the corresponding public key according to address information contained in this transaction, then call *VerifySignatureMPKC()* function of Rainbow algorithm to verify the correctness of signature according to public key. Finally, this transaction is recorded into the blockchain through Proof Of Work (POW) consensus mechanism.

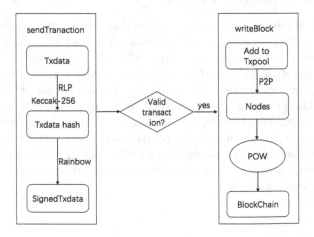

Fig. 4. Transaction Transmission Process.

Here, it should be noted that blockchain nodes need sender's public key when verifying the transaction's signature. So far, there is no standard method of publishing public key. In general, public key is placed in transaction data and sent to the network along with the transaction. In Bitcoin, the signature and public key are combined as a signature script that is a part of the transaction. However, ECDSA used by Bitcoin and Ethereum has a very peculiar nature: public key can be derived from the hash value and signature of transaction. Therefore, Ethereum transactions only contain signature part, and then algorithm is used to derive public key before verifying correctness of the signature.

Since Rainbow algorithm doesn't have the nature as ECDSA and its public key is relatively large, we have added a public key storage server to manage the public key-address pairs information of all users. In this way, when a transaction is sent, the public key is not directly sent out as the part of transaction, but the address generated by public key is encapsulated in the transaction. After that, when verifying the validation of signature, they only need to request the public key storage server for obtaining public key according to address information provided by transaction, then verifying signature.

4   Results

This experiment verifies the correctness of result by building a private chain using the runned geth client. The experimental result shows that after replacing the ECDSA with Rainbow signature algorithm, it does not affect the normal use of its original functions, such as creating an new account, sending a transaction and so on. Moreover, since the Rainbow algorithm is a post-quantum cryptographic algorithm, the Rainbow-based blockchain in the future will be able to resist the attack of quantum computers.

The different choices of parameters o_1, v_1, o_2 in Rainbow algorithm will result in different lengths of public key, private key and signature. The security level

Table 2. The Key and Signature Size of ECDSA and Rainbow Algorithm

Security level (bit)	Algorithm	Private key size (kB)	Public key size (kB)	Signature size (byte)
80	ECDSA	0.010	0.020	40
	Rainbow(13, 17, 13)	19.1	25.1	43
100	ECDSA	0.013	0.026	52
	Rainbow(16, 26, 17)	45.0	59.0	59
128	ECDSA	0.016	0.032	64
	Rainbow(21, 36, 22)	101.5	136.1	79
192	ECDSA	0.024	0.048	96
	Rainbow(34, 63, 34)	434.5	582.9	131
256	ECDSA	0.032	0.064	128
	Rainbow(46, 85, 47)	1073.1	1463.1	178

will vary greatly. In the experiment, this paper refers to several parameter recommendation schemes given by Professor Petzoldt [19] on the finite field $GF(256)$, and compares the key and signature sizes of ECDSA and Rainbow algorithm under different security levels. The specific data is shown in Table 2.

It can be seen from the table that private key and public key of Rainbow signature algorithm are very large. In order to reduce the size of public key, this experiment drew on the special public key construction method in the cyclicRainbow signature scheme [20], and compressed the original Rainbow's public key. The results of public key compression are shown in Table 3.

Table 3. The Key and Signature Sizes of Three Algorithms

Security level (bit)	Algorithm	Private key size (kB)	Public key size (kB)	Signature size (byte)
80	ECDSA	0.010	0.020	40
	Rainbow(13, 17, 13)	19.1	25.1	43
	cyclicRainbow(13, 17, 13)	19.1	10.4	43
100	ECDSA	0.013	0.026	52
	Rainbow(16, 26, 17)	45.0	59.0	59
	cyclicRainbow(16, 26, 17)	45.0	21.7	59
128	ECDSA	0.016	0.032	64
	Rainbow(21, 36, 22)	101.5	136.1	79
	cyclicRainbow(21, 36, 22)	101.5	47.3	79
192	ECDSA	0.024	0.048	96
	Rainbow(34, 63, 34)	434.5	582.9	131
	cyclicRainbow(34, 63, 34)	434.5	185.4	131
256	ECDSA	0.032	0.064	128
	Rainbow(46, 85, 47)	1073.1	1463.1	178
	cyclicRainbow(46, 85, 47)	1073.1	458.3	178

Apart from the size of key and signature, the efficiency of signature algorithm plays an essential role in the blockchain technologies. The ECDSA used in Ethereum has reached a security level of 256 bits. Therefore, this paper compared the signature time and verification time of ECDSA and Rainbow algorithms under the same level. The results are shown in Table 4.

Table 4. The Signature and Verification Time of ECDSA and Rainbow Algorithm

Security Level (bit)	Algorithm	Sign time (ms)	Verify time (ms)	Post-quantum?
256	ECDSA	0.25	0.35	no
	Rainbow(46, 85, 47)	204.78	28.66	yes

As can be seen from the table, the signature verification time of the Rainbow algorithm is obviously much higher than the ECDSA algorithm. At this point, an apples-to-apples comparison of operational speed should't be. The operational speed of two algorithms is shown here for reference only. Nevertheless, regardless of speed, the main selling point of our scheme is its reliance on different computational problems from those used in other branches of cryptography. Considering future attacks of quantum computers, we can sacrifice some time and space in exchange for the security of blockchain.

5   Conclusion

In this paper, we explored the application mode and method of multivariate public key cryptosystem in Ethereum platform. We realized the replacement of the original signature algorithm with *multivariate public key cryptosystem-rainbow scheme* in Ethereum, and verified the feasibility of this scheme by building a private chain. It shows that after replacing the Ethereum's ECDSA with Rainbow signature algorithm, it does not affect the normal use of its functions.

Our design demonstrates that the combination of dedicated multivariate signature scheme and blockchain technologies. Our scheme solves the security problem that blockchain cannot resist quantum computer attacks, and provides more secure and efficient underlying support for the application developed with the blockchain technologies in the future.

Funding Information. This work was supported by National Key R&D Program of China No. 2017YFB0802000.

References

1. Jun, Z., Zhang H.-N., Tang, Y., Li, L.: Blockchain Technical Guide. China Machine Press (2016)
2. Swan, M.: Blockchain: Blueprint for a New Economy. OReilly Media Inc., Sebastopol (2015)
3. Satoshi, N.: Bitcoin: a peer-to-peer electronic cash system (2009). http://www.bitcoin.org/pdf
4. Ethereum White Paper. A next-generation smart contract and decentr-alized application platform (2015). http://github.com/ethereum/wiki/wiki/WhitePaper
5. HYPERLEDGER (2016). http://www.hyperledger.org/BLOCKSTREAM
6. Yong, Y., Fei-Yue, W.: Blockchain: the state of the art and future trends. Acta Automatica Sin. **42**(4), 481–494 (2016)
7. Johnson, D., Menezes, A., Vanstone, S.: The elliptic curve digital signature algorithm (ECDSA). Int. J. Inf. Secur. **1**(1), 36–63 (2001)
8. Shor, P.W.: Polynomial-time algorithms for prime factorization and discrete logarithms on a quantum computer. SIAM J.Comput. **26**(5), 1484–1509 (1997)
9. Divesh, A., Troy, L.: Quantum attacks on Bitcoin, and how to protect against them (2017). arXiv:1710.10377v1quant-ph
10. Quantum-Resistant Ledger (2017). https://github.com/theQRL/QRL

11. Chen, L., Jordan, S., Liu, Y.-K., Moody, D., Peralta, R.: NISTIR 8105 Report on Post-Quantum Cryptography, NIST, 10.6028/NIST.IR.8105 **5** (2016)
12. Post-Quantum Cryptography Round-1-Submissions, NIST (2017). https://csrc. nist.gov/Projects/Post-Quantum-Cryptography/Round-1-Submissions
13. Bernstein, D.J., Buchmann, J., Dahmen, E. (eds.): Post Quantum Cryptography. Springer, Heideberg (2009). https://doi.org/10.1007/978-3-540-88702-7
14. Stark, J.: Making sense of blockchain smart contracts (2018). https://www. coindesk.com/making-sense-smart-contracts/
15. Ding, J., Gower, J.E., Schmidt, D.S.: Multivariate Public key Cryptosystems. Advances in Information Security. Springer, Boston (2006)
16. Patarin, J.: The oil and vinegar signature scheme. In: Dagstuhl Workshop on Cryptography (1997)
17. Ding, J., Schmidt, D.: Rainbow, a new multivariable polynomial signature scheme. In: Ioannidis, J., Keromytis, A., Yung, M. (eds.) ACNS 2005. LNCS, vol. 3531, pp. 164–175. Springer, Heidelberg (2005). https://doi.org/10.1007/11496137_12
18. Buterin, V.: Ethereum go-ethereum source code [EB/OL] (2018). https://github. com/ethereum/go-ethereum
19. Petzoldt, A.: Selecting and Reducing Key Sizes for Multivariate Cryptography (2013)
20. Petzoldt, A., Bulygin, S., Buchmann, J.: CyclicRainbow – a multivariate signature scheme with a partially cyclic public key. In: Gong, G., Gupta, K.C. (eds.) INDOCRYPT 2010. LNCS, vol. 6498, pp. 33–48. Springer, Heidelberg (2010). https://doi.org/10.1007/978-3-642-17401-8_4

Secure Sharing Model Based on Block Chain in Medical Cloud (Short Paper)

Tao Feng[✉], Ying Jiao, and Junli Fang

School of Computer and Communication,
Lanzhou University of Technology, Gansu 730050, China
fengt@lut.cn

Abstract. The cloud storage and sharing system are widely used in medical systems. The unique characteristics of cloud storage enable healthy data being efficiently delivered and retrieved. Nevertheless, traditional medical cloud system suffers two flaws. For one thing, centralized cloud servers are vulnerable to malicious attack and single point of failure. For another, these systems cannot offer a powerful capability to protect medical health data. Blockchain technology is considered to be one of vital technologies of Bitcoin. In this paper, we propose a security model which combines the cloud storage technology with blockchain technology. Our model adopts Delegate Proof of Stake (DPOS) consensus mechanism to ensure that all nodes have unified state in the network. Additionally, the CP-ABE scheme is introduced into the Proxy Re-encryption to store and share medical data which supports the keywords searching. Moreover, we rank medical institutions that different ranks have different duties. In our secure sharing models, there are no central nodes and it is a distributed environment. It not only can reduce the access overhead of the blockchain but also better resist the collusion attack. Furthermore, our security analysis indicates that the proposed scheme achieves provable security under the q-DBDHE assumption in the random oracle model. Then, the comparisons show that our model is more efficient and practical than previous ones.

Keywords: Medical cloud (MC) · Blockchain · DPOS consensus mechanism · Attribute-based Proxy Re-encryption (AB-PRE) · Privacy-preserving

1 Introduction

1.1 Background and Related Work

As everyone pays more attention to health, medical health data is becoming more and more important. Everyone expects the Medical Cloud (MC) to provide desirable health care in a near future. However, MC is still in many concerns remain to be solved for practical applications. In particularly, security storage and sharing issues of medical data have become the biggest concerns in MC. the traditional medical health system stored the user s data through the Semi Trusted Third Party server (DaSCE) in the cloud, which improves the efficiency of storage, retrieval and sharing. However, if DaSCE was attacked or some medical institutions are tempted by high-value sensitive information, the medical data in the DaSCE must be leaked. Researchers in the medical

© ICST Institute for Computer Sciences, Social Informatics and Telecommunications Engineering 2019
Published by Springer Nature Switzerland AG 2019. All Rights Reserved
X. Wang et al. (Eds.): CollaborateCom 2019, LNICST 292, pp. 429–438, 2019.
https://doi.org/10.1007/978-3-030-30146-0_30

cloud have recently explored this problem. Someone has proposed schemes based on medical cloud. He et al. [1] proposed a private cloud platform architecture which includes interoperability services with CCR standards according to the specific requirements, but the architecture has not secure and private. Kyazze's Health Ticket model [2] helps healthcare providers to access users' health data through the web applications and the model uses CP-ABE to protect the user's privacy, but the single encryption mechanism has been unable to protect user's privacy. Hong et al. [3] proposed a hybrid secret sharing scheme based on attribute encryption, which achieved more efficient access control with dynamic policy updating. Seo et al. [4] proposed a scheme which combines traditional proxy re-encryption with ABE, so a user is able to empower designated users to decrypt the re-encrypted ciphertext with the associated attributes of designated users. These solutions can protect medical health data well, but they have some obstacles in sharing data stage. Literature [5] proposed a searchable KP-ABE based proxy re-encryption, the scheme enables a data owner to efficiently share his data to a specified group of users matching a sharing policy and meanwhile, the data will maintain its searchable property, but its communication overhead is relatively large. These schemes are sound but encryption processes are all required to be carried out in the highly centralized cloud severs, which are vulnerable to malicious attack and the single point of failure. This could lead to sensitive health data breaches. Blockchain technology can solve these problems well. Literature [6] proposed a MedRec scheme, it is a novel, decentralized record management system to handle medical data by using the blockchain technology. MedRec use the features of the blockchain and POW consensus mechanisms for authentication and management, as well as ensuring the confidentiality of shared medical data. Fu et al. employed a better encryption algorithm from NTT Service Evolution Laboratory to enforce the decentralizing Privacy. Instead of using POW for protection, they employed Proof-of-Credibility Score to improve the previous system [7]. Shrier and Chang proposed to create a secure environment for storing and analyzing medical data with blockchain technology [8].

1.2 Our Contribution

In this paper, we efficiently address both security storage, sharing and data privacy issues in Medical cloud (MC) by introducing a security model. In our security model, we focus on the important issues mentioned above, i.e., Decentralization, Privacy-preserving, supporting keyword retrieval, collusion resistance, expressiveness and full Security. We simultaneously solve these issues by combined blockchain and MC with the attributed-based proxy re-encryption. In addition, the improved DPOS consensus mechanism is used to ensure that nodes in the network trust each other. Our rigorous security proofs and comprehensive comparisons with other schemes indicate that the secure sharing model is fully secure and efficient. Specifically, our model is characterized by the following attractive features.

2   System Model

In this section, we will illustrate the basic structure of the sharing model, its threat model and its security model.

2.1   Threat Model

In the proposed scheme, it is assumed that the medical institutions and patients in the alliance have valid identity information. Only the owners of medical data are fully trusted; the cloud server is honest but curious. It will abide by the protocol returning the searched ciphertext to the value node R, but it may steal the shared data and information; the shared requester can be malicious and collude with each other to decrypt the data that they don't have permissions.

2.2   System Architecture

System architecture is depicted in Figs. 1 and 2, There are four entities are involved in the scheme: data owner, cloud server, block chain, first-level medical node alliance group (HL1) and second-level medical node alliance group (HL2).

Data Owners: Patients and medical institutions in the alliance can store relevant medical data. Moreover, they need to encrypted data and set sharing permissions structure. When other medical institutions in the alliance wanted to get the data, they need to meet the permissions in order to decrypt the ciphertext and then achieve the original data.

HL1 and HL2:

1. Storage Phase: When the user started a storage request to the general node O_0 in HL1, O_0 broadcast the message to the entire network and the check node C_0 in HL2 verified the identity of user. If the verification steps are successful, O_0 encrypted the user's data using the ABE and stored it in its own database, and then O_0 broadcast the information about the original ciphertext in the entire network again. If over 1/3 of the nodes in the network received this information, O_0 returned to the user a message about accepted the storage request; O_0 send a message about stored the data to the current value node R at this time, R received the message and broadcast to the entire network again. After more than 1/3 of the nodes received the message, R begins to store the data.
2. Sharing Phase: If the medical institution in the alliance wanted to obtain medical data of the certain user. It needs to submit a sharing request to the current value node R at the moment; After received the request, R broadcasts the request information to the entire network, and in HL2, the check node C_1 verified the identity of the institution and determined whether the ciphertext sharing permission was satisfied; If the organization met the sharing permission and more than 1/3 of the nodes received the sharing request, then R use keyword to searched the medical data in the blockchain which was requested. Finally, R will find the corresponding TX block.

Blockchain and Cloud Server:

1. Storage Phase: The ciphertext CT of the original user's data was stored in the cloud server, and the cloud server returned the location information LM of the ciphertext; the public-key PK of R at this time, sharing permission (A, f), the original encryption key, the storage location information LM and the data digest are encrypted and stored in the TX block, then put them into the blockchain according to the structure of the Merkel tree.

2. Sharing Phase: the medical institution wanted to get the data in the alliance and the value node R need to find the corresponding TX block. By using proxy re-encryption for ciphertext CT' and sharing authority structure (A', f'), R can convert the information which is in the TX block and make it satisfied the medical institution. And then, R broadcast this conversion information in HL1. If more than 1/3 of the nodes received this information, it means that the medical data can be shared with the organization; Next, this institution get the CT', the location information LM of the data in the cloud server by decryption and ciphertext CT of the original data. Through these operations, the medical institution can get the plaintext data. In order to ensure the security of the medical data after sharing, the value node R can revoke the sharing request information at any time through the re-encryption algorithm.

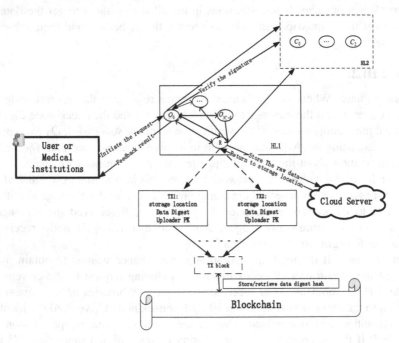

Fig. 1. Storage phase of the security model

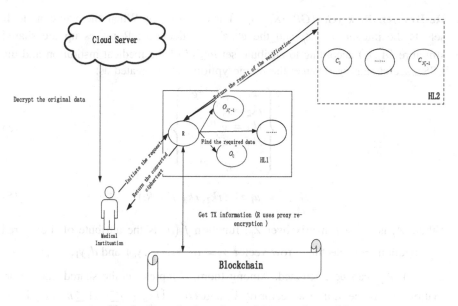

Fig. 2. Data sharing phase of the security model

2.3   Concrete Algorithm

In this section, we will give the specific algorithm construction of our proposed scheme:

1. **Setup** $Setup(\tau, U) \rightarrow (GP, PK, MSK)$: the security parameter of the preset system is τ, the attribute set of the medical institution in the alliance is U. There is a bilinear map $e : G \times G \rightarrow G_T$, G is the additive cyclic group of prime order p and the generator of G is g, $g_1 \in G$. There are the following Hash functions:

$$H_1 : (0,1)^{2k} \rightarrow Z_p; H_2 : (0,1)^{2k} \rightarrow G_T; H_3 : (0,1)^* \rightarrow G;$$
$$H_4 : (0,1)^* \rightarrow G_T; H_5 : (0,1)^k \rightarrow Z_p; H_6 : (0,1)^k \rightarrow G_T \tag{1}$$

With choosing the random number $\alpha, \beta \in Z_p$, calculate: $H_x = g^\beta, x \in U$.
Global parameter: $GP = (p, g, g_1, g^\alpha, e(g,g)\alpha, H_1, \cdots, H_6)$.
Public key: $PK = (g, g_1, g^\alpha, e(g,g)^\alpha, H_x)$.
Master key: $MSK = (g^\alpha, \alpha)$

2. **KeyGen** $keyGen(GP, PK, MSK, u_i) \rightarrow (PK_i, SK_i)$: the value node R input GP, PK, MSK, data owner's attribute set $u_i \subseteq U$ and the medical institution attribute set $u_l \subseteq U$, R selects random number $\lambda \in Z_p$. The public-private key pair is calculated as follows:

$$SK_i = (u_i, K_i = g^\alpha g^{\alpha\lambda}, P_i = g^\lambda, (K_i = H_3(u_i^n)^\lambda)_{u_i^n \in U})(SK_l \text{ same argument}) \tag{2}$$

$$PK_i = g^{SK_i}(PK_l \text{ same argument}) \tag{3}$$

3. **Re-KeyGen** Re $keyGen(GP, SK_i, (A_l, f_l), PK_l) \rightarrow rk_{i \rightarrow l}$: When the value node R selects the integers $\theta \in Z_p$ and the g^θ, g_1^θ is calculated; R makes up the shared structure (A_l', f_l') according to attribute set $u_l \subseteq U$ of the medical institution and the LSSS secret sharing scheme; the re-encryption key is created as:

$$\begin{cases} rk_1 = g^\alpha g^{\alpha\lambda} g_1^\theta \\ rk_2 = g^\theta \\ rk_3 = g^{\lambda H_5(\delta)} \\ rk_4 = C'_{(u_l', f')} \\ R_i = K_i^{H_5(\delta)} \end{cases} \tag{4}$$

$$rk_{i \rightarrow l} = (u_i, rk_1, rk_2, rk_3, rk_4, R_i) \tag{5}$$

Where A_l' is a $a \times b$ matrix over Z_p, function $f'(a)$ is the attribute of the shared organization; By selecting a row vector $\vec{y} = (d, y_1, \cdots, y_n)$, and $d, y_1, \cdots, y_n \in Z_p$. $\vec{\xi}_{a_m} = \vec{y} \cdot A_{a_m}'$ can be calculated. Among them, d represents the shared data information, A_{a_m}' is the m-th row vector of A_l', and $U_l = \{l : f'(a) \subseteq U, 1 \leq m \leq a\}$ is the attribute set in (A_l', f').

4. **Encrypt the Medical Data:**
   (1) Encrypt the original data $Enc_1(D, (A_i, f_i), PK_i) \rightarrow CT_i$: The value node R use CP-ABE to encrypt the user's public key, the original medical data and the shared permission structure, and then the ciphertext CT_i is generated and store it in the cloud server.
   (2) Encrypt Data digest and other information $Enc_2(PK, LM, D_i, t, (A_i, f_i), k_i) \rightarrow CT_i' \rightarrow TX_i$: The system public key PK, the shared structure (A_i, f_i), the storage location LM of the original data in the cloud, the data digest D_i and the key k_i of the decrypt original data is encrypted by R, and then generate the ciphertext CT_i'. R put the CT_i' into the TX block.

5. **Re-Encrypt** $CT_i ReEnc(rk_{i \rightarrow l}, CT_i, PK_l, (A_l', f')) \rightarrow CT_l$: The check node C verifies the identity of the medical institution in the alliance which need to get the shared data, and if the verification is successful, R performs the following calculations:

$$CT_l = (X_1, X_2, (A_l', f'), (Y_l, Z_l)_{l=1}^{N_1^*-1}, \mu) \tag{6}$$

Among them:

$$X_1 = \zeta \cdot e(g, g)^{\alpha \cdot d}, X_2 = g^d, X_3 = g_1^d, \zeta \in G_T \tag{7}$$

$$Y_1 = \frac{(g^\alpha)^{\xi_{a_1}}}{H_1(f'(1))}, \cdots, Y_l = \frac{(g^\alpha)^{\xi_{a_1}}}{H_1(f'(N_1^* - 1))} \tag{8}$$

$$Z_l = g^{\tau_1}, \cdots, g^{\tau_l}, \tau_1, \cdots, \tau_l \in Z_p \tag{9}$$

$$\mu = \frac{e(X_1, rk_1) \cdot e(X_2, rk_2)}{\Pi_{l \in U}(e(Y_l, rk_3) \cdot e(Z_l, R_{f(1)}))^{w_l}}, w_l \in Z_p \text{ and } \prod_{l \in U} w_l \cdot \xi_{a_l} = d \quad (10)$$

6. **IndexGen** $Index(GP, D'_i) \rightarrow ID_i$ and ID_l: When R utilizes the global parameter GP, the data digest D_i of original data, and then the MAC_i is calculated; similarly, we can get MAC_l, ID_i and ID_l in Re-encrypt ciphertext.

7. **Re-Decrypt** Re $Dec(SK_l, CT_l) \rightarrow CT_i$: the value node R checks whether the attribute set u_l matches the shared structure (A_l, f_l); If there is a match, the medical institution can decrypt CT_l uses the CP-ABE to get CT_i, and then the decryption keys k_i can be calculated:

$$k_i = \frac{X_1}{\gamma^{\frac{1}{H(v)}}}, \gamma \text{ is the part of ciphertext } v \in G_T \quad (11)$$

$$CT_i = \frac{A_1 \cdot e(A_3, g^\theta)}{\gamma}, \theta \in Z_p \quad (12)$$

8. **Decrypt the original data ciphertext** $Dec(CT_i, k_i, GP) \rightarrow d$: Using the formula

$$d = \frac{A_1}{\Pi_{i \in U}(e(Y_l, g^\lambda)e(X_2, R_{f(1)}))^{w_i}} \quad (13)$$

3 Security Proof

In this section, the security of proposed sharing model is proved in the random oracle model that it is against chosen plaintext attacks (CPA).

Lemma 4.1: Based on the q-DBDHE assumption, if the scheme in [9] is secure against chosen plaintext attacks (CPA) in the random oracle model, our scheme is secure against CPA.

Proof: Suppose there exists a probabilistic polynomial time adversary A can attack our scheme with a non-negligible advantage ε. We prove that the following q-DBDHE game can be solved by the challenger B with the advantage $\frac{\varepsilon}{2}$.

Initialization: Challenger B randomly picks $x, y \in Z_p$ and multiple hash functions $H_1, H_2, H_3, H_4, H_5, H_6$ to calculate $e(g, g)^z = e(g, g)^x e(g, g)^y$. The global parameters $GP = (p, g, g_1, g^\alpha, e(g, g)\alpha, H_1, \cdots, H_6)$ and $PK = (g, g_1, g^\alpha, e(g, g)^\alpha, H_x)$ are sent to the adversary A.

Inquiry 1:

(1) **Private Key Query:** The adversary A queries for the private key SK_U according to the attribute set U and shared permission structure (A_*, f). If U satisfies the shared permission structure (A_*, f), challenger B chooses to output a value at $\{0,1\}$ and the game ends; If U is not satisfied, Challenger B picks a set of data to make $m = (m_1, \cdots, m_n) \in Z_p, m_1 = -1, m \cdot A_* = 0$.

(2) **Re-encrypt Key Query:** Select the attribute set u_l to determine whether it conforms to the shared permission structure (A_l, f). If u_l meets the shared permission structure (A_l, f), challenger B chooses to output the value at $\{0,1\}$, the game ends. Instead, the private key SK_l is obtained; the re-encrypt key $rk_{i \to l} = (u_i, rk_1, rk_2, rk_3, rk_4, R_i)$ is calculated and sent it to the adversary A.

Challenge: The adversary A selects two data digests D_1, D_2 which has equal length and sends them to the challenger B. The challenger B selected one bit attributes from $\theta \in (0, 1)$ and encrypt it with the shared permission structure (A_*, f). Then B gets the ciphertext CT_* and sent CT_* to the adversary A. If $e(g, g)^{\alpha^{q+1}s}$ and T are equal, CT_* is a valid ciphertext.

Inquiry 2: Repeat Phase 1 adaptively.

Guess: The adversary A submits the guess θ' of θ. When $\theta' = \theta$, the simulator represented challenger B outputs $T = e(g, g)^{\alpha^{q+1}s}$; when $\theta' \neq \theta$, the simulator represented challenger B outputs $T \neq e(g, g)^{\alpha^{q+1}s}$. In the game, the advantage of the adversary A is $\left| \Pr[\theta' = \theta] - \frac{1}{2} \right|$; if $\theta = 0$, it means that the advantage A can't get any useful information and the probability of guessing correctly is 1/2. When $\theta = 1$, it means that the adversary A can get all the information about the ciphertext and the original data, so the advantage is $1/2 + \varepsilon$. Therefore, the advantage of the probabilistic polynomial time adversary in the q-DBDHE game is $\Pr(\theta' = \theta) - \frac{1}{2} = \frac{1}{2}\left(\frac{1}{2} + \varepsilon\right) + \frac{1}{2} \cdot \frac{1}{2} - \frac{1}{2} = \frac{\varepsilon}{2}$. To conclude, if the adversary has non-negligible advantage ε in the constructed game, he can solve the q-DBDHE problem with the non-negligible advantage $\frac{\varepsilon}{2}$. Based on the q-DBDHE assumption, there is no adversary has significant advantage in our security game and our scheme is secure.

4   Analysis and Comparison

1. Privacy Analysis of Medical Data Content

In order to protect medical health data while sharing and storing, our scheme uses DPOS to rank the medical institutions. Moreover, the scheme adopts a combination of the CP-ABE algorithm and the proxy re-encryption algorithm to store and share medical data, which is safer than the symmetrical encryption. The data owners presets the shared permission structure of the medical data, They use the attribute-based proxy Re-encryption algorithm stores the complete ciphertext of original data in the cloud server, and stores important information such as storage location and data digest in the blockchain in order to facilitate the searching and sharing of the medical data. The requesters want to obtain the medical data, they need to find the corresponding block by the keyword searching in blockchain, and then they can find the ciphertext in the cloud server. In our security model, the ciphertext is stored separately, so our model realizes the privacy of medical data content.

2. Collusion Resistance

When the value node R generates the re-encryption key, R could verify the attribute set $u_l \subseteq U$ and share permission structure (A_l, f) of medical institutions through the X_2. In our model, rk_3, rk_4, R_i and $\delta \in G_T$ are associated; rk_1, rk_2, rk_4 and $\theta \in Z_p$ are associated; $\delta \in G_T$ is encrypted by rk_4, shared permissions (A_i, f) and $\theta \in Z_p$. Therefore, when rk_1, rk_2, rk_3, R_i is hacked lead to the original data is changed, the re-encrypted ciphertext will also be invalid according to the above relationship. If the attribute sets, sharing permissions, and rk_4 are tampered, you can verify it by calculating the following formula:

$$e(X_2, H_6(X_1, X_2, (Y_l, Z_l)_{l=1}^{N_1^*-1}, u_i, (A_i, f))) = e(g, g) \tag{14}$$

3. Scheme Comparison

In this paper, we compared the proposed scheme with some of classic cloud storage schemes, as is shown in Table 1. Among the schemes, the scheme of Akinyele [10] and Hong [3] are the single attribute-based encryption cloud storage scheme. The schemes of Seo [4], Shi [11], and Luo [12] use attribute-based proxy re-encryption, but they rely on third parties to complete storage and sharing. In particular, the Seo's solution required multiple data centers, so it is difficult to ensure that the medical data has not tampered during data is transported and stored. Moreover, except for the Shi's solution, other schemes which the ciphertext are not searchable, these schemes have hindered the data sharing. Our solution can realize all the functions on the table at the same time, and select the required information according to the actual situation, so it is more suitable for the practical application of sharing.

Table 1. Comparison of sharing schemes.

Scheme	Key-word search	Attribute encryption	Proxy re-encryption	Attribute-based Proxy re-encryption	Blockchain technology	No third party
[10]	×	√	×	×	×	×
[3]	×	√	×	×	×	×
[4]	×	√	√	√	×	×
[11]	√	√	√	√	×	×
[12]	×	√	√	√	×	×
our	√	√	√	√	√	√

5 Conclusion

In order to ensure the security of medical health data in the process of storage and sharing, we proposed a way to combine blockchain and cloud storage; the attribute-based encryption was introduced into the proxy re-encryption which supports the keywords searching to store and share the medical data in the security situation. This way avoids the problem that some share requesters want to secondary forward shared data. The ciphertext of original data and ciphertext of re-encrypted are stored separately, which has the possibility of preventing the collusion. Through the security proof and privacy preserving analysis, our model has practicality. Compared with other existing models, the proposed model gives a better performance in terms of sharing medical data and privacy preserving.

References

1. He, C., Fan, X., Li, Y.: Toward ubiquitous healthcare services with a novel efficient cloud platform. IEEE Trans. Biomedical Eng. **60**(1), 230–234 (2013)
2. Kyazze, M., Wesson, J., Naude, K.: The design and implementation of a ubiquitous personal health record system for South Africa. Stud. Health Technol. Informatics **206**(206), 29–41 (2014)
3. Cheng, H., Min, Z., Deng-Guo, F.: Achieving efficient dynamic cryptographic access control in cloud storage. J. Commun. **32**(7), 125–132 (2011)
4. Seo, H.J., Kim, H.W.: Attribute-based proxy re-encryption with a constant number of pairing operations. J. Inf. Commun. Convergence Eng. **10**(1), 53–60 (2012)
5. Liang, K., Susilo, W.: Searchable attribute-based mechanism with efficient data sharing for secure cloud storage. IEEE Tran. Inf. Forensics Secur. **10**(9), 1981–1992 (2017)
6. Azaria, A., Ekblad, A., Vieira, T.: MedRec: using blockchain for medical data access and permission management. In: 2nd International Conference on Open and Big Data (OBD), pp. 25–30. IEEE (2016)
7. Fu, D., Fang L.: Blockchain-based trusted computing in social network. In: IEEE International Conference on Computer & Communications, pp. 19–22. IEEE (2017)
8. Kuo, T., Ohno-Machado, L.: Model chain: decentralized privacy-preserving healthcare predictive modeling framework on private blockchain networks. Int. J. Netw. Secur. Appl. **1802**, 01746 (2018)
9. Liang, K., Susilo, W.: Searchable attribute-based mechanism with efficient data sharing for secure cloud storage. IEEE Trans. Inf. Forensics Secur. **10**(9), 1981–1992 (2017)
10. Akinyele, J.A., et al.: Securing electronic medical records using attribute-based encryption on mobile devices. In: 1st ACM Workshop on Security and Privacy in Smartphones and Mobile Devices, pp. 75–86. ACM (2011)
11. Yanfeng, S., Jiqiang, L., Zhen, H.: Attribute-based proxy re-encryption with keyword search. PLoS ONE **9**(12), 116325 (2014)
12. Luo, S., Hu, J., Chen, Z.: Ciphertext policy attribute-based proxy re-encryption. In: Soriano, M., Qing, S., López, J. (eds.) ICICS 2010. LNCS, vol. 6476, pp. 401–415. Springer, Heidelberg (2010). https://doi.org/10.1007/978-3-642-17650-0_28

A Smart Topology Construction Method for Anti-tracking Network Based on the Neural Network

Changbo Tian[1,2], YongZheng Zhang[1,2(✉)], Tao Yin[1,2], Yupeng Tuo[1,2], and Ruihai Ge[1,2]

[1] Institute of Information Engineering, Chinese Academy of Sciences, Beijing 100093, China
{tianchangbo,zhangyongzheng,yintao,tuoyupeng,geruihai}@iie.ac.cn
[2] School of Cyber Security, University of Chinese Academy of Sciences, Beijing 100049, China

Abstract. Anti-tracking network is the effective method to protect the network users' privacy confronted with the increasingly rampant network monitoring and network tracing. But the architecture of the current anti-tracking network is easy to be attacked, traced and undermined. In this paper, We propose smart topology construction method (STon) to provide the self-management and self-optimization of topology for anti-tracking network. We firstly deploy the neural network on each node of the anti-tracking network. Each node can collect its local network state and calculate the network state parameters by the neural network to decide the link state with other nodes. At last, each node optimizes its local topology according to the link state. With the collaboration of all nodes in the network, the network can achieve the self-management and self-optimization of its own topology. The experimental results showes that STon has a better robustness, communication efficiency and anti-tracking performance than the current popular P2P structures.

Keywords: Anti-tracking network · Topology · Neural network · Cyber security

1 Introduction

1.1 Background and Motivation

Along with the popularization and development of network, the Internet has entered into every aspects of our lives. And the Internet has evolved into a global platform for social networking, finance, education, communication, health care and so on. Large amount of personal information is transferred in the network,

Supported by the national natural science foundation of China under grant No. U1736218.

and most of them has huge economic benefits. So, the easy reach of the Internet has posed a serious threat to the online privacy of network users [1].

Even though the end-to-end encryption technology has been developed very mature, but it can only protect the data content of communications against the eavesdropping of the adversaries. The significant information about the identity of the sender and the receiver or the network addresses of the source and the destination are still in danger [2]. The adversaries can easily monitor or eavesdrop the network users' online behavior, and aggregate the data of users' communication to make a big profit.

In order to protect the online privacy of network users, anonymous communication (AC) network emerges as the times require [3]. However, most of the current AC networks focus on the anonymity of network users' identities at the application layer. From the network layer, when confronting with the network tracing and monitoring, they have not too many advantages in tracking-resistance. So, we propose the anti-tracking network which is used to mitigate the network tracing and network monitoring in the network layer. The anti-tracking network is built on the P2P network and the weakness of the P2P network, such as the cut point and key point problem, the problem of topology management and so on [4], have a big impact on the performance of anti-tracking network. Motivated by this, we devote into the research of smart topology construction method to build a smart and robust anti-tracking network.

1.2   Limitation of Prior Art

Anti-tracking network is used to fight against the network tracing and network monitoring. Because the anti-tracking network is built on P2P network, there are some disadvantages which seriously affect the performance of anti-tracking network [5–7].

- Cut point and key point problem: Cut points and key points are the critical threats to the P2P-based anti-tracking networks. The disconnection of cut points will split the network into different blocks. The key points are the core points to transfer messages and they are always the bottleneck of message transmission. So, the attack to the cut points and key points is the common means to undermine the anti-tracking network. If so, the anti-tracking network can not provide good performance to the network users.
- The monitor of C&C channel: As we know, the traditional anti-tracking network needs the controller to construct, manage and optimize the network topology. The frequent communication between the anti-tracking network and the controller may lead to the exposure of the controller's identity [8,9]. Once the controller is traced, the anti-tracking network will be taken over or fall into an unavailable situation.
- The fixed transmission path: Most of the anti-tracking network has the fixed topology structure and fixed message transmission path. This provides tremendous convenience for the adversary to trace the traffic flow. And, the adversary can easily probe the topology structure and destroy the anti-tracking network.

1.3 Proposed Approach

To solve the problems discussed above, we propose a smart topology construction method for anti-tracking network based on neural network, called STon. The basic principle of STon is that we deploy the neural network algorithm on each node of the anti-tracking network. Each node collects its local network state periodically to generate the network state parameters. Then, each node executes the neural network algorithm with the parameters to decide the connection or disconnection with other nodes. Each node only has the ability to adjust its local network topology structure. But, according to the collaboration of all nodes in the anti-tracking network, the network has the ability to adjust and optimize its topology structure by itself. With STon, the anti-tracking network doesn't need the controller to manage or optimize the topology structure any more, it achieves the self-management and self-optimization of topology structure.

To make a straightforward sense of our proposal, we conclude STon with three steps:

- Deployment of neural network in each node.
- Collection of network state parameters.
- Calculate the link state and adjust the topology.

1.4 Contributions

We make three key contributions in this paper as follows.

- We propose a smart topology construction method (STon) for anti-tracking network. STon achieves the self-management and self-optimization of network topology and effectively avoid the emergence of cut points and key points. STon makes the anti-tracking network more robust.
- We propose a parameter collection algorithm (PCA) to collect the local network state and generate the corresponding parameters for the deployed neural network. PCA can effectively collect the network state even if the network topology is dynamic.
- We propose connection judgement algorithm (CJA) which calculates the link state with network state parameters. CJA achieves that each node can optimize its local topology according to its network state. With the collaboration of all nodes in the network, anti-tracking network has the ability to optimize its own topology and always keeps in a stable and robust situation by itself without the management of the controller.

2 The Overview of STon

The main principle of STon is that the nodes in anti-tracking network have the ability to change its link state dynamically according to the network state for the purpose that the network can manage and optimize its topology intelligently and automatically. So, the network does not change its topology arbitrarily, but changes it to a more stable and robust structure. In this way, the maintenance expense and potential risks [10,11] of P2P network would be curtailed greatly. And the anti-tracking performance and robustness of the network would be improved highly. Before the detail discussion of STon, we need to introduce two important concepts as follows.

- **Candidate node.** Candidate nodes are defined as the nodes which can be choosed to calculate the link state by the current node. We denote the neighboring nodes collection of the current node as N, and denote the current node's neighbor' neighbor collection as S. Then the candidate nodes collection $C = \{N, S\}$.
- **Node stable situation.** For the current node u and one of its candidate nodes v, node u calculate with the parameters of node v and get the result. If the result is 1 and $v \in N$, or the result is 0 and $v \in S$, then the current node is in *node stable situation*. Node stable situation means the link state of the current node has been the same with the adviced link state by the neural network, and needs no optimization.

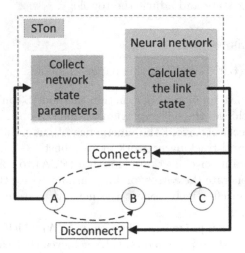

Fig. 1. The overview of STon.

Each node has to deploy the neural network, collect the network state parameters and calculate the link state with candidate nodes. As showed in Fig. 1, there is a simple topology that node A links to node B and node B links to node C. If node A is not in the *stable situation*, the node A needs to collect the network state parameters of node B and node C, then calculates link state with them. In Fig. 1, the link state between node A with other two nodes is subject to the calculation result of the neural network deployed in each node in advance. At last, with the calculation result, the node A updates its local topology.

So, STon has big advantages in the management and optimization of the topology for anti-tracking network. Anti-tracking network with STon will not need the controller's management in case of the traceback of C&C channel of the controller. From the aspect of robustness of network, the topology can change according to the changes of network state. With the parameters of network state, STon prefers to update its topology to a more stable and efficient structure in case of the emergence of cut points or key points. From the aspect of anti-tracking, the dynamic change of topology according to the network state will change the message transmission path which makes the network monitoring and traffic tracing more difficult.

3 Methodology

3.1 Parameter Collection Algorithm

Parameter Selection. How each node adjust its local topology is subject to the parameters calculated by the STon. In order to make sure the network optimizes its topology towards a more robust and anti-tracking structure, we comply with the following rules to select the network state parameters.

- **Robustness.** P2P-based anti-tracking network is an open and distributed platform. Each node can connect or disconnect with the network freely. This process may result in the emergence of cut points and key points which are the potential threats to the network. So, we need to select the parameters conductive to avoid the cut points and key points.
- **Anti-tracking.** STon has the ability to optimize its topology by itself. So, without the communication to the controller, C&C channel is hard to be monitored. Inspired by the infeasibility of monitoring the global Internet, cross-domain communication [12] is proposed to improve the anti-tracking performance. So, we also consider the cross-domain between two neighbouring nodes.
- **Invulnerability.** Invulnerability is the precondition of the availability of anti-tracking network. When some nodes, even the cut points or the key points, are removed, the network can still recover its topology to a robust and stable structure. This power is what the anti-tracking network needs. We also select the parameters which make sure the network has rapid resilience.

In view of the above, we classify the parameters into two categories showed as follows.

- The parameter of network topology. This kind of parameters can be counted directly according to the network topology information and used for the optimization of the network topology.
  - $C\_Domain:$ The domain of current node.
  - $D\_Domain:$ The domain of candidate node.
  - $C\_Degree:$ The degree of current node.

- *D_Degree:* The degree of candidate node.
- *C_CandidateAmount:* The candidate node number of current node.
- *C_NeighborsAvgDegree:* The average degree of all neighboring nodes of the current node.
- *SharingNode:* The sharing node number between the current node and the candidate node. If the two nodes are neighboring nodes, the parameter is 0.
- *DifferenceOfDegree:* The difference of the degree between the current node and the candidate node.

- The parameter of network traffic. This kind of parameters is generated by the traffic information and used for the optimization of traffic load balance. In unit time, each node counts the amount of message transfered by it and calculates the average value to generate the parameters.
  - *C_MessageAvg:* The average transmission quantity of the current node in unit time.
  - *D_MessageAvg:* The average transmission quantity of the candidate node in unit time.
  - *C_NeighborsAvgMessage:* The average transmission quantity of all neighboring nodes of the current node in unit time.
  - *DifferenceOfAvgMessage:* The difference of average transmission quantity between the current node and the candidate node.

The original parameters need to be normalized and limited in the interval [0, 1] for the further calculation of the neural network.

C_Domain and *D_Domain* denote the domain of the current node and the candidate node. We firstly number each domain from $1 \sim n$ and n denotes the total number of all domains. Then the two parameters can be normalized by the Eq. (1) in which i denotes the domain number. Except the two parameters mentioned above, the other parameters have the value of 0 or any positive integer. So, we normalize the other parameters with Eq. (2) in which x denotes the parameter value.

$$f(i) = \frac{i}{n} \tag{1}$$

$$f(x) = \frac{1}{1+x} \tag{2}$$

Parameter Collection Algorithm. Each node uses PCA to collect the network state information and generates the corresponding parameters. For the parameter of network topology, only when the local topology of the current node changes, the current node updates this kind of parameters. For the parameter of network traffic, each node counts the amount of the message transfered by it in each unit time and computes the average value as this kind of parameters. Because the parameter of traffic information changes as the network traffic changes, we need recalculate the parameter of traffic information to get the latest network traffic information in each unit time. Algorithm 1 gives the pseudocode of PCA. In Algorithm 1, we can only collect the basic parameters directively generated by the network topology and network traffic. The other parameters, such as *C_CandidateAmount*, *C_NeighborsAvgDegree*, *SharingNode*, *Difference-OfDegree*, *C_NeighborsAvgMessage*, *DifferenceOfAvgMessage*, need further calculations of the basic parameters from the current node and its candidate nodes.

Algorithm 1. Parameter Collection Algorithm

Input: v: current node. *totalmessages*: the total amount of transfered messages.
Output: P: Parameter collection
 1: **function** UPDATETOPOLOGYPARA(v)   ▷ The function of collecting the parameter of network topology.
 2:     $domain \leftarrow GetDomain(i)$ ▷ Get the parameter of domain.
 3:     $degree \leftarrow GetDegree(i)$ ▷ Get the parameter of degree.
 4:     $P \leftarrow domain, degree$
 5: **end function**
 6:
 7: **function** PCA($v, totalmessages$)
 8:     **while** True **do**
 9:         **if** $TopologyChange(v)$ **then**   ▷ Check whether the topology has been changed. If $True$, optimize the parameters of network topology.
10:             UPDATETOPOLOGYPARA(v)
11:         **end if**
12:         **if** $UnitTime(v)$ **then** ▷ Check whether it's time to update the parameters of network traffic.
13:             $avgmessage \leftarrow totalmessages/totaltimes$ ▷ Calculate the average value of total amount of transfered messages.
14:             $P \leftarrow avgmessage$
15:             $totaltimes + +$ ▷ Accumulate the number of unit times.
16:         **end if**
17:     **end while**
18: **end function**

3.2   Connection Judgement Algorithm

With CJA, the anti-tracking-network can achieve the self-management and self-optimization of topology. In detail, each node asks for the parameters of all its candidate nodes, and executes CJA with its candidate node one by one to calculate the link state. At last, this node updates its local topology according to the calculated link state.

The Structure of the Neural Network. Firstly, we introduce the neural network deployed in each node. We use two RBMs to construct a two-layer neural network. The first RBM is Gaussian-Bernoulli RBM (GBRBM) [13], because the input of the first RBM is real number distributed in the interval $[0, 1]$, but the output value is 0 or 1. The second RBM is Bernoulli-Bernoulli RBM (BBRBM) [13], both of its input and output are 0 or 1. The structure of the proposed neural network is showed in Fig. 2. The input of GBRBM is the parameters collected by PCA, and the output of GBRBM is as the input of BBRBM to calculate the link state.

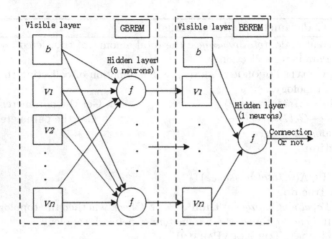

Fig. 2. The structure of neural network.

Parameter Training of Neural Network. In the parameter training of RBM, we usually use Contrastive Diversity (CD) [14] to train the weights between the nodes in different layers and the bias of each layer.

In order to improve the accuracy and efficiency of parameter training, we use genetic algorithm (GA) to optimize the weights of the neural network. The fitness function of GA is defined based on the distribution of nodes, domains and the traffic load of each node. The fitness function is showed in Eq. (3). α, β, γ are the coefficients. d, d_{avg} separately denote the degree of current node and the average degree of its neighboring nodes. num_i denotes the number of nodes in the same domain with the current node. m, m_{avg} separately denote the amount of messages transfered by the current node and average amount of messages transfered by all its candidate nodes.

$$F = \alpha \left(\frac{1}{1 + |d - d_{avg}|} \right) + \beta \left(\frac{1}{1 + num_i} \right) + \gamma \left(\frac{1}{1 + |m - m_{avg}|} \right) \quad (3)$$

Crossover and mutation are the important steps to optimize the computational process of GA. Firstly, we need to calculate the crossover and mutation rates according to the evolution situation. In the optimization process of weights, in order to keep both the items with high fitness value and the diversity of the population in GA, we use Eq. (4) to calculate the crossover and mutation rates.

In Eq. (4), λ_1, λ_2 are the constants in the interval $(0, 1)$. f_{max} denotes the highest fitness in the population of GA. f_{avg} denotes the average fitness of the whole population.

$$p = \begin{cases} \lambda_1 \frac{f_{max}-f}{f_{max}-f_{avg}} & f \geq f_{avg} \\ 1 - \lambda_2 \frac{f_{max}-f_{avg}}{f_{max}-f} & f < f_{avg} \end{cases} \tag{4}$$

If we use Eq. (4) to calculate the crossover rate, f denotes the higher fitness of the two items in crossover calculation. If we use Eq. (4) to calculate the mutation rate, f denotes the fitness of the item in mutation calculation. So, with Eq. (4), when the fitness is too high, the crossover and mutation rate are low so that GA can avoid the premature convergence. When, the fitness is too low, the crossover and mutation rate are high so that GA can expand the item range to search the best solution.

In crossover calculation, we take two different crossover methods to generate two different items. One item prefers a balanced crossover of its parents, but another item prefers crossover with its parent has high fitness. We use g_i and h_i separately denote the genetic value of two items in crossover calculation, and s_i denotes the genetic value of a new item generated by the crossover calculation of g_i and h_i. The crossover calculation is showed in Eq. (5) in which p_c denotes the crossover rate. If we calculate the balanced crossover, we use Eq. (6) to replace the parameters Δ_i and Θ_i in Eq. (5). If we calculate the crossover inclined to the parent with higher fitness, we use Eq. (7) to replace the parameters Δ_i and Θ_i in Eq. (5).

$$s_i = p_c \Delta_i + (1 - p_c)\Theta_i \tag{5}$$

$$\begin{aligned} \Delta_i &= g_i \\ \Theta_i &= h_i \end{aligned} \tag{6}$$

$$\begin{aligned} \Delta_i &= \begin{cases} g_i & f_i \geq f_j \\ max(p_c g_i + (1 - p_c)h_i, g_i) & f_i < f_j \end{cases} \\ \Theta_i &= \begin{cases} g_j & f_j \geq f_i \\ max(p_c g_j + (1 - p_c)h_i, g_j) & f_j < f_i \end{cases} \end{aligned} \tag{7}$$

In mutation calculation, we randomly choose one value from the interval $[x_1, x_2]$ with the probability p_m to replace the genetic value of a item. The upper and lower bounds of the above interval are defined as Eq. (8) in which x_{min} and x_{max} separately denote the minimum and maximum weight of the neural network to keep the mutation calculation in a reasonable range. When the fitness of the item is approximate to the best fitness of the population, the interval of mutation will be small; on the contrary, when the fitness of the item is too low, the interval of mutation will be large. In this way, we not only avoid the impact of mutation to the items with high fitness, but also expand the range of mutation items in case of the premature convergence.

$$\begin{aligned} x_1 &= (1 + \frac{f}{f_{max}})x_{min} \\ x_2 &= (1 - \frac{f}{f_{max}})x_{max} \end{aligned} \tag{8}$$

GA is used to search for the approximate optimal weights for the neural network. When the GA converges, we can use the parameters generated by GA to train the neural network for higher efficiency and fast convergence. The training method of RBM has been discussed detailly in [14], and needs no further elaboration.

Connection Judgement Algorithm. CJA is used to calculate the link state according to the network state. CJA is a two-layer neural network based on RBM. Each node uses CJA to calculate the network state parameters to decide the link state with its candidate nodes. And then, the node updates its local topology according to the calculated link state.

The output of CJA is 0 or 1. If the output is 0, the node will break the connection with the candidate node if they are neighboring nodes. If the output is 1, the node will ask for connection to the candidate node and send its network state parameters to it. If the candidate node receives the parameter sent by the node who asks for the connection, it will also execute the CJA with the received parameters to make its own decision. Only when the output of the candidate node's CJA is also 1, the two nodes will build the connection. Or, the candidate node will refuse the connection. The pseudocode of CJA is showed as Algorithm 2.

4   Experiment and Analysis

We propose STon to achieve the self-management and self-optimization of anti-tracking network's topology. The anti-tracking network with STon has better performance in robustness, load balance and anti-tracking performance. We compare STon with the two popular P2P topologies, ZeroAccess [15] and TDL-4 [16], and analyze the advantages of STon.

ZeroAccess is based on a layered and unstructured P2P topology and its structure is familiar with Gnutella network [17]. So, we use the open source data of Gnutella topology from Stanford university [18] to simulate the ZeroAccess. TDL-4 is structured P2P topology based on Kademlia protocol [19]. We also use the open source date of Kademlia topology from Illinois university [20] to simulate the TDL-4. We use Igraph to simulate the above three P2P topology structures with 6000 nodes.

4.1   Evaluation of Robustness

To evaluate the robustness [21], we firstly give a evaluation formula (9) to quantify the evaluation results.

$$\beta_p = \frac{The\ node\ number\ of\ MCS(G(p))}{The\ node\ number\ of\ G} \tag{9}$$

In formula (9), $G(p)$ denotes the subgraph after remove p percent of the nodes from the original network. $MSC(G(p))$ denotes the maximum connected subgraph of $G(p)$. In the experiment, we use two different ways to remove nodes from the network to compare the robustness.

Algorithm 2. Connection Judgement Algorithm

Input: u:current node. C: candidate nodes collection. N: neighboring nodes collection.

1: **function** CALCULATEPARAMETERS(u, C, N)   ▷ The function of calculating the parameter of network topology.
2:     **for** v *in* C **do**
3:         $parameter = GetParameter(v)$ ▷ Get the parameters of candidate node v.
4:         $connection = RBM(parameter)$ ▷ Calculate the link state.
5:         **if** $connection = 0$ **then**
6:             **if** v *in* N **then**
7:                 $Breaklink(v)$ ▷ Break the connection with node v if they are neighboring nodes.
8:                 $Update(u)$ ▷ Update the network state parameter and candidate nodes collection of current node.
9:             **end if**
10:         **else if** $connection = 1$ **then**
11:             $parameter_u = GetParameter(u)$ ▷ Get the parameter of current node u.
12:             $result = RequestLink(v, parameter_u)$ ▷ Current node ask for connection with the candidate node v.
13:             **if** $result = 1$ **then** ▷ when the calculation result of candidate node u is 1, it means the candidate node also agrees with the connection with current node.
14:                 $BuildConnection(v)$ ▷ Build connection between current node and candidate node.
15:                 $Update(u)$
16:             **end if**
17:         **end if**
18:     **end for**
19: **end function**
20:
21: **function** LISTENCONNECTIONREQUEST(v)   ▷ The function of listening the request of connection.
22:     **while** GetConnectionRequest() **do**   ▷ If there is a request of connection, the current node need to calculate and judge the connection with it.
23:         $parameter_v = GetParameter(v)$
24:         $connection_v = RBM(parameter_v)$
25:         **if** $connection_v = 0$ **then**
26:             $RefuseLink(v)$ ▷ If the calculatoin result is 0, current node refuses to build connection with it.
27:         **else if** $connection_v = 1$ **then**
28:             $BuildConnection(v)$
29:             $Update(u)$
30:         **end if**
31:     **end while**
32: **end function**

- **Random-p removal.** In each round, we remove p percent of nodes from the network randomly.
- **Top-p removal.** In each round, we remove p percent of nodes with highest degree from the network.

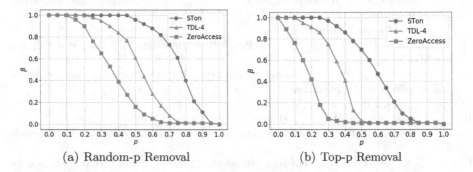

(a) Random-p Removal   (b) Top-p Removal

Fig. 3. The influence of node removal on the robustness of networks

From the experiment results in Fig. 3, no matter in which node removal experiment, STon has the best robustness. Because when some nodes disconnect the network, the network topology will be changed and also may be broken into different blocks. Without the management of the controller, the TDL-4 and ZeroAccess can not management their topologies by themselves, so the topologies of the two P2P networks will be more worse along with the more nodes disconnect from the network. But, STon has the ability of self-management of its topology. STon can perceive the changes of topology and optimize it according to the network state to a stable situation by the calculation of network state parameters. From the two experiments, we can see that the top-p removal has the greater damage to the network, because the nodes with highest degree always have a more important position in network communication. So, TDL-4 and ZeroAccess perform worse in top-p removal. But for STon, the performance of the two experiments decreases not too much. This is because the self-optimization of topology always keeps STon in a stable situation as the network state changes.

4.2   Evaluation of Load Balance

Network load balance is an important evaluation index of quality of service for anti-tracking network [22]. We evaluate the network load of the three topology structures with the following index under the same network size and the same message transmission volume.

- **Load node number:** The number of nodes take part in the message transmission in the network.
- **The highest load:** In each round of message transmission, the amount of transferred message by the node with highest load in the network.

The index of *load node number* is higher, then in the same amount of transferred message, more nodes take part in the message transmission. In this way, the transferred message will be shared to more nodes in case that a few nodes take on the more traffic load. The index of *highest load* is to measure the network load through the worst case.

We set up 20 rounds for message broadcasting and the TTL of the message is 4. After each round, we count the corresponding index of network load to evaluate the load balance performance of the three topology structures.

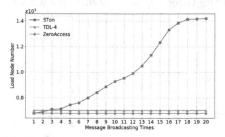 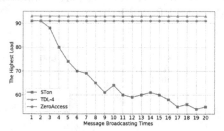

(a) The changes of load node number according to the continuous broadcasting

(b) The changes of the highest load according to the continuous broadcasting

Fig. 4. The performance of network load balance comparision experiment

As illustrated in Fig. 4, TDL-4 and ZeroAccess have no ability of self-optimization. So, if the topology structure has no changes, the network traffic load also has no changes. But, STon has an obvious changes in the index of *load node number* and *the highest load*. This means STon can optimize its topology as the network traffic changes. The ability of self-management and self-optimization of topology will provide huge convenience and advantages to ensure the efficient communication and strong tracking-resistance for anti-tracking network.

4.3 Evaluation of Anti-tracking

Anti-tracking is the priority for anti-tracking network. The monitoring range of the adversary has a direct impact on the intensity of anti-tracking performance. So, we use the number of traced nodes by the adversary to measure the anti-tracking performance. Firstly, we need introduce two indexes for anti-tracking evaluation as follows.

- **TPR: True Positive Rate.** TPR denotes the proportion of the traced target nodes in all target nodes. TPR is used to evaluate the anti-tracking ability of the network. The less target nodes are traced, the stronger anti-tracking performance the network has.
- **FPR: False Positive Rate.** FPR denotes the proportion of the traced target nodes in all the traced nodes. FPR is used to evaluate the difficulty of the adversary to trace the target nodes. Because the adversary can trace a lot of nodes in the network, but may be hard to trace the target nodes.

We randomly choose 50% nodes as target nodes from the network to send message to a specific node. Assume that the adversary can only monitor the traffic flow to trace the target nodes. For convenience, we assign all the nodes into 10 domains equally. We assume the adversary can monitor one or more domains to trace the target nodes. By increasing the monitoring domains, we evaluate the anti-tracking performance of the three topology structures with the index of TPR and FPR.

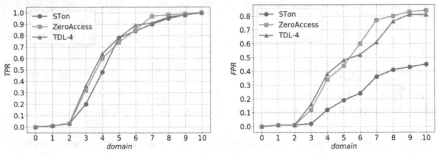

(a) The changes of TPR along with the increase of monitoring domains

(b) The changes of FPR along with the increase of monitoring domains

Fig. 5. The performance of anti-tracking comparision experiment

In Fig. 5, the values of X-axis are the number of domains monitored by the adversary. In Fig. 5(a), along with the increase of monitoring domains, the number of traced target nodes increases exponentially and the performance of the three topology structures is almost the same. This is because the anti-tracking performance is subject to the monitoring range of the network by the adversary. Just think that if the adversary can monitor the whole the Internet, there will be no chance to escape from the network tracing and network monitoring. But in Fig. 5(b), the FPR of STon increases slowly. From the anti-tracking experiment, we can conclude that STon improve the anti-tracking performance by the means of dynamic changes of network topology and transmission path. In this way, the adversay will trace too many unrelated nodes. So, STon makes the adversary to trace the target nodes more difficult.

5   Conclusion and Future Work

In this paper, we propose an smart topology construction method for anti-tracking network based on the neural networks, called STon. STon achieves the self-management and self-optimization of network topology which improve the robustness, communication efficiency and anti-tracking performance of the network. Firstly, we use genetic algorithm to optimize the weights of the neural network and help the neural network converge fastly. After deployed the neural network on each node of the network, each node has the ability to calculate the network state parameters to evaluate the link state. With the calculation result of the neural network, each node can optimize its local topology. With the collaboration of all nodes in the network, the network has the ability of self-management and self-optimization of its topology. This kind of network has stronger robustness, communication efficiency and anti-tracking performance than the current popular network topology structures.

But, there are still some weakness in our work. Firstly, we need to train the neural network previously to make sure the algorithm can suit to the network state in practice. Once the network state has a drastic change, and the network state may be totally different with the training data. Then, the performance of the neural network may be reduced greatly, even lose the efficacy. In the future, we will take further research on the online weight learning and rapid adaption to new network state of the neural network.

Acknowledgements. We thank the anonymous reviewers for their insightful comments. This research was supported in part by the national natural science foundation of China under grant No. U1736218.

References

1. Shirazi, F., Simeonovski, M., Asghar, M.R., et al.: A survey on routing in anonymous communication protocols. ACM Comput. Surv. (CSUR) **51**(3), 51 (2018)
2. Ren, J., Wu, J.: Survey on anonymous communications in computer networks. Comput. Commun. **33**(4), 420–431 (2010)
3. Dixon, L., Ristenpart, T., Shrimpton, T.: Network traffic obfuscation and automated internet censorship. IEEE Secur. Priv. **14**(6), 43–53 (2016)
4. Kang, S.: Research on anonymous network topology analysis. In: 2015 International Conference on Automation, Mechanical Control and Computational Engineering. Atlantis Press (2015)
5. Feinerman, O., Haeupler, B., Korman, A.: Breathe before speaking: efficient information dissemination despite noisy, limited and anonymous communication. Distrib. Comput. **30**(5), 339–355 (2017)
6. Zang, W., Zhang, P., Wang, X., et al.: Detecting sybil nodes in anonymous communication systems. Procedia Comput. Sci. **17**, 861–869 (2013)
7. Mittal, P., Borisov, N.: Information leaks in structured peer-to-peer anonymous communication systems. ACM Trans. Inf. Syst. Secur. (TISSEC) **15**(1), 5 (2012)

8. Caballero, J., Poosankam, P., Kreibich, C., et al.: Dispatcher: enabling active botnet infiltration using automatic protocol reverse-engineering. In: Proceedings of the 16th ACM Conference on Computer and Communications Security, pp. 621–634. ACM (2009)

9. Cho, C.Y., Caballero, J., Grier, C., et al.: Insights from the inside: a view of botnet management from infiltration. In: Usenix Conference on Large-scale Exploits & Emergent Threats: Botnets (2010)

10. Danezis, G.: Designing and attacking anonymous communication systems. University of Cambridge, Computer Laboratory (2004)

11. Kotzias, P., Matic, S., Caballero, J.: CARONTE: detecting location leaks for deanonymizing tor hidden services. In: ACM SIGSAC Conference on Computer & Communications Security. ACM (2015)

12. Yin, T., Zhang, Y., Li, J.: AppBot: a novel P2P botnet architecture resistant to graph-based tracking. In: 2016 IEEE Trustcom/BigDataSE/ISPA, pp. 615-622. IEEE (2016)

13. Yamashita, T., Tanaka, M., Yoshida, E., et al.: To be Bernoulli or to be Gaussian, for a restricted Boltzmann machine. In: International Conference on Pattern Recognition, pp. 1520–1525. IEEE Computer Society (2014)

14. Hinton, G.E.: Training Products of Experts by Minimizing Contrastive Divergence. MIT Press, Cambridge (2002)

15. Kerkers, M., Santanna, J.J., Sperotto, A.: Characterisation of the Kelihos.B Botnet. In: Sperotto, A., Doyen, G., Latré, S., Charalambides, M., Stiller, B. (eds.) AIMS 2014. LNCS, vol. 8508, pp. 79–91. Springer, Heidelberg (2014). https://doi.org/10.1007/978-3-662-43862-6_11

16. Golovanov, S., Soumenkov, I.: TDL4 top bot. Kaspersky Lab Analysis (2011)

17. Ripeanu, M.: Peer-to-peer architecture case study: Gnutella network. In: Proceedings of the First International Conference on Peer-to-Peer Computing, pp. 99–100. IEEE (2001)

18. Leskovec, J.: Stanford Large Network Dataset Collection (2014) [OL]. http://snap.stanford.edu/data/index.html

19. Maymounkov, P., Mazières, D.: Kademlia: a peer-to-peer information system based on the XOR metric. Revised Papers from the First International Workshop on Peer-to-Peer Systems (2002)

20. Godfrey, B.: Repository of Availability Traces (2015) [OL]. http://pbg.cs.illinois.edu/availability/

21. Scott, D.M., Novak, D.C., Aultman-Hall, L., et al.: Network robustness index: a new method for identifying critical links and evaluating the performance of transportation networks. J. Transp. Geogr. **14**(3), 215–227 (2006)

22. Zeng, Z., Veeravalli, B.: Design and performance evaluation of queue-and-rate-adjustment dynamic load balancing policies for distributed networks. IEEE Trans. Comput. **55**(11), 1410–1422 (2006)

A Novel Feature-Selection Approach Based on Particle Swarm Optimization Algorithm for Intrusion Detection Systems (Workshop Paper)

Jianzhen Wang[✉] and Yan Jin

Business College of Shanxi University, Taiyuan 030031, Shanxi, China
aawangjz@163.com, px_happy@163.com

Abstract. This paper proposes a feature selection approach, based on improved Discrete Particle Swarm Optimization (DPSO), to solve the "dimension disaster" problem in data classification; it is named Progressive Binary Particle Swarm Optimization (PBPSO). This feature selection approach is highly problem-dependent and influenced by the locations of particles. It adopts the principle of "partial retention - change - reduction of duplication - update" in the process of selection, and defines a new fitness function describing the correlation between the features and class labels. Experimentation was conducted using of the KDDCup99 data set to evaluate our proposed PBPSO. The experimental results show that 14 features were selected from the original data space with 41 features. Three classic classifiers, namely J48, Naive Bayes and ID3, were then used to further evaluate the performance of the selected features. The classification accuracy rates on the different classifiers achieved using the selected feature subset are similar to those achieved using the original feature set. The training time is, however, significantly reduced. In comparison with other similar algorithms, including Genetic Algorithm GA and Greedy Algorithm FGA. The results show that the PBPSO extracts fewer features, achieves slightly higher classification accuracy, and less time consuming in terms of model training. It has been demonstrated that the PBPSO enhances the practicability of certain classification algorithms in handling high-dimensional data.

Keywords: Feature selection · Discrete particle swarm algorithm · Correlation analysis · Correct classification rate · Modeling efficiency

1 Introduction

With the tremendous growth of computer network technology, various issues of network security are arising accordingly. Firewall is the first gate for network security. Traditional firewall, based on the static security technology, is unable to prevent attacks from the inter-network, attacks bypassing firewall, new attacks and is unable to

Supported by Shanxi Provincial Department of Science and Technology, Natural Science Fund Project, 2016; Shanxi Scholarship Council, Scholarship Fund Project, 2016; State Administration of Foreign Experts, Overseas Training Fund Program.

X. Wang et al. (Eds.): CollaborateCom 2019, LNICST 292, pp. 455–465, 2019.
https://doi.org/10.1007/978-3-030-30146-0_32

effectively defense virus [1]. IDS, Intrusion Detection System, is the second gate for network security, which is able to dynamically monitor inter-network or host computer, to detect various attacks in time and response, and to compensate for the defect of the static security technology.

According to the technology approach adopted, IDS is comprised of misuse detection and anomaly detection [2, 3]. Currently, misuse detection is the major monitoring approach for IDS, and the attacking feature database is its core component. misuse detection can detect attacks of known types with low rate of false alarm and high rate of under reporting, and do nothing for the new unknown attacks, which requires constantly upgrading of feature database to guarantee the completeness of system detection ability. The completeness and accuracy of attacking feature database of misuse detection directly affect the performance of IDS based on misuse detection. Anomaly detection, based on normal behavior, builds feature outline and cannot detect the specific type of attacks with high rate of false alarm and low rate of under reporting, but is able to detect the new unknown attacks. Anomaly detection mostly adopt the statistical analysis or based on the approach of rule description, builds behavior feature outline of normal user in the system. These two detection approaches are complementary in the aspects of applicable objects and ways of detection, and so on. The effective combination of both can offset the defects of each other, improving the performance of intrusion detection.

From key point of computer network or within the host computer, IDS collects data and make classification. Only a small proportion of massive feature of data source has something to do with attacking classification. These massive and redundant features cause enormous drop of classification efficiency and classification accuracy of attacking classifier. Caruana pointed out that variety of feature significantly affected the quality of inductive learning [4]. Extracting effective feature subset from massive features not only improves the performance of learning algorithm, but increases the training speed of algorithm as well. The smaller a feature subset is, the more representative the selected feature might be, the higher the quality of generated rule is. Consequently, feature selection is critical to increase the classification efficiency of network attacking [5], and is the core issue of Intrusion Detection System [6]. The feature selection of intrusion detection in fact is strategy that we are seeking for an optimal point on the aspects of reduction of rate of false alarm and rate of underreporting and improvement of system performance. Effective feature selection is the focus of this paper.

2 Feature-Selection Approach

Choosing some most effective features from a set of features to achieve the objective of reducing the dimension of feature space, this process is called feature selection. The basic task of feature selection is to find out a feature subset from a known features set, in order to describe the known samples in a consistent way [7]. The quantity of feature selection of intrusion detection should be appropriate, neither too many nor too few. Too many features mean strong particularity which is easy to cause under reporting, intensive computation and poor real-time affect the system efficiency. Too few features mean strong universality which is easy to cause false alarm. Before and after feature selection, the distribution of category should be as consistent as possible. The classification accuracy cannot drop obviously.

According to whether depend on machine learning algorithm, feature selection can be divided into two models: filter model and wrapper model [8]. In the filter model, feature selection approach is independent of any inductive learning algorithm. It can select feature subset by using a preprocessing pattern, selected feature subset is independent of any particular algorithm, and then inductive learning. In the wrapper model, feature selection approach directly optimizes the certain particular algorithm, by evaluating algorithms' generalization ability for the selected feature subset in each step to achieve feature selection. Wrapper model regards feature selection as the searching issue within all possible feature space.

Filter model has higher computation efficiency than wrapper model, and is a classification algorithm which is independent of the ultimate choice. But because the adopted evaluation function is likely to lead to incorrect orientation, causing feature selection deviate from the ultimate objective, and less effective. Wrapper model wraps learning algorithm into feature selection algorithm, classification accuracy of subset ultimately selected is pretty higher. But when data size is higher, it needs to take massive computing resources. Feature selection is actually a combinatorial optimization issue, which has proven to be NP difficult problem [9, 10]. Search algorithm and evaluation function are two main components of feature selection algorithm. Adopting some heuristic search algorithm to select a features subset of suboptimal can reduce the computational workload. After the generation of feature subset, use an evaluation function to calculate whether the feature subset is good or bad, and compare the result with previous best one. After several iterations, the best fitted features subset is the ultimate selected result.

This paper focuses on the issue of feature selection for intrusion detection. The data set contains massive data and computation is time-consuming, it is inappropriate to use wrapper model. Therefore, this paper adopts filter model to select feature subset, takes advantage of particle swarm algorithm with fast convergence to search within the feature space, simultaneously introduce the correlation analysis to guide the search of algorithm.

3 Particle Swarm Optimization Algorithm

3.1 Basic Particle Swarm Algorithm

PSO, Particle Swarm Optimization [11] is a global random search algorithm based on swarm intelligence proposed by James Kennedy, an American social psychologist and Russell Eberhart, an electrical engineer in 1995 through simulating birds' migrating and flocking behavior during the process of foraging.

First of all, PSO initialize a group of random particles (random solution), and then find the optimal solution through iteration. In the each iteration, the particles update themselves through tracking two extreme values. One is the optimal solution found by the particle itself, which is called individual extreme value Pi, the other one is the optimal solution found by the whole population, which is called global extreme value Pg. Assume size of particles population is N, particles' current position is represented as $X_i^k = (x_1^k, \cdots, x_n^k, \cdots, x_N^k)$, $x_n^k \in [l_n, u_n]$, $1 \leq n \leq N$, l_n and u_n represent the upper and lower bound of nth dimension respectively. Particles' current speed is $V_i^k = (v_1^k, \cdots, v_n^k, \cdots, v_N^k)$, V_i^k is limited between the maximum value $V_{max}^k = (v_{max,1}^k, \cdots, v_{max,n}^k, \cdots, v_{max,N}^k)$ and minimum value $V_{min}^k = (v_{min,1}^k, \cdots, v_{min,n}^k, \cdots, v_{min,N}^k)$. After particles find the two extreme values above, then update speed and position of themselves according to formulas (1) and (2).

$$V_i^{k+1} = \omega V_i^k + c_1 r_1 (P_i^k - X_i^k) + c_2 r_2 (P_g^k - X_i^k) \tag{1}$$

$$X_i^{k+1} = X_i^k + V_i^{k+1} \tag{2}$$

Where ω is inertia weight, c1, c2 are constant, called learning factors, used to adjust the relative importance of individual extreme value and global extreme value. r1, r2 are random numbers uniformly distributed among (0, 1). P_i^k, P_g^k represent position of individual extreme value and position of global extreme value for particles' kth iteration. Conditions for iteration termination are that either reach the maximum time of iteration or meet the minimum threshold of fitness. The first part of formula (1) is particles' speed in previous step, indicating particles' current state, the second part is the reflection of particle itself, which is the cognitive part, particles adjust their speed and position for next step by thinking the position of themselves, in this way particles have sufficiently strong global search capability to avoid falling into a local minimum, the third part represents that particles update their next step through the information exchange with other particles.

3.2 Discrete Binary Particle Swarm Optimization Algorithm

In 1997, Kennedy and Eberhart proposed Discrete Binary Particle Swarm Optimization (BSPO) of PSO algorithm, which make it into the field of combinatorial optimization [12]. BPSO adopts binary encoded form, constrains each dimension of x_i^k and p_i^k as 1 or 0 within BSPO model, but there is no such constraint for speed v_i^k. The Sigmoid function of speed (formula 3) indicates the possibility of position state changes. Formula for speed update of BPSO is unchanged, but formula for position update is altered to formula (4). Where rand() is random numbers among [0, 1]. Within the discrete binary model, v_{max}^k is preserved, playing the role of constraining the ultimate possibility of X_i^k is 1 or 0. In fact, normally $v_{max}^k i$ s set between ± 4.0, so that there is at least one opportunity making $S(v_{max}^k) \approx 0.0180$, meaning under the condition of upcoming state changing.

$$S(v) = \frac{1}{1 + e^{-v}} \tag{3}$$

$$\begin{aligned} &\text{if } (\text{rand}() \prec S(v_i^k)) \text{ then } x_i^k = 1 \\ &\text{else } X_i^k = 0 \end{aligned} \tag{4}$$

PSO can be directly used to solve continuous problem, while intrusion detection feature selection is non-continuous problem. Consequently, this paper uses BPSO Algorithm, each particle has its own position and speed, and particles' position represents one possible solution for the problem. The implement of algorithm requires the re-definition of particle coding scheme, particles' position and speed, and the updating rules.

4 Feature-Selection Approach Based on BPSO for IDS

4.1 Data Set Selection

This paper adopts KDDCup99 data set [13]. This dataset is a 9 weeks data selected from a simulated U.S. Air Force LAN, which has great similarity with real-world scenarios and is widely used to test the efficiency of intrusion detection system. KDDCup99 data set is divided into marked training dataset and unmarked testing dataset. According to Table 1, training dataset has different probability distribution with testing dataset. Testing dataset contains some types of attacking which do not appear in the training dataset, making intrusion detection more realistic. According to Table 2, training dataset contains one kind of normal identifier class-Normal and 22 kinds of training attacking types. There are another 14 kinds of attacking types appearing only in the testing dataset. In KDDCup99 data set, each connected record contains 41 fixed feature attribute and one kind of class identifier. Identifier is used to indicate that this connected record is either normal or a certain specific attacking type. Within 41 fixed feature attributes, nine of them are discrete and the rest is continuous.

Table 1. Distribution of connection types in 10% KDDCup99 data set

Attack classes	Training data		Testing data	
	Number	Percentage	Number	Percentage
Normal (0)	97278	19.691066	60593	19.481463
Probe (1)	4107	0.831341	4166	1.339425
DoS (2)	391458	79.239142	229853	73.900826
U2R (3)	52	0.010526	228	0.073305
R2L (4)	1126	0.227926	16189	5.204981

4.2 Algorithm Design

Traditional dimension reduction method is a non-supervisory algorithm. Despite dimension reduction of data source can simplify the data source, the low-dimensional data is not completely equivalent to the original data. The key of taking advantage of particle swarm algorithm to solve the issue of feature selection rests on the selection of coding scheme and fitness function [14, 15]. Coding is determined by the essence of the issue and the space where the particle is, the fitness function reflects the connection between practical issues and optimizing algorithm.

Table 2. Sample size in 10% KDDCup99 training dataset

Attack classes	Attack label name
Normal	Normal97278
DOS	Back2203, Land21, Neptune107201, Pod264, Smurf280790, Teardrop979
Probe	Ipsweep1247, Nmap231, Portsweep1040, Satan1589
R2L	Ftp_write8, Guess_passwd53, Imap12, Multihop7, Phf4, Warezclient1020, Warezmaster20, Spy2
U2R	Buffer_overflow30, Loadmodul9, Perl3, Rootkit10
Total	494,020

4.2.1 Coding Scheme

Coding scheme is that for a given network states data set D including N-dimensional feature, the goal of feature selection is to select a feature subset R making objective function optimal [16].This paper, based on the analysis of KDDCup99 standard data set, determines to make natural number coding for particles. Using natural number to represent feature attributes, in this way, coding is simple and easy to implement. Several of features compose of a feature subset, each feature subset is a natural number coding sequence. The natural number coding sequence corresponds to a particle of the population, while each particle corresponds to a feasible solution, the combination of different features attributes of 41 features attributes.

4.2.2 Definition of Particles Position, Speed, and the Updating Rules Within PSO Algorithm

Each particle's position, within PSO algorithm, is a potential solution [17, 18]. Particles' position is the natural number sequence between 1 and 41, numbers of sequence dimension represent numbers of feature attributes. Dimensions of each particle vary from 2 to 41, respectively representing various attributes from 2 to 41. The dimensions are determined by a parameter. For each dimension, use PSO algorithm to optimize, finally make comparison for optimal solutions corresponding each dimension obtained, then select best fitness as the ultimate solution, realize extracting effective features. In the sequence which is represented by particles' position, because sequence of various features in feature subset has nothing to do with ultimate result. To prevent repetitive combination, particles' position coding is arranged from small to big, like (3, 9, 16, 38).

Particles' speed determines the updating way of particles' position. This study proposes rules for position updating: "partially preserved-alter-compare and duplicate checking-updating". In this way, the rules ensure all possibility of combinations of different feature attributes, and avoid the repetitive search, improving the convergence rate for the algorithm. For instance, a particle's current position is (2, 4, 5), preserve 2 unchanged in the next step, and then compare historical position, randomly altering the rest coding and there is no repetition with historical position. In this instance, if there is historical position like (2, 7, 9), there will not be such combination like (2, 7, 9) when 4 and 5 is altered, coding varying from 1 to 41. At initial, the particles' population is randomly generated, the size of particles' population is 30, and the maximum times of iteration are 1000.

4.2.3 Definition of Fitness Function

In the feature selection within filter model, selection of fitness function is very significant [19]. This paper adopts correlation evaluation method, uses the correlation of feature attributes and attacking types to evaluate particles' pros and cons, furthermore define the fitness function. Particles' position within PSO algorithm represents the independent variable in correlation function, and particles' speed is the alteration of attribute number, altering and updating particles' coding in the search process of algorithm iteration. Correlation of various feature attributes and attacking types is the fitness function, and take advantage of joint probability of each attribute and identifier class to measure how great or small the correlation is, use discrete PSO algorithm search to find the most correlated set of solutions as feature subset this study extracts. Fitness function of particles is computed according to formulas (5) and (6). Where i and j contain all attributes of feature attributes set, C is identifier class. The bigger the value of fitness function is, the greater the correlation of the feature attribute and the class is, the higher the fitness of particles is.

$$f = \frac{\sum_j \rho(A_j, C)}{\sum_i \sum_j \rho(A_i, A_j)} \tag{5}$$

$$\rho(A, B) = \frac{P(AB) - P(A)P(B)}{\sqrt{P(A)(1 - P(A))P(B)P(1 - P(B))}} \tag{6}$$

4.3 Experimental Result

Based on the ideas above to program, PSO tool-kit is developed in Matlab [20]. After the running of PSO algorithm main programming, it returns optimal solutions and its corresponding fitness. The experimental result extracts 14 feature attributes to constitute feature subset, out from 41 fixed feature attributes within each connected record in KDDCup99 Data set, reducing feature dimensions, see Table 3.

Table 3. Features subset using BPSO

Features number	Features subset
14	Duration, Protocol_type, Service, Flag, Src_bytes, Dst_bytes, Land, Wrong_fragment, Count, Srv_count, Dst_host_count, Dst_host_diff_srv_rate,Dst_host_same_src_port_rate, Dst_host_srv_diff_host_rate

5 Algorithm Validation Test

Select part of data from 10% KDDCup99 training data set to test algorithm. To keep the classification information of the original data, adopt sampling method without replacement. For classes more than 10,000 samples, randomly select 10 percent of them as the sample, for classes less than 10,000 samples, select them all, ultimately 22 classes are generated, and 57,141 samples, in total, constitute experimental sample collection, see Table 4.

Table 4. Details of sample dataset

Attack classes	Attack label name
Normal	Normal9800
DOS	Back2203, Land21, Neptune10720, Pod264, Smurf28000, Teardrop879
Probe	Ipsweep1247, Nmap231, Portsweep1040, Satan1589
R2L	Ftp_write8, Guess_passwd53, Imap12, Multihop7, Phf4, Warezclient1020, Warezmaster20, Spy2
U2R	Buffer_overflow30, Loadmodul9, Perl3, Rootkit10
Total	57,141

Weka, based on Java, is an intelligent analysis environment used for data mining and knowledge discovery [21]. In this experimental sample collection, use classic classification like J48, ID3 and Naive Bayes provided by Weka platform to build model training learning, respectively taking advantage of original feature attributes of KDDCup99 data set and 14 features attributes after feature selection. Adopting 10-fold cross-validation verify the influence classification result of feature selection algorithm this study proposed has on various classification algorithm [22, 23]. It turns out that after feature selection based on BPSO algorithm, there's slight increase for the rate of correct classification, significantly reducing the time to build a classifier, see Tables 5 and 6.

Table 5. Classification results of features collection

Classification	Sample number	Features number	Correctly classified rate	Classifier build time
J48	57141	41	99.8740%	12.33
ID3	57141	41	91.9983%	7.08
NaiveBayes	57141	41	96.8411%	2.23

Furthermore, analyze feature subset respectively extracted by discrete BPSO algorithm, Genetic Algorithm (GA) and First Greedy Algorithm (FGA) [24, 25], see Table 7. Adopt Weka platform built-in J48 decision tree classifier and Naive Bayes classifier respectively to make classification, verifying operating performance of feature

Table 6. Classification results of features subset

Classification	Sample number	Features number	Correctly classified rate	Classifier build time
J48	57141	14	99.8782%	2.77
ID3	57141	14	91.9983%	4.95
NaiveBayes	57141	14	96.1341%	0.55

selection algorithm based on BPSO and other feature selection algorithm. Experimental result show that the algorithm of this paper can achieve relatively higher rate of correct classification by using fewer numbers of features, and has a big advantage on running time as well, which is an effective feature selection method, according to Tables 8 and 9.

Table 7. Features subset of different algorithms

Algorithms	Features number	Features subset
BPSO	14	duration, protocol_type, service, flag, src_bytes, dst_bytes, land, wrong_ fragment, srv_count, dst_host_count, dst_host_diff_srv_rate, dst_host_same_src_port_rate, count, dst_host_srv_diff_host_rate
GA	19	protocol_type, service, flag, src_bytes, dst_bytes, land, wrong_fragment, num_shells, srv_count, same_srv_rate, diff_srv_rate, srv_diff_host_rate, dst_host_srv_count, dst_host_diff_srv_rate, dst_host_same_src_port_rate, dst_ host_rerror_ rate, count, hot
FGA	15	protocol_type, service, flag, src_bytes, dst_bytes, land, wrong_fragment, root_shell, count, srv_count, diff_srv_ rate, dst_ host_srv_count, dst_ host_srv_ diff_host_rate, dst_host_rerrorr_ rate

Table 8. Classification results of features subset using J48

Algorithms	Sample number	Features number	Correctly classified rate	Time of build model
BPSO	57141	14	99.8782%	2.77
GA	57141	19	99.8530%	4.16
FGA	57141	15	99.9057%	5.31

Table 9. Classification results of features subset using NaiveBayes

Algorithms	Sample number	Features number	Correctly classified rate	Time of build model
BPSO	57141	14	96.1341%	0.55
GA	57141	19	96.0029%	0.83
FGA	57141	15	96.1457%	0.76

6 Conclusion

First of all, analyzes the key issues of feature selection of intrusion detection systems and determines the feature selection mode. Based on the analysis of the basic particle swarm optimization algorithm and the discrete particle swarm optimization algorithm, Proposed an improved feature selection method BPSO-P based on discrete particle swarm optimization. Design the BPSO-P algorithm group natural number coding scheme, define the particle position, velocity and update rules, define the fitness function of evaluating the particle's advantages and disadvantages, using the correlation evaluation method, according to the correlation degree of the particle, 14 feature attributes were selected from all 41 features of KDDCUP99 data set. BPSO-P's coding method and location update rule in this paper can be used not only in the feature selection of intrusion detection, but also can process other similar discrete problems. It has certain application value.

Finally, 57141 data were extracted from the KDDCUP99 data set to construct the experimental sample space. The classification model was built using the classic classifier in the Weka platform. The ten-fold cross-validation method was used to verify the effectiveness of the algorithm. The experimental results show that BPSO-P feature selection algorithm proposed in this paper is applicable to a variety of classifiers, which can slightly improve the correct classification ratio, and the modeling time of the classifier is significantly shortened. Compared with other feature selection algorithms, BPSO-P can obtain a higher correct classification ratio by using fewer feature numbers, which is an effective feature selection method.

References

1. Daoyuan, H., Jinghua, S.: Network security (2004)
2. Anderson, J.P.: Computer security threat monitoring and surveillance (1980)
3. Spafford, E.H.: Crisis and aftermath. Commun. ACM **32**(6), 678–687 (1989)
4. Caruana, R., Freitag, D.: Greedy attribute selection. In: ICML, pp. 28–36. Citeseer (1994)
5. Cox, I.J., Miller, M.L., Bloom, J.A., Honsinger, C.: Digital Watermarking, vol. 53. Springer, Heidelberg (2002)
6. Tataru, R. L., El Assad, S., D'eforges, O.: Improved blind DCT watermarking by using chaotic sequences. In: 2012 International Conference for Internet Technology and Secured Transactions, pp. 46–50. IEEE (2012)
7. Dash, M., Liu, H.: Feature selection for classification. Intell. Data Anal. **1**(1), 131–156 (1997)
8. Kohavi, R., John, G.H.: Wrappers for feature subset selection. Artif. Intell. **97**(1), 273–324 (1997)
9. John, G.H., Kohavi, R., Pfleger, K., et al.: Irrelevant features and the subset selection problem. In: Machine Learning: Proceedings of the Eleventh International Conference, pp. 121–129 (1994)
10. Chen, B., Hong, J., Wang, Y.: The problem of finding optimal subset of features. Chin. J. Comput.-Chin. Edn. **20**, 133–138 (1997)

11. Eberhart, R.C., Kennedy, J.: A new optimizer using particle swarm theory. In: Proceedings of the Sixth International Symposium on Micro Machine and Human Science, New York, NY, vol. 1, pp. 39–43 (1995)
12. Kennedy, J., Eberhart, R.C.: A discrete binary version of the particle swarm algorithm. In: 1997 IEEE International Conference on Systems, Man, and Cybernetics. Computational Cybernetics and Simulation, vol. 5, pp. 4104–4108. IEEE (1997)
13. Tavallaee, M., Bagheri, E., Lu, W., Ghorbani, A.-A.: A detailed analysis of the KDD cup 99 data set. In: Proceedings of the Second IEEE Symposium on Computational Intelligence for Security and Defence Applications (2009)
14. Gong, S., Gong, X., Bi, X.: Feature selection method for network intrusion based on gqpso attribute reduction. In: 2011 International Conference on Multimedia Technology (ICMT), pp. 6365–6368. IEEE (2011)
15. Zhang, X.Q., Gu, C.H.: A method to extract network intrusion detection feature. J. South China Univ. Technol. (Nat. Sci. Edn.) 1, 019 (2010)
16. Li, Y., Fang, B., Guo, L., Chen, Y.: Network anomaly detection based on TCM-KNN algorithm. In: Proceedings of the 2nd ACM symposium on Information, computer and communications security, pp. 13–19. ACM (2007)
17. Zhang, Y., Wang, L., Sun, W., Green, R.C., Alam, M., et al.: Distributed intrusion detection system in a multi-layer network architecture of smart grids. IEEE Trans. Smart Grid 2(4), 796–808 (2011)
18. Wang, X., Sun, L.: Ant algorithm inspired immune intrusion detector generation algorithm. In: 2011 International Conference on Network Computing and Information Security (NCIS), vol. 2, pp. 124–127. IEEE (2011)
19. Shitao, C., Guolong, C., Wenzhong, G., Yanhua, L.: Feature selection of the intrusion detection data based on particle swarm optimization and neighborhood reduction. J. Comput. Res. Dev. 7, 018 (2010)
20. Su, J.-R., Li, B.-Y., Wang, X.-K.: Particle swarm optimization using average information of swarm. Jisuanji Gongcheng yu Yingyong (Comput. Eng. Appl.) 43(10), 58–59 (2007)
21. Group, W.M., et al.: The waikato environment for knowledge analysis. http://www.cs.waikato.ac.nz/ml/weka-2007
22. Xu, J., You, J., Liu, F.: A fuzzy rules based approach for performance anomaly detection. In: Proceedings of the 2005 IEEE Networking, Sensing and Control, pp. 44–48. IEEE (2005)
23. Amudha, P., Karthik, S., Sivakumari, S.: A hybrid swarm intelligence algorithm for intrusion detection using significant features. Sci. World J. (2015)
24. Singh, A., Banafar, H., Pippal, R.S.: Intrusion detection on KDD99cup dataset using K-means, PSO and GA: a review. Probe 300, 300 (2015)
25. Lin, S.-W., Ying, K.-C., Lee, C.-Y., Lee, Z.-J.: An intelligent algorithm with feature selection and decision rules applied to anomaly intrusion detection. Appl. Soft Comput. 12(10), 3285–3290 (2012)

Software Development

Predicting the Fixer of Software Bugs via a Collaborative Multiplex Network: Two Case Studies

Jinxiao Huang and Yutao Ma$^{(\boxtimes)}$ (iD)

School of Computer Science, Wuhan University,
Wuhan 430072, People's Republic of China
ytma@whu.edu.cn

Abstract. Bug triaging is an essential activity of defect repair, which is closely related to the cost of software maintenance. Researchers have proposed automatic bug triaging approaches to recommend bug fixers more efficiently and accurately. In addition to text features, most of the previous studies focused on single-layer bug tossing (or reassignment) graphs, but they ignored the multiplex (or multi-layer) network characteristics of human cooperative behavior. In this study, we build a collaborative multiplex network composed of a tossing graph and an e-mail communication graph in the bug triaging process. By integrating the idea of network embedding and multiplex network measures, we propose a new strategy of random walks. Moreover, we present a bug fixer prediction model that takes structure and text features as inputs. Experimental results on two large-scale open-source projects show that the proposed method outperforms the selected baseline approaches in terms of commonly-used evaluation metrics.

Keywords: Collaborative multiplex network · Network embedding ·
Bug fixer prediction · Structure and text features

1 Introduction

As a necessary activity of software development, defect repair (also known as bug fixing) plays a vital role in software quality assurance. Defect repair usually uses bug tracking systems (such as Bugzilla[1] and JIRA[2]) to manage software bug information and assists developers in fixing reported bugs. Bug triaging is an essential part of defect repair [1], and its primary goal is to go through a list of bug reports and assign bugs which have been confirmed to appropriate developers to fix. Since a large number of duplicate, invalid, or unreproduced bugs are regularly reported to bug tracking systems, accurate, automated bug triaging becomes an urgent problem for open-source software development and maintenance. Ideally, a confirmed bug can be assigned directly to the right developer to fix immediately. However, bug triaging is a time-consuming process

---

[1] https://www.bugzilla.org/.

[2] https://www.atlassian.com/software/jira.

© ICST Institute for Computer Sciences, Social Informatics and Telecommunications Engineering 2019
Published by Springer Nature Switzerland AG 2019. All Rights Reserved
X. Wang et al. (Eds.): CollaborateCom 2019, LNICST 292, pp. 469–488, 2019.
https://doi.org/10.1007/978-3-030-30146-0_33

in practice. For example, a previous study on the Eclipse project[3] showed that it took 40 days on average in the first assignment process, and then it took 100 days or more time in the reassignment process (or called tossing process) [2].

In recent years, many researchers have studied automated bug triaging approaches. In general, these existing methods can be categorized into three main classes: (1) machine learning-based approach [3–6], where classification models are trained based on bug features, such as title, comment, and description; (2) graph (or network)-based approach [2], in which prediction models are built with tossing graph attributes to reduce the tossing path length; and (3) hybrid approach which combines machine learning-based and graph-based approaches. Besides the prediction of the ultimate fixer, some researchers argue that non-fixer developers (also known as tossers) also play a crucial role in the whole bug fixing process. Their contributions include but are not limited to reproducing bugs, commenting bugs, and modifying bug status. This type of developers was called "bug resolution catalyst" by Mani *et al.* [7]. In the bug triaging process, different types of developers work together and collaborate to find the right fixer via deepening the understanding of given bugs.

Social network analysis (SNA) has been widely recognized as a commonly-used tool to analyze the interactions between individuals from network-structured populations in real life and cyberspace. Many previous studies of bug triaging were conducted based on bug tossing graphs, a specific type of social networks, where each node represents a developer and each edge represents an action of bug reassignment (or called tossing). However, most of the previous studies focused on a single-layer tossing graph which has only a single type of relationships between nodes, and they ignored the multiplex (or multi-layer) network characteristics of human cooperative behavior. For example, when different developers collaborate to develop a project, they usually communicate by e-mail or chat by instant messengers (e.g., WhatsApp and WeChat), thus leading to a multiplex network that possesses several layers, each of which represents one type of relationships between nodes.

To leverage more interaction information between developers to predict the right fixer, in this study, we propose a new concept of *collaborative multiplex network*, which is a network composed of different developers and development activities. Different types of activities are represented as different layers of the network to describe various relationships between developers. Because hundreds or thousands of developers are usually involved in a large open-source software project, there has been an increasing concern for the ability of SNA in processing the unprecedented growth of activity data. To facilitate efficient analysis of a complex collaborative multiplex network, we utilize network representation learning (also known as network embedding) to understand the composition of different layers of the network, as well as to analyze the network from different perspectives. Also, we analyze the text information of bug reports, including *summary, status, history*, and some predefined fields. As a result, the combination of structural information and text information enables us to predict fixers more accurately. In brief, the main contributions of this study include:

---

[3] https://www.eclipse.org/.

1. We construct a collaborative multiplex network composed of two everyday developer activities (i.e., bug tossing and e-mail communication) in the bug triaging process. Inspired by the idea of network embedding, we also propose a new random walk strategy designed based on multiplex network measures and network embeddings.
2. By combining the structural information of the collaborative multiplex network and text information extracted by the latent Dirichlet allocation (LDA) model [8], we propose a prediction model to recommend appropriate fixers for target bug reports.
3. We conducted an empirical study on the datasets collected from Eclipse and Gnome[4], and the experimental results indicated that the proposed model outperformed the selected baseline methods.

The remainder of this paper is organized as follows. Section 2 introduces the related work; Sect. 3 presents the background and preliminaries of this work to facilitate understanding the concept of collaborative multiplex networks in bug triaging; Sects. 4, 5, 6 and 7 introduce the proposed prediction model, experimental setups, empirical results, threats to validity, respectively; finally, Sect. 8 concludes this work.

2 Related Work

2.1 Bug Fixer Prediction

Generally speaking, the studies of bug fixer prediction can be divided into two main types, namely text content-based approach and developer relationship-based approach, according to the feature information they used.

Text Content-Based Approach. The existing approaches based on text information usually use machine learning algorithms to predict the ultimate fixer of a given bug. The text information of a bug report mainly includes *title*, *description*, and *comments*. Cubranic had previously extracted keywords from the fields of title and description as training features and used a Naïve Bayes (NB) classification model (or called classifier) to achieve 30% accuracy [9]. Anvik *et al.* [10] then improved the data processing and classification algorithm by Cubranic's work. They filtered out all the records labeled as *invalid*, *wontfix* and *worksform*, deduplicated bug reports, and removed the bug reports processed by those inactive and non-participating developers. Their prediction model achieved an accuracy of 57% for the Eclipse dataset and 64% for the Firefox[5] dataset.

With the rapid development of natural language processing techniques, the topic extraction of text information has also attracted the attention of researchers. For example, Xie *et al.* [11] used the Stanford topic modeling toolbox[6] to group bug reports on the same topic. For new bug reports that have been confirmed, they obtained bug groups (or clusters) according to the model they built and then recommended top-*k* appropriate fixers based on developer experience and skills learned from historical data of fixed bugs. Naguib *et al.* [12] used the LDA model to divide bug reports into

---

[4] https://www.gnome.org/.

[5] https://www.mozilla.org/.

[6] https://nlp.stanford.edu/software/tmt.

different topics. According to the topics and history of each bug report, they created an activity description file (i.e., a profile) for each developer to describe the role and expertise associated with the developer. Eventually, the proposed model recommended the most appropriate fixer by matching developer expertise with extracted bug topics. Xia *et al.* [13] proposed a specialized topic model-based bug triaging approach, which considered the topic distribution of a new bug report when assigning topics to words of the bug report. They evaluated the method on five software projects and demonstrated that it was better than the selected baselines.

Along with the popularity of deep learning, some new approaches based on deep neural networks have also been proposed in recent years. Lee *et al.* [14] applied deep learning-based automatic bug triager to a few industrial software projects. In particular, they built an automatic bug triager using convolutional neural networks (CNNs) and word embedding. The results obtained from both industrial and open-source projects revealed the benefits of the proposed approach. Xi *et al.* [15] presented a sequence to sequence model named SeqTriage. Since the model took into account fixed bugs which developers report themselves and the tossing sequence information, it outperformed the selected baseline methods. Besides, Mani *et al.* [16] considered the data noisy in the description of bug reports, which consists of unstructured text, code snippets, and stack trace making. By using DBRNN-A (short for an attention-based deep bidirectional recurrent neural network model) that learned syntactic and semantic features from long-word sequences in an unsupervised manner, they proposed a bug report representation algorithm to address the problem mentioned above.

Developer Relationship-Based Approach. Developer relationship-based approaches need to construct developer collaboration networks, which are sometimes referred to as tossing graphs. Jeong *et al.* [17] proposed a tossing graph model based on a Markov chain and the bug tossing process among developers. The experimental result indicated that the reassignment rate of new defects was reduced by about 72% when taking the structural features of the graph into account. Wu *et al.* [18] proposed a method based on the k-nearest neighbor (KNN) algorithm by ranking developer expertise. After constructing a developer collaboration network, the method ranks developers in terms of network measures, such as degree, out-degree, frequency, PageRank, betweenness, and closeness. Their empirical results showed that two network measures, out-degree and frequency, were more effective in predicting appropriate fixers. Besides, Zhang *et al.* [19] proposed an approach named KSAP using KNN search and heterogeneous proximity. KASP recommends possible fixers for a given bug report via automatically building a heterogeneous network of a bug repository and extracting meta-paths of developer collaborations in the network.

2.2   Network Embedding

In recent years, unsupervised learning-based network node representation (i.e., network embedding) methods have been proposed and proven to be more effective in capturing latent structural features than standard network metrics [20]. For single-layer networks, inspired by the idea of Word2Vec, each network node can be regarded as a word, and the sequence of walks on different nodes can be regarded as a sentence. Nodes of such a network are then assigned to low-dimensional representations in a similar way to utilizing the skip-gram model [21] in Word2Vec.

Until now, researchers have proposed a few network embedding methods that embed nodes of a (single-layer) network to vectors and other low-dimensional representations while preserving the network structure. DeepWalk [22] is the first approach applying deep learning techniques which have achieved success in natural language processing to network analysis. It obtains the context sequence of a node by random walks and then optimizes the probability of neighbors around the node. Finally, DeepWalk outputs embedding results by using the skip-gram model. However, this method does not have any limitation on the direction and length of the search of neighbors, thus resulting in relatively high computational complexity.

To overcome the above shortcoming of DeepWalk, Node2Vec [23] sets two parameters p and q to control the width and breadth of random walks. Similarly, the large-scale information network embedding (LINE) method [24] extends the random walk strategy to the first-order and second-order similarity-induced weighted random walk, which can meet the embedding requirements of large-scale networks. Besides, Wang et al. [25] proposed a structural deep network embedding method, called SDNE, which exploits the first-order and second-order proximity jointly to preserve the local network structure and global network structure. For more information about other network embedding approaches, please refer to the survey made by Cui et al. [20]. Unfortunately, most of the existing methods of network embedding focus on single-layer network and do not consider multiplex networks.

Collaborative human activities such as distributed collaborative writing with wikis and software development, which usually take place on multiple layers rather than on a single one, can be better modeled by multiplex networks [26]. Multiplex networks, whose edges indicate various types of interactions belonging to different layers, represent a significant advance of network science in describing real-world networked systems [27]. Liu et al. [28] defined three Node2Vec-based random walk strategies on multiplex networks, including network aggregation, result aggregation, and layer co-analysis. Inspired by a specific random walk model, Guo et al. [29] investigated a new navigation strategy on multiplex networks. Significant analytical expressions were derived for the mean first-passage time and the average time to reach a node on these networks, using the spectral graph theory and stochastic matrix theory. Considering the information of multi-type relations, Zhang et al. [30] combined different types of relations while maintaining their distinctive properties by using a high-dimensional common embedding and a lower-dimensional additional embedding for each type of relation. Matsuno et al. [31] proposed an embedding method for multiplex networks named MELL, which was able to capture and characterize each layer's connectivity. In particular, this method exploited the overall structure effectively and was also capable of embedding both directed and undirected multiplex networks.

3 Preliminaries to This Study

3.1 Bug Tossing Graph and E-mail Communication Graph

Bug Report and Tossing Graph. Bug reports are one of the most valuable assets in the bug tracking system of an open-source software project. Each reported bug report is a semi-structured document that contains all the information about a software bug, which can be used to help developers find and fix the bug. Figure 1 illustrates an example of a bug report whose ID is 1532[7] in the Eclipse project.

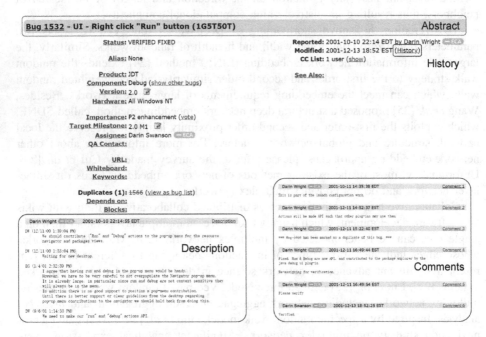

Fig. 1. An example of a bug report with ID 1532 in the Eclipse project.

As shown in Fig. 1, the *abstract* field present the primary information (or attributes) of the bug directly. For example, *product* and *component*, which are two necessary pre-defined attributes in this filed, describe the primary and secondary categories, respectively, of a bug. The *history* field is a table which details the bug repair process. Figure 2 displays the modified history of the bug. There are five columns in the table, namely *Who*, *When*, *What*, *Removed*, and *Added*. The values of *Removed* and *Added* in a row represent a change to the value of *What*. According to modification records of the *assignee* field, we can extract bug tossing paths of resolved bug reports to form a tossing graph. Besides, a bug report provides a detailed description of the bug and developer comments in the natural language form to help find appropriate fixers.

---

[7] https://bugs.eclipse.org/bugs/show_bug.cgi?id=1532.

Back to bug 1532

Who	When	What	Removed	Added
jeffmcaffer	2001-10-11 00:09:16 EDT	Assignee	Darin_Swanson	Darin_Wright
darin.eclipse	2001-10-11 14:35:38 EDT	Status	NEW	ASSIGNED
darin.eclipse	2001-10-12 22:48:16 EDT	Priority	P1	P2
darin.eclipse	2001-12-11 14:52:46 EST	Target Milestone	---	2.0 M1
darin.eclipse	2001-12-11 15:22:40 EST	CC		Darin_Swanson
darin.eclipse	2001-12-11 16:49:44 EST	Assignee	Darin_Wright	Darin_Swanson
		Status	ASSIGNED	NEW
darin.eclipse	2001-12-11 16:49:54 EST	Status	NEW	RESOLVED
		Resolution	---	FIXED
Darin_Swanson	2001-12-13 18:52:25 EST	Status	RESOLVED	VERIFIED

Fig. 2. The modified history of the bug 1532.

E-mail Communication Graph. Software developers always communicate with each other by e-mail to develop open-source software projects. Figure 3 illustrates an e-mail "Using ACTF on Linux"[8] in the mailing list of the accessibility tools framework[9] (ACTF), which is a subproject of the Eclipse Project. Developers can follow any e-mail in a mailing list after subscribing to the mailing list. As shown in Fig. 3, the fields *From* and *Date* record the sender and time of the e-mail, respectively. The *Follow-ups* field at the bottom of the figure indicates the developer who responded to this e-mail (i.e., Kentarou Fukuda). After entering the link in the *Follow-ups* field, we can see more information about the follow-up e-mail. After analyzing records in the archive of the ACTF project, we can construct an e-mail communication graph by extracting possible e-mail communication paths, each of which contains different developers with e-mail addresses corresponding to *From* and *Follow-Ups*.

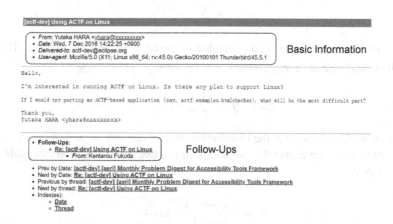

Fig. 3. An example of an e-mail in the mailing list of the ACTF project.

---

[8] https://www.eclipse.org/lists/actf-dev/msg00477.html.

[9] https://www.eclipse.org/actf.

3.2   Multiplex Network Measures

First of all, we introduce some notations of multiplex networks. A multiplex network system (MNS) consists of N nodes and $M(M \geq 2)$ layers, each of which is a network that has the same nodes V but different edges [27]. The adjacency matrix of layer α of the MNS system is defined as $A^{[\alpha]} = \left\{ a_{ij}^{[\alpha]} \right\} (\alpha \in [1, M])$. If there is an edge between nodes i and j on layer α, $a_{ij}^{[\alpha]} = 1$, otherwise 0. Then, the whole system can be expressed as $MNS = \{A^{[1]}, \cdots, A^{[M]}\}$. If we take the weight of each edge into consideration, the weighted adjacency matrix of layer α is defined as $W^{[\alpha]} = \left\{ w_{ij}^{[\alpha]} \right\}$, and the whole system can be represented as $MNS = \{W^{[1]}, \cdots, W^{[M]}\}$. The definitions of other multiplex network measures are given in Eqs. (1)–(6).

Degree of node i on layer α: the number of links of node i to other nodes on layer α. This metric represents a developer's activity level in a certain way of collaboration. Thus, the degree of node i in a multiplex network is a vector $\mathbf{k}_i = (k_i^{[1]}, \cdots, k_i^{[M]})$.

$$k_i^{[\alpha]} = \sum_j a_{ij}^{[\alpha]}. \tag{1}$$

Overlapping degree of node i: the sum of the degree of node i on all the layers of a multiplex network. This metric represents a developer's activity level in the whole multiplex network.

$$o_i = \sum_\alpha k_i^{[\alpha]}. \tag{2}$$

Strength of node i on layer α: the weighted degree of node i on layer α. Thus, the strength of node i can be represented as a vector $\mathbf{s}_i = (s_i^{[1]}, \cdots, s_i^{[M]})$.

$$s_i^{[\alpha]} = \sum_j w_{ij}^{[\alpha]}. \tag{3}$$

Entropy of multiplex degree: the distribution of the degrees of node i among various layers. This metric represents the uniformity of the degree distribution of a node across different layers.

$$H_i = - \sum_{\alpha=1}^{M} \frac{k_i^{[\alpha]}}{o_i} \ln(\frac{k_i^{[\alpha]}}{o_i}). \tag{4}$$

The first (clustering) coefficient for node i: the ratio of the number of 2-triangles with a vertex at node i to the number of 1-triads centered at node i. Due to the popular saying, "the friend of your friend is my friend," clustering coefficient is an essential network metric to measure the tendency of nodes to form triangles. In this study, a 2-triangle is defined as a triangle whose edges belong to two different layers, and a 1-triad centered in i is also defined as a triangle composed of nodes j, i, and k, in which both edge e_{ji} and edge e_{ik} are on the same layer.

$$C_{i,1} = \frac{\sum_\alpha \sum_{\alpha' \neq \alpha} \sum_{j \neq i, m \neq i} (a_{ij}^{[\alpha]} a_{jm}^{[\alpha']} a_{mi}^{[\alpha]})}{(M-1) \sum_\alpha k_i^{[\alpha]} (k_i^{[\alpha]} - 1)}. \tag{5}$$

Interdependence of node i: the multiplex contribution of node i to the reachability of each unit of a multiplex network. Reachability is also a crucial characteristic in graph theory and network science. In Eq. (6), σ_{ij} is the total number of shortest paths between nodes i and j in the multiplex network, and φ_{ij} is the number of shortest paths between the two nodes which make use of links on two or more layers.

$$\lambda_i = \sum_{j \neq i} \frac{\varphi_{ij}}{\sigma_{ij}}. \tag{6}$$

4 Bug Fixer Prediction Approach

4.1 Overall Framework

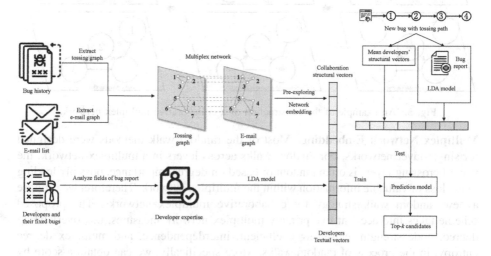

Fig. 4. The overall framework of our method.

The overall framework of our bug fixer prediction approach consists of three parts (see Fig. 4). The first part is *structural information processing*, which has three steps: (1) constructing a collaborative multiplex network; (2) calculating the measures of the multiplex network; and (3) using a new random walk strategy to obtain the structural information of all developers. The second part is *text information processing*, which has two steps: (1) collecting and preprocessing bug reports; and (2) obtaining text vectors of all bugs and developers by the LDA model. The third part is *prediction model*, which takes the structure features of developers and text features of bug reports as inputs and outputs possible k bug fixers. More details of the three parts, please refer to the following subsections.

4.2   Structural Information Processing

Building a Collaborative Multiplex Network. According to the definition of multiplex networks, we take the Eclipse project as an example to introduce the construction of a collaborative multiplex network (see Fig. 5). First, we removed duplicated and null records when building the tossing graph and e-mail communication graph. Second, we preserved the common nodes (i.e., the same developers) in the two graphs and removed other nodes and their corresponding edges. We then summed up the number of edges between each pair of nodes as the weight of the edge between the nodes. For example, in Fig. 5, the weight of the edge between *Denis* and *Olivia* is two. Third, we generated the collaborative multiplex network after mapping each developer in the two graphs into a unified node ID.

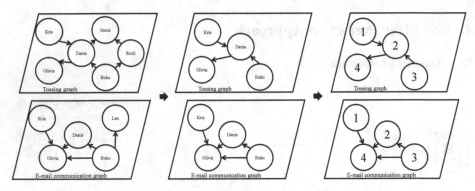

Fig. 5. An example of the construction of a collaborative multiplex network.

Multiplex Network Embedding. Most of the random walk methods were designed for single-layer networks. For random walks across layers in a multiplex network, the way of crossing layers is often random or based on degree importance, possibly leading to the loss of valuable information within the multiplex network. Therefore, we propose a new random walk strategy for collaborative multiplex networks. The proposed scheme takes into account five primary multiplex network measures, i.e., overlapping degree, node strength, clustering coefficient, interdependence, and multiplex degree entropy, in the process of random walks. More specifically, we can obtain a score by weighting these measures, which is used to choose the next-step node to generate a sequence of nodes when sampling node sequences in layer α of the multiplex network.

Suppose i and j denote the current node and the next-step node, respectively, on the same layer α. The score of node j is defined as follows:

$$score_j = (\omega_1 * o_j + \omega_2 * s_j^{[\alpha]} + \omega_3 * H_j + \omega_4 * C_{j,1} + \omega_5 * \lambda_j) * w_{ij}^{[\alpha]},$$
$$s.t. \sum_{k=1}^{5} \omega_k = 1$$

$$(7)$$

where $\omega_k \in [0, 1]$ is the weight of a multiplex network measure and $w_{ij}^{[\alpha]}$ represents the weight of the edge between nodes i and j. Nodes v_i are then generated according to the following distribution:

$$P(v_i = p | v_{i-1} = q) = \begin{cases} \frac{score_p}{Z} & \text{if } q \text{ has a link to } p \\ 0 & \text{otherwise} \end{cases}. \tag{8}$$

where Z is a normalizing constant. We set the same objective function as Node2Vec [23], described as follows:

$$\max_f \sum_{v \in V} [-\log \sum_{v \in V} \exp(f(u) \cdot f(v)) + \sum_{n_i \in N_s(u)} f(n_i) \cdot f(u)], \tag{9}$$

where $f : V \to \mathbb{R}^d$ is a mapping function from nodes to vection representations and $N_S(u) \subset V$ is a set of the neighbours of node u.

By employing the embedding algorithm based on the random walk strategy (see **Algorithm 1**), we can obtain the embedding result of each node in the multiplex network, which can be used as structural features of developers in this study.

Algorithm 1. The multiplex network embedding algorithm

Input: Two-layer collaborative multiplex network G, Dimensions d, Walks per node r, Walk length l, Context size k, Parameter weight vector ω

Output: Mapping function f for layer α

1: $G_s = CountScore(G, \omega)$ // Update G with each node's score calculated using Eq. (7)

2: Initialize $walks$ to Empty

3: **for** $iter = 1$ **to** r **do**

4:    **for all** $nodes\ u \in V$ **do**

5:        $walk = RandomWalk(G_s, \alpha, u, l)$

6:        Append $walk$ to $walks$

7: $f = StochasticGradientDescent(k, d, walks)$

8: **return** f

$RandomWalk(G_s, \alpha, u, l)$

1: Initialize $walk$ to $[u]$

2: **for** $walk\_iter = 1$ **to** l **do**

3:    $V_{curr} = GetNearestNeighbors(walk[-1], G_s, \alpha)$ // Layer α is also a graph $(V, W^{[\alpha]})$

4:    Find node s with the highest score in V_{curr}

5:    Append s to $walk$

6: **return** $walk$

4.3 Text Information Processing

A previous study [32] showed that the *summary, product, component, description,* and *comments* fields in a bug report are significant textual descriptions of a bug. Therefore, we collect and preprocess the above fields of each fixed bug and then integrate them into a text representation (or called text information). Finally, we obtain text features of each bug after inputting the text information to the LDA model [8].

Text Preprocessing. As mentioned above, we first clean the text information of each bug report by using Gensim[10]. Moreover, numbers, punctuations, and special characters are removed, and stop words and stems for long texts are deleted. More details of text preprocessing, please refer to previous studies [9–13, 32].

Text Feature Extraction. Considering the success of topic models in automatic bug triaging, in this study, we also utilize the LDA model to extract text features of bug reports. The LDA model can capture themes (or topics) of each bug in the whole dataset in the form of a probability distribution, and it clusters (or groups) bugs according to the topics extracted from the text information. Besides, the topics of bugs fixed by a developer can represent the expertise or skills of the developer. Similarly, we input all bugs fixed by a developer to the LDA model, and the output of the LDA model is used to represent the professional skills of the developer.

4.4 Fixer Prediction Model

After extracting structure and text features, we train a fixer prediction model, which is essentially a multi-class classification model, for new bug reports. In theory, the fixer prediction model can be trained by any classification algorithm. For example, support vector machines (SVMs) have been used as a standard classification model and proven to be effective in automatic bug triaging in many previous studies [2, 10, 17, 32]. In this study, we utilize a multilayer perceptron (MLP), which is a typical class of feedforward artificial neural networks, to train the fixer prediction model.

5 Experimental Setups

5.1 Research Questions

In this study, we attempt to answer the following two research questions.

RQ1: Does the proposed network embedding (structure features learning) method perform better than the selected baseline approaches?

The first research question aims to test the effectiveness of the proposed random walk strategy designed based on multiplex network measures and network embeddings. Since it is hard to evaluate network embedding results obtained by different approaches directly, we evaluate the efficacy of the approaches under discussion on two binary

---

[10] https://radimrehurek.com/gensim.

classification tasks, i.e., link prediction and node classification. Note that we perform these two tasks on the layer of bug tossing regarding the primary goal of this study.

RQ2: Does the proposed bug fixer prediction (multi-class classification) model outperform the selected baseline approaches?

The primary goal of the second research question is to test the effectiveness of the proposed bug fixer prediction model. We will compare the performance of different classification models when inputting the same features. In the context of this research question, a bug's fixer is the ultimate developer who fixes the bug.

5.2   Data Collection

The experimental datasets used in this study were collected using Bugzilla, a popular bug tracking system. In the whole lifecycle of each defect, its status is ever-changing. Therefore, in this study, we selected only fixed bugs, whose statuses were "RESOL-VED" or "CLOSED" and bug resolution was "FIXED," to crawl their *abstract, description, comments, product, component*, and *history* fields. Finally, we collected 200,000 bugs (record number from 1 to 357553) and 200,000 bugs (record number from 93 to 782996) from the Eclipse project and the Gnome project, respectively.

Large-scale open-source software projects often set up mailing lists for developers to communicate with each other via e-mail. A developer can send e-mails through a mailing list to inform any developer who has subscribed to the mailing list. The projects of Eclipse and Gnome have a large number of mailing lists and e-mails. As shown in Fig. 3, each e-mail contains *From, Follow-Ups, Date, Follow-Ups-Date*, and other fields. We crawled 30,338 and 1,748,687 e-mail records created before August 2017 from public subprojects in the two projects, respectively.

We then constructed two collaborative multiplex networks following the procedures introduced in Subsect. 4.2. According to the definition of multiplex networks, the two-layer collaborative multiplex networks were smaller than the combination of a tossing graph and an e-mail communication graph. The statistics of the two constructed network are shown in Table 1, where TG, ECG, and LSCC denote tossing graph, e-mail communication graph, and the largest strongly connected component, respectively.

Table 1.   Statistics of the experimental datasets.

Dataset	#Nodes	#Edges (TG/ECG)	Transitivity (TG/ECG)	#LSCC Nodes (TG/ECG)
Eclipse	716	6,954 (4,041/2,913)	0.067/0.054	323/594
Gnome	916	20,310 (1,280/19,030)	0.029/0.186	115/893

5.3   Baseline Approaches

We use the following four network embedding (structure features learning) methods as baseline approaches to answer RQ1.

DeepWalk. DeepWalk (Perozzi *et al.* 2014) [22] assumes that the space formed by the corresponding vectors of nodes can accurately represent the actual relationship between nodes in a network. It transforms network nodes into a linear sequence, regards the hierarchical softmax of the skip-gram model as an objective function, and finally obtains the corresponding vector of each node.

LINE. LINE (Tang *et al.* 2015) [24] is an improved network embedding method based on DeepWalk. It preserves the local and global properties of a network by taking into account the first-order proximity and second-order proximity. Moreover, this approach can be applied to different types of networks and is useful for large-scale network embedding.

Node2Vec. Inspired by the idea of maximizing the probability of the neighbors of network nodes, Node2Vec (Grover *et al.* 2016) [23] combines the depth-first search and breadth-first search. It uses return parameter p and in-out parameter q to explore the neighbors of nodes flexibly. At the same time, this approach satisfies the local and global attributes of a network, thus making random walks relatively controllable.

PMNE. PMNE (Liu *et al.* 2017) [28] proposes three patterns based on Node2Vec, which combine all the layers of a multiplex network. *Network aggregation* merges nodes and edges on multiple layers directly to form a new network. Node2Vec takes the new network as an input. *Result aggregation* embeds each layer of a multiplex network with Node2Vec and then concatenate s node vectors on different layers to obtain the final embedding result. *Layer co-analysis* adds a parameter r to Node2Vec to determine whether it crosses layers in the random walk process. The final sequence of nodes is a cross-layer sequence embedded by the skip-gram model.

As for RQ2, the proposed MLP model uses the *softmax* function as an activation function for the output layer. Because the SVM algorithm and Cosine similarity have been widely used as classification models in many previous studies, we also choose them as baseline models for comparison in this study.

5.4   Configurations of Tasks and Parameters

To answer RQ1, we used five-fold cross-validation in the link prediction and node classification tasks for bug tossing. In the link prediction task, the cosine similarity between two nodes represented by embedding vectors determines whether there is a link between the two nodes. In our experiments, the decision rule is that a cosine similarity value greater than 0.5 indicates a link. Besides, we randomly selected the same number of non-existent edges from the existing network as negative samples for training, and the negative sample size was set to five.

In the node classification task, more specifically, a multi-label classification task, embedding vectors of nodes were inputted to an SVM model [33] implemented by the tool sklearn[11]. The SVM model outputs a binary classification result to determine whether the target developer corresponding to a given node is a skilled developer in fixing software defects.

The parameter weight vectors ω were set to [0,0,0.3,0.4,0.3] and [0,0,0.9,0,0.1] for Eclipse and Genome, respectively. The weights were obtained from their respective largest strongly connected componnets. The embedding dimension of each method was

---

[11] https://scikit-learn.org/stable.

set to 200. Since LINE has two embedding settings, we set each of the LINE embedding dimension to 100 and concatenated them directly to form the final embedding. Besides, the window size of random walks was set to ten, and other parameters of our method used in the experiments were set as the same as Node2Vec unless specified otherwise.

To answer RQ2, we employed five-fold incremental learning [2, 13, 32] to compare the performance of different classification models. The topic number of the LDA model was set to 200. We also used the tool sklearn to implement the MLP model with default parameter settings. Note that we optimized the log-loss function of this model using stochastic gradient descent (SGD).

5.5 Evaluation Metrics

To answer RQ1, we utilize the area under the curve (AUC) [34] as an evaluation metric, which has been used by a previous study [23]. As with previous work [13, 16] that studied RQ2, we choose *Accuracy@k* as an evaluation metric to measure how many fixers are hit by the top *k* recommend developers.

6 Experimental Results

6.1 Answer to RQ1: Node Representation Capability

Table 2 shows the experimental results of the two tasks on the Eclipse and Gnome datasets. NA, RA, and CA represent network aggregation, result aggregation, and layer co-analysis, respectively, of the PMNE method. The best result is highlighted in bold.

Table 2. Results of link prediction and node classification in term of AUC (mean ± s.d.).

Approach	Link prediction		Node classification	
	Eclipse	Gnome	Eclipse	Gnome
DeepWalk	0.639 ± 0.007	0.482 ± 0.009	0.720 ± 0.123	0.536 ± 0.022
LINE	0.708 ± 0.011	0.581 ± 0.009	0.720 ± 0.000	0.510 ± 0.000
Node2Vec	0.639 ± 0.007	0.482 ± 0.009	0.704 ± 0.016	0.518 ± 0.012
PMNE (NA)	0.644 ± 0.011	0.630 ± 0.008	0.794 ± 0.019	0.519 ± 0.012
PMNE (RA)	0.691 ± 0.009	0.582 ± 0.011	0.817 ± 0.012	0.531 ± 0.043
PMNE (CA)	0.707 ± 0.010	0.641 ± 0.004	0.818 ± 0.016	0.527 ± 0.015
Ours	**0.731 ± 0.004**	**0.656 ± 0.002**	**0.823 ± 0.007**	**0.625 ± 0.065**

As shown in Table 2, our method achieves the best results in both link prediction and node classification tasks. Because DeepWalk, LINE, and Node2Vec are used for single-layer networks, they cannot leverage useful information from the other layer in the collaborative multiplex network. Therefore, in the two tasks, the results of the three methods were, in general, worse than those of PMNE and our approach. Although the PMNE method merged two-layer embedding results, its result was still worse than that of our approach. The main reason for the difference is that PMNE does not consider multiplex network measures when designing the random walk strategy. The results indicate that these network measures can represent the connectivity and transitivity of nodes in the whole multiplex network better. Due to limitations of space, we do not show the results of parameter sensitivity.

6.2 Answer to RQ2: Fixer Prediction Performance

In this experiment of multi-class classification, the Eclipse dataset contains 531 fixers and 98,301 bug reports, and the Gnome dataset has 603 fixers and 19,701 bug reports. We compared the prediction performance of different models in two cases: considering "S" (short for structural features of developers) and considering "S + T" (short for both structural features of developers and text features of bug reports). The main results of the two datasets using five-fold incremental learning are presented in Tables 3 and 4, respectively. Note that the value of k ranges from one to five. The best result is highlighted in bold.

Table 3. *Accuracy@k* values of different models on the Eclipse dataset (mean ± s.d.).

Model	Top-1	Top-2	Top-3	Top-4	Top-5
DeepWalk	0.585 ± 0.006	0.706 ± 0.007	0.749 ± 0.008	0.775 ± 0.009	0.792 ± 0.008
Node2Vec	0.580 ± 0.002	0.708 ± 0.008	0.751 ± 0.009	0.776 ± 0.010	0.793 ± 0.010
LINE	0.593 ± 0.009	0.718 ± 0.009	0.760 ± 0.010	0.784 ± 0.009	0.800 ± 0.009
PMNE (NA)	0.581 ± 0.009	0.712 ± 0.003	0.756 ± 0.004	0.782 ± 0.003	0.798 ± 0.003
PMNE (RA)	0.561 ± 0.014	0.689 ± 0.007	0.729 ± 0.008	0.751 ± 0.009	0.766 ± 0.008
PMNE (CA)	0.593 ± 0.007	0.726 ± 0.005	0.772 ± 0.007	0.798 ± 0.007	0.815 ± 0.006
Ours	**0.600 ± 0.007**	**0.729 ± 0.003**	**0.775 ± 0.003**	**0.800 ± 0.002**	**0.817 ± 0.002**
Cosine	0.064 ± 0.004	0.102 ± 0.003	0.145 ± 0.002	0.163 ± 0.001	0.177 ± 0.001
SVM	0.597 ± 0.007	**0.729 ± 0.003**	0.774 ± 0.001	0.799 ± 0.001	0.816 ± 0.001
MLP	**0.614 ± 0.005**	0.720 ± 0.007	**0.799 ± 0.005**	**0.813 ± 0.002**	**0.830 ± 0.002**

In each of the two tables, the first part that ranges from the 2nd row to the 8th row represents the case of "S," and the second part that ranges from the 9th row to the 11th row represents the case of "S + T." The structure features extracted by each of the five approaches were inputted into an MLP classification model to predict k possible fixers. As shown in Tables 3 and 4, the proposed network embedding method outperforms the four baseline approaches in both the two datasets. In particular, for the Eclipse dataset, our method achieved a 60.0% accuracy when recommending only one developer ($k = 1$). If $k = 5$, the prediction accuracy increased to 81.7%. The results further demonstrate the effectiveness of our method that learns structure features from multiplex networks.

In the case of "S + T," we inputted the same features set, including structure features obtained using our method and text features extracted by the LDA model, to three classification models. As shown in Tables 3 and 4, the MLP model performs

Table 4. *Accuracy@k* values of different models on the Gnome dataset (mean ± s.d.).

Model	Top-1	Top-2	Top-3	Top-4	Top-5
DeepWalk	0.551 ± 0.004	0.642 ± 0.002	0.677 ± 0.002	0.705 ± 0.003	0.730 ± 0.004
Node2Vec	0.552 ± 0.005	0.641 ± 0.002	0.675 ± 0.003	0.705 ± 0.005	0.726 ± 0.006
LINE	0.555 ± 0.004	0.635 ± 0.002	0.670 ± 0.002	0.699 ± 0.003	0.723 ± 0.004
PMNE (NA)	**0.561 ± 0.005**	0.648 ± 0.004	**0.687 ± 0.004**	0.714 ± 0.005	0.734 ± 0.005
PMNE (RA)	0.551 ± 0.010	0.639 ± 0.008	0.676 ± 0.006	0.705 ± 0.006	0.723 ± 0.005
PMNE (CA)	0.558 ± 0.005	0.647 ± 0.002	0.685 ± 0.003	0.715 ± 0.003	0.737 ± 0.002
Ours	0.560 ± 0.006	**0.651 ± 0.002**	**0.687 ± 0.002**	**0.716 ± 0.003**	**0.740 ± 0.004**
Cosine	0.047 ± 0.005	0.087 ± 0.003	0.136 ± 0.002	0.143 ± 0.002	0.155 ± 0.002
SVM	0.562 ± 0.004	0.647 ± 0.002	0.685 ± 0.003	0.713 ± 0.003	0.735 ± 0.004
MLP	**0.586 ± 0.007**	**0.683 ± 0.004**	**0.731 ± 0.005**	**0.756 ± 0.004**	**0.775 ± 0.003**

better than the other two models. When k was equal to one, the accuracy of the MLP model was, on average, increased by 3.5% compared with that of the SVM model. Moreover, the improvement increased to 3.6% when k reached five. However, the concatenation of structure features and text features did not contribute to a significant improvement in the performance of bug fixer prediction (see the difference between "Ours" and "MLP"), which deserves further investigation on feature combination and dimension reduction.

7 Threats to Validity

Although this study achieves some useful results on the Eclipse and Genome projects, there are still potential threats to the validity of the study that may affect the results, mainly including the internal validity and external validity.

The *internal validity* concerns the explanation (or causality) of the results within the context of this study. It is hard to evaluate network embedding results directly. As with a few previous studies [22–24, 28], we evaluated different methods' embedding results in the link prediction and node classification tasks under the assumption that better node representations contribute to higher performance in the tasks. Besides, the parameters of the baseline approaches were set as default. Therefore, computational optimization or parameter fine-tuning may change the experimental results.

The *external validity* focuses on the generalizability of the proposed network embedding and fixer prediction approaches outside the context of this study. First, due to the strict definition of multiplex networks [27], i.e., a multiplex network's layers have different types of edges with the same nodes, the conclusions of this study do not apply to single-layer tossing graphs [17] or heterogeneous information networks [19]. Second, the performance of our methods on other large-scale software projects is yet to be tested. Therefore, their advantages over the selected baseline approaches on other software projects remain unexplored. Third, since commonly-used network embedding and classification algorithms were selected as the baseline methods in our experiments, we are unable to determine whether the proposed approaches can outperform some recently-proposed approaches, such as graph convolutional networks [35].

8 Conclusion and Future Work

Software bug triaging is a necessity in software development and maintenance. In this paper, we study the problem of automatic bug triaging from the perspective of multiplex networks rather than from single-layer tossing graphs. Due to the multi-layer network characteristics of human cooperative behavior in bug triaging, this study constructs a collaborative multiplex network composed of two layers corresponding to bug tossing and e-mail communication. We then present a new random walk strategy based on some multiplex network measures (e.g., overlapping degree, node strength, and the entropy of the multiplex degree) to generate network embeddings for nodes, which can be used as structural features of developers. Besides, we propose a bug fixer prediction model that takes structural features of developers and text features of bug reports as inputs. According to the experiments on two large-scale open-source software projects with a large number of bug reports and e-mails, we have two conclusions. On the one hand, the proposed network embedding algorithm based on the random walk strategy performed better than four standard network embedding methods in the link prediction and node classification tasks. On the other hand, the proposed prediction model outperformed the selected baseline approaches in predicting the right fixers for target bug reports.

In addition to testing the generalizability of the proposed approach in more large-scale software projects, our future work includes two aspects. First, we will extend the collaborative multiplex network to k-layer collaborative networks where $k \geq 3$ by leveraging other available social relationships between developers such as "Follow" on GitHub[12]. Second, due to the complexity of the proposed network embedding algorithm, we will investigate more efficient deep feature learning algorithms to extract structure features of nodes in multiplex networks that have greater than or equal to three layers.

Acknowledgment. This work was partially supported by the National Key Research and Development Program of China (No. 2018YFB1003801), National Science Foundation of China (Nos. 61832014, 61672387, and 61572371), and Natural Science Foundation of Hubei Province of China (No. 2018CFB511).

References

1. Aberdour, M.: Achieving quality in open source software. IEEE Softw. **24**(1), 58–64 (2007)
2. Bhattacharya, P., Neamtiu, I., Shelton, C.R.: Automated, highly-accurate, bug assignment using machine learning and tossing graphs. J. Syst. Softw. **85**(10), 2275–2292 (2012)
3. Helming, J., Arndt, H., Hodaie, Z., et al.: Semi-automatic assignment of work items. In: The 5th International Conference on Evaluation of Novel Approaches to Software Engineering (ENASE), pp. 149–158. SciTePress (2010)

---

[12] https://github.com/.

4. Anvik, J., Murphy, G.C.: Reducing the effort of bug report triage: recommenders for development-oriented decisions. ACM Trans. Softw. Eng. Methodol. **20**(3), 10:1–10:35 (2011)
5. Shokripour, R., Anvik, J., Kasirun, Z.M., et al.: Why so complicated? simple term filtering and weighting for location-based bug report assignment recommendation. In: The 10th Working Conference on Mining Software Repositories (MSR), pp. 2–11. IEEE (2013)
6. Jonsson, L., Borg, M., Broman, D., et al.: Automated bug assignment: ensemble-based machine learning in large scale industrial contexts. Empirical Softw. Eng. **21**(4), 1533–1578 (2016)
7. Mani, S., Nagar, S., Mukherjee, D., et al.: Bug resolution catalysts: identifying essential non-committers from bug repositories. In: The 10th Working Conference on Mining Software Repositories (MSR), pp. 193–202. IEEE (2013)
8. Blei, D.M., Ng, A.Y., Jordan, M.I.: Latent dirichlet allocation. J. Mach. Learn. Res. **3**, 993–1022 (2003)
9. Murphy, G., Cubranic, D.: Automatic bug triage using text categorization. In: The 16th International Conference on Software Engineering & Knowledge Engineering (SEKE), pp. 92–97. KSI Research Inc. and Knowledge Systems Institute Graduate School (2004)
10. Anvik, J., Hiew, L., Murphy, G.C.: Who should fix this bug? In: The 28th International Conference on Software Engineering (ICSE), pp. 361–370. ACM (2006)
11. Xie, X., Zhang, W., Yang, Y., et al.: Dretom: developer recommendation based on topic models for bug resolution. In: The 8th International Conference on Predictive Models in Software Engineering (PROMISE), pp. 19–28. ACM (2012)
12. Naguib, H., Narayan, N., Brügge, B., et al.: Bug report assignee recommendation using activity profiles. In: The 10th Working Conference on Mining Software Repositories (MSR), pp. 22–30. IEEE (2013)
13. Xia, X., Lo, D., Ding, Y., et al.: Improving automated bug triaging with specialized topic model. IEEE Trans. Softw. Eng. **43**(3), 272–297 (2017)
14. Lee, S.R., Heo, M.J., Lee, C.G., et al.: Applying deep learning based automatic bug triager to industrial projects. In: The 11th Joint Meeting on Foundations of Software Engineering (ESEC/FSE), pp. 926–931. ACM (2017)
15. Xi, S., Yao, Y., Xiao, X., et al.: An effective approach for routing the bug reports to the right fixers. In: The 10th Asia-Pacific Symposium on Internetware (INTERNETWARE), p. 11. ACM (2018)
16. Mani, S., Sankaran, A., Aralikatte, R.: Deeptriage: exploring the effectiveness of deep learning for bug triaging. In: The ACM India Joint International Conference on Data Science and Management of Data (COMAD/CODS), pp. 171–179. ACM (2019)
17. Jeong, G., Kim, S., Zimmermann, T.: Improving bug triage with bug tossing graphs. In: The 7th Joint Meeting of the European Software Engineering Conference and the ACM SIGSOFT Symposium on the Foundations of Software Engineering (ESEC/FSE), pp. 111–120. ACM (2009)
18. Wu, W., Zhang, W., Yang, Y., et al.: Drex: developer recommendation with k-nearest-neighbour search and expertise ranking. In: The 18th Asia-Pacific Software Engineering Conference (APSEC), pp. 389–396. IEEE (2011)
19. Zhang, W., Wang, S., Wang, Q.: KSAP: an approach to bug report assignment using KNN search and heterogeneous proximity. Inf. Softw. Technol. **70**, 68–84 (2016)
20. Cui, P., Wang, X., Pei, J., et al.: A survey on network embedding. IEEE Trans. Knowl. Data Eng. **31**(5), 833–852 (2018)
21. Guthrie, D., Allison, B., Liu, W., et al.: A closer look at skip-gram modelling. In: The 5th International Conference on Language Resources and Evaluation (LREC), pp. 1222–1225. European Language Resources Association (2006)

22. Perozzi, B., Al-Rfou, R., Skiena, S.: Deepwalk: online learning of social representations. In: The 20th ACM SIGKDD International Conference on Knowledge Discovery and Data Mining (KDD), pp. 701–710. ACM (2014)
23. Grover, A., Leskovec, J.: node2vec: scalable feature learning for networks. In: The 22nd ACM SIGKDD International Conference on Knowledge Discovery and Data Mining (KDD), pp. 855–864. ACM (2016)
24. Tang, J., Qu, M., Wang, M., et al.: LINE: large-scale information network embedding. In: The 24th International Conference on World Wide Web, pp. 1067–1077. ACM (2015)
25. Wang, D., Cui, P., Zhu, W.: Structural deep network embedding. In: The 22nd ACM SIGKDD International Conference on Knowledge Discovery and Data Mining (KDD), pp. 1225–1234. ACM (2016)
26. Gómez-Gardenes, J., Reinares, I., Arenas, A., et al.: Evolution of cooperation in multiplex networks. Sci. Rep. **2**, 629 (2012)
27. Boccaletti, S., Bianconi, G., Criado, R., et al.: The structure and dynamics of multilayer networks. Phys. Rep. **544**(1), 1–122 (2014)
28. Liu, W., Chen, P.Y., Yeung, S., et al.: Principled multilayer network embedding. In: The 2017 IEEE International Conference on Data Mining Workshops (ICDMW), pp. 134–141. IEEE (2017)
29. Guo, Q., Cozzo, E., Zheng, Z., et al.: Levy random walks on multiplex networks. Sci. Rep. **6**, 37641 (2016)
30. Zhang, H., Qiu, L., Yi, L., et al.: Scalable multiplex network embedding. In: The 27th International Joint Conference on Artificial Intelligence (IJCAI), pp. 3082–3088. IJCAI Oganization (2018)
31. Matsuno, R., Murata, T.: MELL: effective embedding method for multiplex networks. In: Companion of The Web Conference 2018 on The Web Conference 2018 (WWW Companion), pp. 1261–1268. ACM (2018)
32. Wu, H., Liu, H., Ma, Y.: Empirical study on developer factors affecting tossing path length of bug reports. IET Softw. **12**(3), 258–270 (2018)
33. Cortes, C., Vapnik, V.: Support-vector networks. Mach. Learn. **20**(3), 273–297 (1995)
34. Fawcett, T.: An introduction to ROC analysis. Pattern Recognit. Lett. **27**(8), 861–874 (2006)
35. Ghorbani, M., Baghshah, M.S., Rabiee, H.R.: Multi-layered Graph Embedding with Graph Convolutional Networks. Computing Research Repository (CoRR), arXiv: 1811.08800 (2018)

Maintainable Software Solution Development Using Collaboration Between Architecture and Requirements in Heterogeneous IoT Paradigm (Short Paper)

Wajid Rafique[1,2], Maqbool Khan[1,2], and Wanchun Dou[1,2(✉)]

[1] State Key Laboratory for Novel Software Technology,
Nanjing University, Nanjing, People's Republic of China
rafiqwajid@smail.nju.edu.cn, maqbool@163.com, douwc@nju.edu.cn
[2] The Department of Computer Science and Technology, Nanjing University,
Nanjing, People's Republic of China

Abstract. Internet of Things (IoT) has been tremendously involved in the development of smart infrastructure. Software solutions in IoT have to consider lack of abstractions, heterogeneity, multiple stakeholders, scalability, and interoperability among the devices. The developers need to implement application logic on multiple hardware platforms to satisfy the fundamental business goals. Moreover, long-term maintenance issues due to the frequent introduction of new requirements and hardware platforms pose a vital challenge in IoT solution development.

Numerous techniques have been devised to satisfy the issues mentioned above for ubiquitous and smart infrastructure. However, these techniques lack in providing a comprehensive approach in dealing with the above challenges. In this paper, we argue that fundamentally, there is no difference between the architecturally significant requirements and the architectural design decisions in IoT solution development. The architecture revolves around the requirements gathered by the analyst at the requirements gathering phase. We stress that the requirements elicitation process must consider the software architectural assessment for maintainable software development. By adopting this perspective, we identify areas where both requirements and architecture communities collaborate to effectively increase the user acceptability, maintainability, and fulfill the heterogeneous needs of IoT solutions.

Keywords: Software architecture · IoT · Requirement Engineering · IoT solution development · Maintainability

1 Introduction

Rapid progress in IT has made the ubiquitousness a reality where individuals are widely using smart sensors, gesture control gadgets, and wearable devices

© ICST Institute for Computer Sciences, Social Informatics and Telecommunications Engineering 2019
Published by Springer Nature Switzerland AG 2019. All Rights Reserved
X. Wang et al. (Eds.): CollaborateCom 2019, LNICST 292, pp. 489–508, 2019.
https://doi.org/10.1007/978-3-030-30146-0_34

in everyday life [1]. Nowadays, smart devices/things have the capability to connect with the internet and control the real-world infrastructure. These smart devices/things are denoted by the Internet of Things (IoT) and are widely being deployed in everyday life during the past few years. IoT provides advanced services by employing a global internet infrastructure including homes, manufacturing, aviation, agriculture, health-care, and many other areas of life. The things in IoT have a unique identity, connected by wireless network connections, and can be remotely controlled [1]. IoT has revolutionized the human lifestyle by enabling decision-making capabilities in the devices with very less human interaction.

Figure 1 illustrates an IoT scenario which uses traditional cloud and mobile edge computing for successful IoT implementation. The outermost layer corresponds to the actuators and sensors embedded in the IoT devices which use internet and gateways for the communication to offload the compute-tensive tasks to the edge infrastructure. The traditional cloud data center infrastructure is at the core of IoT which acts as the centralized data repository. A seamless IoT operation is governed by the software solutions in the IoT devices. A typical architecture of IoT consists of a mini processor, actuators, and sensors. IoT has been deployed in networked systems where smart devices collect data using sensors and pass it to the physical systems to control the real-world infrastructure. IoT uses IPv6 network addressing scheme which can accommodate a huge number of IoT devices with larger address space as compared to approximately 4.3 billion device space of IPv4 [2].

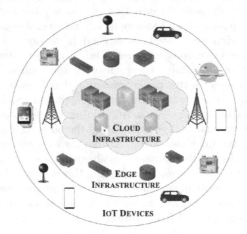

Fig. 1. An IoT service orchestration example using traditional cloud and mobile edge computing.

Software solutions in IoT are the fundamental component in handling the IoT services. They comprise up of architectural components used in a specific configuration while the interaction among these components depends on the underlying software architecture. These components denote the state of the system while the links between them describe the interaction pattern among them [3]. Moreover, the architectural configurations provide the underlying structure of the software design components. Furthermore, the architectural design explains the configuration of the software and hardware components and their interaction to orchestrate services from IoT. Software requirements provide the basis for the architectural development of an IoT software solution. These can be represented by the Architectural Design Decisions (ADDs) to illustrate the structure of a software solution.

Due to the gigantic proliferation of IoT, the need for standardized software architecture development has become a vital challenge [4]. Recently, many new software development life cycles aligned with the requirements of rapid application development and evolution have been introduced. Heterogeneity in IoT makes maintainable software development as a complex task. Traditional software architectural patterns suffer in IoT solution context which relies heavily on the functional requirements. However, ADDs in IoT depend mostly on the nonfunctional requirements of scalability, interoperability, programmability, and maintainability.

Therefore, the study of correlation among software architecture and the requirements in IoT is of vital importance. Both the solution architect and the requirements' analyst work on their specific part of the problem separately, where the architect concentrates on the development perspective, whereas the requirements' analyst apprehends the customers' view. The requirements translate the system in terms of "What" and "How," statements where "What" represents the functionality of the product to be developed and "How" corresponds to the design of the system. Hence, there is still a need to study areas where requirements and architecture are strongly associated [5].

Requirement Engineering (RE) in IoT concentrates on the elicitation of the intended user-goals from IoT that are specified in the form of functional requirements, quality attributes, and constraints. The underlying functions of requirements are distributed among agents like humans, available solutions, or the solutions that need to be developed [5]. The requirements comprise up of diverse characteristics because of the heterogeneity in the IoT infrastructure. They should satisfy the following goals.

- The problem domain must be represented in the form of precise formal statements.
- The problem statements should completely fulfill the intended functional requirement of the business.
- The relationship among different problem statements must be analyzed and documented.
- The stakeholders involved in the problem and the solution domain must be explicitly identified.

Figure 2 illustrates the characteristics of IoT including programmability, intelligence, unique identification, and internet access. The interoperability in IoT denotes its property to operate with multiple other platforms including

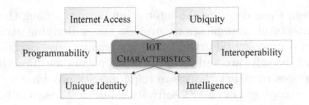

Fig. 2. Characteristics of IoT.

cloud infrastructure, physical devices, and other computing systems. The traditional architectural pattern selection tools analyze, make design decisions, and document them according to software requirements. However, these tools may not be equally effective in the IoT software development domain [5]. The analysis of the user requirements is performed from the top to bottom and further refined until the properties of the desired solution are established [6]. Recent research in the field of software engineering has changed the perspective of considering software architecture as only an abstract entity to a wider scope of architectural knowledge [5]. Additionally, new trends stress the importance of ADDS for developing maintainable software. In this research, we discuss different approaches which establish the collaboration among requirements and the architecture in the IoT paradigm. We present the Architecturally Significant Requirements (ASRs) that can be transformed to the ADDs and explain the architectural choices that are appropriate for effective software development in the IoT paradigm. Furthermore, we provide different models on the collaboration of requirements and the architecture. Based on the above discussion, we present the following contributions in this paper.

- We compare different perspectives of the software community on how software requirements and architecture contribute to the software development process in the heterogeneous IoT application domain.
- We propose that the requirements and architecture are the main building blocks for developing maintainable software and discuss how key characteristics are lost if software requirements and architecture are not considered concurrently.
- We present a systematic discussion on how different models can be used in the software requirements and architecture evolution and ascertain how a maintainable IoT solution can be developed using these models.

Table 1 illustrates the key terms and their description used in this research. Rest of the paper is organized as follows, Sect. 2 discusses the related work on different techniques used in the software architecture development for IoT. Section 3 provides the novel characteristics of IoT which pose challenges in maintainable architecture development. Section 4 explains insights into the approaches used in simultaneous software requirements and architecture development. Section 5 discusses different models to translate problems into corresponding solutions in IoT, whereas Sect. 6 includes the effect of requirements on ADDs. Furthermore,

Table 1. Key terms and their explanation.

Term	Explanation
ADD	Architectural Design Decision
CBSP	Component-Bus-System-Property
ASR	Architectural Significant Requirements
RE	Requirement Engineering
COTS	Commercial-of-the-shelf
IoT	Internet of Things
XP	Extreme Programming
JSF	JavaServer Faces
JMS	Java Message Service
MDD	Model Driven Development
KIWIS	I will Know it When I see it
ADRQ	Architectural Design Design and Requirement Repository

Sect. 7 provides a discussion on the cross-benefit analysis of software requirements and the architecture finally, Sect. 8 concludes the paper and provides some future insights.

2 Related Work

Software architecture is the collection of design decisions which presents a high-level structure of a software system including its components and their interaction [7]. The software architecture paradigm has been considered as structure-oriented in the past, however, with the development of smart infrastructure, it has been transformed towards the knowledge-oriented domain. The architecture is not a solution structure whereas, it is a collection of design decisions which tranced towards a structure [7]. Khan et al. discuss the similarities between the nonfunctional requirements and the architecture of the software. However, their approach lacks in presenting a solution for the heterogeneous IoT domain [8].

Michael Jackson devises optative and indicative problem frames and assigns frequently occurring requirements to a particular frame to document the available software specifications [9]. The indicative corresponds to the problem domain, and optative denotes the selected choices according to the underlying machine specifications. The problem domain is definite, which is represented by the indicative properties, e.g., the requirement of storing the temperature sensor's data by the IoT device. Whereas, the optative corresponds to the requirements, which are the explanations of what the client needs to be true in the problem side, e.g., the interval between consecutive data transfers of an IoT sensor. The machine specifications and the actual behavior of the machine at its interface are different. Limitations on the behavior of the hardware and specifications describe the difference between architecture, requirements, problem domain, and the solution.

Janson et al. propose an Archium model which maps the software architecture to a set of ADDs [10]. The COMPACT model proposed by Marquez et al. extracts components from the nonfunctional requirements [11]. However, COMPACT does not utilize any formal criteria to select design decisions. An improvement of COMPACT has been presented in [12], which utilizes a semantic recommendation system and provides architectural components from the business scenarios. It assists in architectural decision making by bridging the gap between software architecture and the requirements.

A web-based tool has been developed by [13], which assists in selecting architectural pattern and style from an architectural repository, however, it fails in addressing quality attributes in selecting architectural styles and patterns. Cai et al. [14] propose Model Driven Development (MDD) for mobile services in the cloud, they demonstrate that the current software service architectures start in a non-sequential manner and their limitations are identified during finalization of the architecture. This methodology often needs reconsideration, which increases cost and time. MDD for IoT has been proposed in [15] named as FARASAD framework. Similarly, an MDD methodology and SOA framework for architecture development and software artifacts generation have also been proposed in [3]. However, MDD tends to develop the solution at a higher level of abstraction, which makes it difficult to handle the low-level requirements of IoT solutions. Moreover, these technologies do not stress the need of ASRs for IoT solution development. Most of the times, the requirement analysis and the modeling teams include different individuals. Thus, it is difficult to translate the domain knowledge into the models.

These studies provide awareness of the relationship between software architecture and the requirements where the requirements represent the problem domain whereas the architecture illustrates the solution paradigm. As it has been discussed in the related work that different authors use ADD tools to select the appropriate architectural styles and patterns. However, a lack of holistic approach has been observed in the field of IoT architectural pattern selection from the requirements which poses novel challenges. The architectural selection problem in IoT depends on communication protocols, resource limitations, interoperability, scalability, and cloud support. Therefore, we discuss the architectural style and pattern selection from different perspectives.

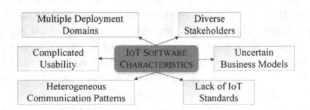

Fig. 3. IoT solution characteristics.

3   Characteristics of IoT Software Solution

Most of the IoT software solutions have been developed without the complete realization of the business and market because of a rapid IoT evolution during the past few years [1]. A common approach used by most of the IoT businesses is to start with a small-scale solution with the flexibility to innovate in order to cater to the huge business investment constraints. Large-scale development having entire features starts upon the acceptance of the product in the market. Figure 3 illustrates the characteristics of IoT solutions which have been discussed in the following.

3.1   Multiple Deployment Domains

IoT solutions need to be deployed on different distributed layers due to multiple IoT hardware constraints, including lower bandwidth, storage, and computation power. The resource limitation also instigates that the data security and privacy requirements are handled in a distributed way, hence, they are mostly provided on the network infrastructure. Moreover, different programming languages are used to develop IoT solutions without having a common code base. Nevertheless, with different build tools, frameworks, versatile platforms, and release cycles, everything must have to run smoothly. Similarly, IoT solutions need data management and storage capabilities to deal with the big data generated by huge IoT infrastructure. Sometimes, the data is classified and filtered before transferring to the cloud storage. In this context, NoSQL comes into play to efficiently manage time-series and high volumes of data.

3.2   Complicated Usability

Smart homes, health-care, and wearable IoT devices are extensively being employed to provide state-of-the-art services to the users. Most of the IoT applications are developed considering the business needs whereas, neglecting the users' perspective of the IoT. The categorization of the requirements according to the involved users and the IoT devices must be extensively performed to understand user needs from the IoT applications. In this regard, the IoT software solutions should be designed in a way that the end users encounter fewer usability problems.

3.3   Lack of IoT Standards

Conway's law in the IoT domain illustrates that the independent and parallel activities in different IoT business solutions provoke many functionally similar solutions which do not follow a standardized development environment [16]. Things work well in a limited paradigm, however, face problems while operating under a broader business context. There are a few IoT standards in the market because of the continuous evolution of the IoT infrastructure. Moreover, many competing IoT development activities are going on around the world, which makes it difficult to enforce standardized IoT solution development.

3.4   Diverse Stakeholders

A diverse range of stakeholders, including versatile domain experts, legal advisers, standardization bodies, third-parties, and infrastructure owners make the requirement gathering a cumbersome process in IoT. Consequently, numerous feasible solutions can be eliminated due to minimal reasons. Extensive technology knowledge even for a smaller solution is inevitable, e.g., development of smart temperature sensors in a heat treating furnace requires deep metallurgical knowledge of the heat treatment process to control the temperature in different parts of the furnace.

3.5   Uncertain Business Models

The business models in IoT change over time because the number of users, the connected devices, and the functionalities varies after deployment. A distributed runtime environment having a versatile set of communication patterns also pose uncertainty in the deployment models. The presence of multiple other IoT solutions increases complexity in designing a solution. Moreover, interaction among architects from other solution domains is also imminent, which poses a significant overhead in IoT solution development.

3.6   Heterogeneous Communication Patterns

Protocols are necessary for moderation when devices communicate with each other. IoT needs novel communication protocols because it has been predicted that the level of heterogeneity of IoT will be much higher than the internet [2]. There is a greater need for communication protocols that enable inter-device communication. Moreover, successful software solutions need to consider heterogeneous communication patterns in IoT.

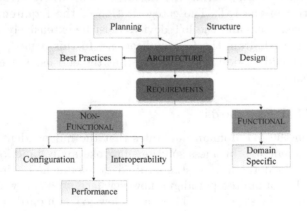

Fig. 4. The characteristics of IoT architecture and its dependence on requirements.

Most of the IoT solutions consider only a limited deployment paradigm which suffers in providing the solution for a global perspective. The above characteristics illustrate that the IoT software development undergoes numerous challenges due to the heterogeneity and lack of standardized development environments which must be addressed in developing a maintainable solution.

4   Software Requirements and Architecture in IoT

In the IoT domain, the requirements of IoT-big data, computational offloading, and resource limitation constraints need to be particularly addressed during the software development process [8]. Figure 4 illustrates the requirements and architecture modeling in an IoT solution development paradigm. It demonstrates that the functional requirements comprise up of domain-specific illustrations, whereas nonfunctional requirements depict configuration, interoperability, and performance. Furthermore, the architecture includes structure, design, and associated best practices in the software. The solution architecture must be aligned with the functional and nonfunctional requirements to enable the usability and maintainability of the IoT solutions. Many attempts have been put forward to evolve software architecture together with the requirements, including problem domains model [17], twin-peak model, and Component-Bus-System-Property (CBSP) approach [18].

The problem domain model relies on extracting individual domain models from the requirements. It represents the problem in terms of frames which increase the efficiency of the overall application development process and instigates the reuse of different frames, which reduces future development effort [17]. The domain modeling approach utilizes the object-oriented perspective for modeling the components of the problem and their relationship. The problem is specified in terms of multilevel abstract-layered representation, which illustrates the problem from multiple perspectives. These models are then developed as running software by the application developers.

Gunbacher et al. propose CBSP an architectural development approach which relates the requirements to the software architecture [18]. A hierarchical taxonomy is utilized to associate requirements with the architecture. A set of general requirements are provided to the CBSP method, which provides intermediate decisions about the architectural styles to be used.

Table 2. Relationship between RE and architecture design.

Requirement engineering	Architecture design
Goal-oriented RE	Pattern-based design
Use case-oriented RE	Architectural style-based design
Sociology and linguistics bases RE	Attribute-based design
Aspects-oriented RE	Component-based design
Sequence constrained business requirements	Product line-based design

IoT poses a versatile set of challenges which needs to be addressed in designing a solution, including the integration of software with heterogeneous platforms, big data needs, scalability, and versatile nature of communication device constraints. Moreover, the architecture is dependent on the software requirements, thus every statement in the requirement document must be represented in the architectural design of the IoT solution.

4.1   RE and Architectural Design

Requirements and the architecture are the integral components of the IoT solutions where requirements are considered as the analysis of the problem domain, whereas the architecture relates to the solution paradigm. IoT requirements consist of limited resources, interoperability among devices, scalability, and heterogeneity, which must be particularly addressed during the architectural development process. In designing an IoT solution, attention must be given to the ASRs which represent the essential design decision of the underlying solution. RE and software architecture play a pivotal role in developing the software structure as illustrated in Table 2. It represents the type of RE process used during the elicitation and the associated architectural design that can be employed.

Practically, both requirements and the architecture emerge separately however, there is a need to explore areas of collaboration among these two processes. Different architectural designs consist of many challenges which relate to the specific solution classes. It is always better to have an early understanding of the user requirements in the IoT solution development, consequently, it will be easier to achieve customer satisfaction towards the solution. Similarly, prior understanding of the architecture provides the basis to discover further constraints related to requirements and the architecture, it also helps to evaluate the system's deployment feasibility [6]. The waterfall process model creates the system architecture that confines the software team to do unavoidable changes in the requirements, which creates a bottleneck in updating the software architecture with evolving requirements. The spiral model was introduced to deal with these challenges, it resolved many deficiencies of the waterfall model and offered incremental software development which helps the developers to flexibly evaluate and change the requirements according to the project risks. The spiral process model concentrates on the need for the development of stable and maintainable software architecture. This model facilitates the developers in a way that they can work on requirements and architecture concurrently [7].

Twin-Peak Model. Figure 5 illustrates the twin-peak model, which enables requirements and architectural specifications in increments to fulfill the needs of the evolutionary software development in the IoT domain. The requirements can be associated with the architecture using a continuous evolution. They are translated to the software components in the architecture, whereas the interaction among the components is moderated by the requirement constraints. Requirements specification, component development, and configuration are carried out continuously until a final architecture is developed. A final assessment of the architecture is performed to ascertain that the architecture fulfills all the required specifications of the business logic. This model is an extension of the Stephen Mellor and Paul ward development model, which they proposed for real-time platforms [19]. Therefore, the twin-peak model has the ability to capture the needs of smart devices in the IoT paradigm. Change control in software development is one of the fundamental property which can efficiently be addressed by using the twin-peak model. Analysis and identification of core software requirements are extremely necessary for stable software architecture in a changing requirements scenario. Different processes are used to develop software systems in this context Commercial-of-the-Shelf (COTS) components can be utilized to re-using built-in products at an earlier stage of the requirements.

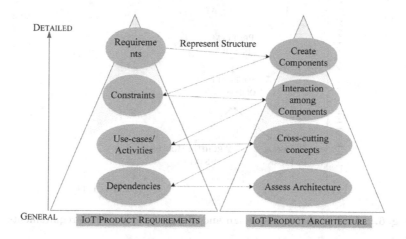

Fig. 5. Twin-peak model for translating IoT requirements to the architecture.

Twin-peak model has been widely used by software development organizations to deal with requirements specification and design issues concurrently. Independent consideration of software requirements and the architecture introduces many challenges which pose restrictions on the developers and provoke repeated software modifications. Agile software development model has the ability to deal with the changing software requirements. The underlying mechanism in agile is also based on the twin-peak model, which emphasizes strong interaction among architecture and the requirements domain. According to Barry Boehm, the twin-peak model has the following management concerns [20].

- **I will know it when I see it (KIWIS):** The requirements tend to change in the process of software development based on the user feedback on the releases. The twin-peak model can detect the changes at an early stage by using incremental modeling.
- **COTS:** Twin-peak model stresses the reuse policy by modifying the available COTS packages which reduce extra effort and cost.

- **Rapid change:** Twin-peak model employs highly adaptive and iterative modeling technique, moreover, it facilitates in incorporating the changes provided by the user during the development life-cycle.

The above discussion demonstrates that the twin-peak model facilitates efficient IoT solution development. It enforces reuse by employing multiple available design patterns and architectural styles which can be customized to adjust in the required context.

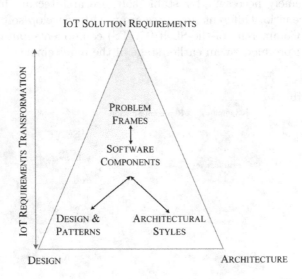

Fig. 6. Selection of solution design and architecture from IoT requirements.

Figure 6 illustrates how requirements can be translated to the design and architecture in IoT solution development. Initially, the requirements are represented by the problem frames, which further translates to the software components. Architectural styles and patterns are adopted by the developers according to the underlying software components. A predetermined architecture poses limitations on the underlying problem, alternatively, rigid requirements pose limitations on the architecture and design choices.

4.2 Weaving the Development Process

Extreme Programming (XP) approach has been used to stress the need for exploring possible implementations of a given problem iteratively [21]. This approach focuses more on front-end software development activities, architectures, and requirements. Therefore, large-scale projects can be efficiently managed if the requirements are comprehended at an early stage, and the choice of architecture is aligned with the requirements. The XP focuses on the production of code, whether it is at the expense of requirements or the architecture. Alternatively, a separate focus on requirements or architecture imposes scalability issues which can harm iterative development and modularity in IoT. Integrating the twin-peak model with the tested and derived components from reliable prototypes can also help in the development of large-scale applications in increments.

Comprehensive problem analysis helps in the reduction of time to market, high-quality, and cost-effective solutions. An efficient development life-cycle allows the concurrent evolution of the requirements and the architecture in order to produce the desired product. A concise consideration of the software architecture provides a clear understanding of the problem from the developers perspective. Moreover, the resultant architecture provides an accurate representation of the user requirements. IoT solutions need to consider the following questions.

- What are the stable requirements and how they can be selected in the context of rapidly changing requirements?
- What type of changes can be expected in the software architecture?
- How can the architecture and requirements be managed to minimize the evolving change impact because of the heterogeneous nature of the IoT devices?

The twin-peak model follows the characteristics of evolutionary software development. Thus, an answer to the above questions will help in identifying ASRs and further maintainable architecture development. There is still a need for a rapid software development process which ensures fast and incremental delivery in the IoT paradigm.

5   Translating Problems into Solutions

A challenging task in software engineering is how to devise a solution that satisfies the present customer's demands and addresses the needs for further evolution using a maintainable architecture. RE and architecture development are the most important activities in the software development life-cycle. The core objectives of an IoT solution can be ascertained during the requirements gathering process which ensures the unambiguity, correctness, and consistency of the requirements so that they provide a baseline for further development, validation, and evolution. The software architecture is explicitly defined, and a baseline is prepared on which subsequent development activities can be planned.

5.1   Problem Exploration Using RE

Problem exploration is concerned with the elicitation of the goals a user needs to accomplish from an underlying IoT device. When developing an IoT solution, an interplay exists between the problem domain and the solution because of the trade-off between the implementation of certain requirements over the others. However, the architecture depends on both the implementable and non-implementable requirements. The RE process explores the problem domain iteratively as further subproblems are identified during the implementation.

IoT solutions depend on design decisions during the architectural development process. These design decisions invoke multiple other design decisions based on the product requirements, which can be characterized in the following.

1. **Existence decision:** These decisions are represented in the implementation of the software system. Moreover, they show up as a quality of the system, e.g., "The temperature sensor solution will consist of three layers."
2. **Property decision:** These decisions have a high impact on the architecture, and they act as the design guidelines for the underlying system. These design decisions can be replaced by new design decisions, e.g., "IoT data will be offloaded to the cloud after 2 ms intervals."
3. **Executive decision:** These design decisions are not directly represented in the design of the solution. However, they are related to environmental factors including political, personal, financial, cultural, and technological constraints, e.g., "The IoT solution will be deployed by using SOA architecture."

ADDs have a high impact on developing a maintainable software solution for IoT. The relation between design decisions plays a pivotal role in the evolution and maintenance of the underlying IoT solution [22]. For instance, if we plan to develop a Java application and decide to use JavaServer Faces for implementation, it limits the use of Java Management Servlets and constrains the use of JavaServer Pages. Similarly, if we use publish-subscribe architectural style, it limits the decision to use peer-to-peer style and constraints with the decision of choosing the client-server architecture.

5.2   Discussion on Problems and Solutions in IoT

The software architect segregates the elicited requirements and identifies those which are not playing any role in the architecture. For example, the requirement to use a matrix-based display to illustrate the speed of a vehicle does not play any role in the software architecture development hence, we eliminate this requirement in the architecture level discussion. Therefore, architecture development only involves ASRs. Conflicting requirements may often appear in the IoT solution development, which needs special attention as IoT involves a versatile set of devices having different configurations. Heterogeneous nature of IoT, big data needs, and mobile platforms often provoke conflicting requirements. Seemingly, performance constraints in a particular situation employ an immense impact on the architecture of a software system. Architectural style selection directly affects the problem as the use of a style provoke new requirements which need additional design decisions.

In this discussion, we conclude that ASRs and ADDs have a strong relationship thus, a maintainable solution must consider both of them concurrently.

6   ADDs and Requirements in IoT

The problem space constitutes the specifications of the solution to develop, its structure, and the domain. ADDs use problem rather than the solution domain which allows the owner who has the core knowledge of the problem to assist in the requirements elicitation phase.

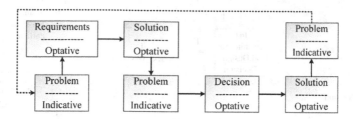

Fig. 7. Indicative and optative properties [23].

6.1   Indicative and Optative Statements

ASRs and ADDs can be represented by indicative and optative statements. They put constraints over the design decisions, and sometimes themselves are constraints over the other design decisions. The description of the problem domain involves indicative specifications. Figure 7 illustrates the process of opting requirements from the problem domain to the problem indicative, and subsequently, the problem indicative can further help in gathering effective requirements for the further phases. In this figure, requirements are extracted from the problem domain, and a loop is formed for the evolutionary software development, which adds experience with every delivery of the product.

Considering an example of using IoT motion tracker, if the hardware has already been selected and its properties are defined then we only need to build its architecture whereas the constraints are only applicable to the requirements. Alternatively, if we have not yet selected the hardware, the ADDs need to consider the hardware as well as the software architecture. In the first situation, the properties of the hardware were given as a part of the problem (indicative), therefore, it constrains the use of software architecture. Whereas, in the second scenario, the properties of the intended hardware need to be chosen (optative) which is part of the solution. Both ASRs and ADDs strongly affect the software system including the preferences for the desired implementation and elimination of the features that are not desirable.

6.2   Architectural Decision Loop

The decision loop illustrates the relationship between ADDs, as shown in Fig. 8 that has been extended from the [23]. It represents that a design decision introduces additional design decisions, which also depends on the previous design decisions hence, creating a decision loop [24]. By using the architectural decision loop ADDs introduce new requirements, and for those requirements, new ADDs need to be considered. Taking an example of flood traffic analysis on an IoT network, multiple use cases can solve this problem, however, we use broadcasting of the alarm when a flooding packet is observed. This endorse further requirements

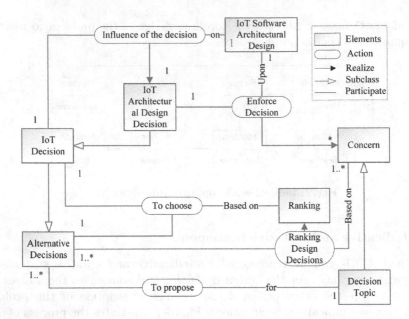

Fig. 8. Architectural decision loop for IoT solutions [23].

of flooding threshold definition, detection technique, and broadcast method to be used. Therefore, the threat broadcast on flood traffic becomes a design decision which has provoked various other design decisions. Another such instance is the storage of IoT generated data, as the IoT devices are limited in capacity, the system keeps track of the storage and transfers the data to the cloud when it exceeds the prescribed limit. Therefore, the decision of the cloud storage invoke new requirements of latency, bandwidth, data rate, and time interval will be provoked. In this regard, we consider this condition as an architectural design decision loop as new requirements will have to follow this design decision.

6.3   Repository of ADDs and Requirements

A solution to select the ADDs and ASRs has been to devise a repository denoted as ADD and Requirement (ADRQ) repository. User's intention dominates the choice of ASRs and ADDs while exploiting the repository. The relationship between the RE to architecture concerning the ADRQ repository has been elaborated in Table 3. Software architect and requirements analyst has domain-specific criteria to contemplate the ADRQ repository, as shown in Table 3. The requirements analyst stores the elicited requirements in the ADRQ in the same way, the solution architect stores the architectural statements in the repository. Requirements that are elicited as well as ADDs should be explicitly documented and stored in the repository to denote the specifications for implementation of the solution.

Table 3. The comparison of RE and architecture in an ADRQ repository.

Requirements domain	ADRQ repository	Architecture domain
Requirements elicitation	Formation of statements	Choice of architecture
Requirements negotiation	Cost-benefit analysis	Architectural exchange analysis
Requirements description	Documenting statements in the repository	Architectural design
Requirements validation	Relate repository statements with clarity	Architecture evaluation
Requirements document	Writing down the repository statements	Architectural explanation
Requirements administration	Organizing the repository	Knowledge management of the architecture

Both architectural requirements and ADDs can be documented using different techniques, including formal language specification, unified modeling language, entity-relationship, and sequence diagrams. The documentation process is extremely necessary to keep track of the software requirements and ADDs efficiently. Both requirements and architecture should analyze the quality of the content which can capture the relationship among ADDs and requirements.

7   Discussion

In this section, we provide a cross-benefit analysis of software requirements and the architecture.

7.1   Requirement Elicitation for Smart Devices

RE is concerned with the elicitation of the goals that a user wants to achieve from the software system. The RE process may involve focused groups, interviews, prototyping, and use cases development. Every requirement is given a relative weight by requirement negotiation process where the software architect selects a particular architecture using the trade-off analysis. In software architecture, the requirements are not processed as they are elicited, but they are less formally represented as they are elicited. Validation is an important component of RE and software architecture. The architecture community has devised various approaches for architectural assessment and their impact on software quality [25]. Moreover, multiple techniques are used for requirements validation, such as the informal technique of review and inspection. Usually, scenario-based methods are used both in architectural assessment and requirements validation.

7.2 Cross-fertilization

In this research, we discuss how software requirements and the architecture community can benefit from each other's experience for effective IoT solution development. The software architecture life-cycle stresses the need for constant interaction among stakeholders to understand their requirements. Business goals and stakeholders' requirements play a major role in architecture development. ADDs and related architectural knowledge plays an important role in architecture management. IoT application development suffers from many challenges, including modifiability, traceability, rationale, and evolution management. Knowledge frameworks can be developed for architectural knowledge management, which also corresponds to the requirements' management. Goal-oriented RE involves goals during the requirements management, whereas, architectural knowledge management includes areas such as traceability, conflicts discovery, and exploring new design variations.

Currently, both requirements and the architectural knowledge management are considered as different information paradigms, however, effective IoT solutions need to consider the similarities of both the fields. We realize that both areas have been addressing the same problem from different perspectives. This study finds that the requirements and architectural knowledge management for IoT solutions need further consideration because of the lack of standard development environments. Further exploration in this field will open new horizons for better requirement management for the IoT architecture where both communities can learn from each other's experience. The illustration of ADRQ repository elaborates that architecture development is not only the responsibility of the software architect, however, ASRs shape the architecture, which also involves the requirement managers concurrently. A maintainable architecture cannot be developed without the consideration of expertise from both the fields.

8 Conclusion

Internet of things utilizes smart infrastructure, big data, communication technologies, and heterogeneous platforms to enable ubiquitousness. The heterogeneity in IoT provokes IoT solutions to integrate with diverse software and hardware platforms. It becomes a critical challenge to develop a maintainable solution that satisfies the requirements of heterogeneous IoT needs. We provide a comprehensive analysis of how software requirements and architectural design decisions can help in developing a maintainable software system. We argue that the architectural design decisions and architecturally significant requirements are on an equal level of significance. This paper plays a key role in characterizing the relationship between architectural design decisions and architecturally significant requirements and recognize them as significant for IoT solution development.

This research opens new horizons towards tighter collaboration between these two paradigms to satisfy the heterogeneous needs of IoT solutions. The analysis of the elicited requirements should be performed by explicitly considering the architecture of the software. Consequently, we can extract architecturally significant requirements which can further be used to develop the architecture. Architectural design decisions play a key role in software evolution and maintenance. Therefore, we should use a proper blend of architecturally significant requirements and architectural design decision to develop maintainable solutions to satisfy heterogeneous IoT demands.

8.1 Future Research

New research directions in the field of IoT architecture modeling can be explored by identifying the significant requirements towards the interdependencies of heterogeneous hardware and software systems. Moreover, these dependencies can be defined in terms of big data needs, communication latency, and bandwidth requirements for IoT solutions.

We are further extending this research by facilitating IoT solution developers by automatic code generation, which reduces cost and time in software development. In this regard, a layered RESTful framework can be employed, which provides platform-specific APIs. Different layers in the RESTful architecture interact to deploy a hardware-specific solution.

Acknowledgment. This research is supported by the National Science Foundation of China under Grant No. 61672276 and 61702277 and the Collaborative Innovation Center of Novel Software Technology and Industrialization, Nanjing University.

References

1. Salman, O., Elhajji, I., Chehab, A., Kayssi, A.: Iot survey: an SDN and fog computing perspective. Comput. Netw. (2018)
2. Zanella, A., Bui, N., Castellani, A., Vangelista, L., Zorzi, M.: Internet of things for smart cities. IEEE Internet Things J. **1**(1), 22–32 (2014)
3. Sosa-Reyna, C.M., Tello-Leal, E., Lara-Alabazares, D.: Methodology for the model-driven development of service oriented iot applications. J. Syst. Architect. **90**, 15–22 (2018)
4. Swaminathan, J.M.: Big data analytics for rapid, impactful, sustained, and efficient (RISE) humanitarian operations. Prod. Oper. Manag. **27**(9), 1696–1700 (2018)
5. Venters, C.C., et al.: Software sustainability: research and practice from a software architecture viewpoint. J. Syst. Softw. **138**, 174–188 (2018)
6. Uikey, N., Suman, U.: A lifecycle model for web-based application development: incorporating agile and plan-driven methodology. Int. J. Comput. Appl. **117**(19), 28–36 (2015)
7. Sarker, I.H., Faruque, F., Hossen, U., Rahman, A.: A survey of software development process models in software engineering. Int. J. Softw. Eng. Appl. **9**(11), 55–70 (2015)
8. Özdemir, V., Hekim, N.: Birth of industry 5.0: making sense of big data with artificial intelligence "the internet of things" and next-generation technology policy. OMICS J. Integr. Biol. **22**(1), 65–76 (2018)
9. Jackson, M.: Problem frames and software engineering. Inf. Softw. Technol. **47**(14), 903–912 (2005)

10. Jansen, A., Bosch, J.: Software architecture as a set of architectural design decisions. In: Proceedings of 5th Working IEEE/IFIP Conference on Software Architecture(WICSA), Pittsburgh, Pennsylvania, pp. 109–120 (2005)
11. Márquez, G., Astudillo, H.: Selecting components assemblies from non-functional requirements through tactics and scenarios. In: Proceedings IEEE 35th International Conference of the Chilean Computer Science Society (SCCC), Valparaíso, Chile, pp. 1–11 (2016)
12. Marquez, G., Astudillo, H.: Selection of software components from business objectives scenarios through architectural tactics. In: Proceedings 39th IEEE/ACM International Conference on Software Engineering Companion (ICSE-C), Buenos Aires, Argentina, pp. 441–444 (2017)
13. Capilla, R., Nava, F., Pérez, S., Dueñas, J.C.: A web-based tool for managing architectural design decisions. ACM SIGSOFT Softw. Eng. Notes 31(5), 4 (2006)
14. Cai, H., Gu, Y., Vasilakos, A.V., Xu, B., Zhou, J.: Model-driven development patterns for mobile services in cloud of things. IEEE Trans. Cloud Comput. 6(3), 771–784 (2018)
15. Nguyen, X.T., Tran, H.T., Baraki, H., Geihs, K.: FRASAD: a framework for model-driven IoT application development. In: Proceedings IEEE 2nd World Forum on Internet of Things (WF-IoT), pp. 387–392 (2015)
16. Kwan, I., Cataldo, M., Damian, D.: Conway's law revisited: the evidence for a task-based perspective. IEEE Softw. 29(1), 90–93 (2012)
17. France, R., Rumpe, B.: Model-driven development of complex software: a research roadmap. In: Proceedings Future of Software Engineering, pp. 37–54. IEEE Computer Society (2007)
18. Grunbacher, P., Egyed, A., Medvidovic, N.: Reconciling software requirements and architectures: the CBSP approach. In: Proceedings 5th IEEE International Symposium on Requirements Engineering, pp. 202–211 (2001)
19. Mohammadi, N.G., Heisel, M.: A framework for systematic analysis and modeling of trustworthiness requirements using i* and BPMN. In: Katsikas, S., Lambrinoudakis, C., Furnell, S. (eds.) TrustBus 2016. LNCS, vol. 9830, pp. 3–18. Springer, Cham (2016). https://doi.org/10.1007/978-3-319-44341-6_1
20. Rosa, W., Madachy, R., Clark, B., Boehm, B.: Agile software development cost modeling for the US DoD. In: SEI Software and Cyber Solutions Symposium, pp. 1–29. Software Engineering Institute (2018)
21. Beck, K., Boehm, B.: Agility through discipline: a debate. Computer 36(6), 44–46 (2003)
22. Shahbazian, A., Lee, Y.K., Le, D., Brun, Y., Medvidovic, N.: Recovering architectural design decisions. In: Proceedings IEEE International Conference on Software Architecture (ICSA), pp. 95–9509 (2018)
23. De Boer, R.C., Van Vliet, H.: On the similarity between requirements and architecture. J. Syst. Softw. 82(3), 544–550 (2009)
24. Fitzgerald, B., Stol, K.-J.: Continuous software engineering: a roadmap and agenda. J. Syst. Softw. 123, 176–189 (2017)
25. Barnes, J.M., Garlan, D., Schmerl, B.: Evolution styles: foundations and models for software architecture evolution. Softw. Syst. Model. 13(2), 649–678 (2014)

Type-Based Modelling and Collaborative Programming for Control-Oriented Systems (Short Paper)

Weidong Ma[1,2]([⊠]) and Zhaohui Luo[2]

[1] Institute of Electronic Engineering,
China Academy of Engineering Physics, Mianyang, China
mawd.sjtu@gmail.com
[2] Department of Computer Science, Royal Holloway,
University of London,
Egham, UK
Zhaohui.Luo@hotmail.co.uk

Abstract. Domain-specific languages (DSL) are more expressive and thus tackle complexity better, making software development easier and more efficient. DSL can automate the production of quality code that based on the proper abstraction of the system. This paper proposes a type-base approach to requirement modelling, called CosRDL, to Implementing a trusted real-time embedded system. A set of rules and formal methods are defined to build CosRDL models for embedded systems, from which the model may be verified apart the specification. CosRDL is described as abstract of event-driven behaviors that support communication between active objects (processes) to support concurrency and collaborative computing. The control processing and properties can be described by CosRDL syntax as an model extension and to make system implementation model. Meanwhile, a case study is presented to figure out how to apply the approach of CosRDL modelling for control systems.

Keywords: Modelling · Domain-specific · Type theory ·
Embedded system · Collaborative computing

1 Introduction

Embedded systems are used in many fields including mobile phone, automation, aeronautics, and so on. Many embedded systems are timed sensitive, application-specific, tightly constrained and system-in-a-system, so that most of them are safety critical systems. These systems are stimulated by some asynchronous events, and the components in the embedded systems need collaborate with

W. Ma—The work has been supported mainly by a project with foundational funds of China Academy of Engineering Physics (Grant No. 060608-2017).

X. Wang et al. (Eds.): CollaborateCom 2019, LNICST 292, pp. 509–517, 2019.
https://doi.org/10.1007/978-3-030-30146-0_35

each other, waiting for the occurrence of external or internal events. For examples, time event is triggered by timer, and a data process task is executed by an arrival event of a data packet from network. After an event was triggered, the components need perform the appropriate actions or operations to manipulate the hardware or generate a new event that triggers other components. It is a classical reactive system that continuously interacts with the physical world.

The design complexity of embedded systems includes high degree of parallelism, sufficient design freedom and constraints, and multiple optimization objectives. Because of its design complexity, the software engineers have to improve productivity by promoting the level of abstraction of embedded systems. Therefore, the model abstracted from the system has more reachable the actual problem domain from the requirements and hides the implementation details. In embedded software development, the domain-specific modelling (DSM) also raises the level of abstraction beyond the programming codes by providing solution scheme and domain concepts. We may use the DSM model to generate the final products. The DSM methodology usually focuses on specific domains so that enables providing better productivity and code quality.

This paper define a modelling languages and development framework for control-oriented embedded systems. The embedded system is designed from the models that is easy understandable, and the specification documentations is conveniently created. According to the defined model, we could implement the designs and correct codes, and finish the debugging, testing, validation and verification on the code level. A control-oriented system requirements description language called CosRDL, is proposed. It is an approach to modelling for control-oriented system in the event-driven framework. The CosRDL-based model has three levels: CosRDL requirements model, CosRDL syntax, and CosRDL system model. It is very proper to develop for control-oriented applications.

2   Related Work

The model-based approaches help abstract away unnecessary details and increase the potential for efficient validation and verification, and easy reuse and evolution. There are several modelling languages such as UML [9], MARTE [2], and SysML [4] etc. Architecture Analysis and Design Language (AADL) is developed for the specification, analysis, automated integration and code generation of critical computer systems. Some researchers have been efforts to establish an effective relationship between AADL and MARTE [7,8]. The paper [5] proposes to extend hybrid MARTE statecharts based on MARTE and the hybrid automata. The formal syntax and semantics of hybrid MARTE statecharts are submited from labeled transition systems (LTS) or live transition systems.

The Spacecraft Requirements Description Language, called SPARDL, which is proposed by Wang, is designed as a requirement modelling language for periodic control systems (PCS) [10–12]. It can specify the features to implement the design, such as periodic driven behaviors, procedure invocations, timed guard, mode transition, and other basic element modes that represents the observable states in periodic control system.

The process algebras CCS and CSP were proposed to model asynchronous processes, describing concurrent, running at indeterminate speed, and can be modelled for embedded system. Hybrid CSP (HCSP) is to extend CSP for describing hybrid systems, which uses differential equations for modelling continuous time-domain environment. The syntax of HCSP can be described as follows [1,3]:

$$P ::= \text{skip} \mid x := e \mid \text{wait } d \mid ch?x \mid ch!e \mid P; Q \mid B \to P \mid P \sqcap Q \mid P^*$$
$$\mid \,[]_{i \in I} io_i \to P_i \mid \langle F(\dot{\mathbf{s}}, \mathbf{s}) = 0 \& B \rangle \mid \langle F(\dot{\mathbf{s}}, \mathbf{s}) = 0 \& B \rangle \trianglerighteq []_{i \in I}(io_i \to Q_i) \quad (1)$$
$$S ::= P \mid S \| S$$

- x is variables, and $\mathbf{s}$ is vectors, respectively
- B is boolean and e is arithmetic expressions
- d is a non-negative real constant
- ch is the channel name, io_i stands for a communication event, and either $ch_i?x$ or $ch_i!e$
- P, Q, Q_i are sequential process terms, and S stands for an HCSP process term.

3 Modelling of the Control-Oriented Systems

3.1 The Development Based on CosRDL

In generally, the system designers write requirements in natural language using Word, Tex etc. Requirements documents written in natural language are prone to ambiguity and no proper formal syntax structure. The CosRDL-based development of control-oriented systems that submits in the paper, is showed in Fig. 1.

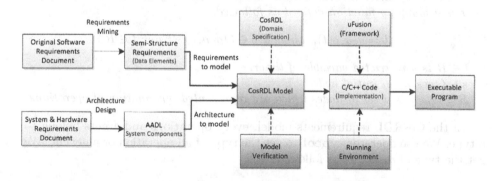

Fig. 1. CosRDL-based development.

The development process is begun from the original software requirements document and system requirements document. The original requirements document can translate into semi-structure requirements by requirement mining. The approaches are using key words of domain-specific fields in control system, so that the semi-structure requirements document keeps the exact semantics of the requirements document. For the system and hardware requirements, it is described by AADL (architecture analysis and design language). For the software requirements, we use CosRDL-based model to describe the control systems.

The CosRDL-based model has three levels: CosRDL requirements model, CosRDL syntax, and CosRDL system model. CosRDL requirements model is designed to define the key elements of the software system that include operations, events and the mapping between events and operations. CosRDL syntax defines a syntax of CCS/CSP style to a model of formal semantics. CosRDL system model is defined for software reuse based on designed components. Once the model has been designed by CosRDL syntax, it can be transformed from CosRDL to C Codes.

3.2 CosRDL Requirements Model

The CosRDL requirement model is defined as follow:

Definition 1. *The CosRDL requirement model is a domain-specific model with 7 objects: an operation set, an event environment set, a type set, an internal action set τ, a mapping function σ, an initial node s, and a set of termination nodes S:*

$$CosRDL_{req} ::= (Oprn, Envr, Type, \tau, \sigma, s, S) \tag{2}$$

- $Oprn = \{a_1, a_2, ..., a_{N_a}\}$ *is a set of operations for a control system.*
- $Envr = \{e_1, e_2, ..., e_{N_e}\}$ *contains communicating events which come from external channels.*
- *Type is a set of types that gives a computing semantic.*
- τ *is a set of internal variables that can not be directly observed in user space.*
- σ *is a mapping function defined as followed:*

$$b = \sigma(a, e, t), \ \ where \ a, b \in Oprn, e \in Envr, t \in R$$

- $t \in R$ *is a restricted variable of timer.*
- $s \in Oprs$ *is an initial node.*
- $S \subseteq Oprn$ *is a set of nodes which are represented termination of operations.*

In the CosRDL requirements model, every operations and events belong to a type. We use operator **typeof** to get the type of an operation or an event. We get the type of a_i and e_i as followed:

$$(\text{event type})Ty_{e_i} : \text{typeof}(e_i)$$
$$(\text{opration type})Ty_{a_i} : \text{tpyeof}(a_i)$$

The type is very important because it not only have formal grammars, but also clarified operational semantics. For examples, we can define a type $\mathbb{N}$ based on $\mathbb{Z}$ that combine with predicate subtypes:

$$\textbf{type} \quad \mathbb{N} = \{x : \mathbb{Z} | x \geq 0\} \tag{3}$$

That means if we have a object $p \in \mathbb{N}$, and once we meet $p < 0$ that must occur some error based the type definition of $\mathbb{N}$.

In the control-oriented systems, the signals of input and output that mostly are voltage or current, usually have special boundary, such as a range of voltage [0.00 v, 5.00 v]. Thus we can define a type of signals $\mathbb{VOL}_\mathbb{A}$ as

$$\text{type} \quad \mathbb{VOL}_\mathbb{A} = \{x : \mathbb{R} | x \geq 0 \quad \& \quad x \leq 5.00\} \tag{4}$$

If all operations or input/output signals are defined by basic types and predicates, we have the right type of the model. Every design and programming must based on the types and then any error maybe discovered in time.

The set of events is an external input/output events, and its type has a real semantics meaning, such as the data of position, speed, accelerator and others.

Every node $a \in Oprn$, if a has more than 2 input from other nodes, we must decide the relation of the input actions. Two operator $\otimes$ (or &) and $\oplus$ (or $+$) was defined as: $\otimes$ means if all input is triggered, then the node is activated; $\oplus$ means if one input is triggered, then the node is activated.

The $CosRDL_{req}$ can be described by a directed acyclic graph (DAG), see Fig. 2. Control systems model with directed acyclic graphs have a wide range of applications. It is closely linked to various control systems that operate in chronological order, such as cars, rail transportation, and aircraft. Usually such systems do not have a loop back to the past scene, the sequence of events and operations are one-way. The operating mechanism of such a system is completely constrained by the external environment and internal timers.

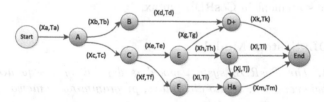

Fig. 2. DAG model of $CosRDL_{req}$.

3.3   CosRDL Syntax

Definition 2. *A formal language for describing hybrid systems, called CosRDL, is defined by the events and its execute operations to modelling the control system. The CosRDL syntax describes as follows:*

$$P ::= SKIP \mid STOP \mid \lambda.P \mid P; Q \mid P \parallel Q \mid P \square Q \tag{5}$$
$$\lambda ::= (ch?(x : A), t) \mid (ch!(v : A), t) \mid \varepsilon \mid \tau \tag{6}$$

- **SKIP** *is an empty statement or represents successful termination.*
- **STOP** *is a termination statement, and represents the process that communicates nothing (or deadlock).*

- λ is an event that executes by input/output actions or empty $(\lambda = \varepsilon)$.
- P and Q are processes or tasks, and is an abstraction of a group of operations.
- $P;Q$ is represented a sequential execution.
- A ranges over a type.
- ch ranges over a channel name, and x, v ranges over the set of communicable data values.
- t is a restricted timer bind the event of x or v.
- $P \parallel Q$ behaves as if P and Q run independently.
- $P \Box Q$ is a external choice of P or Q.
- τ is a set of invisible actions in the internal of the system.

If $\lambda = (ch?x, t)$, we define the operation $\otimes$ and $\oplus$ for all $x \in Envr$ as follows:

$$(x_1, t_1) \otimes (x_2, t_2) = [x_1 \& x_2), \text{Max}(t_1, t_2)] \tag{7}$$

$$(x_1, t_1) \oplus (x_2, t_2) = [(x_1 | x_2), \text{Min}(t_1, t_2)] \tag{8}$$

Where $x_1 \& x_2 = $ True means that both events x_1 and x_2 happen, and $x_1 | x_2$ that x_1 or x_2 happens.

We use *labelled transition system* to define the semantics. A transition of form

$$P \xrightarrow{(ch?x,t)} Q \tag{9}$$

is taken to express the ability of P to perform the event that inputs x at timer t from channel ch, and thereafter behave like the process Q (execute output v in time t on channel ch). In CSP, there is an *internal* choice syntax $P \sqcap Q$, and we do not use the statement in CosRDL syntax.

3.4   CosRDL: System Model

Definition 3. *The CosRDL system model is defined by a sequence of active objects, a global events set, a data dictionary, programming framework and global clocker:*

$$CosRDL_{system} ::= (ActiveObj, Evts, DataDict, uFrm, t) \tag{10}$$

- *ActiveObj is a set of active objects, which can be run concurrently.*
- *Evts is a set of global events that used by the ActiveObj.*
- *uFrm is the uFusion programming framework.*
- *DataDict is a set of variables that mainly have the global scope in system.*
- *t is a global clocker.*

An active object has its own private thread that executes all of its works, and it has private data and methods that can be invoked by other callers through event-trigger mechanics.

Definition 4. *The active object is a set including three tuples:*

$$ActiveObj ::= (Oprs, EvtQueue, pri) \tag{11}$$

- *Oprs* is a set of some operations that process related events.
- *EvtQueue* is an event queue.
- *pri* is a priority used by system scheduler.

The *ActiveObj* and *uFusion* are running by event-trigger model that introduced by [6]. We can design the event process function by using directly C/C++ codes, or using simulink/stateflow, pseudocodes etc.

4 Case Study

A case study is presented that figure out how to use CosRDL to build an abstract model. A simplified model of an aircraft was built that showed in Fig. 3.

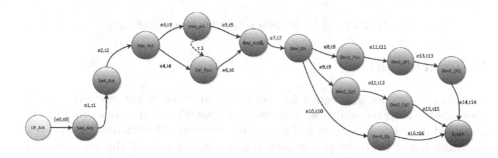

Fig. 3. A simplified CosRDL model of an aircraft electronic system

There are many nodes that represent the specific operations of phases in the system. Each node has to process some actions or operations based on event triggers coming from outer-environment or inner-timer. The Fig. 3 can be modelled in CosRDL as follows:

$$Oprs = \{LP_{Act}, Lau_{Act}, Swt_{Act}, Sep_{Act}, Dev2_{wk}, Cell_{POn}, Ree_{Act}, Dev_{On},$$
$$Dev1_{Pon}, Dev1_{Dt1}, Dev1_{Dt2}, Dev2_{Cp1}, Dev2_{Cp2}, Dev3_{Dy}, End\}$$

$$Envs = \{e_0, e_1, e_2, \ldots, e_{16}\}$$

$$Type = \{\text{typeof}(e_0), \ldots, \text{typeof}(e_{16}), \text{typeof}(LP_{Act}), \ldots, \text{typeof}(End)\}$$

$$Ts = \{t_0, t_1, t_2, \ldots, t_{16}\}$$

$$s = LP_{Act}, \quad S = \{End\}$$

$$s;$$

$$(e_0, t_0).Lau_{Act};$$

$$(e_1, t_1).Swt_{Act};$$

$$(e_2, t_2).Sep_{Act};$$

$$(e_3, t_3).Dev_{wk}[ch!(v : A)] \parallel e_4(t_4).Cel_{Pon}[ch?(x : A)]];$$

$[(e_5, t_5) \& (e_6, t_6)].Ree_{Act};$

$(e_7, t_7).Dev_{On};$

$\{(e_8, t_8).Dev1_{Pon}; (e_{11}, t_{11}).Dev1_{Dt1}; (e_{13}, t_{13}).Dev1_{Dt2}; \} \parallel$

$\quad \{(e_9, t_9).Dev2_{Cp1}; (e_{12}, t_{12}).Dev2_{Cp2}; \} \parallel \{(e_{10}, t_{10}).Dev3_{Dy}; \}$

$[(e_{14}, t_{14}) + (e_{15}, t_{15}) + (e_{16}, t_{16})].End.$

Where Dev_{wk} and Cel_{Pon} communicate in channel. Dev_{wk} has an output action along the channel ch with $ch?(x : A)$ and Cel_{Pon} has an action to accept a value on channel ch with $ch!(v : A)$. In the same time, We may refined in some restriction for e_k and t_k and define the types of all values, then execute model checking for the software system. For examples, we define a verified function **checktype** to verify the valid of the event e_k and the operation a_k in every step of the operation, such as:

$$(e_1, t_1).Swt_{Act}[\text{checktype}(e_1, t_1); \text{checktype}(Swt_{Act})];$$

5   Conclusions

The CosRDL model is designed for model-driven development environment. It supports the more reusability and efficient analysis of control systems that based on model-driven development and program framework. Traditionally, embedded programs have been developed in ad hoc time-sensing ways. If the requirements were changed, the CosRDL requirement model would be modified and automatically be translated into the system model, and the system model bind with a program framework. The CosRDL requirement model is built by engineers from the system specification to describe the system behavior through operations, events and functional mapping. The CosRDL system model is translated from CosRDL requirement model to expressed by actived objects, events, data dictionary and program framework, which have more reusability and extensibility. The CosRDL syntax defined a formal language for described the hybrid systems, and the method is more expressive and tackle complexity better, especially for the domain-specific field such as railway control and flight control systems etc.

Acknowledgements. The first author thanks for discussions of related work of the DSL model of embedded systems with prof. Geguang Pu and Weika Miu, and for discussions of formal modelling and hybrid CSP with prof. Naijun Zhan and Shuling Wang.

References

1. Chaochen, Z., Ji, W., Ravn, A.P.: A formal description of hybrid systems. In: Alur, R., Henzinger, T.A., Sontag, E.D. (eds.) HS 1995. LNCS, vol. 1066, pp. 511–530. Springer, Heidelberg (1996). https://doi.org/10.1007/BFb0020972

2. Espinoza, H., Cancila, D., Selic, B., Gérard, S.: Challenges in combining SysML and MARTE for model-based design of embedded systems. In: Paige, R.F., Hartman, A., Rensink, A. (eds.) ECMDA-FA 2009. LNCS, vol. 5562, pp. 98–113. Springer, Heidelberg (2009). https://doi.org/10.1007/978-3-642-02674-4_8

3. He, J.: From CSP to hybrid systems. In: A Classical Mind. Embedded system, Programming, Software. Prentice Hall International Ltd., Hertfordshire (1994)

4. Khan, A.M., Mallet, F., Rashid, M.: Combining SysML and Marte/CCSL to model complex electronic systems. In 2016 International Conference on Information Systems Engineering, pp. 12–17. IEEE, Los Angeles, April 2016

5. Liu, J., Liu, Z., He, J., Mallet, F., Ding, Z.: Hybrid marte statecharts. Front. Comput. Sci. **7**(1), 95–108 (2013)

6. Ma, W., Deng, Y., Xu, L., Lin, W., Liu, Z.: COSRDL: an event-driven control-oriented system requirement modeling method. In: Bi, Y., Chen, G., Deng, Q., Wang, Y. (eds.) ESTC 2017. CCIS, vol. 857, pp. 103–117. Springer, Singapore (2018). https://doi.org/10.1007/978-981-13-1026-3_8

7. Mallet, F., André, C., DeAntoni, J.: Executing AADL models with UML/Marte. In: 2009 14th IEEE International Conference on Engineering of Complex Computer Systems, pp. 371–376. IEEE, Potsdam, June 2009

8. SAE: Architecture analysis and design language (AADL)

9. Samek, M.: Practical UML Statecharts in C/C++, Programming for Embedded System. Embedded system, Programming, Software, 2nd edn. Elsevier Inc., Oxford (2008)

10. Wang, Z., et al.: SPARDL: a requirement modeling language for periodic control system. In: Margaria, T., Steffen, B. (eds.) ISoLA 2010. LNCS, vol. 6415, pp. 594–608. Springer, Heidelberg (2010). https://doi.org/10.1007/978-3-642-16558-0_48

11. Wang, Z., et al.: A novel requirement analysis approach for periodic control systems. Front. Comput. Sci. **7**(2), 214–235 (2013)

12. Yang, M., Wang, Z., Pu, G., Qin, S.: A novel requirement analysis approach for periodic control systems. Sci. China Inform. Sci. **55**(12), 2675–2693 (2012)

Predicting Traffic Flow Based on Encoder-Decoder Framework

Xiaosen Zheng, Zikun Yang, Liwen Liu, and Li Kuang[✉]

School of Computer Science and Engineering,
Central South University, Changsha 410075, China
kuangli@csu.edu.cn

Abstract. Predicting traffic flow is of great importance to traffic management and public safety, and it has high requirements on accuracy and efficiency. However, the problem is very challenging because of high-dimensional features, spatial levels, and sequence dependencies. On the one hand, we propose an effective end-to-end model, called FedNet, to predict traffic flow of each region in a city. First, for the temporal *trend, period, closeness* properties, we obtain low-dimensional features by downsampling high-dimensional input features. Then we perform temporal fusion to get temporal aggregations of different spatial levels. Next, we generate traffic flow by upsampling the fused features which are obtained by combining the corresponding temporal aggregation and the output of the previous upsample block. Finally, the traffic flow is adjusted by external factors like weather and date. On the other hand, we transfer the original task into a sequence task and then use teacher forcing to train our model, which make it learn the sequence dependencies. We conduct extensive experiments on two types of traffic flow (new-flow/end-flow and inflow/outflow) in New York City and Beijing to demonstrate that the FedNet outperforms five well-known methods.

Keywords: Traffic flow prediction · Encoder-Decoder framework ·
Skip connection · Teacher forcing

1 Introduction

Predicting traffic flow in a city is of great importance to traffic management and public safety. For example, massive crowds of people streamed into a strip region by different vehicles like the bike, taxi, bus, subway etc. at the 2015 New Year's Eve celebrations in Shanghai, resulting in a catastrophic stampede. If we can predict the traffic flow with high accuracy and efficiency, then adopt emergency measures, such tragedies can be mitigated even prevented.

New-flow is the transportation flow originating from a region at a given time interval. End-flow is the transportation flow terminated in region. Intuitively, new-flow and end-flow track the origins and final destinations of the transportation. These thus summarize the movements of transportations and are enough for traffic management and risk assessment, as shown in Fig. 1.

© ICST Institute for Computer Sciences, Social Informatics and Telecommunications Engineering 2019
Published by Springer Nature Switzerland AG 2019. All Rights Reserved
X. Wang et al. (Eds.): CollaborateCom 2019, LNICST 292, pp. 518–533, 2019.
https://doi.org/10.1007/978-3-030-30146-0_36

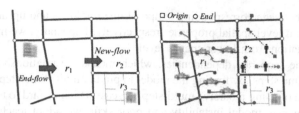

Fig. 1. Traffic flow in a region [1].

Although recently published works consider spatial dependencies, temporal dependencies and external influence, model them properly and get the state-of-the-art accuracy, simultaneously predicting the traffic flow in each region of a city is still challenging, affected by the following aspects:

1. **High-Dimensional Features.** A city usually has a very large size, containing many regions, so the dimension of the input matrix will be high. And for citywide traffic prediction, the output matrix will have the same size with the input matrix. So, previous mentioned state-of-the-art models, which are based on deep neural networks, usually obtain high-dimensional features in hidden layers. First, from the perspective of auto-encoder, if the dimension of feature is too high, it will be difficult for the model to learn useful information from the input and get more general representations [2]. Second, using these high-dimensional features usually requires more parameters and computation.
2. **Spatial Levels.** To capture the city-wide spatial dependencies, we stack some convolution layers because one convolution layer only accounts for near spatial dependencies. However, if we only consider the output of the final convolution layer which contains coarse semantic information of city-wide spatial dependencies, we will lose too much detail information from low-level spatial dependencies like distinct-wide spatial dependencies, especially when we use stride-2 convolution.
3. **Sequence Dependencies.** Some external factors like events may tremendously change the traffic flow in continuous time steps. Although we employ external component, we cannot collect all the information due to many realistic limitations. If we train the model by one-time-step predicting, then the model will focus on the next time step and is not robust enough to tackle some unexpected continuous volume change. For this issue, we consider the relationship among multiple future time steps as sequence dependencies.

To tackle these challenges, we propose an effective model, called FedNet, to collectively predict traffic flow in every region more accurately and more efficiently. The primary contributes of this paper can be summarized as follows:

1. FedNet adopts the encoder-decoder framework to obtain the low-dimensional features by downsampling the high-dimensional features for each temporal property, which leads it to learn more general representations and reach higher accuracy while needs fewer parameters and computation.
2. Not only consider temporal properties, but we also take the influence of spatial properties into account. Inspired by Skip Architecture [3], we add some skip

connections between corresponding temporal fusion blocks and upsample blocks to model different level spatial properties respectively. Especially, we make use of the detail information from lower spatial level.

3. We model the sequence dependencies, which means the relationship among multiple future time steps, by forcing the model to predict multi-time-step at the training stage. Instead of using recursive multi-step forecast which is hard to train because of slow convergence, model instability and poor skill, we adopt teacher forcing [4], which *works by using the actual output from the training dataset at the current time step y(t) as input in the next time step X(t + 1) rather than the output generated by the network.*

2   Related Work

Traffic Flow Prediction. For individual-scale traffic flow prediction, some previous work mainly predicts massive individuals' traces based on people's location history [5, 6], which requires massive computation. For road-scale, some researchers focus on predicting travel speed and traffic volume on the road [7–9]. For region-scale, there are previously published works like FCCF [1], which naturally focus on the individual region instead of the city and need a complex method to find irregular regions. However, such tasks that focus on part of the city are not always necessary for applications like traffic management which needs the information of the overall situation. Recently, researchers have started to focus on city-scale traffic flow prediction, tried to adopt deep learning methods and proposed some effective models like DeepST and ST-ResNet [10, 11]. These DNN-based models firstly partition the city using a grid-based method. However, all these methods are different from ours where they did not tackle the challenges of high-dimensional features, spatial levels, and sequence dependencies.

Deep Learning. To capture spatial dependencies, the convolution neural network has been successfully applied to various problems like image classification [12]. For capturing temporal dependencies, recurrent neural networks based on the long short-team memory unit has been successfully used to various sequence learning task [13]. To capture spatial-temporal dependencies, researchers recently proposed a convolutional LSTM network [14]. However, this network exists gradient vanishing problem, so it cannot model very long-range temporal dependencies. Also, training becomes more difficult as depth increases. Instead, ST-ResNet employs residual learning that enables networks to have a deep structure and a parametric-matrix-based fusion mechanism to model the spatial-temporal dependencies of traffic flow [15]. Though it shows state-of-the-art results, it has massive parameters and requires huge computation, which limits its application. Also, it did not consider modeling different spatial level properties and explore the sequence dependencies of traffic flow predicting task.

Encoder-Decoder Framework. The idea of the encoder-decoder framework is simple: An encoder processes the input and emits a fixed-dimension context. Then a decoder generates the output based on the context. For machine translation, researchers proposed the encoder-decoder or sequence to sequence architecture to map a variable-length sequence to another variable-length sequence for machine translation which obtained state-of-the-art translation [13]. In computer vision field, the convolution encoder-decoder framework is widely applied, especially for some problems that must generate an image output but not a label such image segmentation, style transfer and super-resolution [3, 16, 17]. To the best of our knowledge, no prior work studies predicting traffic flow based on the encoder-decoder framework.

3 Preliminary

In this section, we first present several preliminaries and define our problem formally.

Definition 1 (Region [11]). *There are many definitions of a location in terms of different granularities and semantic meanings. In this study, we partition a city into an H * W grid map based on the longitude and latitude where a grid denotes a region.*

Definition 2 (New-Flow/End-Flow [1]). *The movement of a transportation can be recorded as a trajectory $\mathcal{T}$, which is a sequence of time-ordered points, $\mathcal{T}: p_1 \to p_2 \to \ldots \to p_{|\mathcal{T}|}$, where each point $p_i = (a_i, b_i, t_i)$ has a geospatial coordinate position (a_i, b_i) and a timestamp t_i, and $|\mathcal{T}|$ is the number of point in $\mathcal{T}$. Likewise, the movement of crowds can be represented by a collection of trajectories P. Specifically, for a region $g(i,j)$, the two types of flow at timestamp t, namely new-flow and end-flow, are defined respectively as*

$$x_t^{new,i,j} = |\{\mathcal{T} \in P : (a_1, b_1) \in g(i,j), t_1 = t\}|$$
$$x_t^{end,i,j} = |\{\mathcal{T} \in P : (a_{|\mathcal{T}|}, b_{|\mathcal{T}|}) \in g(i,j), t_{|\mathcal{T}|} = t\}|$$

where $(a_i, b_i) \in g(i,j)$ means that point p_i lies within region $g(i,j)$. A simple example of new-flow and end-flow in every region is as shown in Fig. 2. At the tth time interval, new-flow and end-flow in all $I * J$ regions can be denoted as tensor $X_t \in \mathbb{R}^{2*I*J}$ where $(X_t)_{0,i,j} = x_t^{new,i,j}, (X_t)_{1,i,j} = x_t^{end,i,j}$.

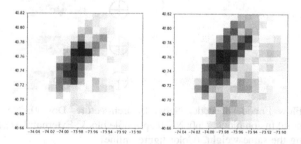

Fig. 2. The taxi new-flow and end-flow example of New York City. (The deeper red means higher traffic volume) (Color figure online)

Problem 1. Given the historical observation $\{X_t|t = 0, 1, \ldots, n-1\}$ predict X_n.

4 Model Architecture

In this section, we describe the architecture of our proposed FedNet, as shown in Fig. 3. FedNet is comprised of four components: an encoder component, a fusion component, a decoder component, and an external component. Referring to previous work, we also turn the traffic flow like new-flow and end-flow into 2-channel image-like matrices according to Definitions 1 and 2, and then divide the input sequence into three fragments: *trend, period, closeness* according to the analyzation [10, 11]. The encoder component captures the spatial dependencies of the input sequence *trend, period, closeness* respectively. The fusion component contains two sub-components: temporal fusion sub-component and the spatial fusion one. The temporal fusion sub-component outputs temporal aggregations of different spatial levels. The spatial one is used to combine corresponding temporal aggregation with the output of previous the upsample block. The decoder component generates the traffic flow output by upsampling the fused features. The traffic flow is further adjusted by the external component that processes the external factors (e.g. holidays) and combines traffic flow with external features.

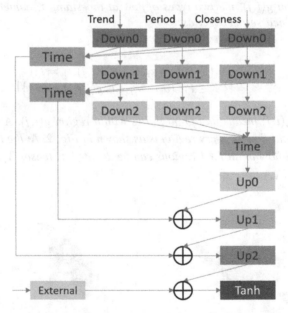

Fig. 3. FedNet (Flow Encoder-Decoder Network) architecture. Down0: No. 0 downsample block; Time: Temporal fusion block; Up0: No. 0 upsample block; External: External block. Same color means sharing the same weight. (Color figure online)

4.1   Encoder Component

The *trend, period, closeness* fragments share the same encoder component that comprises some downsample blocks, which are composed of stride-2 convolution layer, batch normalization layer and leaky relu layer, as shown in Fig. 4.

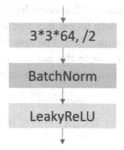

Fig. 4. Downsample block structure. 3*3: kernel size; 64: channel number; /2: Stride-2; BatchNorm: Batch Normalization.

Downsample Blocks Sharing. We share one group of downsample blocks among *trend, period, closeness* instead of using three groups because it is obvious that the spatial pattern of a city is relatively stable among *trend, period, closeness* fragments as shown in Fig. 5. This structural change cuts down the amount of parameter, leads the model to learn more general representations and reduces the risk of overfitting.

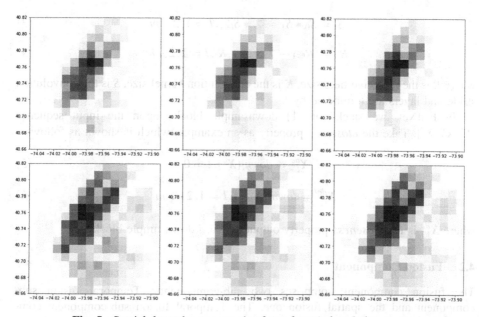

Fig. 5. Spatial dependency example of *trend, period and closeness*.

Stried-2 Convolution. A stack of convolution layers can capture the spatial dependencies among regions in the city. For serval benefits, we use the stride-2 convolution to downsample the input.

The first benefit is about feature extraction. An autoencoder whose output dimension is less than the input dimension is called under complete. We can obtain most salient features of the training data from the under complete autoencoder because it is forced to learn an under complete representation. Motivated by under complete autoencoder, we consider stride-2 convolution can help us get more general representations.

The second benefit is about computation. The task of traffic flow prediction needs a real-time reaction, so we want to reduce the computation as much as possible while ensuring effectiveness. We use flops of convolution to measure the computation of the model as follows

$$FLOPs = 2(C_{in}K^2 + 1)H'W'C_{out} \tag{1}$$

where $H'W'$, the output size of stride-n convolution, is the $1/n^2$ of normal convolution, so the FLOPs will also be the $1/n^2$ [18]. C_{in} and C_{out} are input channels and output channels respectively. And K means kernel size.

The third benefit is about effective receptive field size. Citywide traffic flow prediction requires each pixel in the output to have a large effective receptive field in the input. For example, each 3×3 convolution layer increases the effective receptive field size by only 2. But using stride-2 convolution layer, each layer increases the effective receptive field more efficiently as follows

$$R_l = K_l, l = 0 \tag{2}$$

$$S_l = S_0 * S_1 * \ldots * S_{l-1}, l = 1, 2, ..m \tag{3}$$

$$R_l = (R_{l-1} - 1) * S_l + K_l, l = 1, 2, ..m \tag{4}$$

where R is the receptive field size, K is the convolution kernel size, S is the convolution stride and layers are numbered by l.

In FedNet, we stack $(m+1)$ downsample blocks upon the input sequence $[X^t, X^p, X^c]$. Take the *closeness* property as an example, which is shown as follows

$$X_l^{dc} = down_l(X^c), l = 0 \tag{5}$$

$$X_l^{dc} = down_l(X_{l-1}^{dc}), l = 1, 2, \ldots m \tag{6}$$

where X_l^{dc} is the *closeness* property output of No. l downsample block.

4.2 Fusion Component

The fusion component comprises two sub-components: Temporal fusion sub-component and the spatial fusion one. The Temporal fusion sub-component comprises some temporal fusion blocks, which are composed of the concatenate layer, one by one convolution layer and leaky relu layer, as shown in Fig. 6. The spatial fusion one is composed of some skip connections as shown in Fig. 3. Like downsample blocks sharing above, we share only one temporal fusion block among different spatial level, because we want the model to capture a general temporal pattern of *trend, period, closeness*, which is independent to specific spatial level. This structural change also cuts down the amount of parameter, leads the model to learn more general representations and reduces the risk of overfitting.

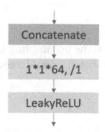

Fig. 6. Temporal fusion block structure. 1*1: kernel size; 64: channel number; /1: Stride-1.

1*1 Convolution. Instead of using parametric-matrix-based fusion [11], which requires a different size for different input feature and is unstable with weight initialization methods, we adopt one by one convolution [19] as our temporal fusion method. One by one convolution was first introduced by Lin et al. [20] to generate a deeper network without simply stacking more layers. However, in our paper, we majorly consider it as a feature transformation method. *Although 1*1 convolution is a 'feature pooling' technique, there is more to it than just sum pooling of features across various channels/features maps of a given layer.* Because this transformation is learned through the (stochastic) gradient descent, so we can use it to learn the different influence of *trend, period, closeness* according to the training data instead of manual setting specify weights.

In this sub-component, for every spatial level, we first concatenate three downsample output and then pass the intermediate output to 1*1 convolution layer that is followed by a non-linear activation layer like leaky relu, as shown as follows

$$X_{m-l}^{time} = time\left(X_l^{dt}, X_l^{dp}, X_l^{dc}\right), l = 0, 1, \ldots m \tag{7}$$

where X_{m-l}^{time} is the temporal aggregation of No. $(m-l)$ spatial level.

Skip Connection. To capture the city-wide spatial dependencies, we stack some convolution layers in the encoder because one convolution layer only accounts for near spatial dependencies. However, if we only consider the output of the final convolution layer which contains coarse semantic information of city-wide spatial dependencies, we will lose too much detail information from low-level spatial dependencies like distinct-wide spatial dependencies, especially when we use stride-2 convolution. Inspired by Skip Architecture, we add some skip connections between corresponding temporal fusion block and upsample blocks to model these spatial properties respectively. Especially, we make use of the detail information from lower spatial level. This sub-component is also learned end-to-end to refine the traffic flow prediction, as shown as follows

$$X_l^s = X_{m-l}^{time} + X_{l-1}^u, l = 1, \ldots m \qquad (8)$$

where X_l^s is the spatial fused feature of No. l skip connection.

4.3 Decoder Component

The decoder component comprises some upsampling blocks, which is composed of the interpolate layer, convolution layer, batch normalization layer, and leaky relu layer, as shown in Fig. 7.

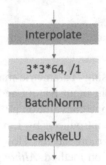

Fig. 7. Upsampling component block structure.

Instead of using transposed convolution that causes Checkboard Artifacts [21], we use factor-2 nearest-neighbor interpolation [22] to upsample the input feature until getting the expected size output, which is simple yet effective as follows

$$X_l^u = up_l(X_l^s), l = 0, 1, \ldots m \qquad (9)$$

$$X_{dec} = X_m^u \qquad (10)$$

where X_l^u is the output of No. l upsample block and X_{dec} is the output of the final upsample block.

4.4 External Component

External encoder component is composed of the linear layer, dropout layer, and leaky relu layer, as shown in Fig. 8.

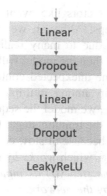

Fig. 8. External component structure.

Referencing previous work [10, 11], we know that traffic flow can be affected by many external factors like the date. In our experiments, we mainly consider date features, which can be obtained directly, like is_month_start. Also, we use weather features that can be approximated by the forecasting weather. Then, we stack two linear layers to process external input which is the feature vector that represents the external factors. Finally, we use the output of external component X_{ext} to adjust X_{dec} by summing them up as follows

$$\widehat{X_t} = \tanh(X_{dec} + X_{ext}) \tag{11}$$

4.5   Model Training

We finally present the training method of our model. FedNet is trained end to end. Especially, to tackle some hard task, at training stage, we transform the one-time-step prediction problem into a multi-time-step sequence prediction problem, and then adopt Teacher Forcing and design a new loss function as shown in Fig. 9. At inferencing stage, for the sake of comparing, we only perform one-time-step prediction and use f_RMSE (factored Root Mean Square Error) as the metric.

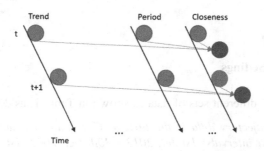

Fig. 9. Sequence predicting and teacher forcing training.

Teacher Forcing. Some external factors like events may tremendously change the traffic flow in continuous time steps. Although we employ external component, we cannot collect all the information due to many realistic limitations. If we train the model by one-time-step predicting, then the model will focus on the next time step and is not robust enough to tackle some unexpected continuous volume change. For this issue, we consider the relationship among multiple future time steps as sequence dependencies. To address this issue, we model the sequence dependencies by force the model to predict multi-time-step at the training stage. Instead of using recursive multi-step forecast which is hard to train because of slow convergence, model instability and poor skill, we adopt teacher forcing, which *works by using the actual output from the training dataset at the current time step y(t) as input in the next time step X(t + 1) rather than the output generated by the network.*

For one time-step training, our model is trained to minimize the MSE (mean square error) between the predicted flow matrix and the ground truth:

$$L_t^s = \frac{1}{z} \sum_i (x_i - \widehat{x_i})^2 \tag{12}$$

where $\widehat{x_i}$ and x_i are the predicted value and the ground truth, respectively; z is the number of all predicted values.

For multi-time-step training, we define the corresponding loss as the average loss of $(j + 1)$ time-step.

$$L_t^m = \frac{1}{j+1} (L_t^s + L_{t+1}^s + \ldots + L_{t+j}^s) \tag{13}$$

To evaluate our model, we design the factored Root Mean Square Error as

$$factor = \frac{H * W}{available} \tag{14}$$

$$f\_RMSE = \sqrt{factor * \frac{1}{z} \sum_i (x_i - \widehat{x_i})^2} \tag{15}$$

where *available* is the amount of available regions and $H * W$ is the amount of all regions.

5   Experiments

5.1   Experiment Settings

Datasets. We use 4 different sets of data as shown in Table 1, as detailed as follows.

- TaxiBJ [11]: *Trajectory data is the taxicab GPS data and meteorology data in Beijing from four intervals: 1st Jul. 2013 - 30th Oct. 2013, 1st Mar. 2014 - 30th Jun. 2014, 1st Mar. 2015 - 30th Jun. 2015, 1st Nov. 2015 - 10th Apr. 2016. Using*

Definition 2, we obtain two types of crowd flows. We choose data from the last four weeks as the testing data, and all data before that as training data.

- BikeNYC [11]: *Trajectory data is taken from the NYC Bike system in 2014, from Apr. 1st to Sept. 30th. Trip data includes: trip duration, starting and ending station IDs, and start and end times. Among the data, the last 10 days are chosen as testing data, and the others as training data.*
- CitiBikeNYC: Trajectory data is taken from the NYC Citi Bike System in 2014, from Apr. 1st to Sept. 30th. Among the data, the last 10 days are chosen as testing data, and others as training data. Among the data, the last 10 days are chosen as testing data, and others as training data.
- TaxiNYC: Trajectory data is taken from the Taxi & Limousine Commission System in 2014, from Apr. 1st to Sept. 30th. Among the data, the last 10 days are chosen as testing data, and the other as training data. Among the data, the last 10 days are chosen as testing data, and the others as training data.

Table 1. Datasets

Attribute	Dataset			
	BikeNYC	TaxiBJ	CitiBikeNYC	TaxiNYC
Data type	Bike GPS	Taxi GPS	Bike GPS	Taxi GPS
Location	New York	Beijing	New York	New York
Gird map size	(16, 8)	(32, 32)	(16, 16)	(16, 16)
Time span	4/1/2014 - 9/30/2014	7/1/2013– 10/30/2013 3/1/2014– 6/30/2014 3/1/2015– 6/30/2015 11/1/2015– 4/10/2016	4/1/2014– 9/30/2014	4/1/2014– 9/30/2014
Time interval	1 h	30 min	1 h	1 h
Available time Interval	4392	22459	4392	4392
Holidays	20	41	20	20
Weather	\	16 types (e.g. Sunny)	\	\
Temperature/°C	\	[− 24.6, 41.0]	\	\
Wind/mph	\	[0, 48.6]	\	\

Baselines. We compare our model with six different baselines as detailed as follows.

- ARIMA: *Auto-Regressive Integrated Moving Average (ARIMA) is a well-known model for understanding and predicting future values in a time series.*
- SARIMA: *Seasonal ARIMA.*

- VAR: *Vector Auto-Regressive (VAR) is a more advanced spatial-temporal model, which can capture the pairwise relationships among all flows, and has heavy computational costs due to the large number of parameters.*
- DeepST: *a deep neural network (DNN)-based prediction model for spatial-temporal data.*
- ST-ResNet: a deep spatial-temporal residual network to collectively predict traffic flow of every region, which shows state-of-the-art results on crowd flow prediction.

Hyper Parameters. For input, we fix trend, period, closeness to one week ago, one day ago and one hour ago, which have the same fragment length 1. For teacher forcing, the amount of predicting time step is 4. Our model is implemented with PyTorch 0.4.1, a popular Deep Learning Python library [23]. The stride-2 convolutions of all down-sample blocks use 64 kernels of size 3 * 3, the convolution of time block use 64 kernels of size 1 * 1 and those of upsample blocks use 64 kernels of size 3 * 3. We select part of the data as training data and then use it to train the model, the rest of the data like the final 10 days' data is the test set. The batch size is 32. We use Adam [24] with the default learning rate 0.001 with a fixed number of epochs (e.g. 100 epochs) and the batch size is 32, and decide whether to update the parameters based on the validation score.

5.2   Experiment Results

Table 2 shows the results of our models and other baselines on BikeNYC and TaxiBJ. Being different from BikeNYC, TaxiBJ is another type of traffic flow, including inflow and outflow [11]. Comparing with the previous models, FedNet_ETS_T, which adopts the encoder-decoder framework, temporal fusion, spatial fusion, and teacher forcing, has 9.00% and 7.01% lower RMSE respectively. Table 3 shows the results of our model on CitiBikeNYC and TaxiNYC. Comparing with the previous best model, FedNet_ETS_T has 9.92% and 3.00% lower RMSE respectively. These results demonstrating the effectiveness of our model.

Table 2. Comparisons with baselines on BikeNYC and TaxiBJ. The results of ARIMA, SARIMA, VAR, ST-ANN, and DeepST are taken from (Zhang et al. 2017).

Model	RMSE	
	BikeNYC	TaxiBJ
ARIMA	*10.07*	*22.78*
SARIMA	*10.56*	*26.88*
VAR	*9.92*	*22.88*
DeepST	*7.43*	*18.18*
ST-ResNet	6.33	16.69
FedNet_ET	5.90	16.22
FedNet_ETS	5.83	15.73
FedNet_ETS_T	**5.76**	**15.52**

Table 3. Comparisons with baselines on CitiBikeNYC and TaxiNYC.

Model	RMSE	
	CitiBikeNYC	TaxiNYC
ST-ResNet	8.57	22.52
FedNet_ET	7.84	24.55
FedNet_ETS	7.84	22.47
FedNet_ETS_T	**7.72**	**21.85**

5.3 Ablation Studies

Considering previous works [10, 11] have approved the effectiveness of temporal fusion and external features, so we majorly discuss the effectiveness of the encoder-decoder framework, spatial fusion, and teacher forcing.

- Encoder-Decoder Framework: For BikeNYC and CitiBikeNYC, comparing to ST-ResNet, FedNet_ET brings 6.79% and 8.52% lower RMSE respectively, which shows the effectiveness of the encoder-decoder framework. However, for TaxiBJ, we get less improvement, and the result of TaxiNYC even becomes worse, which shows it is hard for a simple encoder-decoder framework to tackle hard dataset which has a higher RMSE on baseline models.
- Spatial Fusion: For TaxiBJ and TaxiNYC, comparing to FedNet_ET, FedNet_ETS brings 3.02% and 8.47% lower RMSE respectively, which shows the effectiveness of spatial fusion. However, for BikeNYC and CitiBikeNYC, we get relatively the same result, which shows spatial fusion is unnecessary for an easy dataset which has a lower RMSE on baseline models.
- Teacher Forcing: For TaxiNYC, comparing to FedNet_ETS, FedNet_ETS_T brings 2.76% lower RMSE, which is nearly twice as much improvement comparing to the improvement on the other datasets which is 1.20%, 1.34%, 1.53% respectively. The overall result demonstrates the effectiveness of teacher forcing, and the result on TaxiNYC shows that modeling sequence dependencies is more effective on the dataset that has a higher RMSE on baseline models.

6 Conclusion and Future Work

In this paper, combining the benefits of the end to end encoder-decoder framework, spatial fusion, and teacher forcing, we propose an effective model, called FedNet, to predict traffic flow in each region of a city. We conduct extensive experiments on two types of traffic flows (new-flow/end-flow and inflow/outflow) in New York City and Beijing to demonstrate that the FedNet outperforms five well-known methods. These results confirm that our model is better and more applicable to the traffic flow prediction. The code and datasets will be released at GitHub.

In the future, we will explore appropriate fusion mechanisms for multiple vehicle data (e.g. taxi, bike, bus, subway). Also, we will consider the multi-time-step predicting task at both training stage and inferencing stage, which is much harder.

Acknowledgement. The research is supported by National Natural Science Foundation of China (No. 61772560), and Natural Science Foundation of Hunan Province (No. 2019JJ40388).

References

1. Hoang, M.X., Zheng, Y., Singh, A.K.: FCCF: forecasting citywide crowd flows based on big data. In: Proceedings of the 24th ACM SIGSPATIAL International Conference on Advances in Geographic Information Systems, p. 6. ACM (2016)
2. Deep Learning Book Homepage. http://www.deeplearningbook.org/. Accessed 06 Mar 2019
3. Long, J., Shelhamer, E., Darrell, T.: Fully convolutional networks for semantic segmentation. In: Proceedings of the IEEE Conference on Computer Vision and Pattern Recognition, pp. 3431–3440 (2015)
4. What is Teacher Forcing for Recurrent Neural Networks? https://machinelearningmastery.com/teacher-forcing-for-recurrent-neural-networks/. Accessed 06 Mar 2019
5. Fan, Z., Song, X., Shibasaki, R., Adachi, R.: Citymomentum: an online approach for crowd behavior prediction at a citywide level. In: Proceedings of the 2015 ACM International Joint Conference on Pervasive and Ubiquitous Computing, pp. 559–569. ACM (2015)
6. Song, X., Zhang, Q., Sekimoto, Y., Shibasaki, R.: Prediction of human emergency behavior and their mobility following large-scale disaster. In: Proceedings of the 20th ACM SIGKDD International Conference on Knowledge Discovery and Data Mining, pp. 5–14. ACM (2014)
7. Abadi, A., Rajabioun, T., Ioannou, P.A.: Traffic flow prediction for road transportation networks with limited traffic data. IEEE Trans. Intell. Transp. Syst. **16**(2), 653–662 (2015)
8. Silva, R., Kang, S.M., Airoldi, E.M.: Predicting traffic volumes and estimating the effects of shocks in massive transportation systems. Proc. Natl. Acad. Sci. **112**(18), 5643–5648 (2015)
9. Xu, Y., Kong, Q.J., Klette, R., Liu, Y.: Accurate and interpretable bayesian mars for traffic flow prediction. IEEE Trans. Intell. Transp. Syst. **15**(6), 2457–2469 (2014)
10. Zhang, J., Zheng, Y., Qi, D., Li, R., Yi, X.: DNN-based prediction model for spatial-temporal data. In: Proceedings of the 24th ACM SIGSPATIAL International Conference on Advances in Geographic Information Systems, pp. 92. ACM (2016)
11. Zhang, J.B., Zheng, Y., Qi, D.K.: Deep spatio-temporal residual networks for citywide crowd flows prediction. In: Thirty-First AAAI Conference on Artificial Intelligence, pp. 1655–1661 (2017)
12. Krizhevsky, A., Sutskever, I., Hinton, G.E.: ImageNet classification with deep convolutional neural networks. In: Advances in Neural Information Processing Systems, pp. 1097–1105 (2012)
13. Sutskever, I., Vinyals, O., Le, Q.V.: Sequence to sequence learning with neural networks. In: Advances in Neural Information Processing Systems, pp. 3104–3112 (2014)
14. Shi, X.J., Chen, Z., Wang, H., Yeung, D.Y., Wong, W.K., Woo, W.C.: Convolutional LSTM network: a machine learning approach for precipitation nowcasting. In: Advances in Neural Information Processing Systems, pp. 802–810 (2015)
15. He, K., Zhang, X., Ren, S., Sun, J.: Deep residual learning for image recognition. In: Proceedings of the IEEE Conference on Computer Vision and Pattern Recognition, pp. 770–778 (2016)

16. Badrinarayanan, V., Kendall, A., Cipolla, R.: Segnet: a deep convolutional encoder-decoder architecture for image segmentation. IEEE Trans. Pattern Anal. Mach. Intell. **39**(12), 2481–2495 (2017)
17. Johnson, J., Alahi, A., Fei-Fei, L.: Perceptual losses for real-time style transfer and super-resolution. In: Leibe, B., Matas, J., Sebe, N., Welling, M. (eds.) ECCV 2016. LNCS, vol. 9906, pp. 694–711. Springer, Cham (2016). https://doi.org/10.1007/978-3-319-46475-6_43
18. Molchanov, P., Tyree, S., Karras, T, Aila, T., Kautz, J.: Pruning convolutional neural networks for resource efficient transfer learning. arXiv preprint arXiv:1611.06440 (2016)
19. One by One [1 x 1] Convolution – counter-intuitively useful https://iamaaditya.github.io/2016/03/one-by-one-convolution/. Accessed 06 Mar 2019
20. Lin, M., Chen, Q., Yan, S.: Network in network. arXiv preprint arXiv:1312.4400 (2013)
21. Deconvolution and checkerboard artifacts. https://distill.pub/2016/deconv-checkerboard/. Accessed 06 Mar 2019
22. Nearest-neighbor_interpolation. https://en.wikipedia.org/wiki/Nearest-neighbor_interpolation. Accessed 06 Mar 2019
23. Pytorch. https://pytorch.org/. Accessed 06 Mar 2019
24. Kingma, D., Ba, J.: Adam: a method for stochastic optimization. arXiv preprint arXiv:1412.6980 (2014)

Algorithms, Networks and Testbeds

An Influence Maximization Algorithm Based on Real-Time and De-superimposed Diffusibility

Yue Ren[1], Xinyuan Zhang[1], Liting Xia[1], Yongze Lin[1,2], Yue Zhao[1], and Weimin Li[1(✉)]

[1] School of Computer Engineering and Technology,
Shanghai University, Shanghai, China
randomvar788@gmail.com, zxy_zhangxinyuan@163.com,
xia_lt@163.com, yongze_lin@163.com,
{yxzhao,wmli}@shu.edu.cn
[2] Shanghai Key Laboratory of Computer,
Software Evaluating and Testing, Shanghai, China

Abstract. Influence maximization is to find a small number of seed nodes in the network that maximize their influence on the network. Existing algorithms select a seed node with the greatest influence. This will inevitably have an influence on mutual coverage, which will have a more or less negative impact on the final results and reduce the performance of the algorithm. In this paper, Node Diffusibility is proposed, and it is updated in real time and eliminated the deviation caused by its overlay. On the basis of traditional calculation of node influence, more attention was paid to the influence of a node's neighboring nodes rather than to the characteristics of the nodes themselves. The proposed algorithm was evaluated by experiments conducted on selected real data sets. Compared with the classical ranking-based algorithms, MaxDegree and PageRank, the proposed algorithm achieved better results in terms of efficiency and time complexity.

Keywords: Social network · Influence maximization · Diffusibility

1 Introduction

With the continuous development of network technology, social networks have become more and more widely used in real life, which has changed the way people communicate or share information. A social network is a complex network that consists of many individuals and their connections. When a person gets a product or a message, he could recommend it to others. Some of them would accept the message and spread to more people nearby under the effect of "Word of Mouth". In this way, the message will be spread from several individuals to some groups. The social information platform is booming and its market value is increasing. For example, it has a strong practical significance in virus marketing [1, 2] and public opinion control. How to spend the least cost to get the most extensive dissemination range, namely to obtain the maximum influence has become the most important thing for information publishers. This is also

© ICST Institute for Computer Sciences, Social Informatics and Telecommunications Engineering 2019
Published by Springer Nature Switzerland AG 2019. All Rights Reserved
X. Wang et al. (Eds.): CollaborateCom 2019, LNICST 292, pp. 537–548, 2019.
https://doi.org/10.1007/978-3-030-30146-0_37

the most critical part of the information dissemination process. Based on the social communication model, this paper will simulate the process of information diffusion in social networks and discuss the influence maximization [3, 4].

The spread and diffusion of social networks have a long history of social science. In recent years, many scholars have conducted deep research on these topics. Social networks have become a research hot spot at present, mainly including the information dissemination modeling in the social network [5], community detection, the calculation of user influence, and the study of the influence maximization. Richardson et al. [6] introduced the issue of influence maximization and defined it specifically in social networks. Kempe et al. [7] studied this problem in detail and abstracted it into a discrete optimization problem to simulate the information transmission process. Many algorithms, such as Greedy algorithm [8, 9] and Heuristic algorithm [10, 11], are been used to solve the problem of influence maximization in social networks. The algorithm of influence maximization is to select some high-impact seed nodes through some appropriate methods and maximize the influence by spreading the messages from these seed nodes.

In the study of the influence maximization algorithm for social networks, Kemple and Kleinberg proposed Greedy Algorithm, which selects the node that can bring the maximum influence benefits each time. However, there exists a problem during the process of influence maximization. The selected seed nodes with the largest influence inevitably have the influence of mutual coverage. In order to address these issues node diffusibility is defined. Then, based on the traditional calculation of node influence we paid more attention to the influence of a node's neighboring and updated the diffusion in real time instead of just to the characteristics of the node itself. Finally, an algorithm is proposed to maximize the influence of real-time diffusibility based on the Linear Threshold Model [12].

The rest of this paper is organized as follows. Section 2 introduces the related work. Section 3 presents a new concept, the algorithm framework, and two optimization methods. Section 4 presents the experimental results. Finally, Sect. 5 concludes this study by highlighting our main contribution and future research work.

2 Related Work

Kempe et al. [7] first established the model of influence maximization, which aims at finding the most influential K nodes on a specific dissemination model. They pro-posed Greedy Algorithm, and simulated the information dissemination process of K rounds in the whole network diagram. The marginal influence of nodes was calculated for selecting seed nodes in each round, and the most influential node could be gained. However, this process is very time-consuming, and the local optimum cannot reach the optimal result of the final dissemination.

Set Covering Greedy Algorithm [13] is another Influence Maximization Algorithm. Once a node is selected as a seed node, all its neighboring nodes will be marked as covered. The algorithm chooses the uncovered node with the highest degree each time, that is, the node with the largest coverage. However, the coverage mentioned here is not equal to activation, so the experimental results are not good for influence maximization.

Heuristic algorithm based on node centrality is a method to reduce the complexity. To evaluate the centrality of nodes in the network [14], many algorithms are proposed, such as Degree Centrality [15, 16], Closeness Centrality [17], Betweenness Centrality [18] and PageRank [19, 20]. Degree Centrality is the most common and simplest measurement. The greater the Degree Centrality of the node, the more important the node is in the network [15]. Closeness Centrality is another index to measure the centrality of nodes by calculating the path length of each node to other nodes. If the path length of one node to other nodes is small, the influence of this node may be greater, also the information diffused by this node will disseminate more easily [17]. Betweenness Centrality is related to the shortest paths of two nodes in the network. If plenty of these shortest paths pass through one node, this node is considered to have high Betweenness Centrality [18]. However, PageRank is different from each of the three ways mentioned above [19]. It's used to evaluate the influence of Web pages. It can also be understood as a method to measure the importance of nodes. Kitsak et al. [21] proposed k-core algorithm to evaluate the dissemination influence of nodes, and proposed Maximum Core Algorithm Based on Coverage and Maximum Degree Algorithm. K- core decomposition measures the centrality of one node by its location in the network. If the centrality of a node is large, it can be gained that this node is in the core position of the network, and its influence may be greater. Cao Qiuxin et al. [22] proposed Core Covering Algorithm, which combined the k-core algorithm and degree centrality to calculate the influence of each node. However, these traditional node centrality index always ignore the characteristics of its neighboring nodes. Degree Discount [3] is an optimization of it. Chen et al. pointed out that when some of one node's neighboring nodes are seed nodes, the degree of the node should be discounted to avoid the overlap of influence.

In addition, there exists some Influence Maximization Algorithm Based on Community Discovery [23]. In social networks, people will form many communities be-cause of various interests and hobbies. Social networks can be divided into many small aggregation areas according to certain characteristics through some behaviors of people. Heuristic algorithm is not always so effective. In addition, the greedy algorithm adds seed node every time and calculates the marginal impact of all inactive nodes, which makes the algorithm run for a long time. Therefore, a better evaluation of node influence needs to be studied. In this paper, we pay attention to the influence of a node's neighboring nodes and eliminates the superimposed influence between neighboring nodes. The aim of this study is to achieve better results with the less computational time cost.

3 Influence Maximization Algorithm Based on Real-Time and De-superimposed Diffusibility

In this section, node diffusibility, a new metric that measures the importance of the node, is defined. It takes the overall impact of the node and its neighbors into account. Loss coefficient is added to simulate the loss caused by information diffusion. Based on experiments, it is found that the nodes with larger diffusibility have higher diffusion range coincidence. Also, node diffusibility is updated in real time to get the most realistic dissemination process. Besides, eliminating the negative effect caused by diffusibility superposition is also considered to get more precise conclusions.

3.1 Node Diffusibility

In an information dissemination network, each node has a different situation and status. Thus, these nodes play different roles in information dissemination. Therefore, it is of great significance to judge the status and importance of a node in the network. Traditional node importance metrics, such as Degree Centrality and Node Influence, usually focus on some factors directly related to one node while ignoring the features of the relevant nodes connected with it. Generally, there exists a fact that the degree of a certain node is very large, but the degree of its neighboring nodes is relatively small. Thus, its influence cannot reach a high level.

To solve the above problems, a new metric Node Diffusibility was proposed. Based on the traditional nodes influence, we considered the influence of the neighboring nodes of one node. The influence of the node spreading i layers is positively correlated with the influence of its neighboring node spreading $i - 1$ layers ($i > 1$). According to the simulation experiments, the necessary condition for one node to be activated is that the gained influence from the surrounding activated nodes reaches its own threshold. So the diffusion of information over each layer must be accompanied by a certain loss. To simulate the loss caused by dissemination, a variable called Loss Coefficient was defined to quantify it.

The estimation formula of node diffusibility is as follows:

$$db(u, i) = db(u, i - 1) + \sum_{v \in U'} db(v, i - 1) \times ls \times b(u, v) \tag{1}$$

$$db(u, 1) = \sum_{v \in U'} b(u, v) \tag{2}$$

where $db(u, i)$ represents the diffusibility of node u spreading i layers; U' is the neighboring node of u; the ls represents the loss coefficient; $b(u, v)$ represents the effect of the active node u on the neighboring node v, calculated by $1/(d(v))$; $d(v)$ represents the degree (in-degree in the directed graph) of the node v.

Algorithm 1. Node Diffusibility Calculating (NDC)

Input: graph: G(V, E),Θ, size of initial dissemination set: k, loss coefficient: ls, n: consider node spreading n layers
Output: initial dissemination set: s
1. Set $s_0 = \emptyset$
2. **For each** node u in graph G do
   $b_{uv} \leftarrow 1/indegree\ of\ u$ /*calculate the effect of the active node u on the neighboring node v*/
3. **For each** node u in graph G **do**
   For each node v in neighbors of node u **do**
   For each i in n: /* consider node u spreading n layers */
      $db(u, i) \leftarrow db(u, i - 1) + db(v, i - 1) \times ls \ast b_{uv}$ /*db(u,i) represents the diffusibility of node u spreading i layers */
   End For
   End For
   End For
4. Sort nodes in G by its value of $db(u,n)$
5. Select *top-k* nodes with large diffusibility to join the set s_0

Algorithm 1 is node diffusibility calculating algorithm (NDC). The effect of node can be calculated, and the loss coefficient is defined to simulate the loss of effect caused by dissemination. The algorithm selects top k nodes that have larger diffusibility. Though we need to consider several layers of dissemination, the time complexity of NDC is $O(E)$ by memorization. The space complexity is mainly consumed on the storage of the network, which is $O(E)$. E is the number of edges.

3.2   Influence Maximization Based on Real-Time and De-superimposed Diffusibility

In order to apply the diffusibility in the dissemination model, some verified experiments were carried out. By combining with the Linear Threshold Model, the top-k nodes of the diffusibility were selected as the seed nodes, and the number of nodes that can be activated could be gained. Through experiments, it is found that the diffusion range of the nodes with large diffusibility is high. Thus, the following two improvements were propose:

(1) Update the node diffusibility in real time

As known that each seed node has an influence on its neighboring nodes. And several such influences will contribute a part of the total influence of the seed node. Considering the following situation, one node v can reach node u after being diffused through n layers. After the node u is selected as a seed node, it is obvious that the node u does not have the ability to provide a contribution value for the influence of the node v. Therefore, under the premise of maintaining the original diffusibility base, the influence contribution value of node u on node v should be subtracted. The specific formula is as follows:

$$db(v, i) = db(v, i) - \sum_{v \in U'} b(v, u) \times ls^i \qquad (3)$$

The result of this formula indicates the influence of node v which can diffuse to node u in i layers.

(2) Eliminate the superposition effects of diffusibility

Obviously, the effect of the activated node u on node v is through the indirect dissemination of the nodes that are on the path of node u to node v. Consider the following situation, node u has been selected as the seed node, assuming that node u has an effect on node v through node p, this effect is the indirect impact of node u on node v, which is included in the direct impact of node p on node v. Therefore, we need to subtract the partially superposed influence of node u on node v when calculating the diffusibility of node p. The specific formula is as follows:

$$db(p, c) = db(p, c) - db(u, c - i) \times ls^{i+1} \qquad (4)$$

Algorithm 2. Influence Maximization Algorithm Based on Real-time and De-superimposed Diffusibility (RDD)

Input: graph: G(V, E),Θ, size of initial dissemination set: k, loss coefficient: ls, n: consider node spreading n layers
Output: initial dissemination set: s
1. Set s_0=∅
2. **For each** node u in graph G do
   $b_{uv} \leftarrow 1/indegree\ of\ u$ /*calculate the effect of the active node u on the neighboring node v*/
3. **For each** node u in graph G **do**
   For each node v in neighbors of node u **do**
     For each i in n: /* consider node u spreading n layers */
       $db(u,i) \leftarrow db(u,i-1)+db(v,i-1) \times ls*b_{uv}$ /*db(u,i) represents the diffusibility of node u spreading i layers */
     End For
   End For
   End For
4. **Loop** following steps for k times
5. **Select** node u with the largest diffusibility to join the set s_0
6. **Recursion** following steps for n depth: /* update the node diffusibility in real time*/
   Parameters: node u, depth i
   For each node v in neighbors of node u **do**
   $db(v,n) = db(v,n) - b_{uv} * ls^i$
   Recursion with set parameters u to v
   End For
   End Recursion
7. **Recursion** following steps for n depth: /*eliminate the superposition effects of diffusibility*/
   Parameters: node now, depth i
   For each node v in neighbors of node now **do**

   $db(v,n) = db(v,n) - db(u,n-i) \times ls^{i+1}$

Recursion with set parameters now to v
End For
End Recursion
8. **End Loop**

The result of this formula (4) indicates the influence of node p which can diffuse to node u in c layers, and node u can diffuse to node v in i layers.

When a node is selected as a seed node, the nodes within n layers should be updated as above. The pseudo algorithm is shown in Algorithm 2.

Algorithm 2 is influence maximization algorithm based on real-time and de-superimposed diffusibility (RDD). This algorithm is designed based on Algorithm 1 by updating the node diffusibility in real time and eliminating the superposition effects of diffusibility, which makes influence maximization more effective. The average time complexity of RDD is $O(E*(E/V)^{(n-1)})$, and the space complexity is $O(E)$. E is the number of edges. V is the number of nodes. n is the number of layers considered. RDD consumes little time than traditional heuristic algorithms like MaxDegree when n is not large, but it is much faster than Greedy Algorithm.

4 Experiments

4.1 Data Set

The experiment was conducted to verify the effectiveness of the algorithm proposed.

The first data set is Gnutella peer-to-peer network, which is derived from data sets published in the social networking field for various tests [24]. It is a snapshot of a series of Gnutella peer-to-peer file sharing networks. Nodes represent hosts in the Gnutella network topology. And edges represent connections between Gnutella hosts. The second data set is PGP network [25], which is a list of edges of the giant component of the network of users of the Pretty-Good-Privacy algorithm for secure information interchange. The data set is described in Table 1.

Table 1. The information of data set

	Gnutella p2p network	PGP network
Nodes	8717	10680
Edges	31525	24316
Average clustering coefficient	0.0067	0.26598
Number of triangles	1142	164.9K
Fraction of closed triangles	0.002717	0.377912

The effectiveness of the algorithm is reflected by the number of nodes that the selected seed nodes can affect through dissemination in final, which means the range that nodes can influence.

4.2 Results and Analysis

Experiments were conducted based on the linear threshold model. And the formula of buv is $buv = \frac{1}{d(v)}$. The value of the threshold is set as 0.8 for each node.

Considering the different number of layers, the results are shown in Figs. 1 and 2, respectively, with the loss coefficient being 0.2. It can be seen that only one layer of dissemination is considered to be less effective. The effect is much more remarkable on Gnutella p2p network. For 2–4 layers, the differences are insignificant. This is because the effect is weakened after the transmission of multi-layers. Therefore, there is no need to consider too many layers.

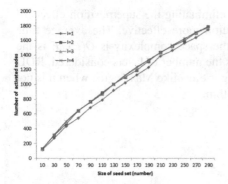

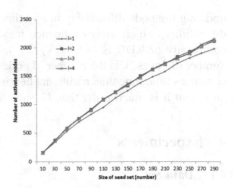

Fig. 1. The algorithm effectiveness of different layers on Gnutella p2p

Fig. 2. The algorithm effectiveness of different layers on PGP

Considering the different value of loss coefficient, the result is shown in the Figs. 3 and 4 when the number of layers is 2. It can be seen that the effect of three different value of the loss coefficient is insignificantly different. On PGP network, the difference of effect among each loss coefficient is much smaller. The reason is that the algorithm RDD has been optimized. Loss coefficient has less effect on the algorithm. As for the Gnutella p2p network, when the loss coefficient is 0.2 the dissemination is slightly better than others, the loss coefficient is set as 0.2 in other experiments of this paper.

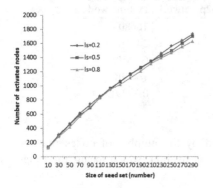

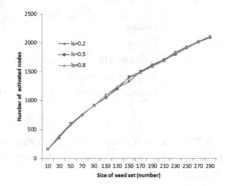

Fig. 3. The algorithm effect of different loss coefficient on Gnutella p2p

Fig. 4. The algorithm effect of different loss coefficient on PGP

Test the Pre-optimized Algorithm (NDC) and the Optimized Algorithm (RDD)
The loss coefficient is set to 0.2 on these two data set, and the effect is shown in Figs. 5 and 6 when the number of layers is 2. It can be seen that the overlap of influence has a large effect on the result when there are more nodes selected in the seed set.

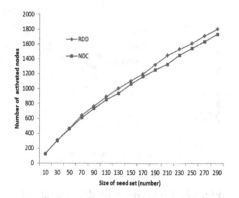

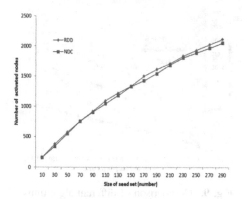

Fig. 5. The algorithm effect on Gnutella p2p ($ls = 0.2$)

Fig. 6. The algorithm effect on PGP ($ls = 0.2$)

When the loss coefficient is large, the optimization still maintains good performance. But the performance before the optimization is greatly reduced as shown in Figs. 7 and 8. On PGP network, when the loss coefficient is 0.2, the influence has no significant effect. If we set the loss coefficient to 0.8, the optimization performs better.

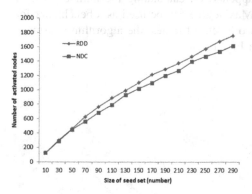

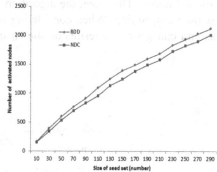

Fig. 7. The algorithm effect on Gnutella p2p ($ls = 0.8$)

Fig. 8. The algorithm effect on PGP ($ls = 0.8$)

Comparison of Different Algorithms' Effect

We compared the proposed algorithm with two existing classical ranking-based algorithms, MaxDegree and PageRank. And the results are shown in Figs. 9 and 10, respectively. For Gnutella peer-to-peer network, the effectiveness of the algorithm is obviously better than the two existing algorithms. The difference between RDD and PageRank's effectiveness is not great on PGP network, but PageRank needs matrix calculation, which consumes a lot of space.

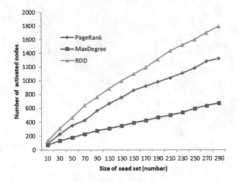
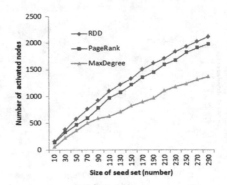

Fig. 9. Comparison of different algorithms' effect on Gnutella p2p

Fig. 10. Comparison of different algorithms' on PGP

Comparison of Time Complexity

When the threshold is set to 0.8 and the number of layers to 2, we can gain the comparisons of the time complexity among MaxDegree, PageRank and proposed algorithm. We found that the cost of time mainly happened in calculating the number of final activated nodes. The algorithm MaxDegree only calculates out-degree of nodes one time, and the cost of time mainly happened on calculating the number of final activated nodes. Therefore, the algorithm MaxDegree can be used as a benchmark for this time-consuming. When considering two layers of nodes, the algorithm consumes less and can get better results as shown in Fig. 11.

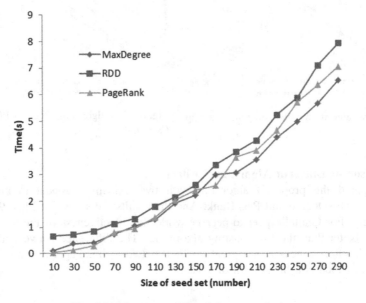

Fig. 11. The comparison of time complexity

5   Conclusion

This paper proposed a new concept, node diffusibility, and a measure metric of node influence. Node diffusibility takes the overall impact of the node and its neighbors into account. Moreover, in order to apply the diffusibility in the dissemination model, an influence maximization algorithm based on real-time and de-superimposed diffusibility was proposed. The algorithm reduces the coincidence of influence of seed node effectively. And the related experiments verified that the method based on the linear threshold model is effective. The results demonstrated that our proposed algorithm works well.

Our future work will focus on the effects of the algorithm on special networks such as weighted graphs, the influence of information timeliness on the result. Also, the influence of node characteristics on the effects of dissemination will be taken into account.

Acknowledgment. The research presented in this paper is supported by the National Key R&D Program of China (No. 2017YFE0117500) and the National Natural Science Foundation of China (No. 61762002).

References

1. Leskovec, J., Adamic, L.A., Huberman, B.A.: The dynamics of viral marketing. ACM Trans. Web (TWEB) **1**(1), 5 (2007)
2. Bhattacharya, S., Gaurav, K., Ghosh, S.: Viral marketing on social networks: an epidemiological perspective. Stat. Mech. Appl., Physica A (2019)
3. Chen, W., Wang, Y., Yang, S.: Efficient influence maximization in social networks. In: Proceedings of the 15th ACM SIGKDD International Conference on Knowledge Discovery and Data Mining, ACM, pp. 199–208 (2009)
4. Aslay, C., Lakshmanan, L.V.S., Lu, W., et al.: Influence maximization in online social networks. In: Proceedings of the Eleventh ACM International Conference on Web Search and Data Mining, ACM, pp. 775–776 (2018)
5. Zhang, Y.C., Liu, Y., Zhang, H.F., et al.: The research of information dissemination model on online social network. Acta Phys. Sin. **60**, 050501 (2011)
6. Richardson, M., Domingos, P.: Mining knowledge-sharing sites for viral marketing. In: Proceedings of the eighth ACM SIGKDD international conference on Knowledge discovery and data mining, ACM, pp. 61–70 (2002)
7. Kempe, D., Kleinberg, J., Tardos, É.: Maximizing the spread of influence through a social network. In: Proceedings of the ninth ACM SIGKDD International Conference on Knowledge Discovery and Data Mining, ACM, pp. 137–146 (2003)
8. Goyal, A., Lu, W., Lakshmanan, L.V.S.: Celf++: optimizing the greedy algorithm for influence maximization in social networks. In: Proceedings of the 20th International Conference Companion on World Wide Web, ACM, pp. 47–48 (2011)
9. Sánchez-Oro, J., Duarte, A.: Iterated greedy algorithm for performing community detection in social networks. Future Gener. Comput. Syst. **88**, 785–791 (2018)
10. Liu, G., Wang, Y., Orgun, M.A., et al.: A heuristic algorithm for trust-oriented service provider selection in complex social networks. In: 2010 IEEE International Conference on Services Computing, IEEE, pp. 130–137 (2010)

11. He, Q., Wang, X., Huang, M., et al.: Heuristics-based influence maximization for opinion formation in social networks. Appl. Soft Comput. **66**, 360–369 (2018)
12. Pathak, N., Banerjee, A., Srivastava, J.: A generalized linear threshold model for multiple cascades. In: 2010 IEEE International Conference on Data Mining, IEEE, pp. 965–970 (2010)
13. Estevez, P.A., Vera, P., Saito, K.: Selecting the most influential nodes in social networks. In: 2007 International Joint Conference on Neural Networks, IEEE, pp. 2397–2402 (2007)
14. Ma, Q., Ma, J.: Identifying and ranking influential spreaders in complex networks with consideration of spreading probability. Physica A Stat. Mech. Appl. **465**, 312–330 (2017)
15. Opsahl, T., Agneessens, F., Skvoretz, J.: Node centrality in weighted networks: generalizing degree and shortest paths. Soc. Networks **32**(3), 245–251 (2010)
16. Freeman, L.C.: Centrality in social networks conceptual clarification. Social Networks **1**(3), 215–239 (1978)
17. Okamoto, K., Chen, W., Li, X.-Y.: Ranking of closeness centrality for large-scale social networks. In: Preparata, Franco P., Wu, X., Yin, J. (eds.) FAW 2008. LNCS, vol. 5059, pp. 186–195. Springer, Heidelberg (2008). https://doi.org/10.1007/978-3-540-69311-6_21
18. Goh, K.I., Oh, E., Kahng, B., et al.: Betweenness centrality correlation in social networks. Phys. Rev. E **67**(1), 017101 (2003)
19. Ding, Y., Yan, E., Frazho, A., et al.: PageRank for ranking authors in co-citation networks. J. Am. Soc. Inf. Sci. Technol. **60**(11), 2229–2243 (2009)
20. Frahm, K.M., Shepelyansky, D.L.: Ising-PageRank model of opinion formation on social networks, p. 121069. Stat. Mech. Appl., Physica A (2019)
21. Kitsak, M., Gallos, L.K., Havlin, S., et al.: Identification of influential spreaders in complex networks. Nat. Phys. **6**(11), 888 (2010)
22. Cao, J.X., Dong, D., Xu, S., et al.: A k-core based algorithm for influence maximization in social networks. Chin. J. Comput. **38**(2), 238–248 (2015)
23. Wang, Y., Cong, G., Song, G., et al.: Community-based greedy algorithm for mining top-k influential nodes in mobile social networks. In: Proceedings of the 16th ACM SIGKDD International Conference on Knowledge Discovery and Data Mining, ACM, pp. 1039–1048 (2010)
24. Leskovec, J., Kleinberg, J., Faloutsos, C.: Graph evolution: densification and shrinking diameters. ACM Trans. Knowl. Discovery from Data (ACM TKDD) **1**(1), 2 (2007)
25. Boguná, M., Pastor-Satorras, R., Díaz-Guilera, A., et al.: Models of social networks based on social distance attachment. Phys. Rev. E **70**(5), 056122 (2004)

Evaluation of Underlying Switching Mechanism for Future Networks with P4 and SDN (Workshop Paper)

O. A. Fernando$^{(\boxtimes)}$ ⓘ, Hannan Xiao ⓘ, and Xianhui Che ⓘ

University of Hertfordshire, Hatfield, UK
{w.k.fernando,h.xiao,x.che}@herts.ac.uk

Abstract. Software Defined Networking (SDN) was introduced with a philosophy of decoupling the control plane from the data plane which facilitates network management while ensuring programmability in order to improve performance and monitoring. OpenFlow which enabled SDN was first introduced to match twelve header fields whilst at current it matches forty one which is expected to grow exponentially. Therefore future networks must have the ability to flexibly parse packets through a common interface. Programming Protocol independent Packet Processing (P4) was introduced to achieve the aforementioned by programming the underlying switch, providing instructions and utilizing APIs to populate the forwarding tables. A P4 programmed switch will forward packets through a parser into multiple stages of match+action tables to find the destination node which is considered the most efficient mechanism for routing. This paper takes into the account the latest platform developed for service providers, Open Networking Operating System (ONOS) to deploy two environments configured in the aforementioned technologies in order to test their performance. Four case studies were drawn which were simulated in Mininet which incorporated SDN + P4 switches. A significant increase of performances were recorded when compared with the performance of cases using SDN only.

Keywords: SDN · P4 · ONOS · Mininet

1 Introduction

By understanding and evaluating the trend of the internet and users intent, it has become evident that the future access of networks will be carried out via utilizing a smart hand held device compared to a red-brick personal computer [13,14]. Cellular network play a crucial part on the aforementioned statement where the users access the medium on-the-go as a habit. The use and application of such technologies has paved the way for researchers to explore new avenues of applications in IoT. They can be listed as mobile cloud computing, vehicular

© ICST Institute for Computer Sciences, Social Informatics and Telecommunications Engineering 2019
Published by Springer Nature Switzerland AG 2019. All Rights Reserved
X. Wang et al. (Eds.): CollaborateCom 2019, LNICST 292, pp. 549–568, 2019.
https://doi.org/10.1007/978-3-030-30146-0_38

networking, edge computing etc. [1]. The heterogeneity of applications executing on user devices requires higher access time and availability of the network over latency. According to a comprehensive research by Mobile and wireless communication Enablers for Twenty-twenty Information Society (METIS) have presented the following key performance indicators (KPIs) for the future networks.

- 1000 times higher mobile data volume
- 10 to 100 times higher typical user data rate
- 10 to 100 times higher number of connected devices
- 10 times longer battery life
- 5 times reduced E2E latency, reaching a target of 5 ms for road safety applications [2]

According to [2] most of the delay derive from the internet. In order to achieve the said requirement of latency, more efficient network architectures, signalling and air interface designs must be taken into consideration. The current networks can not accommodate the above mentioned KPIs due to incapable fundamental designs and centralised routing mechanisms [1] etc. Therefore a new underlying switching/forwarding mechanism must be inherited in order to achieve the KPIs presented by METIS [2] to reduce the latency of the core and increase it's performance.

This research consists of technologies and software which will be later discussed in an in-depth manner. Software Defined Networking (SDN), Programming Protocol independent Packet Processing (P4), Mininet, iPerf, Open Networking Operating System (ONOS) and the GUI of ONOS are among them. SDN was introduced as a mechanism of decoupling, disassociating the data plane from the control plane which provides more efficiency breaking away from the decentralization of the predecessor networks. SDN also improves network performance and enables network monitoring.

P4 is a high level programming language, which is domain-specific with a number of constructs designed for the sole purpose of optimizing network's forwarding plane. P4 is an open-source language maintained by a non-profit organization, which goes under the name P4 Language Consortium [15]. The language was originally described and presented in the white paper titled Programming Protocol-Independent Packet Processors [5].

The research will be based on understanding the functionality of the aforementioned two technologies and evaluating the performance. System design or the test bed will be discussed later with illustrations at Sect. 2. In brief, two environments will be designed with the same variables and resources with the exception of the underlying controller. A network which consists of a SDN controller and an independent environment with P4 switches enabled with a SDN controller are the two. Test results, data and statistics are collected by running various experiments. The said experiments are designed to be line with the ISO OSI model, which will be explained in detail at Sect. 2. Data capture is conducted utilizing a well-known software, Wireshark [16].

Wireshark is a free, open-source software designed for packet analysing. Wireshark equips a GUI for ease of understanding where as a terminal CLI based option is also available. Wireshark has the ability to capture packets as described earlier that can be used for education, troubleshooting, protocol usage, port activities and for conducting various analysis on the network. Whilst conducting the experiments as mentioned above, Wireshark will be activated running on an Ethernet port in promiscuous mode in order to capture the traffic passing through the port. These traffic, data and statistics are later used in the research for analysis.

1.1 Related Work

Future Network Requirements. Future of networking and communication will occupy the space of the current paradigm as predicted by the year 2020. As predicted by technological giants and experts the 5th generation (5G) will be the foundation of the future networking and internet. Due to the complexity and heterogeneity of tomorrow's communication METIS have presented six Horizontal Topics (HT) which can be used to build the foundation of network and communication for tomorrow. The HT's are as follows [18].

- Direct device-to-device communication (D2D)
- Massive machine communication (MMC)
- Moving Networks (MN)
- Ultra-dense networks (UDN)
- Ultra-reliable communication (URC)
- Architecture (Arch)

Table 1 presents a brief summary and a description of the topics that will make future networks possible. Or in a sense, they provide research avenues for both academia and industry to evaluate the current network, invest and implement in features that will enable tomorrows communication possible. As per the author's at [4] *et al.* presents three major use cases or case studies for 5G, which can stated as deduced from the above categories. Although the requirements are similar for the categories, the terminologies given are different. They are

- Enhanced Mobile Broadband (eMBB)
- Ultra-reliable low-latency service (URLLC)
- Massive machine-type communication (mMTC)

By understanding the terminology, it is clear that the above three was derived from the original six aforementioned. Although the requirements for each of the above stated remains the same from the previous, the above are specifically for an environment which facilitates 5G. It is arguable if the future of network presented by various author's were only for 5G or does it falls under the category of 5G and beyond, but following is related research that were conducted in the realm of 5G and future networking.

Related Work. Following is a description of significant work conducted in the realm. Author's at [19] presented a novel approach, known as Softbox. The novel approach was able to reduce the signalling overhead, data plane delay and CPU usage. The author's utilized a P4 core in order to reduce the SDN signalling overhead with a redesigned virtual core. The architecture also facilitates a future networking requirement where the author's were able to achieve a significant reduction in delay.

Research presented by [20] follows a novel approach where the author's distinguishably remark and account the traffic which is present in the network at the time of applying optimization algorithms. Although this research is not in-line with fronthaul or C-RAN, the same logic of accounting traffic which is present in the network is taken into consideration.

Theoretical framework presented by [4] utilizes three different controllers for the future cellular networking infrastructure. Although the paper is in review of the latest applications of technologies, this research understands the utilization of a centralized controller to accommodate future traffic needs. It's application of three different controllers may create traffic overhead in the network. However application of P4 is not present in this framework.

Research presented by [21,22] represents the future of the network in an architecture. This architecture also known as SELFNET utilizes SDN controllers, actuators and sensors in order to carry out functions in the control plane. As stated previously this research encourages the application of a controller to the core of the network but as a flavour of SDN configured using P4. Since P4 has the ability to provide programmability to the forwarding plane, the architecture which ever one presented could benefit from it's application.

1.2   Research Gap and Motivation

The P4 programming language and it's components were delivered in a way to overcome drawbacks of OpenFlow. As per the author's [5] P4 intend to be OpenFlow 2.0. The research is to understand the two potential supporting pillars of future networks and to understand the equilibrium of the two and how it could potentially support the KPI's of future networking and requirements of the software which runs on the network.

To the best of our knowledge, a research has not been conducted in the realm of understanding the performance matrices of the two underlying switching mechanisms. To the best of our knowledge no research has evaluated the two enablers of future networks, SDN independently and SDN with P4. To the best of our knowledge, experiments have not planned nor conducted in accordance with the ISO OSI layer. The experiments will be described in the Sect. 4 in detail with illustration for the ease of understanding.

The primary motivation for the research was derived in-order to understand the performance of the two technological enablers for the networking and the equilibrium of the two. As the gap was derived from referring to the most recent research, the motivation is to understand the performance at it's equilibrium where the P4 has the ability to compliment the performance of a SDN aware

Table 1. Description of Horizontal Topics (HTs) along with the requirements as presented by METIS and elaborated by [18]

HT	Description	Requirements
D2D	Direct communication between devices User plan traffic is hidden, doesn't traverse through the network Minimum interference	Increase coverage Fall-back connectivity Max spectrum utilisation Max capacity Offload backhaul
MMC	Provides two way connectivity to a large number of devices	Data rate Latency Cost
MN	Provide coverage for devices that are part of jointly moving	Communicate with the environment Location awareness
UDN	High traffic demands via infrastructure densification	Increase capacity of radio links Increase energy efficiency of links Better exploitation of spectrum Cost effectiveness Reduced interference Multiple access nodes
URC	Provide high availability	High availability Cost effective Reliability Short response latency
Arch	Platform integrating centralized and decentralized approaches	Heterogeneity Target independence

environment. P4 will deliver independence from underlying protocol and hardware having the ability to provide reconfigurability to the network. Since P4 is designed to conduct the routing based on a match+action table has the ability to compliment the performance of the network. Another motivation can be derived as the need to increase the performance and the productivity of the core network that can reduce the latency of the network as a whole. As per the literature [2], more latency occurs at the core network rather than the latency at the edge or at the end of the network. Hence the motivation was derived.

Since the application of P4 holds merit for networking for tomorrow, more research will follow in future to further support our hypothesis and statistics. The research in future was also considered as a motivation for carrying out this research as a stepping stone. The future work utilizing the P4 enabled SDN environment will be outlined in Sect. 5.

1.3   Contribution

The contribution of the paper are as follows.

- An in-depth analysis of the factors/data/statistics contributing towards increasing performance of the network.
- Experiments benchmarking the ISO-OSI Layer to further clarify and justify the intended use of experiments.
- To the best of our knowledge the two forwarding mechanisms in the data plane have never been tested or evaluated with equal resources given to facilitate a core network for a service provider.
- To the best of our knowledge these data/statistics have not been collected while noise is present in the network.

Structure of the paper is as follows. Section 2 represents the design and the methodology of the experiments which follows a description of the technologies utilized in the domain. Section 3 illustrates a detailed description of the system model. Section 3.1 describes the experiments conducted. Section 4 is a description of the data and an analysis that follows with conclusion and future work in Sect. 5.

2   Design and Methodology

As previously mentioned briefly, the research will consist of two environment with the exception of SDN and P4 against an environment configured with SDN only. The design of the topology is a simple ring with two core switches and two edge switches. An illustration can be found at Figs. 4 and 5. The illustration is self-explanatory for the description provided above. The experiment will consist of independent variables, environments or software such as ONOS, Mininet, Iperf and VLC-wrapper in order to conduct experiments whilst the depending variable will be a SDN flavoured switches in one instantiated environment, P4 switches configured in a SDN environment in the later.

The topology was designed using a python script which is capable of pushing the configuration to Mininet in order to simulate a networking environment. A custom python script was used for the SDN only environment and the bmv2 was used for the later to instantiate P4 switches in the ONOS environment. Since the topology is also an independent variable, the configuration is uniform across both environments.

2.1   System Platforms

Mininet. Mininet [12] is a tool developed at Stanford University which is an open-source, easy-to-deploy and a light-weight network emulator capable of providing a programmable interface to define and build networks and configurations with virtualized elements. It's original intention stands today to alleviate the cost of experimentation by utilizing virtualized resources and software and to perform network testing extensively [6]. Since Mininet has the ability to rapidly prototype large networks and its functions on a single physical computer, this tool has attracted its popularity with the research community to conduct experiments and tests. Tests and experiments not limited to but specializing in OpenFlow [7].

Open Networking Operating System (ONOS). In the recent years, SDN attracted attention from both academia and industry. OpenFlow allows network operators and administrators to replace expensive commodity proprietary hardware with open-source operating systems that has the ability to evolve and scale in time. A such OS has the ability to manage, monitor and programme network switches that facilitates applications and services across a wide range of hardware [8].

To facilitate the above and the KPIs for future networks and applications that is forecast to run on the hardware, ONOS [3] was developed and was launched in April 2013. ONOS is an open source SDN network operating system built for service provider networks [10]. ONOS provides the control plane for a SDN network components such as switches, links etc. and running software, programmes, applications or modules to facilitate and provide communication services to hosts and neighbouring networks [11]. ONOS provides high scalability, high performance and resilience and highly scalable option which makes it the best choice for building next generation SDN and Network Functions Virtualization (NFV) solutions. The GUI provides a global view of the network and its applications whilst maintaining its priority on performance and resilience. Development of ONOS paves the operators and administrators with the ability to vendor neutral control of data plane resources with provisioning capabilities which includes route calculations [9].

ONOS has two APIs, southbound and northbound while its core is responsible for maintaining the network state as mentioned earlier without compromising on the performance. ONOS interacts with the network devices via southbound APIs and Northbound APIs offer services to the applications. ONOS provides three network abstractions at different levels. Flow Rules is responsible for configuring the forwarding logic in devices by abstracting the protocol, Flow Objectives abstract the pipelines of the device and the third level is Intents where it abstracts the topology [10]. Figure 1 is a representation of the different tires of ONOS architecture differentiating the modules and their functions.

ONOS can be configured to run a distributed system (clusters) across multiple servers, allowing it use the CPU and memory of all the underpinned servers whilst maintaining performance and fault tolerance in the face of server failure. This ability of ONOS provides the capability of potential live updates/upgrades without having to reduce/gracefully regrade performance of the system. These updates/upgrades could vary from hardware upgrades to software updates [11].

Methodology is as follows. The environment is pushed utilizing the Mininet API with ONOS as the controller. The distinction between the two environments is detailed in the Table 2. The experiment column will be further explained at Sect. 3. Case study as described in Sect. 2.2 is designed in order to experiment the two platforms which can easily highlight the intended layer in ISO OSI structure. The underlying topology is unique and uniform in both instances.

The experiments which were conducted in both environments were planned meticulously to be in lined with the industry standard. Which is ISO OSI layer. The said statement can be illustrated using the Fig. 2. The experiments were

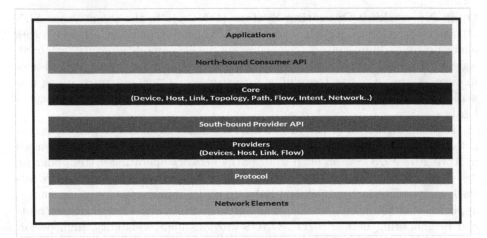

Fig. 1. The illustration represents the ONOS with differentiated tires of functionalities as presented at [11]

Table 2. A summary of the experiments that are conducted in the research, outlining the variable, software and platforms used.

Case	Experiment	ISO OSI Layer	Platform	Software	Data gathered
Case 1	LLDP	Layer II	Ubuntu 16.04 ONOS Mininet	Wireshark	No of Packets Undiscovered Packets
Case 2	ICMP	Layer III		Ping Wireshark	End to End Delay
Case 3	UDP	Layer IV		x-Term Iperf Wireshark	Transmission Delay Throughput
Case 4	Video Streaming	Layer V, VI, VII		x-Term VLC wrapper Wireshark	Quality of Image

built on top of the one which was conducted previously. i.e whilst UDP is passing through the network a separate ICMP is stream and a LLDP stream is present in the background.

2.2   Case Study

The main motivation or the objective of this research is to evaluate the performance of the two forwarding mechanisms that have been presented in literature. Evaluation is conducted in many ways by following several in-depth analysis.

SDN is widely used in current internet infrastructure and forecast to grow even more so with the application and availability of 5G. Whereas P4, a novel approach aims at out performing OpenFlow whilst opening the possibility to achieve the KPIs with respect to the performance inside the core network.

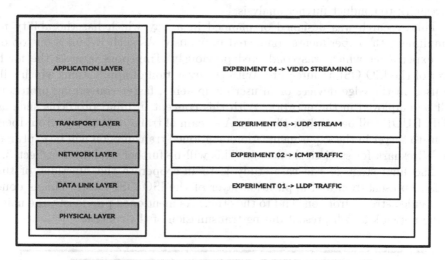

Fig. 2. A visual representation of the experiments which were described in Table 2 are to be in line with ISO OSI layer of communication.

The topology, as illustrated at Fig. 5 is a representation of the underlying network which is configured using python which was pushed towards Mininet. The network consists of four switches, two as edge and two at the core. Two hosts are connected at either ends of the network to the two edge devices. These two hosts (not illustrated) resembles the functionality of the servers, DB, Content Data Centres etc.

The case studies are as follows. There are four primary case studies involved in this research. Each case study involves one or two experiments in their respective environments, which totals the number of experiments to eight. A summary of the experiments along with the software used on each case study is illustrated in Table 2. Following is a description of the experiments conducted.

A core network consists of traffic which is created autonomously without the intention of the administrators. Which is considered as noise, elephant traffic, periodic updates etc. in literature. This traffic is a crucial factor and a metric to consider when an optimization theory is calculated or implemented on the network. Hence the network this research has employed, consists of such traffic simulated in Mininet. The first experiments wraps around the concept of the aforementioned. This experiment functions at the link layer of the network which will be further explained at Sect. 3.

In order to reduce the latency at the core of the network, End-to-End delay must be accounted as a primary experiment. This statistic will significantly provide evidence, which will illustrate whether the medium or the content will be available to the user with the lowest possible latency. Whist conducting the experiment, traffic previously mentioned (LLDP) is also available in making the data realistic. This experiment will be in-lined with the network layer (Layer III) of the ISO OSI layer. As mentioned previously, traffic will be captured by Wireshark to conduct further analysis.

This research was designed or planned in a way which has the ability to compliment the experiments conducted previously. As such it builds on top of the experiment which was conducted previously. Transport layer is the forth layer of the ISO OSI architecture. With the evolution of applications which will be used in the edge devices or in user equipments, faster converging protocols will be employed in the network. With this concept in mind protocols such as UDP, RUDP will be employed heavily. A stream of traffic will be sent from Iperf client to server in the experiment. Aforementioned transmission will be captured via Wireshark for statistical analysis. This will be further explained at Sect. 3.

The final stage of the case study is to in-cooperate the functions of the session, presentation and application layer of the ISO OSI Layer. This is done via a video stream from one end to the other. As mentioned previously, the noise in the network is still present during transmission of the content.

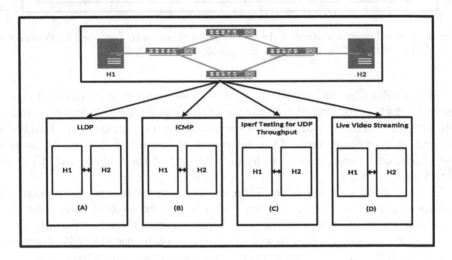

Fig. 3. The experiments conducted under the ring topology utilizing the two distinct variables to test the hypothesis.

3 System Model

In order to test and evaluate the two underlying switching mechanisms, two VMs were deployed using VmWare [17]. Each of this virtual machines are given 16 GB of RAM, 60 GB HDD and 4 CPU cores with Ubuntu 16.04 LTS as the guest operating system. Wireshark was installed on both VMs monitoring the

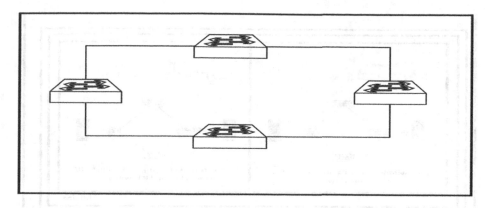

Fig. 4. The underlying network architecture for the core designed to test the two forwarding mechanism.

virtual Ethernet ports that are configured using the Mininet. The topology was described and fed to Mininet using a python script and ONOS was installed in both instances with the exception of one environment configured to operate P4 switches with the former configured to operate under OpenFlow.

Figure 4 is a representation of the environment which was used in order to carry out the tests. It consists of four switches connected in a ring topology with equal weight and bandwidth in each link. The exception as mentioned above is the differentiation of the forwarding mechanism. SDN or SDN+P4. Two Hosts are connected at either ends to the two edge switches. Since the illustrated environment is a representation of the core network, the experiment seeks to answer the KPIs, for the future networks. Hosts in the network are an illustration of a server, end point, processing agent, UE etc. but for the purpose of the experiment the aforementioned hosts are capable of a PC's processors which is supported by Mininet. Figure 5 represents the two environments with variable (P4 or SDN) difference.

Figure 3 represents the experiments which were conducted in order to test the hypothesis of the best underlying forwarding/switching mechanism for the core network of a service provider. These experiments are in-lined with the KPIs presented in section I towards future networks. The list of experiments that have conducted on the environment can be found at Table 2. An illustration of the said experiments in line with the ISO OSI layer can be found at Fig. 2.

Case Study I. The following is an elaboration of the experiments conducted in a detailed manner. Figure 3(a) illustrates the first experiment conducted. The application of a controller requires periodic updates to be sent over the network in order to keep track of links, hosts, servers, elements, traffic etc. This traffic is mandatory for the function of the environment. The future networks requires crucial availability of the medium, hence this type of traffic is mandatory. The periodic traffic ensures that the services and servers are aware/live and kept

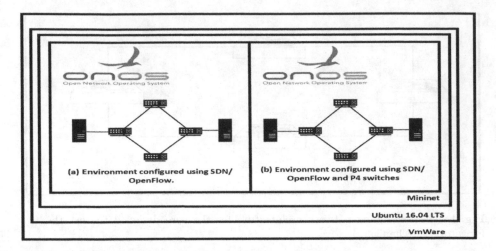

Fig. 5. Illustrated description of the two environments. (a) Represents the environment which is configured using OpenFlow. (b) Represents the environment configured using P4 switches. As illustrated ONOS is acting as the controller with Mininet emulating the network with Ubuntu 16.04 LTS as the guest OS on VmWare.

at ready state. These updates must be accounted for when an improvement algorithm is being placed in the network. Hence this traffic is a crucial factor for administrators. Wireshark was used in order to monitor and capture the LLDP packets travelling inside the network.

Case Study II. Figure 3(b) represents the experiment where a continuous stream of ICMP messages were sent from H1 towards H2. The controllers will decide the best route for the stream to traverse. The selected route is visible via accessing the ONOS GUI. A total of 1300 packets are transmitted from H1 to H2. Wireshark with sudo privileges posses the capability to listen to traffic at a given Ethernet port. Packets are collected at the destination node utilizing Wireshark. Above experiment is conducted on both environments, SDN and SDN + P4.

Case Study III. Figure 3(c) represents the third test/experiment which was conducted in the network. An Iperf test was carried out where H1 acts as the Iperf Server and H2 as the Iperf Client. The future network requirements will provide new avenues for various applications to run on the network and on the host devices. In the instance of such higher data rates must be employed with highly efficient transmission protocols. Hence protocols such as UDP, RUDP and other protocols of same resemblance will have more merit. In order to test the latency and support the hypothesis a UDP stream is generated via accessing the x-term of the hosts utilizing the Mininet simulator. Data transmission can be monitored via accessing the Wireshark with sudo privileges listening to the relevant Ethernet port. One of an additional advantage is that the protocol functionality along with the port information can also be viewed using Wireshark.

Case Study IV. Forth test compliments the third experiment and have the ability to support the hypothesis even better. Since Iperf sends a randomly generated stream of UDP data between a client and a server, a live video stream amongst the two hosts will carry actual UDP data. The transmission is conducted utilizing the vlc-wrapper by accessing the x-term of hosts. In the experiment H1 will be considered the content network or the content provider whilst H2 will be considered the service or the server/edge server/user equipment/host requesting the content. Wireshark with sudo privileges as mentioned above has the ability to listen to live stream of traffic passing in the network with port information. The test results are qualitative in the underpinned experiment whilst previous tests are consisting quantitative data. The quality of the video is examined by understanding and capturing the frequency of frame lag in the video from original. Displaced pixels and frames arriving late will also be monitored and recorded. Total number of UDP packets will also be recorded in order to test and evaluate the quality of the video.

4   Data and Analysis

The following is a discussion of the data which was gathered at the end of each experiment and the analysis that follows of the results. The results which are presented here are in the same order as it is shown in the Table 2 and the Fig. 3. The distinction of the environment along with the variables that were used to configure the aforementioned is illustrated at Fig. 5. The data were collected utilizing a well-known tool Wireshark as previously mentioned.

4.1   Traffic in the Idle State

The data were collected utilizing the network monitoring tool Wireshark. Upon sending the network configuration file to the Mininet API, by default LLDP packets are generated due to the design of the controller. These packets serve a purpose to the controller, in which the controller is fully aware of the changes in the network since the network devices advertise information about themselves to their neighbours. These traffic is a crucial factor for future networking since the aforementioned traffic will be present in the network at any given time.

Figure 6 represents the traffic in the environment configured with SDN when there's no traffic is available and in idle state where as Fig. 7 represents the same traffic when a P4 switch is present in an environment with SDN.

It is a clear representation of the traffic which is passing through the network when it is in idle state. The Wireshark has the ability to listen to traffic at a given time in a given specific port. By careful observation of Fig. 6, we can observe points where the LLDP have recorded one packet instead of two. These points are highlighted in the plot as well. They are (54,1), (57,1), (64,1), (104,1)

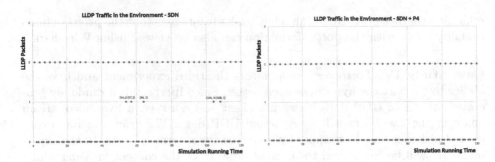

Fig. 6. LLDP traffic in SDN   **Fig. 7.** LLDP traffic in SDN+P4

and (108,1). Although it may seem like a drop in the network, the ambiguity of the network could cause delay or service unavailability in the future applications which requires trivial access and availability of the content and medium. It is evident that the environment when configured with the SDN and P4 has a constant pattern. Since the match+action table consists of neighbour information and routing information the future networks will not have to face moments of ambiguity.

For the purpose of this research, simulation time was 120 s. Hence the noted points of ambiguity in the network is as low as four points. If a higher sample size was chosen with more nodes connected to the controller, more results can be observed. But for the purpose of this research, the chosen sample size is 120 s.

4.2 ICMP

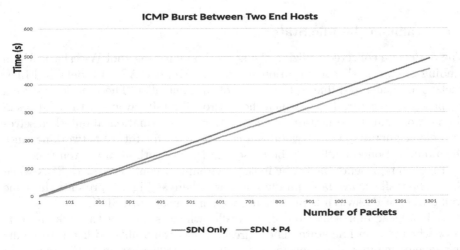

Fig. 8. Illustration of the ICMP bursts in the two environments for 1300 packets (Color figure online)

ICMP is traffic is sent from H1 towards H2 utilizing the Mininet CLI. The traffic can also be generated using the x-term, but for the purpose of the experiment traffic is generated using a simple command in the Mininet CLI. The logic behind the experiment is that the minimum time spent on the process will provide the future environments with the lowest form of latency. Since the networks of tomorrow requires faster traverse of traffic in the core of the network, this experiment can provide feedback and evidence to support.

Figure 8 represents the ICMP burst between the two end hosts in the same graph with SDN only environment in blue and SDN + P4 in amber. It is evident that SDN + P4 requires a smaller time frame (452 s) to traverse the ICMP packets to the end host where as SDN only environment requires a higher time (492 s) comparatively to the latter. Destination host was discovered after 3 s in the SDN environment where as the SDN + P4 environment consumed 0.23 s. Although the time gap is not significantly greater, the future network requires 5 times reduced latency, refer Sect. 1.

Mathematical difference between the two is as little as 40 s. This difference can be observed in a more significant scale if the sample size was increased. But for the purpose of this experiment a sample size of 1300 packets were chosen. If more number of packets were captured containing ICMP traffic more of a difference will be able to identify. Although this is the case, the route request time will have no effect. This is because it represents the time which is required by the controller to define the route for the packets to traverse. Increasing the sample size will have no effect on the end result since it directly speaks of the effectiveness of the controller.

4.3 UDP

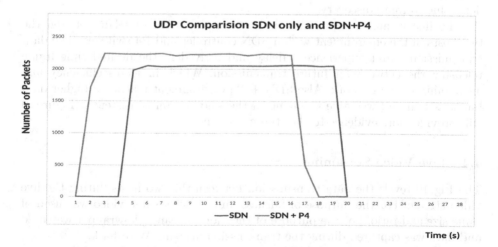

Fig. 9. Illustration of the UDP stream of between the two hosts

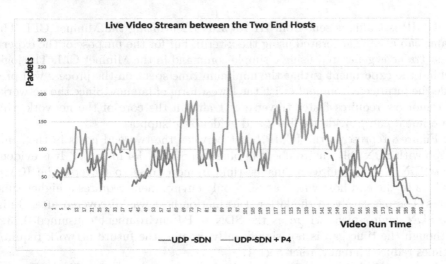

Fig. 10. Live video stream UDP capture utilizing wireshark

Figure 9 is a representation of a capture file which was derived from Wireshark to the traffic which was generated using x-term in the Mininet for an Iperf test of a UDP stream. Out of the two hosts, H1 carried out the Iperf server functionality whilst H2 as the client. A data burst of 25 Mb was sent for the duration of 15 s in order to make the noise in the network create effect and a larger data burst would make the noise negligible.

The line of blue in the Fig. 9 represents the stream of UDP traffic in the environment configured using SDN and a delay of 4 s can be observed which resulted the stream to end with a delay of 3 s. The Data stream started with a delay due to route discovery.

The line in amber represents the data transmission of UDP between the two hosts in the environment with a SDN controller and P4 switches. The data transmission didn't experience a delay and arrived in the desired time frame releasing the network for future transmission. Which indicates efficiency and availability of the network. Also SDN + P4 environment reached a higher data burst as well and was able to maintain the said stream consistently. Figure 10 will provide more evidence to the statements above.

4.4   Live Video Streaming

The Fig. 10 revels the data transmission between the two hosts during the live video stream. For the purpose of fairness and equality same video was used of same size and ratio. For the purpose of the video stream, vlc-wrapper was used and data was captured during the transmission utilizing Wireshark.

As in previous diagrams, SDN is represented using blue lines whilst amber represents the UDP stream of SDN + P4 switches. As represented the blue line of the diagram tend to have a significant drop or below the expected rate

Original Frame in the Video at the Source	Frame at the Receiving End

Fig. 11. Live video stream between the two hosts, demonstrating the quality of the frames in the environment configured with SDN

compared to amber line. This cause for the video to experience distorted pixels and become low in quality at unfrequented times. However the video stream which is represented in amber seems to have significant performance since the video show no disoriented pixels or frames with video arriving at the destination as the same time (with an insignificant delay) as it is being displayed at the local source. In both these scenarios background traffic was present in order to simulate a real-life environment. The high points in the Fig. 10 seems to be overlapping with each other but a significant difference is visible at the start of the video where the link tends to be busy with existing traffic. Still the SDN + P4 achieved the first high data burst compared to SDN only environment making the video more accessible/high in quality to the destination. This is because the application of P4 switches and its function of the match+action table assist the controllers with route discovery and routing.

The above paragraph can be further justified by the Figs. 11 and 12. The Fig. 11 represents the video stream of the environment configured using SDN. Left hand two images represents the video displayed locally whilst the right hand side is the video at the destination. As captured, the video is of low quality with disoriented pixels visible on the frame. The low points of the Fig. 10 represents these disoriented images. Figure 9 shows a delay in the start of UDP stream to occur. The third and fourth images of the Fig. 11 can be used as evidence to further support the findings. The image on the right (fourth) can be seen in a mode of transition (trees on the adjacent left hand image are visible) from the existing frame of the video. Hence the significant delay in delivering the packets can be observed.

Figure 12 represents the video stream in the environment configured in SDN + P4. As shown in the figure quality of the picture shows a significant

Original Frame in the Video at Source	Frame at the Receiving End

Fig. 12. Live video stream between the two hosts, demonstrating the quality of the frames in the environment configured with SDN+P4

improvement compared to the one configured in SDN only. The frames seem to arrive at the destination with a least significant delay. By close inspection of the images from left to the images on right in the Fig. 12 a slight delay of frames can be observed. But this is insignificant compared to the delay of frames which are arriving at the destination in the Fig. 11. This is further supporting the Figs. 8, 9 and 10. With the background traffic, the controller seems to be complemented with the effect, programmability the P4 has offered.

By further understanding the data that were gathered, following conclusions can be derived. Compared to the SDN only case study, a decrease of 92% can be observed in the time controller spent on destination host discovery. Also a total of 7% reduction in the case study SDN + P4 can be observed in the total E2E compared to the SDN only environment. UDP transmission delay has a significant reduction in SDN + P4 environment of which is 70%. The above statistics significantly improved the quality of the video feed in the last experiment. 8% increase of quality can be marked in the SDN + P4 environment compared to the SDN only case study. Hence the quality of the video was observed. The statistics are all leading up to confirming that the future of networking can benefit greatly from applying a fabric of SDN + P4 as the underlying switching mechanism. The experiments conducted, data gathered and the calculated statistics are all providing evidence to the statement above.

5   Conclusion and Future Work

By a series of test and experiments expanding over the ISO OSI layer of the two environments with four use cases, we can conclude the performances of the environment of SDN + P4 switches stands out superior to the environment without P4. Hence it is wise to incorporate P4 switching mechanisms in the core of the network for a service provider to better utilize resources and provide services with minimal latency and minimal ambiguity.

Following this research, we aim to utilize the environment to further run experiments with a fully functioning core which includes various services and databases. We also aim to simulate the aforementioned in real equipments as oppose to Mininet to further support the findings of this research.

References

1. Wang, H., Chen, S., Xu, H., Ai, M., Shi, Y.S.N.: A software defined decentralized mobile network architecture toward 5G. IEEE Network **29**(2), 16–22 (2015)
2. Monserrat, J.F., Mange, G., Braun, V., Tullberg, H., Zimmermann, G., Bulakci, Ö.: METIS research advances towards the 5G mobile and wireless system definition. EURASIP J. Wirel. Commun. Network. **2015**(1), 53 (2015)
3. ONOS project. https://onosproject.org/. Accessed 19 Mar 2019
4. Li, R.: Intelligent 5G: when cellular networks meet artificial intelligence. IEEE Wirel. Commun. **24**(5), 175–183 (2017)
5. Bosshart, P., et al.: P4: programming protocol-independent packet processors. ACM SIGCOMM Comput. Commun. Rev. **44**(3), 87–95 (2014)
6. Muelas, D., Ramos, J., de Vergara, J.E.: Lopez assessing the limits of mininet-based environments for network experimentation. IEEE Network **32**(6), 168–176 (2018)
7. De Oliveira, R.L.S., et al.: Using mininet for emulation and prototyping software-defined networks. In: 2014 IEEE Colombian Conference on Communications and Computing (COLCOM), pp. 1–6 (2014). Organization IEEE
8. Berde, P., et al.: ONOS: towards an open, distributed SDN OS. In: Proceedings of the Third Workshop on Hot Topics in Software Defined Networking, pp. 1–6 (2014). Organization ACM
9. Giorgetti, A., Secondini, M., Cugini, F., Sgambelluri, A., Castoldi, P.: ONOS MetroApp for filtering effect assessment in metro optical networks. In: 2018 European Conference on Optical Communication (ECOC), pp. 1–3 (2018). Organization IEEE
10. Sanvito, D., et al.: ONOS Intent Monitor and Reroute service: enabling plug & play routing logic. In: 2018 4th IEEE Conference on Network Softwarization and Workshops (NetSoft), pp. 272–276 (2018). Organization IEEE
11. ONOS project. https://wiki.onosproject.org/. Accessed 20 Mar 2019
12. Mininet. http://mininet.org/. Accessed 24 Mar 2019
13. Cisco Visual Networking Index: Forecast and Methodology, 2016to2021, Cisco Public, (2017). Cisco
14. Cisco The Zettabyte Era: Trends and Analysis, Cisco Public (2017). Cisco
15. P4 Language Consortium. https://p4.org/. Accessed 24 Mar 2019
16. Wireshark. https://www.wireshark.org/. Accessed 24 Mar 2019
17. VM-Ware Workstation. https://www.vmware.com/uk/products/workstation-pro/workstation-pro-evaluation.html. Accessed 24 Mar 2019
18. Osseiran, A., et al.: Scenarios for 5G mobile and wireless communications: the vision of the METIS project. IEEE Commun. Mag. **52**(5), 26–35 (2014)

19. Moradi, M., Lin, Y., Mao, Z.M., Sen, S., Spatscheck, O.: SoftBox: a customizable, low-latency, and scalable 5G core network architecture. IEEE J. Sel. Areas Commun. **36**(3), 438–456 (2018)
20. Luong, P., Gagnon, F., Despins, C., Tran, L.-N.: Joint virtual computing and radio resource allocation in limited fronthaul green C-RANs. IEEE Trans. Wirel. Commun. **17**(4), 2602–2617 (2018)
21. Jiang, W., Strufe, M., Schotten, H.D.: Intelligent network management for 5G systems: the SELFNET approach. In: 2017 European Conference on Networks and Communications (EuCNC), pp. 1–5 (2017)
22. Jiang, W., Strufe, M., Schotten, H.: Autonomic network management for software-defined and virtualized 5G systems. In: European Wireless 2017; 23rd European Wireless Conference, pp. 1–6 (2017). Organization IEEE

Quantum Based Networks: Analysis of Quantum Teleportation Protocol and Entanglement Swapping (Workshop Paper)

Preeti Kandwal$^{(\boxtimes)}$ [iD], William Joseph Spring [iD], and Hannan Xiao [iD]

University of Hertfordshire, Hatfield, UK
{p.kandwal,j.spring,h.xiao}@herts.ac.uk

Abstract. In this paper we consider the quantum teleportation and entanglement swapping protocols used in quantum based networks for passing information between a sender and receiver. For the teleportation protocol we observe and identify relationships that exist between Einstein-Podolsky-Rosen (EPR) Bell states employed as quantum resources, measured sender values and the gates employed at the receiver side. For the entanglement swapping protocol we consider input and output EPR states and the relationship between the two. We include a review of the concepts and our findings from the analysis carried out.

Keywords: Teleporation · Entanglement · Entanglement swapping ·
Bell states · Quantum networks and communication ·
Quantum applications

1 Introduction

Quantum networks have been in existence since DARPA's 2003 Quantum Network [19] and have experienced substantial development during the last two decades. Examples include SECOQC - Secure Communication based on Quantum Cryptography Network [33], the TOKYO Network [38] and the Generic Network and Networks in Classical communication [7]. Distances of 2000 km are now being achieved [21,46], using entanglement, teleportation, and entanglement swapping. Recent developments in technology are opening up new and exciting possibilities for the practical application of quantum concepts to networks and distributed systems with the potential for realising a quantum based internet together with quantum based cloud resources [13,15,21,24,34].

Quantum teleportation is an important tool that is used in establishing a global platform for secure quantum networks and communication and distributed quantum applications [10,44]. The sharing of information between a sender and a receiver via quantum based networks and distributed systems employs the use of quantum entanglement [18,23], local operations with classical communication

© ICST Institute for Computer Sciences, Social Informatics and Telecommunications Engineering 2019
Published by Springer Nature Switzerland AG 2019. All Rights Reserved
X. Wang et al. (Eds.): CollaborateCom 2019, LNICST 292, pp. 569–582, 2019.
https://doi.org/10.1007/978-3-030-30146-0_39

(LOCC) [8,31,44] together with a classical communication channel. Teleportation is a fundamental resource which can be utilised in many applications such as quantum repeaters [12], quantum networks [7] and quantum computing based on measurements [36].

From an experimental point of view we do not have pure quantum system due to decoherence; however, in theory quantum computing is considered a major breakthrough in technology. Quantum entanglement and quantum teleportation play a significant role in a variety of models for quantum communication and distributed networks [9,11,31,44]. Entanglement swapping [30,32] using polarised qubits [32] have laid the foundation for the development of quantum repeaters [12] enabling long distance quantum communication.

However, to the best of our knowledge, the analysis of the quantum teleportation and entanglement swapping protocols has not been generalised in the literature, although analysis of specific inputs have been presented. This motivates us to generalise the analysis for both protocols; such generalised analysis will facilitate further analysis of applications such as quantum-based networks with quantum repeaters that rely on the quantum teleportation and entanglement swapping protocols.

The rest of the paper is organised as below. In Sect. 2 we briefly introduce the quantum teleportation protocol and present our generalised analysis and observations. In Sect. 3, we present our generalised analysis of entanglement swapping and observations. Finally we conclude the paper in Sect. 4.

2   Quantum Teleportation

Quantum based research, both theoretical and experimental have now moved into a 'second global wave' with academia and industry combining to develop and advance quantum technology. Companies such as IBM [1], Google [2], Toshiba [3], Intel [4] and Microsoft [5] are each actively involved in the quantum revolution. With time and technology, one of the most outstanding achievement has been in the distance achieved for networks using teleportation [29,35,42,45,46]. In 1998, the first successful teleportation was observed approximately across a distance of one meter [42] at the California Institute of Technology. In 2006, Quantum teleportation between different quantum systems (light and matter) was experimentally achieved by Sherson et al. [39], increasing the possibility for improved quantum memories [26,40]. Such developments involving memory and distance are now possible together with the possibility for the development of a quantum internet [27]. Success followed in 2012 when an experiment [29] achieved over 143 km of quantum teleportation between the two Canary Islands of La Palma and Tenerife. This led to the establishment of metropolitan area networks using optic modes leading to unconditional security [20] over long distance quantum networks.

Recent breakthroughs [45] in the area of long distance quantum teleportation have improved quantum communication achieving success in establishing quantum communication across a free space distance of 1200 km (by free space is meant no interference from the environment which is practically difficult to achieve, and is carried in space). Using free space for the purpose of quantum communication reduces the chances of channel loss because the travel path for each photon is predominantly in empty space [37], as a result no disturbance is experienced in establishing quantum communication.

2.1 Teleportation

We commence this section with the brief introduction of the teleportation protocol itself. The quantum teleportation protocol is used in quantum networks for teleporting an unknown state from one location to another location. It is used to teleport or transfer any unknown state between a pair of users sharing an entangled Bell state (Fig. 1).

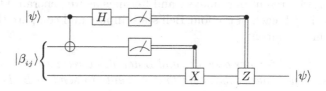

Fig. 1. Quantum teleportation protocol [17]

Generating Bell States: Bell states are the maximally entangled states of two qubits. Bell state is generated using a Hadamard gate, $\mathbb{H}$ along with a Controlled NOT or CNOT gate. The following circuit diagram illustrates how one can generate Bell states.

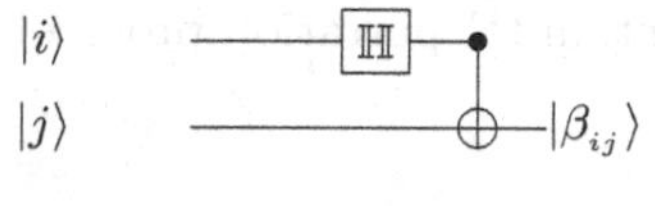

$$|i\rangle \quad \text{---}\boxed{\mathbb{H}}\text{---}\bullet\text{---}$$
$$|j\rangle \quad \text{-------}\oplus\text{---}|\beta_{ij}\rangle$$

Fig. 2. Bell states generation [17]

For any two qubits $|i\rangle$ and $|j\rangle$ with $i, j \in 0, 1$, we define the associated Bell state as:

$$|\beta_{ij}\rangle = \frac{1}{\sqrt{2}}\left(|0j\rangle + (-1)^i |1\bar{j}\rangle\right) \tag{1}$$

in which $\bar{j}$ represents the opposite of j, e.g., if $j = 0$ then $\bar{j} = 1$ and vice versa. We therefore have four Bell states in total in which $ij \in \{00, 01, 10, 11\}$ (Fig. 2).

For example, if we input the qubits $|0\rangle$ and $|0\rangle$ to the circuit, then the Hadamard gate changes the state of $|00\rangle$ to $\frac{1}{\sqrt{2}}\left((|0\rangle + |1\rangle)|0\rangle\right) = \frac{1}{\sqrt{2}}(|00\rangle + |10\rangle)$, to which the CNOT gate is applied generating $\frac{1}{\sqrt{2}}(|00\rangle + |11\rangle)$. The four Bell states are

$$|\beta_{00}\rangle = \frac{1}{\sqrt{2}}(|00\rangle + |11\rangle)$$

$$|\beta_{01}\rangle = \frac{1}{\sqrt{2}}(|01\rangle + |10\rangle)$$

$$|\beta_{10}\rangle = \frac{1}{\sqrt{2}}(|00\rangle - |11\rangle)$$

$$|\beta_{11}\rangle = \frac{1}{\sqrt{2}}(|01\rangle - |10\rangle)$$

2.2 A Generalised Analysis of the Teleportation Protocol

In this section we present our analysis and findings as we generalise the teleportation protocol with each of the four Bell state inputs and compare the patterns that emerge in the output.

Theorem 1. *Let A denotes a sender and B denotes a receiver. Let $|\psi\rangle = \alpha |0\rangle + \beta |1\rangle$ denotes an unknown qubit state that A wants to send to B. Let $|\beta_{ij}\rangle$ with $i, j \in \{0, 1\}$ denote a general Bell state. Then following measurement at A with respect to the basis $B = \{|kl\rangle\}_{k,l \in \{0,1\}}$ the photon at B is found to be in one of four states*

$$|\bar{\psi}\rangle = \begin{cases} \alpha |j\rangle \pm (-1)^i \beta |\bar{j}\rangle, & i, j \in \{0, 2\} \\ \beta |j\rangle \pm (-1)^i \alpha |\bar{j}\rangle, & i, j \in \{1, 3\} \end{cases} \tag{2}$$

resulting in recovery of $|\psi\rangle$ at the receiver's side following the application of $\mathbb{Z}^{i+k} \mathbb{X}^{j+l}$ to the receiver's part of the shared Bell state resource.

Proof. Using Eq. (1) and applying the operator $(\mathbb{H} \otimes \mathbb{I})_0 CNOT$ at the senders side to the unknown state $|\psi\rangle$ with shared Bell state resource $|\beta_{ij}\rangle$ generates the given result for $|\bar{\psi}\rangle$ in quantum teleportation protocol.

$$|\psi_1\rangle = |\psi\rangle \otimes |\beta_{ij}\rangle$$

$$|\psi_1\rangle = (\alpha |0\rangle + \beta|1\rangle).\frac{1}{\sqrt{2}}(|0j\rangle + (-1)^i |1\bar{j}\rangle)$$

$$= \frac{1}{\sqrt{2}}\{\alpha|0\rangle(|0j\rangle + (-1)^i |1\bar{j}\rangle) + \beta|1\rangle(|0j\rangle + (-1)^i |1\bar{j}\rangle)\}$$

$$= \frac{1}{\sqrt{2}}(\alpha |0\rangle |0j\rangle + (-1)^i\alpha |0\rangle |1\bar{j}\rangle + \beta |1\rangle |0j\rangle + (-1)^i\beta |1\rangle |1\bar{j}\rangle)$$

$$|\psi_2\rangle = (\text{CNOT} \otimes \mathbb{I}) |\psi_1\rangle$$

$$= \frac{1}{\sqrt{2}}(\alpha |0\rangle (|0j\rangle + (-1)^i |1\bar{j}\rangle) + \beta |1\rangle (|1j\rangle + (-1)^i |0\bar{j}\rangle))$$

$$|\psi_3\rangle = (\mathbb{H} \otimes \mathbb{I} \otimes \mathbb{I}) |\psi_2\rangle$$

$$= \frac{1}{\sqrt{2}}.\frac{1}{\sqrt{2}}(\alpha(|0\rangle + |1\rangle)(|0j\rangle + (-1)^i |1\bar{j}\rangle) + \beta(|0\rangle - |1\rangle)(|1j\rangle + (-1)^i |0\bar{j}\rangle))$$

$\frac{1}{2}(\alpha\,|00j\rangle + (-1)^i\alpha\,|01\bar{j}\rangle + \alpha10j + (-1)^i\alpha\,|11\bar{j}\rangle + \beta\,|01j\rangle + (-1)^i\beta\,|00\bar{j}\rangle - \beta\,|11j\rangle - (-1)^i\beta\,|10\bar{j}\rangle)$

$= \frac{1}{2}\big(|00\rangle\,(\alpha\,|j\rangle + (-1)^i\beta\,|\bar{j}\rangle) + |01\rangle\,((-1)^i\alpha\,|\bar{j}\rangle + \beta\,|j\rangle) + |10\rangle\,(\alpha\,|j\rangle - (-1)^i\beta\,|\bar{j}\rangle) + |11\rangle\,((-1)^i\alpha\,|\bar{j}\rangle - \beta\,|j\rangle)\big)$

$= \frac{1}{2}\big(|00\rangle\,(\alpha\,|j\rangle + (-1)^i\beta\,|\bar{j}\rangle) + |01\rangle\,(\beta\,|j\rangle + (-1)^i\alpha\,|\bar{j}\rangle) + |10\rangle\,(\alpha\,|j\rangle - (-1)^i\beta\,|\bar{j}\rangle) - |11\rangle\,(\beta\,|j\rangle) - (-1)^i\alpha\,|\bar{j}\rangle\big)$

We now measure with respect to the basis $|\{k, l\}\rangle_{k,l \in \{0,1\}}$ identifying the corresponding receiver states as shown in Table 1.

Table 1. Quantum teleportation protocol with classical values and corresponding outputs.

Classical (k, l)	$|kl\rangle$	Corresponding operation
(0, 0)	$|00\rangle$	$(\alpha\,|j\rangle + (-1)^i\beta\,|\bar{j}\rangle)$
(0, 1)	$|01\rangle$	$(\beta\,|j\rangle + (-1)^i\alpha\,|\bar{j}\rangle)$
(1, 0)	$|10\rangle$	$(\alpha\,|j\rangle - (-1)^i\beta\,|\bar{j}\rangle)$
(1, 1)	$|11\rangle$	$-(\beta\,|j\rangle - (-1)^i\alpha\,|\bar{j}\rangle)$

Based on the above generalisation we note that the following formula for teleportation holds.

$$|\psi\rangle \xmapsto{\;|\beta_{ij}\rangle\;} |kl\rangle\,\mathbb{X}^{j+l}\mathbb{Z}^{i+k} \tag{3}$$

where $|\beta_{ij}\rangle$ is any of the Bell state; $|i, j\rangle$ represents the qubits in Bell state; and k, l represents the classical values after measurement. Hence for any $|\beta_{ij}\rangle$ and (k, l), Bob (receiver) needs to apply $\mathbb{X}^{j+l}\mathbb{Z}^{i+k}$; we note that the superscripts are $mod2$. By substituting the ij values of the entangled Bell state in the Table 1 the reciever can reconstruct the original quantum state, $|\psi\rangle$.

Example 1. Let us consider the case, where $|\beta_{ij}\rangle = |\beta_{00}\rangle$ and using Table 1 we receive the below information on following the protocol:

$|00\rangle\,(\alpha\,|j\rangle + (-1)^i\beta\,|\bar{j}\rangle) \implies |00\rangle\,(\alpha\,|0\rangle + (-1)^0\beta\,|1\rangle) = |00\rangle\,(\alpha\,|0\rangle + \beta\,|1\rangle) = |00\rangle\,|\psi\rangle$

$|01\rangle\,(\beta\,|j\rangle + (-1)^i\alpha\,|\bar{j}\rangle) \implies |01\rangle\,(\beta\,|0\rangle + (-1)^0\alpha\,|1\rangle) = |01\rangle\,(\beta\,|0\rangle + \alpha\,|1\rangle) = |01\rangle\,\mathbb{X}\,|\psi\rangle$

$|10\rangle\,(\alpha\,|j\rangle - (-1)^i\beta\,|\bar{j}\rangle) \implies |10\rangle\,(\alpha\,|0\rangle - (-1)^0\beta\,|1\rangle) = |10\rangle\,(\alpha\,|0\rangle - \beta\,|1\rangle) = |10\rangle\,\mathbb{Z}\,|\psi\rangle$

$|11\rangle \{-(\beta\,|j\rangle + (-1)^i \alpha\,|\bar{j}\rangle)\} \implies |11\rangle \{-(\beta\,|0\rangle - (-1)^0 \alpha\,|1\rangle)\} = |11\rangle \{-(\beta\,|0\rangle - \alpha\,|1\rangle)\} = |11\rangle (\alpha\,|1\rangle - \beta\,|0\rangle) = |11\rangle \,\mathbb{XZ}\,|\psi\rangle$

2.3 Observations

Combining all four Bell states together we obtain the following table:

Table 2. Quantum teleportation protocol for all four Bell states with classical values and corresponding quantum operators.

$|\beta_{ij}\rangle$	Input Bell state $|\beta_{00}\rangle$		Input Bell state $|\beta_{01}\rangle$		Input Bell state $|\beta_{10}\rangle$		Input Bell state $|\beta_{11}\rangle$	
$|ij\rangle$	$|00\rangle$	$|\psi\rangle$	$|01\rangle$	$|\psi\rangle$	$|10\rangle$	$|\psi\rangle$	$|11\rangle$	$|\psi\rangle$
$|i\bar{j}\rangle$	$|01\rangle$	$\mathbb{X}\,|\psi\rangle$	$|00\rangle$	$\mathbb{X}\,|\psi\rangle$	$|11\rangle$	$\mathbb{X}\,|\psi\rangle$	$|10\rangle$	$\mathbb{X}\,|\psi\rangle$
$|\bar{i}j\rangle$	$|10\rangle$	$\mathbb{Z}\,|\psi\rangle$	$|11\rangle$	$\mathbb{Z}\,|\psi\rangle$	$|00\rangle$	$\mathbb{Z}\,|\psi\rangle$	$|01\rangle$	$\mathbb{Z}\,|\psi\rangle$
$|\bar{i}\bar{j}\rangle$	$|11\rangle$	$\mathbb{XZ}\,|\psi\rangle$	$|10\rangle$	$\mathbb{XZ}\,|\psi\rangle$	$|01\rangle$	$\mathbb{XZ}\,|\psi\rangle$	$|00\rangle$	$\mathbb{XZ}\,|\psi\rangle$

We observe the patterns from Table 2 for the teleportation protocol and find that given an entangled state $|\beta_{ij}\rangle$ and measurement outcomes (k, l) on the senders side, the corresponding state on the receivers side would be as follows:

Table 3. General form of teleportation.

$|\beta_{ij}\rangle$	$k=0, l=0$	$k=0, l=1$	$k=1, l=0$	$k=1, l=1$
$|\beta_{00}\rangle$	$|\psi\rangle$	$\mathbb{X}\,|\psi\rangle$	$\mathbb{Z}\,|\psi\rangle$	$\mathbb{XZ}\,|\psi\rangle$
$|\beta_{01}\rangle$	$\mathbb{X}\,|\psi\rangle$	$|\psi\rangle$	$\mathbb{XZ}\,|\psi\rangle$	$\mathbb{Z}\,|\psi\rangle$
$|\beta_{10}\rangle$	$\mathbb{Z}\,|\psi\rangle$	$\mathbb{XZ}\,|\psi\rangle$	$|\psi\rangle$	$\mathbb{X}\,|\psi\rangle$
$|\beta_{11}\rangle$	$\mathbb{XZ}\,|\psi\rangle$	$\mathbb{Z}\,|\psi\rangle$	$\mathbb{X}\,|\psi\rangle$	$|\psi\rangle$

Note: Based on the qubits used in our Bell state and measured values (k, l), we can define the corresponding quantum operator at the receiver's end.

We can apply the required quantum operator and recreate the information based on the shared Bell states and corresponding measurement outcomes (Table 4).

Or we can rewrite Table 3 in the form of below relationship that holds for input and corresponding output:

$$|\beta_{ij}\rangle \xrightarrow{\text{QTP}} |ij\rangle\,|\psi\rangle \pm |i\bar{j}\rangle\,\mathbb{X}\,|\psi\rangle \pm |\bar{i}j\rangle\,\mathbb{Z}\,|\psi\rangle \pm |\bar{i}\bar{j}\rangle\,\mathbb{XZ}\,|\psi\rangle \qquad (4)$$

Where $\bar{i}$ and $\bar{j}$ are the negation of i and j respectively, i.e., if $i=0$ then $\bar{i}=1$ and vice versa and similarly for j, if $j=0$ then $\bar{j}=1$ and vice versa.

Table 4. Operators applied to recreate the information in specific cases of Bell states.

$\|\beta_{ij}\rangle$	$\|\beta_{00}\rangle$	$\|\beta_{01}\rangle$	$\|\beta_{10}\rangle$	$\|\beta_{11}\rangle$	Teleported state
$\|ij\rangle$	$\|00\rangle$	$\|01\rangle$	$\|10\rangle$	$\|11\rangle$	$\alpha\|0\rangle + \beta\|1\rangle \rightarrow \|\psi\rangle$
$\|i\bar{j}\rangle$	$\|01\rangle$	$\|00\rangle$	$\|11\rangle$	$\|10\rangle$	$\alpha\|1\rangle + \beta\|0\rangle \rightarrow \mathbb{X}\|\psi\rangle$
$\|\bar{i}j\rangle$	$\|10\rangle$	$\|11\rangle$	$\|00\rangle$	$\|01\rangle$	$\alpha\|0\rangle - \beta\|1\rangle \rightarrow \mathbb{Z}\|\psi\rangle$
$\|\bar{i}\bar{j}\rangle$	$\|11\rangle$	$\|10\rangle$	$\|01\rangle$	$\|00\rangle$	$\alpha\|1\rangle - \beta\|0\rangle \rightarrow \mathbb{X}\mathbb{Z}\|\psi\rangle$

Example. Let $i = j = 0$ then

$$|\psi\rangle \xrightarrow{\;|\beta_{ij}\rangle\;} |kl\rangle\, \mathbb{X}^{j+l}\mathbb{Z}^{i+k}\,|\psi\rangle$$
$$= |00\rangle\, \mathbb{X}^{(0+0)mod2}\mathbb{Z}^{(0+0)mod2}\,|\psi\rangle + |01\rangle\, \mathbb{X}^{(0+1)mod2}\mathbb{Z}^{(0+0)mod2}\,|\psi\rangle +$$
$$|10\rangle\, \mathbb{X}^{(0+0)mod2}\mathbb{Z}^{(0+1)mod2}\,|\psi\rangle + |11\rangle\, \mathbb{X}^{(0+1)mod2}\mathbb{Z}^{(0+1)mod2}\,|\psi\rangle$$
$$= |00\rangle\, \mathbb{X}^0\mathbb{Z}^0\,|\psi\rangle + |01\rangle\, \mathbb{X}^1\mathbb{Z}^0\,|\psi\rangle + |10\rangle\, \mathbb{X}^0\mathbb{Z}^1\,|\psi\rangle + |11\rangle\, \mathbb{X}^1\mathbb{Z}^1\,|\psi\rangle$$
$$= |00\rangle\, \mathbb{I}\,|\psi\rangle + |01\rangle\, \mathbb{X}\,|\psi\rangle + |10\rangle\, \mathbb{Z}\,|\psi\rangle + |11\rangle\, \mathbb{Z}\mathbb{X}\,|\psi\rangle$$

3   Entanglement Swapping

3.1   Introduction

We now present a brief introduction to the entanglement swapping protocol and swapping process itself. Entanglement swapping [6,14,25,28,47] refers to the activity of swapping entanglement from a pre-existing pair of entangled photons to a corresponding pair of non entangled photons. This is a key resource used in quantum networks to establish entanglement between two quantum entities such as a pair of routers on a quantum network.

Suppose we have 4 photons namley A, B, C and D with two entangled states. Photon A and photon B are entangled in one state and photons C and D are entangled in another state. We assume that there exists Bell state entanglement between the pairs A-B and C-D. This implies that any measurement on photon A will affect the state of photon B and vice-versa and similarly any observation on photon C will affect the state of photon D and vice versa.

In entanglement swapping, by operating a Bell measurement on A and C we establish entanglement between B and D. We note that in establishing entanglement between B and D we lose the previously shared entanglement links between A and B and between C and D.

3.2   A Generalised Analysis of Entanglement Swapping

Theorem 2. *Let satellite S and station 1 and station 2 be as shown in Fig. 3. Let* $|\beta_{ij}\rangle_{AB}$ *denote one pair of an arbitrary entangled Bell states between photons A and B and* $|\beta_{kl}\rangle_{CD}$ *denote a second pair of arbitray entangled Bell states between photons C and D. Then the state for the system is given by (Fig. 4):*

$$|\psi\rangle_{ABCD} = |\beta_{ij}\rangle_{AB} \cdot |\beta_{kl}\rangle_{CB} \tag{5}$$

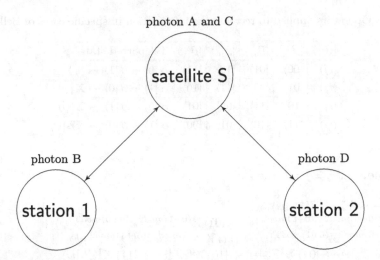

Fig. 3. Pre entanglement swapping: entanglement exists between photons A-B and C-D.

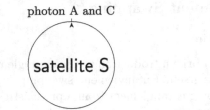

Fig. 4. Post entanglement swapping: initial entangled states are now separable and new entangled states established between photons A-C and B-D respectively.

$$
= \begin{cases}
|\beta_{00}\rangle_{AC} |\beta_{i+k,l}\rangle_{BD} + (-1)^k |\beta_{01}\rangle_{AC} |\beta_{i+k,\bar{l}}\rangle_{BD} + |\beta_{10}\rangle_{AC} |\beta_{i+k+1,l}\rangle_{BD} + \\
(-1)^k |\beta_{11}\rangle_{AC} |\beta_{i+k+1,\bar{l}}\rangle_{BD} \\
\qquad\qquad\qquad\qquad \textit{(for j=0)} \\
(-1)^{i+k} |\beta_{00}\rangle_{AC} |\beta_{i+k,\bar{l}}\rangle_{BD} + |\beta_{01}\rangle_{AC} |\beta_{i+k,\bar{l}}\rangle_{BD} + (-1)^{i+k+1} |\beta_{10}\rangle_{AC} |\beta_{i+k+1,\bar{l}}\rangle_{BD} + \\
(-1)^k |\beta_{11}\rangle_{AC} |\beta_{i+k+1,l}\rangle_{BD} \\
\qquad\qquad\qquad\qquad \textit{(for j=1)}
\end{cases}
$$

$$(6)$$

Hence measuring with respect to the Bell basis at the satellite leads to a corresponding Bell state between the two stations in terms of photon B and photon D.

Proof. Let $|\psi_{ABCD}\rangle$ denote the state for the four photons at A, B, C and D. Since there exists an initial entanglement between photons A-B and C-D which is defined by two Bell states, $|\beta_{ij}\rangle_{AB}$ and $|\beta_{kl}\rangle_{CD}$ respectively, it follows that

$$|\psi_{ABCD}\rangle = |\psi_{AB}\rangle \cdot |\psi_{CD}\rangle$$

$$= \tfrac{1}{\sqrt{2}}|\beta_{ij}\rangle_{AB} \cdot \tfrac{1}{\sqrt{2}}|\beta_{kl}\rangle_{CD}$$

$$= \tfrac{1}{2}(|0j\rangle_{AB} + (-1)^i|1\bar{j}\rangle_{AB}) \cdot (|0l\rangle_{CD} + (-1)^k|1\bar{l}\rangle_{CD})$$

$$= \tfrac{1}{2}(|0j\rangle_{AB}|0l\rangle_{CD} + (-1)^k|0j\rangle_{AB}|1\bar{l}\rangle_{CD} + (-1)^i|1\bar{j}\rangle_{AB}|0l\rangle_{CD}$$
$$+ (-1)^{i+k}|1\bar{j}\rangle_{AB}|1\bar{l}\rangle_{CD})$$

NOTE: For simplicity we omit the constant scalar multiples but note that we will be working with normalised states throughout.

$$= |0j0l\rangle_{ABCD} + (-1)^k|0j1\bar{l}\rangle_{ABCD} + (-1)^i|1\bar{j}0l\rangle_{ABCD} + (-1)^{i+k}|1\bar{j}1\bar{l}\rangle_{ABCD}$$
$$= (|00\rangle_{AC}|jl\rangle_{BD} + (-1)^k|01\rangle_{AC}|j\bar{l}\rangle_{BD} + (-1)^i|10\rangle_{AC}|\bar{j}l\rangle_{BD}$$
$$+ (-1)^{i+k}|11\rangle_{AC}|\bar{j}\bar{l}\rangle_{BD})$$

In terms of the states at the satellite (photons A and C) we obtain the following:

$$= (|\beta_{00}\rangle + |\beta_{10}\rangle)_{AC}|jl\rangle_{BD} + (-1)^k(|\beta_{01}\rangle + |\beta_{11}\rangle)_{AC}|j\bar{l}\rangle_{BD}$$
$$+ (-1)^i(|\beta_{01}\rangle - |\beta_{11}\rangle)_{AC}|\bar{j}l\rangle_{BD} + (-1)^{i+k}(|\beta_{00}\rangle - |\beta_{10}\rangle)_{AC}|\bar{j}\bar{l}\rangle_{BD}$$
$$= |\beta_{00}\rangle_{AC}|jl\rangle_{BD} + |\beta_{10}\rangle_{AC}|jl\rangle_{BD} + (-1)^k|\beta_{01}\rangle_{AC}|j\bar{l}\rangle_{BD} + (-1)^k|\beta_{11}\rangle)_{AC}|j\bar{l}\rangle_{BD}$$
$$+ (-1)^i|\beta_{01}\rangle|\bar{j}l\rangle_{BD} - (-1)^i|\beta_{11}\rangle_{AC}|\bar{j}l\rangle_{BD} + (-1)^{i+k}|\beta_{00}\rangle_{AC}|\bar{j}\bar{l}\rangle_{BD}$$
$$- (-1)^{i+k}|\beta_{10}\rangle_{AC}|\bar{j}\bar{l}\rangle_{BD}$$
$$= (|\beta_{00}\rangle_{AC}|jl\rangle_{BD} + (-1)^{i+k}|\beta_{00}\rangle_{AC}|\bar{j}\bar{l}\rangle_{BD}) + ((-1)^k|\beta_{01}\rangle_{AC}|j\bar{l}\rangle_{BD} + (-1)^i$$
$$|\beta_{01}\rangle_{AC}|\bar{j}l\rangle_{BD}) + (|\beta_{10}\rangle_{AC}|jl\rangle_{BD} - (-1)^{i+k}|\beta_{10}\rangle_{AC}|\bar{j}\bar{l}\rangle_{BD})$$
$$+ ((-1)^k|\beta_{11}\rangle_{AC}|j\bar{l}\rangle_{BD} - (-1)^i|\beta_{11}\rangle_{AC}|\bar{j}l\rangle_{BD})$$
$$= |\beta_{00}\rangle_{AC}(|jl\rangle_{BD} + (-1)^{i+k}|\bar{j}\bar{l}\rangle_{BD}) + |\beta_{01}\rangle_{AC}((-1)^k|j\bar{l}\rangle_{BD} + (-1)^i|\bar{j}l\rangle_{BD})$$
$$+ |\beta_{10}\rangle_{AC}(|jl\rangle_{BD} - (-1)^{i+k}|\bar{j}\bar{l}\rangle_{BD}) + |\beta_{11}\rangle_{AC}((-1)^k|j\bar{l}\rangle_{BD} - (-1)^i|\bar{j}l\rangle_{BD})$$
$$= |\beta_{00}\rangle_{AC}(|jl\rangle + (-1)^{i+k}|\bar{j}\bar{l}\rangle)_{BD} + |\beta_{01}\rangle_{AC}((-1)^k|j\bar{l}\rangle + (-1)^i|\bar{j}l\rangle)_{BD}$$
$$+ |\beta_{10}\rangle_{AC}(|jl\rangle - (-1)^{i+k}|\bar{j}\bar{l}\rangle)_{BD} + |\beta_{11}\rangle_{AC}((-1)^k|j\bar{l}\rangle - (-1)^i|\bar{j}l\rangle)_{BD}$$

$$= |\beta_{00}\rangle_{AC}(|jl\rangle + (-1)^{i+k}|\bar{j}\bar{l}\rangle)_{BD} + |\beta_{01}\rangle_{AC}((-1)^k|j\bar{l}\rangle + (-1)^i|\bar{j}l\rangle)_{BD} +$$
$$|\beta_{10}\rangle_{AC}(|jl\rangle + (-1)^{i+k+1}|\bar{j}\bar{l}\rangle)_{BD} + |\beta_{11}\rangle_{AC}((-1)^k|j\bar{l}\rangle + (-1)^{i+1}|\bar{j}l\rangle)_{BD} \tag{7}$$

From Eq. (7) we note the following two cases in terms of the Bell states where all subscripts (sum of subscripts) are mod 2.

1. For $j = 0$
$$|\psi\rangle_{ABCD} = |\beta_{00}\rangle(|\beta_{(i+k),l}\rangle) + |\beta_{01}\rangle((-1)^k|\beta_{(i+k),\bar{l}}\rangle) + |\beta_{10}\rangle(|\beta_{(i+k+1),l}\rangle) +$$
$$|\beta_{11}\rangle((-1)^k|\beta_{(i+k+1),\bar{l}}\rangle)$$

578   P. Kandwal et al.

2. For $j = 1$

$$|\psi\rangle_{ABCD} = |\beta_{00}\rangle \left((-1)^{i+k} |\beta_{(i+k),\bar{l}}\rangle\right) + |\beta_{01}\rangle \left(|\beta_{(i+k),l}\rangle\right)$$
$$+ |\beta_{10}\rangle \left((-1)^{i+k+1} |\beta_{(i+k+1),\bar{l}}\rangle\right) + |\beta_{11}\rangle \left((-1)^{i+1} |\beta_{(i+k+1),l}\rangle\right)$$

We present the possible input and output Bell states that occur in Table 5.

Table 5. All possible inputs for entanglement swapping using Bell states with swapped output.

Initial Bell states		Result (swapped entanglement)							
$\|\beta_{00}\rangle_{AB}$	$\|\beta_{00}\rangle_{CD}$	$\|\beta_{00}\rangle_{AC}$	$\|\beta_{00}\rangle_{BD}$	$\|\beta_{01}\rangle_{AC}$	$\|\beta_{01}\rangle_{BD}$	$\|\beta_{10}\rangle_{AC}$	$\|\beta_{10}\rangle_{BD}$	$\|\beta_{11}\rangle_{AC}$	$\|\beta_{11}\rangle_{BD}$
$\|\beta_{00}\rangle_{AB}$	$\|\beta_{01}\rangle_{CD}$	$\|\beta_{00}\rangle_{AC}$	$\|\beta_{01}\rangle_{BD}$	$\|\beta_{01}\rangle_{AC}$	$\|\beta_{00}\rangle_{BD}$	$\|\beta_{10}\rangle_{AC}$	$\|\beta_{11}\rangle_{BD}$	$\|\beta_{11}\rangle_{AC}$	$\|\beta_{10}\rangle_{BD}$
$\|\beta_{00}\rangle_{AB}$	$\|\beta_{10}\rangle_{CD}$	$\|\beta_{00}\rangle_{AC}$	$\|\beta_{10}\rangle_{BD}$	$-\|\beta_{01}\rangle_{AC}$	$\|\beta_{11}\rangle_{BD}$	$\|\beta_{10}\rangle_{AC}$	$\|\beta_{00}\rangle_{BD}$	$-\|\beta_{11}\rangle_{AC}$	$\|\beta_{01}\rangle_{BD}$
$\|\beta_{00}\rangle_{AB}$	$\|\beta_{11}\rangle_{CD}$	$\|\beta_{00}\rangle_{AC}$	$\|\beta_{11}\rangle_{BD}$	$-\|\beta_{01}\rangle_{AC}$	$\|\beta_{10}\rangle_{BD}$	$\|\beta_{10}\rangle_{AC}$	$\|\beta_{01}\rangle_{BD}$	$-\|\beta_{11}\rangle_{AC}$	$\|\beta_{00}\rangle_{BD}$
$\|\beta_{01}\rangle_{AB}$	$\|\beta_{00}\rangle_{CD}$	$\|\beta_{00}\rangle_{AC}$	$\|\beta_{01}\rangle_{BD}$	$\|\beta_{01}\rangle_{AC}$	$\|\beta_{00}\rangle_{BD}$	$-\|\beta_{10}\rangle_{AC}$	$\|\beta_{11}\rangle_{BD}$	$-\|\beta_{11}\rangle_{AC}$	$\|\beta_{10}\rangle_{BD}$
$\|\beta_{01}\rangle_{AB}$	$\|\beta_{01}\rangle_{CD}$	$\|\beta_{00}\rangle_{AC}$	$\|\beta_{00}\rangle_{BD}$	$\|\beta_{01}\rangle_{AC}$	$\|\beta_{01}\rangle_{BD}$	$-\|\beta_{10}\rangle_{AC}$	$\|\beta_{10}\rangle_{BD}$	$-\|\beta_{11}\rangle_{AC}$	$\|\beta_{11}\rangle_{BD}$
$\|\beta_{01}\rangle_{AB}$	$\|\beta_{10}\rangle_{CD}$	$-\|\beta_{00}\rangle_{AC}$	$\|\beta_{11}\rangle_{BD}$	$\|\beta_{01}\rangle_{AC}$	$\|\beta_{10}\rangle_{BD}$	$\|\beta_{10}\rangle_{AC}$	$\|\beta_{01}\rangle_{BD}$	$-\|\beta_{11}\rangle_{AC}$	$\|\beta_{00}\rangle_{BD}$
$\|\beta_{01}\rangle_{AB}$	$\|\beta_{11}\rangle_{CD}$	$-\|\beta_{00}\rangle_{AC}$	$\|\beta_{10}\rangle_{BD}$	$\|\beta_{01}\rangle_{AC}$	$\|\beta_{11}\rangle_{BD}$	$\|\beta_{10}\rangle_{AC}$	$\|\beta_{00}\rangle_{BD}$	$-\|\beta_{11}\rangle_{AC}$	$\|\beta_{01}\rangle_{BD}$
$\|\beta_{10}\rangle_{AB}$	$\|\beta_{00}\rangle_{CD}$	$-\|\beta_{00}\rangle_{AC}$	$\|\beta_{10}\rangle_{BD}$	$-\|\beta_{01}\rangle_{AC}$	$\|\beta_{11}\rangle_{BD}$	$\|\beta_{10}\rangle_{AC}$	$\|\beta_{00}\rangle_{BD}$	$\|\beta_{11}\rangle_{AC}$	$\|\beta_{01}\rangle_{BD}$
$\|\beta_{10}\rangle_{AB}$	$\|\beta_{01}\rangle_{CD}$	$\|\beta_{00}\rangle_{AC}$	$\|\beta_{11}\rangle_{BD}$	$\|\beta_{01}\rangle_{AC}$	$\|\beta_{10}\rangle_{BD}$	$\|\beta_{10}\rangle_{AC}$	$\|\beta_{01}\rangle_{BD}$	$\|\beta_{11}\rangle_{AC}$	$\|\beta_{00}\rangle_{BD}$
$\|\beta_{10}\rangle_{AB}$	$\|\beta_{10}\rangle_{CD}$	$\|\beta_{00}\rangle_{AC}$	$\|\beta_{00}\rangle_{BD}$	$-\|\beta_{01}\rangle_{AC}$	$\|\beta_{01}\rangle_{BD}$	$\|\beta_{10}\rangle_{AC}$	$\|\beta_{10}\rangle_{BD}$	$-\|\beta_{11}\rangle_{AC}$	$\|\beta_{11}\rangle_{BD}$
$\|\beta_{10}\rangle_{AB}$	$\|\beta_{11}\rangle_{CD}$	$\|\beta_{00}\rangle_{AC}$	$\|\beta_{01}\rangle_{BD}$	$-\|\beta_{01}\rangle_{AC}$	$\|\beta_{00}\rangle_{BD}$	$\|\beta_{10}\rangle_{AC}$	$\|\beta_{11}\rangle_{BD}$	$-\|\beta_{11}\rangle_{AC}$	$\|\beta_{10}\rangle_{BD}$
$\|\beta_{11}\rangle_{AB}$	$\|\beta_{00}\rangle_{CD}$	$-\|\beta_{00}\rangle_{AC}$	$\|\beta_{11}\rangle_{BD}$	$-\|\beta_{01}\rangle_{AC}$	$\|\beta_{10}\rangle_{BD}$	$\|\beta_{10}\rangle_{AC}$	$\|\beta_{01}\rangle_{BD}$	$\|\beta_{11}\rangle_{AC}$	$\|\beta_{00}\rangle_{BD}$
$\|\beta_{11}\rangle_{AB}$	$\|\beta_{01}\rangle_{CD}$	$-\|\beta_{00}\rangle_{AC}$	$\|\beta_{10}\rangle_{BD}$	$-\|\beta_{01}\rangle_{AC}$	$\|\beta_{11}\rangle_{BD}$	$\|\beta_{10}\rangle_{AC}$	$\|\beta_{00}\rangle_{BD}$	$\|\beta_{11}\rangle_{AC}$	$\|\beta_{01}\rangle_{BD}$
$\|\beta_{11}\rangle_{AB}$	$\|\beta_{10}\rangle_{CD}$	$\|\beta_{00}\rangle_{AC}$	$\|\beta_{01}\rangle_{BD}$	$-\|\beta_{01}\rangle_{AC}$	$\|\beta_{00}\rangle_{BD}$	$-\|\beta_{10}\rangle_{AC}$	$\|\beta_{11}\rangle_{BD}$	$\|\beta_{11}\rangle_{AC}$	$\|\beta_{10}\rangle_{BD}$
$\|\beta_{11}\rangle_{AB}$	$\|\beta_{11}\rangle_{CD}$	$\|\beta_{00}\rangle_{AC}$	$\|\beta_{00}\rangle_{BD}$	$-\|\beta_{01}\rangle_{AC}$	$\|\beta_{01}\rangle_{BD}$	$-\|\beta_{10}\rangle_{AC}$	$\|\beta_{10}\rangle_{BD}$	$\|\beta_{11}\rangle_{AC}$	$\|\beta_{11}\rangle_{BD}$

We formulate the entanglement swapping as follows:

$$|\psi\rangle_{AB.CD} = \sum_{k=0}^{3} |\beta_{(i+k) \bmod 4}\rangle_{AC} \cdot |\beta_{(j+(-1)^{(i+j)}.k) \bmod 4}\rangle_{BD} \tag{8}$$

We note $|\psi\rangle = |\beta_i\rangle \cdot |\beta_j\rangle = |\beta_i\rangle_{AB} \cdot |\beta_j\rangle_{CD}$ where i and j corresponds to pairs of Bell states for which we wish to use entanglement swapping. $i, j \in \{0, 1, 2, 3\}$, in which $\{0, 1, 2, 3\}$ are decimal representations corresponding to the binary values $\{00, 01, 10, 11\}$ respectively. Additions for subscripts are calculated in $mod4$.

3.3 Observations

We note that we swapped the entanglement from particles A-B and C-D to particles A-C and B-D and lost the initial entanglement between AB and CD. We observe from Table 5 that we have 16 combinations of inputs for which we can perform entanglement swapping, but irrespective of the different inputs we obtain only 4 possible unique outputs. The results are presented in Table 6. We also note that we get the outcome as a combination of input state (i.e, the output is similar to the input entangled states). For four different inputs we have the same output, a combination of the four states; for example,

$$|\beta_{00}\rangle\cdot|\beta_{00}\rangle,\ |\beta_{01}\rangle\cdot|\beta_{01}\rangle,\ |\beta_{10}\rangle\cdot|\beta_{10}\rangle,\ |\beta_{11}\rangle\cdot|\beta_{11}\rangle =$$
$$|\beta_{00}\rangle\cdot|\beta_{00}\rangle \pm |\beta_{01}\rangle\cdot|\beta_{01}\rangle \pm |\beta_{10}\rangle\cdot|\beta_{10}\rangle \pm |\beta_{11}\rangle\cdot|\beta_{11}\rangle.$$

We now consider which swapped state is going to be utilised between B-D for the purpose of communication from the initial combination of Bell states, between A and B and between C and D.

The following table presents pairs of input states and their corresponding possible output (swapped) states subject to measurement at AC.

Table 6. Combination of different entangled Bell states input and corresponding swapped entangled states.

Initial entangled states ($|\beta_{AB}\rangle\cdot|\beta_{CD}\rangle$)	Swapped entangled states ($|\beta_{AC}\rangle\cdot|\beta_{BD}\rangle$)
$|\beta_{00}\rangle\cdot|\beta_{00}\rangle\|\|\beta_{01}\rangle\cdot|\beta_{01}\rangle\|\|\beta_{10}\rangle\cdot|\beta_{10}\rangle\|\|\beta_{11}\rangle\cdot|\beta_{11}\rangle$	$|\beta_{00}\rangle\cdot|\beta_{00}\rangle \pm |\beta_{01}\rangle\cdot|\beta_{01}\rangle \pm |\beta_{10}\rangle\cdot|\beta_{10}\rangle \pm |\beta_{11}\rangle\cdot|\beta_{11}\rangle$
$|\beta_{00}\rangle\cdot|\beta_{01}\rangle\|\|\beta_{01}\rangle\cdot|\beta_{00}\rangle\|\|\beta_{10}\rangle\cdot|\beta_{11}\rangle\|\|\beta_{11}\rangle\cdot|\beta_{10}\rangle$	$|\beta_{00}\rangle\cdot|\beta_{01}\rangle \pm |\beta_{01}\rangle\cdot|\beta_{00}\rangle \pm |\beta_{10}\rangle\cdot|\beta_{11}\rangle \pm |\beta_{11}\rangle\cdot|\beta_{10}\rangle$
$|\beta_{00}\rangle\cdot|\beta_{10}\rangle\|\|\beta_{01}\rangle\cdot|\beta_{11}\rangle\|\|\beta_{10}\rangle\cdot|\beta_{00}\rangle\|\|\beta_{11}\rangle\cdot|\beta_{01}\rangle$	$|\beta_{00}\rangle\cdot|\beta_{10}\rangle \pm |\beta_{01}\rangle\cdot|\beta_{11}\rangle \pm |\beta_{10}\rangle\cdot|\beta_{00}\rangle \pm |\beta_{11}\rangle\cdot|\beta_{01}\rangle$
$|\beta_{00}\rangle\cdot|\beta_{11}\rangle\|\|\beta_{01}\rangle\cdot|\beta_{10}\rangle\|\|\beta_{10}\rangle\cdot|\beta_{01}\rangle\|\|\beta_{11}\rangle\cdot|\beta_{00}\rangle$	$|\beta_{00}\rangle\cdot|\beta_{11}\rangle \pm |\beta_{01}\rangle\cdot|\beta_{10}\rangle \pm |\beta_{10}\rangle\cdot|\beta_{01}\rangle \pm |\beta_{11}\rangle\cdot|\beta_{00}\rangle$

Replacing each Bell state with its corresponding subscript value, (that is, $|\beta_{00}\rangle$ becomes 0, $|\beta_{01}\rangle$ becomes 1, $|\beta_{10}\rangle$ becomes 2 and $|\beta_{11}\rangle$ becomes 3), we observe:

Table 7. Updated Table 6 using the terminology used in proposed formula.

Initial entangled states				Swapped entangled states
0.0	1.1	2.2	3.3	$0.0 + 1.1 + 2.2 + 3.3$
0.1	1.0	2.3	3.2	$0.1 + 1.0 + 2.3 + 3.2$
0.2	1.3	2.0	3.1	$0.2 + 1.3 + 2.0 + 3.1$
0.3	1.2	2.1	3.0	$0.3 + 1.2 + 2.1 + 3.0$

Note: We have dropped the 'minus' sign because it does not have any observable effect [31].

Throughout we note as AC increases from 0 to 3, BD increases in steps of 1 mod 4 for the first and third lines in Table 7 but decreases in steps of 1 mod 4 for the other two lines.

Example 2. For any given pair of initial entangled states we can deduce the swapped entangled states between the particles by utilising the formula given in Eq. (8).

For example

$$
|i\rangle_{AB} \cdot |j\rangle_{CD} = |0\rangle_{AB} \cdot |0\rangle_{CD}
$$
$$
= |\beta_{00}\rangle_{AB} \cdot |\beta_{00}\rangle_{CD}
$$
$$
= |\beta_{(0+0)mod4}\rangle_{AC} \cdot |\beta_{(0+(-1)^{(0+0)}.0)mod4}\rangle_{BD} + |\beta_{(0+1)mod4}\rangle_{AC} \cdot |\beta_{(0+(-1)^{(0+0)}.1)mod4}\rangle_{BD}
$$
$$
+ |\beta_{(0+2)mod4}\rangle_{AC} \cdot |\beta_{(0+(-1)^{(0+0)}.2)mod4}\rangle_{BD} + |\beta_{(0+3)mod4}\rangle_{AC} \cdot |\beta_{(0+(-1)^{(0+0)}.3)mod4}\rangle_{BD}
$$
$$
= |\beta_{0mod4}\rangle_{AC} \cdot |\beta_{0mod4}\rangle_{BD} + |\beta_{1mod4}\rangle_{AC} \cdot |\beta_{1mod4}\rangle_{BD} + |\beta_{2mod4}\rangle_{AC} \cdot |\beta_{2mod4}\rangle_{BD} +
$$
$$
|\beta_{3mod4}\rangle_{AC} \cdot |\beta_{3mod4}\rangle_{BD}
$$
$$
= |\beta_0\rangle_{AC} \cdot |\beta_0\rangle_{BD} + |\beta_1\rangle_{AC} \cdot |\beta_1\rangle_{BD} + |\beta_2\rangle_{AC} \cdot |\beta_2\rangle_{BD} + |\beta_3\rangle_{AC} \cdot |\beta_3\rangle_{BD}
$$
$$
= |\beta_{00}\rangle_{AC} \cdot |\beta_{00}\rangle_{BD} + |\beta_{01}\rangle_{AC} \cdot |\beta_{01}\rangle_{BD} + |\beta_{10}\rangle_{AC} \cdot |\beta_{10}\rangle_{BD} + |\beta_{11}\rangle_{AC} \cdot |\beta_{11}\rangle_{BD}
$$

Similary we can check all other pairs and get final entangled states as given in Table 5.

4   Conclusion, Future Work and Applications

In this work we have analysed the teleportation and entanglement swapping protocols and have identified relationships between inputs and their corresponding outputs. We have summarised our observations in both tables and as generalised formulae, relating inputs to outputs. We are currently developing applications that employ the above results within a quantum network setting. These includes ring signatures, voting protocols [16,22,41,43] and long distance communication. Details will follow shortly.

References

1. Meet IBM Q. https://www.research.ibm.com/ibm-q/
2. Quantum A.I. research at google. https://research.google.com/pubs/QuantumAI. html/
3. Quantum information. https://www.toshiba.eu/eu/Cambridge-Research-Laboratory/Quantum-Information/
4. Qutech quantum institute enters into collaboration with Intel. https://www. tudelft.nl/en/2015/tu-delft/qutech-quantum-institute-enters-into-collaboration-with-intel
5. Station q - worldwide consortium for the advancement of topological quantum computation. https://stationq.microsoft.com/
6. Quantum teleportation of patterns of light (2017). https://www.sciencedaily.com/ releases/2017/09/170921121147.htm
7. Quantum network - Wikipedia (2018). https://en.wikipedia.org/wiki/Quantum_network
8. Bennett, C.H., Brassard, G., Crépeau, C., Jozsa, R., Peres, A., Wootters, W.K.: Teleporting an unknown quantum state via dual classical and Einstein-Podolsky-Rosen channels. Phys. Rev. Lett. **70**(13), 1895 (1993)
9. Bennett, C.H., Shor, P.W.: Quantum information theory. IEEE Trans. Inform. Theory **44**(6), 2724–2742 (1998)

10. Bouwmeester, D., Pan, J.W., Mattle, K., Eibl, M., Weinfurter, H., Zeilinger, A.: Experimental quantum teleportation. Nature **390**(6660), 575–579 (1997)
11. Braunstein, S.L., Van Loock, P.: Quantum information with continuous variables. Rev. Mod. Phys. **77**(2), 513 (2005)
12. Briegel, H.J., Dür, W., Cirac, J.I., Zoller, P.: Quantum repeaters: the role of imperfect local operations in quantum communication. Phys. Rev. Lett. **81**(26), 5932 (1998)
13. Castelvecchi, D.: IBM's quantum cloud computer goes commercial. Nat. News **543**(7644), 159 (2017)
14. De Riedmatten, H., Marcikic, I., Van Houwelingen, J., Tittel, W., Zbinden, H., Gisin, N.: Long-distance entanglement swapping with photons from separated sources. Phys. Rev. A **71**(5), 050302 (2005)
15. Devitt, S.J.: Performing quantum computing experiments in the cloud. Phys. Rev. A **94**(3), 032329 (2016)
16. Dolev, S., Pitowsky, I., Tamir, B.: A quantum secret ballot. arXiv preprint quant-ph/0602087 (2006)
17. Eastin, B., Flammia, S.T.: Q-circuit tutorial. arXiv preprint quant-ph/0406003 (2004)
18. Eisert, J., Plenio, M.: Introduction to the basics of entanglement theory in continuous-variable systems. Int. J. Quant. Inform. **1**(04), 479–506 (2003)
19. Elliott, C.: The DARPA quantum network. In: Quantum Communications and Cryptography, pp. 83–102 (2006)
20. Furusawa, A., Sørensen, J.L., Braunstein, S.L., Fuchs, C.A., Kimble, H.J., Polzik, E.S.: Unconditional quantum teleportation. Science **282**(5389), 706–709 (1998)
21. Gibney, E., et al.: One giant step for quantum internet (2016)
22. Hillery, M., Ziman, M., Bužek, V., Bieliková, M.: Towards quantum-based privacy and voting. Phys. Lett. A **349**(1–4), 75–81 (2006)
23. Horodecki, R., Horodecki, P., Horodecki, M., Horodecki, K.: Quantum entanglement. Rev. Mod. Phys. **81**(2), 865 (2009)
24. IBM: Quantum cloud. https://www.ibm.com/cloud/why-ibm/
25. Jennewein, T., Weihs, G., Pan, J.W., Zeilinger, A.: Experimental nonlocality proof of quantum teleportation and entanglement swapping. Phys. Rev. Lett. **88**(1), 017903 (2001)
26. Julsgaard, B., Sherson, J., Cirac, J.I., Fiurášek, J., Polzik, E.S.: Experimental demonstration of quantum memory for light. Nature **432**(7016), 482–486 (2004)
27. Kimble, H.J.: The quantum internet. Nature **453**(7198), 1023–1030 (2008)
28. Kirby, B.T., Santra, S., Malinovsky, V.S., Brodsky, M.: Entanglement swapping of two arbitrarily degraded entangled states. Phys. Rev. A **94**(1), 012336 (2016)
29. Ma, X.S., et al.: Quantum teleportation over 143 kilometres using active feed-forward. Nature **489**(7415), 269–273 (2012)
30. Megidish, E., Halevy, A., Shacham, T., Dvir, T., Dovrat, L., Eisenberg, H.S.: Entanglement between photons that never co-existed. In: Frontiers in Optics, p. FTh2C-4. Optical Society of America (2012)
31. Nielsen, M.A., Chuang, I.L.: Quantum computation and quantum information. Quantum **546**, 1231 (2010)
32. Pan, J.W., Bouwmeester, D., Weinfurter, H., Zeilinger, A.: Experimental entanglement swapping: entangling photons that never interacted. Phys. Rev. Lett. **80**(18), 3891 (1998)
33. Peev, M., et al.: The secoqc quantum key distribution network in vienna. New J. Phys. **11**(7), 075001 (2009)

34. Pirandola, S., Braunstein, S.L.: Unite to build a quantum internet. Nature **532**, 169–171 (2016)
35. Pugh, C.J., et al.: Airborne demonstration of a quantum key distribution receiver payload. In: CLEO: Applications and Technology, p. ATu4B-5. Optical Society of America (2017)
36. Raussendorf, R., Briegel, H.J.: A one-way quantum computer. Phys. Rev. Lett. **86**(22), 5188 (2001)
37. Ren, J.G., et al.: Ground-to-satellite quantum teleportation. arXiv preprint arXiv:1707.00934 (2017)
38. Sasaki, M., et al.: Field test of quantum key distribution in the tokyo QKD network. Opt. Express **19**(11), 10387–10409 (2011)
39. Sherson, J.F., et al.: Quantum teleportation between light and matter. Nature **443**(7111), 557–560 (2006)
40. Simon, C., et al.: Quantum memories. Eur. Phys. J. D **58**(1), 1–22 (2010)
41. Singh, S.K., Srikanth, R.: Generalized quantum secret sharing. Phys. Rev. A **71**(1), 012328 (2005)
42. Tindol, R.: Caltech physicists achieve first bona fide quantum teleportation—caltech. http://www.caltech.edu/news/caltech-physicists-achieve-first-bona-fide-quantum-teleportation-291
43. Vaccaro, J.A., Spring, J., Chefles, A.: Quantum protocols for anonymous voting and surveying. Phys. Rev. A **75**(1), 012333 (2007)
44. Van Meter, R.: Quantum Networking. Wiley, Hoboken (2014)
45. Yin, J., et al.: Satellite-based entanglement distribution over 1200 kilometers. Science **356**(6343), 1140–1144 (2017)
46. Yin, J., et al.: Quantum teleportation and entanglement distribution over 100-kilometre free-space channels. Nature **488**(7410), 185–188 (2012)
47. Zukowski, M., Zeilinger, A., Horne, M.A., Ekert, A.K.: "Event-ready-detectors" bell experiment via entanglement swapping. Phys. Rev. Lett. **71**(26), 4287–4290 (1993)

NTS: A Scalable Virtual Testbed Architecture with Dynamic Scheduling and Backpressure

Youbing Zhong[1,2,3], Zhou Zhou[1,2,3](✉), Da Li[4], Wenliang He[1,2,3], Chao Zheng[1,2,3], Qingyun Liu[1,2,3], and Li Guo[1,2,3]

[1] Institute of Information Engineering, Chinese Academy of Sciences, Beijing, China
zhouzhou@iie.ac.cn
[2] School of Cyber Security, University of Chinese Academy of Sciences, Beijing, China
[3] National Engineering Laboratory of Information Security Technologies, Beijing, China
[4] Department of Electrical and Computer Engineering, University of Missouri, Columbia, USA

Abstract. Experimental platforms perform a key role in evaluating the proof-of-concept and innovations. Nowadays, researchers from academia and industries rely on expensive physical testbeds to evaluate their experiments, while there are very limited software testbeds in market, which usually not available or costly. In addition, the applications of existing traffic generators are restricted to their single function and performance in network area. It has come to a point that lack of validation and testing tools has tremendously jeopardized the innovation in this field. In this paper, we propose NTS, which is a scalable software-based virtual testbed architecture. The scheduling and management framework can dynamically schedule resource of services. The scheduling algorithm adopts the concept of cost proportional fairness scheduling, which takes the evaluated traffic proportion and packet arrival rate into account. By leveraging container technology, the resources of services are restrictedly managed and fully isolated without tampering the OS kernel's scheduling mechanisms. Another advantage of the proposed testbed architecture is that the software can generate most kinds of backbone network traffic and can also be extended easily for customized protocol or traffic patterns. Our experiments show that the virtual testbed is generic scalable and cost-efficient, which is suitable and affordable for researchers in the field of network.

Keywords: Resource scheduling · Testbed · Docker container · Virtualization

1 Introduction

Due to the increasingly huge number of applications on the Internet, the network is becoming more and more complex and congested. Many researchers are spending vast amount of efforts in this area to address with the challenges. With the help of new

This work is partially supported by National Key R&D Program 2016 (Grant No. 2016YFB0801300), Strategic Priority Research Program of the Chinese academy of Sciences (Grant No. XDC02030000) and Youth Innovation Promotion Association CAS.

X. Wang et al. (Eds.): CollaborateCom 2019, LNICST 292, pp. 583–599, 2019.
https://doi.org/10.1007/978-3-030-30146-0_40

network technologies, such as Software-Defined Networking (SDN) [1] and Network Function Virtualization (NFV) [2], Internet service providers (ISPs) and application service providers (ASPs) adopt virtualization solutions to reduce equipment investment. Institutions and enterprises also propose different kinds of novel network technologies. For instance, the Intel DPDK [3] provides high throughput I/O in high speed network to accelerate packet forwarding. Accordingly, there are also some traffic generating tools available for testing network, such as pktgen [4] and UDPGen.

However, access to real internet online platforms to capture backbone traffic are very limited to many researchers, especially for those from academia. On the other hand, traffic simulation tools usually provide limited functionalities, which are not suitable for innovative protocols and applications. In the meanwhile, the tools often fail to mimic the content based on user-defined mode and real-world traffic load. As the consequence, many new algorithms and architectures, which require network traffic with the above-mentioned patterns, can be hardly evaluated using existing tools. As the existing tools lack of the ability to simulate real-world traffic and evaluate the results, academia and industries have realized the demand and importance of redesigning new architecture of testbed to facilitate various research needs.

Fortunately, the emergence of physical testbeds [5], which is one of most popular options, is a significant improvement. The physical testbeds usually are able to simulate multiple types of protocols by generating specified traffic. With abundant hardware resources, the physical testbeds are also able to simulate very complex, large-scale, and hybrid backbone traffic. However, while presenting a wide variety of advantages, the physical testbeds also have following drawbacks: First, these physical testbeds are very expensive, which is not affordable for universities and institutions from academia. Second, the physical testbeds are usually developed for a few scenarios and they are very hard or impossible to adjust for many needs. Last but not least, NFs also have heterogeneous processing requirements, which results in evaluation using physical testbeds not being suitable completely.

With the advent of container technologies like Docker [6], individuals can easily build traffic generators to mimic real application [7]. Even though OS scheduler can efficiently manage system resources, it doesn't have the knowledge of packet arrival rate and traffic proportion cost, resulting in serious performance degradation during the evaluation of NF. By leveraging cgroups [8], the scheduling of generators process can be exposed to the OS without modifying OS scheduler, reducing onerous work to customize scheduler in OS, which might lead to unnecessary maintenance overhead and inaccurate results.

Based on above-mentioned facts, many researchers proposed to exploit virtualization to facilitate building a cost-efficient and flexible testbed. As a matter of fact, some networking hardware vendors have developed virtual testbed and include their commercial products in the market. Usually, the solutions are based on real-world application traffic emulation running on top of hypervisors and the network functions are provided by NFV. At the low-level, application simulations are divided into VMs. At the high-level, all application simulations are connected by virtual network function with the help of NFV or SDN. Several solutions even provide the abstraction network topology for the underlining test environment like Mininet [9]. With all these appealing features like portability, flexibility and hardware accelerated performance, these solutions are unaffordable due to high commodity prices.

After analyzing state-of-the-art solutions, we propose a novel architecture for testbeds to simulate network traffic load generated by real-world applications, namely Network Traffic Simulator(NTS). The architecture takes both task-based application service scheduling and packet arrival rate into consideration. The focuses of our proposed architecture are on the control and scheduling problem of application simulation and traffic generation. NTS has following features: (i) generating real traffic load through interaction between services and clients, (ii) leveraging open source software that can be deployed on commodity hardware, (iii) CPU shares adjustment for services based on packet arrival rate and computation cost, (iv) providing scheduling elasticity to achieve backpressure to avoid wasting work and outburst due to congestion, (v) a generic scheduling framework without modifying operation system or kernel.

We aim to define a lightweight, cost-efficient, and extensible traffic simulator with affordability for researchers in network area to easily verify and evaluate new ideas and innovations. The design also considers the possibility to extend with user behavior simulation to generate synthetic network behavior pattern in the future, which can be used as background traffic in network security.

The rest of this paper is organized as follows. In Sect. 2, we discuss the related work. We introduce our proposed testbed in detail in Sect. 3. Section 4 presents the evaluation result and discusses the implication. Finally, we give a conclusion to our work in Sect. 5.

2   Related Work

This section provides the preview of previous work related to our proposal. It consists of three parts: The first part gives the background of the use of testbeds to validate NF, especially for innovative algorithm and architecture in network scope; The second part describes the deficiency of existing OS scheduler for service scheduling; And the last part mainly encompasses works that have exploited the area of testbed.

2.1   Background

Evaluation serves as a very important and challenging part for any new proposed methods, frameworks or systems in many research fields. In the area of network, whether the evaluation input can reflect the real-world applications and the collected metrics are good and accurate enough for the evaluation influence the result. This means that the effectiveness of simulation depends on whether testbed can fairly simulate various network protocol features. In other words, it is dependent on the traffic load that testbed generates.

For ASPs and ISPs, QoS related metrics are critical for the evaluation and adoption of any innovative network solutions. Performance degradation of QoS damages the reputation of their services and operations, causes customer complains, eventually result in losing market share and business profits. Another challenge is that it is very risky to evaluate new solutions in production networks, given the concerns on service outage and interruption. Additionally, because of restrictions to access privileged resources and privacy protection of user data, NF validations that need massive online internet traffic are limited and infeasible for many researchers.

However, with the application of container technologies and NFV, there is a potential possibility to solve these problems.

To solve these challenges, our proposal provides the traffic load generation and exploits virtualization to reduce cost and minimize the impact on production during evaluation.

2.2 The Deficiency of OS Scheduler for Virtual Testbed

Network function evaluation includes: (1) function validation, and (2) performance evaluation. For instance, firewalls and content audit system commonly need to detect the correctness of protocol identification and blocking effectiveness during tests.

Linux provides completely fair scheduling (CFS) [10] in the default mode since kernel 2.6.23. It manages CPU resource allocation for all running processes and aims to maximize overall CPU utilization. Each task under CFS maintains a fair chance to get certain CPU shares and the time-slice is determined by the run-time of contending tasks. Thus, CFS presents a fair CPU proportion shares to all tasks.

However, the fairness scheduling is not suitable for service emulation. Intuitively, different types of services have different computation costs due to the characteristics of the service. Fairness scheduling won't take this into consideration. Furthermore, users' requirements are diverse during evaluation. For example, if two simulation services, which generate different kinds of traffic, have the similar computation cost with different sizes of traffic loads (one has twice traffic load than the other), then we hope the schedule can match the traffic loads between the two. Similarly, if the service has twice computation cost than the second, then we expect it has twice CPU run-time at the same traffic load. Obviously, we can introduce the weight or prioritization factor to supplement the deficiency of fairness.

Unfortunately, lack of enough information for the default CPU scheduler to allocate resources according to the computation cost and traffic load pose the hardness of scheduling resources on the basis of cost-proportional fairness [11]. As mentioned above, CFS scheduler usually provides a fair allocation of time-slice, but it cannot provide rate-cost fairness if services have diverse computation costs. To achieve this, the core of NTS should ingest more information to allocate CPU resources in priority or weight mode.

Cost-proportional fairness scheduling differs from Round-Robin [12] and Max C/I. It is a trade-off between throughput and fairness, which not only seeks to maximize throughput for the services at given traffic load but also ensures that all the contending services needed during a test to obtain a minimal CPU share keep running in the worst scenarios. What's more, we can adapt cost-proportional scheduling to meet diverse experiment demands. This scheduling method also ensures that the winner among application emulations will not impede others.

2.3 Exploration of Testbed

For network research, a testbed is often used to evaluate the function and performance of NFs. As a result, the major function of a testbed is to generate various network traffic load based on protocol types. Despite the adoption of NFV and SDN, it is still a huge challenge to provide traffic emulation solution, which can mimic real-world services for evaluation due to the following reasons: Firstly, the rapid evolvement of Internet protocols increases the hardness to simulate traffic load conforming to the features of services. Secondly, traffic emulation needs to be flexible enough to support diverse protocols. Lastly, the huge throughput and privileged access of backbone networks also hinder the simulation. Consequently, parts of existing works focus on designing and building high throughput packet generators. In the meanwhile, some of the works are aimed to build mathematical models to produce traffic loads similar to the statistical characteristics of real-world network traffic. As alternative solutions, others achieve the goal indirectly by designing capture and storage systems to store internet traffic and replay under test environment. We select the works [11,20], which are representative and closely related to our proposal.

In [13], the authors presented a flexible high-throughput packet generator, which uses only a single CPU core by running on top of packet processing framework called DPDK. In the experiments, the generator could saturate 10GBE links using packets with minimum sized and provide the highest possible flexibility by Lua scripts. By leveraging the high-performance hardware, [14] described an open-source traffic generator, which has highly accurate inter-packet delays. [15] proposed a virtual testbed solution using software agents to emulate the activity of users thus generating similar network activity automatically. The experiments are evaluated through the validation of a network-monitoring tool for Voice over IP (VoIP). [16] defined methods to generate connections to simulate the statistical patterns of real network.

For the related work focused on packets capture, storage and replay, [17] showed a system using a modified network driver with the help of Non-Volatile Memory express (NVMe) technology and Storage Performance Development Kit (SPDK) framework, which is capable of capturing, timestamping and storing 40Gbps network traffic. [18] presented a novel framework, namely "Record and Deterministic Replay" architecture to log the traffic and then replay during the test. [19] researched the feasibilities of using packet header fields to partition network traffic for efficiently enabling distributed packet capturing and processing. In [20], FloSIS was proposed, which was a highly scalable software-based flow storing and indexing system. [21] employed network simulator to build the infrastructure and capture bandwidth traces in the wild and replays the traces reproducibly. Although the traffic generators using this approach can provide high throughput, it just constructs the packet and send out without considering any interactive information. Most of time, researchers cannot modify the content according to demand. Network activity pattern emulation is usually simple application relatively. Capturing and storing traffic loads need significant investment in solid state disk (SSD) or hard disk and it also take times to get the data.

In [22], it introduced a global testbed, namely PlanetLab. As the next generation of federated testbed, it aimed to federate multiple testbeds that owned and operated by autonomous organizations. However, it was subjected to members of the organization.

In the field of wireless network, Nils Aschenbruck *et al.* presents a new software-based approach that essentially combines mobility modeling with link control to facilitate evaluation of routing protocols and node mobility in testbeds [23]. In [24], Matthias *et al.* proposes a security testbed for the evaluation of wireless sensor network.

For theses many reasons, we propose a scalable software-based virtual testbed called NTS, which can generate real-world interactive traffic with high throughput. Also, the proposed virtual testbed can simulate most types of existing well-known protocols on the internet. Furthermore, by leveraging backpressure, the management framework of NTS can reallocate CPU resources for services dynamically based on cost-proportional policy.

3   Virtual Testbed Architecture

In a common testing environment, the devices, such as DPI, proxies or network content audit system, are deployed in series or parallel. The traffic load is mirrored or through by one or a few switch ports. For the sake of validation of system functions, the traffic generator must output a specified type of traffic, which has features similar to protocol under test. What's more, the operation platform should be able to schedule different kinds of protocol emulators in such a way that users can specify the requirement for CPU resources. However, operating system's scheduler doesn't have enough information of emulation applications. As a result, the NTS should be able to convert the scheduling requirements of application emulators to a format understood by the OS.

Although each container is isolated respectively, all of them run on the top of same CPU. The control platform of NTS needs to know the resource requirements of each traffic generator to avoid exhausting CPU resources, as well as monitoring the average process time of each service emulator. Furthermore, it also needs to estimate how many CPU shares to allocate for each generator. As for the evaluation indexes of testbed, it focuses on the correctness in function and throughput in performance in the field of network. The services queues are modeled as M/M/1 queue based on the statistical analysis. With the help of queueing theory, we can approximately calculate the resource quota.

To be aware of workload of various traffic generators in NTS, the scheduler needs to include network specific parameters in the scheduling algorithms. For instance, the scheduling algorithm needs to change the priority of a generator based on its computation cost. One possible implementation is to modify OS scheduler directly. However, it is a troublesome task that may lead to unnecessary maintenance overhead or introduce bugs, which will affect the stability and efficiency of the system. Also, using this approach means that a change of the scheduling priority requires a system call, which consumes CPU resources heavily if changes are frequent. Our proposed NTS adopts cgroups, which is a standard userspace primitive provided by Linux OS to schedule process. For simplicity, NTS monitors packet arrival rate and process cost and allocate CPU shares accordingly.

3.1   Overview of NTS

As shown in Fig. 1, the architecture of NTS mainly consists of four modules: (1) NTS manager, (2) services simulation composed of a series of service containers and optional network containers (e.g. BGP container), (3) various analog clients corresponding to services, and (4) backpressure (not included in the figure). Commonly, each service container is responsible for only one protocol simulation. The network containers are used for stimulation of network protocol or generation of tunnel traffic. We can deploy network simulator (e.g. Mininet) and devices under test between analog clients and services emulation to set up a virtual network topology environment. The basic workflow of NTS is simple: According to the parameters in the configuration file, analog clients make requests to services. By this means, it generates interactive real-world Internet traffic of different protocol. This way also offers users the chance to adapt evaluation indexes, such as protocol type or traffic proportions for various protocols, to meet test requirement. By leveraging flexible configuration, NTS can simulate a variety of hybrid traffic to meet most kinds of evaluation scenarios.

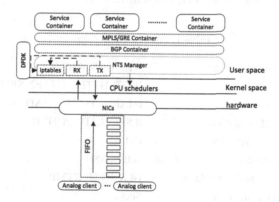

Fig. 1. The NTS architecture

To reduce context switches, NTS manager is allocated to a dedicated set of cores and is responsible for deciding which service container is to launch. NTS can also adopt DPDK optionally to accelerate packet forwarding with the help of user space protocol stack [25]. When the request packets from the analog clients arrive at the NIC, the RX does a look up in the iptables to transmit the packet to an appropriate application emulation in bridge mode, or directly send the packet to services in the host mode. Vice versa to the TX.

3.2   Traffic Simulation

As the core module of NTS, service simulation contains many types of application emulations. Each service based on a real-world application emulation is implemented in its own process and exposes ports from container without publishing them to host.

Moreover, most of service containers are constructed with open source software, reducing onerous task tremendously. Each analog client can perform basic operation. For the sake of reduction of deviation in the stage of resource evaluation, we have simplified clients. In other words, compared to real client, it only has one or two commonly used functions with single-mode. We can also specify the running time, execute count and so on in the configuration file for each one.

After establishing communication between services and analog clients, NTS can generate real interactive internet traffic. Through mount mode of volume provided by container technology, we can modify the content of traffic arbitrarily. This design brings great convenience to our experiment, especially for the function evaluation of network devices (e.g. content audit system). Besides, we can also decide which version of the protocol to mimic according to the test requirements. To the simulation of encrypted traffic, we can specify the certificate with different algorithms and length of secret keys. What's more, we have built diverse service applications for single specific protocol emulation to explore the difference of underlying servers. Every container is set up a threshold of CPU resources on the basis of calculated quota initially. The main supported protocols for emulation are listed in Table 1.

Table 1. Protocol Emulation

Common emulation	NTS, DNS, Radius
Web emulation	HTTP, HTTPS, HTTP2, SPDY
Mail emulation	IMAP(s), POP3(s), SMTP(s)
Tunnel emulation	IPSEC, L2TP, PPTP, IKE
File transfer emulation	FTP(s)
Remote connection emulation	Telnet, SSH
Stream media emulation	HLS, RTSP, RTMP
Proxy emulation	Socks
Instant message emulation	XMPP, VoIP, H.323
Network emulation	GRE, MPLS, BGP

In addition, researchers can deploy their application emulation in container mode to generate backbone network traffic without interfering network devices in the system, which provides chances for the researchers to obtain privileged access traffic without impacting the infrastructure. NTS provides a flexible and cost-efficient traffic simulator with various protocols to evaluate novel algorithms, tools, and systems in network research.

3.3 Resources Estimation

Each time, NTS manger needs to set up the initial threshold, which is similar to slow start threshold (ssthresh) in TCP Congestion Control, for every application emulation in start-up phase. Although we can use the default mode, meaning to employ whole CPU shares for allocation, it is easily to overload the system because of resource exhaustion. For instance, if two services start at the same time in default mode but one requires more process time per packet and gains high priority, then the heavy one will hinder another because of contention. Besides, operators do not have information to generators when configuring parameters. If the parameters are set up so big that exceed peak, contending generators will occupy vast majority of resource, leading to boot failure or errors of others. Furthermore, presetting threshold for generators diminishes the number of resource reallocation times, reducing resource overhead.

By leveraging queueing theory, we can formalize the problem of estimation using a queue model. We assume that the set of application emulations can be represented as disjoint sets. In this paper, we only take CPU into account. As mentioned before, different application emulations have various computation costs and per-packet costs. In addition, the analog clients are normalized to perform simple single-mode operation to reduce impact. We treat these costs as variables. The application emulation services are modeled as M/M/1 queues. Using the standard formula for an M/M/1 process time, the average time spent in the service j by a traffic simulation is:

$$C_j = 1/(1 - \lambda_j/\mu_j) \tag{1}$$

λ_j is the arrival rate of packets at j^{th} service (the client packet delivery rate), and μ_j is the process rate. These two number can be easily obtained from directory /proc/pid/net (pid is service container process id). In this paper, the initial threshold is set at the base that total CPU resource account for not more than 50%.

$$\sum threshold_i \leq 0.5 * Total_C PU_s hares \tag{2}$$

$$threshold_i = \frac{C_i * s_i}{\sum C_i * s_i} \tag{3}$$

s_i is the tuning parameter set in the configuration file. For simplicity, we select the minimum instead. In addition, only selected service containers to be run are taken into account.

3.4 Application Emulations Scheduling

Since multiple containers are likely to be available for scheduling to run at the same time, NTS must determine which service to schedule at any point in time. In our proposal, we leverage Linux's existing scheduling framework rather than designing an entirely new scheduler for application emulation. Furthermore, we tune the OS scheduler to provide cost-proportional fairness. Figure 2 shows how the NTS scheduler works. NTS manager governs OS scheduler via crgoups and assigns running simulated services to shared CPU cores ultimately.

If services are busy waiting for packets, the overall performance of the testbed will be very poor as it is a shared CPU environment. It is critical to design the management framework so that only services with packets available for them to process will be activated. NTS manager provides a relatively simple policy to trigger a service: once an operator configures parameters and specifies the types of protocols, manager will

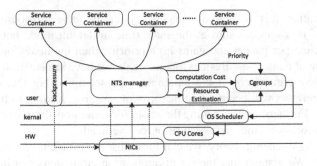

Fig. 2. Scheduling architecture of NTS

execute command (e.g. docker run) to start matched container with specified ports and other arguments, then service will be scheduled to run. This provides an efficient mechanism to trigger services.

For services with lots of packets to process, NTS supports preemption. The preemption decision and interaction with manager are arbitrated by the shared flag array set by backpressure. After processing a batch of packets, NTS manager will check the flag list to decide which state to keep. If the value in flag array is not set, the corresponding service will continue to run; if the value is not set and the parameter indexes (set in configuration file) has reached, the services will hold on (keep cpu ratio in balance); only if the value is set or there are no resources available, the service will be blocked until notified by the manager. This provides a flexible way for the NTS manager to indicate which service should be swapped out without the help from the kernel's CPU scheduler.

NTS manager provides mechanisms for application emulation to monitor arriving packets to estimate its CPU shares and adjust its scheduling weight accordingly. In this way, NTS manager can dynamically tune the scheduling weights for each service in order to meet operator evaluation demand.The packet arrival rate for a service can be easily measured. We measure the service time to process a packet inside each service using self-developed lib. NTS manager monitors all activated services to get a rate array. For simplicity, we maintain a histogram of timings and employ the median value to avoid outliers.

For service i on a shared core, the load is:

$$load(i) = \lambda_i * S_i \tag{4}$$

λ is the packet arrival rate and S is service time. Then we can calculate the total load on the core m:

$$total\,load(i) = \sum_i^n load(i) \tag{5}$$

and assign CPU shares for service i on core m is:

$$share(i) = priority_i * \frac{load(i)}{total\,load(m)} \tag{6}$$

After figuring out the result, manager can modify the CPU shares directly without interrupting containers by writing the file located in /sys/fs/cgroup/cpu,cpuacct/docker-containerID (docker-containerID is created when service container launched). The allocation of CPU shares provides cost proportional fairness to each service. Besides, we can tune the priority to generate different proportional traffics indirectly for various evaluation scenarios. Comparing with adjusting the CPU priorities exposed by OS scheduler, this method provides a more intuitive control.

A key goal of NTS manager is to avoid blocking all generators. We can describe the situation as follows: when two or more services are triggered, NTS manager monitors new packets arrival rate of each service and reallocates CPU resources based on cost proportional fairness scheduling. However, if there is no idle CPU to utilize, all running analog clients will still send out excessive packets and services will be blocked, resulting in increased errors and performance reduction. We avoid this through backpressure, which ensures the NTS can detect bottlenecks quickly and minimizes the performance degradation due to blocking.

After allotting CPU shares to services, NTS manager communicates with other modules in the system. When the CPU surplus is not enough, NTS manager will drop extra packet and send a flag to analog clients, preventing request packet arrival rate from rising by increasing time interval. NTS manager maintains states of each running service, and in this case, it moves the service's state from uphill to steady. When the time expires, manager will stop all of running services, then the state moves to initialization. The state transition diagram is shown in Fig. 3.

4   Experimental Evaluation

To reducing hardware cost, our experiment uses four commercial computers and a 10GE switch device. We deployed two type of analog client, network simulator and NTS server, separately on each of the computers. All of them are connected by switch. In our

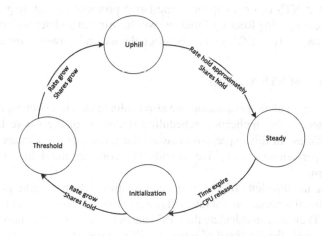

Fig. 3. NTS state diagram

experiments, we choose Mininet to simulate the network topology in all the tests. Each computer is equipped with a 2.4 GHz Intel Xeon E5-2680 processor and 128GB RAM. Each node is connected back-to-back with 10 Gbps dual-port DPDK compatible NICs. The OS is Centos 7.2 with kernel version 3.10.0-693.el7.x86_64.

4.1 Traffic Generation

Before proceeding with the NTS manager, we first validate whether the emulation can generate traffic that matches the protocol. In this stage, we select two kind of analog client each time. We start our emulators according to specified parameters and dump each kind of traffic to file in order respectively. In this paper, we adopt Wireshark to check the correctness of simulated traffic, protocol version and so on. Besides, to verify the function of content modification, we firstly examine the packet content before encryption. Secondly, we adopt available clients on the internet to validate cipher text. Part experimental results are show in Table 2.

Table 2. Protocol validation

Protocol	HTTP(s)	HTTP2	POP3(s)	IMAP(s)	SMTP(s)	FTP(s)
Traffic generation	•	•	•	•	•	•
Content modification	•	•	•	•	•	•
Algorithm type	•	•	•	•	•	•
Key length	•	•	•	•	•	•
Version	•	•	•	•	•	•

Furthermore, we also employ NTS during the function test of audit content system for two month. Compared to the result of online Internet traffic, they are almost the same except that NTS can not support some latest protocol version (e.g. TLS1.3). In addition, after configuring Routing Table on switch, Mininet and network container, we can find route packet (e.g. BGP packet) between device and network container.

4.2 Evaluation of NTS Manager

Apart from traffic emulation evaluation, we also evaluate the effectiveness of NTS manager that influences the application scheduling decisions of the native Linux kernel scheduling policies. In this paper, we measure the throughput to evaluate NTS manager's overall performance every five seconds. We compare the default OS scheduler with our system.

To estimate the threshold of each service emulation, we start traffic generators one by one and count the packet arrival rate and process rate. Besides, we set tuning parameter the same. Then we can calculate the CPU shares and evaluate the threshold approximately. In this way, the threshold of services will be proportion to their actual computational cost.

Due to the high proportion in traffic and widespread use on internet, we select HTTP and HTTPS for evaluation. As for other kinds of traffic generators, we can evaluate them in the same way. To minimize the influence of other variables, the content and underlying servers of selected traffic emulation are same, as well as the configuration. In addition, we deploy the traffic generators in host mode, which can reduce the overhead of resource for looking up the iptables.

Apart from backpressure, one important optimization we apply to NTS is "Redundancy Estimate and Pre-allocation". In practice, we cannot evaluate resource requirement accurately, leading to the allocation of CPU shares inaccurately. We note that lightweight excessive assignment of the resource has a slight impact on the performance compared to inadequacy, which blocks generators and causes NTS manager to experience a marginal degradation in throughput and connections. Furthermore, frequent assignment increases the overhead of resource, leading to small amplitude degradation when involuntary switching.

To alleviate the unavoidable defect, we first adopt a buffering resources allocation, namely redundancy estimate, by referring to the existing optimization method in the scope. In this paper, we not only take the packet arrival rate and processing cost into account but also think about the throughput above. With the increasing magnitude of throughput gradually diminishing during the initial phase, we can estimate the computational cost based on queuing theory. We monitor the variation trends of throughput discontinuously and assign resources for activated emulation services with proximately ascensional range, resulting in redundant shares slightly. Once throughput do not arise anymore, we keep the CPU shares for a moment. This way could mitigate the impact of unbefitting allocation of CPU weights.

In addition, we also employ pre-allocation in NTS manager during the ascent stage. We could estimate the resources required to process packets for next time based on output and update the cgroup's weights of running services. That's to say we estimate the load at the present and compute the growth rate to predict the CPU shares approximately. Furthermore, once we detect that the output does not increase any more, we revert to the original method.

In this paper, we collect each service container state data every five seconds during the experiment with the help of docker technology (e.g. docker stats) to check their CPU shares. In all cases, the services specified in the configuration file are triggered by NTS manager.

To evaluate the impact of threshold to NTS, we also set different initial tuning parameter and change the threshold proportion indirectly.

Figure 4 shows that NTS with backpressure can achieve improvement of throughput as much as 12.5% compared to operation system. It also shows that NTS can adjust services initial threshold by tuning the parameter directly according to evaluation requirement. In addition, it can also improve CPU utilization. By combining these, NTS with backpressure improves the overall throughput and can generate various proportional traffic.

For the default scheduler, the achieved throughput differs tremendously compared to NTS. What's more, we can observe that the value varies quickly without law. As mentioned above, OS scheduler just provides completely fairness scheduling.

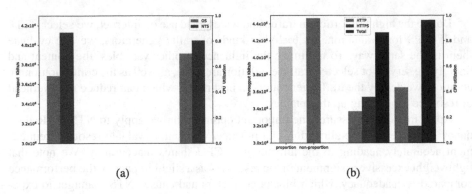

Fig. 4. Throughput comparison

When contending CPU resources, services obtains CPU shares alternately. This leads to an inevitable context switch and amounts of overhead. As a result, the throughput goes up and down.

On the contrary, by leveraging backpressure, NTS will determine whether to process the additional packets depending on the residual resources. It also allocates CPU shares based on packet arrival rate and process cost. This way refrains from resource contention and avoid an outbreak of errors, maintaining throughput in a relative stationary status for a period. We can also observe that the value fluctuates in a small margin. This is because the variation in per-packet processing cost of services result in an inaccurate estimate of processing cost and thus an inappropriate CPU shares allocation. We could mitigate the impact of variable packet processing cost by profiling services precisely and frequently. We could also maintain a histogram of times to average the packet process cost. However, this can be costly because it consumes significant amount of CPU resources. This is why we use redundancy estimate and pre-allocation mentioned above to alleviate the penalty from the variability and get a relatively smooth and better throughput.

We consider two different initial threshold setting. Due to the high proportion in traffic and widespread use on Internet, we select two types from them, namely HTTP and HTTPS, for evaluation. The threshold proportion is set to be 0.22:0.28 at first and then set to be 0.35:0.15 for HTTP and HTTPS. The two analog clients and configurations are same except access port. There is no modification for the rest. As showed in Fig. 4(b), once allocating the initial resources according to the set threshold proportion rather than their actual computation cost, the aggregate throughput and CPU utilization has improvement with small margin. Besides, compared to the threshold of cost proportional fairness, HTTP obtains more CPU resources, which is opposite to the former situation. In addition, if we set the proportion unfairly, the lightweight and prior service container will occupy mostly CPU resources. Accordingly, it also obtain higher throughput performance.

On the one hand, if we take cost-proportion fairness into account and allot initial resources for service container, each container have the same probability to obtain more resources to process arrival packet. With the help of backpressure, all of them will keep balance finally and fluctuate slightly. On the other hand, if the service container start from high base, namely owning adequate initial resource, it has the priority during resource allocation, resulting in reduction of available shares of CPU. In addition, compared to HTTPS, HTTP is more lightweight and need fewer computation cost to process packet. Although HTTPS has limited shares to process packet, impacting the overall throughput, the throughput of HTTP service container could offset the part loss and improve the overall performance.

By this way, NTS can adjust the initial shares and priority to generate various proportion hybrid traffic. What's more, it can also preempt the shares for lightweight service emulator to improve throughput. The experiment result show that: NTS design with backpressure and cost-proportion fairness scheduling can support a number of different traffic emulators. It effectively supports heterogeneous emulation application and still provides superior performance.

5 Conclusion

In this paper, we have presented a proposal for the generation of network traffic load that behaves like most of the real interactive traffic of the Internet. Such a proposal can improve the development of experimental studies that require network traffic for practitioner in network scope. It enables the definition of virtual testbed by making use of container technologies. Besides, it can be extended easily according to evaluation scenarios and requirement. What's more, our proposal doesn't think about the problem of ethical concerns related to information disclosure and has no impact to online network.

As the key part of our proposal, we adopt the notion of cost-proportion fairness scheduling to improve the performance. It not only takes packet arrival rate into account but also considers processing cost. By carefully tuning the scheduler weight and employing backpressure to efficiently evict excessive load, NTS has substantial improvement in throughput and dramatically reduces overhead. Furthermore, it adopts the redundancy mechanism and pre-allocation to mitigate the fluctuation because of improper allocation of CPU. It also demonstrates how a management framework can efficiently tune the OS scheduler in a relatively simple way to meet our goal.

The technical viability of our proposal is rooted in the feasibility of virtualization. By leveraging existing standard user space primitive provided by OS, namely cgroups, and accompanying virtual file system, rather than modifying scheduler itself, NTS manager could compute the load and assigns the CPU shares with low overhead.

The experiment results shows that: NTS is a lightweight, cost-efficient and extensible network traffic stimulator with affordability for researchers in network area. Next work, we consider the possibility to extend with user behavior simulation to generate synthetic network behavior pattern, which can be used as background traffic in network security.

References

1. Xia, W., Wen, Y., Foh, C.H., Niyato, D., Xie, H.: A survey on software-defined networking. IEEE Commun. Surv. Tutorials **17**(1), 27–51 (2015)

2. ETSI, N.F.V.: Network functions virtualisation (nfv). Management and Orchestration, vol. 1, V1 (2014)
3. Intel: Data plane development kit (2018)
4. Olsson, R.: Pktgen the Linux packet generator. In: Proceedings of the Linux Symposium, Ottawa, Canada, vol. 2, pp. 11–24 (2005)
5. Goel, U., Wittie, M.P., Claffy, K.C., Le, A.: Survey of end-to-end mobile network measurement testbeds, tools, and services. IEEE Commun. Surv. Tutorials 18(1), 105–123 (2016)
6. Merkel, D.: Docker: lightweight Linux containers for consistent development and deployment. Linux J. 2014(239), 2 (2014)
7. Olson, M., Christensen, K., Lee, S., Yun, J.: Hybrid web server: traffic analysis and prototype. In: 2011 IEEE 36th Conference on Local Computer Networks, pp. 131–134. IEEE (2011)
8. Menage, P.: Linux kernel documentation: Cgroups (2017)
9. Yan, J., Jin, D.: Vt-mininet: Virtual-time-enabled mininet for scalable and accurate software-define network emulation. In: Proceedings of the 1st ACM SIGCOMM Symposium on Software Defined Networking Research, vol. 27. ACM (2015)
10. Molnar, I.: Linux kernel documentation: CFS scheduler design (2017)
11. Kulkarni, S.G., et al.: NFVnice: dynamic backpressure and scheduling for NFV service chains. In: Proceedings of the Conference of the ACM Special Interest Group on Data Communication, pp. 71–84. ACM (2017)
12. Kanhere, S.S., Sethu, H., Parekh, A.B.: Fair and efficient packet scheduling using elastic round robin. IEEE Trans. Parallel Distrib. Syst. 13(3), 324–336 (2002)
13. Emmerich, P., Gallenmüller, S., Raumer, D., Wohlfart, F., Carle, G.: MoonGen: a scriptable high-speed packet generator. In: Proceedings of the 2015 Internet Measurement Conference, pp. 275–287. ACM (2015)
14. Rotsos, C., Sarrar, N., Uhlig, S., Sherwood, R., Moore, A.W.: OFLOPS: an open framework for openflow switch evaluation. In: Taft, N., Ricciato, F. (eds.) PAM 2012. LNCS, vol. 7192, pp. 85–95. Springer, Heidelberg (2012). https://doi.org/10.1007/978-3-642-28537-0_9
15. Muelas, D., Ramos, J., López de Vergara, J.E.: Software-driven definition of virtual testbeds to validate emergent network technologies. Information 9(2), 45 (2018)
16. Weigle, M.C., Adurthi, P., Hernández-Campos, F., Jeffay, K., Smith, F.D.: Tmix: a tool for generating realistic TCP application workloads in ns-2. ACM SIGCOMM Comput. Commun. Rev. 36(3), 65–76 (2006)
17. Julián-Moreno, G., Leira, R., de Vergara, J.E.L., Gómez-Arribas, F.J., González, I.: On the feasibility of 40 gbps network data capture and retention with general purpose hardware. In: Proceedings of the 33rd Annual ACM Symposium on Applied Computing, pp. 970–978. ACM (2018)
18. Shalabi, Y., Yan, M., Honarmand, N., Lee, R.B., Torrellas, J.: Record-replay architecture as a general security framework. In: 2018 IEEE International Symposium on High Performance Computer Architecture (HPCA), pp. 180–193. IEEE (2018)
19. Gad, R., Kappes, M., Mueller-Bady, R., Medina-Bulo, I.: Header field based partitioning of network traffic for distributed packet capturing and processing. In: 2014 IEEE 28th International Conference on Advanced Information Networking and Applications (AINA), pp. 866–874. IEEE (2014)
20. Lee, J., Lee, S., Lee, J., Yi, Y., Park, K.: Flosis: A highly scalable network flow capture system for fast retrieval and storage efficiency. In: USENIX Annual Technical Conference, pp. 445–457 (2015)
21. Frömmgen, A., Stohr, D., Fornoff, J., Effelsberg, W., Buchmann, A.: Capture and replay: reproducible network experiments in mininet. In: Proceedings of the 2016 ACM SIGCOMM Conference, pp. 621–622. ACM (2016)

22. Kim, W., Roopakalu, A., Li, K.Y., Pai, V.S.: Understanding and characterizing planetlab resource usage for federated network testbeds. In: Proceedings of the 2011 ACM SIGCOMM Conference on Internet Measurement Conference, pp. 515–532. ACM (2011)
23. Aschenbruck, N., Bauer, J., Bieling, J., Bothe, A., Schwamborn, M.: Let's move: adding arbitrary mobility to WSN testbeds. In: 2012 21st International Conference on Computer Communications and Networks (ICCCN), pp. 1–7. IEEE (2012)
24. Nils, A., Jan Bauer, J.B.A.B.M.S.: WSNLab - a security testbed and security architecture for WSNS. In: 2011 IEEE 36th Conference on Local Computer Networks, pp. 4–7. IEEE (2011)
25. Zheng, C., Tang, Q., Lu, Q., Li, J., Zhou, Z., Liu, Q.: Janus: a user-level TCP stack for processing 40 million concurrent TCP connections. In: 2018 IEEE International Conference on Communications (ICC), pp. 1–7. IEEE (2018)

Collaborative Applications for
Recognition and Classification

GeoCET: Accurate IP Geolocation via Constraint-Based Elliptical Trajectories

Fei Du[1,2], Xiuguo Bao[3], Yongzheng Zhang[1,2(✉)], and Huanhuan Yang[3]

[1] Institute of Information Engineering, Chinese Academy of Sciences, Beijing, China
{dufei,zhangyongzheng}@iie.ac.cn
[2] School of Cyber Security, University of Chinese Academy of Sciences, Beijing, China
[3] National Internet Emergency Center, CNCERT/CC, Beijing, China

Abstract. The geographical location of the IP device is crucial for many network security applications, such as location-aware authentication, fraud prevention, and security-sensitive forensics. Since most data mining-based methods are subject to the privacy protection policies, the delay-based measurement methods have broader application prospects. However, these methodologies are relying on heavyweight traffic on networks and high deployment costs. Besides, the worst case errors in estimation made by delay-based measurement methods render them ineffective. In this paper, we propose an accurate IP geolocation approach called GeoCET. This methodology only requires a small number of one-way delays (OWDs) to locate the targets, combining with elliptical trajectory constraints and maximum log-likelihood estimation technique. We introduce polynomial regression to fit the delay-distance model and enhance the accuracy of the localization. To evaluate GeoCET, we leverage real-world data which come from China, India, Western United States, and Central Europe. Experimental results demonstrate that GeoCET performs better for all existing measurement-based IP geolocation methodologies.

Keywords: Network security · IP geolocation ·
Delay-based measurement · Constraint-based elliptical trajectories

1 Introduction

Knowing the geographical location of Internet devices have an extensive range of applications, examples include delivery of local news and advertising, Internet anti-fraud (e.g., fraud signup, collision attack, brushing and spamming), credit card fraud detection, load balancing, resource allocation [9,10]. Particularly for law enforcement agencies, it is necessary to determine the location information very accurately as quickly as possible in order to satisfy all the requirements for an attacker's forensic strategy [24].

© ICST Institute for Computer Sciences, Social Informatics and Telecommunications Engineering 2019
Published by Springer Nature Switzerland AG 2019. All Rights Reserved
X. Wang et al. (Eds.): CollaborateCom 2019, LNICST 292, pp. 603–622, 2019.
https://doi.org/10.1007/978-3-030-30146-0_41

Our **goal** is to develop a high precision lightweight geolocation approach to locate active IP addresses on the Internet efficiently. Additionally, *IP geolocation* means determining the real-world location of an Internet-connected device. However, what makes this work challenging is that there is no one-to-one mapping between IP addresses and geographic locations. The dynamic assignment of IP addresses makes IP geolocation more difficult. On the other hand, because the propagation characteristics of the Internet are sharply influenced by factors such as the circuitous route, network congestion and queueing delay, it is more challenging to locate Internet devices. Besides, most Internet devices do not have the ability to self-positioning (e.g., Global Positioning System (GPS) or other location techniques [3]), other mobile devices may choose to hide location information due to privacy protection.

In the last years, the IP geolocation methods are based on static sources of information, such as registries and databases (e.g., [1,2]). However, with the adoption of IPv6, such databases become more difficult to update and maintain, the accuracy of these databases is in general not excellent. Some studies show that errors in the order of several thousand kilometers are possible [23].

For this reason, the device to be localized is mainly through network delay measurements (e.g., [8,27]). These methods for geolocation primarily measure end-to-end latency from a set of nodes with known locations of nodes to be geolocated using active probes (e.g., by using the Internet Control Message Protocol (ICMP), Ping or traceroute). Then, delays are converted into distances according to a previously defined delay-distance model, which assume that there is an existent correlation between network latency and geographical distance. (e.g., linear relationships include: *bestline*, $\frac{2}{3}c$ [22], $\frac{4}{9}c$ [16] or $\frac{3}{4}c$ [15]; non-linear relationships include probability distributions and hybrid strategies [5,6,25].) Finally, the coordinates of the target are inferred using geometrical techniques, such as [14,21,26] and [28]. Nevertheless, these methods do not achieve good accuracy, as inferences and approximations characterize the geolocation process, their accuracy is strongly dependent on the location of the landmark nodes to the target nodes. Therefore, these methods require a large number of available landmark nodes, relying on heavyweight traceroute-like or Ping-like probe packets on networks.

This paper proposes a novel accurate approach to IP geolocation—GeoCET. The GeoCET methodology considers two categories of nodes in the network: *Targets*, i.e., nodes with unknown geographic location that we aim to geolocate and respond to probes; *Analyszs*, i.e., nodes with known geographic location and the ability to send probe packets and receive response packets and perform localization operators. Then, we partition these nodes to "Observers" and "Landmarks". In prior literature, "Observers" sometimes referred to as "Vantage points", similar to Landmarks with probe capability.

The main contributions of this paper are summarized as follows.

– Presenting GeoCET, a novel approach for IP geolocation, which only relies on lightweight network load and reduces the number of feasible geographic coordinates to infer geographic location using elliptical trajectory constraints and maximum log-likelihood estimation technique.

- Constructing spoofed packets using the landmark's IP addresses to measure a target node, the one-way delay (OWD) links formed naturally can improve the localization accuracy. The flexibility and scalability of our scheme can effectively reduce the deployment of network resources.
- Evaluating GeoCET through detailed experiments on the real-world network, with nodes based in China, India, Western United States, and Central Europe. The evaluation involves analyzing the algorithm's accuracy and processing time, and other factors that affect the efficacy of GeoCET's results.

The rest of the paper is organized as follows. Section 2 presents the most relevant work in the field. Section 3 describes the delay-distance model and the detail of GeoCET algorithm. An empirical evaluation of GeoCET and a security discussion are presented in Sects. 4 and 5 respectively. Finally, Sect. 6 concludes the paper, and future work is outlined.

2   Related Work

In this section, we review related work which is closer in spirit to our proposed geolocation approach.

The constraint-based-geolocation (CBG) [14] used the limit of *"bestline"* to compensate for the detour and bloat of routes on the Internet. However, since it is difficult to predict whether a route from a monitor node to a target node is detoured, CBG is usually useful only when the target node is close to the monitor node. Another geolocation system that used information about intermediate routers is Topology-based Geolocation (TBG) [16].

Li et al. [19] developed a simple IP address mapping scheme GeoGet, a large number of web servers are used as passive landmarks, and the target maps to the geographic location of the landmark with the shortest delay. In order to control the measurement overhead, a multi-step detection method is used to optimize the geographical location of the target. The Octant [26] framework used a variety of information to locate the target node. It divides all information into positive and negative constraints to narrow the prediction area and improve localization accuracy. A positive constraint refers to an area where the target node may be located, and a negative constraint refers to a node cannot be located. It does not locate the position of the target node at a specific coordinate but represents its possible position as a surface determined by a Bézier curve. Since the network delay does not conform to the ideal delay transmission model, Octant introduces a "height" dimension to represent the access delay of the last hop.

The Spotter [18] algorithm is based on a detailed statistical analysis of the relationship between network delay and geographic distance and uses a probabilistic method to derive a general delay distance model, which can be achieved by the parameter estimation. In the case of multiple nodes, the delay distribution represents the joint probability of the independent normal distribution, and the parameter estimation method of the normal distribution is relatively simple. Compared to the same kind of active measurement method (relying on a large amount of network load), Posit [11] only requires a small amount of Ping measurement, combined with computational useful statistical embedding technology to locate the target node. Consequently, the computational complexity of the Spotter and Posit is small. Hillmann et al. [15] presented a new approach for optimizing the Landmark position for active measurements—Dragoon. For a reasonable Landmark selection is crucial for highly accurate localization services, the goal is to find landmarks close to the target in terms of infrastructure and hop count. Besides, they introduced an improved approach to adaptability and more accurate modeling of the geolocation process. Whereas, the number of samples and representativeness are important factors affecting the accuracy of estimation.

CPV [4] has been proposed as a delay-based mechanism that verifies clients' geographic locations, and they introduced a new OWD-estimation algorithm and evaluated its practicability by the probability distribution of one's absolute error. Compared with the round-trip halving, the one-way delay is more accurate in many scenarios.

GeoCET differs from the approaches as mentioned above, because it uses a lightweight network load to achieve higher accuracy and is easy to deploy and implement. Computational complexity also has significant advantages over similar measurement-based IP geolocation methodologies. We will describe in detail in the next section.

3   GeoCET Geolocation Methodology

This section presents some definitions about this paper, application scenario, and the detail of the GeoCET algorithm.

3.1   Notations and Definitions

We present the relevant concepts and the formalized description of the problem.

Measurement Delay (x): refers to the round-trip delay directly measured between nodes or the time interval between the request package and response package, which mainly refers to the propagation delay [17] between nodes, ignoring the transmission delay and processing delay. e.g., the interval between the request SYN packet and the response ACK packet of the TCP protocol, the packet sending of UDP protocol on higher port and the delay of the response packet.

In this paper, we use **one-way delay** (OWD) as the measurement delay. Let R be the number of value collected, and let $x_i = \{x_{i,1}, x_{i,2}, ..., x_{i,R}\}$ be the set of one-way delay between node i and the target.

Steady-State Delay ($\hat{x}$): we assume that there is a steady state of delay between network nodes, i.e., when the expansion of delay caused by network load and processing time of intermediate nodes is excluded, the propagation delay between any two nodes is a specific value. Given that the network is a dynamic system, the delay between nodes is also dynamic, so the minimum value in multiple measurements is chosen to be the steady-state delay between the two nodes. Let us define $\hat{x}_i = \min(x_i)$, then $\hat{x}_i$ is used for computing the steady-state delay between node i and the target.

Problem. In this paper, we ask the following question: is it possible to design an algorithm to achieve a high-precision IP geolocation algorithm with a fine-grained city block scale? In addition to being accurate and fast response time, such algorithms should also be scalable to networks of different application scenarios, and flexible in its use of computing resources.

For theoretical analysis purposes, we consider the following **scenario**. There are analysis nodes set $\mathcal{A}$ to measure target nodes set $\mathcal{T}$ ($\mathcal{T} = \{t_1, t_2, ..., t_l\}$), $\mathcal{A} = \mathcal{V} \cup \mathcal{L}$. where $\mathcal{V}$ ($\mathcal{V} = \{i_1, i_2, ..., i_m\}$) is a subset of analysis nodes as *observers* to send probe packets, and $\mathcal{L}$ ($\mathcal{L} = \{j_1, j_2, ..., j_n\}$) is a subset of analysis nodes as landmarks receive response packets of target nodes. Analysis nodes set $\mathcal{L}$ are used as *landmarks* and their distribution is over a small scale area (e.g., within 50 km), it satisfies the normal distribution. The network topology connectivity of analysis nodes set $\mathcal{A}$ can be approximated as the cyberspace with a 2-dimensional Euclidean model.

Ciavarrini et al. [7] derive the Cramér-Rao low bound (CRLB) of IP geolocation with delay-distance model. They proved that the distance between the landmarks related to the geolocation and the target should not be too large. Consequently, we limit the geolocation scenario to a range of 50 km.

The GeoCET algorithm will estimate the geographic location of each target node using only these steady-state delay measurement vectors from a set of analysis nodes.

3.2 Delay-Distance Model

According to the steady-state delay between the analysis nodes, combined with the geographical location of the known nodes, it can be drawn that the conversion relationship between the distances and delays of the analysis nodes. We define $r = [r_1, r_2, ..., r_N]^T$ the vector of measured distances between target and the analysis nodes, and $d = [d_1, d_2, ..., d_N]^T$ the vector of real distances between target and the analysis nodes. Ranging information can be modeled as in Eq. (1):

$$r = d + \delta \tag{1}$$

with $\delta = [\delta_1, \delta_2, ..., \delta_N]^T$ is the vector of errors associated to the ranging phase, when δ is not a zero vector.

There is often a certain degree of error in the end-to-end direct measurement delay or the estimated relative delay. The conversion function calculated based on the steady-state delay between the analysis node and the neighbor nodes (which can be regarded as neighbor nodes between the analysis nodes) can eliminate some errors, so we use the steady-state delay to locate the target IP address.

When the observer is far away from the target IP, the delay is easily affected by factors such as network load and routing policies, and the delay measurement value is prone to be too large, which makes it difficult to obtain accurate distance constraints based on the *bestline* method. It makes the distance of the cyberspace violate the triangular inequality of the Euclidean space in the measurable region.

Additionally, the factors affecting delay accuracy also include node jitter, coordinate drift, non-shortest route, malicious attacks, and link delays and so on.

Therefore, we limit the distance between the *observer*, the target IP and the analysis nodes on a relatively small scale to minimize the impact of the delay error. In theory, the principle is satisfied: (1) in the measurable region, the distance in the cyberspace must conform to the triangular inequality of the European space; (2) the propagation delay occupies a large proportion in the steady-state delay, so that the conversion relationship between the steady-state delay and the distance can be obtained by the least squares method.

Considering the non-linear relationship of the delay distance, we use a polynomial regression model [20] to solve the delay-distance conversion relationship. Suppose the conversion relationship is polynomial (2):

$$f_\rho(\hat{x}) = \rho_1 \hat{x}^n + \rho_2 \hat{x}^{n-1} + \rho_i \hat{x}^{n-i+1} + \ldots + \rho_{n+1} + \epsilon \tag{2}$$

where n is the degree of polynomials, $\hat{x}$ is the steady-state delay, ρ_i is the conversion coefficient, and $f_\rho()$ is the distance calculated from the delay. Since the regression function is linear in terms of the unknown coefficients $\rho_1, \rho_2, \ldots$. Therefore, for least squares analysis, the computational and inferential problems of polynomial regression can be completely addressed using the techniques of multiple regression.

Conveniently, the polynomial regression model (2) can be expressed in matrix form in terms of a design matrix $\mathbf{X}$, a distance vector f_ρ, a coefficient vector $\vec{\rho}$, and a vector $\vec{\epsilon}$ of random errors. Which when using matrix notation is written as:

$$\vec{f_\rho} = \mathbf{X}\vec{\rho} + \vec{\epsilon} \tag{3}$$

The vector of estimated polynomial regression coefficients is

$$\widehat{\vec{\rho}} = \left(\mathbf{X}^T \mathbf{X}\right)^{-1} \mathbf{X}^T \vec{f_\rho} \tag{4}$$

Since $\mathbf{X}$ is a Vandermonde matrix, the invertibility condition is guaranteed to hold if all the $\hat{x}_i$ values are distinct. This is ordinary least squares estimation (OLSE) solution [13].

3.3   Position Estimation Using Elliptical Trajectory Constraints

In contrast to delay-based and statistical-based methods, our algorithm's expectation is to locate the target IP address in a relatively small region (e.g., block in the city). Unlike machine learning-based methods (e.g., [12, 26]), there is no need to explicitly define population and geographic data as input to the algorithm. We only consider the known locations of analysis nodes (as viewed landmarks and observers) in the infrastructure contained in the geographically constrained region C, where we expect to exploit regional information with high Internet resource density.

Therefore, given the set of possible coordinates (*lat, lng*) in the region C found by constraint-based geolocation, which embeds into the cyberspace with a 2-dimensional Euclidean model by the elliptical trajectory.

We define the set of Internet resource nodes (described in Sect. 4), aim to use the observer node i, the landmark nodes set $\mathcal{L}$ to geolocate the target node t. The main process of the GeoCET algorithm is as follows.

(1) Clock synchronization is performed on the analysis nodes involved in the location target node t.
(2) We perform end-to-end mutual measurement on nodes in node i and set $\mathcal{L}$, measure the steady-state delay in the current network situation, and calculate the delay-distance conversion relationship $\vec{f}_\rho$ (in Eq. (3)) and polynomial regression coefficient vector $\widehat{\vec{\rho}}$ (in Eq. (4)).
(3) The node i spoofs one's IP address with node j ($j = 1, 2, ..., n$) to send probe packets to the target node t, the target node t responds to the response packet to the corresponding IP node j, respectively. The link sequence of the packet is: node i → node t → node j, computing its one-way steady state delay $\hat{x}_{i,t,j}$, i.e., $\hat{x}_{i,t} + \hat{x}_{t,j}$.

   We combine the delays $\hat{x}_{i,j}$ of nodes i and j to analyze whether $\hat{x}_{i,t,j}$ is greater than $\hat{x}_{i,j}$, if $\hat{x}_{i,t} + \hat{x}_{t,j} \not> \hat{x}_{i,j}$, i.e., the delay distance violates the triangular inequality of Euclidean space, ignoring the measured value of the link.
(4) In contrast to previous work, we do not adopt the intersection area of N circles as the candidate area of the target node, but exploit the elliptical trajectory intersection area, which takes the nodes i and j as the focus, and the distance sum after the delay conversion is constant, as shown in Equation (5) and Fig. 1.

$$\zeta_{i,t} = \bigcap_{j=1}^{n} E_{i,j} \left\{ (F_i, F_j), |F_i T| + |T F_j| = 2a, (2a > |F_i F_j|) \right\} \qquad (5)$$

where a is a constant, $E_{i,j}$ is an ellipse with F_i and F_j as the focus, the trajectory of the moving point $T(x, y)$ is the possible position of the target, $\zeta_{i,t}$ is the intersection of multiple elliptical trajectories, The center of the region $\zeta_{i,t}$ is taken as the target node geolocation, denoted as $\ell_{i,t}$. Other variables are as follows.

$$F_i = (-c, 0), F_j = (c, 0), T = (x, y)$$
$$|F_i F_j| = 2c = f_\rho(\hat{x}_{i,j})$$
$$|F_i T| = \sqrt{(x + c)^2 + y^2} = f_\rho(\hat{x}_{i,t})$$
$$|T F_j| = \sqrt{(x - c)^2 + y^2} = f_\rho(\hat{x}_{t,j})$$
$$2a = \sqrt{(x + c)^2 + y^2} + \sqrt{(x - c)^2 + y^2} = f_\rho(\hat{x}_{i,t,j})$$

The intersection points of the elliptical trajectories that have been modeled between the target node and analysis nodes using the probe packet paths is shown in Fig. 2, in the case (c), due to the symmetry caused by the collinearity of the analysis nodes in the geometric space, the localization of the target node is determined to be false positive. When elliptical trajectories intersect straight lines, there is a false positive position in case (d) but not in the case (b). Therefore, it is necessary to avoid the phenomenon of multi-node collinearity as much as possible.

(5) By traversing multiple observer nodes i in set V, we will get a set of candidate regions Ω_t of the target node t, $\Omega_t = \{\ell_{1,t}, \ell_{2,t}, ..., \ell_{d,t}\}$, $|\Omega_t| = d$, then, use the statistical algorithm to find the location of the target node t, $\hat{\ell}_t$, by maximizing the log-likelihood given measurements $\ell_{k,t}$ from the analysis nodes and to target node.

$$\hat{\ell}_t = \underset{\ell_t \in \Omega_t}{\arg\max}\, \hbar_i\,(\ell_t) = \underset{\ell_t \in \Omega_t}{\arg\max} \sum_{i=1}^{d} \log P\,(\ell_{i,t}|\hat{\omega}_i) \tag{6}$$

where $P\,(\ell_{i,t}|\hat{\omega}_i)$ is the posterior probability,

$$P\,(\ell_{i,t}|\hat{\omega}_i) = \frac{P\,(\hat{\omega}_i|\ell_{i,t})\,P\,(\ell_{i,t})}{\sum P\,(\hat{\omega}_i|\ell_{i,j})\,P\,(\ell_{i,j})} \tag{7}$$

The $\hat{\omega}_i$ is the coordinate (lat_i, lng_i) of the observer node i, then $P\,(\ell_{i,t})$ indicates the prior possibility of a candidate region. The set of of analysis nodes that lie in the constrain region, C.

An example of the scenario using GeoCET methodology can be found in Fig. 1. Considering that only four analysis nodes are needed to build an intersection region using the one-way delay, the computational complexity of our proposed algorithm is very low, and the traffic generated by the measurement is negligible.

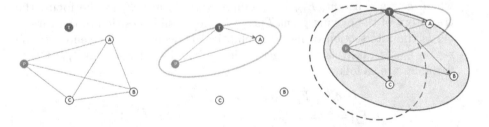

Fig. 1. (Left) - Example: probe node is P, analysis nodes are A, B, C, and the target node is T. (Center) - The P spoofing A's IP address measures T, $delay_{PT} + delay_{TA} = 2\beta\,(delay_{PT} + delay_{TA} > delay_{PA})$, β is a constant, and the candidate trajectory of T is an ellipse with P and A as the focus. (Right) - P spoofs one's IP address through A, B and C to measure the target T separately. The intersection of the three elliptical trajectories is the position area of T.

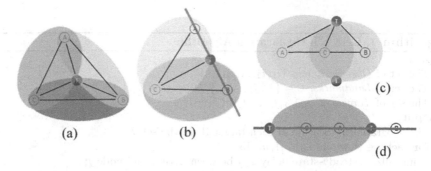

Fig. 2. Different cases of intersection: (a) One intersection point of multiple elliptical trajectories. (b) One intersection point of multiple elliptical trajectories and a straight line. (c) Two intersection points of multiple elliptical trajectories. (d) Two intersection points of elliptical trajectory and multiple lines.

3.4   GeoCET Geolocation Algorithm Summary

The complete GeoCET geolocation methodology is presented in Algorithm 1. The nodes in the set $\mathcal{A}$ ($\mathcal{A} = \mathcal{V} \cup \mathcal{L}$) are required to be an approximately uniform distribution with known geographic location, the networks are connected to each other, and the space constructed by the steady-state delay $\hat{x}$ conforms to the 2-dimensional Euclidean space.

To prevent overfitting and multiple feasible solutions, we carefully select the analysis nodes that participate in building the polynomial regression model. In practice, we construct a steady-state delay matrix $\mathbf{M}$ through multiple measurements in batches, minimizing the effects of cumulative errors.

Usually, $m < n$, we need fewer observers than landmarks. In the best case, where m is 1, and n is merely 3. This GeoCET algorithm achieves high precision with fewer probe packets, and the traffic on these networks is negligible.

In order to make the algorithm have a satisfactory convergence speed, the errors or outliers should be eliminated from the set $\mathcal{V}$ and $\mathcal{L}$.

GeoCET comprises two high-level capabilities (in Fig. 3): *Delay-distance generation* takes a geographic region that a target IP address belongs to as input, and generates a parameter vector of polynomial regression (PR) model for localization. *Candidate landmark localization* takes the target IP address and PR model as input and generates the target IP positions in the specified geographic region as output.

4   Evaluation

To validate and evaluate our GeoCET geolocation methodology, we exploit four datasets. In this section, we compare GeoCET with prior work and analyze relevant experimental results.

Algorithm 1. GeoCET Geolocation Algorithm

Input:

The set of *Observers*, $\mathcal{V} = \{i_1, i_2, ..., i_m\}$, $|\mathcal{V}| = m$.

The set of *Landmarks*, $\mathcal{L} = \{j_1, j_2, ..., j_n\}$, $|\mathcal{L}| = n$.

The set of *Targets*, $\mathcal{T} = \{t_1, t_2, ..., t_l\}$, $|\mathcal{T}| = l$.

Output:

The geographical location of each target IP in the set $\mathcal{T}$.

1: **for** each $i \in [1, m]$ and $j \in [1, n]$ **do**
2:     initialize a steady-state delay $\hat{x}_{i,j}$ between node i and node j;
3:     build a steady-state delay matrix $\mathbf{M} = (\hat{x}_{i,j})_{m \times n}$;
4:     determine the delay-distance conversion polynomial regression function $\vec{f}_\rho$ and the conversion coefficient vector $\widehat{\vec{\rho}}$ using Equation (3) and (4);
5: **end for**
6: **for** each $t \in [1, l]$ **do**
7:     use Equation (5) to resolve the each t intersection regions Ω_t;
8:     **while** $(|\Omega_t| > 1)$ **do**
9:         select the maximum log-likelihood estimation $\hat{\ell}_t$ from Ω_t using Equation (6) and (7);
10:     **end while**
11:     **if** $(\Omega_t \neq \phi)$ and $(|\Omega_t| = 1)$ **then**
12:         the element ℓ_t in Ω_t is the geographic location of node t;
13:     **end if**
14: **end for**

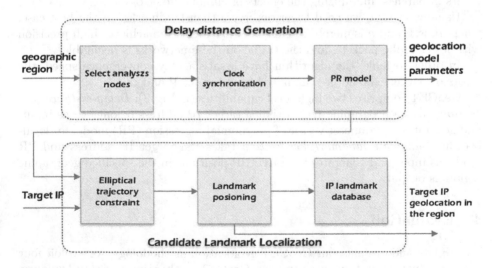

Fig. 3. GeoCET Components.

4.1 Experimental Data

We use a set of measurements collected from 361 analysis nodes with ground truth location knowledge. These nodes include: 75 cloud server nodes for Alibaba Cloud lease and their accurate locations are verified using codes written in Python and accessed the Google Map API, and volunteers provide the accurate location of 286 servers. Figure 4 shows the geographical distribution of the analysis nodes.

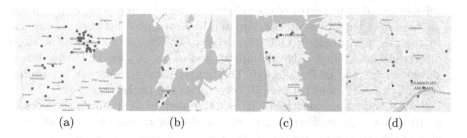

(a)   (b)   (c)   (d)

Fig. 4. Analysis nodes come from four different regions: (a) analysis nodes in China; (b) analysis nodes in Mumbai; (c) analysis nodes in Silicon Valley and (d) analysis nodes in Frankfurt.

In the area where the analysis nodes are being, we collected more than 40,000 active IP addresses based on the principle of crowdsourcing. These IP addresses have fine-grained location information, i.e., latitude and longitude coordinates in the WGS84 coordinate system. Table 1 shows the specific information of the target nodes.

Table 1. Target nodes come from different regions of the world.

Different regions	Target nodes (crowdsourcing)
Beijing, Tianjin, Hebei, Shanxi, China	32,719
Mumbai, India	1,768
Silicon Valley, Western United States	2,574
Frankfurt, Central Europe	3,693

Among these target nodes, IP addresses in China cover different scenarios where the analysis nodes are dense or sparse; IP addresses in Mumbai are relatively complex in network topology; IP addresses in Silicon Valley belong to high-speed network connectivity; moreover, the geographical distribution of the analysis nodes and target nodes in Frankfurt is approximately uniform.

4.2 Implementation

We implemented GeoCET algorithm in C and Python. The probing packets are marked with the characteristic words as the fingerprint in the content field.

Each packet contains the IP address of the target node (reflection device) and the original packet transmission time, which is on the path from the observer to landmark nodes. Our implementation has six components (Fig. 3). All experiments described in this paper are run on analysis servers with Intel Xeon (Skylake) Platinum 8163 at 2.5 GHz, 16 GB memory and 40 GB hard drives. Below, we discussed the primary components of parallelizing GeoCET computing across multiple servers.

(1) PR model. This component uses a vector of one-way delays (OWDs) to solve the coefficient vector of the polynomial regression model, as polynomials have broader representation capabilities in a global network. Compared to the round-trip delays, One-way delays (OWDs) can mitigate the effect of network instability, path asymmetry and so on. It uses TCP-based measurements instead of Ping-based. The fundamental reasons are (1) routers that block ICMP, and (2) firewall constraints the packets.

(2) Elliptical trajectory constraint. It uses the method of spoofing the peer IP address and requires distributed collaboration for measurement. The geometry of the elliptical trajectory is the optimal choice for this mechanism.

(3) IP landmark database. The database maintains an IP address corresponding to the physical location information of the network entity, in addition to the latitude and longitude coordinates of the GPS, and also includes a semantic description of the geographic location. The network entity landmark database is dynamic.

4.3 Metrics

To measure the performance of GeoCET, we use two metrics: *accuracy* and *processing time*. We discuss the false positive rate of GeoCET, which can be used to determine GeoCET's precision.

The *accuracy* of GeoCET is measured by its positioning error, the distance between GeoCET's position $g(x_i)$ and ground truth d. The value of root mean square error (RMSE) is used to calculate the metric as follows:

$$RMSE\left(\boldsymbol{x}, g\right) = \sqrt{\frac{1}{m}\sum_{i=1}^{m}\left(g\left(x_i\right) - \boldsymbol{d}\right)^2}$$

For *processing time*, we quantify the processing speed of each component in GeoCET, which can depend on various factors such as the adopted communication technologies. Since the processing time is a relative value, we define the measured average of a set of data in the same network environment as the evaluation metric.

$$PT = \lambda\frac{1}{m}\sum_{i=1}^{m}\left(t_{DDG}^i + t_{CCL}^i\right)$$

where t_{DDG}^i is the measurement time of *Delay-distance Generation* component, t_{CCL}^i is the computation time time of *Candidate Landmark Localization* component, λ is the adjustment factor of the network environment.

4.4   An Example: Delay-Distance Model

In the delay-based measurement method, a large number of errors may result due to the non-linear relationship between the network distance and the geographical distance. For a more explicit expression, the scatter plot of the delay-distance is shown in Fig. 5, which only use the steady-state delay between the analysis nodes in datasets.

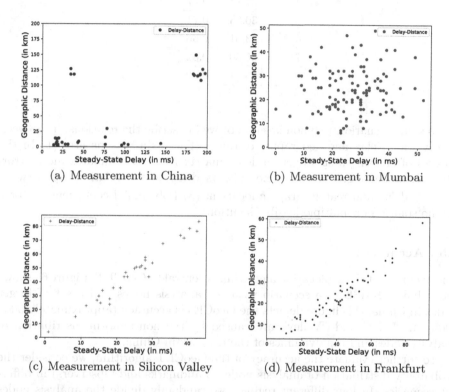

(a) Measurement in China   (b) Measurement in Mumbai

(c) Measurement in Silicon Valley   (d) Measurement in Frankfurt

Fig. 5. Example: Scatter plot of delay and distance from four datasets.

We solve polynomial regression function $\vec{f_\rho}$ in Python environment, the specific index is shown in Table 2. In general, the closer the $R^2\text{-}score$ coefficient is to 1, the smaller the value of root mean square error (RMSE), the better the fitting effect of the corresponding polynomial. As can be seen from Table 2, we choose a polynomial fit of $degree = 5$. The conversion relationship is: $f_\rho(\hat{x}) = 9.67954503e\text{+}00\hat{x}^5 - 1.78578444e\text{-}01\hat{x}^4 + 1.22928376e\text{-}03\hat{x}^3 - 3.27890994e\text{-}06\hat{x}^2 + 2.74087855e\text{-}09\hat{x} - 112.21036574$.

In addition, in Fig. 5, the delay-distance relationship corresponding to the measurement dataset in Mumbai conforms to the normal distribution, and a linear function can represent the delay-distance relationship corresponding to the measurement dataset in Silicon Valley, and the measurement dataset in Frankfurt corresponds to the delay-distance relationship can be described by a second-order polynomial function, i.e., $degree = 2$.

Table 2. Polynomial conversion relationship from measurement dataset in China.

degree	RMSE	R^2-score
1	53.80	0.12
2	40.22	0.51
3	39.98	0.51
4	37.73	0.57
5	30.83	0.71
6	33.51	0.66
7	35.50	0.62
8	35.21	0.62

In some scenarios, polynomials do not well describe the relationship between steady-state delay and geographic distance. The main reasons are: (1) In the process of creating a steady-state delay matrix $\mathbf{M}$, it accumulates more error. (2) Polynomial regression does not always describe the relationship between network delay and real geographic location. (3) Polynomial coefficient vector $\widehat{\rho}$ has no solution or multiple feasible solutions.

4.5 Accuracy

The accuracy of the geolocation algorithm is central to GeoCET. Figure 6a shows the value of RMSE in a scenario with ten analysis nodes and a set of target nodes in China, this figure depicts the GeoCET's accuracy (approximately 500–1000 m). "Peak" and "Valley" are caused by the non-uniform distribution of analysis nodes and the dynamics of the network in China.

To further evaluate the accuracy of the GeoCET algorithm, we consider the probability distribution of analysis nodes (Landmarks and Observers) in different scenarios. In four different regions, we randomly divide the analysis nodes and target nodes into five groups. In the same measurement environment, we compared the GeoCET algorithm to Octant [26], Spotter [18], Posit [11] and Dragoon [15]. We did not get the source codes of these related algorithms. For the comparison of experiments, we implemented the core functions of the related algorithms based on the description in the literature. Taking the mean value of multiple measurements of five sets of data as input, Fig. 7 shows the cumulative probability distribution function (CDF) of errors of correlation comparison algorithms.

We find that the GeoCET outperforms the other algorithms in these four datasets. Regarding Dragoon, it is sensitive to the performance of the network, and the performance difference is significant in different networks. The Posit algorithm has a higher accuracy than Spotter and Octant, but still less accuracy than the GeoCET algorithm. Table 3 shows the comparison results of the median errors for these algorithms.

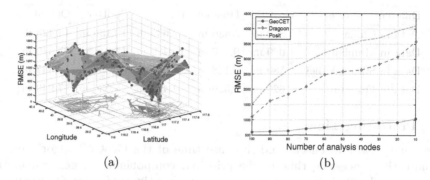

(a)   (b)

Fig. 6. (a) Accuracy: 3D representation in China and (b) Accuracy when varying the number of analysis nodes.

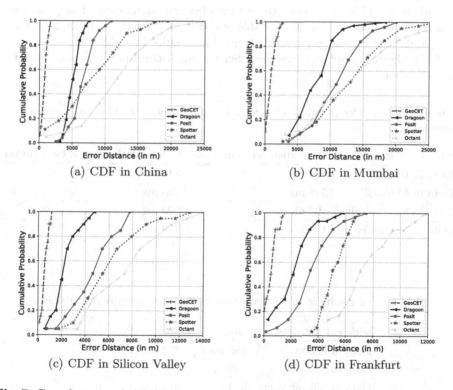

(a) CDF in China   (b) CDF in Mumbai

(c) CDF in Silicon Valley   (d) CDF in Frankfurt

Fig. 7. Cumulative probability distribution of localization error for different methodologies in four datasets.

Table 3. The results of five algorithms in different measurement datasets.

Different datasets	GeoCET	Dragoon	Posit	Spotter	Octant
Data in China	870 m	5,436 m	7,630 m	10,136 m	14,423 m
Data in Mumbai	1,029 m	9,130 m	13,429 m	14,011 m	17,510 m
Data in Silicon Valley	580 m	3,128 m	4,685 m	7,331 m	8,347 m
Data in Frankfurt	620 m	2,536 m	4,422 m	5,536 m	7,949 m

4.6 Processing Time

To evaluate the bottlenecks and response time of the GeoCET algorithm, we evaluate the processing time of the principal components. In general, in the same geographical region, we compare the response times of different algorithms to discover the bottlenecks of the algorithm and the implementation that can optimize and improve.

Table 4 compares the processing time of two components on the same set of data sets. The first component of the measurement time overhead on a large proportion, factors affecting its performance include network access, routing policies, network bandwidth and so on, these times become significant. The processing time of the second component is stable and does not fluctuate much. Fast CPU and parallelization can reduce this time. The results in Table 5 show that our GeoCET algorithm outperforms the other two algorithms in terms of positioning response time.

Table 4. The processing time of GeoCET's components in different measurement datasets.

Different datasets	Delay-distance generation	Candidate landmark localization
Data in China	329 ms	345 ms
Data in Mumbai	548 ms	350 ms
Data in Silicon Valley	93 ms	300 ms
Data in Frankfurt	110 ms	329 ms

Table 5. The results of three algorithms in different measurement datasets.

Different datasets	GeoCET	Dragoon	Posit
Data in China	659 ms	892 ms	1,872 ms
Data in Mumbai	898 ms	1,201 ms	2,412 ms
Data in Silicon Valley	343 ms	980 ms	1,024 ms
Data in Frankfurt	510 ms	829 ms	1,548 ms

5   Discussion

As mentioned, It is clear that identifying the delay-distance model $\vec{f_\rho}$ and the nature of noise $\vec{\epsilon}$ is essential, as they have a profound impact on localization accuracy. According to the CRLB of a delay-distance model [7], their results show that the localization accuracy and the number of landmarks involved can be relevant, and their distance from the target cannot be too large. We used OWDs to alleviate the circuitousness of paths in the delay-distance model, and achieved the measurement work at the nearest city of the target nodes by leasing server nodes.

However, the proposed GeoCET method is limited: (1) The polynomial regression model and the elliptical trajectory constraints need to satisfy the characteristics of the 2-dimensional European space, i.e., the geometric structure (in the local environment of measurement) of the triangle inequality cannot be violated (TIV). (2) If the target node manipulates the response delay of the probe packet, it will forge the real position and deceive the geolocation algorithm. We have left this to future work.

We assumed that an IP geolocation method is to work on a global scale. It makes sense to understand GeoCET's coverage. Table 6 shows the coverage with the GeoCET algorithm in different regions. Across these four cities, GeoCET achieves more than 79.1% coverage.

Table 6. GeoCET's coverage in measurement data from different regions of the world.

Regions	Target IP nodes	GeoCET	Coverage
Beijing, Tianjin	1,247	963	77.2%
Mumbai	768	540	70.3%
Silicon Valley	576	496	86.1%
Frankfurt	693	600	86.6%

In China, our GeoCET identified 963 out of 1,247 target IP nodes, most IP nodes that cannot be located are due to (1) the delay measurement results violate the triangle inequality, (2) the PR model cannot describe the local delay-distance relationship, and (3) the negative constraint of the analysis node selection on the measurement. In Mumbai, GeoCET finds 540 out of 768 IP addresses for a 70.3% coverage. Of the ones that GeoCET missed, about 28 nodes did not respond to the probe packets, and the remaining nodes had a longer delay and were excluded as outliers. In Silicon Valley and Central Europe, the GeoCET can localize 86.1% and 86.6% the target IP addresses respectively. In addition to some unresponsive nodes, some of the target nodes are farther away from the analysis node than the initial threshold. We then manually inspected the remaining uncovered target nodes but not identified by GeoCET, tried and repeated multiple iterations in different periods or reselected the analysis nodes, and it turns out that our algorithm can solve more than 80% of the uncovering nodes.

Finally, we evaluated GeoCET's flexibility and scalability. The GeoCET is flexible enough to support extended functionality or improve its scalability. The GeoCET algorithm relies on fewer analysis nodes than other algorithms, which uses the intersection of the elliptical trajectories, its constraint is stronger than the triangulation method, and its stability is better on a real data set. For scalability, GeoCET can be stretched to larger areas, and many of its components can be parallelized. When the distribution of analysis nodes is sparse or the number of nodes is small, the localization accuracy and stability of GeoCET are better than similar algorithms. This phenomenon is also highlighted by Fig. 6b.

6   Conclusion

In this paper, we describe a novel accurate method for IP geolocation, namely, GeoCET. Our methodology estimates geographic location using elliptical trajectories intersection combined with maximum log-likelihood estimation technique. We also use a polynomial regression to fit the delay-distance model. It mitigates the effects of noisy distance estimation from measurements.

We assess the performance of GeoCET using four datasets of latency measurements collected from hundreds of nodes on the Internet where they are distributed in different regions of the world such as the China, India, Western United States, and Central Europe. Experimental results show that GeoCET can identify the geographic location of target nodes with a median error of 500–1000 m and 300–800 ms processing time. We compare it with implementations of the current existing measurement-based IP geolocation methodologies on the same datasets, and these results highlight the efficient performance of our approach and lower deployment costs.

As our future work, we will investigate better probability distributions for delay-distance data which can capture the behavior of noise in latency measurements. Then, we plan to extend the testing scope of the GeoCET method to cover more regions around the world to verify its scalability and stability.

Acknowledgment. We thank the anonymous reviewers whose comments helped improve the paper. We also thank the volunteers who provide the right location nodes. This work has been supported by the National Key Research and Development Program of China (grant no. 2016YFB0801300, 2016YFB0801304 and 2017YFB081701).

References

1. Apnic - query the apnic whois database. http://wq.apnic.net/apnic-bin/whois.pl
2. Maxmind: Detect online fraud and locate online visitors. http://www.hostip.info/
3. Skyhook: Location technology and intelligence. https://www.skyhookwireless.com/
4. Abdou, A., Matrawy, A., Van Oorschot, P.C.: CPV: delay-based location verification for the internet. IEEE Trans. Dependable Secure Comput. **14**(2), 130–144 (2017)
5. Allman, M., Beverly, R., Trammell, B.: Principles for measurability in protocol design. ACM SIGCOMM Comput. Commun. Rev. **47**(2), 2–12 (2017)

6. Bajpai, V., Eravuchira, S.J., Schönwälder, J.: Dissecting last-mile latency characteristics. ACM SIGCOMM Comput. Commun. Rev. **47**(5), 25–34 (2017)
7. Ciavarrini, G., Greco, M.S., Vecchio, A.: Geolocation of internet hosts: accuracy limits through cramér-rao lower bound. Comput. Networks **135**, 70–80 (2018)
8. Ciavarrini, G., Luconi, V., Vecchio, A.: Smartphone-based geolocation of internet hosts. Comput. Networks **116**, 22–32 (2017)
9. Dan, O., Parikh, V., Davison, B.D.: Improving IP geolocation using query logs. In: Proceedings of the Ninth ACM International Conference on Web Search and Data Mining, pp. 347–356. ACM (2016)
10. Ding, S., Luo, X., Yin, M., Liu, Y., Liu, F.: An IP geolocation method based on rich-connected sub-networks. In: 2015 17th International Conference on Advanced Communication Technology (ICACT), pp. 176–181. IEEE (2015)
11. Eriksson, B., Barford, P., Maggs, B., Nowak, R.: Posit: a lightweight approach for IP geolocation. ACM SIGMETRICS Perform. Eval. Rev. **40**(2), 2–11 (2012)
12. Eriksson, B., Barford, P., Sommers, J., Nowak, R.: A learning-based approach for IP geolocation. In: Krishnamurthy, A., Plattner, B. (eds.) PAM 2010. LNCS, vol. 6032, pp. 171–180. Springer, Heidelberg (2010). https://doi.org/10.1007/978-3-642-12334-4_18
13. Gergonne, J.: The application of the method of least squares to the interpolation of sequences. Historia Mathematica **1**(4), 439–447 (1974)
14. Gueye, B., Ziviani, A., Crovella, M., Fdida, S.: Constraint-based geolocation of internet hosts. IEEE/ACM Trans. Networking (TON) **14**(6), 1219–1232 (2006)
15. Hillmann, P., Stiemert, L., Rodosek, G.D., Rose, O.: Modelling of IP geolocation by use of latency measurements. In: 2015 11th International Conference on Network and Service Management (CNSM), pp. 173–177. IEEE (2015)
16. Katz-Bassett, E., John, J.P., Krishnamurthy, A., Wetherall, D., Anderson, T., Chawathe, Y.: Towards IP geolocation using delay and topology measurements. In: Proceedings of the 6th ACM SIGCOMM Conference on Internet Measurement, pp. 71–84. ACM (2006)
17. Laki, S., Mátray, P., Hága, P., Csabai, I., Vattay, G.: A model based approach for improving router geolocation. Comput. Networks **54**(9), 1490–1501 (2010)
18. Laki, S., Mátray, P., Hága, P., Sebők, T., Csabai, I., Vattay, G.: Spotter: a model based active geolocation service. In: 2011 Proceedings IEEE INFOCOM, pp. 3173–3181. IEEE (2011)
19. Li, D., et al.: IP-geolocation mapping for moderately connected internet regions. IEEE Trans. Parallel Distrib. Syst. **24**(2), 381–391 (2013)
20. Magee, L.: Nonlocal behavior in polynomial regressions. Am. Stat. **52**(1), 20–22 (1998)
21. Padmanabhan, V.N., Subramanian, L.: An investigation of geographic mapping techniques for internet hosts. In: ACM SIGCOMM Computer Communication Review, vol. 31, pp. 173–185. ACM (2001)
22. Percacci, R., Vespignani, A.: Scale-free behavior of the internet global performance. Eur. Phys. J. B-Condens. Matter Complex Syst. **32**(4), 411–414 (2003)
23. Shavitt, Y., Zilberman, N.: A geolocation databases study. IEEE J. Sel. Areas Commun. **29**(10), 2044–2056 (2011)
24. Shue, C.A., Paul, N., Taylor, C.R.: From an IP address to a street address: using wireless signals to locate a target. In: Proceedings of the 7th USENIX Conference on Offensive Technologies, p. 8. USENIX Association (2013)

25. Trammell, B., Kühlewind, M.: Revisiting the privacy implications of two-way internet latency data. In: Beverly, R., Smaragdakis, G., Feldmann, A. (eds.) PAM 2018. LNCS, vol. 10771, pp. 73–84. Springer, Cham (2018). https://doi.org/10.1007/978-3-319-76481-8_6
26. Wong, B., Stoyanov, I., Sirer, E.G.: Octant: A comprehensive framework for the geolocalization of internet hosts. In: NSDI, vol. 7, p. 23 (2007)
27. Zhao, F., Luo, X., Gan, Y., Zu, S., Cheng, Q., Liu, F.: IP geolocation based on identification routers and local delay distribution similarity. Concurrency and Computation: Practice and Experience, p. e4722 (2018)
28. Ziviani, A., Fdida, S., de Rezende, J.F., Duarte, O.C.M.: Improving the accuracy of measurement-based geographic location of internet hosts. Comput. Networks **47**(4), 503–523 (2005)

Wi-Fi Imaging Based Segmentation and Recognition of Continuous Activity

Yang Zi, Wei Xi$^{(\boxtimes)}$, Li Zhu, Fan Yu, Kun Zhao, and Zhi Wang

Xi'an Jiaotong University, Xi'an, China
ziyang783282949007@gmail.com, weixi.cs@gmail.com, zhuli@gmail.com,
fanfanyyy1997@gmail.com, pandazhao1982@gmail.com, zhiwang.xjtu@gmail.com

Abstract. Automatic segmentation and action recognition have been a long-standing problem in sensorless sensing. In this paper, we propose CHAR, a continuous human activity recognition system to solve these problems in a different way. We've noticed that these challenges have been solved in image processing field, so CHAR could effectively perform action segmentation and recognition after WiFi imaging. The key idea behind Wi-Fi imaging is that different body part reflects transmitted signal, the receiver receives the combination of them, and then we separate the received signals from different directions and get the signal intensity in each direction to get the heat map showing the shape of the object. The imaging sequence contains multiple pictures records a continuous action at different time, and we can easily separate and recognize the action based on IC^2(image classification), a classification framework we proposed. We implement CHAR using commodity WiFi devices to evaluate its performance under different environment. The results show that the imaging result is better than prior works, facilitating CHAR to achieving an average recognition accuracy, i.e., >95%.

Keywords: Activity recognition · CSI · Wi-Fi imaging

1   Introduction

Human activity recognition is an importance technic in current applications, such as the human-computer interaction, somatic game, and health-care. Recent solutions fall into three categories: camera-based [1], sensor-based [2,3] and wireless-based [4,5] approaches.

Camera based approaches are able to guarantee high resolution for activity recognition. However, those approaches have fundamental limitations, including the line-of-sight detection, good illumination, and potential privacy leakage. On the other hand, sensor-based approaches usually require targets to carry on sensors, which is inconvenient in daily usage. Different from above solutions, leveraging wireless signals to achieve device-free activity recognition becomes promising, such as WiSee [4], E-eyes [6], and WiHear [7].

© ICST Institute for Computer Sciences, Social Informatics and Telecommunications Engineering 2019
Published by Springer Nature Switzerland AG 2019. All Rights Reserved
X. Wang et al. (Eds.): CollaborateCom 2019, LNICST 292, pp. 623–641, 2019.
https://doi.org/10.1007/978-3-030-30146-0_42

Those approaches are based on the observation that different human activities introduce different multi-path distortions in wireless signals, which can be used as the fingerprints of those activities. Nevertheless, there are still two drawbacks on the wireless signal based approaches. First, they usually can only distinguish activities in coarse granularity, e.g., [8,9]. Moreover, they often request specific facilities (e.g. USRP [4], GPS clock [10] or RFID [11,12]) to eliminate the impacts of ambient noises.

Recent advance in the research of WiFi networks proposes to utilize the Channel State Information(CSI) to realize fine-grained fingerprinting for activity recognition. CSI is sensitive to channel variances and position changes, which makes itself possible to capture the change as the experimenter performs action. However, CSI fingerprint based device-free activity recognition remains challenging. First, to perform continuous activity segmentation using CSI is extremely difficult. Second, CSI reflects the change of the channel, but its changes are difficult to match the corresponding specific movements. So when the receiver receives a continuous signal which contains two or more actions, it is difficult to distinguish them.

Another challenge for fingerprint based activity recognition is the device incompatibility. Due to the imperfect manufacturing process, different devices exhibit different signal gains. The variant gains make different CSI values once we change transmitting or receiving devices to detect the same activity. Hence, if some devices are changed, it is necessary to retrain the model for updating the fingerprint database.

The third challenge is to eliminate random disturbance caused by environmental noises and electromagnetic interferences. These two negative factors may result in unpredictable errors. Since the errors do not follow specific distributions, it is hard to eliminate or zero them by repeating trainings. In other words, even if a user performs a standard action identical to the one operated in the training phase, the CSI may still have a large difference from the fingerprint in the database.

In this paper, we propose a novel approach to solve the 3 aforementioned challenges. We've noticed that these challenges have been solved in image processing field, so is it applicable in our research? The answer is Yes and irrelevant to the existing fingerprint approaches. Instead, we propose a novel approach to perform Wi-Fi imaging first on which highly precise human activity recognition is implemented afterwards. The difficulty is how to perform WiFi imaging. Our basic idea is similar to optical imaging systems where images are typically formed by measuring the incoming signal intensities from each azimuth and elevation angle. Therefore, in our perception region, if we can get the signal strength from every direction, then we will get a heat map shows the shape of the object. After we obtain the imaging sequence using the phase shift across antennas, we can easily split continuous action imaging sequence. In order to better classify the heat map, we propose a new classification method called IC^2. The final classification result can be obtained from the IC^2.

Our contributions are summarized as follows:

1. CHAR proposes a novel approach to perform imaging using Wi-Fi signals and achieves preferable effect.

2. CHAR solves the problem of continuous motion segmentation by Wi-Fi imaging.
3. CHAR builds a bridge between wireless and pictures. Our extensive experiments show that CHAR is highly accurate in action recognition and insensitive to the diversity of individual users.

2   Related Work

In the literature, researches related to human activity recognition can be divided into two categories: Received Signal Strength Indicator (RSSI) based and Channel State Information (CSI) based approaches. In classification region, SVM (support vector machine) and CNN (convolutional neural networks) have been widely used and proved to have good performance.

2.1   RSSI Based

RSSI is sensitive to ambient movements, allowing it to produce a set of patterns for identifying locations [13] and human activities [14–16]. The work proposed in [14] employs RSSI measurements to obtain images of moving objects. The authors in [17] use kernel distance-based radio tomographic to locate a moving or stationary person. The authors in [18] design an RSSI based recognition system over mobile phones, identifying 7 different gestures. RSSI based recognition systems usually fail to recognize delicate motions because RSSI is too coarse to perform fine-grained detections [18].

2.2   CSI Based

CSI is also susceptible to human activities, such as walking, falling, presence and movements of part of human body. Because of its fine-grained WiFi signature, CSI is capable to support highly accurate activity recognition. Utilizing CSI, WiHear [7] detects lip and mouth movements. E-eyes [6] recognizes a set of human activities by leveraging CSI values as fingerprints. FCC [19] achieves device-free crowd counting using CSI. WiFall [8] detects people falls using CSI. The authors in [20] propose a stationary presence and mobile user detection scheme. CARM [9] utilizes the amplitude of CSI to recognize activities. ARM [10] uses both amplitude and phase of CSI to achieve gesture recognition.

2.3   Classification

Classification is one of the most active research and application areas of machine learning. The literature is vast and growing [21]. Traditional classification approaches, such as SVM (Support Vector Machine), DT (Decision Tree), have been widely applied for classification tasks, and exhibit great performance [21]. With the advent of convolutional neural networks (CNN), many researchers use it for classification problems. The work proposed in [22] employs CNN to Sentence

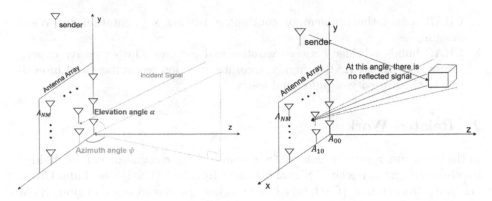

Fig. 1. Imaging system   **Fig. 2.** Overview of imaging approach

Classification. The authors in [23] design a Classifier to Image Classification. In recent years, researchers have tried to achieve better classification performance by increasing the depth of CNN. The VGG [24] uses a 19-layer neural network and the Resnet [25] uses more than one hundred layers of network structure. Apart from the factor of depth, researchers have proposed other different aspect of architecture design, such as STN [26] and CBAM [27]. These modules can be inserted into existing convolutional architecture, and achieve better performance (Fig. 2).

3 Preliminary

In IEEE 802.11n standard, wireless communication uses OFDM modulated signals, which are transmitted over multiple orthogonal subcarriers, and each subcarrier have different frequencies [28]. For one subcarrier of frequency, the transmitted model in frequency domain can be expressed as:

$$Y(f) = H(f) \times X(f) + N(f). \tag{1}$$

Where $X(f)$ is the signal transmitted on subscarrier f, $Y(f)$ is the received signal, $N(f)$ is the additive white Gaussian noise vector and is the channel estimated result. If we have P subcarriers, we can get channel matrix $H = H(f)_{f=1...p}$ which is called the Channel State Information (CSI). CSI reflects the environment influences to the signal includes amplitude attenuation and phase shift. That is to say, the CSI phase measures the phase shift of the WiFi link between the transmitter and the receiver. What's more, the CSI can be easily obtained by COTS Intel 5300 NIC [29].

4 Design

In this section, we describe the processing flow of CHAR and address the associated challenges. CHAR includes the three main stages: WiFi imaging using CSI information received by commercial NICs, continuous action segmentation of image sequences, action recognition using IC^2.

4.1 CHAR's Imaging Algorithm

In this paper, we propose a novel approach to perform imaging using Wi-Fi signals. CHAR's approach is similar to optical imaging systems where images are typically formed by measuring the incoming signal intensities from each azimuth and elevation angle [30]. That is the transmitted signal can effectively "light up" reflective objects and the receiver uses the reflections to image the objects. Hence there is no need for distance computation and it can be implemented on commercial Wi-Fi APs. However this is not easy to accomplish in practice. because the receiver receives a linear of combination of reflections from multiple regions representing different body parts on each of its antennas. In an optical system, a lens is used to physically separate the received signals from different directions. CHAR, in contrast, uses multiple antennas and phase differences analysis to separate signals. In the rest of this section, we first recommend our image system which includes a two-dimensional antenna array as receiver and a directional antenna as transmitter, and then describe our image algorithm.

System Construction. CHAR is a system that captures human figure at first and then conduct activity recognition using these figures. The whole process includes transmitting Wi-Fi OFDM signals, receiving the reflections from different body parts, and processing these reflections to capture the human figure. CHAR's prototype consists of a directional antenna as transmitter and a two-dimensional antenna array as receiver as shown in Fig. 1. The antenna arrays along the x-y plane, and the antenna is located at the origin. There are a total of N and M antennas along the x-axis and y-axis respectively, of which the distance between two adjacent is d. To describe the direction of a reflected signal which can be received by the antenna array, two parameters are necessary. First, the angle between the signal and the X axis called azimuth angle. Second, the angle between the signal and the x-z plane called elevation angle.

CHAR's Imaging Algorithm. CHAR performs imaging using multiple antennas as Wi-Fi receiver which receives a linear combination of the multiple reflections from different directions, in other words, from different body parts (i.e., azimuth and elevation angles). Therefore, our key idea is to separate the received signals from different directions and get the signal intensity in each direction.

Consider a reflection signal $S(\Psi_k, \alpha_k)$ from the kth propagation path which represent a signal coming from a part of the body, arrives at the receiver from the azimuthal angle and the elevation angle α_k. The complex attenuation at the antenna in the origin of the signal after traveling along kth propagation path is denoted by γ_k. The attenuation at the second antenna in the array is the same except for an additional phase shift accumulated due to additional distance traveled by the signal which depends on d, Ψ_k and α_k.

Take two antenna A_{00} and A_{nm} of our antenna array as an example, we compute the phase shift between them. From basic physics, a distance difference Δd will introduce a phase shift $e^{-j\frac{2\pi\Delta d}{\lambda}}$, where λ is the signal wavelength.

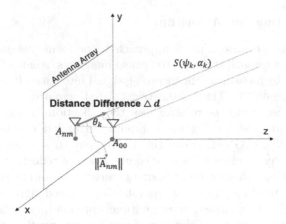

Fig. 3. Calculate the phase shift between antenna A_{00} and A_{nm}

Thus, as shown in Fig. 3, for signal $S(\psi_k, \alpha_k)$, the phase shift between antenna A_{00} and A_{nm} is given by:

$$\Phi_{n,m}(\psi_k, \alpha_k) = \gamma_k e^{-j\frac{2\pi \Delta d_{n,m}(\psi_k, \alpha_k)}{\lambda}} \tag{2}$$

where $\Delta d_{n,m}(\psi_k, \alpha_k)$ is the distance difference traveled by the signal between A_{00} and A_{nm}, as shown in the Fig. 3. According to trigonometric identities, we can derive the following equations:

$$\Delta d_{n,m}(\psi_k, \alpha_k) = \| A_{nm} \| \cos(\theta_k) \tag{3}$$

$$\cos(\theta_k) = \frac{S(\psi_k, \alpha_k) \cdot A_{nm}}{\| S(\psi_k, \alpha_k) \| \| A_{nm} \|} \tag{4}$$

Where θ_k is the angle between the signal and the x-y plane, A_{nm} is the vector from the origin to the antenna element A_{nm}, $S(\psi_k, \alpha_k)$ is the signal vector, and the $(\cdot)$ operations is the dot product between two vectors. The coordinate of A_{nm} can be expressed as (nd, md, 0), where d is the distance between adjacent antennas, therefore, A_{nm} can be expressed as:

$$A_{nm} = [nd, md, 0]_T \tag{5}$$

where (T) is transpose operation of the vector. Similarly, the signal $S(\psi_k, \alpha_k)$ from the azimuthal angle ψ_k and the elevation angle α_k can be expressed as:

$$\frac{S(\psi_k, \alpha_k)}{\|S(\psi_k, \alpha_k)\|} = [cos(\alpha_k)cos(\psi_k), sin(\alpha_k), cos(\alpha_k)sin(\psi_k)]^T \tag{6}$$

Combining all the above formula into Eq. 1, we can get the phase shift between antenna A_{00} and A_{nm}:

$$\Phi_{n,m}(\psi_k, \alpha_k) = \gamma_k e^{-j\frac{2\pi(ndcos(\alpha_k)cos(\psi_k)) + mdsin(\alpha_k))}{\lambda}} \tag{7}$$

That is, ψ_k and α_k will introduce a specific phase shift at different antenna. Suppose the size of antenna array is $N \times M$, and take the antenna in the origin as reference, the phase shift between each antenna and reference antenna can be write as:

$$\Phi(\psi_k, \alpha_k) = \begin{bmatrix} 1 & \cdots & \Phi_{0,M-1}(\psi_k, \alpha_k) \\ \vdots & \ddots & \vdots \\ \Phi_{N-1,0}(\psi_k, \alpha_k) & \cdots & \Phi_{N-1,M-1}(\psi_k, \alpha_k) \end{bmatrix} \quad (8)$$

the receiving signal due to kth path can be expressed as $a(\psi_k, \alpha_k)$, where denotes the complex attenuation at the antenna in the origin along the path and $a(\psi_k, \alpha_k)$ is a vector accumulated elements in the matrix by column, it can be expressed as:

$$a(\psi_k, \alpha_k) = [1...\Phi_{N-1,0}(\psi_k, \alpha_k)\Phi_{0,1}(\psi_k, \alpha_k)...\Phi_{N-1,1}$$
$$(\psi_k, \alpha_k)...\Phi_{0,M-1}(\psi_k, \alpha_k)...\Phi_{N-1,M-1}(\psi_k, \alpha_k)]^T \quad (9)$$

The vector $a(\psi_k, \alpha_k)$ is called steering vector which represents the phase shift between different antennas theoretically. Because there are multiple propagation paths, we have multiple steering vectors. The overall steering matrix A is defined as:

$$A = [a(\psi_1, \alpha_1), a(\psi_2, \alpha_2), a(\psi_L, \alpha_L)] \quad (10)$$

L represents the number of propagation path and the dimensions of A is $(N \times M) \times L$. The receiver receives a linear combination of the multiple reflections from different path, so the received signal can be expressed as:

$$x = A\Gamma \quad (11)$$

where A is the steering matrix and $\Gamma = [\gamma_1, \gamma_1, ..., \gamma_L]^T$ represents the complex attenuations along L propagation paths. The standard MUSIC algorithm can be used for one-dimensional angle estimation, but it still applies to two-dimensional case.

In our scenario, when we get the vector X through experimental measurements, we can use the MUSIC algorithm to get the steering matrix A, and then we can easily derive the azimuth and elevation angle. The key idea behind the MUSIC algorithm is that the eigenvector of xx^H corresponds to the eigenvalue zero represents noise subspace, If they exist, then they are orthogonal to the steering vector A which represents signal subspace. For simplicity, we omitted the formula deduction process, and if you are interested, you can refer to [].

However, directly using the above-mentioned measured vector x does not give a good result. It is theoretically proved that in order to obtain an eigenvector corresponding eigenvalue is zero of the matrix xx^H, the measured vector should be a matrix whose rows and columns are both larger than the number of multipaths [31]. A straightforward method is to use multiple measurements/packets to form a measurement matrix X, of which each column represents the result of a single measurement. However, in this paper, we want to observe the influence of the human activity on multiple packets, so we proposed an idea to obtain

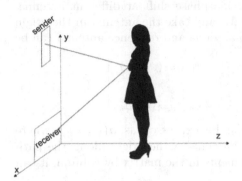

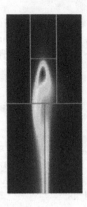

Fig. 4. Reflection off human body   **Fig. 5.** Body segmentation

an imaging picture using only one data packet. We can increase the number of physical antennas to increase the accuracy. But building a physical array is very expensive and not suitable for real situations.

OFDM uses multiple subcarriers to transmit information, and the frequency of each subcarrier is different. Since the frequency interval of the subcarriers is small, the phase shift generated between the subcarriers is negligible for signals in a certain direction, which means that the steering matrix of different subcarriers is the same. In order to distinguish the phases of different subcarriers, the Tof (Time of Flight) is introduced and the phases of different subcarriers can be expressed as formula 12 [31]:

$$\Omega(\tau_k) = e^{-j2\times\pi\times f_\delta\times\tau_k} \tag{12}$$

Finally, the steering vectors of different subcarriers of different antennas can be expressed as the kron product of formula 8 and formula 6.

Then, we can follow the classic MUSIC algorithm to solve the problem.

In one packet transmission, we can get the phase shift across different subcarriers of different antennas, For example, we use a 5300 NIC that can report the CSI of 30 subcarriers. We can get the following measurement matrix:

$$Xmatrix = \begin{bmatrix} csi_{0,0,1} & \cdots & csi_{0,0,30} \\ \vdots & \ddots & \vdots \\ csi_{N-1,M-1,1} & \cdots & csi_{N-1,M-1,30} \end{bmatrix} \tag{13}$$

Finally, transform X0 into one-dimentional column vector X:

$$Xmatrix = [csi_{0,0,1} \cdots csi_{N-1,M-1,30}] \tag{14}$$

With the above measurement matrix, the following algorithm can be used to get the final imaging results.

Algorithm summary:

1. Construct sample covariance matrix $R = \frac{1}{P}\sum_{i=1}^{P} XX^H$, where P is the number of subcarriers.

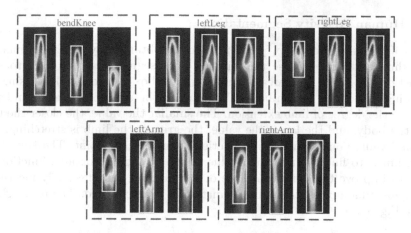

Fig. 6. The bounding box of human body changing as moving

2. Perform eigenvalue decomposition of the matrix R. Order eigenvectors of R according to eigenvalues. Let eigenvectors corresponding to L largest eigenvalues span signal subspace S, and remaining eigenvectors span noise subspace G.
3. Construct spatial spectrum

$$Pmusic(\psi, \alpha) = \frac{1}{a(\psi,\alpha)^H GG^H a(\psi,\alpha)}$$

Through the above steps, we can get the spatial spectrum Pmusic, which represents the possibility of the existence of a signal in each direction. Pmusic can be understood as the intensity of the signal in each direction called heat map.

4.2 Continuous Human Activity Segmentation

When human performs continuous activity, a set of image sequences can be obtained according to the imaging algorithm mentioned above, and many existing image processing algorithms can be used for continuous action segmentation. In this paper, a simple algorithm is proposed to verify the feasibility of continuous activity segmentation based on our heat map.

CHAR uses the body's reflection signal to measure the angle of each part. However at some point, our receiving antenna can only receive reflection from only some parts of the body. As the Fig. 4 shows, because the propagation of the signal satisfies the law of reflection, most parts of body's reflected signals can't be received by the receiver. However, because the chest is large and convex, its reflection signal is always the strongest. As shown in Fig. 5, we confirm the center of the image according to the strongest reflection position, and then divide a picture into the following six parts. The upper part of the chest represents the head, the left and right sides of the chest respectively represent the left and right arms, and the lower part of chest are the effect of the left and right legs respectively.

4.3 Human Activity Segmentation

A set of image sequences $p_1, p_2, ..., p_N$ can be obtained by using the imaging algorithm, and then we use the minimal area segmentation method to split the action [32]. First, the area of the bounding box is calculated by using the bounding box of the human body. The value of the area is used as an index to measure the degree of limb extension. The smaller the value, the closer the limb is to the body, and the larger the value, the greater the limb is stretching. The minimal value point is used as the action segmentation point. The key of the algorithm is to find the minimum value of the bounding box area function. In order to improve the noise resistance of the method and effectively locate the minimum value points, the smooth function is first executed. The result shows as the Fig. 6.

Smooth Body Bounding Box Area Function. Assume that Bt(x, y, w, h) is the minimum enclosing rectangle of the human body in the t-th frame, referred to as the human bounding box, where (x, y) represents the coordinates of the upper left corner of the human bounding box, and w and h respectively represent the surrounding width and height of the box. $S(t) = B_t^w \times B_t^h$ denotes the area function of the bounding box. The area of the human bounding box changes as the person moves.

In order to overcome the influence of the missing character extraction, find the essential regularity of the area function, we apply the local weighted smoothing method to smooth the are function, the steps are as follows:

1. Set the width of the local smoothing window to L. The smoothing target point is in the middle of the window. There are two neighbors on the left and right sides, and the localized weighted linear regression is performed on the target point. The regression model is $f(t) = \alpha_0 + \alpha_1 t$, where α_0 and α_1 are constant terms and primary coefficients, respectively. The performance indicator function is $J(\alpha_0, \alpha_1) = \frac{1}{L} \sum_{i=1}^{L} w_i (S_i - f(t_i))^2$, where S_i is the area value of the i-th point in the smoothing window, and the initial weight function is $w_i = (1 - |\frac{t-t_i}{d(t)}|^3)^3$, t is the target position, t_i is the i-th neighbor position of the t point in the smoothing window, and $d(t)$ is the farthest distance from the neighboring data point in the window.
2. Calculate the residual $r_i = S_i - f(t_i)$ of each data point in the window based on the weighted regression data.
3. Calculate the weight of each data point in the window, and define the weight as

$$w_i = \begin{cases} ((1 - (\frac{r_i}{6M})^2)^2 & r_i < 6M \\ 0 & r_i \geqslant 6M \end{cases} \tag{15}$$

where r_i is the residual of the i-th data point, and M is the median of the absolute values of the L residuals, which is used to measure the degree of dispersion of the residual. If $r_i < 6M$, the corresponding weight is close to 1, if $r_i \geqslant 6M$, the weight is 0.

4. Re-execute the weighted linear regression function of step 1 and setting iterations being 5, using the regression model as the smoothing model.

After smoothing, most of the fluctuation points can be eliminated, making the area function more regular.

Action Segmentation. Let $S'(t)$ be the area function after smoothing. If t' satisfies the inequality

$$(S'(t'+1) - S'(t')) \times (S'(t') - S'(t'-1)) \leqslant 0 \tag{16}$$

Then, $S'(t')$ is an extreme value of the function $S'(t)$

Considering the incompleteness of the action at the start and end point, and in order to reduce the impact of insufficient smoothing, the extreme points calculated by equation(16) are subjected to secondary filtering in the space-time domain:

1. The area of the start frame and the end frame of the video is added to the set of extreme points, and the maximum or minimum value is determined according to the trend of change of $S'(t)$.
2. Each extreme point S_i is checked in turn. If the time interval between S_i and the adjacent extreme point S_{i-1} is less than the threshold T_t, and their area difference is less than T_s, Then S_i is regarded as the interference point. According to multiple experiments, T_t is set to 0.2 s (that is, 25 frames/s, 5 frames apart), and T_s is set to $0.1 \times min(S_{i-1}, S_i)$.

After filtering twice, the attribute value is judged by the extreme point, if $(S'(t'+1) - S'(t')) > 0$ is satisfied, it is a minimum value point. After obtaining the minimum value point of the area function, the frame sequence between the extracted minimum value points is sequentially divided into separate action segments, thereby achieving action segmentation.

4.4 IC^2-Based Activity Recognition

CHAR can obtain image sequences by using Wi-Fi imaging method. The framework of our classifier is showed in Fig. 7. The above-mentioned continuous motion segmentation algorithm can divide the sequence of pictures into several sequences according to the actions performed. Each sequence represents a complete action and we call it a sample. We process the input data through STN (Spatial Transformer Network) before the VGG19.

In traditional image classification, input data is a serials of samples which each sample is a three channel colored picture. Our input data is a set of consecutive action sequences represented in heat map format. Each sample is a 51 * 61 * 16 pixel picture which 51 being width, 61 being height and the number of each action being 16. In order to match the input channel of pictures, we transform the dimensionality to 272 * 61 * 3 while holding the amount of pixels unchanged.

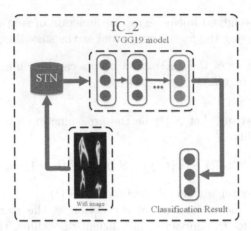

Fig. 7. Framework of IC^2

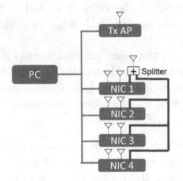

Fig. 8. System overview

Fig. 9. Imaging result (left: CHAR, right: Wision)

5   Implementation

We implemented our system using off-the-shelf Intel 5300 Wi-Fi NICs. We employed Linux CSI tool [68] to obtain the PHY layer CSI information for each packet. Our transmitter is directional antenna on the NIC, whose model is SCWL-2425-15D65VHPB-001. Its horizontal lobe width is 20° and the vertical lobe width is 70°. The object stands at a position two meters away from the antenna, and the beam of the antenna can cover the whole body of the person. Therefore, the use of directional antennas can effectively eliminate the effects of other objects.

Our receiver is a two-dimensional antenna array, the size of which is 4 × 4 using eight NICs. Because we use the phase difference between antennas to calculate the direction of arrival of the signal, different antennas should be synchronized. However, due to hardware errors, the antenna between different NIC has CFO, SFO, PDD and so on. We use the method proposed in Phaser[d] to calibrate the phase. Since the clock sources of different NIC are different, it is difficult to be calibrated. We send the signal of one antenna of one NIC to the other through the power splitter. We use the data of the sacrificed antenna to calibrate the phase between different NIC. So if we use 4 network cards can form a 3×3 receiving antenna array as shown in Fig. 8. The phase difference between different antennas of the same NIC can be calibrated by software. For more detailed principles, please refer to Phaser. In the following evaluation, we use 8 network cards to form a 4×4 receiving antenna array, in which one antenna data is not used.

6   Evaluation

We evaluate our prototype in an office building. First, CHAR uses a 2-D antenna array to evaluate the ability to image objects. Next, CHAR demonstrates the ability to identify different human activities using imaging results.

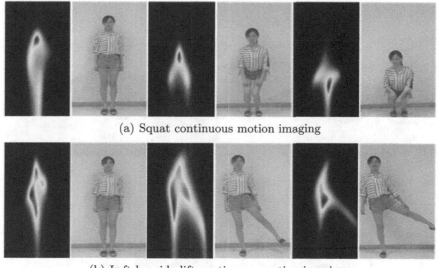

(a) Squat continuous motion imaging

(b) Left leg side lift continuous motion imaging

Fig. 10. Human figures obtained with CHAR

6.1   Imaging Using 2D Antenna Arrays

According to the analysis of 4.2, the reflected signal propagation conforms to the law of reflection. So in order to obtain the reflection signal of more body parts, we use two directional antennas as transmitting, which are placed at coordinates (10, 70) and (10, 140) respectively. We use 4×4 antenna array as receiver whose coordinate is (0, 0) and the distance between every two adjacent antennas is half wavelength. CHAR sends OFDM symbols which contain multiple subcarriers and the central frequency is 2.4 G.

Experimenter stands at a location of two meters away from the receiving antenna. In order to receive signal from different body part, experimenter should make a slight movement in situ, collects the data of two seconds, and achieve WiFi imaging using the algorithm proposed above in which multiple data packets are used for better imaging results. We compared the imaging results of CHAR and Wision [30]. In the specific implementation, the two systems sent the same data, and the imaging results are shown in Fig. 9.

Result: Due to the movement of the experimenter, different body parts will introduce a reflection signal, and the imaging result are shown in Fig. 10. We can see that the strongest reflection area is located in the chest part, and the reflection of the head and limbs is weak, but Wision's resolution is very low and in which different parts of the body can not be distinguished.

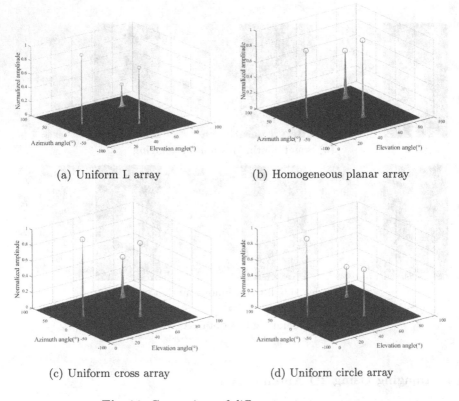

(a) Uniform L array   (b) Homogeneous planar array

(c) Uniform cross array   (d) Uniform circle array

Fig. 11. Comparison of different antenna arrays

6.2   Imaging Human Activity

To evaluate the human activity imaging performance of CHAR, we design five different actions namely left hand raising, right hand raising, left leg lifting, right leg lifting and squating. We have 5 participants and everyone preforms the five actions above for ten times.

In order to see the imaging results of continuous motion, we used the information of the subcarriers shown in 4.1 for imaging. We can see that the imaging result changes as object performs actions with different data packets. For each motion, we choose the results of some representative packets. As shown in Fig. 10, figures on the left shows the imaging results of our system and those on the right shows the actual actions of the user. For the squatting action, we can see that as experimenter moves down, the strongest reflection point keeps moving down; for left leg lifting, we can see the change of a leg raised to the side. Different changes can be observed for the five simple actions.

6.3   Comparison of Different Antenna Arrays

In Sect. 4.2.2, this article describes several arrays of different shapes that can be used for 2D DOA estimation. In order to study the performance and effects of various arrays, MATLAB was used in this section for simulation experiments. In the experiment, the number of signals to be tested is $D = 3$, the signal-to-noise ratio is $SNR = 10\,\mathrm{dB}$, the number of snapshots is N = 100, and the azimuth and elevation angles of the three sources are: $(-18°., 18°), (18°)., 27°), (46.8°, 57.6°)$. The two-dimensional spectrum search is performed in the range of azimuth angle $-90°$ to $90°$ and pitch angle 0 to 90°, and the angle search interval is 0.05°. Except for a uniform circular array, the distance between adjacent antennas is $\lambda/2$, and the radius of the circular array is λ. Using this distance can effectively resist the phase ambiguity problem, and the specific principle is beyond the scope of this paper. The circular array has 8 array elements, and the plane array, cross array and L array have 9 array elements. The 2D MUISC results for the four different arrays are shown in Fig. 11.

The X axis represents the azimuth angle, the Y axis represents the pitch angle, and the Z axis represents the magnitude of the MUSIC spectrum obtained. It can be understood as the signal strength of the angle, and the circle represents the estimated angle information. Comparing the four graphs, it can be found that in the case where the number of antenna elements is similar, the spectrum of the uniform circular array and the uniform cross array is sharper, and the plurality of spectral peaks are relatively uniform, indicating that its angle measuring ability is stronger. However, in reality, the uniform planar array has a smaller aperture and a smaller footprint, and the theoretical model is closer to the real scene. Therefore, a uniform planar array is used in the actual experiment.

Overall, we have sufficient resolution for our imaging systems to meet imaging requirements. Although the uniform L-array performs well, the angular accuracy and stability are very strong, but its array aperture is large, and the actual area occupied is large. Therefore, it is quite different from the signal propagation

Actual \ Estiimated	Left hand raising	Right hand rasing	Left leg lifting	Right leg lifting	Squating
Left hand raising	0.85	0.1	0.05	0	0
Right hand	0.15	0.8	0	0.05	0
Left leg lifting	0.05	0.05	0.9	0	0
Right leg lifting	0	0.05	0	0.95	0
Squating	0	0	0	0	1

Fig. 12. Confusion matrix of activity classification with SVM

Actual \ Estiimated	Left hand raising	Right hand rasing	Left leg lifting	Right leg lifting	Squating
Left hand raising	0.922	0.035	0.043	0	0
Right hand	0.05	0.913	0	0.037	0
Left leg lifting	0.028	0.03	0.942	0	0
Right leg lifting	0	0.022	0	0.978	0
Squating	0	0	0	0	1

Fig. 13. Confusion matrix of activity classification with IC^2

model and is not suitable for the actual scene. Uniform planar arrays have poor overall performance. Uniform circular arrays and uniform cross arrays have good direction finding accuracy and stability, and can perform two-dimensional direction finding on multiple incoherent sources.

6.4 Activity Recognition

We test our data in five different actions and each action contains 500 samples. 80% are used as training sets and 20% test sets. The parameters for IC^2 are set as follows, learning rate 0.01, epoch 100 and batch 75.

Confused Matrix Comparison. The confused matrix shows both SVM and IC^2 can get at least 80% classification accuracy. As Figs. 12 and 13 show, especially in squat moving which can capture more representative features than other moving actions. Accuracy can reach up to 1 and no misclassification. We analyze the statistics through comparing the squat moving with other moving actions, the previous action can track the reflected signal from chest up and down with moving which can lead to strong representative features. The worst case is classifying the right hand raising action which the accuracy is 80%. Because classification is based on continues sequences partition, arm and leg can not reflect strong signals due to their physical shapes.All CNN based classification approaches are beyond 91%.

Classification Accuracy Comparison. Both SVM and IC^2 can reach up to very high accuracy when the number of classification is small. Figure 14 shows that as the number increases, IC^2 begins to show more advantages than SVM. The average accuracy of IC^2 still maintains in high level even the difficulty increased. During our test, We observe that IC^2 network is much more robust than SVM. For different test samples, once the loss is converged in training data set, the evaluation accuracy will always maintain in very high level rather than SVM that has very fluctuation.

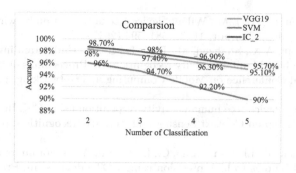

Fig. 14. Accuracy comparison between SVM, VGG19 and IC^2

7   Conclusion

Indoor wireless sensing has spawned numerous applications in a wide range of living, production, commerce, and public services. The increase of mobile and pervasive computing has sharpened the need for accurate, robust, and off-the-shelf indoor continuous action recognition schemes. CHAR can easily solve automatic segmentation and action recognition problem using WiFi imaging which is achieved using the transmitted signals reflected from different body parts. We propose a novel approach using these reflections to realize Wi-Fi imaging. The evaluations demonstrate that CHAR can reach an average 95% high matching accuracy under a wide variety of environment.

References

1. Harville, M., Li, D.: Fast, integrated person tracking and activity recognition with plan-view templates from a single stereo camera. In: Proceedings of the 2004 IEEE Computer Society Conference on Computer Vision and Pattern Recognition, CVPR 2004, vol. 2, p. II. IEEE (2004)
2. Fullwood, D., Kalidindi, S., Adams, B., Ahmadi, S.: A discrete fourier transform framework for localization relations. Comput. Mater. Continua (CMC) **9**(1), 25 (2009)
3. Kwapisz, J.R., Weiss, G.M., Moore, S.A.: Activity recognition using cell phone accelerometers. ACM SigKDD Explor. Newsl. **12**(2), 74–82 (2011)
4. Pu, Q., Gupta, S., Gollakota, S., Patel, S.: Gesture recognition using wireless signals. GetMobile: Mob. Comput. Commun. **18**(4), 15–18 (2015)
5. Liu, W., Luo, X., Liu, Y., Liu, J., Liu, M., Shi, Y.Q.: Localization algorithm of indoor wi-fi access points based on signal strength relative relationship and region division. Comput. Mater. Continua **55**(1), 071–071 (2018)
6. Wang, Y., Liu, J., Chen, Y., Gruteser, M., Yang, J., Liu, H.: E-eyes: device-free location-oriented activity identification using fine-grained wifi signatures. In: Proceedings of the 20th Annual International Conference on Mobile Computing and Networking, pp. 617–628. ACM (2014)
7. Wang, G., Zou, Y., Zhou, Z., Wu, K., Ni, L.M.: We can hear you with Wi-Fi!. IEEE Trans. Mob. Comput. **15**(11), 2907–2920 (2016)

8. Wang, Y., Wu, K., Ni, L.M.: WiFall: device-free fall detection by wireless networks. IEEE Trans. Mob. Comput. **16**(2), 581–594 (2017)
9. Wang, W., Liu, A.X., Shahzad, M., Ling, K., Lu, S.: Understanding and modeling of wifi signal based human activity recognition. In: Proceedings of the 21st Annual International Conference on Mobile Computing and Networking, pp. 65–76. ACM (2015)
10. Xi, W., et al.: Device-free human activity recognition using CSI. In: Proceedings of the 1st Workshop on Context Sensing and Activity Recognition, pp. 31–36. ACM (2015)
11. Yang, L., Chen, Y., Li, X.-Y., Xiao, C., Li, M., Liu, Y.: Tagoram: real-time tracking of mobile RFID tags to high precision using COTS devices. In: Proceedings of the 20th Annual International Conference on Mobile Computing and Networking, pp. 237–248. ACM (2014)
12. Ding, H., et al.: Device-free detection of approach and departure behaviors using backscatter communication. In: Proceedings of the 2016 ACM International Joint Conference on Pervasive and Ubiquitous Computing, pp. 167–177. ACM (2016)
13. Zhao, Y., Patwari, N., Phillips, J.M., Venkatasubramanian, S.: Radio tomographic imaging and tracking of stationary and moving people via kernel distance. In: 2013 ACM/IEEE International Conference on Information Processing in Sensor Networks (IPSN), pp. 229–240. IEEE (2013)
14. Wilson, J., Patwari, N.: Radio tomographic imaging with wireless networks. IEEE Trans. Mob. Comput. **9**(5), 621–632 (2010)
15. Zhao, Y., Patwari, N.: Noise reduction for variance-based device-free localization and tracking. In: 2011 8th Annual IEEE Communications Society Conference on Sensor, Mesh and Ad Hoc Communications and Networks, pp. 179–187. IEEE (2011)
16. Han, J., Qian, C., Yang, P., Ma, D., Jiang, Z., Xi, W., Zhao, J.: GenePrint: generic and accurate physical-layer identification for UHF RFID tags. IEEE/ACM Trans. Netw. **24**(2), 846–858 (2016)
17. Sigg, S., Blanke, U., Tröster, G.: The telepathic phone: frictionless activity recognition from WiFi-RSSI. In: 2014 IEEE International Conference on Pervasive Computing and Communications (PerCom), pp. 148–155. IEEE (2014)
18. Sigg, S., Shi, S., Buesching, F., Ji, Y., Wolf, L.: Leveraging RF-channel fluctuation for activity recognition: active and passive systems, continuous and RSSI-based signal features. In: Proceedings of International Conference on Advances in Mobile Computing and Multimedia, p. 43. ACM (2013)
19. Xi, W., et al.: Electronic frog eye: counting crowd using WiFi. In: IEEE INFOCOM 2014-IEEE Conference on Computer Communications, pp. 361–369. IEEE (2014)
20. Zhou, Z., Yang, Z., Wu, C., Shangguan, L., Liu, Y.: Towards omnidirectional passive human detection. In: Proceedings IEEE INFOCOM, pp. 3057–3065. IEEE (2013)
21. Kotsiantis, S.B., Zaharakis, I., Pintelas, P.: Supervised machine learning: a review of classification techniques. Emerg. Artif. Intell. Appl. Comput. Eng. **160**, 3–24 (2007)
22. Kim, Y.: Convolutional neural networks for sentence classification. arXiv preprint arXiv:1408.5882 (2014)
23. Girshick, R.: Fast R-CNN. In: Proceedings of the IEEE International Conference on Computer Vision, pp. 1440–1448 (2015)
24. Simonyan, K., Zisserman, A.: Very deep convolutional networks for large-scale image recognition. arXiv preprint arXiv:1409.1556 (2014)

25. He, K., Zhang, X., Ren, S., Sun, J.: Deep residual learning for image recognition. In: Proceedings of the IEEE Conference on Computer Vision and Pattern Recognition, pp. 770–778 (2016)
26. Jaderberg, M., Simonyan, K., Zisserman, A., et al.: Spatial transformer networks. In: Advances in neural Information Processing Systems, pp. 2017–2025 (2015)
27. Woo, S., Park, J., Lee, J.-Y., So Kweon, I.: CBAM: convolutional block attention module. In: Proceedings of the European Conference on Computer Vision (ECCV), pp. 3–19 (2018)
28. Shen, W.-L., Lin, K.C.-J., Gollakota, S., Chen, M.-S.: Rate adaptation for 802.11 multiuser mimo networks. IEEE Trans. Mob. Comput. **13**(1), 35–47 (2014)
29. Halperin, D., Hu, W., Sheth, A., Wetherall, D.: Predictable 802.11 packet delivery from wireless channel measurements. ACM SIGCOMM Comput. Commun. Rev. **41**(4), 159–170 (2011)
30. Huang, D., Nandakumar, R., Gollakota, S.: Feasibility and limits of Wi-Fi imaging. In: Proceedings of the 12th ACM Conference on Embedded Network Sensor Systems, pp. 266–279. ACM (2014)
31. Kotaru, M., Joshi, K., Bharadia, D., Katti, S.: SpotFi: decimeter level localization using WiFi. In: ACM SIGCOMM Computer Communication Review, vol. 45, no. 4, pp. 269–282. ACM (2015)
32. Wang, L., Suter, D.: Learning and matching of dynamic shape manifolds for human action recognition. IEEE Trans. Image Process. **16**(6), 1646–1661 (2007)

Multiuser Detection Using Hybrid ARQ
with Incremental Redundancy
in Overloaded MIMO Systems
(Workshop Paper)

Muhammad Kashif[1], Zakir Ullah[1], Muddesar Iqbal[2(✉)], Leila Musavian[2],
Sohail Sarwar[3], Xinheng Wang[4], Shahid Mumtaz[5], Zia Ul-Qayyum[6],
and Haji Muhammad Safyan[7]

[1] Department of Electrical and Computer Engineering,
Center for Advanced Studies in Engineering (CASE), Islamabad, Pakistan
[2] School of Computer Science and Electronic Engineering, University of Essex,
Essex, UK
m.iqbal@lsbu.ac.uk
[3] SEECS, National University of Sciences and Technology (NUST),
Islamabad, Pakistan
[4] Department of Electrical and Electronic Engineering, Xi'an Jiaotong University,
Suzhou, China
[5] Instituto de Telecomunicações, Lisbon, Portugal
[6] Allama Iqbal Open University, Islamabad, Pakistan
[7] GCU, Lahore, Pakistan

Abstract. Multiple Input and Multiple Output (MIMO) systems use
multiple antennas at both transmitter and receiver ends for increasing
link capacity and spectral efficiency. However, combining schemes used
for such systems face critical issues such as presence of interference, signals to interference and noise ratios (SINRs) and complexity. To overcome the asserted issues; in this paper linear multiuser detection techniques are employed in over loaded MIMO systems where the number
of transmit antennas (N_t) is greater than number of receiver antennas
(N_r), using Hybrid Automatic Repeat request with Incremental Redundancy (HARQ IR). The primary aim of this research is to enhance bit
error rate (BER) and throughput by transforming an overloaded MIMO
systems ($N_t > N_r$) into critically loaded system ($N_t = N_r$) or under
loaded MIMO systems ($N_t < N_r$) by simple retransmission method.
Simulation results show unprecedented performance compared to con-
temporary approaches in term of throughput and BER.

Keywords: HARQ · Incremental Redundancy · Multiuser detection ·
MIMO

This work has been partially funded by the European Union Horizon 2020 research and
innovation programme under the Marie Sklodowska-Curie grant agreement No.823903,
(RECENT).

X. Wang et al. (Eds.): CollaborateCom 2019, LNICST 292, pp. 642–653, 2019.
https://doi.org/10.1007/978-3-030-30146-0_43

1   Introduction

Fifth generation (5G) systems are moving towards the concept of "device centric systems (DCS)" [1] in which many devices are transmitting and receiving at the same time. For handling such situation, massive MIMO (Multiple Input and Multiple Output) [2] is required that deploys multiple transmitters and receivers at both ends to enhance data rate and throughput under the conditions of interference, fading and multipath. It is well known that MIMO maximizes the spectral efficiency and is widely implemented in different wireless standards such as IEEE 802.11n WLAN [3], IEEE 802.16 WiMAX [4] and LTE [5]. However, complexity and performance gets affected, especially in overloaded scenario when there are more transmitter antennas than receiver antennas, i.e. $(N_t > N_r)$ [6–8].

In order to detect multiuser data in overloaded MIMO system, detection algorithms such as joint maximum likelihood (JML) can be used [9]. However, situation becomes more complex when transmitting antennas increases, leading it to complex situation where it is difficult to implement in practical scenario. To resolve this issue, low complex MUD (multiuser detection) techniques are proposed for overloaded conditions [6–8]. However, these techniques are still intricate in terms of computation and require a lot of processing to be implemented in practical scenarios.

Different hybrid automatic repeat request (HARQ) schemes are also proposed for using in conjunction with MIMO systems to further enhance throughput and reduce computational complexity. In HARQ chase combining (HARQ CC) [10] every retransmission contains the same packet i-e the data bit and parity bit while on the other hand in HARQ Incremental Redundancy (HARQ IR) [11] different information bits are transmitted from the previous one, using multiple set of coded bits. As a result these multiple coded bit results in improved performance at the receiver end. Moreover, reliability is increased by retransmitting incremental redundancy packets on requirement basis only. Similarly, Zahid et al. [12] focused on an overloaded MIMO scenario and presented schemes of converting an overloaded MIMO systems $(N_t > N_r)$ into critically loaded MIMO systems $(N_t = N_r)$ or under loaded systems $(N_t < N_r)$ by combining all retransmissions at receiver end using HARQ [13] and HARQ Chase Combining (CC) [10] techniques.

The very focus of this research is to utilize HARQ IR scheme in overloaded MIMO system for enhancing data rate, throughput and at the same time using a simple and low complex technique for detection purpose. For this purpose, a scheme is proposed considering the concept of stacking retransmission. Multiple packets are transmitted at the same time and if the packets are decoded incorrectly at the receiver end, then transmitter sends additional redundancy bits only until either decoding is succeeded or maximum number of retransmission is reached. Here, all versions of redundant bits of the same packet are combined at the receiving end. Furthermore, transmitters whose data are correctly received remain idle in the next time slot. Simulation results of the proposed scheme clearly show enhanced throughput and reduced BER as compared to existing schemes.

The rest of the paper is organized as follow; Sect. 2 includes related study, Sect. 3 describes system model whereas proposed methodology is given in Sect. 4. Section 5 is comprised of simulation analysis establishing that the proposed technique is useful in terms of BER and throughput efficiency. Finally, Sect. 6 concludes the paper.

2 Related Study

Literature survey focuses on overloaded MIMO systems. Moreover, use of sub-optimal detection techniques with simplistic implementation and optimal performance is highly desired and discussed. Two of the well known linear detection techniques such as ZF [14] and MMSE [14] significantly degrade in case of overloaded systems. In [14], low complex MIMO detection schemes have been proposed but their performance and complexity increased drastically as the number of users increases. Similarly by using other detection techniques like V-BLAST algorithms [15]; due to matrix singularity fail in overloaded conditions [6]. In [15], network coding technique is used after the summation of two packets received. Thus, by using this approach error propagation issue which is vital in V-BLAST greatly reduced. However, in overloaded MIMO systems, V-BLAST schemes are not able to detect data successfully. Various other suboptimal group-wise detection techniques [6,7] are also proposed for overloaded systems. The soft decisions that are used internally provides a good solution for detection in overloaded systems that uses block chain architecture. This method has some limitations like as we increased the group size both its computation and performance comprises. Some of the heuristic based approaches are also anticipated for overloaded systems like ant colony optimization (ACO) [16] and genetic algorithms (GA) [17].

HARQ IR is a more sophisticated protocol in terms of error detection and correction as compared to HARQ CC [18]. Recently, in [19], a linear precoder was premeditated followed by HARQ detection at the receiver end by stacking all the received vectors from all re transmission. However this scheme had some limitation that they had considered only the case of critically loaded conditions where the number of transmitters equal to the number of receivers. This concept discussed in [19] has been extended to overloaded MIMO systems in addition to critically loaded MIMO systems with the number of transmitters exceeding the number of receivers. The concept of virtual receive antenna at receiver side has been used for efficient detection of data received, analysis of the Throughput and BER in proposed model.

3 System Model

In this paper, an uplink Overloaded MIMO channel is considered. Multiple users are assumed which are denoted by U. We define $N_t = \sum_{u=1}^{U} N_t^u$ as the total number of transmit antennas across all users. This equation determines the total number of Tx antennas across all users. This means that each user has a provision of single antenna for data transmission. The proposed model is presented in Fig. 1.

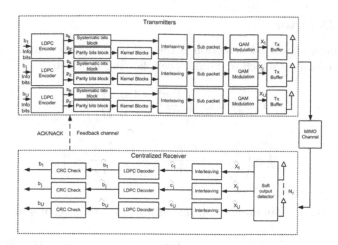

Fig. 1. HARQ IR MIMO Architecture.

In this system model, a packet constitutes of $\boldsymbol{b_j} = (b_{(j,1)}.....b_{(j,k)}.....b_{(j,K)})$ where K represents the bits which include both the info bits and CRC bits for each transmitter and $j = 1, 2.....U$. The bits are then encoded by Low Density Parity Check (LDPC). LDPC block is constituted using two different kinds of block i-e Systematic and Parity bit block followed by kernel blocks. In kernel blocks different priorities are assigned related to order in which packets are transmitted. The coded bits are re ordered by interleaver to form a sub packet. Coded bits are then modulated through QAM modulation and transmitted over the wireless channel.

The received signal $\boldsymbol{y} \in \mathbb{C}^{N_r \times 1}$ is given by

$$y = \sum_{j=1}^{N_t} h_j x_j + v, \tag{1}$$

$$y = Hx + v, \tag{2}$$

where $\boldsymbol{h_j}$ is the jth column of the channel matrix $\boldsymbol{H}$ of size $N_r \times N_t$, $\boldsymbol{x} \in \mathbb{C}^{N_t \times 1}$ is the overall transmitted vector and $\boldsymbol{v} \in \mathbb{C}^{N_r \times 1}$ is the complex Additive White Guassian Noise (AWGN). The received signal is given by

$$Y = HX + V, \tag{3}$$

where $\boldsymbol{Y} \in \mathbb{C}^{N_r \times L}$, $\boldsymbol{X} \in \mathbb{C}^{N_t \times L}$ and $\boldsymbol{V} \in \mathbb{C}^{N_r \times L}$. The channel is considered as frequency-flat Rayleigh fading model. Furthermore, channel properties of a wireless communication link is known at the receiver which is well known as Channel state information (CSI).

Soft- output Multi user detection either optimal or suboptimal is used to reduce CCI due to multiple users. Following two different detection schemes have been used.

3.1 JML Detector

Joint Maximum likelihood detection is the estimate of $\{x(t)\}$ and is defined to be sequence of values which maximize the following function:

$$L(C_p^u) = \log\left(\frac{P[c_p^u = 1|y, H]}{P[c_p^u = 0|y, H]}\right), \tag{4}$$

$$= \log\left(\frac{\sum_{x \in X_p^1} exp(-\frac{1}{\sigma_v^2}||y - Hx||^2)}{\sum_{x \in X_p^0} exp(-\frac{1}{\sigma_v^2}||y - Hx||^2)}\right), \tag{5}$$

where $u = 1, 2, ...U$.

Applying the maximum log approximation [23] to (5) results in

$$L(C_p^u) = \frac{1}{\sigma_v^2}(min_{x \in X_p^0}||y - Hx||^2 - min_{x \in X_p^1}||y - Hx||^2), \tag{6}$$

However, (6) is complex to implement and its complexity increases exponentially with the increase in number of transmitting antenna.

3.2 Suboptimal MMSE Detector

The MMSE linear detector, however, has low complexity and yet provides acceptable performance. The received signal vector of the MMSE detector is given by

$$\widehat{X}_{MMSE} = (H^H H + \sigma_v^2 I)^{-1} H^H y, \tag{7}$$

where I is the identity matrix. The MMSE detector [22], outputs the LLR of the pth coded bit of the uth user's j^{th} antenna as

$$L(C_p^u, j) = \frac{1}{\sigma_{j,u}^2}(min_{x \in \Omega_p^0}||\widehat{x}_j^u - x||^2 - min_{x \in \Omega_p^1}||\widehat{x}_j^u - x||^2), \tag{8}$$

for $j = 1, 2, ...N_t^u$, $u = 1, 2, ...U$, where Ω_p^0 and Ω_p^1 represents the set of symbols in Ω whose p^{th} bit equals to 1 or 0, $\widehat{x}_j^u = \frac{(\widehat{X}_{MMSE})_j^u}{D_j^u}$ is soft MMSE estimate of uth user's j^{th} transmitted symbol, $D_j^u = (j + \sum_{u=1}^{u-1} N_t^u, j + \sum_{u=1}^{u-1} N_t^u)^{th}$ diagonal element of D, $D = ([I + \sigma_v^2(H^H y)^{-1}])^{-1}$ and $\sigma_{j,u}^2 = \frac{1 - D_j^u}{D_j^u}$ is the noise variance.

Zahid et al. [12] in his work used the concept of HARQ CC and combined all the vectors at receiver end by considering them as a single virtual receive antenna [16]. We proposed a different approach by modifying his method and used the concept of HARQ IR in overloaded MIMO system. HARQ IR is a promising technique that has the potential of achieving enhanced performance both in terms of BER and throughput as compared to HARQ CC as also highlighted through simulation results. Secondly, HARQ IR architecture differs from HARQ CC in that HARQ IR needs additional signaling since the retransmission number need to be communicated to the receiver.

4   Proposed Scheme

In this section, HARQ IR scheme in overloaded MIMO system using LDPC code is proposed. HARQ IR is the extended version of HARQ CC. In contrast to HARQ CC, HARQ IR retransmission is not necessarily identical to previous transmission. Instead multiple set of coded bits are generated which are a combination of multiple set of parity bits. For each negative acknowledgment from the receiver, additional parity bits are re transmitted. These multiple parity bits are different from each retransmission resulting in a higher coding and diversity gain as compared to HARQ CC. The working procedure of the proposed model is shown in Fig. 2.

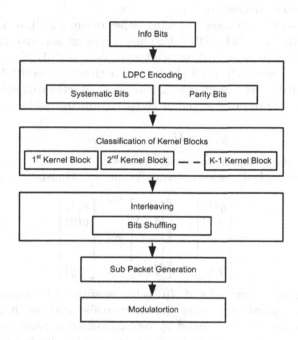

Fig. 2. Proposed HARQ IR Architecture.

Information bits encoded by LDPC encoder is given by $C = \{S; P\} = \{s_0, s_1, ...s_k; p_0, p_1, ...p_z\}$, where, $s_0, s_1, ...s_k$ are the systematic bits of kth order and $p_0, p_1, ...p_z$ are the parity bits of zth order. Parity bit blocks which constituted the kth kernel block set Ψ_k, (for $k = 1, 2, ..5$) are given as follows:

First kernel blocks: $\Psi_1 = \{PB_1\}$, where PB_1 denotes the parity bits in block 1
Second kernel blocks: $\Psi_2 = \{PB_2\}$, where PB_2 denotes the parity bits in block 2
Third kernel blocks: $\Psi_3 = \{PB_3\}$, where PB_3 denotes the parity bits in block 3

Fourth kernel blocks: $\Psi_4 = \{PB_4\}$, where PB_4 denotes the parity bits in block 4

Fifth kernel blocks: $\Psi_5 = \{PB_5\}$, where PB_5 denotes the parity bits in block 5

The parity bits in each block are shuffled. Here, if a packet is wrongly decoded by receiver then it will send negative ACK to sender for requesting of retransmission of first kernel block. If packet is still erroneous then it will send second kernel block and this process is repeated till fifth kernel block. After fifth kernel block transmission, the packet is considered as lost if still not correctly decodable.

The interleaved encoded bits are then modulated using quadrature amplitude modulation (QAM) as $\boldsymbol{x}^u = (x_1^u, ..., x_j^u, ..., x_{Nt}^u)^T$ and finally transmitted employing MIMO transmission.

At receiver, soft MUD detection using either optimal JML or Linear MMSE detection is carried out with LDPC decoding. If packet is correctly received, an ACK else a NACK is sent back to sender. In case of NACK, parity bits are retransmitted incrementally until the packet is either correctly decodable and positive acknowledgment is sent or maximum limit of retransmissions is reached.

Utilizing (2), the received signal at the gth (re)transmission can be written as given in

$$\boldsymbol{y}(g) = \boldsymbol{H}(g)\boldsymbol{x}(g) + \boldsymbol{v}(g), \tag{9}$$

where $g = 1, 2, ...G$ is the retransmission number.

Similarly, the stacked received vectors [21] after G transmissions can be written as

$$\boldsymbol{r} = \begin{bmatrix} \boldsymbol{y}(1) \\ \boldsymbol{y}(2) \\ . \\ . \\ \boldsymbol{y}(g) \end{bmatrix} = \begin{bmatrix} \boldsymbol{H}(1) \\ \boldsymbol{H}(2) \\ . \\ . \\ \boldsymbol{H}(g) \end{bmatrix} \boldsymbol{x} + \begin{bmatrix} \boldsymbol{v}(1) \\ \boldsymbol{v}(2) \\ . \\ . \\ \boldsymbol{v}(g) \end{bmatrix}. \tag{10}$$

One of the major drawbacks of (10) is the wastage of resources (in terms of link bandwidth, transmitting power and resource allocation at the receiver end). This wastage of resources is caused by retransmission of same data during all retransmissions. To cater for this situation i-e to avoid multiple retransmission of the same packet, Scheme HARQ IR is proposed as explained in following section.

4.1   HARQ IR Stacking

Consider a case of over loaded MIMO system, i.e., $N_t > N_r$. In this Scheme, at first transmission, i.e., at time $t = 1$, all users send their packets. Transmitters whose packets are correctly received remain idle in the next time slot, whereas the transmitters of erroneous packets send their packets again in next retransmission. This method has an added advantage that it reduces co-channel interference and hence improves throughput. Co-channel interference is reduced due to the fact that those users whose data is correctly received are not available in next time slot and hence result in reduced system loading

The received signal vector from erroneous user is given by

$$\overline{\boldsymbol{y}}(1) = \boldsymbol{y}(1) - \sum_{u=1}^{U} \boldsymbol{H}(1)\boldsymbol{x}(1). \tag{11}$$

Similarly, during second time interval, the correctly decoded users remain silent while the erroneous decoded ones are requested for re-transmission. This re-transmission is carried out by incrementally transmitting parity bits of kernel blocks. Here, the received signal vector is given as

$$\overline{\boldsymbol{y}}(2) = \overline{\boldsymbol{H}}(2)\boldsymbol{x}(2) + \boldsymbol{v}(2). \tag{12}$$

After this, received signal vectors, i.e., $\overline{\boldsymbol{y}}(1)$ and $\overline{\boldsymbol{y}}(2)$ are stacked together for creating virtual receive antenna, as given by

$$\boldsymbol{r} = \begin{bmatrix} \overline{\boldsymbol{y}}(1) \\ \overline{\boldsymbol{y}}(2) \end{bmatrix}. \tag{13}$$

Now, MUD is employed on vector $\boldsymbol{r}$ for generating soft estimates as decoder's input. This process continues till the transmission of parity bits of last kernel block. Moreover, packet is considered lost if maximum G is reached and correct decoding is not resulted.

5   Performance Analysis

The proposed scheme is evaluated in this section and compared with HARQ CC [12] in order to confirm its effectiveness using bit error rate (BER) and throughput as performance parameters in various simulations scenarios. In simulations, four users are considered. For packet encoding, LDPC code is used with the rate of $R_c = 1/2$. Similarly, 16-QAM is used as modulation whereas both JML and linear MMSE are used as detectors. The default simulation parameters are enlisted in Table 1.

5.1   Bit Error Rate (BER) Analysis

For a 4×1 Over loaded MIMO system (i.e., four transmitters and single receiver), employing soft output detection scheme (JML and MMSE) and using BER performance as a parameter is presented in Figs. 3 and 4. Figure 3 shows BER performance of HARQ IR and HARQ CC using JML detection during $G = 2$, 3 and 4, respectively. JML detection compares received signal with all possible transmitted signal vectors and then estimates the transmitted symbol vector which is modified by channel matrix $\boldsymbol{H}$. In the proposed scheme, as shown in Fig. 3, it is clearly observed that HARQ IR outperforms HARQ CC for each transmission and lower BER is achieved when G is 2, 3 and 4. For each case of retransmission at different SNR (Eb/No (dB)), BER of HARQ IR is less than BER of HARQ CC. This means that fewer bits are found in error

Table 1. Default simulation parameters

Parameter	Value
Number of transmitters (N_t)	4
Number of receivers (N_r)	1
Number of retransmission (G)	4
Modulation type	16-QAM
Channel model	Uplink
Packet size (Info bits + CRC)	576
Encoder	LDPC
Encoder rate (R_c)	1/2
Number of kernel blocks	5

in HARQ IR than in HARQ CC. Furthermore, it is also attested that BER decreases with the increase in SNR. Moreover, in proposed scheme, co-channel interference is reduced resulting in system reduction i-e shifting of system from overloaded to under loaded or critically loaded. When compared the HARQ IR with HARQ CC, HARQ CC retransmits the same message in each retransmission while HARQ IR has an advantage that if message is not correctly decoded it requests only for retransmission of kernel blocks incrementally. This incremental retransmission results in improved BER. Furthermore, BER is also improved with increasing the diversity order. Also as shown, when G is 4, enhanced performance of the scheme is observed as compared to the performance when G is 2 and 3.

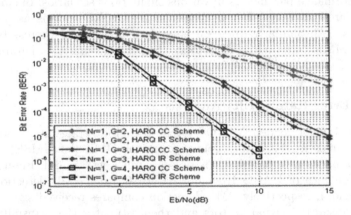

Fig. 3. BER comparison of HARQ IR and HARQ CC with JML detection.

Figure 4 shows BER performance of HARQ IR and HARQ CC using the Scheme and with linear MMSE during $G = 2$, 3 and 4 respectively. Here also,

HARQ IR attested improved performance in comparison to HARQ CC. Moreover, in terms of spectral efficiency HARQ IR perform better than HARQ CC due to the fact that HARQ IR adapts its error correcting code redundancy to varying channel conditions. MMSE detection mitigates the effect of noise by taking into account the interference from other symbols and noise. Higher values of G means higher number of retransmission and more reduction of system loading due to reduction in correctly decoded users. Hence resulting in improved SNR.

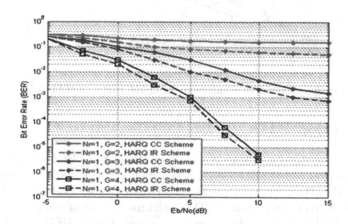

Fig. 4. BER comparison of HARQ IR and HARQ CC with MMSE detection.

5.2 Throughput Analysis

The most important aspect of this work is to improve throughput especially in noisy wireless channel. It is calculated for each retransmission using (14).

$$\delta = \frac{\log_2(\omega R(1 - P_{rate}))}{N_{avg}} \ (b/s/Hz), \tag{14}$$

where N_{avg} is the maximum number of retransmission, P_{rate} is drop packet rate and R is the code rate. Figure 5 shows throughput comparison of HARQ IR with HARQ CC when G is 4. Throughput analysis is achieved by implementing both the detection schemes, i.e., JML and MMSE in the proposed scheme.

As shown in Fig. 5, HARQ IR throughput is much better than HARQ CC. For example, at SNR of 10 Eb/No (dB), throughput of Scheme HARQ IR proposed is 0.75 as compared to HARQ CC which is 0.45 with JML detection, it means throughput efficiency is improved by 20% for HARQ IR as compared to HARQ CC. Similarly, for MMSE detection throughput of HARQ IR is 0.46 in contrast to HARQ CC which is 0.4. This improved performance of HARQ IR is due to the fact that instead of retransmitting whole packet as practiced in HARQ CC, it retransmits additional parity bits only.

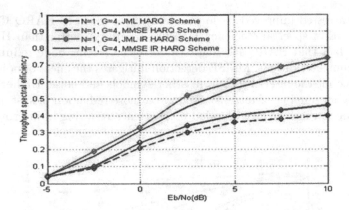

Fig. 5. Throughput comparison of HARQ IR and HARQ CC.

6   Conclusion

In this paper, a detection scheme has been implemented with the combination of HARQ IR in overloaded MIMO system in which through simple retransmission, overloaded MIMO system is reduced to critically or under loaded MIMO system. This scheme help in using linear MUD algorithms instead of using complex MUD set of rules. Performance of the scheme is evaluated using BER and throughput and compared with HARQ CC and better results are achieved with the proposed scheme by adding no complexity to the system. Hence, the approach may be considered to be used in LTE and other advanced wireless systems.

For our future work as we observe in this paper, an error free feedback with perfect channel state information is assumed which is practically impossible. Moreover, CRC detection is considered as error free, we will consider both these factors as well in our future work.

References

1. Shakir, M.Z., Ismail, M., Wang, X., Qaraqe, K.A., Serpedin, E.: From D2D to Ds2D: prolonging the battery life of mobile devices via Ds2D communications. IEEE Wirel. Commun. **24**(4), 55–63 (2017)
2. Larsson, E.G., Van der Perre, L.: Massive MIMO for 5G. IEEE 5G Tech Focus, vol. 1, no. 1 (2017)
3. Uthansakul, M., Uthansakul, P.: Experiments with a low-profile beamforming MIMO system for WLAN applications. IEEE Antennas and Propag. Mag. **53**(6), 56–69 (2011)
4. Siadari, T., Rezha, F., Shin, S.-Y.: Applied MIMO based on Hadamard transform in IEEE 802.16 WiMAX system. In: IET International Conference on Information and Communications Technologies (IETICT), pp. 582–586, April 2013
5. Badic, B., Balraj, R., Scholand, T., Bai, Z., Iwelski, S.: Impact of feedback and user pairing schemes on receiver performance in MU-MIMO LTE systems. In: IEEE Wireless Communications and Networking Conference (WCNC), pp. 399–403, April 2012

6. Zarikoff, B.W., Cavers, J.K., Bavarian, S.: An Iterative groupwise multiuser detector for overloaded MIMO applications. IEEE Trans. Wireless Commun. **6**(2), 443–447 (2007)
7. Krause, M., Taylor, D.P., Martin, P.A.: List-based group-wise symbol detection for multiple signal communications. IEEE Trans. Wireless. Commun. **10**(5), 1636–1644 (2011)
8. Colman, G., Willink, T.J.: Overloaded array processing using genetic algorithms with soft-biased initialization. IEEE Trans. Veh. Tech. **57**(4), 2123–2131 (2008)
9. Grant, S.J., Cavers, J.K.: Performance enhancement through joint detection of co channel signals using diversity arrays. IEEE Trans. Commun. **46**(8), 1038–1049 (1998)
10. Chase, D.: Code combining-a maximum likelihood decoding approach for combining an arbitrary number of noisy packets. IEEE Trans. Commun. **33**, 385–393 (1985)
11. Wu, Y., Xu, S.: Energy-efficient multi-user resource management with IR-HARQ. In: IEEE 75th Vehicular Technology Conference (VTC Spring), pp. 1–5, May 2012
12. Rauf, Z., Martin, P.A., Taylor, D.P.: Multiuser detection of overloaded systems employing HARQ. In: IEEE International Conference on Communication Systems (ICCS), pp. 300–304, Nov. 2012
13. Lin, S., Costello, D.J.: Error Control Coding, 2nd edn. Prentice Hall (2004)
14. Bai, L., Choi, J.: Low Complexity MIMO Detection. Springer, Boston (2012). https://doi.org/10.1007/978-1-4419-8583-5
15. Zhang, S., Nie, C., Lu, L., Zhang, S., Qian, G.: MIMO physical layer network coding based on VBLAST detection. In: IEEE International Conference on Wireless Communications and Signal Processing (WCSP), pp. 1–5, October 2012
16. Tasneem, K.T., Martin, P.A., Taylor, D.P.: Iterative soft detection of cochannel signals using ant colony optimization. In: IEEE International Symposium on Personal, Indoor and Mobile Radio Communications (PIMRC), pp. 1617–1621, September 2012
17. Obaidullah, K., Miyanaga, Y.: Efficient algorithm with lognormal distributions for overloaded MIMO wireless system. In: IEEE Signal and Information Processing Association Annual Summit and Conference (APSIPA ASC), pp. 1–4, December 2012
18. Stanojev, I., Simeone, O., Bar-Ness, Y., Kim, D.H.: Energy efficiency of non-collaborative and collaborative hybrid-ARQ protocols. IEEE Trans. Wirel. Commun. **8**(1), 326–335 (2009)
19. Liang, X., Zhao, C., Ding, Z.: Sequential linear MIMO precoder optimization for Hybrid ARQ retransmission of QAM signals. IEEE Commun. Lett. **15**(9), 913–915 (2011)
20. Larsson, P., Johansson, N.: Multi-user ARQ. In: IEEE Vehicular Technology Conference (VTC 2006-Spring), Melbourne, Australia (2006)
21. Larsson, P.: Multicast multiuser ARQ. In: IEEE Wireless Communications and Networking Conference (WCNC08), Las Vegas, USA (2008)
22. FertI, P., JalMn, J., Matz, G.: Capacity-based performance comparison of MIMO-BICM demodulators. In: SPAWC, pp. 166–170 (2008)
23. Miiller-Weinfurther, S.H.: Coding approaches for multiple antenna transmission in fast fading and OFDM. IEEE Trans. Signal Process. **50**(10), 2442–2450 (2002)

Towards Efficient Pairwise Ranking for Service Using Multidimensional Classification

Yingying Yuan[1], Jiwei Huang[2(✉)], Yeping Zhu[3], and Yufei Hu[4]

[1] State Key Laboratory of Networking and Switching Technology,
Beijing University of Posts and Telecommunications, Beijing 100876, China
`yuanyingying@bupt.edu.cn`
[2] Department of Computer Science and Technology,
China University of Petroleum - Beijing, Beijing 102249, China
`huangjw@cup.edu.cn`
[3] Chinese Academy of Agricultural Sciences, Beijing 100081, China
`zhuyeping@caas.cn`
[4] Beijing Boyu Kaixin Machinery Equipment Co., Ltd., Beijing 102600, China
`yufeihu1996@outlook.com`

Abstract. With the growing popularity of services which meet the divergent requirements from users, service selection and recommendation have drawn significant attention in services computing community. Service ranking is the most important part in service selection and recommendation. Although there have been several existing approaches of service ranking which is basically rating-based, suffering from the heterogeneity of ranking criteria from users. Moreover, the efficiency of such comparison-based approaches is the bottleneck in reality. To attack these challenges, an efficient pairwise ranking scheme with multidimensional classification is proposed in this paper, which also fully considers the context information of service and users. Furthermore, the scheme is able to mitigate data sparsity of users similarity matrix and improve accuracy. Next, we introduce a random walk model for ranking formulation, and propose a Markov chain based approach to obtain the global ranking. Finally, the efficacy of our approach is validated by experiments adopting the real-world YELP dataset.

Keywords: Service ranking · Multidimensional classification · Pairwise ranking · Markov model

1 Introduction

Nowadays, with the rapid development of service-oriented architecture (SOA), an increasing amount of functionally similar service have been published on the Internet, which makes the selection of suitable service a complex task. To achieve this goal, recommendation techniques have been applied to help users satisfy

© ICST Institute for Computer Sciences, Social Informatics and Telecommunications Engineering 2019
Published by Springer Nature Switzerland AG 2019. All Rights Reserved
X. Wang et al. (Eds.): CollaborateCom 2019, LNICST 292, pp. 654–666, 2019.
https://doi.org/10.1007/978-3-030-30146-0_44

their needs and preferences. Recommendation systems are all over e-commerce system, social network, advertising recommendation, search engine, etc. To satisfy user requirements, Quality-of-service (QoS) criteria are considered as one of the most important factors in the field of service recommendation. Furthermore, the importance of service recommendation is the selection of service. Since users may have different needs and preferences in various contexts, (e.g. users' favorite service may change over time and place.) the selection of suitable service for users is still a challenging problem.

In most recommendation processes, users indicate their preferences for the service through rating. Typically, the utility function is estimated based on prior user ratings, which is applied to predict the service relevant to the specified user [2], then the top-k services are picked out and recommended to the user. So the ranking method shows its importance. However, in many real world applications, it is quite difficult to aggregate the ratings from multiple users, since different users may have different criteria with can be closely correlated with their preferences, and thus "the trust level" of service ratings from different users should be considered very carefully in service raking.

The variety of context information should also be taken into account when service ranking. There are several factors that need to be considered, such as functionality, location, constraints, price, performance, availability, etc., making the service ranking be a very complex multidimensional mathematical problem. With the growing number of the dimension, the search space to solve the problems grows exponentially. Therefore, the efficiency problem in service ranking, which seeks to solve the problem with acceptably low complexity, is another challenge for researchers.

In this paper, a context-based multidimensional classification model is presented, enhancing the high-efficiency and accuracy of ranking. The multidimensional property can be formulated as the process of service ranking. Firstly, we classify users and obtain the context-based service of the nearest neighbors of the users, and then a pairwise comparison method is applied within the ranking process. Comparisons between of service are formulated as the stochastic process of random walk, and thus, ranking results can be obtained by rated the steady-state probabilities of the underlying Markov chain.

The main contributions of our work are listed as below. Firstly, a context-based multidimensional classification method is presented, which is quite helpful for improving the accuracy of ranking aggregation as well as dramatically reducing the computational complexity. Secondly, we apply the pairwise comparison model to ranking aggregation, which is robust to the variety of ranking criteria and preferences from different users. Finally, we conduct experiments based on real-world large-scale service rating data to empirically validate the effectiveness and efficiency of our approach.

The remainder of this paper is organized as follows. Section 2 presents the basic concepts and the related work used. In Sect. 3, we propose a pairwise ranking method with multidimensional classification, and its properties and capabilities are discussed. In Sect. 4, we implement our approach and conduct real-data-based experiments to demonstrate its accuracy and efficacy. Finally, we conclude this paper in Sect. 5.

2   Related Work

2.1   Existing Problems

The algorithms about ranking can also be divided into two categories: ranking with implicit feedback (PRIF) [6–9] and ranking with explicit feedback (PREF) [13,14]. The main algorithm of PREF is Collaborative Filtering [1,3,5], and the foremost of PRIF is Bayesian Personalized Ranking (BPR) [16], which converts the OCCF problem into a ranking problem.

One of the most successful technologies for recommendation systems called Collaborative Filtering, has been developed and improved over the past decades, and several relevant algorithms were designed and delivered for conduct service ranking. For example, Shi et al. [14] proposed Extended Collaborative Less-Is-More Filtering (xCLiMF) model, which could be seen as a generalization of the CLiMF method. The key idea of the xCLiMF algorithm is that it builds a model by optimizing Expected Reciprocal Rank, an evaluation metric that generalizes Reciprocal Rank (RR) in order to incorporate user' explicit feedback.

The above implicit feedback model based on ranking learning is mostly based on the two-dimensional matrix of user services, without considering the context information, such as time and place. For example, the location information that a user interacts with the system when looking for a restaurant is important contextual information. Adomavicius and Tuzhilin et al. [2] pointed out earlier that integrating context information into the ranking would be conducive to improving the accuracy of ranking, and proposed the widely cited concept of "context-aware recommendation system". In the field of context-aware, different scholars have proposed various solutions, such as context pre-filtering, context post-filtering, TimeSVD, tensor decomposition model [4,9], etc. The first two methods are hybrid methods based on collaborative filtering, whose drawback is that it may cause loss of information. The latter two are model-based methods, which lead to executable algorithms with high time complexity and do not develop.

In our paper, we study the problem from a totally different angle of classification. We focus on its implicit context information and rating, and group into different classes.

2.2   Collaborative Filtering

Now, we introduce traditional collaborative filtering and classification algorithm.

Most collaborative filtering system apply the user-based technique, also called user to user approach. Collaborative filtering systems predict a user interest in new service based on the recommendations of other users with similar interests. Instead of performing content indexing or content analysis, collaborative filtering systems entirely depend on interest rankings from members of a participating community.

In the user-based approach [13], a number of users are selected based on their similarity to the active users. A prediction for the active users is made by calculating a weight average of the ratings of the selected users. The similar formula is expressed by $sim(a, u) = \cos(\boldsymbol{a}, \boldsymbol{u})$, where a and u are two users. Therefore, a prediction for the rating assigned by user a, who is computed as follows: $P(a_i) = \bar{r}_a + k \sum_{u=1}^{N}(r_{u,i} - \bar{r}_a) \times sim(a, u)$, where $k = \frac{1}{\sum_{u \in \hat{S}} \times |sim(a,u)|)}$, $\hat{S}$ is the similar set of current user a, and $\bar{r}_a$ and $\bar{r}_u$ are the average ratings of user a and user u respectively. Note that if no one has rated service i, the prediction is equal to the average of all the ratings that user a has made.

2.3 Classification

Early research work on clustering usually assumed that there was one true clustering of data. However, complex data are typically multifaceted and can be meaningfully clustered in many different ways. Clustering algorithms [10,11] usually employ a distance metric based (e.g., Euclidean) similarity measure in order to partition the database such that data points in the same partition are more similar than points in different partitions.

Two main of the challenges in cluster analysis are: first to select an appropriate measure of similarity to define clusters, and second to specify the optimal number of clusters in the data set. In this direction, clustering algorithms have been developed which prove to perform very satisfactorily in clustering and finding the number of clusters [9,10]. The present work, a clustering algorithm which tackles these two important problems and is able to partition a data set and the optimal number of clusters existing in the data set.

In this paper, we present our clustering approach that is based on hierarchical clustering. We firstly introduce the concepts used in the classification as follows.

(1) **Neighbors:** Two similar users are called neighbors. In other words, we set user a and user u be neighbors if their similarity greater than a threshold value θ. Let $SIM(a, u)$ be a similarity function that is closeness between the pair of users a and u. Function value is between 0 and 1, with larger values indicating that the users are more similar. To sum up, given a threshold θ between 0 and 1, a pair of users a, u are defined to be neighbors if the following holds: $SIM(a, u) \geq \theta$.

(2) **Link:** Let us define $link(a, u)$ to be the number of common neighbors between a and u. If $link(a, u)$ is large, then it is more probable that a and u belong to the same classification. Therefore, we use link to merge users into a single cluster. The link-based approach adopts a global approach to the clustering problem and it is very robust.

(3) **Criterion Function:** Since we are interested in each cluster to have a high degree of connectivity, we would like to maximize the sum of $link(a, u)$ for data point pairs a, u belonging to a single cluster, at the same time, minimize the sum of $link(a, u)$ for a, u in different clusters. This leads us to the criterion function that we would like to maximize for the k clusters. We'll discuss this issue in detail at Sect. 3.

3   Multidimensional Classification Model

The multidimensional classification problem is a generalization of the recently-popularized task of multi-label classification, where each data instance is associated with multiple class variables. In this section, we describe classification model based on multidimensional similarity and ranking.

3.1   Classification

Multiple classification brings an ability to view a type from more than one perspective. Users have many influencing factors and preferences when rating, such as time, place, weather, etc. Generally, users preferences are represented by users explicit ratings or implicit context information. In this section, we consider the perspective of ratings as dimensions.

We let $D_1, D_2, ...D_n$ be dimensions, each dimension D_i being an perspective of a rating $R_{u,i}$, for example, ratings that a user provided for same service are two dimensions in March 2019 and February 2019.

Then, we define the multidimensional space for these dimensions as a cartesian product $Space = D_1 \times D_2 \times ... \times D_n$. Therefore, the user preference for the service should be combined with the ratings and dimensional space, shown as Eq. (1).

$$D_1 \times D_2 \times ... \times D_n \rightarrow Ratings \tag{1}$$

For example, there is a three-dimensional space $Space = Service\ demand \times Date \times Place$, the ratings given by users can be seen as a 3*3 matrix in three dimensions, of course the matrix is sparse. In this paper, we set up a matrix of user to service supporting user preference, $A = [r_{u,s}]_{m*n}$, where $r_{u,s}$ is the rating of service s assigned by user u, m is the number of users, and n is the number of service. The matrix of User-Service is illustrated by Fig. 1, and $r_{u,i}$ is defined as,

$$r_{u,i} = \begin{cases} r, & r \in [1,5], if\ \ ratings\ \ exit \\ 0, & otherwise \end{cases} \tag{2}$$

In the above example, the rating in 3-dimensional space $Space = Service\ demand \times Date \times Place$, is denoted as $r_{u,s}^{|S| \times |D| \times |P|}$, where S represents the service demand dimension, D represents the date dimension, and P represents the place dimension.

In this paper, $r_{u,s}^{|S|}$ can be represented as a vector $S =< s_1, s_2, ...s_n >$, where each vector represents a user demand dimensional attribute $r_{u,s}^{|D|}$ can be represented as a vector $D =< d_1, d_2, ...d_m >$, where each vector represents service dimensional attribute and similarly $r_{u,s}^{|P|}$ can be represented as a vector $P =< p_1, p_t, ...p_n >$. 3-dimensional rating can be supposed to product of 3 vectors. The extension of the multidimensional profiling approaches proposed in this section to N-dimensional data is straightforward.

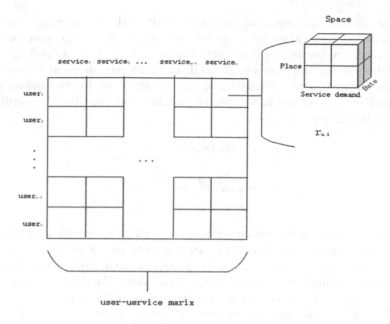

Fig. 1. User-Service matrix

Similar procedure can generate a matrix with a given factor number $k =<$ $k_1, k_2, ..., k_i, ...k_n >$ for the user-service matrix, where k_i is a vector in i dimension and n is the number of dimensions.

The profiles of a user u and a service s in latent factor spaces are represented as follows,

$$k = \prod_{i=1}^{n} k_i, 0 \le |k_i| \le |1|$$ (3)

The profiles created by the N-dimensional vector can essentially preserve the multidimensional semantic relations in the data. Thus, the value of matrix $r_{u,s}^{|K|}$ is defined as,

$$r_{u,s}^{|K|} = \begin{cases} r.k, & r \in [1,5], if \quad ratings \quad exit \\ 0, & otherwise \end{cases}$$ (4)

Next, we present an improved collaborative algorithm integrated with the multidimensional approach proposed and classifying users according to the method. Traditionally, collaborative systems try to predict the rating of a service based on users' history data. It works by finding users with similar preference and recommending similar services to users.

The standard collaborative algorithm [2] works with the following procedure: First, formulate user rating into user-service matrix, differently, user rating in our approach are created by the multidimensional method. Second, generate user neighborhoods based on a predefined similarity measurement between any two users, such as Jaccard similarity or Cosine similarity. In our approach, the cosine similarity algorithm is adopted to calculate users similarity according to the rating in different dimension.

$$
\begin{aligned}
sim(a, u) = \cos(\boldsymbol{a}, \boldsymbol{u}) &= \frac{\boldsymbol{a} \cdot \boldsymbol{u}}{|\boldsymbol{a}|_2 * |\boldsymbol{u}|_2} \\
&= \frac{\sum_{s \in S_{au}} r_{a,s} r_{u,s}}{\sqrt{\sum_{s \in S_{au}} r_{a,s}^2} \sqrt{\sum_{s \in S_{au}} r_{u,s}^2}}
\end{aligned}
\tag{5}
$$

The Eq. (5) calculates similarity between two users a and u, where $S_{a,u}$ represents service sets that have been rated by both user a and u.

We compute a user final similarity based on their preferences combined Eq. (5). Each rating has a corresponding dimension. The dimension D_i determines the similarity between users. The final similarity of users is calculated jointly by different dimensions. Suppose the rating under the multi-dimension $D_i, i \in [0, n]$ of service s assigned by user u is $r_{u,s}^{\sum_{i=1}^{n} |D_i|}$. We take the dimensional variable as the vector of the User-Service matrix, then the similarity between different dimension D_i can be calculated by Eq. (6).

$$
sim(a, u) = \frac{\sum_{s \in S_{au}} (r_{a,s}^{\sum_{i=1}^{n} |D_i|} r_{u,s}^{\sum_{i=1}^{n} |D_i|})}{\sqrt{\sum_{s \in S_{au}} r_{a,s}^2} \sqrt{\sum_{s \in S_{au}} r_{u,s}^2}}
\tag{6}
$$

The user similarity is classified by agglomerative clustering method that we assign each user to its own cluster. The rationale for the above criterion formula E_l is as follows,

$$
E_l = \sum_{i=1}^{k} n_i \cdot \sum_{a,u \in N} \frac{link(a, u)}{n_i^{1+2f(\theta)}}
\tag{7}
$$

where N denotes user sets. The concept of $link$ has been discussed in Sect. 2. It may seem that since one of our goals was to sums up the $links$ between pairs of users a and u in the same cluster and maximize $link(a, u)$. However, it may not be easy to determine an accurate value for function $f(\theta) = \frac{1-\theta}{1+\theta}$. We select the optimal θ according to the OSTU. The optimal θ is the minimum number of links between the final clusters and the maximum number of links within clusters.

Next, the best clustering of users were those that resulted in the highest values for the criterion function. Since our goal is to find a clustering that maximizes the criterion function, we use a measure similar to the criterion function in order to determine the best pair of clusters to merge at each step of clustering algorithm.

Then, we define the goodness measure $g(a, u)$ for merging a, u as follows,

$$g(a, u) = \frac{link(N_a, N_u)}{(n_a + n_j)^{1+2f(\theta)} - n_a^{1+2f(\theta)} - n_u^{1+2f(\theta)}} \tag{8}$$

$link(N_a, N_u)$ is the number of neigbours about two user sets N_a and N_u, n_a and n_u are the numbers of the two user sets. The pair of clusters for which the above goodness measure is maximum is the best pair of clusters to be merged at any given step. In general, it is a good candidate for merging.

3.2   Comparison-Based Ranking

Ammar and Shah [15] have brought to the fore the problem of comparison-based ranking. They presented detailed mathematical models of ranking from the entropy point of view. In this paper, we study the problem from other point of view of ranking based on multidimensional classification. Comparing on ranking and rating, ranking has better evaluation accuracy and efficiency.

In order to obtain service ranking, we select some users to rate the service, and we use a comparative ranking model to focus on the final ranking. This paper adopts a model obtain the users ranking of service evaluation based on Markov decision processes.

The pairwise comparison model reflects the relationship between different services. In this section, we sort the user ratings for the services, and compare in pair all user ratings, and finally obtain a comparison matrix, defined as a comparison matrix as follows,

$$B = [P_{ij}]_{n*n}, i \in n \tag{9}$$

Here, P_{ij} is the frequency of service i being rated higher than service j in all user ratings. We let P_{ij}^l denote the outcome of the l-th comparison of the pair i and j, such that $P_{ij}^l = 1$ if service j is preferred over (ranked higher) than j and 0 otherwise.

$$P_{ij}^l = \begin{cases} 1, with \quad probability \quad \dfrac{P_{ji}}{P_{ij} + P_{ji}} \\[2mm] 0, with \quad probability \quad \dfrac{P_{ij}}{P_{ij} + P_{ji}} \end{cases} \tag{10}$$

As Eq. (10) shows, if $P_{ij}^l = 1$ which represents the service i is ranked higher than service j for most users, Therefore, it is more likely to recommend service i to users when there is no other factors to consider.

The relationship between the services can be denoted as a directed graph $G = (V, E)$, where V represents the set of services used to be ranked, and E represents the weight of compared services in pairs.

Here, the transmission from service i to service j can be denoted as (i, j, q_{ij}). q_{ij} indicates the probability service i is ranked higher than j, which can be obtain by the fraction of times that service i ranks higher than service j when compared. Therefore we can obtain the value of q_{ij} by the following equation,

$$q_{ij} = \frac{1}{k} \sum_{l=1}^{k} P_{ij}^{l} \tag{11}$$

where k is the number of comparisons between i and j. We let $q_{ij} = q_{ji} = 0$ if the pair has not been compared.

In this model, each comparision can be denoted by a random walk process, and we propose a Markov model-based approach to derive the service ranking. With the random walk model, in order to obtain the service ranking, the random walk can be regarded as a discrete-time Markov chain (DTMC) [12].

We solve this Markov chain in the following step. First, we use $\pi = [\pi_1, \pi_2, ...\pi_n]$ represent the steady-state probabilities in DTMC, which have the relationship as $\sum_{i=1}^{n} \pi_i = 1$. Therefore, the steady-state probabilities can be obtained from the following equations,

$$\begin{cases} \pi \cdot p = \pi \\ \sum_{i=1}^{n} \pi_i = 1 \end{cases} \tag{12}$$

4   Evaluation

4.1   Data Set

We select Yelp Open Dataset in Dataset Challenge to implement experiment. The dataset itself contains almost 5 million reviews from over 1.1 million users on over 150,000 businesses from 12 metropolitan areas.

In this section, due to the huge amount of data, we select four cities to implement experiment, i.e., Gastonia, Mississauga, Henderson, and Toronto, the numbers of services in cities are 500, 2000, 3000, 20000.

For example, in Gastonia, we calculate users similarity based on multidimensional classification model. Then, we mark neighbors and *link* (that the number of common neighbors between two users), and perform clustering method based on users similarity and Criterion Function (7,8). Next, we divide users of Gastonia into 6 groups according our classification method (Eq. (1)). In the next process, we establish a Markov chain based on rated for each classification group to obtain the business ranking. When recommending service to users, we determine users' groups at first, and then recommend top service by ranking.

4.2   Evaluation Index

To verify the effectiveness of our algorithm, three methods are used as contrast experiments: collaborative filtering (CF), direct pairwise ranking (PR), pairwise ranking after classification (CR). Comparing a traditional CF (Eq. (5)) to a direct pairwise ranking, one can see that the effect of multidimensional classification model on improving ranking accuracy. In many scenarios, users pay more attention to the services with higher rankings, we selected an index kendall tau distance for evaluating the quality of ranking.

The Kendall tau rank distance is a metric that counts the number of pairwise disagreements between two ranking lists. The larger the distance, the more dissimilar the two lists are. In this section, we use the concept of Kendall tau distance to verify the error rate of our ranking. The Kendall tau distance between two lists τ_1 and τ_2 is computed by,

$$K(\tau_1, \tau_2) = \sum_{i,j \in P} \bar{K}_{i,j}(\tau_1, \tau_2) \tag{13}$$

where P is the set of unordered pairs of distinct elements in τ_1 and τ_2, $K_{i,j}$ $(\tau_1, \tau_2) = 0$ if i and j are in the same order in τ_1 and τ_2, $K_{i,j}(\tau_1, \tau_2) = 1$ if i and j are in the inverted order in τ_1 and τ_2. For example, the Kendall tau distance between $\{0, 3, 1, 6, 2, 5, 4\}$ and $\{1, 0, 3, 6, 4, 2, 5\}$ is 4.

Next, we define error rate as follows,

$$Error \quad rate = \frac{K(\tau_1, \tau_2)}{N_S} \tag{14}$$

where N_S is the total number of pairs of services.

4.3 Experimental Results

The Ranking Performance: For a user, we calculate the error rate between service ranking and the real ranking by Kendall tau distance.

For example, the error rate is calculated with a random selected 9 users in Gastonia (the number of services is 500) as shown Fig. 2. Obviously, compared with other methods, our method (CR) has high classification accuracy and its error probability is less. Compared with CF, CR decreases the error average rate by 0.37% for each user. It seems that the sample size is in Fig. 3, where reason is that Gastonia is a small-scale city, and the improvement is not so significant too small to be making accurate classification.

In Fig. 3, we prove the impact of different number of services on error rate through experiment data. It turns out that the average error rate decreases with the increase of the number of service all of three methods, but obviously CR has more dependent on the number of services. Large-scale service sets are more friendly to classification results and lower error rates. When the number of services rises from 500 to 20000, compared with CF, CR decreases the error rate average by 1.27%.

Matrix Density: In the experiment, the compare matrix (Eq. (9)) we obtained is sparse in the ranking, but the density of sparse matrix has increased after classification. Experimental results show, the density of sparse matrix increased

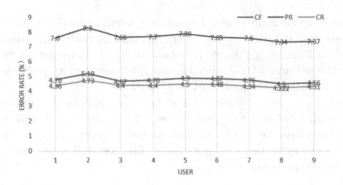

Fig. 2. The error rate of 9 users in Gastonia.

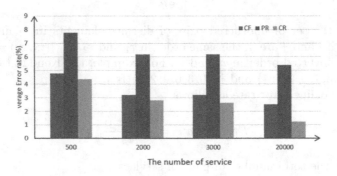

Fig. 3. The average error rate of CF and CR.

from 0.032% to 0.05% in Gastonia developing 0.5-fold. As shown in the Fig. 4, the density matrix of CF and PR does not change as the number of services increases, but there is an incremental gradient in density by CR method and large-scale services having a larger increase. It turns out that reduce the sparsity of the matrix by classification and reduce the computational complexity.

Time Complexity: It is assumed that there are n services rated by m users. During the procedures of computing similarity and partial ranking, each two services need to be compared in our approach, so the computational complexity is $O(|N_{S_u}|^2)$, where the N_{S_u} represents the number of ranked services by user u. The iterative algorithm is adopted in our algorithm, whose computational complexity is $O(n^2)$.

In multidimensional classification model, the time complexity of classification becomes $O(n log n)$ on average, and that is $O(n^2 * log n)$ in the worst case. Along with ranking process, we has total time complexity of $O(n log n + w^2)$, where w is the number of services in a group. The run-time efficiency comparison between the two methods is shown in the Fig. 5.

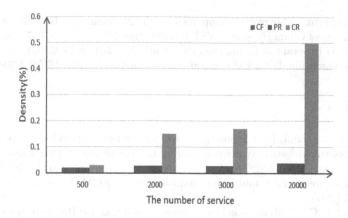

Fig. 4. Matrix density.

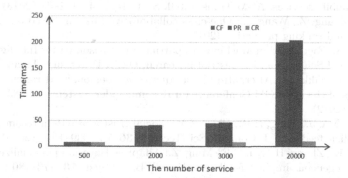

Fig. 5. Time complexity.

5 Conclusions

In this paper, we study the fundamental ranking problem in service recommendation from a pairwise comparison viewpoint. Random walk model is applied to formulate the comparisons among the rating data collected from multiple users, and Markov chains are used for ranking aggregation and calculation. A multidimensional classification approach is designed according to user data (e.g., time, place, weather, etc.) and is combined with the comparison-based model. With the classification technique, the ranking calculation can be personalized and its accuracy can be significantly enhanced. Also, since the data can be classified into multiple small groups, the computational workload and the sparse in matrix can be dramatically reduced. Finally, we adopt real-world dataset collected by Yelp and demonstrate the efficacy of our approach empirically. This work is expected to provide a computationally efficient methodology of service ranking for personalized recommendation. We believe that, with the rapid development of classification models and data analytics techniques, there will be several avenues for our future work to further improve the accuracy and performance of the service ranking approaches.

Acknowledgment. This work is supported by the National Key Research and Development Program of China (Nos. 2018YFB1003800 and 2016YFC0303707), the National High-tech R&D Program of China (863 Program) (No. 2013AA102305), and the Fundamental Research Funds for the Central Universities (No. 2462018YJRC040).

References

1. Maihami, V., Zandi, D.: Proposing a novel method for improving the performance of collaborative filtering systems regarding the priority of similar users (2019)
2. Adomavicius, G., Tuzhilin, A.: Incorporating contextual information in recommendation systems using a multidimensinal approach. ACM Trans. Inf. Syst. **23**(1), 103–145 (2005)
3. Aggarwal, C.C.: Content-based recommender systems. In: Recommender Systems, pp. 139–166 (2016)
4. Biancalana, C., Gasparetti, F.: An approach to social recommendation for context-aware mobile services. ACM Trans. Intell. Syst. Tech. **4**(1), 1–31 (2013)
5. Li, G., Zhang, Z., Wang, L.: One-class collaborative filtering based on rating prediction and ranking prediction (2017)
6. Rendle, S.: Factorization Machines, Department of Reasoning for Intelligence, The Institute of Scientics and Industrial Research, Osaka University, Japan (2010)
7. Takcs, G., Tikk, D.: Alternating least squares for personalized ranking. In: Proceedings of the 5th ACM Conference on Recommender Systems, pp. 83–90. ACM, Dublin (2012)
8. Guo, L., Ma, J., Jiang, H.R., Chen, Z.M.: Social trust aware item recommendation for implicit feedback. J. Comput. Sci. Technol. **30**(5), 1039–1053 (2015)
9. Pan, W.K., Zhong, H., Xu, C.F., Ming, Z.: Adaptive Bayesian personalized ranking for heterogeneous implicit feedbacks. Knowl. Based Syst. **73**, 173–180 (2015)
10. Liu, T., Zhang, N.L.: A novel LTM-based method for multi-partition clustering HKUST (2012)
11. Bafna, P., Shirwaikar, S., Pramod, D.: Task recommender system using semantic clustering to identify the right personnel. VINE J. Inf. Knowl. Manag. Syst. **49**, 181–199 (2019)
12. Huang, J., Chen, Y., Lin, C., Chen, J.: Ranking web services with limited and noisy information. In: ICWS 2014, Anchorage, AK, USA, pp. 638–645 (2014)
13. Pinela, C.: Recommender systems-user based and item-based collaborative filtering (2017)
14. Shi, Y., Karatzoglou, A., Baltrunas, L., Larson, M.: XCLiMF: optimizing expected reciprocal rank for data with multiple levels of relevance. In: Proceedings of the 7th ACM Conference on Recommender Systems, Hongkong, pp. 431–434 (2013)
15. Ammar, A., Shah, D.: Ranking: compare, don't score, Allerton, Monticello, USA, pp. 776–783 (2011)
16. Freudenthaler, Z. Gantner, Z.: BPR: Bayesian personalized ranking from implicit feedback. In: Proceedings of the 25th Conference on Uncertainty in Artficial Intelligence, Canada, pp. 452–461 (2009)

Smart Transportation

Intelligent-Prediction Model of Safety-Risk for CBTC System by Deep Neural Network

Yan Zhang[1], Jing Liu[1(✉)], Junfeng Sun[2], Xiang Chen[2], and Tingliang Zhou[2]

[1] Shanghai Key Laboratory of Trustworthy Computing, East China Normal University, Shanghai, China
jliu@sei.ecnu.edu.cn
[2] R&D Institute, CASCO Signal Ltd., Shanghai, China

Abstract. Safety-risk estimation aims to provide guidance of the train's safe operation for communication-based train control system (CBTC) system, which is vital for hazards avoiding. In this paper, we present a novel intelligent-prediction model of safety-risk for CBTC system to predict which kind of risk state will happen under a certain operation condition. This model takes advantages of popular deep learning models, which is Deep Belief Networks (DBN). Some risk prediction factors is selected at first, and a critical function factor in CBTC system is generated by statistical model checking. Afterwards, for each input of samples, the model utilizes DBN to extract more condensed features, followed by a softmax layer to decouple the features further into different risk state. Through experiments on real-world dataset, we prove that our new proposed intelligent-prediction model outperforms traditional methods and demonstrate the effectiveness of the model in the safety-risk estimation for CBTC system.

Keywords: Risk estimation · Deep learning · Communication-based train control system · Statistic model checking

1 Introduction

Communications-based train control (CBTC) system is the latest generation automatic train control system in the world, which is widely used in urban rail transit transportation [1]. There is no denying that CBTC system is a safety-critical system, whose failure could result in loss of life, significant property damage, or damage to the environment [15]. Safety risk estimation not only is a necessary requirement of CBTC system, but also is effective means to identify the hazardous operation conditions that may lead to a risk state. Risk estimation is a technique for identifying the operational safety of a system using either a qualitative or quantitative method, which have been utilized in safety management system. Generally, multiple system parameter factors need to be considered to explore the nonlinear relationship between them and the safety-risk state.

© ICST Institute for Computer Sciences, Social Informatics and Telecommunications Engineering 2019
Published by Springer Nature Switzerland AG 2019. All Rights Reserved
X. Wang et al. (Eds.): CollaborateCom 2019, LNICST 292, pp. 669–680, 2019.
https://doi.org/10.1007/978-3-030-30146-0_45

One of the main challenges for safety-risk assessment for CBTC system is uncertainty in system operation. The difference of running environment and the unreliability of system components would lead to the large deviation of pre-determined running state, which cannot be avoided or estimated in the system. However, traditional risk assessment models suffer from several limitations. Fault tree analysis [17], Failure mode and effects analysis (FMEA) [21] and Bayesian network analysis [14], all belong to static modeling analysis, would not have satisfactory results due to the uncertainty cannot be considered in the process. A second challenge stems from the need to effectively capture the correlations between multiple CBTC system safety-risk states. Considering that the different safety-risk states are parameter change of system operation, analyzing safety-risk states as independent of one another will lead to suboptimal models.

Recently, with the development of artificial neural networks, deep learning is currently the most popular method for data representation learning, time series data prediction, and image recognition, etc. Deep Neural Networks (DNNs) can be very effective in learning features from data in an unsupervised fashion without prior knowledge [7,16]. In addition, DNNs are also a well-established approach in traffic flow prediction [13], automatic driving fault prediction [4], and track circuit fault prediction [24]. These applications show that DNN has a good prospect in fault or risk prediction. The data record in CBTC system contains uncertainty information, which is another representation of the random behavior of the system. DNN can learn system features from these data to effectively solve the uncertainty problem. Meanwhile, DNN can capture the correlation between different safety-risk states.

In this paper, we proposed a deep intelligent-predictive model for hazard risk assessment in CBTC system. The model is implemented by deep neural network (DNN), considering a variety of influential factors. More specifically, a Deep Belief Network (DBN) is trained to predict which kind of risk state will happen from some safety-related factors. As a result, the proposed intelligent-predictive model has the advantage of simultaneously achieving two important desiderata: consideration of uncertainty and Capture of risk state correlation. A selection and generation method of risk factors is proposed, where one of risk factors about safety critical function, movement authority (MA), is obtained from Statistical Model Checking (SMC) [5]. Compared with traditional methods like numerical methods [3], as a kind of formal method, SMC samples behaviors of the system model and resolves the safety critical problem more efficiently.

The rest of this paper is structured as follows: Sect. 2 reviews related studies on risk assessment. Section 3 defines safety risk prediction problem and give the model framework. Our intelligent-predictive model is described in Sect. 4. Section 5 presents the experiment and result. Finally, we conclude this study with future work in Sect. 6.

2   Related Work

Safety risk analysis and evaluation has been long considered as key functional component in urban rail transit operation.

Huang *et al.* proposed to employ FTA in railway traffic system safety. In this model, they mainly considered traffic accidents caused by human errors and hardware failure, and proposed the fuzzy fault-tree model, which simulated the failure probability of each unit of the system by defining fuzzy sets in probability space [12]. Zhang *et al.* illustrate and analyze Interval Signal Control Function for Train Control Center case using Fuzzy-FMECA method, where in this method, FMECA is used to abstract the potential failure modes in such function and FAHP is to determine risk weight [23]. The formal method is mainly used for system safety verification, and focus on safety-critical applications. Mathieu Comptier *et al.* analyzed the safety of the Octys CBTC system interlocking infrastructure using formal proofs, Event B. They modeled verified it with Atelier B tool [6]. Hybrid I/O Automaton (HIOA) framework is very effective for hybrid system verification. Mitra *et al.* designed a supervisory pitch controller for a model helicopter system and verified some safety property based on HIOA [18].

In addition, some artificial intelligence methods are also applied to solve the collision prediction problem. Nefti and Oussalah proposed using Artificial Neural Networks (ANNs) architecture to deal with the prediction problem of the system fault. By taking irregularities in the positioning of rails as input and using a wavelet transformation technique to reduce the dimensionality, the ANN can predict the safety ratio of the rails. Moreover, they found out the best structure of ANN for predicting railway safety and evaluated performances [19].

Deep learning algorithms was proposed in 2006 [9, 10], and so many researches are published on the basis of it. Huang *et al.* [13] proposed a deep architecture to predict traffic flow, which is a multi-task regression DBN to incorporate multitask learning (MTL). In addition, to make MTL more effective, the weights in the top layer were grouped to make the experimental results better. Jinyong Wang and Ce Zhang utilized a deep learning model in software reliability and faults prediction problem. This model is made up of recurrent NN (RNN) encoder–decoder. The comparison among exist models shows that their model has better prediction performance [22].

3 Problem Definition

Our overall research goal is to build an effective intelligent-prediction model to predict the safety-risk state classification, taking as input some risk-influencing factors.

Safety-Risk Estimation. We define the four safety-risk states in line with common hazards listed in IEEE standard 1474.1-2004 [1]:

- Normal (H0)
- Collision between two trains (H1)
- Derailment of train (H2)
- Train-to-structure collisions (H3)

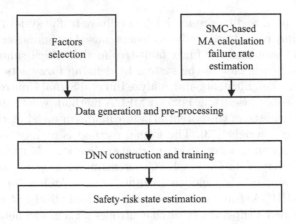

Fig. 1. Procedures for forecasting CBTC hazard risk

Figure 1 shows the implementation procedures for safety-risk prediction of CBTC system based on deep learning. First, we should have a feature selection process. After extensive investigations in published research [8,11], we built a set of risk-influencing factors. Eight factors that are most correlated with risk state are chosen. Meanwhile, for the MA calculation failure probability, we used the statistic model checking (SMC) method to calculate. Second, we generate and pre-processing a dataset, included normalizing them and dividing them into training and test datasets, the former to train DNN and the latter to participate in prediction. Afterward, we build DNN and train it with dataset. Once the training is over, the test dataset was fed to the trained DNN to forecast the safety-risk state at current situation.

4   An Intelligent-Prediction Model to Safety-Risk for CBTC System

In this section, our proposed safety-risk intelligent-prediction model is given in detail. We present a deep neural network model using DBN in this model.

4.1   Selecting Risk Factors

The prediction factor should include four kinds, such as *equipment, facilities, procedures, people* [1]. For the above four risk states, we selected eight factors that have the most closely related influence on them. They are listed in Table 1, with category and range value.

For the factor G, MA is the authority for a train to enter and travel through a specific section of track, in a given travel direction. It is the most influential factor associated with collision events. The Zone Controller (ZC) is the core subsystem of the CBTC system and is responsible for calculating the MA of the train on the track. Generally, taking the train head as the starting point and

Table 1. List of safety risk prediction factors that influence hazard

Category	Factor variable	Range
Facilities	Communication delay (A)	0.5 s ~ 2 s
	Maximum number of trains (B)	10 ~ 40 trains
Equipment	Train speed (C)	±0.5 km/h ~ ±60 km/h
	Train location accuracy (D)	±5 m ~ ±0 m
People	Working time (E)	0 h ~ 10 h
	Passenger flow (F)	3 ~ 4 w/h
Procedures	MA calculation failure rate (G)	$<10^{-8}$
	MA calculation time (H)	0.07 s ~ 1 s

considering current state of relevant equipment on track, ZC calculates MA, and calculation results will be transmitted to the train to adjust its driving behavior. This end point is called end of authority (EOA), which is determined by the MA. The most likely cause of train collision is that the train has wrong information about the end of the current travel range, and results in an incorrect speed control command. Therefore, in each sampling point, once the MA calculation error, the train in this state must have an accident. However, it is not easy to judge whether the current MA is wrong, and a better method is to use MA calculation failure rate at current system parameters.

4.2 Calculating MA Failure Rate

For the purpose of obtaining MA calculation failure probability by SMC, MA calculation scenario simulation samples need to be realized by establishing a CAL_EOA module. Generation of the wrong MA is a rare event in ZC system. In order to obtain its failure probability, we convert it into a formal verification problem about safety requirements. Now, we use Statistical Model Checking (SMC) method estimates MA failure rate [5]. Statistical model checking is a simulation-based model checking approach to verify properties specified in a temporal logic [2]. In this paper, we estimated the MA failure probability by establishing a CAL_EOA model and defining a temporal logic formula for safety requirements.

Before estimation, we should give the formal definition of this problem in the system.

Definition 1. *Given a CAL_EOA model M, and a safety requirement property ϕ, statistical model checking estimation is to verify whether M satisfy ϕ with greater than or equal to a probability θ, that is $M \models P_{\geq\theta}(\phi)$.*

And the safety requirement we considered is : *MA calculation failure does not occur.*

Considering the simple case, five key sensors are involved in the calculation of the MA. As long as the value of each sensor is guaranteed to be correct at each moment, the MA calculation will not failure. We described the requirement utilizing BLTL. That is described as:

$$\psi = F^{100}G^1(\phi_0(t) \wedge \phi_1(t) \wedge \phi_2(t) \wedge \phi_3(t) \wedge \phi_4(t)) \tag{1}$$

where $\phi_i(t)$ is:

$$\phi_i(t) = InvalidValueDetected(t) \tag{2}$$

Section 4.2 states that within 100 cycles, at any moment, five sensors would not produce invalid values and wrong MA would not be generated, where $InvalidValueDetected(t)$ follows the Bernoulli distribution.

SMC method use random sampling of system execution paths. Unlikely the classical statistical model checking, the improved SMC is merged with importance sampling and cross-entropy method to reduce sample state space. The basic idea is based on Monte Carlo method, which generate N random simulations sequence $\chi_1, \ldots, \chi_N$, followed Bernoulli distribution. Importance sampling is an effective technique to reduce samples space in the application of SMC [20]. Importance sampling starts by introducing a weighting function $W(\chi_i)$ on the observed random variables, without changing their expectancy $E(\chi_i)$ and reducing their variance. Therefore, finding a good weighting function distribution is a crucial problem. Suppose we have a weighting function and random variables χ_i with optimal density f_*, the general idea can be written as:

$$E(\chi_i) = \frac{1}{N} \sum_{i=1}^{N} B(\chi_i \models \psi)W(\chi_i) \tag{3}$$

The weighting function and optimal density are:

$$W(\chi_i) = \frac{f(\chi_i)}{f_*(\chi_i)} \tag{4}$$

$$f_*(\chi_i) = \frac{B(\chi_i)f(\chi_i)}{E(\chi_i)} \tag{5}$$

The cross-entropy method can select the appropriate members that minimize Kullback-Leibler divergence from the optimally biasing, through sampling from the original unbiased distribution. We got the appropriate distributions using the cross-entropy method. Once the density distributions had been decided, the probability was calculated. MATLAB/Simulink is used for model implementation platform.

4.3   Network Architecture

Our proposed DNN model is constructed by DBN. More specifically, stacking RBMs to form a DBN and using a *softmax* regression layer at the output layer, and we can perform supervised fine-tuning on the whole network.

RBM and DBN. Deep Learning is a class of machine learning algorithms, which proposed by Hinton *et al.* in recently year [9]. DBN model is a probabilistic generative module and composed of stochastic variables. It is a combination of a number of Restricted Boltzmann Machines (RBMs). An RBM consists of two layers, that is, one layer of binary stochastic hidden units and one layer of binary stochastic visible units, where each sub-network's hidden layer serves as the visible layer for the next. Generally, they obey a Bernoulli distribution or a Gaussian distribution. All visible layer units are full-connected to all hidden layer units and no connection within the layer. Corresponding energy function $E(\mathbf{v}, \mathbf{h}; \theta)$ and conditional probability distributions $p(h_j|\mathbf{v}; \theta), p(v_i|\mathbf{h}; \theta)$ are given as following:

$$E(\mathbf{v}, \mathbf{h}; \theta) = \sum_{i=1}^{|V|} \frac{(v_i - b_i)^2}{2\sigma_i^2} - \sum_{j=1}^{|H|} a_j h_j - \sum_{i=1}^{|V|} \sum_{j=1}^{|H|} \frac{v_i}{\sigma_i} w_{ij} h_j \tag{6}$$

$$p(h_j|\mathbf{v}; \theta) = sigm(\sum_{i=1}^{|V|} w_{ij} v_i + a_j) \tag{7}$$

$$p(v_i|\mathbf{h}; \theta) = N(\sigma_i \sum_{j=1}^{|H|} w_{ij} h_j + b_i, \sigma_i^2) \tag{8}$$

where σ is the standard deviation vector of normal distribution visible units, and $N(\mu, \sigma^2)$ is the normal distribution with mean μ and variance σ.

Our network has three hidden layers containing 256 units each. Between each adjacent layer is an RBM, which is stacked to form a DBN. In our network, we have three RBMs. This configuration was obtained after many experiments and produced the best results for the current problem. The complexity of the research problem and dataset determined the size of our neural network altogether. The network structure that is too large or too small can not effectively improve the experimental performance.

Input and Output. Corresponding to the Table 1, the dimension of a sample in our dataset is eight, which corresponds to the eight safety-related factors we selected. Suppose $\mathbf{I}$ is the input sample vector of DBN, and the input layer unit is eight:

$$\mathbf{I} = (A, B, C, D, E, F, G, H) \tag{9}$$

Each unit refers to one of sample data features.

For output, we used *softmax* unit in the output layer to implement the task of hazard classification. The *softmax* layer contains 4 units, one for the normal state and three for each hazard. Suppose vector $\mathbf{O}$ is the output vector, $\mathbf{O}$ is composed of the likelihood of safety risk hazard o_k occurred. The greater the value, the greater the likelihood that this hazard will occur.

The $\mathbf{O}$ could be denoted as

$$\mathbf{O} = \{o_0, o_1, o_2, o_3\} \tag{10}$$

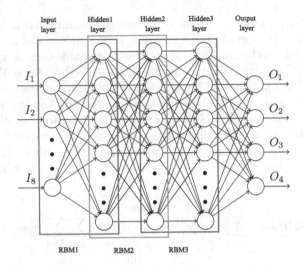

Fig. 2. The structure of intelligent-prediction model for safety-risk. The model is built by a DBN with three RBMs.

where o_0 refers to no collision occurred and system as a normal state, o_1 refers to collision between two trains, o_2 means derailment of train and y_3 is train to structure collision. The outputs of last hidden layer are the inputs to the *softmax* output layer. They give the probability of each category o_k as

$$P(Y = o_k) = \frac{e^{sigm(\mathbf{w}_k\mathbf{v}+\mathbf{a}_k)}}{\sum_{k=0}^{3} e^{sigm(\mathbf{w}_k\mathbf{v}+\mathbf{a}_k)}} \tag{11}$$

This DBN architecture is illustrated in Fig. 2.

5   Experiment and Results

In this section, we present the details of experiments on our intelligent-estimation model. We first introduce the dataset and evaluation metrics in experiments, and show the results of the model as well as compared models.

5.1   Dataset

We gathered datasets from a resourceful train control signal system company we cooperated, CASCO Ltd., and divided it into two parts, consisting of training and test. datasets. The total dataset has 15000 samples. The training dataset has 12500 samples and the test dataset has 500 samples. Our dataset is an unbalanced dataset. There are 12960 samples in H0, 682 samples in H1, 705 samples in H2 and 653 samples in H3. 86.4% of samples are in the normal state, while only 13.6% are in the risk states.

The dataset we received needs some extra preparation steps specific to our problem. The first step is to make the data comparable in the model. Data comparable preparation works by proper data normalization. We use

$$x = \frac{x_i - x_{min}}{x_{max} - x_{min}} \tag{12}$$

to have a mean of zero, or to be centered, with a standard deviation of one. It can ensure that all data values obeys normal distribution.

5.2 Evaluation Metrics

In our experiments, the evaluation metrics include Accuracy, Precision, Recall. They are computed as

$$Accuracy = \frac{1}{n} \sum_{k=1}^{m} \mathbb{I}(f(\mathbf{x_k}) = y_k), \tag{13}$$

where $\mathbb{I}$ is Indicator function, y_k is the real value and y_k' is a prediction value.

$$Precision = \frac{TP}{TP + FP} \tag{14}$$

$$Recall = \frac{TP}{TP + FN} \tag{15}$$

Precision and Recall were based on the results of the confusion matrix, in which TP is true positive, FP is false positive, TN is true negative, and FN is false negative.

5.3 Results and Discussion

In our experiment, a group of 500 samples from dataset are used to estimate the hazard risk prediction performance of our intelligent model. Table 2 shows the confusion matrix for the safety-risk prediction task on test dataset with 500 samples, and Table 3 shows evaluation metrics results on five groups.

Table 2. Confusion Matrix for the safety-risk prediction task on test dataset with 500 samples.

True	Predicted			
	H0	H1	H2	H3
H0	430	1	2	1
H1	2	19	-	1
H2	1	1	15	2
H3	1	-	1	23

Table 3. Model evaluation metrics results in five group experiments

Group	Accuracy	Precision	Recall
1	0.976	0.948	0.947
2	0.972	0.937	0.939
3	0.972	0.937	0.937
4	0.968	0.929	0.925
5	0.973	0.946	0.936
Mean	0.972	0.947	0.930

The test dataset was divided into 4 kinds of state, of which 485 samples were identified successfully, and the confusion matrix is shown in Table 2. The row means the true category and the columns delegate the prediction category. For all classification, the accuracy is 0.972 for five times. In the test dataset, most of the samples belong to the normal state data that were accurately classified, a total of 430 groups. However, for the collision between two trains and train-structure collision, there are some misclassification. The misclassification of H1 as H3 and the misclassification of H3 as H1 may be due to the judgment of the end point type is different in the EOA calculation, the former is the end of the train, and the latter is the turnout, the end of the railway or buffers. The communication delay could lead to the misclassification of H2 as H1. The most likely cause is the interlocking system in the two cases cannot receive the control command in time and cannot be interlocked. Table 3 is the evaluation metrics results in five group of test datasets. As we can see in Table 3, the mean of accuracy is 0.972 and it is stable in such experiments. Recall in these experiments is 0.930, which means that the intelligent prediction model can handle unbalanced datasets.

To a large extent, the most likely cause is that we consider multiple influential factors and utilized a multilayer neural network, where made our model more precise. This result shows that using our predictive model can make for the decline of occurrence of a hazard and the deep neural network is very effective in train collision classification. Taken together, these results suggest that our intelligent-prediction model is effective in system hazard risk prediction by considering multiple influential factors and using deep learning.

6   Conclusion

In this paper, we proposed a novel intelligent-prediction model, in which the model was learned from historical operation parameter samples in CBTC system, to predict which kind of risk state will occur. The design of intelligent-prediction model takes advantage of popular DBN. More importantly, we use a formal method, statistical model checking, to calculate one of prediction factors, the MA failure rate. Finally, experiments on real-world dataset validated the performance of our new proposed intelligent-prediction model and demonstrated the effectiveness of the deep learning framework in the safety-risk estimation for CBTC system. Without relevant domain knowledge, the dependence with the considered hazards can be learned by DNN from the dataset. It is shown that the proposed novel can significantly predict the hazard risk in the CBTC system.

In future work, more prediction factors and types of hazards will be taken into account, which can potentially improve prediction performance. We are also interested in exploring the relationship between a hazard and spatial-temporal data, and other deep learning algorithms may help solve it.

Acknowledgment. This paper is partially supported by funding under National Key Research and Development Project 2017YFB1001800, NSFC 61572195, NSFC 61802251 and Shanghai SHEITC Project 2017-GYHLW-01036.

References

1. Ieee standard for communications-based train control (cbtc) performance and functional requirements. IEEE Std 1474.1-2004 (Revision of IEEE Std 1474.1-1999), pp. 1–45 (2004). https://doi.org/10.1109/IEEESTD.2004.95746
2. Agha, G., Palmskog, K.: A survey of statistical model checking. ACM Trans. Model. Comput. Simul. **28**(1), 6:1–6:39 (2018). https://doi.org/10.1145/3158668, http://doi.acm.org/10.1145/3158668
3. Baier, C., Haverkort, B., Hermanns, H., Katoen, J.P.: Model-checking algorithms for continuous-time markov chains. IEEE Trans. Softw. Eng. **29**(6), 524–541 (2003)
4. Berriel, R.F., et al.: Heading direction estimation using deep learning with automatic large-scale data acquisition. In: 2018 International Joint Conference on Neural Networks (IJCNN), pp. 1–8. IEEE (2018)
5. Clarke, E.M., Zuliani, P.: Statistical model checking for cyber-physical systems. In: Bultan, T., Hsiung, P.-A. (eds.) ATVA 2011. LNCS, vol. 6996, pp. 1–12. Springer, Heidelberg (2011). https://doi.org/10.1007/978-3-642-24372-1_1
6. Comptier, M., Deharbe, D., Perez, J.M., Mussat, L., Pierre, T., Sabatier, D.: Safety analysis of a CBTC system: a rigorous approach with event-b. In: Fantechi, A., Lecomte, T., Romanovsky, A. (eds) International Conference on Reliability, Safety and Security of Railway Systems, vol. 10598, pp. 148–159. Springer, Cham (2017). https://doi.org/10.1007/978-3-319-68499-4_10
7. Ekanadham, C.: Sparse deep belief net models for visual area v2. In: Advances in Neural Information Processing Systems, vol. 20, pp. 873–880 (2008)
8. Ferrari, A., Itria, M.L., Chiaradonna, S., Spagnolo, G.O.: Model-based evaluation of the availability of a CBTC system. In: Avgeriou, P. (ed.) SERENE 2012. LNCS, vol. 7527, pp. 165–179. Springer, Heidelberg (2012). https://doi.org/10.1007/978-3-642-33176-3_12
9. Hinton, G.E., Osindero, S., Teh, Y.W.: A fast learning algorithm for deep belief nets. Neural Comput. **18**(7), 1527 (2006)
10. Hinton, G.E., Salakhutdinov, R.R.: Reducing the dimensionality of data with neural networks. Science **313**(5786), 504–7 (2006)
11. Hordvik, S., Øseth, K., Blech, J.O., Herrmann, P.: A methodology for model-based development and safety analysis of transport systems. In: ENASE, pp. 91–101 (2016)

12. Huang, H.Z., Yuan, X., Yao, X.S.: Fuzzy fault tree analysis of railway traffic safety. In: International Conference on Transportation and Traffic Studies, pp. 107–112 (2000)
13. Huang, W., Song, G., Hong, H., Xie, K.: Deep architecture for traffic flow prediction: deep belief networks with multitask learning. IEEE Trans. Intell. Transp. Syst. **15**(5), 2191–2201 (2014)
14. Jensen, F.V., et al.: An Introduction to Bayesian Networks, vol. 210. UCL press, London (1996)
15. Knight, J.C.: Safety critical systems: challenges and directions. In: Proceedings of the 24th International Conference on Software Engineering ICSE 2002, pp. 547–550. ACM, New York (2002)
16. Krizhevsky, A., Sutskever, I., Hinton, G.E.: Imagenet classification with deep convolutional neural networks. In: International Conference on Neural Information Processing Systems, pp. 1097–1105 (2012)
17. Lee, W.S., Grosh, D.L., Tillman, F.A., Lie, C.H.: Fault tree analysis, methods, and applications: a review. IEEE Trans. Reliab. **R-34**(3), 194–203 (1985)
18. Mitra, S., Wang, Y., Lynch, N., Feron, E.: Safety verification of model helicopter controller using hybrid input/output automata. In: Maler, O., Pnueli, A. (eds.) HSCC 2003. LNCS, vol. 2623, pp. 343–358. Springer, Heidelberg (2003). https://doi.org/10.1007/3-540-36580-X_26
19. Nefti, S., Oussalah, M.: A neural network approach for railway safety prediction. In: IEEE International Conference on Systems, Man and Cybernetics, vol. 4, pp. 3915–3920 (2004)
20. Srinivasan, R.: Importance Sampling: Applications in Communications and Detection. Springer, Heidelberg (2013). https://doi.org/10.1007/978-3-662-05052-1
21. Stamatis, D.H.: Failure Mode and Effect Analysis: FMEA from Theory to Execution. ASQ Quality Press, Milwaukee (2003)
22. Wang, J., Zhang, C.: Software reliability prediction using a deep learning model based on the RNN encoder-decoder. Reliab. Eng. Syst. Saf. **170**, 73–82 (2018)
23. Zhang, Y.P., Xu, Z.J., Su, H.S.: Risk assessment on railway signal system based on fuzzy-FMECA method (2013)
24. Zhu, T., de Pedro, J.M.M.S.: Railway traffic conflict detection via a state transition prediction approach. IEEE Trans. Intell. Transp. Syst. **18**(5), 1268–1278 (2017)

A Platform Service for Passenger Volume Analysis on Massive Smart Card Data in Public Transportation Domain

Weilong Ding[1,2(✉)] 🄳, Zhe Wang[1,2], and Zhuofeng Zhao[1,2]

[1] School of Computer Science and Technology,
North China University of Technology, Beijing 100144, China
dingweilong@ncut.edu.cn
[2] Beijing Key Laboratory on Integration and Analysis of Large-Scale Stream
Data, Beijing 100144, China

Abstract. In current public transportation of modern cities, the passenger volume analysis counts the bus passengers in multiple perspectives, and it is significant to optimize the bus scheduling and evaluate transportation capacity. On the smart card data of passengers taking buses, traditional solutions have inherent limitations about long processing delay, inaccuracy result and poor scalability. In this paper, the spatio-temporal correlation with business restrictions is considered, and an effective platform service for passenger volumes analyses are proposed on massive smart card. Our service has been applied in practical usage for three types of passenger volume, and holds minute-level latencies on weekly data with nearly linear scalability in extensive conditions.

Keywords: Spatio-temporal data · Smart card data · Behavior analysis · Passenger volume · Platform service

1 Introduction

Nowadays, smart cards solutions have been adopted extensively in urban environment, and generate massive offline historical data [1]. The large data makes it possible for official governors to achieve intelligent analysis [2]. In public transportation domain, the *passenger volume* analysis counts the bus passengers in multiple perspectives. It is a significant indicator to find hot spots in a city, optimize the bus scheduling, and evaluate transportation capacity in the intelligent transportation system (ITS) [3].

Traditionally, the smart card data with typical spatio-temporal attributes are stored in data warehouse or relational database after necessary data cleaning [4, 5], and the passenger volume is achieved through statistic linear models. Most of those methods are done by interactive SQL (structural query language) or predefined store procedure on small data samples [4, 6]. However, it faces inherent limitations on massive spatio-temporal data. (1) First, the executive latency is intolerable when the involved data size is huge. With the simplified assumptions, traditional methods on small samples [7] only achieve short-term predictive values for limited locations [8] (e.g., prediction for given stations in a periodic five minutes). It suffers long time through database that large

© ICST Institute for Computer Sciences, Social Informatics and Telecommunications Engineering 2019
Published by Springer Nature Switzerland AG 2019. All Rights Reserved
X. Wang et al. (Eds.): CollaborateCom 2019, LNICST 292, pp. 681–697, 2019.
https://doi.org/10.1007/978-3-030-30146-0_46

volume of data has to be centralized loaded and scanned many times during the query execution. The I/O of such analyses even cost more time than that of computation itself [9]. As a result, the release of the routine report for passenger volumes is always delayed in metropolises. (2) Second, the analytical accuracy is low in practice because the business spatio-temporal correlation has not been fully considered. Traditional methods always focus on the holistic statistic characteristics to fit the historical observations, and neglect specific passenger behaviors in temporal or spatial perspective. In fact, how to describe those behaviors restricts the accuracy essentially [10]. (3) Third, the analytical scalability during calculation is extremely poor when the data size increases or the infrastructure updates. In either case, traditional methods have to pursue higher-level hardware or software in "scale-up" to redeploy the applications accordingly. It also implies a great deal of financial and man-power expenses.

In this paper, we propose a novel platform service for passenger volume analyses on massive smart card data. The contributions can be summarized as follows. (1) Three types of bus passenger volume, getting-on, getting-off and transfer, are defined by business spatio-temporal characteristics. It is the necessary condition for the accurate analyses. (2) On massive smart card data, each type of bus passenger volume is efficiently achieved with horizontal scalability. Modeled as Hadoop MapReduce jobs, the analyses procedure holds minute-level latencies on weekly data in extensive conditions. (3) Available in a practical project of public transportation domain, our work has brought benefits due to the visualization of the bus passenger volume.

This paper is organized as follows. Section 2 shows the background including motivation and related works. Section 3 elaborates the platform service and the volume analyses for multiple passenger behaviors. Section 4 quantitatively demonstrates effects from the experiment and case studies in various conditions. Section 5 summarizes the conclusion.

2   Background

2.1   Motivation and Assumption

Our work was initiated by *Passenger Big Data Analysis Platform* in Beijing. We cooperated with *E-hualu*, one of the leader Chinese companies in intelligent traffic domain, to deploy a bus scheduling system for more than 30 new night-bus lines in late 2014. The goal of this project is to optimize public transits through Big Data technologies to alleviate traffic jams, improve air quality, and bring regional integration with peripheral *Tianjin* city and *Hebei* province.

In Beijing until the end of 2015, more than 30 thousand buses of nearly one thousand lines adopted smart card readers and 44 million cards had been released to citizens, which would generate 15 thousand records with about tens of gigabyte data daily. Such data from buses has been accumulated day by day as massive historical data. As the data unit, a record of smart card data is typical spatio-temporal union, and contains 13 attributes in Table 1 including entities, timestamps and spatial attribute-groups.

The regular business reports for bus service are released from our system to evaluate the traffic management and passenger guidance in a macroscopic viewpoint.

Table 1. The record structure of smart card data.

Attribute	Notation	Type
card_ID	Identity of smart card	Entity
line_ID	Identity of bus line	
bus_ID	Identity of bus	
begin_time	Timestamp of getting-on	Time
end_time	Timestamp of getting-off	
from_station_ID	Identity of getting-on station	Space
from_station_name	Identity of getting-on station	
from_station_longitude	Longitude of getting-on station	
from_station_latitude	Latitude of getting-on station	
to_station_ID	Identity of getting-off station	
to_station_name	Name of getting-off station	
to_station_longitude	Longitude of getting-off station	
to_station_latitude	Latitude of getting-off station	

For example, in rush hours the early warnings and vehicle dispatching could be made for certain busy lines due to their too long departure frequency. Traditionally, such historical data was processed periodically through data warehouse and statistic models after its capture and storage, but the delay during the analysis is too long to endure. For instance, such a monthly report of Beijing usually requires more than half a month to complete. Accordingly, it is required to pursue efficient analyses solution, not only for optimizing bus departure intervals or passenger on-board time, but also for the better data management. That is the just motivation of our work.

In this paper, there are two assumptions.

First, a record must contain the timestamps of both getting-on and getting-off. If one is excluded, it should be inferred by the other one before further processing [11, 12]. In Beijing, there are two charge kinds due to the smart card readers on buses. One is charged by travel counts and a card is read once in a trip at the getting-on time of passengers; the other is charged by travel distances and a card is read twice in a trip at both getting-on and getting-off times of passengers. All the data in this work was generated from the readers of the latter type. It is a sound assumption because such charging is popular progressively. For example, according to the official policies, all the buses in Beijing had updated their readers for distance charging since December 12th 2014.

Second, the fallacious records have been eliminated in advance. Due to the uncertain conditions of devices or storage, the raw data has two main defects. (1) The temporal attributes among the records are inconsistent. For example, we do not know whether 2001-01-01 or 2015-05-31 is the factual date if both values appear in the same record. (2) The missing or illegal records bring business confusion. For example, a bus may seem run too much time without any rest if the records in certain time are lost. Therefore, low data quality is the inevitable obstruct for data analysis [13]. Here, we employ dedicated data cleaning method [14] on massive spatio-temporal data to guarantee temporal consistency and semantic legality.

2.2 Related Work

As a hot topic in public transportation domain, the research about bus passenger volume can be classified in three categories according to the involved technology.

Database is the widely used technology for bus passenger volume analysis. The smart card data is maintained in the persistent storage, and the passenger volume is calculated by interactive SQL or predefined store procedure [4]. Through geographical database, Long et al. [6] uncovered the passengers' commuting pattern in Beijing, and compared their trips with the expensed time and geographical distance in different perspectives. On GTFS (General Transit Feed Specification) data in database, Tao et al. [10] demonstrated a multi-step method to examine the spatio-temporal dynamics of travel behaviors among bus passengers. But those works only concern the limited data instead of the holistic ones in wider time ranges. It would suffer long processing latency due to the heavy IO of loading and scan during analytical processing [9].

Statistic model is also adopted for bus passenger volume prediction. In some time intensive conditions, it can reduce the executive delay dramatically. During the short-time prediction for passenger volume, such models rely on the characteristic of samples. On smart card data, Ma et al. [4] built trip probability models of involved stations, and proposed DBSCAN joint algorithm to identify historical travel patterns and regularities. Zhou et al. [11] proposed OD (origin-destination) matrix to estimate public passenger volume in probability view. Zhang et al. [7] proposed a Kalman filter model to forecast short-term passenger volume on smart card data, vehicle location data and station video data. The accuracy can hold well, but benefits on limited data samples in practice. Moreover, as typical time series approaches, all these works above only exploit time characteristics without spatial consideration. It makes it impossible to exhaustively evaluate bus passengers' behaviors.

Big Data technology is popular nowadays especially on large volume data in scalable Cloud environment [15]. Hadoop ecology has been applied in the transportation domain, with the help of highly utilized virtual resources. Through Hadoop distributed file system, UrbanCPS [16] and coMobile [17] store data from heterogeneous sensors, and predict traffic speeds with human mobility in urban areas. Moreover, in a private Cloud, Xiong's work [3] integrates the transportation data in multiple perspectives. Through Hadoop MapReduce on smart card data and bus GPS data, Zhang et al. [1, 12] analyzed the passenger density to infer crowdedness and evaluate the vehicle scheduling. With analogous solutions, Wang et al. [18] estimated boarding stop time and bus arrival time. Moreover, SMARTBUS [19] shows a composite solution in multiple Hadoop layers. All those works prove their effectiveness in specific business, but none of them considers bus passenger volume analysis yet.

In brief, on massive data of smart card data, challenges still remain to analyze passenger volume efficiently. Therefore, we introduce platform service via Big Data technologies.

3   Bus Passenger Volume Analyses in the Platform Service

3.1   Methodology

We designed a platform service whose architecture is illustrated as Fig. 1.

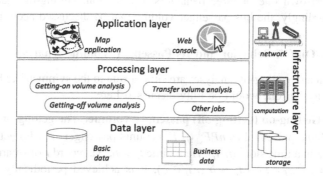

Fig. 1.   The service architecture.

The *data layer* maintains the required data. The *basic data* is the essential auxiliary for analyses in the relational database, including locations of station, profile of bus lines and vehicle id, etc. The *business data* is the spatio-temporal records captured from the smart card readers, which would regularly load into the distributed file system after data cleaning. Compared with the basic data, the business data has much larger size (i.e., terabyte vs. megabyte level) with higher updates frequency (i.e., daily vs. monthly).

The *processing layer* provides run-time environment to calculate business analyses like bus passenger volumes. Such analyses are built and submitted by domain experts as calculative jobs, and run as parallel tasks.

The *application layer* shows the results of business analyses with pre-defined configurations. The *map application* visualizes the results in online maps of multiple perspectives. For bus passenger volumes, the results could be demonstrated in a map as the granularity of stations, bus lines, and road network. The *web console* sets the configurations of the whole service, manages the business analyses, and monitors the status of each layer.

The *infrastructure layer* supplies the virtualized resources from a private Cloud. The resources like computation, storage, and network are accommodated elastically on demand.

In fact, it is a typical architecture for Big Data analysis in the public transportation domain, where we focus on the bus passenger volume analyses in this following part.

From Table 1, the smart card data is formally defined first.

Definition 1: Smart card data. The smart card data is generated when a passenger's card is read by reader on the bus. A record as the unit can be represented as $r = (p, b, s_n, t_n, s_f, t_f)$. Here, p is a passenger's card, b is the taking bus, s_n (s_f) is the getting-on (getting-off) station, and t_n (t_f) is the getting-on (getting-off) timestamp at s_n (s_f).

For any station $s \in S$, its *passenger volume analyses* counts the number of passengers in any time slot δ_i, where S is the station set. Divided by the fixed interval length θ, δ_i, is the ith time slot of a day. For example, when $\theta = 1$ h, $|i| = 24$, $\delta_0 = [0:00\text{–}1:00)$, $\delta_1 = [1:00\text{–}2:00)$, ..., $\delta_{23} = [23:00\text{–}24:00)$; the passenger volume would be a 24-dimensional vector, whose element is the count in a δ_i at s. In fact, a passenger must own one of three behaviors at a station: getting-on, getting-off and transfer. Accordingly, the bus passenger volume can be discussed accordingly.

3.2 Getting-On/Off Behavior and Its Passenger Volume Analysis

The getting-on and getting-off analyses are similar due to the symmetrical behaviors, so that only the former one would be fully discussed here.

Definition 2. Getting-on (getting-off) passenger volume. The getting-on (getting-off) passenger volume presented as nPF_s^δ (fPF_s^δ) counts passengers P who get on (off) any bus at station s in a time slot $\delta(t_l, t_r)$. Here, time $t_r > t_l$, $\exists$ a record r of smart card data, r. $p \in P$, $r.s_n = s$ ($r.s_f = s$), $r.t_n \in \delta$ ($r.t_f \in \delta$). It is achieved periodically with a fixed interval length $\theta = |\delta| = t_r - t_l$. Usually, θ is set as 30 min, 1 h or 2 h in practice.

Referring certain location (i.e., station) at given time interval (i.e., time slot), those volumes as an aggregation evaluation reflect the hot degree of that station. The spatio-temporal continuity of individual passengers is kept in the records, but the moving of buses is required in the analysis. A certain bus always runs more than one round-trip in a day, and it is would stop and start at any station in each trip. The time when the bus started (stopped) brings the passengers' getting-on (getting-off) behaviors. However, only some passenger's times instead of that of buses are kept in the records. Therefore, the first difficulty comes from the gap of different temporal semantics. As Fig. 2, there are two trips of a certain bus at a station in a day. The getting-on timestamps of passengers would be gathered in clusters according to the time of bus start in each trip (i.e., t_{s1} and t_{s2} here).

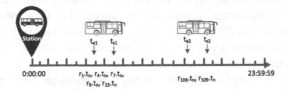

Fig. 2. The moving of a bus at a station.

Therefore, it remains three problems for getting-on (getting-off) passenger volume analysis: how to discriminate each trip of any bus; how to infer a bus's stop and start time at any station; how to sensibly build nPF_s^δ (fPF_s^δ) if waiting period of bus at a station overlaps two adjacent time slots (e.g., if a bus stopped when $t_e = 8:58$ and started when $t_s = 9:01$, the ridership during $[t_s, t_e)$ overlaps the time slots $\delta_7 = [7:00\text{–}8:00)$ and $\delta_8 = [8:00\text{–}9:00)$).

To solve those problems, we observe the characteristics of data, and propose the following Algorithm 1 with the symbols in definition 1. The algorithm is based the observations below. For a bus b at station s, a passenger's getting-on time must be earlier than b's start time in a probability larger than 50%; that time of all getting-on passengers in the same trip must cluster according to b's start time; in the same trip of b, all those times must be statistically positive-skewed because the median of those timestamps is smaller than their mean value. In the line 3–7, getting-on timestamps of different trips are clustered under auxiliary business conditions. In practice, we employ the empirical $\gamma = 420$ (i.e., 7 min), because we have learned from the official documents, a bus of Beijing spends at least 14 min for a round-trip. In the line 9–13, to infer the start time of bus b at station s, we have to alleviate the skewness of getting-on timestamps by logarithm transformation (i.e., function $\ln()$), where $\mathrm{EXP}(x) = e^x$. For those positive-skewed timestamps, their logarithmic values roughly conform to the normal distribution. Due to the normality knowledge, we know 68% of g_i would not larger than $m_g + sd_g$. Therefore, t_s defined in line 12 is a sound approximation, because the start time of bus is larger getting-on timestamps of passengers in a probability more than a half.

Algorithm 1. *Bus trips recognition*
Input: records of smart card data in a bus ordered by the getting-on timestamp
Output: trips of the bus b at station s and the bus start time t_s in each trip

```
1    for a record rᵢ
2      b= rᵢ.b; s= rᵢ.sₙ;
3      if (rᵢ.tₙ - rᵢ₋₁. tₙ) < γ
4        put rᵢ to the same trip with rᵢ₋₁;
5      else
6        put rᵢ to a new trip;
7      end if
8    end for
9    for a trip of b at s
10     for any rᵢ, gᵢ=ln(rᵢ.tₙ);
11     on those gᵢ, get their mean mg and standard deviation sdg;
12     b's start time tₛ = EXP (mg + sdg)
13   end for
```

Through the Algorithm 1 above, the getting-on passenger volume analysis can be modeled as a two-step procedure in Fig. 3. Each step can be implemented as a Hadoop MapReduce job. Here, the vertical left part of either step works as a map task and the right one is a reduce task; each step requires only one-pass processing on the data.

The first step as the upper part of the Fig. 3 is to achieve the getting-on passenger volume of every single bus. Here, each record would be extracted by its attributes. The timestamp of getting-on is divided to *date* and *time*. After grouping by the composition of station id, bus id and date, Algorithm 1 is invoked. As a result, the passenger volume of each bus are achieved and ordered by the station id. For example, when θ is set as 1 h, and a output could be <3, 00028294, 20151208, 0, 0, 0, 0, 0, 0, 13, 0, 0, 25, 0, 0, 0, 18, 0, 0, 0, 0, 0, 0, 0, 0, 0, 0>. It means the bus 0028294 at station 3 on Dec.8th 2015 had three trips when the counts were 13 in [6:00, 7:00), 25 in [9:00, 10:00) and 18 in [13:00, 14:00).

The second step as the lower part of Fig. 3 is to achieve the getting-on passenger volume of all the buses. In this step, the inputs are achieved from the first step. After grouping by the composition of station id, bus id and date, the final result is the vector addition in respective time slot. For example, when θ is set as 1 h, and an output could be <3, 20151208, 0, 0, 0, 0, 0, 64, 85, 105, 128, 256, 204, 230, 242, 189, 205, 143, 145, 252, 286, 259, 235, 102, 82, 35>. It means the count for station 3 at each time slot of one hour on Dec.8th 2015.

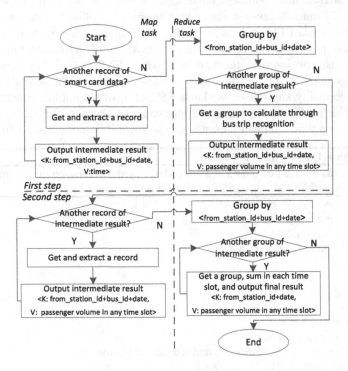

Fig. 3. Getting-on passenger volume analysis.

Here, considering some waiting periods of bus at a station overlap two adjacent time slots δ_i, δ_{i+1}, we regard the ridership belongs to either δ_i if $t_s \in \delta_i$ or to δ_{i+1} if $t_s \in \delta_{i+1}$. It is sound because the getting-on behaviors of passengers depend on the start of a bus.

Therefore, all three problems mentioned have been solved. Analogously, the **getting-off passenger volume** could be achieved, where the getting-off timestamp (i.e., $r_i.t_f$) of passengers and the stop time of buses are focused instead. With the similar logarithm transformation, the inferred bus stop time $t_e = \text{EXP}(m_g + sd_g)$ with the same confidence 68%. It is sound because the getting-off timestamps are also positive skewed and smaller than stop time in a probability more than a half.

3.3 Transfer Behavior and Its Passenger Volume Analysis

Then, the third type of passenger volume is discussed.

Definition 3. Transfer passenger volume. The transfer passenger volume presented as xPF_s^δ in any time slot $\delta(t_l, t_r)$ counts passengers P who gets off any bus b_j at s_f and gets on another bus b_k at s_n within a time duration no more than ε. Here, time $t_r > t_l$, $\exists$ two records r_f, r_n of smart card data, $r_f.p = r_n.p \in P$, $r_f.s_f = s_f$, $r_n.s_n = s_n$, $r_f.t_f \in \delta$, $r_n.t_n \in \delta$. It is achieved periodically with a fixed interval length $\theta = |\delta| = t_r - t_l$. Usually, θ is set as 30 min, 1 h or 2 h in practice, and the threshold $0 < \varepsilon < \theta$. The station s_f and s_n are either geographical neighbors or the same one.

Referring a location pair (i.e., getting-off and getting-on stations) at given time duration (i.e., time slots), the transfer passenger volume faces analogous condition as that of getting-on passenger volume. Because transfer behavior consists of a getting-off behavior and a successive getting-on one like Fig. 4, it could be achieved directly from the method in Sect. 3.2. However, it would be inefficient to merge two independent analyses for integral results. Accordingly, we focus on the dedicated method in this section.

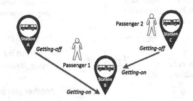

Fig. 4. The transfer behaviors of passengers.

Algorithm 2. *Transfer behaviors recognition and counting*
Input: records of smart card data group by passenger
Output: the transfer behavior of each passenger
1   **for** two successive records r_{i-1}, r_i of passenger p
2      $r_{i-1}.p = r_i.p = p$; $b_f = r_{i-1}.b$; $b_n = r_i.b$; $s_f = r_{i-1}.s_f$; $s_n = r_i.s_n$; $t_f = r_{i-1}.t_f$; $t_n = r_i.t_n$;
3   **if** $(b_f \neq b_n)$
4   **if** (distance $(s_f, s_n) < \eta$) and $((t_n - t_f <= \Gamma)$
5   a transfer behavior of p appears at station s_n and at the time t_n;
6   **end if**
7   **end if**
8   **end for**

Besides the same problems with the getting-on volume analysis, the transfer passenger volume analysis remains other two ones. One is how to define the spatial neighborhood of any station. The transfer behavior only makes sense at the getting-on station. The other is how to depict temporal closeness of any passenger for a transfer between his getting-off behavior and the successive getting-on one. Too long delay would not appropriately reflect the passengers' real intention.

To solve those problems, we propose the Algorithm 2 with the symbols in definition 1. The algorithm to find a transfer behavior is based the definition of spatial neighborhood and temporal closeness in the line 3–5. For a transfer behavior of a passenger, the getting-off bus must be different with the getting-on one; while the getting-off station could be same with the getting-on one. Threshold η of spatial neighborhood restricts the max cartographic distance between two stations, and threshold Γ of temporal closeness implies the longest period duration two behaviors. Here, we regard the count of transfer behavior as the result at the time t_n with the station s_n.

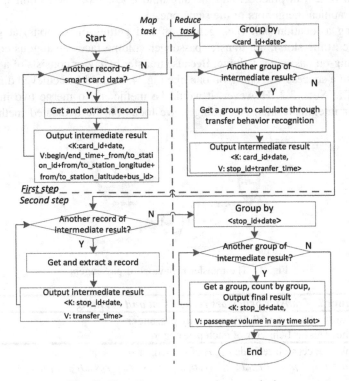

Fig. 5. Transfer passenger volume analysis.

Through the Algorithm 2, the transfer passenger volume analysis can be modeled as two-step procedure in Fig. 5. Each step can be implemented as a Hadoop MapReduce job. Here, the vertical left part of either step works as a map task and the right one is a reduce task; each of which requires only one-pass processing on the data.

The first step as the upper part of the Fig. 5 is to find the transfer behaviors of passengers. Here, each record would be extracted by its attributes. The timestamp of either getting-on and or getting-off is divided to *date* and *time*. The date of getting-on and getting-off are identical. After grouping by the composition of card id and date, the algorithm 2 is i. The thresholds could be set empirically: $\eta = 1000$ m and $\Gamma = 20$ min. It comes from the facts in the official documents: in Beijing for a bus transfer, 95% passengers expect to wait less than 20 min; only 16% passengers would endure to walk more than 1000 m to the next getting-on station. As a result, if θ is 1 h, an output could be <3, 00000370A80456014EBE774FE6D150C1, 20151208, 8, 1>. It means a passenger using that card had a transfer behavior at station 3 at the 8th time slot, i.e., [7:00, 8:00) on Dec.8th 2015.

The second step as the lower part of Fig. 5 is to achieve the transfer passenger volumes of all the passengers. In this step, the inputs are achieved from the first step. After grouping by the composition of station id and date, the final result is the vector addition in respective time slots. For example, if θ is set as 1 h, a output could be <3, 20151208, 0, 0, 0, 0, 0, 26, 52, 75, 82, 126, 124, 123, 130, 98, 105, 93, 75, 82, 96, 89, 75, 82, 68, 23>. It shows the transfer passenger volume at station 3 in 24 time slots on Dec.8th 2015.

4 Evaluations

4.1 Settings

The executive performance and practical effects are evaluated respectively by extensive experiments and case studies in this section.

In our private Cloud as the service infrastructure layer, four Acer AR580 F2 rack servers via Citrix XenServer 6.2 are utilized in the infrastructure layer, each of which own 8 processors (Intel Xeon E5-4607 2.20 GHz), 64 GB RAM and 80 TB storage. Six virtual machines are used to build our platform service, each of which owns 4 cores CPU, 4 GB RAM and 1.2 TB storage with CentOS 6.6 x86_64 operating system. As the Fig. 1, the data layer consists of MySQL 5.1 and HDFS; the processing layer is the customized Hadoop MapReduce 2.6.0; the application layer would be further exploited in the Sect. 4.3.

We employ the smart card data of Beijing on eight days in 2013, which contains 24263142 records on 7349 buses of 233 lines involving 3581 stations. All the data was generated from the readers charging by travel distance, and each record contains 13 attributes as Table 1. The data has been cleaned in advance through dedicated method [14], and has been divided into eight parts by the original dates as the experiment inputs.

To analyze the passenger volume, two different methods have been implemented in our platform service for comparison. One is our method termed as BD (Big Data). The counterpart is a statistic estimation [11] termed as ODE (Origin-destination Estimation) in the current productive environment.

4.2 Experiments

We evaluate the performance of two methods to analyze passenger volume in the experiments below.

Experiment 1. The data of different size is used as the input. The getting-on and transfer passenger volume are executed through both BD and ODE, and note their average executive times in each condition. The result is showed as Fig. 6 where the left is the getting-on passenger volume analysis and the right is the transfer one.

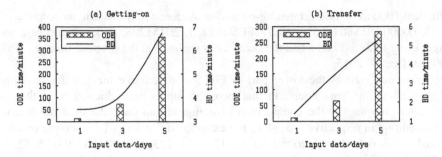

Fig. 6. The passenger volume analyses through two methods

When the input size increases, the executive time of both methods rises, but ODE has much longer time than BD in two orders of magnitude for either analysis. In average, the input record size of one day is about 1 million. The executive time through ODE grows sharply when the input is more than 5 million, while that of BD rises almost linearly. On the input of 3-day data, BD costs minute-level time, while the ODE requires more than 5 h. The lower latency of BD comes from the parallel execution of two-step procedure in either passenger volume analysis. But through ODE, the analysis requires multiple passes to sort data, and has to run on a single machine without parallelism. As a result, ODE only suits small size data, while BD has much lower latencies on massive data.

In the following parts, only BD is evaluated for its efficiency and scalability.

Experiment 2. The data of one day is appended to the input in each test, and the executive times for getting-on passenger volume analysis through BD are noted. For the comparison on each input size, the interval length θ is set as 10-min, 1-h and 4-h respectively. The result is presented in Fig. 7(a). The average executive time on fixed one million records in each test can be deduced as Fig. 7(b).

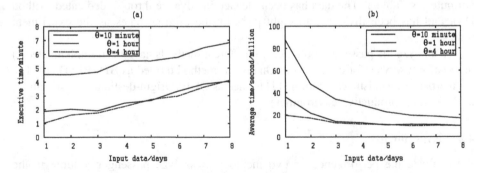

Fig. 7. The getting-on passenger volume analyses at 3 intervals on 8 inputs.

The getting-on analysis through BD method is proved scalable on the increasing data. On the one hand, when input scales at any interval length, the increment of executive time surpasses the linearity. In Fig. 7(a), the time is kept minute-level and not doubled even when the input size grows eight folds. That trend can be demonstrated clearly in another perspective of Fig. 7(b), where the average executive time on fixed input size declines to the steadiness about 10 s. It shows that the processing capacity of BD method is stable and horizontally scalable. On the other hand, on the input of the same size, the executive time varies by interval lengths. The longer interval length implies lower latencies, because our analysis relies on the interval length: shorter interval length implies more dimensions in result vector due to definition 2, and requires more calculation delay. It is interesting that when input scales, the capacity on fixed size converges at any interval length like Fig. 7(b), which also proves its horizontal scalability.

In a similar way, the transfer passenger volume analysis is evaluated next.

Experiment 3. The data of one day is appended to the input in each test, and the executive times for transfer passenger volume analysis through BD method are noted. For the comparison on each input size, the interval length θ is set as 10-min, 1-h and 4-h respectively. The result is presented in Fig. 8(a). The average executive time on fixed one million records in each test can be deduced as Fig. 8(b).

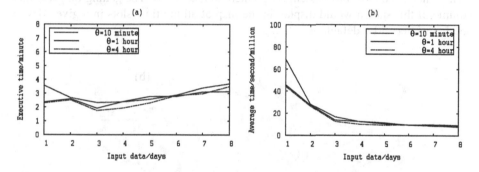

Fig. 8. The transfer passenger volume analyses at 3 intervals on 8 inputs.

The transfer analysis through BD method is also proved scalable on the increasing data. On the one hand, when input scales at any interval length setting, the executive time of the analysis keeps steadily. In Fig. 8(a), that time fluctuates between one and four minutes even when the input grows eight folds. Compared with that of getting-on analysis, the execution here is relatively faster, because transfer behavior appears much fewer than getting-on and requires lesser time. As Fig. 8(b), the executive time on fixed input size declines to a steadiness about less than 10 s. The same value with that of getting-on analysis shows the scalable capacity of BD method again. On the other hand, on the input of the same size, the executive time has little difference at three interval lengths setting because the intermediate results in the experiment are too small to manifest their variance. The capacity on fixed input size also converges at any interval length when input scales as Fig. 8(b), which proves its scalability either.

With the three experiments above, our analysis in platform service proves minute-level latencies on weekly historical data with horizontal scalability.

4.3   Case Studies

We evaluate the practical effects in the application layer of service by case studies next. The getting-on passenger volume is exhibited first.

Case 1. The jobs of getting-on passenger volume are submitted successively to *web console* to execute. After their completion, the visual results are available in *map application*. As an example, when a station named *Beijing West Railway Station* is selected in the map, the profile emerges including id, name and GPS location, and the hyperlink of getting-on passenger volume is also enabled in a pop-up window.

The analysis jobs are governed full life-cycle in our service via the *web console*. In this case as the Fig. 9(a), the second job of the getting-on passenger volume analysis is being submitted to the console. After the code package has been uploaded, the console would check source code to assist the job configuration (e.g., the executive entrance from the candidate Java main classes is auto-prompting), and then assigns to the processing layer. For any station, the passenger volume would be visualized in the *map application*. As In this case as the Fig. 9(b), the station *Beijing West Railway Station* is a transportation hub and close to a railway station. Some buses are in 7 * 24 h service around there, and most bus passengers go there to take trains. The getting-on passenger volume of this station would display in the map at all the time slots in a given day at one hour interval by default.

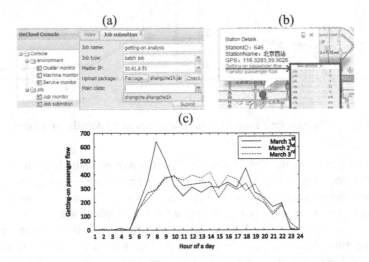

Fig. 9. The getting-on passenger volume of station Beijing West Railway Station.

Moreover, the synthetic views can be generated in our platform service. In this case, such a view as the Fig. 9(c) demonstrates the comparison of getting-on passenger volume on three successive days. We found the result on any of three days keeps steadily high since 8:00 to 19:00 just when the trains are usually busy. All those exactly match the real situations from the local official statistics.

Next, the effects of transfer passenger volume are evaluated in another case.

Case 2. The jobs of transfer passenger volume analysis are submitted successively to *web console*. After their completion, the visual results are available in *map application*. As an example, when a station named *Chinese Academy of Agricultural Science* is selected in the map, the profile emerges, and the hyperlink of transfer passenger volume is also enabled in a pop-up window.

The jobs' status is available in JSON (JavaScript Object Notation) format in our service and also visualized in *web console*. In this case as Fig. 10(a), the newly submitted jobs are noted as successfully completed in a history table. Even during the jobs' run-time, the console provides graphical interface to suspend or kill them. In this case as the Fig. 10(b), the station *Chinese Academy of Agricultural Science* lies in a junction of three trunk roads where more than 12 bus lines pass-by around two adjacent stations. It also can reach to two subway stations within 800 m. Therefore, many bus passengers go there for a transfer. The transfer passenger volume would display in the map at all the time slots in a day at one hour interval by default.

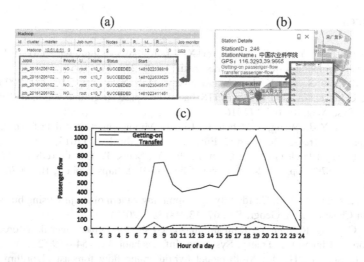

Fig. 10. Two kinds of passenger volume of station Chinese Academy of Agricultural Science.

Moreover, a synthetic view as the Fig. 10(c) is generated in the platform service to compare two kinds of passenger volume on a given date March 4th. We found the value of transfer volume is about 1/8-1/5 than that of getting-on and owns the same rush hours. It reflects the fact that transfer behavior is much smaller than getting-on one but shares the similar temporal trends. In either type of passenger volume in this workday, we can find the morning rush hours are from 7:00 to 9:00 and evening ones are from 17:00 to 20:00. All those exactly match the traffic report published by Beijing Traffic Commission.

With the two case studies above, our method achieves convenient effects and effective results in practical situations.

5 Conclusion

In public transportation domain, we propose a novel platform service to analyze multiple passenger volumes on massive smart card data. For any analysis, our service can hold minute-level latency on historical weekly data and keep nearly linear scalability in extensive conditions. It also shows practical effects and exact results in authentic cases. In the future, we would introduce more domain analyses in our service, such as bus arrive time prediction at given station and bus transit speeds prediction between two directly adjacent stations.

Acknowledgements. This work was supported by the Youth Program of National Natural Science Foundation of China under Grant 61702014, the General Program of Beijing Natural Science Foundation under Grant 4192020, and Top Young Innovative Talents of North China University of Technology under Grant XN018022.

References

1. Zhang, J., Zheng, Y., Qi, D., Li, R., Yi, X., Li, T.: Predicting citywide crowd flows using deep spatio-temporal residual networks. Artif. Intell. **259**, 147–166 (2018)
2. Chen, M., Mao, S., Liu, Y.: Big data: a survey. Mob. Netw. Appl. **19**, 171–209 (2014)
3. Xiong, G., et al.: A kind of novel ITS based on space-air-ground big-data. IEEE Intell. Transp. Syst. Mag. **8**, 10–22 (2016)
4. Ma, X., Wu, Y.-J., Wang, Y., Chen, F., Liu, J.: Mining smart card data for transit riders' travel patterns. Transp. Res. Part C: Emerg. Technol. **36**, 1–12 (2013)
5. Tang, N.: Big data cleaning. In: Chen, L., Jia, Y., Sellis, T., Liu, G. (eds.) APWeb 2014. LNCS, vol. 8709, pp. 13–24. Springer, Cham (2014). https://doi.org/10.1007/978-3-319-11116-2_2
6. Long, Y., Zhang, Y., Cui, C.: Identifying commuting pattern of Beijing using bus smart card data (in Chinese). Acta Geogr. Sin. **67**, 1339–1352 (2012)
7. Zhang, C., Song, R., Sun, Y.: Kalman filter-based short-term passenger flow forecasting on bus stop (in Chinese). J. Transp. Syst. Eng. Inf. Technol. **11**, 154–159 (2011)
8. Zhou, J., Sun, Y., He, L.: Multi-model hybrid traffic flow forecast algorithm based on multivariate data. In: Sun, Y., Lu, T., Xie, X., Gao, L., Fan, H. (eds.) ChineseCSCW 2018. CCIS, vol. 917, pp. 188–200. Springer, Singapore (2019). https://doi.org/10.1007/978-981-13-3044-5_14
9. Dugane, R.A., Raut, A.: A survey on big data in real time. Int. J. Recent Innov. Trends Comput. Commun. **2**, 794–797 (2014)
10. Tao, S., Rohde, D., Corcoran, J.: Examining the spatial–temporal dynamics of bus passenger travel behaviour using smart card data and the flow-comap. J. Transp. Geogr. **41**, 21–36 (2014)
11. Zhou, X., Yang, X., Wu, X.: Origin-destination matrix estimation method of public transportation flow based on data from bus integrated-circuit cards (in Chinese). J. Tongji Univ. (Nat. Sci.) **40**, 1027–1030 (2012)
12. Zhang, J., Yu, X., Tian, C., Zhang, F., Tu, L., Xu, C.: Analyzing passenger density for public bus: inference of crowdedness and evaluation of scheduling choices. In: 17th International IEEE Conference on Intelligent Transportation Systems (ITSC 2014), pp. 2015–2022. IEEE, (Year)

13. Carey, M.J., Jacobs, S., Tsotras, V.J.: Breaking BAD: a data serving vision for big active data. In: Proceedings of the 10th ACM International Conference on Distributed and Event-based Systems, pp. 181–186. ACM, Irvine (2016)
14. Ding, W., Cao, Y.: A data cleaning method on massive spatio-temporal data. In: Wang, G., Han, Y., Martínez Pérez, G. (eds.) Advances in Services Computing: 10th Asia-Pacific Services Computing Conference, APSCC 2016, Proceedings, pp. 173–182. Springer International Publishing, Cham (2016). https://doi.org/10.1007/978-3-319-49178-3_13
15. Pelletier, M.-P., Trépanier, M., Morency, C.: Smart card data use in public transit: a literature review. Transp. Res. Part C: Emerg. Technol. **19**, 557–568 (2011)
16. Zhang, D., Zhao, J., Zhang, F., He, T.: UrbanCPS: a cyber-physical system based on multi-source big infrastructure data for heterogeneous model integration. In: Proceedings of the ACM/IEEE Sixth International Conference on Cyber-Physical Systems, pp. 238–247. ACM, Seattle (2015)
17. Zhang, D., Zhao, J., Zhang, F., He, T.: coMobile: real-time human mobility modeling at urban scale using multi-view learning. In: Proceedings of the 23rd SIGSPATIAL International Conference on Advances in Geographic Information Systems, pp. 1–10. ACM, Bellevue (2015)
18. Wang, Y., Ram, S., Currim, F., Dantas, E., Saboia, L.A.: A big data approach for smart transportation management on bus network. In: 2016 IEEE International Smart Cities Conference (ISC2), pp. 1–6. IEEE (2016)
19. Ram, S., Wang, Y., Currim, F., Dong, F., Dantas, E., Saboia, L.A.: SMARTBUS: a web application for smart urban mobility and transportation. In: Proceedings of the 25th International Conference Companion on World Wide Web, pp. 363–368. International World Wide Web Conferences Steering Committee, Montreal (2016)

Reliable Collaborative Semi-infrastructure Vehicle-to-Vehicle Communication for Local File Sharing

Bassem Mokhtar[1,2], Mohamed Azab[3(✉)], Efat Fathalla[4],
Esraa M. Ghourab[1], Mohamed Magdy[5], and Mohamed Eltoweissy[3]

[1] Electrical Engineering Department, Alexandria University, Alexandria, Egypt
bmokhtar@alexu.edu.eg, esraa.M.Ghourab@mena.vt.edu
[2] Computer Engineering Program, School of Engineering and Applied Sciences,
Nile University, Giza, Egypt
[3] Computer and Information Sciences, Virginia Military Institute,
Lexington, VA 24450, USA
mazab@vt.edu, eltoweissymy@vmi.edu
[4] Department of Electrical and Computer Engineering,
Old Dominion University, Norfolk, VA, USA
effat_samir@mena.vt.edu
[5] College of Computing and Information Technology,
Arab Academy for Science, Technology and Maritime Transport,
Alexandria, Egypt
mmagdy@aast.edu

Abstract. Recently, Vehicular Cloud Communication (VCC) has been gaining momentum targeting intelligent and efficient data transmission. VCC is a type of mobile ad-hoc network comprising heterogeneous vehicles sharing their resources to perform collaborative activities. In this paper, we propose a new semi-infrastructure file-browsing in order to provide Network as a service (NaaS) enabling internet-independent browsing. In our scenario, a central management platform plays the role of controlling and managing the selection of relaying vehicles supporting the source to destination file transmission procedure. Nagel-Schreckenberg rules for traffic cellular automata (CA) are used as the basis for our scenario simulation. Nagel-Schreckenberg rules simulate the behavior of a group of hypothetical vehicles moving across a highway. We study the reliability and efficiency of file transfer in such settings. Simulation results show that the number of selected relays required to establish the network highly impacts the probability of successfully sending the requested files. In addition, the distances between the selected relays influence the network throughput and the probability of network failure. Moreover, the density of relays strongly affects the overall delay that occurs due to the continuous re-transmission of the selected files among different hops.

Keywords: Vehicular Cloud Communication (VCC) ·
Nagel-Schreckenberg rules · Network as a service (NaaS) ·
Collaborative file sharing

© ICST Institute for Computer Sciences, Social Informatics and Telecommunications Engineering 2019
Published by Springer Nature Switzerland AG 2019. All Rights Reserved
X. Wang et al. (Eds.): CollaborateCom 2019, LNICST 292, pp. 698–711, 2019.
https://doi.org/10.1007/978-3-030-30146-0_47

1 Introduction

In the last few decades, substantial resources have been added to vehicles, including computational power, sensing capabilities, and data storage and analytics [1]. Currently, vehicle resources are underutilized, due, in part, to limited service and resource management models [2]. Recently, Vehicular Cloud Communications (VCC) has received significant attention as a host for various infotainment services [3]. Vehicles can communicate with other vehicles directly forming vehicle-to-vehicle communication (V2V) model, or communicate with fixed equipment next to the road, referred to as Road Side Unit (RSU) forming vehicle to infrastructure communication (V2I) model [4, 5]. Nowadays, there are many vehicle-to-vehicle (V2V) applications such as emergency braking, velocity adjustment to avoid accidents, effective transportation to avoid passage congestion, hazardous location notifications transmitted to the road/side station [6–8].

Apparently, the growth of population and the increase of traffic issues made people spend more time on the road. Browsing new files, videos, do some research, or even read articles might be a good way to expend the time on the road. However, the continuous usage of the mobile internet for browsing purposes might cost a lot, and sometimes cause higher data congestion which influences the speed of data transfer. From this context, we propose a novel local-communication-based browsing as a service for enabling internet-independent browsing among moving vehicles.

The paper is proposing an idea for Network as a Service (NaaS), that utilizes the VANETs concept to provide an entertainment services for the passengers on highways that may stay on the road for several hours with limited access to the cellular network like (4G). For simplicity the proposed scenario and the presented results, we consider a hypothetical idea using emulator. In the future extensions we will address the same scenario with real data representing actual traffic.

In this scenario, we assume a group of vehicles are moving across a long highway and have plenty of time for browsing files. The proposed approach depends on constructing network via a hierarchical management framework in order to provide data routing for multi-hops V2V communications. Our approach adopts the concept of data Storage for browsing as a Service, where the mobile communicating networked vehicles maintain different types of data that might be requested by other vehicles at real time. Therefore, there is a tremendous need in such networking environment to locate and construct reliable paths to fulfil the requests in a timely manner.

For simulation purposes, we assume a group of vehicles moving across a two lanes highway. Nagel-Schreckenberg traffic flow model for Cellular Automata (CA) is used. Nagel-Schreckenberg model is a well-known model investigates some features commonly found in real traffic problems, such as the transition between free flow and a jammed state, and shocks (due to driver overreaction) [10, 11]. By applying Nagel-Schreckenberg rules, velocities and positions of these hypothetical vehicles are calculated and updated frequently without any crashing across the simulated highway.

The proposed scenario exploits a cloud management platform, which plays the role of establishing a multi-hop network from the surrounding vehicles that act as communication relays/hops. These vehicular relays are responsible for delivering the requested file from the source vehicle to the destination of the requester vehicle.

The numbers and positions of theses selected relays are highly influencing the network and the probability of successfully receiving the requested files. Consequently, the cloud management platform should determine carefully which relays could be used for establishing the vehicular network. The appropriate selection of these relays reduces the number of hops, which definitely minimizes the chance of networking failure.

Therefore, our main contributions in this paper can be summarized as follows:

- A novel localized file sharing model on a vehicular cloud management platform exploiting semi-infrastructure V2V communication and vehicular resources; and
- Autonomous Cellular Automata (CA) model based on ad-hoc multi-hop V2V network guided by real-time dynamic vehicle location updates.

The paper organization is as follows. Section 2 illustrates the proposed semi-infrastructure system model and the networking strategy for the local offline browsing scenario. Section 3 describes the vehicular traffic flow model and the suggested methods for selecting the routing path. Section 4 presents the obtained numerical results that illustrate the influence of relay selection on the system. Finally, the paper concludes in Sect. 5.

2 V2V Communication Framework for Local WiFi-Based File-Sharing

The proposed system is composed of a user side mobile application, a cloud backend or management cloud platform, and the vehicle computational and storage device, which is assumed to be raspberry PIs controllers. In the presented scenario, we implement a mobile application to enable users traveling on the road to access the proposed offline browsing VCC service. The proposed system aims to limit the internet access for cost reduction purposes. Therefore, the internet access would be for management purposes only which are sending the request to browse and receiving the list of available file only. All heavy computations and data transfer are done locally over WiFi under the control of a cloud management platform. The aforementioned application continuously registers the user GPS location, and the available list of files for sharing. The expected amount of traffic involved in such updates is no more than a few bytes and can be neglected if compared to the heavy file transfer traffic conducted over WiFi.

We assume that all travelling vehicles are capable of bidirectional transmission and will participate in the proposed network. Further, we assume a semi-infrastructure less network, so relying on the RSU is only considered for network construction only. Cloud connection are established through RSUs to handle network management traffic only. Heavy traffic is transmitted directly between travelling cars.

Our scenario starts when one of the registered users requests to browse the list of available files on the road. The requester application sends a notification to the cloud management application on the backend. Once received, the management system selects all files available for sharing only from the vehicles within reasonable communication range to the requester. Once received, the requester will have a fixed amount of time to select the files to be downloaded. Once selected, the management system starts to select the list of vehicles that will participate as relays to construct the network between the requester and the source file vehicles. This process is depicted in details in Fig. 1. Each of these vehicles will receive a directed connection establishment instruction defining his role in the connection process between source file and the requester vehicles. The management system will monitor the connection for any interruptions or connection termination signal. In the case of connection interruption, the entire process will be repeated.

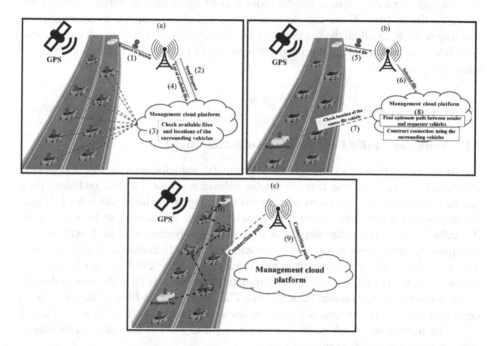

Fig. 1. Communication Network Architecture for Reliable V2V Communication

2.1 Networking Strategy

As mentioned before, the proposed system consists of a set of vehicles equipped with Raspberry PIs controllers with WiFi 802.11p modules enabling wireless communication. The hierarchical management framework in our approach consists of two main levels, which are a set of Road Side Units (RSUs) or cellular service providers and the management cloud platform. Each RSU serves a certain number of vehicles at a section of the highway. The storage capacity and the types of stored data are two related attributes defined at the cloud management side. The data communication in the proposed scenario depends on bidirectional wireless communication technologies. For communication between vehicles and RSUs and between RSUs and the cloud platform, WiFi protocols are used. While, the network topology in this scenario is defined as a linear multi-hop network that comprises a set of vehicles to form a multi-hop V2V data communication path between the sender (S) and requester (R) vehicles. The communication between vehicles can be established within the communication range defined by the IEEE 802.11p.

At the beginning, all of the online vehicles on the road send their information including their positions, velocities, and any of the required data to the cloud platform through the nearby RSUs. For the browsing process, users desire to browse send requests to browse via their mobile application to the nearby RSUs, which directly forward these notifications to the cloud management platform. After that, the cloud replies with the available files during the requested time slot. After that users send the cloud again when they choose the data files according to their preferences within the available list of files. Then, the cloud performs some calculations to determine the possible paths to fulfill all the requests sent by the vehicles. Accordingly, the cloud will send RSUs all of these recommended paths to begin establishing and monitoring the file-sharing network.

3 System Model

3.1 Vehicular Traffic Flow Cellular Automata Model

The used simulation model describes a group of vehicles moving on a highway, composed of two crossable lanes. Vehicles behavior across the road including their updated velocities and positions are calculated using a modified version of Nagel-Schreckenberg traffic flow model. The simulated road is assumed to be with length (L) cells. Each cell in that hypothetical road is equivalent to 2 m length, and is occupied by either zero, or one that represents the vehicle existence at different time instants. The model constrains that the vehicles velocity can't exceed a specified maximum velocity (Vmax). During the simulation, any vehicle (i) in the road is defined by its position (Xi) and current velocity (Vi). The empty sites in front of the ith vehicle; i.e. gap between any two consecutive vehicles is denoted by $d_i(t) = X_i + 1 - X_i - 1$ [10]. The movement of vehicle (i) from time step t to t + 1 is then defined by Nagel-Schreckenberg model four rules as follow:

$$\textbf{Acceleration:} \ V_i(t) = \min(V_i(t) + 1, V_{max}) \tag{1}$$

$$\textbf{Deceleration:} \ V_i(t) = \min(d_i(t), V_i(t)) \tag{2}$$

$$\textbf{Randomized barking probability (p):} \ V_i(t+1) = \max(V_i(t) - 1, 0) \tag{3}$$

$$\textbf{Movement:} \ X_i(t+1) = X_i(t) + V_i(t+1) \tag{4}$$

At each discrete time step $t \rightarrow t + 1$, both the position, and velocities of all the vehicles must be updated.

During the vehicles journey across the road, they might change their location from one lane to the other. The rules for updating the vehicles location with respect to the road lanes is as follows [12]:

$$\textbf{Incentive criterion:} \ d_i < \min(V_i + 1, V_{max}) \tag{5}$$

$$\text{Safety constraints: } d_{pred} > d_i \tag{6}$$

$$d_{succ} > d_{safe} \tag{7}$$

where dpred and dsucc are the gaps between the targeted vehicle (i) and the preceding vehicle and the succeeding vehicle in the target lane respectively; and dsafe is the maximum possible gap of the preceding and succeeding vehicles in the target lane. Figure 2, shows a detailed flow chart of the described traffic flow model.

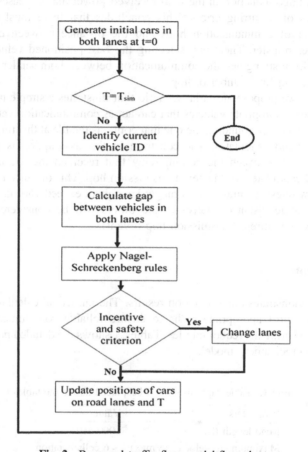

Fig. 2. Proposed traffic flow model flow chart

3.2 Path Selection Mechanism

When a certain vehicle sends a request to browse to the cloud, it starts connecting the requester vehicle (R) to the source-file vehicle (S). In case of the long distances between S and R, the network will use the surrounding vehicles to act as vehicular communication relays/hops. In our simulation model, we assume that all the surrounding vehicles around both S and R are valid online vehicles and can act as communication relays at any time.

Nevertheless, the main issue depends on what is the most appropriate vehicle to act as a communication relay/hop. The main factor affects selecting the best relay is the position of those vehicles from each other. If the selection process depends on minimizing the distance link between each relay, this might result in the usage of several communication hops, leading to increase the overall system transfer delay with slow communication.

On the other hand, selecting the vehicles positions that lead to maximize the communication link between each hop, leads to increase the Signal-Noise Ratio SNR which causes a huge reduction in the total received power and increases significantly the probabilities of occurring errors. This concludes that there must be a tradeoff between number of communication hops and the distance between every hop for successfully files transfer. Therefore, selecting the best positioned vehicles acting as relays could help in strengthen the communication between both sender and requester vehicles while using few number of hops.

In this paper we propose an initial scenario that illustrates a simple mechanism for selecting the most appropriate vehicles that can act as communication vehicular relays. All the possible relays surrounding the one that contains the file at this time instance are assumed to be valid candidates. The constrain in this assumption is related to the distance of the link between the current relay that received the file and all of the suggested valid candidates for the next transmission hop. This distance must be within the acceptable wireless communication range; i.e. cannot exceed 150 m. The relay that exists in an average distance relative to the others will be considered as the best selected one for the current transmission hop (event).

4   Evaluation

This section demonstrates our simulation results. The numerical calculations focus on the selection of most appropriate paths to ensure reliable communication between vehicles during sharing the requested files. Tables 1 shows the detailed parameters used in the Nagel-Schreckenberg model.

Table 1. Table captions should be placed above the tables.

Parameters	Value
Road length (L)	1000 cells
Maximum car velocity (Vmax)	~6 cells/iteration
Probability of parking (P)	0.6
Simulation total time	500 iteration

Our numerical results obtained for the vehicles moving across a two lanes road. The cloud start selecting all the possible paths between the source and requester vehicles, then determine the optimal routing path between them. As per the number of lanes increase, the number of existing vehicle increase leading to increase the possibilities of finding paths.

The proposed model estimates the total road capacity per each iteration. From this information, we can determine the expected computational power within the whole road at any time instant as shown in Fig. 3. As mentioned before, we assume that every vehicle on the road to be equipped with a low power controller like Raspberry Pi that is responsible for controlling the network. Therefore, in this scenario we can exploit such controllers for performing small tasks or controlling the traffic among the vehicles.

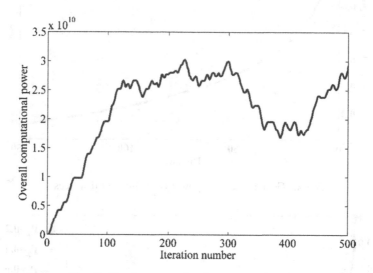

Fig. 3. Total computational power per iteration

Generally, it is well known that wireless transmission across different distances highly influences the received signal power. In fact, the relation between the received power and the transmission distance link is inversely proportional as shown in Fig. 4. The received power is exponentially reduced with increasing the transmission link between the sender and receiver. This depicts that reducing the transmission distances is better for power constrained devices.

Figure 5 depicts the influence of increasing the communication hops on the probability of successful file reception in our assumed model. This figure shows that under different circumstances of the transmission media which increases the probability of error per each link, the probability of successful transmission is highly reduced with the increase of number of hops. This concludes constructing a network using high number of hops increases the probability of networking failure, thus losing the communication between vehicles.

Moving to our proposed scenario, as mentioned previously, there is a cloud management platform, which is responsible for managing the networking between the source file vehicle S and requester vehicle R using the surrounding relays. We assume that the request to browse signal is sent to the cloud management platform from the first vehicle in the road at a certain iteration. In order to study the effect of sending files over large distances, we assume that the source file vehicle is located at end of this road.

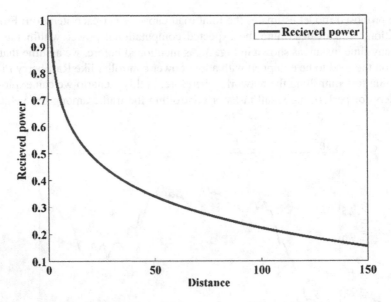

Fig. 4. General received power over different distances

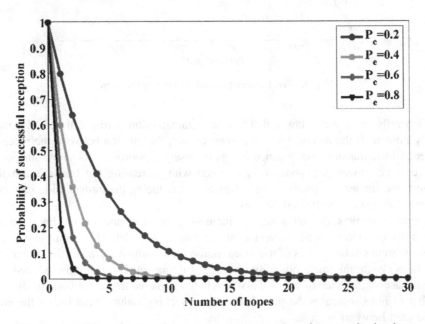

Fig. 5. Probability of successful reception versus number of communication hops

Using the previous assumption, the distance between both vehicles is found to be very long that the file cannot be sent directly. Therefore, the cloud management platform starts selecting the communication relays from the surrounding vehicles to establish the multi-hop network. Figure 6 shows three cases for the relay selection between both the requester R and sender S vehicles.

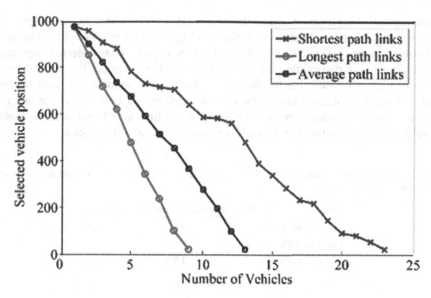

Fig. 6. Selected paths between S and R vehicles

The first case studies selecting the nearest relays from each other to reach the shortest possible link between every two consecutive relays. Minimizing the distance between the selected relays guarantees transferring higher signal power, therefore a reliable communication. However, the simulation results in this case, shows that it requires around 21 relay at different iterations to establish the required network between S and R. Despite the high throughput that can be reached in this case, the probability of transmitting the sharable file between S and R successfully is reduced as discussed before in Fig. 5.

Meanwhile, using few vehicles to share the file between the same S and R may lead to send the file at relatively longer distances. In the second case study, the selected relays between S and R are picked based on the maximum achievable distance link between the relays without exceeding 150 m before the received signal power depletes. As shown in Fig. 6, selecting relays between R and S located at relatively long distances from each other results in reducing the number of the needed hops to be only 7 relays. Reducing number of relays results in increasing the distance link between each relay, therefore the average received power of the file is highly reduced leading to increase the probability of error, as illustrated before in Fig. 5.

The above studied cases show that there is a tradeoff between number of selected relays and their positions from each other. For the best relays selection, the afore-mentioned algorithm in Sect. 3 is used. Selecting vehicles located in average distances from each other, achieves constructing the required network using less number of relays located in moderate distance from each relay. Figure 6, shows that about 11 relays could be used for establishing this optimum path between the same R and S studied in the other two cases. Table 2, shows number of required vehicles and average distance between relays for the mentioned three cases which are shortest, longest, and optimum paths. Moreover, it is found that the total delay added to the original file transferring time between both S and R, depends highly on the number of used relays in the network as shown in Table 2. We assume that every relay selected required a delayed time for re-transmitting the received file to the next node. Based on the simulation results, it's found that the first case which is the shortest link path required around 44 ms extra delay added to the overall transmission time due to the usage of large numbers of vehicles as relays. While this delay time is reduced in case of using less relays for constructing the network between both S and R vehicles.

Table 2. Comparison between the studied three cases for selecting the communication relays between S and R vehicles.

Case	Number of hops	Overall delay (ms)
Shortest path	21	44
Longest path	7	8.4
Optimal path	11	14.4

Projecting the mentioned issues across the network, Figs. 8 and 9 show how the variation of the relays number affects both the throughput and increases the probability of error per links. Throughput or network throughput is the rate of successful message delivery over a communication channel. These messages belong to be delivered over a physical or logical link, or it can pass through a certain network node. Throughput is usually measured in bits per second (bit/s or bps), and sometimes in data packets per second (p/s or pps) or data packets per time slot.

Simply, throughput is the average rate of successful message delivery over a communication channel. It is a measure of how many units of information a system can process in a given amount of time. It is applied broadly to systems ranging from various aspects of computer and network systems to organizations. The system throughput or aggregate throughput is the calculated by adding the data rates that are delivered to all nodes in a network. However, the throughput of a communication system may be affected by various factors, including the available processing power of the system components the speed with which some specific workload can be completed, and response time between a single interactive user request, receipt of the response, and the distance between the transmitter nodes.

Figure 7 presents the throughput in case of differently selected relays of our system model with respect to the signal to noise ratio (SNR). It is clearly shown that the throughput of the short selected path is the highest one compared with either the long or the optimal paths. As shown in Fig. 6, the shortest link path includes multi-vehicle relays, thereof the link reliability increased which guarantee that the data arrived correctly to the destination. On the other hand, the long path includes less number of vehicles, which means that the distance between each node is higher than the distances between nodes in the shortest one. As the distance increase the throughput decrease and the probability of error increased too. Consequently, optimizing the number of the used vehicles with respect to the distances between each relay results in aggregating the maximum achievable throughput.

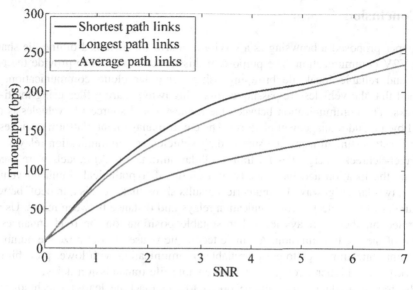

Fig. 7. Throughput Vs SNR

As mentioned in the previous section, if the actual throughput was less than the expected amount, therefore the network is effected and there is higher probability that the requested file fail to reach the destination correctly. Figure 8 shows the probability of error for the available three paths with respect to different hops invariant signal to noise ratio values. As the number of hops increases the reliability of the system increase, then the immunity to prevent errors occurrence increase too, therefore the probability of error decreases. That's why, the longest path suffers from the highest probability of error and the shortest path have an advantage of increasing the ratio of the corrected data reach to its destination node. From this context, our optimized path has an acceptable probability of error with low complexity of multi-vehicle relays.

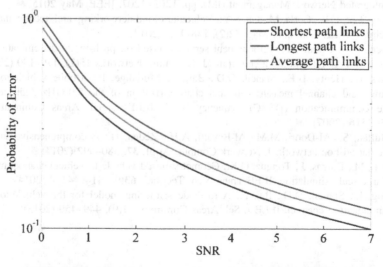

Fig. 8. Probability of error per each link for the three studied cases

5 Conclusion

This paper proposed a browsing as a service scenario for localized offline file sharing using V2V communication. The purpose of this novel service is to provide the users quick and reliable local file browsing using vehicular cloud communication. We assumed that the vehicles are passing across a highway, sharing files using multi-hop networks. The communication between the requester and source file vehicles is controlled by a cloud management platform. The cloud management platform manages the network establishment using the surrounding vehicles as communication relays.

Nagel-Schreckenberg rules for traffic cellular automata (CA) models were used to calculate the location and the velocity of a group of hypothetical simulated vehicles across a two-lane highway. The numerical results show that there is a tradeoff between the number of the selected communication relays and distance between relays. Using a moderated number of relays located in suitable positions on the road enhances the process of the file transmission. A simple technique is used to optimize the number of used communication hops to ensure reliable communication with lower probability of network failure, higher throughput and acceptable file transmission delay.

The recommendation for future work is to use machine learning techniques for predicting the best relays for the "near" optimum paths to reduce cloud management overhead.

Acknowledgements. Authors would like to express their appreciation for the "IoT and Cyber Security lab", SmartCI, Alexandria University, Egypt; for supporting and hosting the activities related to this manuscript.

References

1. Truong, N.B., Lee, G.M., Ghamri-Doudane, Y.: Software defined networking-based vehicular adhoc network with fog computing. In: 2015 IFIP/IEEE International Symposium on Integrated Network Management (IM), pp. 1202–1207. IEEE, May 2015
2. Lee, E., Lee, E.K., Gerla, M., Oh, S.Y.: Vehicular cloud networking: architecture and design principles. IEEE Commun. Mag. **52**(2), 148–155 (2014)
3. Baiocchi, A., Cuomo, F.: Infotainment services based on push-mode dissemination in an integrated VANET and 3G architecture. J. Commun. Networks **15**(2), 179–190 (2013)
4. Cheng, L., Henty, B.E., Stancil, D.D., Bai, F., Mudalige, P.: Mobile vehicle-to-vehicle narrow-band channel measurement and characterization of the 5.9 GHz dedicated short range communication (DSRC) frequency band. IEEE J. Sel. Areas Commun. **25**(8), 1501–1516 (2007)
5. Al-Sultan, S., Al-Doori, M.M., Al-Bayatti, A.H., Zedan, H.: A comprehensive survey on vehicular ad hoc network. J. Network Comput. Appl. **37**, 380–392 (2014)
6. Boban, M., Barros, J., Tonguz, O.K.: Geometry-based vehicle-to-vehicle channel modeling for large-scale simulation. IEEE Trans. Veh. Technol. **63**(9), 4146–4164 (2014)
7. Cheng, L., Stancil, D.D., Bai, F.: A roadside scattering model for the vehicle-to-vehicle communication channel. IEEE J. Sel. Areas Commun. **31**(9), 449–459 (2013)

8. Cheng, X., Yao, Q., Wen, M., Wang, C.X., Song, L.Y., Jiao, B.L.: Wideband channel modeling and intercarrier interference cancellation for vehicle-to-vehicle communication systems. IEEE J. Sel. Areas Commun. **31**(9), 434–448 (2013)

9. Dhar, P., Gupta, P.: Intelligent parking Cloud services based on IoT using MQTT protocol. In: International Conference on Automatic Control and Dynamic Optimization Techniques (ICACDOT), pp. 30–34. IEEE, September 2016

10. Bette, H.M., Habel, L., Emig, T., Schreckenberg, M.: Mechanisms of jamming in the Nagel-Schreckenberg model for traffic flow. Phys. Rev. E **95**(1), 012311 (2017)

11. Bouadi, M., Jetto, K., Benyoussef, A., El Kenz, A.: The investigation of the reentrance phenomenon in cellular automaton traffic flow model. Physica A Stat. Mech. Appl. **469**, 1–14 (2017)

12. Zhu, H.B., Lei, L., Dai, S.Q.: Two-lane traffic simulations with a blockage induced by an accident car. Physica A Stat. Mech. Appl. **388**(14), 2903–2910 (2009)

A Decentralized and Anonymous Data Transaction Scheme Based on Blockchain and Zero-Knowledge Proof in Vehicle Networking (Workshop Paper)

Wei Ou[⊠], Mingwei Deng, and Entao Luo

Hunan University of Science and Engineering, Yongzhou, China
ouwei1978430@163.com

Abstract. Data transaction in internet of vehicles is a transaction occurs between vehicle owner and data buyer. Blockchain is a new technology that brings decentralized ledger system for user, which means users could make payment without the third party. There are several projects combined internet of vehicles and Blockchain, however, none of them realize a trustworthy anonymous data transaction. In this paper, we first propose the concept of Super Nodes to guarantee data authenticity, then we construct the anonymity for the transaction base on *zero-knowledge Succinct Non-interactive Argument of knowledge* (zk-SNARKs) and DAP from Zerocash. Moreover, a smart contract is deployed for mutual benefits. Simulation experiment shows this scheme is practical.

Keywords: Internet of vehicles · Blockchain · Zero knowledge · Smart contract

1 Introduction

In recent years, with continuous growth of car ownership, road carrying capacity has reached saturation in many cities, and traffic safety, travel efficiency, and environmental protection have become increasingly prominent. As an important field of in-depth integration of informatization and industrialization, internet of vehicles (IoV) is of great significance to promote integration and upgrade of the automobile, transportation, information and communication industries, and reshape of relevant industrial ecology and value chain systems.

Blockchain is a new technology that first proposed by bitcoin [1]. It describes a decentralized ledger without participation of the third party. In such ledger, it cannot be tampered once data is confirmed. That is achieved by a novel consensus mechanism, called Proof of Work (PoW), and timestamp server. PoW describes a safe accounting

Supported by the construct program of applied characteristic discipline in Hunan University of Science and Engineering.

X. Wang et al. (Eds.): CollaborateCom 2019, LNICST 292, pp. 712–726, 2019.
https://doi.org/10.1007/978-3-030-30146-0_48

system that solves the Byzantine Problem by introducing a computing power competition of distributed nodes to ensure data consistency and ledger consensus. The node who wins the competition will broadcast a "block" in whole network, which contains all transactions he collects and a timestamp to avoid double spending. After more than 10 years of development, consensus mechanisms in Blockchain has from the beginning of a single POW into Proof of gaining (PoS), Delegated Proof of Stack (DPoS), Practical Byzantine Fault Tolerance (PBFT), and other common mechanism occurring together. Moreover, Ethereum introduced smart contracts for Blockchain in 2014, which are Blockchain-based programs that directly control digital assets [2]. Concretely, a smart contract is a computer program that automatically enforces contract terms, is deployed on a shared, replicated ledger. It could maintain its status, control its assets and respond to incoming external information or assets. The digital form means that the contract has to be written into computer-readable code. As long as the participations agree, the rights and obligations established by the smart contract are performed by a computer or computer network. And all these agreements and its realization would be recorded in Blockchain.

There are several projects that combined IoV and Blockchain, such as Smartcarchain and Carblock. They expect that Blockchain and its decentralized characteristic could return the data ownership to data producer, general speaking, the vehicle owners, which means they can freely dispose those data that collected by their vehicles. It gives users an incentive to collect more data. And the more data users collect, the more valuable data are. Automotive and transportation companies are all interested in these data, because they can be analyzed to build better, more targeted products and services, thus earning more profits. This kind of demand for data makes data transaction important. Carblock proposed a data transaction method through smart contract, eliminating the participation of the third party [3]. However, such a method requires buyer to deploy two smart contracts for verifying data and transaction. That may not convenient to a buyer.

Moreover, the anonymity is a feature that users care about. In 2014, based on Bitcoin system, Zcash [4] proposes a new scheme to make an anonymous payment in blockchain system by using zero knowledge proof. This scheme realizes strong anonymity for a payment in Blockchain. It brings us to do research in anonymity of data transaction in IoV, however, there has been no relevant research so far.

In this paper we propose a decentralized anonymous data transaction scheme for vehicle networking based on Blockchain. This scheme allows a data buyer to buy the data that collected by vehicle sensors from a seller. Concretely, it achieves two goals: (i) decentralization: there is no third party in our transaction; (ii) anonymity: transaction participants and relevant information (including transfer amount) are invisible to others; To do this, we provide a construction of the scheme and design a simulation experiment to test its performance.

The rest of this paper is organized as follow. Section 2 is an overview of our scheme, we describe the concept of *Super Nodes* and main steps of our scheme; Sect. 3 provides technical background including *zk-SNARKs* and DAP scheme; Sect. 4 gives the formal construction of our scheme; Sect. 5 shows the result of simulation experiment; last, we summarize our contribution and discuss the future work.

2 Overview

Our scheme is an extension based on *Zerocash*, which is a blockchain that supports anonymous payment. It describes such a system: every node in the system could deposit their base currency (e.g., bitcoin) in an escrow to mint a coin in *Zerocash* ledger, this new coin is bound to the address public key of the node. The minting process will generate some secret values, only someone who knows the corresponding address private key and some secret values can use it; to use the coin, the node who owns the address private key and the secret values will broadcast a transaction: I "destroy" my old coin to mint two new coins that one of them or both of them are bound to the target address public key, which is bound to the receiver, and the total value of two new coins is equal to the value of the old coin; besides, in order to avoid additional infrastructure and assumption, the transaction contains a ciphertext of the secret values of new coin, which is encrypted by receiver's encryption public key; lastly, the coin receiver scans the transaction in the ledger and use his encryption private key to decrypt the ciphertext until he finds the transaction for him. Then, he can use the coin with his address private key and the secret values he gets from the ledger. This system achieve anonymity by introducing *zk-SNARKs*, which is a cryptology that allows anyone check a proof of a statement in a short time (we show details in Sect. 3.1).

We realize such a system could use for the data transaction in vehicle networking. Every buyer and seller can join such a system by deposit any digital currency to an escrow, thus achieving the goal of anonymous transaction. However, this transaction is just a currency transfer, it only meets the requirement for sellers rather than mutual benefit. Namely, this system cannot guarantee that a buyer obtains the data he wants. To solve the problems, we construct the concept of *Super Nodes*.

2.1 Super Nodes

Super Nodes are some nodes that run by some trusted third party, they have all function of normal nodes such as transaction broadcasting, transaction check and consensus reaching, meanwhile they also have some special functions.

- **Data checking and storage.** A vehicle owner could upload data to the *Super Nodes* through networking protocol interface from corresponding vehicle sensor, note that these data are encrypted by data encryption public key that the hardware generated, which guarantee that the *Super nodes* can't "see" these data. When a *Super Node* receive the data, it will verify its authenticity by checking if they come from vehicle sensors, then storages and compresses them if verify success. This function enables *Super Node* to become a de-centralized server, and data in server are authentic.
- **dataID generating.** After the process of data check and storage, every *Super Node* will generate a *dataID* for the data and a cyphertext of data uploader's address public key (encrypted by an encryption public key). *dataID* is a hash of corresponding data and encrypted by the uploader's encryption public key (note this is a key pair different from data encryption key), due to that every *Super Node* processes the same procedures, different *Super Node* will generate same *dataID* if they

received same row data. Consequently, they can make a consensus through Practical Byzantine fault tolerance [5] among all *Super Nodes*. After that, the *dataID* is broadcasted to whole Blockchain system, to make the consensus that append it in the public ledger. In this way, every buyer could verify the *dataID* for confirming the authenticity of data by simply checking the public ledger.

- **Data retrieval.** Anyone in the system can get the encryption of data by the corresponding *dataID* from *Super Nodes*. However, only the one who owns data encryption private key could get the origin data. Note that there is no constructed of private communication channel such as that a seller sends the data to a buyer individually, therefore we don't have to add additional infrastructures or worry about being eavesdropped.

2.2 Steps

With *Super Nodes,* which we show function component in Fig. 1, a seller could upload his data, and a buyer could confirm the authenticity and get the data. However, this is still not enough to make an anonymous data transaction, because the data is encrypted by the seller's data encryption public key, the buyer must to know the data encryption private key for getting the data.

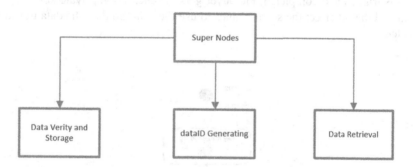

Fig. 1. Function of *Super Nodes*

So far, we have converted the issue that money to data to the issue that money to private key. So how can we make the money-to-key transaction in Blockchain? We find a solution: *Hashed-Timelock Contract (HLTC)* [6]. *HLTC* is a technology used for cross-chain payment. It requires the payer to set a smart contract about a cryptographic puzzle (usually is a hash value of sha256 function), anyone trigger the contract and solve the puzzle (e.g., support the preimage of a hash value) could get the money that the payer deposit to an escrow. The key point of *HLTC* is make sure only the recipient knows the answer of the puzzle.

With *Super Nodes* and *HLTC*, we can finally extend *Zerocash* system to make an anonymous data transaction. Here, we show main steps of data transaction; algorithms construction is in Sect. 4.

Step1: Info Sending. If a buyer wants to buy a seller's data, the seller should firstly send some information to the buyer. Which including *(i) dataID*; *(ii)* hash of data decryption private key. The buyer checks *dataID* in the ledger. If it does exist in the ledger, the buyer confirms the authenticity of data. But he cannot get the data immediately, because the data is encrypted and he don't know the decryption key. The hash is a required item for smart contract deployment after coin transfer.

Step2: Anonymous Payment. The buyer now needs deposit corresponding amount of digital currency for data in escrow to mint a coin A. After that, he mints another coin B that is bound to the receiver's address public key and transfer the value of coin A to coin B. Next, we modify the origin scheme of *Zerocash*: we broadcast the transfer of coin value but we don't broadcast the ciphertext of the secret values of coin B.

Step3: Smart Contract. So far, the seller still doesn't get the coin because he doesn't know the secret value and the buyer doesn't get the data because he doesn't know the data encryption private key. So, the buyer first encrypts the secret value of coin B by the receiver's encryption public key. Then, the buyer creates such a hash lock smart contract using hash that he obtains in Step1: if someone can support the pre-image of the hash, which is the data encryption private key, he will get the ciphertext of the secret values.

This is an overview of our construction, we show sketch in Fig. 2. If the smart contract is trigged and completed, the buyer gets the encryption private key to decrypt the data and the seller get the secret values to use the coin. So that, the data transaction completed.

Fig. 2. Steps of our data transaction

3   Background

3.1   zk-SNARKs

We used the zero-knowledge Succinct Non-interactive Argument of Knowledge (zk-SNARK) as our main cryptographic technology to make an anonymous data transaction in this paper. In this section, we will give three components of zk-SNARKs and we refer the reader to [7, 8] for concrete protocol and implementation.

Arithmetic Circuit

An arithmetic circuit is consisted of wires with specific values and *bilinear gate* with only addition and multiplication. Given a finite field $\mathbb{F}$, an $\mathbb{F}$-*arithmetic circuit* takes input that are element in $\mathbb{F}$, and its gates output elements in $\mathbb{F}$. Considering we have an input $x \in \mathbb{F}^n$ and an auxiliary input $a \in \mathbb{F}^h$, we have the definition of arithmetic circuit satisfiability that analogous to the boolean case as follows:

Definition 3.1. *The circuit satisfaction problem of a circuit* $C: \mathbb{F}^n \times \mathbb{F}^h \rightarrow \mathbb{F}^l$ *with bilinear gate is defined by the relation* $\mathcal{R}_C = \{(x, a) \in \mathbb{F}^n \times \mathbb{F}^h : C(x, a) = 0^l\}$; *and its language is* $\mathcal{L}_C = \{x \in \mathbb{F}^n : \exists a \in \mathbb{F}^h, C(x, a) = 0^l\}$.

Note that a is what we want to obtain in zk-SNARKs, which we called *witness*.

Quadratic Arithmetic Program

zk-SNARKs leverages quadratic arithmetic programs (QAPs) [9] to converted any arithmetic circuit to corresponding sets of polynomials. The main idea of QAPs is that converting circuit to three basic sets of polynomials and a target polynomial, these polynomials must meet such a fact: there is a product of three basic polynomials sets and some coefficients could divide the target polynomial. We give the formal definition of a QAPs below:

Definition 3.2. *A quadratic arithmetic program of size m and degree d over* $\mathbb{F}$ *is a tuple* $(\vec{A}, \vec{B}, \vec{C}, Z)$, *where* $\vec{A}, \vec{B}, \vec{C}$ *are three vectors, each of them is m + 1 polynomials in* $\mathbb{F}^{\leq d-1}[z]$, *and* $Z \in \mathbb{F}[z]$ *has degree exactly d.*

And as we mentioned above, a QAPs induces a satisfaction problem:

Definition 3.3. *The* **satisfaction problem** *of a size-m QAP* $(\vec{A}, \vec{B}, \vec{C}, Z)$ *is the relation* $\mathcal{R}_{(\vec{A}, \vec{B}, \vec{C}, Z)}$ *of pairs* (x, s) *such that (i)* $x \in \mathbb{F}^n$, $s \in \mathbb{F}^m$, *and* $n \leq m$; *(ii)* $x_i = s_i$ *for* $i \in [n]$(*i.e., x extends s*); *(iii) the polynomial* $Z(z)$ *divided the following one:*
$$\left(A_0(z) + \sum_{i=1}^{m} s_i A_i(z)\right) \cdot \left(B_0(z) + \sum_{i=1}^{m} s_i B_i(z)\right) - \left(C_0(z) + \sum_{i=1}^{m} s_i C_i(z)\right).$$ *We denote by* $\mathcal{L}_{(\vec{A}, \vec{B}, \vec{C}, Z)}$ *the language of* $\mathcal{R}_{(\vec{A}, \vec{B}, \vec{C}, Z)}$.

So far, we have the definition of arithmetic circuit and QAPs. Due to that the QAPs is a result of encoding arithmetic circuit, we can combine the Definitions 3.1, 3.2 and 3.3 to obtain a complete definition of QAP:

Definition 3.4. *A QAP Q over field* $\mathbb{F}$ *consist of three sets of m + 1 polynomials* $\vec{A} = \{a_k(x)\}$, $\vec{B} = \{b_k(x)\}$, $\vec{C} = \{c_k(x)\}$, *for* $k \in \{0 \ldots m\}$, *and a target polynomials* $t(x)$. *Suppose F is a function that takes as input n elements of* $\mathbb{F}$ *and output n' elements, for a total of* $N = n + n'$ *I/O elements. Then we say that Q computes F if:* $(s_1, \ldots, s_N) \in \mathbb{F}^N$ *is* *valid assignment of F's inputs and outputs, if and only if there exist coefficients* $(s_{N+1}, \ldots, s_m)$ *such that* $t(x)$ *divides* $p(x)$, *where:*

$$p(x) = \left(a_0(x) + \sum_{k=1}^{m} s_k \cdot a_k(x)\right) \cdot \left(b_0(x) + \sum_{k=1}^{m} s_k \cdot b_k(x)\right) - \left(c_0(x) + \sum_{k=1}^{m} s_k \cdot c_k(x)\right).$$

In other words, there must exist some polynomial $h(x)$ *such that* $h(x) \cdot t(x) = p(x)$. *The size of* Q *is* m, *and the degree is the degree of* $t(x)$.

Verifiable Computation (VC)

A verifiable computation (VC) [10] for $\mathbb{F}$-*arithmetic circuit* $C: \mathbb{F}^n \times \mathbb{F}^h \to \mathbb{F}^l$ allows a prover to generate a non-interactive proofs for the language $\mathcal{L}_C$ using the public parameters that generated by VC, and anyone can use another generated public parameter to verify these proofs. Moreover, the verification process only requires a short time. Concretely, a VC contains three set of polynomial-time algorithms: KeyGen(), Compute() and Verify(). Below we defined the three algorithms:

- $(EK_F, VK_F) \leftarrow \text{KeyGen}(F, 1^\lambda)$: *The public key generation algorithm takes the function F, which is exact* $\mathbb{F}$-*arithmetic circuit C, and a security parameter* λ *as inputs; Then it output a public evaluation key* EK_F *and a public verification key* VK_F.
- $(y, \pi) \leftarrow \text{Compute}(EK_F, x)$: *The proof computation algorithm takes evaluation key* EK_F *and x to output* $y \leftarrow F(x)$ *and a non-interactive proof* π *for y's correctness.*
- $b \leftarrow \text{Verify}(VK_F, x, \pi, y)$: *The proof verification algorithm takes verification key* VK_F, *x and a proof* π *as input. It outputs* $b = 1$ *if* $y \leftarrow F(x)$.

The three algorithms defined above are main part of VC scheme. Note that this system that we defined is actually not public verifiable, the verification key VK_F should be hidden in some *designated verifier* otherwise the scheme is vulnerable to attack. To avoid such issue, we introduce the concept of **Zero-knowledge Verifiable computation**, which required the verifier learns nothing about the prover's input beyond the output of computation. Concretely, we change the proof computation algorithm Compute() and the proof verification algorithm Verify().

- $(\pi) \leftarrow \text{Compute}(EK_F, x, a)$ *The proof computation algorithm takes evaluation key* EK_F *and* $(x, a) \in \mathcal{R}_C$ *(see Definition 3.1) as input to output a non-interactive proof* π *for the statement* $x \in \mathcal{L}_C$.
- $1 \leftarrow \text{Verify}(VK_F, x, \pi)$ *The proof verification algorithm takes verification key* VK_F, *x and a proof* π *as input to outputs* $b = 1$ *if it is convinced that* $x \in \mathcal{L}_C$.

With this change, *evaluation key* EK_F *and verification key* VK_F could be public in system, thus allowing anyone to check the *proof* π. That is a very applicable scheme for blockchain system, because it allows every node in the system to check a transaction and thus making consensus in the chain. Such a scheme also referred to as a non-interactive zero-knowledge proof. From these definitions, we give the properties that zk-VC scheme should satisfy:

- **Correctness.** *For any function F, and any input u to F, a honest prover could always convince the verifier that he knows the witness a. Namely, if we run* $(EK_F, VK_F) \leftarrow \text{KeyGen}(F, 1^\lambda)$ *and* $(\pi) \leftarrow \text{Compute}(EK_F, x, a)$, *we will always get* $1 \leftarrow \text{Verify}(VK_F, x, \pi)$.

- **Security.** For any function F and any probabilistic polynomial-time adversary $\mathcal{A}$, $\Pr[(\hat{u}, \hat{\pi}) \leftarrow \mathcal{A}(EF_K, VK_F) : \mathrm{x} \notin \mathcal{L}_C \text{ and } 1 = \text{Verify}(VK_F, \hat{u}, \hat{\pi})] \leq \text{negl}(\lambda)^1$.
- **Efficiency.** KeyGen() is assumed to be a one-time operation whose cost is amortized over many calculations, however, we required a cheaper Verify() than evaluating F.

3.2 Dap

The main payment scheme used in this paper is *Decentralized Anonymous Payment* (DAP) scheme, which is proposed by *Zerocash*. As we described in Sect. 2, this is a scheme making anonymity in a payment. Here, we provide basic components of DAP. We refer the interested reader to [4] for complete scheme.

DAP scheme is consisted of a tuple of polynomial-time algorithms: Setup, CreateAddress, Mint, Pour, Receive.

- **Setup.** This algorithm is executed by a trusted third party. It requires to input a security parameter, then it will output a public parameter pp, which includes the *public knowledge* of zk-SNARKs (see Sect. 3.1).
- **CreateAddress.** This algorithm is executed by users in the system. Each user can generate at least one pair (a_{pk}, a_{sk}), where $a_{pk} = (\text{addr}_{pk}, \text{pk}_{enc})$, and $a_{sk} = (\text{addr}_{sk}, \text{sk}_{enc})$. Concretely, addr_{sk} is a random number, and $\text{addr}_{pk} := \text{PRF}_{a_{sk}}^{\text{addr}}(0)^2$, they are an address key pair bound to the user; Encryption key pair $(\text{pk}_{enc}, \text{sk}_{enc})$ is generated based on a *key-private encryption scheme* [11], it is used for encryption. Note a user may generate any number of key pairs.
- **Mint.** This algorithm is executed by a payer. It requires to input public parameter pp, a coin value v, and a destination address public key addr_{pk}, then it will outputs a coin c and a TX_{mint}. Here, we give concrete steps to mint a coin (*i*) the algorithm generates three random value ρ, r, s; (*ii*) the algorithm compute $\text{sn} := \text{PRF}_{a_{sk}}^{\text{sn}}(\rho)$, $k := \text{COMM}_r(\text{addr}_{pk} \| \rho)^3$ and $\text{cm} := \text{COMM}_s(v \| k)$. (*iii*) the algorithm outputs the minting result: a coin $c := (\text{addr}_{pk}, v, \rho, r, s, \text{cm})$ and a mint transaction $TX_{mint} = (v, k, s, \text{cm})$. Note that anyone could verify if cm is a coin commitment of a coin with value v by checking that $\text{cm} := \text{COMM}_s(v \| k)$ is equal to cm and no one can discern the coin owner or a serial number sn, because they don't know the address key addr_{pk} and the secret value ρ. As before, $TX_{mint} = (v, k, s, \text{cm})$ is added in ledger only by the payer deposits the correct amount of basecoin to escrow.
- **Pour.** This algorithm is executed by a payer to spend a coin. This is an operation to transfer the values of a set of input coins to another set of new output coins, the total value of input coins is equal to the total values of the output coins. Suppose a payer

---

[1] Negligible function.

[2] PRF() is a pseudorandom function.

[3] COMM() is a statistically-hiding non-interactive commitment scheme, which satisfy the verifiability: given $c := \text{COMM}_r(s)$, one who knows r and s can verify that $\text{COMM}_r(s)$ is equal to c.

with address key pair $\left(\text{addr}_{\text{pk}}^{old}, \text{addr}_{\text{sk}}^{old}\right)$ wants to pay the coin $c^{old} = \left(\text{addr}_{\text{pk}}^{old}, v^{old},\right.$ $\left.\rho^{old}, r^{old}, s^{old}, \text{cm}^{old}\right)$ to a recipient. To do this, the payer produces two new coins c_1^{new} and c_2^{new} targeted at two address public key $\text{addr}_{\text{pk},1}^{new}$ and $\text{addr}_{\text{pk},2}^{new}$ with the value meet $v_1^{new} + v_2^{new} = v^{old}$ (note one of them is recipient's address public key and another may give value of 0 for hiding the concrete transfer amount); Take inputs as public parameter pp, the Merkle-tree root rt, an old coin c^{old}, an old addresses secret key $\text{addr}_{\text{sk}}^{old}$, a authentication path path_{old} from cm^{old} to root rt, two new values v_1^{new} and v_2^{new}, two new addresses public key $\text{addr}_{\text{pk},1}^{new}$ and $\text{addr}_{\text{pk},1}^{new}$, and some transaction information. For each $i \in \{1, 2\}$, the algorithm proceeds as follows: (i) the algorithm generates three random value $\rho_i^{new}, r_i^{new}, s_i^{new}$; (ii) the algorithm computes $k_i^{new} := \text{COMM}_{r_i^{new}}\left(\text{addr}_{\text{pk},i}^{new} \| \rho_i^{new}\right)$, $c_i^{new} := \left(\text{addr}_{\text{pk},i}^{new}, v_i^{new}, \rho_i^{new}, r_i^{new}, s_i^{new}, \text{cm}_i^{new}\right)$. (iii) the algorithm computes a zk-SNARKs proof π for the following NP statement:

"*Given a Merkle-tree root* rt, *serial number* sn^{old}, *and coin commitment* cm_1^{new}, cm_2^{new}, *I know coins* c^{old}, c_1^{new}, c_2^{new}, *and secret key* $\text{addr}_{\text{sk}}^{old}$ *meet:*

a. *The coins satisfy: for* c^{old} *it holds that* $k^{old} = \text{COMM}_{r^{old}}\left(\text{addr}_{\text{pk}}^{old} \| \rho^{old}\right)$ *and* $\text{cm}^{old} = \text{COMM}_{s^{old}}\left(v^{old} \| k^{old}\right)$; *Similarly for* c_1^{new} *and* c_2^{new}.
b. *The address secret key matches the public key:* $\text{addr}_{\text{pk}}^{old} = \text{PRF}_{\text{addr}_{\text{sk}}^{old}}^{\text{addr}}(0)$.
c. *The serial number is computed correctly:* $\text{sn}^{old} := \text{PRF}_{\text{addr}_{\text{sk}}^{old}}^{\text{sn}}\left(\rho^{old}\right)$.
d. *The coin commitment* cm^{old} *appears as a leaf of a Merkle-tree with root* rt.
e. *The values added up:* $v_1^{new} + v_2^{new} = v^{old}$.

With all these processes, the algorithm outputs a transaction $\text{TX}_{pour} = \left(\text{rt}, \text{sn}^{old},\right.$ $\left.\text{cm}_1^{new}, \text{cm}_2^{new}, \text{info}, \pi, C_1, C_2\right)$, where C_1 is a ciphertext that is the encryption of the plaintext $\left(v_1^{new}, \rho_1^{new}, r_1^{new}, s_1^{new}\right)$ under pk_{enc} (similar to C_2); two new coins c_1^{new}, c_2^{new}. As before, TX_{pour} is rejected by the ledger if the serial number sn^{old} appears in a previous TX_{pour}, therefore avoiding double spending. Note to use a coin c_i, the payer must know following required items: value v_i, three rand ρ_i, r_i, s_i and the corresponding address secret key addr_{sk}.

- **Receive.** This algorithm is executed by the recipient. Take a public parameter pp, a pair of recipient key $(a_{\text{pk}}, a_{\text{sk}})$, and the current ledger, the algorithm scan the transaction TX_{pour} in the ledger to find and decrypt the ciphertext C_i (using his sk_{enc}), thus obtaining the required secret values to use the coin.

Anonymity of DAP is mainly reflected in pour transaction, because of zk-SNARKs, the payer doesn't have to reveal the identity of both sides, transaction amount and account balance in public. Moreover, the buyer can not trace the coin flow of the coin he mints in pour transaction, because he doesn't know the serial number of the coin.

4 Construction of Decentralized and Anonymous Data Transaction Scheme

In this section, we show how to construct a decentralized and anonymous data transaction scheme using DAP and smart contract. First, we define some basic notion and notation for what we will use in the construction. Then, we will use them to construct our algorithms.

4.1 Basic Notion and Notation

Payer. A *payer* is a node in Blockchain. We use *payer* to denote a data buyer. Namely, the side that pays in payment. In construction, we sometimes use *he* or *him* for convenience.

Recipient. A *recipient* is a node in Blockchain. We use *recipient* to denote a data seller. Namely, the side that receives in payment. In construction, we sometimes use *she* or *her* for convenience.

dataID. A *dataID* is generated by *Super Nodes* from data. Concretely, a *dataID* is obtained by hashing the data and encrypt the result with uploader's *encryption public key*.

ID. It contains a *dataID* and a cyphertext of uploader's *address public key*.

Address. A user may join the system whenever they generate an *address key pair* $(addr_{pk}, addr_{sk})$ and publishes the public key $addr_{pk}$ in the system. The private key $addr_{sk}$ is keep by the user to receive the coins sent to him. Note that a user can generate any number of *address key pairs*.

Coins. A coin c contains a *coin commitment* cm, a *coin value* v, a *serial number* s, and a *coin address* $addr_{pk}$. cm is a string generated by some cryptographic function (see Sect. 3.2) and it will be appended to the ledger if coin c is minted; v is the denomination of c, namely, the amount of the basecoins (e.g., bitcoin); s is a unique string binding with the c to avoid double spending; $addr_{pk}$ is the *address public key* of coin owner, representing who owns c.

Ledger. Our scheme is based on a digital currency system such as Bitcoin. Here, we refer to basecoin as *Basecoin*. Our ledger L is a sequence of transaction and it's append-only. Moreover, it contains transaction of *Basecoin* and two types of new transaction.

λ. It represents an adjustable security parameter to produce a set of global public parameter pp.

Data Encryption Key. It contains (E_{pk}, E_{sk}), where E_{pk} is *data encryption public key* used for encrypting the data, and E_{sk} is *data encryption secret key* used for decrypting the data.

Encryption Key. It is a key pair generated by *key-private encryption scheme*. It consists of *encryption public key* pk_{enc} and *encryption private key* sk_{enc}.

Hash. We use *hash* to denote the hash function Hash256.

New Transaction

- *Mint.* A mint transaction TX_{mint} is a statement: a coin with commitment cm and value v is minted. It contains a *coin commitment* cm, a coin value v and two value k and s. Namely, $TX_{mint} =: (cm, \ v, \ k, \ s)$.
- *Pour.* A pour transaction TX_{pour} is a statement: an old coin is be "destroyed", two new coins is be minted and the value of old coin is transferred to the two new coins. It contains a Merkle tree root rt, the serial number of old coin sn^{old}, two new *coin commitment* cm_1^{new} and cm_2^{new}, and a proof π that prove the transaction initiator owns the old coin, a public value. Note that at least one of cm_1^{new} and cm_2^{new} is bound to the recipient's address public key and the total value of the two coins should equal to old coin. Namely, $TX_{pour} =: \left(rt, \ sn^{old}, cm_1^{new}, cm_2^{new}, \pi, info\right)$.

List. For given time T, there are three lists beyond the ledger as public knowledge:

- $IDList_T$. This is a list for all *ID* generated by *Super Nodes*.
- $cmList_T$. This is a list for all coin commitments appearing in mint and pour transactions in L_T
- $snList_T$. This is a list for all serial numbers appearing in pour transaction in L_T.

Note that *ID* contained in *IDList_T* are not only required to make consensus in the *Super Nodes*, but also in whole blockchain system.

Merkle Tree Overs Coin Commitment and dataID. For given time T, there is an $Tree_T$ over $cmList_T$ and rt_T is its root. Besides, we use $Path_i$ to denote a valid authentication path for leaf cm_i with respect to rt_T.

4.2 Algorithms Construction

Our scheme is a tuple of polynomial-time algorithms (GenerateID, GetID, VerifyID, Setup, CreateAddress, Mint, Pour, VerifyTransaction, Recieve) and a smart contract. The algorithm details of DAP have showed in Sect. 3.2, here we only briefly summarize.

- $(dataID, C_{pk}) \leftarrow$ GenerateID$(data, addr_{pk}, pk_{enc})$. On input a data set, a $addr_{pk}$ and a pk_{enc}, the algorithm computes the result of $hash(data)$ and then outputs *dataID*, which is a ciphertext that is encrypted with pk_{enc} on the result, and C_{pk} is a ciphertext that $addr_{pk}$ encrypted using pk_{enc}.
- $(dataID) \leftarrow$ GetID$(IDList_T, addr_{pk}, sk_{enc})$. On input an *IDList_T*, a $addr_{pk}$ and a sk_{enc}, this algorithm will decrypt every C_{pk} in *IDList_T* using sk_{enc} to outputting *dataID* that corresponding to his $addr_{pk}$.
- $(b1) \leftarrow$ VerifyID$(dataID, IDList_T)$. On input a *dataID* and a *IDList_T*, the algorithm will scan *IDList_T*, and outputs $b1 = 1$ if the *dataID* appears in the *IDList_T*.
- $(pp) \leftarrow$ Setup(λ). On input a security parameter λ, the algorithm outputs a public parameter pp, which contains public parameter for zk-SNARKS and some pseudorandom values.

- $(\mathrm{addr}_{pk}, \mathrm{addr}_{sk}) \leftarrow \text{CreateAddress}(pp)$. On input the public parameter pp, algorithm outputs an *address key pair* addr_{pk} and addr_{sk}.
- $(c, \mathrm{TX}_{mint}) \leftarrow \text{Mint}(pp, v, \mathrm{addr}_{pk})$. On input the public parameter pp, coin value v and destination *address public key* addr_{pk}, the algorithm outputs a new coin c and a *mint* transaction TX_{mint}.
- $(c_1^{new}, c_2^{new}, \mathrm{TX}_{pour}) \leftarrow \text{Pour}(pp, \mathrm{rt}, c^{old}, \mathrm{addr}_{sk}^{old}, \mathrm{path}_{old}, \mathrm{cm}^{old}, v_1^{new}, v_2^{new}, \mathrm{addr}_{pk,1}^{new},$ $\mathrm{addr}_{pk,2}^{new}, \mathrm{info})$. On input a public parameter pp, a Merkle tree root rt, a coin c^{old}, an *address public key* addr_{pk}^{old}, a authentication path path_{old} from commitment cm^{old} to root rt, two coin values v_1^{new} and v_2^{new}, two new *address pubic key* $\mathrm{addr}_{pk,1}^{new}$ and $\mathrm{addr}_{pk,2}^{new}$, and some transaction string info, the algorithm outputs two new coin c_1^{new}, c_2^{new} and a *pour* transaction TX_{pour}.
- $(b2) \leftarrow \text{VerifyTransaction}(pp, \mathrm{TX}_{mint}/\mathrm{TX}_{pour}, L)$. On input a public parameter pp, a TX_{mint} or a TX_{pour} and a ledger L_T in time T, the algorithm outputs $b2 = 1$ if the transaction is valid.
- $(\mathrm{coinsSet}) \leftarrow \text{Recieve}(pp, \mathrm{addr}_{pk}, \mathrm{addr}_{sk}, L_T)$. On input a public parameter pp, an *address key pair* $(\mathrm{addr}_{pk}, \mathrm{addr}_{sk})$ and a ledger L_T in time T, the algorithm outputs a set of coins coinsSet.

4.3 Smart Contract Construction

Our smart contract is a *HLTC*. In Pour, four random values $(v_i^{new}, \rho_i^{new}, r_i^{new}, s_i^{new})$ are generated for a new coin c_i^{new}, they are required items to use the coin (another required item is addr_{sk}, see algorithm Pour). However, in our algorithm, we didn't reveal them to recipient or public. Which means even if a TX_{pour} was broadcast by *payer* and verified, the *recipient* still can't get the *coin* that *payer* mints for *her*, because the *payer* didn't get data. Therefore, after a TX_{pour} was broadcast, *payer* deploys a smart contract in blockchain to get data. Here, we give the steps of the smart contract deployment.

1. *Payer* input two initial values: $hash(\mathrm{E}_{sk})$, C_v, addr_{pk}. Where $hash(\mathrm{E}_{sk})$ is a hash value of the data's *data encryption private key* E_{sk}, *payer* obtains it before the payment (see Sect. 2); C_v is a ciphertext of the four random value $(v_i^{new}, \rho_i^{new}, r_i^{new}, s_i^{new})$ that generated by *payer* in Pour and encrypt by pk_{enc} of *recipient*.
2. *Payer* deploys such a contract: if someone could provide a preimage of $hash(\mathrm{E}_{sk})$, the provider will be return C_v; the preimage (i.e., E_{sk}) will be encrypted by pk_{enc} of *payer*, and be sent to *payer*.

This smart contract be triggered when someone input a preimage of $hash(\mathrm{E}_{sk})$, namely, E_{sk}. Obviously, because of the property of hash function, only *recipient* can give the preimage, which means only *recipient* could get C_v, and only *recipient* could decrypt C_v, because *she* is the only one who owns the decryption key sk_{enc}. Meanwhile, E_{sk} is sent to payer after encryption. So far, payer gets *data encryption private key* E_{sk}, *he* can download the encryption data from Super Nodes, and uses E_{sk} to decrypt it, thus obtaining the row data; As for *recipient*, with C_v, *she* can get the secret values by decrypt C_v using *her* sk_{enc}, in this way, recipient finally get the coin that *payer* mints for *her*, because *she* has all required items: four random values and $addr_{sk}$ targeted at the coin. We show the flow of smart contract in Fig. 3.

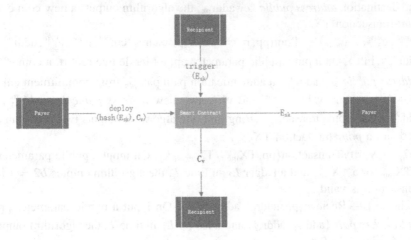

Fig. 3. Smart contract

We use asymmetric encryption in our smart contract to ensure safety. As we describe above, all message be returned and sent are encrypt by the receiver' encryption public key, which means even if the message is eavesdropped by a probabilistic polynomial-time adversary, this adversary has probability Pr[successful decryption] ≤ negl.

5 Experiment

To test validity of our scheme, we design several experiments. First, we test the basic algorithm of our scheme, including CreateAddress, Mint, Pour, smart contract and GenerateID. Second, we give three different size of data to test the performance of GenerateID algorithm, because this algorithm's performance with respect to the size of data. Our code is written in java, and all of our experiments were conducted on same machine (Inter Core i5-6300 @ 2.30 GHz with 12 GB of RAM).

Table 1 shows performance of specific algorithms in our scheme, and Table 2 shows performance of correspondent algorithms in Zcash. Similar to Zerocash, we didn't maintain the Merkle tree in our experiment, because that is not responsibility to our algorithm. And note we generate a big result in every basic algorithm of Zerocash, which brings big latency. In reality, the time consumption could be lower. Our smart contract is self-triggered, concretely, we automatically input the preimage of data encryption secret key's hash.

Table 1. Performance of our algorithm

Create address	Time	360 ms
	$addr_{pk}$	816B
	$addr_{sk}$	947B
Mint	Time	1.5 ms
	Coin c	1068B
	TX_{mint}	196B
Pour	Time	6 min 1.2 s
	TX_{pour}	2856B
SmartContract	Time	0.3 ms
	E_{sk}	846B
GeneralID	Time	5.6 s
	data	1M

Table 2. Performance of Zcash algorithm

Create address	Time	326.0 ms
	$addr_{pk}$	343B
	$addr_{sk}$	319B
Mint	Time	23 μs
	Coin c	463B
	tX_{mint}	72B
Pour	time	2 min 2.01 s
	tX_{pour}	996B[16]

Figure 4 shows performance of GenerateID with different size of data inputting. As it shows, latency of our algorithm grows with the data size grows. Property of hash function results in this performance, the latency will get lower if we change the way to generate dataID.

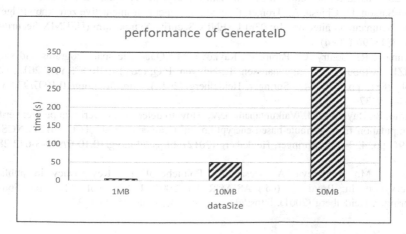

Fig. 4. Performance of algorithm GenerateID

6 Conclusion

We propose a new data transaction scheme that brings decentralization and anonymity for data sellers and data buyers. Concretely, our scheme enables the data transaction be completed only with an information sending by seller and a smart contract deployment by buyer, which is simple and convenient to both sides. Moreover, we introduce the DAP scheme to provide anonymity for transaction, experiment shows that our scheme has almost same performance as Zerocash, which means this is a practical scheme in data transaction.

In the future, we want to improve the performance of our scheme. The first aspect is simplifying transaction process such as eliminating the information sending step for sellers. The second aspect is zk-SNARKs, it takes a long time to compute a proof for each pour transaction, if we can shorten time of this part, we can give a more practical scheme for users among IoV. Moreover, our scheme builds a verification relationship (using zk-SNARKs) rather than trust relationship, which means we can't avoid a failed transaction caused by human behavior. The establishment of trust relationship in system is our important research direction in future.

References

1. Nakamoto, S.: Bitcoin: a peer-to-peer electronic cash system (2008)
2. Buterin, V.: A next-generation smart contract and decentralized application platform. white paper (2014)
3. CarBlock: A global transportation data protocol with decentralized applications. white paper (2018)
4. Sasson, E.B., Chiesa, A., Garman, C., et al.: Zerocash: decentralized anonymous payments from bitcoin. In: 2014 IEEE Symposium on Security and Privacy, pp. 459–474. IEEE (2014)
5. Castro, M., Liskov, B.: Practical Byzantine fault tolerance. OSDI, vol. 99 (1999)
6. https://bitcointalk.org/index.php?topic=193281.msg2224949#msg2224949
7. Parno, B., Howell, J., Gentry, C., et al.: Pinocchio: nearly practical verifiable computation. In: 2013 IEEE Symposium on Security and Privacy, pp. 238–252. IEEE (2013)
8. Ben-Sasson, E., Chiesa, A., Tromer, E., et al.: Succinct non-interactive zero knowledge for a von Neumann architecture. In: 23rd USENIX Security Symposium (USENIX Security 14), pp. 781–796 (2014)
9. Gennaro, R., Gentry, C., Parno, B., Raykova, M.: Quadratic span programs and succinct NIZKs without PCPs. In: Johansson, T., Nguyen, P.Q. (eds.) EUROCRYPT 2013. LNCS, vol. 7881, pp. 626–645. Springer, Heidelberg (2013). https://doi.org/10.1007/978-3-642-38348-9_37
10. Parno, B., Raykova, M., Vaikuntanathan, V.: How to delegate and verify in public: verifiable computation from attribute-based encryption. In: Cramer, R. (ed.) TCC 2012. LNCS, vol. 7194, pp. 422–439. Springer, Heidelberg (2012). https://doi.org/10.1007/978-3-642-28914-9_24
11. Bellare, M., Boldyreva, A., Desai, A., Pointcheval, D.: Key-privacy in public-key encryption. In: Boyd, C. (ed.) ASIACRYPT 2001. LNCS, vol. 2248, pp. 566–582. Springer, Heidelberg (2001). https://doi.org/10.1007/3-540-45682-1_33

Recommendation and Social Computing

Accuracy-Guaranteed Event Detection via Collaborative Mobile Crowdsensing with Unreliable Users

Tong Liu[1,2]($\boxtimes$), Wenbin Wu[1], Yanmin Zhu[3,4], and Weiqin Tong[1,2]

[1] School of Computer Engineering and Science, Shanghai University, Shanghai, China
{tong_liu,wenbinw,wqtong}@shu.edu.cn
[2] Shanghai Institute for Advanced Communication and Data Science,
Shanghai University, Shanghai, China
[3] Department of Computer Science and Engineering,
Shanghai Jiao Tong University, Shanghai, China
yzhu@sjtu.edu.cn
[4] Shanghai Key Lab of Scalable Computing and Systems, Shanghai, China

Abstract. Recently, mobile crowdsensing has become a promising paradigm to collect rich spatial sensing data, by taking advantage of widely distributed sensing devices like smartphones. Based on sensing data, event detection can be conducted in urban areas, to monitor abnormal incidents like traffic jam. However, how to guarantee the detection accuracy is still an open issue, especially when unreliable users who may report wrong observations are considered. In this work, we focus on the problem of user recruitment in collaborative mobile crowdsensing, aiming to optimize the fine-grained detection accuracy in a large urban area. Unfortunately, the problem is proved to be NP-hard, which means there is no polynomial-time algorithm to achieve the optimal solution unless P = NP. To meet the challenge, we first employ a probabilistic model to characterize the unreliability of users, and measure the uncertainty of inferring event occurrences given collected observations by Shannon entropy. Then, by leveraging the properties of adaptive monotonicity and adaptive submodularity, we propose an adaptive greedy algorithm for user recruitment, which is theoretically proved to achieve a constant approximation ratio guarantee. Extensive simulations are conducted, which show our proposed algorithm outperforms baselines under different settings.

Keywords: Collaborative mobile crowdsensing · Event detection · User recruitment · Adaptive greedy algorithm

1 Introduction

With the popularization of mobile devices equipped with rich embedded sensors and wireless communication modules, mobile crowdsensing [7,8,15] has emerged as a promising data sensing and collecting paradigm. Taking advantage of widely

© ICST Institute for Computer Sciences, Social Informatics and Telecommunications Engineering 2019
Published by Springer Nature Switzerland AG 2019. All Rights Reserved
X. Wang et al. (Eds.): CollaborateCom 2019, LNICST 292, pp. 729–744, 2019.
https://doi.org/10.1007/978-3-030-30146-0_49

distributed mobile devices, fine-grained event detection over an urban area can be conducted via collaborative sensing, which can support services such as traffic jam monitoring [18]. In this work, we consider a typical mobile crowdsensing system, consisting of a central *platform* built in cloud and a set of collaborative *users* equipped with sensing devices. The platform is responsible for recruiting some users to participate in event detecting, within a given budget. Then, the recruited users perform detecting during their movement. Finally, the platform infers all event occurrences in the monitored area, based on the observations reported by recruited users.

It is still an open issue that how to guarantee the detection accuracy, in terms of considering the unreliability of users and the budget constraint. Here, detection accuracy measures the deviation between ground truth and inference of event occurrences. On one hand, certain costs are incurred on users for detecting, such as energy consumption, bandwidth usage and interaction time. Thus, given a fixed budget, the number of recruited users is significantly limited. On the other hand, observations reported by different users have different accuracy levels, which may be influenced by device hardware or user experience. Which users are recruited and what observations are collected make a big difference on the fine-grained detection accuracy could be achieved. Considering these two aspects, users should be carefully selected by the platform, to satisfy the budget constraint and optimize the detection accuracy at the same time.

Recently, some works have paid efforts to figure out the problem of quality-aware data collection in mobile crowdsensing, which are the most related with our work. Different metrics are considered to measure data quality. A certain attained value of each user is considered to measure the quality of information in [13]. Data utility is measured by data granularity and quantity in [23] and prediction uncertainty and data density in [29], respectively. Yang *et al.* [30] consider the distance between measurements and true values estimated as the centroid of the measurements, to measure the quality of each user. Most other works [10,11,26–28,31] focus on designing truthful incentive mechanisms for quality-aware users, which model the quality of each user as a constant real value. Moreover, a few works [21,31] have noticed the unreliability of users. Zheng *et al.* [31] assume qualities of users follow certain multinomial distributions. A discrete probabilistic effort matrix is used in [21] to model the deviation between measurements and ground truth. Moreover, expectation maximization (EM) based algorithms are proposed to estimate the qualities of users. However, these works ignore digging how the unreliability of users influences the quality of data collection, e.g., fine-grained detection accuracy in our work, and accordingly proposing efficient user recruitment approaches.

In this work, we study the problem of user recruitment in collaborative mobile crowdsensing to provide event detection services, with the objective to optimize the detection accuracy under a fixed budget constraint. In addition, we consider unreliable users, whose observations may variously deviate from ground truth. Thus, multiple users should be recruited to detect one event, which can collaboratively improve the detection accuracy. Different from previous works, we aim to propose an optimal user recruitment approach, by formally analyzing the relationship between the unreliability of recruited users and the fine-grained accuracy achieved given the observations collected from users.

However, the problem is particularly difficult due to the following challenges. *Firstly*, the more users are recruited, the higher detection accuracy could be achieved in intuition. However, the number of recruited users is significantly limited by the budget constraint. *Secondly*, observations of an unreliable user are nondeterministic before the user is recruited, which makes the platform hard to estimate the value of each user in terms of improving the overall detection accuracy. *Thirdly*, the improvement of detection accuracy made by the observations collected from a user is varying, which is also related with the observations have been collected from others. *Finally*, as the problem is formally proved to be NP-hard, there does not exist a polynomial-time algorithm to achieve the optimal solution if P $\neq$ NP.

To meet the challenges, we propose an adaptive greedy algorithm for user recruitment in a budgeted mobile crowdsensing system in this paper. We first employ a probabilistic matrix to model the unreliability of each user, which consists of true-positive, false-positive, true-negative, and false-negative detection probabilities. Then, the probability of an event occurrence is estimated given the collected observations based on the Bayesian rule. Moreover, Shannon entropy is employed to measure the uncertainty of the estimation, which represents the detection accuracy. Next, by taking advantage of the properties of adaptive monotonicity and adaptive submodularity, we put forward an adaptive greedy algorithm, in which users are sequentially recruited according to the expectation of accumulated entropy reduction obtained by their observations. Our proposed algorithm is theoretically proved to achieve near-optimal performance with a constant approximation ratio guarantee. Extensive simulations are conducted to evaluate the performance of our proposed algorithm, compared with baselines. The comparative results show that our algorithm can achieve high detection accuracy under different settings.

The main contributions of this paper are summarized as follows:

- First, we employ a probabilistic model to characterize the unreliability of users, and Shannon entropy to measure the uncertainty of estimations on event occurrences. Moreover, the relationship between the detection accuracy achieved by collected observations and the unreliability of recruited users is formally established.
- Second, we propose an adaptive greedy user recruitment algorithm, which is proved to achieve approximately optimal performance with a constant approximation ratio guarantee.
- Third, we perform comprehensive simulations to evaluate our proposed algorithm, compared with baselines. The results show that our algorithm can achieve better performance under different settings.

The rest of the paper is organized as follows. Section 2 reviews related work. The system model, formal problem formulation and preliminary definitions are presented in Sect. 3. In Sect. 4, we illustrate the design details of our proposed user recruitment algorithm, and its optimization analysis. Section 5 evaluates the performance of our algorithm compared with baselines via extensive simulations. Finally, we conclude our work in Sect. 6.

2   Related Work

With the proliferation of mobile sensing devices like smartphones, mobile crowd-sensing has attracted a lot of attention from industry and academia. Many useful applications have been developed to collect various sensing data from crowds for environment monitoring [16,17,22], smart transportation [18,25], health-care [5,9,20], and social interaction [1,3,4]. How to collect high-quality sensing data and extract accurate information is a fundamental issue for the success of mobile crowdsensing. Recently, quality-aware data collection has attracted some research efforts. In this section, we briefly review related works and point out the difference and contributions of our work.

The concept of Quality-of-Information (QoI) is first introduced into query-based mobile crowdsensing by [13]. QoI is formally formulated as a function of the required value of each query and the attained value of each user. An energy-efficient algorithm and a dynamic pricing scheme are proposed for deciding participants and allocating credits to participants respectively. Followed by [23], Song et al. propose a QoI-aware energy-efficient participant selection method, where QoI is measured by data granularity and quantity. Different from these two works, we use a probabilistic matrix to model the unreliability of users, and the data quality, i.e., fine-grained detection accuracy, is measured by the uncertainty of the estimations inferred based on observations of users.

Given the QoI of each user, reverse combinatorial auction-based incentive mechanisms are proposed for both single-minded and multi-minded users in [10], to maximize the profit defined on the accumulated QoI of selected users. Similarly, a few other works [11,26–28,31] have proposed quality-aware incentive mechanisms to encourage users to contribute high-quality data. Most of these works model qualities of users as known, certain and additive real values. They focus on how to guarantee the truthfulness of strategic users. In our work, we consider unreliable users who may contribute incorrect observations, and focus on discovering the truth with high certainty based on unreliable observations. We also propose an adaptive algorithm for greedily recruiting valuable users, while providing proper incentives to users is beyond the scope of our work.

Both Yang et al. [30] and Peng et al. [21] propose approaches to estimate qualities of users according to their measurements and then provide incentives based on their qualities. In [30], the quality of users is measured by the deviation of their measurements and ground truth, which is estimated as the centroid of the measurements. This truth discovery method is also employed in [11]. In [21], a probabilistic effort matrix is used for modeling the quality of each user, and an EM algorithm is proposed to estimate effort matrixes of users as well as ground truth. Developed by [14], data qualities of users, which are assumed following multinomial distributions, can also be estimated by an EM algorithm. Moreover, a context-quality classifier is trained to discover the truth and a greedy-based algorithm is proposed for user selection. In [29], Xu *et al.* consider the platform can actively orchestrate queries for collecting annotation data, and data utility is measured by both prediction uncertainty and data density. A threshold-based method is proposed for online participant selection.

Similar with [21], we model the unreliability of users by a discrete probabilistic matrix. Different from the previous works, we focus on how to accurately discover ground truth with high certainty, given the observations collected from unreliable users under a fixed budget constraint.

3 Preliminaries and Problem Formulation

3.1 System Model

A typical mobile crowdsensing system is consisted of a central platform located in cloud and a universal set of mobile users equipped with smart devices, i.e., $\mathcal{U} = \{u_1, u_2, \cdots, u_K\}$, where K is the number of users. The platform is responsible to recruit some users to collect observations of event occurrences. For sake of describing the locations of events and users, we partition the whole detected area into fine-grained grids with equal size (e.g., a square of $200\,\text{m} \times 200\,\text{m}$). The set of all grids is denoted by $\mathcal{G} = \{g_1, g_2, \cdots, g_N\}$, where N is the number of grids. We use a Boolean variable X_n to denote whether there is an event occurring in grid g_n. Thus, the ground truth of event occurrences in the whole area can be expressed as $\mathbf{X} = \{X_n \in \{0,1\}, \forall 1 \leq n \leq N\}$.

As users are mobile, we consider the trajectory of each user during the period of event detection is reported to the platform at the beginning. The trajectory of user $u_k, \forall 1 \leq k \leq K$ can be denoted by a set of grids, i.e., $\mathcal{G}_k \subseteq \mathcal{G}$, as shown in Fig. 1. If user u_k is selected as a participant by the platform, all the grids in $\mathcal{G}_k$ will be detected by u_k. The set of observations collected by u_k can be represented by $\mathcal{D}_k = \{D_{k,n} \in \{0,1\}, \forall g_n \in \mathcal{G}_k\}$, where $D_{k,n} = 1$ means an event is detected by u_k in grid g_n. In addition, some costs are paid by participants, like power consumption and human-device interaction. We denote the cost of user u_k participating in event detection is c_k.

Unreliable Users. In our work, we consider unreliable users, who may report wrong observations to the platform, caused by device hardware, sensing contexts, or user experience. Thus, the observations of users are uncertain, even given the ground truth of event occurrences. To characterize the stochastic nature of detection results collected by users, we model each user is associated with a certain level of detection accuracy, denoted by a matrix of probabilities, i.e.,

$$\mathbf{P}_k = \begin{bmatrix} p_k^{\mathrm{T}} & 1 - p_k^{\mathrm{T}} \\ p_k^{\mathrm{F}} & 1 - p_k^{\mathrm{F}} \end{bmatrix}. \tag{1}$$

Here, p_k^{T} and p_k^{F} respectively represent the true-positive and false-positive detection probabilities, i.e.,

$$p_k^{\mathrm{T}} = \Pr(D_{k,n} = 1 | I_n = 1), \forall 1 \leq n \leq N,$$
$$p_k^{\mathrm{F}} = \Pr(D_{k,n} = 1 | I_n = 0), \forall 1 \leq n \leq N.$$

The detection probability matrix of each user is different and can be effectively estimated from the historical detecting records by the EM algorithm proposed in [21,31]. As it is not the focus of our work, we assume that the detection probabilities of all users are known by the platform for simplicity.

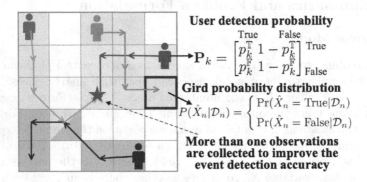

Fig. 1. Illustration of our collaborative mobile crowdsensing system model. Some users are recruited to collect observations along their trajectories for event detection. Different users have different accuracies represented by detection probabilities, while each grid is associated with a random variable to characterize the uncertainty of event occurring inference based on collected observations.

User Recruitment. In this work, we consider the platform sequentially recruits users, unless the total costs of recruited users exceed a given budget. Note that observations are collected once a user is recruited, and then the platform continues recruiting the next one. We use $I_k \in \{0,1\}$ to indicate whether user u_k is recruited or not, and denote $\mathbf{I} = \{I_k \in \{0,1\}, 1 \leq k \leq K\}$. Moreover, we denote $\mathcal{D}_n$ as the set of observations collected in grid g_n by all recruited users, i.e., $\mathcal{D}_n = \{D_{k,n} | I_k = 1 \text{ and } g_n \in \mathcal{G}_k, \forall 1 \leq k \leq K\}$, and we denote $\mathbf{D} = \{\mathcal{D}_n, \forall 1 \leq n \leq N\}$.

Given the set of recruited users indicated by $\mathbf{I}$ and their observations $\mathbf{D}$, we define a *realization* $\phi \triangleq \{(u_k, \mathcal{D}_k)\}$, indicating to what extent various users are recruited and their observations are collected. In addition, we use $\varPhi$ to denote a random realization, in which the value of $\mathbf{I}$ is not determined. Then, the probability distribution over realization ϕ can be calculated as $\Pr(\varPhi = \phi) = \prod_{I_k=1} \Pr(\varPhi(u_k) = \phi(u_k))$, where $\phi(u_k) \triangleq \mathcal{D}_k$. After a user is recruited by the platform, the set of observations collected so far is updated, which is represented by a *partial realization* ψ. We define $\mathrm{dom}(\psi)$ representing the recruited users given a partial realization ψ, i.e., $\mathrm{dom}(\psi) = \{u_k | \exists (u_k, \mathcal{D}_k) \in \psi\}$. A partial realization ψ is consistent with a full realization ϕ (denoted by $\phi \sim \psi$), if $\mathcal{D}_k$ is the same for all $u_k \in \text{dom}(\psi)$. Moreover, ψ is called a *subrealization* of ψ', if ψ and ψ' are both consistent with ϕ and $\text{dom}(\psi) \subseteq \text{dom}(\psi')$.

Detection Accuracy. Given the observations collected by participants in grid g_n, whether there is an event occurring in g_n can be estimated. We use a random variable $\hat{X}_n$ to denote the estimation, which is associated with a probability distribution $P(\hat{X}_n|\mathcal{D}_n) = \Pr(\hat{X}_n = 1|\mathcal{D}_n)$. When a new observation $D_{k,n}$ in grid g_n is reported by user u_k, the probability can be updated according to the Bayesian rule [24] as

$$P(\hat{X}_n|\mathcal{D}_n \cup D_{k,n}) = \Pr(\hat{X}_n = 1|\mathcal{D}_n \cup D_{k,n}) \tag{2}$$

$$= \begin{cases} \dfrac{p_k^{\mathrm{T}} \cdot P(\hat{X}_n|\mathcal{D}_n)}{p_k^{\mathrm{T}} \cdot P(\hat{X}_n|\mathcal{D}_n) + p_k^{\mathrm{F}} \cdot (1 - P(\hat{X}_n|\mathcal{D}_n))}, & \text{if } D_{k,n} = 1, \\[3mm] \dfrac{(1 - p_k^{\mathrm{T}}) \cdot P(\hat{X}_n|\mathcal{D}_n)}{(1 - p_k^{\mathrm{T}}) \cdot P(\hat{X}_n|\mathcal{D}_n) + (1 - p_k^{\mathrm{F}}) \cdot (1 - P(\hat{X}_n|\mathcal{D}_n))}, & \text{if } D_{k,n} = 0. \end{cases}$$

Note that the Bayesian rule can be applied here because we assume the detection probabilities of users are independent from each other.

We denote the joint probability distribution over the discrete-valued random vector $\hat{\mathbf{X}} = [\hat{X}_1, \hat{X}_2, \cdots, \hat{X}_N]$ as $P(\hat{\mathbf{X}})$. With the observations collected in all grids, there exists

$$P(\mathbf{x}|\mathbf{D}) = \Pr(\hat{\mathbf{X}} = \mathbf{x}|\mathbf{D}) = \prod_{n=1}^{N} \Pr(\hat{X}_n = x_n|\mathcal{D}_n), \tag{3}$$

where $\mathbf{x} = \{x_1, x_2, \cdots, x_N\}$ and $x_n \in \{0,1\}, \forall 1 \le n \le N$.

The fine-grained detection accuracy of the whole area can be measured by the reduction of the uncertainty of estimations $\hat{\mathbf{X}}$ in all grids, given all observations $\mathbf{D}$ collected by recruited users. Specially, *Shannon entropy* [21] is a commonly used criterion to measure the uncertainty of random variables. Given the joint probability distribution of $\hat{\mathbf{X}}$, its entropy can be calculated as

$$H(\hat{\mathbf{X}}|\mathbf{D}) = -\sum_{\mathbf{x}} (P(\mathbf{x}|\mathbf{D}) \cdot \log P(\mathbf{x}|\mathbf{D}))$$

$$= -\sum_{\mathbf{x}} \left[\prod_{n=1}^{N} \Pr(\hat{X}_n = x_n|\mathcal{D}_n) \cdot \sum_{n=1}^{N} \log \Pr(\hat{X}_n = x_n|\mathcal{D}_n) \right]$$

$$= \sum_{n=1}^{N} \left[-\sum_{x_n \in \{0,1\}} \Pr(\hat{X}_n = x_n|\mathcal{D}_n) \cdot \log \Pr(\hat{X}_n = x_n|\mathcal{D}_n) \right]$$

$$= \sum_{n=1}^{N} H(\hat{X}_n|\mathcal{D}_n). \tag{4}$$

Then, the entropy reduction obtained by the observations $\mathbf{D}$ is $H(\hat{\mathbf{X}}) - H(\hat{\mathbf{X}}|\mathbf{D})$.

3.2   Problem Formulation

In this work, we consider the problem that how the platform recruits a proper subset of unreliable users given a fixed budget constraint, aiming to optimize the fine-grained detection accuracy of the whole area. Given the system model built in the last subsection, the problem can be formally formulated as follows,

$$\max_{\mathbf{I}} f(\mathbf{I}, \varPhi) \tag{5}$$

$$s.t. \quad \sum_{u_k \in \mathcal{U}} c_k \cdot I_k \leq \eta,$$

$$I_k \in \{0, 1\}, \forall 1 \leq k \leq K,$$

where $f(\mathbf{I}, \varPhi) \triangleq \mathbb{E}[H(\hat{\mathbf{X}}) - H(\hat{\mathbf{X}}|\mathbf{D})]$, representing the expectation of the entropy reduction obtained by recruiting users indicated by $\mathbf{I}$, and η is the budget on the total costs of recruited users.

This problem is a stochastic 0-1 integer programming problem. We prove its NP-hardness in Theorem 1.

Theorem 1. *The user recruitment problem with a fixed budget is NP-hard.*

Proof. The decision version of this problem is that given a set of users and their trajectories, whether a subset of users can be found to achieve a given detection accuracy requirement, and the total costs of the users are no larger than η.

Then, we prove the NP-hardness of our problem by reducing a classical NP-hard problem, *vertex cover problem* [2], to our problem in polynomial time. An instance of the decision version of the vertex cover problem is, given an undirected graph $G = (V, E)$, whether a subset of n vertexes $V' \subseteq V$ can be found, such that for $\forall uv \in E, u \in V' \vee v \in V'$ exists.

Next, we construct an instance of our problem, and show that the instance of the vertex cover problem can be transformed to the instance of our problem. We transform vertex set V and edge set E into the set of users $\mathcal{U}$ and grids $\mathcal{G}$, respectively. For $\forall uv \in E$, the corresponding grid is included in the trajectories of the users corresponding to u and v. For each user $u_k \in \mathcal{U}$, we set $p_k^{\mathbb{T}} = 1$, $p_k^{\mathbb{F}} = 0$, and $c_k = 1$. The detection accuracy requirement is set as $\sum_{g_n \in \mathcal{G}} H(\hat{X}_n | \mathcal{D}_n) = 0$. Thus, as long as grid g_n is included in the trajectory of a recruited user, there exists $H(\hat{X}_n | \mathcal{D}_n) = 0$. Also, we set $\eta = n$. Then, the instance of our problem is equal to select n users, the union of whose trajectories cover all grids.

Now, a solution of the instance of the vertex cover problem can be transformed to the solution of the instance of our problem. Specially, if the corresponding users in $\mathcal{U}$ for each $u \in V'$ are recruited (denoted by $\mathcal{U}'$), the detection accuracy requirement can be achieved, as any grid is included in the trajectories of at least one user in $\mathcal{U}'$.

Thus, any instance of vertex cover problem is polynomial-time reducible to an instance of our problem. As vertex cover problem is NP-hard, we prove that our problem is NP-hard as well.

Unfortunately, there does not exist a polynomial-time algorithm to solve the user recruitment problem, unless P = NP. In the following, we design an adaptive greedy algorithm, which is proved to achieve a constant approximation ratio guarantee.

3.3 Preliminaries

In this subsection, we present the definitions of two important properties: *adaptive monotonicity* and *adaptive submodularity*, which are generalizations of monotonicity and submodularity [19] to adapt random realization. If the objective function of a stochastic 0-1 integer optimization satisfies these two properties, a good performance with a constant approximation ratio can be achieved by conducting an adaptive greedy algorithm.

Definition 1 (Conditional Expected Marginal Benefit [6]). *Given a partial realization ψ and an item e, the conditional expected marginal benefit of e conditioned on ψ is*

$$\Delta(e|\psi) = \mathbb{E}\left[F(dom(\psi) \cup \{e\}, \Phi) - F(dom(\psi), \Phi)|\Phi \sim \psi\right],$$

where the expectation is computed with respect to $p(\phi|\psi) = \Pr(\Phi = \phi|\Phi \sim \psi)$.

Definition 2 (Adaptive Monotonicity [6]). *A function $F : 2^E \times O^E \to \mathbb{R}$ is adaptive monotone with respect to distribution $p(\phi)$ if, for any partial realization ψ and for any $e \in E$, we have*

$$\Delta(e|\psi) \geq 0.$$

Definition 3 (Adaptive Submodularity [6]). *A function $F : 2^E \times O^E \to \mathbb{R}$ is adaptive submodular with respect to distribution $p(\phi)$ if, for any partial realization ψ and ψ', where ψ is a subrealization of ψ' (i.e., $dom(\psi) \subseteq dom(\psi')$), and for any $e \in E \setminus dom(\psi')$, we have*

$$\Delta(e|\psi) \geq \Delta(e|\psi').$$

4 Adaptive Greedy Algorithm

In this section, we first propose an adaptive greedy algorithm for the user recruitment problem, and then theoretically prove that the performance of our algorithm achieves a constant approximation ratio guarantee.

4.1 Algorithm Design

The basic idea of designing the algorithm is to greedily select the user, who achieves the most entropy reduction and has the least cost at the same time. Specially, users are sequentially recruited according to the following rule,

$$u_{k^*} = \arg\max_{u_k} \frac{\Delta(u_k|\psi)}{c_k}, \tag{6}$$

where $\Delta(u_k|\psi) = \mathbb{E}[H(\hat{\mathbf{X}}|\mathbf{D}) - H(\hat{\mathbf{X}}|\mathbf{D} \cup \mathcal{D}_k)]$, denoting the expectation of the entropy reduction obtained by observations collected from u_k, given partial realization ψ. As observations $\mathcal{D}_k$ are unknown before u_k is recruited, the expectation can be computed by considering any possible value of $\mathcal{D}_k$ and its probability respectively, i.e.,

$$
\begin{aligned}
\Delta(u_k|\psi) &= \mathbb{E}\left[\sum_{g_n \in \mathcal{G}_k} (H(\hat{X}_n|\mathcal{D}_n) - H(\hat{X}_n|\mathcal{D}_n \cup \{D_{k,n}\}))\right] \\
&= \sum_{g_n \in \mathcal{G}_k} \mathbb{E}[H(\hat{X}_n|\mathcal{D}_n) - H(\hat{X}_n|\mathcal{D}_n \cup \{D_{k,n}\})] \\
&= \sum_{g_n \in \mathcal{G}_k} [\Pr(D_{k,n} = 1) \cdot \Delta H(\hat{X}_n|D_{k,n} = 1) \\
&\qquad\qquad + \Pr(D_{k,n} = 0) \cdot \Delta H(\hat{X}_n|D_{k,n} = 0)].
\end{aligned}
\tag{7}
$$

Here, $\Pr(D_{k,n} = 1) = P_n \cdot p_k^{\mathrm{T}} + (1 - P_n) \cdot p_k^{\mathrm{F}}$, and $\Pr(D_{k,n} = 0) = P_n \cdot (1 - p_k^{\mathrm{T}}) + (1 - P_n) \cdot (1 - p_k^{\mathrm{F}})$.

The details of our proposed adaptive greedy algorithm for user recruitment are illustrated in Algorithm 1. We first initialize the probability distribution of each grid as uniform distribution without any priori information in line 1. Line 3 to 15 are repeatedly executed to sequentially recruit users, according to the rule in (6). Observations are collected once a user is recruited as shown in line 9, and then the probability distribution of each grid within the trajectory is updated according to (2). If the budget constraint cannot be satisfied by recruiting any user left, the algorithm ends. The time complexity of our algorithm is $O(K^2 N)$.

4.2   Optimization Analysis

Theorem 2. *Let $\mathbf{I}^o$ indicate the set of recruited users returned by Algorithm 1, and $\mathbf{I}^*$ indicate the set of recruited users which achieves the maximal entropy reduction. Then, for any budget η, we have*

$$
f(\mathbf{I}^o, \Phi) \geq (1 - 1/e)f(\mathbf{I}^*, \Phi)
\tag{8}
$$

Proof. First, we define function $\hat{f}(\{(u_k, \mathcal{D}_k)\}) = H(\mathbf{X}) - H(\hat{X}|\mathbf{D})$, which is monotone submodular as shown by Krause and Guestrin [12]. Obviously, there is $f(\mathbf{I}, \phi) = \hat{f}(\{(u_k, \mathcal{D}_k)|I_k = 1, \phi(u_k) = \mathcal{D}_k\})$ under realization ϕ.

Then, we prove this theorem, by proving f is adaptive monotone and adaptive submodular. Adaptive monotonicity is readily proved as $f(\cdot, \phi)$ is monotone for each ϕ. To prove adaptive submodularity, we aim to show $\Delta(u_k|\psi' \leq \Delta(u_k|\psi)$ for any ψ, ψ' such that $\psi \subseteq \psi'$ and any $u_k \notin \mathrm{dom}(\psi')$. We define a coupled distribution p over pairs of realizations $\phi \sim \psi$ and $\phi' \sim \psi'$ such that $\phi(u_k) = \phi'(u_k)$ for all $u_k \notin \mathrm{dom}(\psi')$. Formally, $p(\phi, \phi') = \prod_{u_k \in \mathcal{U} \backslash \mathrm{dom}(\psi)} \Pr[\Phi(u_k) = \phi(u_k)]$ if $\phi \sim \psi, \phi' \sim \psi'$, and $\phi(u_k) = \phi'(u_k)$; otherwise, $p(\phi, \phi') = 0$. Next, we calculate $\Delta(u_k|\psi'$ and $\Delta(u_k|\psi)$ using p as follows,

Algorithm 1. Adaptive Greedy User Recruitment Algorithm

Input: A set of users $\mathcal{U}$, detection probabilities of each user $\mathbf{P}_k$, cost of each user c_k, budget η.

Output: A set of recruited users indicated by $\mathbf{I}$.

1: $I_k = 0$, $\mathcal{V} \leftarrow \emptyset$, $\psi \leftarrow \emptyset$, $P(\hat{X}_n) = 0.5$;
2: **while** $\sum_{u_k} c_k \cdot I_k < \eta$ and $\mathcal{U} \setminus \mathcal{V} \neq \emptyset$ **do**
3:     **for** each $u_k \in \mathcal{U} \setminus \mathcal{V}$ **do**
4:         Calculate $\Delta(u_k | \psi)$ according to (7);
5:     **end for**
6:     Select $u_{k^*} = \arg\max_{u_k \in \mathcal{U} \setminus \mathcal{V}} \frac{\Delta(u_k | \psi)}{c_k}$;
7:     **if** $\sum_{u_k} c_k \cdot I_k + c_{k^*} \leq \eta$ **then**
8:         $I_{k^*} = 1$;
9:         Collect observations $\mathcal{D}_{k^*}$;
10:         $\psi \leftarrow \psi \cup \{(u_{k^*}, \mathcal{D}_{k^*})\}$;
11:         **for** each $g_n \in \mathcal{G}_{k^*}$ **do**
12:             Update $P(\hat{X}_n)$ according to (2);
13:         **end for**
14:     **end if**
15:     $\mathcal{V} \leftarrow \mathcal{V} \cup \{u_{k^*}\}$;
16: **end while**
17: **return** $\mathbf{I}$;

$$f(\text{dom}(\psi') \cup \{u_k\}, \phi') - f(\text{dom}(\psi'), \phi') = \hat{f}(\psi' \cup \{(u_k, \mathcal{D}_k)\}) - \hat{f}(\psi')$$
$$\leq \hat{f}(\psi \cup \{(u_k, \mathcal{D}_k)\}) - \hat{f}(\psi)$$
$$= f(\text{dom}(\psi) \cup \{u_k\}, \phi) - f(\text{dom}(\psi), \phi),$$

where the inequality holds due to the submodularity of $\hat{f}$. Thus, we have

$$\Delta(u_k | \psi') = \sum_{(\phi, \phi')} \left[p(\phi, \phi') \cdot (f(\text{dom}(\psi') \cup \{u_k\}, \phi') - f(\text{dom}(\psi'), \phi')) \right]$$
$$\leq \sum_{(\phi, \phi')} \left[p(\phi, \phi') \cdot (f(\text{dom}(\psi) \cup \{u_k\}, \phi) - f(\text{dom}(\psi), \phi)) \right]$$
$$= \Delta(u_k | \psi).$$

According to Theorem 5.2 in [6], if a function f is adaptive monotone and adaptive submodular, and π is a greedy policy, then for any policy π^*, there exists $f(\pi) \geq (1 - 1/e) f(\pi^*)$. Thus, we can conclude that

$$f(\mathbf{I}^o, \Phi) \geq (1 - 1/e) f(\mathbf{I}^*, \Phi).$$

5   Performance Evaluation

In this section, we evaluate the performance of our proposed adaptive greedy algorithm (marked as AG in figures) by conducting comprehensive simulations.

5.1   Methodology and Setups

In our simulations, we compare our algorithm with three greedy-based baseline algorithms, which are illustrated in the following:

1. *Random Algorithm (RD)*. Users are randomly selected by the platform, until the budget could not be satisfied if any one more user is recruited.
2. *User-Greedy Algorithm (UG)*. This algorithm sequentially selects users with the most observations per cost, i.e., $|\mathcal{G}_k|/c_k$, under the budget constraint.
3. *Grid-Greedy Algorithm (GG)*. This algorithm sequentially selects users with the highest accumulated entropy of all grids past through, i.e., $\sum_{g_n \in \mathcal{G}_k} H(\hat{X}_n)$.

Three metrics are employed to measure the performance achieved by our proposed algorithm and these three baselines. First, we compare the *entropy* achieved given the observations of recruited users selected by different algorithms, i.e., $H(\hat{\mathbf{X}}|\mathbf{D})$. Then, we employ two criterions, *precision* and *recall*, to measure the accuracy of event inference achieved by different algorithms. We infer there is an event occurring in grid g_n if $P(\hat{X}_n|\mathcal{D}_n) \geq 0.8$. If ground truth $X_n = 1$, then we consider the event is accurately inferred. Otherwise, an event is detected by mistake, or it is not found. Specifically, precision is calculated as the ratio between the number of accurately detected events and the number of estimations with $P(\hat{X}_n|\mathcal{D}_n) \geq 0.8$, while recall is calculated as the ratio between the number of accurately detected events and the number of events.

The default setting of all parameters in our simulations is illustrated as follows. All simulations are performed on a square area divided into $20 * 20$ grids (i.e., $N = 400$). Events randomly occur in 40 grids of them. There are 500 collaborative users in the system. For each user u_k, the true-positive and false-positive detection probabilities are randomly generated within $[0.5, 1]$ and $[0, 0.5]$ respectively, and cost c_k is uniformly distributed between \$0 and \$5. We limit the upper bound of the number of grids past by a user as 10. To generate the trajectory of a user, we first randomly choose a grid as the starting point. Next, the user may stay in the grid or move towards any direction[1]. For each grid, $P(\hat{X}_n)$ is initialized as 0.5. The default value of budget is set as 400. All simulation results are the average of 20 runs.

5.2   Performance Comparison

In this subsection, we evaluate the performance achieved by our adaptive greedy algorithm and the three baselines, by varying the number of users, the budget, and the number of events.

The performance achieved by different algorithms, when the number of users varies from 400 to 800, is plotted in Figs. 2, 3, and 4, respectively. We can find that generally the more users available in the system, the better performance

---

[1] We consider there are eight directions: northward, southward, westward, eastward, northwestward, northeastward, southwestward, southeastward.

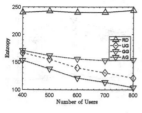

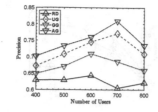

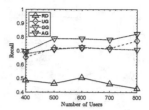

Fig. 2. Entropy vs. number of users.

Fig. 3. Precision vs. number of users.

Fig. 4. Recall vs. number of users.

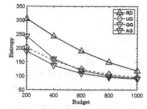

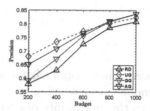

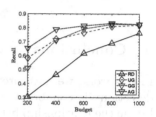

Fig. 5. Entropy vs. budget.

Fig. 6. Precision vs. budget.

Fig. 7. Recall vs. budget.

achieved by each algorithm. Apparently, our algorithm outperforms the baselines in terms of the three metrics, no matter how many users there are. The user-greedy algorithm performs secondly, better than the other two baselines, because users with more observations per cost are recruited. When there are 700 users, entropy achieved by our algorithm is 15% lower than the user-greedy algorithm, and precision and recall are 5.2% and 8.3% higher than the user-greedy algorithm, respectively.

In Figs. 5, 6, and 7, we evaluate the performance achieved when the budget varies from 200 to 1000. Intuitively, the more budget is provided to recruited users, the higher detection accuracy can be achieved, while the marginal increment is reduced. We can find that our algorithm outperforms the baselines, except achieves a little lower precision than the user-greedy algorithm when the budget is less than 800. It may be caused by recruiting users with low detection accuracy, who report wrong observations in grids without events occurring. Specially, when budget is 200, our algorithm obtains 12% and 27% higher recall than the user-greedy algorithm and the grid-greedy algorithm, respectively.

We also vary the number of events from 10 to 50, to compare its impact on the performance of different algorithms, as shown in Figs. 8, 9, and 10. It can be found that precision achieved by the four algorithms increases when there are more events occurring, as the number of events detected by mistake deceases. On the other hand, entropy and recall have no obvious variation trend with the increase of number of events. Specially, when there are 40 events, entropy achieved by our algorithm is 12.5% and 17.3% lower than the user-greedy algorithm and the grid-greedy algorithm.

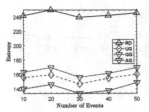

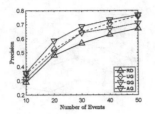

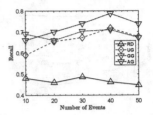

Fig. 8. Entropy vs. number of events.

Fig. 9. Precision vs. number of events.

Fig. 10. Recall vs. number of events.

6   Conclusions

In this work, we have proposed a new approach for accuracy-guaranteed event detection via collaborative mobile crowdsensing with unreliable users. We first bridge the relationship between the uncertainty of event detection given observations of recruited users and the unreliability of recruited users, by building probabilistic models and applying the Bayesian rule. Then, leveraging the adaptive monotonicity and the adaptive submodularity, we propose an adaptive greedy algorithm for user recruitment, which is rigorously proved to achieve $(1 - 1/e)$-approximated performance. Extensive simulations are performed, whose results show that our algorithm outperforms the baselines in terms of achieving low entropy and high detection accuracy under different settings. When the budget is very limited, e.g., 200, our algorithm achieves at least 12% higher detection accuracy than the baselines.

Acknowledgements. This research is supported by NSFC (No. 61772341, 61472254, and 61802245), STSCM (No. 18511103002 and No. 16010500400), and KQJSCX20180329191021388. This work is also supported by the Program for Changjiang Young Scholars in University of China, the Program for China Top Young Talents, the Program for Shanghai Top Young Talents, Shanghai Engineering Research Center of Digital Education Equipment, SJTU Global Strategic Partnership Fund (2019 SJTU-HKUST), and the Shanghai Sailing Program (No. 18YF1408200).

References

1. Bao, X., Choudhury, R.R.: MoVi: mobile phone based video highlights via collaborative sensing. In: International Conference on Mobile Systems, Applications, and Services, pp. 357–370 (2010)
2. Cormen, T.T., Leiserson, C.E., Rivest, R.L.: Introduction to algorithms. Resonance **1**(9), 14–24 (2009)
3. Cox, L.P., Dalton, A., Marupadi, V.: SmokeScreen: flexible privacy controls for presence-sharing. In: International Conference on Mobile Systems, Applications, and Services, pp. 233–245 (2007)
4. Eagle, N., Pentland, A.: Social serendipity: mobilizing social software. IEEE Pervasive Comput. **4**(2), 28–34 (2005)

5. Gao, C., Kong, F., Tan, J.: HealthAware: tackling obesity with health aware smart phone systems. In: International Conference on Robotics and Biomimetics, pp. 1549–1554 (2009)
6. Golovin, D., Krause, A.: Adaptive submodularity: theory and applications in active learning and stochastic optimization. J. Artif. Intell. Res. **42**, 427–486 (2011)
7. Guo, B., et al.: Mobile crowd sensing and computing: the review of an emerging human-powered sensing paradigm. ACM Comput. Surv. (CSUR) **48**(1), 7 (2015)
8. Guo, B., Yu, Z., Zhou, X., Zhang, D.: From participatory sensing to mobile crowd sensing. In: 2014 IEEE International Conference on Pervasive Computing and Communications Workshops (PERCOM Workshops), pp. 593–598. IEEE (2014)
9. Reddy, S., Parker, A., Hyman, J., Burke, J., Estrin, D., Hansen, M.: Image browsing, processing, and clustering for participatory sensing: lessons from a dietsense prototype. In: The Workshop on Embedded Networked Sensors, pp. 13–17 (2007)
10. Jin, H., Su, L., Chen, D., Nahrstedt, K., Xu, J.: Quality of information aware incentive mechanisms for mobile crowd sensing systems. In: ACM International Symposium on Mobile Ad Hoc Networking and Computing, pp. 167–176 (2015)
11. Jin, H., Su, L., Nahrstedt, K.: Theseus: incentivizing truth discovery in mobile crowd sensing systems. In: ACM International Symposium on Mobile Ad Hoc Networking and Computing, p. 1 (2017)
12. Krause, A., Guestrin, C.: Near-optimal observation selection using submodular functions. In: AAAI 2007, pp. 1650–1654 (2007)
13. Liu, C.H., Hui, P., Branch, J.W., Bisdikian, C., Yang, B.: Efficient network management for context-aware participatory sensing. In: 2011 8th Annual IEEE Communications Society Conference on Sensor, Mesh and Ad Hoc Communications and Networks (secon), pp. 116–124. IEEE (2011)
14. Liu, S., Zheng, Z., Wu, F., Tang, S., Chen, G.: Context-aware data quality estimation in mobile crowdsensing. In: INFOCOM 2017 - IEEE Conference on Computer Communications, pp. 1–9. IEEE (2017)
15. Ma, H., Zhao, D., Yuan, P.: Opportunities in mobile crowd sensing. IEEE Commun. Mag. **52**(8), 29–35 (2014)
16. Maisonneuve, N., Stevens, M., Niessen, M.E., Steels, L.: NoiseTube: measuring and mapping noise pollution with mobile phones. Environ. Sci. Eng. **2**(6), 215–228 (2009)
17. Mendez, D., Perez, A.J., Labrador, M.A., Marron, J.J.: P-sense: a participatory sensing system for air pollution monitoring and control. In: 2011 IEEE International Conference on Pervasive Computing and Communications Workshops (PERCOM Workshops), pp. 344–347. IEEE (2011)
18. Mohan, P., Padmanabhan, V.N., Ramjee, R.: Nericell: rich monitoring of road and traffic conditions using mobile smartphones. In: Proceedings of the 6th ACM Conference on Embedded Network Sensor Systems, pp. 323–336. ACM (2008)
19. Nemhauser, G.L., Wolsey, L.A., Fisher, M.L.: An analysis of approximations for maximizing submodular set functions–I. Math. Program. **14**(1), 265–294 (1978)
20. Oliver, N., Floresmangas, F.: HealthGear: automatic sleep apnea detection and monitoring with a mobile phone. J. Commun. **2**(2)(2007)
21. Peng, D., Wu, F., Chen, G.: Pay as how well you do: a quality based incentive mechanism for crowdsensing. In: ACM International Symposium on Mobile Ad Hoc Networking and Computing, pp. 177–186 (2015)
22. Rana, R.K., Chou, C.T., Kanhere, S.S., Bulusu, N., Hu, W.: Ear-phone: an end-to-end participatory urban noise mapping system. In: Proceedings of the 9th ACM/IEEE International Conference on Information Processing in Sensor Networks, pp. 105–116. ACM (2010)

23. Song, Z., Zhang, B., Liu, C.H., Vasilakos, A.V.: QoI-aware energy-efficient participant selection. In: Eleventh IEEE International Conference on Sensing, Communication, and Networking, pp. 248–256 (2014)

24. Stone, J.V.: Bayes' Rule: A Tutorial Introduction to Bayesian Analysis. Sebtel Press, Sheffield (2013)

25. Thiagarajan, A., et al.: VTrack: accurate, energy-aware road traffic delay estimation using mobile phones. In: ACM Conference on Embedded Networked Sensor Systems, pp. 85–98 (2009)

26. Wang, H., Guo, S., Cao, J., Guo, M.: MeLoDy: a long-term dynamic quality-aware incentive mechanism for crowdsourcing. IEEE Trans. Parallel Distrib. Syst. $\mathbf{PP}$(99), 1 (2018)

27. Wang, J., Tang, J., Yang, D., Wang, E., Xue, G.: Quality-aware and fine-grained incentive mechanisms for mobile crowdsensing. In: IEEE International Conference on Distributed Computing Systems, pp. 354–363 (2016)

28. Wen, Y., et al.: Quality-driven auction-based incentive mechanism for mobile crowd sensing. IEEE Trans. Veh. Technol. $\mathbf{64}$(9), 4203–4214 (2015)

29. Xu, Q., Zheng, R.: When data acquisition meets data analytics: a distributed active learning framework for optimal budgeted mobile crowdsensing. In: INFOCOM (2017)

30. Yang, S., Wu, F., Tang, S., Gao, X., Yang, B., Chen, G.: Good work deserves good pay: a quality-based surplus sharing method for participatory sensing. In: IEEE International Conference on Parallel Processing, pp. 380–389 (2015)

31. Zheng, Z., Yang, Z., Wu, F., Chen, G.: Mechanism design for mobile crowdsensing with execution uncertainty. In: IEEE International Conference on Distributed Computing Systems, pp. 955–965 (2017)

Context-Aware Point-of-Interest Recommendation Algorithm with Interpretability

Guoming Zhang[1,5], Lianyong Qi[2], Xuyun Zhang[3], Xiaolong Xu[4], and Wanchun Dou[1(✉)]

[1] State Key Laboratory for Novel Software Technology,
Nanjing University, Nanjing, China
kelvinzhang@smail.nju.edu.cn, douwc@nju.edu.cn
[2] School of Information Science and Engineering,
Qufu Normal University, Qufu, China
lianyongqi@gmail.com
[3] Department of Electrical Computer Engineering,
The University of Auckland, Auckland, New Zealand
xuyun.zhang@auckland.ac.nz
[4] School of Computer and Software, Nanjing University
of Information Science and Technology, Nanjing, China
njuxlxu@gmail.com
[5] Health Statistics and Information Center of Jiangsu Province, Nanjing, China

Abstract. With the rapid development of mobile Internet, smart devices, and positioning technologies, location-based social networks (LBSNs) are growing rapidly. In LBSNs, point-of-interest (POI) recommendation is a crucial personalized location service that has become a research hotspot. To address extreme sparsity of user check-in data, a growing line of research exploits spatial-temporal information, social relationship, content information, popularity, and other factors to improve recommendation performance. However, the temporal and spatial transfers of user preferences are seldom mentioned in existing works, and interpretability, which is an important factor to enhance credibility of recommendation result, is overlooked. To cope with these issues, we propose a context-aware POI recommendation framework, which integrates users' long-term static and time-varying preferences to improve recommendation performance and provide explanations. Experimental results over two real-world LBSN datasets demonstrate that the proposed solution has better performance than other advanced POI recommendation approaches.

Keywords: Point-of-interest recommendation · Interpretability · Location based social network

© ICST Institute for Computer Sciences, Social Informatics and Telecommunications Engineering 2019
Published by Springer Nature Switzerland AG 2019. All Rights Reserved
X. Wang et al. (Eds.): CollaborateCom 2019, LNICST 292, pp. 745–759, 2019.
https://doi.org/10.1007/978-3-030-30146-0_50

1   Introduction

Geographical location information has played an increasingly important role in people's lives with the popularization of smart terminals and development of geolocation technologies. Location-based social networks (LBSNs), combined with location-based services and online social networks, are emerging rapidly. In LBSNs, users can share their check-in activities as they visit point-of-interests (POIs) (e.g., supermarkets, restaurants, attractions, and hotels). Massive check-in data can be used to mine users' visit preferences and introduce personalized POI recommendation system, which not only helps users explore new areas and discover new POIs but also enables POIs to increase the revenue through smart location services (e.g., location-based advertising services). As a smart service based on big data [1,2], POI recommendation has recently attracted increasing attention from academics and industry [3–5].

POI recommendation is more complicated than traditional recommendation system. Information such as distance, time, social relationships, category, and popularity of POI must be considered in addition to user preferences and location attributes [5]. Moreover, a user check-in matrix has higher sparseness than a user-item matrix in traditional recommendation systems [6].

To alleviate data sparsity, existing approaches mainly utilize auxiliary information such as time, geographical location, and social relationship. The temporal and spatial transfers of user preferences are seldom mentioned. In current POI recommendation algorithms, user interest is assumed static, but people's interest actually change over time. The visit preferences of people usually change along with their workplace or accommodation. The POIs that they are interested in may also change after beginning a relationship. At the same time, people have static preferences because some interests are retained for a long time on the one hand. For example, users who like reading books tend to go to bookstores. On the other hand, some static interests are related to people's rational choice in nature. For example, people usually prefer to visit nearby POIs and famous POIs. In addition, the interpretability of the recommendation results is an important factor in the recommendation systems as it can increase the credibility of the recommendation. However, current research has overlooked this factor. Existing advanced POI recommendation algorithms typically take model-based methods to mine visit preferences of users by integrating auxiliary information, such as matrix factorization, which experiences difficulty in distinguishing the influence of different factors and explaining recommendation results.

In light of the above discussion, we propose a collaborative filtering POI recommendation approach (HWREC) in this study. The proposed approach uses improved Hawkes process to integrate user's long-term static and time-varying preferences, capitalizing on multiple contextual information, including spatial clustering, spatial distance, spatial sequence transformation, temporal, and POI popularity information, to improve performance of recommendation. More significantly, HWREC can explain recommendation results in several aspects according to the preferences and historical check-in records.

The remainder of this paper is organized as follows. Section 2 describes the preliminaries of the POI recommendation task. Section 3 presents the proposed POI recommendation method in detail. Section 4 evaluates the effectiveness of the proposed method. Section 5 reviews related work. Finally, Sect. 6 concludes this study.

2   Preliminaries

2.1   Notation

In a LBSN, assume a set of N users represented as $U = \{u_1, u_2, \ldots, u_N\}$ and a set of M POIs represented as $L = \{l_l, l_2, \ldots, l_M\}$. Each POI has a geographic coordinate $g = <longitude, latitude>$. The POIs can be clustered into K POI clusters by the coordinates, denoted as $C = \{c_l, c_2, \ldots, c_K\}$. Each check-in activity is a tuple $<u, l, t>$ that represents user $u \in U$ visiting POI $l \in L$ at time t.

2.2   Problem Statement

The goals of POI recommendation task in this study are to recommend to each user with top-k new POIs that he/she may be interested in but has not visited before by learning users' personalized preferences from their history check-in activities, and explain the recommendation results.

3   Methodology

In this section, we describe the proposed HWREC method in detail.

3.1   Select Candidate POIs

To reduce the commutating complexity of the proposed solution, we first select candidate POIs for users. Candidate POIs are obtained from similar users, which makes this method a user-based collaborative filtering approach. Similar users are believed to share similar behaviors. We analyze user behaviors according to the geospatial aggregation phenomenon of their check-in POIs [7] and then extract user features to compute similarity among users. The feature representation of a user is defined as follows:

Definition 1. *User feature representations. A vector of check-in frequencies in each POI cluster of a user.*

First, we determine clusters of POIs in a certain geographic area by applying the density-based spatial clustering of applications with noise (DBSCAN) algorithm whose inputs are geographic coordinates of POIs. The DBSCAN allocates a cluster to each POI and obtains noise POIs that do not belong to any cluster. The features of a user u_i are then expressed according to Eq. 1 expressed as follows:

$$F_i = \{f_0, f_1, f_2, \ldots, f_K\}(0 \le i \le N) \tag{1}$$

where f_0 indicates the check-in frequency of user u_i at noise points. f_1 to f_c indicate the respective check-in frequency of user u_i in clusters 1 to c. The check-in frequency of the user u_i in the cluster j is defined as Eq. 2:

$$f_j = \frac{k}{n}(1 \le j \le m) \tag{2}$$

where n_i is the total number of check-in records for user u_i. Similarly, the check-in frequency of the user u_i at the noise point is defined as Eq. 3:

$$f_0 = \frac{k_0}{n_i} \tag{3}$$

Finally, the similarity among users can be calculated as follows:

$$S_{ij} = \sum_{q \in Q} min(f_{iq}, f_{jq}) \tag{4}$$

where Q is a set of clusters that users u_i and u_j have visited. The index q must be positive, so the noise points will not be taken into account. According to Eq. 4, we can identify a group of similar users for each user, and the candidate POIs can be selected from his/her similar users' historical check-ins.

Algorithm 1 illustrates the functionality of candidate POI selection.

Algorithm 1. Candidate POIs Selecting

Input: Users U, POIs L with coordinates g
Output: Candidate POIs set P_i of each user
1: Run DBSCAN on L to get Clusters $C = \{c_l, c_2, \ldots, c_K\}$
2: **for** each $u_i \in U$ **do**
3:     calculate check-in count n_i
4:     **for** each $c_i \in C$ **do**
5:         calculate check-in count k_i in cluster c_i
6:         set check-in frequency $f_i = k_i/n_i$
7:     **end for**
8:     set user feature $F_i = \{f_0, f_1, f_2, \ldots, f_K\}$
9: **end for**
10: **for** each $u_i \in U$ **do**
11:     **for** each $u_j \in U$ **do**
12:         set $S_{ij} = \sum_{q \in Q} min(f_{iq}, f_{jq})$
13:     **end for**
14:     sorting S_{ij} in descending order
15:     get Candidate POIs P_i from top 1 similar user.
16: **end for**
17: **return** $P = \{P_1, P_2, \ldots, P_N\}$

3.2 Improved Hawkes Process

The Hawkes process is a linear self-excited point process model proposed by Hawkes in 1972 [8]. The model is widely used in various fields, such as economic analysis and forecasting and social network modeling. This model believes that previous events affect the probability of occurrence of future events, and the incentives of past events are positive, additive, and decay over time. We introduce the Hawkes process to model the spatio-temporal sequence of users' check-in records. The equation is as follows:

$$\lambda_{ul_k}(t) = \mu_{ul_k} + \sum_{l_i \in H_u} \alpha_{l_i l_k} e^{-\delta(t-t_{l_i})} \tag{5}$$

where $\lambda_{ul_k}(t)$ is the intensity of user u visiting POI l_k, μ_{ul_k} is the basic intensity (probability) of u visiting l_k, $\alpha_{l_i l_k}$ is the excited degree of historical check-in $<u, l_i>$, $e^{-\delta(t-t_{l_i})}$ indicates the time decay of the historical check-in $<u, l_i>$, and H_u is the set of POIs that user u has visited. The left part of the formula can be considered as long-term preferences of a user, and the right part can be considered as time-varying preferences.

Each user can have a personalized Hawkes process to estimate the probability of visiting candidate POIs based on his/her historical check-ins to obtain the top-k recommended POIs. The way of solving the parameters in Hawkes process is described in the following sections.

3.3 Basic Intensity μ_{ul_k}

The basic intensity μ_{ul_k} can be calculated in different ways. Considering that the distances from a user to POIs and the popularity of POIs are critical information, we utilize the improved Huff model to integrate distance and popularity to compute the basic intensity μ_{ul_k}.

The Huff model was proposed by David Huff. It attributes the attraction of a mall to customers in two factors [9]: (1) the area size of the mall and (2) the geographical distance between the mall and the customer. The original Huff model is expressed as follows:

$$P_{ij} = \frac{S_j d_{ij}^{-\gamma}}{\sum_{j=1}^{M} S_j d_{ij}^{-\gamma}} \tag{6}$$

where S_j represents the area size of mall j, d_{ij} is the distance between customer i and mall j, and γ is the distance attenuation coefficient.

In our study, the Huff model is improved to adapt to LBSN check-in datasets. The equation is expressed as follows:

$$P_{ij} = \frac{v_j^{\beta} Haversine(d_{ij}^{-\gamma})}{\sum_{j=1}^{M} v_j^{\beta} Haversine(d_{ij}^{-\gamma})} \tag{7}$$

where v_j denotes the total number of check-ins of POI l_j, which reflects the POI popularity, and the exponential distribution v_j^{β} is used instead of S_j, where β is an elasticity coefficient. $Haversine(d_{ij})$ is used to calculate the Haversine distance between the last check-in location of user u_i and the candidate POI l_j, and γ is the distance attenuation coefficient. Haversine distance is the great-circle distance between two points on a sphere given their longitudes and latitudes.

The Huff model is further normalized by the sigmod function to obtain the basic intensity μ_{ul_k} of improved Hawkes process:

$$\mu_{ul_k} = \frac{1}{1 + e^{-P_{ij}}} \tag{8}$$

3.4   Excited Degree $\alpha_{l_i l_k}$ and Time Decay Coefficient δ

The excited degree $\alpha_{l_i l_k}$ of historical check-in $<u, l_i>$ with respect to future check-in $<u, l_k>$ can be calculated by a POI transition graph.

Definition 2. *POI-to-POI Transition Graph [4]. Graph $= (L, E)$, where L is the set of vertices, and E is the set of edges. Each vertex $l_i (l_i \in L)$ represents a POI. Each POI has an out-degree, defined as $OutDegree(l_i)$, which represents the number of transitions from l_i to other POIs. Each edge $(l_i, l_j) \in E$ represents a transition $l_i \rightarrow l_j$. The number of transitions contained in each edge is defined as $EdgeWeight(l_i, l_j)$.*

Definition 3. *Transition probability. The transition probability of $l_i \rightarrow l_j$ is defined as $TP(l_i \rightarrow l_j)$, and calculated as follows:*

$$TP(l_i \rightarrow l_j) = \begin{cases} \frac{EdgeWeight(l_i, l_j)}{OutDegree(l_i)}, & \text{if } (OutDegree(l_i) > 0) \\ 0, & \text{other} \end{cases} \tag{9}$$

The excited degree $\alpha_{l_i l_k} = TP(l_i \rightarrow l_k)$ can be obtained by Eq. 9.

The time decay coefficient δ is a free parameter, we will discuss the tuning method of δ and analyze its value in the experimental section.

The detailed algorithm is illustrated in Algorithm 2.

Algorithm 2. POI Recommendation Based on Hawkes Process

Input: Users U, POIs L, check-in time T
Output: $top - k$ POIs for each user
1: Run Algorithm 1 to get candidate POIs $P = \{P_1, P_2, \ldots, P_N\}$ for each user
2: **for** each $u_i \in U$ **do**
3:    **for** each $l_k \in P_i$ **do**
4:       calculate $Haversine(d_{ik}^{-\gamma})$ between user u_i and candidate POI l_k
5:       calculate popularity v_k for POI l_k
6:       calculate basic intensity $\mu_{u_i l_k}$ according to equation 7 and 8
7:       **for** each $l_m \in H_{u_i}$ **do**
8:          set $\alpha_{l_m l_j} = TP(l_m \rightarrow l_j)$
9:       **end for**
10:       calculate visit preference of l_k according to equation 5
11:    **end for**
12:    recommend to u_i with top-k POIs according to visit preference.
13: **end for**

---

4   Experiments

4.1   Dataset

Two datasets are used in our experiments.

Gowalla Dataset. The Gowalla dataset used in this experiment is obtained from Stanford University's public dataset collection site[1]. The check-in data cover different parts of the world, and the data densities vary from place to place, which makes data mining inconvenient. In the experiment, the Manhattan area of New York City, where user check-in is denser and data quality is higher, is selected as the study area. The geographic range is latitude 40.60° to 40.85° N and longitude 73.89° to 75.05° W. The contents of each check-in record in the dataset include user ID, POI ID, geographic coordinate of POI, and check-in time. The users whose check-in times are less than 5 and the POIs that have been visited less than 10 times are filtered out. After preprocessing, the dataset contains 59,336 check-in records made by 1,612 users at 2,299 POIs, and the check-in time span is from February 2009 to October 2010.

Foursquare Dataset. Foursquare is a mobile service website based on user geographical location information. It encourages mobile phone users to share information about their current geographical location with others. In the experiment, the Tokyo check-in dataset of Foursquare provided by [10] is used. The contents of each check-in record in the dataset include user ID, POI ID, category ID of POI, category name of POI, geographic coordinate of POI, and check-in time. After filtering out users who have checked in less than 10 times and the POIs that have been visited less than 10 times, the dataset contains 357,147

---

[1] http://snap.stanford.edu/data/loc-gowalla.html.

check-in records made by 2,293 users at 7,866 POIs, and the check-in time span is from April 2012 to February 2013.

Table 1 shows the statistics of the two datasets.

Table 1. Statistics of dataset

Dataset	Number of users	Number of POIs	Number of check-in records	Average number of check-ins	Check-in matrix density
Gowalla	1612	2299	59336	36.81	1.60%
Foursquare	2293	7866	357147	155.75	1.98%

4.2   Evaluation Metrics

For each user, the top 80% of the check-in data (sorted by check-in time in ascending order) are used as the training data, whereas the remaining 20% are used as the testing data. The visited probabilities of a user to the candidate POIs are calculated according to the proposed HWREC algorithm, and the top-k POIs sorted by visiting probability are recommended to the users.

To evaluate the performance of the proposed method, two metrics are used [11], namely, precision and recall, and the equations are defined in 10 and 11, respectively.

$$Precision = \frac{\sum_u |R_u \bigcap T_u|}{\sum_u |R_u|} \tag{10}$$

$$Recall = \frac{\sum_u |R_u \bigcap T_u|}{\sum_u |T_u|} \tag{11}$$

where R_u represents a set of POIs recommended for user u, and T_u represents a set of POIs that actually visited by user u in the testing data.

4.3   Baseline Methods

We compare the proposed HWREC with the following baseline algorithms.

- HUFF. It is the basic intensity of HWREC, which uses the distance and popularity information of POIs to obtain the long-term static preferences of users.
- AMC. It is the time-influencing part of HWREC, which uses additive Markov process to calculate the time-varying preferences of users.
- ASVD++ [12]. It is a combined model which improves the accuracy of top-k recommendation by utilizing the advantages of latent factor and neighborhood method. In this experiment, the number of user check-ins is normalized as implicit scores of $<user, POI>$ pairs when calculating.

- AOBPR [13]. It is an advanced Learning-to-Rank based algorithm for top-k recommendation, which studies the preferences of users from implicit feedback.
- LORE [4]. This algorithm integrates several contextual information, such as social relationships, spatial distance, POI popularity, and time information; it achieves better results compared with many other advanced methods, such as CoRe [14] and USG [15]. The Foursquare dataset does not contain social relationship information, so the similar users calculated in Sect. 3.1 are used instead in the experiment.

4.4   Parameter Settings

In the experiment, the radius of neighborhood and density threshold of DBSCAN clustering algorithm are set to 100 and 2, respectively.

The improved Huff model has two parameters: distance attenuation coefficient γ and elastic coefficient β of POI popularity. Parameter γ is set to 2 according to the modified Huff model in [9]. Parameter β is set to 3.5 in the Gowalla dataset and 5 in the Foursquare dataset.

The excited degree $\alpha_{l_i l_k}$ of historical check-in $<u, l_i>$ is calculated according to the method presented in Sect. 3.4. The time decay coefficient δ is set to -0.5 in the Gowalla dataset and -0.001 in the Foursquare dataset. A smaller δ indicates a lower decay rate. The time differences between historical events and current events are calculated in scale of hours.

For the two free parameters, β and δ, we search for the optimal values by tuning the parameters alternately. First, β is fixed, and δ is tuned to obtain the best recommendation accuracy. Next, δ is fixed, and β is tuned to obtain the best recommendation accuracy. In general, this process is repeated 3 to 5 times to achieve the best results.

4.5   Parameter Discussion

Two free parameters are used in our proposed algorithm: elastic coefficient β of POI popularity and time decay coefficient δ. Figures 1 and 2 show the effect of these parameters on the Gowalla and Foursquare datasets in terms of precision and recall, respectively. The experiment compares the average accuracy and recall of top-k (k = 1, 2, 3, 4, 5) recommendations when the parameters are varied.

The performance is poor in the both datasets when parameter $\beta \leq 2$ because the distance coefficient γ is fixed to 2. The best performance for the Gowalla dataset is obtained when $2.5 \leq \beta \leq 4$, after which the average accuracy and recall decrease slightly. On the Foursquare dataset, the best performance is achieved when $5 \leq \beta \leq 6$, and the performance changes are imperceptible thereafter. Therefore, the value of β can be generally selected from 3 to 5, which indicates that user check-in probability has an exponential relationship with the popularity of a POI. It also reflects actual phenomena, for example, the number of visitors who travel to famous attractions is usually dozens of times that of ordinary ones.

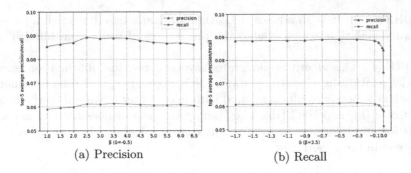

Fig. 1. Influence of β and δ on recommendation of Gowalla dataset

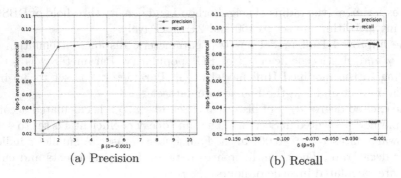

Fig. 2. Influence of β and δ on recommendation of Foursquare dataset

Parameter δ differs significantly between the two datasets. On the Gowalla dataset, the recommendation performance drops significantly when $\delta > -0.1$. When $\delta = 0$ (no decay), the result is the worst. When $\delta \leq -0.3$, not much difference is observed between the performances. On the Foursquare dataset, the best performance is obtained when $\delta = -0.001$. When $\delta = 0$ (no decay), the performance is slightly lower than the best value. When the value of δ decreases, the performance changes are minor because the time decays of historical check-ins on the Foursquare dataset are considerably lower than those on the Gowalla dataset. Therefore, the value of $|\delta|$ should be smaller on the datasets with lower time decays.

4.6 Performance Comparison

Figures 3 and 4 compare the proposed algorithm HWREC and other baseline methods on the Gowalla and Foursquare datasets, respectively. The results indicate that the accuracy decreases as the value of k increases, whereas the recall increases as the value of k increases. This is because the visit probability of recommended POIs decreases as the value of k increases.

Figures 3 and 4 demonstrate that the proposed HWREC is far superior to matrix factorization based ASVD++ and Learning-to-Rank based AOBPR.

These algorithms consider only the check-in counts of users and do not use spatial and temporal information. Although the top-1 recommendation performance of the proposed HWREC is slightly lower than HUFF in the Gowalla dataset, the overall performance of HWREC is significantly better than the HUFF, which considers only static preferences of users, and the AMC, which considers only time-varying preferences of users. The LORE uses distance, popularity, time, and social relationship information, but HWREC achieves better results, particularly on the Gowalla dataset.

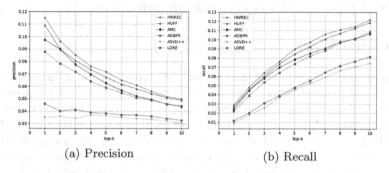

(a) Precision   (b) Recall

Fig. 3. Recommendation performance with respect to top-k values on Gowalla dataset

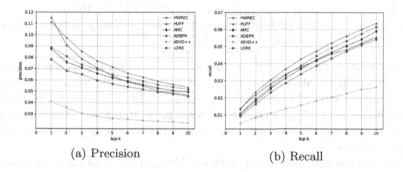

(a) Precision   (b) Recall

Fig. 4. Recommendation performance with respect to top-k values on Foursquare dataset

4.7 Interpretability

Different from existing methods, the proposed HWREC algorithm considers both static preferences and time-varying preferences, so it can easily explain the recommendation results.

First, let's consider the long-term static preferences. In the location-based mobile applications, such as Meituan, when you search for POIs according to the keywords, it will show you a list of POIs sorted by popularity or distance. In our proposed method, the popularity and distance of POIs are reflected in the static preferences part. We can tell users that "we recommend the POI to you according to its distance (e.g., 2 km from you) and popularity (e.g., 1000)."

Second, we consider the time-varying preferences. The influence of historical check-ins is related with multiple factors, including check-in count, check-in time and transition probability. For each POI that is recommended to users, an explicit score of every historical check-in can be calculated by the time-varying preferences part of the proposed method. Then we can tell users that "we recommend the POI to you because you have visited POIs a, b, and c (a, b, and c, are sorted by their scores in descending order)." Furthermore, we can provide the information, such as check-in count, check-in time, and transition probability, related with the score, which can enhance the explanation.

5   Related Work

POI recommendation has attracted lots of attention from academics and industry, and related works include collaborative filtering (CF) approaches [16], matrix factorization-based algorithms, geographical distance-based models, social relationships-based methods, and context-based method, etc. Different methods are suitable for different check-in datasets. For example, the CF method, which recommends POI by calculating similarity of users or POIs, is widely applicable. The geographical distance-based method, which is applicable for datasets with precise geographic locations, leverages the distance between users and POIs to characterize user behaviors. The social relationship-based methods can be applied to datasets that contain friend information of users. The recommendation is performed by mining the similarity between users and their friends. We summarize the related works as follows.

(1) Collaborative filtering (CF) methods. Most existing POI recommendations are based on CF algorithms [16,17], which assume that similar users usually visit similar POIs. There are two types of CF algorithms, user-based CF [17] and item-based CF (a POI is considered as an item) [16]. The former compares the similarity among users, whereas the latter compares the similarity among POIs.

(2) Geographical distance-based methods. Geographic location is an important factor for POI recommendation. POIs that are closer to the users tend to be visited. A study [18] analyzes the distance distribution of the users' check-in locations, and the results reveal that the distances of adjacent check-in locations present a power-law distribution. In [7], data sparsity is alleviated by modeling user activity areas and POI impact areas. The literature [14] uses kernel density estimation to analyze the influence of the 2D geographical coordinates of POIs to improve recommendation performance.

(3) Social relationship-based methods. The social relationship (e.g., friendship) between users is an important factor in the location based social networks. Friends tend to share common preferences. In [19], a friend-based CF method using the common check-in records of friends to recommend POIs is proposed. However, given that few users share information about check-in POIs, the improvement of recommendation performance is limited by only using social relationships [20].

(4) Time-aware methods. Time is an important factor for POI recommendations because the places users tend to visit vary with the time of the day. The literature [21] proposes a time-aware POI recommendation by considering the temporal influence of user activities.

(5) Content-based methods. Users can rate and comment on POIs in LBSNs. Modeling users' comments on the POIs [3] is useful to understand the preferences of users accurately and improve the recommendation performance.

(6) Methods integrated with multi-factors. The visit preferences of users are influenced by many factors, single-factor based recommendation algorithm can not archive good performance. Most studies have attempted to integrate geospatial information, time effects, social relationships, content information, popularity, and other factors to improve the recommendation performance [22].

In this study, we propose a new approach to model interests of users from both long-term static preferences and time-varying preferences. Unlike existing methods, our approach can provide satisfactory explanations for recommended POIs.

6   Conclusion

In this study, we propose a context-aware POI recommendation approach with interpretability based on improved Hawkes process. The proposed method exploits users' long-term static and time-varying preferences by using multiple context information to alleviate the problem of data sparsity and provide explanations to users for recommendation results in several aspects. Context information include spatial clustering, spatial distance, spatial sequence transformation, temporal, and POI popularity information. We conduct experiments over two real-world LBSNs datasets and compare our model with several baselines. The experimental results demonstrate that the proposed solution achieves better performance than other advanced POI recommendation algorithms.

In the future work, we intent to improve the performance and interpretability of POI recommendation by integrate more auxiliary information, such as POI category, comments of POI, etc. to the static and time-varying preferences of our model. Moreover, the recurrent neural network which is excellent at sequence modeling can be explored to mine the check-in sequences of users to study the time-varying preferences. Further, the time-varying part of our proposed model can be improved to do online POI recommendation based on deep reinforcement learning.

Acknowledgment. This work is supported in part by the National Science Foundation of China under Grant No. 61672276, the National Key Research and Development Program of China under Grant No. 2017YFB1400600, Jiangsu Natural Science Foundation of China under Grant No. BK20171037, and the Collaborative Innovation Center of Novel Software Technology and Industrialization, Nanjing University.

References

1. Wang, X., Yang, L.T., Liu, H., Deen, M.J.: A big data-as-a-service framework: state-of-the-art and perspectives. IEEE Trans. Big Data **4**(3), 325–340 (2018)
2. Wang, X., Yang, L.T., Chen, X., Deen, M.J., Jin, J.: Improved multi-order distributed HOSVD with its incremental computing for smart city services. IEEE Trans. Sustain. Comput. (2018)
3. Liu, B., Fu, Y., Yao, Z., Xiong, H.: Learning geographical preferences for point-of-interest recommendation. In: Proceedings of the 19th ACM SIGKDD International Conference on Knowledge Discovery and Data Mining, pp. 1043–1051. ACM (2013)
4. Zhang, J.-D., Chow, C.-Y.: Spatiotemporal sequential influence modeling for location recommendations: a gravity-based approach. ACM Trans. Intell. Syst. Technol. (TIST) **7**(1), 11 (2015)
5. Aliannejadi, M., Crestani, F.: Personalized context-aware point of interest recommendation. ACM Trans. Inf. Syst. **36**(4), 45 (2018)
6. Yu, Y., Chen, X.: A survey of point-of-interest recommendation in location-based social networks. In: Workshops at the Twenty-Ninth AAAI Conference on Artificial Intelligence, vol. 130 (2015)
7. Lian, D., Zhao, C., Xie, X., Sun, G., Chen, E., Rui, Y.: GeoMF: joint geographical modeling and matrix factorization for point-of-interest recommendation. In: Proceedings of the 20th ACM SIGKDD International Conference on Knowledge Discovery and Data Mining, pp. 831–840. ACM (2014)
8. Liniger, T.J.: Multivariate Hawkes processes. Ph.D. thesis, ETH Zurich (2009)
9. Li, Y., Pan, H., Tian, L.: Modification of Huff model and its application in urban commercial network planning: a case of Changzhou city, Jiangsu province. Arid Land Geography **37**(4), 802–811 (2014)
10. Yang, D., Zhang, D., Zheng, V.W., Yu, Z.: Modeling user activity preference by leveraging user spatial temporal characteristics in LBSNs. IEEE Trans. Syst. Man Cybernet. Syst. **45**(1), 129–142 (2015)
11. Karypis, G.: Evaluation of item-based top-n recommendation algorithms. In: Proceedings of the Tenth International Conference on Information and Knowledge Management, pp. 247–254. ACM (2001)
12. Koren, Y.: Factorization meets the neighborhood: a multifaceted collaborative filtering model. In: Proceedings of the 14th ACM SIGKDD International Conference on Knowledge Discovery and Data Mining, pp. 426–434. ACM (2008)
13. Rendle, S., Freudenthaler, C.: Improving pairwise learning for item recommendation from implicit feedback. In: Proceedings of the 7th ACM International Conference on Web Search and Data Mining, pp. 273–282. ACM (2014)
14. Zhang, J.-D., Chow, C.-Y.: Core: exploiting the personalized influence of two-dimensional geographic coordinates for location recommendations. Inf. Sci. **293**, 163–181 (2015)
15. Ye, M., Yin, P., Lee, W.-C., Lee, D.-L.: Exploiting geographical influence for collaborative point-of-interest recommendation. In: Proceedings of the 34th International ACM SIGIR Conference on Research and Development in Information Retrieval, pp. 325–334. ACM (2011)
16. Bao, J., Zheng, Y., Mokbel, M.F.: Location-based and preference-aware recommendation using sparse geo-social networking data. In: Proceedings of the 20th International Conference on Advances in Geographic Information Systems, pp. 199–208. ACM (2012)

17. Cheng, C., Yang, H., Lyu, M.R., King, I.: Where you like to go next: successive point-of-interest recommendation. In IJCAI, vol. 13, pp. 2605–2611 (2013)
18. Yin, H., Cui, B., Sun, Y., Zhiting, H., Chen, L.: LCARS: a spatial item recommender system. ACM Trans. Inf. Syst. (TOIS) **32**(3), 11 (2014)
19. Ye, M., Yin, P., Lee, W.-C.: Location recommendation for location-based social networks. In: Proceedings of the 18th SIGSPATIAL International Conference on Advances in Geographic Information Systems, pp. 458–461. ACM (2010)
20. Cheng, C., Yang, H., King, I., Lyu, M.R.: Fused matrix factorization with geographical and social influence in location-based social networks. In: AAAI, vol. 12, pp. 17–23 (2012)
21. Yuan, G., Cong, G., Ma, Z., Sun, A., Thalmann, N.M.: Time-aware point-of-interest recommendation. In: International ACM SIGIR Conference on Research and Development in Information Retrieval, pp. 363–372 (2013)
22. Ren, X., Song, M., Junde, S.: Point-of-interest recommendation based on the user check-in behavior. Chin. J. Comput. **1**, 28–51 (2017)

Detecting Overlapping Communities
of Nodes with Multiple Attributes
from Heterogeneous Networks

Kamal Taha[1]([⊠]) and Paul D. Yoo[2]

[1] Khalifa University, Abu Dhabi, UAE
kamal.taha@ku.ac.ae
[2] Birkbeck College, University of London, London, UK

Abstract. Many methods have been proposed for detecting communities from heterogeneous information networks with general topologies. However, most of these methods can detect communities with homogeneous structures containing nodes with only a single attribute. Investigating methods for detecting communities containing nodes with multiple attributes from heterogeneous information networks with general topologies has been understudied. Such communities are realistic in real-world social structures and exhibits many interesting properties. Towards this, we propose a system called DOMAIN that can detect overlapping communities of nodes with multiple attributes from heterogeneous information networks with general topologies. The framework of DOMAIN focuses on domains (i.e., attributes) that describe human characteristics such as ethnicity, culture, religion, demographic, age, or the like. The ultimate objective of the framework is to detect the *smallest* sub-communities with the *largest* possible number of domains, to which an active user belongs. The smaller a sub-community is, the more specific and granular its interests are. The interests of such a sub-community is the union of the interests and characteristics of the single domain communities, from which it is constructed. We evaluated DOMAIN by comparing it experimentally with three methods. Results revealed marked improvement.

Keywords: Social networks · Heterogeneous information networks · Community detection · Overlapping communities · Multi-domain community

1 Introduction

To be empirically studied, a large number of complex scientific problems need to be depicted as a network representation. Such problems are not limited to specific scientific fields. For example, complex scientific problems in the following fields have been successfully studied after being depicted as a network representation: ecosystems [1, 7, 10, 13, 30], biological systems [4, 5, 6, 16, 23, 25, 26, 33], scientific citations [22], and information systems [3, 8, 14, 15, 19, 29, 32, 34, 35, 38]. However, problems related to social media ecosystem (e.g., Facebook, LinkedIn, Twitter, forums, and blogs) are the most successfully and efficiently studied ones. Detecting community structures is one of the most studied social media ecosystem problems. Each social

© ICST Institute for Computer Sciences, Social Informatics and Telecommunications Engineering 2019
Published by Springer Nature Switzerland AG 2019. All Rights Reserved
X. Wang et al. (Eds.): CollaborateCom 2019, LNICST 292, pp. 760–779, 2019.
https://doi.org/10.1007/978-3-030-30146-0_51

network has a specific community structure. Such structure can be studied for understanding the dynamics of the network. There are numerous reasons for detecting such communities from social networks. For example, there may be a need for classifying the members of some social media network into communities that reflect the organization of the society. A society can be organized into unions that reflect some social criteria. Example of such unions are social groups, colleagues, families, and villages. Such classification is useful in identifying many features that can be used for community membership prediction. It also helps in understanding the dynamics of the members of a community. A cohesive community is defined as a group of densely connected individuals via some common social characteristics such as interests. A "good" community is widely defined as cohesive, compact, and strongly connected internally, but sparsely connected with the remaining parts of the network.

Current methods cluster nodes based on two types of information: network data and attribute data. The network data depicts the relationships between some objects. The attribute data characterizes the objects. These methods employ different techniques that cluster nodes by grouping them either based on their network structural data or attribute data. Most of the methods that cluster nodes based on network structure employ probabilistic generative models to infer the posterior memberships of a community [3, 9, 10, 21, 33, 36]. Most of the methods that cluster nodes based on attribute data can be classified as: (1) methods use the connections between nodes (i.e., link structure) to perform the clustering [3, 11, 13, 28], (2) methods use node attributes to detect the network's communities [4, 37], and (3) methods use both link structure and node attributes to perform clustering [2]. The methods under the first classification overlook the nodes' attributes, which hold important clustering characteristics. The methods under the second classification overlook the important structural relationships between nodes. The methods under the third classification combine the structural and attribute information so that nodes are grouped not only based on the density of their connectivity, but also their common attribute similarities. A large number of these methods detect communities from heterogeneous information networks, which are realistic and exhibits interesting properties. For example, an academic network may include multiple heterogeneous attributes such as author names, journal/conference names, and keywords. However, many of these methods detect communities with only certain topological structures [1, 9, 12–14, 18, 29, 30, 34]. To overcome this, a number of methods have been proposed for detecting communities from hetcrogeneous information networks with general topologies [20]. However, most of these methods can detect communities with homogeneous structures containing nodes with only a single attribute. That is, they may not detect a community of nodes with multiple attributes. Towards this, we propose in this paper a system called DOMAIN (Detecting Overlapping Multi-Attributed Information Nodes) that can detect overlapping communities of nodes with multiple attributes from heterogeneous information networks with general topologies.

The framework of DOMAIN focuses on attributes that describe human characteristics such as ethnicity, culture, religion, demographic, age, or the like. We use the term "domains" to refer to such attributes. Heterogeneous multi-domain communities are realistic and resemble many real-world communities. For example, a multi-domain community formed from the domains ethnicity, religion, age, and demography can represent a portion of individuals from a specific ethnic group, who follow a specific religion, who live in a specific neighborhood, and belong to a specific age range. Such a community is realistic in real-world community structures and exhibits many interesting properties. Therefore, DOMAIN aims at detecting the smallest overlapping sub-communities with the largest possible domains, to which active users belong. This is because, the smaller a sub-community is, the more specific and granular its interests are. The interests of such a sub-community is the union of the interests and characteristics of the single domain communities, from which the sub-community is constructed. The main contributions of this paper are summarized as follows:

1. Proposing a methodology for extracting the set of dominant keywords (e.g., buzzwords) from the messages associated with a specific social group to act as a potential representative of the social group.
2. Proposing a graphical model that represents cross-communities and their ontological relationships. The model accounts for all sub-communities with multiple domains that exist due to the interrelations between communities.
3. Proposing a novel and efficient methodology for identifying the smallest sub-communities with the largest number of domains, to which active users belongs.
4. Evaluating our proposed method by comparing it experimentally with three other methods.

2 Concepts Used in the Paper

We call an information network a heterogeneous information network, if the number of attributes and number of links of its nodes are $|N| > 1$ and $|L| > 1$, respectively; otherwise, the information network is a homogeneous information network. We use the term "domain" to refer to a common characterizing attribute of the nodes of a community within a heterogeneous information network. A domain (i.e., a characterizing attribute) defines a community based on a specific and known social group characteristic such as ethnicity, religion, belief, demography, culture, pursuit, area of activity, or the like. We use the term Lone-Domain Community (LDC) to refer to a group of individuals who share a single common domain. For example, individuals, who belong to a specific ethnic group form a LDC. We formalize the concept of LDC in definition 1.

Definition 1 - Lone-Domain Community (LDC): LDC is an aggregation G of individuals within an information network G = (V, E) with schema (A, R), where each $x, y \in G \, (x \neq y)$ share one single common attribute mapping $\partial: V \rightarrow A$ and link type mapping $\psi: E \rightarrow R$. That is, a LDC is defined by a common characterizing attribute mapping A, with links as relations from R.

The smaller a community is, the more specific and granular its interests are. Towards this, we introduce a granular class of communities called Multi-Domain Community (MDC), which is formed from two or more LDCs. Thus, a MDC is a group of individuals who share multiple common domains (e.g., ethnicity, religion, etc.). The size of a MDC is usually smaller than each of the LDCs forming it. An Overlapping Multi-Domain Community (OMDC) is a MDC formed from the intersection of two or more LDCs with different domains within a heterogeneous information network. That is an OMDC is an aggregation of individuals who share common cross-communities (i.e., inter-communities) domain characteristics. Therefore, an OMDC can be formed from the overlapping of two or more LDCs that belong to different domains.

In general, an OMDC is a granular class of communities formed from two or more LDCs with different domains. As an example, an OMDC can be a portion of individuals who belong to a same ethnic group $ETH(x)$, who also follow a same religion $REL(y)$, and are also descendants from a same national origin $ORG(z)$. Thus, this OMDC is formed from the intersection: $ETH(x) \cap REL(y) \cap ORG(z)$. Intuitively, the characteristics of an OMDC are more granular and specific than the characteristics of each of the LDCs, from which the OMDC is formed. In the framework of DOMAIN, an OMDC is represented by *the set of the overlapped LDCs*, from which the OMDC is formed.

We model OMDCs and their hierarchical relationships using a graphical representation called Overlapping Multi-Domain Communities Graph (OMDCGraph). In an OMDCGraph, each LDC is represented by a node. An OMDC formed from the overlapping of two LDCs C_1 and C_2 is represented by a node $\{C_1, C_2\}$. The ontological relationship between the node $\{C_1, C_2\}$ and each of the nodes C_1 and C_2 is represented by the link connecting them. An OMDCGraph accounts for all the OMDCs that exist due to the interrelations between LDCs of different domains. We formalize the concept of OMDCGraph in Definition 2.

Definition 2 - Overlapping Multi-Domain Communities Graph (OMDCGraph): An OMDCGraph is a graphical representation of the ontological relationships between cross-communities OMDCs. It consists of a pair of sets (V, E). V is a finite set of nodes depicting LDCs of various domains and the OMDCs formed from the overlapping of these LDCs. E is a set of edges depicting the binary relations on V. An OMDC at a hierarchical level n consists of at least n LDCs. If two OMDCs contain at least one common LDC (i.e., an overlapping LDC), they are linked by an edge to denote their class-subclass relationship. The subclass has its own characteristics while inheriting the characteristics of its parent class. The set of edges E that denotes class-subclass relationships in an OMDCGraph is formalized as follows:

$E = \{edge(OMDC_i, OMDC_j): OMDC_i, OMDC_j \in V; OMDC_i \cap OMDC_j \neq 0;$ $OMDC_i$ resides at hierarchical level n and $OMDC_j$ resides at hierarchical level $n+1$ of the OMDCGraph}.

For the sake of easy reference, we present in Table 1 abbreviations of the concepts proposed in the paper.

Table 1. Abbreviations of the concepts proposed in the paper

Abbreviation	Description
LDC	Lone-Domain Community
MDC	Multi-Domain Community
OMDC	Overlapping Multi-Domain Community
OMDCGraph	Overlapping Multi-Domain Communities Graph

3   Motivation and Outline of the Approach

3.1   Motivation

In real-world setting, there are always new members wishing to join existing and established communities. This requires a methodology for efficiently identifying all existing communities that share the interests of active users. That is, this process requires a methodology for detecting the LDCs, with which the active user shares domains. Each of the different LDCs, to which this user belongs, has the characteristics of a special domain. A sub-community that possesses all these domains, is the most reflective to the characteristics of the user. That is, the smaller a multi-domain community is, the more reflective it is to the characteristics of its members. Therefore, our proposed method in this paper attempts to identify the smallest and most granular multi-domain sub-communities for a user. A granular multi-domain sub-community (i.e., an OMDC) is a subclass of all the LDCs, to which the user belongs. An OMDC is formed from the intersection of two or more LDCs. The characteristics of an OMDC are more granular and specific than the characteristics of each of the LDCs, from which the OMDC is constructed. Intuitively, the size of an OMDC is smaller than each of the LDCs, from which it is constructed.

Identifying the OMDC, to which a user belongs, requires a method that can detect communities of nodes with multiple attributes from heterogeneous information networks with general topologies. Investigating such methods has been understudied. Most such existing methods can detect communities with homogeneous structures containing nodes with only a single attribute. That is, most these methods cannot detect a community of nodes with multiple attributes. Towards this, we introduce our proposed system DOMAIN. The system focuses on characterizing attributes (i.e., domains) that describe human characteristics such as ethnicity, culture, religion, demographic, age, or the like. The ultimate objective of DOMAIN is to detect the smallest sub-communities with the largest possible domains, to which active users belong.

3.2   Outline of the Approach

The following are the sequential processing steps taken by DOMAIN for detecting the smallest sub-communities with the largest possible number of domains, to which an active user belongs:

(1) *Constructing a Training OMDCGraph (Sect. 4):*
   (a) Collect messages from explicitly declared LDCs of different domains to be used as training datasets. Each set of messages associated with a specific LDC will be used by the system as a training dataset with respect to the LDC.
   (b) Extract a set of *candidate* keywords (e.g., buzzwords) from the messages associated with each LDC to act as a *potential* representative of the LDC.
   (c) Filter the candidate keywords of each LDC to identify the *dominant* ones (the ones that have frequent occurrences in a significant number of messages associated with the LDC). The identified set of dominant keywords will be used by the system as a representative of the LDC.

    (d) Construct the training OMDCGraph as follows:

        i. *Construct the root level of the graph:* Each LDC with a unique domain is represented by a node at the root level of the graph.

        ii. *Construct level 1 of the graph*: If there is a significant number of *common* dominant keywords associated with a set S of root LDC nodes, the set converges at level 1 of the graph. The convergence node represents an OMDC, which is represented by the set S.

        iii. *Construct the remaining levels of the graph:* Each combination of OMDC nodes located at level n of the graph converge at level $n + 1$ to form a new OMDC node, if: (1) there exist at least one common LDC in all the OMDC nodes in the combination, and (2) the combination does not include more than one LDC with the same domain. The convergence node is represented by the set of all the LDCs in the combination. This process continues until no new OMDC can be formed at a new level.

(2) *Identifying the LDCs to which an active user belongs (Sect. 5):*

    (a) Extract the dominant keywords from the messages associated with the active user using the same techniques described in steps 1-b and 1-c.

    (b) If the active user and a root LDC node have significant common dominant keywords associated with their messages, the active user belongs to this LDC.

3) *Identifying the smallest OMDC with the largest number of domains to which the active user belongs (Sect. 6):*

    (a) Mark the root nodes identified in step 2-b.

    (b) The active user's smallest OMDC is located at the convergence of the *longest paths* originated from the marked nodes described in step 3-a. The active user belongs to all the LDCs comprising this convergence OMDC.

4 Constructing a Training OMDCGraph

4.1 Extracting the Dominant Keywords from the Training Messages Dataset Associated with a LDC

After extracting the set of candidate keywords (e.g., buzzwords) from the messages associated with a LDC, DOMAIN filters these keywords to keep only the dominant ones (the ones that have frequent occurrences in significant number of the messages associated with the LDC). This is because a keyword is uninformative, if it occurs in a few messages or/and it has few occurrences in the messages. To overcome this, DOMAIN keeps only the candidate keywords that have frequent occurrences in a significant number of messages associated with the LDC. This set of identified dominant keywords will be used by DOMAIN as a representative of the LDC.

    DOMAIN identifies the dominant keywords by associating each keyword with a score that reflects its dominance status with regards to the other keywords. It assigns a pairwise beats and looses indicator for each candidate keyword that occur in the messages associated with the LDC. A beat-loose table is constructed as follows. The entries of the table are (k_i, k_j) where k_i denotes keyword i while k_j denotes keyword j.

Let n_i be the number of times that the number of mentioning of k_i in the messages associated with the LDC is greater than that of k_j. Let n_j be the number of times that the number of mentioning of k_j in the messages is greater than that of k_i. If $ni > n_{j,}$ entry (k_i, k_j) will assigned the indicator symbol "+". Otherwise, it will be assigned the indicator "−". If $n_i = n_j$, entry (k_i, k_j) will assigned the indicator symbol "0". We now formalize the concept of pairwise score of a keyword in Definition 3:

Definition 3 – Pairwise score of a keyword: *Let the denotation $k_i > k_j$ means that the number of times the number of mentioning of k_j in the messages associated with a LDC is greater than that of k_i. The pairwise score of the keyword k_i equals:* $\left|\{k_j \in K_{LDC} : k_i > k_j\}\right| - \left|\{k_j \in K_{LDC} : k_j > k_i\}\right|$, *where K_{LDC} denotes the set of all candidate keywords in the messages associated with the LDC.*

Finally, the keyword k_i will be given a dominance score S, which is computed as follows. Let N_b be the number of times that k_i *beat* all other keywords. Let N_l be the number of times that k_i *lost* to all other keywords. The dominance score of k_i (S_{ki}) equals: $S_{ki} = N_b - N_l$. The summation of the dominance scores of all keywords is zero. If m is the number of keywords, the highest possible dominance score is $(m - 1)$, while the lowest possible dominance score is $-(m - 1)$. Each keyword is given a normalized dominance score $\bar{S}$. The keywords, whose normalized dominance scores are greater than a threshold β are considered dominant. The rest of the keywords are excluded and considered uninformative. As shown in Eq. 1, β is the value that is less than the mean of the normalized dominance score by the standard error of the mean.

$$\beta = \frac{1 - \sqrt{\sum_{\forall k_j \in K_{LDC}} (\bar{S}_{k_j} - \frac{1}{|K_{LDC}|})^2}}{|K_{LDC}|} \tag{1}$$

Example 1: To illustrate the process of identifying the dominant keywords, we present a simplistic hypothetical example of 10 keywords that co-occur in 3 messages as shown in Table 2. Table 3 shows the pairwise score S and dominance score $\bar{S}$ of each keyword computed based on the number of occurrences of the keyword in the 3 messages shown in Table 2.

Table 2. Distribution of the 10 hypothetical keywords in the 3 messages shown in Example 1

	k_1	k_2	k_3	k_4	k_5	k_6	k_7	k_8	k_9	k_{10}
m_1	2	4	0	0	3	0	1	2	4	1
m_2	0	2	2	3	4	2	0	0	1	3
m_3	3	5	1	4	5	2	3	1	2	0

Table 3. The pairwise scores of the 10 keywords presented in Table 2 and described in Example 1 computed based on their *beats* and *looses* indicators. The table shows also the dominance scores and normalized dominance scores of the 10 keywords.

Keyword	k_1	k_2	k_3	k_4	k_5	k_6	k_7	k_8	k_9	k_{10}
k_1	0	+	−	+	+	−	−	−	+	−
k_2	−	0	−	−	0	−	−	−	−	−
k_3	+	+	0	+	+	+	+	0	+	+
k_4	−	+	−	0	+	−	−	−	−	0
k_5	−	0	−	−	0	+	−	−	−	−
k_6	+	+	−	+	−	0	+	−	0	+
k_7	+	+	−	+	+	−	0	0	+	0
k_8	+	+	0	+	+	+	0	0	+	−
k_9	−	+	−	+	+	0	−	−	0	−
k_{10}	+	+	−	0	+	−	0	+	+	0
S	+1	+8	−8	+4	+6	−2	−3	−5	+2	−3
$\bar{S}$	0.11	0.2	0	0.15	0.17	0.08	0.06	0.04	0.13	0.06

4.2   Constructing the Training OMDGraph

In this section, we describe the process of constructing a graphical representation of the ontological relationships between the training OMDCs. That is, we describe the process of constructing an Overlapping Multi-Domain Social Graph (OMDCGraph) that depicts the ontological relationships between the training OMDCs. Each LDC with a unique domain is represented by a node and placed at the root level of the OMDC-Graph. This node itself is represented by the dominant keywords (recall Sect. 4.1) in the messages associated with the LDC.

Level 1 of the OMDCGraph is constructed as follows. The paths originating from a subset S of the set of root nodes converge at level 1 of the graph to form a new OMDC node, if: the frequency of messages associated with each LDC node $N \in S$ that have occurrences of dominant keywords found in the messages associated with each other LDC node $N' \in S$ is significant. The new convergence OMDC node is represented by the set S of nodes. This node inherits the characteristics of each of the LDCs in the set S. Let $F_{N_i}^{N_j}$ be the frequency of messages associated with node N_j that contain occurrences of dominant keywords found in the messages associated with node N_i. $F_{N_i}^{N_j}$ is considered significant, if it is greater than β', which is a heuristically determined threshold. In the framework of DOMAIN, one of the following two frequency formulas is used based on application-specific requirements:

(1) Let M_k be the number of messages containing occurrences of keyword k. The following formula is preferred, if we want to diminish the impact of rare events. That is, if we do not want to consider the occurrences of k for which $M_k = 1$ as twice significant as the occurrence of k for which $M_k = 2$:

$$F_{N_i}^{N_j} = \log\left(1 + \frac{|M^{N_j}|}{|M_{N_i}^{N_j}|}\right)$$

- M^{N_j}: The set of messages associated with node N_j.
- $M_{N_i}^{N_j}$: The set of messages associated with node N_j that contain occurrences of dominant keywords in the messages associated with node N_i.

(2) The following formula is preferred, if the sizes of messages are relatively close. Specifically, it is preferred, if we want to disregard the *size* of messages containing common dominant keywords relative to the overall size of messages:

$$F_{N_i}^{N_j} = \log\left(1 + \frac{MAX|K_{N_i}^{N_j}|}{|M_{N_i}^{N_j}|}\right)$$

- $MAX|K_{N_i}^{N_j}|$: Maximum number of occurrences of the dominant keywords in the messages associated with node N_j in a message associated with node N_i.

The remaining levels of the OMDCGraph are constructed as follows. All unique combinations of OMDC nodes located at level n of the graph are enumerated. Let ς be the set of all these different combinations at level n. Each subset $\acute{s} \subseteq \varsigma$ converge at level $n + 1$ to form a new OMDC node, if: (1) there exist at least one common LDC in all the OMDC nodes $\in \acute{s}$, and (2) $\acute{s}$ does not include two or more LDCs with the same domain. The convergence OMDC node is represented by the set of LDCs in $\acute{s}$. The node inherits the characteristics of each LDC in $\acute{s}$. This process concludes when there is no new OMDC node can be formed at a new level. An OMDCGraph accounts for *all* the OMDCs that exist due to the interrelations between LDCs of different domains.

Example 2: From the messages that belong to some social media, consider that DOMAIN identified the seven LDCs shown in Table 4, which fall under four different domains. Consider that DOMAIN constructed the OMDCGraph shown in Fig. 1 using the techniques described in Sect. 4. Each OMDC node at level 2 of the graph is formed from the convergence of two OMDC nodes at level 1 that have at least one common LDC and do not have two or more LDCs with the same domain. For example, the OMDC node {REL(y), ETH(x), NBHD(y)} at level 2 resulted from the convergence of the following two OMDC nodes at level 1, which include the common LDC node ETH (x) and do not include more than one LDC with the same domain: {ETH(x), NBHD(y)} and {ETH(x), REL(y)}. This convergence node {REL(y), ETH(x), NBHD(y)} is represented by the set of LDCs forming it and it denotes the portion of individuals who follow the same religion REL(y), who also belong to the same ethnic group ETH(x), and who also live in neighbourhood NBHD(y).

Table 4. Seven hypothetical LDCs with four different domains used in the construction of the OMDCGraph in Fig. 1 and described in Example 2

LDC	Domain	Description
NBHD(x), NBHD(y)	Neighbourhood-based	Users who live in neighbourhood NBHD(x) and NBHD(y)
REL(x), REL(y)	Religion-based	Users who follow religions REL(x) and REL(y)
ETH(x), ETH(y)	Ethnicity-based	Users who are descendants of ethnicities ETH(x) and ETH(y)
ORG(x)	Region-based	Users from national origin (ORG(x))

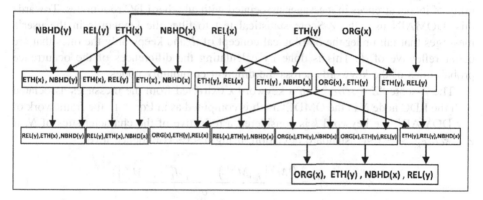

Fig. 1. A training OMDCGraph constructed based on the information described in Example 2

5   Identifying the LDCs to Which an Active User Belongs

As described in Sect. 4.2, each LDC with a unique domain is represented by a node and placed at the root level of the training OMDCGraph. As described in Sect. 4.1, each of these LDC nodes is represented by the set of dominant keywords extracted from the messages associated with it. From the set of LDC nodes, OMDCGraph identifies the subset, to which as active user belongs. It determines that the active user belongs to a LDC, if the messages associated with the user contains significant number of keywords, whose *ontological concepts* fall under the dominant keywords of the LDC. An ontology describes the concepts in a domain of discourse. Let k "kind of" k' means that class k is a subclass of class k' in an ontology. k' is the highest general superclass of k in a defined ontology hierarchy. k shares the same domain, cognitive characteristics, and properties of k'. DOMAIN labels all nodes in an ontology with the label of the root node.

First, DOMAIN fetches the user's messages for keywords, whose ontological concepts fall under the ontological concepts of the dominant keywords of each root LDC node in the OMDCGraph. Consider that d_i is one of these nodes. Each of the dominant keywords representing d_i is considered a root ontology. Then, DOMAIN fetches the user's messages for keywords, whose ontological concepts fall under the root ontologies of d_i. That is, it fetches the user's messages for keywords that fall under each of the ontological concept of the dominant keywords of d_i. Consider that the word "entertainer" is one of the dominant keywords of d_i.

The user is considered to belong to the LDC represented by the node d_i, if the number of keywords in the user's messages that fall under the ontological concept of d_i is greater than a heuristically determined threshold. However, some of the keywords in the user's messages that fall under the ontological concepts of the dominant keywords of d_i may not be reflective of the community represented by d_i. This happens when these keywords are associated with many *other* LDC root nodes. To overcome this, the DOMAIN considers a keyword as reflective of d_i if the probability of its occurrences in the messages associated with d_i is statistically significantly different from the probability of its occurrences in messages associated with all other LDC root nodes. Towards this, DOMAIN uses the Z-Score statistical test to filter the keywords in the user's messages that fall under the ontological concept of d_i and keeps only the ones that are better reflective of d_i. This is done by calculating the differences of the occurrence probabilities of the keywords across the different community nodes.

The Z-score "$Z - score_k^N$" of a keyword k extracted from the messages associated with the LDC node N in the OMDCGraph is computed as in Eq. 2. In the framework of our DOMAIN, the keyword k is considered a reflective of the characteristics of N, if $Z - score_k^N > $ "-1.96" standard deviation, using a 95% confidence level.

$$Z - score_k^N = \frac{\left(|M_k^N| / |M^N|\right) - \left(|M_k^{N'}| / |M^{N'}|\right)}{\sigma} \tag{2}$$

- M_k^N: Set of messages associated with LDC node N that contain occurrences of the keyword k.
- $M_k^{N'}$: Set of messages associated with all other LDC nodes N' that contain occurrences of the keyword k.
- M^N: Set of messages associated with LDC node N.
- $M^{N'}$: Set of messages associated with all other LDC nodes N'.
- σ: population's standard deviation.

DOMAIN is built on top of Stanford CoreNLP [12] and Protégé [24]. DOMAIN uses Stanford CoreNLP for generating keyword lemmas and recognizing named entities in the messages associated with the user. It uses Protégé for ontology alignment and the matching between the keyword lemmas in the user's messages and the dominant keywords in the training dataset (i.e., the dominant keywords representing the root nodes in the training OMDCGraph). That is, DOMAIN uses Protégé for capturing the correspondences between the keywords in the user's messages and the training dominant keywords. Ontology matching (i.e., ontology alignment) is the procedure of identifying the correspondences between different concepts. DOMAIN through Protégé checks if there is a match between a dominant keyword and a keyword (or its respective ontological sub-categories) extracted from the user's messages.

6 Identifying the Smallest OMDC with the Largest Number of Domains to Which an Active User Belongs

To identify the smallest OMDC with the largest number of domains to which an active user belongs, DOMAIN performs the following:

(1) It marks the *root* LDC nodes in the OMDCGraph, to which the active user belongs (recall Sect. 5 for how OMDCGraph identifies these root LDC nodes).

(2) It traverses through the paths of the OMDCGraph starting from the marked root LDC nodes to identify the OMDC nodes, at which *all* the paths convergence at each level of the graph. That is, by navigating the paths originating from the marked nodes, OMDCGraph identifies the OMDC nodes located at the convergences of *all* the paths at each level.

(3) From among the different OMDCs identified in step 2, the smallest OMDC with the largest number of domains, to which the active user belongs, is the one located at the convergence of all the *longest* paths originating from the marked root nodes. That is, this OMDC node is positioned at the intersection of *all longest paths* originating from the marked root nodes.

If all longest paths originated from n root nodes, the user's smallest OMDC located at the convergence of these paths is usually formed from m LDCs, where $m > n$. That is, if DOMAIN identified n *explicit* LDC root nodes for the user (using the techniques described in Sect. 5), the user's smallest OMDC with the largest number of domains is likely to contain greater than n LDCs. The extra LDCs (i.e., the $m - n$ LDCs) are identified *implicitly* by DOMAIN based on the structure of the OMDCGraph and the interrelations between the different OMDC nodes. The user's messages may not contain keywords that directly refer to these extra LDCs.

Example 3. Consider that DOMAIN traversed the paths of the OMDCGraph shown in Fig. 1 and described in Example 2 in order to identify the smallest OMDC with the largest number of domains, to which an active user belongs. Using the techniques described in Sect. 5, consider that DOMAIN identified the following explicit LDC nodes, to which the active user belongs: (1) neighborhood NBHD(x), and (2) national origin ORG(x). First, DOMAIN would mark the root LDC nodes NBHD(x) and ORG(x) as shown in the OMDCGraph in Fig. 2. Then, starting from the marked two root nodes, DOMAIN would navigate through the paths to identify the convergence OMDC nodes as shown in Fig. 2. For easy reference, the path originating from NBHD(x) is marked with dotted red and the path originating from ORG(x) is marked with dashed blue. There can be several convergence OMDC nodes at different levels of the graph, but there is only one convergence node in this particular example. As Fig. 2 shows, the smallest OMDC with the largest number of domains, to which the active user belongs is the following:

$$\{\text{ORG}(x), \text{ETH}(y), \text{NBHD}(x), \text{REL}(y)\}$$

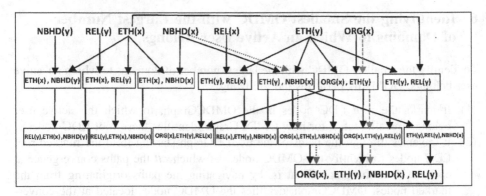

Fig. 2. The convergence of the longest paths originating from the root nodes in the OMDCGraph that indicates the smallest OMDC, to which the user described in Example 3 belongs.

This OMDC is located at the convergence of the longest paths originating from the root nodes NBHD(x) and ORG(x). The following observations can be drawn from the result:

- The paths originated from only *two* root LDC nodes and that the active user's smallest OMDC node contains *four* LDC nodes. That is, from the user's two *explicitly* identified LDCs, DOMAIN could identify the user's smallest OMDC, which contains four LDCs. Two of them are *implicitly* inferred by the system.
- The two extra implicitly identified LDCs (i.e., ETH(y) and REL(y)) are inferred by DOMAIN based on the structure of the OMDCGraph and the interrelations between the different OMDCs.

Every time DOMAIN identifies the smallest OMDC for a user, it will enhance the training dataset and OMDCGraph accordingly. Let N be the smallest OMDC node identified by DOMAIN for an active user u. DOMAIN will enhance the training dataset by updating it as follows. It will add the list of messages associated with u to the list of messages associated with each LDC node $N' \in N$. That is, the list of training messages associated with each N' will be incremented by including the list of messages associated with u. Accordingly, DOMAIN will update and optimize the following: (1) the number of keywords' occurrences in the messages associated with each $N' \in N$ (e.g., recall Table 2), and (2) the pairwise score S and dominance score $\bar{S}$ (recall Table 3) of each keyword in the messages associated with each $N' \in N$. For the sake of conserving computation time, we advocate updating the pairwise score S and dominance score $\bar{S}$ only at certain intervals (i.e., update points). That is, the update is based on *all* OMDCs identified between intervals and not based on each one of them individually.

7 Experimental Results

We implemented DOMAIN in Java. We ran the system under Windows 10 Pro using Intel(R) Core(TM) i7-6820HQ processor. The machine has 2.70 GHz CPU and 16 GB RAM. We evaluated DOMAIN by comparing it experimentally with Sharma et al. [27]. Sharma et al. [27] uses the concept of group accretion, which is the process of increasing the size of a group by adding new more members. It uses the communication paths in a network to measure the degree of relationships between a group and a person outside the group. Given a group with n members, [27] predicts the likelihood of a new member outside the group for being absorbed in the group, where the size of the group will be incremented to $n + 1$. The authors proposed three different methods inspired by dyadic link prediction (DLP) techniques and sociology theories. Each of these methods assigns a score to each group to reflect its similarity (i.e., affinity) with the person outside the group. The first method is called GKS. It extends the Katz method [17], which enumerates network paths. GKS makes predication by employing a DLP-inspired unsupervised path counting. The second method is called BRWS. It uses a semi-supervised learning approach inspired by network alignment algorithms. It identifies each cycle that passes through each group and the remaining groups. The third method is called GLPS. It employs a semi-supervised method inspired by hypergraph label propagation techniques. We evaluated and compared the accuracy of communities detected by DOMAIN, GKS, BRWS, and GLPS in terms of F1-score and Adjusted Rand Index (ARI), with reference to a ground-truth dataset. F1-score is the harmonic average of precision and recall, and is computed as shown below:

$$F1 - \text{socre} = 2 \cdot \frac{\text{precision} \cdot \text{recall}}{\text{precision} + \text{recall}}$$

ARI computes the expected similarity of all pair-wise comparisons between two clusters (e.g., between a ground-truth community and a community detected by a method), as shown in the formula below:

$$ARI = \frac{\text{index} - \text{expected index}}{\text{maximum index} - \text{expected index}}$$

- Index $= \sum_{ij} \binom{n_{ij}}{2}$
- Expected index $= \left[\sum_i \binom{a_i}{2} \sum_j \binom{b_j}{2} \right] / \binom{n}{2}$
- Max index $= \frac{1}{2} \left[\sum_i \binom{a_i}{2} + \sum_j \binom{b_j}{2} \right]$

We evaluated and compared DOMAIN, GKS, GLPS, and BRWS using the DBLP dataset [31]. We adopted the same experimental setup and the same dataset used for evaluating GKS, GLPS, and BRWS as described in [27]. We used the following same experimental setup described in [27]: (1) the same training and test periods of main splits, (2) the same metrics, and (3) the same DBLP dataset. Below are brief descriptions of the mentioned DBLP, split periods, and metrics:

- The DBLP dataset [31] was extracted from publications in 22 different computer science subfields from 1930 to 2011.
- The dataset was divided to different splits as shown in Table 5. As shown in the table, each split is marked with a fixed end year of the training dataset. Papers published between the years 2004 and 2007 are used for the training while papers published between the years 2008 and 2010 are used for the testing.
- The metrics used for the evaluation are defined as follows:

$$\text{Precision}@\,N_{top}\,(IA) = \frac{\text{Number of groups correctly predicted using IA process from top} - N_{top}\text{ list}}{N_{top}}$$

$$\text{Recall}@N_{top}\,(IA) = \frac{\text{Number of collaborations correctly predicted using IA process from top} - N_{top}\text{ list}}{\#\text{ of actual IA generated groups}}$$

- IA: Incremental accretion.
- N_{top}: The top sorted N unique set of IA.
- $Top\text{-}N_{top}$: The highest scoring in the sorted N unique set of IA.

As Table 5 shows, we divided the dataset into the same training and test periods (splits) as described in [27]. These divisions are the same ones used by Sharma et al. [27] in evaluating GKS, BRWS, and GLPS. Table 6 shows the prediction accuracy of the methods based on the divisions of the dataset shown in Table 5, using the per-group metrics Precision@N_{top}(IA) and Recall@N_{top}(IA) for $N_{top} = 100$ as described in [27]. The values shown in Table 6 for GKS, BRWS, and GLPS are the same ones listed in [27].

Table 5. Dividing the dataset into the same training and test periods (splits) as described in [27]

Boundary Yr	Split No.	Train	Test
2007	Main Split	2004–2007	2008–2010

Table 6. The prediction accuracy of the methods using the per-group metrics Precision@N_{top}(IA) and Recall@N_{top}(IA) for $N_{top} = 100$ as described in [27]. The values shown in the table for GKS, BRWS, and GLPS are the same ones listed for these methods in [27].

	GKS	GLPS	BRWS	DOMAIN
AvgPrecision@100(IA)	0.0210	0.0349	0.0355	0.147
AvgRecall@100(IA)	0.3176	0.6034	0.6050	0.6083

We also compared the accuracy of the four methods for detecting the DBLP communities in terms of F1-score (Fig. 3) and ARI (Fig. 4).

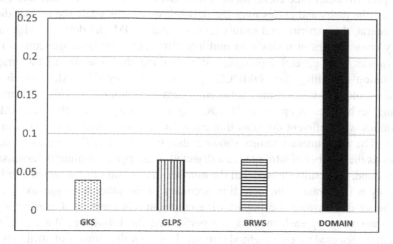

Fig. 3. The accuracy of each method for detecting the DBLP communities in terms of F1-score

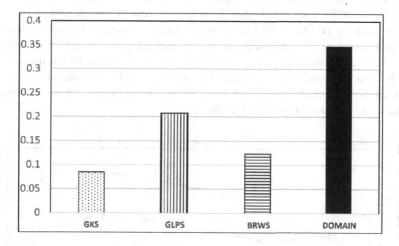

Fig. 4. The accuracy of each method for detecting the DBLP communities in terms of ARI

8   Discussion of the Results

As Table 6 and Figs. 3 and 4 show, DOMAIN outperformed the GKS, BRWS, and GLPS methods in terms of AvgPrecision@100(IA), AvgRecall@100(IA), F1-score, and ARI. We attribute the performance of DOMAIN over the other three methods to its good predictive capabilities and also the limitations of these three methods. In general, the GKS method did not perform well, while the GLPS method performed well compared to the BRWS and GKS methods. Based on our observations of the experimental results, we attribute the poor performance of the GKS method to several limitations, mostly related to Katz score employed by the method. We attribute the relative performance of the GLPS method over BRWS method to the fact that the later considered the paths and cycles over the network of groups while the former did not.

In general, the experimental results revealed that DOMAIN detected with marked accuracy communities of nodes with multiple attributes from heterogeneous information networks with general topologies. We attribute this, mainly, to the graphical representation modelling (i.e., OMDCGraph) employed by DOMAIN, which represents the ontological relationships between *all* cross-communities. This is because the modelling techniques adopted in OMDCGraph account for all the multi-attribute communities with different domains that exist due to the interrelations between communities. The experimental results showed also that DOMAIN's detection accuracy increases as the number of attributes in a detected overlapped community increases. On the other hand, the results showed that the number of attributes in a detected overlapped community is irrelevant to the detection accuracy of the other three methods.

To better demonstrate the impact of a community's number of attributes on its detection accuracy by each method, we performed the following. We classified the communities detected by each method into sets based on the number of attributes in the communities. For each of the four methods, each set includes the communities detected by the method that have the same number of attributes. Then, we computed the overall average F1-score for each set. Figure 5 shows the results. As the figure shows, the detection accuracy of DOMAIN increases constantly as the number of attributes in a community increases. We attribute this to the capability of DOMAIN to detect the smallest sub-communities with the largest possible domains, to which users belong. This is because, the smaller a community is, the more specific and granular its interests are, which is evident in the dataset used in our experiments. These interests are included in the profiles of users in the dataset.

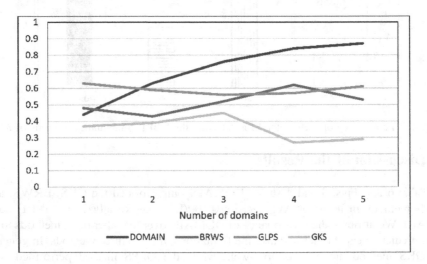

Fig. 5. The overall average F1-score for each set of detected communities that have the same number of attributes.

9   Conclusion

We proposed in this paper a system called DOMAIN that can detect communities of nodes with *multiple attributes* from heterogeneous information networks with general topologies. The framework of DOMAIN focuses on attributes (i.e., domains) that describe human characteristics such as ethnicity, culture, religion, demographic, or the like. Detecting such heterogeneous multi-domain sub-communities is crucial for understanding and analysing the structures and dynamicity of real-world social networks.

DOMAIN aims at detecting the smallest OMDC with the largest possible number of domains, to which an active user belongs. The smaller a sub-community is, the more specific and granular its interests are. The interests and characteristics of such an OMDC is the union of the interests and characteristics of the LDCs, from which it is constructed. DOMAIN identifies the user's smallest OMDC with the largest number of attributes as follows. It models training OMDCs using a graphical representation called OMDCGraph, which represents the ontological relationships between the OMDCs. In the graph, each LDC is represented by a node at the root level. The paths from some root nodes converge at level 1 of the graph to form a new OMDC node, if the frequency of messages associated with these nodes that contain common dominant keywords is significant. Each OMDC node at level $n+1$ of the graph is formed from the convergence of two or more OMDC nodes at level n that have at least one common LDC and do not have two or more LDCs with the same domain. The user's smallest OMDC with the largest number of domains is located at the convergence of the longest paths originating from root nodes representing LDCs that have significant matches with the user.

We evaluated DOMAIN by comparing it experimentally with the three methods proposed by Sharma et al. [27]. The experimental results showed that DOMAIN outperformed the three methods in terms of AvgPrecision@100(IA), AvgRecall@100 (IA), F1-score, and ARI. The results showed that DOMAIN's accuracy increases as the number of attributes in an overlapped detected community increases. We attribute this to the strong graphical representation modelling (i.e., OMDCGraph) employed by DOMAIN. This is because OMDCGraph accounts for all cross-communities with different domains that exist due to the interrelations between communities. However, the results showed that DOMAIN achieves modest results when the percentage of incomplete users' profiles in a detected community is rather large. We will investigate this shortcoming in a future work.

References

1. Aggarwal, C., Xie, Y., Yu, P.: Towards community detection in locally heterogeneous networks. In: SDM, pp. 391–402 (2011)
2. Akoglu, L., Tong, H., Meeder, B., Faloutsos, C.: PICS: parameter-free identification of cohesive subgoups in large attributed graphs. In: Proceedings of the SIAM International Conference on Data Mining, 2012, USA, pp. 439–450 (2012)

3. Al Zaabi, M., Taha, K., Martin, T.: CISRI: a crime investigation system using the relative importance of information spreaders in networks depicting criminals communications. IEEE Trans. Inf. Forensics Secur. 10(10), 2196–2211 (2015)
4. Al-Aamri, A., Taha, K., Homouz, D., Al-Hammadi, Y., Maalouf, M.: Analyzing a co-occurrence gene-interaction network to identify disease-gene association. BMC Bioinformatics 20, 70 (2019)
5. Al-Aamri, A., Taha, K., Homouz, D., Al-Hammadi, Y., Maalouf, M.: Constructing genetic networks using biomedical literature and rare event classification. Sci. Rep. 7, 15784 (2017)
6. Al-Jarrah, O., Yoo, P., Taha, K., Muhaidat, S.: Randomized subspace learning for proline cis-trans isomerization prediction. IEEE/ACM Trans. Comput. Biol. Bioinform. 12(4), 763–769 (2015)
7. Boden, B., Ester, M., Seidl, T.: Density-based subspace clustering in heterogeneous networks. In: ECML/PKDD, 2014, pp. 149–164 (2014)
8. Berlingerio, M., Pinelli, F., Calabrese, F.: Abacus: frequent pattern mining-based community discovery in multidimensional networks. Data Min. Knowl. Disc. 27(3), 294–320 (2013)
9. Chen, Y., Wang, X., Bu, J., Tang, B., Xiang, X.: Network structure exploration in networks with node attributes. Physica A Stat. Mech. Appl. 449, 240–253 (2016)
10. Chai, B., Yu, J., Jia, C., Yang, T., Jiang, Y.W.: Combining a popularity-productivity stochastic block model with a discriminative content model for general structure detection. Phys. Rev. E 88, 012807:1–012807:10 (2013)
11. Cheng, H., Zhou, Y., Yu, J.X.: Clustering large attributed graphs: a balance between structural and attribute similarities. ACM Trans. Knowl. Disc. Data 5, 12:1–12:33 (2011)
12. CoreNLP: Stanford University. https://stanfordnlp.github.io/CoreNLP/. Accessed Oct 2018
13. Camacho, J., Guimerà, R., Amaral, L.: Robust patterns in food web structure. Phys. Rev. Lett. 88, 228102 (2002)
14. Dan, S., Fusco, J., Shank, P., Chu, K., Schlager, M.: Discovery of community structures in a heterogeneous professional online network. In: System Sciences (HICSS), Hawaii USA, pp. 3262–3271, January 2013
15. Adly, F., et al.: Simplified subspaced regression network for identification of defect patterns in semiconductor wafer maps. IEEE Trans. Ind. Inform. 11(6), 1267–1276 (2015)
16. Guesmi, S., Trabelsi, C., Latiri, C.: Community detection in multi-relational bibliographic networks. In: Hartmann, S., Ma, H. (eds.) DEXA 2016. LNCS, vol. 9828, pp. 11–18. Springer, Cham (2016). https://doi.org/10.1007/978-3-319-44406-2_2
17. Katz, L.: A new status index derived from sociometric analysis. Psychometrika 18(1), 39–43 (1953)
18. Loe, C.W., Jensen, H.J.: Comparison of communities detection algorithms for multiplex. Phys. A 431, 29–45 (2015)
19. Taha, K., Yoo, P.: A system for analyzing criminal social networks. In: IEEE/ACM International Conference on Advances in Social Networks Analysis and Mining (ASONAM 2015), Paris, France, August 2015
20. Murate, T., Ikeya, T.: A new modularity for detecting one-to-many correspondence of communities in bipartite networks. Adv. Complex Syst. 13(1), 19–31 (2010)
21. Newman, M.E.J., Clauset, A.: Structure and inference in annotated networks. Nat. Commun. 7, 11863 (2015)
22. Newman, M.E.J.: Scientific collaboration networks: II. Shortest paths, weighted networks, and centrality. Phys. Rev. E 64, 016132 (2001)
23. Yoo, P., Muhaidat, S., Taha, K.: Intelligent consensus modeling for proline cis-trans isomerization prediction. IEEE/ACM Trans. Comput. Biol. Bioinform. 11(1), 26–32 (2014)
24. Protégé: Stanford Center for Biomedical Informatics Research, Stanford University. https://protege.stanford.edu/. Accessed Oct 2018

25. Al-Dalky, R., Taha, K., Al Homouz, D., Qasaimeh, M.: Applying Monte Carlo simulation to biomedical literature to approximate genetic network. IEEE/ACM Trans. Comput. Biol. Bioinform. 13(3), 494–504 (2016)
26. Taha, K.: GRtoGR: a system for mapping go relations to gene relations. IEEE Trans. Nanobiosci. 12(4), 1–9 (2013)
27. Sharma, A., Kuang, R., Srivastava, J., Feng, X., Singhal, K.: Predicting small group accretion in social networks: a topology based incremental approach. In: IEEE/ACM International Conference on Advance in Social Networks Analysis and Mining (ASONAM), 2015, pp. 408–415 (2015)
28. Taha, K.: Determining semantically related significant genes. IEEE/ACM Trans. Comput. Biol. Bioinform. 11(6), 1119–1130 (2014)
29. Taha, K., Elmasri, R.: SPGProfile: speak group profile. Inf. Syst. (IS) 35(7), 774–779 (2010)
30. Taha, K.: Disjoint community detection in networks based on the relative association of members. IEEE Trans. Comput. Soc. Syst. 5(2), 493–507 (2018)
31. Tang, J., Zhang, D., Yao, L.: Social network extraction of academic researchers. In: 7th IEEE ICDM, Nebraska, USA, 2007, pp. 292–301 (2007)
32. Taha, K.: Automatic academic advisor. In: 8th IEEE International Conference on Collaborative Computing: Networking, Applications and Worksharing (IEEE CollaborateCom), Pittsburgh, USA, October 2012
33. Taha, K.: Extracting various classes of data from biological text using the concept of existence dependency. IEEE J. Biomed. Health Inform. (IEEE J-BHI) 19(6), 1918–1928 (2015)
34. Taha, K., Yoo, P.: SIIMCO: a forensic investigation tool for identifying the influential members of a criminal organization. IEEE Trans. Inf. Forensics Secur. 11(4), 811–822 (2015)
35. Wang, X., Liu, J.: A layer reduction based community detection algorithm on multiplex networks. Phys. A 471, 244–252 (2014)
36. Yang, T., Jin, R., Chi, Y., Zhu, S.: Combining link and content for community detection: a discriminative approach. In: 15th ACM SIGKDD International Conference on Knowledge Discovery and Data Mining, 2009, France, pp. 927–936 (2009)
37. Yang, J., McAuley, J., Leskovec, J.: Community detection in networks with node attributes. In: IEEE International Conference on Data Mining, 2013, USA, pp. 1151–1156 (2013)
38. Zhu, G., Li, K.: A unified model for community detection of multiplex networks. In: Benatallah, B., Bestavros, A., Manolopoulos, Y., Vakali, A., Zhang, Y. (eds.) Web Information Systems Engineering –WISE 2014, vol. 8786, pp. 31–46. Springer, Cham (2014). https://doi.org/10.1007/978-3-319-11749-2_3

Dynamical Rating Prediction with Topic Words of Reviews: A Hierarchical Analysis Approach

Huibing Zhang[1], Hao Zhong[1], Qing Yang[2($\boxtimes$)], Fei Jia[1], Ya Zhou[1], and Fang Pan[3]

[1] Guangxi Key Laboratory of Trusted Software,
Guilin University of Electronic Technology, Guilin 541004, China
zhanghuibing@guet.edu.cn
[2] Guangxi Key Laboratory of Automatic Measurement Technology and Instrument,
Guilin University of Electronic Technology, Guilin 541004, China
gtyqing@hotmail.com
[3] Teaching Affairs Office, Guangxi Normal University, Guilin 541004, China

Abstract. Social commerce is an important part of the social network which contains a large number of user behaviors and user relationships. Users generate reviews, social relations, user-product or product-product mapping information that can reflect an evolution of product characteristics and user preferences in using social commerce. It is a popular topic by using these information to conduct rating prediction in the field of intelligent recommendation. In this paper, optimizing the rating prediction based on topic analysis in two aspects. On the one hand, in the process of data preprocessing, constructing a dynamic hierarchical tree of topic words (DHTTW), which can not only capture the change of users' preferences for product property, but also reflect the impact of different product property on users' preferences at the same time. Based on DHTTW, designing the mapping rules from user reviews to DHTTW to generate user preference vectors. On the other hand, in the process of prediction, proposing a prediction method named combination of gradient boosting decision tree and multi-class linear regression (GBDT-MCLR), which further improves the accuracy of rating prediction.

Keywords: Social commerce · Reviews · Rating prediction · Dynamic Hierarchical Tree of Topic Words · Multi-Class Linear Regression

1 Introduction

Social commerce is an integration of e-commerce and social networks, which is a developmenttendencyinthefuture. As an important part of the Internet of Things, social commerce achieves the deep integration of users and products by using user behavior (for example reviews) and user relationship. Reviews

© ICST Institute for Computer Sciences, Social Informatics and Telecommunications Engineering 2019
Published by Springer Nature Switzerland AG 2019. All Rights Reserved
X. Wang et al. (Eds.): CollaborateCom 2019, LNICST 292, pp. 780–798, 2019.
https://doi.org/10.1007/978-3-030-30146-0_52

in social commerce websites are users' evaluations of quality, performance, and price about products in a specific space–time environment, which reflect the basis of user rating and preference slightly. Therefore, reviews can be used to predict user rating and recommend certain products to them that satisfy their preferences. Here, the key is to extract topic features from reviews and achieve a mapping between topic features and rating value. The mapping mechanism must be established between reviews and the dynamic hierarchical relationship of topic words to describe an accurate meaning of reviews well under a specific space-time condition.

Traditional methods represent user preferences and product property by extracting topic features from reviews, which generate a topic distribution of reviews by performing topic analysis on reviews. And then obtain the relationship between each topic and real rating by using prediction model. However, in the process of data preprocessing, these methods only consider the topic distribution of reviews [1,2] but ignore the dynamic changes in the probability of topic words in different time windows and lack the description of hierarchical relationship between topic words. Thus, they can neither adapt well to the change in user preferences nor describe the effect of different properties of products on user rating. In the process of user rating prediction, using LR (linear regression), GBDT (gradient boosting decision tree), RF (random forest) and other prediction algorithms to predict. Based on recent research [3,4], a rating prediction method is proposed in this work by using DHTTW and GBDT-MCLR. The main contributions of the paper as follows:

(1) A review–preferences dynamic mapping method based on time windows was designed. On the basis of dynamic topic model (DTM) [5], excavating the potential change rule of topic words in different time windows, and exhibiting the evolution of user preference for product property by the change in probability of topic words for a timely rating prediction.

(2) A DHTTW constructing method of topic words of reviews was proposed. On the basis of dynamic changes in topic words, fusing the similarity and intensity of mutual information between topic words in a specified time window to establish hierarchical relationship. That is, a topic generated different hierarchical trees of topic words in different time windows, such that the hierarchy of topic words could dynamically represent the effect of topic words on user rating.

(3) A method for generating user preference vector based on DHTTW of topic words was proposed. Reviews were mapped to DHTTW in a specified time window to generate a topic vector of reviews. Using the vector to represent user preferences such that all reviews in different time windows were mapped to a vector space with the same dimension.

(4) A prediction method named GBDT-MCLR is proposed. In view of the discreteness of rating data [6], There is still much improvement when using GBDT-LR for predicting. Before rating prediction based on user preference vectors, clustering all preference vectors. Based on the idea of regression, generating a fitting function in each class. So that the GBDT-LR can adapt to the discrete data to a certain extent.

The remainder of this paper is organized as follows. Section 2 introduces relevant research. Section 3 describes the meaning of a dynamic analysis of topic words, constructs a hierarchical tree, and summarizes the process of the model and algorithm. Section 4 presents the construction details of the dynamic hierarchical tree of topic words, the mapping of user reviews to the tree structure, the generation rules of user preference vectors, and the improvement method of GBDT+LR prediction model. Section 5 conducts an experimental analysis of real datasets. Finally, Sect. 6 presents the conclusion of this work.

2   Related Works

There are two ways of recommendation for users: based on user location information [7–9] and user rating. Traditional methods for rating prediction in an intelligent recommendation system analyze a user's historical rating behavior and predict user rating on unrated products through a collaborative filtering method [10] without analyzing a user review text. With the development of topic discovery [11], sentiment analysis [12], user opinion mining [13], and other technologies of word prediction [14,15]. For example, Tang et al. [16] generates user preference vectors by analyzing the sentimental intensity of review texts, and predicts user ratings by combining the neural network prediction model. Seo et al. [17] uses convolutional neural network to analyze the features of user reviews, correlates users and product according to the features of user reviews by using matrix decomposition method, and finally makes rating prediction. In the research of this paper, the focus is topic analysis technology on user reviews, a rating prediction based on text topic discovery has become the focus of research in recent years.

Ma et al. [18] used LDA (Latent Dirichlet Allocation) model to conduct topic analysis on reviews, generate topic words, calculate a distribution probability of each topic word, manually annotate the sentiment intensity of topic words, generate corresponding word vector in accordance with topic words in reviews, and predict user rating. Ji et al. [19] considered a structural information among users, reviews, and products to propose a topic propagation model on the basis of user–review–product structure for describing user characteristics, products properties, and finally predicting user rating on the basis of random walk. Fang et al. [20] proposed a topic gradient descent model to conduct a topic analysis by using LDA model. The characteristic of topic was expressed by the probability distribution of topic words, and a latent factor was assigned to each topic. The latent factor was dynamically assigned in accordance with the proportion of topic in user review set. Finally, rating was predicted in accordance with the performance value of reviews on each topic. Zhang et al. [21] argued that if topic of review is limited to review text it cannot fully reveal the complex relationship between reviews and ratings. Thus, they proposed a method for integrating a topic and latent factor model, which enables them to complement each other linearly during user rating prediction to improve the accuracy of prediction. McAuley et al. [22] proposed an HTF (Hypersonic Tunnel Facility) model to explore the hidden relationship between user rating and reviews, which used LDA model to analyze all reviews published by each user and all reviews for each product. So it obtained characteristic matrixes of each user and product, and finally input the two characteristic matrixes into SVD (Singular Value Decomposition) model to obtain predicted value of user rating on the product. Zhang et al. [23] conducted a topic analysis based on HTF model. It represented reviews as a set of topic vectors in accordance with the topic words, and normalized these topic vectors to obtain the characteristics of each user and product. Then, it predicted user ratings of products on the basis of each vector and its corresponding rating by using three models: RF, LR, and GBDT. During the experiment, the RMSE value of score prediction was the smallest when LR was used, and the MAE value of score prediction was the smallest when GBDT was used. Therefore, the combination of GBDT and LR has become another focus of research.

Blei et al. [24] first proposed the concept of hierarchical topic, but did not consider the hierarchical relationship between the topic words. None of the above mentioned studies has considered the dynamic changes in the probability of topic words and the hierarchical relationship between topic words. Consequently, these studies have failed to dynamically adapt to the change in user preference and distinguish the effect of different topic words on user rating, thereby leading to a certain amount oferror in predicting user rating. Paranjpe et al. [25] first proposed the method of combining GBDT and regression model. Gupta et al. [26] applies the algorithm to CTR (Click Through Rate). When combining GBDT and regression model, Wang et al. [27] spliced the extracted features with the original features to increase the dimension of features, thereby reducing the prediction error. However, the prediction effect of LR on discrete data is still unsatisfactory.

3 Model and Algorithm

The definitions of relevant symbols are displayed in Table 1.

Table 1. Relevant symbol definitions in the present work.

Reviews	$R = \{R_1, R_2, ..., R_m\}$
Topics	$T = \{T_1, T_2, ..., T_K\}$
Topic words	$W_i = \{W_{i1}, W_{i2}, ..., W_{iN}\}$
Time windows	$t = \{t_1, t_2, ..., t_n\}$
Hiberarchy of words	$H_{t_n,i} = \{H_{t_n,i1}, H_{t_n,i2}, ..., H_{t_n,iN}\}$
Preference vector	$U^m = \{U_1^m, U_2^m, ..., U_K^m\}$
Divide reviews	$R^1, R^2, ..., R^n$
Ratings	$G = \{G_1, G_2, ..., G_m\}$
New features	$\{U^m, u^m\}$
Classes	$C = \{C_1, C_2, ..., C_l\}$
Final feature	$\{U^m, u^m, C_l\}$

Figure 1 illustrates the process of rating prediction model based on dynamic and hierarchical analysis of topic words.

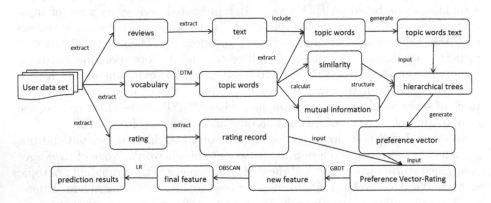

Fig. 1. Process of rating prediction

Firstly, considering the dynamics of user preferences, dividing user reviews set $R = \{R_1, R_2, ..., R_m\}$ into different subsets $R^1, R^2, ..., R^n$, that correspond to time windows. Using the DTM to generate a uniform set of topic $T = \{T_1, T_2, ..., T_K\}$ and a distribution of topic words $W_i = \{W_{i1}, W_{i2}, ..., W_{iN}\}$ in each time window. The probability value of each topic word in each time window was also calculated. So a change of user preferences for product property could be expressed by probability value changes. Secondly, considering a difference in the effect of each topic word on user rating, a hierarchical tree of topic words was constructed by combining similarity and intensity of mutual information between topic words. Among these words, a hierarchy that corresponds to the set of topic word $W_i = \{W_{i1}, W_{i2}, ..., W_{iN}\}$ in the time window t_n was $H_{t_n,i} = \{H_{t_n,i1}, H_{t_n,i2}, ..., H_{t_n,iN}\}$. Different weights were given to topic words in accordance with their hierarchies. To characterize the effect of topic words on user rating, a deeper hierarchy (a fine granularity) indicated a significant influence on user rating. Finally, user review R_m was mapped to the hierarchical tree of topic words to obtain the number of topic words and average depth, then it calculated the performance value U_K^m of reviews on each topic. A user preference vector $U^m = \{U_1^m, U_2^m, ..., U_K^m\}$ that corresponds to the user review R_m was formed by traversing K topics. Finally, U^m and G were inputted into GBDT for feature analysis, it will generate new feature vectors $\{U^m, u^m\}$, using DBSCAN (Density-Based Spatial Clustering of Applications with Noise) to cluster the new feature vectors and get l classes. Finishing linear fitting for each class of reviews $\{U^m, u^m, C_l\}$. The corresponding value of $\{U^m, u^m, C_l\}$ in the fitting function is used as the predicted value of user rating. The work will evaluate the prediction results on the basis of two kinds of errors, namely, mean absolute error (MAE) and root mean square error (RMSE). The process is presented in Algorithm 1.

Algorithm 1. Rating Prediction based on Dynamic and Hierarchical Analysis of the Topic Words of Reviews.

Input: user dataset
Output: MAE and RMSE of prediction results
1: Divide(R,n)//Division of review set
2: DTM($R^1,R^2,...,R^n,K,N$)//Dynamic topic analysis of reviews
3: GetPro(W_{iN},n)//Dynamic analysis of topic words
4: GetTree($W_{i1},W_{i2},...,W_{iN}$)// Hierarchical analysis of topic words
5: GetUser($R_m,H_{t_n,i}$)//Generate preference vector
6: GBDT(U^m,G)//Feature analysis and processing
7: DBSCAN(U^m,u^m)//Clustering new features generated by GBDT
8: LR($C_1,C_2,...,C_l$)//Linear fitting for each class
9: Predic(U^m,u^m,C_l)//Prediction based on new feature and classes of feature

---

4   Algorithm Design and Implementation

4.1   Dynamic Analysis of Topic Words

The beginning of the research work, preprocessing the set of reviews $R = \{R_1, R_2, ..., R_m\}$, to get the review sets $R^1, R^2, ..., R^n$ in each time window. Then inputing $R^1, R^2, ..., R^n$ into the DTM, obtaining the topic set $T = \{T_1, T_2, ..., T_K\}$ of reviews and the set of topic words $W_i = \{W_{i1}, W_{i2}, ..., W_{iN}\}$ under the ith topic. The change of user preferences in different time windows was described by the dynamic nature of topic words: the probability of a topic word is different in each time window, thereby indicating that the users' concern about the product was dynamic.

For topic i in the time window t_n, $P_{t_n,W_{iN}}$ represents the probability of occurrence of topic word W_{iN}. The calculation method is expressed in Formula (1).

$$P_{t_n,W_{iN}} = C_{t_n,W_{iN}} / \sum_{j=1}^{N}(C_{t_n,W_{ij}}), \tag{1}$$

where $C_{t_n,W_{iN}}$ represents the number of occurrences of the topic word W_{iN} in the time window t_n, the definition of $C_{t_n,W_{iN}}$ is as Formula (2).

$$C_{t_n,W_{iN}} = \begin{cases} C_{t_n,W_{iN}} + 1, W_{iN} \in R^n; \\ C_{t_n,W_{iN}}, W_{iN} \notin R^n. \end{cases} \tag{2}$$

Calculating the probability values of all topic words in each time window by Formula (1) and Formula (2). Thus, the probability distribution of the topic word W_{iN} is presented as follows:

$$P_{n,W_{iN}} = \{P_{t_1,W_{iN}}, P_{t_2,W_{iN}}, ..., P_{t_n,W_{iN}}\} \tag{3}$$

The dynamics of user preference was described by the probability values of topic words in different time windows, such that user rating prediction could reflect the dynamics of user preference in different time windows, thereby enhancing the rating prediction timeliness and authenticity.

4.2   Dynamic and Hierarchical Analysis of Topic Words

The hierarchical relationship between the topic words is determined by similarity and mutual information of the topic words in the specified window. And the DHTTW is constructed accordingly: the larger the mutual information of the topic word, the more likely it becomes the upper layer concept. Therefore, it is necessary to compare the mutual information strength of each topic word to determine the upper and lower position of topic words. At the same time, using the similarity between the topic words as the constraint condition for constructing the hierarchical relationship. So that the topic words with high similarity are distributed in the same branch of the hierarchical structure, while the topic words with low similarity are distributed in different branches of the hierarchical structure. The influence of the topic words on the user's rating is characterized by the hierarchy in DHTTW.

Calculating the intensity of mutual information of each topic word in time window t_n by Formula (6), and the results were ranked in descending order. Obtaining an ordered set of topic words $W_i^{'} = \{W_{i1}^{'}:MI(t_n, W_{i1}^{'}), W_{i2}^{'}:MI(t_n, W_{i2}^{'}), ..., W_{iN}^{'}:MI(t_n, W_{iN}^{'})\}$ under topic i, and $MI(t_n, W_{i1}^{'}) > MI(t_n, W_{i2}^{'}) > ... > MI(t_n, W_{iN}^{'})$. Selecting the topic word $W_{i1}^{'}$ with the highest intensity of mutual information as the upper concept of hierarchical structure and deleting $W_{i1}^{'}$ from the set $W_i^{'}$. Selecting $W_{i2}^{'}$ as the candidate word of the hierarchical structure. If the relation between $W_{i2}^{'}$ and $W_{i1}^{'}$ satisfied the requirement of Definition 1, then $W_{i2}^{'}$ was added to the hierarchical structure as lower concept of $W_{i1}^{'}$ and was deleted from the set $W_i^{'}$. If the relation between $W_{i2}^{'}$ and $W_{i1}^{'}$ failed to satisfy the requirement of Definition 1, then $W_{i2}^{'}$ remains in $W_i^{'}$, selecting $W_{i3}^{'}$ as the candidate word of the hierarchical structure.

Definition 1. *Discriminating hierarchical relations of topic words* W_{ia}, W_{ib} *in time window* t_n

(1) *In Formula (4), satisfy* $SIM(R^n, W_{ia}, W_{ib}) < \alpha$, *where* α *is the tuning parameter.*
(2) *In Formula (6), satisfy* $MI(t_n, W_{ia}) < MI(t_n, W_{ib})$.

According to Definition 1, the hierarchical relationship among the topic words is judged in turn, until the set $W_i^{'}$ is empty. The same method was adopted to construct hierarchical tree for all topics in different time windows. Generating K hierarchical trees in each time window. The hierarchical tree of topic i in the time window t_n was $H_{t_n, i} = \{H_{t_n, i1}, H_{t_n, i2}, ..., H_{t_n, iN}\}$, where $H_{t_n, i1} \neq H_{t_n, i2} \neq ... \neq H_{t_n, iN}$, and $H_{t_1, iN} \neq H_{t_2, iN} \neq ... \neq H_{t_n, iN}$. Therefore, the hierarchies of topic words in hierarchical tree were different, and the hierarchy of the same topic word changed with time. The similarity between two topic words W_{ia} and W_{ib} in topic i in time window t_n is calculated as follows:

$$SIM(R^n, W_{ia}, W_{ib}) = \frac{(E_{W_{ia}, R^n} E_{W_{ib}, R^n})}{\sqrt{(E_{W_{ia}, R^n})^2}\sqrt{(E_{W_{ib}, R^n})^2}}, \tag{4}$$

where E_{W_{ia},R^n} represents the space vector formed by TF-IDF (Term Frequency–Inverse Document Frequency) value of topic word W_{ia} in each user review within a set of review R^n; therefore, $E_{W_{ia},R^n} = \{E_{W_{ia},R^n,1}, E_{W_{ia},R^n,2}, ..., E_{W_{ia},R^n,m'}\}$. The element $E_{W_{ia},R^n,m'}$ of the vector represents TF-IDF value of topic word W_{ia} in the m'th review within the set of review R^n. The calculation formula is expressed in Formula (5).

$$E_{W_{ia},R^n,m'} = \frac{F_{W_{ia},R^n,m'}}{\sum_{k=1}^{N} F_{W_{ik},R^n,m'}} log \frac{|R^n|}{|\{j : W_{ia} \in R_j^n\}|},\qquad(5)$$

where $F_{W_{ia},R^n,m'}$ represents the number of occurrence of topic word W_{ia} in the set of user review R^n, $|R^n|$ represents the total number of review texts, and $|\{j : W_{ia} \in R_j^n\}|$ represents the total number of texts containing the word W_{ia}.

Under topic i in time window t_n, the intensity of mutual information of topic word W_{ia} referred to the accumulation of point mutual information between topic word W_{ia} and other topic words. As shown in Formula (6):

$$MI(t_n, W_{ia}) = \sum_{k=1}^{N} PMI(t_n, W_{ia}, W_{ik})\qquad(6)$$

The calculation formula of point mutual information of two topic words is as follows:

$$PMI(t_n, W_{ia}, W_{ib}) = log \frac{P_{t_n,(W_{ia},W_{ib})}}{P_{t_n,W_{ia}}P_{t_n,W_{ib}}}\qquad(7)$$

According to Formula (1), $P_{t_n,W_{ia}}$ represented the probability of occurrence of topic word W_{ia} in time window t_n. The probability that the topic words W_{ia} and W_{ib} occurred at the same time window t_n is expressed by $P_{t_n,(W_{ia},W_{ib})}$.

The construction pseudo code of topic words hierarchical tree of under time window t_n is defined in Algorithm 2.

4.3   Construction of User Preference Vector

In time window t_n, the corresponding hierarchy of each topic word in $W_i = \{W_{i1}, W_{i2}, ..., W_{iN}\}$ under topic i was $H_{t_n,i} = \{H_{t_n,i1}, H_{t_n,i2}, ..., H_{t_n,iN}\}$. Topic word W_{iN} was given a weight by using hierarchy $H_{t_n,iN}$. The number of topic words S_{i,t_n} under topic i in the record r of user review set R^n is calculated using Formula (8).

$$S_{i,t_n} = \begin{cases} S_{i,t_n} + 1, \exists W_{iN} \in r; \\ S_{i,t_n}, \exists W_{iN} \notin r. \end{cases}\qquad(8)$$

The number of topic words $S_{t_n} = \{S_{1,t_n}, S_{2,t_n}, ..., S_{K,t_n}\}$ under each topic contained in reviews could be obtained by traversing K topics.

The average depth of each user review on hierarchical tree of topic was calculated in accordance with topic words in user review r, which contains the topic

---

Algorithm 2. Construction algorithm of the hierarchical tree of topic words.

Input: a set of topic words $W_i = \{W_{i1}, W_{i2}, ..., W_{iN}\}$

Output: The hierarchy of topic words $H_{t_n,i} = \{H_{t_n,i1}, H_{t_n,i2}, ..., H_{t_n,iN}\}$ that corresponds to $W_i = \{W_{i1}, W_{i2}, ..., W_{iN}\}$

1: **GET** W_i' By Formula (6)

2: $H_{t_n,i} = [], Node = []$

3: $H_{t_n,i}[1] = 1, Node[1] = W_{i1}'$

4: **FOR**(j=2;j$\leq$N;j++)

5:    $SIM(R^n, W_{i1}', W_{ij}')$//By Formula (4)

6:    **IF** $SIM(R^n, W_{i1}', W_{ij}') < \alpha$

7:       **THEN** $H_{t_n,i}[j] = 1, Node[j] = W_{ij}'$

8: **END FOR**//The first hierarchy is end

9: **FOR**(temp=1;temp$\leq$N;temp++)

10:   **IF** $H_{t_n,i}[temp] = 1$

11:      **THEN** $M_1 = M_1 + 1$

12: **END FOR**

13: $M_1 \rightarrow num$

14: $M_1 \rightarrow sum$

15: **FOR**(j=1;j$\leq$num-1;j++)

16:   $index1 = findindex(W_i', Node[j])$

17:   $index2 = findindex(W_i', Node[++j])$

18:   $H_{t_n,i}[index1] = 2, Node[index1] = W_{iindex1}'$

19:   **FOR**(k=index1+1;k$\leq$index2-1;k++)

20:      $SIM(R^n, W_{iindex1}', W_{ik}')$//By Formula (4)

21:      **IF** $SIM(R^n, W_{iindex1}', W_{ik}') < \alpha$

22:        **THEN** $H_{t_n,i}[k] = 2, Node[k] = W_{ik}'$

23:      **END FOR**

24: **END FOR**//The second hierarchy is end

25: **FOR**(temp=1;temp$\leq$N;temp++)

26:   **IF** $H_{t_n,i}[temp] = 2$

27:      **THEN** $M_2 = M_2 + 1$

28: **END FOR**

29: $M_1 + M_2 \rightarrow sum$

30: **IF** $sum < N$

31:   $M_2 \rightarrow num$

32: **Repeat**

---

word set W_i and the corresponding hierarchies of topic words in hierarchical tree $H_{t_n,i}$, as expressed in Formula (9).

$$L_{i,t_n} = \sum_{j=1}^{N} (H_{t_n,ij}(\exists W_{ij} \in r))/S_{i,t_n} \tag{9}$$

The average depth of reviews under the topic hierarchical tree was obtained by traversing K topics, where $H_{t_n,ij}$ represents the hierarchy of topic word W_{ij}

under topic i in time window t_n, and L_{i,t_n} represents the average depth of user review r under the hierarchical tree of topic i.

Based on the number of topic words $S_{t_n} = \{S_{1,t_n}, S_{2,t_n}, ..., S_{K,t_n}\}$ of each topic contained in reviews and the average depth $L_{t_n} = \{L_{1,t_n}, L_{2,t_n}, ..., L_{K,t_n}\}$ of reviews under hierarchical tree, the user review R_m was assumed to be in time window t_n, and the user preference U_K^m for topic K is calculated as follows:

$$U_K^m = e^{L_{K,t_n}} \times ln(1 + S_{K,t_n}), \tag{10}$$

where U_K^m is calculated individually to obtain user preference vector $U^m = \{U_1^m, U_2^m, ..., U_K^m\}$, which corresponds to user review R_m. The method fully considers the different effects of S_{t_n} and L_{t_n} on user preference.

4.4   Rating Prediction Model

The input of the prediction model were user preference–rating set $\{U^m, G_m\}$, where U^m represents preference vector generated by the ith user review, and G_m represents rating value that corresponds to review R_m.

This paper presents a prediction algorithm called GBDT-MCLR. Firstly, GBDT carries out feature analysis on user preference-rating set $\{U^m, G_m\}$ and generates new feature $\{U^m, u^m\}$. The process of element u^m generation of feature $\{U^m, u^m\}$ is as follows:

(1) According to the relationship between feature vector U^m and decision value G_m, GBDT model constructs a specified number of RT(Regression Decision Tree) based on residual learning. Expressing the decision value of each RT by $f(U^m)$.
(2) Suppose the number of RT is q, it will get $u^m = \{u_1^m, u_2^m, u_3^m ..., u_q^m\}$. Each element u_q^m of $\{u_1^m, u_2^m, u_3^m, ..., u_q^m\}$ is calculated by Formula (11).

$$u_q^m = f_q(U^m) \tag{11}$$

Secondly, using DBSCAN algorithm to cluster the set of feature vectors $\{\{U^1, u^1\}, \{U^2, u^2\}, ..., \{U^m, u^m\}\}$, and obtaining the set of classes $C = \{C_1, C_2, ..., C_l\}$. The training process of the MCLR model is as follows:

(1) In each class C_l,
(2) Setting the feature weight vector to W_l, and the error to θ_l
(3) Determining the loss function according to the parameters W_l and θ_l, and obtaining the minimum value of the loss function.
(4) Using the least square method to solve the loss function and getting the minimum value. Determining the parameters W_l and θ_l.

Finally, when predicting the rating based on $\{U^m, u^m\}$, judging the class C_l of $\{U^m, u^m\}$, and calculating the corresponding rating value of $\{U^m, u^m\}$ according to the parameters W_l and θ_l of class C_l. The calculation method is as follows:

$$G'_m = W_l\{U^m, u^m\} + \theta_l \tag{12}$$

5   Experiment and Results

5.1   Data Set and Evaluation Standard

Test data were extracted from Amazon.com. Two product categories, namely, inch-tablet and remote streaming media player, were selected. The corresponding reviews are listed in Table 2.

Table 2. Amount of user review data for different products.

Product name	Product code	Total review number
Inch-Tablet	B00TSUGXKE	74615
Media-Player	B00ZV9RDKK	108930

Note: The data set contains all user reviews for each product from 2015 to 2017. Among them, the product numbered B00TSUGXKE belongs to the product with frequent updates, while the product numbered B00ZV9RDKK updates slowly. Each record in the user data contains user's review and ratings of product. Product codes are used to represent the products in the experiment.

In the present work, the result of rating prediction was evaluated by using MAE, RMSE, Recall and F-score. The formulas of MAE, RMSE, Recall and F-score are presented in Formula (13), Formulas (14), Formulas (15) and Formulas (16).

$$MAE = \frac{1}{m} \sum_{i=1}^{m} |(y_i' - y_i)| \tag{13}$$

$$RMSE = \sqrt{\frac{1}{m} \sum_{i=1}^{m} (y_i' - y_i)^2} \tag{14}$$

$$Recall = (\frac{m_1'}{m_1} + \frac{m_2'}{m_2} + \frac{m_3'}{m_3} + \frac{m_4'}{m_4} + \frac{m_5'}{m_5})/5 \tag{15}$$

$$F - score = \frac{(\frac{m_1'+m_2'+m_3'+m_4'+m_5'}{m}) * Recall * 2}{(\frac{m_1'+m_2'+m_3'+m_4'+m_5'}{m}) + Recall} \tag{16}$$

The m is the total number of reviews, among them, the rating mechanism sets user rating with positive integer 1–5. m_1', m_2', m_3', m_4', m_5' are the correct predictions of the number of 1, 2, 3, 4, 5, respectively. m_1, m_2, m_3, m_4, m_5 are the actual number of 1, 2, 3, 4, 5, respectively. y_i' is the predicted rating, y_i is the actual rating.

5.2 Test Analysis

Test on the DHTTW Construction. In this paper, we set the number of topics $K = 5$, the number of topic words $N = 50$, the number of time windows $n = 3$, and the similarity threshold $\alpha = 0.1$. Selecting B00TSUGXKE as an example of the construction of the dynamic hierarchical tree of topic words, specifying the topic T_1. According to the method of constructing the hierarchical tree of topic words proposed in Chapter 4, the dynamic hierarchical analysis of topic words under the topic T_1 is carried out. Part of the hierarchical trees under three time windows are shown in Fig. 2, respectively.

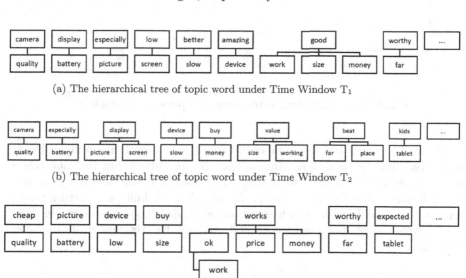

(a) The hierarchical tree of topic word under Time Window T_1

(b) The hierarchical tree of topic word under Time Window T_2

(c) The hierarchical tree of topic word under Time Window T_3

Fig. 2. Example-dynamic hierarchical tree of topic world

As shown in Fig. 2, the topic words extracted from user reviews are divided into two categories, one is the user's daily language, such as "ok", "money", "good", etc. and the other is the user's descriptive vocabulary for goods, such as "camera", "quality", "battery", "screen", etc. It can be clearly seen from the Fig. 2 that the descriptive vocabulary of a product is at or above the second hierarchy of the hierarchical tree. The more such vocabulary users use in their reviews, the more they like the product. Meanwhile, descriptive vocabulary, such as "quality" and "battery", has the same influence on users'ratings in every time window. Vocabulary such as "device" and "screen", has a declining influence on users' ratings. Vocabulary such as "work" and "price", has an increasing influence on users' ratings. Generally speaking, the dynamic hierarchical tree of topic words can reflect the change of the impact of keywords on user ratings.

To prove that the hierarchical tree of topic words proposed in this work changed dynamically, the number of time windows n was set to 3. In each time window, the proportions of topic words in topic T_1 of two categories of products in different hierarchies are displayed in Fig. 3.

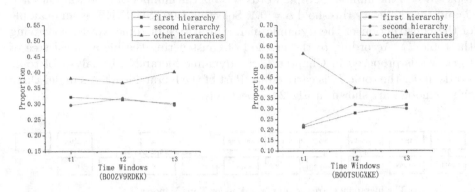

Fig. 3. The hierarchical distribution of topic words in topic T_1

Figure 3 presents that the number of topic words in each hierarchy of hierarchical tree differ in each time window, thereby indicating that the hierarchical tree of topic words changes with time. The change in the hierarchy of topic words described the change in user preference slightly. Thus, user rating prediction based on the dynamic and hierarchical analysis of topic words would adapt to the evolution of user preferences and enhance the timeliness of the rating prediction.

Comparison of Prediction Results Based on DHTTW. At the same time, in order to prove the effectiveness of DHTTW, three prediction models, LR, GBDT and RF, are used to predict rating. The product code chosen in the experiment is B00TSUGXKE. The similarity threshold ∂ of the DHTTW was set to 0.025, the number of time windows n to 3; in addition, the number of topics K was set to 5, and the number of topic words N to 50. The comparison with the method [23] is shown in Fig. 4.

Figure 4 displays that the method for rating prediction based on the dynamic and hierarchical analysis of topic words proposed in this work was superior to the method for analyzing reviews based on the LDA model in four evaluation indexes, namely, MAE, RMSE, Recall and F-score. The optimization degrees of rating prediction results of two categories of products were different because the hierarchical analysis on topic words of two products could describe the influence of different topic words on user rating, thereby enhancing the practicality of the rating prediction work. Thus, DHTTW can reduce the error of rating prediction of two products on the basis of the LDA prediction model. The dynamic analysis of topic words result in timely rating prediction to reflect the changing rule of user preferences well in products. So the effect of DHTTW is obviously better than that of LDA.

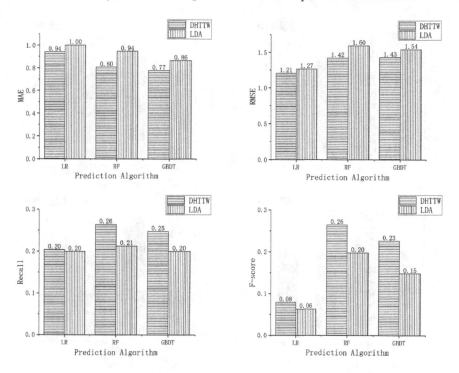

Fig. 4. Comparison of rating prediction results

Test on the GBDT-MCLR. As shown in Fig. 4, the prediction algorithm-LR performs best on RMSE and the prediction algorithm-GBDT performs best on MAE. On the basis of DHTTW, the GBDT-LR algorithm mentioned [27] and the GBDT-MCLR algorithm are tested. The experimental parameters are shown in Fig. 4, the experimental results are shown in Fig. 5.

As shown in Fig. 5, compared with GBDT and LR models alone, the prediction results with using GBDT-LR model are not much improved. The reason is that LR model can not achieve expected results in predicting discrete data. Therefore, the GBDT-MCLR algorithm proposed in this paper can make the GBDT-LR algorithm adapt to discrete rating data to a certain extent, thus making MAE and RMSE worthwhile to be effectively reduced. However, for Recall, GBDT-MCLR is not as effective as GBDT, but the difference is no more than 0.05. For F-score, this indicator has increased 0.1. This is because the GBDT-MCLR algorithm essentially uses the GBDT algorithm to optimize the LR algorithm, so it can be improved compared to the LR algorithm.

Test on the Different Number of Data. Figure 6 shows the variation of the rating prediction error of the same product under different number of user reviews. The product code chosen in the experiment is B00ZV9RDKK. User reviews in each time window are randomly selected for 20%, 40%, 60% and 80% to verify the prediction error of the algorithm under different number of user reviews.

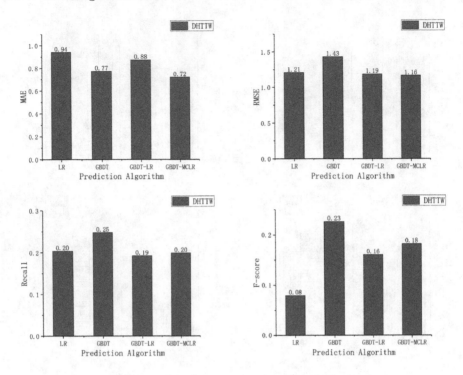

Fig. 5. Comparison of rating prediction results

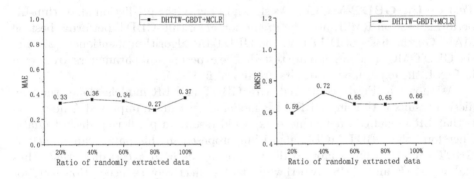

Fig. 6. Ratio of randomly extracted data

As shown in Fig. 6, for the same product, the error of rating prediction tends to be stable under the different number of user reviews, which indicates that the prediction model is stable and suitable for user rating prediction of each product. At the same time, we can see from Figs. 5 and 6 that the predicted errors of user ratings for different products are different, because the data sets come from real e-commerce websites, and the quality of user reviews for different products can not be guaranteed.

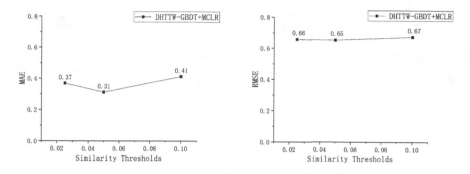

Fig. 7. Rating prediction results under different similarity thresholds

Test on the Similarity Threshold. With the increase of similarity threshold, the proportion of topic words in the first hierarchy of hierarchical tree increased, whereas those in other hierarchies decreased continuously. Thereby indicating that a small similarity threshold denotes additional topic words that were divided into the lower structure of the same word of upper concept, and an apparent hierarchical structure between topic words. When the hierarchical structure between topic words was apparent, the effect on the result of rating prediction is demonstrated in Fig. 7.

Figure 7 exhibits that an apparent hierarchical structure of topic words indicates an improved MAE and RMSE values of rating prediction results, but the improvement was insignificant. This result was due to a small similarity threshold resulted in additional topic words that were divided into the lower structure of the same upper concept. Therefore, a gradual increase in topic words was at high hierarchies. In real life, each word that users use to review a product has different effects on user rating, but the effect will be similar in several hierarchies. Thus, if additional topic words are found at high hierarchies, the method for analyzing reviews with the hierarchical tree of topic words cannot improve the rating prediction result well.

Test on the Number of Time Windows. To verify the effect of different numbers of time windows on rating prediction, the number of time windows was set to 3 (in year), 6 (in half a year), and 12 (in quarter) for the test. The number of topic K was set to 5, the number of topic words N to 50, and the similarity threshold ∂ was set to 0.025. The rating prediction results of two categories of products under different numbers of time windows are illustrated in Fig. 8.

Figure 8 depicts that the dynamic and hierarchical analysis of topic words could be conducted in a small time range with the increase in the number of time windows. The rating prediction result of B00TSUGXKE was clearly improved, but that of B00ZV9RDKK was only slightly improved because it belonged to the slowly updating product. User preference for such products changed slowly over time, thereby causing minimal change in the hierarchical tree of topic words. Therefore, the improvement in rating prediction result was minimal when

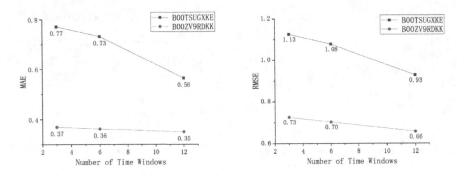

Fig. 8. Rating prediction results under different time window numbers

conducting the dynamic and hierarchical analysis of topic words in a fine time range. User preference for B00TSUGXKE change rapidly, thus resulting in the apparent change in the hierarchical tree of topic words over time. Given a small time interval, adapting to changes in user preferences and the significance rating prediction effect had been improved.

6   Conclusions

As a typical application of social network, the study of social commerce focuses on the dynamic characteristics of time and space. The method for rating prediction based on dynamic and hierarchical analysis of topic words proposed in this work started from the topic discovery of reviews to conduct a dynamic analysis of topic words, which could adapt to the dynamics of user preference for products. The hierarchical trees of topic words was constructed on the basis of dynamics of topic words. Different hierarchies of topic words could describe the influence of different topic words contained in reviews on user rating. The mapping rule from reviews to the hierarchical tree of topic words and the generation method of the user preference vector were designed. The dynamic and hierarchical analysis of the topic words were conducted for realistic and timely rating prediction, thereby reducing the error caused by the unified analysis of topic words.

In the future, we will focuson dynamically selecting the number of time windows. That is, selecting the appropriate number of time windows dynamically to describe the change rule of user preference well for products with different change cycles and achieve improved rating prediction results.

Acknowledgments. This work is supported by National Natural Science Foundation (61662013, U1501252, U1711263, U1811264,61662015, 61562014); Guangxi Innovation-Driven Development Project (Science and Technology Major Project)(AA17202024); The Guangxi Natural Science Foundation (2017GXNSFAA198372, 2016GXNS-FAA380149); The Funds of Guangxi Key Lab of Trusted software Project (kx201511); The Teacher Growth Fund of the Education Development Foundation of Guangxi Normal University (EDF2015005); The Funds of Graduate student innovation program Guilin University of Electronic Technology (2017YJCX56, 2019YCXS045).

References

1. Brody, S., Elhadad, N.: An unsupervised aspect-sentiment model for online reviews. In: Proceedings of Human Language Technologies: Conference of the North American Chapter of the Association of Computational Linguistics, Los Angeles, California, USA, 2–4 June 2010, pp. 804–812 (2010)

2. Titov, I., McDonald, R.T.: Modeling online reviews with multi-grain topic models. In: Proceedings of the 17th International Conference on World Wide Web, WWW 2008, Beijing, China, 21–25 April 2008, pp. 111–120 (2008)

3. Tang, X., Xiang, K.: Hotspot mining based on LDA model and microblog heat. Libr. Inf. Serv. **58**(5), 58–63 (2014)

4. Shin, S.-J., Moon, I.-C.: Guided HTM: hierarchical topic model with Dirichlet forest priors. IEEE Trans. Knowl. Data Eng. **29**(2), 330–343 (2017)

5. Bingyu, L., Cuirong, W., Cong, W.: Microblog community discovery algorithm based on dynamic topic model with multidimensional data fusion. J. Softw. **28**(2), 246–261 (2017)

6. Cena, F., Gena, C., Grillo, P., Kuflik, T., Vernero, F., Wecker, A.J.: How scales influence user rating behaviour in recommender systems. Behav. Inf. Technol. **36**(10), 985–1004 (2017)

7. Yin, Y., Chen, L., Xu, Y., Jian, W.: Location-aware service recommendation with enhanced probabilistic matrix factorization. IEEE Access **6**, 62815–62825 (2018)

8. Yin, Y., Xu, Y., Xu, W., Min, G., Yu, L., Pei, Y.: Collaborative service selection via ensemble learning in mixed mobile network environments. Entropy **19**(7), 358 (2017)

9. Gao, H., Zhang, K., Yang, J., et al.: Applying improved particle swarm optimization for dynamic service composition focusing on quality of service evaluations under hybrid networks. Int. J. Distrib. Sens. Netw. **14**(2), 1550147718761583 (2018)

10. Koren, Y., Bell, R.: Advances in collaborative filtering. In: Ricci, F., Rokach, L., Shapira, B. (eds.) Recommender Systems Handbook, pp. 77–118. Springer, Boston (2015). https://doi.org/10.1007/978-1-4899-7637-6_3

11. Jo, Y., Oh, A.H.: Aspect and sentiment unification model for online review analysis. In: Proceedings of the Forth International Conference on Web Search and Web Data Mining, WSDM 2011, Hong Kong, China, 9–12 February 2011, pp. 815–824 (2011)

12. Titov, I., McDonald, R.T.: A joint model of text and aspect ratings for sentiment summarization. In: Proceedings of the 46th Annual Meeting of the Association for Computational Linguistics, ACL 2008, Columbus, Ohio, USA, 15–20 June 2008, pp. 308–316 (2008)

13. Zhang, W., Xu, M., Jiang, Q.: Opinion mining and sentiment analysis in social media: challenges and applications. In: Proceedings of HCI in Business, Government, and Organizations - 5th International Conference Held as Part of HCI International 2018, HCIBGO 2018, Las Vegas, NV, USA, 15–20 July 2018, pp. 536–548 (2018)

14. Goulart, H.X., Tosi, M.D.L., Gonçalves, D.S., Maia, R.F., Wachs-Lopes, G.A.: Hybrid model for word prediction using Naive Bayes and latent information. CoRR, abs/1803.00985 (2018)

15. Keith, T., Debra, Y., Kathleen F.M., Christopher A.P.: Topic modeling in fringe word prediction for AAC. In: Proceedings of the 11th International Conference on Intelligent User Interfaces, IUI 2006, Sydney, Australia, January 29–February 1 2006, pp. 276–278 (2006)

16. Tang, D., Qin, B., Liu, T., Yang, Y.: User modeling with neural network for review rating prediction. In: Proceedings of the Twenty-Fourth International Joint Conference on Artificial Intelligence, IJCAI 2015, Buenos Aires, Argentina, 25–31 July 2015, pp. 1340–1346 (2015)
17. Seo, S., Huang, J., Yang, H., Liu, Y.: Interpretable convolutional neural networks with dual local and global attention for review rating prediction. In: Proceedings of the Eleventh ACM Conference on Recommender Systems, RecSys 2017, Como, Italy, 27–31 August 2017, pp. 297–305 (2017)
18. Ma, C., Chen, W.: A review topic analysis method for rating prediction. J. Chin. Inf. Process. **2**, 209–216 (2017)
19. Ji, Y., Li, Y., Shi, C.: Aspect rating prediction based on heterogeneous network and topic model. J. Comput. Appl. **37**(11), 3201–3206 (2017)
20. Fang, G.-S., Kamei, S., Fujita, S.: Rating prediction with topic gradient descent method for matrix factorization in recommendation. Int. J. Adv. Comput. Sci. Appl. **8**(12), 469–476 (2017)
21. Zhang, W., Wang, J.: Integrating topic and latent factors for scalable personalized review-based rating prediction. IEEE Trans. Knowl. Data Eng. **28**(11), 3013–3027 (2016)
22. McAuley, J., Leskovec, J.: Hidden factors and hidden topics: understanding rating dimensions with review text. In: Proceedings of the 7th ACM Conference on Recommender Systems, pp. 165–172. ACM (2013)
23. Zhang, R., et al.: Review comment analysis for predicting ratings. In: Dong, X.L., Yu, X., Li, J., Sun, Y. (eds.) WAIM 2015. LNCS, vol. 9098, pp. 247–259. Springer, Cham (2015). https://doi.org/10.1007/978-3-319-21042-1_20
24. Blei, D.M., Griffiths, T.L., Jordan, M.I., Tenenbaum, J.B.: Hierarchical topic models and the nested Chinese restaurant process. In: Advances in Neural Information Processing Systems 16, NIPS 2003, Vancouver and Whistler, British Columbia, Canada, 8–13 December 2003, pp. 17–24 (2003)
25. Paranjpe, D.: Learning document aboutness from implicit user feedback and document structure. In: Proceedings of the 18th ACM Conference on Information and Knowledge Management, CIKM 2009, Hong Kong, China, pp. 365–374, 2–6 November 2009
26. Gupta, M.S.: Predicting click through rate for job listings. In: Proceedings of the 18th International Conference on World Wide Web, WWW 2009, Madrid, Spain, pp. 1053–1054, 20–24 April 2009
27. Wang, Y., Feng, D., Li, D., Chen, X., Zhao, Y., Niu, X.: A mobile recommendation system based on logistic regression and gradient boosting decision trees. In: 2016 International Joint Conference on Neural Networks, IJCNN 2016, Vancouver, BC, Canada, pp. 1896–1902, 24–29 July 2016

An Efficient Mutual Authentication Framework with Conditional Privacy Protection in VANET

Ying Wang, Jing Hu, Xiaohong Li$^{(\boxtimes)}$, and Zhiyong Feng

College of Intelligence and Computing, Tianjin Key Laboratory of Advanced
Networking (TANK), Tianjin University, Tianjin 300350, China
{joycewang,mavis_huhu,xiaohongli,zyfeng}@tju.edu.cn

Abstract. Vehicular Ad Hoc Network (VANET) is a special application
of traditional Mobile Ad Hoc Network (MANET) in traffic roads, which
has attracted extensive attention due to its important role in intelligent
traffic and road services. In order to ensure the safety of road traffic
and protect the privacy of users, it is of vital importance to provide
effective anonymous authentication in VANET. In this paper, we propose an efficient mutual authentication framework with conditional privacy protection (EMAPP), which can achieve the security authentication
from vehicles to infrastructure and vehicles to vehicles. In the proposed
framework, we are combined with pseudo ID and temporary pseudonym
to protect the privacy of vehicles, and use the identity-based signature
scheme to achieve authentication between vehicles and infrastructure. At
the same time, with the assistance of the roadside unit (RSU), we utilize an online/offline signature scheme to achieve authentication between
vehicles in the same RSU area and different RSU area. Our scheme has
reusability, and we have conducted a performance evaluation. Without
expensive and time-consuming operations such as bilinear pairing and
mapping to point (MTP) functions, our framework can produce better
performance and is appropriate for practical application. In addition,
we also use the Internet Security Protocol and Application Automatic
Authentication (AVISPA) tools to provide formal security analysis.

Keywords: VANET · Authentication ·
Conditional privacy protection · AVISPA · Formal proof

1 Introduction

In order to reduce the occurrence of traffic accidents and develop road entertainment services, people have focused on the development of intelligent transportation systems (ITS). Therefore, Vehicular ad hoc network (VANET), which is
an important component of ITS, has developed rapidly in the past two decades
[2]. In VANET, the vehicles equipped with On-Board Units (OBU) and infrastructure deployed along roads, called roadside units (RSU), form the nodes of

© ICST Institute for Computer Sciences, Social Informatics and Telecommunications Engineering 2019
Published by Springer Nature Switzerland AG 2019. All Rights Reserved
X. Wang et al. (Eds.): CollaborateCom 2019, LNICST 292, pp. 799–815, 2019.
https://doi.org/10.1007/978-3-030-30146-0_53

the network. And there are two types of communication in VANET: vehicle-to-vehicle (V2V) communication and vehicle-to-infrastructure (V2I) communication, which are based on the Dedicated Short Range Communication (DSRC) [15] protocol.

The main purpose of VANET is to improve road safety by exchanging safety information. When safety information is transmitted in wireless channels, it can be easily eavesdropped, modified and deleted by malicious attackers. Therefore, in the face of these security attacks, the authentication of messages becomes a key security service for communication between vehicles and between vehicles and infrastructure in VANET. However, the traffic information exchanged in VANET may contain the drive's personal privacy, such as the driver's true identity, daily route, home address, etc. Some criminals may use the collected private information to hurt the driver. Therefore, the true identity of the vehicle should also be protected during the authentication process. At the same time, the illegal vehicle should also have the right to be revoked and exposed to their true identity.

At present, there are numerous research work related to the authentication problem in VANET, among which the widely adopted schemes are roughly divided into three categories: PKI-based authentication, ID-based authentication, and certificateless scheme. [8,10,12] are all PKI-based authentication schemes, but the common problem of these schemes is that additional communication is required to manage vehicle certificates and certificate revocation, which may impose heavy communication and computation costs on the network. [4,6,9,11,17] are all ID-based authentication frameworks. Among them, [9,17] adopt identity-based signature (IBS) and online/offline signature (IBOOS) schemes. By putting the pseudonym generated by the vehicle itself and the offline signature obtained by the vehicle from the RSU into a set, and broadcasting the set to the vehicles in the RSU area, the vehicles in the area can confirm the legal identities of other vehicles through the set, thus completing the authentication between the vehicles. However, as the number of certified vehicles increases, the set will also gradually increase, and the set needs to be updated after each successful verification of the vehicle, which will result in great communication overhead and high storage requirements for the vehicle. In addition, the framework is also vulnerable to impersonation attacks and Sybil attacks. Some vehicles may use pseudonyms and offline signatures of other vehicles in the set to communicate under the identities of other vehicles. Also, since the pseudonym of the vehicle is independently generated by itself, illegal vehicles may generate multiple pseudonyms, creating the illusion of multiple vehicles. In response to the problems in [9,17], we improved the scheme and proposed a different authentication process.

In this paper, we propose an efficient mutual authentication framework with conditional privacy protection (EMAPP). In the proposed framework, we adopt an identity-based signature scheme to ensure the authenticity and integrity of the message in the authentication process between the vehicle and the roadside unit, and through the identity-based online/offline signature scheme, with the assistance of the RSU, the identity authentication between vehicles is realized.

In addition, the vehicle can independently generate temporary pseudonyms to protect its privacy during the communication process. However, when the vehicle commits illegal activities, TA can track the vehicle according to the information source, restore its true identity and revoke the vehicle from the network, thus realizing conditional privacy protection. In addition, EMAPP is reusable, eliminates the need for expensive and time-consuming bilinear pairing and point mapping operations, and does not require the storage of key certificates and pseudonym sets, which greatly reduces the performance requirements of the vehicle.

Our framework is formally verified by using the formal tool AVISPA, and its performance is evaluated by quantitative calculation in terms of computational costs and communication overhead. The results show that the proposed EMAPP is secure and can achieve security objectives such as identity authentication, non-repudiation, identity privacy protection, traceability, etc. It can also resist Sybil attack, impersonation attack, modification attack, replay attack and repudiation attack. Our framework also achieves lower message latency and is more suitable for large-scale VANET.

The rest of this paper is organized as follows: in Sect. 2, some related work are reviewed. Section 3 describes some necessary preliminaries knowledge. Section 4 describes the proposed scheme. Section 5 provides a security analysis of the scheme. Section 6 provides a performance assessment of the proposed and other schemes. Section 7 concludes the paper.

2   Related Work

Currently, there are many jobs that can implement anonymous authentication in VANET, and these tasks can be divided into three categories: the public key infrastructure (PKI) based authentication, the identity (ID) based authentication and certificateless scheme.

– the PKI based authentication:

In 2004, Hubaux et al. [8] first proposed that PKI technology can be used to protect transmission messages in the vehicles. In 2007, Raya and Hubaux et al. [10] proposed an anonymous authentication scheme for VANET based on anonymous certificates. However, this scheme requires each vehicle to be preloaded with a large number of anonymous public/private key pairs and corresponding public key certificates, thus requiring huge storage space to store the keys. In 2008, Lu et al. [12] proposed an effective conditional privacy preservation (ECPP) scheme using temporary anonymous certificates to solve the problem of large storage space for vehicles. In short, PKI-based authentication schemes require additional communication to manage vehicle certificates and certificate revocation on and computational overhead.

– the ID based authentication:

Liu et al. [11] used the identity-based signature method of bilinear pairing to let the proxy vehicle verify the validity of the signatures on other vehicle messages in batch, and RSU then checked the verification results of the proxy vehicle in batch. However, this scheme is vulnerable to sybil attacks, and if there is at least one invalid signature in the verification batch, the batch verification may fail. He et al. [6] proposed an identity-based signature scheme without bilinear pairing to reduce the computational complexity of bilinear pairing functions. Vehicles can also use self-generated pseudonyms to communicate anonymously with other vehicles and RSU. However, this scheme is also vulnerable to sybil attacks and global positioning system (GPS) spoofing attacks because no information is provided to prove the credibility of the location provided by the vehicles. Ons Chikhaoui et al. [4] proposed the use of temporary tickets to maintain the privacy of vehicles. This scheme obtains certificates and corresponding private keys from a trusted authority (TA) in the offline phase, and forms tickets by signing the certificates in the online phase to realize authentication between vehicles and RSU as well as between vehicles. However, this scheme needs to generate a set of certificates for vehicles in advance, and also needs to use a public key certificate to ensure that vehicles can safely obtain new certificates and private keys from TA before the current certificate set is used up, thus requiring higher storage requirements.

- **certificateless scheme:**

Horng and Tzeng et al. [7] proposed a provably secure CCPPA scheme based on certificateless cryptography. In this scheme, part of the private key of the user (vehicle and RSU) is generated by the Trusted Key Generator Center (KGC), while the complete private key is formed by the user selecting a secret value and combining part of the keys, so KGC cannot obtain the user's private key. In addition, Yang et al. [14] proposed a certificateless conditional privacy protection authentication scheme in 2019. The scheme does not use hash mapping to points and l batch message authentication.

3 Preliminaries

In this section, we will introduce the system model, security goals, and the signature schemes to be used in the authentication process, such as the signature scheme BNN-IBS between the vehicle and the RSU, and online/offline signature scheme without key escrow between vehicles.

3.1 System Model

As shown in Fig. 1, VANET typically consists of three parts: trusted third-party TA, roadside infrastructure RSU, and OBU-equipped vehicles.

- **TA** is a trusted authority in VANET. It has powerful computing and storage capabilities and is responsible for generating the primary initial parameters for RSUs and OBUs in the region. Each car must be registered with the TA before joining the network, so the TA can store the real information of the vehicle, and it is also the only party that has the right to reveal the user's

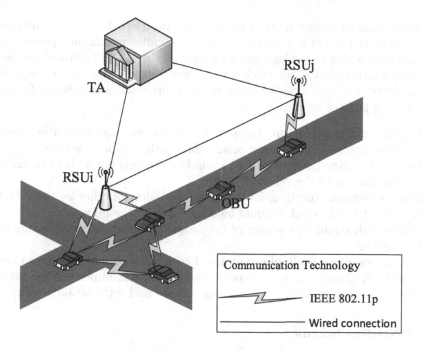

Fig. 1. System model.

identity. If there is malicious and false information in the road network, the TA can track and identify the information source to resolve the dispute. In addition, the TA is considered unable to compromise with its opponents and is fully trusted by all parties in the system.

– **RSU** is an infrastructure distributed on the roadside. It communicates securely with the TA via a wired link and communicates with the OBU via the DSRC protocol, so he is semi-trusted. RSU will obtain the revocation list from TA, assist TA in verifying the legality of the vehicle identity within its area, and give the vehicle verification certificate so that the vehicle can communicate with other verified legal vehicles. In addition, it can also provide services such as Web and TCP to OBU. Each RSU is equipped with a Tamper Proof Device (TPD) to increase the reliability of the VANET.

– **OBU** is the internal processing unit of the vehicle. It enables vehicles to wirelessly communicate with other vehicles and RSUs based on the DSRC protocol and uses TPD to store their sensitive information. When the vehicle is driving, it broadcasts information such as location, time, speed, vehicle path and traffic conditions to other vehicles and RSUs. If it receives false information or suffers some attacks during vehicle communication, it can report to TA through RSU.

3.2 Security Goals

In VANET, in order to protect the security of users' information, users must authenticate their identities anonymously. However, if some vehicles send out fraudulent messages, there must be a trusted authority that can track and reveal the actual identities of the vehicles, which is also called conditional privacy protection. Besides, due to the high-speed changes of the VANET network topology and other characteristics, the efficiency and feasibility of the scheme must also be considered, so the safety objectives of the proposed scheme should focus on the following points:

- **Message authentication:** the receiver of the message should be able to verify the integrity of the message and the legitimacy of its source.
- **Identity privacy protection:** TA should be the only party that can disclose the true identity of the vehicle.
- **Identity revocation:** In order to protect the safety of other legitimate vehicles, misbehaving vehicles should be expelled from the network.
- **Non-repudiation:** The sender of the message should not deny having sent that message.
- **Defense against multiple attacks:** The scheme should be able to resist a variety of attacks, such as identity analysis attack, impersonation attack, Sybil attack, modification attack, replay attack and repudiation attack.

3.3   BNN-IBS Scheme

The BNN-IBS [13,16] scheme is based on elliptic curve cryptography, and it dose not use time-consuming and expensive bilinear pairing and mapping to point hash functions. It mainly includes the following four steps:

- **Setup:** TA generates system parameters, including master key sk and corresponding public key PK, and publishes the system parameters to the network, sk keeps the secret.
- **Extract:** TA calculates the private key rk of the RSU and the private key vk of the OBU based on the master key sk and the given ID.
- **Sign:** Given the ID, the corresponding private key and the message m, a signature $\sigma(m)$ is generated, and it is a triplet containing the public key.
- **Verify:** Given the signature $\sigma(m)$, the corresponding public key and the message m, after the relevant calculation, the signature is accepted if the answer is yes and rejected otherwise.

3.4   Online/Offline Signature Scheme Without Key Escrow

The identity-based cryptography (IBC) scheme has serious security issues due to key escrow, and the scheme [5] avoids key escrow problems by adopting the idea of Certificateless Cryptography (CLC). It mainly includes the following steps:

- **Setup:** TA generates system parameters and publishes them to the network.
- **Extract:** The RSU extracts the signature private key and public key according to the master key.

- **Off-sign:** A probabilistic algorithm that calculates an offline signature $\sigma_{off}(ID)$ by entering system parameters, the corresponding ID and a signature private key.
- **On-sign:** Given the message m and the offline signature $\sigma_{off}(ID)$, it outputs online signal $\sigma_{on}(\sigma_{off}(ID)\|m)$, and give the full signature.
- **Verify:** An auxiliary algorithm that outputs an acceptance or rejection after verification by inputting the message m, the ID, the public key and the full signature.

4   The Proposed Framework

Our framework can be described from four phases: the system initialization phase, the R2V authentication phase, the inner-V2V authentication phase and the cross-V2V authentication phase. The symbols used in our scheme are listed in Table 1. Table 2 describes the general operations of the framework.

Table 1. The used notations

Notations	Description
TA	The trusted authority
E/F_q	An elliptic curve E over a finite field F_q
q	The field size
p	A large prime number
P	A point of order p on the curve E
G	A cyclic group of order p under the point addition "$+$" generated by P
sk, PK	The private key and public key of TA
ID_i, ID_{vj}	The identity of RSU_i, the identity of OBU_j
GC_i	The geographical coordinates of RSU_i
rk	The private key of RSU
PID_i	The pseudo identity of the OBU_i
vk	The private key of OBU
rt, prt	The temporary private key and public key of RSU
$\sigma_{ri}(), \sigma_{vj}()$	The signature of RSU_i and the signature of OBU_j
T	The time stamp of R2V authentication
n	A random number
vt, pvt	The temporary private key and public key of OBU
t	The time stamp of V2V authentication
PS_i	The pseudonym of OBU_i
RID	The real identity of the OBU
TID	The signature ID of offline signature, $TID = PS\|\sigma^*(PS)$
$\sigma^*()$	The signature does not contain the public key
$\sigma_{off}, \sigma_{on}$	The offline and online signature
$qr, result$	The query request, the query result

4.1 System Initialization

1. TA establishes the network parameters through the BNN-IBS setup algorithm, and then publishes the parameters $\{E/Fq, G, P, q, p, PK, H_1, H_2\}$ to the network, sk as its master key, $PK = skP$ as its master public key, and keep sk secret.
2. TA sets the identity of the RSU as the connection between its geographic coordinates and the serial number of the RSU. The identity of RSU is $ID_i = GC_i\|SQN$. Then it calculates the private key rk of the RSU through the key extraction algorithm in the BNN-IBS scheme, and sends $< ID_r, R_s, rk >$ to the RSU through a secure channel, the RSU can verifies the validity of rk by verifying $R_s + cPK = rkP$. R_s is defined in [16].
3. TA calculates the private key vk of the OBU through the key extraction algorithm of the BNN-IBS, and calculates the pseudo identity PID_i of the OBU by using PK:
   - Choose at random $w \in Z_p^*$, and compute
   - $PID_1 = wP$
   - $PID_2 = ID_v \oplus H_1(wPK)$
   - $PID_i = < PID_1, PID_2 >$
4. TA sends $< PID_i, R_v, vk >$ to OBU safely, and OBU can verifies the validity of vk by verifying $R_v + cPK = vkP$.

Table 2. Operations of the proposed EMAPP

R2V authentication	
Step 1. $RSU_r \Rightarrow *:$	$< ID_r, T, prt, \sigma_{r1}(ID_r\|T\|prt), n_r >$
Step 2. $OBU_i \rightarrow RSU_r:$	$< PS_i, T, \sigma_v^*(PS_i), \sigma_{v1}(\sigma_v^*(PS_i)\|T), n_r >$
Step 3. $RSU_r \rightarrow OBU_i:$	$< PS_i, \sigma_{off}(TID), T, \sigma_{r2}(\sigma_{off}(TID)\|T), n_r >$
Inner V2V authentication	
Step 1. $OBU_i \rightarrow OBU_j:$	$< PS_i, \sigma_i(PS_i), t, \sigma_{on}(\sigma_{off}(TID_i)\|t), n_i >$
Step 2. $OBU_j \rightarrow OBU_i:$	$< PS_j, \sigma_j(PS_j), t, \sigma_{on}(\sigma_{off}(TID_j)\|t), n_i >$
Cross V2V authentication	
Step 1. $OBU_i \rightarrow OBU_j:$	$< PS_i, \sigma_i(PS_i), t, \sigma_{on}(\sigma_{off}(TID_i)\|t), n_i >$
Step 2. $OBU_j \rightarrow RSU_j:$	$< (PS_j, \sigma_j(PS_j), T, \sigma_{on}(\sigma_{off}(TID_j)\|T), n_j, qr) >$
Step 3. $RSU_j \rightarrow OBU_j:$	$< PS_j, \sigma_{off}(PS_j\|PS_i), T, result, \sigma_{rj}(result\|T), n_j >$
step 4. $OBU_j \rightarrow OBU_i:$	$< PS_j, PS_i, ID_j, \sigma_{on}(\sigma_{off}\|ID_j), t, \sigma_{vj}(PSj\|t), n_i >$

4.2 R2V Authentication

1. The RSU calculates the temporary key $rt = H_2(rk\|Tr_1)$ according to the private key rk, Tr_1 is the validity period, and the corresponding public key $prt = rtP$. Then RSU calculates σ_{r1} through BNN-IBS algorithm, and periodically broadcasts the messages $< ID_r, T, prt, \sigma_{r1}(ID_r\|T\|prt), n_r >$ within its range, T is the current time interval.

2. The OBU firstly calculates the temporary key $vt = H_2(vk\|Tr_2)$ according to the private key vk, Tr_2 is the validity period, and the corresponding public key $pvt = vtP$. Then, after receiving the message, the OBU performs the following steps:
   - OBU checks the freshness of T.
   - If T is fresh then the OBU verifies GC_r in ID_r through GPS.
   - If GC_r is correct, the OBU verifies σ_{r1} through the BNN-IBS algorithm.
   - If the verification passes, the OBU generates pseudonym

$$PS_i = < T_{start}\|Enc_{prt}(PID)\|ID_r\|T_{end} >$$

   and signature σ_{v1}, T_{start} is the time when the pseudonym is generated, and T_{end} is the validity period of the pseudonym. Then the OBU sends the RSU the message:

$$< PS_i, T, \sigma_v^*(PS_i), \sigma_{v1}(\sigma_v^*(PS_i)\|T), n_r >$$

   Note that according to the BNN-IBS scheme, the signature is a triple containing the public key, but in this case, $\sigma_v^*(PS_v)$ is a two-tuple that does not contain the public key.
3. Once the RSU receives the message sent by the OBU, it performs the following steps:
   - the RSU first checks whether the T is fresh.
   - If T is fresh, the RSU obtains the PID in the pseudonym and the real ID of the OBU according to the parameters in the TPD, $ID_v = PID_2 \oplus H_1(skPID_1)$, then the RSU checks whether the vehicle is in the control revocation list (CRL) according to the obtained ID_v.
   - If it is, the OBU is rejected. If not, the σ_{v1} is verified by the BNN-IBS verification algorithm.
   - If σ_{v1} passes the verification, the RSU stores the PS_v and sends the PS_v and the PID to the TA. Then TA obtains the real ID of the vehicle according to the PID, and searches the record according to the ID to check whether it has used the pseudonym before. If not, it stores the pseudonym and PID. If there is, it updates the pseudonym and checks whether the pseudonym used before is expired. If not, the pseudonym used before will be revoked from the network.
   - Next, RSU uses its own temporary private key rt, generates the offline signature $\sigma_{off}(TID)$ according to the signature scheme [5], where $TID = \sigma_v^*(PS_i)\|PS_i$ is the signature ID. Then the RSU send the message

$$< PS_i, \sigma_{off}(TID), T, \sigma_{r2}(\sigma_{off}(TID)\|T), n_r >$$

   to the OBU. If the signature σ_{r2} is valid, the OBU will store the $\sigma_{off}(TID)$.

4.3   Inner V2V Authentication

1. OBU_i generates online signature and sends a message to OBU_j, the message is:

$$< PS_i, \sigma_i(PS_i), t, \sigma_{on}(\sigma_{off}(TID_i)\|t), n_i >$$

Note that $\sigma_i(PS_i)$ is a triple containing the public key pvt.
2. After receiving the message, OBU_j performs the following steps:
   - OBU_j checks the ID_r in the pseudonym to confirm whether OBU_i is in the same area as itself.
   - If it is, it first verifies the $\sigma_i(PS_i)$, and then verifies the online/offline signature by using the public key prt.
   - If the verification passes, it will reply to the message:

$$< PS_j, \sigma_j(PS_j), t, \sigma_{on}(\sigma_{off}(TID_j)\|t), n_i >$$

OBU_i will verify the identity of OBU_j in the same way.

4.4   Cross V2V Authentication

1. OBU_i sends a message to OBU_j, the message is:

$$< PS_i, \sigma_i(PS_i), t, \sigma_{on}(\sigma_{off}(TID_i)\|t), n_i >$$

2. When OBU_i and OBU_j are not in the same area, OBU_j sends RSU_j the inquiry request message

$$< (PS_j, \sigma_j(PS_j), T, \sigma_{on}(\sigma_{off}(TID_j)\|T), n_j, qr) >$$

qr contains PS_i, $\sigma_i(PS_i)$, t and $\sigma_{on}(\sigma_{off}(TID_i)\|t)$.
3. RSU_j queries other RSUs to check the validity of the OBU_i, if the OBU_i is a legitimate vehicle, RSU_j will return the inquiry result and give the vehicle OBU_j a ticket that can prove itself. The RSU_j sends the message to the OBU, the message is:

$$< PS_j, \sigma_{off}(PS_j\|PS_i), T, result, \sigma_{rj}(result\|T), n_j >$$

$\sigma_{off}(PS_j\|PS_i)$ is generated by the RSU_i in where OBU_i is located.
4. If the OBU_i is legal, OBU_j will send the message

$$< PS_j, PS_i, ID_j, \sigma_{on}(\sigma_{off}(PS_j\|PS_i)\|ID_j), t, \sigma_{vj}(PSj\|t), n_i >$$

to OBU_i, OBU_i can verify that OBU_j is a legitimate vehicle after getting the signature $\sigma_{on}(\sigma_{off}(PS_j\|PS_i)\|ID_j)$.

5   Security Analysis

In this section, we use the Internet Security Protocol and Application Automated Authentication (AVISPA) formalize our work and analyze security requirements presented before.

5.1   Formal Security Validation

The formal tool AVISPA [1] describes the security protocols and checks their security properties using HLPSL language. It contains four back-ends, OFMC, CL-AtSe, SATMC and TA4SP. Because V2V communication depends on R2V communication, we formally verified V2V communication process with AVISPA.

Part of the code after the formalization of our framework is given in Fig. 2. It provides entities authentication and secrecy of the message. Figure 3 shows the verification results of the inner-V2V communication under the OFMC model and the CL-AtSe model, which shows that the communication process is SAFE. The results of the cross-V2V communication are illustrated in Fig. 4.

```
RCV(IDr.Ks.T.H1(IDr.Ks.T))=|>State':=2/\N1':=new()
     /\PS1':=IDr.{IDv}_Ks
     /\TID1':=H2(PS1'.inv(Ku))/\secret(IDv,id,{B,R})
     /\SND(PS1'.TID1'.H2(TID1'.T).N1'.T)
RCV(PS1'.H1(TID1'.PS1'.inv(Ks)).T.H1(H1(TID1'.PS1'.inv(Ks)).T).N1')
   =|>State':=3/\N2':=new()
     /\SND(PS1'.Ku.TID1'.T2.H2(H1(TID1'.PS1'.inv(Ks)).T2).N2')
     /\witness(B,C,c_b_tid,TID1')
```

Fig. 2. Partial code for formal verification.

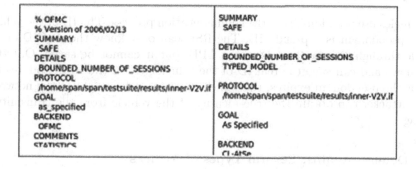

% OFMC	SUMMARY
% Version of 2006/02/13	SAFE
SUMMARY	
SAFE	DETAILS
DETAILS	BOUNDED_NUMBER_OF_SESSIONS
BOUNDED_NUMBER_OF_SESSIONS	TYPED_MODEL
PROTOCOL	
/home/span/span/testsuite/results/inner-V2V.if	PROTOCOL
GOAL	/home/span/span/testsuite/results/inner-V2V.if
as_specified	
BACKEND	GOAL
OFMC	As Specified
COMMENTS	
STATISTICS	BACKEND
	CL-AtSe

Fig. 3. Results of inner-V2V communication.

5.2   Message Authentication

All RSUs and OBUs will sign the outgoing message. When processing a secure message, the receiving vehicle must verify the validity of the online/offline signature in order to check the legitimacy of the latter.

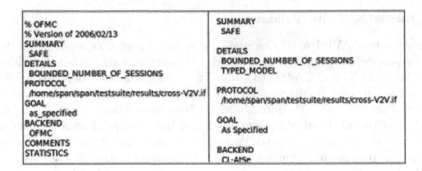

Fig. 4. Results of cross-V2V communication.

5.3   Identity Privacy Preservation

All vehicles use pseudonyms in the communication process. The ID of the vehicle in the pseudonym is a pseudo ID. The RSU can only know the real ID of the vehicle through the parameters in the TPD, but it cannot be saved. Only the TA knows and can save the real ID of the vehicle. When the RSU updates the key, or the pseudonym expires, the vehicle must re-authenticate to the network, so no attacker can obtain the true identity of the vehicle from the transmitted message.

5.4   Traceability

All vehicles use pseudonyms in the communication process. The ID of the vehicle in the pseudonym is a pseudo ID. The RSU can only know the real ID of the vehicle through the parameters in the TPD, but it cannot be saved. Only the TA knows and can save the real ID of the vehicle. When the RSU updates the key, or the pseudonym expires, the vehicle must re-authenticate to the network, so no attacker can obtain the true identity of the vehicle from the transmitted message.

5.5   Defense Against Several Types of Attacks

1. **Impersonation attack:** every vehicle in the network must get the online/offline signature of the RSU before communicating with other vehicles, and the identity of the vehicle must be verified again before verifying the online/offline signature, thus ensuring that the vehicle identity will not be being impersonated.
2. **Sybil attack:** a malicious vehicle may create the illusion of multiple vehicles by generating multiple pseudonyms. However, in our scheme, each vehicle must be certified by RSU and TA before communicating with other vehicles. The TA saves the vehicle's real ID, pseudo ID and currently used the pseudonym, which has a valid period. If the vehicle applies for a new

pseudonym before the expiration date of the pseudonym, the TA will revoke the old pseudonym from the network, thus ensuring that multiple pseudonyms will not coexist in the network at any time for each ID. Therefore our plan can prevent the Sybil attack.

3. **Replay attack:** each vehicle and RSU include a timestamp and a random number in each message, they send to detect the replay of the message.
4. **Modification attack and repudiation attack:** Our scheme adopt an identity-based signature scheme. And according to the above analysis, it can resist modification attacks and denial attacks.

6   Performance Evaluation

We compare the proposed EMAPP with ACPN [9] and MADAR [17] in terms of computational cost and communication overhead. Table 3 shows the time and size measurement for different operations, which is used to estimate the computational overhead and communication cost of the framework.

Table 3. Time and size measures of operations for evaluation.

Scheme	Operation	Time (ms)	Size of signature
BNN-IBS [3]	Sign	0.442	100B
	Verify	1.326	
Online/offline	Sign/verify(online)	0.066	80B
signature [5]	Offline	0	80B
ECDSA [17]	Sign	1.24	64B
	Verify	2.33	
IBOOS [9]	Sign/verify(online)	0.19	60B
	Offline	0	40B

6.1   Computation Cost

Due to the reusability of our framework, we can adopt a more efficient signature scheme to improve the performance of the proposed EMAPP. In order to better compare the proposed EMAPP with other schemes, in the experiment, we first used the same signature scheme as ACPN and MADAR to generate digital signatures for our framework. In Table 4, EMAPP-Y represents the computational overhead incurred when our scheme adopts ECDSA and IBOOS signature schemes, and EMAPP-N represents the computational overhead incurred when we adopt BNN-IBS scheme and online/offline signature scheme in Table 3.

As can be seen from the table, when the signature schemes are the same, our framework only has about $1 - 2\,ms$ more computational overhead than ACPN and MADAR, but our framework can resist impersonation attacks. The proposed

Table 4. Computation costs of OBU and RSU for different schemes (ms).

Phase	Subject	ACPN	MADAR	EMAPP-Y	EMAPP-N
R2V	OBU	5.900	6.600	7.140	3.536
	RSU	4.810	4.860	4.810	2.210
inner-V2V	Sender	0.190	0.380	2.710	1.458
	Receiver	0.190	0.380	2.710	1.458
cross-V2V	Sender	0.190	4.850	2.710	1.458
	Receiver	5.000	3.760	3.950	1.900
	RSU	3.570	2.860	6.280	3.226

EMAPP adds a process of verifying the pseudonym of the vehicle in the communication process, preventing other vehicles from posing as the identity of the vehicle when the offline signature and pseudonym are leaked. In addition, when our framework adopts BNN-IBS signature scheme and online/offline signature scheme, the computational overhead required is reduced by approximately half. Therefore, our framework has the possibility to further reduce the computational cost.

Besides, there are two kinds of V2V communication in EMAPP, which have different computation costs. In order to understand the influence of the proportion of vehicles participating in inner-V2V or cross-V2V communication on the overall computation costs, we use the same method as [9] to analyze the total cost of each communication process. In the procedure of vehicle-roadside communication, the computation delay T_{R2V} is calculated as:

$$T_{r2v} = 2T_{rsu\_sign} + 2T_{v\_verify} + 2T_{v\_sign} \\ + T_{rsu\_verify} + T_{rsu\_offsign}$$

In the procedure of inner-V2V authentication, the computation delay T_{inner} is calculated as:

$$T_{inner} = T_{snd\_onsign} + T_{rcv\_onverify} + T_{rcv\_verify} \\ + T_{rcv\_onsign} + T_{snd\_onverify} + T_{snd\_verify}$$

In the procedure of cross-V2V authentication, the computation delay T_{cross} is calculated as:

$$T_{cross} = T_{snd\_onsign} + T_{rcv\_onsign} + T_{query} \\ + T_{snd\_verify} + T_{rcv\_sign} + T_{snd\_onverify}$$

where T_{query} is the process of communication between receiver and the RSU, and its calculation is as follows:

$$T_{query} = T_{rcv\_onsign} + 2T_{rsu\_onverify} + 2T_{rsu\_verify} \\ + T_{rsu_offsign} + T_{rsu_sign} + T_{rcv_verify}$$

we can define γ as the proportion of vehicles participating in inner-regional communication. The value of γ can be calculated by $N_{inner}/(N_{inner} + N_{cross})$, and the ratio of vehicles who use cross-regional communication is $1-\gamma$. Therefore, the average computation delay of V2V authentication is calculated as:

$$T_{v2v} = \gamma\Delta T_{inner} + (1 - \gamma)\Delta T_{cross}$$

Figure 5 illustrates the effect of the proportion of inner-regional communication on the total calculation cost in different schemes. The results show that with the increase in the proportion of internal communication, the computation cost will be lower and lower, that is, the authentication efficiency will be higher and higher. We can also see that when the framework adopts a more efficient signature scheme, the efficiency of V2V communication is less affected by γ.

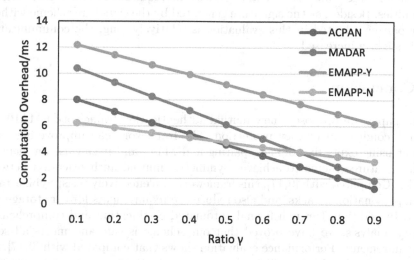

Fig. 5. Comparison on Computation Overhead (V2V).

6.2   Communication Cost

We estimate the communication cost by the length of the message. For the convenience of comparison, we use the length of some parameters in [17], such as the ID of RSU, the ID of OBU, the random number and timestamp, so we mainly consider the lengths of pseudonyms and signatures to compare the communication overhead. In our scheme, we select the same curve parameters as [3], which utilizes a 160-bit field for ECC to achieve the security level of 80 bits. For these settings, the random number is 20B, and an elliptic curve is 40B. Therefore, the pseudonym length is 56B, the signature length generated by BNN-IBS is 100B, and the signature length generated by the online offline signature scheme is 80B, as shown in Table 3. We chose the longest message at each stage for comparison. Table 5 lists the communication costs of the three schemes in different stages, where n is the number of certified vehicles.

Table 5. Communication costs of different schemes (byte).

Phase	ACPN	MADAR	EMAPP-Y	EMAPP-N
R2V	$64+92n$	$64+88n$	160	236
inner-V2V	112	156	180	236
cross-V2V	368	224	360	472

In Table 5, because ACPN and MADAR update the set of pseudonyms and offline signatures after each successful authentication, when the number of vehicles successfully authenticated increases continuously, their communication costs will also increase linearly. Our scheme gets rid of the set, so our scheme is more suitable for large-scale VANET and reduces the requirements for vehicle storage capabilities. Besides, as the signature generated by the signature scheme without linear pairing adopted in this evaluation is relatively long, the communication load is slightly increased.

7 Conclusion

In this paper, we propose a new mutual authentication framework EMAPP for VANET conditional privacy protection. The framework can improve efficiency without using expensive bilinear pairing and MTP, and it can use an identity-based signature scheme to achieve asymmetric mutual authentication between vehicles. Compared with [9,17], this framework can effectively resist Sybil attacks and impersonation attacks, and also reduce the requirements for car storage efficiency. In addition, through formal automated certification and comprehensive security analysis, we have proved that our scheme is safe and meets all security requirements. Performance evaluation shows that compared with [9,17], our framework also has higher efficiency in communication cost and computational load. As future work, we will explore how to reduce message length and further improve efficiency in terms of communication costs.

Acknowledgement. This work is supported in part by National Natural Science Foundation of China(Nos. 61572349, 61872262).

References

1. Armando, A., et al.: The AVISPA tool for the automated validation of internet security protocols and applications. In: Etessami, K., Rajamani, S.K. (eds.) CAV 2005. LNCS, vol. 3576, pp. 281–285. Springer, Heidelberg (2005). https://doi.org/10.1007/11513988_27
2. Bariah, L., Shehada, D., Salahat, E., Yeun, C.Y.: Recent advances in VANET security: a survey. In: 2015 IEEE 82nd Vehicular Technology Conference (VTC2015-Fall), pp. 1–7, September 2015. https://doi.org/10.1109/VTCFall.2015.7391111

3. Chikhaoui, O., Ben Chehida Douss, A., Abassi, R., Guemara El Fatmi, S.: Towards the formal validation of a ticket-based authentication scheme for VANETS. In: 2018 32nd International Conference on Advanced Information Networking and Applications Workshops (WAINA), pp. 496–501, May 2018. https://doi.org/10. 1109/WAINA.2018.00134

4. Chikhaoui, O., Chehida, A.B., Abassi, R., Fatmi, S.G.E.: A ticket-based authentication scheme for VANETs preserving privacy. In: Puliafito, A., Bruneo, D., Distefano, S., Longo, F. (eds.) ADHOC-NOW 2017. LNCS, vol. 10517, pp. 77–91. Springer, Cham (2017). https://doi.org/10.1007/978-3-319-67910-5_7

5. Liu, D., Zhang, S., Zhong, H., Shi, R., Wang, Y.: An efficient identity-based online/offline signature scheme without key escrow. Int. J. Netw. Secur. **19**, 127–137 (2017). https://doi.org/10.6633/IJNS.201701.19(1).14

6. He, D., Zeadally, S., Xu, B., Huang, X.: An efficient identity-based conditional privacy-preserving authentication scheme for vehicular ad hoc networks. IEEE Trans. Inf. Forensics Secur. **10**(12), 2681–2691 (2015). https://doi.org/10.1109/ TIFS.2015.2473820

7. Horng, S.J., Tzeng, S.F., Huang, P.H., Wang, X., Li, T., Khan, K.: An efficient certificateless aggregate signature with conditional privacy-preserving for vehicular sensor networks. Inf. Sci. **317**, 48–66 (2015). https://doi.org/10.1016/j.ins.2015.04. 033

8. Hubaux, J.P., Capkun, S., Luo, J.: The security and privacy of smart vehicles. IEEE Secur. Priv. **2**(3), 49–55 (2004). https://doi.org/10.1109/MSP.2004.26

9. Li, J., Lu, H., Guizani, M.: ACPN: a novel authentication framework with conditional privacy-preservation and non-repudiation for VANETs. IEEE Trans. Parallel Distrib. Syst. **26**(4), 938–948 (2015). https://doi.org/10.1109/TPDS.2014.2308215

10. Liu, X., Fang, Z., Shi, L.: Securing vehicular ad hoc networks. In: 2007 2nd International Conference on Pervasive Computing and Applications, pp. 424–429, July 2007. https://doi.org/10.1109/ICPCA.2007.4365481

11. Liu, Y., Wang, L., Chen, H.: Message authentication using proxy vehicles in vehicular ad hoc networks. IEEE Trans. Veh. Technol. **64**(8), 3697–3710 (2015). https:// doi.org/10.1109/TVT.2014.2358633

12. Lu, R., Lin, X., Zhu, H., Ho, P., Shen, X.: ECPP: efficient conditional privacy preservation protocol for secure vehicular communications. In: IEEE INFOCOM 2008 - The 27th Conference on Computer Communications, pp. 1229–1237, April 2008. https://doi.org/10.1109/INFOCOM.2008.179

13. Bellare, M., Namprempre, C., Neven, G.: Security proofs for identity-based identification and signature schemes. J. Cryptol. **22**, 1–61 (2009). https://doi.org/10. 1007/s00145-008-9028-8

14. Ming, Y., Cheng, H.: Efficient certificateless conditional privacy-preserving authentication scheme in VANETs. Mob. Inf. Syst. **2019**, 19 (2019). https://doi.org/10. 1155/2019/7593138

15. Oh, H., Yae, C., Ahn, D., Cho, H.: 5.8 GHz DSRC packet communication system for ITS services. In: Gateway to 21st Century Communications Village. VTC 1999-Fall. IEEE VTS 50th Vehicular Technology Conference (Cat. No. 99CH36324), vol. 4, pp. 2223–2227, September 1999. https://doi.org/10.1109/VETECF.1999.797333

16. Yasmin, R., Ritter, E., Wang, G.: Provable security of a pairing-free one-pass authenticated key establishment protocol for wireless sensor networks. Int. J. Inf. Secur. **13**, 453–465 (2014). https://doi.org/10.1007/s10207-013-0224-7

17. Sun, C., Liu, J., Xu, X., Ma, J.: A privacy-preserving mutual authentication resisting DoS attacks in VANETs. IEEE Access **5**, 24012–24022 (2017). https://doi.org/ 10.1109/ACCESS.2017.2768499

Covering Diversification and Fairness for Better Recommendation (Short Paper)

Qing Yang[1]ⓘ, Li Han[1], Ya Zhou[2], Shaobing Liu[2], Jingwei Zhang[2]ⓘ,
Zhongqin Bi[3], and Fang Pan[4(✉)]

[1] Guangxi Key Laboratory of Automatic Measurement Technology and Instrument,
Guilin University of Electronic Technology, Guilin 541004, China
[2] Guangxi Key Laboratory of Trusted Software,
Guilin University of Electronic Technology, Guilin 541004, China
[3] College of Computer Science and Technology,
Shanghai University of Electronic Power, Shanghai 200090, China
[4] Teaching Affairs Office, Guangxi Normal University, Guilin 541004, China
panfang@mailbox.gxnu.edu.cn

Abstract. Smart applications are appealing an accurate matching
between users and items, in which recommendation technologies are
applied widely. Since recommendation serve for two roles, namely users
and items, accuracy is not the only focus, the diversification and fairness
should also be paid more attention for improving recommendation performance. The tradeoff among the accuracy, diversification and fairness on
recommendation is bringing a big challenge. This paper proposed a novelty recommendation model to ensure the recommendation performance,
which introduces a multi-variate linear regression model to cooperate
with the collaborative filtering method. This study utilizes an improved
similarity metrics to discover the closeness between users and item categories under the help of the collaborative filtering methods, and exploits
the micro attribute information of items by a multi-variate linear regression model to decide the final recommended items. The experimental
results show that our proposed method can provide better recommendation accuracy, diversification and fairness than the recommendation
based on pure collaborative filtering method.

Keywords: Diversified recommendation · Recommendation fairness ·
Recommendation evaluation

1 Introduction

Many smart services, copious merchandise, and other items are being pushed
to users by mobile applications, electronic commerce, etc. The accompanying
challenge is how to discover those items matching users' real needs. The classical recommendation methods transform users' historical information into a

X. Wang et al. (Eds.): CollaborateCom 2019, LNICST 292, pp. 816–825, 2019.
https://doi.org/10.1007/978-3-030-30146-0_54

vector model for describing users or items, and then apply a similarity computation based on the vector model to find those similar users/items for a specific user/item, who are finally exploited to predict scores for this specific user/item. But those micro recommendation factors, such as item attributes, can often play an important role for recommendation acceptance. On the other hand, users often have diversified requirements, but the strict ranking mechanism for recommendation limits the recommendation diversification. For example, when a movie fan is labelled by a tag of action movie, most of the items in his/her recommendation list will be action movies. In addition, from the angel of the recommended items, each item wish to gain the recommendation opportunities, but the global ranking often causes that most of items can not be recommended for a low prediction score or less attention, the recommendation fairness are not introduced well.

This paper put forward a novelty recommendation model to provide both recommendation diversification and recommendation fairness, which also considers the item attributes for improving recommendation performance. The major contribution of this paper is to make full use of both users' historical information and item attributes to design a novelty recommendation strategy, the former is responsible for predicting those missing scores and then deciding the concrete item categories that have a high relevance with users, and the latter is applied to obtain the final recommended items in the limited categories by a multivariate linear regression model. The proposed recommendation strategy gains better recommendation performance when giving consideration on both recommendation diversification and fairness.

2 Related Work

Two popular recommendation strategies are recommendation based on collaborative strategy and recommendation based on classification-aided decision. Collaborative filtering is the most classical recommendation technology driven by collaborative strategy, which includes user-based collaborative recommendation [1], item-based collaborative recommendation [2,3] and model-based collaborative recommendation [4–6]. Their primary strategy is to model users/items as vector model and then to apply similarity metrics to find similar objects for identifying those items well matched with users. Computing efficiency is also a focus of recommendation based on collaborative filtering, [7] realizes a distributed and scalable collaborative filtering algorithm on cloud computing platform.

Classification-driven recommendation often uses classification results to generate recommendation lists. [8] proposes a novelty information entropy metric, which is based on a new split criterion and a new construction method of decision trees and can avoid local optimums. [9] introduces multi-label classification for approximate nearest neighbor search, which obtains better prediction accuracy for large label space. [10] put forwards a method that can extend random forest to any data set and obtains better performance on multi-dimensional data sets than traditional random forest methods. [11] introduces the recommendation technology for location-based services.

3 Problem Statement

In this section, we will discuss the problem about recommendation covering diversification and fairness. Usually, recommendation diversification requires that a user should enjoy items in different categories, and recommendation fairness requires that each item should have enough opportunities to be recommended. The traditional recommendation problem is that you have a set of ratings S that are done on a set of items I by a group of users U, you should output a list of items RI for a specific user u, in which each item $i \in RI$ has a high predicted rating for the user u than those items $j \in I \wedge j \notin RI$.

In order to give consideration to both recommendation diversification and fairness, a set of categories, C, are introduced to our recommendation problem, each item $i \in I$ belongs to a specific category $c \in C$. The attributes of items, which can show the popularity of items, such as sales, price, etc., are also covered for recommendation. The recommended items depends on a function $T(u, c)$ which tells the closeness between a user u and a category c, namely those items that will be recommended should satisfy two conditions, one is that the item should be in the categories that have a high score on closeness with the specific user u, and the other is that the item should have a high predicted rating for the user u in its category. The formal definition for recommendation covering diversification and fairness can be defined as Definition 1.

Definition 1. Recommendation covering diversification and fairness *Given a set of items I, a set of categories C, a group of users U and their ratings on items S, and a function $T(u, c)$ for computing the closeness between users and categories. The constraints are that each item $i \in I$ belongs to a category $c \in C$, and each item also has some attributes to show their popularity, such as sales, price, etc. Each score $s \in S$ is a triple, $<u, i, g>$, to show a real number g, namely the rating on the item i exerted by the user u. Recommendation covering diversification and fairness aims at finding those close categories with a specific user u by $T(u, c)$ and then applying the predicted rating and their popular attributes to decide those output items for each found category.*

In the above definition, recommendation diversification is provided by computing the closeness between users and categories, which can ensure that the items in different categories can be output, and recommendation fairness is improved by the final recommendation decision on the popular attributes of items.

4 Recommendation Model and Proposed Method

4.1 Recommendation Framework

In order to improve the recommendation diversification and recommendation fairness, we design a recommendation framework that is composed of four parts. The first step is to design the similarity metrics to find the similar users, and the second step is to provide a closeness function $T(u, c)$ and to compute the closeness between users and categories. The third step is to introduce multi-variate linear regression on the item attributes to compute their popularity, which will also consider the recommended times and the corresponding recommendation weights for each item, and the top-n popular items in top-m close categories will be initially filtered out. The final step is responsible for computing the global weights of the filtered items from the third step and outputting top-k items. The recommendation framework is illustrated in Fig. 1.

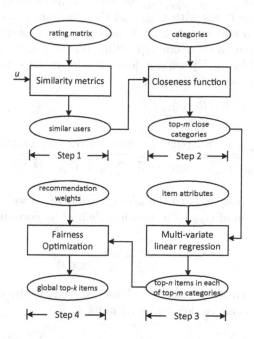

Fig. 1. The recommendation framework.

4.2   Computing Closeness Between Users and Categories

The part is responsible for finding similar users and then computing the closeness between users and categories. In order to find those similar users, we introduce weighted common scoring items $w_{ab}(i)$, which is based on the item similarity matrix H_{nn}. H_{nn} is constructed from the rating matrix by computing the similarity of any item vectors, $w_{ab}(i)$ is defined as Formula 1.

$$w_{ab}(i) = \frac{Max(|I(a \cap b)|, \gamma)}{\gamma} * \frac{(r_{a,i} + r_{b,j})}{2} * \frac{\sum_{g_j \in G_{ab} \wedge j \neq i} h_{i,j}}{n - 1} \tag{1}$$

I is a set of items. $I(a \cap b)$ denotes the number of those items which are bought by both user a and user b. γ is a constant represented by a positive integer. $r_{a,i}$ denotes the rating that user a assigns to an item i. Obviously, $\frac{r_{a,i}+r_{b,i}}{2}$ is to increase the weights of those items that are assigned a high rating by both a and b, and to reduce the weights of those items that are assigned a low rating by a and b.

G_{ab} is an item set holding those items that are rated by both a and b, and n is the cardinal number of G_{ab}. $\sum_{g_j \in G_{ab} \wedge j \neq i} h_{i,j}$ is to sum all similarity between the specific item i and all items $j \in G_{ab} \wedge j \neq i$. The above value is used to indicate whether a category is a common preference of both user a and user b. Intuitively, a big value output by $\sum_{g_j \in G_{ab} \wedge j \neq i} h_{i,j}$ means that the category holding the item i have more common items with G_{ab}, and this category is more likely to be a preference for user a and user b. $w_{ab}(i)$ can compute the weights for similarity between a and b based on those corresponding item similarity. Depending on the weights contributed by $w_{ab}(i)$, we can define the Pearson Correlation Coefficient between user a and user b as Formula 2.

$$
\begin{aligned}
Sim(a,b,w) &= \frac{cov(R_a, R_b; w)}{\sigma(R_a; w)\sigma(R_b; w)} \\
&= \frac{\sum_{g_i \in G_{ab}} w_{ab}(i)(r_{a,i} - m(a;w))(r_{b,i} - m(b;w))}{\sqrt{\sum_{g_i \in G_{ab}} w_{ab}(i)(r_{a,i} - m(a;w))^2}\sqrt{\sum g_i \in G_{ab} w_{ab}(i)(r_{b,i} - m(b;w))^2}}
\end{aligned}
\tag{2}
$$

Here, $m(b; w)$ corresponds to the average value of all weighted ratings that are done on each item of G_{ab} by a, which is defined as Formula 3.

$$
m(a; w) = \frac{\sum_{g_i \in G_{ab}} w_{ab}(i) r_{a,i}}{\sum_{g_i \in G_{ab}} w_{ab}(i)}
\tag{3}
$$

According to both item ratings and user similarity, the closeness between users and categories can be defined as Formula 4.

$$
T_{a,c_k} = \frac{\sum_{i=1}^{n} r_{a,c_k,i}}{\sum_{j=1}^{m} \sum_{i=1}^{n} r_{a,c_j,i}} + Sim(a,b,w)\frac{\sum_{i=1}^{n} r_{b,c_k,i}}{\sum_{j=1}^{m} \sum_{i=1}^{n} r_{b,c_j,i}}
\tag{4}
$$

The expected rating of i contributed by a, namely $p_{a,i}$, can be computed as Formula 5.

$$
p_{a,i} = \overline{r_a} + \frac{\sum_{b \in NSIM_a} sim(a,b,w) \times (r_{b,i} - \overline{r_b})}{\sum_{b \in NSIM_a} sim(a,b,w)}
\tag{5}
$$

$NSIM_a$ corresponds to the set holding the nearest neighbors of user a. $\overline{r_a}$ and $\overline{r_b}$ represent the average rating contributed by a and b respectively.

4.3   Ranking Items on Diversification

In this section, we introduce a multi-variate linear regression model to cooperate with collaborative filtering method for further optimization on recommendation outputs, in which both users macro behavior information and their micro attribute information are given a full consideration. When we obtain the closeness between users and categories, the attributes of those items in the top-k categories will be input into the multi-variate linear regression, which is defined as Formula 6.

$$F = f(x_{i,j}) = \omega^T x_{i,j} + d \tag{6}$$

Here, $x_{i,j}$ denotes the j_{th} attribute of the i_{th} item, such as sales, price, rating, etc. F can be understood as the quantitative popularity of items. The least square approach is used for deciding the optimal parameters of the regression model, and the minimal Euclidean distance is used as the evaluation metric.

The rating of each item on popularity, F, can be computed by the least square method. For giving consideration to the fairness of those unrecommended items, we introduce the item rating on the fairness, which is defined by both the recommendation times of items and the item rating on popularity and expressed as Formula 7. In Formula 7, the recommendation times of items is denoted as *times*, F is the item rating on popularity and FS is just the item rating on the recommendation fairness. The rating on the recommendation fairness aims at making those items in the long tail to gain the referral opportunities, which can avoid the recommendation overfitting effectively.

$$FS = \frac{log(2)}{log(1 + times)} F \tag{7}$$

4.4 A Comprehensive Ranking Algorithm

This section will design a comprehensive ranking algorithm based on the information provided by both the multi-variate linear regression model, which makes recommendation contributions by micro item information, and the collaborative filtering method. The great advantage for our proposed recommendation algorithm is that it can make the tradeoff among the recommendation accuracy, diversification and fairness. The whole recommendation process is presented in Algorithm 1.

5   Experiments and Analysis

In this section, we designed experiments on the real data set to verify our proposed recommendation method. The data set is an open data set on shopping and is composed of 12,000 records contributed by 213 users on 2352 items. The data set covers 18 categories, and each record consists of the following information, *title, category, sales, price*, and *rating*. All program is coded in Python and Matlab.

$$Accuracy = \frac{RightNum}{OutputNum} \tag{8}$$

$$Coverage = \frac{OutputCategories}{AllCategories} \tag{9}$$

$$Fairness = \frac{2 * Accuracy * Coverage}{Accuracy + Coverage} \tag{10}$$

Algorithm 1. *A Comprehensive Recommendation Algorithm*

Input: user a and b,
    user-item rating matrix R,
    common rating item set G_{ab},
    item similarity matrix H_{nn},
Output: the top-k recommended item list
1: $p = 0, G_1 = G_{ab}$;
2: get g_i from G_1, $G_1 = G_1 - g_i, p + +$;
3: **repeat**
4:    $G_2 = G_{ab}, w_{ab}(i) = 0, q = 1$;
5:    **repeat**
6:       get $h_{i,k}$ from H, $i \neq k \wedge g_k \in G_2$;
7:       $q + +, G_2 = G_2 - g_k$;
8:       $w_{ab}(i) = w_{ab}(i) + h_{i,k}$;
9:    **until** $q \geq |G_{ab}|$
10:   $w_{ab}(i) = \frac{w_{ab}(i)}{n-1} * \frac{Max(|I(a \cap b)|, \gamma)}{\gamma} * \frac{(r_{a,i} + r_{b,j})}{2}$;
11: **until** $p \geq |G_{ab}|$
12: computing the weighted average $m(a; w)$ by Formula 3;
13: computing the similarity between users $Sim(a, b, w)$ by Formula 2;
14: computing the closeness between users and categories T_{a,c_k} by Formula 4;
15: computing the prediction rating between users and items $p_{a,i}$ by Formula 5;
16: computing the linear regression scoring of each item F by Formula 6;
17: computing the final recommendation score of each item FS by Formula 7;
18: generating the final top-k items according to the FS value of each item in each
    category;
19: **return** top-k items.

5.1 Experimental Evaluation

We introduce the recommendation accuracy and the category coverage as the evaluation metrics, which are defined in Formulas 8 and 9. Here, **OutputNum** denotes the number of the recommended items by our proposed method, and **RightNum** denotes the number of items that should be recommended and also are in the output list. **AllCategories** denotes the total number of the categories covering all items, and **OutputCategories** denotes the number of the categories that are related with those recommended and accepted items. Both accuracy and coverage are merged into the fairness for recommendation, which is a trade-off between the recommendation accuracy and recommendation coverage and is defined in Eq. 10. Cross validation is introduced for experimental evaluation, the ratio between the training set and the testing set is 8 to 2.

5.2 Experimental Results and Analysis

We made an experimental comparison between our proposed method (abbr. CTT) and the collaborative filtering method(abbr. CF), and the experimental results are presented in Figs. 2, 3 and 4. Our proposed method has a slight fall in the recommendation accuracy than the collaborative filtering method, but outperforms the collaborative filtering method on both the recommendation coverage and the recommendation fairness. The reason of a lower accuracy by our method is due that we reduce the recommendation time of those popular items that are covered by those categories with high closeness to users. The above measure contributes a little to the higher coverage and fairness, on the other hand, the integration of classification and micro attributes is very helpful to improve the recommendation performance.

We also designed a group of experiments to verify the recommendation performance under different data volume, and the experimental results are presented in Figs. 5, 6 and 7. When increasing the amount of data, both the recommendation accuracy and coverage have an obvious rising, which is due that more data can contribute more accurate relationships between users and items. But when the data amount becomes bigger, the recommendation fairness shows a small decrease, which is because the number of the recommended items is fixed though the base of the candidate items becomes bigger.

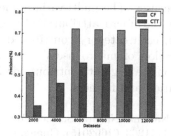

Fig. 2. Performance Comparison on Precision

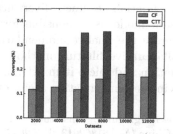

Fig. 3. Performance Comparison on Coverage

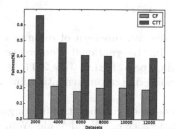

Fig. 4. Performance Comparison on Fairness

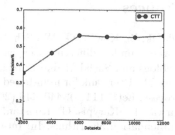

Fig. 5. Performance Comparison on Precision

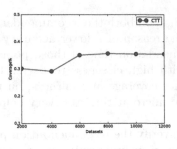

Fig. 6. Coverage

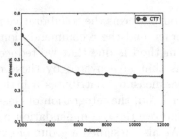

Fig. 7. Fairness

6 Conclusions

This paper provided an integration mechanism between the multi-variate linear regression and the collaborative filtering method for improving the recommendation performance, which presents a good performance for balancing the recommendation accuracy, diversification and fairness. The multi-variate linear regression model is responsible for considering the micro attributes of items to generate the final recommendation results in each category contributed by the collaborative filtering methods. The unification of macro users' behavior information and micro item attribute information make great contributions for improving recommendation accuracy, diversification and fairness.

Acknowledgments. This study is funded by the National Natural Science Foundation of China (No. 61862013, 61462017, U1501252, U1711263, 61662015), Guangxi Natural Science Foundation of China (No. 2018GXNSFAA281199, 2017GXNSFAA198035), Guangxi Key Laboratory of Automatic Measurement Technology and Instrument (No.YQ19109) and Guangxi Key Laboratory of Trusted Software (No. kx201915).

References

1. Szlávik, Z., Kowalczyk, W., Schut, M.C.: Diversity measurement of recommender systems under different user choice models. In: International Conference on Weblogs and Social Media, Barcelona, Catalonia, Spain. DBLP, July 2011
2. Gao, M.: User rank for item-based collaborative filtering recommendation. Inform. Process. Lett. **111**(9), 440–446 (2011)
3. Sarwar, B., Karypis, G., Konstan, J., et al.: Item-based collaborative filtering recommendation algorithms. In: International Conference on World Wide Web, pp. 285–295. ACM (2001)
4. He, T., Chen, Z., Liu, J., et al.: An empirical study on user-topic rating based collaborative filtering methods. World Wide Web-Internet Web Inform. Syst. **20**(4), 815–829 (2017)
5. Jia, D., Zhang, F., Liu, S.: A robust collaborative filtering recommendation algorithm based on multidimensional trust model. J. Softw. **8**(1), 806–809 (2013)
6. Koren, Y.: Factorization meets the neighborhood: a multifaceted collaborative filtering model. In: ACM SIGKDD International Conference on Knowledge Discovery and Data Mining, pp. 426–434. ACM (2008)

7. Zhao, Z.D., Shang, M.S.: User-based collaborative-filtering recommendation algorithms on Hadoop. In: Third International Conference on Knowledge Discovery and Data Mining, pp. 478–481. IEEE Computer Society (2010)

8. Wang, Y., Xia, S.T., Wu, J.: A less-greedy two-term Tsallis entropy information metric approach for decision tree classification. Knowl.-Based Syst. **120**, 34–42 (2017)

9. Tagami, Y.: AnnexML: approximate nearest neighbor search for extreme multi-label classification. In: The ACM SIGKDD International Conference, pp. 455–464. ACM (2017)

10. Aggarwal, C.C.: Similarity forests. In: ACM SIGKDD International Conference on Knowledge Discovery and Data Mining, pp. 395–403. ACM (2017)

11. Zhang, J., Yang, C., Yang, Q. et al.: HGeoHashBase: an optimized storage model of spatial objects for location-based services. Front. Comput. Sci. (2018). https://doi.org/10.1007/s11704-018-7030-3

Author Index

Printed in the United States
By Bookmasters